MW00574529

# For Europe Revisited

The French Volunteers of the Waffen SS, 1943-1945

Robert Forbes

 **Helion & Company Limited**

**This edition is dedicated to Mouse,**
**who has brought joy and love to my life**

Helion & Company Limited
Unit 8 Amherst Business Centre
Budbrooke Road
Warwick
CV34 5WE
England
Tel. 01926 499 619
Email: info@helion.co.uk
Website: www.helion.co.uk
Twitter: @helionbooks
Visit our blog at blog.helion.co.uk

Published by Helion & Company 2022
Designed and typeset by Mary Woolley (www.battlefield-design.co.uk)
Cover designed by Paul Hewitt, Battlefield Design (www.battlefield-design.co.uk)

Text © Robert Forbes 2022
Images © as individually credited
Maps drawn by George Anderson © Helion & Company 2022

Every reasonable effort has been made to trace copyright holders and to obtain their permission for the use of copyright material. The author and publisher apologize for any errors or omissions in this work, and would be grateful if notified of any corrections that should be incorporated in future reprints or editions of this book.

ISBN 978-1-913336-18-9

British Library Cataloguing-in-Publication Data.
A catalogue record for this book is available from the British Library.

All rights reserved. No part of this publication may be reproduced, stored in a retrieval system, or transmitted, in any form, or by any means, electronic, mechanical, photocopying, recording or otherwise, without the express written consent of Helion & Company Limited.

For details of other military history titles published by Helion & Company Limited contact the above address or visit our website: http://www.helion.co.uk.

We always welcome receiving book proposals from prospective authors.

# Contents

# Acknowledgements

My life-long interest in the French volunteers of the Waffen-SS started with the purchase of a copy of *Historia* while on a school trip to France. I was surprised to read that French volunteers were among the last defenders of the Führer bunker and wondered how this was possible after the terrible bloodletting between France and Germany during the First World War. Then, on another school trip to France, I came across and purchased a paperback copy of *La Division Charlemagne* by Jean Mabire in a hypermarket. Imagine my surprise because I could never see the likes of Tesco or Sainsbury in this country stock a similar book about the British Free Corps. The book proved a revelation. Not only was it full of information unavailable elsewhere, but it listed the names of many veterans interviewed. Somehow I had convinced myself that few had survived the massacre in Pomerania. I still have that paperback from all those years ago, although it's well-worn now from constant reading. Learning that Mabire had written two other books on the same subject, I ordered them by post.

Next I chanced upon a rather tatty copy of *Ashes of Honour* by Christian de La Mazière from a stall at a weekly market held in my hometown of Amersham. Here was a firsthand account of somebody who had served with 'Charlemagne' and fought in Pomerania. I was captivated.[1]

*Les Hérétiques* by Saint-Loup, referenced by Mabire, was much harder to find, but I stumbled across a used copy in the History Bookshop in Friern Barnet, North London. Tucked out the way, this musty-smelling bookshop offered a rather unique shopping experience for the collector and the curious alike. Moreover, the staff often greeted me with a warming cup of tea upon entry, which was gladly received. Sadly, when this purveyor of books moved to new premises in central London it never quite felt the same. Anyway, I noted there were numerous differences in the stories told by Mabire, de La Mazière and Saint-Loup.

As an avid reader of *Siegrunen*, I eagerly awaited the publication of *Charlemagne's Legionnaires* by Richard Landwehr, the first major English language work on the French volunteers of the Waffen-SS, which I obtained thanks again to the History Bookshop, but this book left me wanting more. And this is when I decided to write the book I wanted to read about the subject. Originally, I had intended to repeat the same story evoked by Saint-Loup and Mabire, highlighting the differences, but the book took on a new life as I received generous assistance and advice from many veterans, as well as many knowledgeable correspondents.

I remain indebted to the following veterans of 'Charlemagne' who assisted me: Jacques Bonnafont, André Bayle, Robert Blanc, Georges Blonay, Jean Castrillo, Rene Cessil, Jean

---

1   The front cover image of *Ashes of Honour* I desperately wanted to use on my original self-published edition but feared copyright infringement.

Chatrousse, Maurice Comte, Noël Cornu, Paul Denamps, Jules Dissent, André Doutart, Henri Fenet, Michel de Genouillac, Robert Girard, Henri-Georges Gonzales, Jean Grenier, Jean Halard, Daniel Le Goff, Robert Lacoste, François de Lannurien, Louis Levast, Jean Malardier, Christian Martres, Pierre Méric, Raymond Mercier, Jean del Missier, Yves Peyret, Paul Pignard-Berthet, Jean-Jacques Pillet, Yvon Prunnenec, Jean-Louis Puechlong, Yves Rigeade, Philippe Rossigneux, Pierre Ruskone, Marc Sainteuil, Jean Sepchat, and Robert Soulat. Others requested anonymity. I have respected their wishes. But you know who you are.

I must pay particular thanks to Robert Blanc, Michel de Genouillac, Raymond Mercier and Robert Soulat for their support, time, hospitality and generosity over the years.

I must also make mention of François Faroux, who served with the NSKK. He greatly encouraged and supported me with the second edition of the book and through some dark times. To say thank you just does not seem enough. For almost twenty years François has been a good friend and confidante.

I also extend thanks to Henri Raga who also served with the NSKK, Nelly who provided me with her rather unique and interesting story as a French nurse of the Waffen-SS and Pierre Duthilleul, who added a personal insight into the BILOM.

Historian Henri Mounine also assisted me, providing much information and many new leads. He read and edited my original manuscript three times and although we may have gone our own ways later he still deserves recognition. I was saddened to learn of his untimely death. Through historian Eric Lefèvre, I gained an understanding of the *Milice française* [French Militia] that my original manuscript lacked. He also provided me with a great deal of unrivalled biographical information.

Lorraine Smith, my gothic princess, proofread the original manuscript numerous times, even though she had absolutely no interest in the subject. Sadly she passed away a few years ago. I hope she now finds the peace she never could in this life.

The writing of the book was a time I will never forget and while almost all of the veterans and my original contacts have now 'joined the Great Army', for such is the nature of time, I still cherish each and every meeting, phone call, letter and email. Looking back at that time there were disappointments. Learning of my book, Pierre Méric contacted me by post, but I never received his letter. Thankfully I was able to meet him before he too passed away and his story is included in this revised edition. Also I met a veteran of the Assault Gun Company of 'Charlemagne' but was never able to interview him. A missed opportunity because, disappointingly, information on that particular unit still remains sparse. Lastly, the wife of Jean de Vaugelas agreed to an interview, but later declined because she felt it would be too painful to relive the family's wartime years, which I fully understood and respected.

It was never my intention to see *For Europe* published again in any format, but when Duncan Rogers of Helion Books floated the idea of a reissue of *For Europe* I agreed on condition that I could revise it. There were several reasons for my decision. The first is Grégory Bouysse, who almost single-handedly reawakened my obsessive interest in the subject. His books have provided some clarity on previously obscured details and much needed biographical information. Through Grégory Bouysse, I met Dominique Berrardelli, who has also been of great help to me. Thank you both for your support and time.

Second, mistakes did creep into my work, even though I strive for accuracy. I relied heavily on eyewitness sources, much of which I was not able to double-check. So this new edition attempts to correct mistakes I made, for example that of Pierre Méric's final rank in the Waffen-SS, which was Oberjunker. That was important to him, which makes it important to me.

Third, since the publication of *For Europe* by Helion Books there have been a veritable deluge of books on the same subject, some of which are not so good and some of which are excellent, bringing new information on the subject, but alas not to those who can only read English. So this new edition attempts to redress this situation.

Finally, leafing through my archive I had to chuckle to myself when I came across a letter from Raymond Mercier who questioned me on how I had somehow managed to sum up the actions of the LVF in the first winter in one sentence. Admittedly, it was longer than one sentence, but the point was made. So this new edition expands on the subject of the LVF. Raymond, this I have now corrected for you, albeit belatedly.

My thanks also go out to the following friends and family who have supported me through the last few difficult years: my stepmother Rhoda, my brother Sean, Bod who sometimes masquerades as Tim Dyson, Phil O'Grady, Mark Best and Matthew King, who has rescued me time and time again. Thank you again one and all for being there.

Anthony Joseph and Marcin Sasal also wished to be name-checked. There you go!

Please note that in previous editions of this work I employed pseudonyms extensively. Because most of their real names are now in the public domain I have updated my work accordingly, but I have retained some pseudonyms for those whose real names have not been disclosed. I still believe that is the correct thing to do for their families.

# Introduction

29 April 1945, Berlin[1]

A little before midday, in Saarlandstrasse I [Uscha. Malardier] fetched under fire a machine gun that its crew, granddads of the Volkssturm, who had abandoned it during a mad rush withdrawal, did not seem in any great hurry to go and collect. Thereupon, feeling like a hero, I volunteered to remain as the file closer in the course of a withdrawal along Friedrichstrasse. The majority of my section stayed with me.

My platoon, which withdrew thanks to a lull, was set on some moments later by two machine guns whose positions I located immediately. Without taking time to clear my throat, I yelled out at the top of my voice so as to be heard over the fracas around me: "MG *en batterie*! Fire at will at the two machine gun positions fifty metres in front of us". As in the majority of its interventions, the MG 42 did not have to spit out its 1300 rounds per minute; very quickly the enemy fire stopped, either our lads had hit the bull's eye or Ivan thought that it would be better to withdraw before the irresistible [MG] 42. I then gave the order to rejoin the platoon but spotting some twenty paces from us a group of Kalmouks emerging from a porch, as peacefully as if they were going for a walk, I took time to send them the *bonjour d'Alfred* in the form of a Sturmgewehr burst of continuous fire. I saw them fall, but, immediately, from the same embrasure other rogues who had spotted me started to fire in my direction. Then, so as not to remain blocked there, considering I had done what I had to, I decided to withdraw in turn, by going through the courtyard of the building and that of the next one where I expected to find comrades. Alas! They had left already and as soon as I ventured a peep into the road it was Ivan who learnt of me rather than ours [who] were not opposite any more... Thus, if I wanted to get out of this tight spot I had to beat a retreat through the back ways. However, before putting my plan into operation, I took several paces back inside the corridor to take cover as well as to observe methodically with binoculars the side of the road in my view, hoping anxiously to spot some friendly presence.

At that moment, a bit set back from the carriage entrance of a building next to that from where I had just been set on, I spotted Rostaing [his company commander] who, it seemed to me, was peacefully doing his exercises, slapping himself on the back and thighs. He was some metres from the enemy!

---

1    Malardier, letter to the author, 21/2/99, abridged.

Although I knew of his legendary qualities of coolness and imperturbability I could not help but be a little astounded for several moments. Then, very quickly, on seeing the white and ochre cloud forming around him, I simply understood that he was shaking off the rubble dust in which his uniform was covered. In fact, afterwards, he told me that he had just been hit by a falling balcony.

When the fire resumed from the corridor next to that where he was trying to give back human form to the 'fellow of plaster' who had emerged from the rubble of the debris, Rostaing immediately interrupted his exercises. I saw him slip along the wall so as to place himself as close as possible to the enemy corridor. From the shelter of the dead angle, he threw a grenade into the doorway and ran in, Sturmgewehr spitting continuous fire. As soon as he entered I crossed the road and rushed in behind him, yelling out his name so as to warn him that I was coming to the rescue.

At first sight the corridor was empty, perhaps Ivan had cleared off before the grenade explosion. But no! Near the door opening onto the courtyard, I spotted a small Kalmouk whose arms were full of bottles and I don't know what provisions, peacefully coming through the cellar door. Having spotted us, he opened his mouth in surprise, let go of his spoils, and in less time than one could say it, fled through the double door left open to the courtyard…

Then, from the far end of the courtyard, we heard voices; one could say a confab of at least ten Russians judging by the different tones of the voices. Therefore, to ward off a re-newed attack, I took the pin out of a grenade and, taking cover against the wall, I opened the door and threw the gadget… Then I sprayed the courtyard with some Sturmgewehr bursts. Unfortunately, as I discovered when I ventured a peep through the door, I had without doubt caused them more fright than real harm, having not thrown the grenade far enough, because they were taking off to the far end of the courtyard towards a way of withdrawal located beforehand—of which all good soldiers would make sure—where I saw them rush jostling each other, some hobbling, without a doubt hit in the legs by my fire.

I then looked for Rostaing and I spotted him on his knees in a corner of the corridor near the carriage entrance. Was he wounded? I approached him and discovered that he was bending over one of our comrades stretched out on the tiled floor in a pool of blood… Before this awful sight, the idea suddenly came to me that it was perhaps us who had struck him down and it was with relief that I heard him murmur: "Ah! It's you, lads, I was expecting you!" I immediately recognised our comrade. It was Rosfelder, a brave Alsatian *adjudant*, who had not wanted his late thirties to make him a 'Etapenschwein'. Despite this handicap of age, he had managed to come to Berlin with 'his' youngsters. Rostaing spoke to him in a voice that I did not know he had, a voice that was low, soft, tender, almost imploring: "Hold on, old brother, we'll get you out of here, we'll get you back." Rosfelder, alas, who had been hit in the stomach, continued to lose a lot of blood that we could not stop. And now we know that he is going to die in several moments. He opened his mouth several times as if he wanted to speak to us, but we heard no longer any words that he seemed to want to tell us, and which only made his lips tremble in a spasmodic movement. Bent over him, we finally deciphered some words that he managed to articulate: "Meine Frau! Meine Frau!" Rostaing took his hand and pressed it into his, and me, eyes full of tears, I caressed with my trembling fingers his bloodless brow, very sticky with sweat. I felt at that point his head lift in one last start of life. Rostaing, who could not feel this movement from Rosfelder, whose strength revealed all his hopelessness as well as the last willpower to push back death, nevertheless saw on our comrade's face the full horror of this fight, and he could not, no more than me already, hold back the tears, nor control the sobs that nervously shook his body of *dur à cuire* [a 'tough nut'].

Both of us, then, to show better that we were not going to abandon him, we bent a bit closer over the one who had betrayed *soldatenglück* [the luck of a soldier] of which he had often spoke when evoking his long military career.

We bent over almost touching his face, our gazes fastened on his whose intensity, that I had trouble seeing through my tears, grew from moment to moment and became so unbearable that I had to force myself not to look away.

Some seconds went by which seemed to us very long, then his head fell back and on his lips, suddenly still, we could no longer read his moving supplication of "Meine Frau! Meine Frau!" I wiped his face with the back of my hand and my blurred eyes believe they saw his mouth part as if he was going to be able to confide to us distinctly his last message for the one with whom he had shared his life.

Leaving the body of Rosfelder where it lay, Malardier and Rostaing went back to the fighting. The three of them were wearing the field-grey uniform of the Germany Army and collar insignia of the SS runes, but on their left sleeve was a *tricolore* shield. Yes, they were French. And they were volunteers serving with the Waffen-SS, the armed branch of the SS, which is not to be confused with the mainly political and bureaucratic Allgemeine-SS (General SS) or the SS-Tokenkopfverbände (SS Deaths Head Units) used to guard the concentration camps.[2]

This book is the story of the more than seven thousand Frenchmen like Rosfelder, Malardier, and Rostaing who served in the ranks of the Waffen-SS. Frenchmen of whom author Jean-François Deniau of the French Academy observed:

*Les dates d'engagement des Français qui ont choisi de servir dans la SS mèritent réflexion: très tard, en 1944, alors que l'Allemagne a déjà perdu évidemment la guerre. Quant aux âges des volontaires, dix-huit à vingt ans pour la plupart.*[3]

---

2    While Totenkopf troops were assimilated into the Waffen-SS as the nuclei of new units or as reinforcements for existing units, it must be noted that at no time did Frenchmen of the Waffen-SS ever serve in any concentration or extermination camp.
3    Deniau Jean-François, *Mémoires de 7 vies* (Paris: Plon, 1954).

# 1

## Defeat, Politics and the LVF

---

### Defeat and Armistice

In the summer of 1940, few would have expected the French Army, the 'greatest army in Europe', to be defeated by that of Germany, but it was and after only six weeks of blitzkrieg. It was a disaster. On 14th June 1940, the victorious German Army entered Paris, which had been proclaimed an open city days before. Christian de la Mazière, who would later serve with the French division of the Waffen-SS, said of the armies of Germany and France:[1]

> And Germany was triumphant. Wherever her armies went they were victorious. I must say that the German Army at that time made a great impression on young people. The sight of those German soldiers, stripped to the waist... Let me remind you, if I may, that I am the son of a soldier, I am a soldier myself, and I had in me a great sense of responsibility, of hierarchy, discipline. A disciplined army is very important for people like us. For the first time we saw an army which was all we had dreamed ours might be. The French Army was made up of rather sloppy recruits, not exactly the kind of soldier that puts fear into the heart of the mob. It is a terrible thing to say, but it must be said. It is the truth.

On 17th June 1940, President Lebrun called upon Marshal Pétain, the eighty-four-year-old hero of Verdun, to form a new government. He accepted.[2] Later that day he addressed the nation:

> Frenchmen, having been called upon by the President of the Republic, I today assume the leadership of the government of France. Certain of the affection of our admirable army that has fought with a heroism worthy of its long military traditions against an enemy that is superior in number and in weapons, certain that by its magnificent resistance it fulfilled its duties to its allies, certain of the support of veterans that I am

---

1     Ophuls Marcel, *The Sorrow and the Pity* (St. Albans: Paladin, 1975), pp.49-50.
2     On 12th July 1940, Pétain named himself Head of the State.

proud to have commanded, I give to France the gift of my person in order to alleviate her suffering.

In these painful hours, my thoughts go out to the unfortunate refugees who, in an extreme penury, are furrowing our roads. I express to them my compassion and my concern. It is with a heavy heart that I say to you today that the fighting must stop.

I spoke last night with the enemy and asked him if he is ready to seek with us, soldier to soldier, after the honorable fight, the means to put an end to the hostilities. May all Frenchmen rally to the government over which I preside during this difficult ordeal and calm their anxieties, so that they can better listen only to the faith they have in the destiny of the homeland.

Within less than a week of his broadcast, on 22 June, to limit the disaster of the defeat, Pétain had signed an armistice with Germany. Compared to the fate suffered by other conquered nations, Czechoslovakia and Poland, and even the likes of Holland and Belgium, the armistice terms imposed on France seemed almost moderate. France was divided into two, separated by a demarcation line. The French government would have complete sovereignty over the unoccupied zone, the so-called 'free' zone, which consisted of some two-fifths of the country and would also facilitate the administration of the occupied zone by the Germans. She was granted a Metropolitan army of one hundred thousand men. Moreover, her Navy and Empire remained intact and there was no mention of Alsace-Lorraine.[3]

The government installed itself at the town of Vichy in the unoccupied zone. Pétain enjoyed popular support from the French people. 'For the present, he was the father who would protect them from the worst'.[4] He was adored. The cult of Pétainism grew swiftly. His picture was everywhere to be seen. He spoke of a 'National Revolution', a political programme to remake a new France, and in contrast to the parliamentary chaos of the Third Republic, which was made responsible for the shameful defeat and the present ruin of France, he would build an authoritarian state. Against the former republic's values of Liberty, Equality, and Fraternity, he preached those of Work, Family and Country. To promote a new morality, he stressed discipline, order, and respect for authority.

Most members of the Vichy government adopted towards the Germans a policy of *attentisme*, 'wait and see'. Then, on 30 October 1940, days after meeting Hitler at Montoire and shaking hands, Pétain said on the radio:

It is in all honour and in order to maintain the unity of France, a unity of ten centuries within the framework of the constructive activity of the new European Order, that I am today pursuing the path of collaboration... This collaboration must be sincere... Until today I have spoken to you in the language of a father. Today I speak to you in the language of a leader. Follow me. Put your faith in France eternal.

---

3    Alsace-Lorraine was later annexed to the Reich. Also, *départements* Nord and Pas de Calais were placed under German military administration in Belgium.
4    Dank Milton, *The French Against the French* (London: Cassell, 1978), p.28.

For Pétain, collaboration signified joint arrangements between the occupiers and the occupied. It was a necessity to *éviter le pire*. Simply put, it was survival. He foresaw economic and administrative collaboration, which he said was inevitable, but not military collaboration.[5]

However, by early 1941, a number of nationalist political parties, some of which pre-dated the 39-40 war, had emerged in the occupied zone, based in Paris, which desired a closer union with Germany than that envisaged by Vichy. Sometimes described as the 'Ultras', they flayed Vichy for its continuing policy of *attentisme*.

Raymond Mercier, who would serve with *Légion des Volontaires Français contre le Bolchevisme*, said of the political climate of this time:

> In June 1940, we were all struck down, irrespective of political colour. The huge majority of French people followed the *Maréchal*. The activist minority (those who thought and who acted) were split into three strands: Vichy, London and Paris. But this was very schematic, because it was evident that the situation wasn't seen in the same way if you lived in Paris or Nice.

## Party politics

Of all the Paris-based collaborationist parties, the *Parti Populaire Français* [French Popular Party] was, by far, the largest and the most important. Its leader was Jacques Doriot, born on 26 September 1898 in Bresles, near Beauvais. In 1915, at the age of seventeen, he left home. Thereafter the working-class area of Saint-Denis in Paris became his home and, in time, the seat of his political triumph.

Doriot started political life as a socialist, joining the *Jeunesses Socialistes de France* [Socialist Youth of France] in 1916, but four years later he became a 'convert' to Communism. A superb orator, he enjoyed a spectacular rise through the French Communist Party (PCF). By 1924, he was at the head of the *Jeunesses communistes* [Communist Youth] and a member of the Central committee of the party, but he was also in prison at la Santé, Paris, for antimilitarist activities. His release came in May 1924 when he was elected to parliament after a most brilliant election campaign.

1929 saw Doriot first break with Communist doctrine and discipline. In favour of co-operation with the Socialists on the common problems of the rights of workers, he found himself shunned by the 'top brass'.[6] He withdrew from the leadership. Nevertheless, he was re-elected to the Chamber of Deputies as a Communist and, in 1931, became the Mayor of Saint-Denis.

In February 1934, the party sent its militants into the streets to fight alongside Rightist organisations against the government. One reason for this call to action was 'a desire to exhibit a display of force against what was called the 'Social-Fascism' of the Socialist Party'.[7] But Doriot still saw the Socialists as allies in the war against Fascism. He was vocal. By June 1934, the party

---

5    Of note is that some historians (for example see E. Jackel, *Frankreich in Hitler's Europe*; A. Milward, *The New Order and the French Economy*; R.O. Paxton, *Vichy France: Old Guard and New Guard, 1940-1944*) have concluded that it was first and foremost the French and not the Germans who wanted to collaborate.
6    Dank, *The French against the French*, p.49.
7    Ibid.

could no longer tolerate his heresies and expelled him for indiscipline. And yet, one month later, the party adopted the policies of Doriot by signing an agreement on 'unity of action' with the Socialists. He was bitter. And so began his march to personal power. He became a most virulent anti-Communist.

On 22 June 1936, some two years after his expulsion from the PCF, Doriot officially created the *Parti Populaire Français* (PPF). His platform for the new political party was Socialistic, nationalistic, and peculiarly French. Strangely enough, his power base was the Communists of Saint-Denis, most of who were disaffected with the party because of its rigid discipline. Also, unemployment was rife.

The PPF proved a great success and, by 1937, had an estimated 200,000 supporters, many of whom had followed Doriot from the path of Communism. With Doriot at the helm, the party continued to drift to 'international Fascism'. His hold over the party was absolute.

In 1938, to 'save the peace', the PPF decided to support Hitler's demand on Czechoslovakia. For the nationalists in its ranks, this decision was the final straw. Resignations tore apart the party. In this way, the PPF all but disappeared as a political force of the Right.

At the start of hostilities Doriot was posted to the *24e Régiment Régional de Garde* at Senalis with the rank of *sergent-chef*. He would be cited at the *ordre de l'Armée* and be awarded the *Croix de guerre avec étoile de vermeil*.

Recruitment poster for JPF.
(Author's collection)

The overwhelming defeat and occupation of 1940 brought unexpected prosperity to Doriot, even if Vichy held him 'at arm's length' and German support was slow in coming. Restricted to the Occupied zone, the PPF did operate in the Unoccupied zone under the title of *Mouvement Populaire Français* (MPF). According to the police, at the start of 1941, the PPF counted 4000 members in the Occupied zone, of which 2700 were Paris-based. The PPF was only allowed to operate in the Occupied zone with 'authorised status' from 28 December 1941, by which time Doriot was in German uniform.

The PPF counted a number of youth movements: the most important was the *Union populaire de la Jeunesse française* (UPJF). In May 1942 the UPJF joined forces with eight smaller youth organisations to form the *Jeunesses Populaires Françaises* (JPF) under the presidency of 'Vauquelin' [real name des Yvetots]. The JPF was against communism, capitalism, Jews, described as 'the direct causes of the degeneracy of our people' and 'instruments of propagation of capitalism', Freemasons as well as those responsible for the disastrous war. With a rallying cry of *Tenue, Force, Audace*, the JPF wanted to rebuild France and 'fight on the same front as the German youth, against Bolshevism, the common enemy...'[8]

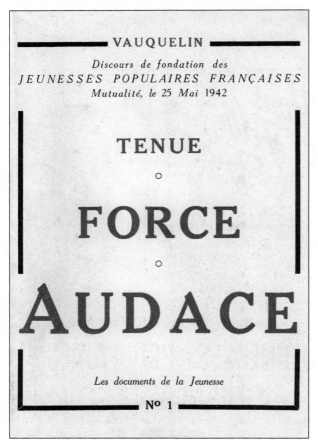

Booklet *Tenue, Force, Audace*. (Author's collection)

8    Vauquelin, *Discours de fondation des J.P.F.* (Les documents de la Jeunesse, 1942)

The PPF's biggest rival was the *Rassemblement National Populaire* [National Popular Rally] or RNP. Established by Marcel Déat on 1 February 1941, the RNP brought together former Socialists and trade unionists with former combatants of the *Union Nationale des Combattants* (UNC), as well as members of Deloncle's *Mouvement Social Révolutionnaire* (MSR). Although most of the executive members of the RNP were of leftist persuasion, the new movement actually promoted a National Socialist programme. For them, socialism was essentially anti-Marxist.

As for Marcel Déat himself, he began political life as a socialist. The First World War, in which he distinguished himself, leaving as a *simple soldat* and returning as a *capitaine* with *la Légion d'honneur* and five citations, also made him a pacifist. In the post war years, he went into teaching. He became the president of the *Fédération des étudiants socialistes* [Federation of the socialist students]. 1926 saw him stand as a candidate of the socialist *Section Française de l'Internationale Ouvrière* [French section of the Workers' International] and enjoy electoral success.

In 1933, Déat called for a revision of Marxism that he labeled Neo-Socialism. To defeat fascism, he argued that the SFIO had to abandon all talk of class struggle and win middle-class support. Also he no longer advocated parliamentary democracy as a means of bringing about socialism, but dictatorship. This, of course, was heresy to the vast majority of members of the SFIO. He was expelled. A number of like-minded 'neo-socialists' left with him to form their own party, the *Parti socialiste de France*. Déat became its *secrétaire général*. He was still anti-Fascist.

From January to June 1936, Déat held office as a cabinet minister, but the 1936 elections and the parliamentary failure of the '*néos*' and his own personal failure before a Communist marked the start of his shift toward the right. In 1939, he got himself elected *député* for Angoulême on a ticket that called itself the 'Anti-Communist Rally'. And yet his famous editorial *mourir pour Dantzig* of 4th May 1939, which argued to plunge Europe into war because of Danzig 'was going a bit too far', placed him in the ranks of the 'Pacifists'.

Then war came and defeat. Déat now emerged as an enthusiastic supporter of Hitler, National Socialism and collaboration. He was sincere, but ambitious. He believed in the 'revolutionary mission of Germany' and his programme advocated the rebuilding of a France integrated in the 'new Europe'. In this way, France would restore its greatness and legitimate influence. He argued that 'the material necessity compelled Collaboration'. However, during the late summer months of 1940, he failed in his efforts to convince Marshal Pétain to establish a *grande parti unique* [large single party] as a means of integrating France into Hitler's 'new European Order'. His hopes disappointed, he went off with his typewriter to Paris from where he sniped at the Vichy regime in his editorials. Months later, for want of this *grande parti unique*, he formed his own, the *Rassemblement National Populaire*.

The *Mouvement Social Révolutionnaire* was founded on 1st September 1940 by Eugène Deloncle, a decorated World War One veteran and former head of the *Comité Secret d'Action Révolutionnaire* (CSAR), a right wing group which was violently opposed to the Popular Front government, made up of an alliance of left-wing groups. Arrested and imprisoned, Deloncle was eventually released without charge. The MSR 'wanted to build a New Europe in cooperation with national socialist Germany and all the other European nations liberated like them from liberal capitalism, Judaism, Bolshevism and Freemasonary...' Slow to organise, the MSR attracted a number of former militants of the CSAR. Its membership peaked in 1941 at one thousand four hundred members.

The RNP had its own militia, the *Milices Nationales-Populaires* (MNP), for the purposes of security and propaganda, but when the MSR amalgamated with the RNP it brought with it its own militia, the uniformed *Légion nationale populaire* (LNP), which became the 'shock troops' of the movement. By June 1941, the RNP claimed that the LNP had six brigades in Paris, with a total number of 10,000 militants throughout France. However, the real number was considerably smaller, perhaps no more than 800. A red tie was worn, which, according to Déat, was a 'souvenir of Socialism'.

JNP emblem.
(Author's collection)

Like the PPF, the RNP had a youth branch which was called the *Jeunesses Nationale Populaires* (JNP). Membership peaked at 2500 and was predominantly Paris-based.

In the autumn of 1941, the internal conflict between Déat and Deloncle, who wanted to take control of the RNP, came to a head. Déat removed Deloncle. In this way, the RNP lost much of the right-wing support and militancy Deloncle had brought to it. In 1942, Déat tried once more to form a single party, the *Front Révolutionnaire National* (FRN). The refusal of Doriot to integrate the PPF was a blow to the success of the FRN.

Although he enjoyed little support from the Germans Déat continued to call for greater collaboration with Germany. Indeed, according to one commentator:[9] 'He would serve them [the Germans]. He would give them his soul.'

Membership of the RNP as a whole is difficult to estimate but is generally believed to have been between 20,000 and 25,000.

The oldest party was the *Parti Franciste,* which was founded on 29 September 1933. The party leader was Marcel Bucard. Born in 1895, he was a highly decorated World War One veteran who was cited ten times, and also a holder of the *Croix de guerre* and *Légion d'Honneur*. He finished the war as a *capitaine* aged only twenty-two and remained haunted by the *esprit du front*.

The trappings and ideology of the *Parti Franciste* was modelled upon Italian Fascism rather than German Nazism. The party manifesto of 1933 ended with these words: 'Let's be clear: our Francisme is to France what Fascism is to Italy. We are not displeased to state it!' The *Parti Franciste* dreamed of a *deuxième révolution française* where 'order would eventually prevail over

9    Delperrié de Bayac Jacques, *Histoire de la Milice* (Paris: Fayard, 1969), p.59.

liberty, the national *corps* and the hierarchic society over individualism, the totalitarian State over all the forces of dissolution'.

Like other political parties of the right, the *Parti Franciste* had a youth branch, which was called the *Jeunesse Franciste*. Its party militia was known first as the *Corps Franc*, which was renamed in 1943 as the *Légion Franciste*. The party also adopted a blue shirt whose shade was the lightest of all.

Bucard's military background, as well as his incendiary speeches captivated his adherents. His hold over them was total. Originally destined for the priesthood, his Catholic background had undoubtedly appealed to those of a more religious disposition. Indeed some *cérémonies francistes* were adorned with Catholic pomp. Bucard's personal bodyguard, termed the *Main Bleue* (Blue Hand), was made 'responsible for keeping agitators at a good distance'.

In June 1936, the party was banned and its membership subsequently dwindled away. Bucard was mobilized in 1939 and fought bravely, leading his men into Switzerland to avoid capture. Many of his former Francistes died for France, dispelling the myth that his party was some sort of fifth column. He returned to France in December 1940 and relaunched his party months later. Membership of the party peaked at 7000. The Germans 'authorized' the party in May 1941.

Bucard was a supporter of the National Revolution and the Maréchal. He was violently anti-Marxist and at the time of the German-Soviet Pact, anti-German, but the German invasion of the Soviet Union in June 1941 changed everything.

There were a myriad of other political parties, which were all on the right of the political spectrum and favoured collaboration.

Headed by Pierre Costantini, a highly decorated World War One pilot, the *Ligue Française* or to give it its full name *Ligue Française d'epuration, d'entraide sociale et de collaboration européenne* was founded in September 1940. 'For Costantini, capitalism and Marxism were fruits from the same tree: Judaism, whose allies were the freemasons and the English'.[10] He regarded the English attack at Mers-el-Kébir as a war crime and declared war on England. Following the German attack on the Soviet Union, he changed the name of the party to the *Ligue Française antibritannique et antibolchevique*. The youth branch of the *Ligue Française* was the *La Ligue des Jeunes de France et de l'Empire*, which failed to attract many adherents. In fact, the *Ligue* had few adherents, perhaps somewhere between 2,000 and 3,000 in October 1941.

One of the smallest and most extreme parties was the *Front Franc*, which was violently anti-Semitic and pro-German. It was founded in Sepember 1936 by Jean Boissel, a highly decorated and severely disabled World War One veteran. Arrested in 1939 as a suspected member of the fifth column, he was released during the summer of 1940. His party numbered only several hundred adherents. Jean-Jacques Boissel, the party leader's second son, volunteered for the NSKK in October 1942. He had just turned eighteen.

Just as extreme was the *Parti Français National Collectiviste* (PFNC) which was first known as the *Parti Français National Communiste*. The party leader was Corsican Pierre Clémenti. The party was violently anti-Semetic and Clémenti ended up in prison for 92 days in 1939 for racial

10    Lambert  Pierre P. and Le Marec Gérard, *Partis et mouvements de la collaboration, Paris 1940-1944* (Paris: Jacques Grancher, 1993), pp.119-120.

defamation. It too had a youth branch, the *Jeune Front*. Membership never exceeded more than a couple of hundred.

The last was *Le Feu*, which was launched in January 1941. Initially cloaked in mystery, the party was the brainchild of Maurice Delaunay, a former deputy of Calvados. On 10 July 1940, he was at Vichy and voted to give full power to Maréchal Pétain. Membership figures are not known.

There was also the influential *Groupe Collaboration*, which was not a political party as such, but an instrument of propaganda. Founded by Alphonse de Châteaubriant on 24 September 1940, it differed from the likes of the RNP and the PPF in so much as its aims were principally cultural and intellectual rather than political. European in outlook, with a strong spiritual ethos, this organisation 'supported the moral regeneration which the National Revolution was to bring to a Europeanised France'.[11]

In its support for an alliance between France and Germany, the *Groupe Collaboration* arranged lectures, screened German films, promoted German literature, and organised public discussions and other social events. Authorised to function in the 'Unoccupied' zone on 29 December 1941, its middle class and wealthy membership may have peaked at the significant total of 100,000 by mid-1943. Its popularity some commentators have ascribed to its theoretical non-political aspect.

Less reserved in its pro-German attitude was its youth branch *Les Jeunes de L'Europe nouvelle* [The Youth of The New Europe] founded in May 1941 and authorized by the Germans on 20 November 1941. The president of the JEN was writer Marc Augier, who had started political life on the left. He wrote under the pen name of Saint-Loup. The *national chef* was Jacques Schweizer, a barrister and pre-war militant of the *Jeunesse patriote* [Patriot Youth].[12] When Augier left to join the LVF Schweizer succeeded him. The JEN operated in both zones. Lyon became a stronghold of the JEN. Starting from July 1942, the JEN published an exclusive bulletin for its militants. The garcons wore a marine blue shirt, while the girls wore a white blouse and marine blue skirt. Its insignia was the life rune.

In June 1942, the JEN decided to conduct a 'vast campaign of propaganda' throughout France. The result was a resounding success and, according to Schweizer, not quite what they expected. Even so, membership peaked at a little over 1500. On the 7 and 8 November 1942, the JEN held a congress in Paris, which 150 delegates from both zones attended. On 14 December 1942, the second anniversary of the return of the ashes of Napoleon II, the JEN hosted a vigil at Les Invalides to celebrate the lifes of Emperor Napoleon and his son and to thank the generous Führer for finally reuniting them. The vigil was attended by representatives from all the youth movements, JNP, JPF, JF and LF.

The JEN also attempted to recruit young Frenchmen serving in the NSKK of the Luftwaffe, those working in Germany and prisoners of war. In this way, the JEN created a section within the NSKK and sections in the POW camps, like Stalag VIII C which published a review called *Sous l'étendard de l'Europe*. Later the JEN actively recruited for the Waffen-SS and some of the NSKK section passed to the Waffen-SS. As the civil war gripped hold of France tighter and

11    Kingston, *Collaboration in France* (Oxford: Berg, 1989) p.67, edited by Hirschfeld Gerhard & Marsh Patrick.
12    François Mitterrand, the former president of France, was also a member of the *Jeunesses Patriotes*.

tighter, JEN militants hardened their position. Indeed, some sections were even attached to the SD and armed for active duty against the resistance.

Each of the political parties had its own newspaper or periodical. In the Occupied Zone the PPF published the daily newspaper *Le Cri du peuple de Paris* or more simply *Le Cri du peuple*. In July 1941, its circulation was between 20,000 and 25,000. In the Free Zone the PPF continued to publish the pre-war *L'Émancipation nationale*. Another daily, *Le Petit Parisien*, whose circulation was 680,000 in November 1940, supported Doriot. Some issues even hit an impressive 900,000. Déat wrote for the daily newspaper *L'Oeuvre*. The *Parti Franciste* published *Le Franciste*. Weekly newspaper *La Gerbe*, founded by Alphonse de Châteaubriant in July 1940 and whose chief editor was Marc Augier, regularly sold 100,000 copies. *La Gerbe* was closely associated with the *Groupe Collaboration*.

The collaborationist parties were political rivals, constantly at war among themselves for political advantage. They were tolerated by the occupying power and, when it suited, supported.[13] They never represented a serious threat to Vichy.[14]

### *Légion des Volontaires Français contre le bolchevisme* (LVF)

On Sunday 22 June 1941, Nazi Germany invaded the Soviet Union. The French collaborationist parties greeted the unheralded invasion with great excitement. That same day, Doriot, the *chef* of the PPF who was attending the first PPF congress of the Free zone in Lyon, said: "France cannot simply be a spectator in the decisive battle which has begun and whose issue will determine the fate of the entire continent." He proposed the creation of a *Légion antibolchevique française* to 'participate by the side of the soldiers of Europe in the decisive battle against Bolshevism'. Full of enthusiasm, he went to the Vichy Government and the Germans for approval.

A similar idea of a *Légion de l'Europe unie* came to Déat and Deloncle, *chefs* of the RNP and the MSR respectively, who were furious that Doriot had stolen a march on them. They too sought approval from the Vichy government and the Germans. Deloncle wrote to the *Maréchal* while Déat contacted Otto Abetz, the German Ambassador in Paris, who also received an offer from Russian émigrés who wished to organize their own legion in the war against Bolshevism.

Otto Abetz, who supported the creation of a legion of French volunteers, immediately contacted his superiors in Berlin for a decision.

Doriot continued to champion the idea of French volunteers participating in the European crusade against Bolshevism. At a PPF meeting in Nice on 28th June 1941 he argued:[15]

13  It is interesting to note that 'German individuals or agencies supporting French collaborationist interests were often working for the promotion of their own careers or political importance' (Kingston, *Collaboration in France*, p.54).
14  It was the Germans who kept the Vichy regime 'in power'. Arguably, Germany, which desired economic rather than political collaboration from France, had more 'need' of the Vichy regime than the collaborationist parties. Through Vichy and its civil servants, the French economy worked to support the German war effort. Indeed, by the autumn of 1943, France had become the most important supplier of raw materials, foodstuffs and manufactured goods to Germany. Moreover, for the first two years of the Occupation, Vichy, through the Police, had kept order in France. Also, the Germans remained suspicious of the nationalist sentiment of some collaborationist parties.
15  *Une etude des renseignments généraux sur la LVF* of 12 January 1942, AN F60 235.

The war against communism cannot leave us indifferent. Although our country cannot intervene officially in this struggle, we demand the right for volunteers to fight at the side of the Spanish, Finnish, and Romanians.

That same day, more importantly, Doriot publicly announced at Marseille that he would participate in this war against communism, but he only wanted grassroots activists to follow him. The cadres of his party should remain in France to continue the 'essential political fight'.[16]

The response from the Vichy government was cautious, stating in an official communiqué of 1 July that no objection would be raised to Frenchmen who enlisted 'to participate in the European struggle against Communism'. And, days later, Vichy suspended the law that prohibited French citizens to serve outside the French Army. Thus the creation of a legion would remain a purely 'private' affair, but Vichy did prevent NCOs and officers of the Armstice Army from joining up. Thus, the only cadres that could be recruited were reservists.

Unbeknown to the political parties, Secretary of State Jacques Benoist-Méchin, with the approval of Admiral Darlan, the Vice-President of the Council, and even that of the Marshal, proposed to German Ambassador Otto Abetz the raising of a legion destined to fight in the East. This proposal was politely rejected.

On 5 July 1941, Otto Abetz received a telegram from Ambassador Ritter stating that the Reich agreed 'to enlist French nationals as volunteers in the struggle against the Soviet Union', but not White Russians. And yet Hitler had showed little enthusiasm when the idea of a French legion first came before him. He had no need of such 'foreign brothers', expecting a quick victory over the Soviet Union. Moreover, since June 1940, he held a very poor opinion of the fighting quality of the French soldier. Nevertheless, he was finally won round by the propaganda benefits to be gained from having a French contingent in the united European crusade against Bolshevism and finally gave his approval on 1 July. However, he did set two conditions: the legion must remain a 'private' initiative of the political parties of the Occupied Zone, independent of the Vichy government; and enlistment would be restricted to no more than 10,000, which was later upped to a maximum of 15,000. In this way, the Vichy government could not demand anything in return for its support and the French contribution would remain strictly symbolic.

On 6 July, Otto Abetz met with party leaders Bucard, Costantini, Déat, and Doriot at the German Embassy on rue de Lille in Paris and told them that Hitler had agreed to the principle of a legion of French volunteers.[17] That evening Doriot held a meeting with his supporters at a packed Salle Wagram.

On 7 July, the same four party leaders as well as Boissel and Clémenti met with representatives of the German military at the Majestic Hotel in Paris to discuss the practical issues. Also present at this meeting were embassy official Westrick, who represented Otto Abetz, and Eugène Deloncle, who was accompanied by his friend *Général de division* Hassler in the capacity as 'technical advisor'. Deloncle wanted Hassler to command the legion. Curiously, the decisions reached at this meeting were more political than military, spawning a *comité commun* on which all the party leaders present at the meeting sat, which quickly became titled the *comité central*, with Deloncle as president.

16   Lefèvre Eric and Jean Mabire, *Par-40° devant Moscou Les Français de la L.V.F. 1941* (Paris: Grancher, 2004), p.9.
17   Lefèvre Eric and Jean Mabire, *La LVF 1941: Par-40° devant Moscou* (Fayard, 1985), p.67.

That same day, Otto Abetz held a press conference to support the official communiqué signed by Boissel, Bucard, Clémenti, Costantini, Déat, and Doriot, which appeared in the press and was aired on the radio:

*Avec l'assentiment de M. le maréchal Pétain, chef de l'État français, et l'acquiescement du Führer, les mouvements français soussignés ont décidé, en plein accord, de participer à la croisade contre le bolchevisme. Ils constituent immédiatement une 'légion de volontaires français' pour représenter la France sur le front russe et y prendre part en son nom au combat pour la défense de la civilisation européenne. Les engagements sont acceptés aux sièges et dans toutes les permanences des groupements soussignés, ainsi qu'au bureau central 12, rue Auber (IX).*

Chosen by Otto Abetz to serve as the *bureau central* of the LVF, the address on rue Auber in Paris once belonged to the Soviet travel agency Intourist. Volunteers could also sign up at the offices of the political parties. To enlist, they had to prove first and foremost that they were French, of Aryan origin, had completed their military service and were without a criminal conviction (as defined by Article 6 of the Statutes of the LVF). However, foreigners who had served in either the French Foreign Legion or units of the French Army could exceptionally join the legion.

Volunteers also had to meet a number of other requirements. They had to be between the ages of 18 and 45, although the age limit for officers was 50.[18] They had to be at least one metre sixty tall. They had to be of good health, with normal vision in at least one eye, no pre-existing problems with hernias or varicose veins, and no more than two missing or decayed teeth. They were also required to undergo a medical to confirm if they met the requirements or not, although notable exceptions were later made for the more politically inclined who were outside the age range.

The Germans also insisted that there was no place for POWs in the Legion of French volunteers.

The communiqué regarding the *légion de volontaires français*, which was soon renamed the *Légion des Volontaires Français contre le Bolchevisme* or more simply LVF, was repeated the following day. The PPF newspaper *Le Cri du people* carried an editorial from Doriot, in which he now argued:

In helping to crush Bolshevism, the *légion de volontaires français* gives France the opportunity to resume her place as a major European power. The soldiers who depart are on the threshold of a struggle for the rebirth of our country.

The newspaper also urged its readers to join the legion in a 'crusade against Bolshevism' to defend European civilization. Newspaper *L'Oeuvre* announced that Alsatian General Hassler would assume command of the LVF, which came as a total surprise to him; he would claim later that he had not been approached beforehand even though he had spent the previous day

18    Lefèvre and Mabire, *La LVF 1941: Par-40° devant Moscou*, p.94. According to Giolitto Pierre, *Volontaires français sous l'uniforme allemand* (Paris: Perrin, 1999), officers were to be no older than 40.

in the presence of his friend Deloncle at Hotel Majestic. Anyway, Hassler bluntly refused the command and left Paris that evening.

Hassler explained his reasons for refusal in a letter he wrote to the cabinet of Marshal Pétain dated 26th July. Firstly, he had become concerned that the LVF was not a 'national movement authorized and encouraged by Vichy', but rather the 'desire of several political groups'. Secondly, as a reserve officer, he was still at the disposal of the Vichy government's Ministry for War and, as such, could not accept a military command without its formal authority. Thirdly, there was no question of taking a command side by side with the Germans while the odious demarcation line existed and while officers and soldiers of his division remained in captivity. He finished his letter with the statement: 'My name is not de Gaulle! I have only one leader, the Marshal, and one flag, the tricolore flag!'

In contrast to Hassler, various influential religious and intellectural figures came out in support of the LVF. Cardinal Baudrillart, the Rector of the Institut Catholique de Paris, had rejoiced at the news of the creation of a legion of volunteers to fight the Bolshevik virus. He wrote in his notebook on 8 July 1941: 'It's now about crusades against the Soviets'. He readily agreed to become a patron of the LVF at the end of November 1941, joining *Le Comité d'honneur de la LVF*.[19] His support for the LVF and its Legionnaires was unwavering and very flattering. Indeed, in an interview he gave to Maurice-Ivan Sicard, who ran the press office of the PPF, he declared:[20]

It's not only the military honour of France that the Legion defends. Don't forget that the volunteers also help to maintain the spiritual power of France, and that, fighting for their family and their homeland, they are fighting at the same time for the Christain civilization of the West, long threatened by Communist barbarism.

The Cardinal continued:

Both as a priest and a Frenchman, I would dare say that these legionnaires rank among the best sons of France… In truth, this Legion constitutes in its own way a new chivalry. These legionnaires are twentieth-century crusaders. May their weapons be blessed! Christ's tomb will be delivered!

Meanwhile, more recruitment offices opened in the Occupied Zone. On 9 July, Deloncle had sixty opened in Jewish-owned shops that the LNP had occupied. Soon there would be over three hundred and twenty recruitment offices, of which two-thirds were located in the Parisian region. The following day, the first one was opened in the Free Zone in Marseille. The central bureau and LVF recruitment offices quickly became the targets of vandalism.[21] Protection was forthcoming from the political parties as well as the police, which some people misinterpreted as proof that the LVF was official and not just a private initative.

19  Baudrillat topped the list of patrons of the LVF published in *Le Matin* of 4 December 1941.
20  *Le Cri du Peuple* of 4 December 1941 and repeated in *L'Émancipation nationale* of 14 December 1941.
21  Between 8 and 20 July thirteen LVF recruitment offices were attacked. See Mabire and Lefèvre, *La LVF: Par-40° devant Moscou*, p.89.

On 11 July, the mass meeting planned by the political parties at the Vélodrome d'Hiver, a large glass-roofed sports stadium on rue Nélaton in Paris, was pushed back to the 18 at the request of the German military authorities.

By the 14th the press was already discussing the possibility of creating an armoured division! On 16 July, *L'Oeuvre* announced that over 10,000 volunteers had already come forward and that 'the French volunteers, dressed in French uniform, will fight with French arms under the colours of France'. The figure of 10,000 was clearly an exaggeration, though.

Again on 17 July, the Paris press confirmed that the 'units of volunteers will be dressed in French uniform'. Also, on that same day, newspaper *Paris-Soir* published the statutes of the new Legion.

On 18 July, the mass meeting of militants planned by the political parties at Vélodrome d'Hiver went ahead. It was the first such meeting in Paris. Estimates of the audience vary from 8,000 to 15,000, of which one-quarter were women. Some militants, including the nineteen-year-old Raymond Mercier of the RNP, were already wearing a homemade tricolore armband with the letters LVF.[22]

The militants heard their leaders speak in turn: Boissel, Clémenti, Costantini, Déat, Doriot and lastly Deloncle. Clémenti's speech was poorly received. Costantini announced that he would enlist in the 'Air Force of the Legion'. Déat applauded both the Maréchal and Hitler for agreeing to the formation of the Legion. Doriot proclaimed France's determination to recover the glory of French arms in Russia after Napoleon's disaster and swore to accompany the first volunteers into combat.[23]

Deloncle announced the formation of an LVF division consisting of a regiment of heavy and one of light tanks, a motorised artillery regiment and a squadron of aircraft. He concluded: "Europe is on the march, nothing will stop it!"

Bucard did not attend the mass meeting at the Vélodrome d'Hiver, Paris. On 9 July, he 'informed the people of France that he would not participate' in the reunion. On 21 July, party newspaper *Le Franciste* described the reunion as an 'internal political manoeuvre'. Publicly, the party continued to give its full consent and support to the 'anti-Soviet crusade', whereas, privately, Bucard and his party lieutenants advised against enlistment. Nevertheless, a handful of *francistes* would serve in the ranks of the LVF.[24]

The volunteers were promised again and again by the likes of Déat that they would fight in French uniform. On 22 July, the *comité central* reiterated this scenario and also clarified that only volunteers who had completed their military service would be accepted as combatants, while those aged between 18 and 21 would be recruited into the support services (drivers, grooms, secretaries...).

On 23 July, the central committee released to the press that volunteers would receive the same benefits as other foreign volunteers 'participating in the war against the USSR'.

The question of the release of a French prisoner for each volunteer that stepped forward remained very dear to the *comité central*, but it could not exact a definitive answer out of the Germans.

22    Raymond Mercier was born on 30 December 1921 in Paris.
23    For more details of this meeting and the content of the speeches see *Une etude des renseignments généraux sur la LVF* of 12 January 1942, AN F60 235.
24    See Deniel Alain, *Bucard et le Francisme* (Paris: Jean Picollec, 1979), pp.189-190.

On 24 July, the *comité directeur* of the RNP, including both Déat and Deloncle, announced that it would enlist en bloc in the LVF. This decision provoked an influx of volunteers from the LNP. Even so some claim that Déat and Deloncle ordered six hundred of their militants to enlist or be kicked out of the party. Not to be outmaneuvered, Doriot repeated at a PPF meeting in Bordeaux that he had decided to leave with the first volunteers.[25]

Two days later on 26 July, the first recruitment posters produced by the central committee of the LVF appeared on the walls of Paris, which proclaimed:

> If you want your country to resume its place in the world
> If you want to defend Western civilization
> If you want to participate in the construction of a humain and just European order
> Fight Bolshevism with us under the French flag
> Enlist in the *Légion des Volontaires Français contre le Bolchevisme*

The Germans turned over *caserne* [barracks] Borgnis-Desbordes at 16 avenue de Paris, Versailles, for the use of the LVF as its 'central depot', which was relocated in December to Quartier de la Reine, rue Carnot, Versailles.

On 4 August, a *sous-comité* was formed in Marseille to conduct propaganda and recruitment in the Free Zone through the Paris central commitee. Simon Sabiani, the leader of the local PPF and arguably one of Doriot's most loyal supporters, was appointed the *secrétaire général*. This *sous-comité* proved very active and even managed to open a recruitment office in Alger.

On 11 August, Vichy Ambassador Fernand de Brinon, wrote to Admiral Darlan, Vichy's Foreign Minister, to determine the government's attitude to the LVF.

On 17 August, Berlin ordered the legion to be formed without further delay and Otto Abetz was tasked with organizing the matter with the military authorities.

On 20 August 1941, the press announced that the sixty-year-old Colonel Labonne would now assume command of the LVF. A product of Saint-Cyr, he served with *tirailleurs sénégalais* in Sudan, Senegal and Morocco. In 1918, he commanded the 1st Battalion of the prestigious *régiment d'infanterie coloniale du Maroc* on the Western Front. In the pre-war years, he held a number of desk jobs, retiring as the military attaché in Turkey. In the 'shooting war', he commanded the *18e régiment de tirailleurs sénégalais* in Tunisia, after which he was demobilized and repatriated.

Some have claimed Colonel Labonne had little field experience as a commander. This is unfair. If anything, he was a little 'rusty'. He was an intellectual and a distinguished military historian of the Napoleonic period.

On 21 August 1941, the creators of the LVF learnt from the mouth of the German ambassador that the volunteers would have to wear the German uniform, in accordance with the Hague conventions. They decided to keep this news quiet.

On that same day, Admiral Darlan anwered the letter of 11 August sent by de Brinon. He clarified that the government was favourable to the creation of a legion of French volunteers and foresaw some political advantages that could be gained from it. Nevertheless, he declared that Vichy was unable to do more than just comment favourably on the LVF 'unless the government

25    *Une etude des renseignements généraux sur la LVF* of 12th January 1942, AN F60 235.

and the High Command of Germany inform us officially, and in advance, of their desire to see France represented among the forces fighting Bolshevism…' The collaborationist parties reacted angrily. Déat wrote in *L'Oeuvre*: '*Il faut que Vichy sorte de son attentisme*' [Vichy must get out of its *attentisme*].

On 26 August 1941, in Berlin, Colonel Labonne met Generaloberst Fromm, the commander of the German Reserve Army. Two days later, at Spala, he saw General der Kavallerie Kurt von Gienanth, the military governor of the General-Government.[26]

Meanwhile, on 25 August, the press finally announced that volunteers were to report to *caserne* Borgnis-Desbordes in Paris. Four *appels* [call-ups] were planned. The first, which included all officers, was planned for 27 August. The second was planned for 31 August.

The first volunteers from the Free Zone crossed the demarcation line on 26 August and were 'severely controlled by the French authorities'.[27]

On 27 August, the scene which greeted the new arrivals at *caserne* Borgnis-Desbordes was one of chaos. According to an official report, 'the organizers seemed to lack direction and initative'. It did not matter, though, for this was a new beginning. Each volunteer was allocated a registration number.

At the end of the afternoon a ceremony was held with great pomp. Present were leading German and French dignitaries, including Ambassador Fernand de Brinon and Laval, as well as party leaders Déat, Clémenti, Costantini and Deloncle, who wore the 'uniform' of the LNP. Doriot was absent, although he sent two representatives instead. A French flag was raised as the *Marseillaise* was sung. Unexpectedly, the Germans invited the French dignitaries to inspect the barracks, which did not last long, after which they left. Raymond Mercier was present and recalls:[28]

> Notably, the atmosphere was one of celebration. For us, or at least for me, this magnificent day seemed to be the start of a new era. I was behind a volunteer dressed as a postman and wearing the Military Medal. We matched the dignitaries pass and Ambassador de Brinon stopped to compliment the Military Medal. It was then that we heard shots.

To explain, as the dignitaries entered the gateway out onto avenue de Paris a man fired five times at point-blank range. Laval and Déat were hit but lived. The would-be assassin was, in fact, a volunteer of the LVF. Disgusted by the actions of the collaborationists, he had joined the LVF with the express intention of killing a prominent collaborator in an attempt to rouse the French from their apathy.[29]

26    According to Saint-Loup, *Les Volontaires* (Paris: Presses de la Cité, 1963), p.24, on 28 August 1941, in Breslau, Colonel Labonne met with General der Infanterie Halm, commanding the VIII. Armeekorps. This is repeated by Bene, but not confirmed by any other source.

27    Lefèvre & Mabire, *Par -40 devant Moscou*, p.24.

28    Mercier, letter to the author, 23/1/2002.

29    The assassin was called Paul Colette. However, Laval himself saved Colette from the death sentence. He did not wish to make a martyr of him. In the early 90s, Colette was decorated with the *Légion d'Honneur*.

On 28 August, the volunteers went before German Army doctors. 1,679 were seen and 800 were rejected, mainly for poor teeth. The suggestion has been made that the selection process was applied rigorously due to the idea that the Germans were trying to limit the number recruited. Abetz, for one, was unhappy with this rigorous approach to selection. Subsequent medical examinations had the same percentage of rejections, though.

On 3 September, the LVF received its flag from Deloncle, who declared the flag as 'the emblem of valiant men' who would fight 'to defend civilisation'. This tricolore flag bore the legend HONNEUR ET PATRIE. Otto Abetz and Doriot attended the ceremony, as well as 120 uniformed militants of the RNP bussed in from Paris.

The following day, the first LVF contingent of 25 officers and 803 other ranks left *caserne* Borgnis-Desbordes for the Deba training camp in Poland.[30] Among them was PPF leader Doriot. He was one of the few political party leaders to keep his promise to go with the first volunteers into combat.[31]

## Volunteers

The volunteers ranged in age. Some were as young as 15 years of age. On the other hand, Callas de Gournay was 57. The volunteers came from all walks of life. Their motives were varied. Those of anti-Communism and 'the need to realise, through himself, the reality of his thoughts' drove Pierre Soulé to enlist in August 1941. An announcement of support from a Papacy official swept away the last scruples he might have had. Besides, he wanted to 'help Marshal Pétain in his mission'.

Pierre Soulé was born on 3 May 1916 in Bordeaux. His father was the co-founder of the Communist Party at Bordeaux, but when he left 'these monsters' they murdered him. Ever since, he had considered Communism as a horror. In 1936, as a *scout de France*, he left for Spain on a bicycle for a month-long holiday. It was there that the 'horrible crimes' committed by the Republicans drove him towards armed struggle.

In 1937, Pierre Soulé returned home to France to do his military service and was assigned to the *126e Régiment d'Infanterie* at Brive. Since Napoleon the First, the *126e* had been wrapped in tradition. Two years later, he was plunged into war. He saw action in the ill-fated French offensive of September 1939 and was wounded in the region east of Deux-Ponts in a 'corner infested with German pillboxes'.

After a month of hospitals, Soulé was sent on leave to convalesce. He was still in his uniform caked with German mud and in his trousers cut by the doctors. He was without shoes. At the end of October, he returned to the *126e* in Alsace.

In February 1940, Soulé was called upon, because of his 'Spanish interlude', to train soldiers in anti-tank warfare. It was farcical. A mock-up tank of wood was used. The only weapon at their disposal was the old and ineffectual 25mm anti-tank gun. He also noted that a number of

---

30 The town is now called Nowa Dęba.

30  The town is now called Nowa Dęba.
31  Lefèvre and Mabire, *La LVF 1941: Par-40° devant Moscou*, p.177. This is confirmed by Mercier, who left with the first contingent (letter to the author, 6/9/2001). He saw Doriot on soup duty, with a mess tin in each hand. Incorrectly, according to Littlejohn David, *Foreign legions of the Third Reich*, volume 1 (San Jose: Bender publishing, 1979), p.149, Doriot went with the second contingent on 20 September.

officers aged between 40 and 60 were incapable of climbing aboard the tank to attack it with grenades or magnetic mines. Like many, he realised that France was unprepared for war.

In May 1940, the *126e* was sent to Tergnier on the Saint-Quentin canal. Soulé volunteered for the *groupe franc* of his battalion and was accepted. Patrols along the canal brought about the capture of two prisoners, but also the loss of a comrade who fell into the water. And then the retreat began. The *126e* saw constant action to the end. On 25 June 1940, the *126e* followed orders and laid down its weapons near Bellac and Limoges. Soulé was proud that his regiment, still in battle order, was one of the few to have fought to the very end. Because of this he wore with glory and honour the *Croix de guerre* that Marshal Pétain awarded to all the men of the *126e*. Subsequently, he was demobilised. He returned to nothing.

In August 1941, Pierre Soulé finally learnt that Germany was fighting against 'Russian dictatorship' and that French volunteers were being accepted for this fight for 'European humanity'. He enlisted in the LVF.

Others wanted to participate in building a new European order. *Lieutenant* C. wrote to his family in February 1942 that 'we're working for a new Europe'.[32] Simon Nicolaï wrote to his wife:[33]

> You probably think I'm mad, I don't think I am. I'm an idealist. I wanted, like thousands of friends who have come here with me, to participate in the crusade against Bolshevism for a new Europe. I may not see the result, but others, you, might see a change, another world will be born of this crusade. For that men are needed, I wanted to be a part of it because it's not in my habit to send others in my place.

Lieutenant Ourdan, who enlisted in the LVF in September 1941, was of the same opinion:[34]

> The struggle against Bolshevism is indispensable. Considering the European character that it's necessary to give to this struggle, the presence of a French expeditionary corps in Russia is one of our unquestionable duties if France wishes to participate in the reconstruction of a new Europe, and if it wants to regain the title of a great power.

Not unexpectedly, many of the volunteers, approximately one in three, were idealistic militants of the collaborating political parties. Many were those from the MSR and the PPF.

Raymond Mercier was from the *Jeunesses Nationales Populaires* (JNP), the youth movement of the RNP. He was the JNP *chef de section* for the XIX° *arrondissement* (district) of Paris with some thirty adherents. Mercier said of his childhood and the 1939-1940 war:

> I was brought up in the cult of the memory of the soldiers of 1914-1918 and was called Raymond to preserve the memory of an uncle of the same name killed on the field of honour. I did not participate in the 1939-1940 war; I belonged to the class of 1941, which was not called up. I wanted to join up, but my mother was opposed; I was a

32   Giolitto, *Les Volontaires Français sous l'uniforme Allemand*, p.80.
33   *L'Emancipation nationale* of 1st November 1941.
34   *Rapport du lieutenant Ourdan*, p.21.

minor and had need of her permission.[35] Nevertheless, we had expected a long war and I thought I would be called up for military service in 1941. In the meantime I undertook the *Préparation Militaire Supérieure* (PMS). When my platoon practiced arms drill at fort Vincennes I was unaware that we were under the window of General Gamelin's office. Defeat came sooner. The defeat of 1940 was the end of a world. French people today cannot imagine what we felt. For me, in 1938, 1939 and up to May 1940, the French Army was the best in the world. I was tempted to try and join the British army but was dissuaded by the shameful sight of the flight of the state-employed teachers who had abandoned the children entrusted to them. My personal reaction was not only to rebuild our country, but also reconstruct it.

The collapse of May-June 1940 was both military and political. Regarding the latter, Mercier said:

> The time had come for a break with the past. Since the armistice some friends and I came to certain conclusions, without agreeing on their consequences. Internally, it was therefore necessary to rebuild the political foundations of the nation. To speak of our old political partie was derisory. Our old divides were outdated. We all agreed about a revival built at first on a national solidarity more or less authoritarian and more or less socialist. However, when it came to external politics, we were divided. Personally I approved of the politics of Montoire.
>
> So when the *Rassemblement National Populaire* was created, I found that it responded perfectly to my perspective; in its internal policy, the RNP was a union of former militants of the left with esprit national and former militants of the right with the spirit of social progress, and, in its foreign policy, the RNP was unequivocal in support of the politics of collaboration. I joined the RNP, but I noted that within the RNP, the MSR had kept its own existence and I thought this formation corresponded more to my personal leanings. Thus, I passed to the MSR while retaining my position within the JNP as the *chef de section* for the XIX° *arrondissement* of Paris.

Of an anti-communist tradition, Mercier welcomed the news of the German invasion of the Soviet Union and recalls:

> I was an active militant in the JNP and MSR when the thunderclap of 22 June broke. The invasion had the immense merit of clarifying the political situation. In the ranks of the RNP in my section of the XIX° *arrondissement* of Paris, traditionally left-wing, I knew of only one resignation from an adherent after 22 June 1941. In the ranks of the MSR there were only anti-bolsheviks. In right-wing circles, rare were the supporters of the USSR at that time. And a number of us thought that the struggle on two fronts would respond better to our ideal view of political combat. Moreover, militant activity was becoming monotous: we were going round and round and I was holding my

---

35   His father had died in 1936.

never-ending weekly reunions in front of the same militants and always preaching to the converted.

The creation of the LVF filled Mercier with joy because political combat became military combat, explaining:

> The youth of my generation was freed from the obsession of 'those of 14' who had been heroes. We were constantly reminded of their sacrifices. We thought in ourselves that if we had been twenty in 1914 we would have done our duty too. Now, we had the occasion to show what 'those of 41' were worth.

The LVF offered Mercier much more:

> First, to show that Franco-German reconciliation was possible because we could form battalions marching for our common civilisation. Next, to contribute to the destruction of the Bolshevik scourge; my father had extended his 1914 war by a year to participate in the Siberian Mission of the French Army sent to Vladivostock in 1919. And to show that 'those of 41' were not unworthy of their fathers.

And so it was with great enthusiasm that Mercier enlisted in the LVF at the recruiting office on rue Auber, Paris. This time, his mother, who did not oppose his 'going to war', gave her written consent. His mother and his brother positively disapproved of his 'collaborationism' and was scandalised by his decision to enlist, but they respected his decision.[36]

Parental permission was not the only obstacle Mercier had to overcome and explained:

> To gain admittance to the LVF, I needed to have done my military service.[37] I had no wish to end up as a groom or a farrier. I wanted to fight. Eugène Deloncle was the the president of the LVF, so I presented myself at the central office of the MSR, 80 rue Saint Lazare and demanded an audience. I was received by Dr. Landrieu, Deloncle's 'orderly officer', who took my case in hand. I was *bachelier és lettres* and attended the Faculty of Law and the Sorbonne. A priori, I had to know how to write and could be of more use as a journalist than a kitchen hand. Now, the war correspondents of the LVF would be under the authority of our comrade Jean Fontenoy, the *chef de la propaganda du RNP*, who would have need of such young and determined collaborators. Thus, the problem was resolved. However, Dr. Landrieu told me in confidence that a young man full of confidence would be much more useful as Deloncle's secretary rather than in Russia and, in any case, the LVF would return from the East through Syria... I was not convinced. In August Dr. Landrieu told me that the LVF would certainly not see the light of day because the Vichy government refused to take charge of the disability pensions. I awaited events and passed on my functions of *chef de section* JNP to a comrade.

---

36  Without approving in the slightest of his enlistment his mother and elder brother would correspond with him to the end.
37  Later this stipulation was dropped.

Nevertheless, for Mercier, joining Fontenoy was 'the means to an end' and there was no question of this. On 27 August 1941, he was present at *caserne* Borgnis-Desbordes when an assassination attempt was made on the life of Laval. Despatched to Deba, he was saddened by the necessity of having to wear the uniform of the victor. He was assigned to the 1st Platoon of the 3rd Company of the I. Bataillon of the LVF.

Georges Blonay, who was born in Paris in 1922 into a Communist family, was also from the RNP. He said of his reasons to enlist in the LVF:

> Before the war, [I was a] militant in the *Jeunesses socialistes* of the S.F.I.O. (the French section of the International worker). I sold *le Populaire* and stuck up posters against the law of two years mandatory military service. Marxist, pacifist, fighting against the rearmament of my country, I regretted in 1936-38 that I was too young to join the International Brigades in Spain.
>
> Shocked by the signing of the German-Soviet pact in 1939, which was approved by the French Communist party, then shattered by our defeat, [and] disgusted by the conduct and the lies of our rulers and governments of the Third Republic after the armistice, it was for me the 'turn-around'. Behind Marshal Pétain, the way of collaboration seemed to me the best means of allowing France to recover and to have the possibility of regaining its place in Europe in case of a German victory.
>
> At the start of 1941, like my father, I joined the newly created RNP (which I would leave in 1943 for Francisme). What first attracted me to the RNP was its pro-European socialist commitment. The start of the German war against the USSR, which betrayed us in 1939, changed for me the stakes in the conflict. I could no longer be a passive spectator to this war.
>
> The LVF offered me the possibility to act and to overcome the humiliation of having been defeated. I enlisted and left with the first contingent.

Like Mercier, Blonay also had to overcome the obstacle of parental consent, which was eventually granted. It proved much easier to convince his good friend André Fortet, also a member of the RNP, to follow him. Like Mercier, Blonay served in the 1st Platoon of the 3rd Company of the I. Bataillon.

For the ultra-right political parties, military collaboration in the form of the LVF was a heaven-sent opportunity for closer ties with victorious Germany and the establishment of an authoritarian regime in France which would secure its place within a German Europe. Jean Vanor, Deloncle's assistant, who served in the Propaganda Company, declared on 26 November 1941:

> The LVF is the surest guarantee of Franco-German friendship. It acts against Bolshevik barbarism and for the future peace alliance of our dear countries. By working, fighting, and if need be dying with honour and loyalty in its ranks, we will fullfil the wishes of the Führer and the *Maréchal*, and we will serve France immortal and Europe of tomorrow.

Jean Sepchat volunteered for the LVF in August 1941. Born on 29 September 1913 in Saint-Germain-près-Hermet, he joined the PPF in 1936, but left at the time of the Munich agreement, like many others. Having failed EOR training, he was mobilized in 1939 as a *caporal* in the *16e bataillon de chasseurs à pied* (16e BCP) and was seriously wounded in the foot by a piece of shrapnel that September during the Saar Offensive. He went from hospital to hospital, missing the fighting of May 1940, and was eventually demobilized. He said of volunteering for the LVF:

> I enlisted out of fear of seeing Europe submerged by Bolshevism, coupled with the sincere hope of a durable reconciliation with the hereditary enemy whose prodigious achievements, especially economic and social, had impressed me and who, after having inflicted on us the most crushing defeat in our history, had spared us.

His father came to Versailles to try and annul his enlistment, but it was in vain; his son was twenty-seven-years-old. Jean would serve with the 7th Company of the II. Bataillon, then with the 1st Company of the I. Bataillon and, finally, with the Headquarters Company. However, many of the recruits had no desire to see closer ties with *les Boches*.

The volunteers were from all political horizons. Some were from the extremist *Front Franc*: Henri Bossut and Gullermin would both serve with the LVF and both would die on the Eastern Front.

*Adjudant* [warrant officer] R. wrote to his father that 'he hoped France would emerge from its great misfortunes thanks to the French National Socialists'.[38] However, few volunteers regarded themselves as genuine National Socialists.

Many, perhaps one third of the volunteers were career soldiers. One such career soldier was Yves Rigeade, who was born on 8 February 1915 in Montguyon (department Gironde). From 1936 to 1938, he served with the *26e Régiment d'infanterie* (RI) at Nancy and, from 1938 to 1939, with the *149e Régiment d'infanterie de forteresse* (RIF) on the Maginot line. When war broke out he was transferred to the *132e RIF*. Taken prisoner at Colmar in June 1940, he escaped the following month. Thereupon he rejoined the *26e RI* then stationed in his region. His reaction to the defeat of May 1940 was one of disbelief. In his eyes, France had the best weapons, the best officers and the strongest army in the world and yet it had been defeated in ten days. It was a catastrophe. Before this *debâcle* he felt such an overwhelming sense of helplessness.

In August 1941, Yves Rigeade volunteered for the LVF. He was a supporter of Marshal Pétain and a traditionalist[39] who wanted to preserve civilisation from Communism. He saw his enlistment in the LVF as a continuation of the struggle against the greatest enemy of civilisation he had begun as a militant of the pre-war *Jeunesses patriotes*. He left with the second contingent to Deba.

On 1 October 1941, twenty-year-old Yves Peyret volunteered for the LVF.[40] He was a supporter of the National Revolution and Marshal Pétain. He was neither a militant of a political party or a career soldier. He had volunteered for Army service, but was declared unfit, even as an auxiliary, because of excessive short sight in one eye. This defect he had had since birth. Disappointment overwhelmed him.

From the sidelines, Peyret looked on as France went to her defeat. He blamed the *Front populaire* government, the Communists and the English for sabotaging the French Army.

---

38    Giolitto, *Les Volontaires Français sous l'uniforme Allemand*, p.84.
39    To his dying day, Rigeade remained a traditionalist.
40    Yves Peyret was born on 22 May 1921 in Germany.

He believed that the English who had disembarked in such a cowardly way at Dunkirk had abandoned France. His attitude towards England hardened after the incidents at Mers-el-Kébir in July 1940 and Dakar in September 1940. In this way, he came to realise that the real enemy of France, its hereditary enemy, was England and not Germany.

Finding himself at a loose end after completing the first year of a law degree, Peyret enrolled in a leadership school [*école de cadres* in French] of the *Chantiers de la Jeunesse*. However, when the LVF was created, he saw this as a means, albeit indirectly, of fighting against England, the allies of Soviet Russia. His father, a *chef d'escadrons de cavalerie* [Cavalry Major], tried to stop him leaving, accusing him of deserting an 'elite', but his son was not to be persuaded.

Yves Peyret encountered in the ranks of the LVF many former French sailors who, like him, were disgusted by the behaviour of their allies of 1939 and wanted to avenge their murdered comrades. He arrived at Deba with the third contingent on 12th October and was sent to the Eastern Front on the 30th of the same month with the *train de combat* of the 13th Company. He only received a rifle one or two days before he departed and learnt how to use it on the train.

Not all of the volunteers were French by birth. According to Article 12 of the statutes of the LVF, foreigners who had served in the Foreign Legion or fought in the French Army could exceptionally join the legion. Germans and Austrians who had seved with the French Foreign Legion were to be found in the ranks of the LVF. Georges Stein of Baltic origin, who was born in Saint-Petersburg in 1905, was one of the first to volunteer and was accepted because of his previous service with the Foreign Legion. Some volunteers were of Italian descent, like Tazzioli and Marcel Lena, a militant of the Paris PPF.

There was also a sprinkling of White Russian émigrés. Wladimir Tibakh, the son of a White Army General, had fought for France in 1940.[41] Dimitri-Vassilievitch Koptev, who was in his mid-forties, had previously served as a lieutenant with the lancers in the Tsar's Imperial Guard and, in 1940, was appointed as an *officier de réserve à titre étranger* in the French Army and posted to the *6e Étranger* in the Levant. He was admitted into the LVF with the rank of *lieutenant*.

Michael Zulukidse, a Georgian prince, travelled to Versailles with forty other ex-Czarist officers. They were admitted and 'remained in the regiment for three weeks until the German command told them that they had to be withdrawn because they were not French born'.[42]

As many as 300 Russian émigrés attempted to enlist in the LVF by the end of November 1941, but 'due to a ban on accepting such cadres into the Wehrmacht, most of them were not accepted'.[43] A few Armenian emigrants also tried to enlist.

The definition of 'Aryan origin' was extended to include French citizens from Maghreb [Northwest Africa] and the French West Indies.[44]

Also recruited into the ranks of the LVF, as with every army the world over, were adventures, social misfits, fugitives on the run from the authorities, the hungry, as well as the unemployed

---

41    Born in China in 1920, Wladimir Tibakh arrived in France in 1933 after his mother remarried. He fought for France in 1940, was captured and escaped.

42    Munoz, Antonio, *The East Came West: Muslim, Hindu and Buddist volunteers in the German Armed Forces 1941-1945* (New York: Axis Europa Books, 2002), p.183. The real reason for their dismissal may not have been their place of birth.

43    Beyda, edited by Stahel David, *Joining Hitler's Crusade* (Cambridge: Cambridge University Press, 2018), p.310.

44    Lefèvre and Mabire, *La LVF 1941: Par-40° devant Moscou*, p.89.

who had joined for money. Indeed, according to *Lieutenant* Ourdan, 85% of the platoon he commanded had enlisted for the money, 10% partly for the money and partly out of ideological conviction, and the remaining 5% out of ideological conviction alone.[45]

For Édouard Contat, the LVF was a place of refuge, far away from his father. He was apolitical.

Marcel Nantoy, an orphan, volunteered with the intention of deserting. Unable to cross the Pyrenees to join the Free French, he convinced himself that the best way forward was to join the LVF, desert and reach London via Moscow! After finding a sense of camaraderie and a reason to live he never quite expected, he did not desert his new comrades.

Another with a remarkable story to tell was Roland Verfaillie, born on 18 July 1922 in Ypres in Belgium. His family immigrated to France and settled down in Seine-et-Oise. He was preparing for the Arts et Métiers in 1939 when war broke out but could not enlist because of his age. At the start of 1941 he volunteered to go and work in Germany, where he grew restless. Quite by accident he learnt of the creation of the LVF and thought it was the opportunity he had been waiting for, and perhaps a way of obtaining French nationality which he craved. He was among the first to present himself at Versailles, receiving registration number 245. He would serve with the I. Bataillon.

Some volunteers were underage. The fifteen-year-old Léon Vatchnadzé managed to join up with his older brother thanks to the connivance of his parents, who were Georgian immigrants and fiercely hated their fellow countryman Stalin.[46] Similarly, Léon Merdjan of Georgian origin was fifteen. René Bourg of the JPF was sixteen.[47]

Over 3000 volunteers were accepted into the LVF in the first three months of its existence.

**Broken promises**

At Deba in Poland, two unpleasant surprises awaited the French volunteers of the LVF. They were met on the train platform by Colonel Labonne and his *adjoint, capitaine* Antoine Casabianca, who were both in German uniform.[48] Their reaction was, of course, one of total surprise and, for some, one of indignation. For others it was an unexpected honour. Some argued that the French who had fought with Franco had donned the Spanish uniform.

Because France was not at war with the Soviet Union the Germans would not entertain the idea of sending the French volunteers to the front in French uniform.[49] This was strictly in accordance with the international rules of land warfare that 'require volunteers from non-belligerent countries to wear the uniform of the army in which they were fighting'. However, the LVF was permitted to wear French Army khaki at home.[50]

Robert Girard, the former *chef de la section de l'UPJF* of Saint-Denis in Paris who was profoundly nationalist, was saddened by the necessity of having to don the German uniform,

---

45   *Rapport du lieutenant Ourdan*, p.14.
46   Lefèvre and Mabire, *La LVF 1941: Par -40 devant Moscou*, p.127.
47   René Bourg was born on 28 March 1925 in Paris.
48   Casabianca was a World War One veteran who had been decorated with the *Légion d'honneur*.
49   Following the German invasion of the Soviet Union, France did break off diplomatic relations with the Soviet Union but did not go to war.
50   A dark blue uniform is also reported as sometimes being worn in France. Only a tricolore shield inscribed with the word 'France' or an early version with 'LVF' (probably of French origin) worn on the upper right arm would distinguish their nationality

more so when he was required to take the oath of loyalty to Hitler, which was the second surprise for the French volunteers.[51] The French press said nothing of these developments for weeks.

The training regime now started under the auspices of a *Ausbildungsstab* [training headquarters] commanded by Major Hammerschmidt who had at his disposal 213 officers, NCOs and men, including sixty interpreters furnished by three Wehrkreise [military regions]. 'The regiment would be entirely dressed, equipped and armed exactly like any other horsedrawn infantry regiment of the German Herr. Food would also be the same'.[52]

The first contingent would form the I. Bataillon. The fanion of the I. Bataillon bore the arms of Saint-Denis, the power base of Doriot's PPF. On 17 September, Otto Abetz visited Deba and talked in private with *sergent* Doriot. Abetz proposed the creation of a *comité d'honneur de la Légion* and a visit from a representative of the Government. They finished off by discussing the release of the volunteers' imprisoned parents. Indeed, days before, on 13 September 1941, *L'Émancipation nationale*, the MPF [PPF] weekly in the Free Zone, had announced that Hitler had agreed to this following the intervention of the party, which was, of course, not true.

On 20 September, the second contingent of 786 volunteers (17 officers, 150 NCOs and 619 men) arrived at Deba, Poland. There were considerably more Doriotists in this contingent. They would form the II. Bataillon under the command of *commandant* Girardeau. Fourteen more officers arrived on 24 September and 3 October.

Monseigneur de Mayol de Lupé celebrates mass at Debra on 5 October 1941 after which the two battalions of the LVF swear an oath of loyalty to Adolf Hitler. (Rigeade)

51    According to Lefèvre & Mabire, *La LVF 1941: Par -40 devant Moscou*, p.161, Robert Girard volunteered for the LVF on 18th August 1941, the date of his twentieth birthday. However, according to Bouysse, Girard was born on 18 February 1921 in Saint-Denis.
52    Lefèvre & Mabire, *Par -40 devant Moscou*, p.23.

On 5 October 1941, after mass celebrated by Monseigneur de Mayol de Lupé, the two battalions of the LVF swore an oath of loyalty to Adolf Hitler 'as the commander of German and Allied Armies in the struggle against Bolshevism' in the presence of General der Infanterie Halm, now commanding Wehrkreis [Military District] VIII. General Halm closed the ceremony with a speech in French, after which La Marseillaise was played and sung, followed by Deutschland Über Alles and the Horst Wessel Lied. Some legionnaires refused to swear the oath. They felt betrayed.[53]

Monseigneur de Mayol de Lupé would become one of the most celebrated and photographed characters of the LVF.

## Monseigneur de Mayol de Lupé[54]

Jean de Mayol de Lupé was born in Paris on 21 January 1873, the seventh child of an ultra-legitimist family. His father, Comte Henri de Lupé, after being in the service of the King of Naples, had returned to fight for France in 1870. His mother, Elisabeth de Caracciolo-Girifalco, was born into the Neapolitan aristocracy. Aged seventeen, Jean entered the Benedictine abbey of Ligugé in the province of Poitou and on 10th June 1900 was ordained a priest of the Benedictine Order.

In 1914, he was mobilised as a military chaplain in the *1re division de cavalerie* and was captured on 28 September 1914. Freed and repatriated as an ecclesiastic on 16th October 1916, he volunteered again for front-line duties and arrived back at the front with the *33e D.I.* on 16th March 1917. He then served with the *9e Régiment de chasseurs à cheval*. He saw action in the Champagne and in the sector of Verdun and was badly wounded in 1918 at Esmery-Hallon (Somme). He was awarded the *Croix de guerre* with six citations. Following the war he continued to serve as a military chaplain and went to Bessarabia, Bulgaria, Syria, where on 16 June 1920 he was made a *chevalier de la Légion d'honneur*, and lastly Morocco. After a long illness, he was discharged from military service in 1927 as a *capitaine* with thirteen citations as well as a disability pension of 40%.

On 17 October 1934, he was made a canon by the powerful chapter of the cathedral of Lucera in Italy. From that day forward he was entitled to the position of Roman Prelate to his Holiness and the honorary title of Monsignor which he valued greatly. His aristocratic ancestry, his diplomatic talents and his knowledge of languages were recognised as the perfect credentials of an envoy and he was assigned a number of cultural missions. In 1934, he went to Munich on behalf of the *ministère de l'Éducation nationale*. He went back with a certain professor Lichzmann and was introduced to various German personalities including some dignitaries of the new regime. And so began his 'conversion' to National Socialism. In 1938, he attended the Nuremberg Rally where he met and began a friendship with professor Otto Abetz who years later would become the German ambassador to occupied France. That same year, such was the

53  According to Danke, *The French against the French*, p.195, they were immediately sent to punishment battalions. According to Delarue Jacques, *Trafics et crimes sous l'Occupation* (Fayard, 1968), p.182, they were sent to 'fortresses' in West Prussia or the Baltic islands, where they served prison sentences in such conditions that several perished.
54  See Bail, article *Monseigneur, Historia hors série 32*, pp.138-143.

esteem in which the military and political authorities held him that he was made an *officier de la Légion d'honneur.*[55]

In August 1939, the *2e bureau* appealed to his great sense of patriotism by asking him to go to Italy to gauge Mussolini's attitude in the event of a Franco-German war. He agreed and met with important ecclesiastic and secular personalities in Rome and Naples. On his return, he reported that Italy, in the event of war, would side with the enemy.

When war came Mgr. de Mayol de Lupé requested to get back into harness as a stretcher-bearer on account of his age. Cardinal Verdier prevented him from doing so. The German victory left him heavy at heart and determined to have nothing to do with the German authorities. Abetz visited him, and while the conversation was courteous, it was without warmth. However, the arrest of some of his close friends and acquaintances prompted him to appeal to the German authorities for their release. The Germans did respond to his request, although not all were released, but in return asked him to become the General Chaplain of the LVF. He refused, but agreed, nevertheless, to spend a month in an untitled capacity with the LVF and to bless its first detachments based in Poland.

On 12 October, the third LVF contingent of 21 officers, 125 NCOs and 498 men arrived at Deba. They would form the bulk of the regimental headquarters company, the 13th Company (Infantry Gun) and the 14th Company (Anti-tank).

On 17 October, sixty 'undesirables', including eight officers, were returned to France.[56] Some had refused to wear the German uniform. Among them was one of the few militants of the *Front Franc* to have joined the LVF. Another was a former Seminarian who would go on to join the N.S.K.K.

On the same day, Labonne sacked Colonel Ducrot and his assistant *Capitaine* Bondi, who had been critical of him, even though they had only arrived on the 12th. This day would also be remembered for the accidental death of André Texier of the II. Bataillon. Colonel Ducrot would leave the very same day but return again with the 5th contingent on 6 December. Colonel Ducrot was a product of Saint-Cyr and Verdun veteran.

On 19 October, after mass celebrated by Monseigneur de Mayol de Lupé, the third contingent of the LVF swore an oath of loyalty to Adolf Hitler in the presence of Generalleutnant von Trotha, who commanded Division z.b.V. 432.

On 22 October, the LVF, designated by the Germans *Infanterieregiment 638 des Heeres* (IR 638), was ordered to Smolensk, Russia.

On 25 October, French Ambassador Fernand de Brinon visited the LVF at Deba where he watched a manueuvre and gave a speech. Colonel Labonne handed a letter to de Brinion, addressed to Pétain, in which he promised that the LVF would 'add new pages of glory to the golden book of our brave army'. Lieutenant Ourdan of the 13th Company wrote of this visit:[57]

> This visit, I have to say, is a great comfort for the legionnaires, both officers and soldiers. But this visit had the great mistake of being too quick and consequently very incomplete.

---

55   To be considered for promotion to *officier* in the order of the *Légion d'honneur*, it is necessary to have been a *chevalier* of this same order for at least eight years. Also, promotion to *officier* has to be merited.
56   Lefèvre & Mabire, *Par -40 devant Moscou*, p.25.
57   *Rapport du lieutenant Ourdan*, p.9.

In late October, to help finance its social work, the LVF issued a commemorative stamp called the 'Bear block', which featured a white polar bear with a red star being put to the sword. In the top right hand corner of the stamp is the Vichy axe with the legend 'LVF' inscribed across the axe head. 25,000 to 30,000 stamps were sold.

*Commandant* Baud, who commanded the I. Bataillon, suddenly and inexplicably departed the LVF. Labonne replaced him with *Capitaine* Leclercq, who commanded the 4th Company. This was just the start of an officer merry-go-round which would plague the first incarnation of the LVF.

## The Eastern Front

The LVF was transported by rail to Smolensk. The headquarters staff left Deba on 28 October. That same day, the fourth contingent of 3 officers and 224 NCOs and men arrived at Deba. They were immediately clothed, equipped and armed. The I. Bataillon (companies 1-4) left on 29 October and the II. Bataillon (companies 5-8) two days later on 31 October. The fifth and last convoy, comprising elements of the regimental companies and men of the newly arrived fourth contingent, left on 1 November.[58] In total, 2,352 men were deployed. The LVF left on trains blessed by Monseigneur de Mayol de Lupé, who now returned to Paris.

The first elements of the LVF arrived at Smolensk on 1 November. It was bitterly cold and snow was on the ground. The last elements arrived on the 5th, during which time it had got colder and colder. The *légionnaires* lacked proper winter clothing. Moreover, many were suffering from dysentery. The officers and men of the fourth contingent now swore their oath of loyalty, after which they were shared out among the regiment.

Colonel Labonne relieved the company commander of the 13th Company, Capitaine Zègre, after it simply abandoned one 75mm gun and managed to overturn another gun, injuring four horses, two of which were shot. Lieutenant Ourdan of the 13th Company left soon after, so did Capitaine Bouyol, the company commander of the 14th Company, who was an active militant of the MSR. The Colonel also expelled lieutenants Zinani and Dubec, officer cadets Balay and Fertinel, and, finally, *Capitaine* Tixier, the company commander of the Headquarters Company. Officially, they were purged because of their incomptency but this was just a pretext. Back at Deba a plot had been hatched to remove the Colonel and install another officer more able to command the Legion!

*Capitaine* Mariotti, a holder of the prestigious *chevalier de la Légion d'honneur* who was well into his sixties but no longer able to 'make a campaign', asked to be evacuated and was returned to France.

The various units of the LVF departed Smolensk between the 6 and 11 of November and made their way on foot to the front before Moscow in temperatures as low as minus forty degrees below zero. The I. Bataillon was the first to leave, followed by the II. Bataillon. The *légionnaires* suffered from the cold and hunger. Indeed, some 400 dropped out before trucks from the VII. Corps eventually 'collected' them. Colonel Labonne dismissed *commandant* Hugla, who had

---

58    Lefèvre & Mabire, *La LVF 1941: Par -40 devant Moscou*, p.71. Also see the *Rapport du lieutenant Ourdan*.

a long and distinguished military career behind him in the Colonial Army, for 'following his troop instead of commanding it'.

On 19 November, the LVF was attached to the German 7th Infantry Division of the VII. Corps. Jean Sepchat was evacuated when his old wound reappeared. He would rejoin months later. Suffering from terrible diarrhea and a high temperature, Robert Girard of the 2nd Company was also evacuated.

Generalleunant von Gablenz commanding the 7th Infantry Division desperately wanted to deploy the Legion but recognized that the long march had taken its toll on the men and equipment. To improve its mobility, he furnished the Legion with horses and carts, which were either lost or still en route. Turning his attention to the undertrained 13th Company and 14th Company, he arranged for German officers and NCOs to provide additional training.

On 24 November, regimental headquarters, the Headquarters Company and the four companies of the I. Bataillon left Nowo-Michailowskoje, where they had been resting, and made their way on foot to the front seventeen kilometers away. As chance would have it, the paths of Generalfeldmarschall von Kluge, commanding the 4th Army, and the LVF crossed at Golowinka, where the headquarters of the 7th Infantry Division was located. The regimental headquarters and Headquarters Company, complete with the flag presented by Deloncle on 3 September, paraded for von Kluge, after which he exchanged a few words with Colonel Labonne. Photographs were taken of the parade.

At nightfall, the I. Bataillon entered the front line. Moscow was only seventy kilometres away. The men had to spend the nights out in the open. The cold became terrible. There were more casualties from frostbite than enemy action, but the frost also struck at the troops' weapons, unprotected by anti-freeze lubricants. Machine pistols and machine guns were rendered unreliable.

Questionably, battalion headquarters, the medical post, and three of the four company headquarters were set up in the village of Wygljadowka, making it an obvious target, more so because the German troops of the III. Bataillon of the 19th Regiment had occupied it three days before.

In the early morning hours of 27 November, positions held by the 1st Company were attacked by Russian patrols, which were repulsed, but the battalion commander, *commandant* Leclercq, totally fell apart and Colonel Labonne had him relieved of command. *Chef de bataillon* de Planard was appointed as the new battalion commander. Shortly after, the commander of the 1st Company, who proved more and more of a nervous disposition, was also replaced. Lieutenant Genest, who was a product of Saint-Cyr promotion 'de Bournazel', took over.[59]

On 28 November, Wygljadowka was hit by artillery fire. Lieutenant Koptev, commanding the 3rd Company, *Sergent* Delannois of the 3rd Company and a runner were wounded. All three were quickly evacuated. Koptev would be missed.

On 30 November, the eve of the attack by the I. Bataillon, Colonel Labonne communicated a letter from Marshal Pétain dated 5 November in response to his letter of 26 October, part of which read as follows:

59   Curiously, as an *officier d'active*, Lieutenant Genest was prohibited from volunteering for the LVF.

In taking part in this crusade which Germany is leading, thus acquiring a right to the gratitude of the world, you are helping to protect us from the Bolshevik peril: thus, it's your country that you are protecting, while at the same time saving the hope of a reconciled Europe.

This letter from Marshal Pétain, which also described the LVF as 'a definite part of our military honour', was well received.[60] Some viewed this letter as official approval for the LVF from the Vichy Government, which had looked on the creation of a legion of French volunteers favourably, but thereafter adopted an air of ambiguity toward the LVF. Despite this personal blessing from Pétain the LVF still remained a purely 'private' enterprise and had no official status.

## The Attack of 1 December 1941

At 13:00 hours on 1 December, the 1st Company (Lieutenant Genest) and 2nd Company (Lieutenant Dupont) of the I. Bataillon attacked towards the village of Djukowo. Each company was reinforced by a machine-gun platoon from the 4th Company. The temperature was minus 22 degrees below zero. The 1st Company advanced first and through a wood. Six men were wounded by mines just after the line of departure.[61] The 1st Company continued forward, reaching a clearing where it became pinned down by heavy enemy fire.

The 2nd Company started out in turn and overran the first enemy positions. It pushed forward from the south-east, outflanking the enemy holding up the 1st Company. The first to fall in the 2nd Company was probably *adjudant* René Faive, a forty-year-old from Lorraine and member of *La Ligue française*. The 1st Company resumed its advance, overrunning the enemy line of defence. *Sergent-Chef* Klinger knocked out a machine-gun position with a grenade. The enemy now withdrew.

The 1st Company came to a second clearing, swept by enemy machine-gun fire, and suffered heavy losses. Brothers Pierre and Robert Pushmann, Parisian MSR militants aged 17 and 20 respectively, were killed by the same burst of machine-gun fire.[62] Once across the clearing, the 1st Company ran into a line of buried petrol bottles which exploded, spewing flames. Several men were injured. René Pillault, an eighteen-year-old PPF militant from the Somme, died from burns received.

The 2nd Company continued to push forward, but now ran into mines, causing a few casualties and creating confusion. Towards 14:30 hours, the first elements reached the edge of the wood south-east of Djukowo, followed soon after by the rest of the reinforced company. It had reached its first objective. Through whirlwinds of snow, Djukowo could be seen barely 1000 metres away, across a frozen lake, which Stukas proceeded to bomb. The 1st Platoon pushed on, reaching the road to Djukowo, but it too ran into a line of buried petrol bombs, as previously encountered by the 1st Company, seriously burning several men, including the platoon commander. Thereupon the platoon withdrew in disorder back to the road where it took

60    The text of this letter appeared in the French press on 6 November 1941.
61    The mines may have been sown by the Germans and not lifted prior to the French attack.
62    To honour the memory of the fallen brothers, the MSR organised a religious ceremony on 8 April 1942 which party leader Deloncle and Colonel Labonne attended. Their father would later join the NSKK.

up a defensive position in foxholes abandoned by the enemy. The thirty-one-year old *adjudant* Charlot of the 4th Company attached to the 2nd Company was killed. He was replaced by the forty-three-year-old *sergent-chef* Maurice Pernel, who wore no less than fifteen medal ribbons! He was a member of the RNP.

Meanwhile, the 1st Company, which numbered no more than forty men and was to the left of the 2nd Company, pursued the Russians through the wood, reaching the side of the frozen lake, where it took up defensive positions.

The war diary of the German 7th Infantry Division read: 'For its first engagement, the French Legion performed well'. The two companies suffered 12 killed and 55 wounded. One Red Army soldier was captured and sent to the rear. Without shelter during the night, the men suffered badly from the cold and more than thirty men were evacuated with severe frostbite.

On 2 December, enemy artillery fire killed one *légionnaire* and wounded thirty-four. On 3 December, the 2nd Company was shelled and sustained more casualties. *Sergent-chef* Esterie was hit and killed when he went to help a wounded comrade, *légionnaire* Maurice Dousett. The two of them were MSR militants of La Garenne-Colombes.

Towards 08:00 hours, the 3rd Company, held in reserve, was moved up to support the right flank of the I. Bataillon along the south-east edge of the forest. Their movement was spotted by the Russians who heavily bombarded the battalion between 08:00 and 10:00 hours. Caught out in the open, the men of the 3rd Company dived for cover. Remarkably, the 3rd Company sustained no casualties from the shelling, but when it continued on two *légionnaires* were soon wounded by a mine. The 3rd Company occupied a front 1,500 metres long.

That same day, after resting for a week, the 5th Company and 7th Company of the II. Bataillon also entered the front line to relieve the I. Bataillon and II. Bataillon of the 19th Regiment. Two platoons of the 6th Company were deployed to guard battalion headquarters; one platoon was still moving up to the front with the regiment's horse-drawn *train*. The three machine-gun platoons of the 8th Company were divided up to provide support to the front-line units.

On 4 December, Mercier, who had fallen sick of exhaustion during the march to the front, rejoined the 3rd Company. The departure of Lieutenant Koptev, wounded and evacuated on 28 November, had unsettled the company. Moreover, his successor, Lieutenant Douillet was not liked and failed to stamp his authority. He did not know how to speak to his men and was rarely seen. He soldiered on to the end, even though his feet were frost-bitten.

On the night of 4 December, a patrol from the 3rd Company managed to capture fourteen Russians, including a political commissar. They were sent to battalion headquarters for interrogation. During the day the I. Bataillon evacuated a further seventy-seven men with frostbite. The II. Bataillon fared better, even though the cold had single-handedly decimated the 7th Company in two days; two sections only counted three men!

On 5 December, more men were evacuated from the 1st Company and 2nd Company, which left them with a combined strength of twenty-six men! The 3rd Company counted thirty men. So numerous were the losses from frostbite that the Germans now doubted the combat value of the LVF and decided to relieve it. The diary of the 7th Infantry Division remarked: 'Although all its elements demonstrate good will, the Legion remains nevertheless 'a Legion'. It has much to learn to become operational'.

During the night, the I. Bataillon came under increasing mortar and artillery fire. The enemy began probing patrols against the weak French defensive line, which were repulsed, often after bitter hand-to-hand fighting. More probing attacks followed. This time some French outposts, believed to be held by the 3rd Company, were overrun. The defenders withdrew hastily more than two kilometers, level with battalion headquarters. The outposts were eventually retaken and contact was re-established with the 61st Regiment on the right. Twenty-one-year-old Georges Larger was later awarded the Iron Cross 2nd Class for repulsing several attacks.

Around 06:30 hours on 6 December, artillery fire killed Lieutenant Dupont (commander of the 2nd Company) and Lieutenant Tenaille (orderly officer, I. Bataillon) who were popular officers. One source wrote of their deaths:[63]

> Lieutenants Dupont and Tenaille just fell side by side, killed by the same shell, a short distance from headquarters. With them disappeared the first LVF, highly politicised, and which will not be born again from its tomb of snow.

Dupont was a PPF militant who had switched to the MSR shortly before volunteering for the LVF. Tenaille, a nephew of Deloncle, was a MSR militant. According to the newspaper *La Gerbe* of 8 January 1942, Tenaille died crying out: 'I'm hit. It's for the MSR and for France'. The death of the two lieutenants profoundly affected the legionnaires. Some lost morale.

The Russians now probed the 2nd Company. The French, supported by accurate and intense German artillery fire, managed to throw them back.

On the afternoon of 6 December, the I. Bataillon was relieved. Its front line units numbered eighty men. The remnants of the 1st Company and 2nd Company comprised a weak platoon under Lieutenant Blancard, while the 3rd Company could muster two platoons under *Sergent* Veyrieras[64] and *adjudant* Guilleux, whose losses had been filled with the remnants of platoon Cousin. The 4th Company (mortars and machine guns), which had been split up to support the three infantry companies counted twenty-five men out of the one hundred and eight who had entered the front line on 24th November.

Also on the same day, thirty-two-year-old *caporal* Francisque (called Francis) André of the 7th Company was wounded by shellfire. He had started political life as a communist but in 1937 joined the PPF, becoming one of Doriot's 'most loyal and ruthless supporters'.[65]

The II. Bataillon was relieved on 8 December. There was a single incident of note: ten Russians deserted to the 1st Platoon of the 5th Company as it prepared to withdraw. The deserters were taken to the rear.

Frostbite had decimated the front line units of the II. Bataillon. For example, in one platoon of the 5th Company, one section comprised one man out of ten, while another section comprised four men, of which two were sick.

---

63  Saint-Loup, *Les Volontaires*, p.77.
64  Guillaume Veyrieras was born on 25 December 1905 in Paris. Demobilised in 1942, he managed to re-enlist in the LVF one year later with the rank of *sous-lieunant* according to Mabire Jean, *La Division Charlemagne* (Fayard, 1974), p.197.
65  Francis André would gain notoriety when he formed the *Mouvement national anti-terroriste*, MNAT, at Lyon in late 1943 to avenge assassinated comrades. The 'movement' enjoyed the support of the SiPo-SD, who granted its men the status of auxiliary police. Arrested in Italy at the end of the war, André was brought before the *cour de justice* of Lyon. Accused of one hundred and eighty assassinations, he was found guilty and condemned to death on 19 January 1946 and shot on 9 March 1946.

The LVF was ordered to regroup at Nowo-Michailowskoje. On 10 December, *Capitaine* Lacroix, although wounded, replaced de Planard as the commander of the I. Bataillon. This appointment also brought him promotion to *Commandant*.

The cost to the LVF of front front line duties from 24 November to 8 December was over 450 casualties, which included around 50 who were killed or died later of wounds received, 120 wounded and 200 frostbitten, and a further 100 evacuated due to sickness during and after the attack. Also, one *légionnaire* by the name of Constantin Klimakoff, a member of the large Russian community of Nice, was shot by firing squad for desertion.

Many of the wounded and frostbitten would have limbs amputated. Jean-Marie Benovar had both legs amputated and totally lost the use of his right arm. Also, the shrapnel lodged in his brain was never removed. Jean Bellec, who was wounded during the night of 2nd December, had both legs amputated. *Caporal-chef* Bunoz of the 3rd Company had one leg amputated. There were many more.[66]

### Reorganisation

Caught up in the Soviet's winter counter-offensive to remove the immediate threat to Moscow, the LVF was ordered westwards. The LVF now made its way back along the Moscow-Smolensk highway, the very same route it had travelled weeks before to reach the front line. By the end of December, after a march of some one hundred kilometers, the LVF had assembled at Wyrutowo. In early January 1942, it was transported by truck from nearby Zarjewo back to Smolensk. The I. Bataillon continued on to Liesno while the II. Bataillon went to Saolscha.

Few had good words to say about the performance of the LVF. In a report dated 23 December 1941, the 7th Infantry Division thanked the LVF for its presence, which had permitted it to rest its units, albeit briefly, but criticised the officers as 'incapable and recruited according to political criteria'. The same report concluded: 'The Legion is not fit to be engaged'. The report about the LVF of 24 January 1942 submitted to the Oberkommando der Heeres [OKH] was more damning, stating that the Legion had lost much of its material and equipment through negligence and that the 'Frenchmen understood nothing about caring for horses'. It concluded:

> The moral attitude of the Legion is doubtful. The troops have no confidence in its officers and discipline leaves something to be desired.

Notably, Reich Minister of Propaganda Joseph Goebbels wrote that 'the Frenchmen had in no way distinguished themselves on the Eastern Front'. Such criticism of the LVF is unfair. The LVF was ill equipped against the cold Russian winter and many of its troops had received little or no training; the fourth contingent of 3 officers and 224 NCOs and men to arrive at Deba was sent direct to the Eastern Front without having fired a single shot or participated in a single exercise, while the fourth platoon of the 13th Company commanded by Lieutenant Ourdan only had three weeks of training at Deba before it too was dispatched to the front.

Labonne was blamed for deploying the LVF to the front too quickly and has even been accused of hurrying to Russia 'to cover himself in glory'. This too is unfair. It was the German

---

66   See Lefèvre & Mabire, *La LVF 1941: Par –40 devant Moscou*, p.382.

military authorities who decided and ordered the LVF to be deployed in the full knowledge that it was not battle ready.

Also, and importantly, many officers and NCOs lacked the necessary leadership skills required of them. Most of the officers were reservists and some were aged over sixty. To underline this issue, after the LVF had been pulled back to reorganize, Colonel Labonne drew up a list of a further seven officers to be returned immediately. Lieutenant Ourdan of the 13th Company was critical of some promotions, which seemed to be influenced by MSR party leader Deloncle rather than ability. In his report he cites one example of a reserve sergeant, who held the rank of *sous-lieuentant* in the MSR and who was enlisted into the LVF as a sergeant, but days after his enlistment was promoted to *sous-lieutenant*. Likewise, the promotion of Doriot to *sous-lieutenant*, who had only reached the rank of sergeant during the First World World War, is questionable.

Turning to the military professionalism of the NCOs, Lieutenant Ourdan of 13th Company was just as critical in his report:[67]

> No NCO knew their job; it's also, according to the Germans themselves one of the causes of our defeat, the general insufficieny of the training of our NCOs. During my stay with the Legion I have done many times the work that normally falls to an NCO.

Ultimately, the Germans themselves should accept some if not most of the responsibility for the poor performance of the LVF. They permitted a poorly trained and poorly equipped unit to be hurriedly deployed in harsh winter conditions.

Now that the German command recognized that the LVF had to be reorganised it acted quickly. To help the Frenchmen look after the horses in their care, it decided to bring in former Soviet POWs, for the most part of Ukrainian origin, and a German veterinarian. The German liaison staff was increased and also provided with a doctor.

In mid-February 1942, the two battalions of the LVF were transported to training camp Kruszyna, which was part of Truppenübungsplatz Mitte near Radom, Poland. The men were thoroughly deloused and stripped of all equipment. NCOs who had proved themselves in combat were promoted to officer.

On 3 March 1942, General der Kavallerie von Gienanth decorated five Frenchmen of the LVF with the Iron Cross 2nd Class. Four of the recipients were officers, including Colonel Labonne and the commander of the I. Bataillon *Commandant* Henri Lacriox, and one was from the ranks. Three more legionnaires, who were in hospital, also received the same award.

The reorganisation began in earnest. The 13th Company (Infantry Gun) was dissolved as was the 14th Company (Anti-tank) which had handed over its remaining guns to the 7th Infantry Division when it was relieved. In this way, Yves Peyret of the 13th Company was now assigned to the 2nd Platoon of the 1st Company under *Capitaine* Cartaud.

The Germans expelled NCOs and legionnaires over the age of thirty, officers over the age of forty, all men of colour, all former white émigrés and all former German volunteers of the Foreign Legion.

67   *Rapport du lieutenant Ourdan*, p.9.

On 3 March 1942, General der Kavallerie von Gienanth decorated five Frenchmen of the LVF with the Iron Cross 2nd Class. (Rigeade)

One constant thorn in the side of the LVF was the bitter rivalry that existed between the militants of the MSR and the PPF. The Germans now told the Frenchmen to renounce all political activity or leave the LVF. The majority of those from the MSR now took the opportunity to return to France. In this way, the PPF became predominant.

This 'purge' thinned the ranks of the two battalions to some 750 officers and men, who were formed into the new I. Bataillon. Colonel Labonne, no longer at the head of a regiment, reacted angrily to these developments, but was soon recalled to Paris. He would resign in June. *Commandant* Lacroix retained the command of the battalion.

Many of those purged or wounded and declared unfit for active service subsequently joined other formations of the German war machine, including the Waffen-SS following the approval of the Vichy government. Some even became agents for the SiPo-SD, the German secret police.

The new I. Bataillon comprised three infantry companies and a headquarters company with a signals platoon, anti-tank platoon and mortar platoon. A fourth infantry company was formed but very quickly disbanded. The men were now granted leave. In June, the battalion incorporated 220 new volunteers of the first *renfort*. When the I. Bataillon was eventually deployed again it was a very different battalion from that formed the year before.

### The III. Bataillon

Meanwhile, the LVF formed the III. Bataillon (companies numbered 9 to 12), an artillery battalion and a *colonne légère d'infanterie régimentaire* at camp Deba in Poland from the four contingents to arrive between December 1941 and February 1942.[68] The new recruits numbered approximately 1,400 of which 200 were coloured (North African Arabs). However, the 12th Company was disbanded at the end of December 1941 due to insufficient manpower. In March 1942, the 15th Company (Arab) was formed, but was quickly dissolved.

Again many of the recruits were political militants, but this time adherents of the PPF outnumbered those of the MSR. The command of this new battalion went to Colonel Ducrot, who swore the oath of loyalty for the battalion on 28th December 1941 in the presence of Generalleutnant Von Trotha.

For the German High Command, there was no question of employing the LVF as a regiment again and ordered the artillery battalion and *colonne légère d'infanterie régimentaire* to disband. Moreover, the artillery battalion was grossly understrength and only comprised a battery.[69]

The recruits had two medicals, first with a French doctor and then one with a German doctor, and again many were rejected for the slightest things. Some were rejected for political reasons. In this way, by 10 April 1942, only 624 volunteers remained of the 1425 that had arrived at Deba. The purge at Deba had been as harsh as that at Kruszyna.

The III. Bataillon comprised a headquarters company and three infantry companies (now numbered 9 to 11). The headquarters company comprised a signals platoon, a PAK platoon and a mortar platoon.

*Sous-lieutenant* Jacques Martin, who had arrived at Deba with the 5th contingent, was appointed the commander of the PAK Platoon. He was born on 12 June 1918 in Carpentras. Aged eighteen, greatly influenced by his teachers, he wanted to join the Communist Youth, but a political epiphany in 1940 changed everything. He trained as a teacher before his compulsory military service. After passing the PMS, he attended EOR training and was commissioned *aspirant* in 1939. Posted to the *8e Régiment d'Artillerie* in Nancy, he was then assigned in late 1939 to the *209e Régiment d'Artillerie*. He did his duty during the war. After the defeat of June 1940, he was maintained in the Armstice Army in the *35e Régiment d'Artillerie* at Limoges. Demobilised in January 1941, he went into teaching, but needed more. He volunteered for the LVF in September 1941 and admitted with the rank of *Sous-lieutenant*. At Deba, he trained with the artillery battalion and when that was dissolved he became the commander of the Anti-Tank Platoon.

*Sous-lieutenant* Verney commanded the Mortar Platoon of the Headquarters Company. Not only was this thirty-nine-year old a reserve infantry officer, but also a priest, ordained in 1929.[70] He served in the *chasseurs à pied* during 1939-40. In 1941, he volunteered for the LVF with orders on him from Archbishop Besançon and was appointed to command the Mortar Platoon of the 12th (heavy) Company, and when that company was disbanded thereafter the Mortar Platoon of the Headquarters Company of the III. Bataillon. He left the LVF in September 1942 and returned to France. One year later, he was back with the LVF as auxiliary chaplain of the I. Bataillon.

---

68  The 5th contingent left Versailles on 1 December 1941 with 942 volunteers. The 6th contingent left on 15 December with 200 volunteers. The 7th contingent left on 5 January 1942 with 102 volunteers. The 8th contingent left on 19 February with 181 volunteers.

69  The Artillery Battalion is often referred to as the 15th Battery.

70  Just Albert Verney was born on 23 November 1902 in Franche-Comté and was appointed *sous-lieutenant de réserve d'infanterie* on 13 August 1938.

At the head of the 10th Company was *Lieutenant* Maurice Berret, who was born on 28 July 1914 in Blainville-sur-l'Eau. In 1936, he was admitted to the *École spéciale militaire de Saint-Cyr* and, on 1 October 1938, was promoted to *Sous-lieutenant d'active* in the infantry and posted to the *23e régiment de tirailleurs algériens* (23° RTA). He served with the same regiment from 1938 to the defeat of June 1940. In late 1941, he volunteered for the LVF, making him one of the few *officiers d'active* to serve with the LVF. He would hold various commands and, on 1 July 1943, was promoted to *Capitaine*. On 30 March 1944, he was awarded with the Iron Cross 2nd Class.

*Lieutenant* Georges Flamand commanded a platoon of the 11th Company. He was in his forties and a veteran of the Great War.[71] He enlisted in the LVF in late 1941 with the rank of *lieutenant*. He took over command of the company as of 7 June 1942. Wounded in the autumn of that year, he was returned to France to recover.

Noteworthy headquarters staff included Orderly Officer and PPF militant Michel Auphan. Born on 21 April 1920 in Marseille, he enlisted in the Air Force in 1939, attended the *École de l'Air*, graduated and was commisioned as a *sous-lieutenant*. He served as a pilot in the *Groupe de Reconnaisance 1/36*. Demobilised in 1941, he wanted to further his military career and fight Bolshevism. In September of that year, he joined the short-lived *Légion des aviateurs contre le bolchevisme*, which never quite got off the ground, and passed to the LVF. He left France with the 5th contingent for Deba.

*Lieutenant* Justin Jautard and *Commandant* Max Lelongt were First World War veterans. Lelongt was awarded the *Crox de guerre* with a brigade citation in 1915. Jautard was assigned first to the Artillery Battalion, but when that was dissolved he was appointed the Supply Officer. He was well regarded, but sometimes 'too brutal' towards the men. As for Lelongt, he was the chief medical officer. He volunteered for the LVF in December 1941, leaving behind his business and his family.

The elderly and colourful Mgr. de Mayol de Lupé was also assigned to the III. Bataillon. On his return to Paris after blessing the first detachments of the LVF as well as the trains that transported them to the Eastern Front he learnt that the situation of one of his friends still held captive, Mme Simonnet, had not improved. Then another friend, Pierre d'Harcourt, was arrested. He intervened on behalf of his friend as well as many Jewish families, but the Germans repeated their blackmail demand for him to become the General Chaplain of the LVF.

Undecided, Mgr. de Mayol de Lupé went to canon Jourdain, a declared enemy of the Germans, who told him not to hesitate as it was a question of French lives. He then wrote to Cardinal Sibilia in Rome asking for advice and permission, which was duly granted. Still beset by misgivings about donning the field grey uniform, he also consulted with Cardinal Suhard, who reassured him by replying: "Come on, it's only a contingency!"

Mgr. de Mayol de Lupé's decision to leave was also swayed by his anti-Bolshevism. He too viewed the attack on the Soviet Union as a religious crusade against atheist Bolshevism. He brought along with him his secretary Henri Cheveau, born on 2 August 1907 in Paris, who would follow him to the end. He left Paris for the Deba training camp on 19 December 1941.

In a letter to the Führer dated 18 April 1942, he asked again for the release of Mme Simonnet, Harcourt and fourteen prisoners from his village, claiming that they were all ardently Franco-German. He also asked the Führer to honour the agreement made that for each legionnaire who

---

71    Georges Flamand was born on 5 March 1901 in Héricourt in Haute Savoie.

had enlisted one prisoner of war would be released. But he also revealed in this letter that he was proud to have sworn an oath to him.

Now with no overall French commander, the two battalions of the LVF were employed separately and exclusively on anti-partisan operations to the rear of Army Group Centre. There was no question of returning them to front line duties again.

On 26 January 1942, Jean Malardier, who was born on 1 October 1919 in the 13th department of Paris, enlisted in the LVF. Before the war he was not a militant of a political party. Underweight when called up for military service he was placed in the *service auxiliaire*. In June 1940, he was called up again, but it was too late for him to meet the Germans on the field of battle. For him, defeat came as no surprise:

> Being interested in military and political questions since the arrival in power of the Front Populaire in 1936, [and] much to the alarm of my employers (la Société Lyonnaise de Dèpots et de Credit in Lyon) and my family circle, I foresaw defeat. Now I jumped at the opportunity to denounce the flaws of our democratic system and its allegiance to Anglo-Saxon politics whose first principal, I recall, was always the humbling of Europe.

In defeat, Malardier did not pass to the Armistice Army. He became a fervent supporter of Marshal Pètain, recognising in him 'the man lawfully vested with all the powers by the representatives of the Third Republic'. Of his decision to enlist in the LVF, he said:

> It seemed evident to me that the German attack on Russia justified itself out of the necessity to push back, as far as possible, the Eastern frontiers of Europe threatened by Slav expansionism. Thus I jumped at the opportunity which was offered to all European people to share in this action... I believed and I believe Napoleon more than ever that 'Europe will be federated or Cossack'. On the philosophical plane I felt none of the difficulties many of my comrades reported.

After completing his training at Kruszyna, Poland, Malardier was posted to Russia and assigned to the Headquarters Company of the I. Bataillon.

Meanwhile, the 9th contingent left Versailles on 9 April 1942, not before it had laid a wreath at the monument to the dead of the *Grande Guerre*. It was seen off by *Président du Comité central* Pierre Costantini.

In early May 1942, Henri-Georges Gonzales enlisted in the LVF at Marseille, his place of residence, where he was born on 8 September 1920. The young Gonzales was not interested in politics but that all changed in 1937 when a friend took him along to the headquarters of the PPF. He became friends with Simon Sabiani, the Marseille mouthpiece of the PPF. When war was declared in September 1939 he was not mobilised to his annoyance so he tried to enlist in the Foreign Legion with two friends. He was accepted and so was one of his friends, but his other friend was rejected; due to an accident he was missing two toes. All three of them promptly left the recruitment office! Because of his friend's missing two toes he would not get to fight the Germans.

Gonzales enlisted in the LVF out of a spirit of adventure, out of ideals, for he had a visceral hatred of Communism, and also out of friendship for Simon Sabiani. 'His political leader', as he described Sabiani, was virulently anti-Communist. Moreover, his father, who had been mobilised in 1939, was now back home and he had no wish to leave his mother all alone.

Gonzales travelled up to the Versailles barracks of the LVF in the company of André Juin, also an inhabitant of Marseille. They became close friends and, although they would serve side by side for years in the 2nd Company of the I. Bataillon of the LVF and later in the Engineer Company of 'Charlemagne', Gonzales never got to learn of Juin's reasons for enlisting.[72]

At Versailles, Gonzales underwent a medical examination and passed. Thereupon he exchanged his civilian clothes for a French Army uniform. Although he wanted to fight Communism 'in the colours of his homeland', he realised that this was out of the question because the Germans were abiding by the international rules of land warfare.

While based at Versailles Gonzales visited Paris for the first time. He was a little ashamed to see the city overrun with disorderly servicemen of the German Army, but he never questioned his decision to enlist. He would fight with them against those that had become the common enemy.

From Versailles, Gonzales was sent to camp Kruszyna near Radom, Poland, where he received three months intense training and then came the moment to swear the oath of loyalty to Adolf Hitler. The ceremony was full of incident as Gonzales remembers:

> The company was formed in a square. A German General, whose name I have forgot, pulled out his sabre and after some minutes of oratorical palaver asked us to swear an oath of loyalty.[73] At that moment the whole group to which I belonged left the ranks as a sign of refusal. The General choked and ordered the German instructors to surround us. And they shut us up in a building whose doors and windows were nailed up. We were left there all night. The following morning, a German Sergeant came and asked us if we had changed opinion. 'No!' half replied. 'Yes!' replied the other half to which I belonged. Some days after these events we left for Russia.

As for those who continued to refuse, they were sent to work in salt mines in Silesia.

Gonzales was assigned to the 2nd Company of the I. Bataillon operating in Byelorussia. Death was never far away. On a resupply mission he experienced his first encounter with death when two scouts stepped on a home-made land mine. The bodies of both were horribly mutilated. Hate gripped him and he readily admitted that he would have killed any 'human form of Russian appearance in front of him'. Such was Gonzales' brutal introduction to partisan warfare.

**Partisan Hunters: May-December 1942**

On 10 May 1942, the III. Bataillon of the LVF left Deba for the front and disembarked on 15 May at Poschinok, some sixty kilometres south-west. Through appalling rivers of mud it took the battalion three days to move to Balutino. Attached to the 221st Security Division, the French battalion relieved the 974th Landesschützen-Bataillon. By 20th May, the four

72  André Juin would meet his death on Belgard plain in March 1945.
73  The German general was General der Infanterie Halm.

companies occupied a front of some four to five kilometres from Pawlowa to Djatlowka opposite encircled Soviet regular units as well as partisans.

On 2 June 1942, the 9th and 10th companies attacked as part of Operation 'Volost' and took their objectives. *Sergent* Pierre Soulé of the 9th Company was advancing towards a village when his platoon came under heavy fire. His friend René Toussaint was killed and the medical orderly, who went about his duty without regard for his safety, was also seriously wounded. In total, four men were killed and seven wounded. Another of those killed was François Sabiani, the son of Simon Sabiani, the leader of the PPF in Marseille. Days before he wrote a letter destined for Doriot:

> Chef,
> I die for my ideal. I hope and I'm certain that this ideal will not be betrayed. Continue to fight. We are still behind you. I'm counting on you, because my Country needs you. *PPF vaincra. La France vivra.*
>
> François Sabiani

Among the wounded was twenty-year-old *caporal* Jean Cossard from Marseille, who was serving with the 1st Platoon of the 10th Company. He was subsequently decorated with the Iron Cross 2nd Class.

On 4 June, after a day of rest, the attack resumed with the 11th Company, which made ground, but came under increasing fire and when the partisans counterattacked it found itself encircled. Thanks to the leadership of both *Capitaine* Demessine and de Mayol de Lupé, the company managed to break out under the cover of night, but the day had cost the company eight dead and missing, as well as countless wounded.

Concerned that Colonel Ducrot was proving incapable of command, the Germans immediately had him removed and replaced by *Capitaine* (later Major) Demessine. The attack continued on 11 June, but the enemy had already evacuated their positions. Even so, some heavy weapons were captured. The following day, Dudrowka was taken without resistance, bringing the attack to an end.

On 16 June 1942, at Bolotowa, the command post of the III. Bataillon, Oberst Wiemann of the 44th Security Regiment decorated five deserving Frenchman with the Iron Cross 2nd Class, including de Mayol de Lupé, *Capitaine* Demessine, Doctor *Lieutenant* Molinié and *Aspirant* Seveau.

The III. Batallion was now moved to Gomel and then onto Krasnopolje, some one hundred kilometres north of Gomel. In July and August, the battalion participated in two small operations named 'Viereck' and 'Eule' without much to show for its efforts. Henceforth, the battalion was attached to the 45th Security Regiment.

On 8 August, *Sous-lieutenant* Martin of the III. Bataillon wrote to the German liaison headquarters requesting a transfer to another battalion. In his letter he stated:

> Undeniably, the III. Bataillon has currently lost all aspect of a military unit and taken on that of a horde, or a caravan of gypsies. Pillage and theft are tolerated and even the battalion commander [*Capitaine* Demessine] sets an example.

He recorded numerous examples of his battalion commanders' behavior which displayed a 'lack of honour and uniform'. Other officers also wrote letters of complaint about *Capitaine* Demessine to the German liaison headquarters. Martin was later transferred to the I. Bataillon after a confrontation with Demessine who had got wind of his letter.

At the end of August, the battalion was assigned to relieve the 743rd Security Battalion and take over guard duty along the vital railway line between Unetscha and Kritschew. The legionnaires were dispersed along some sixty kilometres of track.

In September, Hauptmann Katzian replaced Oberstleutant von Kirschbaun as the Chief-of-Staff of the German liaison. He would stay with this battalion until the end of the campaign in Russia. The first replacements were also received, in total one hundred and twenty-five men, who had left Versailles for training at Kruszyna on 18 June 1942. The days proved an endless succession of patrols, fire fights and explosions. Notably, on the night of 9 October, eight Frenchmen guarding a post at Korenez were attacked by some fifteen partisans, but they manged to fight them off.

In late November, the III. Bataillon was finally relieved of guarding the railway line and sent to the zone Niwnoje-Strushenka-Shastkoff. On 26 November, the *section d'intervention*, reinforced by some twenty-five Russian police of the Ordnungsdienst, violently clashed with partisans while on patrol to the village of Krutojar, six kilometres north-east of Niwnoje. French losses were heavy: three dead, six wounded and six missing. The 9th Company and thirty or so Russian police now attempted to occupy the village but were 'vigorously welcomed' by the partisans and fell back to Niwnoje. That same night the partisans attacked Niwnoje, which had been hastly prepared for defense. The French managed to fight them off with the support of mortars. On 28th November, the 9th Company and one company from the 1st Battalion/8th Police Regiment occupied Krutojar without incident. Once again, the partisans had disappeared into the shelter of the forests.

### The I. Bataillon

As for the reorganised I. Bataillon, it left the training camp of Kruszyna on 17 July 1942 to occupy its new post at Borisov in the Minsk region and was attached to the 286th Security Division. After one week of rest, on 27 July, the battalion was on the move again to Murovo. In August, it participated in Operation 'Grief' [Griffin] but saw very little action. Although the majority of partisans managed to get out of the encirclement, the operation was still deemed a success with some 800 partisans killed and 600 taken prisoner, along with many captured small arms and two serviceable tanks. With that said the battalion commander was still of the opinion that 'we were being left in complete isolation, ignored by all' so much so it was starting to have a bad effect on morale.[74]

At the start of September 1942, the I. Bataillon was moved to Tolotchin, from which it launched more anti-partisan sweeps, all with the same disappointing results; suspect villages were already empty when the Frenchmen arrived. The battalion moved to winter quarters around Borisov on 18 September 1942.

74    Letter dated 28 September 1942 from the battalion commander to de Brinon.

In September 1942, Alfred Falcy joined the 2nd Company as a platoon commander. Born on 26 June 1912 in Saint-André-de-Boëge in Haute-Savoie, he was commissioned *sous-lieutenant de réserve* in 1938 and subsequently served with the elite *chasseurs alpins*. He volunteered for the LVF in 1942.

Disaster struck the 2nd Company on 4 October when a demi-section [two sections or half a platoon] was ambushed by partisans between Vydritsa and Denissovitchi in the clearing of Kalinine. A rescue party was sent, only to find twenty horribly mutilated corpses, two of which were actually still alive. One died later of his wounds, while the other, René Bourg, survived. Notably, one of those killed was André Albietz whose father, Auguste, was also serving with the LVF [and would later be transferred to the Waffen-SS].

Elements of the I. Bataillon, including *sous-lieutenant* Alfred Falcy's platoon of the 2nd Company, then participated in Operation 'Karlsbad' (12-23 October) in the forest south of Wydriza. Other units involved in this anti-partisan sweep included 1. SS-Infanterie-Brigade (mot), SS Sonderkommando Dirlewanger, (lituauische) Schutmannschaft Bataillon 255 and I. Bataillon/Kosaken Abteilung 102. The results of this rather large-scale operation were frustrating; one report stated that by 18th October only 316 'bandits' had been killed, although this number had risen to 1051 by 24 October, while German losses were minor.

On 25 October, twenty-five KVK II were awarded. Most went to the Headquarters Company.

On 6 November, the first snow fell. On 16 November, two platoons of the 1st Company and a Cosssack detachment scored a notable success when they attacked the village of Somry, putting some sixty partisans out of action. Three members of the 1st Company were awarded the Iron Cross 2nd Class, including the Company commander.

Later that month, *Sous-lieutenant* Martin of the III. Bataillon was posted to the I. Bataillon and took over command of its PAK Platoon from *Sous-lieutenant* Le Marquer,[75] whereupon he was appointed as the interim commander of the Headquarters Company, replacing *Capitaine* Hays, who, in Martin's words, was 'completely incapable'. Moreover, he had reservations about two fellow officers and the companies they commanded; he found the 2nd Company a 'little slack', typified by the time a German General visited Wydriza and company commander *Capitaine* Henri Poisson was not even shaved, while the 3rd Company was a bit derided because of the antics of its company commander.

On 9 December, in a bizarre twist, battalion commander *Commandant* Lacroix, who had long been suspected of harbouring political ambitions, issued a communiqué in which he expressed his view that the 'real role' of the LVF was to overthrow the Vichy Government after its glorious return to France. The Germans reacted quickly and four days later relieved him of his command and sent him back to France. As a parting shot he issued a note, affirming that he was leaving the legion to dedicate himself to the interests of the legionnaires, who he reminded to remain politically viligant. *Capitaine* Henri Poisson assumed temporary command of the battalion.

---

75  Born on 14 June 1921 in Casablanca, Jean-Louis Le Marquer joined the LVF in 1941 with the rank of *aspirant*. Assigned to the 4th Company, he saw action before Moscow and was promoted to *Sous-lieutenant* in December 1941. In November 1942, he was appointed as the commander of the Propaganda Platoon of the I. Batallion, but found himself in trouble for alleged ill-discipline and was returned to France in the spring of 1943. He joined the Waffen-SS later that year and was assigned to SS-Standarte Kurt Eggers with the rank of Oberjunker. He was promoted to Untersturmführer on 14 May 1944.

In mid-December, the two battalions of the LVF greatly benefited from the influx of officers from the recently dissolved *Légion Tricolore*.

## *La Légion Tricolore*

Meanwhile, back in France, with the approval of the Vichy Government, the LVF was transformed into *La Légion Tricolore*. The principal architect of this politically inspired move was Jacques Benoist-Méchin, the young Vichy Secretary of State to the *Chef de gouvernement*. A brilliant intellectual, he was a 'man of letters in his books, in his speech, and in his life'.[76] His monumental *Histoire de l'armeé allemande* was published in 1938 which was favourable towards the German Army, triumphant Nazism and Hitler.

Benoist-Méchin wrote on 17 November 1941:

> A defeated country can take up three positions, against its conqueror, for its conqueror, or with its conqueror. I am against, as indeed France has shown herself to be against, the first position, because in a whole succession of circumstances she has not reacted. On the other hand, France is not agreed to be for the conquering power. I am a partisan of the third formula: with the conqueror.

A partisan of a New Europe in which France would play an important role thanks to its colonial Empire, Benoist-Méchin worked hard for military co-operation with Germany. Born of this was his idea of *La Légion Tricolore* modelled on the Spanish Blue Division. In April 1942, when Laval returned to power, Benoist-Méchin was tasked with the creation of *La Légion Tricolore*.

President Laval had much to gain from the creation of *La Légion Tricolore*. He would then have at his disposal a new Legion that could be employed in France against the Resistance and in Africa against those colonies that had gone over to de Gaulle. Moreover, through *La Légion Tricolore*, he hoped to control not only the 'ultras' of Paris, but also Joseph Darnand and the SOL. He knew that they could 'not remain uninvolved in a government initiative which corresponded to their views and ideal'.[77]

Benoist-Méchin went about the creation of *La Légion Tricolore* with great enthusiasm and formed a team of collaborators in his own image. To progress the project, he requested a meeting with Oberst Kossmann, the Chef des Stabes Militärbefehlshaber Frankreich, who proved evasive, but who pointed him in the direction of General Matsky, said to be in charge of foreign formations incorporated into the Wehrmacht. General Matsky sent his Chief-of-Staff, Colonel Mayer, to meet Benoist-Méchin in Paris. The meeting took place on 21 June 1942.

Benoist-Méchin handed a memorandum to Colonel Mayer, which proposed that the existing French battalions, referring to the LVF, be amalgamated with new forces to form a *grande unité*, which would fight in German uniforms at the front, but be authorised to wear the French uniform in France. Mayer seemed receptive and concluded the meeting with the encouraging words: "I think your projects will be accepted by General Matsky."[78] Benoist-Méchin was now of the opinion that he finally had German approval for the creation of *La Légion Tricolore*.

76  Aron Robert, *The Vichy Regime 1940-44* (London: Putnam, 1958), p.281.
77  These words are actually those of Darnand from his speech at Lyon on 12 July 1942.
78  Lefèvre Eric and Jean Mabire, *La Légion perdue* (Paris: Jacques Grancher, 1995), p.168.

Benoist-Méchin also entered into negotiations with representatives of the political parties that had created the LVF. He respected the fact that the *chefs* of the political parties had shown real courage to argue in favour of the Legion at a time when Vichy deliberately ignored its existence and also that their militants filled the ranks of the Legion. He would write later that to oust them would be both awkward and unjust. So he decided to take control of the *Comité central de la LVF*, assuming the presidency as the government delegate. To water down the 'northern' influence, he brought onto the *Comité central* Darnand, the *inspecteur* of the SOL, and Jean-Marcel Renault, the *chef* of the JFOM, as representatives of the two most active organisations in the Free Zone.

On 22 June 1942, the *Comité central de la LVF*, meeting at hotel Matignon in Paris, announced the dissolution of the LVF and its transformation into *La Légion Tricolore*. Costantini, the president in office, handed over power without complaint to Benoist-Méchin. Statutes for the *La Légion Tricolore* were agreed unanimously. The *Comité central de la Légion Tricolore* replaced the *Comité central de la LVF* with Benoist-Méchin now as president. Notably, according to Article 3 of its statutes, *La Légion Tricolore* 'can be engaged on any front where the national interest is at stake'.

General Galy was duly appointed the *Commissaire Général de la Légion Tricolore*.

Support for *La Légion Tricolore* was forthcoming from the Vichy government, as well as German Ambassador Otto Abetz and SS-Brigadeführer Carl Oberg, the Higher SS and Police Leader (HSSPF) of France.

On 6 July 1942, General Bridoux, the Vichy Secretary of State for War, put his name to a circular that authorised officers and men of the metropolitan Armistice Army and the transitional Army in North Africa to enlist in *La Légion Tricolore*.

The following day, a Ministry of Interior circular to the *préfets* started: 'It's with the approval of the government that the *Légion des Volontaires français contre le Bolchevisme* has been transformed into *Légion Tricolore*.' The circular proceeded to call upon the *préfets* to support the recruitment offices of *La Légion Tricolore* and to encourage those civil servants expressing a desire to enlist.

To encourage recruitment, the Vichy government passed Law N° 704 on 18 July 1942, published in the *Journal officiel* on 8 August 1942.[79] According to Article 1, the French State would guarantee the benefits granted by *La Légion Tricolore* to its members. According to article 3:

> The officers, non-commissioned officers and men of *La Légion Tricolore* may be decorated with the *Légion d'honneur* or the *Médaille militaire* under the conditions provided for by the regulations in force. Citations including the attribution of a medal will be awarded to those who particularly distinguish themselves.

That medal was the *Croix de guerre légionnaire*. The first awards of this new medal followed soon after on 27 August 1942.

*La Légion Tricolore* took over the LVF's barracks in Versailles for recruits from the Occupied Zone and, in July, opened up *Caserne des Augstines* in Guéret (department Creuse) for recruits

---

79   This law has often been misrepresented, from creating *La Légion Tricolore* to official recognition of the *Croix de guerre légionnaire*. This law makes no specific mention of the *Croix de guerre légionnaire*, though.

from the Free Zone and French North Africa. This depot, a former hospital, dated back to the 17th Century. Colonel Puaud was appointed to command the recruits recruited in the Free Zone and French North Africa.

## Edgar Puaud[80]

Born on 29 October 1889 in Orléans, Edgar-Joseph-Alexandre Puaud joined the Army in 1907. At the end of his four-year contract he went back to civilian life but returned to the flag a year later. In May 1914, *sergent* Puaud of the *133e régiment d'infanterie* was 'recognised eligible' for attendance at the *école militaire d'infanterie de Saint-Maixent*. However, because of the threat of war, he never got to go to the infantry military school. On 5 August 1914, the Ministry of War decided that those NCOs recognised eligible for the military schools of Saint-Maixent, Saumur, Fontainebleau, Versailles and Vincennes were to be promoted to *aspirant* (published in the *Journal officiel* on the 8th). This included Puaud.

On 1 September 1914, Puaud was promoted to *sous-lieutenant à titre temporaire*. By the end of the war, he held the rank of *capitaine à titre définitif* and his chest was ablaze with medals. He was the proud holder of the *Croix de guerre* with seven citations, including two *à l'ordre de l'armée*, the *Croix de guerre des T.O.E.* with two bronze stars and the *Croix de Chevalier de la Légion d'honneur*. He was later awarded the *médaille des evades* instituted by law in 1926 for the *guerre* 1914-1918.

After the war Puaud served with the *13e bataillon de chasseurs mitrailleurs* (BCM) of the *armée du Rhin* [Army of the Rhine]. From 1926 to 1937, he served in Morocco, obtaining three more citations. His posts were many and some were administrative. Notably he served with the *1er régiment étranger d'infanterie* [Foreign Legion] from 1926 to 1927 and with the *3e régiment étranger d'infanterie* from 1934 to 1937. In 1934, he was promoted to *chef de bataillon*.

In 1937, *chef de bataillon* Puaud was posted to Tonkin and the *5e régiment étranger d'infanterie*.

He returned to France in 1940[81] and, after the armistice, took command of the camp of Septfonds in the Tarn-et-Garonne, where he did his utmost to protect the foreign volunteers, including many of Germanic origin, sought by the German authorities.

He went on to command the *3e bataillon du 23e régiment d'infanterie*, garrisoned at Montauban. A witness who served under *Commandant* Puaud described him as a *'super anti-collaborateur'*. Indeed, he refused to shake hands with the German officers of the armistice commission who came to inspect his weapons arsenal. Like many, he dreamt of revenge and had hidden a weapons cache in Montech forest to use against the 'Boches' when the time came.[82]

In July 1942, Puaud, the patriot, enlisted in *La Légion Tricolore* and was promoted to temporary Colonel. After the departure of Lieutenant-Colonel Tézé, he was appointed the *Commissaire général adjoint* of *La Légion Tricolore*.[83] His promotion to Colonel was confirmed on 25 November 1942. In early 1943, he became the *délégué général militaire de la LVF* in France.

---

80   The author wishes to express his thanks to Eric Lefèvre for the information concerning Puaud.
81   According to Ory Pascal, *Les collaborateurs* (Paris: Le Seuil, 1977), p.245, Puaud returned from Indo-China in May 1940 to do battle with the Germans. As such, this remains unconfirmed.
82   See H.L., p.134, *Historia hors série* 32.
83   Roch, *La Division Charlemagne*, p.170.

## From hope to despair

Joseph Darnand, the Inspector-General of the SOL, threw his considerable weight behind the new Legion. At a ceremony held in Lyon on 12 July, Darnand stated that 'whereas the activities of the SOL would be confined mainly to France, *La Légion Tricolore*, should the necessity arise, would fight on the side of the Axis in Europe and in Africa'. With serious words heavy with meaning, Darnand told his adherents that they had to be represented in *La Légion Tricolore* and that they 'will prove in its ranks that they are sons of France agreeing to every sacrifice as soon as the homeland demands it'.

Jean Bassompierre, along with a handful of other SOL *chefs*, volunteered for *La Légion Tricolore*. Before coming forward, Lieutenant Bassompierre had hesitated. A traditionalist, he was anti-German but 'he had always been anti-Communist'. Darnand had spoken to him about the fate of Poland 'which had been fully absorbed by a tyrannical conqueror' and explained that France must not suffer the same fate. Darnand added that these 'new barbarians from Asia' had to be prevented from submerging one day 'our old continent'. The anti-Bolshevist struggle and the independence of France in the eventuality of a German victory were the reasons that silenced Bassompierre's lingering scruples. Before leaving, with the approval of Laval, he held propaganda meetings at Nice, Marseille, Toulouse, Lyon, Limoges, in the principal cities of the Southern zone. Received by Marshal Pétain, Bassompierre was embraced and told: "You are the youth of France."

On 10 August 1942, a governmental decree stated that volunteers for *La Légion Tricolore* would receive French Army rates of pay, enjoy French Army pension rights and be allowed to wear the French uniform.

On 12 August 1942, Clémenti, the party leader of the PFNC, and his secretary Eric Labat enlisted in *La Légion Tricolore*. [Both would go on to serve with the LVF. In the absence of Clémenti, his party disintegrated].

On 25 August 1942, Benoist-Méchin, accompanied by General Galy and Colonel Puaud, inspected the 200 to 250 volunteers of *La Légion Tricolore* assembled at Guéret. Benoist-Méchin was presented to each officer by Puaud. The volunteers were then sent to Versailles to participate in the celebrations planned for 27 August in Paris. However, the German military authorities were not expecting them and put them through a medical, of which three-quarters did not pass as fit for service on the Eastern Front. The volunteers from Guéret were separated from those from the Occupied Zone and confined to barracks, which to one commentator, started to resemble a prison.

This turn of events confounded Benoist-Méchin who was convinced it was all a misunderstanding. He sought clarification from Oberst Kossmann, who, like the German command, was totally unaware of the Legion's new statutes. Nevertheless, they agreed that the volunteers from Guéret would have a new medical the following week.

On 27 August 1942, a number of ceremonies were held in Paris to mark the first anniversary of the formation of the LVF. *La Légion Tricolore* recruits from Guéret participated in the ceremonies but they were required to return to barracks by one in the afternoon following a last minute intervention by the furious German military authorities. They wore for the very first time a new badge on their right breast chosen by Benoist-Méchin, which featured a gold embroidered imperial eagle holding four lightning bolts in its talons.

The first ceremony was held at cathedral Notre-Dame, where mass was celebrated in memory of the dead of the LVF. Among the dignitaries present were Admiral Platon, representing the head of state, Ambassador de Brinon, representing the head of government, Secretary of State Benoist-Méchin, and Otto Abetz, German Ambassador to France.

The next ceremony was held in la cour d'honneur de l'Hôtel des Invalides in the presence of various representatives of the Maréchal, the services, and the head of government, as well as three members of the central committee of *La Légion Tricolore*, including Darnand. Colonel Puaud read aloud the names of the dead. General Galy awarded the *Croix de guerre légionnaire* to four recipients, including Mgr. Jean de Mayol de Lupé and Colonel Roger Labonne, who wore his German uniform even though he had been dismissed from the LVF months before. The four of them had previously been decorated with the Iron Cross 2nd Class.

Tricolore fanions for the first battalions of the proposed 'French Division' were then ceremoniously entrusted to *légionnaires* by Colonel Puaud. The design of the new standards harked back to the days of the First Empire.

In the afternoon, Benoist-Méchin and General Galy visited Suresnes hospital to present awards to seriously wounded *légionnaires*. At the same time, Colonel Puaud, accompanied by six *légionnaires*, laid three wreaths on the Tomb of the Unknown Soldier.[84] The wreaths were donated by the Vichy Government, the central committee and the volunteers.

Arguably, the celebrations of 27 August, while a success, proved the end for *La Légion Tricolore* whose existence the German military authorities could no longer ignore. Indeed, the Germans refused to arm *La Légion Tricolore* recruits on their return to Guéret, who now spent their days on sport or in the classroom. Morale dropped. Some deserted.

The end came weeks later. On 17 September 1942, the Wehrmacht officially informed the Vichy Government that it was not prepared to accept an autonomous Legion into its midst and demanded the disbandment of *La Légion Tricolore*.[85]

*La Légion Tricolore* was duly disbanded by law N° 1113 of 28 December 1942, signed by Pierre Laval and published in the *Journal officiel*. The reason was simple. Germany did not want to contribute to the reconstruction of well-equipped and well trained French forces which might prove dangerous for German interests one day.[86] Indeed, if the LVF was to come under French control, the Germans would have no power to prevent it being withdrawn from Russia. Such a prospect was intolerable. The French volunteers had to remain under German authority.

Besides, from the outset, the Legion had been forged on an 'illusion', on a 'false impression'.[87] The source of the misunderstanding stemmed from the meeting on 8 July 1942 between Benoist-Méchin and Colonel Mayer, whose opinion had been taken as approval from the German military authorities, when in fact he was solely on a fact-finding mission and had 'no mandate to promise in the name of the OKW'.[88]

---

84    Many sources state that on 27 August 1942 *La Légion Tricolore* was inaugurated at the Tomb of the Unknown Soldier in Paris. This is incorrect. There was no such inauguration.

85    Ory, *Les Collaborateurs*, p.245. Some sources also record this same day when Hitler intervened and ordered *La Légion Tricolore* to be disbanded because it violated the armistice convention.

86    Bene, Krisztián, *La collaboration militaire française dans la Seconde Guerre mondiale* (Éditions Codex, 2011), p.176.

87    Delperrié de Bayac, *Histoire de la Milice*, p.136.

88    General Galy, October 1942.

On 5 October 1942, *La Légion Tricolore* had reported its strength at 54 officers, 118 NCOs and 595 men (including 105 Moroccans), but what now for its recruits? They were offered the option of returning to civilian life or transferring to the resurrected LVF. In fact, before *La Légion Tricolore* was even officially disbanded, a number of officers and *aspirants* had already decided to sign up for the LVF and were undergoing basic training in Poland, including Bassompierre, Boudet-Gheusi, Lafargue, Panné, Prévost and Simoni. Many other officers would subsequently sign up for the LVF, be it weeks or months later, including Audibert, Bénétoux, Gaillard, Huot, Obitz, Salle, Schlisler, and Vincent.[89] At least eighty men passed to the LVF. One of those was Jacques Gagneron, who had previously served with the *1er Régiment d'Infanterie*.[90] He was admitted with the rank of *caporal*.

And so, in mid-December 1942, the first batch of officers and *aspirants* from *La Légion Tricolore* arrived in Russia. Five officers and *aspirants* were assigned to the I. Batallion.

On donning the German uniform for the first time, *Capitaine* Jean Bassompierre would later admit to shedding a tear. He only managed to overcome his repugnance by repeating to himself the following words of Marshal Pétain to the *légionnaires* of the LVF: "You protect the same frontiers of France from Bolshevism by going to fight far from your homeland."

One or two days before Christmas day 1942, Bassompierre arrived at the village of Wydriza (which is also spelt Vydritsa) to take over the command of the 2nd Company of the I. Batallion. Henri-Georges Gonzales was appointed his orderly.

*Capitaine* Jean Boudet-Gheusi and *Sous-lieutenant* Robert Lafargue were also assigned to the I. Batallion. Boudet-Gheusi replaced *Sous-lieutenant* Martin at the head of the Headquarters Company in January 1943. Thereupon, Martin became the commander of the Anti-Tank [PAK] Platoon and, on 26 January 1943, was awarded the KVK II. Lafargue was appointed as commander of the Mortar Platoon of the Headquarters Company.[91]

Born on 26 July 1904 in Tarbes, Jean Boudet, called Boudet-Gheusi, studied law at the *Faculté de droit d'Aix-en-Provence*. Armed with the *brevet de PMS*, he attended EOR training at Saint-Maixent. Promoted to *sous-lieutenant de réserve* in 1930, he was posted to the elite *22e bataillon de chasseurs alpins* (22° BCA). After the defeat of 1940, he joined the *Légion Française des Combattants*, and then passed to the SOL, becoming *chef-départemental-adjoint* for department Alpes-Maritimes. Responding to Darnand's appeal, he volunteered for *La Légion Tricolore*. On 15 August 1942, he was promoted to the rank of *Capitaine*.

Three officers, who were all *active*, and one *aspirant* from *La Légion Tricolore* were assigned to the III. Batallion. They arrived on a sleigh at the headquarters of the III. Batallion on 18th December 1942. *Capitaine* Madec took over the reins of the 11th Company, *Capitaine* Dewitte that of the 10th Company and *Lieutenant* Neveux a platoon of the 11th Company. Notably, Neveux, who was only twenty-three, had graduated from Saint-Cyr, promotion *Marne et Verdun*, won the *Croix de guerre* with two citations fighting against the Germans in 1940, and

89 Notably, at least 41 officers who enlisted in *La Légion Tricolore* before it was officially dissolved signed up for the LVF [and some of those later passed to the Waffen-SS]. And yet, curiously, according to Littlejohn, *Foreign Legions of the Third Reich: volume 1*, p.156, only nine officers joined the LVF.
90 Jacques Gagneron was born on 21 March 1925 in Châteauroux (department Indre). He would later distinguish himself while serving with 'Charlemagne' in Pomerania.
91 Robert Lafargue was born on 20 August 1906 in Paris.

also distinguished himself in the Levant in 1941. Appointed to command the 11th Company on 28 January 1943, he bravely led the company until 16 February 1944 when he was wounded.[92]

## December 1942–May 1943

On 19 December 1942, the III. Bataillon of the LVF participated in Operation 'Ankara I', along with the 791st Security Battalion, the 1st Battalion of the 8th Police Regiment, and Ostbataillon 604. So disappointing were the results of the week-long sweep[93] that the follow-up Operation 'Ankara II' was planned with a start date of 17 January 1943. There was one 'casualty', though. A report from the commander of the 36th Security Regiment was highly critical of the French battalion, remarking that 'there are a few officers who are able to exert a good influence on the men' and 'there are only a few good NCOs'. The report also criticised the German liaison staff, before concluding 'its fighting value is questionable'. Capitaine Dessine paid the price of this report as battalion commander and was relieved of his command.

On 7 January 1943, the III. Bataillon received 109 replacements from the *3e renfort* which had left Versailles on 8 October 1942 for three months training at Kruszyna. Among them was Éric Labat who was assigned to the 9th Company. He would write a book about his time with the LVF called *Les places étaient chers*.

Operation 'Ankara II' was initiated as planned with the same units deployed in 'Ankara I', as well as a battery of three captured Russian 76.2mm guns. The operation went well and finished on 21 January 1943 with all objectives having been achieved. The results of 'Ankara II' were much more satisfactory: enemy losses were estimated at 150, which included 41 executed after capture by *Geheime Feldpolizei* [secret field police] attached to the operation. The French battalion suffered two dead.

The III. Bataillon then participated in Operation 'Klette II' (22 January–9 February 1943) which was much more ambitious as the 2nd Panzer Army planned to encircle and annihilate partisans centered in the forest of Mamajewka. The 707th Infantry Division was also made available for this operation. The French battalion, as part of Kampfgruppe von Geldern, held the line of encirclement to the west and south west of the forest between the 1st Battalion of the 8th Police Regiment and a reinforced company from the 791st Security Battalion. The legionnaires dug emplacements in the frozen ground and waited for the partisans to make their move. Patrols were constantly sent out. The temperature dropped to 21 below zero.

On 28 January 1943, Major Panné of *La Légion Tricolore* became the new battalion commander, replacing *Capitane* Madec who was acting as the temporary battalion commander after Demessine was relieved of command. On 4 February, Kampfgruppe von Geldern moved east, reaching its objective, without any partisan interference. That night a French patrol captured four partisans but one legionnaire was wounded. The following day, Kampfgruppe von Geldern further tightened the encirclement, again without any contact, only to learn that some 1300 partisans had broken through the lines of the 707th Infantry Division. The operation duly fizzled out and the exhausted French battalion was relieved. The operation was deemed a

---

92    Transferred to the Waffen-SS, Neveux would play no active role because of his wounds. After the war, he found religion, becoming a Trappist monk.

93    187 able-bodied men were rounded up for forced labour. There is no mention of a single partisan killed or of arms captured.

success, despite the escape of a large number of partisans, boasting 441 killed, 178 deserters, and 126 prisoners. German losses were 14 killed and 32 wounded, as well as 156 cases of frostbite, of which a good number were legionnaires. On 16 February, General von Schenckendorff thanked the French battalion and Ostbataillon 604 in writing, noting they 'had shown themseves worthy of their German comrades'.

Two weeks of rest followed at Mglin. Major Panné made a number of changes within the battalion and twenty-eight-year-old former *enseigne de vaisseau de 1re class de réserve* Raymond Gaillard was appointed the commander of the Headquarters Company.[94]

Back in France, on 11 February, the Vichy Government, through Law N° 95, finally recognised the LVF as an official organisation 'having public utility'. Admittedly this gave the legionnaires certain benefits, but few cared about this development.

Because of the detoriating situation of Army Group Centre, the III. Bataillon was hurriedly moved to Ordjonikidzegrad to construct a new defensive line, one hundred kilometres behind the front line, along with six other security units. The French battalion was attached to Oberbaustaub 18, but still reported to the 221st Security Division.

On 5 March, the III. Bataillon left Ordjonikidzegrad for the city of Trubschewsk, beside the river Desna, where the legionnaires were put to work again building fortifications. The battalion was attached to Reiterverband Trubschewsk, a cavalry unit of regimental strength, also composed of infantry. Patrols broke the monotony of digging. There was some partisan activity which inevitably led to casualties.

Atmospheric photograph of LVF cemetery at Smorki. (Rigeade)

94   Raymond Gaillard was born on 2 September 1914 in Athis-Mons (department la Seine-et-Oise).

The Frenchmen were stationed along the Desna for almost three months. On 11 May, the battalion received 60 replacements, which belonged to the *5e renfort* despatched from Versailles to Kruszyna on 29 January. Four days later, *lieutenant* Roger Audibert, who was an architect by profession, arrived and was assigned as a platoon commander in the 11th Company.[95] This *officier de réserve du train* won the *Croix de guerre* during 1939-40. He enlisted in the *Légion Tricolore* and signed up for the LVF on 11 January 1943. *Sous-lieutenant* Jean Wagner arrived later still and was given command of a platoon in the 9th Company. This twenty-nine-year-old Alsatian had served previously with the rank of *Aspirant* in the *2e Régiment de Tirailleurs Marocains* (2RTM).[96] He too had enlisted in the *Légion Tricolore* and subsequently the LVF.

At the end of May, the III. Bataillon was relieved of its long guard along the Desna, assembled and sent to Mogilev where it was reunited with the I. Bataillon. The III. Bataillon was also attached to the 286th Security Division whose headquarters was at Orsha.

The past six months had also been eventful for the I. Bataillon. On 22 December, *Chef de bataillon* Jean Simoni was appointed as the new battalion commander. He had served previously with the Foreign Legion and passed from *La Légion Tricolore* to the LVF.

On Christmas night 1942, the stables some one hundred metres from the village of Wydriza, where the headquarters of the 2nd Company was located, caught fire and was consumed so quickly that none of the horses could not be saved. Gonzales described this as an unlucky start for the new company commander *Capitaine* Bassompierre. Fortunately, another horse was stabled nearby which Gonzales sometimes rode to the small hamlet of Grosgorono, some three kilometers from Wydriza, occupied by a platoon of the 2nd Company under *Adjudant* Auguste Albietz.

Suffering from a bout of rheumatism, Gonzales was transported to battalion headquarters at Smorki where he was treated by the fearsome Capitaine Fluery who sent him packing with orders to rejoin his company by foot. However, at Smorki, he did meet two others who treated him kindlier and whose paths would cross again.[97]

In early January 1943, the new battalion commander turned his attention to a partisan concentration positioned around the village of Stych (or Sytsch) to the south of the 3rd Company's positions. Partisan strength was estimated at three hundred. The I. Bataillon launched an operation on 6 January with all available forces, elements from three companies, supported by twenty local police and mortars. On the 8th, they attacked and captured Stych. The operation was deemed a success with fifty partisans killed or wounded, and a large cache of weapons captured or destroyed. This was not enough for the battalion commander, though, who also had four villages razed and thirty civilians shot on the pretext they were partisan sympathisers.

95   Roger Aubert was born on 15 September 1917 in Marseille.
96   Jean Wagner was born on 14 July 1913 in Molsheim.
97   The first person was a medical orderly called Rouillon who Gonzales would meet again after the war in 1949 at the Grand Hôtel de Louvre, Paris, where Rouillon was working as a concierge. Born in 1916, Rouillon volunteered in 1936, trained at a medical school for Colonial troops and served in Tonkin for three years. Repatriated in 1940 and demobilized, he was one of the very first to volunteer for the LVF and served with the 2nd Company during the first winter. He was decorated with the *Croix de guerre légionnaire*, the KVK-II, the EK-II as well as, according to Soulat, the EK-I. He would pass to 'Charlemagne'. The second was called Pons who he would meet again some two years later after the disaster on Belgard plain and who tried to convince him to change into civilian clothes, which he categorically refused to do.

After a fairly quiet two months, the partisans started to harass the I. Bataillon again. On 1 April, a platoon from Bassompierre's company attacked the partisan held village of Murovo (also spelt Murowo), but was pushed back, with the loss of one dead and one wounded. Bassompierre proved himself once again as an exemplary officer, rescuing two of his units surrounded by overwhelming enemy numbers. Two weeks later, the French battalion attacked again with greater forces and captured the village *sans grands combats*.

Soon after, the partisans attacked Murovo. A platoon was sent as reinforcements with weapons and ammunition. While crossing the Berezina in a boat Giordano from Cherbourg, who had served in the Navy, was shot in the head and fell into the water. His body could not be found, despite an extensive search. A little later, Gonzales of the 2nd Company attended a commemoration organised by *Capitaine* Bassompierre for those killed in the region. Just as his *Capitaine* read out Giordano's name a villager came running up with the news that his body had just been discovered! It was not far from the spot he fell into the water.

With the agreement of his *Capitaine*, Gonzales of the 2nd Company, employed a 'panenka', a young Russian girl, called Anna which developed into a relationship.

On 10 April, Bassompierre wrote to *chef de bataillon* Simoni, expressing his concerns once again about the poor morale and incompetence of a great number of his men. He listed five reasons for this:

1. The countless deceptions since the creation of the LVF
2. The incomprehension of their compatriots
3. The rejection by their family
4. The political and military situation of their country especially after the treachery of November 1942
5. The prolonged cantonment in a sector far from the front with very few military operations

Bassompierre recommended that the battalion should be withdrawn immediately, reorganised, all undesirables ruthlessly dismissed, starting with several officers, as well as all legionnaires morally or physically unfit, whereupon this new regenerated battalion be assigned to a 'real combat sector'.

## The *Chef de bataillon* Simoni Report

On 11 May, *Chef de bataillon* Jean Simoni was relieved of his command and returned to France. Back home he wrote a damning report about the I. Bataillon. Indeed, according to the report, only 40% of NCOs and men 'were determined to fight'. The remaining 60%, which he called parasites, were 'determined not to fight.'

Simoni continued that two of the company commanders are 'radically incapable due to their almost total lack of serious military knowledge' and have 'no serious notion' of commanding a platoon, yet alone a company in combat. He lambasted a certain number of *adjudants* for not knowing their job, as well as the *Sergents* and *Sergent-Chefs*, who he described as a non-entity, 'without prestige and without authority'. In contrast, he was full of praise for the platoon commanders, with the notable exception of *Lieutenant* Le Marquer. Thus, the LVF was, in his opinion, 'only a militia, belonging to the mediocre battalions of gardes mobiles of 1870' that was incapable of front-line duty for fear of being massacred or disbanded.

If that were not bad enough, Simoni wrote that the majority of all ranks looked on their presence in Russia as an opportunity to 'eat better than in France' and 'the possibility to live lazily, well-supplied with women and vodka'! And yet, Simoni had commanded them for over four months and, ultimately, could be blamed for failing to instill the highest standards of military bearing.

Further on in his report, Simoni noted that his men were happy to return to the battalion after leave because they 'no longer had anything in common' with their countrymen, explaining that wherever they went they always received the same icy welcome and that most have fallen out with their family. He added that they felt unanimously rejected by the country, and completely abandoned by the Vichy Government and especially by its organs. He attributed the principal reason for this to the wearing of the German uniform. Regarding the future of the Battalion, he reiterated the recommendations of Bassompierre.

The war continued for the I. Bataillon, now under the temporary command of *Capitaine* Poisson. On 22 May, a reinforced patrol of some 150 men, including one platoon of the 2nd Company and two of the 3rd Company, was ambushed near the village of Kotovo by a partisan group numbering between seven hundred and one thousand, armed with ten heavy machine-guns and six mortars. The patrol, which was led by *lieutenant* Dagostini, managed to break through the encirclement by setting fire to the village, but suffered heavy losses of seven killed and twelve seriously wounded.[98] For his brave actions that day commanding the rearguard, Gobin of the 2nd Company was awarded the Iron Cross 2nd Class and the *Croix de guerre légionnaire*.[99]

Ten days later, a patrol returned to village of Kotovo to find no partisans and shot several civilians who refused to divulge the whereabouts of the French dead and wounded. *Lieutenant* Dagostini was subsequently tried by a court martial for the summary executions, found guilty, condemned to death, but later acquitted. His only 'punishment' was immediate repatriation to France.[100]

On the night of 27-28 May 1943, *Sous-lieutenant* Martin of the PAK Platoon of the Headquarters Company was wounded during a reconnaissance mission at Sapolje, but continued to lead his unit. For this action, he was awarded the *Croix de guerre légionnaire avec étoile de bronze*.

On 30 May 1943, the day he turned eighteen, Jean Grenouillet enlisted in the LVF.[101] He said of his decision to enlist:[102]

98   Saint-Loup, *Les Volontaires*, pp.204-214.
99   Lucien Gobion was born on 9 March 1903 in Orléans (department Loiret). His citation dates the ambush to 17 May 1943, see Bouysse Grégory, *Encyclopédie de l'ordre nouveau: Français sous l'uniforme allemande partie II: sous-officiers & hommes du rang de la Waffen-SS* (Lulu, 2019).
100  Two sources also make mention that Dagostini was charged with rape. See Chevallet, Franck and Martin, Gérard, *Pour la France, pour l'Europe* (Amazon, 2018), p.61, and Valla Jean-Claude, *La Milice. Lyon 1943-1944* (Paris: Pygmalion, 2000).
101  Jean Grenouillet was born on 30 May 1925 in Périgueux (department Dordogne).
102  Letter to the author, 12/4/98, abridged.

I always wanted to enlist in the French Army, at the time the LVF was a French Regiment and we hoped to be victorious. It must be put in context; we wanted to serve... I enlisted on the advice of a French field officer, a friend of my parents. I was their only son. I waited to my eighteenth birthday, 30 May 1943, to enlist in the LVF; yet my father did not really approve, then my parents were very proud. I had been thinking of this idea for a long time, belonging to the *amis de la LVF*.

My motives were also political and philosophical because the national and domestic enemy was atheistic Communism and Bolshevism. I believed in the New France of Marshal Pétain, the new Europe. This battle was for me an obvious fact. As France was not at war with the URSS, to fight in the uniform of the Wehrmacht posed me no problem.

Moreover, my father was a *combattant volontaire* of 14-18, a volunteer in 39, a prisoner in 40, liberated in 42 as a former combatant of 14-18, [and] he came back with the evident idea that France and Europe could only be reborn with Marshal Pétain and Germany, like the great majority of French people at the time. Furthermore, the context of the time, contrary to what is said today, was that the great majority of French people accepted the politics of the Marshal...

He left Versailles for Poland with the 9e *renfort*, which had paraded through the streets of Paris with the *8e* renfort on 19 June 1943.

From July 1941 to May 1943, 10,738 volunteers signed up for the LVF, of which only 6429 were retained. In that same period, the LVF had lost a total of 169 killed and 550 wounded.

On 4 September 1942, in response to German demands, Vichy introduced the *Service du travail obligatoire* [Compulsory Work Service] or STO. On 16 February 1943, Vichy passed a new law that modified the regulations of the STO. The 'young people' of the classes of 1940, 1941 and 1942, that is to say those born between 1920 and 1922, were now required to work in Germany (or France) for two years. The LVF, with the full agreement of Vichy and the Germans, used exemption from the STO as a means of recruitment. Posters appeared which appealed specifically to the 'young people' of the classes of 1940, 1941 and 1942 offering the LVF as an alternative to the STO. No figures are available of how many opted for the LVF rather than become a worker. The number was undoubtedly very few.

## June 1943-August 1943

On 9 June 1943, a detachment of fifteen men from the Signals Platoon and the 10th Company of the III. Bataillon sent to repair sabotaged telephone lines was ambushed. Help was sent only to find a burnt out truck and the bodies of their comrades, stripped naked and robbed. Some had been mutilated. This was the battalion's greatest loss of life in a single event since its arrival in Russia the previous year. They were buried in Mogilev cemetery. Lieutenant Alaineau, acting company commanding of the 10th Company, did not cover himself in glory and was relieved of command and demobilized at the end of July 1943.[103]

---

103  PPF militant, Paul Alaineau would set up the *Groupe de Sécurité* in Enghien in July 1944 to protect and if need be evacuate the families of militants of the collaborationist parties.

On 14 June, a delegation of French dignitaires from the *comité central de la LVF* and journalists, including Ambassador Fernand de Brinon, Robert Brasillach who was the editor of newspaper *Je suis partout*, and Edgar Puaud, the *délégué général militaire de la LVF* in France, visited the III. Bataillon. There was much pomp and ceremony. The delegation also visited the I. Bataillon. The total strength of the two battalions stood at some 1500.

On 17 June, some one hundred men of the *6e renfort* arrived. The replacements were much needed. Among them were *aspirant* Philippe Rossignol and *légionnaire* Jean-Marie Croisile.

Born on 2 June 1919 in St. Cloud, the 16th department of Paris, Philippe Rossignol enlisted at the end of 1938 for three years in the Air Force. He did not see action against the Germans, explaining that 'the armistice came too early'! He said of the defeat of May 1940:

> Unfortunately defeat was 'deserved' through a lack of military preparation and because of the almost general 'defeatism' in some political classes. I would have left for England if I had had the opportunity.

After the Armistice he was sent to Senegal, where he served out the rest of his contract. Returning to France, he enlisted in the Armistice Army with the rank of *caporal-chef*. He attended EOR training, but the invasion of the Free Zone by the Germans in November 1942 returned him to civilian life and unemployment. Out of religious anti-Communism, this devout catholic enlisted in *La Légion Tricolore*, which brought him promotion to the rank of *Aspirant*. He went across to the LVF. After basic training at Kruszyna, he was sent to the front and posted to the 9th Company as a platoon commander. He went on to become Puaud's Orderly Officer[104] and receive promotion to *Sous-lieutenant*. He was not a militant of a political party; he was and remained a monarchist throughout his life.

As for Jean-Marie Croisile, he was born on 14th May 1922. In June 1940, he had attempted to flee on bike from the Germans only to end up at Clermont-Ferrand where he registered as a refugee. On 19th July he joined the *Compagnons de France* and was sent to Randan for training. He worked his way up through this youth movement. On the day that *Maréchal* Pétain visited the camp to encourage the new adherents he was promoted to *chef d'équipe*, which was followed by promotions to *chef de chantier*, then *second assistant de compagnie* and finally *premier assistant*. This was not enough, though.

On 10 January 1941, wanting to enlist in the Army, which was a former shadow of itself, Croisile signed up and was posted to the *6e Bataillon de chasseurs alpins* at Grenoble. On 8 March 1941, he participated in a parade and march-past in honour of *Maréchal* Pétain who was visiting the city. Then came the 'supreme honour' of mounting guard in front of the *hotel du Parc* which was serving as the official residence of the Pétain government.

In June 1941, Croisile volunteered to go and fight in Syria against the English, their former ally who had betrayed his country at Calais and Dunkirk, and then stabbed her in the back at Mers-El-Kébir in July 1940. Immediately transferred to the *159e Régiment d'infanterie alpine*, he was then amalgamated with other volunteers to form the *33e Bataillon de marche de chasseurs*. The battalion was trained at La Valbonne and due to depart for the Levant on 5 July, which was

104  Dates of Rossignol becoming Puaud's Orderly Officer vary: January 1944, June 1944 and as late as July 1944.

pushed back several days. This delay, however, saw the end of the fighting in Syria. The battalion was disbanded and he was returned to the 6e BCA.

Because of his political leanings, which he did not hide, he was considered to have *mauvais esprit* and felt increasingly depressed and isolated. He welcomed the German crusade against Bolshevism and was of the opinion that 'England and the United States had betrayed our world, our civilisation, by allying themselves with Bolshevism'.

When the unoccupied zone was invaded the 6e BCA was deployed in the city of Grenoble to guard all the important positions, which were handed over to the Italians. General Laffargue commanding the garrison of Grenoble refused to obey the order to demobilise and moved the battalion into defensive positions at Vié. Excited by the promise of combat, the *chasseurs* awaited the Italians. However, the General finally came to the conclusion that all resistance was futile and ordered the battalion to disband. Croisile returned home to spend Christmas with the family.

Restless, Croisile knew that he had to make a decision. There were many options available to him at that time: the Gendarmerie, the *Garde nationale*, the *Légion Tricolore* and even the *Forces Françaises de l'Interieur* (FFI). For him, the greatest threat to Europe was Bolshevism. He felt that it was his duty to come to her defence. His father, a militant anti-communist, was receptive to his son's decision. Thus, on 23 February 1943, accompanied by his father, he enlisted in the *Légion Tricolore*. Upon his arrival in Russia he was assigned to Rossignol's Platoon of the 9th Company.

The war against the partisans continued without mercy. On 18 June 1943, the partisans ambushed a patrol from the 10th Company, killing five legionnaires. Again the bodies were stripped of their uniform and horribly mutilated. The war continued. Sometimes two or three partisans were killed and sometimes it was legionnaires who lost their lives. On 3 July, three Frenchmen who wandered too far from their quarters were assasinated. The war continued. On 17th July, a patrol from the 10th Company seized the village of Kolbovo as planned. Finding nothing, it pushed on and suddenly came under heavy fire. It withdrew in good order to the village, which it vigorously defended, killing or wounding thirty partisans while it suffered five killed. The war continued. On 23 July, while clearing mines, two legionnaires were killed outright and one died the following day. *Lieutenant* Raymond Gaillard was also wounded in the face. He was decorated with the *Croix de guerre légionnaire*.

On 25 July, the III. Bataillon was moved to Krugloje, attached to the 122nd Security Regiment and strengthened by the arrival of the *7e renfort* with 56 volunteers. Among the newcomers was *lieutenant* Michel Bisiau. Born on 20 July 1914, he was a reserve officer in the cavalry and then in the colonial infantry. He was promoted to *lieutenant* during the Phoney War and was serving with the *7e régiment de tirailleurs sénégalais* (7e RTS) when the Allies attempted and failed to capture the port of Dakar in September 1940.[105] A fervent member of the PPF, he joined the LVF in 1943. On his arrival in Russia, he replaced Gaillard as head of the Headquarters Company.

This new sector proved 'hotter' than the previous one. On 1 August, elements of the 9th Company holding the miserable forest hamlet of Dubovoje were attacked by partisans but fought them off. The partisans left behind twenty bodies on the field of battle. The French counted ten wounded. On the 7th of the same month, Seveau's platoon of the 11th Company came under attack at Orechowka. The battle lasted several hours, after which the partisans retired. The French suffered yet more wounded.

---

105  Darkar was in French West Africa, now Senegal.

Days later on the 11th, partisans ambushed a French supply column. *Sergent* Pierre Soulé suddenly found himself in the thick of battle. He saw comrades fall one by one. Out of ammunition, Ackerman crawled towards a dead soldier to restock, but was hit in the head. *Caporal* de Polignac was hit first in the heel and then in the head. *Lieutenant* Auphan, firing a machine-gun, ran out of ammunition and beckoned Soulé to join him. After finding some ammunition Soulé joined the *Lieutenant*, becoming his loader. Auphan then gave him the order to get on a horse and go and alert battalion, which he managed to do. Nevertheless, the partisans inflicted heavy losses on the Frenchmen; twenty-one killed, four missing and some forty wounded. Indeed, French losses might have been worse if part of the convoy had not managed to break out of the partisan encirclement. The newly arrived *Capitaine* Estel was killed. *Lieutenant* Audibert of the 11th Company was wounded. Evacuated, he would rejoin the LVF in early 1944 as the company commander of the 7th Company. Soon after *Lieutenant* Auphan became the adjutant-major of the I. Bataillon.[106]

*Capitaine* Maurice Berret succeeded Dewitte at the head of the 10th Company. Berret had been with the III. Bataillon since December 1941 and served as its *officier adjoint* since December 1942. On the night of the 21 August, a platoon of the 10th Company stationed at Pawlowitschi fought off a partisan attack, killing ten of them at the cost of two wounded. Russian peasants later told the Frenchmen that the partisans had lost twenty-three dead as well as a large number of wounded.

As a result of this attack and other costly failures against well-fortified and defended French posts, the partisans changed tactics and resorted to planting improvised explosives on roads and other areas regularly patrolled and used by the French.

On 27 August 1943, the LVF celebrated the second anniversary of its formation with a number of events in Paris. After a religious ceremony, the Legion received a new Colour from General Bridoux, the Vichy Secretary of State for War, at a ceremony in the *Cour d'Honneur* at the *Hôtel des Invalides*, Paris. The Colour, symbolically of the 1879 regulation pattern for all French Army regiments, bore the legend HONNEUR ET PATRIE which appeared on French regimental Colours and the two battle honours of 1941-1942 DJUKOWO and 1942-1943 BÉRÉSINA.

The *Croix de guerre légionnaire* was awarded to current and former legionnaires of the LVF, some of whom were now serving with the German Naval Police. Medals were also posthumously awarded to families of legionnaires killed on the Eastern Front. This was was followed by a parade before German and French dignitaires. *Lieutenant* Martin and René Bourg, who had been wounded and lost a leg while serving with the LVF, participated in the ceremony.

At 19:00 hours, Fernand de Brinon, the French Ambassador and also the president of the Central Committee of the LVF, laid a wreath at the tomb of the Unknown Soldier. This was followed by the inauguration of the *Foyer des Anciens Combattants de la Légion* in a former hotel at 5 rue de Tilsitt. The two battalions of the LVF in Russia celebrated the anniversary as best they could.

Meantime, back in France, two German military organisations, the NSKK and the Waffen-SS, had officially started to recruit French volunteers, who might have otherwise opted for the LVF.

---

106    Curiously, according to Soulé, after the events of 11th August, Auphan was not well regarded by *Commandant* Panné who had him transferred to Regiment Headquarters. Auphan was appointed as Oberleutnant on 1 May 1944 backdated to 1 April 1944.

## 2

## The NSKK, Waffen-SS and Sennheim Camp

---

### NSKK Motorgruppe Luftwaffe

The Nationalsozialistisches Automobil Korps [National Socialist Motor Car Corps] or more simply the NSAK was set up on 1st April 1930 to transport around Nazi Party formations and top officials. The NSAK was renamed the Nationalsozialistisches Kraftfahrkorps [National Socialist Motor Corps] or NSKK and established as a branch of the SA on 1 May 1931.

When Hitler became Chancellor in January 1933 the NSKK was expanded and later in the year took over all German motor clubs and civilian motoring organisations. Following the elimination of the SA leadership in the Night of the Long Knives, the NSKK absorbed the Motor SA, the SA's own transport service, and on 23 August 1934 was declared an independent organisation of the Nazi Party. It proved a great success and after the reorganization of 1934 it counted some 350,000 members.

The NSKK controlled and promoted all motoring activites, including car exhibitions, racing car and motorbike events, and also propagated National Socialist ideology. It ran driving and motor mechanics courses with an 'eye for eventual military application of the knowledge'.[1] By 1939, the NSKK counted 500,000 members.

The war brought the NSKK new responsibilities, including the transportation of equipment, supplies and personnel for the military. With much of its membership now serving in the motorized formations of the German Army, the victories of 1940 placed an additional burden on the already overstretched NSKK. Consequently, the NSKK looked for new manpower sources and started to recruit from the occupied countries of Western Europe, namely Belgium and Holland. The recruitment drive met with some success in the Flanders region of Belgium: according to German sources, some 2500 Flemings enlisted in 1941 and a further 1500 in the following year. The majority of Flemish, Walloon and Dutch recruits were placed under the control of the Luftwaffe while some worked for the Organisation Todt.

From the start of the occupation a small number of Frenchmen had managed to enlist and serve in the NSKK as individual volunteers. For example, Charles-Gilbert Robba, born on 30 January 1914, enlisted in the NSKK in 1941. He was trained at Vilvoorde, Belgium, after which

---

1    Lepage, *Hitler's Armed Forces Auxiliaries*, p.108.

he was sent to Poland with a munitions convoy that 'melted away en route like snow in the sun'. After eight days on the road, he found himself back at Diest, Belgium. Some of his compatriots were 'more or less demobilised', returning to France as workers, while 'others vanished into thin air'.

During the winter of 1941-1942, an all-French unit of the NSKK with a German cadre was engaged on the Eastern Front in the region of Leningrad. This is all the more surprising because the NSKK did not officially open its ranks to French volunteers until early 1942.[2]

Pierre Costantini, the head of political party *Ligue Française* and member of the central committee of the LVF, paved the way for the official recruitment of French volunteers for the NSKK. In the late summer of 1941, with great enthusiasm, he had set about forming a French branch of the Luftwaffe for the many airmen who had joined the LVF. This new formation was known as the *Légion des Aviateurs Français*, sometimes called the *Aviateurs Volontaires Français*.[3] Without waiting for the agreement of the Germans, Costantini opened offices for this new formation in 5, rue de la Chaussée d'Antin, Paris, a stone's throw from *Ligue* headquarters, and then, from November 1941, in 1, rue Godot de Mauroy, between La Madeleine and the Opera.

Recruit advertisement for CAVA August 1942.

2    Dates of when the NSKK officially opened its ranks to French volunteers vary. The first French volunteers left Paris for the NSKK training centre at Vilvoorde in July 1942 which suggests that the NSKK only opened its door to French volunteers months before.

3    Michel Auphan, a former pilot, volunteered for the *Légion des Aviateurs Français* in September 1941, only to discover that he had in fact signed up for the LVF. See Rentano Bruno & Léguerandais Christophe, *Ces Franciliens qui ont choisi Hitler* (Les Éditions du Lore, 2015), p.111.

Costantini continued to lobby the Germans, wishing to see himself at the head of the squadron he intended to raise. The German response was to open in 1, rue Godot de Mauroy a recruiting office for the *Corps Automobile de Volontaires Antibolcheviques* [Motor Corps of Anti-Bolshevik Volunteers] or more simply CAVA.[4] Recruitment advertisements for the CAVA appeared in the press until August 1942. Soon after, the CAVA was rebranded the NSKK Motorgruppe Luftwaffe.[5]

NSKK Motorgruppe Luftwaffe started life in the summer of 1940 as NSKK Regiment Luftwaffe for the express purpose of delivering munitions to forward airfields in France. The Regiment went through a number of name changes as it expanded to divisional strength before it was named on 11 May 1942 as NSKK Motorgruppe Luftwaffe. In July 1943, NSKK Motorgruppe Luftwaffe was redesignated NSKK Transportgruppe Luftwaffe.[6]

The German decision to open the NSKK to French volunteers apparently had much more to do with propaganda than combat. *Capitaine* Troupeau, the *secrétaire général* of the *Ligue Française*, ran the recruiting office.[7] Troupeau was the brother-in-law of General Bridoux, Vichy's Secretary of State for War. Also of note is that the French NSKK attracted the attention of the French *Deuxieme bureau* and the German Abwehr.[8]

The NSKK recruited throughout the whole of France, although it concentrated its efforts mainly in the Occupied Zone. It ran newspaper advertisements and one such newspaper advertisement read:

> The NSKK (National Socialist Automobile Corps) Motorgruppe Luftwaffe appeals to all automobile drivers who understand and approve of the politics of collaboration for a new Europe united and pacified. Every person aged from 18 to 50 years, driving licence holders or not, can enlist in the ranks of the NSKK.

Other advertisements stated that priority would be given to drivers and former soldiers. *Capitaine* Troupeau wrote to those invalided out of the LVF to encourage them to enlist in NSKK Motorgruppe Luftwaffe. Recruits were required to sign on for the duration of the war.[9]

On 21 July 1942, the first one hundred and fifty French recruits left Paris for the NSKK training centre at Vilvoorde, outside Bruxelles, where they were issued with uniforms and commenced basic military training. They wore the blue-grey uniform of the Luftwaffe with NSKK ranks and insignia, and on the upper left sleeve a tricolore shield surmounted by a

4    Presumably the *Légion des Aviateurs Français* was now dissolved or soon after.
5    Recruitment advertisements for NSKK Motorgruppe Luftwaffe appeared in the press in October 1942.
6    French NSKK volunteer Faroux does not recall this change of designation.
7    According to Littlejohn, *Foreign Legions of the Third Reich vol. 1*, p.161, Troupeau was the prime mover behind the formation of an official French section of the NSKK.
8    For example, French NSKK volunteer Raga knew of two French moles.
9    Lambert Pierre P. and Le Marec Gérard, *Les Français sous le casque allemand* (Paris: Jacques Grancher, 1994), p.71, confirmed by French NSKK volunteers Raga (letter to the author, 16/9/2002) and Faroux (letter to the author, 2/10/2002). According to Littlejohn, *Foreign Legions of the Third Reich vol. 1*, p.161, volunteers were required to sign on for a minimum engagement of two years.

double-headed axe, the *francisque*.[10] The choice of the *francisque* may have been derived from the *francisque* of *Les Jeunes du Maréchal* or the *Ligue Française*. Eventually, the recruits were issued with weapons: French Army Lebel rifles!

The French recruits were grouped together in a training company which numbered 312 men on 11 September 1942, 357 men in October and 281 men in December. Many of the initial French recruits were former *légionnaires* invalided out of the LVF.[11]

By the end of 1942, a first company of about two hundred men, who were largely from the occupied zone, had been raised at Schaffen, some fifty kilometres east of Vilvoorde. Many were young and had enlisted out of a spirit of adventure and a taste for uniforms.[12] A second company of French recruits was subsequently raised at Diest, which was followed by a third. The French companies may have been grouped as a battalion.[13] The third company comprised many former officers of the French Army. The French companies formed part of NSKK-Luftwaffe Regiment 4.

The 1st Company was deployed to Russia in January 1943 and the 2nd Company followed in late February/early March 1943[14] where they were put at the disposal of Luftgau Rostov/Don.[15] The 2nd Company was stationed for some fifteen days at Osnowa airfield, south-east of Kharkov. By the end of March 1943 or at the beginning of April 1943, the two companies were back in Diest.[16] They had suffered some fifty casualties and lost much of their equipment, in particular the Second Company.[17]

### *Les Jeunes du Maréchal*, François Faroux and Henri Raga

Meanwhile, in November 1942, the Pétainist and anti-Communist autonomous youth movement *Les Jeunes du Maréchal* [The Marshal's Youth or Young] launched a newspaper appeal for volunteers for the 'national socialist motorised combat formations'.[18] Created in June 1941

---

10    French NSKK volunteer Raga was welcomed into the NSKK at Vilvoorde by a French Sturmführer who referred to the tricolore badge by saying: "It's a piece of French territory that you wear on your arm!"
11    Léguerandais, *Uniforms* Hors-Série no 29, p.48.
12    Mabire Jean, *La Brigade Frankreich* (Fayard, 1973), p.39.
13    An NSKK battalion contained three companies (Kompanien).
14    French NSKK recruit Raga arrived at Schaffen at the start of March 1943 and noted that the 2nd Company had just left for Russia (letter to the author, 19/9/2001).
15    Of note is that in December 1942 an advance party of 24 or 30 men was sent to the Ukraine.
16    Léguerandais, Christophe, *Hitler's French volunteers* (Barnsley: Pen & Sword Military, 2016), p.65. However, according to Lambert and Le Marec, *Les Français sous le casque allemand*, p.72, the two companies returned to Diest on 24th April 1943, and, according to Mounine, article *Le Bataillon français du NSKK*, it was late April 1943.
17    According to Léguerandais, *Hitler's French volunteers*, p.65, while in Russia the 2nd Company abandoned many of its trucks by order of the company commander and chief engineer to facilitate an early return to Brussels and a peaceful life. According to another source, the trucks passed to the 2nd Company had been abused and run into the ground by their previous owners and this too contributed to the return of the 2nd Company! Lastly, according to Lambert and Le Marec, *Les Français sous le casque allemand*, p.72, the equipment was 'prematurely worn out by the climate and inexperienced personnel'.
18    According to Littlejohn, *Foreign Legions of the Third Reich vol. 1*, p.132, *Les Jeunes du Maréchal* actively recruited for the NSKK. This is disputed by French volunteers of the NSKK Raga (letter to the author, 16/9/2002) and Faroux (letter to the author, 2/10/2002). Moreover, Faroux was a member of *Les Jeunes*

by Jacques Bousquet and authorized in September of the same year, *Les Jeunes du Maréchal* recruited adherents from among high schools and colleges. It operated in both zones. Weeks after it was launched, membership peaked at 1400, mainly centred in Paris, dropping to 483 some months later. Some left to join the *Jeunesses Francistes*, which was more politicised.

That same month, Jean-Marie Balestre and forty-three militants of the youth movement *Les Jeunes du Maréchal* enlisted in the NSKK. The departure of Balestre marked the end of the movement, which had already incurred the wrath of its namesake.

> **Un appel aux jeunes Français pour la lutte contre le bolchevisme et la juiverie anglo-saxonne**
>
> Les Jeunes du Maréchal lancent un appel aux jeunes Français pour qu'ils se groupent dans la lutte contre le bolchevisme et la juiverie anglo-saxonne. Ils les invitent à s'enrôler dans les formations motorisées de combat nationales socialistes. Les engagements sont reçus 3, rue Récamier, Paris (VIIᵉ). Le prochain départ aura lieu le 20 novembre.

*Les Jeunes du Maréchal* recruit for the NSKK in *Le Petit Parisien*, November 1942.

On 18 December 1942, the day he turned sixteen, François Faroux went to the Caserne de la Reine to enlist in the LVF with an identity card which stated that he was eighteen. When he saw the puttees, the disparate uniforms, the pointed caps, he turned around and walked out. This smacked of the French Army of old. Moreover, he was received by a young lieutenant full of sufficiency, who looked at him with a very superior air.

The NSKK recruiting office in rue Godot de Mauroy was much more welcoming. The German officer spoke fluent French, but it was late and the German officer told him to come back. When he explained that he had nowhere to stay the German officer gave him a ticket for a hotel and dinner. The following morning, at nine o'clock sharp, he returned to the NSKK recruiting office and saw the very same German officer. They spoke for around thirty minutes, after which Faroux enlisted, but the next departure of volunteers was scheduled for 10 January 1943. He asked what he should do. The German officer replied that perhaps he should return to his family. He decided to spend a few more days in Paris, before returning home for Christmas and then back to Paris in the New Year.

Although a member of *Les Jeunes du Maréchal*, Faroux was not politically motivated. He needed to get away from home. And with no skills to his name and no job, he chose to sign up for the army rather than enter religion. Moreover, he wished to give the lie to the horror stories

---

*du Maréchal* and he only learnt of the NSKK from a newspaper advertisement. With that said, *Les Jeunes du Maréchal* did launch an appeal for volunteers but whether this constitutes 'actively recruited' is questionable.

of German atrocities on which he had grown up.[19] His father, who had sympathies with the PPF, did not disagree with his son's decision.

Faroux was dispatched to Bruxelles by train and arrived on 12 January 1943. More than six months of recruit training were to follow at Vilvoorde, Diest, Schaffen, and Grammont, west of Bruxelles. The drilling was hard, the discipline tough, and the rations poor. He received rifle and anti-tank weapons training. Most of the instructors were German. A few were from Alsace. Most were convalescents.

Faroux recalls heated, sometimes violent political arguments between the supporters of *Croix de Feu*,[20] Doriot, Déat, and even some former Cagoulards or so they claimed. He did not get involved. He was too young for all of that. Besides his main worry was food, describing the daily rations as plain ridiculous for a growing lad of sixteen.

Faroux also saw Jean-Marie Balestre a number of times at Vilvoorde, but never met him. Balestre was the assistant to the chief Medical Officer, Obersturmführer Rollin.

In March 1943, Faroux swore an oath of loyalty to Hitler. This made him proud, describing the oath as the 'consequence of his engagement'. At the end of March, he attended a training course for medical orderlies at Forest, a suburb of Bruxelles. It was a veritable refuge for homosexuals and all too quickly did he understand why he had been sent there! Thus to keep his virtue intact, each evening after soup, he returned to sleep with his 'Column'.[21] Thankfully the course only lasted two weeks, after which he was promoted to the rank of Obersturmmann. Henceforth, he wore the badge of caduceus on the lower right arm.

Meanwhile, on 2 February 1943, the nineteen-year-old Henri Raga volunteered for the NSKK. He came from a nationalist and military family but was shaped by the events that marked France from 1936 up to his enlistment. He was a staunch anti-Communist and anti-German nationalist. His reaction to the defeat of June 1940 was one of incomprehension and sadness:

> I desired to fight, but *Maréchal* Pétain, who I respected, was doing his utmost to keep France out of the conflict. In July 1940, with some comrades of my age, we tried to reach the 'free' zone from where we hoped to travel and join the Army in England or failing that the one in Africa but could not cross the guarded demarcation line.

As time passed Raga became less and less anti-German; French pre-war propaganda had started to wear thin. And then the German attack on the Soviet Union on 22 June 1941, which made him realise that this new conflict engaged the whole of Europe, turned him into a Germanophile. The winds of change continued to blow:

> My mediocre and morally uninteresting life I was leading started to weigh heavy on me, while much of the European youth was fighting for an ideal. In August/September 1942, I enlisted in the French Navy to respect a family tradition; my father had served

19   One such story was that the Germans would cut off the hands of the civilian population.
20   Founded in 1928, the *Croix de Feu* [Cross of Fire] grew under the charismatic retired Lieutenant Colonel de La Rocque to number some half a million members by the time it too was banned in 1936. Thereupon the CF became the Parti Social Français, the PSF. The CF was more right-wing than fascist.
21   An NSKK Company contained ten columns, (Kolonnen).

for more than twenty years in the French Navy. But the 'sabotage' of the French fleet in November 1942 freed me from all sentimental connections and I considered that I should finally embark on a project which I thought about for several months, no longer distracted by filial respect.

Raga decided to make contact with the LVF and described what followed:

I came away very disappointed. Firstly, I believed I had found myself in the French Army of old, to which I had no inclination. Secondly, the influence of the political parties of the day within the LVF was too great. Indeed, the officers and NCOs I met were more concerned about the political party to which I belonged rather than my reasons for enlistment and personal convictions, which did not seem to interest them. I was not a member of a political party anway. Thus I contacted the NSKK which seemed to fit my aspirations better. When I told my parents they were disorientated. Of course, my father took the prospect of his son in a German uniform badly and my mother feared for my life, but they were always there for me morally, even after 1945.

On 9 February 1943, Raga with other young Frenchmen left Gare du Nord, Paris, for Vilvoorde, Bruxelles, where he met and made friends with François Faroux. At the start of March 1943, he was sent to Schaffen and was assigned to the forming 3rd Company, 6th Regiment, otherwise the 3/6.[22] Like Faroux, Raga found the training at Schaffen very hard; exercises were conducted in the rain and cold and there was very little to eat. Things improved when he was dispatched to Grammont late April 1943 to complete his basic training.

Raga fully expected to join the other French NSKK companies in Russia, but as previously noted they were returned to Diest at the end of March 1943 or at the beginning of April 1943.

Faroux recalls meeting comrades from the 1st Company and 2nd Company. They spoke of the cold, the snow and the lice. 'We listened to them narrate their campaign, epic and valorous for some, botched and lamentable for others'.

Thereupon the personnel of both the 1st Company and the 2nd Company had the choice to continue or work in German factories. In this way, very few men of the 2nd Company chose to soldier on.

Around the same time as the return of the French companies from Russia, the French battalion was reorganised as the 2nd Battalion, 4th Regiment, otherwise the II/4, under the command of Staffelführer Joseph Seigel.[23] Company 3/6 became Company 4/II under Kompanieführer Sturmführer Hans Ströhle. The remaining personnel of Companies 1/6 and 2/6 were used to form Company 5/II. Company 6/II was commanded by Alsatian Stürmfuhrer Leissner.

Henri Raga was assigned to the 3rd Column of the 4th Company under Kolonneführer Truppführer Rupp (known as 'Riton') and François Faroux to the 4th Column of the 4th Company under Frenchman Kolonnefführer Hauptscharführer André Soyer, who was one of the very few French *chefs*. The three other Columns of the 4th Company were commanded by Voll, Marz and Naegele. André Henriot, the son of Philippe Henriot, who would later become

22  The 6th Regiment was formed in April 1942.
23  According to Raga, letter to the author of 19/9/2001, the French battalion inherited the designation of the 2nd battalion, 4th Regiment from a Dutch battalion disbanded after a tour of duty in Russia.

Vichy's Minister of Information, 'soldiered' in the 3rd Column of the 4th Company. He and Faroux were good friends [and would remain so after the war].

To Raga, Rupp was hard, but fair and open. He recalls the time Rupp assembled the Column and had translated (he did not speak a word of French): "I am Prussian and I don't like the French." The Frenchmen replied to him: "That's lucky, we don't like the Prussians." Then there was the time Staffelführer Seigel organised a competition between the barrack rooms one Sunday morning. The prize was a radio set. Raga recounts:[24]

> Truppführer Rupp came into our barrack room about one hour before the inspection: beds not made, the barrack room not swept, nothing put away! Rupp, self-effacing, did not even react. The officers arrived, led by the Staffelführer, the door opened, and behind every one Rupp, anxious, preparing himself for the worst of reprimands when he heard 'Fine, perfect, very good' said by the Staffelführer. After the officers left, he entered the barrack room and this is what he saw: an enlargement of a photo of the Staffelführer in a quite beautiful frame placed on a table covered with a blanket and several small flowers around the photo. He looked at us all, smiled, and left us saying: "Great swindler." Of course our barrack room won the radio set.

At Grammont, Raga also remembers the time Rupp returned from leave:

> Rupp joined us in our barracks and pulled out from a bag two litres of schnapps which he had brought along from home. We were alone with him, without any officer. We drank the two litres of schnapps while smoking and talking.

And yet another anecodote from Raga, still at Grammont:

> A billet inspection was due to take place one Sunday morning. Another! While preparing the barracks one of us broke a windowpane. Rupp, resigned, left and returned a little later with a glazier. From the courtyard of the billet (a school) he showed the glazier the window with the brozen pane. The glazier looked wide open, very surprised. Rupp looked at him worried then looked at the window; there was no broken windowpane. Rupp looked at the glazier again and hurriedly excused himself and came and asked us how we did it. We had simply replaced the broken casement window with an intact one from a disused room!

In July 1943, when Rupp left to join the Wehrmacht, he had requested a transfer, the members of his Column clubbed together to offer him a gold-rimmed amber cigar holder. He was touched. They would miss him. Raga's training at Grammont and Geraardsbergen would last until October 1943.

Recruits were sent to a driving school at Forest or to the NSKK Motor schule at Tübingen for heavy goods vehicle training. Three courses were run for French recruits at Tübingen during the second half of 1943. The courses would last two months.

---

24    Letter to the author, 19/9/2001.

By 20 May 1943, 1325 French NSKK recruits had been sent to Bruxelles. Faroux and Raga would both serve with the NSKK for 'the duration of the war'. However, some Frenchmen viewed the NSKK as little more than a stepping stone to their ultimate goal of joining the Waffen-SS and, in early March 1943, French NSKK recruits of a company at Vilvoorde began to 'desert' to Waffen-SS barracks or nearby recruitment centres. Among them were Boulmier, Delsart,[25] Fayard, Labourdette, Pierre Molin and Robba.[26]

Christian Martres would follow them at a later date. Born on 20 June 1926 in Vierzon (department Cher), he volunteered for the NSKK and then the Waffen-SS because his family was anti-bolshevist and on good terms with the Germans. Also he harboured a burning desire for military life. The Waffen-SS had fascinated him ever since the day he had witnessed the parade of elements from SS-Division 'Totenkopf' in the streets of Vierzon. The sight of motorcyclists with leather raincoats was etched in his memory. He did not belong to any political party or movement.[27] His father, however, had been a member of the once popular, but short-lived right-wing *Solidarité Française* (SF).[28] Martres declared:[29]

Not without reluctance, my parents agreed to sign my enlistment papers and I found myself incorporated into the motorized formation of the Party. But my desire for action, to participate fully and entirely in the struggle against the enemies of Europe persuaded me to take the plunge. And it was in this way that in the first days of summer 1943[30] with my comrade Jacques Le Maignan de Kérangat we 'deserted' from Vilvoorde and presented ourselves at the Bruxelles Ersatzkommando der Waffen-SS. From there we

25  Paul Delsart was born on 8 July 1919 in Tourcoing (department Nord).
26  Robba was the first or third Frenchmen to volunteer for the French unit of the Waffen-SS. After completing his basic training at Sennheim, he was assigned to run the camp's 'Germanische SS-Werber' [Germanic SS-Recruiter] platoon. Detached to the SS-Hauptampt [Main Office], he subsequently attended a one month preparatory course for officer cadets at SS-Junkerschule Tölz and was appointed Junker on 15th June 1944 (Bouysse, *Encyclopédie de l'ordre nouveau: Français sous l'uniforme allemande partie II: sous-officiers & hommes du rang de la Waffen-SS*). Promotion to Oberscharführer would follow. Shortly after his return to the SS-Hauptampt, he was posted to the nascent French Brigade of the Waffen-SS where he served as a platoon commander in Kompanie 8/57. He was detached again to the SS-Hauptampt in January 1945 and rubbed shoulders with Gamory-Dubourdeau. During the battle of Berlin he led a mixed kampfgruppe in the district of Moabit. Captured by the Russians and handed over to the French authorities, he was condemned to ten years hard labour and also stripped of his French nationality with *interdiction de séjour* (an order denying access to specified places). He died on 20 March 1993.
27  Curiously, when interviewed by the author, Martres stated that he did not belong to any political party and yet when he attended SS-Panzergrenadierschule Kienschlag he recorded on his SS-Aufnahme-u. Verpflichtungsschein that he had been a member of the PPF since 1942.
28  Launched in June 1933 by millionaire François Coty, an anti-Communist, the *Solidarité Française* claimed a total membership of 315,000 in December 1933. However, its fall was just as dramatic and by June 1934, because of financial problems and internal dissension, the SF was in shambles. During that period it was, according to police authorities, the largest right-wing movement in France. After 1934 the SF limped on with a hardcore of militants. Banned in June 1936 as a paramilitary league, the SF reconstituted itself as the *Amis de la Solidarité Française* [Friends of French Solidarity]. Like all of the other major French right-wing parties of the interwar period, the SF had its own uniformed 'shock troops'.
29  Mounine Henri, *Cernay 40–45* (Ostwald: Editions du polygone, 1999), p.252.
30  Martres enlisted in the Waffen-SS on 5 August 1943.

were sent to the SS-Vorschule at Schotten and ten days after to Sennheim, to the 2nd Company.

Martres had served with the NSKK some seven months, obtaining the rank of Obersturmmann. Jacques Le Maignan de Kérangat was born on 1 July 1924.

In the end, after a war of words between the NSKK and the Waffen-SS, this transference was encouraged; an SS representative came to Vilvoorde and appealed for volunteers.[31] In mid-September 1943, Costamagna decided there and then to enlist in the Waffen-SS. In fact, eight out of the ten men in his room signed up. He was the first.

Born on 15 July 1926 in Nice (department Alpes-Maritimes), Fernand Costamagna joined the youth movement UPJF aged fifteen. He attended political talks on Communism, Fascism, as well as the history of France and Europe. Every Sunday morning, he went out to sell the PPF's newspapers. He also guarded public events organised by the party. At the end of May 1943, he enlisted in the NSKK. He simply said of the decision:[32]

> My enlistment was essentially motivated by anti-communism. Although my parents were not politically engaged, I knew that they had no sympathy for communism.

Costamagna was sent to Vilvoorde for basic training. He was also employed to fill in holes after air raids on the Luftwaffe airbase at Evere. He described this task as 'not very exhiliating', even if he was entitled to extra rations. The Waffen-SS offered him adventure.

Those Frenchmen volunteering for the Waffen-SS from the NSKK and at the recruiting centres of SS-Ersatzkommando Bruxelles and Antwerpen were first sent to SS-Ausbildungslager (otherwise called SS-Vorschule) Schotten in the scenic setting of a chateau. As its designation suggests, Schotten was a training and preparatory depot whose primary role was to welcome the volunteers to the Waffen-SS and then form them into a convoy which could then be sent on to a unit or a training establishment. Thus, most volunteers passed through Schotten within a matter of weeks, unless they were unlucky enough to arrive there just after a convoy had left. No more than two companies were ever present at Schotten at any one time.

In the short time available to the training personnel at Schotten to prepare the volunteers, the former 'Leibstandarte' NCOs and officers could do little more than issue their 'pupils' with an assorted range of equipment, begin their physical (sports) training programme and enlighten them on close order drill. But the volunteers noted that they were still without weapons.

By SS standards, the depot 'regime' was very relaxed; each and every day the volunteers could go out into the town. Nevertheless, the depot was permanently guarded. Charles Robba recalled that 'after eight days at Schotten some even obtained permission to return home in the North to settle some family matters'. The departure of his convoy was marked by 'a ceremony full of the usual decorum' organised in a Flemish town.[33] Later he reflected about Schotten: 'A life of luxury compared to what awaited us at Sennheim.'

---

31   Mabire, *La Brigade Frankreich*, p.42. Curiously, Faroux and Raga do not recall the Waffen-SS approaching them.
32   Costabrava Fernand, *Le soldat Baraka* (Self-published, 2007), p.41.
33   In fact, each departure was marked in a different Flemish town.

From Schotten, the French volunteers were sent on to SS-Ausbildungslager Sennheim near Cernay in Alsace. Sennheim was the name given to Saint-André Institute (or school) built after the Great War as an orphanage housing handicapped children and the mentally sick, but now employed as a training camp.

By early July 1943, some fifty NSKK deserters had arrived at Sennheim. They were incorporated into international companies of Germanic volunteers. Under the watchful eye of German, Flemish, and Dutch NCOs, they underwent basic training. Emphasis was placed on sports and physical activities.

And yet there was still no official agreement between Vichy and the German authorities authorising recruitment of French volunteers by the Waffen-SS, despite some political activity of late.

## The Waffen-SS

The notion of foreign volunteers was not new to the Waffen-SS. The victories of 1940 provided the Waffen-SS with a vast new recruiting ground and volunteers were accepted from the so-called 'Nordic' countries of Norway, Denmark and Sweden, and from the 'Germanic' areas of North Western Europe such as Holland and Flanders. In this way, the Waffen-SS formed two new regiments, 'Nordland' and 'Westland'.

The German attack on the Soviet Union on 22 June 1941 brought offers of military support from most of the occupied countries, as well as from the Independent State of Croatia, and neutral Spain. On 29 June, Hitler gave his approval to the formation of legions of foreigners who wished to participate in the 'European crusade against Bolshevism'. The Waffen-SS was made responsible for the legions from the Germanic countries and the Wehrmacht for those from the Non-Germanic countries, including France.

Similar to the NSKK, from the start of the occupation a number of French citizens had managed to enlist in the Waffen-SS as individual volunteers. During 1942, many of those who volunteered their services for the Waffen-SS enlisted as 'Flemings born in Northern France', hence called Ch'timi.[34] Of the estimated three hundred 'private enlistments', many served with the premier Waffen-SS divisions 'Totenkopf' and 'Wiking'. At least two Frenchmen served with 'Leibstandarte Adolf Hitler'.[35]

Times had now changed and faced with huge losses on the Eastern Front, Germany was in need of fresh manpower. RF-SS Himmler, who was constantly struggling with the Wehrmacht for new recruits, turned his attention to France and wrote to Hitler on 12 December 1942, proposing the creation of a French unit within the Waffen-SS.

On 30 January 1943, Hitler authorised the recruitment of French volunteers by the Waffen-SS. The French volunteers were to form a regiment by the name of 'Charlemagne'. Himmler was instructed accordingly.

34    A Ch'timi is a native of the *Pas-de-Calais* and the adjoining *Départment du Nord*.
35    According to H.L., Chapter 30000 Français sous l'uniforme allemande, *Historia* hors série 32, p.113, a French Unterscharführer from Nice, who was wounded with the Sturmbrigade in Galicia in August 1944, met one of his compatriots in a Prague hospital, who was serving with 'Hitler's personal bodyguard' but refused to say how he had managed it.

On 19 March 1943, Dr Ernst Achenbach, who worked in the German Embassy in Paris, reported in a telegram that officials representing SS-Brigadeführer Carl Oberg, the Höherer SS und Polizeiführer [HSSPF] Frankreich,[36] had contacted and discussed the formation of a French regiment of the Waffen-SS with different French groups, including Darnand, the *chef* of the *Milice française*, and Doriot, the head of the PPF. However, only Doriot was ready to commit himself to this new formation so long as it was a matter of participating in the European National Socialist revolutionary army and not a process of germanisation.

Achenbach also reported that the German Ambassador had discussed the matter in a prudent manner with a number of officials of the Vichy Government who were friends of his. Secretary of State Marion and Ambassador Fernand de Brinon did not dismiss the idea of a 'pure SS regiment' but favoured a scenario whereby the regiment was presented to the public as an 'additional elite formation to reinforce the *Légion des Volontaires Français contre le Bolchevisme* (LVF)'. They argued that members of the regiment could then declare that they belonged to a French institution, that of the LVF. They added that the regiment should be placed 'within the framework of the French volunteers against Bolchevism'. In this way, the French Government could also participate in recruitment and it would negate competition between the LVF and the Waffen-SS, which would trouble public opinion and might 'sabotage' the LVF, without a 'real and important formation of the Waffen-SS' to take its place.

Undoubtedly such a solution would have given Vichy some influence, if not control, over the new regiment, but the telegram went on to state that the Ambassador may have been persuaded, but Oberg was not, declaring that he had received an unequivocal order which he was not prepared to override. He would press ahead with the formation of a French Regiment of the Waffen-SS.

A recruiting office, called Ersatzkommando Frankreich der Waffen-SS, was opened at 24 avenue du Recteur-Poincaré in Paris. It was run by SS-Hstuf. Alfred Nikles. SS-Schtz. Jean-Marie Balestre, one of the leading figures of the ultra-collaborationist Vichy youth movement *Les Jeunes du Maréchal* who had now deserted the cause of the NSKK for that of the Waffen-SS, worked out of the same office as a *referent* (reporter) for Ergänzungsstelle der Waffen-SS Frankreich. He took up this post on 17 May 1943.[37]

Henri Breuvart, the Secretary General of *Les Jeunes du Maréchal*, who had enlisted in the Waffen-SS in October 1943, was also assigned to the Ersatzkommando der Frankreich in Paris. He worked alongside Jean Duffaure, François Anger, Charles Van Dyck and Jean-Pierre Chapuis. Breuvart held the rank of Unterscharführer.

36    As the head of the SS and police, the HSSPf was responsible for internal security.
37    Balestre would later claim that he enlisted in the 'German Army' on the order of 'his *chefs* of the Resistance' and that his role was to help Jews to escape. He further claims that in 1944 he was arrested by the Germans as he was about to dynamite the Waffen-SS recruiting office and sent to Dachau. However, in response, if he was caught red-handed in the act of dynamiting the Ersatzkommando Frankreich der Waffen-SS in Paris, the Germans would have undoubtedly sent him before a firing squad rather than to Dachau. In addition, some sources have a less honourable explanation for his arrest. Nevertheless, after the war, on his repatriation to France, he was denounced, arrested and interned at Fresnes prison in Paris for two years. Yet, when the *Cour de justice* judged his case, he was exonerated of collaboration; testimonials from the Minister for war veterans, from the Minister for the Armed forces and from the Minister for Defence revealed that he had been resisting since 1942. (*Le Point* N° 736, October 1986.)

The young fanatic Jean-François Bardot from Versailles also briefly worked at the Ersatzkommando Frankreich der Waffen-SS in Paris.[38] He had served with the LVF for two years, which he had joined on the very first day of recruitment. He said of his journey to the Waffen-SS:[39]

> Law student, holder of the baccalauréat, I adhered to the Franciste party at the start of 1939. I maintained my membership after the Occupation, although there was not a great deal of activity, Bucard being a prisoner of war. I then belonged to the MSR where I was *secrétaire* but did not have any political activites. I joined the LVF on 27 August 1941. I was convinced that the Legion would fight in French uniform as it had been stipulated. Arriving in Poland, we had to don the German uniform on the orders of our *chefs*. I swore an oath of loyalty to the Führer. I fought on the Eastern Front from the month of November 1941 to the end of July 1943. Wounded in the leg by shrapnel, I was decorated with the *Croix de guerre légionnaire*, the Iron Cross, the East Medal and French and German wound badges.

Barbot had his leg partially amputated. After a short period of convalescence in several hospitals, notably at Garches, he then decided to join the Waffen-SS and was assigned to the Ersatzkommando Frankreich der Waffen-SS in Paris. He wrote articles for the French SS newspaper entitled *Devenir* and also organised film screenings at which he spoke. Bardot held the rank of Unterscharführer.

Towards 1000 hours on Monday 15 March 1943, André Bayle from Marseille, aged only sixteen and a half, stepped into Ersatzkommando Frankreich der Waffen-SS and volunteered for the European Waffen-SS.[40]

European in outlook, Bayle wanted to defend Europe from the Reds, the enemy of Europe, and from the Anglo-Amercians, who were also anti-European. In 1936, he attended the Olympic Games in Berlin with his parents and was totally seduced by what he saw in Germany, including Hitler, who had only been in power for some three years. 'The population seemed happy in a grandiose, organised and clean environment. Pensions were already instituted, as well as Social Society. Calm reigned'.[41] This was in contrast to the economical, and political chaos back in France. He blamed the Popular Front government for the moral decline of the country and for her defeat in May 1940. Nevertheless, he did not belong to any political party.

He was proud of the Colonial Empire and the Navy, which the armistice had safeguarded, but the brutal English attack on the Navy at Mers-el-Kébir, the aborted assault on Dakar, and the seizure of colonies in Central Africa were not the friendly acts of a former ally. In this way, they 'deprived France of the defence of its empire, leaving it to the mercy of the firstcomers: the English and their loyal supporter de Gaulle'.[42]

A Sea Scout, Bayle had wanted a career in the Navy, but that was out of the question after the fleet was scuttled at Toulon on 27 November 1942. He was stunned that the sailors had not

38    Bardot was born on 16 May 1923.
39    Rentano & Leguérandais, *Ces franciliens qui ont choisi Hitler*, pp.120-121.
40    André Bayle was born on 20 May 1926 in Marseille.
41    Bayle André, *De Marseille à Novossibirsk*, (Histoire et Tradition, 1992), p.12.
42    Bayle, *De Marseille à Novossibirsk*, p.33.

fought to the bitter end, like so many before them. They had 'spoilt' their honour and that of the French Navy and no excuse could absolve them.[43]

With Toulon, the time had now come for Bayle to act and participate in the war of his generation. Attentisme was not for him. On the morning of 10 March 1943, he saw some young French workers leaving for Germany and thought to himself, 'Why them and not me? I'm off!' He rallied to the camp of Europe, a united Europe against Bolshevism, which the Waffen-SS best represented.

After the formalities at the recruitment office, Bayle was sent to Clignancourt barracks, Boulevard Ney, Paris. Two days later, he left for Sennheim in Alsace. Also among the first to volunteer and sign up for the duration of the war was Henri Kreis, whose father was Swiss. Another French volunteer said of his decision to enlist:

> In 1940, the German soldiers had filled me with admiration and horror. In 1943, they began to inspire pity in me. I knew that they were facing the entire world and I had a feeling that they were going to be defeated.
>
> After Stalingrad and El Alamein, we hardly ever saw any more tall blond athletes. In the streets of Paris, I passed pale seventeen or eighteen-year-old adolescents with helmets too large for them and old Mausers of the other war. Sometimes also old men with sad eyes. We called them mockingly: the *Bismarck-Jugend*...
>
> But suddenly reappeared small groups of soldiers true to the legend. Tall, silent, solitary, [with] both hardened and childish features. They returned from hell and the Devil was their only friend. On their collar the two 'lightening flashes' of the Waffen-SS.
>
> I knew that the French were not admitted to this 'Germanic elite'. But I refused to be respected [any] less than a Norwegian or a Dutchmen. Why would I not have the right to fight in what I knew to be the best army in the world?
>
> When I learnt that Degrelle's Walloons were going over to the SS, I guessed that the doors were going to open for us as well. I was among the first to enlist ... [44]

Notably, the French volunteers were registered as Walloons because the Vichy Government had still not approved the recruitment of French volunteers by the Waffen-SS.

## Vichy gives its rubber stamp of approval

On 20 June 1943, Reich Ambassador Rudolf Schleier, who had replaced the disgraced Otto Abetz, reported in a telegram that he had officially informed *chef du Gouvernement* Laval that the creation of a Waffen-SS regiment of French volunteers would now begin. He also pressed Laval to ensure for this regiment 'the same concessions as those in force for the LVF'.[45] Also, during the discussions they had about the subject of the formation of the Waffen-SS regiment, mention was made of the *francisque* as collar insignia. As events would soon prove, Laval yielded to the demands of the Germans.

---

43    Bayle, *De Marseille à Novossibirsk*, p.38-39.
44    Delatour, chapter SS et Français pourquoi?, *Historia* hors série 32, p.118.
45    Telegraph that Minister Schleier sent to Berlin on 20th June 1943.

On 28 June 1943, Foreign Minister von Ribbentrop met with Ambassador de Brinon and discussed the 'necessity' to create one or two French divisions of the Waffen-SS. De Brinon stated that he would take a personal interest in the creation of such a division.

On 13 July 1943, General Bridoux, Vichy's *sous-secrétaire d'état à la defense nationale*, wrote in his journal:[46]

> Laval disclosed to the *conseil* [Council of Ministers] his last talks in Paris; we also talked to him about the possibility of recruiting French units of SS. The Germans are willing to call for volunteers from prison camps and groups of French workers in Germany. Laval intends to publish a law authorizing Frenchmen to enlist in such formations to fight communism outside national territory.

Finally, on Wednesday 22 July 1943, Laval passed Law No. 428 concerning voluntary service in anti-Bolshevist formations. The Law consisted of three articles and read as follows:[47]

| | |
|---|---|
| Article 1 | The French are allowed to enroll voluntarily in French units formed by the German Government (Waffen-SS) for the purpose of fighting Bolshevism outside of France. |
| Article 2 | The members of this unit who actually fight outside state [national] territory shall be entitled to all the benefits promised to the *Légion des volontaires français contre le bolchevisme*. |
| Article 3 | This law shall be published in the *Journal Officiel* and be enforced as a State law. |

Law No. 428 was published in the *Journal Officiel* one day later.

Thus, for the first time, French volunteers could 'officially' enlist in the Waffen-SS and in a wholly French unit. Except for those of Jewish blood and those who had incurred a *condamnation infamante*,[48] all Frenchmen, bachelors or married men, could enlist. Volunteers were required to be physically fit for the demands of military training, a minimum height of 1.65m, and between the ages of seventeen and forty. The height restriction was later lowered to 1.60m.

Recruitment offices, which were attached to regional *Kommandos der Ordnungspolizei*, opened across the country at Angers, Bordeaux, Châlons-sur-Marne, Clermont-Ferrand, Dijon, Limoges, Lyon, Marseille, Montpellier, Nancy, Orléans, Potiers, Rennes, Rouen, Saint-Quentin and Toulouse.[49] More would open at Besançon, Brive and Périgueux. In the north of the country recruitment offices opened in Bruay-en-Artois, Calais, Douai, Lens, Lille, Roubaix and Tourcoing. The recruitment offices would soon become targets for the resistance.

---

46   Merglen, *Soldats français sous uniformes allemands*, p.78.
47   Ertel Heinz and Schule-Kossens Richard, *Europäische Freiwillige im Bild* (Osnabrück: Munin Verlag, 1986), p.301, with slight modifications.
48   A sentence involving exile or a loss of civil rights.
49   Newspaper advertisement in *Le Petit Parisien* of 11 September 1943, see Mounine, *Cernay*, pp.40-45, 255. The KDOs reported to the HSSPF. Thus, as Lefèvre argues, the recruitment process was entirely controlled by the SS-HA 'without regard for French demands' (*Axe & Alliés* hors série no 1).

The response was a flurry of activity. On 6 August 1943, SS-Ustuf. Fernand Rouleau, a Walloon officer attached to Ersatzkommando Frankreich, announced at a press conference held in Paris that more than 1,500 volunteers had already come forward for the medical with little propaganda and that the first battalion already existed, soon to be followed by the first regiment.

The Waffen-SS was presented as 'an indissoluble community of European youth fighting for the maintenance of its cultural values and its civilisation' against Bolchevist nihilism. The same theme of a united European youth against Bolchevism would be repeated in propaganda material.

It was also announced that volunteers that showed the required aptitude could be admitted to officer and NCO training schools of the Waffen-SS and that admittance would not be determined by diplomas or university desgrees. Futhermore, former officers and NCOs would have the opportunity of regaining their previous ranks and receiving commands if they demonstrated the required capacity and aptitude at the Waffen-SS officer and NCO schools.

The press conference was widely reported in the collaborationist press.[50] Posters of various designs appeared which encouraged volunteers to join the French Division of the Waffen-SS! One read: 'The victims of the Anglo-American terrorist raids shout VENGEANCE. Frenchmen! Avenge your dead... Defend your families'.

The 2000th volunteer came forward on 12 August. Even so, the number of volunteers fell short of what the German authorities expected. After signing up, volunteers were required to attend a *conseil de revision* [recruitment board] held at 4, square du Bois-de-Boulogne, Paris. The first board was held on 13 August 1943 and every two to four weeks thereafter. The board was later moved to avenue Victor-Hugo.[51] Those that passed the board were sent to Caserne de Clignancourt, boulevard Ney, Paris, and then onto Sennheim.

To 'tidy' the paperwork of those 'Frenchmen' who had already enlisted, the Waffen-SS authorities had them sign their enlistment papers again.[52] No longer were they Walloons.

Many of the initial volunteers after the publication of Vichy's statutory 'seal of approval' were adherents of the Paris-based collaborationist political parties. Of the first 'official' convoy of French volunteers of the Waffen-SS to arrive at SS-Ausbildungslager Sennheim in early August 1943, half were members of the *Jeunesse franciste*, the youth branch of Marcel Bucard's *Parti Franciste*.

In the summer of 1943, during the *camp des Mille* gathering at Semblançay, near Tours, Bucard had tried to dissuade several tens of his *francistes* from volunteering for the Waffen-SS, but had met with little response.[53] Indeed, 'Bucard had magnified his memories of a former combatant so much that the young *francistes* now believed that nothing could replace military glory, whatever the uniform'.[54] For some, the downfall of Mussolini and Fascism had been their final motive for enlisting in the Waffen-SS. Even so the *francistes* promised to wear their blue

---

50   For example, see *Le Petit Parisien* of 8 August 1943.
51   The boards would continue until at least May 1944.
52   Bayle, *De Marseille à Novossibirsk*, pp.46-48.
53   Mabire, *La Brigade Frankreich*, p.50. However, Bucard would very quickly change his tune. On 14 August 1943, *Le Franciste* described the SS as the 'purest elements in the militant order of European fascist doctrine'. Also, according to Deniel, *Bucard et le Francisme*, p.204, Bucard and his lieutenants actively encouraged a number of their supporters to enlist so that they could start to colonise the French Waffen-SS.
54   Mabire, *La Brigade Frankreich*, p.50.

Various recruitment posters for the SS

shirt of France under their Waffen-SS uniform! Pierre Bousquet and Henri Simon were two such *francistes* Bucard could not talk out of volunteering for the Waffen-SS.

Pierre Bousquet and his whole family had joined the Party before the war.[55] As the years passed, his importance within the Party grew and by the time he volunteered for the Waffen-SS he was a member of its *Bureau national* and the leader of the *conseil national* of the *Jeunesse franciste*. This was a far cry from when he was a young kid selling the party newspaper in the streets.[56] Although he hailed from Alsace, he was *tricolore* and in 1939 was a *Sergent aviateur* ready to do battle with the Germans. To Bousquet, the poor performance of the French Army against the Germans in 1940 was a crushing blow and after that debacle 'he no longer believed in the French Army'.[57]

The crushing defeat also turned the world of Henri Simon upside down. Born on 18 May 1919 in the department Vosges in the region of Lorraine, he was raised in the cult of heroic patriotism. Despite the pacifist words of the primary school teacher, he dreamt about the stories of *assault à la fourchette* [assault with 'pig-sticker' fixed]. Besides, his first name of Henri was in memory of an uncle, a *sous-lieutenant d'infanterie*, who had fallen in combat in Alsace.

By the age of twelve, Simon was already interested in politics and a reader of *L'Action Française* [the newspaper of the right wing movement *L'Action Française* headed by Charles Maurras].

---

55   Pierre Bousquet was born on 2 November 1919 in Tours.
56   His future wife was a member of the women's section of the *Francistes*.
57   Mabire, *La Brigade Frankreich*, p.50.

Little by little, the thoughts of Maurras impregnated his spirit. The Stavisky scandal and the bloody night of 6 February 1934 reinforced his disgust for parliamentary democracy.[58]

In 1938, Simon enlisted in the French Navy, becoming a *quartier-maître des fusiliers-marins* [a leading seaman in the Marines]. Of the defeat, he would never forget the picture of a *capitaine de cor-vette* [a lieutenant commander] 'clearing off with the flag in an oil cloth' or that of 'an officer of a ship's crew, a former hero of Dixmude,[59] who was crying his eyes out because he had lost his bags'.[60] This spectacle of such abandon and such refusal of community interest aroused in him contempt towards his compatriots. At heart, he was still the young boy who admired the *poilu* of the 14-18 war.[61]

Defeat also brought captivity, but he was out within one month after he volunteered to work for the Germans. Fluent in German, Henri Simon became an interpreter and worked for the *Militärverwaltung* [the administrative arm of the *Militärbefehlshaber in Frankreich* - the military command in France] at the city port of Lorient, Brittany. A nationalist through and through, he clashed with Breton separatists and, on one occasion, got into a fight with Dutch Schutzkommando of the Organisation Todt guarding a *Breiz Atao* meeting.[62] For this, he was punished with one month's imprisonment.

And then, one day during the summer of 1941, while passing through square Alsace-Lorraine, Simon came upon the office of the *Parti Franciste*. On display was a *grand* portrait of a robust man sporting a chestful of military decorations, 'proof of valorous acts during the war of his elders'. Simon stood there in awe of this man on the portrait who was, of course, Marcel Bucard, the leader of the *Parti Franciste*. Thereupon Simon became a *franciste*. He went on to run a *section départementale* in the West. He later reflected that the portrait of Marcel Bucard became the 'most deciding object of his destiny'.[63] Convinced that France was slipping into civil war, Simon had no desire to police his countrymen and thus volunteered for the Waffen-SS.

Pierre Bousquet and Henri Simon were on the first official convoy of French Waffen-SS volunteers to arrive at Sennheim. On this same convoy were volunteers from the *Jeunesses Nationale Populaires* (JNP), the *Jeunesses Populaires Française* (JPF), *Les Jeunes de L'Europe Nouvelle* (JEN), and *La Ligue des Jeunes de France et de l'Empire*.

The recruitment of French volunteers for the Waffen-SS offered Doriot one more opportunity to find favour with the German authorities and perhaps political power. Ambitious, Doriot still lived in hope of coming to power. However, his short-term aspirations were dealt a blow on 21

---

58    As a result of the financial scandal, the Right had taken to the streets and, with the Communists fighting side by side, attempted to storm the Chamber of Deputies and bring down the Republic. The insurrection was defeated by a handful of Police at the cost of 16 dead and 655 wounded.
59    This is a reference to the Battle of the Yser that took place during October 1914.
60    Mabire, *La Brigade Frankreich*, p.51.
61    *Poilu* translates as hairy; while on active service French privates did not shave. *Poilu* is the French equivalent of 'Tommy' in the British Army.
62    Literally 'Brittany always', this slogan became the title of a Breton separatist review in 1927 and, later, the title of a Breton separatist newspaper. The last issue of *Breiz Atao*, 27th August 1939, had prophesied French military defeat and that France 'would then have to resign itself to making concessions and collaborating with the Axis, or be subjected in turn to the coup de grâce.'
63    Cera, *Les raisons de l'engagement de volontaires francais sous l'uniforme Allemand*, p.129. The notion that Simon came to *francisme* after the armistice is also recounted by Mabire, *La Brigade Frankreich*, p.51. However, in contrast, according to Gaulois, *Der Freiwillige*, 10/97, Simon joined the *Parti Franciste* at a young age.

September 1942 in a letter from Ribbentrop to Otto Abetz: to maintain social order in France, Hitler preferred Laval to Doriot. Undeterred, he held a 'Congress of Power' in Paris from the 4 to the 8 of November 1942. 7,200 delegates attended. However, they may have represented no more than 25,000 members. When Laval banned its closing ceremony at the Velodrome d'Hiver the delegates, in a show of force, paraded along the Champs-Elysées, clashing with the police.

The PPF promised to send 600 men into the Waffen-SS. Many were from its youth branch, the JPF. A student by the name of Charles Laschett, born on 2 March 1920, was the sole representative of *Le Front Franc*. His father, Maurice, figured among those in charge of this 'party' numbering only several hundred adherents.

Few were the number of volunteers who were not adherents of a political party, but even they spoke of similar, if not the very same, motives for enlisting. For one volunteer, the international Waffen-SS offered an opportunity to find his dream of European Socialism:[64]

> My father was a (primary school) teacher. An honest and simple bloke with ideas of his milieu: socialism, peace and Europe ... Thanks to him, I discovered Romain Rolland and Germany. I believed the most important thing was to get along among neighbours.
>
> I joined the 'youth hostels'. I discovered there the open air, the sun, friends who came from other countries with their guitars and their songs, and friendship.
>
> I was mobilised in 1939. I waged war in an atmosphere of disorder and cowardice which would not stop until the defeat... I returned to my region, a small sub-prefecture on the banks of the Loire. My father still continued to read *L'Oeuvre*, just like before the war. He admired Marcel Déat. I found he was right sometimes, but the masquerade imitated from the Germans did not really tempt me. Those coloured shirts, those shoulder-belts, those *bérets basques* that seemed to me small and mean, in a word French. What interested me was Europe. Not Germany, Europe. [And] Socialism that spanned a whole continent.
>
> I was still not a militarist, but I believed we had to win the war against the communists who I had never liked, and against the capitalists I had always detested. The LVF did not tempt me because of its *tricolore* side. And besides it had too many regulars and *doriotistes*. In the Waffen-SS, I hoped to find an international army and a sort of socialism in poverty, courage and voluntary discipline.

Nicholas Montignac, a novelist and member of the *Groupe Collaboration* in his mid-thirties, arrived at Sennheim in August 1943. After his mother left the family home when he was aged seven, he was brought up by his father, a hero of the battle of Verdun, who often told him stories of the Great War. Politically, he detested Communism, which he regarded as the 'most ignoble barbarism there was'.[65] As a fervent patriot, he feared German expansionism, even though he appreciated some of the aethestic qualities of the Nazi regime, but the seemingly invincible French Army reassured him.

---

64    Delatour, chapter SS et Français pourquoi?, *Historia* hors série 32, pp.116-117.
65    Lormier Dominique, *SS Français* (Paris: Éditions Jourdan, 2018), p.71.

Mobilised at the start of October 1939, Montignac served and fought bravely with the *57e régiment d'infanterie*. Defeat angered him, which he blamed on the tactical errors made by some commanders, the military unpreparedness of the country, as well as the 'blindness and profound mediocrity of our politics'.[66] Disgusted by the corrupt, improvident, and decadent Republic, he wholeheartedly supported Pétain and the National Revolution.

Soon after his demobilization in July 1940, Montignac joined the Group. He admired the discipline of the occupier and believed that collaboration with Nazi Germany was a 'logical sequence at the end of the republican regime'.[67] The common enemy was Communism. He thought about joining the LVF but injured his leg falling from a horse. He hated the enemies of the Reich all the more after learning of the death in an Allied air raid of a German woman journalist he had met and befriended just before the outbreak of war. He finally opted for the Waffen-SS.

Some volunteers were from the *1er Régiment de France* (1er R.d.F.). Created by Law N° 413 of 15th July 1943, published in the *Journal Officiel* of 28th July 1943, the 1er R.d.F. was, in the words of Laval of 15th June 1943, 'the promise and hope of our new army'; France had been without an army ever since the dissolution of the Armistice Army on 27th November 1942. Even though Vichy had wanted to raise several divisions, the Germans only authorised the formation of a single regiment. The 1er R.d.F., however, was placed under the direct authority of the head of government and not the head of State. Vichy defined the role of the regiment as 'keeping alive military values in France' but did not rule out its use against the internal enemies of the regime.

A total of some three hundred officers volunteered for the sixty-five posts available. In this way, the 1er R.d.F. filled with former cadets of military schools Saint-Cyr, Saint-Maixent, Poitiers, Versailles and Saumur whose studies had been cut short by the dissolution of the Armistice Army. Also, such was the influx of students into the 1er R.d.F. that the press dubbed it the *'régiment des bacheliers'*.[68] Jews and freemasons were refused admission to the regiment. The recruitment of men for the ranks proved much more difficult, though. Despite the best efforts of Vichy, which included a package of financial incentives, only 1500 volunteers came forward, of which only 800 joined the regiment. The majority of the volunteers were conservatives, often from military families. Even though agreements were made between the SS-Hauptamt and the 1er R.d.F. to facilitate the engagement of men in the French Waffen-SS,[69] few 'went over'.

At Sennheim, the French volunteers were assigned to the 1st Company under the command of SS-Ostuf. der Reserve Martin Laue, a former minister in the Reformed Church. Laue had declared to the French volunteers upon their arrival at Sennheim: "To serve France was a duty, but to serve Europe in the Waffen-SS is an honour!"

The 1st Platoon was almost exclusively made up of 'deserters' from the NSKK.

By September 1943, French recruits had filled out the 2nd Company under SS-Oscha. Lang. Notably, the majority of the new intake arrived from Germany. Some were former POWs. Months earlier, in July, German authorities earmarked a sum of 100,000 Reichsmarks to finance

---

66    Lormier, *SS Français*, p.93.
67    Ibid.
68    The French word *bachelier* describes a person who has passed the *baccalauréat* [secondary school examination giving university entrance qualification].
69    See report with reference SAM/36003, CARAN.

the recruitment of French workers and POWs in Germany for the Waffen-SS.[70] The Germans attempted to recruit prisoners of all ranks and employed the likes of First World War hero and collaborator Christian du Jonchay to win them over. Du Jonchay approached *Commandant* Pierre Debray in Oflag IV-D and invited him to join him. Debray politiely responded: "Not being on the same side of the barbed wire, we cannot feel the same way." There was a further exchange of words, but Debray was not to be won over.[71]

Free worker Lucien Hennecart required no persuasion whatsoever to volunteer.[72] After having tried and been disappointed by all the pre-war French fascist parties, he became a 'Hitlerian'.[73] Nonetheless, when war came he immediately rallied to the flag. Well, to him, 'France is France'. During May 1940, this convinced fascist fought the Germans, but his old F.M. was no match for the tanks and airplanes of the enemy.

Made a prisoner because somebody senior put his hands up for him, Hennecart ended up in a Stalag in Germany. Behind barbed wire, he was not attracted to either de Gaulle or Pétain. He believed the former was too far away and the latter too weak. Indeed, he wrote to Brasillach:[74] 'The war is lost, but I would like to die with weapons in my hands.'

Becoming a free worker,[75] Hennecart now found himself in a kommando, but soon tired of 'pushing a wheelbarrow'. Learning that prisoners could enlist in the Waffen-SS, the thirty-five-year-old decided to see 'how it was going on the other side of the barbed wire'.[76]

Arguably, twenty-two-year-old Pierre Roesch was an idealist,[77] coming to the Waffen-SS years after he first tried to gain admittance:

> I did not belong to any political party but from my fourteenth year I was already won over by the cause of National Socialism and before that I had always been a Germanophile. I was nevertheless a monarchist but not of *Action Française*.
>
> I had no desire to make war or play at soldiers. It was quite simply the call of blood and race. Since 1815 I was descended from a Prussian who, wounded, remained at Paris and got married there. Thus I could not be anything else, for better or for worse
> …
>
> I never believed at all that I was a fanatic. I simply believe I was a convinced National Socialist. My enlistment was not only the sole product of my germanophilia

70  Bundesarchiv, Potsdam, R55-1237.
71  Debray, *Souvenirs*, p.42-43.
72  See Mabire, *La Brigade Frankreich*, p.67 and Delatour, paragraph *Plutôt au front qu'au stalag* [Rather at the front than in the stalag], *Historia* hors série No 32, pp.118-119. And although the latter is anonymous, there is some similarity between the two. Hennecart was born on 27 May 1908 in Paris.
73  Mabire, *La Brigade Frankreich*, p.67.
74  Brasillach was a journalist who wrote for the Fascist Parisian newspaper *Je Suis Partout*.
75  From early 1943, for every French worker who arrived in Germany, one French prisoner of war could volunteer to become a *freiarbeiter* [free worker]. Vichy was against this change of designation because the prisoners were no longer protected by their status.
76  Delatour, *Plutôt au front qu'au stalag*, *Historia* hors série No 32, p.119. In contrast, according to Mabire, *La Brigade Frankreich*, p.67, Hennecart was told that he did not have the right to enlist in the Waffen-SS. However, this did not deter him and so he took the train to Görlitz where there was a Waffen-SS recruiting office. The rest was just a formality. When he departed a Gestapo agent was waiting for him outside. Already a *SS-Freiwillige*, he was not sent back to his stalag.
77  Pierre Roesch was born on 1 March 1921 in Paris.

and my support without for restriction for National Socialist ideology more of a great admiration for the Führer. Whereas even [SS-Uscha. Philippe] Merlin[78] [of Abteilung IV, ideological training] had ambitions for France (not for the Republic, nor tricolore...)

From the start I had requested my integration into a purely German unit but paradoxically my impeccable knowledge of the German language stopped me. They had need of me as an interpreter. Thus I ended up by only having personal relations with the Germans. The French eventually regarded me as such and all too quickly as a 'fanatic'.

My enlistment in the SS dates from 1941. In France, on holiday in a small, charming village whose name I forget there was billeted an SS unit whose commander played chess with me and of which a very young SS-Ustuf. (Ernst Ritter of Magdebourg) came for walks with me to practice French. It was over a game of chess that I asked the commander if I could enlist in his unit. It took three weeks for his reply: "Today impossible, but later, soon, you can."

His presence at Sennheim was brief, ending when he was posted to SS-Ergänzungsstelle Nordost at Königsberg. Roesch believes that Merlin was responsible for this. Because of his impeccable German Roesch found himself in great demand when Merlin was not available, even by the likes of the camp commander SS-Oberführer Fick, but this situation was not agreeable to Merlin, who wanted to remain the sole German speaker at Sennheim. Roesch was posted back to Sennheim on 15 April 1944.[79]

Not all recruits were idealists like Roesch. Some were victims of blackmail. Ending up in the suburbs of Vienna, an S.T.O.[80] worker explained:[81]

[It was] an idiot job. A nasty ambience. The majority of the workers were Polaks. People I can't stand. The only distraction, on Sunday: walks along the Danube. With a friend, a lad from Levallois[82], we found ourselves two small, kind 'birds'. But it was forbidden to frequent with German females, especially if they were engaged to soldiers at the front. One day the feldgendarmes fell on us. We ended up at the Gestapo. It seemed that we were 'race defilers'. A right fine mess. We risked years of work camps. Arrived a bloke in uniform who told us everything could be sorted out. We just had to enlist and they would forget about it. Thus, rather than end up in the nick, we both signed...

S.T.O. worker Camille Rouvre was also backmailed into joining the Waffen-SS.[83] One day at the factory he was caught by his foreman making love to a young German girl. When the

78    See Mouine, *Cernay*, pp.318-322.
79    Merlin committed suicide on the night of the 24-25 January 1944.
80    On 16 February 1943, under a law instituting the *Service du Travail Obligatorie* (S.T.O.) Laval and the Vichy government made labour service obligatory for all French males born in 1920, 1921 and 1922.
81    Delatour, chapter SS et Français pourquoi?, *Historia* hors série 32, p.119.
82    Levallois is a suburb of Paris.
83    See Lupo, Georges, *Levée d'écrou* (1948), pp.125-126. Camille Rouvre was born on 23 July 1923 in Troo (department Loir-et-Cher).

foreman started to bawl him out in German he lost his temper and punched him in the face. Two Gestapo agents and a policeman arrived and threatened him with the concentration camp. Then an Oberscharführer of the SS arrived who spoke very good French. This NCO told him that he could only avoid the concentration camp by enlisting in a French formation of the SS, adding that if this formation was not to his liking he could return to France. Rouvre signed up on 13 January 1944. Two days later, he was accompanied to Sennheim.

Victor Degraeve, an S.T.O. worker at Duisburg, was arrested by the German Police in October 1943 for giving blue overalls to a French prisoner who wanted to escape. To avoid punishment, he enlisted in the Waffen-SS. On 15 November 1943, he received orders to go to Sennheim.[84]

There were also some romantics among the volunteers. To them, the Waffen-SS offered a gigantic adventure that no French political party could and also a break with the world around them. One such volunteer, a romantic seventeen-year-old philosophy student who had discovered National Socialist Germany through the bearded prophet Alphonse de Châteaubriant[85] and his book *Gerbe des forces*, explained:[86]

> I was against the bourgeois order, that of my parents and my teachers. I believed in all the myths of revolution and youth. My enlistment in the Waffen-SS was above all a rupture with the old world. I wanted to scandalise, why deny it? I have to say I succeeded perfectly...

In September 1943, nineteen-year-old national socialist Jean del Missier arrived at Sennheim camp in the uniform of the NSKK.[87] In May of that year, he had signed up for the NSKK and was sent to Vilvoorde, Belgium, but as soon as enlistment in the Waffen-SS was made official for Frenchmen he left the NSKK for the Waffen-SS. He wanted to be a *combattant contre le bolchevisme* in an elite unit and there was absolutely no question of him joining the LVF whose internal squabbles, which reminded him of the Third Republic, 'made him sick'. He did not belong to any political party and nor did his parents. Also, his parents did not criticize his choice.

At Sennheim, Jean del Missier was assigned to the 1st Platoon of the 5th Company commanded by German SS-Ostuf. Sommer. He noted:

> My instructors were in the image of the Waffen-SS: European. My section commander was a Flemish Rottenführer and my platoon commander an Oberscharführer from Luxembourg.

---

84   Rentano and Leguérandais, *Ces Franciliens qui ont choisi Hitler*, p.129. The source of this material is from his interview with Military Security at the end of the war and the possibility exists that he misled his interviewers about his real reasons for enlisting.

85   A Christian intellectual, but also a champion of collaboration and an admirer of Hitler, Châteaubriant headed the strongly spiritual and Europeanist *Groupe collaboration*. Châteaubriant also published the weekly newspaper *La Gerbe* which had one of the largest circulations of the collaborationist newspapers or magazines.

86   Delatour, chapter SS et Français pourquoi?, *Historia* hors série 32, p.116.

87   Jean del Missier was born on 8 September 1924 in Amiens (department Somme).

At Sennheim, all commands were given in German. Many struggled with the language. Laue, whose mother was French, helped out by giving German lessons. On 13 September 1943, in the somewhat poignant setting of the former chapel, the 1st Company swore the oath of loyalty to Adolf Hitler.

Political affiliations faded. On one October day, SS-Ostuf. Sommer assembled the 5th Company and explained to them that the time to make the final decision had come. They were free to leave if they so wished, but if they chose to remain in the Waffen-SS they would have to give up questions of politics and religion. Some fifteen men left. That same month, the 5th Company swore the oath of loyalty to Hitler. According to del Missier, it was a *cérémonie grandiose*.

The French *freiwillige* felt less and less French, but for all that they did not become German. They felt born into a new European army.[88] Fernand Costamagna, who was attached to the 3rd Company, wrote of their state of mind after months of training which had bonded the French recruits together:[89]

> We Frenchmen wanted, despite the difficulties of the moment and the humiliations resulting from our military defeat of 1940, to prove, by our energy in action, our bravery and our virility, that we were ready and capable of performing acts of courage and making sacrifices in order to improve the image of our country. We wanted to make our contribution to the safety of Europe, against the Bolshevik hordes.

Within the Waffen-SS, Costamagna felt a very real sense of European camarderie. He would remain loyal to his comrades then and throughout his life.

From the start of his training Nicholas Montignac felt like he belonged to an 'extraordinary warrior caste', whose role was to 'fight for the existence and future of Aryan Europe against Bolshevism and plutocracy'. Moreover, 'we were not only knights of the new Europe, but also revolutionary militants who wanted to save France from decadence'. He knew that they were outnumbered, but that mattered not, convinced that they were able to defeat the multitude. For Montignac, the transformation from the dark days of defeat was complete: 'No longer were we the vanquished of 1940'.[90]

Many of the first recruits reacted angrily to the arrival of a convoy of some two hundred of their own countrymen in October 1943. These newcomers, mostly from the South, many of whom were from the *Milice*, including several officers, represented those who had fled shamefully before the Germans in 1940.[91]

---

88   Mabire, *La Brigade Frankreich*, p.71.
89   Costabrava, *Le soldat Baraka*, p.64.
90   Lormier, *SS Français*, p.96.
91   Mabire, *La Brigade Frankreich*, p.71.

**3**

# Darnand, the SOL and the *Milice française*

## Joseph Darnand

Many of these new volunteers were from Joseph Darnand's *Milice française*. His story and that of the *Milice* is closely entwined with the formation of the French Sturmbrigade of the Waffen-SS and, at a later date, the French Division of the Waffen-SS.

Joseph Darnand was born on 19 March 1897 in Coligny, the son of a railway worker. In 1915, at age seventeen, he volunteered for the Army, but was rejected; he was too sickly. It was a terrible blow for him and years later he admitted that he 'cried with anger'. He was not a man to give up and finally on 8 January 1916 he was declared fit for service and joined the *35e regiment d'infanterie*. It was as if he had found his true vocation and quickly rose to the rank of sergeant. Found where where the action was hottest, in thirteen months of combat he won six citations, including two *à l'ordre de l'Armée*, and the Belgium *Croix de guerre*, picking up two wounds in the process.

On 14 July 1918, Darnand, now of the *366e regiment d'infanterie*, took twenty-four prisoners, including a Lieutenant Colonel, during a raid on the German lines. The subsequent interrogation of the prisoners revealed an impending German attack that was smashed. For his exploit, Darnand won the *médaille militaire* [Military Medal] which he received six days later from Pétain in person. This event, according to some commentators, led to a lifelong devotion to the Marshal. Later, in 1927, Darnand was to receive the *Légion d'honneur*. President of the Republic Poincaré even lauded Darnand as one of 'the artisans of victory'.

After the war *adjudant* Darnand hoped for a commission at *École militaire d'infanterie de* Saint-Maixent but his superiors, who appreciated his military virtues but doubted his intellectual abilities, dissuaded him with the assurance that he would have a choice. This assurance came to nothing and it was this deception that embedded the seeds of his hatred of this Republic. On 30 September 1919, he enlisted again, this time for two years. He ended up in Syria and saw action in Cilicie,[1] before returning to France. Realising that he would never be commissioned, he left the army on 26 July 1921 a very bitter man. He was burning to take his revenge. He married

---

1   Cilicie is a region of Turkey along the northern border of Syria which was under a French mandate at the time.

one year later and had two children: a daughter, who died in infancy, and a son, who was named Philippe. Moving to Nice, he set up and ran his own transport company, which became highly successful.

The years between the World Wars saw Darnand drift from one Rightist group to another but it was only in Eugène Deloncle's *Comité Secret d'Action Révolutionnaire* (CSAR), otherwise known as *La Cagoule* ('The Hooded Ones'), that he finally felt at home among men in his own mould, men whose hatred of the present government of Léon Blum and its communist supporters was as strong as his. He was soon the head of the CSAR in Nice.

Convinced that France was now in danger of a communist takeover, which was its call to action, the CSAR and its action squads were responsible for a series of political murders during 1936 and 1937. Darnand became actively involved in gunrunning from Italy to the Côte d'Azur, which his trucks then distributed throughout France.

This gunrunning activity led the CSAR to murder Maurice Juif at Imperia in Italy. A trafficker and go-between for the sale of arms, Juif 'had not been playing fair'. Darnand's complicity in this murder is not known but the subsequent investigation brought about his arrest on 14 July 1938. He found himself in the dock accused of plotting against State Security, gunrunning and criminal conspiracy.

While in prison Darnand was visited by a young reserve officer by the name of Jean Bassompierre. Strapped up tight in his uniform, *Sous-lieutenant* Bassompierre came to show Darnand his 'affection' and 'his loyalty in misfortune'. The two men got on well and would soon become close friends.

Born on 23 October 1914 in Honfleur, Bassompierre studied at the *lycée* Jeanson-de-Sailly before going on to receive his *Diplôme de Sciences Politiques* at the university of Paris. While a student in the Latin Quarter of Paris he became a militant of the right-wing movement *Jeunesses Patriotes* [Patriot Youth].[2] Bassompierre made a name for himself at the time of the Stavisky scandal participating in anti-parliamentary and anti-semitic demonstrations. Two years later, the University suspended him for six months after he disrupted with teargas a lecture by Dr. Jèze, a sworn enemy of the extreme French right. Before the League of Nations, Dr. Gaston Jèze had condemned Mussolini's aggression against Négus Hailé Selassié of Ethiopia.

Politically, after leaving the *Jeunesses Patriotes*, Bassompierre was drawn to the CSAR.[3]

In October 1936, Bassompierre attended military academy Saint-Cyr for *école d'officiers de réserve* [EOR] training and graduated in April 1937 with the rank of *sous-lieutenant de réserve* [Reserve Second-Lieutenant] whereupon he was posted to the the *74e Bataillon Alpin de Forteresse* (74e BAF). That same year, Deloncle, the leader of the CSAR, made the young officer responsible for detecting any possible communist infiltration in his regiment. And it was also Deloncle who put the young idealist and ardent patriot in contact with Darnand. Bassompierre's military service was due to end in October 1938, but he asked to continue his service as a *lieutenant d'active*, which was granted. He continued to serve with the 74e BAF.

---

2    In 1924, Champagne magnate Pierre Taittinger, the deputy for Paris, founded the *Jeunesses Patriotes*. It would remain a significant force on the French right to the mid 1930s.

3    According to Giolitto Pierre, *Volontaires français sous l'uniforme allemand* (Paris: Perrin, 1999), p.536, Bassompierre became one of the first adherents of the CSAR with the number 180. However, his name does not appear on the list of CSAR members later seized by the Police. Nevertheless, he did work actively for the CSAR.

Darnand's service record earnt him the court's leniency and, after six months in detention, he was granted bail on 16 December 1938. Seven months later, the case against him was dismissed through lack of evidence. Darnand's strong defence case and the fact that war was looming are often cited as the reasons behind the prosecution's decision to drop the case rather than any failure on their part.

When war broke out *lieutenant de réserve* Darnand was mobilised to a rear area assignment as a transport officer in the *6e demi-brigade de Chasseurs Alpins*. Irked, the forty-two-year-old Darnand demanded combat duty and was rewarded with being assigned to the *24e bataillon de chasseurs* of the *29e division d'infanterie*. He and his good friend Lieutenant Agnély obtained authorisation from the General commanding the *29e D.I.* to form a *corps franc*, a sort of commando unit whose role was to penetrate German lines in order to gather intelligence. Agnély commanded. Darnand was second in command. In February 1940, the troops of the *corps franc* were greatly surprised to be armed with Italian Beretta sub machine-guns seized from the clandestine CSAR arsenal!

On 8 February 1940, Darnand's commanding officer and friend, Agnély, was killed while on a night patrol at Forbach. Darnand and three volunteers returned to the village under fire and brought back the body of his comrade. For this *coup de main*, Darnand was awarded the *rosette d'officier de la Légion d'honneur* and given command of the *corps franc*, as well as making the front cover of the magazine Match on 21 March 1940.

During the remainder of the so-called 'Phoney War' Darnand continued to distinguish himself time and again by his courage and his audacity. When the Battle of France came he was in constant action with his *corps franc* and was taken prisoner on 19 June 1940 at La Motte-Beuvron, in Sologne. By that time, he had been awarded two further bronze palms for his *Croix de guerre*.[4]

In August, Darnand escaped from his POW camp at Pithiviers. Returning to Nice, he began to plot revenge against the Germans. Soon after, Bassompierre joined him. He too now wanted revenge.

During the war Lieutenant Bassompierre had served on the Alpes front, commanding an outpost at Conchetas, near Saint-Martin-Vésubie. On 20 June 1940, the Italians attacked. In heavy fighting, they were contained everywhere. Among the artisans of this defensive victory was Bassompierre. He fought bravely and was awarded the *Croix de guerre* with one gilt star.[5] On 25 June, after the armistice, he even defied orders and blew up an ammunition dump. In this way, he showed himself to be 'the best officer of his *régiment*'.[6] When he separated from his men he told them not to be afraid to look the occupying forces in the face because 'we are not beaten'. After the Armistice he wanted to continue to serve France but was demobilised on 15 August 1940 at Toulon.

Bassompierre returned to Nice where he met Darnand. He said of this meeting of similar minds:

4    A bronze palm indicates a citation in an Army dispatch.
5    A gilt star indicates a citation in a Corps dispatch.
6    See Charles Ambroise Colin, *Sacrifice de Bassompierre* which is part of Bassompierre Jean, *Frères ennemis* (Paris: Amiot-Dumont, 1948).

We agree at once; we want to continue to serve France; we still have a government; this one speaks to us of National Revolution, prestigious words which restore hope to us. For it is obvious that our military disaster is above all due to the total incompetence of a regime loathed by all honest people. We all hope for a bit of moral decency and social justice. A noble task awaits us: to show the world that we have not become a nation of slaves, that we are still a great country at the head of an intact empire and commanding the most modern navy. The Marshal urges us to undertake this great task; we give ourselves to him heart and soul, to him who is the symbol of a France that does not want to or can not die.

On 29 August 1940, the Vichy Government announced the formation of the *Légion française des Combattants* [Legion of War Veterans] to unite the numerous existing war veterans' organisations. Its president was Pétain and its secretary-general Xavier Vallat. The nationalist Legion exhibited adoration of the Marshal and with its anti-German sentiments dreamed of revenge. Indeed, the Legion was not allowed to function in the Occupied Zone. As such, the Legion can not be considered collaborationist.

After very favourable advice from Pétain, Vallat chose Darnand to run the Legion in the department of the Alpes-Maritimes raised on 6 October 1940. A convinced *maréchaliste*, he agreed. His friend Bassompierre became the *Secrétaire general départemental*. To him, the Legion seemed the source of French revival. In June 1941, he was appointed the *secrétaire régional* for the region of Marseille.

After Pétain's public statement that he had 'entered in all honour in the way of collaboration', Darnand, blinded by his devotion to Pétain, fell into line like the good soldier he was. That devotion was intensified when he was summoned at the end of the year to see Marshal Pétain and told to continue his work in the Legion and denounce the enemies of the New Order. The Marshal told him: "I do not like Jews, I detest Communists and I hate Freemasons."

At the same time Darnand was also wholeheartedly involved in the *Groupes de Protection* created at Vichy by Colonel Groussard, François Méténier and Doctor Martin. Colonel Groussard wrote: 'My task will be to create the nucleus of an anti-German intelligence service under the guise of a subsidiary police force.' As well as being anti-German in nature, the *Groupes de Protection* were anti-Gaullist, but very *Maréchal, nous voilà*. In its ranks were many former *cagoulards* and that included Darnand. In many ways, the *Groupes de Protection* could be regarded as one of the first French 'underground' movements.

The *Groupes de Protection* were made up of two distinct branches: the armed military branch and the civilian branch, the *Centre d'Information et d'Études*. When the Italian authorities refused the formation of the *Groupes de Protection* in the department of Alpes-Maritimes, Darnand was appointed *chef de la 15e region du Centre d'Information et d'Études* on 11 November 1940. However, Darnand resigned his post the following month to devote himself entirely to the Legion. But in that short time Darnand had armed with weapons furnished in secret by the French Army and trained some two hundred and fifty men. More importantly, many *chefs* of the *Groupes de Protection* would become future *Milice* dignitaries. They included Joseph Lécussan and Jean-Baptiste Géromini, a former *Sous-lieutenant* of the *24e bataillon de chasseurs alpins* (24e BCA).

The German invasion of Russia in June 1941 compounded Darnand's commitment to collaboration. By the late summer of 1941, he had become disillusioned by the unwieldy and the unreliable Legion, which had proved slow to give up its anti-German sentiments and the idea of revenge. He was in need of real revolutionaries.[7] Thus, in August 1941, together with other senior members of the Legion, including Bassompierre, he created in the Alpes-Maritimes Department the *Service d'Ordre Légionnaire* [the Order Service of the Legion], the SOL.[8]

The SOL remained a private organisation until the Vichy Government gave its official blessing in January 1942. Named as the *Inspecteur général du SOL*, Darnand relocated to Vichy. He surrounded himself with friends. And again by his side was Bassompierre. He was in charge of Propaganda. Pierre Cance was at the head of the Third Bureau (operations and propaganda). In the months that followed, the SOL spread throughout the unoccupied zone, inaugurated at Annecy on 13 and 14 June 1942, then at Lyon on 11 and 12 July 1942... Membership of the SOL was probably a little over 15,000.[9]

The SOL was an integral part of the Legion but differed in every aspect. Entry to the SOL was limited to those who were naturalised citizens, aged between twenty and forty-five, and not Jewish or members of a secret society. Also, recruits were required to undergo and pass a three month period of probation that included physical training, political education and practical training in the techniques of the maintenance of order. In this way, the recruits would come to know of what was expected of them and sign up 'with full knowledge of the facts'. [And, of course, if the recruits were found wanting their applications could be rejected.]

Once recruited, members of the SOL were given the title of 'Knight of the New France' and assured that this new knighthood 'would draw from the past the strength to build the future'. Their suit of armour was the 'beret of our chasseurs, the khaki shirt of the French Army and a black tie, as a sign of mourning for the Homeland'.[10] On the left arm a white edged black brassard was worn and on the upper right arm heraldic unit insignia of the district of origin.

The doctrine of the SOL was based entirely on twenty-one points codified by three friends of Darnand: Jean Bassompierre, Dr. Durandy,[11] and Noël de Tissot. The points were a series of slogans that positioned the SOL politically against Gaullist dissidence, Jewish leprosy, Bolshevism, and pagan freemasonry. Equally the SOL was for French unity, Nationalism, French purity and Christian civilisation. But what did this mean in practical terms? Its regulations called for the SOL to maintain good order at Legion gatherings, as well as meetings organised by the government. This was deemed as 'very easy, but necessary' and excellent training for more important and difficult tasks. One such task was to provide assistance for the repression of public demonstrations against Marshal Pétain and the Vichy government. Another such task for the political 'shock troops of the National Revolution', as for the Legion of French Combatants,

---

7    Delperrié de Bayac is not the only source to comment that Darnand was also in need of a party (see *Histoire de la Milice*, p.96).

8    Delperrié de Bayac, *Histoire de la Milice*, p.96, and Darnand, speech to the *Haute Courte de Justice* on 3 October 1945 (Delperrié de Bayac, *Histoire de la Milice*, p.97). Curiously, according to Lambet and Le Marec, *Organistaions, mouvements et unités de l'état français*, p.117, Marcel Gombert, Darnand's right-hand man, created the SOL without the knowledge of Darnand.

9    Conclusion reached by Giolitto, *Histoire de la Milice*, p.78. Also see Delperrié de Bayac, *Histoire de la Milice*, p.146.

10   Jean Bassompierre, *Frères enemis*, p.127.

11   Born on 6 May 1910 in Puget-Théniers (department Alpes-Maritimes), Paul Durandy qualified as a doctor and served in Darnand's *corps franc* in 1940. He became the *chef départmental de la Milice* for Alpes-Maritimes in February 1943.

was the surveillance of the population. In short, the SOL was 'to guarantee on all occasions the functioning of the public services'.

The SOL would ensure the triumph of the National Revolution through the personal qualities of its membership. Their life, their attitude and their outward behaviour had to be beyond reproach. They had to be the living embodiment of the Marshal's motto 'Work, Family, Country'. They had to have a 'spirit of strict discipline' and obey orders without question even when their sense and necessity were hard to understand. Its members had to be a veritable rock of order and discipline and must 'never let despair invade their soul'. Furthermore, a SOL circular read that the National Revolution was not about guns or fists, but method and organisation, and not about destroying but building, although this did not rule out the use of force. But the SOL was unarmed. In the final analysis the SOL was the 'young and dynamic force of the Legion' and perhaps *une troupe de choc de réserve*.[12] But Vichy had no need of the SOL because the *gendarmerie*, *la garde mobile* and the police were loyal to the regime and they alone could protect France from what little internal disorder there was.

On 28 June 1942, a delegation of the *comité central* of the *Légion Tricolore* left Paris for Poland. Darnand was at its head. On 1 July, at the camp of Kruszyna, the delegation visited the 1st Battalion of the *Légion Tricolore*.[13] Darnand brought with him a message from Benoist-Méchin, *secrétaire d'Etat* to the *chef du gouvernement*, which spoke of defending French interests as well as a European cause.

It was this visit that convinced Darnand of the greater Russian threat to Europe than that posed by Germany to French national integrity. Thereupon, as a man of action, he saw it his duty to encourage SOL adherents to sign up for military duty on the Eastern Front in the *Légion Tricolore*. In this way, he drew even closer to aligning himself with the German cause in Europe.

That October, Darnand admitted that his values and ideals were not shared by most French people but declared: "We are determined to save France despite public opinion and against it if necessary..."

### The *Milice française*

On 19 December 1942, Hitler summoned Laval and demanded the creation of a police/security force to be used against the growing Resistance groups in France. The SOL was to be the nucleus of such a force. On 5 January 1943, Marshal Pétain announced the transformation of the SOL into the *Milice Nationale* [National Militia]. He granted this new formation a 'certain amount' of autonomy from the Legion in order to faciliate its task as 'the advance guard for the maintenance of order inside French territory in co-operation with the police'.

Weeks later, law N° 63 of 30 January 1943 published in the *Journal Officiel* on the 31st, renamed the *Milice Nationale* to the *Milice française* [French Militia] under the presidency of Pierre Laval. The *Milice française* was described in the annex to article 2 of the law establishing its creation as being 'composed of volunteers morally ready and physically capable not only of supporting the new state by their action, but also to assist in the maintenance of internal order'.

---

12    Delperrié de Bayac, *Histoire de la Milice*, p.113.
13    It should be recalled that on 22 June 1942, the *comité central* of the LVF (*Légion des Volontaires Français*) transformed the LVF into *La Légion Tricolore*. On 18 July 1942, *La Légion Tricolore* was created by law N° 704, which was published in the *Journal officiel* on 17 September 1942.

The law also required that members of the *Milice* be French by birth, not Jewish, nor belong to any secret society, and be volunteers.

On 31 January 1943, at Vichy, Pierre Cance declared to an audience of SOL *chefs* after lunch:

> You're only a minority, but I prefer quality to numbers... I want to be your friend, and I will be your *chef.* The action that is is being taken today is of the upmost importance. It is France that must reap the benefits, and that even dictates your duty.

At a ceremony held in Vichy on 1 February 1943 Darnand was appointed the Secretary General of the *Milice française*. Laval spoke, stressing once again the danger Bolshevism was to Europe. To prevent his country suffering this misfortune, he wanted France to understand that it must be at one with Germany. It is not known if Darnand shared this view but he did see saving France from the danger of Bolshevism as a fundamental part of the revolutionary task of the *Milice*. Indeed, one member of the organisation is recorded as saying that the greatest pleasure of a *Milicien* would be 'to wash his hands in the blood of communists!'

The fight against Bolshevism was but one expression of the political mission of the *Milice* defined by the twenty-one points of the SOL, which it adopted as its own. The *Milice* had to be the best advert for Vichy and the National Revolution. It would attack poverty and hunger, described as the consequences of defeat. It would curb the black market. It would revive and purify the Arts, and 'protect French intellectual heritage'.[14] Indeed, according to Philippe Henriot, the Vichy Secretary of State for Propaganda and Information, the *Milice* would 'return a soul to France'. Nevertheless, *La Milice a pour première tache d'abattre le Communisme*.[15]

The *Milice* also adopted many other attributes from the SOL. The marching song of the SOL, *Le Chant des Cohortes*, became *Le Chant de la Milice*. The *Milice* mirrored the SOL's adminstrative organisation. The *Milice* retained the SOL's three-month probation period. At the end of the period of probation, successful new recruits swore the following oath:

> I undertake upon my honour to serve France, even to the sacrifice of my own life. I swear to devote all my strength to the triumph of the revolutionary ideal of the *Milice française* whose discipline I freely accept.

The general regulations of the *Milice* stated that it was not an organisation in which one could enter or leave on a simple nod. A new recruit could only be accepted by a *chef départemental* subject to the approval of the *secrétaire général*. Resignations could only be pronounced by the *secrétaire général*. In this way, recruits for the *Milice*, like those for the SOL, had to 'understand the importance of their enlistment'.

That was not all the *Milice* and SOL had in common. The *Milice* carried forward the same morality and discipline outlined for membership of the SOL. According to Darnand, *Miliciens* were 'not vulgar henchmen stupidly in love with violence' or 'mad youngsters only longing to play with the revolver'. They were militants not mercenaries. Darnand saw the *Milice* establishing itself through its loyalty, its honesty and its asceticism, and the *Milicien* as being

14  Some commentators have even described the *Milice* as the lofty successor to the Armistice army disbanded in November 1942.
15  Darnand, speech of February 1943.

not only revolutionary in word, but also in action. Article 45 of the *Milice* general regulations remarked that no *Milicien* must take advantage of his position for personal vengeance. Even Pétain set out his own tone for the *Milice*, suggesting that the organisation could win the heart of the population by showing 'an example of discipline and an unblemished private life'.

The *Milice française* was composed of four branches; the *Miliciens*; the *Avant-Garde* (the Youth branch); the *Franc-Garde* (the armed branch); and *Les Miliciennes* (the Womens branch).

The *chef* of the *Avant-Garde* was *Capitaine* Jean-Marcel Renault, the co-founder of the 'recognised' youth movement *Jeunesse de France et d'Outre Mer* [The Youth of France and Overseas] in January 1941. Born on 4 May 1912 in the Nièvre, he had to abandon his preparartory studies for the Arts and Métiers when his father died and find work instead. In 1931 he joined the Merchant Navy. In 1935 he started his career as an officer in the Air Force, working his way up through the ranks. From 17 May to 6 June 1940 he commanded *escadrille de chasse de nuit* 2/13 [night fighter squadron 2/13].[16] Distinguishing himself against the Germans in Belgium, he received the *Croix de guerre* with two citations. Ever since, Renault, the sincere and ardent patriot, remained 'literally hypnotised by German efficiency and force'.[17]

In November 1941 Renault succeeded Henry Pugibert at the head of the *Jeunesse de France et d'Outre Mer*, JFOM. Founded in January 1941 and recognized by the Secrétariat Général à la Jeunesse in July 1942, the JFOM only operated in the Unoccupied Zone. Its *chef* was Pétain. The JFOM held its first congress between 25 and 27 October 1941 in Nice, by which time it claimed a membership of 30,000. The mission of the JFOM was to build the National Revolution and create a new man, who was 'positive, integrated, community minded and enthusiastic'. The JFOM was present at most meetings, rallies and *prestations de serment* organised by the *Légion française des combattants* and the SOL.

To fill the ranks of the *Avant-Garde*, Laval put to Renault that he encourage members of his former movement to enlist in the *Milice*. According to Renault, only one in ten would come across from the JFOM to the *Milice*.[18] Renault would later resign from the *Milice* and join the LVF. His reasons for this are not known. He would pass from the LVF to the French Division of the Waffen-SS.

The sixteen-year-old Georges Garrot, a sincere supporter of Marshal Pétain's National Revolution, passed from the JFOM to the *Avant-Garde*. His involvement consisted for the most part of parading in the streets.

Georges Cazalot, born on 8 September 1927, joined the *Avant-Garde* during the summer of 1943 thanks to his school sports teacher Charpentier, also a *chef de la Milice*, who was highly respected by all. He had fought with the LVF on the Russian Front and been seriously wounded. His medals of the *Légion d'honneur* and the *Croix de guerre* with four *palmes* were testament to his bravery. Cazalot said of him:[19] 'Men like him are neeeded at the rear. They're as useful here

---

16    Lefèvre, conversation with the author. This corrects Delpierré de Bayac, *Histoire de la Milice*, p.205, that Jean Renault was an officer of *l'aviation d'assaut*.

17    Delperrié de Bayac, *Histoire de la Milice*, p.205.

18    And yet according to Lambert  Pierre P. and Le Marec Gérard, *Organisations, mouvements et unités de l'état français, Vichy 1940-1944* (Pars: Jacques Grancher, 1992), p.144, the *Avant-Garde* 'was, especially in the South Zone, composed almost exclusively of the *jeunes* of the JFOM who had preferred to follow their *chef*, Jean-Marcel Renault who had given them the choice between the *Milice* or remaining with the JFOM.'

19    Cazalot Georges, … *Et la terre a bu leur sang!* (Paris: Éditions de l'Homme Libre, 2005), p.17.

to instruct, form, educate and advise the impatient *jeunes*.[20] Two of Cazalot's classmates also joined up. Cazalot, however, wanted to be a *combattant de l'Ordre Européen* and intended to join the Waffen-SS as soon as he turned the age of seventeen.

The creation of a *corps d'élite* called the *Franc-Garde* [Free Guard] was announced by Darnand on 30 January 1943 and placed under the orders of Jean de Vaugelas. On 2 June 1943, the *Franc-Garde* was sub-divided into the *Franc-Garde Permanente* and the *Franc-Garde bénévole* (otherwise *Franc-Garde Non-permanente*). The first unit of the *Franc-Garde Permanente* was created at the camp of Calabres, near Vichy. The Permanent force, as the name suggests, were the 'regulars' who belonged to full-time units which were available for active duty anywhere in the Southern, unoccupied Zone. The *Franc-Garde bénévole* consisted of 'part-timers' who could be mobilised in the event of emergencies or for specific actions. Darnand said of the *francs-gardes*:

> To create the *esprit de corps*, to obtain a very strict discipline and to show to all that the *Milice* is an organisation with nothing to hide, and finally to force those who wear it to appear without fear, the *francs-gardes* will wear a uniform.

As such the *francs-gardes* were the only *Miliciens* to wear full uniform. Its uniform retained much of the flavour of its forerunner, the SOL: khaki shirt (although civilian shirts were sometimes worn), black tie and dark blue trousers. However, the *type basque* beret of the SOL was replaced by the blue-coloured modèle 41 beret, worn *à la manière des chasseurs*, pulled to the right for men and to the left for officers. While on active duty a French (Adrian) army steel helmet was sometimes worn. The badge of the department/province to which they belonged was often worn on the left sleeve. In addition, the *Milice* emblem was worn on the beret and on the right breast pocket of the tunic and shirt.

The *Milice* emblem was a stylised gamma in a circle. The Greek letter gamma, the Zodiac sign of the Ram and thus a symbol of force and rebirth, reflected the revolutionary task of the *Milice*.

The *Franc-Garde* was organised along the hierarchical lines of the SOL: *Main, Dizaine, Trentaine, Centaine* and *Cohorte*. The smallest unit was the *Main*, consisting of four *francs-gardes* and a *chef de main*. Two *Mains* made a *Dizaine* and three *Dizaines* constituted a *Trentaine*, deemed the smallest single unit to participate in the maintenance of order. The largest unit was the *Cohorte*, made up of three *Centaines*. Several *Cohortes*, depending upon their numbers and department configuration, could be grouped into *Centres*.

Regulations insisted that all *Franc-Garde* units had to be placed under the command of 'an officer proven in the military point of view and absolutely certain in the political point of view.' In addition, at every echelon throughout the *Milice*, *chefs* had to give their adherents political training.

The *chefs* and *cadres* of the *Milice* received their political and military training at various *Écoles de cadres* (leadership training schools). The most celebrated was undoubtedly the *École des cadres de la Milice* at the picturesque chateau de Saint-Martin d'Uriage. Established on 1 March 1943, the national school accepted its first entrants on the 25 of the same month. The political training was centred on the twenty-one points of its Manifesto and the military training on the strategic rudiments of the *guerre des maquis* and street fighting. In October 1943, the first *Chef de l'École*

20   Captured by the resistance in late 1944, he was shot.

*d'Uriage*, by the name of du Vair, was replaced by de Vaugelas, the *chef régional de la Milice* for Marseille.

At first, there was great enthusiasm for the *Milice*. Large numbers of recruits stepped forward. They were militants of various past and present right wing and far right movements; ultra-Catholics; fanatical anti-Communists; anti-Semites; former members of the royalist *Action française*; and former service-men. Indeed, some were from movements of the far left. A good number, however, did not belong to any political party.

The *Milice* attracted recruits from all age groups and from all sections of the community. A high percentage of the men came from the urban lower middle and middle class, but a number also hailed from agricultural backgrounds. A high percentage of the *chefs* were from professional backgrounds or intellectuals. Some were former or serving officers and bearers of old noble names who were violently anti-Republican.

What compelled them to come forward? For the most part, they loved France, its people and its way of life. They feared and hated Communism. They supported the Marshal and the National Revolution. They wanted to save France from ruin by maintaining order and fighting Communism. They wanted to rebuild an independent France that was the master of its fate. Most had little regard for Nazi Germany and its policies. In a letter to a friend, a young recruit from the South-West had this to say about joining the *Milice*:[21]

> To tell you the truth we are determined, no matter what, to pull France out of the mess in which it is stuck, without any other help than only our arms, drawing our theories and our strength from what our country holds traditionally French. That is why you see me serving in the ranks of the *Milice*, and devoting my days to developing myself or even developing men capable of serving France…

Nevertheless, not all were convinced idealists. Undoubtedly, the *Milice* attracted a small number of those in search of adventure. For some, the *Milice* meant employment, even clothes and lodging. The wages were good and very large payments were made for denouncements. Also, for some, the *Milice* became a means of avoiding deportation to Germany for labour service.[22]

## The Story of Pierre Méric

Pierre Méric was born on 27 April 1920 in Casteljaloux (department Lot-et-Garonne). Growing up, he was taught to fear Communism. He hated the sight of the huge Red Flag with hammer and sickle which flew from the town hall in place of the national flag. He blamed the weak, dishonest and corrupt Republican government in Spain for plunging this neighboring country, which was Latin and Christian,   into a bloody civil war.

---

21    *Historia* hors série *40: La Milice-La collaboration en uniforme*, p.40. The unnamed author of this letter would end up in the uniform of the Waffen-SS and finish the war fighting with the French *Sturmbataillon* in Berlin where he was seriously wounded by a Russian grenade.

22    Some sources claim that, at a later date, courts offered petty criminals a choice of either serving a prison sentence or serving in the *Milice française*. However, historian Lefèvre vehemently denies this accusation.

Pierre Méric. (Author)

Filled with patriotic zeal, Méric volunteered for the Air Force before he was called up, passing the exam of *personnel navigant* in December 1939, which proved difficult for him, and was posted to the air base at Avord as a cadet pilot. His country was at war and his place was where he could be most useful, and he had a taste for the most exposed. Besides, he was desperate to learn to fly, even though he had never flown before. He would never get the chance before the Phoney War abruptly came to an end. On 10 May 1940, at six in the morning, he was rudely woken by the sound of nearby explosions. Wearing pajamas, he rushed to find shelter. He thought to himself: this is war and the front has caught us napping.

On 17 June 1940, a day which would burn itself into the national memory, Méric listened to Pétain solemnly address the nation about ending hostilities. Profoundly shocked, he did not mind admitting that he cried bitterly. A few days later he was transferred to the nearby air base at Pont-Long, where an incredible disorder reigned. He was employed on guard duty but had no bullets for his carbine!

One day, a staff officer from the base addressed the cadet pilots, Méric among them, and convinced them to work on making the nearby aerodrome at Pau-Idron usable with a promise of their first pilot lessons. After four days of backbreaking manual work, just as they finished off making the aerodrome ready for use, a small squadron of biplanes from the Belgium Army landed. They had worked hard with the promise of pilot lessons, which was so dear to them, only for this now to be revealed as a false pretense. They were disgusted by this deception, which had an enormous impact on the behavior of the majority of them.

Demobilised in August 1940, Méric became an enthusiastic supporter of the National Revolution. He believed that the defeat, however humiliating it was, presented the French people with a unique opportunity to build a new country, an opportunity which would not repeat itself and be lost forever. He joined the LFC, which he saw as the new, ardent, ambitious and uncompromising elite of this desire for change. He marched and paraded in uniform. He saw *Maréchal* Pétain twice at Legion sponsored events. He was proud to wear the badge of the Legion, but disappointed to see the badges of many go missing from their buttonholes, followed by their hearts. As an elitist and visceral anti-communist, he passed from the LFC to the SOL and then to the *Milice*, which also obviated the need to go to Germany under the STO.

Méric attended the fourth training course at Uriage (24 May to 5 June 1943) where he met Paul Pignard-Berthet and Philip Marchèse, who would become good friends while in captivity in Russia. At the end of the course he was promoted to *chef de dizaine*. Mobilized in the *Franc-Garde permamente*, he was posted to the camp des Calabres, near Vichy, where he received weeks of physical training, as well as a brief and intense first aid course. And then it was back to Uriage for more physical training and his first weapons training.

At the end of the course Méric visited Paris for the baptism of a friend's son, but upon his return was accused of desertion. His *chef de trentaine*, who Méric believes was jealous of him, had not sent headquarters details of his leave. He defended himself vigorously against the accusation. Nevertheless, he was still demoted to a simple *franc-garde*. He was not bitter about his punishment, though.

Sent to Nantes, Méric helped with the clear up following Allied air raids. Never would he forget the sight of a German Sergeant performing a controlled explosion of a bomb. He dug large trenches for the dead and helped bury the coffins. Emotion overwhelmed him when he found himself in front of three small children's coffins and their tearful parents.

### Summer of crisis

On 24 April 1943, Paul de Gassowski, the *chef départemental adjoint de la Milice* for Bouches-du-Rhône, was assasinated in Marseille by the Resistance. Days later, also in Marseille, surgeon Buisson, the *chef régional adjoint*, was killed. These two murders marked the beginning of a ferocious campaign of assassinations of *Miliciens* and their families, and bombings of their property. Pierre Dac on Radio London marked them out for assassination.

The situation soon became intolerable. Unarmed, the *Miliciens* could not defend themselves. Again and again Darnand went to President Laval, the nominal *chef* of the *Milice française*, and pleaded for arms. His insistent pleas fell on deaf ears. In point of fact, Laval had no intention, for political reasons, of arming a movement more loyal to Darnand than it was to him. Besides, at that time, he had no need of the *Milice*. The traditional forces of order were still loyal to the Vichy government and he was of the opinion that they were sufficient to maintain order. Moreover, what then of the prospect of 'extremists of the right' with arms? To him, this was dangerous. Indeed, he was concerned that their actions might only inflame the Resistance to commit further excesses against Vichy.

Consequently, many *Miliciens* lost faith in President Laval and reproached him for refusing them weapons. On 26 June 1943, a *Chef départemental* reported:[23]

> If the men lack confidence, it is not in their *chefs*, it is in their possibilities of success: the underhand campaigns just like the indifference - if not the hostility - of the public powers discourages them. Generally they believe that our success is linked to that of the Axis and few are those who do not see Germany defeated.

---

23    Non-referenced document, CARAN, F1 A, 3747.

Faced with a lack of government support and no prospect of arms, many members of the *Milice* now resigned. Recruitment also slowed.

On 13 July 1943, in a change of tact, Darnand tendered his resignation to Laval, explaining that the *Milice* did not have the means to fulfil its mission.[24] On the following day, Pétain refused the resignation and handed it back to him in person. He told Darnand: "You are my best and my most faithful soldier." Darnand said nothing. Moments later, Darnand said to his friends that he could not refuse Pétain.[25]

Deceived by Laval, Darnand now thought of switching sides to the Resistance. He contacted Colonel Groussard, the ex-*chef* of the *Groupes de Protection*, in Geneva.[26] When Groussard asked him to sign a declaration promising to serve under him against the Germans and to obey him under all circumstances, Darnand discontinued all negotiations.

Although he detested de Gaulle, Darnand then turned to London. Through ex-*cagoulard* friends of his in the Resistance, he offered his support to de Gaulle. There was no reply.

Cornered more than ever, with his *Miliciens* still being cut down, Darnand, a man of responsibility, went to the Germans whom he still regarded as *Les Boches*. For their part, the German authorities had always shown great hostility towards the creation of 'stand alone' French military forces. They greatly feared the *revanche* of the French. In addition, many *chefs* of the *Milice* drew their inspiration from Charles Maurras, the leader of the Royalist *Action française*, whose pre-war vehement anti-German sentiments were notorious and whose watchword was 'France only'.[27] Moreover, his ideology was taught as part of the *formation politique* of *Milice* *élèves* [students]. Nevertheless, times had changed. The Germans had need of men to participate in the European battle.

Darnand played the 'SS card.'[28] In August 1943, at the German embassy in Paris, he swore an oath of loyalty to Adolf Hitler and accepted the rank of Obersturmführer in the Waffen-SS.[29] Fritz-Bernd de la Fontaine was present when Darnand swore the path and recalls:

24  Pierre Cance also tendered his resignation.
25  Mabire, chapter *Le serment au Führer*, *Historia* hors série 40*: La Milice-La collaboration en uniforme*, p.45. Curiously, no other source confirms Pétain's praise of Darnand or Darnand's immediate reaction to the refusal of his resignation. Also of interest to note is that, according to Delperrié de Bayac, *Histoire de la Milice*, p.202, Darnand was not serious about resigning. If true, this would suggest his resignation was little more than a political ploy, but the tone of his letter suggests otherwise.
26  According to Mabire, chapter *Le serment au Führer*, *Historia* hors série *40: La Milice-La collaboration en uniforme*, p.46, Darnand sent Cance, the *Délégué Général* of the *Milice*, to Geneva to contact Colonel Groussard. He spent several days with Groussard, but their negotiations soon came to an impasse. They could not agree on who posed the greater threat to France. For Cance, it was the Communists, and, for Groussard, it was the Germans. Thereupon, 'just in case', Groussard drew up a declaration for Darnand to sign, described as 'a token of rallying and almost of repentance'. However, according to Delperrié de Bayac, *Histoire de la Milice*, p.202, the intermediary was a certain Louis Guillaume and Colonel Groussard sent Darnand, through him, 'two pieces of papers'. On the second sheet was written the declaration requiring the signature of Darnand.
27  Throughout the war, Maurras would maintain an anti-German sentiment, although somewhat toned down. He wrote in his book *La Seule France* published in 1941: 'We have only one slogan: France. We are not Germans or English. We are French. Only France or, if you prefer France only...'
28  Delperrié de Bayac, *Histoire de la Milice*, p.206.
29  The rank Darnand accepted at the German embassy in Paris is often misquoted as Sturmbannführer. Bernd de la Fontaine, the 'adjudant' of Franz Riedweg, who was present during the swearing in ceremony, has confirmed in writing to historian Mounine that Darnand did accept the Waffen-SS

After my second injury I was assigned as Franz Riedweg's Orderly Officer. At that time in Paris it was on my officer's sword that Darnand took the oath during a ceremony at the start of the creation of the French Waffen-SS. 'European chivalry' that was the motto!

Darnand's decision was an unequivocal gesture to the Germans, Vichy, and his *Milice*.[30] At his post-war trial he attempted to justify his decision: 'I swore this oath because first it would only apply to me when I was at the front, that is to say on the Eastern Front, since French laws, the laws which would protect those of the LVF, would only apply to us when we were at the front'.[31]

Pierre Méric of the *Franc-Garde permanente* was not won over. On his return to Vichy from Nantes he attended a packed meeting to hear the likes of Darnand, Cance and de Tissot speak passionately about enlisting in the Waffen-SS. His answer was a categorical no. He was newly married. Moreover, he believed that their 'priority mission' was in France where they needed to set up a solid and quick training programme modelled on the successful SS method. And in this way build an efficient fighting force which could be deployed rapidly wherever the maintenance of order was going to be a problem. His choice made, he returned to Uriage where his training resumed.

During a lesson on small arms, Méric nearly killed one of his comrades. He pressed the trigger of a pistol he believed to be empty, but it went off, wounding a comrade facing him on the other side of the table. His comrade survived and when he was moved to Grenoble for an operation Méric asked for and received permission to accompany him so that he could protect him in case of an assassination attempt.

In early October 1943, Darnand, accompanied by high-ranking *Milice* chiefs Gallet and Roleau, met with Ogruf. Gottlob Berger, the Chief of the SS-Hauptamt [SS-Main Office] and the man in charge of Waffen-SS recruitment. This was the first meeting between Darnand and Berger.[32] The upshot of the meeting suggests an arrangement was reached whereby arms would be supplied to the *Franc-Garde* of the *Milice* in return for co-operation from its executive in recruiting members from its ranks for the newly formed French Waffen-SS unit.

Arguably, both sides came away from the meeting content. Darnand could now arm his beseiged *Milicens*, who, for the first time, would be in a position to take the fight to the 'terrorists' in the name of maintaining order. As for Berger, the *Milice* was an ideal source for new recruits and, in particular, potential cadres for the French Waffen-SS unit, which thus far had failed to attract sufficient numbers of former officers and NCOs. The SS-Hauptamt would

rank of Obersturmführer. Besides, the SS rank of Obersturmführer was equivalent to his French Army rank of *lieutenant*. However, in the autumn of 1944, the SS rank of Sturmbannführer was conferred upon Darnand to give him certain parity with Doriot, his political rival who had received the honorary SS rank of Sturmbannführer.

30    Although Darnand would play no active role in the French Sturmbrigade or later in 'Charlemagne', his Waffen-SS appointment should not be viewed as 'purely nominal' (see Mabire, *La Brigade Frankreich*, p.83). As such, at any moment, Darnand could have been called up for active service. Curiously, according to Ministry of Interior report MRU/14/35301 dated 18 December 1943, 'the German authorities had named him [Darnand] inspector of the French Waffen-SS'. This is not true.

31    Charbonneau Henry, *Le roman noir de la droite française* (Robert Desroches, 1969), pp.286-287.

32    Research provided by historian Eric Lefèvre. This corrects the suggested dates of mid to late July 1943 that appear in all previous accounts of this meeting (Delpierré de Bayac, Mabire, and Lambert and Le Marec).

acknowlege this shortfall when it issued an order on 15 October 1943 to recruit ninety former French officers and three hundred veteran NCOs. Berger would have been well aware that most *chefs* of the *Milice* had served in the military as officers or NCOs and fought bravely for their country. And so, on 11 October 1943, eleven senior *chefs* of the *Milice* enlisted in the Waffen-SS.[33] One week later, on 18 October, from *gare de L'Est*, Paris, fourteen left for Sennheim.[34] Darnand saw them off.

## The Officers [35]

The first *chef* to offer his services was Noël de Tissot from Nice, born on 22 December 1914 in Versailles. A mathematics teacher by profession, this family man was of late unemployed. As a reserve artillery NCO,[36] he fought with great courage against the Germans in 1939-40, winning the *Croix de guerre*, but ever since had harboured a deep sense of betrayal. Among the first to join the *Légion des Combattants*, he replaced Bassompierre as the *secrétaire général* of *La Légion* for the Alpes-Maritimes department in June 1941.

In August 1941, while *secrétaire général*, de Tissot was the subject of an 'opinion' put together by the prefect of the Alpes-Maritimes department.[37] The report remarked, generally, that he was aged 27 and married with a child. As for his politics, the report read that he had always been a member of some extreme right wing group and that now he was a PPF militant. As for his personal qualities, he was reported 'serious, reflective, a hard worker and of perfect morality'. And yet some sources claim he was famed for his eccentricity.[38] The report, however, failed to mention that he was fanatically devoted to Darnand and was one of his closest colleagues.

De Tissot passed to the SOL and was appointed *secrétaire général* on 13 March 1942. Together with Bassompierre and Durandy he developed the doctrine of the SOL which was later transported to the *Milice*. When Darnand left Nice for Vichy he followed. It was he who imposed the gamma as the emblem of the *Milice* – Darnand would have preferred a 'stylised grenade'. On 4 February 1943, he was appointed principal private secretary to the *Secrétaire général de la Milice* [Darnand]. His role was to maintain co-ordination between the *Milice* high command and the central administration, but Laval mistrusted him.[39]

33  Delperrié de Bayac, *Histoire de la Milice*, p.213.
34  Lefèvre, *Axe & Alliés* hors série no 1, p.27.
35  According to Mabire, *La Brigade Frankreich*, p.80, there was great enthusiasm among the *chefs* of the *Milice* to enlist and Darnand had to limit those wishing to enlist because he was in need of their services in France. Many, however, were not so ready to don the German uniform. To them, the 'internal enemy' remained the greater threat.
36  Giolitto, *Histoire de la Milice*, p.145. His rank was actually that of *maréchal des logis*, equivalent to that of Sergeant in the British Army, which corrects Mabire, *La Brigade Frankreich*, p.80, that de Tissot was a reserve artillery officer.
37  On 27 August 1941, prefects were asked to 'give a verdict' on the members of the *comités départementaux de La Légion*.
38  For example, see Saint-Loup, *Les Hérétiques* (Paris: Presses de la Cité, 1965), p.17.
39  According to Saint-Loup, *Les Hérétiques*, p.17, de Tissot was an instructor at the *Milice École des cadres* (training school) at Uriage. This is not confirmed by any other source, although he may have given lectures there.

The next *chef* was Pierre Cance, from Bordeaux, a brewer and seller of beer,[40] born on 28 June 1907 in Bousquet-d'Orb (department Hérault). As a reserve infantry *lieutenant* in the *112e Régiment d'infanterie alpine*, he saw action during the 'shooting war' and was decorated with the *Croix de guerre*.[41] He joined the LFC, passed to the SOL, becoming the *Inspecteur régional du SOL* for the region of Montpellier, and, on 4 January 1943, Darnand appointed him as the *Délégué Général* of the *Milice* responsible for its organisation. Cance was Darnand's right hand man who was 'more tempted through direct action than doctrine'.[42]

Like Darnand, Cance had received his political education in the CSAR. Courageous and ambitious, this former military international rugby player, with a matching physique, was a leader of men who inspired great confidence even if he was unrefined when he spoke. 'The emulation between Cance and de Tissot profited all, one with more strength, the other with more flexibility'.[43] Arguably, to put it more simply, if de Tissot was the 'brains' of the *Milice*, then Cance was the 'muscle'. Cance said of his pathway to the Waffen-SS:[44]

I had always been what they call a man of order. I belonged to the middle class, which puts money by, which goes to mass, and which doesn't like foreigners much.

Before the war, I worked as a personnel manager in a small factory in the South-East. I joined Colonel La Rocque's *Parti social français*. I did not like much the lads of the *Action française* who I found too excited.

In 39-40, I did my duty as an *officier de reserve* in an infantry regiment, but I was astounded at the frame of mind of the lads I had to command. Nobody wanted to fight. They only just managed not to be taken prisoner. The defeat seemed crushing to me.

I believed, with the *Maréchal*, that the most urgent thing to do was to give back to our compatriots the sense of duty, service and homeland. I am very *révolution nationale*. I became the local person responsible for the *Légion des combattants* and I led the *service d'ordre légionnaire* of the department. I found Darnand a very good bloke: hero of two wars, that counted a great deal to me. I made some speeches to encourage the most ardent of our men to leave for the *Légion Tricolore* or the *Phalange africaine*. I passed quite naturally from the SOL to the *Milice française*. I was not particularly pro-German or collaborationist. But I remained anti-Communist. When, at the end of summer 1943, they asked for *cadres miliciens* for the Waffen-SS, I thought that it was my duty to leave. How could I urge the others to join without going (there) myself? There I was caught up in the chain of events...

40    Research provided by historian Lefèvre. His trade has often been inaccurately recorded as agricultural engineer or engineer. According to Ministry of Interior report, WEZ 11/31306, dated 18th August 1943, Cance had been an entrepreneur at Montpellier 'where he had realised a rather tidy fortune'.

41    According to Mabire, *La Brigade Frankreich*, p.80, Pierre Cance was a reserve *Captaine*. This is incorrect. In addition, according to Giolitto, *Histoire de la Milice*, p.145, Cance was a former *saint-cyrien* [military cadet of the Saint-Cyr academy]. This is incorrect. In fact, it was in 1929 that Cance was appointed *sous-lieutenant de réserve*. (Research provided by historian Eric Lefèvre.)

42    See Mabire, *La Brigade Frankreich*, p.80.

43    Gaultier Léon, *Siegfried et le Berrichon* (Paris: Perrin, 1991), p.149.

44    Delatour, chapter SS et Français pourquoi?, *Historia* hors série 32, p.121. Although the quote is unidentified it is most certainly Pierre Cance.

Pierre Roesch, who served with the French Sturmbrigade, had a low opinion of Cance, describing him as 'a dirty little climber, capable of anything and everything in his endless intrigues'.

There was also Léon Gaultier from the Berry, born on 1 February 1915 in Bourges. As a member of the PPF during the years of 1936 and 1937 he lectured with François Dochet in small villages of the Berry before tired workers and peasants 'in order to revive France'. In August 1939, he entered the *École spéciale militaire* of Saint-Cy and was commisioned *Lieutenant*. Posted to the *17e Bataillon de Chasseurs Alpins*, he did his duty for France during the 39-40 war. Shortly after the defeat, he worked as an attaché in the Vichy Ministry of Information and Propaganda. Regarded as an intellectual, arts graduate Gaultier said of his decision to enlist: 'This enlistment represented a considerable step. It was the realisation of our political will and our consideration of interior French politics.'

Add to this Henri Joseph Fenet, the 24-year-old *chef départemental de l'Ain*, born on 11 June 1919 in Ceyzériat, Department of Ain. The outbreak of the war found him as a student at the Paris University of Henry IV studying for the entrance exam to the *École normale Supérieure* [teacher training college]. Without hesitation he enlisted, joining the *21e régiment d'infanterie coloniale* [21st Colonial Infantry Regiment] garrisoned in Paris. He had no regrets about abandoning his university studies for military service. In May 1940, after attending *École d'officiers de réserve* [reserve officers school] training, he was commissioned *Aspirant de réserve* [reserve officer cadet] and posted to the divisional anti-tank company of the *3e division d'infanterie coloniale* [3rd Colonial Infantry Division].[45]

In the subsequent hard battles against the Germans Fenet was wounded on 13 June 1940 in the foot and the thigh. He was awarded with the *Croix de guerre* with a silver star for bravery.[46] With defeat came shame and anger at the rotten politicians and senile generals who were responsible, ultimately, for the *debâcle*. For a while he thought about leaving for England but was enticed away when Pétain spoke. He believed him and opted for Vichy.

Passing to the Armistice Army, *aspirant* Fenet served with the *21e régiment d'infanterie coloniale* stationed at Fréjus in southeastern department Var. He volunteered to serve in Syria against the British and was posted to the *batallion de marche d'infanterie coloniale*, which was dispatched, but could not travel beyond Thessalonki. The adhoc battalion was returned to Marseille whereupon Fenet was posted to French West Africa. On 1 October 1941, he was assigned to the 3rd Battalion of the *1er régiment de tirailleurs sénégalais* or 1RTS, becoming a platoon commander in a company garrisoned in the small city of Akjoujt in Mauritania. This posting was to his great satisfaction, for he had little interest in what was happening in France.[47] He craved purity and adventure.[48] The LVF was not for him, nor the *Légion tricolore* which, according to him, had all the defects of the old French Army.[49]

45  This corrects many sources, including Landwehr Richard, *Charlemagne's Legionnaires* (Silver Spring: Bibliophile Legion Books, 1989), p.185, that by May 1940 Fenet held an officer's commission of Lieutenant.
46  The *Croix de guerre* with a silver star represents a mention in dispatches at division level.
47  *Historia N° 613*, p.15. However, in contrast, according to Mabire, *La Brigade Frankreich*, p.28, Fenet was exasperated by the political vacillations of the Vichy Government and its adopted *attentisme* [wait-and-see policy] towards Germany.
48  Mabire, *La Brigade Frankreich*, p.28.
49  Ibid.

In July 1942, Fenet returned to metropolitan France to attend the *École militaire d'infanterie* of Saint-Maixent relocated to Aix-en-Provence.[50] Soon after, in November 1942, the Allies landed in French North Africa and the Germans invaded the free zone. On 29 November, he was demobilised with the rank of *Sous-lieutenant* (Second-Lieutenant).[51] He returned home. He was now at a loss what to do. And then one day his father told him that the local *chef* of the SOL, a retired major, was going to hold a conference and that he had expressed a wish to meet him. Henri Fenet did not attend the conference, but he did make a point of meeting this retired major and it was this meeting that was to define his immediate pathway. The retired major told him:

> France needs young officers like you. For the moment, there's no longer a French Army, but we're trying to assemble decent people because any day there will be a new army. Do you wish to work with me?

Fenet was of the same opinion. He joined the SOL and then the *Milice française* on its creation. He became the *chef départemental de la Milice* for Ain at the end of March or early April 1943. After the German defeat at Stalingrad he came to realise that 'what he was doing in France was serving no purpose'.[52] Rather than combating the 'internal enemy', he now saw himself on the Eastern Front defending Europe against Soviet invasion. In October 1943, he volunteered for the Waffen-SS.[53]

There was also Jean Artus, an instructor at the *École des cadres de la Milice française* at Uriage. Born on 4 April 1916 in Blaye in the Gironde department, he studied politics at the Paris *École des sciences politiques*. Having obtained the *brevet* [certificate] *de préparation militaire supérieure* (PMS), he subsequently attended *École d'officiers de réserve* [reserve officers school] training.[54] On 10 April 1939, he was commissioned with the rank of *aspirant* [officer cadet] and posted to the *24e bataillon de chasseurs alpins* (24e BCA). On 10 October of that same year, he was made up to the rank of *sous-lieutenant de réserve*. During the winter of 1939-40, the 24e BCA put up Darnand's *corps franc*. Never would Artus forget the raids into the forest of Warndt. He was awarded the *Croix de guerre*.

Taken prisoner in June 1940 and demobilised months later in November 1940, Artus joined the *Jeunesse et Montagne* [Youth and Mountain], the Air branch of the Vichy *Chantiers de la Jeunesse* (a sort of State Labour Service).[55] He joined the SOL and in September 1942 was appointed as the *chef-départemental-adjoint* for Alpes-Maritimes. He held the same position in the *Milice*. In May 1943, he took up a position of training instructor at Uriage.

Artus brought along with him his twenty-three-year-old friend Paul Pignard-Berthet who was also an instructor at the *École des Cadres de la Milice*. Paul Pignard-Berthet was born into a military family on 17 May 1920 near Annecy, Haute Savoie. His father was the commander

50  Saint-Maixent formed regular officers, but its entrants were NCOs and reserve officers.
51  Incorrectly, according to Landwehr, *Charlemagne's Legionnaires*, p.185, on 29 November 1942, Fenet was released from a POW camp.
52  *Historia N° 613*, p.15.
53  According to German records, Henri Fenet enlisted on 18 October 1943. That is one week later than that stated by Delperrié de Bayac.
54  Those who passed the yearlong *préparation militaire supérieure* attended, on call up for military service, *École d'officiers de réserve* [reserve officers school] training.
55  *Journal Officiel* of 18 January 1941.

of the 6th Battalion of the *1er Régiment Etranger d'Infanterie* in the Levant. He followed the phenomenal ascension of the National Socialist Third Reich with an anxiety tinged with admiration, while the 'democratic' powers floundered sterilely in their internal contradictions. Enlisting in November 1939, he attended the *École militaire de l'Infanterie et des Chars de Combat* (EMICC) where he was shocked by the morale and the dilapidated state of the equipment of the 'most beautiful army in the world'. The subsequent debacle before the Germans in May 1940 came as no real surprise to him. He was not bitter. He felt that many officers, although willing and well educated, had been suddenly thrust into this responsibility without any idea of command. He was not angry at those of his age, but at those 'puppets' who had declared war against Germany without being prepared for it and who had expected the infantry offensive of the Wehrmacht.

Commissioned with the rank of *Aspirant* in August 1940, Pignard-Berthet was posted as a *Chef de Groupe* to the *Chantiers de la Jeunesse* in the Pyrenees. Demanding to be returned to the Army, which was accepted because of his graduation from the EMICC, he joined the *27e bataillon de Chasseurs alpins*. He served with the 27e BCA for just one month before the Armistice Army was disbanded. He came to the SOL and then passed to the *Milice*, becoming an instructor at Uriage.

Many reasons contributed to his final decision to enlist in the Waffen-SS; he could see that France was slipping inexorably into bloody civil war and did not want to end up firing on his fellow countrymen; he was in sympathy with Germany in general and with National Socialism because of its political and social successes; he had military ambitions; and in particular he feared the dangers of Bolshevism. He was of the opinion that this war could only be resolved on the Eastern Front. Through his actions he hoped to see France regain a place of power within a preponderant Europe. And yet like so many of his comrades he had absolutely no idea about the precise nature of the Waffen-SS. His only information about this European army had been gleaned from hearsay and a few inconsistent written accounts. He honestly viewed his enlistment as a step into the unknown.

Pignard-Berthet also felt that there were other motives behind Darnand's political manoeuvres towards the Germans:

> Darnand sent us to the Waffen-SS, rather like hostages, revealing a sincere wish to collaborate, and, also, to acquire the necessary skills to fulfil the second function: internal and external security of the nation. A man of the traditional French right, he had gone through the Maurrasian school and remained fundamentally catholic. For him, politics was an intellectual and sentimental choice based on images corresponding more to vows than to realities. This the youngest among us understood straight away... National Socialism opened horizons to us going well beyond these concepts.

Max Quiquempois, a sports instructor at the *École des Cadres de la Milice* at Uriage, volunteered for the Waffen-SS, following the visit of a German commission. He was born on 10 September 1916 in Ribérac (department Dordogne).

Not all would be so young. There was Albert Pouget, the *Chef départemental* for Lozère, born on 24 August 1902 in Marchastel (department Lozère).[56] In 1929, reserve *sous-officier* Pouget of the 80° RI was commissioned as *Sous-lieutenant de réserve*. In keeping with his appearance as an ecclesiastic, when asked by a recruitment officer why he was enlisting in the Waffen-SS he had replied: "For the Christian West!"

Also in his forties was Ivan Bartolomei. Born on 11 November 1898 near to Bordeaux, this career soldier had first enlisted aged eighteen in 1916 'for the duration of the war' and was demobilised after the war. Signing up again in October 1925, he served with the rank of *sergent-chef*, then *adjudant*, in the *13e régiment de tirailleurs algériens*. He fought in the closing stages of the campaign in Morocco and his feat of arms on 17 July 1933 on the Haouja-N'oua brought him the *médaille militaire*, conferred by decree of 13 December 1933. In November 1937, he ended this part of his military career when he retired as a *adjudant de chasseurs à pied* [Adjutant in the Light Infantry].

In 1939, after finding himself overlooked by mobilisation, the forty-one-year-old Bartolomei called to order those responsible for this administrative oversight and left for war again. This time his rank was that of *Sous-lieutenant*. Appointed to a pioneer unit, he grew more and more bored as the Phoney War dragged on. Then the Blitzkrieg came to France. He was captured in Flanders on 4 June 1940.

Released as a World War One veteran, Bartolomei attempted to enlist in the LVF but his application was turned down 'through lack of places'! Joining the *Légion des Combattants*, he passed to the SOL, then to the *Milice*, and finally to the Waffen-SS.

There were other *chefs Milicien*:

- Emilien Boyer, born on 3 April 1910 in Carcassone, who had just escaped unhurt from an assassination attempt[57]
- Pierre Crespin, born on 20 September 1891 in Auch[58]
- Jacques de Lafaye, the *chef départemental de la Milice de l'Allier*, born on 26 April 1914 in Paris
- Paul Pruvost, born on 9 January 1901
- Jacques Massot, the *chef départemental de la Milice du Var*, born on 11 January 1897 in Nice[59]
- Pierre Bonnefoy, *chef départmental de la Milice du Vaucluse*
- Jacques Lefèvre, the *chef départemental de l'Aude*, born on 17 February 1902 in Saint-Mandé (departmemt Seine)

According to *Combats*, the *Milice* newspaper, Lefèvre's example inspired seven militants from the same department to follow him.[60]

---

56  His son Georges also served with the *Milice*. Captured at Estivareiles on 22 August 1944, condemned to death on 15 September by the *cour martiale du Puy*, he was executed on 18 September.
57  Details of the assassination attempt appear in *Combats* number 22 of 2 October 1943.
58  Crespin was a highly decorated First World War veteran, winning the *Croix de guerre* with three citations, who had worked his way up to become an officer.
59  Massot attended Sennheim but was subsequently recalled to France in June 1944.
60  *Combats* number 27 of 6 November 1943.

Emilien Boyer. (Author)

On 20 October 1943, two days after the *chefs* of the *Milice* left for Sennheim, the Germans, true to their word, supplied the *Milice* with fifty submachine guns to arm its *Franc-garde*. Darnand continued to pay the quid pro quo: on 6 November 1943, in the pages of *Combats*, the *Milice* newspaper, he published an article, entitled *Alerte miliciens*, appealing for enlistment of *miliciens* in the Waffen-SS. He declared:

> I am determined to take up arms a third time, beside all Europeans, to mutually defend our revolution and the future of our peoples. I will not do this out of despair nor out of bravado, I will leave with the conviction of serving the French cause more usefully than ever.

Darnand argued:

> Europe is in danger. France is threatened with losing its independence. Our civilisation will be enslaved by triumphant Judaism or destroyed by Bolshevism. But nothing is lost if a large enough number of men face the fight...

Continuing, Darnand spoke of their fight on the interior front and its complement on the 'European battlefields'. Turning to the subject of France, he remarked:

> France is a warlike nation; its grandeur will be restored through the heroism of its sons. Several of our comrades understood this a long time ago and have risked, for more than

two years, their life on the Eastern Front. A great number, at the time when the clever ones are going over to the Jewish camp, have just followed their example and reached the training camps where the French Division of the Waffen-SS is being organised. I have decided to join them when, in several months time, they go into the firing line.

Darnand followed this vibrant appeal with a series of personal appearances before mass-meetings of the *Milice*. At Limoges, he distinguished between his 'military' oath to Hitler and his 'political' oath to Pétain.

In November 1943, Darnand made a short trip to Germany. He visited SS-Junkerschule Bad Tölz, SS-Truppenübungsplatz Beneschau [troop training area] in Bohemia and Berlin where he was received by the France-Germany Committee and the Groupe Collaboration. According to *Milice* newspaper *Combats*, when Darnand met a representative of the OFL, he declared:[61]

> The French SS are being recruited from the militants of the National Revolution. They will form a troop officered by French officers, firstly in the service of France and the European idea. The national socialist ideal constitutes the principal motive of their enlistment. It is for this ideal that they will fight on the Eastern Front. They are revolutionary militants whose ambition is to save France from the Communism and the anarchy threatening it.

Darnand also met members of Himmler's entourage, including Ogruf. Gottlob Berger, the Chief of the SS Main Office. Much was agreed. The political parties would have to give up their own 'militias or services of order' to the *Milice*. A French National Socialist party would be created under the patronage of the *Milice* and the Waffen-SS. The *Milice* would fill the high-ranking positions of the French Division of the Waffen-SS, which would integrate the LVF. A second then a third French Division of the Waffen-SS would be created. And, lastly, all political parties in France would be banned following the creation of the National Socialist party.[62]

On 21 November 1943, *chef départemental de la Haute-Savoie* Jacquemin and his *adjoint* Roger Franc were assassinated at Thones. With the agreement of Brigf. Oberg, Darnand authorized reprisals for the first time. On 24 November, at Annecy, the *Milice* took revenge for six comrades killed of late in Savoie, Haute-Savoie and at Lyon. There were other reprisals at Grenoble.

On 28 November 1943, in Nice, Darnand spoke before an audience estimated at 1,200 strong. In the main, they were *miliciens*. His speech would last almost an hour. He evoked the sacrifices of the *Milice*, 33 dead and 25 seriously wounded since April, but proudly acknowledged that the last had already been avenged. He stormed that he no longer wanted them to sacrifice themselves in vain and then warned all enemies that they would pay for their crimes. He denounced the justice system for being too slow and stigmatised the magistrates who feared for their lives. He promised: "I will arm our troops. Today I bring to them the necessary arms! Our last martyrs will be avenged! Our enemies have been warned! We fight!" This was a declaration of war, civil war.

61   *Combats* number 29 of 20 November 1943. This declaration is reproduced in Ministry of the Interior report NJP/1/35303, F1A 3747, CARAN, of 16 December 1943.
62   Delpierré de Bayac, *Histoire de la Milice*, p.215.

Darnand then moved onto the theme of setting up a union of 'European nationalities against Bolshevism'. After announcing that a great number of *Miliciens* had already enlisted in the Waffen-SS, he said: "I too have enlisted. I have taken the oath. Soon, I will join them on the Eastern Front, the only battle, when their training is finished. I am proud to tell our friends and enemies."

He attempted to justify his conduct, recalling his past in the two wars. He declared that the cause of France was linked to that of Europe and that the internal revolution would happen after victory. Finally he concluded:

> We are proud to say that we are going to fight beside the Germans! It is a question of life or death! You will be hanged along with me, we will all be hanged if we do not know how to fight! Be resolute, together we will win!

The auditorium resounded to a storm of applause and cries of 'Vive Darnand!' The whole room rose to its feet. Even those German officers present stood up and applauded.

Pierre de Séverin, who had joined the *Milice* months before, was in the audience. Darnand's speech left him with much to think about as he explained:[63]

> My engagement in the *Milice* corresponded to the chivalrous ideal of my childhood. The purity of our combat against capitalist materialism and communism found its full justification in the creation of this new force. Within the *Milice* I saw that two main trends were emerging: the first, military and nationalist, remained *pétainiste* and wanted to save France from communism; the second, more radical, wanted to make the *Milice* a close ally of Germany to put France in the school of Nazism or fascism. I considered these two trends complementary. I was a French fascist, loyal to the *Maréchal*, fighting against Communism and Anglo-American imperialism. Nevertheless, I was not willing to fight the *résistants*. To kill French [people] was for me contrary to my *milicien* ideal. I dreamt of joining the French engaged alongside the Germans in the struggle against Bolshevism on the Russian Front.
>
> On 28th November 1943, I attended a public meeting at Nice, in the presence of German officers. Darnand, also present, recalled that 33 *miliciens* were dead, struck down by the resistance, 165 wounded. He announced terrible reprisals against all resistance, Gaullist and Communist. Henceforth we were on the slippery slope to civil war in France. Not wanting to spill French blood, I decided to enlist in the LVF to fight Stalin and his Bolshevik soldiers. My choice is final.

The very same reasons also prompted some *Miliciens* to volunteer for the Waffen-SS. However, for some traditionalists, Darnand had gone too far. They now resigned from the *Milice*.

And what was the response to Darnand's personal appeal for enlistment of *Miliciens* in the Waffen-SS? According to one Ministry of Interior report dated October 1943, 200 *Miliciens* had signed up for the Waffen-SS.[64] By February 1944, again according to the Ministry of

---

63  Lormier, *SS Français*, pp.48-50. Pierre de Séverin is undoubtedly a pseudonym.
64  Non-referenced report, F1A 3747, CARAN. *Milicien* Marcel Bargstedt joined the Waffen-SS in the autumn of 1943 and may have been one of the reported 200. His reasons for enlisting are not known,

Interior, the *Milice* had furnished the Waffen-SS with nearly 300 men.[65] Nevertheless, the initial response must have come as a great personal disappointment to Darnand, for his *Milice* in the autumn of 1943 numbered some 29,000 adherents of which 10,000 were 'active'.[66] However, of the 10,000 real militants, perhaps no more than one thousand were *francs-gardes*.[67] Therefore, it could be argued that the *Milice* was starting with a very small pool of 'combat-worthy' men from which to draw recruits for the Waffen-SS. Moreover, the majority of *Miliciens* stubbornly adhered to the idea that the greater danger was from the internal Communists and 'terrorists'. Ironically, the *Miliciens* and *francs-gardes* who now took the field against the 'terrorists' were the most anti-German! The civil war proved brutal and bloody.

Also disappointed in his attempts to recruit for the Waffen-SS was Jacques Doriot, the leader of the PPF. By November 1943, the party had recruited from its membership fewer than 500 of the 600 men promised. Nevertheless, if it were not for the manpower demands of the S.T.O., the PPF would have kept its promise.[68] Notably, a high percentage of those who continued to volunteer were from the PPF Indeed, the following statistics concerning the political party affiliation of 163 recent French volunteers appeared in a German report of 8 December 1943:[69]

38% no party
20% PPF
10% *Milice française*
9% Francisme
4% RNP
19% all other parties

Remarkably 'the headquarters of the Waffen-SS' came to the PPF 'cap in hand'.[70] It demanded of the PPF to find urgently from the members of its party doctors, vets, and medical and veterinary staff for the French unit of the Waffen-SS. Doctors and vets were promised officer ranks even if they had not served as officers in the French Army. An internal PPF circular specified that 'medical auxiliaries of the Army and veterinary auxiliaries who in France are *adjudants* will be

---

though. A member of extreme right-wing parties before the war, he volunteered for military service on 6th September 1939 and by the end of hostilities had worked his way up to the rank of *adjutant de réserve*. He fought in Syria, was captured and was held prisoner for three months by the English whom he greatly resented. See AN F1A 3748, CARAN.

65    Ministry of the Interior report ENE/3/35301, written 21 February 1944, CARAN.
66    Delpierré de Bayac, *Histoire de la Milice*, p.181, based on figures quoted by Francis Bout de l'An, the *directeur de la propagande de la Milice*.
67    According to Ministry of Interior reports LIA/6/31300, dated 10 May 1943, and WEZ 9/31301, dated 18 June 1943, the *Franc-Garde* numbered 920 men and 30 *chefs*. However, in a report dated 19 June 1943, Cance put the number of *francs-gardes* in the zone under Italian control at 6,809. Undoubtedly this figure is exaggerated.
68    The reason for not meeting its target is given in an undated report, see X.C.G./1/35302, CARAN.
69    A certain Stubaf. Zwickler wrote the report. Also of great interest is that the majority of the volunteers were from Paris and the adjoining Ile de France. (28% of the volunteers were from Paris and 9% from Ile de France.)
70    Undated report, see X.C.G. 1/1/35302, CARAN. Presumably 'the headquarters of the Waffen-SS' was the SS-Hauptamt.

assimilated with the rank of *sous-lieutenant* into the French corps of the SS'.[71] The same circular stressed the 'extreme' importance that *le Chef* [undoubtedly Doriot] attaches to 'the efficient participation of the Party in the organisation of the Waffen-SS...'

In December 1943, Darnand went to Paris where he met with several representatives of the SS and took lunch with German Ambassador Otto Abetz.[72]

## The 'sieve' of Sennheim

By 30 September 1943, about 800 French volunteers were undergoing selection at the camp of Sennheim.[73] This figure had risen to about 1100 on 30 October 1943. However, out of the first 1500 French volunteers to attend Sennheim, less than a third were actually admitted into the Waffen-SS.[74]

According to a German communiqué,[75] of those French volunteers who stepped forward for the Waffen-SS during the month of October 1943, 48% were students, farmers and young men between the ages of eighteen and twenty, 39% were workers and 13% had technical and industrial professions.[76] The communiqué also stated that the majority had never belonged to a political party.

Many of those classed as 'workers' were from camps in Germany and from the mines to the north of France. About one third of the volunteers were Parisians, followed by the Southerners who had grown in number and more vocal since the arrival of the *Miliciens*.[77]

Also, according to one historian, a large number of *repris de justice* [ex-convicts] were present.[78] The past of the recruits was investigated where possible. Jacques Lorazo said of this: 'When I think about myself, just a simple volunteer, they went to the *quai des Hollandais* at Dunkirk to investigate me, which had well annoyed the family vis-à-vis the neighbours.' Undoubtedly some convicts did slip through the net, but it's unlikely to have been many. Some historians also claim that many volunteers had only been able to enlist by falsifying their date of birth. Undoubtedly some did, but not many.

Notably, the harsh training regime at Sennheim did not dampen the enthusiasm of some for playing party politics. Indeed, according to Pierre Roesch: 'The struggle between the French political clans was not secret, but open, avowed, strident and bitter. All considered the SS as a simple INSTRUMENT.'

---

71   Ibid. Curiously the report states that Darnand 'holds the rank of *Capitaine* and is the only French SS officer'.
72   *Combats* number 33 of December 1943.
73   Ory, *Les Collaborateurs*, p.266, and Landwehr, *Charlemagne's Legionnaires*, p.30.
74   Mabire, *La Brigade Frankreich*, p.87.
75   The German communiqué is reproduced in the French Ministry of Interior report X.C.G./1/35324, dated 13 December 1943 (F1A 3747, CARAN).
76   Indeed, according to Saint-Loup, *Les Hérétiques*, p.31, 50% of Cance's 1st Battalion of the SS-Sturmbrigade were students.
77   Mabire, *La Brigade Frankreich*, p.87.
78   Ory, *Les collaborateurs*, p.266. Bayle, who served with the French Sturmbrigade, takes great exception to this suggestion (letter to the author), but some members of the Sturmbrigade were dismissed when the volunteers' criminal records turned up at Neweklau.

## Officer and NCO material

The Waffen-SS also attracted a number of former French Army officers and NCOs who were not drawn from the *Milice*. Indeed, former Lieutenant-Colonel Gamory-Dubourdeau was from the PPF and did not disguise the fact that he saw his role as that of preventing Darnand's men from colonising the French Waffen-SS!

Born on 29 January 1885 in Ploudalmézeau, Brittany, Paul-Marie Gamory-Dubourdeau started his long military career in 1902 when he enlisted in the Foreign Legion. In 1911, after attending the *École militaire d'infanterie de Saint-Maixent*, he graduated with the rank of *sous-lieutenant d'active* and was posted to the 2° RIC at Brest. He went on to serve with the Camel Corps in Sudan and Chad and with the *tirailleurs sénégalais* in the trenches of France from 1916 to 1918. His career came to a less than illustrious end when he was demobilised in Morocco as an officer in the Supply Corps. Over the years he amassed a large number of decorations, the most important were the *Croix de guerre* with one palm and three stars and the *Chevalier de la Légion d'honneur*.

In 1932, Gamory-Dubourdeau moved to Casablanca. Haunted by politics, he joined the PPF in 1937 and went on to become the *Secrétaire adjoint* of the party in Morocco. Nevertheless, he remained fiercely loyal to his Celtic homeland of Brittany and led a small autonomous group called *Le Roc breton*. Recalled in 1939, he did his bit again in various transport roles.

After the defeat, he was appointed *inspecteur du PPF* for Morocco and Algeria. He was expelled from Morocco in August 1941 when all political parties were banned in the non-occupied zone. At the end of 1942, he became the head of the PPF Breton study commission. In October 1943, he enlisted in the Waffen-SS, even though Doriot had wanted him to join the LVF instead. His appearance of an 'aryan menhir was going to captivate the Germans'.[79]

Also from Doriot's PPF was Paul Pleyber, born on 19 September 1906 in Paris. He served in the artillery from 1929 to 1931 and in 1934 was commisioned as a *Lieutenant de reserve*. Called to arms in 1939, he served on the Maginot Line with the *70e Régiment d'Artillerie Mobile de Forteresse*. Politics was important to him and in 1937 he joined the newly formed PPF. He enlisted in the Waffen-SS in order to follow in the footsteps of party leader Doriot who had gone to the Eastern Front himself in the ranks of the LVF. Pleyber had been greatly encouraged to do so by his wife, a more ardent supporter of Doriot than he was. Moreover, because of the crisis engulfing the coal industry he was at risk of losing his job as *directeur technique* at Entrepot d'Ivry and he had four children to support. He enlisted in the Waffen-SS on 24 August 1943.

The Corsican Dominique Scapula, born on 10 December 1906, was also a PPF adherent.

Robert Lambert was a member of the *Parti Franciste*. Born on 10 February 1918 in Grand-Verly, he fought on the side of the nationalists during the Spanish Civil War. When he returned to France he signed up on 9 September 1937 for three years with the *3e régiment de Spahis Marocains*. In 1938, he attended Saumur calvary school and returned to his unit the following year. His war was a quiet one guarding the Moroccan border with Spain. He passed to the Armitice Army. One of the first to sign up for the LVF, he was accepted with the rank of *Sergent*.[80] He saw action with the 3rd Company but was invalided out due to health problems.

79    Mabire, *La Brigade Frankreich*, p.93.
80    Lambert received the registration number 74.

He was awarded the Ostmedaille. Enlisting in the Waffen-SS, he arrived at Sennheim on 17 October 1943. He spoke four different languages, as well as two or three Moroccan dialects.

The political origin of the following French officer cadets is not known:

- Henri Maudhuit, born on 6 August 1895 in Paris
- Pierre Brocard, former Air Force pilot, born on 15 August 1916 in Paris
- Jean Croisile, born on 2 September 1894 in Hénin-Liétard
- Edmond Fluhr, born on 29 September 1916
- Isidore Lopez, born on 8 December 1912 in Saint-Denis du Sig, Algeria
- Robert Roy, ex-NSKK, born on 13 June 1900
- Alfred Pieyre de Mandiargues, born on 3 June 1920 in Paris
- Pierre Wable, ex-NSKK, born in 1904 in Amiens

Of note is that the white-haired and rosy-faced Croisile, who was approaching fifty, had enlisted in the Waffen-SS to be with his youngest son, Alain, who had just enlisted too. Jean Croisile was training to be a lawyer when war broke out in 1914. He volunteered. He saw constant action, was wounded five times and was awarded the *Croix de guerre* with four citations, the *Médaille militaire* and the *Légion d'honneur*. He continued to serve after the war, was promoted to *Sous-lieutenant de réserve* and was sent to reinforce the French intervention forces stationed in Odessa, but the city fell to the Bolsheviks before his arrival. He left the military soon after but enlisted again in 1932. Promotion to *Capitaine de réserve* followed. When war broke out for a second time, despite his age and his injuries, he wanted to fight and was eventually posted to a combat role. He fought at Calais, was wounded again and received another citation. Captured and dispatched to Oflag IV/D, he was released in August 1941.[81]

Henri Maudhuit had fought in the trenches of the First World War, winning the *Croix de guerre* with two citations. He fought again in 1940, winning the *Croix de guerre 39-30* with a divisional citation.

The religious Isidore Lopez enlisted in the *Légion Tricolore* with the rank of *Sous-lieutenant* on 25 September 1942 but did not pass to the LVF. His branch was the Engineers. He became an officer in the *Franc-Garde permanente*.

The Waffen-SS recognised that the previous military experience of the former French Army officers could serve as a potential 'building block' from which to train the unit's future encadrement, although it did not reward it like the LVF. Separated from their men upon their arrival at Sennheim, the former officers were quartered in maison Sordi, named after its former proprietor, near Sennheim station.

Stripped of their former French Army rank, although 'promoted' to the rank of Oberscharführer in the interim, the officer candidates of the *Französisch Lehrgang* were tested and educated by their new world. The pace would be furious. Their training was placed under the overall supervision of Stubaf. Welbrock. Although an amputee, his legs having been smashed by a Soviet shell, he was a man of extraordinary energy and he got around in a barouche. Welbrock had fully embraced the Germanic revolution of the Waffen-SS that was only just beginning.

81   For more details of Jean Croisile's long and distinguished military career, as well as his personal life, see Croisile Jean-Marie, *Sous Uniforme Allemand* (Paris: Nimrod, 2018), and Bouysse Grégory, *French in German Uniform Part 1: Officers of the Waffen-SS* (Lulu, 2018) Both are highly recommended.

SS-Ustuf. Hans Reiche. (Author)

Ustuf. Hans-Ulrich Reiche from SS-Ausbildungslager Sennheim, a former embassy attaché at Berne with a gift for languages, was assigned to supervise the French officer candidates on a personal basis. His fair hair and glasses gave him the appearance of a diplomat rather than that of a soldier.[82]

Ustuf. Binder and Ustuf. Kopp were responsible for the political education of the French officer cadets.

Born on 29 May 1907 in Offenburg, Erich Kopp had been a card-carrying member of the NSDAP since 1928; he had received his party card from Goebbels in person. Before the war he served with the SiPo-SD at Freiburg-am-Breisgau. Very energetic, he spoke French well.

Flemish NCOs Uscha. Eeckhout, born on 31 January 1921 in Maldegem, and Uscha. de Lodere, supervised the military and technical training of the French officer cadets. Pignard-Berthet recalls that they received a warm welcome from the German cadres but, on the other hand, their relations were rather distant with the other volunteers, particularly with the Flemings. This contrasts with Bayle who remembers an excellent spirit reigning between the different nationalities.

82   Hans-Ulrich Reiche was born on 1 March 1914 in Hattingen.

At the beginning of October 1943, Gauleiter Robert Wagner paid the French officer cadets a visit. After inspecting the officer cadets who were still in civilian clothing, he asked if any among them had fought in the First World War. Only Jean Croisile came forward. The Gauleiter shook his hand and his hand alone. The others took this gesture of reconciliation very badly.

The group of officer candidates was joined by Doctor Pierre-Auguste Bonnefoy, born on 1 August 1908 in Belley, and by Abel Chapy, born on 1 July 1920. Both were from the *Milice française*.

Pierre-Auguste Bonnefoy studied medicine and graduated in 1934. In 39-40 he served with the rank of *médecin sous-lieutenant de reserve* with the colonial artillery winning the *Croix de guerre* as well as the *Croix du combattant*. A prominent local figure, he joined the LFC, passed to the SOL and then the *Milice*, attending Uriage, after which he was promoted *chef départmental de la Milice du Vaucluse*.

Before the war Chapy was a militant 'among the leagues of the nationalist formations', including the *Jeunesses Patriotes* [Patriot Youth], and came to realise that this nationalism correlated with ideas advocated by National Socialism. Chapy has gone on the record as stating: 'From his seizure of power, Hitler developed, as it were, ideas which were mine.' Yet his sense of country and duty were such that he was moved to enlist. Thus, in 1938, aged eighteen, he signed up. He served in Morocco with the *3e Régiment de Spahis marocains* and then the *Chasseurs d'Afrique*.

Demobilised in June 1941 with the rank of *Aspirant*, Chapy felt great bitterness over having missed the battle for France and her subsequent defeat. He secretly crossed the Demarcation line to return to his native Tours. 'It was with no light heart that he saw the Germans in his country'. In November 1942 he joined the Organisation Todt and was posted to Saint-Nazaire.[83] He absconded and returned home for Christmas.[84]

An admirer of Darnand, Chapy crossed into the Southern zone and came to the *Milice*. Following attendance at its Uriage training school in March 1943 he returned to Tours and organised an underground *Milice Trentaine*, which in theory was still prohibited, being in the occupied Northern zone.

Because of his European and National Socialist convictions, Chapy also decided to volunteer when he heard that many *Milicien* cadres were leaving for the Waffen-SS.[85] There was another reason, that of Nationalism. He detailed:[86]

There were at that time in Alsace about one thousand young Frenchmen who had enlisted in the Waffen-SS and to whom it was essential to give French cadres. The reason? What would the sacrifice of thousands of Frenchmen have served if they had to be integrated in a German unit! For them, [it was an] absolute necessity to have French

---

83  Arguably, Chapy was called up under S.T.O. and decided to volunteer for the OT instead.
84  According to Mabire, *La Brigade Frankreich*, p.87, and Leguérandais, *Uniforms* Hors série 29, p.70, in November 1942, Chapy volunteered for the *Phalange Africaine* raised by Laval and Darnand to defend French Tunisia against the Anglo-Americans, but never left for North Africa. No other source confirms this event.
85  Mabire, *La Brigade Frankreich*, p.87.
86  *Der Freiwillige*, Nr.2/1985 and radio broadcast *Les SS français et l'Europe*, Radio Monte Carlo, 1 February 1971.

officers and fight as Frenchmen. It was quite obvious and important that this formation of young SS Frenchmen could bring by itself an advantage and a role to France. I add that it was essential that France could benefit from our battles and the prestige we were going to win on the Eastern Front.

When asked by the recruiting officer what he was looking for in the Waffen-SS Chapy replied: "The Iron Cross. I need honour." Moreover, Chapy knew Robert Lambert. They had both served in the same regiment of *Spahis Marocains*.

In mid-November 1943, more officer cadets arrived. They included the following:

- René Fayard, born on 17 May 1922 in Paris
- Pierre Hug, born on 24 January 1920 in Vandoeuvre
- Henri Kreis, born on 2 February 1923 in Blois
- Charles Laschett, born on 2 March 1920 in Paris
- Joseph Peyron, born on 1 June 1913
- Michel Potier, born on 25 November 1922 in Maubeuge

Fayard, Hug, Kreis, Laschett and Peyron were all selected from the NCO cadets *Lehrgang*.[87] That they should be considered Waffen-SS officer material is a remarkable achievement. Fayard had served briefly with the NSKK before deserting to the Waffen-SS. Hug had served briefly with the French Army[88] and volunteered for the Waffen-SS on 1 September 1943. Also of note is that his father, a prominent and well respected Army Colonel, would become the *secrétaire général* of the *Comité des amis de la Waffen-SS* when it was created in April 1944. Kreis and Laschett had no previous military service to speak of, while Peyron had spent some time with the Todt, but had not found what he was looking for.

Potier was ex-LVF and was decorated with the Iron Cross, probably 2nd Class.

Like all new recruits, the officer cadets received some form of sports uniform, perhaps the all black two-piece SS tracksuit with a circular black and white SS emblem on the left breast.[89] The fatigue uniform would follow and finally the *feldgrau* SS uniform. Chapy admitted that he shed some tears when he donned the field-grey for the first time and that he was not alone. He recalled that the former French officers and *aspirants* beside him 'were hardly smiling'. For Fenet, the German uniform posed no problem, remarking:[90] 'There was no other possible uniform to fight against the Soviet Union. In a war that atrocious, there was no place for doubts'.

The officer cadets' training was not solely physical. Ustuf. Binder and Ustuf. Erich Kopp took them for the *Weltanschauung*, the central tenet of National Socialism. Ustuf. Binder spelled out this 'world view' through lectures on the laws of heredity and the history of humanity according

---

87   Throughout *La Brigade Frankreich* Mabire affectionaly describes Hug, Kreis, Laschett and Peyron affectionately as the Sturmbrigade's 'Four Musketeers'!

88   According to Leguérandais, *Uniforms* Hors série 29, Hug attended the celebrated military school of Saint-Cyr. His source was undoubtedly the German document of 26 January 1944 which lists the names, the current ranks and the previous ranks of the twenty-six French officer cadets sent to SS-Junkerschule Bad Tölz. The previous rank of Hug is recorded as 'Schule Saint-Cyr'. However, no other source confirms his attendance at Saint-Cyr.

89   See two photographs that appear in Mabire's *La Brigade Frankreich*.

90   *Historia N° 613*, p.16.

to racist laws. The enemies of National Socialism were clearly identified: Communism, egalitarianism, Freemasons, multiparty democracy, capitalism, Judaism and Christianity. The French audience was difficult and demanding. Indeed, many were very thankful for the rest from the otherwise physical demands of the day. But this *Weltanschauung* came as a shock to those like officer cadet Pignard-Berthet who saw in National Socialism a political party like those back in France.

SS-Ausbildungslager Sennheim 'sieved' the French officer cadets in the same way as all French recruits. For whatever reason at least two officer cadets 'dropped out' and returned to France.

From the start of October to the end of December 1943, between eighty and one hundred Frenchmen underwent NCO training. Almost all were from the 1st Company. Ustuf. Bastian, a Volksdeutsche from Eupen-Malmédy in Belgium, commanded the NCO candidates *Lehrgang*. Seriously wounded in the face on the Eastern Front, he wore a black patch across one eye. His *Spiess* was SS-Oscha. Waldemar Holtorf.[91]

The French NCO candidates were billeted in Sennheim church hall. Notably, they became the first French SS Freiwillige to receive a rifle. The training was intense.

There was one incident the French NCO candidates had cause to remember well. Three times, a Norwegian instructor had them march past a local priest and thunder out 'Heil Hitler!' Politely, each time, the priest had replied 'Guten Morgen!' And, each time, the instructor did not acknowledge this. Reported, the incident was investigated. The arrogant Norwegian instructor was returned to his original unit.[92]

At the end of the course, only about a dozen trainees were promoted to the rank of Rottenführer and thirty or so to that of Sturmmann. Nevertheless, the number who had simply failed the course was only about half a dozen. The remainder became Oberschütze.

## Murder

In December, according to official wartime reports, a handful of French volunteers of the Waffen-SS took the law into their own hands.[93]

On 5th December, the press reported that terrorists had killed Roger Verdier in Sainte-Foy-la-Grande hospital, as well as his wife and his sister-in-law. Verdier was a well-known member of the Waffen-SS, allegedly responsible for thirty or more denunciations leading to the arrest of many resistants.[94] On the night of 7th December, four armed men identified as belonging to the Waffen-SS turned up at Sainte-Foy-la-Grande police station. After questioning the gendarmes about the murder of Verdier, the SS men lined them up against a wall and opened fired killing

91  Holtorf is incorrectly identified by Mabire as Hans Ohlendorf.
92  Bayle, *De Marseille à Novossibirsk*, p.54. Bayle was, in fact, one of the French NCO candidates present. Mabire recounts the 'same' incident, *La Brigade Frankreich*, pp.101-102, but curiously there are some major differences; French NCO candidate Bousquet replaces the Norwegian instructor, the priest does eventually reply 'Heil Hitler!' and no action is taken against Bousquet.
93  See *12 December 1943, Meutre des gendarmes de Sainte-Foy-la-Grande par les Waffen SS français*, F1A 3748, CARAN and *15th December 1943, Attaque de la gendarmerie de Saint-Nallxer par les Waffen SS français,* F1A 3748, CARAN.
94  Giolitto, *Volontaires français sous l'uniforme allemande*, p.381.

two and wounding three. The SS men left behind them a piece of paper with the message: 'A la gloire de Verdier'.

On the night of 8 December, five men who were identified as French members of the Waffen-SS stationed at Castillon-sur-Dordogne, turned up at Saint-Nallxer gendarmerie. They questioned the five gendarmes present about the murder of the Verdiers. Not satisfied with the answers, they blamed the gendarmes for not finding the killers and then coldly gunned them down. Four were killed while the last was seriously wounded. The SS men left behind them a note on the gendarmerie door which read: 'En mémoire des Verdier'.

The Frenchmen responsible for the revenge killings at Sainte-Foy-la-Grande who were identified as members of the Waffen-SS were actually members of the 8th Company of the Brandenburg Division training at Castillon.[95] Undoubtedly, the same is true for those responsible for the revenge killings at Saint-Nallxer.

French recruits continued to arrive at Sennheim. Bernand Triqueneaux arrived on 27 December 1943.[96] Born on 20 June 1914 in Reims, he was granted an exemption from military service due to an 'irremediable weakness of constitution'. Nevertheless, he recovered and was mobilized in November 1939. He trained for the artillery at Orléans, then at the prestigious *école d'application de l'artillerie* at Fointainebleau for officer cadets, where he achieved good results. He subsequently participated in the defence of Pont-sur-Seine on 13 June 1940 and retreated with his unit to Dordogne. Demobilized in August of that same year, he returned to Reims. In September 1942, he left for Germany as a worker, but disappointment awaited him. He returned home, was arrested by the German police and sent back to Germany to work. Following his divorce and to secure the release of his young brother who the Germans were holding as a prisoner, he enlisted in the Waffen-SS in July 1943.

Another new arrival was Jean Halard, born December 1926 in the 12th department of Paris, who abandoned his college studies to enlist in the Waffen-SS. Ashamed of the military debacle of 1940, he wanted to show the Germans just how proud he was to be French. Moreover, his enlistment was a statement to the Germans that not all Frenchmen were cowards in the fight against Communism and also that they were not alone in this fight *pour l'Europe*. Notably, unlike many other recruits, he whole-heartedly believed in the ideology of National Socialism.

Roger P. volunteered for the European Waffen-SS on 14 December 1943. Born on 21 July 1912 in Versailles, he described himself as the 'political leader of the RNP for the Parisian region'.

Leave was granted over the festive period (22/12/1943-7/1/1944) for some one thousand volunteers training at Sennheim. Their conduct while on leave was not always exemplary, though. The exploits of some came to the attention of the German Military Administration in Paris that complained in turn to Abteilung III [the justice section] of Sennheim camp. Pierre Roesch recalls of one incident:[97]

95    For details of the killers see Bouysse, *Encyclopédie de l'ordre nouveau: Histoire du SOL, de la Milice française & des mouvements de la collaboration volume 8.*
96    Mouine, *Cernay 40-45*, p.268.
97    Mouine interview with Roesch.

Paul Delsart [pseudonym] hated me to death because I knew about him. While on leave he had attacked, pistol in hand, a chic bar in Paris, at the head of a small commando (group) of bandits disguised like him as SS. This idiot had badly miscalculated his coup: the bar was protected by the SD and the attackers ended up in Fresnes [prison] less than two hours later. At that time, my influence still carried a certain weight and Delsart sent me a 'desperate word' through a [female] friend. He begged me to plead his case, that he had been drinking, that there was nothing else for him to do other than commit suicide, etc… Anyway, he was 'part' pardoned and he never forgave me…

Roesch did not expect such behaviour from a NCO and platoon commander.

## New Year of 1944

On the evening of 6 January 1944,[98] at the end of their leave, the French volunteers of the Waffen-SS assembled at Paris Gare de l'Est for the return journey to Sennheim. Darnand came to see them off. Notably, he was pictured with a group of officer cadets, all of whom were former *Miliciens*, and who were due to attend SS-Junkerschule Tölz days later.

Hundreds were missing at roll call. Some had deserted. Most were behind bars for various offences whilst on leave. On their return to Sennheim they were assigned to the 3rd Training Company at Weiler to resume their training. Their exploits were duly investigated. After taking into consideration that they had rejoined their units rather than deserting which would have been easier, only token punishments were meted out.

By early January 1944, French volunteers had filled six companies at Sennheim.[99] At the head of the 1st Battalion (Companies 1-4) was Swiss officer W-Sturmbannführer Hersche.[100]

Heinrich Hersche was born on 30 September 1889 in Zurich. He served in the Swiss Army from 1910 to 1934, retiring with the rank of Major.[101] He also enjoyed international success as a member of the Swiss national horse-riding team. He was a member of various right-wing and National Socialist parties and came under police surveillance. When war broke out[102] he moved to Germany and found employment as a civilian riding instructor at the SS-Hauptreitschule München [SS-Riding School]. In 1942, he enlisted in the Waffen-SS with the rank of

---

98   Most sources date the return of the French volunteers from leave to 6 January 1944. However, Lefèvre dates their return one day earlier (*Axe & Alliés* hors série no 1, p.26) while Jean del Missier dates his return to 4 January 1944 (Mounie, *Cernay 40-45*, p.274).

99   Mabire, *La Brigade Frankreich*, p.113.

100  Curiously, according to Mabire, *La Brigade Frankreich*, p.113, in early January 1944, the first to enlist finally started their real military training and formed the first *bataillon de marche* and the last to arrive formed a training battalion under Hersche. This is unconfirmed.

101  Bouysse, *French in German Uniform Part 1: Officers of the Waffen-SS*. Dates of Hersche leaving the army vary. According to *Schweizer Soldat*, April 2012, p.46, Hersche, after falling into financial difficulties, decided to do the honourable thing and resign from the army, and was released on 1 January 1936.

102  Bouysse, *French in German Uniform Part 1: Officers of the Waffen-SS*. Dates of Hersche moving to Germany also vary. According to *Schweizer Soldat*, April 2012, p.47, Hersche left for Germany on 13 December 1941.

*Sturmbannführer* and served with an SS Calvary training unit.[103] On 1 December 1943, he was assigned to the SS-Hauptamt and later sent to Sennheim as a training instructor.

The training at Sennheim was hard and manoeuvres were often conducted with live-fire. Louis Blanchere said:[104]

> We were on manoeuvre towards Thann, [in an] undulating and wooded region, [and] a detachment of the Kriegsmarine[105] was holding a sector opposite. At a certain point the order was given to the latter to fire on us; we took cover on the ground and I found myself on a half-frozen stream. I threw myself on the ice, I broke it and I remained for quarter of an hour with icy water going over me. As I wished to realise if the danger was as real as they had told me, I took a stick in my hand and raised it 70cms from the ground; it was instantly broken by bullets which whistled all around us. Three comrades were killed and five or six were wounded. The following week the same exercise was repeated.

Discipline at Sennheim was very strict. Two French volunteers, one of whom was a *Milicien* from Lyon, stole two geese, brought them back to their sleeping quarters and cooked them up. Unfortunately for the two men and del Missier, who witnessed the cooking, the geese belonged to the local NSDAP leader. There was an inquiry. The two thieves were caught and brought before a military tribunal. They were sent to SS-und Polizeilager Danzig-Matzkau. As for 'accomplice' del Missier, he was sentenced to fifteen days close arrest, but the punishment was not executed immediately, only in June 1944 when he was with the French SS-Sturmbrigade in Bohemia-Moravia, finding himself in Neweklau prison. Also, he had to forfeit promotion to Unterscharführer for one year.

In January, some one hundred French NCO candidates were sent to Unterführerschule der Waffen-SS Posen-Treskau, Poland (then Reich territory), for an eight week training course. Among them was Christian Martres, who was promoted to the rank of Sturmmann on 15 January 1944. Three German instructors accompanied them.

On their arrival, much to their surprise, the French NCO candidates were greeted in French by their course supervisor, a young Walloon Oberjunker. In French, he ordered them to stand to attention but they did not react. A second order, quickly followed by a third, was barked out in French. The French NCO cadets stayed as they were. They would only respond to orders in German!

The French NCO cadets were also surprised to meet Moslems on the same course who were dressed in the exact same uniform but wearing an SS fez with the death's head and SS cap eagle. They were from the recently raised 13. Waffen-Gebirgs-Division der SS 'Handschar' (Kroatische Nr.1).

---

103  Identified as *SS-Kavallerie-Ersatz-Abteilung* or *SS-Kavallerie-Ausbildungs-und-Ersatz-Abteilung 8* (Bouysse, *French in German Uniform Part 1: Officers of the Waffen-SS*).

104  Recorded in a non-referenced Ministry of the Interior report, dated 5 February 1944, F1A 3747, CARAN.

105  It should be noted that at no time did French volunteers of the Kriegsmarine, also trained at Sennheim, conduct manoeuvres with their compatriots of the Waffen-SS. (Personal conversation with Soulat.)

All the NCO cadets would receive section commander and even platoon commander training. Yet at the end of the training course only fifty of their number were promoted, for the most part, to the rank of Sturmmann.

## SS-Junkerschule Tölz

Around the same time twenty-six French officer candidates, accompanied by Reiche and Binder, were dispatched to SS Junkerschule Tölz for a special abridged training course (*1. Sonderlehrgang für französische Offiziere*) that ran from 10 January 1944 to 4 March 1944.

Ustuf. Reiche, who spoke excellent French, went in place of Uscha. Eeckhout. On 8 March 1944, Eeckhout was transferred to 6. SS-Freiw. Sturmbrigade 'Langemarck'.

The French officer candidates were (in alphabetical order): Artus, Bartolomei, Brocquat, Cance, Chapy, Croisille, Fayard, Fenet, Fluhr, Gamory-Dubourdeau, Gaultier, Hug, Kreis, de Lafaye, Lambert, Laschett, Maudhuit, de Mandiargues, Peyron, Pignard-Berthet, Pleyber, Pouget, Pruvost, Scapula, de Tissot and Wable.[106]

The course supervisor was SS-Hauptsturmführer Kostenbader, otherwise called 'Koko', holder of the Iron Cross 1st Class, who had transferred to Bad Tölz from a post at NCO school Posen-Treskau.

On their arrival at Bad Tölz, the French officer candidates found themselves 'demoted' from the rank of Oberscharführer to that of Unterscharführer. All would start from a 'level playing field'.

Because the standard of German amongst the French officer candidates left much to be desired instruction was given in French and the time spent learning German was increased by one hour per week to six hours per week. The French officer candidates were permitted to wear French medals and that included those won during the 1940 campaign. And, for the first time, the French tricolore flew with equal status to those flags of the other nations at Bad Tölz.

At the close of the course, the French officer cadets were commissioned as such:

Sturmbannführer: Gamory-Dubourdeau
Hauptsturmführer: Cance
Obersturmführer: Artus, Fenet, de Tissot, Pleyber, Croisile and Maudhuit
Untersturmführer: Brocard, Bartolomei, Gaultier, Lambert, Pignard-Berthet and Scapula
Standartenoberjunker: Fayard, Chapy, Hug, Peyron, Kreis and Laschett

Of those that had served in the French Army, most bettered their former rank. Some promotions do surprise.[107]

---

106 The official report 'SS-FHA. Amt XI (2) Az: 36 o /Amt V/IIa Ref.6/Amt II/Org. IE/III/4 vom 26.1.44' actually spells four of the names incorrectly!!
107 The promotion of Cance to Hauptsturmführer and particularly that of de Tissot to Obersturmführer suggests that the Germans were 'looking after' some of the more influential and senior members of the *Milice*.

Pierre Cance (author's collection)

Found wanting, Pouget and Fluhr were 'promoted' to the NCO rank of Oberscharführer.[108] For Pouget, promotion it was not. The equivalent French Army rank of Oberscharführer is *adjudant* and this NCO rank was well below the commission of *Lieutenant* he once held in the French Army. Alfred Pieyre de Mandiargues and Pruvost also received the rank of Oberscharführer.

Wable and de Lafaye did not complete the course. Wable was returned to Sennheim whereas de Lafaye left the Waffen-SS and rejoined the Milice. He was assigned the *Milice* and was assigned to the *Franc-Garde permanente de Vichy* with the rank of *chef de centaine*, conducting operations against the maquis in the departments of Allier and Côte d'Or during the summer of 1944.

The end of the course also brought the news that Hauptsturmführer Kostenbader had just become an instructor to the French Waffen-SS regiment soon to be assembled in Bohemia-Moravia.[109]

After the training course at Bad Tölz the French SS officers went off for a weeklong stay (perhaps 4 March 1944 to 11 March 1944) at San Martino di Castrozza in the Italian Tyrol

---

108  Edmond Fluhr was appointed *germanische SS Werber* (recruiting-sergeant) on 1 May 1944 and then posted on 2 December 1944 to the *Franz. SS-Grenadier-Ausbildungs und Ersatz Batallion*, the depot and training battalion of 'Charlemagne'.

109  According to Mabire, *La Brigade Frankreich*, p.163, Hstuf. Kostenbader was promoted to Sturmbannführer soon after the end of this course. Bayle does not recall this.

where they could initiate themselves into skiing or, if more experienced, perfect their skills. However, they paled before the Scandinavians.

While his fellow officers were away at Bad Tölz, Doctor Bonnefoy attended a training course at SS-ArztlicheAkademie [SS Medical School] Graz. He was promoted to the rank of Obersturmführer.

Meantime, at Sennheim, more volunteers continued to arrive for basic training. In early 1944, sixteen-year-old Jean Faverau from Beauchamp was working for the Organisation Todt when, dragged along by his comrades, he decided to sign up for the Waffen-SS. Born on 2 July 1927, he had to make a living when his father fell sick in 1943. He found a job as a factory worker at Saint-Cloud, but it paid pittance. In need of more money and wanting to travel, on 15 October 1943, in Paris, he enlisted as a telephonist in the Organisation Todt. Sent to Rastenburg for training, where he spent three weeks, he was forwarded to Kettwig in the Ruhr and then to Berlin, where he enlisted in the Waffen-SS.

Seduced by propaganda and a taste for adventure, free-worker Albert Émile Poignant volunteered for the Waffen-SS on 7 January 1944 at the recruitment office at Stettin. Born on 9 September 1913 in Buc (department Seine-et-Oise), he trained as a miner. From 1934 to 1935 he was called for military service and served with the 150e RI. The following year, and notably, he enlisted in the International Brigades to fight Franco and the Nationalists. On 2 September 1939 he was mobilized and assigned to the 332e RI. He did his duty when war came and was captured on 20 June 1940. Sent to Stalag IIC, he was sentenced to one year in prison for having served with the International Brigades, after which he was on the move again to another POW camp. In July 1943, he was transformed into a free-worker and posted to the submarine base at Stettin-Odenwerk.

Didier volunteered for the Waffen-SS in 1944.[110] Like many, his story began with the humiliating defeat of 1940:

> I was all the more traumatized by the defeat of 1940 in which I was too young to fight by only a few months. I thought a little naively that I could have somehow changed the outcome of the fight. Aged twenty in 1942, business employee and feeling bad about myself, I felt the need to return to war. I had to find a cause to 'serve'. It was a word very used at the time.

To calm his warrior instincts, he joined the *Jeunes du Maréchal*, but it proved not enough for him: initially he had supported 'father' Pétain, but he soon came to realise that the maréchal 'kept our minds in a vanquished mentality'. When the Allies invaded North Africa he thought that French forces should have resisted them. Thereupon, in his own words, he became openly fascist, more so after the Grand Council of Fascism voted Mussolini out of power. He militated in one of the nationalist parties, wore a colour shirt and read newspaper *Je suis partout*, but was troubled by the onset of the civil war between the collaborators and the resistance, for he had no desire to spill French blood. Recruitment posters for the Waffen-SS, a 'new European Army fighting against Bolshevism', very much caught his eye and his imagination, he now reasoned:

110 Lormier, *SS Français*, p.13, and Delatour, chapter SS et Français pourquoi?, *Historia* hors série 32. Didier might be a pseudonym.

'The only possible place for a French fascist was in the Waffen-SS on the Eastern Front against the Soviet Reds'.[111] Moreover, nobody could ever accuse him of being an opportunist; he knew that Germany had already lost the war.

The recruitment posters for the Waffen-SS also caught the attention of others, like Édouard, who had enlisted in the Army in 1936 aged eighteen, serving first with the tirailleurs in Morocco, a time he fondly recalls. Deployed with his regiment back to the mainland in 1939, he fought bravely against the Boches, winning the *Croix de guerre*, and managed to avoid capture. The armistice shocked him. He thought about leaving for North Africa to continue the fight, but apathy got the better of him.

Dragged along by a friend to a Doriot event, Édouard liked what he heard and saw and thus began his politicization, so much so that he soon became openly fascist, even though he did not join a party. When the LVF was created Édouard volunteered but was rejected because of bad teeth. He managed to save a little money and visit a dentist to get treatment. He tried a number of jobs, but none pleased him. Called up for the S.T.O., he went into hiding and even thought about joining a maquis, but the 'magnificent posters' for the Waffen-SS was the turning point for a new path. Profoundly anti-communist, he decided to try and enlist in this elite army, convinced that it had need of recruits more than ever and that standards would be less severe than the LVF, and was accepted.

S.T.O. worker Masson volunteered for the Waffen-SS following a visit from recruiters. As a worker at Magdeburg, he had been treated well by his co-worker, an old Social Democrat of the old school, and been impressed by the discipline of the German people, stating that 'there was not much difference a German worker and a French worker'. Even so, he had quickly become fed up. The Waffen-SS gave him the opportunity to fulfill his desire to 'see the country'.

Arriving at Cernay, he spoke in French to some Alsatians, one of whom alerted him to the fact that it was forbidden to speak French. Asked where he was going, he replied Sennheim. He was then asked if he knew what's out there. He replied: "Yes. There are Waffen-SS." His interlocutor questioned him further: "But why are you going to Sennheim?" He replied: "To join the Waffen-SS." There was total silence. Such was his welcome.

Disaster struck on 10 February 1944 when ten French volunteers of the 3rd Training Company were killed in an explosion while unloading ammunition from a train.[112] An eleventh died the following day from his injuries. The names of the dead are:

- Albert Cottin
- Jules Delebasse
- André Delebrouck
- André Moncelet, born on 28 March 1919 in Paris
- Marcel Morel, born on 21 May 1926
- Lucien Prignot
- Louis Rougier

111  See Lormier, *SS Français*, p.14.
112  Lefèvre, *Axe & Alliés* hors série no 1, p.28. Mounine dates the accident to 10 January 1944 and numbers the dead at nine, *Cernay 40-45*, pp.275-276. Leguerandais, *The European Volunteer* Number 1, p.47, and Anon., *Trente Trois* numero 1 also date the accident to 10 January 1944. Bouysse dates the accident to 9 February 1944.

- Jacques Seguin
- Robert Virrion, born on 12 February 1922
- Louis Grangeri

Enter Skorzeny. French volunteers of the Waffen-SS were recruited for the SS-Sonderverband z.b.v. (and later the SS-Jagdverbände). The total number of Frenchmen who went on to serve in the ranks of Skorzeny's Special Forces is not known. However, between 25 and 28 February 1944, fifty-three Frenchmen at Sennheim were proposed for the SS-Sonderverband z.b.v. Some had served previously in the French Army and even in the Russian Army.

On 22 February 1944, Breton nationalist Yvon Prunennec, born on 28 February 1922 in Bordeaux, volunteered for the Waffen-SS at the Rennes recruiting office. He said of his formative years:

> I was not against the Germans. My teacher was not anti-German. I had friends who had been in Germany in 1938. They had been well received and well treated. In August 1939, for fear of war, they were advised that it would be better to go home. I was not in favour of war against Germany because I was a Breton nationalist, I had been a member of the PNB since 1937, and because of France's hypocrisy, summed up best by the expression 'do as I say and not what I do'. France had seized Alsace-Lorraine and yet it was complaining about the German occupation of Sudatenland. And the majority of Austrian people wanted the annexation. In France it was lies, lies.
>
> [I remember] a discussion with my half-sister, a teacher, who was married to a French officer of the Colonial Army. She had been in Senegal for two years. She was in favour of war. I was not. [It was] a lively discussion. She grabbed me. I took her by the arms and she fell on her knees. Her husband, who was present, did not say a word. A few weeks after the declaration of war she said to me that I was a traitor. This I did not accept. My mother sided with my sister. She was anti-Boche and anti-Nazi. I never used the word Boche. My mother and half-sister did.
>
> I did not fight against the Germans in the 39-40 war. I was too young. And yet I had received mobilisation papers in 1939, but I was only seventeen and a half. I was morally and physically older than my age.
>
> In May 1940, my schoolteacher told the class to return home to their families. I heard on the radio about the fighting on the Somme. [President] Renault said we are the strongest and we will win and, yet weeks later, catastrophe.

He tried to embark for England but was thwarted by the speed of the German advance. He was impressed by the bearing and appearance of the German soldiers he met:

> Suddenly a new German column stopped on the right side of the street. Ten or so Germans 'joined' us in a bar, asking for cigarettes, cigars and sweets. The owner, who was afraid, gave them everything. Suddenly the Germans said: "How much?" Surprised, she gave them receipts and they gave her Marks. She gave them French change. Appel! The Germans left. The lady said: "Ah bien ça alors!"
>
> I reflected. The Germans looked good. They were tall, strong and not hungry. And they were wearing good uniforms. And yet the newspapers and radios were reporting

that the German soldiers were hungry and in paper uniforms. So this was not true. And they had paid too. Later we met more German soldiers and all were of the same good appearance.

Contact with the occupying German forces only accentuated his already strong German sympathies. He wanted to serve, but the 'French' LVF was not for him. He chose instead the European Waffen-SS. Sent to Sennheim, he trained with the 5th Company under SS-Hauptsturmführer Hartmann at Weiler. In June 1944, he was transferred to the 1st Company.

On 25 February 1944, a report submitted by SS-Obersturmführer Laue proposed French volunteers for officer and NCO training after three weeks of basic training. Some details of the report are worthy of note. Jean Aimé-Blanc, a student who had served five years with the French Air Force as *sergent*, was proposed for officer training. Nikolas Osseletsky was proposed for the position of Stabsscharführer [Senior NCO]. Born on 14 September 1906, he had served twelve years in the French Air Force.

The following were proposed as section commanders:

- Roland Gussenburger, a member of the *Milice*
- Emile Benso, four years in the French Artillery and also a member of the *Milice*
- Georges Nicouleau, served 10 months in the French Navy and 9 months in the German Navy as a guard
- Georges Ogier, served 10 months with the NSKK and a member of the *Franciste* party
- Maurice Dubus, served 10 months with the OT

The following were proposed as instructors and much later as section commanders:

- Louis Lavelle, served 10 months with the French Navy, and *chef politique* of the JPF
- Dante Giorgi, served one year with the NSKK and a member of the *Franciste* party
- Bernand Ossello, no military service and did not belong to any political party

That same month of February, Fernand R. and Louis Senecaut both volunteered for the Waffen-SS. Born on 19 November 1916 in Calais, Fernand R. fought for France and was captured on 24 June 1940. Sent to Germany, he was released in October 1943.

As for Senecaut, he was born on 26 November 1912 in Roubaix and first fought Communism as a member of the *Croix de Feu* from 1932 to 1936. He fought in 1939-40, was captured and sent to a 'POW camp at Hohenstein' [presumably Stalag I-B], where he volunteered to work as a translator. In January 1941 he was sent to Königsberg, working as an office clerk. On 27 June 1941, he volunteered to fight in Russia, but was refused because he was still a POW. He tried again in March and September 1942, but again was refused. In December of that same year, he joined the *Milice française* and worked with the Gestapo of Königsberg to defeat the Gaullists and Communists. Signing up for the Waffen-SS in February 1944, he was called up at the end of May 1944 and left for Sennheim.

On 5 April 1944, a *Comité des Amis de la Waffen-SS* was established under the chairmanship of Vichy Secretary of State Paul Marion, a former member of the Communist Party and the PPF. Marcel Déat, Jacques Doriot and Joseph Darnand also sat on the committee. The role of the committee was to maintain contact between the combatants and its friends and comrades in France and provide them with 'all possible material and moral assistance'.[113] The committee was only recognized by the German authorities on 17 July, by which time it could do no good.

On 25 April 1944, Roger Roberti signed up for the Waffen-SS at Nantes. Born on 15 January 1926 in Saint-Nazaire, Roberti was a member of the JNP. Two reasons prompted him to enlist. The first was the defeat of 1940. Like many, he could not believe that the country had been defeated so quickly by a 'young, bronzed and healthy army'. The second reason was the allied terror air raids on Saint-Nazaire and especially on Nantes, which left a deep and lasting impression on him. The family home was badly damaged and the family was forced to move. Moreover, in the wake of the air raids, he helped out finding victims buried under rubble. His father advised him against joining up, but nothing was going to hold him back. He said of arriving at Sennheim:[114]

> What impressed me the most on my arrival was the youth, the cleanliness, the organisation, a strict discipline, in short the impression of entering a Germanic world previously unknown to us.

After one month of this regime, Roberti noted that 10 to 15% of the volunteers had terminated their contract. Roberti swore his oath of loyalty at a ceremony he described as 'very impressive'. It was a momentous step as he recalls:[115]

> After the taking the oath we were considered different, like fully-fledged SS. We finally had the feeling of belonging to this Order, to this Knighthood whose trials, it seems, were too hard for us Frenchmen.

**The Swiss Connection**

In April 1944, SS-Untersturmführer Büeler arrived at SS-Ausbildungslager Sennheim to pick up the reins of the 2nd Company.[116] Heinrich Büeler was born into a German-speaking Swiss family on 12 December 1901 in Cochin, India, which was under British colonial rule at the time. In 1907, he went to live with his grandfather in Winterthur. He studied law at the universities of Zurich and Hamburg, before attending La Sorbonne, Paris, for three semesters. Not surprisingly he was fluent in German, French and English. More exams followed. He eventually settled in Zurich as a lawyer.

---

113  AN F 60 1688.
114  Mounine, *Cernay 40–45*, p.304.
115  Mounine, *Cernay 40–45*, p.308.
116  Curiously, according to Mabire, *La Brigade Frankreich*, p.114, Ustuf. Büeler commanded the 3rd and the 4th Companies.

At the age of twenty, Büeler joined the Communist youth. Some years later, he discovered National Socialism. Becoming a member of the *Front National*, he defended young Swiss National Socialists in court. He was soon considered an enemy of the state and, in June 1941, was arrested. The payment of a fine of 20,000 Swiss francs brought him his release. With his practice in ruins, he left Switzerland and crossed into Germany.

In October 1941, at the age of thirty-nine, Dr. Büeler decided to join the Waffen-SS. He underwent basic training at Sennheim. In April 1942, he was posted to the SS-Hauptamt in Berlin where he took up an administrative post in the Waffen-SS library department under Dr. Franz Riedweg. In April 1943, he was awarded the KVK II. In September 1943, Büeler attended the SS-Junkerschule at Bad Tölz and graduated with the rank of Untersturmführer in April 1944 whereupon he was returned to Sennheim.

The *Spiess* of the 2nd Company was SS-Oscha. Johann Neubauer, born on 31 December 1918 in Wels, Austria.[117]

In May 1944, André Doutart of the RNP enlisted in the Waffen-SS. He was born on 13 June 1923 in Geneva, but of French nationality. This connoisseur of jazz enlisted out of hatred for Communism, hatred born of Stalin's ban on jazz music and purge of musicians, and of the death of musician Parnakh in the Gulag. He arrived at Sennheim on 3rd June 1944 and was assigned to the 1st Company.

## The Story of Marc Sainteuil

Also in May 1944, up and coming Parisian actor Marc Sainteuil volunteered for the Waffen-SS and was accepted. His decision was all the more remarkable because he was a *résistant* for the first two and a half years of the occupation, explaining that he had wanted to erase the shameful defeat.[118] But the geopolitical situation in 1944 was quite different to that at the end of 1940. He explained:

> It was no longer a matter of a Germanic Greater Reich dominating the whole of Europe. Germany needed the help of the countries of Western Europe no longer for a total victory enabling it to dictate its terms but to obtain, if the Anglo-American landing failed, a separate peace with the USA and England. This was not a utopia. Churchill was all too aware of the Soviet danger and wanted a landing in Greece in such a way to cut off the advance of the Soviet armies. Of course such a peace was only possible with the eviction of Hitler.
>
> Also, we were going more and more inexorably towards a disenchanted, senseless, [and] material world, a world without sorrow and a world without joy. Both my father and I were moral and spiritual 'human animals' who believed that it was the quality of the 'personal being' that counted. We were not politically minded.[119]

---

117  SS-Oscha. Johann Neubauer should not be confused with the SS-Ustuf. of the same surname who commanded the transport of the 1st Battalion of the French SS-Sturmbrigade in Galicia.

118  Curiously, during his time as a *résistant*, Sainteuil never heard of the word *résistant* or De Gaulle.

119  In late 1936, at the age of sixteen, Marc Sainteuil had joined the PPF, which he saw as both a national and popular movement. Disappointed by the party's obvious lack of ideals and vision of the future, he resigned months later. Never again would he flirt with a political party.

The SS was the only means in existence through which I could start to realise my desire: to make the world enchanted and enchanting again. I wanted to pass in the road Egyptian, Greek, Khmer, Roman or Gothic statues. I wanted to be sitting in the Metro beside a Giotto, a Vermeer. I wanted to pay my taxes to an important person like Eschyle or Shakespeare. I was born immortal. I 'joined' the war so that everybody would know it. All this was for me simple and realistic.

I enlisted against two materialisms: the collectivism of Marxism and the capitalism of the Anglo-Americans.

Also he had become alarmed by the Gaullist government of Algiers behaving like the governments of the Third Republic that had led France to defeat in 1940.

There were a number of other reasons to help explain his decision to enlist. First, he had fond childhood memories of Germany. In 1936, his father, a prominent figure in the *Comité France-Allemagne* founded by former combatants of the 14-18 war in the spirit of reconciliation, took him to the Olympic Games held in Berlin as a present for his unexpected exam success.[120] The Games were a great success for Germany and he never forgot the spirit of youth of the Germans. Also, like many, he respected Hitler for the way he had revived his people between 1933 and 1939. Then the occupation followed. The discipline and bearing of the occupying German troops greatly impressed him. But that was in the past and so were the victories of 1940-41. Germany could no longer win the war by itself. He reasoned that Napoleon had employed the services of foreign volunteers. He wished to help and help in the ranks of the Waffen-SS, whom he described as *les forces vives* and viewed as an 'embryo of Europe'. The LVF, which he described as a 'patriotic French movement of struggle against Marxist communism', was not for him because he also wished to fight the 'supreme capitalism represented by the USA'.

Secondly, prominent authors and journalists such as Jacques Chardonne, Henry de Montheriant and Robert Brasillach, and sculptor Aristide Mailloi, regarded by Sainteuil as the greatest sculptor of the twentieth century, had committed to collaboration. Indeed, cultural life had continued to flourish under the occupation.[121]

Lastly, the possibility of victory was slim when Sainteuil enlisted in May 1944. And yet this did not dissuade him from enlisting. In fact, he felt that he should enlist regardless of the consequences, even if it meant defeat or losing his life. *Attentisme* was not for him.

Parents and friends alike were surprised by his decision. His mother cried. His father, who did not share his son's convictions, said to him: "If you believe that it is your duty, do it. I only ask that you go and see Benoist-Mechin." Benoist-Mechin was a Vichy Secretary of State and a good family friend. Thus, he went to see Benoist-Mechin who said to him: "Don't leave. What are the reasons? I cannot tell you." He left, thinking to himself: another one playing the *double-jeu*. This he described as lamentable.

---

120  After the *coup de Prague* in 1938, his father, concerned that German foreign policy had become aggressive and a threat to France, shelved *Le Comité*. Moreover, his father was hostile to the anti-Christain character of National Socialism.

121  For example, the major philosphical work *L'Etre et le Néant* by Jean-Paul Sartre was published in 1943. The collaboration in the arts is the subject of many books, but not this one. Nevertheless, the enlistment of Frenchmen like Sainteuil should be placed and perhaps best understood within the context of this rich and intense cultural life.

He was sent to Sennheim. On or around 20 June 1944, he learnt of the landings in Normandy. He immediately circulated among his fellow French volunteers a petition to fight on the Normandy front with the proviso that under no circumstances were they to be engaged against French troops. 70 to 75 of the 200 French volunteers present at Sennheim at that time signed the petition. However, the others thought he was going too far or had enlisted to fight solely the Soviet Union and Communism. Nothing came of his petition or so he thought.

The wearing of the *feldgrau* posed him no problems. He was a soldier and as such was expected to wear a uniform. And as a soldier he had to obey his commanders. Thus, the oath he swore to Hitler, a direct link between the soldier and the supreme commander, only strengthened this obligation. Be that as it may, he and his comrades did not hero-worship the Führer. They believed that the 'Ein Volk, Ein Reich, Ein Führer' of 1933-42 was well in the past. Moreover, the oath did not give them the feeling of having entered a kind of Hitlerian monastic order.

At the end of his training at Sennheim, instead of leaving with his comrades, he was assigned to the political department and made an instructor. This was a posting he did not want. Sent to Neweklau for NCO training, he was promoted to the rank of Unterscharführer, but the racism of the political training he found crass and refused to teach. He asked to be transferred to the Special Forces. He would serve with Skorzeny.

Roger Godard, a free worker at Frankfurt am Main, signed up for the Waffen-SS on 15 May 1944 after being threatened with internment in a camp. Besides he was hungry and wanted to get back to his beloved France. Sent to Sennheim, he escaped but was captured in the Vosges.

French volunteers continued to arrive and be trained at Sennheim until its closure on 28 November 1944. At the end of May 1944, days before the *embarquement* in Normandy, twenty-year-old Parisian student Jean-Jacques Pillet volunteered for the Waffen-SS.[122] His parents had told him to wait and do nothing, but he could not sit by and see Germany continue to suffer in isolation without showing his solidarity. For his ideals were those of Germany. He believed that Germany would, if victorious, create a new Europe. And if Germany was defeated then he could console himself with his show of solidarity. Rejecting the French spirit of political 'clanism', he wanted to enlist in an exclusively German movement rather than the LVF. As for regrets, he had none, but remained convinced to his dying day that he would have regretted making a decision not to enlist.

On his arrival at Sennheim, Pillet was sent on to the village of Weiler, some ten kilometres from the main camp, where he was quartered in a former factory. Two or three days followed of administrative formalities, which also, and curiously, saw the first attempts to desert, but the cadres were alert to this and prevented them, sometimes at gun point.

Pillet was assigned to the 2nd Company of Ustuf. Büeler and moved to a villa. He counted himself lucky when one night the empty villa across the river was bombed from the air and totally destroyed. And yet the villa occupied by him and two companies of French Waffen-SS volunteers was not touched. It seemed to him that the bombers had been fed the wrong intelligence.

Pillet spent six weeks at Weiler, which was time enough to complete his basic training. The majority of his instructors were Flemish, but there was also a Volksdeutsche from Romania and a German who had lost an arm in combat. He recalls of one particular march:

122  Jean-Jacquet Pillet was born on 8 September 1924 in Saint-Mandé.

My company, on manoeuvre in the field, was granted a rest period in the shade of cherry trees. Hungry, the men could not resist the bountiful fruit and gorged themselves. Soon after, back on their way, they started to fall out with stomach pains. The cherries which had begun to ferment were their undoing. In this way, the whole company was incapacitated!

Jacques Evrard, born on 7 May 1924 in Paris, volunteered for the Waffen-SS in June 1944 shortly after the Allied landings in Normandy. He was a militant of the PPF. By volunteering for the Waffen-SS, he was seeing his political commitment through to the end. He left for Sennheim on 27 June 1944 where he was assigned to the 2nd Company of Ustuf. Büeler and sent to Weiler. The Company was made up of some 80 to 100 Frenchmen, including an important group of *Miliciens* from Limoges, as well as Dutch and Flemings.

At the start of August, the training companies quartered at Weiler were moved to Sennheim. Pillet and Evrard were assigned to an Unterführerlehrgang which also received political and racial education delivered by Büeler and Kopp in a former chapel. Pillet recalls that they had little to learn because 'they were convinced!' Evrard had much more to say on the subject:[123]

The so-called political education focused on the history of the NSDAP and the SS; the evocation of the European idea and the wrongdoings of Communism. We had to write an essay on the reasons for our enlistment. The military situation was rarely mentioned, except for big events (like the capture of Paris). Besides, to tell you the truth, we didn't care… The racial education, for its part, evoked the great human races, the Jews (but without excess)… They also emphasised eugencis and the dangers of race mixing.

On 8 September 1944, Pillet and a 20 to 30 strong group of men went in search of *résistants* in the neighbourhood of Sennheim. One French Waffen-SS volunteer was hit in the head by a bullet.

In late September, six 'French training companies', numbering over one thousand men, were sent to the newly formed Franz. SS-Grenadier Ausbildungs-und Ersatz bataillon at Greifenberg in Pomerania, north-west Poland.[124] While en route by train to Greifenberg, Pillet witnessed one French Waffen-SS volunteer commit murder. At one stop, a French POW insulted a group of Waffen-SS volunteers. One of them was so enraged that he shot the French POW dead.[125]

At Greifenberg, Pillet was assigned to the Stammkompanie [depot company] of the Franz. SS-Grenadier Ausbildungs-und Ersatz-bataillon. In this way, he found himself on administrative duties with three or four others recording the new arrivals. He went on to attend a *Lehrgang* run at Greifenberg after which he was promoted to Sturmmann.

123  Mouine, *Cernay 40-45*, pp.306-307.
124  Mabire, *La Brigade Frankreich*, p.442.
125  After the war, the French *gendarmerie* investigated this murder. The outcome of its inquiry is not known to the author.

# 4

## The Sturmbrigade

---

### Evolution of the French unit of the Waffen-SS

The French unit of the Waffen-SS underwent a series of title and number changes.

On 16 September 1943, on the Führer's orders, the SS-FHA called for the establishment of the Französisches SS-Freiw. Grenadier Regiment [French SS Volunteer Grenadier Regiment].[1] Two days later, on 18 September 1943, the SS-FHA noted: 'The Führer has ordered the formation of a French SS volunteer grenadier regiment. The planned formation of a French SS volunteer division has been set aside for the time being'.[2]

This French SS Volunteer Grenadier Regiment was to have a structure of two battalions, each with four companies. In addition, and notably, the regiment had two infantry gun companies and two anti-tank gun companies.[3] The Stabskompanie [Headquarters Company] was to consist of the following:

| | |
|---|---|
| Nachrichtenzug | [Signals Platoon] |
| Pionierzug | [Engineer Platoon] |
| Reiter-(Aufklärungs-)Zug | [Horse-mounted Reconnaissance Platoon] |

By SS-FHA order of 22 October 1943,[4] which numbered all Waffen-SS formations and infantry regiments into a numerical sequence according to their chronological dates of formation, the French Regiment became the 8. Franz. SS-Freiw. Gren. Rgt.[5] Curiously, the order lists the

---

1   Lefèvre, *Axe & Alliés* hors série No 1, p.24.
2   SS-FHA, Amt II Org.Abt. Ia/II Tgb. Nr. 1297/43 g.Kdos, 18.9.43.
3   See Chevallet & Martin, *Pour la France, pour l'Europe*, p.190, and Yerger Mark, *Waffen-SS commanders, Krüger to Zimmermann* (Atglen: Schiffer, 1999, p.168. The former is dated October 1943, the latter is undated. Normally, each infantry regiment comprised one infantry gun company and one anti-tank company.
4   SS-FHA Amt II Org.Abt. Ia/II Tgb. Nr. 1574/43 g.Kdos, 22.10.43, Anlage 3: III. Brigaden und Sturmbrigaden.
5   However, Angolia John, *Cloth Insignia of the SS* (San Jose: Bender publishing, 1983, 2nd printing), p.491, shows the same designation, but without the number.

136

French Regiment under 'Brigaden und Sturmbrigaden'. This suggests that the French Regiment, although it still carried the designation of a regiment, had Brigade status.

On 9 November 1943, SS-Ostubaf. Hans-Joachim Woith took command of the French Regiment, which, curiously, appears in official documentation as the Franz.SS-Freiw.Gr.Rgt.7.

Shortly after, on 12 November 1943, the SS-FHA again ordered the renumbering of the Waffen-SS infantry regiments and the Franz. SS-Freiw. Rgt became the Franz. SS-Freiw. Rgt 57.[6] Notably, this time the French Regiment appeared under 'Regimenter'.

On 22 January 1944, the SS-FHA ordered that all non-German infantry regiments of the Waffen-SS (SS-Freiw.-Gren.Rgter) should have nationality as well as a progressive numeration within that nationality added parenthetically to their titles. In this way, the French Regiment became the Franz. SS-Freiw.Rgt.57 (französisch Nr.1).[7]

On 1 February 1944, SS-Ostubaf. Hans-Joachim Woith left his post to become the commander of SS-Pz.Gren.Rgt.19 of the 9. SS-Panzer-Division 'Hohenstaufen'.[8]

In March 1944, the French volunteers were ordered to form a motorised heavy artillery regiment with the title and number of Schw.Franz.SS-Freiw.Artillerie Rgt.(mot.) 500.

The artillery regiment was to be organised as follows and with such field post numbers:

| | |
|---|---|
| Headquarters and Headquarters Battery | Nr. 11 003 |
| I. schw. Abt. (Heavy Battery) | Nr. 13 847 |
| II. schw. Abt. (Heavy Battery) | Nr. 12 175 |
| III. schw. Abt. (Heavy Battery) | Nr. 14 049 |
| Artilleriekolonne (Artillery Column) | Nr. 13 847 |

In April 1944, an Observation Battery, field-post number 06 386, was added to the regiment.

For artillery training, the newly promoted French officers were dispatched to SS-Artillerieschule II Beneschau, one of the many training schools located within Truppenübungsplatz Beneschau, south of Prague.

In mid-March, at the conclusion of their training at Posen-Treskau, the French NCO cadets were sent to artillery school Beneschau.[9]

The French officers and NCOs alike had no enthusiasm for the artillery training. It was with sadness that the NCOs replaced their white epaulettes of the Infantry for the vermilion-piped epaulettes of the Artillery. In protest, many NCOs went sick or went down with the strangest of medical complaints. This seriously disrupted the training and came as a great surprise to the instructors.

The officers, for their part, protested in a manner more befitting their rank. Cance wrote to Darnand, Pleyber wrote to Doriot and the young Oberjunken wrote direct to RF-SS Himmler himself. Gamory-Dubourdeau went off to Berlin intent on 'having it out man to man' with Ogruf. Berger.[10]

---

6    SS-FHA Amt II Org.Abt. Ia/II Tgb. Nr. II/9542/43 geh, 12.11.43, Anlage 4: III. Regimenter.
7    SS-FHA, Amt II, Org.Abt.Ia/II, Tgb.Nr. 166/44 g.Kdos of 22.1.1944.
8    Woith was subsequently killed in action on 30 June 1944.
9    Curiously, Bayle, one such French NCO, does not speak of meeting the officers at Beneschau.
10   Mabire, *La Brigade Frankreich*, p.160.

Equipment, straight out of the factory, was supplied to the forming French Artillery Regiment: semi-tracked lorries, and 105mm and 155mm guns.

Several days after their arrival at Beneschau, the French officers were joined by Ostuf. Pierre Michel. He too had acquired his rank at SS Junkerschule Tölz, but in a platoon of Germanic officer cadets. Regarded as a National Socialist fanatic, he was welcomed with some reservation. Born on 15 February 1919 in Paris,[11] Michel, a student engineer, entered the *École spéciale militaire de Saint-Cyr* in 1938. On 2 September 1939, he was commissioned as a *Sous-lieutenant d'active* and posted to the *503e régiment de chars de combat* (503e RCC), which was disbanded soon after, and was transferred to the *3e Compagnie* of the *46e Bataillon de chars de combat* (46e BCC). Wounded on 30 May 1940 and captured, he managed to escape. He was awarded the *Croix de guerre*.

After a stint with the Armistice Army, Michel joined the LVF, becoming the company commander of the 2nd Company. In late August 1942, he resigned from the LVF, whereupon he joined the NSKK. On 5 July 1943, after some five months with the NSKK, he volunteered for the Waffen-SS, bringing along with him from the NSKK several like-minded illuminate and was sent to SS-Ausbildungslager Schotten.

Among the first Frenchmen to arrive at Sennheim on 2 August 1943, Michel attended the officer cadets' course run from 1st September to 17 October 1943. Assigned to SS Ausbildungs-und Ersatz-Battalion 11 at Graz on 17 October 1943, he was sent to SS Junkerschule Tölz on 20 October, attending the *3. Lehrgang für germanische Offiziere*, which ran to March 1944. He graduated with the rank of Obersturmführer.

Even with the arrival of Michel the French Sturmbrigade of the Waffen-SS remained desperately short of officers. Stubaf. Gamory-Dubourdeau asked the PPF to send urgently officers or *aspirants*, preferring those who had received their rank before the war.[12] The PPF was his party.

In March 1944, officer candidates Martres, Oschner and Roy were dispatched to SS-Pionier-Schule Hradischko while James Royer, Jacques Sarrailhé, Jean-Marie Stehli and Georges Wagner were sent for Infantry Gun training with SS-IG. Ausb.u.Ers.Btl. 1, Breslau-Lissa.[13]

## The French Sturmbrigade

In late March 1944, perhaps as a result of the protests, the French volunteers were formed into the Französische-SS-Freiwilligen-Sturmbrigade [French SS Volunteer Assault Brigade][14] abbreviated to the Franz.SS-Freiw.- Sturm-Brig. with the proposed following structure:

11   Potsdam archives. However, according to Mabire, *La Brigade Frankreich*, p.161, Pierre Michel retained a great passion for his pagan homeland of Brittany.
12   Undated report, see X.C.G. /1/35302, CARAN.
13   *SS*-Infanteriegeschütz-Ausbildungs und Ersatz Bataillon 1 [Infantry Gun Training and Replacement Battalion 1].
14   SS-FHA Amt II, Org.Abt.Ia/II Tgb.Nr. II/4611/44 geh, stamped 23 March 1944, The French Sturmbrigade has appeared with a variety of designations, though; Mounie, *Cernay 40-45*, Franz. SS-Sturmbrigade Nr. 8; Lambert, *Les Français sous le casque allemand* and Angolia, *Cloth Insignia Of The Waffen-SS*, p.491, 8. Franz. SS-Freiwilligen Sturmbrigade; Mabire, SS-Sturmbrigade Nr. 7 Frankreich; and Saint-Loup, SS-Sturmbrigade Nr. 7. In response to those titles carrying number 7, in September 1944, number 7 was officially allocated to the Dutch Brigade 'Landstorm Nederland'. Therefore, its use

| 1 Stb.u.Stbs.Kp.Panz.Gren. Btls. | [Headquarters Staff and Company] |
|---|---|
| 4 Panz.Gren.Kp. | [Panzergrenadier Company] |
| 1 schw.Pan.Jäg.Kp. | [Heavy Anti-Tank Company] |
| 1 Fla.Kp. | [FLAK Company] |
| 1 Krad-Schütz.Zg. | [Motorcycle Platoon] |
| 1 Erk.Zg. | [Reconnaissance Platoon] |

The PAK Company was to be equipped with twelve guns and the FLAK Company with nine 3.7cm light anti-aircraft guns. The French Sturmbrigade was to be furnished with eighteen German liaison and headquarters staff to oversee its formation and later to 'ensure the perfect transmission and execution of commands' when deployed. Headed by SS-Hstuf. Kostenbader, the staff included a San.Offz [Medical Officer], a Führer.d.Verw [Administrator Officer] and three translators.

Told that they were leaving to form a Sturmbrigade instead, the NCOs literally jumped with joy. The 'sick' miraculously recovered. They had been SS-Kanonier for some three weeks. The NCOs went on to attend Panzer as well as Engineer training. In this way, they became 'ultra-trained'.[15]

The French SS-Sturmbrigade was now assembled in the village of Networschitz, several kilometres from Beneschau. More than 1,000 men arrived from SS-Ausbildungslager Sennheim.

To perform administrative duties, French-speaking 'German' personnel, many of whom were Alsatians or natives of Lorraine, were transferred to the forming French SS-Sturmbrigade. For the most part, they were furious about the posting, but all would knuckle down to their duties.

By early April 1944, five companies had been formed with such a command:

| 1st Company (infantry) | Maudhuit |
|---|---|
| 2nd Company (infantry) | Artus |
| 3rd Company (infantry) | Fenet |
| 4th Company (heavy) | Michel |
| 5th Company (PAK) | Pleyber |

The infantry companies had more than 200 men each.

Maudhuit was quickly replaced by Ostuf. de Tissot at the head of the 1st Company. Later on, Ustuf. Pignard-Berthet was detached from the 2nd Company and assigned to the 1st Company

by the French unit should be regarded with great suspicion. Moreover, the number 7 does not appear in the SS-Soldbuch or on the identity disc of French SS volunteers. And yet certificates for medals won in Galicia show the use of number 7 (see Bayle, *De Marseille à Novossibirsk*, p.100), but are they post war reproductions? Furthermore, as far as many veterans were concerned, the French SS-Sturmbrigade never carried the official number of 7. Nevertheless, the number 8 also cannot be found in the SS-Soldbuch or on the identity disc of French SS volunteers. Also see footnote 28.

Also, some sources name the Sturmbrigade 'Frankreich' (the German word for France). In response to this, at no time was the French Sturmbrigade ever officially called 'Frankreich' or even 'Brigade Frankreich'. However, 'Brigade Frankreich' was employed because many French SS volunteers could not report the full unit name in German! Even so the French SS volunteers often contented themselves with just saying 'Sturmbrigade'.

15    Bayle, *De Marseille à Novossibirsk*, p.79.

with orders to take over the supervision of the training. Ustuf. Brocard was assigned to the 5th Company.[16]

Officers and NCOs were also appointed to other positions of command in the various support and heavy units. Croisile went to the Headquarters services.

Jean del Missier was assigned to the 2nd Platoon of the 2nd Company. Jean Tramet, who was a former member of the LVF, was assigned to the 5th Company.[17]

To supervise the continued training, Kostenbader placed a young German officer in each company. Some had combat experience. After some initial suspicion and friction between the French company commanders and their German supervisors, things were quickly smoothed out and they jointly set about the business of training.

As in many other non-German Freiwilligen Waffen-SS units, German NCOs were also brought in to various posts for their stabilising influence, but their number is unknown. Karl Rapp, a former member of the premier 'Leibstandarte SS Adolf Hitler' Division, served as *Spiess* [company sergeant major] in the 5th Company.

Stubaf. Gamory-Dubourdeau was appointed to command the French Sturmbrigade. Although he was the most senior and the highest-ranking former French Army officer to volunteer for the Waffen-SS, his selection at the grand age of fifty-eight does surprise, even if he did attend and pass out from Bad Tölz. Perhaps one explanation for his selection is that the Waffen-SS authorities, who, undoubtedly, were well aware of his political fidelity, wished to play him off against the large number of officers from the *Milice*.

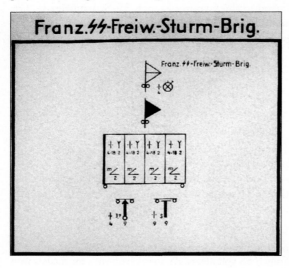

Proposed structure for the French Sturmbrigade

As of May 1944, the structure proposed for the Franz.SS-Freiw.- Sturm-Brig. consisted of a single battalion.[18] Nevertheless, two battalions were formed and issued field post numbers:

16   Documentation from Neweklau dated 26 May 1944.
17   Jean Tramet would later serve with the FLAK Company of 'Charlemagne'.
18   NARA Records Group 242, Publication T78, roll 409.

| Stab I u. 1.-4. Kompanie | Nr. 41 592 |
|---|---|
| Stab II u 5.-8. Kompanie | Nr. 35 411 |

The Sturmbrigade also fielded a small Feldgendarmerie unit. Oberscharführer Georges Loistron and Oberscharführer Alfred Pieyre de Mandiargues were assigned to the unit. Loistron was ex-LVF and had served with the rank of *caporal* in the 2nd Company during the winter of 1941 and been demobilised in 1942, whereas Alfred Pieyre de Mandiargues was a former member of the *Franc-Garde bénévole* of Toulouse, like his younger brother Jacques who also volunteered for the Waffen-SS and served with the Sturmbrigade.[19] Oscha. Loistron served as the Spiess of the unit and was thoroughly detested. Command of the 1st Battalion went to Hstuf. Cance.[20]

## FLAK Company of the Sturmbrigade

On 1 April 1944, the 3rd Company left Sennheim to join the SS-Sturmbrigade. After journeying for three days, it arrived at Neweklau. The 3rd Company came with the tag of 'a sort of disciplinary unit'. This was not unfounded. In its ranks were a number of 'hotheads' whose exploits while on leave in France that Christmas and New Year had not gone unpunished. Nevertheless, this company, for all its ills, was well trained. It became the 6th Company of the Sturmbrigade.[21]

After some permutations, the 6th Company was designated the FLAK Company of the French SS-Sturmbrigade. German instructor SS-Ustuf. Jauss then asked Ostuf. Maudhuit to take command of this unit, and to organise its recruitment and training. In a matter of days, he set up the FLAK Company. And although some volunteers left to join the companies formed before their arrival, others did their utmost to fill the posts made vacant. In this way, the FLAK Company realised its full 'complement' of 1 officer, 36 NCOs, and 111 men, for a total of 148 soldiers.

After completing his basic training at Sennheim, Bernard Triqueneaux, who had joined the Waffen-SS to secure the release of his younger brother, was assigned to the FLAK Company as a secretary.

Also on the books of the FLAK Company were former French Army officers Crespin, Croisile, Roy, and de Lareinty-Tholozan.[22] All held the rank of Oberscharführer and all were waiting to take up their appointment. Nevertheless, the rank and file of the FLAK Company never saw them.

---

19   Alfred Pieyre de Mandiargues was born on 3 June 1920 in Paris and Jacques on 16 March 1924 in Paris.
20   It is not known when Cance assumed command of the 1st Battalion. However, SS-Gruppenführer Oberg wrote in a letter to the Reichsführer-SS of 25 May 1944 that Cance commanded the '1. Franz. Waffen-SS-Batl.' (see BDS Paris FS Nr. 47947 25.5.44).
21   Soulat, *Historique de la Division Charlemagne*, p.26.
22   Born on 20 December 1895 into one of France's oldest noble families, Foulques de Lareinty-Tholozan had served in the First World War during which he made a name for himself, becoming a Russian prince! See Bouysse, *Encyclopédie de l'ordre nouveau: Français sous l'uniforme allemande partie II: sous-officiers & hommes du rang de la Waffen-SS*. He volunteered for the Waffen-SS at the end of June 1943 and left in April 1944. Arrested when liberation came, he was brought before the courts, found guilty and executed at Narbonne on 6 September 1944.

Once formed, the FLAK Company began its training, but its personnel, 'as a direct consequence of the defeat of 1940', did not wish to serve under former French Army officers.[23] However, Maudhuit persevered and did his best, but on 22 or 23 April 1944 he was relieved of command and replaced by Führerbewerber Jean Guignot, a former highly decorated French Foreign Legion *Capitaine*, who had attended Saint-Cyr between 1930 and 1932.[24]

To give Guignot support, the young, dynamic Oberjunker Fayard was assigned to the company and appointed the commander of the 1st Platoon.

On 25 April 1944, the FLAK Company set out by civilian trains to Munich to attend a training course with the SS-Flak.Ausb.u.Ers.Regt. [SS-Flak Training and Replacement Regiment]. Arriving three days later on 28 April, the FLAK Company moved into barracks Freimann on Ingolstaderstrasse, which would be its home for the next three months.

Although the Germans endeavoured to screen accurately each volunteer some of dubious loyalty and morality entered the ranks of the Sturmbrigade. While at Networschitz the Sturmbrigade received the criminal records of its recruits. All those who had received *condamnations infamantes* were expelled.

The Sturmbrigade also shed itself of those guilty of theft. In three months, some twenty volunteers, for the most part seasoned ex-criminals, were sent without a second thought to concentration camps. Among them was a common law criminal who, whilst on leave in France, went back to his old ways and was responsible for several robberies from Jews.

Fenet came to suspect that a saboteur was disrupting his company. He was right. The saboteur was quickly exposed and arrested. The evidence against him was overwhelming: foolishly, he had kept a sort of diary of his acts of subversion. Fenet decided to have him sent to Prague for court martial. Until such time as he could be moved, he was kept under lock and key in a hut best described as ramshackle. The prisoner soon made his escape, but the guard from the same company by the name of Maurette calmly shouldered his rifle and shot him dead. Headquarters immediately promoted Maurette to the rank of Sturmmann! This precedent worried Fenet. Such was his concern that he had a message relayed to all his men that they were not to start taking pot shots at prisoners to gain promotion to Sturmmann!

To supplement their meager rations at Networschitz the French volunteers took to hunting game. One time Christian Martres was happily tucking into what he thought was rabbit only to discover that it was in fact fox. The liver, which had proved hard, had given away the animal's true identity.

In May, following the arrival of new volunteers who would form the 2nd Battalion, Networschitz became overcrowded and the 1st Battalion was moved to Neweklau, some 10kms away. Besides, the wretched conditions at Networschitz were paralysing the training and seriously affecting morale. The accommodation at Neweklau was considered better.

There was no respite at Neweklau, training continued day and night. Continuous drill. Continuous inspections. Route marches. Platoon maneuvers. Then company maneuvers. Then battalion maneuvers. And all were conducted with live ammunition. As a result some volunteers were injured and evacuated to hospitals in Prague, where they were treated by French nurses, also volunteers for the Waffen-SS.

23    See Gaulois, article *La SS-Französische Flakbatterie*.
24    Jean Guignot was born on 20 September 1901 in Belfort.

Ostuf. Fenet came close to death in a 'live' exercise when his command post in a farmhouse was attacked by a *corps franc* led by Oberjunker Kreis. A bullet actually went straight through the death's head on his cap!

Also, one beautiful, quiet Sunday a French SS volunteer writing to his family was accidentally killed by another cleaning his weapon nearby. His death was lamented.

Maurice Manfredi was wounded during the training at Neweklau. In 1942, this nineteen-year-old Marseillais volunteered for the paramilitary OT-SK (Organisation Todt-Schutzkommando) and served in Guernsey and Jersey. In September 1943, he volunteered for the Waffen-SS and was accepted after completing his basic training at Sennheim.[25]

Pignard-Berthet acquired the nickname of 'Tito', the partisan leader; following a night exercise with a *demi-compagnie* he had to set traps, in the manner of partisans, to break up the march of the battalion. Twice, acting on his own initiative, he brilliantly ambushed the units on the move whilst maintaining an elastic defence of a village in which his men had taken refuge.

As the weight of the volunteers dropped their morale heightened. The timely arrival of the French SS-Sturmbrigade at Neweklau had also contributed to the considerable rise in morale. And when Fenet learnt that a volunteer by the name of Vallebout, serving in the Heavy Platoon, had lied about his age to gain enlistment he offered him the opportunity to return home. Without hesitation the volunteer chose to remain with his comrades!

In May 1944, a number of French and Walloon officer candidates entered SS-Panzergrenadierschule Kienschlag in Bohemia-Moravia to attend the 1. Kreigs-Waffen-Junkerlehrgang.[26] The course would last until 9 September 1944. One such officer candidate was Christain Martres, a graduate of the NCO school at Posen-Treskau.

The platoon leader of the French officer candidates was SS-Ustuf. Kleindienst, who had once served with Waffen-SS Division 'Leibstandarte Adolf Hitler'. Martres remembers him as a playboy; although Kleindienst would often go into Prague late at night, he was always the first to report for duty the following morning!

On 22 May 1944, SS-Ostuf. Robert Jauss was appointed as the Chef der Wallonisch-französischen Inspektion [Head of the Walloon-French Inspection] of Lehrgruppe [Training Group] IV at Kienschlag. Jauss said that his 'transfer to Kienschalg was based on his French language skills' and it was here that he caught the attention of Gamory-Dubourdeau.[27]

In early June 1944, Martres interrupted his officer training to return home.[28] His parents, innocent civilians, had been killed on 27 April 1944, victims of an English bomber downed by FLAK. Thanks to Kleindienst, Martres, who only had a fatigue uniform, went home in a complete service uniform. His donning of the *feldgrau* for the first time left him unmoved except for, perhaps, a touch of pride in the wearing of the 'runes'.

At the end of the course the following Frenchmen graduated: Pierre Albert, Jean Ambroise, Aimé Berthaud, Jean Brazier, Philippe Colnion, Guy Counil, Pierre Crespin, Roger Erdozain, Serge Krotoff, Robert Lefèvre, Christian Martres, Claude Ochsner, Robert Roy, James

---

25   Manfredi was subsequently listed as missing-in-action with 'Charlemagne' in Pomerania, 1945.

26   The number of officer cadets who started this course at SS-Panzergrenadierschule Kienschlag is not known, but seventeen graduated, including Martres. Curiously, Lefèvre dates the start of the course to 30 June 1944, *Axe & Alliés* hors série no 1, p.31.

27   BAK, Z42 VI/1090, Spruchkammerakte Jauss, Vernehmung am 28.05.1947.

28   Strangely enough, Martres arrived in Paris on 6 June 1944.

Royer, Jacques Sarrailhé, Jean-Marie Stehli and Georges Wagner. Most received the rank of Oberjunker. Notable exceptions were Crespin, Krotoff and Roy who were promoted to Obersturmführer, and Lefèvre, Ochsner and Wagner who were promoted to Standartenjunker. Roy was recommended to command an IG.-Kr [Infantry Gun Company].[29]

Meanwhile, back in France, at 0930 hours on 13 June 1944, Otto Abetz, the German ambassador to Occupied France, met with Doriot, Déat, Bucard, Knipping (Darnand's *délégué du Maintien de l'Ordre en zone Nord*), de Brinon (the *président du Comité de la LVF*) and Marion (the *président des Amis de la Waffen-SS*). The French side took the lead, insisting that since the invasion 'all members of the LVF and the Waffen-SS wish to fight, not in Russia, far from their homeland, but on French soil, to defend their homeland against the internal and foreign enemy'.[30] Abetz supported this request, noting that the French volunteers would probably fight with more zeal 'for their very existence against their mortal enemies, the gaullists, and against their Anglo-American allies'. However, support was not forthcoming from the military authorities and all such plans were soon abandoned.[31]

As of 30 June 1944 the Sturmbrigade had a total troop strength of 1,688 (30 officers, 44 NCOs and 1,614 men). This figure included those French volunteers at Neweklau, Networschitz and Munich, but not those undergoing training at Sennheim or at any other training establishment.[32] Indeed, by the end of January 1944, two sources agree that 2,480 Frenchmen had enrolled in the Waffen-SS[33] and, by that August, the figure had increased to 3,000.[34] Notably, the Sturmbrigade still remained desperately short of officers and NCOs despite the best recruitment efforts of the SS-Hauptamt.

29    Curiously, according to official documentation dated 7 September 1944, most of the graduates were returned to the 8. Frz.SS-Frw. Sturmbrigade, which no longer existed as such.
30    Telegram of 13 June 1944 from Abetz to Ribbentrop, see Brunet Jean-Paul, *Jacques Doriot* (Paris: Balland, 1986). And yet, according to Delperrié de Bayac, *Histoire de la Milice*, pp.381-383, Abetz took the lead, calling on all the *groupements nationaux* to agree to fight in Normandy. Continuing, Abetz 'saw in the units that could be formed in this way a start point of a future Franco-German military alliance'. Then, and importantly, it was Abetz who called for the return of the LVF and for the 'immediate return of the 'Sturmbrigade des Waffen SS'.
31    Delperrié de Bayac, *Histoire de la Milice*, p.381-383. And yet, according to Mabire, *La Brigade Frankreich*, pp.183-184, at the end of June 1944, the French officers learnt that the Sturmbrigade was to be sent to France and employed against the maquis. Incensed, Stubaf. Gamory-Dubourdeau gave them his word that they would be employed as soldiers and not 'cops', and on the Eastern Front and nowhere else. He kept his word; he created such a fuss at the SS-Hauptamt [SS Main office] that the order was revoked.
32    Curiously, according to Michaelis, Rolf, *French units in the Waffen-SS* (Atglen: Schiffer Military History, 2016), p.23, 'fifty-five French officers and NCOs, most from the militia, were recruited for training or retraining according to German regulations at the newly established SS Grenadier School in Sophienwalde'. Grenadierschule der SS Sophienwalde was established in June 1944, but no other source confirms that French officers and NCOs were sent to Sophienwalde at or around that time.
33    See Ory, *Les Collaborateurs*, p.266, and Neulen, *An Deutscher Seite*, p.110. Curiously, according to Burrin, *La France à l'heure allemande, 1940-1944*, by January 1944, some 6,000 Frenchmen had volunteered for the Waffen-SS, of which one half had been accepted.
34    Saint-Loup, *Les Hérétiques*, p.31, and although this figure is not dated, the engagement of the 1st Battalion of the French SS-Sturmbrigade before Sanok in August 1944 is talked about in the very same breath. Furthermore, Littlejohn repeats the figure of 3,000 (*Foreign Legions of the Third Reich vol. 1*, p.159).

Introduced for wear in July 1944 was the official SS 'tricolore' sleeve shield.[35] This sleeve shield differed noticeably from its official LVF counterpart with curved sides and the word 'FRANCE' at the top. However, privately made insignia was worn prior to its official introduction and it is considered extremely likely that this practice continued. According to regulations from the SS-FHA, the national sleeve shield was to be worn on the left sleeve directly under the SS sleeve eagle. However, most wore the shield on the forearm. Strangely enough, when the first French sleeve shields (unquestionably the official SS pattern versions) were received it was the German instructors who were first to sport them, whereas the Alsatian NCOs held out for as long as possible.[36]

Discipline remained harsh. During a sweep for enemy paratroopers, Rottenführer Simon, a platoon commander in the 2nd Company who had attended NCO school Posen-Treskau, found himself before a charging doe. He did not hesitate to shoot it down. As punishment he had his command taken from him and was transferred to the 2nd Battalion.

On that same sweep, men from the 4th Company went hunting even though it was prohibited. This became known and 'went all the way up to Prague'. Put under close arrest, Company commander Ostuf. Michel had his command taken from him. Punishment was also meted out to the NCO candidates of the company who had to give up any idea of promotion. Furthermore, all were fined twenty marks!

On 12 July 1944, undoubtedly as a result of the hunting incident, Michel was transferred to SS-Pz.Gren.Ausb.u.Ers.Btl.35 at Bruss as the Kompanieführer of the A.u.E.Kp. [Training and Replacement Company] of the Sturmbrigade.[37] SS-Panz.Gren.Ausb.u.Ers.Btl. 35 was the interim Ersatz unit for the French Sturmbrigade.[38]

There were other events worthy of note.[39] Picture the scene of Oberjunker Kreis of the 5th Company standing in the middle of a road, with his legs wide apart, watching over his platoon conduct an exercise in crossing a road under enemy fire. Suddenly behind him came the sound

---

35   Angolia, *Cloth Insignia Of The SS*, p.492.

36   Mabire, *La Brigade Frankreich*, p.173.

37   This A.u.E.Kp. is also identified in wartime documentation as the Stammkompanie of the Sturmbrigade.

38   Michel was ordered back to the Sturmbrigade on 1 September 1944 but did not go because he was admitted into Treptow hospital on 5 September 1944 suffering from irritable bowel syndrome.

39   The first edition of this book also recounted the affair of Bussang pass, which can be found in both the pages of Saint-Loup (*Les Hérétiques*, pp.42-44) and Mabire (*La Brigade Frankreich*, pp.439-422), but really does beg belief. Because of this it has now been relegated to a footnote. According to Saint-Loup, following an alert in July 1944, a *compagnie de marche* of Frenchmen, Norwegians, Flemings and Dutchmen was hastily formed at Sennheim under Stubaf. Hersche to defend Bussang pass from American paratroopers. Although they did not find any American paratroopers, they did surprise and capture forty armed masquisards (members of the maquis) without a fight. Lined up in the main square of Thillot, a village at the foot of Bussang pass, Hersche informed them that since they were *francs-tireurs* they would be shot according to regulations. Suddenly changing his mind, Hersche asked all those who wanted to join the Waffen-SS to take one step forward. Thirty-five maquisards did so. Hersche screamed at the five who stood fast to get lost and not to fall into his hands again! This he repeated several times. Of the forty, ten now remained. Concluding, Hersche told them to go and join their new comrades and to try and fight with a little more energy than earlier! The arrival of the maquisards at Neweklau aroused great curiosity. Assigned to Ostuf. de Tissot's 1st Company, they would serve loyally when the time came in Galicia.

      However, Mabire is not in full agreement. He replaces Hersche by a 'Prussian' Hauptsturmführer. He names the village Le Tillot. He numbers the masquisards captured at nearly 100. He numbers

of a car horn. He paid the car no attention and continued on with the exercise that lasted some time. With the exercise finished, he turned round and waved the car on. It was only then that he realised that no less a person than the Reichsführer-SS himself was in the car! Kreis presented his men to Himmler who then drove off to Neweklau. Now expecting the worst on his return to barracks, Kreis drew out the training. When he did finally venture back awaiting him was an order to report at once to Hstuf. Kostenbader. Far from being reprimanded, Kostenbader passed on to him Himmler's congratulations! There was an article in the regulations that prohibited the passage of vehicles across an exercise in progress.

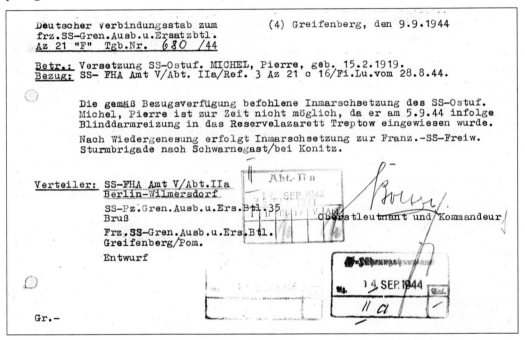

Pierre Michel went into hospital on 5 September 1944.

the masquisards determined to enlist in the Waffen-SS at 30 or so. And he states that the former masquisards would serve in Pomerania.

In reply to both Saint-Loup and Mabire, a local historian of Le Thillot has stated there was no such incident and there was nowhere near the same number of *franc-tireurs* in Le Thillot and the surrounding area. However, one villager did volunteer for the Waffen-SS, but that was before the summer of 1944. (Research provided by Mounine, letter to the author.) Also, Pignard-Berthet, at that time a platoon commander serving with de Tissot's 1st Company, does not recall the systematic incorporation of former maquisards into the company (letter to the author). Nevertheless, many former *franc-tireurs* did enlist in the ranks of the Waffen-SS.

By July, the 7th Company had begun to form. Ustuf. Pignard-Berthet received its command, but it was an appointment he accepted only on condition that he left for the front at the head of the 1st Platoon of the 1st Company, which he had trained.[40] Pierre Million-Rousseau, who was also ex-*Milice*, became Pignard-Berthet's assistant.[41]

On 13 July, the Sturmbrigade was ordered to make ready a battlegroup for employment on the Eastern Front with the 18.SS-Freiw.Panz.Gren.Div 'Horst Wessel'.[42] The battlegroup was to be titled the 1st Battalion of the Sturmbrigade under the command of Hstuf. Cance with a proposed structure of:

| | |
|---|---|
| 1 Stb.u.Stbs.Kp.Panz.Gren. Btls. | [Headquarters Staff and Company] |
| 3 Panz.Gren.Kp. | [Panzergrenadier Company] |
| 1 schw.Pan.Jäg.Zg. | [Heavy Anti-Tank Platoon] |

The three grenadier companies were commanded by de Tissot, Artus and Fenet. The Anti-Tank Platoon commanded by Oberjunker Kreis was equipped with three 7.5cm PAK guns. SS-Ustuf. Reiche was ordered to accompany the 1st Battalion as Verbindungsführer [Liaison Officer] with four assistants.

The same order of the 13th July also restructured the II. Bataillon of the Sturmbrigade as follows:

| | |
|---|---|
| 1 Stb.u.Stbs.Kp.Panz.Gren. Btls. | [Headquarters Staff and Company] |
| 3 Panz.Gren.Kp. | [Panzergrenadier Company] |
| Fuhr.schw.Kp. (mot) | |
| 8cm Gr.W. Zg. (mot) | [8cm Mortar Platoon] |
| 2 Gesch.Zg. (mot Z) | [Infantry Gun Platoon] |

The remaining fourth Kompanie was designated as a Stammkompanie [Depot Company] whose role was to induct recruits, issue uniforms and equipment, and start to acclimatise the recruit to military life.

SS-Ostuf. Jauss was appointed as the Führer des Verbindungs-und Ausbildungsstabes [leader of the liaison and training staff]. This was at the personal request of Gamory-Dubourdeau.[43]

The 1st Battalion was heavily reinforced prior to its departure, although the precise nature of that reinforcement is unclear. The Panzervernichtungstruppe of Pleyber's 5th Company, described as a close combat tank destruction unit, would accompany the 1st Battalion into battle.[44] This unit, apparently of platoon strength, lacked the necessary equipment required for

40 Yvon Prunennec states that he was transferred to the Company commanded by Pignard-Berthet, but numbers the Company as the 5th.
41 Million-Rousseau's rank may have been that of Unterscharführer. He was born on 7 November 1921 in Lyon.
42 SS-FHA Amt II Org.Abt. Ia/II Tgb. Nr. II/10943/44 geh.
43 Geiselhöring, *Hans Robert Jauss Jugend, Krieg und Internierung*, p.88.
44 Mabire, *La Brigade Frankreich*, p.187. Prior to going into battle, the Panzervernichtungstruppe was attached to de Tissot's 1st Company. In the fighting that ensued no other elements of the 5th Company, except for the PAK Platoon, are mentioned.

its role, though. Also, those elements of the 1st Battalion 'not quite up to scratch' were replaced by some of the best volunteers arriving from Sennheim.[45]

Before the 1st Battalion was deemed as combat ready it had to undergo a manoeuvre under the critical eye of an impressive group of Waffen-SS Gruppenführer. The results were very favourable. After the manoeuvre, a grand parade was held at Neweklau. At its close Hstuf. Kostenbader called together the French SS volunteers and congratulated them for the first and last time. He added that of all the SS Freiwillige he had trained the French had been the best.

Elation for one officer and disappointment for another marked the days running up to the departure of the 1st Battalion for the Eastern Front. Hstuf. Cance appointed Oberjunker Chapy to the command of the Panzervernichtungstruppe which he intended to use in the meantime as a sort of *corps franc* for the Battalion. Chapy was elated.

The officer disappointed was Ostuf. Artus. Cance summoned Artus, commanding the 2nd Company, and after praising him as one of his best officers, told him that he would be staying behind at Neweklau to serve as Stubaf. Gamory-Dubourdeau's assistant and to oversee the formation of the 2nd Battalion of the Sturmbrigade. Cance reasoned that Artus would be the heart of the 2nd Battalion, as such its real commander. Concluding, Cance assured Artus that soon he would join the 1st Battalion at the front with the new recruits from Sennheim. Ustuf. Gaultier became the new commander of the 2nd Company.[46]

The Feldgendarmerie unit was now disbanded. Cance, who feared that one of their men would put a bullet into the widely detested Oscha. Loistron if deployed to the front, took the precaution of leaving him behind.[47]

Before the departure for the Eastern Front the *Amis de la Waffen-SS* visited the French volunteers. With them they brought reasonable quantities of sardines and French wine. Also the short stay of thirty young French nurses of the Waffen-SS is fondly remembered. One such French nurse was Nelly, who recalls that they received a warm welcome. She said of her enlistment:[48]

In June 1940, I had just turned nineteen. My family and I supported Marshal Pétain, the hero of the 1914 war. The armistice had just been signed when I met a young German NCO of the Wehrmacht; for both of us it was love at first sight. His regiment stayed six days at Moulins. When we separated he asked my parents for permission to correspond with me; he spoke rather good French. My father was Flemish and very pro German, thus no difficulties in that respect all the more so because he was very much on the right.

In 1941 his regiment was stationed at Brest. On 15 April, he came to my parents to spend part of his leave (unauthorised) and we were engaged. Claus was of Danish origin. Back home, in Schleswig-Holstein, he had taken steps so that we could marry, but it was still not possible.

45   Pignard-Berthet, letter to the author.
46   According to Bayle, *De Marseille à Novossibirsk*, p.91, Gaultier was nicknamed 'Play-Boy' because of his presence and elegance. However, in 1944, the expression 'Play-Boy' was not in common use. Therefore, he may have acquired this nickname at a later date.
47   Mabire, *La Brigade Frankreich*, p.170.
48   Letter to Jean Castrillo, 26/10/2004.

Nelly and her German fiancé 15 April 1941. (Nelly)

On 26 August, he left for Russia. Claus taught me what National Socialism was and told me before we separated: "If I die in this war (he had a premonition) think always that I died not only for my country, but also for yours, for Europe." On 4 February 1942, he was killed at Smolensk. He had just turned twenty-four and I was twenty-one. It was his mother who had informed me. I was out of my mind with grief. Then a friend of my father suggested I join the JEN where his daughter was. We became very good friends. It was here that I regained a little the strength of life without him, among soldiers who came to the JEN.

Then there were enlistments, several of our comrades joined the Abwehr and the Waffen-SS, and when I was told that women could enlist in the German Red Cross I was one of the first, we must have been three or four from the JEN. In 1943, it must have been towards the end [of the year] that we had signed our enlistment in the German Red Cross in the offices of the Waffen-SS in Paris, in the 16th [district] I think. On 2 November 1943, we left for Belgium, to Spa, for training. I had no previous training as a nurse.

Like all those joining the Waffen-SS, Nelly also swore an oath of loyalty to Hitler. For her, the oath represented 'loyalty to our engagement, to the fight against Bolchevism and especially to Europe'. She wore the uniform of the German Red Cross and on her coat lapel a JEN badge.

Nelly in the uniform of the German Red Cross. Note the JEN badge on her coat lapel (right). (Nelly)

On 9 February 1944, she left Spa for Germany, continuing her training at Nieder-Weisel hospital, curiously a civilian hospital. The air raids on nearby Frankfurt left the hospital with 'much work' and Nelly with thoughts for the victims and also of retaliation, hoping that the Germans would bombard England likewise, because that 'is the only way they will understand'. In this 'first test' some of her comrades were found wanting. In a letter to her parents she expressed her determination to continue:[49]

> If we leave for Russia it is through ideals and we know very well the life that awaits us, I assure you that I prefer to be in a Lazarette and in a big city than being at Nieder-Weisel. We are not in the German Red Cross to avoid the alerts and the bombardments. Believe me that I might have some hard days ahead, but never will I regret the path I have chosen and I want to fight until victory, in the difficult moments the memories of Claude will always support me.

49    Nelly, letter to her parents, 22/3/1944.

Nelly and colleague. (Nelly)

Nelly was at Nieder Weisel for some three months, after which she was sent to Berlin for an exam. Passing the exam, she was then posted to an SS hospital in Prague.[50] She was one of eight such French nurses there. The wounded SS soldiers were surprised that the nurses attending them were French, but very happy to have them, all the more because the French nurses amused them greatly, being unable to speak German fluently. Moreover, Nelly spoke German with a French accent!

There were no more than sixty French nurses of the Waffen-SS.

Before his departure to the front one French volunteer wrote a farewell letter to his parents:

My dear parents
I presume that you have received my letter in which I informed you that I have signed up with the Waffen-SS for the duration of the war. I always had this idea, and I also

50  According to Bayle, *De Marseille à Novossibirsk*, p.87, the French Waffen-SS nurses would also leave for the Eastern Front. This is not correct.

know that you hold a different view. But, dear parents, one should never act against his ideals.

Perhaps your home is forever closed to me, but if anything ever happens to you I will be the first to rush to your aid, if it is not already too late. Remember that, despite everything, I will love you always. A child must always love his parents; they have enough difficulty getting us far enough that we can later earn our own keep.

I will soon be going to the front and I believe that as Frenchmen who have worked continuously and hard, you will someday be able to be proud to have given your son for his ideal - the defence of France and all of Europe.

My dear old parents, I do not believe that in the end you will have anything to reproach me for.

Finally, on 29 July 1944, the reinforced 1st Battalion of the French SS-Sturmbrigade under Hstuf. Cance left Neweklau on foot for Beneschau railway station. The very next day the battalion boarded trains and departed. Destination: the Eastern Front.[51]

Rttf. Simon came to see off his comrades from Beneschau railway station. Suddenly he saw Ustuf. Lambert, who he knew through Francisme. Lambert proposed to Simon that he would conceal him until they reached the front after which Simon could show himself. Simon refused. He was not authorised to leave and this smacked of desertion. Moreover, Gamory-Dubourdeau had promised him a command and a promotion in the 2nd Battalion.[52]

The strength of the reinforced 1st Battalion of the French SS-Sturmbrigade is reported as 20 officers and 980 other ranks.[53] Only the nucleus of the 2nd Battalion, apparently several hundred volunteers in two grenadier companies was now left at Networschitz whose training continued under Artus and Hstuf. Kostenbader.[54]

51    Mabire, *La Brigade Frankreich*, p.198. However, according to Saint-Loup, *Les Hérétiques*, p.38, and repeated by Littlejohn, *Foreign Legions of the Third Reich vol. 1*, p.161, the date of departure was 18 July 1944 which would put the arrival of the 1st Battalion at the front much earlier than most sources agree upon.
52    Simon was later transferred to the Engineer Company of 'Charlemagne'. Much to his regret, other reasons kept him from going to Pomerania and Berlin. Bayle wrote: 'In this way, Simon's voluntary service became sterile.'
53    Bayle, *De Marseille à Novossibirsk*, p.121, and confirmed in correspondence to the author, 1997. Mabire in *La Brigade Frankreich* uses a figure that fluctuates between 1,000 and 1,200.
54    One of the companies may have been commanded by Ustuf. Brocard.

## Command roster of the reinforced 1st Battalion of the 'Französische SS-Freiwilligen-Sturmbrigade' in Galicia August 1944

| | |
|---|---|
| Commander: | Hauptsturmführer Pierre Cance (wounded 22 Aug'44) |
| | Obersturmführer Jean Croisile (at Tarnow) |
| German Liaison Officer: | SS-Untersturmführer Reiche (killed 22 Aug'44)[55] |
| German Liaison Officer: | SS-Untersturmführer Binder (killed 22 Aug'44) |
| Orderly Officer: | Untersturmführer Scapula (killed 22 Aug'44) |
| Medical Officer: | Obersturmführer Bonnefoy |
| Kriegsberichter[56]: | Untersturmführer Le Marquer (killed 22 Aug'44) |

### Headquarters Company

| | |
|---|---|
| Commander | Obersturmführer Jean Croisile |
| | Oscha. Emilien Boyer |
| Engineer Platoon: | Oberscharfuhrer Lopez (wounded) |
| Signals Platoon: | Oberscharführer Czulowski (killed 22 Aug'44) |
| Transport: | Obersturmführer Henri Maudhuit |
| | SS-Untersturmführer Gustav-Adolf Neubauer[57] |

### 1st Company

| | |
|---|---|
| Commander: | Obersturmführer Nöel de Tissot (Missing in Action 21 Aug'44) |
| | Oberjunker Abel Chapy |
| | Obersturmführer Henri Maudhuit |
| Medical Officer: | Unterscharführer Jonquières (killed 10 Aug'44) |
| 1st Platoon: | Untersturmführer Pignard-Berthet (wounded 10 Aug'44) |
| | Unterscharführer Ruault |
| Assistant: | Oberjunker Pierre Million-Rousseau (wounded 10 Aug'44) |
| 2nd Platoon: | Oberjunker Pierre Hug (wounded 10 Aug'44) |
| 3rd Platoon: | Oberscharführer Paul Mulier (wounded 10 Aug'44) |
| | Unterscharführer Maurice Carré |
| | Untersturmführer Ivan Bartolomei (takes over on 17 Aug, wounded on 19 Aug) |
| | Unterscharführer Maurice Carré |
| 4th (Heavy) Platoon: | SS-Oberscharführer Kastner |
| Attached Platoon: | Oberjunker Abel Chapy |
| Assistant: | Oberscharführer Grossman (killed 14 August 1944) |
| | Unterscharführer Anger |

---

55   According to Lefèvre, *Axe & Alliés* hors série No 1, p.33, Reiche was the Battalion's *adjudant-major*.
56   Le Marquer was accompanied by a reporter photographer by the name of Pierre Briandet, who was born on 19 July 1944. Once at the front Le Marquer offered his services to Cance who took him on as *adjutant de bataillon*, but he sometimes proved to be overly assertive (see testimony of Boyer).
57   Gustav-Adolf Neubauer was born on 13 November 1895 in Freiburg.

## 2nd Company

| | |
|---|---|
| Commander: | Untersturmführer Léon Gaultier (wounded 10 Aug'44) |
| | Untersturmführer Ivan Bartolomei (evacuated 14 Aug'44) |
| | Obersturmführer Pleyber (to PAK 16 Aug'44) |
| | Untersturmführer Lambert (killed 22 Aug'44) |
| | Untersturmführer Ivan Bartolomei |
| | |
| 1st Platoon: | Unterscharführer Jacques Lefèvre (to 3rd Company) |
| 2nd Platoon: | Oberjunker Joseph Peyron (killed 15 Aug'44) |
| | Unterscharführer André Bayle |
| 3rd Platoon: | Oberscharführer Charles |
| 4th (Heavy) Platoon: | Untersturmführer Ivan Bartolomei (company commander 10 August '44) |

## 3rd Company

| | |
|---|---|
| Commander: | Obersturmführer Henri Fenet (wounded 22 Aug'44) |
| | Oberjunker Abel Chapy (arrested 28 Aug'44, Tarnow) |
| | Unterscharführer Lefèvre[58] |
| | |
| 1st Platoon: | Untersturmführer Lambert (to 2nd Company 16 Aug'44) |
| | Unterscharführer Max Quiquempois |
| 2nd Platoon: | Untersturmführer Lambert |
| 3rd Platoon: | Unterscharführer Delsart |
| 4th (Heavy) Platoon[59]: | Oberjunker Laschett (captured 21-22 Aug'44) |
| Assistant | Oberscharführer Couvreur |

## Attached

| | |
|---|---|
| | Obersturmführer Pleyber (to 2nd Company 14 Aug'44) |
| Anti-tank Platoon: | Oberjunker Henri Kreis |

58  Mistakenly, Mabire records Lefèvre's rank as Oscha. which was the rank he would attain in 'Charlemagne'. Lefèvre's younger brother also served with the Sturmbrigade.
59  Correction based on the memoires of Fernand Costamagna who served in this platoon.

# 5

## The Sanok Sector

---

### Military Situation in Galicia

On 13 July 1944, the 1st White Russian Front and the 1st Ukrainian Front went over to the offensive and inflicted a series of body blows on the German Army Group designated as North Ukraine. To begin with, on 16 July, the German XIII Corps was encircled. Then, on 18 July, the Russian 1st Guards Tank Army, striking between the Fourth and First Panzer Armies, reached Rava Russkaya. Also on that same day the Third Guards Tank Army passed north of Lwów while the newly committed 4th Tank Army closed in on the city from the east. The city would finally fall a week later.

The 22 July was disastrous for the 4th Panzer Army. To the North, the 1st White Russian Army punched through Chelm in the morning and by nightfall elements were beyond Lublin, some 40 miles away. In addition, to the South, not only was the gap between the 4th Panzer Army and the First Panzer Army now thirty miles wide, but the spearheads of the 1st Guards Tank Army had reached the San river near Jaroslaw against no resistance. In danger of being outflanked and encircled, 4th Panzer Army reported to Army Group that it could only save itself by immediate withdrawal behind the Vistula and San rivers. Two days later, on 24 July, the 3rd Guards Tank Army and Cavalry-Mechanised Group Baranov had also approached the San on the stretch between Jaroslaw and Przemysl.

When the 4th Panzer Army finally received permission to withdraw on 25 July 1944 it was too late. The Russians already had bridgeheads across the Vistula and on that day the 1st Guards Tank Army and the 3rd Guards Tank Army burst across the San between Jaroslaw and Przemysl and fanned out. While the 1st Guards Tank Army stabbed north-west toward an open stretch of the Vistula on both sides of Baranów, the 3rd Guards Tank Army pushed south-west toward Krosno, west of Sanok.

To try and plug the gap between the 4th Panzer Army and 1st Panzer Army, the 17th Army was activated late July 1944 and initially provided with two and half divisions. By 31 July, its headcount had risen to five 'divisions'. That day marked the first signs of the Russian offensive faltering as the Armies outran their supply lines and also the first day of a counterattack by Army Group North Ukraine aimed at clearing the entire San-Vistula triangle. Although both the 17th Army and 4th Panzer Army made gains, the counterattack petered out in two days, with little disruption to the Russians. Throughout early August 1944 the Russians continued

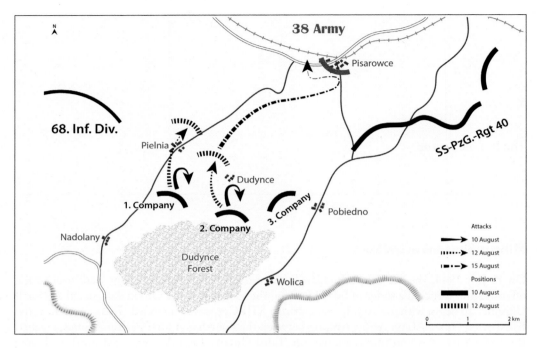

Sanok Sector, 10-15 August 1944.

to advance through Krosno, Sedziszów Mlp, Mielec and Sanok in the area of the 17th Army. It was to this 'fluid' front in Galicia, Southern Poland, that the 1st Battalion of the French SS-Sturmbrigade was sent.

**The preliminaries**

On 5 August 1944, after a weeklong journey by rail without incident, the Battalion finally arrived at the town of Turka. Situated between Sambor (or Sambir in Ukrainian) and Uzhgorod, near to the source of the Dnestr, Turka was some ninety kilometres east of Sanok. The troops disembarked. Their first priority was to clean their weapons, which was quickly carried out. Towards the end of the afternoon, the three grenadier companies set off on foot. They marched for some six hours through the hills of the Beskides before bivouacking for the night. Each company set up in a 'hedgehog' around which the Engineer Platoon under Oscha. Lopez erected barbed wire entanglements. Before nightfall Cance assembled his officers to inform them that the Battalion would be fighting with the 18. SS-Freiwilligen-Panzer Grenadier Division 'Horst Wessel' in a sector to the west of Sanok. On the following morning, the officers told their men in turn of this attachment.

At 1000 hours, the companies marched off again due north in the direction of Sanok. The vehicles started out in turn escorted by the tracked vehicles of the PAK Platoon. They climbed hill after hill. The dust and the heat soon became unbearable. Their bodies were covered in sweat. Their equipment and weapons became heavier and heavier and dug into their flesh. Their singing gradually ceased.

They came to a 'real' road that was nothing more than a gullied earth track. They were passed by ambulances and columns of Russian prisoners dressed in dust-coloured rags going to the rear and by convoys of vehicles and tanks from the Waffen SS, on which rode its exhausted infantry support, going back up to the front. The battalion covered some fifty-five kilometres before stopping at last around midnight in a bombed-out village surrounded by forest. And there were no stragglers! Patrols went out as this area could no longer be termed 'friendly'.

During the night Ostuf. Bonnefoy, the Battalion's chief medical officer, went off in an ambulance to attend to a local who had been knocked down by a German vehicle. The ambulance was soon back and a stretcher was brought out. Even though the local actually turned out to be a partisan who had blown a leg off while laying a mine Bonnefoy had him evacuated to a military hospital. He was strictly adhering to his moral responsibility as a doctor to save life.

Ironically, for the rest of the night, the partisans made a nuisance of themselves around the bivouac. The French volunteers warded them off with machine-guns, their first shots fired in anger.

Outside of the bivouac a greater danger lurked in the night: mines. A truck carrying ammunition in which Oberjunker Peyron was travelling ran over a mine, but he was lucky enough to escape with only minor injuries.[1]

That night Cance decided to attach Oberjunker Chapy's Platoon to Ostuf. de Tissot's 1st Company.

'Horst Wessel' sent trucks to speed up the arrival of the desperately needed French reinforcements. The truck journey on the following day, 7 August, took the Battalion across anti-tank ditches, streams and the San river, all spanned by makeshift bridges, to another nameless village where the French SS volunteers accommodated themselves for the night. The front was near now.

No movement is reported on 8 August 1944, but gunfire and mortar explosions could now be heard. Sanok could be seen with binoculars. That evening, Cance was paid a visit by Obf. Trabandt, the commander of 18. SS-Freiwilligen-Panzer Grenadier Division 'Horst Wessel', who explained to him just how serious the situation was and that it was deteriorating hourly. To the west of Sanok a huge hole had been torn in the lines held by the Wehrmacht. Kampfgruppe Schäfer of 18. SS-Freiwilligen-Panzer Grenadier Division 'Horst Wessel' had been called in to deal with the breach.

Kampfgruppe Schäfer was based on SS-Panzergrenadier-Regiment 40 and led by SS-Stubaf. Ernst Schäfer, a Knight's Cross holder, although it seems that Trabandt was in direct command of the Kampfgruppe. Formed as a result of the Russian offensive of June 1944, the Kampfgruppe had been rushed to Southern Poland where it had been in constant action ever since.

By 8 August, despite committing in vain all his last reserves, Trabandt had still not managed to completely plug the breach and the left flank of his sector was still wide open. Indeed, now faced with the Russians attacking through his left flank and the strength of his infantry companies reduced to 40, 30 and as little as 25 men, Trabandt felt he would no longer be able to hold onto his present positions. Thus it was with great relief that he welcomed the arrival of

1    Mabire, *La Brigade Frankreich*, p.229. However, according to Bayle André, *San et Persante* (Self-published, 1994), p.59, the same incident came to pass on 13 August 1944, Peyron's 2nd Platoon of the 2nd Company was actually travelling in the lorry, and Peyron was left stunned by the explosion; he had not been wearing his helmet and had bashed his head.

the 1st Battalion of the Sturmbrigade with some 1,000 men. One official wartime source lists the 1st Battalion of the French SS-Sturmbrigade as the IV. Battalion of Kampfgruppe Schäfer.[2]

Trabandt asked Cance to engage a company straightaway. Ostuf. Fenet's 3rd Company was put at his disposal. It assembled and set off immediately. Reporting to Kampfgruppe headquarters, Fenet was given concise orders by Trabandt: firstly, to try and establish contact with friendly troops to the left of the positions of the Kampfgruppe, and, secondly, if unable to do so, then to cover its left flank. Because the situation was so confused, Fenet was told to wait for dawn before starting out. In the meantime, the French Company was held in reserve.

Morning came, bringing with it a slight delay for the 3rd Company impatient to get going. Fenet did not waste the 'time now on his hands'. He asked his NCOs to remind the men of how to handle safely the panzerfäusts they had just drawn.[3]

The demonstrations were interrupted by another piece of rocket equipment in the armoury of the German Army, the Nebelwerfer. When a nearby battery opened up the Frenchmen immediately dived to the ground; they had never heard the Nebelwerfer firing before.

The 3rd Company finally set off mid-afternoon on 9 August 1944 and advanced across terrain that alternated from open to woods. Suddenly the company came to a stretch of open ground that it could not possibly avoid without considerable delay. Ostuf. Fenet decided to push straight on and gave the appropriate orders. As the first Frenchmen started across this stretch, Russian guns and mortars opened up and shells soon started to rain down. Zigzagging and advancing by successive dashes as if on exercise, the company made it across at the cost of only two casualties: both were slightly wounded.

As soon as the two wounded were dressed, Ostuf. Fenet pushed on and soon made contact with the company holding the extreme left of the Kampfgruppe's front.[4] Commanded by Ostuf. Tämpfer, the last surviving officer, this company, once 200 strong, had been hit badly and now stood at only 20 to 25 men. Tämpfer had just beaten off another attack and had dispatched a patrol to reconnoitre the ground opposite his positions. Before continuing, Fenet decided to await the return of this patrol. Some hours later, the patrol was back, reporting that it had 'found nothing'.

Concluding that it now seemed impossible to establish contact with neighbouring friendly troops, Fenet set about carrying out the second part of his orders. Setting off again, his company soon took up a covering position that sealed off a small valley. Fenet ordered patrols from the 1st Platoon under Ustuf. Lambert into a hamlet opposite, while the rest of the company dug

---

2    This is confirmed by Mounine and Tieke Wilhelm, *Horst Wessel* (Winnipeg: J.J. Fedorowicz Publishing, 2015), although they use slightly different designations for 'Horst Wessel'. According to Mouine, letter to the author, the French Battalion was the 'IVth Bataillon des Kampfgruppes der 18. SS-Div' while according to Tieke the French Battalion was attached to 'Kampfgruppe 18.SS-Pz.Gren.Div.' (*Horst Wessel*, p.41). While on the subject of designations Tieke often uses that of 'Battalion Cance' in *Horst Wessel* to describe the French Battalion. No veterans who served in Galicia recollect this. However, it was normal German practice to name a unit after its commander.

3    The launching tube of the panzerfäust actually carried the warning *Achtung! Feuerstrahl* (Beware of Jet flame). This was to protect the unwary user from the potentially dangerous jet of flame that extended rearwards from the tube when fired. In fact some men had actually been burnt alive by the rearwards flame.

4    Tieke identifies the company as the 1. Kompanie of SS-Panzergrenadier Regiment-40 (*Horst Wessel*, p.49).

in. Their positions received sporadic mortar fire. The patrols reported back that the sector was infested with Russians who seemed to be growing in strength. Night fell. More patrols were dispatched. Two orders in quick succession, the first to prepare to leave the position that was countermanded by the second, were the only events in an otherwise quiet night for the company.

On the following day, a dawn patrol from the 1st Platoon of the 3rd Company into the same hamlet drew fire. Section commander Strmm. Delattre was killed outright. After silencing the Russian snipers, the patrol returned with his body. Platoon commander Ustuf. Lambert buried him. Twenty-year-old Strmm. Delattre was probably the Sturmbrigade's first killed in action.[5]

On 9 August 1944, while the 3rd Company was undergoing its baptism of fire, the rest of the battalion spent the whole day on a frustrating succession of marches and partisan alerts.[6] The two other companies marched for twelve hours non-stop. Throughout the day patrols were sent into reported partisan-occupied villages and yet all returned with no sightings.

The first brush with the partisans came after nightfall. One tractor of Kreis' PAK Platoon, which had broken down crossing a river, was fired upon. Fortunately nobody was hurt. The village from which the shot came was surrounded and searched, but again no partisans were found. Back on its way again, far worse was to follow for the PAK Platoon when one of its men, Courcol, standing up in his tractor, was half decapitated by barbed wire strung across the road. And still there was no sign of the partisans.

## 10 August 1944 and 2nd Company

On 10 August 1944, the 1st Company and 2nd Company went into line. They had orders to capture Dudyńce and establish contact with the 208th Infantry Division in the area to the west of Pielnia.[7]

By midday, the two companies were well into Dudyńce forest and under intermittent mortar fire. Separating, de Tissot's 1st Company moved off to the left and Gaultier's 2nd Company to the right. Led by Oberscharführer Charles' Platoon and Gaultier himself, the 2nd Company advanced towards the edge of the forest. Despite a skirmish with unidentified enemy forces and gunfire still ringing out, Gaultier decided to press on in order to carry out his orders to the letter.

Reaching the edge of the forest, Gaultier gave orders to Bartolomei to support the attack of the 1st Company to dislodge the Russians from the forest opposite. Ahead of Gaultier was a hill that would serve as an excellent observation post, but to reach it a stretch of exposed ground had to be traversed. Somewhat recklessly, Gaultier, accompanied by Bartolomei and a section

---

5    Gilbert Delattre was born on 31 May 1924 in Saint-Amand, although there are several *communes* in France with this name.
6    Mabire, *La Brigade Frankreich*, pp.247-249. Curiously, according to Bayle, *San et Persante*, p.51, the whole battalion was already in line and under fire. The 2nd Company took its first casualty; SS Freiwillige Quinton was seriously wounded in the leg, which was partly severed.
7    Tieke, *Horst Wessel*, p.49. Unfortunately Mabire does not record what exact orders the two companies had received but implies that they were to relieve front-line units of the Wehrmacht. And as the companies advanced, it seems they passed the very units they were due to relieve, which had evidently pulled back too early. Ustuf. Pignard-Berthet, the commander of the 1st Platoon of the 1st Company, was particularly critical of this untimely withdrawal which did not bode well. Also, Mabire states the premature withdrawal of the Wehrmacht units as a contributory factor to the failure of the French Battalion that day.

of men, ventured across this stretch of ground and were suddenly caught in the open by Russian mortars that marked the beginning of a ferocious bombardment. Many were hit. Gaultier was seriously wounded in the chest and the loins. He was dragged back to cover, continuing to give orders and asking for Bartolomei to take his place. He was evacuated.[8]

Taking what cover could be found when the bombardment begun, Bartolomei was soon awake to another danger as any movement he made was greeted by a sniper's bullet. Thus it took him an hour to crawl back to the edge of the forest where he discovered that the 2nd Company had moved on. All alone, pistol in hand, he wandered around the forest for three hours before stumbling upon a German sentry who directed him to his unit.

Ustuf. Bartolomei now took command of the 2nd Company. One third of the company was missing, but not all of those missing were actually casualties. Uscha. Lefèvre's platoon would reappear three days later.[9] During its absence from the battalion, it had joined and fought with a German unit, stopping several Russian attacks, which might explain why Lefèvre returned with the Iron Cross.[10]

The day of 10 August had been one of frustration for Uscha. Bayle, who led a section, which never advanced beyond the edge of Dudyńce forest. Without orders and coming under increasingly accurate mortar fire, Bayle decided to withdraw. Several men were lightly wounded by shellfire as they retreated through the forest.

Bartolomei received a visit from Cance. The battalion commander seemed concerned. The cause of his concern was the 1st Company that had been badly hit. Three-quarters of its cadre was already out of action.

## 10th August 1944 and 1st Company

For its part, the reinforced 1st Company, on separating from the 2nd Company, also advanced to the edge of Dudyńce forest, but along a gully that afforded it shelter from the Russian bombardment. Its objective was a farm atop a hill that lay beyond a huge cornfield, but the gully opened out at the edge of the forest.[11]

First to heave themselves out of the gully and make their way across the cornfield to no or little enemy fire were the men of the 1st Platoon under Ustuf. Pignard-Berthet. Accompanying the platoon were the company commander Ostuf. de Tissot and the twenty-three-year-old company doctor Uscha. Henri Jonquières.[12] When they arrived near the farm they saw a horse roaming about. De Tissot started to draw water for it from a well, but this humane gesture

---

8    Gaultier's wounds were such that he would play no further part in the war. Still hospitalised, on 21 November 1944, he was assigned to the depot and training battalion of 'Charlemagne'.

9    Incorrectly, Mabire, *La Brigade Frankreich*, p.265, identifies Lefèvre's Platoon as the company's heavy platoon with mortars and heavy machine-guns.

10   Mabire, *La Brigade Frankreich*, p.265. However, according to Saint-Loup, *Les Hérétiques*, p.20, Lefèvre's Platoon 'disappeared' after the attack on 12 August and reappeared two days later with some Iron Crosses.

11   Mabire, *La Brigade Frankreich*, p.269. Undoubtedly this is the same hill referred to by Tieke, *Horst Wessel*, p.50, southwest of Pielnia, but there is no mention of a farm on this dominating height.

12   Incorrectly, Tieke, *Horst Wessel*, p.49, lists Jonquières serving with the 2nd Company. Born on 28 August 1920 in Paris, Henri Jonquières served with the Colonial Army. Demobilised, he went on to join the *Franc-Garde permanente* of the *Milice* and held the rank of *chef de dizaine*.

seemed to serve as a trigger that unleashed the response from Russian gunners and infantrymen alike. The first to be killed was Uscha. Jonquières who had gone to the head of the 'scouts' (and who was possibly pushing beyond the farm with them).[13]

The 1st Platoon attempted to manoeuvre but was blown to pieces before it even had the opportunity to fire a single shot. Ustuf. Pignard-Berthet was wounded twice and out of action, as were his three section commanders, Atama, Cran and Jacquet, and his assistant Million-Rousseau, who had only been transferred to the 1st Platoon just as the 1st Battalion was going up to the front. Atama would lose an eye and a leg.[14] Uscha. Ruault now assumed command of the platoon.

Next to jump off was Hug's 2nd Platoon, followed by Mulier's 3rd Platoon and then Kastner's 4th Heavy Platoon. A warm reception greeted each platoon as it jumped off. The 2nd Platoon, advancing to the left of the 1st Platoon, suffered heavy losses. There were dead and wounded everywhere. Hug was seriously wounded, as was Mulier, whose stomach had been ripped open by a piece of shrapnel. All was confusion.

Now it was the turn of the platoon under Chapy to jump off, but he delayed its entrance into this abattoir until he had personally spoken to de Tissot. As he made his way across the cornfield to the farm he had to dive for cover again and again. He found de Tissot in the farm. De Tissot gave him a situation report. It was not good. Not only was his company badly hit and disorganised it was all alone, having no contact with friendly units to the left or to the right where Gaultier's 2nd Company was supposed to have been. Moreover, through a lack of defensive artillery support, the Russians could be seen massing in the valley below in readiness to attack once their barrage had finished.

De Tissot and Chapy urgently set about deploying the Company: on the right spur, the 3rd Platoon under Uscha. Maurice Carré, Mulier's assistant; in the centre, around the farm serving as a command post, Oscha. Kastner's Platoon as well as the remnants of the 1st and 2nd Platoons; and on the wooded left spur Chapy's Platoon. Returning to his men, Chapy brought them out and across the cornfield to their position with the loss of only two wounded. One of those wounded, section commander Uscha. Dupin, a former legionnaire of the LVF, refused to be evacuated and rejoined his men. He finally let himself be evacuated on 14 August.

The Russians approached. The machine-guns of the Frenchmen started rattling. Chapy went to his map case and discovered that he was lucky not to be wounded; a piece of shrapnel had cut through his large map of Europe and his message pad, only to be stopped by his curvometer that it had crushed.

By 1900 hours, the Russian fire had eased off, though it had become more accurate and shell after shell now ripped into the farm. Later, at an unrecorded time, de Tissot gave the order to pull back to Dudyńce forest, although the order never reached Chapy and his platoon. Three

13  According to Lupo, *Levée d'écrou*, p.129, Jonquières was killed by mortar shrapnel whereas according to Mabire, *La Brigade Frankreich*, p.270, a sniper put a bullet through his head. Incorrectly, Tieke, *Horst Wessel*, p.49, records that Jonquières was only wounded.
14  Mabire, *La Brigade Frankreich*, p.270. Atama is undoubtedly a pseudonym for Uscha. Robert Amata from Paris. Because of his wounds he was discharged from the Waffen-SS in January 1945 at Wildflecken. Curiously, according to Rentano & Leguérandais, *Ces Franciliens qui ont choisi Hitler*, p.115, he was seriously wounded on 28 August 1944, by which time the 1st Battalion of the Sturmbrigade had been pulled out of front line duties.

runners carrying the order were sent to him by de Tissot, but unfortunately the first two were wounded and the third could not get through.

Meantime, concerned about his growing isolation and the depletion of ammunition, Chapy sent a runner to the farm who managed to get through and report back that it was deserted. Only then did Chapy realise his predicament and to make matters worse he had just spotted three Russian tanks not far from his position. He gave the necessary order and his platoon disengaged and hurried off towards the forest. It was now getting dark. A sense of loneliness prevailed. It seemed as though the 1st and 2nd Companies had disappeared into thin air. They did chance upon several German soldiers from the Wehrmacht, who were also lost and did not know the whereabouts of the headquarters of the French Battalion. Chapy searched on and finally came across comrades from Oberjunker Peyron's Platoon who directed them to the southern edge of Dudyńce where Battalion Headquarters was believed to be.

Battalion Headquarters had been set up in a log dug-out south-west of Dudyńce forest between two hills, near to the road leading to Sanok and near to the village of Wolica where the field hospital of the 'Horst Wessel' Division was located. Throughout that first day of combat Battalion Headquarters resembled and served more as a first-aid post than a command post. Medical officer Dr. Bonnefoy and his orderlies had been busy treating the wounded since early afternoon. There had been a constant to and fro of ambulances and trucks evacuating the wounded from the Battalion's first-aid post to the field hospital at Wolica.

'By the close of play', Hstuf. Cance was furious. The day had been most unsatisfactory. Casualties had been heavy, especially among the cadre, losing one company commander, six platoon commanders and about twenty section commanders.[15] Casualty figures vary, but may have been as high as sixty-five.[16] Among those killed were Gilbert Delattre (3rd Company), Robert Colombi (3rd Company), Roger Cantareul (3rd Company) and Pierre Colombi (3rd Company). The French SS Freiwilligen had paid a heavy price for their baptism of fire. If truth were told, the French Battalion had not covered itself with glory.

Cance now decided to keep the 3rd Company on its present positions, send the 2nd Company back up to the front line and keep the 1st Company in reserve due to its crippling losses. Chapy's Platoon was held in reserve near the command post. The next day he planned to counterattack.

## 11 August 1944

On the whole, 11 August 1944 passed rather uneventfully for the 1st Battalion.[17] Appreciating that the exhausted Battalion still required time to rest, accustom itself to its surroundings

---

15    Mabire, *La Brigade Frankreich*, p.284.

16    According to Mabire, *La Brigade Frankreich*, p.284, about twenty volunteers were killed, but gives no figure for those wounded. Tieke, *Horst Wessel*, p.49, records that five volunteers from the 2nd Company were killed and that over sixty wounded passed through the hands of Dr. Bonnefoy and his orderlies. Lefèvre confirms these numbers (article TK 18/33 Région Grand-Ouest, no 13). Bayle states sixty dead and wounded.

17    Mabire, *La Brigade Frankreich*, p.295. Curiously, according to Tieke, *Horst Wessel*, p.51, 'an infantry attack supported by tanks on the heights southwest of Pielnia was repelled by Kompanie de Tissot with artillery support'. This is confirmed and perhaps repeated by Bayle, *San et Persante*, p.57, who also writes that the 2nd Company repulsed a major Soviet attack and inflicted heavy losses. The author has not been able to reconcile these differences.

and reorganise following the terrible blood-letting of the previous day, Cance had no other choice than to postpone the counterattack planned for that day. Instead the 2nd Company was called upon to send out patrols. One patrol led in person by the new company commander, Untersturmführer Bartolomei, clashed with the enemy approximately 500 metres from his command post, but this time the Frenchmen came out on top: Twenty Russians were killed. 'Bartolomei had just equalised the score'.[18] Bartolomei hoped to do even better during the counterattack being prepared for 12 August.

The Frenchmen were on the receiving end of a Russian ruse when they welcomed into their positions some young children who had appeared from Russian lines. The children were trembling with fear or so it seemed. Sent to the rear, they discreetly slipped back to Russian lines. And thanks to their little spies, the Russians were able to bombard the French positions systematically and with precision.

That same day, the PAK Platoon attempted to set up one of its three guns on an exposed hill in the sector of either the 3rd Company or 2nd Company and immediately drew heavy Russian fire.[19] The gun was destroyed, one of the gun crew was killed and five were seriously wounded. What a disaster! The gun had not even fired a single shot.

Trabandt, Schäfer and a German Colonel from the Wehrmacht came to congratulate Cance and the French volunteers on their bearing and courage, while lamenting their inexperience.

During the night the 3rd Company was relieved and occupied new positions for the planned attack on 12 August.

## 12 August 1944

The assault on 12 August 1944 to align the front to the Cracow/Sanok railway was to be led by Kampfgruppe Schäfer and the French Battalion and was promised massive artillery and Nebelwerfer support. The initiative for this attack seems to have come from Oberführer Trabandt and Lieutenant-General Wirtz of the 96th Infantry Division, elements of which had started to arrive in the sector of Kampfgruppe Schäfer.

The French Battalion was to take the village of Dudyńce and then push on northwards to Pisarowce. The 3rd Company was to safeguard the right flank of the battalion's disposition and hence the left flank of the front held by Kampfgruppe Schäfer. H-hour was fixed for midday.

During the morning the German and French SS soldiers moved up to their starting positions on the edge of Dudyńce forest. One hour before the attack, the German artillery opened up. The attack started at the appointed hour. The 2nd Company captured the village of Dudyńce without a fight and occupied positions abandoned by the Russians but had to abandon them.[20]

---

18   Mabire, *La Brigade Frankreich*, p.295. Tieke also wrote of this in *Horst Wessel*, p.51: 'a Russian combat patrol approaching Kompagnie Bertholomei was recognized early, lured into an ambush and annihilated'.

19   According to Mabire, *La Brigade Frankreich*, pp.292-293, the PAK gun was set up in the sector of the 3rd Company, whereas, according to Tieke, *Horst Wessel*, p.51, it was in the sector of the 2nd Company. Also, according to Lefèvre, *Axe & Alliés* hors série no 1, p.38, this incident happened on the morning of 15 August and not 11 August.

20   Lefèvre, *Axe & Alliés* hors série no 1, p.37. According to Saint-Loup, *Les Hérétiques*, p.19, the Russians withdrew before the irresistible attack of the 2nd Company, leaving absolutely nothing behind them,

The 1st Company, which was on the left, took the village of Pielnia and held it against violent Russian counterattacks.[21] The attack could not be continued, though.

From artillery observation posts, officers of 'Horst Wessel' and commanders of neighbouring Wehrmacht divisions followed the attack. The latter were surprised to learn from Obf. Trabandt that this attack was conducted by French volunteers placed of late under his command. In this way, they 'learnt of the efficient presence of French volunteers facing Bolshevism and *pour L'Europe*'.[22]

As for the 3rd Company, although it was to protect the right flank of the battalion's disposition, Fenet ordered his men to advance and take up position from where they could best support their comrades of the attack companies. In so doing, the 3rd Company revealed itself and was shelled savagely by mortars and artillery, yet it somehow managed to maintain its support through this storm of steel.

The day's satisfactory proceedings for the 3rd Company were marred by a self-inflicted injury and while this particular individual from Couvreur's Platoon got his wish to be evacuated, a court martial and the concentration camp awaited him. Nobody would miss him. The 2nd Company was relieved that night or around midday on the following day.[23]

## 13 August 1944

Outside of burying the dead, the battalion's units rested. During the night the three companies were on the move again to new positions to relieve battered and exhausted German units believed to be from the 68th Infantry Division.

Lieutenant-General Wirtz of the 96th Infantry Division wrote to the Kommandeur of 'Horst Wessel': 'The Frenchmen of the I./Französische SS-Freiwilligen Sturmbrigade participated with Kampfgruppe Kobold in the attack of 12 August 1944 on Pielnia. They particularly distinguished themselves by their offensive spirit and their bravery. I consider them worthy of a distinction.'

## 14 August 1944

In the early morning, the 2nd Company took up residence in former Russian positions on a hill from where German combat troops could be seen advancing towards enemy positions that they took easily. The 2nd Company received some sporadic mortar fire that was of no consequence.

---

no equipment, no wounded and no dead. And yet, according to Tieke, *Horst Wessel*, p.52, after storming the Russian front line, the 2nd Company captured the village of Dudyńce, but was thrown out.
21   Tieke, *Horst Wessel*, p.52. No other source mentions the 1st Company fighting off Russian counterattacks, though.
22   Bayle, *De Marseille à Novossibirsk*, p.97.
23   According to Saint-Loup, *Les Hérétiques*, p.19, at 2100 hours, Bartolomei received the order to hand over the conquered positions to troops of the Wehrmacht whereupon the 2nd Company took up position on a rocky height to the south of the 3rd Company. In contrast, according to Mabire, *La Brigade Frankreich*, p.300, the 2nd Company spent the night out in the field, 'sharing their holes with Russian corpses' and was relieved around midday on the following day.

The command of the 2nd Company changed hands once again.[24] Owing to his deteriorating health, Ustuf. Bartolomei, old 'Barto', who was in the late forties, asked to be relieved of his command. Since his arrival at the front, Bartolomei had only managed to hold out by dint of will. Ostuf. Pleyber, the Heavy Company commander, to all intents and purposes 'unemployed', was given the command of the 2nd Company. This gunner inspired little confidence among the infantrymen, though.[25]

Russian artillery continued to inflict casualties. Needlessly caught in the open, Oberjunker Chapy was wounded by shrapnel, but turned down evacuation, but his assistant, Oberscharführer Grossman, was killed outright. Jean-Louis Bonnegarde and Bernand Desgardins were also wounded. Desgardins was evacuated.[26]

In need of an 'efficient assault platoon' to support a tank attack on Pisarowice,[27] a village located alongside the Cracow-Sanok railway, the Germans came to the French Battalion. Bartolomei and Cance chose the 2nd Platoon of the 2nd Company, that of Oberjunker Peyron, because of its competence and its dynamism over the past few days: it had particularly distinguished itself on the 12th. For the mission the platoon was brought up to full strength, that is to say three sections of twelve men each, plus two radio operators.[28]

At nightfall, after receiving final instructions delivered by Chapy, Peyron's 2nd Platoon of the 2nd Company set out. With the platoon was Pleyber, the new company commander. Inexplicably, the two officers had told the NCOs and the men nothing of the mission. The platoon would march till daybreak on the 15th.

## 15 August 1944

Two French battalion units saw action and achieved success. The first was Chapy's Platoon attached to the 1st Company. In the early hours of 15 August, Stubaf. Schäfer of 'Horst Wessel' called upon the French Battalion to help a neighbouring company of his Kampfgruppe cut off by partisans. Ustuf. Kammer, the company commander, had asked his regiment for help, but Schäfer went straight to the Frenchmen.[29] The 1st Company supplied Chapy's Platoon for the rescue mission, which immediately set off and managed to cut its way through some two kilometres of hostile terrain to reach Kammer's Company just after daybreak.

Kammer's situation was not good. The partisans, who occupied a dominating height one hundred metres away, had his company pinned down and had inflicted many casualties; his

24  Bayle, *De Marseille à Novossibirsk*, p.99. However, Mabire records the change of command of the 2nd Company one day earlier (see *La Brigade Frankeich*, p.303).
25  Ibid.
26  Bernand Desgardins was born on 6 November 1926 in Paris and enlisted in the Waffen in spring 1943.
27  Bayle, letter to the author 19/3/97.
28  According to Mabire, *La Brigade Frankeich*, p.309, this attack was Cance's last effort to reach the Cracow-Sanok railway line because he was expecting an order to be relieved on 15 August. This is not wholly accurate. See Bayle, *De Marseille à Novossibirsk*, p.99. This attack was confined solely to the 2nd Platoon of the 2nd Company and was not an entire company action as intimated by Mabire, and Tieke, *Horst Wessel*, p.54.
29  According to Bender Roger James and Taylor Hugh Page, *Uniforms, organization and history of the Waffen-SS*, volume 4 (San Jose: Bender publishing, 1982), p.174, Schäfer only turned to the Frenchmen because he had no men available. As such this sentiment is not expressed by Mabire.

company was no stronger than that of a platoon. The breakout would hinge upon the capture of the height.

Bayonets fixed, around one hundred screaming French and German soldiers of the Waffen-SS raced towards the height, from which the enemy hurriedly fell back. Although the rest of the rescue mission proved delicate, Chapy brought Kammer and his company safely back. Not one further man was lost.

When a volunteer reported to Chapy that he had lost two boxes of ammunition and a machine-gun barrel crossing a road Chapy ordered him to return and collect them. The volunteer hesitated but went on his way after Chapy grabbed a rifle. The volunteer was back minutes later with the recovered items and was offered a conciliatory cigarette from Chapy.

Oberjunker Peyron's 2nd Platoon of the 2nd Company was also in action.[30] By daybreak, after a night of many inexplicable and pointless detours, the platoon was ordered to halt along a road in a sort of basin bordered by cornfields. To Bayle, the officers seemed lost. Although gunfire and the noise of clanking armour could be heard, the front seemed far away. The weather was splendid. As Peyron and Pleyber went off to a nearby village in ruins to find their bearings the platoon deployed itself leisurely and lazily.

Suddenly shots rang out from the east, shattering the peace, but the platoon remained untroubled by this development. At that very same moment, Peyron and Pleyber came running back from the village, shouting in alarm, which could not be made out at first: "The Russians! The Russians!" They pointed to the Russians surrounding the platoon through the cornfields bordering the road to the east. The men quickly equipped themselves again and regrouped. Without any order being given, the Frenchmen fixed bayonets and watched over the cornfields. Hit in the hollow of his shoulder, a young grenadier went down besides Uscha. Bayle and died without a noise.

Ordered forward by Peyron, the platoon followed him into the cornfields. The Frenchmen started to run. They broke the encirclement at bayonet point and their momentum carried them further forward. The Russians fled. The very young volunteer Sacomont was killed.[31] Others fell, wounded or dead. The Germans were quick to provide artillery and mortar support, but the Frenchmen were running so fast that they were hit by their own rolling fire support, which could not keep up with them!

The charge continued through increasing enemy and friendly fire. The Frenchmen broke into the village of Pisarowce but were held up by a machine-gun in a grove. Trévisan was hit in the back by shrapnel from friendly mortar fire and called out for help. Uscha. Bayle went to him and was ordered away by Oberjunker Peyron with the words: "It's not your job!" Bayle left Trévisan who slipped into a stream where he died moments later.[32]

---

30    Bayle, *De Marseille à Novossibirsk*, pp.99-103. However, Tieke, *Horst Wessel*, p.54, provides a slightly different version of events. After Pisarowice fell to Kompanie Pleyber, the Russians counterattacked from two directions and surrounded the company, which broke out to the south-west, reaching the rail road station west of the village where it dug in. And it was during this breakout that Oberjunker Peyron and *freiwillige* Trévisan were killed. In response to Tieke, the author has used Bayle's account because he was an eyewitness.

31    Denis Sacomont was born on 14 October 1926 in Marseille.

32    René Trévisan was born on 16 September 1923 in Saint-Donat-sur-l'Herbasse.

Oberjunker Peyron attacked the machine-gun nest with five others. Hearing an incoming mortar salvo, Uscha. Bayle held back the others, but Peyron continued to rush forward alone and was killed instantly by mortar shrapnel which also destroyed the Russian machine-gun position. He was the first French officer of the Waffen-SS to be killed in action.[33]

Uscha. Bayle now took over the command of the platoon and, despite the absence of firm orders, he sensibly continued to charge forward. After ejecting the Russians from Pisarowice, the platoon took up defensive positions on a nearby level crossing over the Cracow-Sanok railway to the west of the village.

The time was about 1000 hours. It was only then that Uscha. Bayle thought about their isolated and very precarious situation. They were without officers, orders, or means of communication and were only lightly armed. They would not be able to repel the inevitable Russian counter-attack.

A Panzer Major, whose tanks were now approaching the platoon's positions, came and asked to speak to the person in charge of this small knot of troops. Uscha. Bayle immediately presented himself and gave his name, rank and unit. The Panzer Major smiled and congratulated the Frenchmen on their 'Blitzkrieg', explaining that they had reached the objective and that he was supposed to have supported their attack! Henceforth, Bayle's nickname was 'Blitzkrieg'.

The Panzer Major asked Uscha. Bayle for his *Soldbuch* so he could propose him for the Iron Cross 2nd Class. Directed by the German officer to a radio antenna among the ruins of Pisarowice some three hundred metres away, Bayle was able to make radio contact with the headquarters of Kampfgruppe Schäfer as well as Hstuf. Cance who was there quite by chance. After making a résumé of the action and detailing his precarious geographical situation, Bayle received orders from Cance to withdraw and rejoin the battalion.

At 1500 hours, the platoon handed its position over to panzergrenadier of the German 'armoured Regiment' and, in two groups taking different routes, pulled back to Wolica where the battalion was assembling. Bayle led one group and his good friend Uscha. Bruhat the other.[34]

Both groups somehow met up on the way back and shortly after made contact with the Battalion. Of the 40 who had set out on the mission, only 25 returned. On the following day, the bodies of those killed on 15 August, including that of Joseph Peyron, were brought back and laid to rest. The dead were buried in a clearing near the village of Wolica.[35]

Early on 16 August, now that the so-called Sanok pocket was sealed, the French Battalion returned the sector to the Wehrmacht. The Waffen-SS and the Wehrmacht 'passed each other without a word'.[36] As the platoons filed into Wolica the French Battalion counted its losses. The casualty figures differ. Mabire records the losses of the 1st Company as 60, the 2nd Company

33  According to Bayle, *De Marseille à Novossibirsk*, p.103, Peyron had been a little deaf ever since his earlier brush with death when a mine blew up a lorry in which he was travelling. Consequently, he may not have heard the incoming mortar salvo. Besides, 'he persisted in not wearing his helmet'.
34  Born on 14 December 1920 in Marseille, Raymond Bruhat had served in the Armistice Army from 1940 to 1942. Anti-Communist, he was a supporter of Pétain and Europe. He was not affiliated to any political party, even though his parents worked for Simon Sabiani, the vice president of the PPF and Doriot's right hand man. Bayle wrote of Bruhat's decision to enlist in the Waffen-SS: 'In this way, he continued the engagement of Sabiani's son by honouring his sacrifice, while thanking the Father.'
35  Saint-Loup, *Les Hérétiques*, p.38. However, Bayle, in a letter to the author dated 19/3/97, stated that he is not so convinced that it was Wolica, but did add that it could easily have been.
36  Mabire, *La Brigade Frankreich*, p.314.

as 50 and the 3rd Company as 20 dead or wounded.[37] Saint-Loup lists the losses as 35, 30, and 20 respectively.[38] Elsewhere Saint-Loup states that the battalion now counted less than 800 men.[39] This implies that the battalion lost in excess of 200 men. Total losses were therefore as low as 85 or as high as 200. However, Mabire does not make mention of the losses suffered by the PAK Platoon and the support services, whereas the latter might. As for the wounded, few, if any, would later return to duty with the battalion while still in Galicia. Kampfgruppe Schäfer was also relieved. It was needed elsewhere.

37    Mabire, *La Brigade Frankreich*, pp.314-315, and repeated by Tieke, *Horst Wessel*, p.55.
38    Saint-Loup, *Les Hérétiques*, p.40.
39    Saint-Loup, *Les Hérétiques*, p.51.

**6**

# The Mielec Sector

---

## A new mission and a new sector

Cance had much to think about. With the exception of the 3rd Company, he was greatly worried by the rashness of his battalion and in particular by de Tissot, the impulsive company commander of the 1st Company, who 'lacked real military experience'.[1] To calm him down, Cance called upon Bartolomei, back to health after several days of rest, and appointed him to the 1st Company as a platoon commander.

Cance also made a number of other changes: Ostuf. Pleyber was returned to the PAK and Ustuf. Lambert was moved from the 3rd Company to the command of the 2nd Company.[2]

On 16 August 1944,[3] the French Battalion was transported by lorry to the sector of Mielec, one hundred kilometres north-west of Sanok. It remained attached to Kampfgruppe Schäfer, which was also deployed to the same sector.

On the night of its arrival the French Battalion went into line.[4] A vast sector of front-line running along the river Wisloka, south of Sandomierz, on the Kampfgruppe's right flank was entrusted to the battalion. Its frontage was possibly as long as 15 kilometres. The French Battalion relieved troops of the Wehrmacht and this time the switch went smoother than previously at Sanok. Cance positioned from north to south the 1st Company, the 2nd Company and the 3rd Company.

---

1    Mabire, *La Brigade Frankreich*, p.321.
2    Saint-Loup, *Les Hérétiques*, p.49. In contrast, according to Mabire, *La Brigade Frankreich*, p.359, Cance assigned Ustuf. Lambert to the 2nd Company to assist Ostuf. Pleyber. His departure displeased Fenet who considered him an excellent officer and hard to replace. Uscha. Max Quiquempois took up the command now left vacant in the 3rd Company. Born on 10 September 1916 in Ribérac (department of Dordogne), Quiquempois was a former *Milicien*.
3    Lefèvre, *Axe & Alliés* hors série no 1, p.38. However, Bayle, Landwehr, Saint-Loup, and Tieke state 17 August and Mabire 19 August, which seems too late.
4    Lefèvre implies that the French Battalion was deployed along the Wisloka on the night of 18-19 August (*Axe & Alliés* hors série no 1, p.39) while Bayle of the 2nd Company recalls two days of peace before the Russian attack on the 20th.

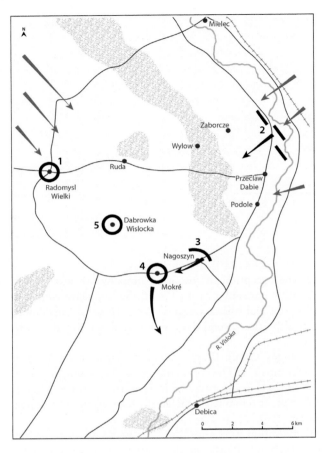

Mielec Sector.
1. The PAK platoon of the French battalion defends Radomyśl Wielki. 2. The three companies of the French battalion in position along the Visloka withdraw. 3. Battalion headquarters withdraws to Nagoszyn and is then forced to withdraw to Mokre. 4. The French battalion fights to the death at Mokre. 5. Chapy and survivors of the 1st Company fight around Dabrówka Wisłocka

To cover this sector, Cance had to spread out his companies thinly on the ground and some of de Tissot's platoons were expected to take over almost one kilometre of front![5] Radio communication was made almost impossible by this gullied and wooded region. Moreover, the river Wisloka could not be considered a serious natural obstacle and could easily be forded. It would be a gross understatement to describe the battalion's disposition as unfavourable although thankfully this sector seemed peaceful enough. In the past fifteen days there had been only one wounded. However, strong concentrations of enemy artillery had been observed to the north-east and south-east of Mielec.

Battalion Headquarters was established in the hamlet of Zaborce. For some, the next two days proved relatively peaceful. Uscha. Bayle of the 2nd Company spent his time sleeping or on patrol. The only danger his men faced was from friendly mortar fire falling short. On one occasion an enemy lookout, sat on the high branches of a tree peacefully smoking, made a friendly sign his way.

5    Indeed, according to Saint-Loup, *Les Hérétiques*, p.51, sixty men were deployed per kilometre.

Indeed, troops of the Wehrmacht and the Red Army fraternised in the late evening when the Soviets came to bathe and swim in the Wisloka. Cigarettes, chocolate and uniform buttons were exchanged.[6]

In contrast, the sector of the 1st Company was under constant sniper fire, and sporadic machine-gun and mortar fire.[7]

Towards midnight on the night of 19-20 August 1944, the 'peace' of the past days was shattered when Soviet artillery bombarded Wehrmacht positions to the left and the right of the French Battalion. The hurricane of fire intensified with the coming of dawn and the entrance of batteries of Katyusha rockets, known as 'Stalin Organs'.[8] The earth trembled, the forests shook and the 'fires set ablaze the whole horizon'. Even though the French Battalion was for the present spared this devastating barrage, it still suffered losses from random shelling. Ustuf. Bartolomei was wounded by shrapnel and evacuated. Uscha. Carré took over the command of the platoon again.

**Radomyśl Wielki**

Meanwhile, the Russians smashed through the 371st Infantry Division to the west of Kampfgruppe Schäfer and pushed westwards towards the town of Radomyśl Wielki.

At 0700 hours on Sunday 20 August 1944, Cance received a telephone call from Stubaf. Schäfer: "Tanks have broken through to the north-east. Send your anti-tank platoon at once to Radomyśl."[9] Off went Oberjunker Kreis and the thirty-strong PAK Platoon.[10] Arriving at Radomyśl at 0900 hours, Kreis received orders to hold the town at all costs until 1600 hours or die trying.[11] He had to smile at the pompous title of 'Kreiskommandant [battle commandant] of Radomyśl' bestowed upon him.

Empowered, Kreis commandeered all personnel and equipment retreating through Radomyśl. With the assistance and 'gentle persuasion' of six formidable Feldgendarmes, his command had grown in size to around one hundred men with the support of a Sturmgeschütz before the Russians attacked at midday exactly.

Infantry attacks came in first. Kreis was everywhere. The defenders held their ground. Eventually they may have faced a whole Soviet infantry regiment.[12] Just after 1500 hours, Soviet

6   Saint-Loup, *Les Hérétiques*, p.51. Of note is that troops of the French Battalion may have also been present at these exchanges (see Landwehr, *Charlemagne's Legionnaires*, pp.39-40).
7   Mabire, *La Brigade Frankreich*, pp.325-326.
8   Mabire, *La Brigade Frankreich*, p.329. However, according to Saint-Loup, *Les Hérétiques*, p.52, the Russians unleashed the bombardment at dawn on the 20th.
9   Saint-Loup, *Les Hérétiques*, p.53, repeated by Landwehr, *Charlemagne's Legionnaires*, p.41. Tieke may have slightly different wording but the meaning is just the same (*Horst Wessel*, p.60). In contrast, according to Mabire, *La Brigade Frankreich*, p.335, Oberjunker Kreis and his PAK Platoon had arrived in a panic-stricken Radomyśl the previous evening.
10  There is no agreement on the armament at the disposal of the PAK Platoon. According to Tieke, *Horst Wessel*, p.60, and repeated by Landwehr, *Charlemagne's Legionnaires*, p.42, Kreis had three 7.5cm anti-tank guns at his disposal, whereas, according to Mabire, *La Brigade Frankreich*, p.335, Kreis had left his two remaining anti-tank guns at the disposal of 'Horst Wessel' and his men had drawn panzerfäuste.
11  Saint-Loup, *Les Hérétiques*, p.54. However, according to Mabire, *La Brigade Frankreich*, p.338, Kreis received orders to hold until 1900 hours, but Mabire does not specify as to when Kreis received them.
12  Mabire, *La Brigade Frankreich*, p.337. Presumably this is based on the eyewitness account of Kreis.

tanks entered the battle.[13] The defenders fought back with panzerfäuste. Minutes later, the first tanks were blazing, but the defenders had paid a great price and now conducted a fighting withdrawal from house to house. They made a last stand in the cemetery.

Faced with another tank attack, the defenders seemed lost when their supply of panzerfäuste ran out. Just at that moment, as if by miracle, a German formation of Stukas appeared and pounced like hawks on the Soviet tanks. Direct hit after direct hit. Explosion after explosion. Saved!

The afternoon seemed without end. Desperately the defenders clung to the cemetery. The ending at Radomyśl was either one of victory or one of good military sense.

According to Mabire,[14] at 1830 hours, German reinforcements of infantry and even several panzers arrived. Stubbornly the Soviets came again with tanks. The defenders were still holding the cemetery when 1900 hours came and went. Oberjunker Kreis welcomed the passing hour with great relief, which meant that he had fulfilled his orders to hold until 1900 hours.

Soon after, panzerfäust in hand, Oberjunker Kreis boldly confronted a Soviet tank. Both man and steel giant fired almost simultaneously. He was seriously wounded. And yet he still noted that his aim had been true. The Soviet tank was burning.

Pulled under cover by his men, Kreis ordered section commander Nisus to take command of the PAK Platoon. He grew delirious. The pain was too much and the prospect of losing an arm too horrible. He wanted to commit suicide.[15] More German reinforcements arrived. The situation stabilised. The PAK Platoon had held Radomyśl to the bitter end. This was victory. However, according to Tieke, far from standing fast, Oberjunker Kreis had to give the order to pull back when the promised reinforcements did not materialise.[16]

By its defence of Radomyśl, the PAK Platoon brought time for the French Battalion and for part of Kampfgruppe Schäfer whose situation, gloomy enough as it was, could have been considerably worse if Radomyśl had passed into enemy hands earlier. Nevertheless, in combat there is always a price to pay and in this case that price was the decimation of the PAK Platoon.

**The most terrible night**

Let us now return to the French SS companies in position along the river Wisloka. All knew that they too would find themselves on the receiving end of the hurricane of fire the Russians had unleashed over the positions either side of theirs. The wall of explosions neared. Suddenly the bombardment was upon them. It was hell. Shells screamed down. The ground trembled from the blasts. Trees were ripped to pieces. Telephone lines were severed. For those sheltering from the death, the end of the barrage could not come soon enough.[17]

---

13   According to Landwehr, *Charlemagne's Legionnaires*, p.42, the defenders faced and 'hurled back' a Soviet tank regiment. This is doubtful.

14   Mabire, *La Brigade Frankreich*, pp.337-341.

15   Kreis was evacuated to a military hospital in Vienna where he quickly regained his appetite for life.

16   Tieke *Horst Wessel*, p.60. Tieke continues that the defenders fell back along the Radomysl-Przeclaw road to west of Ruda where they were integrated into the improvised defensive line of Battalion Riepe of Kampfgruppe Schäfer. Curiously, there is no mention of Kreis' wounding.

17   Remarkably, no casualties are reported.

Soviet snipers now targeted the runners. Two from the 2nd Company were mortally wounded in the space of several minutes. Each platoon closed up.

In the late afternoon of 20 August 1944, because of the deteriorating situation to the northeast, Obf. Trabandt, the commander of 'Horst Wessel', ordered Hstuf. Cance to disengage the three companies of the French Battalion with the utmost urgency from their positions along the river Wisloka to a position defined by the line Radomyśl-Pouby-Przeclaw.[18]

Oberjunker Chapy was called to see company commander Ostuf. de Tissot. When they were alone together de Tissot confided to him: "We've been encircled since this morning."[19] He explained that the Russians had steamrollered through Wehrmacht lines to the 'north and the south of their lines'. Also, he had received orders from battalion to withdraw at 1800 hours.

At the designated time the companies disengaged. Pushed by their commanders, the exhausted men quickly made it to the forest without too much interference. Then came a short period of rest during which night fell. Hstuf. Cance summoned the three company commanders who, like their men, had not slept for two days. The plan of action and the order of march was fixed. The first echelon would be Lambert's 2nd Company, including the headquarters group and Lopez's Engineer Platoon, followed by Fenet's 3rd Company and then by de Tissot's 1st Company bringing up the rear.

The platoons set off one after another into the darkness of the night and were immediately swallowed up. In order of march the echelons slipped through the burning hamlet of Dzilec.[20] Chapy's Platoon, the rearguard, formed a defensive 'hedgehog' position to the east of the hamlet. Although the hamlet came under increasing mortar and artillery fire, no Russians had been spotted yet, but they were thought to be everywhere. A runner finally brought the rearguard the order to withdraw.

## The 2nd Company

The 2nd Company reached its assigned positions, only to find the Russians already there. Battle ensued. In the darkness, confusion set in. The 2nd Company shattered and its survivors retreated south, pursued by the Russians. Bartolomei, who was wounded in the leg by a bullet, attempted in vain to round up the 2nd Company.[21] Some groups gave battle. Outgunned and outflanked, they were forced to withdraw.

Marching with Bartolomei were some thirty survivors of the 2nd Company. Convinced that they had at last outdistanced their pursuers, they stopped. It was now that a Russian patrol intervened. Uscha. Bayle saw the Russians slip into the nearby forest with one of his comrades, seized while attending to nature's needs.[22]

Presently, the Frenchmen came under fire. No casualties are reported. 'To facilitate the withdrawal', Bartolomei decided to separate the thirty survivors with him into two groups, one under himself and the other under Uscha. Bayle. The village of Mokre, where Cance was to

18    Saint-Loup, *Les Hérétiques*, p.54.
19    Mabire, *La Brigade Frankreich*, p.331.
20    Saint-Loup, *Les Hérétiques*, p.55.
21    Presumably Bartolomei was now back with the 2nd Company.
22    The captured soldier was known by sight to Bayle, but not by name.

set up Battalion Headquarters, was indicated as the meeting point. The two groups went their separate ways. By morning, the group led by Bartolomei had joined Battalion Headquarters.

During the night of 20-21 August 1944, Battalion Headquarters withdrew to Ruda and then 800 metres further to Nagoszyn.[23]

## The 1st Company

Last to set off, the 1st Company followed a badly gullied dirt track for some time before coming to a stop when the track crossed a road. Nearby was a small bridge spanning a dry stream and beyond that a village which seemed deserted.[24] The rest of the battalion seemed to have vanished without a trace. The night was heavy with mystery and danger. Uncertainty overtook company commander de Tissot; unsure of which direction to take, he sent out patrols to reconnoitre the vicinity, some of which were dispatched in the direction of where the positions of the 2nd Company were thought to be.

While awaiting the return of these patrols de Tissot heavily fortified the crossroads and rested his exhausted company in the village. Silence descended. The patrols began to return. Nothing had been found. By midnight, two scouts still had not returned.

Sat on the bridge, Chapy and de Tissot awaited the return of the last scouts. They heard the sound of snoring, went to investigate and found a machine-gunner fast asleep. He was harshly awoken. De Tissot then told Chapy to go and inspect the other posts just in case the other men were asleep as well. They parted company. Chapy went first to the cottage serving as a command post and then on to the village where he awoke other lookouts fast asleep. Apparently de Tissot went back to sit on the nearby bridge.

On hearing a convoy approaching the crossroads from the east, Ostuf. Nöel de Tissot went to meet it. Unexpectedly, the convoy was not civilian, but Soviet. Suddenly, gunfire from the post at the eastern edge of the village rent the night. More gunfire followed, then grenade explosions. Mortars joined in. De Tissot disappeared into the night and was never heard from again.[25]

Chapy heard the gunfire and raced back up the village towards the crossroads. On the way, in the light of a mortar being fired, he spotted a Russian soldier and fired at him. Once at the crossroads he came across Oscha. Kastner, commander of the Heavy Platoon, who told him that de Tissot had ordered a withdrawal westwards and that he had already departed. Chapy

---

23    Soulat, *Histoire des volontaires français dans l'armée allemande 1940-1945*, and Lefèvre, *Axe & Alliés* hors série no 1, p.40. Lefèvre also points out that Ruda is not to be confused with the locality of the same name near Radomyzl, presumably Radomyśl. However, according to Tieke, *Horst Wessel*, p.62, on the morning of 21 August, Cance finally arrived with the remnants of his battalion at Dabrówka Wislocka whereupon he received orders from Schäfer to go to Mokre and hold it for twelve hours.

24    Lefèvre believes this village may have been Przeclaw (*Axe & Alliés* hors série no 1, p.40). The author is not so convinced and believes the village is north of Przeclaw and to the west.

25    According to Mabire, *La Brigade Frankreich*, p.379, a French Freiwillige of the 1st Company named Camille Rouvre, who later managed to make it back to French lines, recounted that during the violent firefight at the crossroads de Tissot was killed. And yet, according to Lupo, *Levée d'écrou*, p.136, which also recounts the story of Rouvre, after his capture and subsequent escape, he learnt the sad news of de Tissot's disappearance when he made it back to French lines. Rouvre described de Tissot as a *grand chef* and the best officer of them all. Lastly, according to Tieke, *Horst Wessel*, p.61, de Tissot was captured wounded and then shot by the Russians.

went to the command post and had the company assemble immediately. It abandoned all heavy equipment. Chapy led the 1st Company out of the village and at first northwards, reasoning that the Russians, once they had reorganised, would surely continue westwards along the road.

Liaison officer Camille Rouvre of the 1st Company, occupying a barn with seven other men, was woken from sleep by the sound of gunfire. He heard voices. He could not make out the language, but it was not German or French. He wiped the sleep from his eyes only to see three weapons pointing at him. He got up and raised his arms. Brossard, who was beside him, did not get up and was shot dead.

To alert his comrades in the barn and in another building to the presence of Russians, he risked his life to shout out a warning. This warning saved the thirty-five men of Carré's Platoon, but his comrades in the barn chose to surrender rather than fight it out.

The seven prisoners were taken to a courtyard. Pinte, who spoke some words of Russian, was taken to see a Soviet commissar in his headquarters. He returned, announcing that the commissar had told him that they were to be taken to a field and there shot. One of them started to cry. Rouvre encouraged him as best he could, telling him that as long as there was life there was hope.

The Russians, nine men and an officer, who may have been the commissar, escorted the prisoners to a field. One Russian was shouldering two spades. Rouvre alerted his comrades to save themselves when he gave the signal. The prisoners were made to sit two by two and back to back. The Russians stood in a circle around them. When Rouvre saw the Russians raise their weapons he shouted: "*En avant!*"

Rouvre charged straight ahead. He punched the Russian in front of him with 'all his force of instinct of self-preservation', sending him reeling. He glanced back to see his comrades also in flight. Jumping into a thorn bush, he fell into a pond. This may have saved his life, for bullets whistled above his head. He swam across the pond, which was some fifty metres across, and ran off, avoiding two or three farms on the way where the enemy had to be. He heard gunfire to his left. Some two kilometres on, he crashed out in a potato field to get his breath back.

Rouvre would eventually make it back to French lines, not before he had been captured again and had escaped again. Of the other prisoners, only Alexandre Rouffet also made it back.[26] The others were never heard from again. They were Darnaud, Grossard, Pinte, Van-de-Put, and an unknown medical orderly. Rouvre was welcomed back with open arms by comrades from his company, which Oberjunker Chapy, almost single-handedly and with a good deal of fortune, had managed to extricate from the clutches of the Soviets.

Silently, the company made its escape along a sunken lane lined with hedges. Things went well until two Soviet cavalrymen on the banks of the sunken lane blocked the escape route. Covered by Chapy, the company slipped past in the shadow of the hedge.

Chapy went to the head of the survivors of the 1st Company. Gnawed by fear, the company wearily marched on in complete silence. The village blurred. The hedgerow became open fields which posed greater danger. Guided by Chapy, who was without a map, the company kept going through fields and marshes.

---

26    Born on 1 October 1922 in Talence (department Gironde), Alexandre Rouffet signed up for the Waffen-SS in August 1943, motivated by a desire to avoid the STO and also to marry a German girl he would later claim when interrogated by the Security Services after the war.

Suddenly, the company came under machine-gun fire. The French SS troops advanced towards this MG which they distinctly recognised as German. A voice called out to them in Russian, rooting them to the spot. Chapy shrank from the risk of pushing straight on and bore further west.

Finally, the company came across a road and Chapy decided to head westwards along the roadside ditches. The night was still like thick ink. After several hundred metres a machine-gun burst stopped the company in its tracks. It was a German MG again. This time they approached with caution. Thankfully, the machine-gun was actually manned by their compatriots. The 1st Company had made it back and it was all thanks to Chapy.

The 1st Company had just come across a hedgehog position manned by twenty men from various units under Ustuf. Le Marquer. The hedgehog position was centred on a crossroads between Ruda and Nagoszyn.[27] Cance's command post was situated in a small hamlet one kilometre away and could be contacted by field telephone.

Speaking to Cance, Chapy's first concern was for his company commander, de Tissot, of whom he asked news. Cance had none but did agree to Chapy's request to go and search for de Tissot and told him to take all available elements of the 1st Company. That amounted to between sixty and one hundred men which was too few to break through the Russian lines and too many to infiltrate. Thus, the search was doomed to fail.

With Chapy marching in the lead platoon, the 1st Company set out in the direction of Mielec. They were hungry, thirsty, exhausted and scared. Only the prospect of extricating their *chef* and other missing comrades drove them forward. It was still not light.

The search collapsed very quickly. Half an hour after setting out, the 1st Company ran into about twenty Russian troops who had suddenly emerged from the mist. Chapy's submachine-gun was the first to speak. More and more Russians emerged from nearby woods. The 1st Company now found itself opposite a strong Soviet battalion supported by anti-tank guns. Chapy responded by sending a runner to Cance for orders.

Presently, the 1st Company came under heavy fire and was pinned down. The air was filled with the whine of shrapnel and bullets in all directions. Chapy's good fortune continued; he escaped injury when a bullet blew off his cap, after which he donned his helmet and that was 'holed'.

Day broke. Exposed, the 1st Company came under heavier and more accurate fire. Le Marquer gave what support he could from afar, but the Russians had outflanked the 1st Company and were infiltrating towards the crossroads held by him.

A runner brought Chapy orders to pull back to the crossroads.[28] If the crossroads fell, the battalion's disposition would be irrevocably disrupted. The 1st Company disengaged without a hitch. Chapy was the last to leave.

On the morning of 21 August, one company from SS-Pz.AA 18 (Panzer-Aufklärungs-Abteilung 18) was ordered to counterattack on Przeclaw to release de Tissot's encircled 1st

27   Lefèvre, *Axe & Alliés* hors série no 1, p.40. Alain Croisile was proposed for the Iron Cross 2nd Class, which states he participated in the defence of crossroads Zagredy on 21 August 1944. Undoubtedly, this crossroads and the one depicted by the likes of Mabire and Lefèvre are one and the same. Unfortunately, the author cannot locate the exact location of this crossroads.
28   Mabire, *La Brigade Frankreich*, p.357. However, according to Saint-Loup, *Les Hérétiques*, p.62, with a heavy heart, Chapy gave the sensible and necessary order to fall back.

Company to the north. Although the Kradschützen (reconnaissance troops) courageously battled it out, they were unable to reach their objective or render assistance to their trapped French comrades.[29]

## The 3rd Company

If the night of 20-21 August 1944 proved terrible for the 1st Company, it was worse for the 3rd and yet the night had started promisingly enough when the company made it to its assigned position near to or in the village of Pouby[30] and promptly dug in.[31]

Mid-morning, Laschett's Platoon found itself isolated and encircled.[32] It fought furiously but was unable to extricate itself. An attempt was made to rescue Laschett's Platoon by headquarters staff under Uscha. Hennecart but was beaten back. Three times Ostuf. Fenet attempted to prise open the Soviet ring around Laschett's Platoon and three times he was repelled, with heavier and heavier losses.[33] The end came all too soon for Laschett's Platoon that was forced to surrender when its ammunition ran out.[34] Some twenty men, including Fernand Costamagna, surrendered, many of whom were wounded.

Under mounting Russian pressure, Ostuf. Fenet withdrew. He now had no more than fifty men with him; two platoons had disappeared and one was lost.[35] He too left behind him seriously wounded who did not wish to delay the march of the survivors. Schütze Charpentier was left with a pistol and a flask of water.[36] Towards midday, the survivors of the 3rd Company reached the Battalion's defence line and took up a position to the right of Nagoszyn.[37]

The battle at the crossroads held by Chapy and Le Marquer continued to rage. Lopez's Engineer Platoon was deployed to the crossroads. Chapy was everywhere, an inspiration to all. In dribs and drabs men from all units made it back to the makeshift 'defence line' whose base was the crossroads. All had the same word on the Russians. They were everywhere.

29  Tieke, *Horst Wessel*, p.61. Furthermore, according to Tieke, the encircled company was massacred.
30  According to Saint-Loup, *Les Hérétiques*, p.59, its designated position was Pouby and according to Mabire, p.359, 'a line of defense not far from the village of Poreby'. There's a certain Poręby which is part of the village of Wylów, some seven kilometres west of Ruda and six kilometres northwest of Przeclaw. Tieke positions the 3rd Company northwest of Przeclaw (*Horst Wessel*, p.60). Also, Costamagna of the 3rd Company wrote that he retreated some four to five kilometres (*Le soldat baraka*, p.150), which is the distance from the Wiskola to the village of Wylów.
31  Curiously, according to Tieke, *Horst Wessel*, p.60, three enemy companies supported by armour attacked the 3rd Company, which had to withdraw to the southwest. Lefèvre, *Axe & Alliés* hors série no 1, p.40, repeats that the 3rd Company was attacked by three enemy companies supported by armour but makes no mention that the company had to withdraw. This attack is not confirmed by any other source.
32  Mabire, *La Brigade Frankreich*, p.361 and Costamagna, *Le soldat baraka*, p.150. However, according to Saint-Loup, *Les Hérétiques*, p.72, Laschett's Platoon was left exposed when the Heavy Platoon was struck violently and scattered.
33  Mabire, *La Brigade Frankreich*, p.367.
34  Oberjunker Laschett would die later in the Soviet camp at Tambov in the first weeks of 1945.
35  Mabire, *La Brigade Frankreich*, p.368. Saint-Loup depicts the other platoons of the 3rd Company in fierce and constant battle with the Russians (see *Les Hérétiques*, pp.65-66 and 71-72).
36  Raymond Charpentier was born on 5 February 1924 in Saumur. He survived and passed to 'Charlemagne'.
37  Lefèvre, *Axe & Alliés* hors série no 1, p.41.

The Russians brought up anti-tank guns and mortars and all too soon the Frenchmen came under a continuous hail of fire. The earth was ploughed up. The slightest careless movement brought injury or death. Any object 'sticking out the ground was riddled with shrapnel'.[38] All units counted dead and wounded. Oscha. Lopez was soon wounded.

The Russians closed to within five hundred metres, but the Frenchmen continued to hold them at bay with machine-gun fire. The defenders' ammunition dwindled dangerously.

Continually cut, the telephone lines would only be kept repaired at the cost of wounded and killed. Brennion's signallers performed miracles to keep pace with the rate at which the Russians destroyed their work. Boyer's runners were almost all wounded or killed. Ferraud disappeared carrying a message from Cance to Fenet; he was never heard from again. Boyer's Kübelwagen, carrying ammunition and provisions for the hard pressed troops, was destroyed by a PAK shell. Ostuf. Pleyber was wounded by shrapnel and evacuated.

Towards 1700 hours, elements of the Wehrmacht on the left were seen to withdrawn. At 1745 hours, Le Marquer reported that he could no longer hold. At 1800 hours the order to withdraw was received by Headquarters at Nagoszyn. The units were to withdraw one hour later at 1900 hours.

1900 hours was fast approaching. The 2nd Company pulled back and the 3rd prepared to follow it.[39] The Russian pressure increased. Machine-guns raked the French lines. Suddenly, gunfire was heard to the rear. Battalion Headquarters was engaged in a heavy defensive battle against Russian units that had infiltrated the sieve-like 'defence line'. Cance just evaded capture. All headquarters personnel had to fight. They were delivered by the timely arrival of the disengaging 3rd Company which swept the area of Russians and formed a hedgehog position around the command post.

The seriously wounded had to be evacuated. Oscha. Boyer had them loaded onto a large car found abandoned. At that very moment, SS-Ostuf. Wagner of 'Horst Wessel' turned up and had a small 75mm infantry gun attached to the rear of Boyer's vehicle. A lorry was totally emptied of all its contents and filled with men who were all armed with a machine-gun or machine-pistol, and well stocked with ammunition. This 'armoured battering ram' led the way for those on foot behind it in columns on each side of the road. All told, the Frenchmen and Germans of Battalion Hoyer/Kampfgruppe Schäfer counted some one hundred men.

When the Russians tried to intercept this Franco-German battlegroup of company strength they were met by intense fire and scattered. With the wounded loaded onto the vehicles, the battlegroup continued on its way. The dead were abandoned 'out of necessity to save the greatest possible number of men'.[40]

The small convoy came to a plain. To the right, some five kilometres away, was the village of Mokre and to the left was the village 'sheltering' the *train de combat* of the battalion.[41] Soon after, the small convoy arrived in Mokre.

38   Mabire, *La Brigade Frankreich*, p.381.
39   Presumably the 2nd Company had been reorganised. It would have been missing the group led by Bayle making its way to Mokre.
40   Bayle, *San et Persante*, p.80.
41   *Train de combat* is a French military term that describes the logistical elements, motorised or horse-drawn, that accompany into battle a unit at least of battalion strength. As such, there is no English equivalent.

1900 hours could not come soon enough for the 1st Company on the verge of being overwhelmed. The Russians were now less than three hundred metres away. The crossroads and the hamlet were still under a continuous hail of fire. The minutes passed. The Soviets tried to turn the Frenchmen, but Uscha. Carré was quick to spot and eliminate the threat.

Finally, at 1900 hours, and not a minute before, the 1st Company withdrew. The survivors, no more than thirty, provided themselves with covering fire by walking backwards, firing from the hip. There was no panic.

Le Marquer led the survivors to the small hamlet 'housing' Battalion Headquarters. Chapy brought up the rear. The hamlet was burning. Cance and some headquarters staff were still there. They joined Le Marquer and the survivors of the 1st Company. Leaving the hamlet, they plunged into the relative safety of the woods. Night fell. Totally exhausted, they staggered southwards like automatons. Gunfire rent the night. Fear gripped them and they started to run.

Tired of withdrawing, two unknown machine-gunners from the 2nd Company stayed behind to fight it out. Their sacrifice brought fifteen valuable minutes for the pursued. Harassed by Russian patrols, the survivors swept aside all in their path and managed to make contact with German forces, whereupon they collapsed on the ground under the watchful eye of several Sturmgeschütze. Thus, at high cost, they had fought their way to freedom, temporary though it proved to be.

By the evening of 21 August 1944, the 1st Battalion of the French Sturmbrigade counted 300 combat-fit men at the very most. Each combat company now had the strength of only fifty men.

**Once more into the breach**

Cance called together his company commanders and passed on to them orders he had just received from 'Horst Wessel'. Quite simply the French Battalion was to occupy new defensive positions and stop the Russians.[42]

Cance set about deploying his battered and bruised battalion. First he drove Fenet to his position to await his 3rd Company. Then he organised Lambert's 2nd Company. After wishing Lambert good luck he came to the 1st Company. He instructed Chapy to position the 1st Company between the 3rd Company on the left and troops of Kampfgruppe Schäfer on the right. At the sound of a fusillade Cance jumped into his Kübelwagen and drove back to the command post where he would be needed most.

In vain Ostuf. Fenet waited for his company. Eventually he met up with a group of German soldiers from the Wehrmacht and together they fought off wave after wave of Russians. Morning broke. He was still without his company and battalion had not been in contact. His situation was no different from that of his German comrades. So they continued to hold their ground and return blow for blow. In the end the continued Soviet pressure told and they now found themselves outflanked.

At 1300 hours on 22 August, the Wehrmacht soldiers and Fenet withdrew and made for the small town of Debica to the south. They came across a road and hid as Soviet motorised columns passed by. Incredibly a column of German vehicles then appeared. They raced to the roadside

---

42  The exact location of these new defensive positions is not known, other than being south of those just vacated.

to make their presence known. A lorry stopped for them and they clambered aboard. Suddenly overcome by a terrible tiredness, Fenet fell asleep. He had gone without sleep for two days and two nights.

The lorry took Fenet and the Wehrmacht soldiers all the way to Debica, where he was incorporated into the mixed Kampfgruppe Muller made up of men from the Waffen-SS, the Wehrmacht and the Military Police. At the head of a group of infantrymen, gunners and engineers, he participated in the defence of Debica.[43] However, he was soon wounded by a piece of shrapnel in the shoulder and, against his wishes, evacuated.[44]

After Cance's hurried departure, the 1st Company cautiously advanced into the dark woods, but found neither the 3rd Company nor Schäfer's SS troops, just Russians. Once again the Russians seemed everywhere. Chapy heard the sound of engines. They had to be Russian. In the hope of finding friends, he decided to head towards the sound of the fusillade he had heard just as Cance was giving him orders.

In this way, Chapy and the 1st Company came to a village and the encircled survivors of two platoons of the badly shot-up 3rd Company. At their head was Oscha. Quiquempois. For the past hour, he and the two platoons had been walking round and round the village in search of a way out that the Russians did not have covered. There were none. Hence, he had come to the conclusion that they were completely encircled.

Staying put, Chapy had the village prepared for all-round defence. In support were two FLAK guns manned by the Wehrmacht, but with few rounds left to expend.

With what little ammunition the defenders had, they managed to keep at bay the inquisitive Soviet patrols. Nevertheless, they continued to receive harassing mortar fire.

Not wishing the village to become a trap, Oberjunker Chapy decided that they would have to get out. He was convinced that by dawn it would be too late. He told Quiquempois of his decision who was in full agreement.

Just before dawn on 22 August 1944, the French SS troops assembled, broke out of the village and marched to the sound of gunfire. They encountered no resistance. Unbeknown to them, the Soviets had pulled back during the course of the night.

They pressed on. Sporadic mortar fire continued to fall. Diving to the ground, they were showered with dirt. Day broke. The countryside seemed empty. Eventually they ran into reconnaissance elements of Kampfgruppe Schäfer who directed them to Stubaf. Schäfer at the village of Dąbrówka Wisłocka, some five kilometres away, where Chapy was welcomed by Schäfer who told him he had need of him to bolster his severely depleted command.[45] The situation was desperate; Schäfer had just dispatched all clerical and support staff to plug another hole in the collapsing front.

43  Mabire, *La Brigade Frankreich*, p.407. However, according to Saint-Loup, *Les Hérétiques* p.86, repeated by Landwehr, *Charlemagne's Legionnaires*, p.50, Ostuf. Fenet led a platoon in Kampfgruppe Muller.

44  Mabire, *La Brigade Frankreich* pp.405-408. Curiously, according to Saint-Loup *Les Hérétiques*, p.80-81, and Lefèvre, *Axe & Alliés* hors série no 1, p.42, Fenet fought at Mokre.

45  According to Tieke, *Horst Wessel*, p.61, during the night of 21-22 August, Ustuf. (sic) Chabert (sic) and the remnants of the 1st Company and 3rd Company reached German lines in Mokre, after which they were sent to the French Battalion that had occupied defensive positions south of Nagoszyn to the right of I/39 (1st Battalion of SS-Panzer Grenadier Regiment 39).

Pointing to his mapboard, Schäfer instructed Chapy to hold a position east of Dabrówka Wisłocka. Resupplied, the eighty French SS troops of the 1st Company and 3rd Company immediately set forth. Suddenly, they found themselves before some thirty German soldiers of the Wehrmacht who had abandoned their weapons and were fleeing the battlefield. At their head was a Major. Raising their weapons, the Frenchmen turned them round.[46]

Chapy moved into the abandoned positions and made contact with troops of the Kampfgruppe on both flanks. Hours later, the Frenchmen drove off a strong Soviet patrol with intense fire. Mortar fire then rained down on their positions. The first wounded were evacuated.

Fierce fighting flared up around Dabrówka Wisłocka. The Frenchmen and the Germans were outnumbered at a ratio of one to ten. Soviet assaults died under the fire of machine guns and machine pistols. Soviet tank attacks were broken up and beaten off by Sturmgeschütze. The Soviet air force made an appearance and machine-gunned the village. German FLAK answered and brought one down. Casualty lists mounted.

The Kampfgruppe managed to send a platoon to reinforce the Frenchmen and, in the afternoon, to relieve them with a company totalling thirty very young and exhausted men. Returning to Dabrówka Wisłocka, the Frenchmen could content themselves with another job well done; once again they had plugged another hole left by the Wehrmacht.[47]

**Mokre**

Meantime, Lambert's 2nd Company also became locked in fierce battle. Deployed in the hamlet north of Mokre during the night of 21-22 August, the 2nd Company was attacked in the early hours of 22 August. The Russians were too strong and broke into the northern part of the hamlet. They fortified the isbas they occupied.

To light up the night, Lambert had incendiary bullets fired into the thatched roofs of the isbas, which were soon ablaze. The fire spread quickly and as the Russians tried to evacuate the burning isbas they were mown down by MGs. Others sought refuge in isbas in the southern part of the hamlet held by the French. They were hunted down and dispatched with pistol and entrenching tools. The very success of Lambert's strategy was his undoing, for the fire continued to spread. He had to withdraw.[48]

Withdrawing to new positions, the 2nd Company came across a Russian standing at a crossroads. He was wearing a mixture of Russian and Wehrmacht uniform and had no papers on him. On the orders of Lambert, a Sergeant executed him as a spy. When the 2nd Company was in place Cance questioned Lambert about the Hiwi [Soviet auxiliary volunteer][49] he had left at the crossroads to direct them along the correct route! Cance had posted many such Hiwis to guide the French stragglers back.

---

46  Mabire alleges that machine-gunners of Kampfgruppe Schäfer deliberately fired on this 'unit of runaways' when it returned to the front-line, killing some (see *La Brigade Frankreich*, p.399).
47  According to Saint-Loup, *Les Hérétiques*, p.86, Schäfer honoured Chapy with field promotion to the rank of Untersturmführer. This is now considered very unlikely. See Bouysse, *Encyclopaedia of the New Order: French in German uniform part1: Officers of the Waffen-SS*.
48  Saint-Loup, *Les Hérétiques*, pp.76-77. However, Uscha. Bayle is incorrectly placed with Lambert.
49  Hiwi is the abbreviation for the German word *Hilfswilliger* or in English voluntary assistant or one willing to help. Hiwis were made up of Soviet prisoners, deserters and volunteers from among the local population.

The Russians came again. Outflanked once again, the Frenchmen had to retreat once again. Hit in the legs, a Sturmmann from Brittany beseeched his platoon commander, Hennecart, to put him out of his suffering. 'In the name of a higher charity', Hennecart administered the coup de grâce.[50]

Early on the foggy morning of 22 August 1944, a hedgehog position was formed around the village of Mokre from survivors of the 2nd Company and rearward personnel scraped together and fed into the front line; at most one hundred men.[51] The defenders included the small group of the 2nd Company led by Uscha. Bayle that good fortune had brought safely to Mokre that morning.

Exhausted, the fifteen-strong group led by Bayle had begun to dig in for the night of 21-22 August near a road when Russian trucks appeared. The Russians stopped and noisily set up camp on the other side of the road. The night and a haze were literally all that separated the two!

Moments later, a Russian patrol, in single file, quietly walked straight through the French positions and joined their comrades on the other side of the road. Incredibly the patrol did not raise the alarm. Bayle put this stroke of good fortune down to the Russians thinking they had seen the bodies of dead men in their holes when in fact they were sound asleep! 'The Frenchmen spent the night in the light of enemy flares and the constant hubbub of their chitchat'.[52]

Before daybreak, the Frenchmen left their Russian 'neighbours' and continued on their way through dense fog that made the going very difficult. Incredibly they stumbled upon a road sign showing the way to Mokre. And the village was only three kilometres away!

Through the thickening fog they marched. And, quite by chance, they came to the command post of the battalion. Bayle reported to Cance. The battalion commander was surprised to see him, all the more so when Bayle showed him which way they had come, because he was convinced that 'they were totally encircled'. He ordered Bayle to take up position.

In the early morning hours, Hstuf. Cance and Ustuf. Lambert discussed the subject of counterattacks to 'loosen the Russian vice'.[53] Cance was back and forth between the front line and his command post, a hovel, which increasingly came under attack from Russian patrols that had slipped past the French resistance points. And it was here that Cance received his first wound of the day, a bullet in his left arm. No sooner was he bandaged up than he received orders from Schäfer to defend Mokre for twelve hours.  Assembling his remaining officers, Cance conveyed the orders to them, adding they would carry them out to the last officer!

Then the Russians came. Ustuf. Lambert went to the head of a platoon and counterattacked. Violent hand-to-hand combat raged with bayonet and trenching spade. The Russians broke, but the battle soon continued. The 2nd Company melted away in this inferno, but held the ground retaken from the enemy.

Hit by mortar shrapnel in the abdomen, Ustuf. Lambert suddenly keeled over. He was evacuated to the makeshift first aid post in the village. Cance asked Boyer to get Lambert and

---

50   Saint-Loup, *Les Hérétiques*, p.80.
51   Mabire, *La Brigade Frankreich*, p.409. Eyewitness Boyer states that the defenders numbered 60 men under Le Marquer and Fenet. Tieke repeats the same defenders and commanders (*Horst Wessel*, p.64), whereas Bayle states that the defenders were divided up into three groups under Le Marquer, Reiche and Fenet (*San et Persante*, p.81). As previously discussed, Fenet may have not been at Mokre.
52   Bayle, *De Marseille à Novossibirsk*, p.117.
53   Mabire, *La Brigade Frankreich*, p.409.

the wounded loaded onto a vehicle and get ready to leave at a moment's notice. Boyer responded that his place was with his men. Cance retorted: "It's an order." Boyer made his way to the first aid post and found Lambert in agony. Nevertheless, Lambert recognised him and asked: "Cance, go get Cance, let him give me my Iron Cross before I die". Boyer and medical orderly Maurer loaded Lambert and the other wounded. A shell landed nearby. Lambert's head touched Boyer's left cheek. His head was virtually cold and a thin trickle of blood ran from his mouth. Lambert would die later of his wounds in the field hospital at Lipiny, some fifteen kilometres north of Tarnów.[54]

Oscha. Czulowski was seriously wounded. Having asked for a pistol and a cigarette, he committed suicide on the approach of the Russians.[55] Machine-gunner Mamet was killed changing position. Alain Croisile, the youngest son of Jean Croisile, was seriously wounded in the head and left for dead.[56] Oscha. Pouget may have also met his death at Mokre.[57] Uscha. Bruhat of the 2nd Company, Bayle's friend, was wounded while carrying a wounded comrade on his back and evacuated.

Hstuf. Cance went back to the battle and was wounded again when a grenade exploded at his feet. It left him dazed, but again he had escaped serious injury.

Hordes of Russians continued to surge forward. For hours the battle ebbed and flowed. Ustuf. Le Marquer was everywhere. No sooner had he averted danger at one 'quill' of the hedgehog than he was dashing off to another where danger was arising. Hennecart was wounded and evacuated.

Once again the Russian artillery thundered and the mortars screamed. Isbas went up in flames and plumes of black smoke spiralled into the sky. Reiche, Binder and Le Marquer were blown to pieces in the farmhouse used as a command post.[58]

54    Lefèvre, *Axe & Alliés* hors série no 1, p.40. According to Saint-Loup, *Les Hérétiques*, p.83 and Mabire, *La Brigade Frankreich*, pp.412-413, Lambert's last moments were much more dramatic. Informed of Lambert's mortal wounding, Cance was soon on the scene. Shouldering Lambert, he brought him back through enemy fire to Mokre. Dr. Bonnefoy raced over but could do nothing for him except try and make him comfortable. Lambert asked for the Iron Cross which was later sanctioned. Minutes later, he died in the arms of Dr. Bonnefoy. In reply, the author has used the testimony of Boyer, which is supported by his citation for the Iron Cross 1st Class, which describes how he transported the body of the mortally wounded Ustuf. Lambert, as well as two seriously wounded soldiers, to the first aid post.
55    Born on 22 April 1912 in Paris into a family of Polish origin, Wladislas Czulowski served in 1939-40 with the rank of *aspirant d'active*. He passed from the SOL to the *Milice*, joining the *Franc-Garde permanente* in May or June 1943. He enlisted in the Waffen-SS on 29 November 1943.
56    See Croisile, *Sous uniforme allemande*, pp.343-344. Born on 10 June 1926 in Paris, Alain Croisile enlisted in the Waffen-SS on 30 August 1943 and attended Posen-Treskau.
57    Mabire, *La Brigade Frankreich*, p.411. However, there are, at least, two other versions of where Pouget met his death. According to Saint-Loup, *Les Hérétiques*, p.62, in the early hours of 21 August 1944, Pouget, listed as the heavy platoon commander of the 1st Company, went in search of the missing Ostuf. de Tissot. He was never heard from again. Secondly, according to Bayle, *San et Persante*, p.79, Pouget went off with a small group to destroy or capture a Russian anti-tank gun in the village of Ruda, whereupon he was killed and the small group decimated.
58    Bayle, *De Marseille à Novossibirsk*, p.119. Bayle was an eyewitness. Incorrectly, both Mabire and Saint-Loup recount that Le Marquer, out of ammunition, was seen to fall in hand-to-hand fighting. Moreover, Saint-Loup puts his death in the afternoon. Furthermore, according to Tieke *Horst Wessel*, p.65, Binder, Le Marquer and Reiche fell during the breakout from Mokre. This also has to be incorrect.

## End at Mokre

In the afternoon the situation at Mokre began to look ugly. Not only were the defenders running out of ammunition, but also they had no anti-tank weapons to combat the Russian tanks that had just been sighted. If they were to offer continued resistance they needed to be resupplied and fast. Orderly Officer Ustuf. Scapula and four others went speeding off in a Kübelwagen to the battalion's supply train located at Debica, some thirteen kilometres away. They got through to Debica.[59] Once the Kübelwagen was stacked high with ammunition they started back; there was not a minute to lose.

Approaching Mokre, the Kübelwagen came under enemy infantry and mortar fire. Against all the odds, a bullet struck the nose cone of a panzerfäust attached to the bonnet for ease of use in the event of a chance meeting with enemy armour. In the resulting explosion the German driver and Ustuf. Scapula were killed outright. The three Frenchmen in the rear jumped out and defended themselves as best they could against the Russians who had just appeared. Of the three, only Sturmmann Mesqui would make it back to French lines. His two compatriots, named as Savaiau and Barthet, who he last saw crawling some fifty metres from the Russians, were never heard from again.[60]

As a result of the loss of the Kübelwagen the fire from the defenders of Mokre gradually diminished. They now only fired when they were sure of hitting their target. There was no longer any organised resistance, just isolated pockets of small groups. Overwhelmed and crushed, the ultimate fate of many of these French groups will never be known. Despite the Frenchmen stubbornly contesting each and every inch of ground, the Russians had grown too strong and broke into Mokre itself. There was bloody hand-to-hand fighting in the blazing village.

Once again a grenade landed at the feet of Hstuf. Cance. This time, he was not so lucky. Seriously wounded in the knee, he was taken to the first aid post and then evacuated by ambulance. Thus, the Frenchmen had fought to their last combat officer, but they had held Mokre for twelve hours.[61]

Finally, the defenders received orders to withdraw to the farm containing Battalion Headquarters where they tried to regroup to face the Russian tanks, accompanied by infantry, closing in 'for the kill'.[62] Clearly, this was the end.

---

59    According to Saint-Loup, *Les Hérétiques*, p.85, Ustuf. Bartolomei, who had been evacuated along with the *train de combat* to Debica, shook hands with Ustuf. Scapula during the brief turnaround. However, Mabire has Bartolomei serving as a medical orderly in the first aid post at Mokre (see *La Brigade Frankreich*, p.410).

60    Saint-Loup, *Les Hérétiques*, p.85.

61    Mabire, *La Brigade Frankreich*, p.417, also Saint-Loup, *Les Hérétiques*, p.85. However, according to Boyer's citation for the Iron Cross 1st Class, he took over the command of the French Battalion at 0900 hours, by which time his *chef de bataillon* [Cance] was seriously wounded and all other offices were dead or wounded. This is not true. See Boyer's own testimony (39/45 magazine, No 335, p.56). Curiously, according to Bayle, *De Marseille à Novossibirsk*, p.119, shortly before the end at Mokre, Ustuf. Reiche confided to him the command of those still left. The author has not been able to explain this, although it should be recalled that the battle appears to have been fought in great chaos.

62    This is a conclusion drawn by the author from Bayle, *De Marseille à Novossibirsk*, p.119, as well as letters to the author.

The courtyard of the farm was full of dead, including Reiche, and seriously wounded. Learning of the tank attack, the wounded were gripped by panic. Some tried to run off, but they could not keep on their feet. Pounding the farm with every kind of weapon, the Russian tanks approached. There was no cover for the wounded lying out in the farmyard. Few, if any, escaped death. The defenders fled from the farm.[63]

Chased by bullets and shells, the survivors came to German assault guns camouflaged behind stacks of straw, but they were not engaging the enemy. They were to learn later that the assault guns had totally exhausted their ammunition and were awaiting replenishment. They pressed on. They now passed Army troops launching a counterattack. They gave the Frenchmen a friendly wave.

Quite by chance the survivors met the *train de combat* of the French battalion. 'Croisile asked for news of his son but they preferred to keep silent'.[64]

At or near Debica, the survivors from Mokre took up position where they met comrades from the 1st Company and the 3rd Company under Chapy.

Orders were received to move to a forest location seventeen or eighteen kilometres from Tarnów on the road from Debica to Tarnów.[65] Trucks transported the survivors to the forest location where they met a very small precursory detachment of reinforcements from the 2nd Battalion of the French Sturmbrigade.[66] Now they could rest.

## The *train de combat* finds itself in trouble

However, the fighting was still not over for some elements of the battalion. On the afternoon of 24 August 1944, its *train de combat* of twenty trucks, carrying French and German wounded, found itself encircled. Gunfire could be heard closing in from the north and the south, shells were pursuing the convoy from the east, and Russian troops had cut the road ahead to Tarnów.

Ostuf. Croisile called together the other officers present. Deciding upon a ruse, he hoped to draw off the Russian troops blocking the way westwards by creating diversions on the flanks. He ordered Ostuf. Dr. Bonnefoy to direct the diversion to the north and Ostuf. Maudhuit that to the south.[67] His orders to them were concise: "Assemble all available machine-guns… All combat-fit men… Intense fire for ten minutes and withdraw!"

63   Bayle, *De Marseille à Novossibirsk*, p.120. However, according to Mabire, *La Brigade Frankreich*, p.417, the French SS troops received orders to disengage and then 'withdrew in small groups, trying to delay the Russians again'. In response to this, Bayle, one of the last defenders of Mokre and perhaps the only able-bodied NCO left as the end neared, does not recall any such orders (correspondence to the author, 1997). Also, according to Bayle, the withdrawal was much more chaotic than that depicted by Mabire and little, or no, resistance was offered by the survivors as they retreated to Debica. Curiously, according to Boyer's citation for the Iron Cross, he was the last to leave the battlefield. This is not true. See Boyer's own testimony (39/45 magazine, No 335, p.56) and Bayle, *San et Persante*, p.82. Boyer was evacuating the wounded by car when Mokre fell.
64   Bayle, *De Marseille à Novossibirsk*, p.121.
65   Bayle, *San et Persante*, p.85. These orders were probably received on the evening of 22 August 1944. Undoubtedly the move would have come soon after.
66   Bayle, *San et Persante*, p.85. This remains unconfirmed.
67   Mistakenly, Landwehr identifies Maud'huit with the rank of Untersturmführer (*Charlemagne's Legionnaires*, p.51).

Bonnefoy assembled the clerks, drivers, lightly wounded, and combat-fit men. Maudhuit assumed command of a platoon. They deployed and opened up on the Russian units across the plain gently descending westwards. Maudhuit fought like a man possessed and, when one of his machine gunners was hit, he immediately took over. Just as Croisile had hoped, the ruse worked and the Russians relaxed their grip on the road to Tarnów to reinforce those under attack. The first trucks of the convoy sped off.

Withdrawing to the convoy, Maudhuit was hit and wounded by mortar shrapnel, but a member of his platoon rushed over, shouldered him and threw him onto the last truck of the convoy. At breakneck speed the convoy now belted westwards, sweeping aside weak parties of Russians and dodging artillery fire. Miraculously it made it through.[68]

## Tarnów

At Tarnów, Ostuf. Croisile reorganised the command of the battalion as follows:[69]

1st Company: Oberjunker Chapy
2nd Company: Ustuf. Bartolomei
3rd Company: Uscha. Lefèvre

The combat companies were now only of platoon strength. Indeed, the casualty balance-sheet made very grim reading. Every combat officer had either been killed or wounded. In point of fact, both Chapy and Bartolomei had been wounded, but refused evacuation!

Of the estimated 980 French SS troops engaged some two weeks before, Mabire states '130 killed, 50 or so missing, and more than 660 wounded'.[70] Saint-Loup states that 140 men and NCOs came back and that 'all the others were dead, wounded or missing'.[71] Bayle repeats that there were 140 survivors of which about one hundred were slightly wounded.[72] Tieke records the appalling losses as 7 officers and 90 other ranks killed, 8 officers and 660 other ranks wounded and 40 taken prisoner out of 15 officers and 900 other ranks engaged.[73] Landwehr states 7 officers and 130 other ranks killed, 8 officers and 661 other ranks wounded and 40 men missing, for a total casualty figure of 846.[74] These figures, which differ little, represent a most terrible bloodletting.

68   Saint-Loup, *Les Hérétiques*, pp.86-87. It should be noted that Landwehr also writes of this same action, see *Charelmagne's Legionnaires*, pp.50-52, but the differences are many. Convinced that Landwehr used Saint-Loup as a source, the author chose not to repeat the rewriting of Landwehr. In addition, no other source confirms this action, which is curious.
69   Mabire *La Brigade Frankreich*, p.424, and Lefèvre, *Axe & Alliés* hors série no 1, p.43. Saint-Loup also places Chapy at the head of the 1st (*Les Hérétiques*, p.92). However, Bayle, *De Marseille à Novossibirsk*, p.125, places Oberjunker Chapy at the head of the 3rd and Maudhuit at the 1st.
70   Mabire, *La Brigade Frankreich*, p.421.
71   Saint-Loup, *Les Hérétiques*, p.88.
72   Bayle, *De Marseille à Novossibirsk*, p.121.
73   Tieke, *Horst Wessel*, p.69.
74   Landwehr, *Charlemagne's Legionnaires*, p.53.

Of those Frenchmen captured, sadly many were summarily put to death.[75] Years of rigorous Soviet imprisonment awaited the others from which few would return. As for the wounded, some would never return to active service. Some would take months to recover from their wounds. Albert Poignant, who was serving with the 1st Company, was wounded in the shoulder by mortar shrapnel on 20 August and evacuated. He spent one month in hospital. After eight days leave, which he spent at Stettin, he was posted to the *Companie de déport* at Greifenberg. Ostuf. Pleyber returned to service in early October. However, he had complications and had to be cared for again. Uscha. Bruhat of the 2nd Company only returned to service in January 1945.

Even at the rear death struck. *Freiwillige* Marcel Artinagave, Boyer's orderly, drowned in a nearby river.[76] He had fought bravely on the battlefield. Strmm. Nicholas Montignac made it out of Galicia unscathed, but was later involved in a serious car accident, fracturing both legs, which kept him out of the rest of the war.

On 24 August 1944, the 1st Battalion of the French SS-Sturmbrigade was cited in the divisional orders of 'Horst Wessel'. Days later, the survivors paraded for Obf. Trabandt of 'Horst Wessel' who passed on his congratulations and those of General Graesler, Balck's assistant.[77]

The Frenchmen now had to part from 'Horst Wessel'.[78] The survivors were to be transferred to the SS-Truppenübungsplatz Westpreußen in the former Danzig corridor to be incorporated into the French Brigade of the Waffen-SS.

A number of soldiers would receive awards.[79] Among the recipients of the Iron Cross 1st Class were Henri Kreis, Robert Lambert and Rttf. Marc Briand.[80] Among the recipients of the Iron Cross 2nd Class were André Bayle, Pierre Bonnefoy, Emilien Boyer, Pierre Cance, Abel Chapy, Fernand Costamagna, Robert Cousin, Pierre Couvreur, René Dupont, Henri Fenet, Lucien Hennecart, Henri Jonquières, Jacques Lefèvre, Pierre Maurer,[81] Strmm. Jacques Pieyre de Mandiargues, Paul Pruvost, Henri Queyrat, Henri Quiquempois, Jacques Rousseau and Camille Rouvre (1st Company).

---

75  See Mabire, *La Brigade Frankreich*, p.380, and Saint-Loup, *Les Hérétiques*, p.68.

76  Marcel Artinagave was born on 2 October 1922 in Bordeaux. He was a member of the *Parti Franciste*.

77  Saint-Loup, *Les Hérétiques*, pp.92-93. Notably, no other source confirms this parade for Trabandt.

78  Curiously, according to Mabire, *La Brigade Frankreich*, p.424, the Frenchmen could not stay with the 'Horst Wessel' because they were missing too many officers and NCOs.

79  Sources differ as to the number of awards as well as the date of the awards. According to Saint-Loup, *Les Hérétiques* p.93, Obf. Trabandt left in his wake 40 Iron Crosses, of which 29 were awarded posthumously. According to Bayle, *De Marseille à Novossibirsk*, p.124, in conjunction with Ustuf. Bartolomei, the NCOs 'prepared the citations'. In this way, in September, nominations for over 100 awards of the Iron Cross, including many posthumously, went forward. Moreover, Bayle does not recall a distribution of Iron Cross at Tarnów (correspondence with the author). According to Tieke, *Horst Wessel*, p.69, the surviving officers and NCOs were decorated with the Iron Cross 1st Cross and 58 French volunteers received the Iron Cross 2nd Class. This is incorrect, for example Bonnefoy, Bayle and Maudhuit did not receive the Iron Cross 1st Class. Lastly, according to Mabire, *La Brigade Frankreich*, p.424, 58 Iron Crosses were awarded, including many posthumously, and 20 were later presented with little ceremony on 10 November 1944 at Wildflecken (see *La Division Charlemagne*, p.169).

80  However, according to Soulat, Briand was awarded the Iron Cross 2nd Class (see Bouysse, *Waffen-SS Français* volume 2). Born in 1925, Briand was a law student, who decided that if he died in France it 'would serve nothing at all whereas dying on the Eastern Front would be for a good cause' (Radio Broadcast of 3 February 1944, see Mounine, *Cernay 40-45*, p.268).

81  Pierre Maurer was born on 22 May 1924 in Paris. He was a medical orderly.

Gamory-Dubourdeau would later request in writing the posthumous promotion of Oscha. Pouget to the rank of Unterstürmfuhrer, noting: 'His exemplary death is for his men a model of military virtue'. It's not known if this promotion was granted.

On 1 September 1944, the 1st Battalion of the French Sturmbrigade left Tarnów railway station for the former Danzig corridor. Oberjunker Chapy was no longer with the battalion. He was actually under arrest for murder!

## Abel Chapy

The ill-feeling that had developed between the combatants of the French Battalion and the personnel of the Verwaltung [Supply Corps] came to a head at Tarnów.[82] So infuriated was Chapy when it came to his attention that the supply personnel were interfering with the belongings of the wounded and dead he confronted and warned a certain Unterscharführer Eglé of the Verwaltung. The Alsatian Eglé was a known trafficker.[83] That same day, a grenadier handed Chapy a letter to read from a wounded soldier of the 1st Company hospitalised in Bohemia-Moravia. The wounded soldier wrote that Eglé had refused to take him to a first-aid post. Chapy, who had had enough, decided to take matters into his hands.

In the presence of a number of witnesses,[84] Chapy summarily executed Eglé and had him buried. He then reported his execution of Eglé to Croisile, Maudhuit and Bonnefoy who were at a total loss what to do. They did nothing. Chapy later reported that Eglé had disappeared, but Ostuf. Danke, the German commander of the Verwaltung, went to the headquarters of Kampfgruppe Schäfer and reported the true nature of Eglé's 'disappearance'.[85]

On 28 August 1944, Chapy and the onlookers were arrested and questioned.[86] Joined by three other Frenchmen of the 1st Company,[87] they were sent to Tarnów and then onto a military prison at Cracow.[88]

---

82    According to Mabire, *La Brigade Frankreich*, p.429, the survivors blamed SS-Ostuf. Danke, the German commander of the Verwaltung, for not keeping them sufficiently fed. This seems unfair because the situation was fluid.

83    Incorrectly, Mabire identifies Eglé as German.

84    According to Mabire, *La Brigade Frankreich*, p.431, Oberjunker Chapy was accompanied by Belanger (pseudonym for François Anger), Quarru (pseudonym for Carré) and Delagarde (pseudonym for de Bonnegarde). Carré served with the 1st Company while Anger and de Bonnegarde were members of Chapy's Platoon attached to the 1st Company. However, according to Bayle, *San et Persante*, p.85, Chapy had four accomplices: Carré, Patt, Max Mercier and de Bonnegarde.

85    According to Mabire, *La Brigade Frankreich*, p.435, Danke had much to cover up.

86    Details of Chapy's arrest conflict. According to Mabire, *La Brigade Frankreich*, p.435, six military policemen of 'Horst Wessel' arrested Chapy and the three other Frenchmen'. Then an ugly situation arose when Chapy was surrounded by NCOs of the Verwaltung who were in turn ringed by armed Frenchmen from all three companies. Nevertheless, the situation was quickly diffused by Chapy himself. According to Bayle, *San et Persante*, p.86, the 'arresting officers' were Oscha. Boyer and Uscha. Lefèvre.

87    Mabire, *La Brigade Frankreich*, p.436. However, there is little accompanying detail about the three. Thus, the possibility exists that they were not involved in the execution of Eglé.

88    Mabire, *La Brigade Frankreich*, p.438. However, in October 1988, Chapy told Mounine that he was held in fortress Warsaw. And yet it was Chapy himself who provided Mabire with the details of his adventures.

Months later, Chapy was brought before a military court, not from the new French formation, but from the 28. SS-Freiwilligen Grenadier Division 'Wallonien'. Found guilty, he was sent to the Waffen-SS military prison at Dachau.[89]

89   What became of Chapy is irreconcilable; according to Mabire, *La Brigade Frankreich*, p.438, repeated by Landwehr, *Charlemagne's Legionnaires*, p.55, Chapy's case would only be reopened upon a personal order from Reichsführer-SS Himmler himself. In response, Bayle states that this is simply not true (correspondence to the author). Mabire continues that Chapy would be set free in the last days of the war. Landwehr adds that Chapy then saw action against the Americans in a mixed kampfgruppe with Hitler Youth and others. Again, Bayle states that this is simply not true (correspondence to the author), noting that Chapy was liberated from prison by the Americans and then arrested and locked up again by the French authorities (see Bayle, *San et Persante*, p.86). And yet, in October 1988, Chapy told historian Mounine that he was at large in Hamburg from late 1945 to early 1946 (Mounine, correspondence to the author). Lastly, according to Bouysse, *French in German Uniform part 1: Officers of the Waffen-SS*, Chapy was released in April 1945 and sent to Czechoslovakia to fight. After deserting, he went to Prague to find his fiancée, but was forced to flee in September 1945 after injuring two Russians who were trying to rape his fiancée. He made his way to Hamburg where his fiancée's parents lived and was unable to find them so he returned to France. He took up residence in Sennheim and assumed a new identity but was still arrested on 30 October 1945. This confirms in part what Chapy told Mounine about spending time on the run in Hamburg.

# 7

# End of the LVF

---

For the past year, which had seen the creation of a French unit of the Waffen-SS and the deployment of a battalion to the Eastern Front, the LVF had continued its brutal war against the growing partisan menace behind the front line.

## September 1943-October 1943

In early September 1943, Michel de Genouillac enlisted in *La Légion Tricolore*.[1] Born on 13 July 1921 near the small village of Concoret, Brittany, he attended the military academy of La Flèche and, in May 1940, passed the written entrance examination for the *École Spéciale Militaire de Saint-Cyr*. Weeks later, France went to her defeat. In September 1940, at Valence, after learning that he was not one of the few to gain admittance to Saint-Cyr relocated to Aix-en-Provence, he resumed his studies. Finally, in October 1941, he entered Saint-Cyr.

On 25 November 1942, de Genouillac graduated, receiving the rank of *sous-lieutenant*. His branch was the cavalry. Four days later, on the dissolution of the Armistice Army, he was demobilised. He returned home, where he waited for instructions that would never come. Months later, tired of waiting, he decided to request his enlistment in *Les Chantiers de la Jeunesse*. Assigned to Groupement 7, 'the Proud', he was entrusted with the command of camp 3, established in the mountains of Clergeon, above Rumilly in Haute Savoie. The months passed by. He had much time to reflect. By July 1943, he could no longer tolerate this inaction when the war was entering a decisive phase and decided to enlist in *La Légion Tricolore*. Thereupon, he wrote to the Vichy *Sécretariat à la Guerre* requesting authorisation to enlist. This only came in September. He then left *Les Chantiers de la Jeunesse* which was disintegrating anyway.

De Genouillac's decision to enlist stemmed from a melting pot of reasons: the partisan war and its excesses disgusted him, to him it was a return to barbarity; he did not want to participate in operations in France which could not fail to set him against Frenchmen of good faith, often sharing the same ideals as him; he had sworn an oath of loyalty to Marshal Pétain, and still felt

---

1    Curiously, at this time, *La Légion Tricolore* ceased to exist. When questioned about this, Michel de Genouillac confirmed to the author that he enlisted in *La Légion Tricolore* and not the LVF. One possible explanation for this is that the French authorities were using the 'front' of the *La Légion Tricolore* as a means of recruiting for the 'less attractive' LVF.

bound to this oath (which was regarded as a sacred undertaking at that time); the atmosphere of the 'Government of Algiers' dominated by Communists and Gaullists did not encourage him to join his compatriots who were already there; to him, Communism was the most redoubtable enemy of his country and 'our' civilisation; and since the Germans were losing the war the symbolic help that he would bring to them on the Eastern Front would not delay the liberation of his country.

On 1 October 1943, de Genouillac left for the training centre of Kruszyna in Poland. He arrived days later. At the end of his training period, he was sent to Russia, where he arrived on 1 April 1944. He was assigned to the 3rd Company of the I. Bataillon.

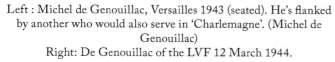

Left : Michel de Genouillac, Versailles 1943 (seated). He's flanked by another who would also serve in 'Charlemagne'. (Michel de Genouillac)
Right: De Genouillac of the LVF 12 March 1944.

In September 1943, while on leave back home in Marseille, Gonzales visited Simon Sabiani, his mentor and good friend. Gonzales brought with him a photo of Sabiani's son, François, in his coffin on a Russian cart.[2] Demoralised, Gonzales revealed to Sabiani his intention not to go back to Russia. They had a long conversation about this. In the end Sabiani managed to convince him to return. So back he went to his comrades of the 2nd Company of the I. Bataillon, as well as his pregnant Russian girlfriend Anna. He was without regrets. Such was his destiny he would later reflect.

When Bassompierre learnt of his orderly's liasions with Anna he transferred him to a village north of the river Berezina called Thernouka, almost opposite Murovo (also spelt Murowo) on the other bank. He was employed in his profession as a carpenter to construct a bridge over the Berezina in collaboration with a Russian engineer, but constantly found himself in conflict with *sous-lieutenant* Mailhé, who was overseeing the project. Nevertheless, Colonel Puaud paid him a visit to inaugurate this bridge, but he was not presentable; once again, he was sleeping off the effects of vodka. His comrades made an excuse for him that he was seriously ill. He was even more surprised to receive a citation from Puaud thanking him for his work!

Jean Mailhé had arrived in Russia in November 1943. Born on 9 September 1912 in Reims, he served France loyally during the 39-40 campaign in the *1e Régiment Étranger* (1er RE) with the rank of *Aspirant* and once more against the Germans in Tunisia in 1943. Captured and sent back to France, he volunteered for the LVF, becoming an instructor alongside Paul Briffaut. Sent to Russia, he served with the 2nd Company and later the 6th Company of the II. Bataillon.[3] Later still, he was awarded the German Kriegsverdienstkreuz [War Merit Cross] 2nd Class.[4]

September was a costly month for the III. Bataillon as a direct consequence of the partisans' change of tactics. On 7 September, a horse-drawn araba of a supply column exploded a mine, instantly killing two legionnaires and wounding five others, who all died later. The following day, a patrol was sent out to recover the two bodies of their comrades killed at the scene of the explosion. However, the partisans had booby-trapped the bodies. Another legionnaire was wounded. He died during the night. On 11 September, a patrol from the 9th Company exploded a mine which killed two and wounded two. *Lieutenant* Prévost rushed to the scene and stepped on another. He died four hours later. *Lieutenant* Gaillard replaced him at the head of the 9th Company. On 18 September, the popular *Adjutant* Sergeant lost his life to a mine. There were more victims of mines; one legionnaire died of his wounds on 23 September and yet another was killed on 30 September.

On 1 October 1943, overall command of the LVF was entrusted to Colonel Edgar Puaud, who had joined the LVF on 17 August 1943. In his first *ordre général* of the same date he stated that it was an honour to take command of the LVF and that it was an honour he had been waiting more than a year for. He continued: 'You have suffered, we will suffer together, but what does it matter since it's for our country and a new, proud, fervent, humane Europe under the

---

2    François Sabiani was killed on 2 June 1942 while serving with the LVF.
3    According to Bouysse, *Encyclopaedia of the New Order: French in German Uniform Part 1: Officers*, Mailhé served with the 6th Company. According to Gonzales, he served with the 2nd Company as a platoon commander.
4    The author originally stated that Mailhe came to the LVF via *La Légion Tricolore*. This is unlikely, given that he fought against the Germans in Tunisia in 1943 (see Bouysse, *Encyclopaedia of the New Order: French in German Uniform Part 1: Officers*).

auspices of the Great German'. He concluded: 'I am counting on you, count on me'. For some soldiers of the LVF, like Pierre Rostaing, Puaud never seemed to be at front and was more of a 'recruiting sergeant'. Many still regarded the larger than life 'Monseigneur' Jean Count de Mayol de Lupé, the General Chaplain of the LVF, as its real commander.

For the past two years, with his pastoral cross hanging on his chest, Mgr. de Mayol de Lupé fought 'his' battle alongside his legionnaires. He won both classes of the Iron Cross and was wounded twice in combat. His photograph appeared frequently not only in the Paris press, but in the German magazine Signal whose front cover he even made, accompanied by the legend: 'From the *Légion d'honneur* to the Iron Cross'. And yet, being a royalist of the old regime, he refused to wear the tricolore badge of the LVF from which OKW had to exempt him. Indeed, he was also authorised to place on his car a white pennant decorated with the fleurs-de-lis.

In June 1943, Mgr. de Mayol de Lupé wrote: 'The world must choose; on the one hand Bolshevist savagery, [an] infernal force; on the other hand Christian civilisation. We must choose at all costs. We cannot loyally remain neutral any longer! It's Bolshevist anarchy or Christian order.'

Linking Adolf Hitler and Christ on the basis of anti-communism, Mgr. de Lupé finished his sermons pledging dual allegiance to 'our Holy Father the Pope and to our venerated Führer Adolf Hitler'. His burning loyalty to National Socialism, which he freely interpreted in his own way, was unquestionable.

Admired by friends and even by those that ridiculed him in private, he enjoyed the confidence of the legionnaires and surprisingly 'managed to fascinate Himmler and the members of his staff'.[5] He was a 'tough guy' who understood the life of the soldier and did not worry about prudishness.

On 20 October 1943, Mgr. de Mayol de Lupé was appointed as the General Chaplain of the LVF, attached to the regimental staff.

## October 1943 to May 1944

Puaud now set about forming the LVF into a regiment with a headquarters and three battalions. The reconstituted II. Bataillon was added to the LVF's order of battle, even though it was and would remain desperately short of manpower. Efforts by the *comité central de la LVF* to recruit career soldiers from the disbanded Armistice Army yielded few results. Undaunted, Puaud pushed ahead with plans to raise a fourth battalion, which would form the base of a second regiment.

On 16 October, the III. Bataillon formed a *section de chasse* [which roughly translates as hunting platoon] under the command of *sous-lieutenant* Seveau to take the fight to the partisans.[6] Attached to the Headquarters Company, the platoon operated independently. The *chasse* was deployed for the first time on 2 November and performed well. It went on to prove its worth again and again, so much so that on the 1 December the commander of the 286th Security

5    La Mazière Christian de, *Ashes of Honour* (London: Tattoo, 1976), p.56.
6    Lefèvre Eric and Jean Mabire, *Sur les pistes de la Russie centrale* (Paris: Jacques Grancher, 2003), p.254. Ruskone believes that the *section de chasse* was formed a little later on 26 October 1943. The date of 16 October appears in Puaud's General Ordre No. 7 of 12 March 1944.

Division awarded Seveau with the Iron Cross 1st Class. Pierre Rostaing and Pierre Ruskone both served in the *section de chasse*.

Born on 8 January 1909 in Gavet (department l'Isère), Pierre Rostaing enlisted in the French Army at the age of eighteen. By the time war broke out, he had completed twelve years' service including tours of duty overseas in the French colonies of Indochina, Morocco, Algeria and Tunisia. The *2e bureau de l'Armée* sent him as a technical advisor to the Finnish Army then at war with Russia. On his return to France, he fought, in vain, against the Germans. A career soldier, he went on to serve in the Armistice Army.

A fervent patriot, Rostaing joined *La Légion Tricolore*, where he wished to continue serving France and its legal government under Pétain.[7] Months later, when *La Légion Tricolore* was disbanded, he hesitated to join the LVF. He detested politics and saw the LVF as an overtly political 'army'. Also, he felt no great enthusiasm to don the uniform of the enemy of yesterday. But being called a coward by his comrades who had already joined the LVF rudely jolted him to sign up. He was no coward. And yet he still had doubts. But the fact that Marshal Pétain, the legal head of State, had given his backing to the LVF eased his patriotic conscience. For Rostaing, the word 'legal' was all-important. His visceral anti-communism and his love of France also won him over to the crusade of the LVF.

With the *6e renfort*, Rostaing left Versailles, the base of the LVF, for the training camp at Kruszyna, Poland. On the completion of his training, he was sent to the Eastern Front and there assigned to the 9th Company of the III. Bataillon. In January 1944, after the departure of the sick and elderly *sergent-chef* Froidevaux, he became Lieutenant Seveau's *adjoint* in the battalion's *section de chasse*.[8] In the months that followed, he was always to be found in the thick of battle. He was tireless. On 20 April 1944, he received the Iron Cross 2nd Class. Earlier that same month, he had appeared in the pages of *Combattant européen* which described him as a conscientious and courageous NCO after throwing himself on and disarming an enemy machine gunner at Raswada on 16 February 1944.

Born in 1921, Pierre Ruskone followed in the footsteps of his father, a veteran of 14-18, and became a militant in the right-wing *Parti Social Français* (PSF) of Colonel de La Rocque.[9] Then war came. He wanted to fight but was too young. On 2 January 1942, having falsified his papers because his parents had refused to sign the *dispense* [certificate of exemption], Ruskone joined the LVF. 'He felt European' and was of the view that France should 'disregard its nationalism

---

7    According to Rostaing Pierre, *Le prix d'un serment* (Paris: La Table ronde, 1975), pp.1-40, he engaged in *La Légion Tricolore* on 13 October 1941, went over to the LVF in early January 1942, left Versailles, the base of the LVF, for the training camp at Kruszyna, Poland, late March 1942, spent more than eight months training at Kruszyna, and joined the LVF in the field in April 1943. However, this schedule is questionable; *La Légion Tricolore* was not created until April 1942. Also of note is that he may have only spent three months at Kruszyna (see page 36 of the same book). Arguably, he engaged in *La Légion Tricolore* on 13 October 1942, and went over to the LVF in early January 1943 after the *La Légion Tricolore* was disbanded. Men of the *6e renfort* joined the LVF in the field in June 1943.

8    Ruskone, letter to the author, 21/3/2001. This corrects the date of 24 December 1943 on which Rostaing became Seveau's *adjoint* (see *Le prix d'un serment*, p.90) and thus also the notion that Rostaing was Seveau's *adjoint* from the outset of the *chasse*, which was formed in October 1943.

9    His father was a member of Colonel de La Rocque's right-wing *Croix de Feu* movement of war veterans that, after the ban on parliamentary pressure groups in 1936, became the *Parti Social Français*.

by integrating itself into a greater European organisation, following the example of Germany'.[10] He left for Deba with the 8th Contingent on 19 February and was assigned to the Headquarters Platoon of the 11th Company, where he served as a runner. After his basic training, he was sent to Russia, arriving in May 1942. He would spend almost the next three years fighting on the Eastern Front.

In late 1943, Ruskone joined the *section de chasse* as Seveau's orderly. In mid-March 1944, he fell sick and was hospitalised at Orcha. Diagnosed with typhus, he was evacuated to Borisov and fought off the illness, after which he returned to the battalion rather than take a period of leave which had been granted.

Yves Peyret of the LVF 1943. (Peyret)

In November, *Capitaine* Bridoux arrived in Russia. After a short stint with the III. Bataillon, he replaced *Capitaine* Bassompierre at the head of the I. Bataillon. Born on 16 November 1911 in Versailles, Eugène-Marie-Jean Bridoux was a product of the celebrated *École spéciale militaire de Saint Cyr*. His branch was the cavalry. He made soldiering his life. During the battle of France he served as a platoon commander with the *10e Régiment de cuirassiers* commanded by a certain Colonel de Gaulle and was wounded twice, winning his *chevalier de la Légion d'honneur*.

10   Rusco Pierre, *Stoi!* (Paris: Jacques Grancher, 1988), p.17.

In defeat, he went across to the Armistice Army and was posted to the headquarters of the 17th Military Division stationed at Toulouse.

Jean Bridoux was one of the few *officiers d'active* to serve in the LVF and, as if to prove his military prowess, within a matter of months he was decorated with the Iron Cross 2nd Class.[11] Notably, his father, General Eugene Bridoux, was the Vichy Under-Secretary of State for National Defence, a post he held from 26 March 1943 to 20 August 1944.[12]

Also, that November, the village of Murovo held by an understrength platoon of Frenchmen under Oberfeldwebel Gobion was attacked by four to five hundred partisans.[13] The attack was repulsed. For his heroic defense of Murovo, Gobion of the I. Bataillon was awarded the Iron Cross 1st Cross, which made him the second soldier of the LVF to receive this award.[14]

That very same night, Gonzales of the 2nd Company was holding a blockhouse in Thernouka across the river Berezina from Murovo. He fired on the opposite bank to dissuade an attack on his village. He was convinced that the attack was organised on information supplied by a deserter named Lopez, who he knew well, adding that his desertion did not come as any surprise to him. At the time of his desertion Lopez was serving with a platoon of the 2nd Company under *sous-lieutenant* Mailhé. On the same night that Lopez deserted his post Gonzales recalls that they heard and saw mortars fired over them onto the village of Murovo.

On 1 December 1943, mass was held in church Notre-Dame-des-Victoires in the 2nd arrondissement of Paris to honour the memory of the first legionnaires of the LVF to die in fighting two years earlier. Members of the *Association des anciens combattants de la LVF* formed a guard of honour outside the church at the end of the ceremony. This Association of Former Combatants of the LVF was created on 18 February 1943 with Guy Servant as its Secretary General. Servant, who was Deloncle's son-in-law, had enlisted in the LVF on 27 August 1941 and, with the rank of *Sous-lieutenant*, fought at Djukowo in December 1941. He was awarded the *Croix de guerre légionnaire* with palm and the Wound Badge in bronze. The Association was to defend the interests of the former combatants, as well as 'give them the training which would enable them to form the necessary cadres in the anti-Communist struggle in France'. One collaborationist newspaper went as far to say that the Association 'would be the base of the French anticommunist edifice'.[15] On 29 July 1943, Servant opened a bar in Paris for the veterans.

In December 1943, Bassompierre was appointed Puaud's Chief-of-staff, but Darnand, now Secretary General for the Maintenance of Order, also had need of him and recalled him at the end of February 1944, concluding his service with the LVF. He returned from Russia decorated with the Iron Cross 2nd Class and the *Croix de guerre légionnaire* which cited his leadership on 1 April 1943.

In early December, the depot of the LVF was relocated from camp Kruszyna to Deba.[16] Soon after, Yves Peyret of the 1st Company was sent to Deba to start officer cadet training. Also on

---

11    Bridoux was awarded the Iron Cross 2nd Class on 17 March 1944.
12    Eugene Bridoux was Vichy Secretary of State for War from 18 April 1942 to 25 March 1943.
13    According to Saint-Loup, *Les Volontaires*, p.310, the partisans also deployed two light armoured cars, one of which was knocked out by a French 37mm PAK gun.
14    Gonzales of the 2nd Company went out on several expeditions with Gobion and noted his courage in the face of battle with the partisans.
15    *Le Petit Parisien* of 20 April 1943.
16    The order was signed on 2 December and stipulated that the relocation should take place before the 11 of the same month.

the same course were Jean de Villefranche, Michel Piffeteau, Antoine Noell (3rd Company), Jacques Moureu, *Sergent* Walter (9th Company) and Jean-Marie Desrumeaux.[17] Commanded by Leutenant Schüler, the platoon of officer cadets numbered between 25 and 30. The instructors were NCOs of the German liaison staff.

In late December the first elements of the II. Bataillon (the 5th Company and headquarters staff) departed Deba for Russia. Officers and NCOs were transferred from the other two battalions, who were already short themselves. *Commandant* Tramu, a reserve *Infanterie Alpine* officer, assumed command of the battalion. *Sous-lieutenant* Veyrieras, who had managed to re-enlist in the LVF after being demobilised in 1942, was appointed the commander of the 5th Company and later the *Adjudant-major* of the II. Bataillon.

Roger Vincent would also command the 5th Company. Born on 6 July 1910 in Versailles, he was appointed as a reserve officer in 1931 and attended the *école militaire et d'application de la cavalerie et du train de Saumur* in 1934-1935, graduating as an *officier d'active* [regular officer]. His branch was the cavalry and he was assigned to the *4e Régiment de Hussards* in 1937 and later still the *6e Régiment de Spahis Algériens* (6e RSA). On 7 October 1942, he enlisted in the *Légion Tricolore* as a lieutenant, which was soon to be dissolved, after which he volunteered for the LVF in April 1943.

The 6th Company and 7th Company of the II. Bataillon would join the 5th Company months later in Russia on 1 March 1944.

That December, Jean Grenouillet arrived in Russia and was assigned to the 11th Company of the III. Bataillon under the legendary *Lieutenant* Neveux. He was transferred in April 1944 to the Headquarters Company of the II. Bataillon.

In the spring of 1944, the LVF became the interest of the politicians again. Doriot attempted to have the LVF brought back to France to fight the maquis and drive the traitors from Vichy. For the first time, the German authorities took the decision to bring the LVF back, but pressure from Laval and de Brinon had the decision reversed.[18]

In January 1944, Alfred Falcy received the command of the 2nd Company. In February 1944, the Ersatzkommando of the LVF was relocated from Deba to Greifenberg.[19] At its head was *Captaine* Georges Cartaud.[20] *Capitaine* Jean Schlisler was appointed as the *officier adjoint*.

Throughout February 1944, the three battalions of the LVF, supported by units of the Wehrmacht and local police, took part in a major anti-partisan sweep in the forest of Somry. The sweep was code-named 'Operation Morocco' in honour of Colonel Puaud. The first two weeks of the operation were quiet; the partisans preferred to withdraw and avoid combat. Gonzales of the 2nd Company recalled:

One of the clearest and most striking souvenirs for me is in early February 1944. Very early in the morning, with *Commandant* Bridoux at the head of our battalion, we

17  Transferred to the Waffen-SS, Jacques Moureu would serve in the Assault Gun Company then the PAK Company of the Panzerjäger Battalion. He attended Kienschlag at the end of November 1944, but thereafter sources differ on his fate.
18  See Brunet, *Doriot*.
19  Its official designation was Ers.Kdo.Frz.I.R.638.
20  His son, Pierre Cartaud, who worked for the SD was killed by the resistance on 7 July 1944. Officers of the SD attended his funeral.

arrived in a small village whose name I have forgotten. The partisans had certainly just left, disturbed by our approach. We learnt from the inhabitants that they had spent the night there getting drunk on vodka. The village bordered a flat plain some 600 to 800 metres from a large forest. I found myself as a scout with my section. *Commandant* Bridoux[21] with the battalion had still not left the village. When we arrived halfway from the forest we came under intense fire from a Maxim machine gun, characterised by its sound of 'taco-taco'. Time to take cover. Thankfully for us, the skirmisher could not see straight.

I spotted horses mounted by riders in a white uniform. They yelled out: "Hourra. Hourra." I thought for a moment that they were going to attack us, but our two 37mm PAK guns under the command of *Commandant* Bridoux opened up with flat trajectory fire. The shells passed over head perhaps some fifty centremes above us. Turning my head, I could clearly see this officer standing upright.

Thankfully, the bulk of the column was still not out in the open; this time the partisans lacked foresight and tactics. Perhaps they felt that they were too weak to attack us. Anyway, some minutes after, heavy mortar fire was not long in being heard. For my part, with my comrades, we felt relieved. The partisans were quick to withdraw when we reached the edge of the forest. We came upon a bewildering sight: disemboweled Russian horses lying on the ground or shattered legs riddled with shrapnel. The partisans had carried off their dead and wounded by abandoning a lot of loot, food and vodka. We had a narrow escape!

Once again the partisans had chosen to withdraw and avoid combat. That all changed on the 16 February when the 10th Company found itself encircled and threatened with annihilation. It was saved by the timely intervention of the *section de chasse*. The company suffered heavy casualties, seven dead and forty wounded (including twenty-three seriously).

The following day, 17 February, the *section de chasse* again distinguished itself, seizing a camp occupied by more than 150 'enemy' and putting them to flight. The very next day, 18 February, *Commandant* Panné was killed.[22] He had been on leave but flown back to personally conduct the operation at the Germans' request. *Capitaine* Berret succeeded him at the head of the III. Bataillon.

Operation 'Morocco' ended soon after. Its German planners deemed the operation a great success and, as 'recognition' for its success, Puaud was awarded with the Iron Cross 2nd Class on 20 February 1944. When back in France accolades were also forthcoming from the Vichy Government, who made him *commandeur de la Légion d'Honneur* on 25 March and promoted him to the rank of *Général de Brigade* on 14 April 1944. However, the Germans authorities did not recognise his new rank and still regarded him as holding that of Oberst.

---

21    According to Bouysse, Bridoux was only promoted to *Commandant* on 1 May 1944, backdated to 1 April 1944.
22    Dates of the ambush of the 10th Company at Rasvada and the death of *Commandant* Panné vary. See Labat Eric, *Les places étaient chères* (Paris: La Table Ronde, 1953), p.252, and Saint-Loup, *Les Volontaires*, pp.359 and 365. The author has used the date of 16 February 1944 for the action at Rasvada which appears on Puaud's General Ordre No. 7 of 12 March 1944.

On 26 February, while returning to its sector east of the Berezina, the I. Bataillon was ambushed by partisans at Devoschizi. The partisans numbered over two thousand. Surprise was total. Nevertheless, after three hours of combat, the battalion managed to extricate itself. The engagement cost the battalion twenty-two dead. Oberfähnrich Paul Briffaut, who fought bravely, was seriously wounded.

Paul Briffaut was born on 8 August 1918 in Hanoi, Vietnam. A deferred conscript, he was still called up and assigned in November 1938 to the *76e bataillon alpin de forteresse*. He attended Saint-Maixent and in October 1939 was commissioned *aspirant de réserve de infanterie* and posted to the prestigous *159e regiment d'infanterie alpine* and then the 16° RTT in the Levant. In 1941, he fought for Vichy France against the British and Gaullists and was awarded the *Croix de guerre* with a citation *à l'ordre de la division*. Defeat and repatriation followed. He was demobilised on 5 April 1942. One year later, in June 1943, he volunteered for the LVF, which welcomed him with the rank of *aspirant*. After training a platoon of officer cadets with Mailhé and participating in most of the LVF's public events that summer, he left for Poland. Two and a half months later, he was sent to the Eastern Front, arriving at the end of November 1943. He was assigned to the 1st Company.

For his actions on 26 February 1944, Briffaut was awarded the *Croix de guerre légionnaire avec palme*, which the Germans followed up with the Iron Cross 2nd Class. Hospitalised, he did not return to duty for some six months. In the meantime, on 15 July 1944, he was promoted to *sous-lieutenant*.

On 27 February 1944, an OKW communiqué credited security troops and the LVF with dispersing strong bolchevist groups, inflicting very heavy losses on them and capturing 'many spoils'. 43 partisan camps, with more than 1,000 blockhouses and supply bases, were reported as destroyed. 1,118 partisans were reported as killed and 1,346 partisans captured. Meanwhile, on 29 February and 1 March 1944, two departures of the *13e renfort* left gare de l'Est Paris for Greifenberg, where the Ersatzkommando of the LVF was located.

In March 1944, Gonzales of the 2nd Company was sent to reinforce the strongpoint of Areskovichy. Some days after his arrival, around the same time that his Russian girlfriend gave birth, he contracted typhus. Immediately transported to Company headquarters, he spent the night in the infirmary. The following day at dawn he was transported to a hospital at Borisov, where he spent twenty-one days in a coma. When he finally woke the first thing he asked for was his hair to be cut because as a child his grandmother had told him that epidemic typhus caused hair loss. Next he asked for a bottle of champagne, which was forthcoming!

Two weeks later, Gonzales was evacuated by train to Warsaw, where he spent one month, and, in the middle of May, he was sent on to a small German village to convalesce.[23] Warmly welcomed by the medical staff, he soon returned to full health. He has fond memories of his stay: the evenings, which were full of music with the staff, as well as the boating trips along the nearby river in the company of a fräulein called Elsa Kourtz, who cried when she accompanied him to the station to see him off.

On the morning of 17 March 1944, a platoon of the 9th Company stationed at the village of Saborje [Zabor'ye], some thirty kilometres north of Bobr, was attacked by some 300 partisans

23   Gonzales is uncertain about the name of the small German village, which was Nasaw or Nasau. Unfortunately, the author cannot locate either.

supported by light tanks. *Adjudant-chef* René Hamard made a sortie with six men to assess the situation. Moving from house to house, they spotted a BT7 light tank surrounded by infantry. After a brief firefight, Hamard fell back to his prepared positions. Faced with a hopeless situation, Hamard decided to attack, which journal *L'Ouest-Éclair* of 18 April 1944 described as a 'final and magnificent decision'. The journal continued:

> Il sort, de nouveau avec six hommes qui se dirigent de face sur le char à travers les incendies allumés dans le tiers du village séparant le blindé du poste, soit environ 300 mètres. À l'approche des français, dès qu'il les aperçoit, le conducteur du char manœuvre de manière à présenter sa mitrailleuse. Les français ne reculent pas et tirent. L'engin parait en difficulté, le moteur gronde. L'ardeur des légionnaires étonne l'ennemi, un vent de déroute souffle, les voltigeurs se dispersent. L'équipage du char, se voyant abandonné, quitte l'engin. Hamard va reconnaitre le char, lance une grenade à l'intérieur : il n'a plus d'occupant.[24]

The partisans fled in disorder, carrying away their dead and wounded. This defence had a positive effect on the locals so much so that they decided to follow the French when they retreated months later.

For this remarkable feat of arms René Hamard became the first Frenchmen of the LVF to be awarded with the Panzervernichtungsabzeichen (tank destruction badge), which he received while in Berlin. He was also decorated with the EKII. Hamard was killed months later. In March, *Capitaine* Martin received the command of the 3rd Company of the I. Bataillon.

Puaud returned to France in late March for a nationwide recruitment drive accompanied by Doriot, Bassompierre, Mayol de Lupé and the writer Marc Augier [nom de plume Saint-Loup]. This 'team of militants', joined by *Capitaine* Demessine of the *comité central de la LVF* responsible for propaganda, spoke at rallies organised in Marseille on 2 April, Lyon on the 5, Paris on the 16 and Nancy on the 19.[25]

The biggest rally was undoubtedly that held in Paris at the Vélodrome d'Hiver, which all the leading collaborationists attended. Demessine, wearing a French uniform, presented the speakers who were writing history 'with their body, their heart, [and] their blood'. When Puaud spoke he stated that he was proud to wear the German uniform to 'save our country, and not only our country, but the whole of Christian civilisation'. He concluded that to rebuild France they have to fight Bolshevism 'hand in hand with the Germans'.

Doriot continued to recruit for the LVF, speaking at a rally in Lille on 30 April 1944, along with François Gaucher, a former lieutenant of the I. Bataillon of the LVF, who Darnand had recalled from Russia in March to become the *délégué général* of the *Milice* for the North Zone.

The officer cadet course at Greifenberg finished at the end of March 1944, after which Peyret went on leave for the third and last time. On his return he was assigned as an instructor to a

---

24  This action is also depicted by Saint-Loup, *Les Volontaires*, pp.371-374 and Croisile, *Sous uniforme allemande*, pp.174-177, although the latter mistakenly identifies the tanks as KV-1s: a photograph confirms that the destroyed tank was a BT7.

25  While in Lyon on 5 April Puaud laid a wreath at the momument to the LVF dead from Lyon in the presence of a number Germam dignitaires.

company of recruits. He remembers three of them well: brothers André[26] and Marius Yi of Korean origin and Lévy, who the Germans did not deem as Jewish because his two grandparents were not Jewish. Towards 15 June 1944, he returned to Russia with his recruits, who were divided up among various companies. Instead of being returned to the 1st Company, Peyret was assigned to the PAK Company.

Back in Russia the partisans were becoming more and more numerous and aggressive. In late April, *Commandant* Bridoux formed a *compagnie de marche* from the best elements of the three infantry companies of the I. Bataillon under the command of *Capitaine* Martin which was put at the disposal of the Fourth Army. The company particapted in Operation 'Kiebitz' around Kembin from 27 April to 6 May, again with little to show for its efforts. Once more the partisans had slipped away. French losses were three dead and twenty wounded. On 12 May 1944, Martin was awarded with the Iron Cross 2nd Class.

Meanwhile, on 1 May, elements of the III. Bataillon (the 9th Company, the *section de chasse*, and a *groupe de mortiers*) participated in Operation 'Spring Festival', a major anti-partisan sweep which had been initiated weeks earlier. In addition to the French battalion, the Germans employed elements of the 95 Infantry Division, the bulk of two Secuity Divisions, Einsatzgruppe Kaminski, Sonder Bataillon Dirlewanger, SS Polizei Regiment 2 and SS Polizei Regiment 24 (operating as Einsatzgruppe Anhalt) and an assortment of local and Latvian security units. The aim of the operation was to destroy partisan forces in the Ushachi region, numbering 18,000. Curiously, the French battalion, which operated along the Berezina, saw little action. Its biggest contribution was the discovery of a veritable arsenal of heavy weapons which had been submerged in a lake. The operation finished on 10 May. French losses were two dead and several wounded. Notably, the Germans later claimed that partisan losses were 7011 dead and 6928 prisoners, with an additional 349 desertions.

In May, the 13th Company of the IV. Bataillon joined the LVF in the field. It was commanded by *Capitaine* Auffray. No other unit of the IV. Bataillon was raised due to a shortage of volunteers, despite the best efforts of Puaud and the 'team of militants'.

On 9 June, a platoon of the 3rd Company, now under the temporary command of *Sous-lieutenant* Rigeade, was ambushed by partisans on its way back from escorting ten soldiers on leave to regiment headquarters at Moliavka. When the platoon did not return help was dispatched, which found twelve corpses, naked and booby-trapped.

On 13 June, elements of the regimental Headquarters Company under *Capitaine* Guiraud and the 3rd Company under *Lieutenant* Martin split into two detachments stumbled into a hornet's nest: a large and organised partisan force around Krutchka preparing to attack the vital arteries of the Orscha-Minsk road and railway line. The detachment under Guiraud, numbering sixty men, was wiped out. There were no survivors. The second detachment under Martin,

26    André Yi was born on 11 September 1925 in Cannes to a Korean father and a French mother. He enlisted in the LVF in November 1943 with number 12647 and served with the 6th Company. Transferred to the Waffen-SS, he was assigned to the 2nd Company of Waffen-Grenadier-Regiment der SS 58. Sent to Pomerania, he was among those who managed to make it out alive. He died on 12 February 2001 in Lorient.

numbering one hundred and thirty men, managed to withdraw under intense fire. The battle cost the LVF 100 killed or missing out of 190 deployed.[27]

Jean Sepchat of the 1st Company was assigned to the medical staff of the Headquarters Company at the request of a Medical *Sergent* who had need of an interpreter to facilitate his reports with the German liaison Feldwebel. He readily admits he had no medical knowledge but managed to keep himself busy. He was not in this role for long; he went on leave, returning to the LVF after the battle of Bobr, to be transferred to the Engineer Platoon.

Roger Pujol, born on 13 March 1926 in Pantin in the northeastern suburbs of Paris, volunteered for the LVF during the summer of 1944. He was a loyal and active member of the PPF, which encouraged him to 'fulfill his duty as a combatant'. Moreover, he wanted to become a 'knight' of the New Europe and believed that 'France could only survive in the new European order by fighting alongside Germany, whose principal enemy was the communism of Soviet Russia'.[28] He was fascinated by the order, discipline and esthetic beauty of the German Army which had conquered Europe in a matter of months and, despite the recent defeat in Africa and the reverses in Russia, he remained convinced of ultimate German victory. Moreover, he saw de Gaulle as a 'remote General dependent on Churchill, a valet of British Imperialism' and there was absolutely no question of joining the resistance, many of whom were communists and foreigners. He would not get to join the LVF on the field of battle.[29]

### 'Their finest hour'

In late June 1944, the entire LVF regiment was assembled at Bobr to be transported back to France. Hours before the planned departure, it suddenly found itself called to action again when Army Group Centre's weak front crumpled under the Red Army's all-out summer offensive.

On 25 June 1944, the I. Bataillon, two companies of the III. Bataillon[30] and the 13th Company of the IV. Bataillon, in total around 600 men, under *Commandant* Bridoux took up a position covering the bridge that carried the strategic Minsk-Moscow highway over the river Bobr, fifty kilometres east of Borisov. The LVF held the position between the cemetery and the highway.

Over the next forty-eight hours of bitter fighting the French Kampfgruppe, supported by Stuka, four Tiger tanks of schwere Panzer-Abteilung 505 and a unit of SS-Police equipped with 75mm anti-tank guns,[31] managed to check attack after attack.

---

27    For more details of this battle see Saint-Loup, *Les Volontaires*, pp.404-411. However, according to Bouysse, *Encyclopédie de l'ordre nouveau: Français sous l'uniforme allemande partie II: sous-officiers & hommes du rang de la Waffen-SS*, Albert Vianello, who was serving with the regimental Headquarters Company, was one of the few survivors of the ambush. Lefèvre Eric and Oliver Pigoreau, *Bad Reichenhall* (Paris: Grancher, 2010), p.119, confirm that Albert Vianello survived the ambush but make no mention that he was serving with the Headquarters Company.

28    Lormier, *SS Français*, p.23.

29    According to Lormier, *SS Français*, p.26, after a short period of training in a barracks in the Paris area, Pujol was sent to Wildflecken. This is unlikely. He was probably sent to Greifenberg first to complete his basic training.

30    The two companies of the III. Bataillon present at Bobr did not actually take up front line positions. The III. Bataillon was only represented by Seveaux's *section de chasse*.

31    Indeed, according to Rostaing, the 'Waffen-SS Polizei Regiment' handed over three of its 75mm anti-tank guns to the LVF.

*Caporal-chef* Malardier of the I. Bataillon distinguished himself at Bobr. When the supply system broke down he volunteered to go to the rear and bring up a convoy of critically needed ammunition and supplies for the hard-pressed battalion. Into a hail of enemy fire he dashed. Some considered the fire impassable. Although wounded, he reappeared with the convoy. He was mentioned in dispatches and proposed for the Iron Cross 2nd Class. Pierre Ruskone, who was serving with the *section de chasse* at Bobr, wrote of one attack:

> Our lines are very quickly overrun. Although I knew there were Tigers to the rear, I had the impression we're done for. The adventure is over ... and Seveau still does not wake! Suddenly, an explosion rings out behind me. The first Russian tank ablaze lights up the sector, allowing the Tigers to better adjust their fire. Soon, five tanks are destroyed. The last three start a prudent retreat, but our anti-tank guns manage to destroy one more and damage another. The fifth gets through the Tiger barrier and will only be destroyed a little further along the road. The Russian attack is a failure; all its engaged tanks are ablaze and its infantry beat a hasty retreat towards its lines taking heavy losses.[32]

Jacques Chavent was awarded the Iron Cross 2nd Class for recapturing from the Russians a PAK gun whose crew had been killed or wounded.

On the morning of 27 June, the Frenchmen were relieved. They pulled back to a new defensive line before Borisov.

The battle of Bobr was undoubtedly the LVF's finest hour. Upwards of forty and perhaps as many as fifty-seven[33] Soviet tanks lay wrecked in front of the French positions: the Tiger tanks were credited with 26 kills, the regimental PAK Company with thirteen and the 3rd Company with one.[34] Victory always comes at a high price. The reported number of LVF killed varies from twenty to forty one.[35] Many were also wounded, including Pierre Ruskone of the *section de chasse* who was hit by shrapnel in his right shoulder, but refused to be evacuated. Testimony to the fighting qualities of the LVF came from no less a source than a Soviet communiqué that spoke of their forces being stopped by the pointless sacrifice of 'two French divisions!'

There was no respite for the exhausted and hungry LVF legionnaires holding the position several kilometres from the town of Borisov that crossed the river Bérésina. This time, without heavy support, they found themselves easily overwhelmed and broken up by Russian tanks. They withdrew to Borisov or failing that attempted to cross the river Bérésina by any means possible. Many were killed. Many disappeared. Mercilessly harassed by the Soviet airforce and closely pursued by its ground forces, they continued to retreat.

32  Rusco, *Stoï!*, p.212.
33  Rusco, *Stoï!*, p.217.
34  Saint-Loup, *Les Volontaires*, p.446.
35  Mabire puts the French 'casualties' (presumably those killed) at forty; Saint-Loup and Lambert forty-one dead and twenty-four seriously wounded; and de Genouillac around twenty killed. According to Rusco, *Stoï!*, p.218, more than half of the six hundred Frenchmen engaged at Bobr were killed or missing. This figure seems exaggerated, though.

The dispersed units of the LVF were assembled at Moritz Lager, south of Minsk. Colonel Puaud gave orders to leave in small groups and reach Vilno, Lithuania, then Greifenberg, Pomerania. *Caporal-chef* Malardier recalled:

> I had to leave Moritz Lager on foot, having not wanted to abandon a medic comrade that *Commandant* Bridoux refused to allow onto the LKW evacuating us on the pretext that he had had a little too much champagne that the quartermaster had provided us with rather than abandon it to the Ivans.[36]

On the afternoon of 30 June, elements of the 9th Company took up defensive positions some seven kilometres from Minsk. The following day, the order to evacuate was received but the two trucks which should have waited for them had already left. Lieutenant Boillot was furious. They set off on foot. The Lieutenant managed to find an empty truck with a driver which transported half of the Frenchmen to Minsk and came back for the rest, which included *Sergent* Jean-Marie Croisile.

The truck carrying Croisile made it to Minsk and joined a column of vehicles ordered to evacuate the city, covered by four Tiger tanks. The column managed to stay ahead of the advancing Russians on the first day. This retreat reminded Croisile of France four years previous.

On the second day the column was forced to stop near the village of Rakov when it came under mortar fire from behind a ridge which ran parallel to the road, about four hundred metres away. The Russians had also sited machine-guns on the peak of the ridge which now started to pour fire on the convoy. Organised into a *groupe de combat*, the Frenchmen attacked the ridge, with supporting fire from a Tiger. They managed to reach the ridge, which the Russians had abandoned, only to come under intense mortar fire. From the ridge, Croisile could see a column of T-34s advancing along a parallel road.

Ordered back to the road, the Frenchmen were pursued by mortar fire. The toll for this action was several dead and wounded. The column resumed its march, but it was short lived. This time the column came under shell fire. One truck was hit. Two 88mm guns engaged Russian tanks, destroying several. The column continued on. Eventually, on the evening of 4 July, the column arrived at Lida from where the Frenchmen embarked for Greifenberg.

*Sous-Lieutenant* de Genouillac and part of the *section de commandement* of the 3rd Company also participated in the fighting at Rakov and Volodzyn before arriving at Lida from where they embarked for Greifenberg on one of the very last trains.

For those groups that did make it to Greifenberg each and every one had a different story to tell of the journey.[37] *Caporal-chef* Gonzales arrived in July 1944 after recovering from typhus. He was happy to find himself among his comrades again. They had news of Anna, the child and her two brothers who were last seen making their way towards Vilno, Lithuania.[38]

At Greifenberg, *Sous-lieutenant* de Genouillac was charged with forming the 4th (Heavy) Company of the I. Bataillon.

---

36   Malardier, letter to the author, 2/9/1999.
37   Ruskone suggests that the Legion was finally assembled at a French monastery in Kaunas where it rested before being transported by rail to Greifenberg on 15 July 1944. This is incorrect.
38   Gonzales does not know what became of Anna, the child and her two brothers.

At the end of July 1944, elements of the LVF left depot Greifenberg for a camp situated at Altwarp on the west bank of the Oder. In August, they were transferred to a training camp at Saalesch (Zalesic), near Bruss, which was in a poor state of repair. The water was polluted and Gonzales suffered from a bout of dysentery. The food was poor as well. 'The bread crunched under tooth because of the sand it contained', recalls Gonzales.

Rumours at Saalesch were rife. According to one rumour, the LVF was to be repatriated to France to fight the maquis. Opinion was divided. For his part, *Caporal-chef* Gonzales was not in agreement; he did not volunteer for the LVF to end up fighting his own countrymen. According to another rumour, the LVF was to be amalgamated with the French Sturmbrigade of the Waffen-SS.

Meanwhile, back at Greifenberg, the depot quickly filled again with French legionnaires of the LVF: stragglers returning from Russia, those who had been delayed returning from leave, new recruits, and the return of those who had 'deserted' to serve in other branches of the German Army.

Jean Grenouillet of the Headquarters Company of the II. Bataillon, who was wounded at Beresino during the June retreat, arrived at Greifenberg in August 1944 and was transferred to the 1st Company under *Sous-lieutenant* Fatin.

### The meeting of two very different worlds[39]

On a sultry Saturday in mid-August 1944,[40] one company of the French Sturmbrigade of the Waffen-SS disembarked at Greifenberg railway station. Commanded by SS-Ostuf. Michel, the company was made up of many volunteers aged seventeen and some as young as sixteen, who were disconsolate about not having been deployed to Galicia with the 1st Battalion. They marched off. Haughtily they sang the German marching song *Panzerlied* whose words they all knew by heart.

From the barracks, the bored French legionnaires of the LVF watched the newcomers arrive. Such was the spectacle the newcomers were putting on that they assumed they were German. That was until they caught sight of the tricolore badge on the left sleeve of their tunic. This surprised them.

The Frenchmen of the Waffen-SS drew up. They awaited the order to dismiss. The Frenchmen of the LVF surrounded them and mocked. Ostuf. Michel made his way to a group of officers, including the 'French Captain who commanded the depot', and saluted.[41] They returned his Nazi salute half-heartedly. He immediately admonished them!

Later that day came the first contact between the youngsters of the Waffen-SS and the 'elders' of the LVF. The SS men were so shocked by the legionnaires. The legionnaires were ragged. Some were even wearing Russian fur 'papachas' and gaudy scarves. Indiscipline was

---

39  See Mabire, *La Division Charlemagne*, p.61-66, and Saint-Loup, *Les Hérétiques*, p.126-128.

40  SS-Panz.Gren.Ausb.u.Ers.Btl. 35 reported on 18 August 1944 that the 'Ausb.-und Stamm-Kompanie franz.' under Michel had relocated to the Ausb.u.Ers.Kdo of the French Legion.

41  Mabire, *La Division Charlemagne*, p.63. Undoubtedly this 'French Captain who commanded the depot' was *capitaine* Cartaud. And yet, according to Saint-Loup, *Les Hérétiques* p.127, it was Colonel Puaud, the LVF commander, who greeted Michel, but there was no warmth in his welcome. This is unlikely; Puaud may have been away in Berlin.

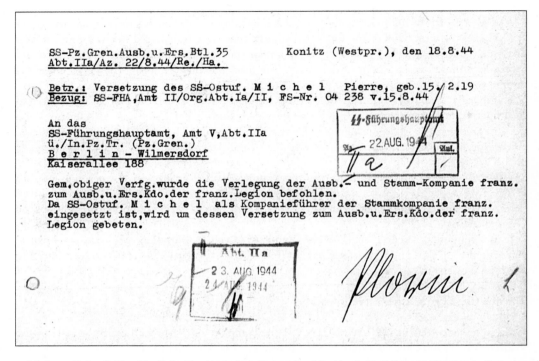

```
SS-Pz.Gren.Ausb.u.Ers.Btl.35          Konitz (Westpr.), den 18.8.44
Abt.IIa/Az. 22/8.44/Re./Ha.


Betr.: Versetzung des SS-Ostuf. M i c h e l  Pierre, geb.15./2.19
Bezug: SS-FHA,Amt II/Org.Abt.Ia/II, FS-Nr. 04 238 v.15.8.44


An das
SS-Führungshauptamt, Amt V,Abt.IIa                    SS-Führungshauptamt
ü./In.Pz.Tr. (Pz.Gren.)
B e r l i n - Wilmersdorf                              22.AUG.1944
Kaiserallee 188

Gem.obiger Verfg.wurde die Verlegung der Ausb.- und Stamm-Kompanie franz.
zum Ausb.u.Ers.Kdo.der franz.Legion befohlen.
Da SS-Ostuf. M i c h e l  als Kompanieführer der Stammkompanie franz.
eingesetzt ist,wird um dessen Versetzung zum Ausb.u.Ers.Kdo.der franz.
Legion gebeten.
```

SS-Panz.Gren.Ausb.u.Ers.Btl. 35 reports the relocation of the 'Ausb.-und Stamm-Kompanie franz.'
under Michel to the Ausb.u.Ers.Kdo of the French Legion. (Author)

rife. Their language was coarse and lewd. The NCOs swore at their men in Russian. And yet the decorations and ribbons on their uniforms did not lie. All were veterans of Russia. Some had been on the Eastern Front since the terrible winter of 1941.

That night, the SS men went to bed early whereas the legionnaires went into town. Without question there was a great gulf between the Frenchmen of the Waffen-SS and the LVF. Next morning, a Sunday, LVF Chaplain Verney celebrated mass in the great ground floor canteen of the barracks. Also in the congregation were the SS men. They were there out of curiosity. In silence, they too listened to the words of Verney nicknamed 'Mickey'.

Suddenly, Ostuf. Michel appeared at the doorway to the canteen and shouted 'Antreten!' His men reacted immediately and dashed to the entrance. In their haste, they knocked over tables and chairs, and pushed aside the legionnaires. Michel now yelled 'Panzeralarm!' Quickly, he briefed them. It was an improvised exercise. He then ordered them to assemble in five minutes time in the square in full combat kit. They obeyed and rushed off.

Now missing part of his congregation, Verney brought mass to a quick end. The legionnaires rushed to the windows just in time to see Michel's Company going through the main gates of the barracks.

According to rumour, the LVF was to be amalgamated with the French Sturmbrigade of the Waffen-SS. If this amalgamation was to have any chance of success, the legionnaires of the LVF had much to learn about the ways of the Waffen-SS, and, in return, the volunteers of the SS had much to learn about the history and the traditions of the LVF.

The LVF had existed for three years. In that time a total of 13,400 volunteers applied to join its ranks. Of this number, 7,600 were rejected, while only 5,800 were accepted. And of the 5800 accepted 3000 were accepted in its first three months of existence. Clearly, recruitment waned as the tide of the war turned against Germany.

The LVF was the brainchild of the Paris-based collaborationist parties, some of whom quickly lost interest in it. The one political party had never 'abandoned' the LVF was the PPF, but its influence over the LVF waned as it too became embroiled in the unfolding conflict between the collaborationists and the 'terrorists'. Nevertheless, the LVF never lost its political character.

Militarily, the LVF, which finally fielded three battalions, contributed very little to the German war machine. Arguably, for the Germans, the LVF remained symbolic, which was their original intention, and often featured in the pages of Signal. Moreover, the first incarnation of the LVF deployed in 1941 has been described as the one of the 'Wehrmacht's least successful foreign formations', but, as previously noted, the German Army should accept some if not most of the responsibility for its poor performance. The reorganised LVF of 1942 was a very different proposition to that of 1941 and the LVF of 1944, no longer plagued by poor officers and NCOs, was different again, attaining a level of professionalism and discipline the other incarnations lacked. The LVF of 1944 proved itself to be an effective fighting force in both the war against the partisans and at the front. The Germans may have only employed the LVF at the front again out of necessity, but this time, importantly, it covered itself in glory.

# 8

## The Formation of 'Charlemagne'

---

### Birth

The decision to amalgamate the LVF and the Sturmbrigade into a single Waffen-SS formation was undoubtedly that of Reichsführer-SS Himmler.[1] On 10 August 1944, the SS-FHA secretly ordered the LVF including its German personnel transferred with immediate effect to the Waffen-SS and merged with the Franz.SS-Freiw.Sturmbrigade at SS-Truppenübungsplatz [SS-training area] 'Westpreußen[2] to form the Französische Brigade der SS [French Brigade of the SS].[3]

Himmler also intended to transfer to the French Brigade of the SS all Frenchmen serving with the Kriegsmarine and the Schutzkommando of the Organisation Todt, more simply the SK, as well as new recruits from among the large number of French workers in Germany.

The command of this French Brigade of the SS went to Oberst Puaud of the LVF and presumably he was told of this when he met Himmler in Berlin.[4] At this meeting Puaud categorically assured Himmler that all his men, without exception, had agreed to enter the Waffen-SS.[5] Needless to say, Puaud had not consulted his legionnaires about entering the Waffen-SS.

1    Of note is that most foreign volunteer units in German service were eventually absorbed into the Waffen-SS. For some units, however, the transfer was largely theoretical.
2    SS-FHA, Amt II Org. Tgb. Nr.2710/44 g. Kdos, 26 August 1944.
3    According to SS-FHA Amt II Org.Abt. Ia/II Tgb. Nr. 10943/44 geh, 13 July 1944, a Französischen Brigade der SS was to be created by merging the Franz.SS-Freiw.Sturmbrigade and the LVF. This is earliest official record of this designation, which also appears in SS-FHA Amt II Org.Abt. Ia/II Tgb. Nr. 12000/44 geh, 1 August 1944.
4    Although the date of this meeting is not known, late August would not seem unreasonable. It should be noted that Puaud was in discussion about the transfer of the LVF to the Waffen-SS weeks before he met Himmler (see letter of 19 August 1944 from SS-Staf. Spaarmann of the SS-Hauptamt to Dr. Reichel at the Foreign Office).
5    Mabire, *Entretien avec le général Krukenberg, Historia* hors série 32, p.131. Contrary to what has often been said and written about Puaud, he was not a soldier who sought promotion at all costs. Indeed, at the end of his last leave, saying goodbye to his wife, he told her: "My duty is to be beside my men!"

At this meeting or a later meeting with Himmler at the SS-Hauptamt in Berlin, Puaud received the following assurances:[6]

- The Brigade would fight under the French flag
- The Brigade would not be engaged as far as possible on a front where it might find itself exposed to fighting against other Frenchmen
- The volunteers would be free to practice Christian religions
- In the case of a German victory the integrity of French national territory and its colonies would be scrupulously guaranteed

On 1 September 1944, Colonel Puaud was promoted to Oberführer[7] and the personnel of the LVF were transferred to the Waffen-SS.[8] On the same day, as though a gesture of farewell, 127 French and German personnel of the LVF were proposed for the Kriegsverdienstkreuz 2. Klasse [KVK II]. The decorations were awarded three months later.

The LVF depot at Greifenberg in Pomerania (called Ers.Kdo.Frz.I.R.638 and Ausb.u.Ers. Kdo.) now became that of the French Brigade of the Waffen-SS and home to the Franz. SS-Grenadier-Ausbildungs und Ersatz-Bataillon [the French SS-Grenadier Training and Replacement Battalion].[9] Command of the battalion went to Swiss SS-Obstubaf. Hersche.[10]

6   Soulat, *Historique de la Division Charlemagne*, p.16.
7   Although the rank of Oberführer was not equivalent to Puaud's Vichy Government recognised rank of *Général de brigade*, the rank of Oberführer did represent promotion from his German recognised rank of Oberst (Colonel) whose equivalent Waffen-SS rank was that of Standartenführer.
8   Lefèvre, *Axe & Alliés* hors série no 1, pp.44-45 and Mabire, *La Division Charlemagne*, p.81. Curiously, Landwehr is the only source to comment that on 1 September 1944 the French SS Division (sic) 'Charlemagne' was ceremonially established at the NCO school at Greifenberg (*Charlemagne's Legionnaires*, p.56). In reply, this is doubtful; Puaud only returned to the LVF on 10 September and any such ceremony would not have gone ahead without his presence.
9   According to Mounine, *Cernay, 40-45*, p.313, Greifenberg was initially designated 5. Franz. Ausb.u.Ers.Kdo. In reply, Mercier, who served in a temporary administrative capacity with one of the training companies, can only recall the designation of Franz. Ausbildungs und Ersatz-Bataillon der SS. Also, the date Ersatz Kommando Franz. I.R. 638 was renamed is unclear. According to Roch, *La Division Charlemagne*, p.50, the Franz. SS-Grenadier-Ausbildungs und Ersatz-Bataillon was formed at Greifenberg in early September 1944. This designation was very much in use in early September 1944 (see documentation from Greifenberg/Pom regarding the transfer of Ostuf. Michel dated 9 September 1944). And yet, curiously, on 1 August 1944, the SS-FHA reported the Franz. SS-Gren.Ausb.u.Ers. Btl., Greifenberg/Pom as the Ersatztruppenteil for the Franz. Brigade der SS (SS-FHA, Amt II/Org. Abt.Ia/II, Tgb.Nr.II/12000/44 geh).
10  Hersche was promoted to Obersturmbannführer der Reserve on 21 June 1944. He left Sennheim on 10 August 1944 to take command of the Franz. SS-Grenadier-Ausbildungs und Ersatz-Bataillon at Greifenberg.

The French Brigade of the Waffen-SS was planned with the following order of battle:[11]

Stab der Brigade
Grenadier-Regiment 1
    Stab und Stabskompanie [Headquarters and Headquarters Company]
    I.Bataillon
    II.Bataillon
    Infanterie-Geschütz-Kp.        [Infantry Gun Company]
    Panzerjäger-Kp.            [Tank-Hunter Company]
Grenadier-Regiment 2
    Stab und Stabskompanie
    I.Bataillon
    II.Bataillon
    Infanterie-Geschütz-Kp.
    Panzerjäger-Kp.
1 Artillerie-Abteilung         [Artillery Battalion]
1 Pionier-Kompanie           [Engineer Company]
1 Panzerjäger-Abteilung      [Tank-Hunter Battalion]
1 Nachrichten-Kompanie      [Signals Company]
1 Sanitäts-Kompanie         [Medical Company]
1 Krankenkenkraftwagen-Zug  [Ambulance Platoon]
1 Veterinär-Kompanie        [Veterinary Company]
2 Feldersatz-Kompanie       [Field Replacement Company]
1 Feldgendarmerie-Trupp (mot.)  [Military Police Troop]
1 Feldpostamt (mot.)        [Field Post Office]

On 10 September 1944, Puaud arrived back at Saalesch.[12] He was in the uniform of a Waffen-SS Oberführer and wearing the Iron Cross First Class. Before his assembled legionnaires he told them that he had seen RF-SS Himmler in Berlin. According to Puaud, the RF-SS 'knew all about the heroism they had shown during the retreat from Russia'. Because of this, the RF-SS had decided to exempt them from swearing a new oath and to admit them with their ranks into the Waffen-SS. Puaud then added that the tradition of the LVF would remain and that 'this incorporation was only administrative'. Of the incorporation, he had this to say:[13]

11    See the official organigram for the Franz. Brigade der SS reproduced in Scherzer Veit, *Sous le Signe SS* (Bayreuth: Verlag Veit Scherzer, 2018), p.168.
12    Mabire, *La Division Charlemagne*, p.81.
13    Labat, *Les places étaient chéres*, p.255. Mabire also recounts Puaud's speech, but there are some notable additions, in particular that the legionnaires of the LVF had been admitted into the Waffen-SS on 1 September 1944 and that not only would they keep their ranks, but their commanders and flag too (*La Division Charlemagne*, pp.81-82). Regarding the employment of 'Charlemagne' in the coming counteroffensive to free France, clearly both the Reichsführer and Puaud were convinced that the legionnaires would fight against the the Western Allies. Arguably, this would seem to contradict the assurance Puaud received from the Reichsführer that the 'Brigade would not be engaged as far as possible on a front where it might find itself exposed to fighting against other Frenchmen'.

It will permit the creation of a complete French Division, which will participate in the fight on all fronts, and I asked the Reichsführer that the division 'Charlemagne' be admitted to participate in the counteroffensive that will recapture France from the Anglo-American armies.

Sources and documents vary as to the subsequent status, title, and naming of the French Brigade of the Waffen-SS. Indeed, it has appeared with the following designations:

- Waffen-Grenadier-Brigade der SS 'Charlemagne'[14]
- Waffen-Grenadier-Brigade der SS (franz. Nr. 1)[15]
- Waffen-Grenadier-Brigade der SS 'Charlemagne' (franz. Nr. 1)[16]
- SS-Sturmbrigade 'Charlemagne'[17]
- Waffen-Grenadier Division der SS 'Charlemagne' (Französische Nr.1)[18]

14  Appears on reports produced by the Brigade dated 10 and 11 of October 1944 (see p.11 and 14 of issue # 87 of magazine *39/45*) and reports from concentration camp Stutthof dated 30 and 31 of October 1944. Also, Mercier of Fahrschwadron A saw this designation used (letter to the author, 23/1/2002). Furthermore, there is the report from the Rekrutenkompanie [Recruit Company] at Leisten dated October 1944 (also on p.11 of issue 87 of magazine *39/45*) that is headed with the designation Waffen-Brigade SS 'Charlemagne'. The omission of the word 'Grenadier' was probably nothing more than a simple error because that of Waffen-Grenadier-Brigade der SS 'Charlemagne' also appears on the same report. And, lastly, Littlejohn in *Foreign legions of the Third Reich: Volume 1* states that the new formation was known as the Waffen-Grenadier-Brigade 'Charlemagne' (p.169). His omission of 'der SS' was probably little more than an oversight, for on page 161 of the same book we read: 'In September 1944 Himmler announced that the Assault Brigade and the LVF were to be amalgamated as a Waffen-Grenadier-Brigade of the SS...'

15  Angolia, *Cloth Insignia of the SS*, p.491. Angolia dates this designation to September 1944, but adds that the name 'Charlemagne was added shortly thereafter.

16  SS-FHA, Amt II Org.Abt. Ia/II Tgb. Nr. 4213/44 g. Kdos, 13 November 1944, and the Waffen-SS promotions list of 30/1/45, with specific reference to the November 1944 promotions of Doriot to Hstuf. and then to Stubaf. Again of interest to note is that different authors have stated this designation, but again with various dates of introduction and employment: Angolia states from September 1944 to February 1945, *Cloth Insignia of the SS*, p.491; Bayle states from 13 November 1944 to 10 February 1945, *De Marseille à Novossibirsk*, p.77; *Europäische freiwillige* gives from September 1944 to November 1944, p.286; and lastly from September 1944 to November 1944 according to Klietmann Dr. K.-G., *Die Waffen-SS eine Dokumentation* (Osnabrück: Verlag 'Der Freiwillige' G.m.b.H. 1965), pp.285-289. Landwehr appears to repeat Klietmann, citing for the duration of the early formation period, defined as a little more than two months, thus from September 1944 into November 1944 (see *Charlemagne's Legionnaires*, p.56).

17  This title appears on a short report dated 14 October 1944 from concentration camp Stutthof. In response to this report, the individual who wrote it probably did so in ignorance of the correct title of 'Charlemagne'. Therefore, this title should be discounted.

18  According to Klietmann, the designation Waffen-Grenadier Division der SS 'Charlemagne' (Französische Nr.1) was employed from November 1944. Also see Verordnungsblatt der Waffen-SS, 1 December 1944. And yet the designation Waffen-Grenadier-Brigade der SS 'Charlemagne' (franz. Nr. 1) was still in use early February 1945 (see the official documentation dated 1.2.45 reproduced in *San et Persante*, p.134). Moreover, Soulat, then serving with the Headquarters Company of the Brigade, does not recall any such conversion in November or December 1944 (personal conversation).

Notably, few of the designations are supported by orders emanating from the SS-FHA in Berlin. For example, the use of Waffen-Grenadier-Brigade der SS 'Charlemagne' appears to have been widespread but is unsupported. However, in summary, from August 1944 until February 1945, the French formation was titled the Französische Brigade der SS, the Waffen-Grenadier-Brigade der SS 'Charlemagne' and [perhaps lastly] the Waffen-Grenadier-Brigade der SS 'Charlemagne' (franz. Nr. 1).

Much has been said of the name 'Charlemagne'. According to Mabire,[19] in late September 1944, when *Milice* chief Darnand met Ogruf. Berger of the SS-Hauptamt in Berlin to discuss issues around the future deployment of the *Miliciens* into the Waffen-SS, Darnand floated the idea of naming the French unit of the Waffen-SS 'Jeanne d'Arc' [Joan of Arc]. To him, the name sounded *catholique et français toujours*. Berger did not commit himself.

Mabire states elsewhere that the name of 'Jeanne d'Arc', in memory of a similar named unit that had served on the side of Franco in the Spanish Civil War, was under consideration, but was dropped in favour of 'Charlemagne'.[20] Landwehr explains that the name of 'Charlemagne' was chosen over that of 'Jeanne d'Arc' because 'Charlemagne' was a 'pan European Germanic hero' while Joan of Arc was too provincially French and orientated towards the Catholic religion.[21]

Delperrié de Bayac recounts that, in early October 1944, Darnand left again for Berlin and this time Brigf. Krukenberg received him. During the initial negotiations, Krukenberg told Darnand that RF-SS Himmler had decided that the new unit would receive the name of *Brigade Charlemagne*.[22] Days later, Berger took Darnand to meet Himmler at Birkenwald in Saxony. The meeting lasted some two hours. His host spoke of 'Charlemagne'.[23]

On the weekend of 7-8 October 1944, Darnand met Brigf. Krukenberg once again. In a letter to RF-SS Himmler, reporting on the favourable talks between himself and Krukenberg, Darnand wrote that the insignia and name of the French Brigade was 'Charlemagne'.

Finally, an order from the Führerhauptquartier of 1 October 1944, which has recently surfaced,[24] the French Waffen-Grenadier-Brigade der SS was awarded the name 'Charlemagne'.

In conclusion, during this political 'merry-go-round', the French side appears to have had little or no input into the choice of the name of 'Charlemagne', although it raised no objections to its 'imposition'. Arguably, the pan-European Germanic Emperor was a perfect symbol of Franco-German union.

The Brigade (and later the Division) was based on two grenadier regiments with the initial titles and numbers of Grenadier-Regiment 1 and Grenadier-Regiment 2. The two grenadier regiments were to be set up as a matter of priority and to be ready for use by 30 September 1944. The Nachr.-Kp, the Pi.Kp, the two Fahrschw., the Feldpostamt and the Feldersatz Kompanie were ordered to be formed only when the manpower became available.

---

19    Mabire, *La Division Charlemagne*, p.122.
20    See the photograph section of *La Division Charlemagne*.
21    Landwehr, *Charlemagne's Legionnaires*, p.56.
22    Delperrié de Bayac, *Histoire de la Milice*, p.568.
23    Ibid. However, according to Giolitto, *Histoire de la Milice*, p.476, Himmler was still undecided at this point between 'Jeanne d'Arc' and 'Charlemagne'.
24    An example of this FHA order was recently Internet auctioned and sold by the seller as original. However, some have questioned the authenticity of the order and the auctioned example. Unfortunately, the author has not seen the auctioned example and thus must refrain from passing comment, even if 'Charlemagne' was in use with 'Waffen-Grenadier-Brigade der SS' as early as October 1944.

By SS-FHA order of 11 October 1944, the non-regimental units of the Franz. Brigade der SS received the number 57.[25] This same order showed the Brigade as having two regiments with the titles and numbers of Franz.Freiw.Gren. Rgt der SS 57 and Franz.Freiw.Gren.Rgt.der SS 58.[26] These changes may have only appeared on paper. The designations Grenadier-Regiment 1 and Grenadier-Regiment 2 were still very much in use 'in the field' as late as 27 October 1944.[27]

The two grenadier regiments were later renamed Waffen-Grenadier-Regiment der SS 57 (franz. Nr. 1) and Waffen-Grenadier-Regiment der SS 58 (franz Nr. 2).[28]

Thus, the principal elements of the French Brigade can now be summarised as follows:[29]

> Stab der Brigade
> Wach-und Ausbildungskompanie der Inspektion
> Waffen-Grenadier-Regiment der SS 57 (franz. Nr. 1)
> Waffen-Grenadier-Regiment der SS 58 (franz. Nr. 2)
> Waffen-Artillerie-Abteilung der SS 57
> Waffen-Pionier-Kompanie der SS 57
> Waffen-Panzerjäger-Abteilung der SS 57
> Waffen-Nachrichten-Kompanie der SS 57
> Waffen-Sanitäts-Kompanie der SS 57
> Waffen-Veterinär-Kompanie der SS 57
> Waffen-Feldgendarmerie Trupp (mot.) der SS 57
> Waffen-Feldpostamt (mot.) der SS 57

The French Sturmbrigade was the nucleus for Waffen-Grenadier-Regiment der SS 57 while the LVF was that for Waffen-Grenadier-Regiment der SS 58.[30] The I. Bataillon of the LVF was used as the base for the 1st Battalion of Waffen-Gren. Regt der SS 58, otherwise the I/58. The III. Bataillon of the LVF was used as that for the 2nd Battalion of Waffen-Gren. Regt der SS 58, the II/58. The II. Bataillon of the LVF was broken up and its men used to strengthen the two combat battalions of Waffen-Gren. Regt der SS 58. The PAK Company of the LVF became the 10th Company (anti-tank) of Waffen-Gren. Regt der SS 58, otherwise the 10/58. The LVF also populated the Artillery Battalion, Brigade Headquarters, the Pionier-Kompanie [Pioneer Company or Engineer Company[31]] and the two transport columns.

25   SS-FHA Amt II Org. Abt. Ia/II Tgb. Nr. 3614/44 g. Kdos, 11 October 1944.
26   The exact date on which the regiments took on the 'Freiw' designation is not known. Roch gives the same date of the order.
27   Wartime documentation in the author's collection.
28   The exact date on which the regiments took on the 'Waffen' designation as well as the nationality in brackets after the title has again been difficult to determine. Roch gives 1 December 1944 (based upon Verordnungsblatt der Waffen-SS, 1 December 1944). However, the final and full designations Waffen-Grenadier-Regiment der SS 57 (franz. Nr. 1) and Waffen-Grenadier-Regiment der SS 58 (franz. Nr. 2) were definitely in use by the middle of November 1944 (wartime documentation in the author's collection).
29   Lefèvre, *Axis & Alliés* hors série no 1, p.53. The author has made some slight amendments.
30   The final designations of the Grenadier Regiments are used hereafter.
31   The literal translation of *Pionier* is Pioneer, although it's often translated as combat engineer or simply engineer. During WW2 the British Army employed engineers and pioneers in very distinct roles. The

The reaction of the legionnaires to the transfer to the Waffen-SS was mixed. For *sous-lieutenant* Rigeade of the 3rd Company and *adjudant-chef* Rostaing of the III. Bataillon it was the continual battle against the communist danger threatening Europe that was paramount and not the uniform worn. Rostaing still felt bound to his oath of loyalty and remarked in his book that if, like some, he did a bunk before defeat he could never again look at himself in the mirror while shaving.

*Caporal-chef* Malardier, who passed from the Headquarters Company of the I. Bataillon/LVF to the Headquarters Company of Waffen-Gren. Regt der SS 58, embraced his integration into the ranks of the Waffen-SS.

This too was the reaction of *Caporal* Sepchat when transferred from the Engineer Platoon of the Headquarters Company of the LVF to the Engineer Platoon of the Headquarters Company of Waffen-Gren. Regt der SS 58. In August 1941, he had joined the LVF to defend Europe against Bolshevism and in the sincere hope of a durable reconciliation with the hereditary enemy. And now, some three years later, the very same motives, 'reinforced by the habit of fighting beside our German comrades', led him to accept the Waffen-SS with open arms, adding that 'we did not have a choice'. However, two of his LVF comrades, who regarded the Waffen-SS as out-and-out hostile to the Catholic Church, refused to be transferred.[32]

*Sergent* Mercier was at the Ersatzkommando of the LVF at Greifenberg when he learnt that the LVF was passing to the Waffen-SS and it was with great satisfaction that he greeted his transfer to the SS, for it corresponded exactly to his idea of things of the time. He wore the distinctive SS runes before it was made compulsory.

*Sergent* Blonay of the 3rd Company regarded the transfer of the LVF to the Waffen-SS as a 'sign of confidence in all foreign volunteers after the assassination attempt on Hitler and a sign of defiance towards the Wehrmacht'. Also, he approved of the 'maintenance of the difference between the LVF and the Sturmbrigade by the creation of two distinct regiments'. In this way, each unit would retain its *esprit de corps* and cohesion.

*Sergent* Jean-Marie Croisile of the 9th Company embraced the transfer of the LVF to the Waffen-SS because he saw in the Waffen-SS a manifestation of his own political views. He explained:[33]

> The soldiers [of the Waffen-SS] received political training based principally on the European idea, the community of blood and culture of the European peoples. Our motivations were different; the LVF had been created in 1941 to participate in the battle against Bolchevism. The Waffen-SS fought for Europe... At the age of sixteen, when I started to have a political opinion, it had been European.

*Sous-lieutenant* de Genouillac of the I. Bataillon does not recall his real reaction when he learnt of being assigned to the Waffen-SS. However, certain thoughts were prevailing in his mind at that time; he was not given any choice; a soldier has to obey his commanders; the only possibility was to continue the battle to the end and 'the uniform in which he would be buried mattered

---

Pionier-Kompanie's role was more akin to that of the engineers in the British Army rather than the pioneers. Consequently, the author has chosen to use Engineer rather than Pioneer.

32    Sepchat named the two as T. and R.
33    Croisile, *Sous Uniforme Allemand*, p.237.

little'. Besides, the prospect of being incorporated into an elite unit where he would be well trained and well equipped did not displease him.

*Sous-lieutenant* Rossignol was punished for his 'attitude of refusal but continued to serve.[34]

*Caporal-chef* Gonzales of the 2nd Company was discontented. He had no desire to serve in the ranks of the Waffen-SS. All the same he 'marched'.

*Sergent* Yves Peyret was transferred from the PAK Company of the LVF to the 10/58. His reaction to the transfer was one of betrayal. He explained:

> We lost our flag, we were no longer a French unit of the Wehrmacht with exclusively French officers and commands, but Frenchmen dragooned into a Division whose name was French alone. There was no regard for our contracts of enlistment.

Nevertheless, the contracts of the LVF officers were respected. In this way, between fifteen to twenty officers chose to leave the German Army, but the majority refused to abandon the legionnaires under their command. Between forty and forty-five officers transferred to the Waffen-SS.[35]

Only the officers had the right to choose.[36] This angered *Sergent* Peyret all the more because, as a NCO, he did not. Nevertheless, he too marched.

Despite wanting to serve in the Waffen-SS, Norbert Désiré of the 10th Company of the III. Bataillon, a black *Martiniquais* [inhabitant of Martinique], found himself expelled because of the colour of his skin.[37]

André Thiollier, born 1922, refused to pass to the Waffen-SS and deserted. Captured, he was sent to a concentration camp.[38] Pierre Soulé, who was transferred to Company 9/58 with his equivalent rank of Unterscharführer, was not prepared to accept the order to pass from the LVF to the Waffen-SS because, as a political soldier, it totally changed the ideals for which he was fighting.

In total, no more than seventy-five legionnaires of the LVF, including two NCOs, decided to resist the transfer to the Waffen-SS. This figure is all the more surprising considering the predominant French disposition and trappings of the LVF. But the legionnaires' weariness after up to three years of combat on the Russian front is cited as a contributory factor to their apparent reluctance to fight the inevitable. Moreover, many of the major 'figures' within the LVF had come out strongly in support of the transfer, including the larger than life Mgr. de Mayol de Lupé.

*Sergent* Pierre de Séverin, a fervent Catholic, was shocked when he was told the news of his transfer to the Waffen-SS:

34  Rossignol never explained to the author what form his punishment took.
35  Roch, *La Division Charlemagne*, p.49.
36  Curiously, *Sergent* Jean-Marie Croisile of the 9th Company wrote that he was called to see Lieutenant Wagner, who announced to him the LVF now ceased to exist and that he was being transferred to the Waffen-SS, but if he did not agree with the transfer he could be released and returned to France. See Croisile, *Sous Uniforme Allemand*, p.229.
37  Sent to KZ Stuttof, Désiré was decorated with the KVK II. while in the concentration camp.
38  Rigeade confirmed to the author that Thiollier did not pass to the 4/58 as recorded in *Der Freiwillige*, 10/2001.

Among the most Catholic of us, the shock was harsh. Joining the Waffen-SS was tantamount to tearing up his certificate of baptism. The Waffen-SS was inspired by Germanic pagan rites and myths that the Catholic Church condemned. The chaplain of the LVF, Monseigneur Mayol de Lupé, silenced the most recalcitrant. The pagan character of the SS did not disturb this man of God.[39]

To de Lupé, the transfer from the Wehrmacht to the Waffen-SS was of no cause for concern. In fact, in his opinion, 'National Socialism reflected the will of God and the SS was its armed arm'. Indeed, de Lupé needed little pushing to compare the Reichsführer-SS Heinrich Himmler to the Archangel Saint Michael![40]

For all his prestige, Mgr. de Mayol de Lupé could still not convert the seventy-five legionnaires of the LVF who refused to be remustered to the Waffen-SS. Indeed, one of their number called Richter,[41] the son of a general, stole de Mayol de Lupé's horse and deserted.[42]

In desperation, Puaud summoned Renard,[43] the 'ringleader', and offered him the choice of either transferring to the Waffen-SS or being sent to a concentration camp. Renard still refused to embrace the Waffen-SS. A few days later, the riled Puaud, true to his word, decided to rid himself of Renard and the other 'undesirables'.

Estimates vary of the number of LVF legionnaires transferred into the French Waffen-SS from 1,200 to 2,100.[44]

Although required to wear the Waffen-SS pattern *tricolore* shield on the left upper arm, many former LVF men continued to wear their former Wehrmacht *tricolore* shield on the right upper arm. Sometimes the former LVF shield was worn with the word 'France' turned inwards to conceal it.

The command of Waffen-Gren. Regt der SS 58 went to *Commandant* Bridoux of the LVF. He had a touchy character that did not win him friends. Nevertheless, the Germans near to him

39  Lormier, *SS Français*, p.52.
40  Mabire, *La Division Charlemagne*, p.75.
41  De Genouillac, correspondance to the author throughout 1997. According to Saint-Loup, *Les Hérétiques*, p.141, de Villefranche stole Mgr. Mayol de Lupé's horse. This is incorrect; de Villefranche was killed on 13 June 1944 in Russia. *Elève-officier* Noell identified his body.
42  According to Saint-Loup, *Les Hérétiques*, p.141, the horse-thief was stopped two or three days later by Feldgendarmerie on the frontier of Eastern Prussia. Sent to SS and Police camp Danzig-Matzkau, he was brought before a court and condemned to death! The news of his execution surprised the soldiers of the LVF, especially at a time when desertions were part of daily life. In fact, the horse-thief was actually accused of deserting to the enemy for which there was no pardon. This execution added yet another powerful argument to Puaud's armoury on which he could draw when he attempted to convert the legionnaires opposing the passage to the Waffen-SS. In response to Saint-Loup, de Genouillac, who served with the LVF, knew Richter well and cannot recall his capture yet alone his execution. This suggests that Saint-Loup is incorrect.
43  Michel Renard was born on 17 January 1922 in the 15th arrondissement of Paris.
44  Littlejohn, Landwehr, Soulat and Bayle state 1,200 or about 1,200; de Genouillac states no more 1,500; Mabire states 2,000; and Roch states 2,100 (minus the 15 to 20 officers and 75 men who refused to transfer).

held him in high esteem because of his military training and bearing. It is said he even quoted them passages from the memoirs of Hindenburg. He was a very good horseman.[45]

### Enter the Kriegsmarine

The French volunteers of the Kriegsmarine and Naval Police were also transferred to the Waffen-SS without any form of consultation. The reaction of the first contingents of Kriegsmarine contrasted with the subdued reaction of the legionnaires of the LVF who found themselves in the same position weeks before. Sources speak of a riot, a revolt, and even a mutiny! However, there was no such mutiny, yet alone a riot, but a 'very limited show of discontent' as one witness described the events that unfolded.

In the late evening of 17 September 1944, the French Kriegsmarine volunteers of the 2nd Company of Schiffsstammabteilung 28 arrived by train at Greifenberg station. Waiting on the platform to greet them were French volunteers of the Waffen-SS. Suddenly it dawned on the sailors that they had been simply transferred to the Waffen-SS without any form of consulation. Some grumbled, but discipline prevailed. They went into barracks.

By parade next morning, after a night of great debate, the French volunteers of the Kriegsmarine were split in two. A small number assembled in the *feldgrau*, but the majority remained in blue. Indeed, some of those willing to pass to the Waffen-SS were even wearing its insignia, its epaulettes, and its belt! As for those who wished to remain 'sailors', encouraged by legionnaires of the LVF present, they shouted out their protest, but their demonstration soon quietened down.

In order to calm the former Kriegsmarine volunteers, headquarters dispersed them to different local villages to help the farmers harvest the potato crop.[46]

Uscha. Mercier, a former legionnaire of the LVF, witnessed the sailors arrive at Greifenberg:

> They told me that their vocation was 'the sea' and nothing else. One of them said to me that he had been a naval officer and agreed to be a simple rating, but not an infantryman. A German NCO said to them 'but there are no ships any more', to which one replied 'then put us in the merchant navy'. They were upset about the 'lightness' with which they had been 'landed' from the train, letting them think that it was for

---

45   Later, while at Wildlecken, Bridoux would host a demonstration of horsemanship at the manege each week. Pierre Méric, who arrived at Wildflecken with the *Milice*, attended the demonstrations.

46   Soulat, correspondence to the author 1997-98. There are, however, different versions of how the Kriegsmarine volunteers 'came to be calmed'. According to Mabire, *La Division Charlemagne*, p.103, the wind of 'revolt' died down days later, which was assisted in part by the removal of the agitators to 'concentration camp' Danzig-Matzkau. According to Saint-Loup, *Les Hérétiques*, pp.125-126, it was Chaplain Verney who came to the assistance of the Kriegsmarine volunteers. Firstly he calmed the riot and then heard the grievances and demands of the Officers and NCOs. Puaud was contacted, but only promised them a court martial and the concentration camp. Thereupon, Verney alerted the influential Mgr. de Mayol de Lupé and, following his intervention, the 'leadership of the LVF' finally gave way to the demands of the Kriegsmarine volunteers 'to choose freely between civilian life and the Waffen-SS'. Rostaing states, *Le prix d'un serment*, p.146, that only the threat of seeing themselves hauled before a court martial quashed the mutinous behaviour of the sailors. In response to Mabire, Saint-Loup and Rostaing, they are all incorrect (Soulat, correspondence to the author 1997-98).

a new embarkation and ending up in an infantry barracks. When an LVF officer assembled them, brought them to attention and spoke to them seriously, without threatening them with anything, there was no revolt. Thus: bitterness, most certainly; dissatisifaction, often; protests, sometimes, but no refusal to obey orders or mutinies. They were impregnated with the mentality of the Navy.[47]

Notably, they were Navy through and through. *Matrose* [rating] Soulat, one such French volunteer of the Kriegsmarine transferred without consultation to the Waffen-SS, explained that they felt angry because their officers had not provided them with any prior explanation and that the age-old hostility that has existed between the Navy and the Army world over could also explain their reaction.

And yet the French volunteers of the Kriegsmarine had little history to talk of and few traditions to uphold. Indeed, the tricolore arm shield,[48] held so dear by the legionnaires of the LVF, does not appear to have been worn by their compatriots serving in the Kriegsmarine. Also of importance to note is that the French volunteers of the Kriegsmarine were not recruited for a wholly 'French unit' like that of the LVF or the Sturmbrigade. Thus, their transfer to a 'French unit' may well have been another source of complaint.

It was only in February 1944 that the Kriegsmarine had begun to appeal for French volunteers on an official basis, although before this date a number of individual 'private' enlistments had certainly been accepted from the traditional sea-going regions of Brittany and Normandy. Law N° 159 of 17 March 1944 (published in the *Journal officiel* of 18 March 1944) supplemented that of the 22 July 1943 with the addition of 'the arrangements apply to those who enlist in the Kriegsmarine'.

The main Kriegsmarine recruiting office for French volunteers was located in Boulevard des Alliés (sic), Caen, Normandy. The Kriegsmarine even continued its campaign to recruit Frenchmen for 'the Atlantic defence of France and Europe' after the Anglo-American landing in France and relocated its main recruiting office to 2 bis Rue du Havre, Paris.

After the medical, French Kriegsmarine recruits were gathered at Caen and then sent on to Alsace and SS-Ausbildungslager Sennheim for basic training with Schiffsstammabteilung 28 (SStA 28), which was subordinated to the 8th Schiffstammregiment located at Varel. The command structure of SStA 28 was as follows:

| | |
|---|---|
| **Commander:** | Fregattenkapitän Dr. Schneider (to March 1944) |
| | Fregattenkapitän Schroeder |
| **Adjutants:** | Oberleutnant Dr. Bruckmann |
| | Oberleutnant Frischauf |
| **Administration:** | Leutnant Battenfeld (to December 1944) |
| | Oberleutnant Benz |
| **Medical services:** | Marine-Oberstabsarzt Dr. Goebel |

47   Mercier, letter to the author, 21/9/2001.
48   Under German regulations, foreign volunteers were permitted to wear an arm shield in their national colours.

Eleven training companies of Kriegsmarine recruits of different nationalities were formed under the tutorship of SStA 28. The 3rd Company under Oberleutnant zur See Hoech and the 6th Company under Oberleutnant zur See Polck were French. The 4th Company and 5th Company were Estonian and Latvian.

In general, the recruit's training lasted a period of six to eight weeks and concluded with the solemn swearing in ceremony. During this period the emphasis was on physical training and on mastering the rudiments of the German language. Besides, no weapons and little equipment was available with which to train. Even so, the volunteers trained hard, very hard, under the watchful eyes of their instructors who were all decorated German NCOs carrying wounds. The results were good. If proof were needed of this, there is the time General Hardtmann made an impromptu visit to Sennheim.

After watching an exercise of Naval Companies, General Hardtmann expressed the wish to inspect a little closer those of the company who had most impressed him. When he questioned some of them, to his great surprise, he received no response: none of the 3rd Company of the SStA 28 (French volunteers) could speak German. Turning to the Kommandeur accompanying him, General Hardtmann observed:

> I have been in the Army for more than thirty years and I started under Emperor Guillaume as a young Second Lieutenant in the 4th Guards Artillery Regiment at Potsdam. I can only tell you that your Frenchmen manoeuvre as well as the companies of the Prussian Guard which I had the honour of commanding in the past!

Apart from in the canteen, the French volunteers of the Kriegsmarine had no contact with their countrymen of the Waffen-SS.[49]

At the conclusion of this training period the Kriegsmarine volunteers were immediately forwarded to various garrisons in Germany, including Duisburg, Varel and Mannheim, for weapon and specialist naval training. This further period of training lasted some three months in which they perfected their 'trade' by manoeuvring small boats on lakes or rivers. Thereupon, the French Kriegsmarine volunteers received an assignment aboard a naval unit. Most assignments, if not all, were to the Baltic Fleet and on the smaller vessels in the armoury of the Kriegsmarine.

Only the French Kriegsmarine volunteers of the first four companies of SStA 28 served aboard and, in some cases, saw action at sea. Initially, there were no French NCOs or officers, but it was in combat that some Frenchmen received their first rank.

Well over one thousand Frenchmen are said to have served in the Kriegsmarine, but the figure of two thousand found in some sources is considered doubtful. One such Frenchman who volunteered for and served in the Kriegsmarine was *Matrose* Robert Soulat.

## The Story of Robert Soulat

Born in January 1920 in Paris, Robert Soulat had not completed his secondary education when he enlisted in the *24e Régiment de Tirailleurs Tunisiens* in November 1938. He was stationed

---

49   Indeed, some from both sides recall no contact whatsoever. This lack of contact appears to have no other reason other than that the volunteers of the KM and the Waffen-SS occupied two distinct annexes of Sennheim.

in France at La Roche sur Yon and then Fontenay-le-Comte. By April 1939, he held the rank of *Caporal*. When the Germans invaded he played his part in the defence of his country and was captured on 20 May 1940 between Valenciennes and Cambrai by the 7th Panzer Division. Sent to the huge Stalag VIII-C at Sagan, Germany, it was here that he learnt of the Armistice. His reaction was one of profound sadness but not of surprise. Even so he was relieved that the French population was now spared the horrors of war. In February 1943, he was repatriated.

The *Parti Franciste* had brought about Soulat's liberation from captivity; he had been a member of this nationalist party since November 1934 and, on several occasions, had met Bucard, its leader, whom he greatly admired and respected. Although the party asked nothing of him in return, it made it obvious that on his homecoming a political gesture was expected from him on its behalf. But, on the month of his homecoming, compulsory labour service was made obligatory for French males born in 1920, 1921 and 1922 under a law instituting the *Service du Travail Obligatoire* (STO). Soulat, born in 1920, fell into this category and the French bureaucrats of the STO, aware that he had just returned, proposed to post him to a foundry at Puteaux. He carefully thought over his next move.

Over the past three years of captivity, the Germans, in most cases, had treated him decently and thus he had no reason not to work on their behalf. And although the STO had been kind enough to propose a French posting, Soulat did not want to work in a foundry. He wanted work that was agreeable to him. Then there was the party to consider. This twenty-three-year-old knew that he could not remain neutral. And so, on 15 March 1943, he volunteered for the Organisation Todt as a uniformed Baufernsprecher (telephone engineer).

Soulat was sent to the Organisation Todt signals school at Ponthierry where, with some seventy other French volunteers, he learnt the 'basic theories of electricity, maintaining a field telephone and how to set up a line'.[50] The training lasted three weeks, after which he swore the oath of loyalty. Posted to Paris, he found himself working in a team of specialist civilians 'who had to install and maintain the telephone network in Paris for the Organisation Todt and the NSKK'.[51]

On 4 July 1943, at the end of the fourth and last day of the Tenth *Franciste* Congress, Soulat, as a loyal party member, paraded down the Champs-Eysées in the uniform of the OT.

At the end of 1943, Soulat was posted to Mamers. By early May 1944, the intensification of the Allied air attacks led him to believe that the Invasion was imminent and he chose to take up arms again. Because he had no desire to experience once again the daily suffering of the Infantry, he volunteered for the German Kriegsmarine on 15 May 1944 at the Caen recruiting office. In fact, he was not looking forward to finding himself on water; he could not swim!

At Sennheim, Soulat underwent his basic training in the 6th Company of Schiffsstamm-abteilung 28. He was surprised to make the acquaintance of anti-militarists. He made friends with Pierre Soulier who had served with the OT-SK in Russia in 1943.

On 30 June 1944, the 6th Company was sworn in. The following day, the first of July, the company visited the hill of Hartmannsweilerkopf, the scene of fierce fighting during the First World War. One of the French Kriegsmarine volunteers found the grave of his father killed there in 1915. Their presence on this ground in the uniform of the enemy of yesterday was full of

---

50    Léguerandais, *Hitler's French volunteers*, p.86.
51    Ibid.

symbolic meaning, marking the desire, once and for all, to put an end to the hostility cultivated between their two countries.[52]

The 6th Company was sent to Duisburg, quartered in the FLAK barracks of Duisberg-Wannheim and renumbered the 2nd Company. Days later, the new company commander, Oberleutnant zur See Hochhaus, arrived.

One day, instructor Bootman Fleming asked the 'sailors' of the 2nd Company if they would be happy to be engaged in the west as *infanterie de marche* with their present officers. He was deafened by an ovation of overflowing enthusiasm and had to calm them down using all of his authority. Nevertheless, nothing came of this.[53]

On 16 September 1944, the 2nd Company left Hamm by rail. According to their German officers and NCOs, the French sailors were now bound for a naval depot on the Baltic Sea. One day later, the train pulled into Greifenberg station.

The 2nd Company was among the first French contingents of the Kriegsmarine transferred without consultation to the Waffen-SS. Soulat greeted his transfer with little enthusiasm rather than with open hostility. But it was clear to him that the coming fight, either on land or at sea, would be against Russia and that was a fight he preferred to that in his homeland, for he had no wish whatsoever to fight against his fellow countrymen.

When the time came for the French Kriegsmarine volunteers to exchange their blue naval uniforms for the *feldgrau* almost all kept their beret band as a souvenir of their time in the Kriegsmarine.

On 28 September 1944, some two weeks after their arrival at Greifenberg, those French volunteers of the Kriegsmarine transferred to the Waffen-SS, including Soulat and his friend Serge Vincent from Catalan,[54] were relocated by train to training area 'West Prussia', around Konitz, in the Danzig corridor. Arriving at the small town of Bruss, they disembarked and set off on foot to Saalesch, six kilometres away. Night had fallen by the time they arrived. Saalesch was the journey's end for one half of them. The others were sent on to Leisten (with the Polish name of Lesno). And yet their quarters were not actually in the village, but a further two kilometres away at the camp of Waldlager. Finally, the sailors found rest on straw in accommodation delightfully described as 'hovels'.

The very next morning, Soulat was awoken by Rttf. Labrousse. Thus began his transformation and that of his comrades into grenadier of the Waffen-SS under Oberjunker Martres.[55]

---

52   The memoirs of Robert Soulat.
53   Ibid. The date of this incident was probably early September 1944.
54   Serge Vincent was born on 16 February 1924. He joined the NSKK in November 1942 but was invalided out because of a foot wound received during a training exercise. In early 1943, he joined the *Jeunesse Franciste*, followed by the JNP [Youth movement of the RNP] and then the JEN. In early 1944, he attended the *école des cadres de la Jeunesse Légionnaire Rexiste* at Marcinelles and was sent for training at a Hitlerjugend camp. Thereupon, he decided to remain in Germany and volunteer for the Kriegsmarine.
55   Curiously, according to Soulat, letter to the author, 16/7/98, the KM volunteers at Waldlager were formed into two strong (Zuge) platoons under Oberjunker Martres and Oberjunker Brazier, with Brazier probably assuming the command of the two because of his senority. In response to this, at no time was Martres a *chef de section* of KM volunteers at Waldlager (personal discussion with Martres) and Oberjunker Brazier did not serve with the *Wach-und Ausbildungskompanie* (Martres, letter to the author, 12/7/99). Furthermore, the KM volunteers were placed into the *Wach-und-Ausb.Kp.* which was forming at Waldlager. And yet, according to Soulat, letter to the author, the KM volunteers under

Matrose Georges F. was also transferred from the Kriegsmarine to the Waffen-SS. His experience only differs from Soulat in so much that he was told he was leaving the Kriegsmarine, but his Oberbootsmann added that 'after the end of hostilities and, of course, victory, they will be reintergrated'. Like many of his fellow sailors, he regretted having to part with his blue uniform and in particular his tally. He was transported by train from Duisburg to Bruss. His 'reception committee' was made up of soldiers from the LVF, the Waffen-SS and the Heer.[56]

The Kriegsmarine also began to recruit Frenchmen in early 1943 for a naval police unit to guard the U-Boat base at La Pallice, near La Rochelle, which was called the Kriegsmarinewerft polizei La Pallice [Navy Shipyard Police La Pallice] abbreviated to KMW. The first volunteers were wounded soldiers discharged from the LVF, followed by adherents of political parties MSR, PPF and Franciste. Some were STO who preferred to do their time in this unit rather than in Germany. Frenchmen of the KMW were also employed to guard the German naval base at Saint-Nazaire.[57]

On 30 June 1944, the German commander of the La Pallice U-Boat base gave the Frenchmen of the KMW the choice of defending the base or joining the LVF in Germany. Some of those who stayed were killed during an air attack on 10 August 1944. Some of those who left eventually found their way into 'Charlemagne'. The KMW numbered some 200-300 men.

Details of a second naval police unit composed of Frenchmen to be raised by the Kriegsmarine are rather sketchy. Created at the end of 1941, the Kriegsmarine Wehrftmänner or Wehrmänner was used to guard naval arsenals in Brittany.[58] Their uniform differed to that of the KMW.

Of the French contingents of the Kriegsmarine transferred to the Waffen-SS, only a handful, at most five or six men, were dismissed during the 'weeding out' in October 1944.[59] Thus, between 1,000 and 1,200 former French volunteers of the Kriegsmarine and the Naval Police actually went on to serve in 'Charlemagne'.[60] They were assigned to all units, but large numbers served in the following:

Martres were only told on their arrival at Wildflecken months later that they were going to constitute the *Wach-und-Ausb.Kp.* Thus, the possibility exists that the KM volunteers were not told of their placement until such time as they had proved themselves worthy of the *Wach-und-Ausb.Kp.* Lastly, according to Jean Mabire, *La Division Charlemagne*, p.106, Martres and Brazier had at their disposal a German *Spiess* of SS-Panzer-Grenadier-Regiment 9 'Germania'. However, Martres does not recall a German Spiess at his disposal. Perhaps the German *Spiess* joined the *Wach-und-Ausb.Kp.* after the departure of Martres.

56   See Leguérandais, *Les Volontaires Français dans l'armée allemande*, p.112.

57   There is even a suggestion that French naval police fought at Saint-Nazaire against the British commando raiders.

58   See Littlejohn, *Foreign legions of the Third Reich*, volume 1, pp.166-167, and Léguerandais, *Hitler's French volunteers* and *Les Volontaies Français dans l'armée allemande*, p.81.

59   Soulat, letters to the author, 8/12/97 and 3/1/98. However, according to Saint-Loup, *Les Hérétiques*, p.126, the first French contingents of the Kriegsmarine transferred to the Waffen-SS were offered the alternative of returning to civilian life. In this way, twenty per cent of the first French contingents of the Kriegsmarine drafted into the Waffen-SS chose to leave Greifenberg as 'free workers'. In response to this, whilst at Greifenberg, Soulat does not recall any such offer or the departure of so many of his comrades. Indeed, according to Soulat, the five or six discharged in October were the only such former volunteers of the Kriegsmarine to leave 'Charlemagne'.

60   Mabire and Bayle, *San et Persante*, p.125. The author has dismissed Littlejohn's figure of 640, *Foreign Legions of the Third Reich: vol. 1*, p.170, undoubtedly based on the strength of the first French contingents of the Kriegsmarine recorded by Saint-Loup minus the twenty per cent of those released.

- The Wach-und Ausbildungskompanie der Inspektion [Guard and Education Company of the Inspection]
- The Signals Company
- The Medical Company
- The Engineer Company

Also, many former members of the Kriegsmarine served in the headquarters staff of the regiments and battalions. 5% of Waffen-Gren. Regt. der SS 58 was ex-Kriegsmarine.[61]

Four former members of the Kriegsmarine were assigned to the FLAK Company of the Brigade. They included Strmm. Grimaldi who would later receive the Iron Cross 2nd Class 'for acts of war in the KM'.[62]

## Special Forces

'Some of the new SS men were from the French section of the Army's celebrated Brandenburg Division'.[63] The number of French *Brandenburgers* that joined 'Charlemagne' probably totalled only a handful.[64]

## Auxiliary forces

Frenchmen serving with the paramilitary formations of the German war machine were also absorbed into the Waffen-SS. It is estimated that some 2,000 to 2,300 Frenchmen of the Schutzkommando of the Organisation Todt [or simply the SK] and the Technische Nothilfe ('Teno') served in 'Charlemagne'.[65] And yet little is known of when and where they were placed into 'Charlemagne'. Also not known is their reaction to this. Presumably it too was one of disgruntlement.

In 1941, the *Schutzkommando* [Protection Command] was formed by the Organisation Todt to guard its building sites against theft and sabotage and to supervise its 'employed' workers.[66]

---

61   Lefèvre, cited by Roch, *La Division Charlemagne*, p.51.
62   Anon., *Encadrement de la FLAK*, unpublished article.
63   Littlejohn, *Foreign Legions of the Third Reich: vol. 1*, p.170. Formed in early 1943, the 8th Company of the 3rd Regiment was largely French. It operated on French soil.
64   Arguably, in September 1944, when the Brandenburg division was relieved of its duties as a special operations unit and transformed into a motorised panzergrenadier division, most French *Brandenburgers* chose to join the commando units of the Waffen-SS commanded by Skorzeny rather than 'Charlemagne'.
65   It should be noted that the figure of 2,000 represented a fraction of those Frenchmen actually employed in these paramilitary formations.
66   In 1938, when tasked by Hitler with the construction of the Westwall, Fritz Todt, the *Generalinspektors für das deutsche Strasenwesen* [Inspector general of German roads], responded by mobilising some one thousand private construction firms. This army of workers Hitler christened Organisation Todt. On 4 September 1939, Fritz Todt declared 'that the OT would function in wartime as a fortress construction organisation, employing building firms organised on military lines'. When war came, OT personnel served on all fronts. Their roles were varied; from building bridges, often under fire, to repairing roads damaged in the fighting; from the construction of harbour facilities to dams in marshy regions; from the running of oil-extraction facilities in Estonia to collective farms in the Ukraine. Indeed, the OT

Personnel of the SK wore a brown uniform with black shoulder straps and black ties. To fill its ranks, the SK turned to the recruitment of foreign volunteers because most physically fit German males were already serving in the armed forces. Many Dutch, Flemings, Walloons and, to a lesser extent, French volunteered for the SK. French volunteers wore on the upper right arm a tricolore shield surmounted by the word 'FRANCE' in a yellow cogwheel on a dark blue, or black, background.[67]

Among the Frenchmen to volunteer for the SK was Roger Vigny. 'Captivated by Nazi doctrine, the launching of operation Barbarossa prompted him to enlist. He did so in September 1942 after having falsified his papers; he was in fact only sixteen years old!'[68] With a contingent of French volunteers, he left in October 1942 for the SK training school at Pontivy, Brittany. He recalled:

> The welcome was rather friendly and courteous from the officers and NCOs responsible for our training. That same evening we were handed a sheet on which appeared every command in German translated into French as well as the names of our instructors, all Frenchmen with the rank of SK-Rottenführer or SK-Kameradschaftsführer. They advised us to do our utmost to learn the contents quickly. The following morning, we received training overalls, a personal weapon, helmet, belt, cartridge belt... The ammunition would be distributed to us later. The training was rigorous: it was similar to that followed by all infantrymen. The training course lasted about a month or longer if it proved necessary. At the end, our recompense was the issue of the epaulettes: black with a white border. They were presented after the swearing in ceremony performed on the 'golden flag' of the OT (a swastika ringed by a cogwheel), the company in a U formation in the barracks square. We then received the khaki uniforms of the OT and we marched through the streets of Pontivy, led by the band and the flag.

became responsible for all construction projects behind the front lines. In late 1941, OT Einsatzgruppe 'West' was formed to supervise the nine Oberbauleitungen units operating in France, Belgium and the Netherlands. Located at Lorient, then 33, avenue des Champs Elysées, Paris, OT Einsatzgruppe 'West' was tasked with the realisation of the 'Atlantikwall', the so-called Atlantic Wall, a defensive system of fortification units stretching along the Atlantic coastline of German occupied Europe. Needless to say, it was a massive undertaking requiring steel, concrete and manpower. By 1942, OT Einsatzgruppe 'West' was employing 112,000 German and 152,000 French workers, including 17,000 North African Arabs. Although many French workers were employees of firms under OT contract or genuine volunteers, others had joined to save themselves from deportation to Germany or in order to escape from poverty. Thus, for some, the Organisation Todt was little more than a point of refuge. Also many of the large numbers of non-French workers in France could hardly be described as volunteers. And yet, in November 1942, members of the OT were granted full armed forces status. By 1943, 'West' had grown to 18 Oberbauleitungen and now numbered 291,000 workers of more than twenty nationalities. For the first time, in its ranks were Allied prisoners-of-war. As well as fortifying the Mediterranean coast, OT labourers now repaired the increasingly bombed and sabotaged railway network. Following the Normandy invasion, 'West' retreated in great disorder into Germany.

67    This national shield may have only been introduced for wear late 1943; Frenchmen Roger Vigny and Castrillo, who volunteered for the SK September 1942 and early 1943 respectively, did not wear the French national shield.

68    See Mounine, article *Les Français Schutzkommandos de l'OT*, magazine 39/45, June 1996.

The next day the postings began. Vigny was posted to Saint-Malo and then Cherbourg. In September 1943, one year after joining up, while on leave, bored of the monotony and the routine of guard duties and convinced that there was no opportunity of promotion for Frenchmen, he decided to hand back his Soldbuch and uniform. However, he did not give up the fight and enlisted in the Speer Legion, another German paramilitary formation.

In January 1943, the twenty-eight-year-old Roger Mariage entered the SK. Previous, with the rank of *sergent*, he had fought with the LVF and been seriously wounded. The SK gave him the NCO rank of SK-Haupttruppführer and made him an instructor at Pontivy. On 9 April 1943, the SK training school was relocated from Pontivy to a former camp for French POWs at Château de Beauregard, La Celle Saint-Cloud, outside Paris. By upgrading its facilities, the camp was converted into a model training school. The instructors were from the Waffen-SS.

Most, if not all, of the French collaborationist political parties actively recruited volunteers for the OT and its SK. Numerous *Francistes* enlisted in the various branches of the OT. At the start of 1943, a two hundred strong uniformed contingent of Déat's *Rassemblement National Populaire* enlisted in the SK. The PPF was also well represented in the SK. And it was orders from the PPF that brought loyal party member Jean Castrillo to the SK.

Born on 10 December 1922 in Paris, Jean Castrillo was the son of a businessman. His father, a French resident since 1907, was of Spanish origin, who took French nationality in 1940. His mother, who was born in Paris, was of Alsatian, Flemish and Dutch origin. Politically, his parents were Falangists. During the Spanish Civil War two cousins were shot in Madrid by communist forces under General Miaja. One of them was a fervent Falangist.

In 1936, the year the PPF was founded, his father went into business in Saint-Denis, which became the power base of the PPF, and struck up a friendship with novelist Drieu La Rochelle, who supported the PPF. Before the year was out, his father had entered the PPF and the fourteen-year-old Jean the *Union populaire de la Jeunesse française*, the youth branch of the PPF.[69]

Castrillo served the party as best a young militant could, selling newspapers and billposting. He attended party meetings. He heard Doriot speak, of whom he described as 'a remarkable orator and organiser, a workaholic, with great leadership qualities and great personal courage'. The young Castrillo was devoted to Doriot and the party.

From June 1940 to October 1941, Castrillo attended secondary school, passing his *baccalauréat*. He remained politically active. Like his father, by now the head of the PPF for the XIX° *arrondissement* of Paris, he greatly admired Pétain. The family supported the German led crusade against Communism and believed that Germany needed help, although it was not yet a question of Jean volunteering for the LVF, populated by the PPF, and leaving for the Eastern Front.

Castrillo followed very closely the debut of the LVF on the Eastern Front. When François Sabiani, the son of Simon Sabiani, the 'proconsul of the PPF for Marseille', was killed at the front he hailed him as a hero. Thus in June 1942 he decided to volunteer for the *Chantiers du Maréchal* whose training instructors belonged to the PPF.

Posted to camp des Châteliers near Orléans, Castrillo received one month's instructor training under the supervision of a former NCO of the LVF, who had been wounded during the winter of 1941-42 before Moscow and invalided out. At the conclusion of the one month *stage*,

69   The UPJF later became the *Jeunesses Populaires française* (JPF).

in receipt of his *diplôme de moniteur des Chantiers de la Jeunesse*, he left for the 'lumber' camp at Méry ès Bois in the Cher,[70] where he was put to work clearing the tree plantations of Sologne. By now it was late August 1942.

Castrillo soon found himself in trouble. Along with a youngster of the RNP and a former sailor, anglophobe since Mers-el-Kébir, he led a mutiny against the criminal activities of the *chefs* of this camp, for they were openly trafficking, buying and selling on the black market, and helping themselves to the recruits' food coupons. With the three 'crooks' locked up, the mutineers requested the Chantiers' headquarters at Orléans to come and investigate.

The following morning, four cars arrived from the *préfecture* of the Loiret with an official from the Chantiers. The newcomers talked with the mutineers. They were all smiles. A lorry of *gardes-mobiles* then arrived. The three ringleaders of the mutiny, which included Castrillo, were arrested and sent to a forced labour camp at Vouzeron in the outer suburbs of Vierzon.

Contact with the outside world was forbidden, but at the beginning of November 1942 Castrillo was granted permission to write to his father. At the request of his father the party now came to the rescue. Vauquelin de la Fresnay, head of the JPF, obtained from Doriot permission to go and see Otto Abetz, who ordered the French authorities to release him because he had not stood trial. A car sent by the party collected him.

On his return to Paris, Castrillo attended the PPF 'congress of power' at cinema Gaumont Palace, which opened on 4 November 1942 and ran to 8 November. Under the *tribune d'honneur* was a huge banner which read 'Vichy betrays'. He recalls the speeches of both Doriot and Simon Sabiani, the 'proconsul of the PPF for Marseille', who exhorted the youngsters of the party to follow the example of his son François. Henceforth 'his decision was made'; he would leave to fight with the LVF. Because he was not yet twenty, he could not leave without consent from a parent, which his father gave him. However, at the request of the party, he volunteered for the SK. He considered himself a political *engagé* [enlisted man or volunteer] through and through. Moreover, as a Germanophile, he admitted: 'After Stalingrad, the worse the situation was, the more I considered that I was one with Germany'.

Castrillo was dispatched to La Celle Saint-Cloud and placed into the French training company. The training under company commander Mariage was hard. On 28 May 1943, shortly after the conclusion of recruit training, Castrillo's company swore an oath of loyalty to Hitler as 'commander of European armies'. Black epaulettes were issued.

Castrillo was then granted three days leave, after which he left for Norway in a company composed of equal numbers of Dutch and French volunteers with German officers and NCOs, all of Saxon origin. The Dutch were for the most part members of the youth branch of the NSB (National Socialist Movement) led by Mussert. Half of the French were apolitical and half were, like Castrillo, from the JPF. Many of the recruits had joined to avoid forced labour in Germany or out of a taste for adventure. Only two or three of Castrillo's compatriots were really politicised. One, a young Belgian residing in France, would later join Degrelle and the Walloon Division of the Waffen-SS.

---

70    The camp was installed in the family chateau of De Lesseps, a name made famous by an ancestor who had conceived and constructed the Suez Canal.

Transported by road to Denmark, the company sailed for Oslo on a cruiser of the German Navy. It was assigned to protect a top secret industrial complex south of Bergen, which Castrillo would later learn was involved in nuclear research.

Norway was no longer a quiet tour of duty. Castrillo received his baptism of fire when the company participated in an operation against Norwegian Resistance forces north-east of Bergen. The operation lasted three weeks.

In October 1943, the company was engaged against British commandos who had landed not far from the complex. This was a much more serious test. The British fought fiercely but were rounded up one after the other. Some two hundred British were taken prisoner. The losses suffered by the SK Company were heavy: five dead, ten seriously wounded, and twenty slightly wounded, which included Castrillo, for which he received the wound badge.

On 14 November 1943, the company was relieved. Hopes of leave were dashed when the company was transported across the Baltic Sea on a Norwegian vessel to the port of Memel, where it remained on security duties alongside Latvian Police until April 1944. Castrillo, promoted to SK Mann 1. Klasse in November 1943 and then to SK-Rottenführer in March 1944, recalls a very friendly population, which was warmly anti-Communist. It was a home from home.

On his return to France, Castrillo was granted one month's leave. As to be expected he went to the headquarters of the PPF at 10 rue des Pyramides, Paris, where he received a warm welcome, but also news of the death of two of his comrades of the JPF with the LVF on the Eastern Front. Barthélémy, one of the leading figures in the party, took him into his office and congratulated him on his service record. Castrillo then asked him to facilitate his transfer to the LVF. There was no question of this because Doriot now had need of men in France to take the fight to the terrorists. Castrillo left the SK and joined the *Milice* in June 1944 and was stationed at Lycée Saint-Louis, boulevard Saint Michel, Paris. He would later serve with 'Charlemagne'.

René Binet, a former member of the *Parti communiste français* and perhaps one of the most well-known Frenchmen of the SK, enlisted in the Waffen-SS and was trained at Sennheim. In this way he too later found himself serving in 'Charlemagne'.[71] He was appointed to Abteilung VI (Political training and activities).

The French volunteers of the SK also served in Germany, Yugoslavia and Estonia, where a company of French SK was 'almost totally destroyed during the summer of 1943'.[72]

By 1944, the SK was also guarding POWs, criminals and concentration camp inmates serving in OT detachments. With the liberation of France, the French SK volunteers fled to Germany, and the great majority were transferred to the Waffen-SS and sent to Wildflecken.

In March 1945, all SK companies were disbanded. There may have been as many as 3,000 French volunteers of the Schutzkommando.[73]

Also absorbed into the Waffen-SS were French volunteers of the Technische Nothilfe [Technical Emergency Help] or 'Teno'. The primary war role of 'Teno' was to repair breakdowns

---

71   It should be noted that at least three persons with the name of René Binet served in 'Charlemagne'.
72   Mabire, *La Division Charlemagne*, p.24. Curiously, according to Lambert and Le Marec, *Les Français sous le casque allemande, Europe 1941-1945*, p.143, a French SK company was entirely annihilated in Latvia.
73   Bayle, *De Marseille à Novossibirsk*, p.147.

in vital public services. The 'Teno' recruited French technicians, but faced competition from a rival, the Organisation Todt. Thus, the number of Frenchmen in 'Teno' is believed to be small.

Like their compatriots in the French NSKK, the French 'Teno' volunteers were subordinate to the Luftwaffe and wore its grey-blue uniform with black 'Teno' ranks and insignia. It is not known whether or not the French 'Teno' volunteers were permitted to wear some form of national insignia, but it is considered very likely. Also not known is the actual number of French 'Teno' volunteers who went on to serve in 'Charlemagne', but they could not have amounted to more than a handful.

Frenchmen serving as Hilfswilligen [perhaps best translated as 'voluntary helpers'] or Hiwis also entered 'Charlemagne'. Perhaps the most remarkable was René Bourg. In 1941, at the age of sixteen, he enlisted in the LVF and served with the 2nd Company. On 4 October 1942, he was caught in a partisan ambush in the clearing of Kalinine and left for dead. However, although seriously wounded, he was still breathing when found. Such were his wounds that he had his right leg amputated. He received the Wound badge silver and Infantry Assault badge. In 1943, he was demobilised. He was later awarded the Iron Cross 2nd Class, the *Croix de guerre légionnaire* and the *Médaille militaire*. Remarkably, on 6 June 1944, he volunteered his services once again. Assigned to the 21st Panzer Division, he 'rode shot-gun' on supply columns.[74] He followed the division to Alsace and saw action there with a *Panzerschützen* unit. He was all too happy to enter 'Charlemagne' and was assigned to the Construction Company.[75]

'Chalemagne' also welcomed into its ranks French agents of the *Selbstschutzpolizei* [Self Protection Police] organised by the German Police in the spring of 1943 to assist in the fight against terrorism. Agents were recruited from the *jeunes* of the collaborationist movements and received police, sabotage and radio training at Taverny. In February 1944, the Germans extended the offer of training to members of the political parties authorised in the occupied zone and those willing to 'take sides with the French and German police to maintain order in case of unrest'.[76] The best students could remain at Taverny to become *permanents* [literally 'paid officials'] of the SPP. In the months of April and May 1944, three Kommandos of these full-time *permanents* were sent to Dijon, Toulouse and Rennes. There were some 150 *permanents*, although the Germans planned to install 50 per department. Before it closed its doors, some 5000 *jeunes* had passed through Taverny. Not all were French. They included Italians, Russians, Arabs, and Flemings. After Liberation, some *permanents* of the *Selbstschutzpolizei* found their way into 'Charlemagne'.

Members of the *Groupe spéciale de Paris* (GSP), who had fled from France to a camp in Germany for political refugees, were offered the choice to join the Waffen-SS, work or remain interned. The GSP of the LVF was responsible for guarding Ambassador de Brinon who was the president of the *Comité Central* of the LVF. All of the men of the GSP held the rank of *sergent*. They were armed, mainly with Sten guns. Albert Gauthier said of the choice presented to them:

---

74    Frenchmen also served as Hiwis with other German Army units. For example, Jean de S.C. served with the 17. SS-Panzer-Grenadier-Division der SS 'Götz von Berlichingen'.
75    In February 1945, Bourg too would go to Pomerania with 'Charlemagne'. Wounded again, he was evacuated to Kolberg and then onto Swinemunde. He survived the war. He died on 17 December 2014.
76    Lambert and Le Marec, *Les Français sous le casque Allemand*, p.205.

The majority of the legionnaires refused to enter the Waffen-SS and even the majority of the active legionnaires refused to sign. Unanimously we really wanted to continue the struggle against bolchevism but we did not want to belong to a political army which would have been engaged against other nations at war other than Russia. The spirit of the LVF was to fight bolchevism, but not fight against the English and or the Americans. I preferred to work and was sent to Strasbourg to the Jacquet Factories for several days. Then I was requisitioned by the Organisation Todt who sent me to the region of Delme in Alsace.[77]

Exiled collaborationists also entered 'Charlemagne'. In late August 1944, with fellow party members of the PPF, Raymond Cartaud decided to flee from his native Bordeaux to Germany; as a loyal member of the party since its creation, he feared being captured and executed by the resistance, even though he had served France bravely in both the First World War and 1939-40.[78] Still fit and active, he decided to join the Waffen-SS.

## The French NSKK

Some sources state that the bulk of the French NSKK was absorbed into the Waffen-SS.[79] This is not correct. Nevertheless, individual Frenchmen may have 'deserted' the NSKK for the Waffen-SS, but their number, if any, would have been small.

From the start of October 1943 to mid-November 1943, the 4th Company of the French Battalion of the 4th Regiment was deployed to Crécy-en-Ponthieu in Northern France to transport sand and other construction material for the V1 sites. After handing over their trucks to Flemish NSKK, the Frenchmen returned to Grammont by train.

From December 1943 to the end of November 1944, the headquarters and the three companies (4-6) of the French Battalion of the 4th Regiment of NSKK Transportgruppe Luftwaffe were stationed in Italy. The sejour in Italy took its toll on the men and equipment. There were a number of desertions. In one company which had started with 300 men and 120 trucks it ended with only 100 men and just 3 trucks. Moreover, Sturmführer André Soyer, the Kolonführer of the 4th Column/4th Company, was arrested for various malpractices.

Meanwhile, back in France, the NSKK continued to compete with rival military and paramilitary organisations for its 'fair share' of French recruits, but its efforts appear to have reaped little reward. Even the Allied invasion of France did not deter the NSKK and 'Gruppe TODT' from attempting to recruit drivers, mechanics and electricians for a French section. Volunteers had to be aged 18 to 50 and in very good health.

In early December 1944, after handing over its trucks, the French battalion was posted from Italy to Denmark. The 4th Company was employed on guard duties at Odense. On 28 January 1945, at Odense, battalion commander Staffelführer Seigel first announced the existence of 'Charlemagne'. Thereupon, ninety per cent of the Frenchmen volunteered to join the Brigade but were only 'rewarded' with three days of intensive exercise!

77 Rentano & Leguérandais, *Ces Franciliens qui ont choisi Hitler*, p.106.
78 Notably, his two sons had not followed the same path of collaboration: one joined the resistance in 1941, while the other joined de Gaulle in England in 1943 and fought with the Free French Air Force.
79 For example, see Littlejohn, *Foreign Legions of the Third Reich: vol. 1*, p.165.

French NSKK transferring to Denmark, December 1944. (Francois Faroux)

The battalion was reorganised into two groups.[80] In late February 1945, one group was dispatched to Hungary. The rail journey lasted almost a whole month. The convoy entered Hungary via Sopron, crossed Györ and Komárno and stopped at Tata. Obersturmmann Faroux's Kolonneführer of the 4th Company, French Sturmführer Györ, who was Hungarian born, disappeared shortly after crossing into Hungary. The convoy was then obliged to make its way south because of the Russian advance, finally stopping at Vezprém. The Frenchmen were billeted in the nearby villages of Tótvázsony and Nagyvázsony, which they had to walk between because they had not yet received trucks from the Luftwaffe.

Finally, the group was equipped with trucks, but was plagued with supply and fuel problems. Each soldier was given a jerrycan and a rubber hose and told to siphon fuel wherever possible from knocked out trucks and tanks. During one mission in March Faroux ended up at Balatonfúzfó where he saw Lake Balaton for the first time and was struck by its immensity.

The front was not continuous. Obersturmmann Faroux had two brushes with the Russians. He would never forget the time his convoy was ambushed a few kilometres west of Vezprem. He jumped out of the cab, took up position under the truck and started to return fire. The German Luftwaffe driver, who took his time to take cover, was shot dead and collapsed beside him. The Russians then withdrew. From that day forth he would count each day as a blessing.

---

80    The battalion may have been reorganised into a 'headquarters' and two companies numbered 4 and 5 (Faroux, letter to the author, 14/8/2001).

Then there was the time Faroux was engaged in anti-tank combat.[81] The date was late March 1945, the location was west of Lake Balaton and the situation was Panzeralarm. Armed with panzerfaust, he was commandeered by a German Army officer, incorporated into an emergency anti-tank unit, and sent on foot in search of enemy tanks, which had cut the road to the rear. The lead elements made contact, destroying one tank. The Russians withdrew, but there was no doubt that they would be back. And they were one hour later. Faroux made use of the bushy terrain to approach to within panzerfaust range, took aim at a tank and fired, but nothing happened. Fortunately, he was not discovered. Losing another tank and with the dark setting in, the Russians withdrew.

The group was forced to retreat northwest. Fuel became a nightmare. Thankfully, Faroux chanced upon a stock of B4 at a makeshift airfield in the vicinity of Szombathely, which no longer had planes. He quickly fuelled up, loaded two barrels of B4 and picked up two 'unemployed' mechanics.

The group retreated into Austria by way of Deutschkreuz, a few kilometres south of Sopron, where it had entered Hungary one month previously. The group rested at Bromberg for several days, but it was now no more than a kolonne, having 'melted like butter in the sun'.[82] The crew of NSKK-Scharführer Tregouboff, a white Russian in his fifties, and Faroux soon found themselves alone. On 7 May 1945, they learnt that many German soldiers had surrendered. The following day, they abandoned their truck, changed into civvies and walked west.

Henri Raga did not leave with the first group for Hungary. Suffering from a sore throat, he was admitted into the military hospital at Fredericia. He was diagnosed with diphtheria, even though he had been vaccinated against it when he was young. Inexplicably, in early February 1945, every soldier in the hospital had their blood group tattooed under their left armpit, but he refused outright. Because he was French the hospital orderlies did not insist and contented themselves with etching his blood group on his identity disc.

On 31 March 1945, the second group left Denmark for Hungary. At Flensburg the Frenchmen met some volunteers of the *Britisches Freikorps* [British Free Corps]. The convoy continued through Berlin, then onto the smouldering ruins of Dresden and then westwards. On 18 or 19 April 1945, the group disembarked at Gmünd in the Sudetanland. To celebrate the Führer's birthday on 20 April, the Frenchmen men paraded for the authorities and local population of Gmünd. The journey resumed the next day. After passing through Linz and Graz, the convoy arrived at Salzburg on the evening of 26 April.

The following morning, a violent air raid destroyed Salzburg station. A tank convoy, which had been given priority over the French convoy and was occupying its place, was smashed. The French convoy suffered no damage whatsoever, but two German NCOs, who were former Foreign Legion and spoke French perfectly, were killed. This, however, was the journey's end. On 29 April 1945, the group was demobilised by Hauptsturmführer Ströhle. Some decided to go to Italy.[83] A small number decided to return to Denmark.

81  According to Littlejohn, *Foreign Legions of the Third Reich: vol. 1*, p.165, '…in the closing months of the war one French NSKK unit fought in Hungary against the Russians as an anti-tank formation'. As such, this is not correct.
82  Faroux, letter to the author, 5/9/2002.
83  A small group of eleven made their way on foot to Innsbruck and from there crossed into Northern Italy via the Brenner Pass. A truck then took them to Bolzano, arriving on 3 May 1945. Their meal

Estimates of the number of Frenchmen who served with the NSKK vary from 2,000 to 10,000.[84] The number was nearer 2,000 than 10,000. Also, several Frenchmen are known to have become officers in the NSKK.

## Workers

To swell the ranks of 'Charlemagne', the Waffen-SS tried to attract new recruits from among the large number of French workers in Germany. One of those involved in the recruitment drive was Swiss-born André Doutart who, in mid-August 1944, after the conclusion of his recruit training at Sennheim, had been posted to the SS recruiting office in Stuttgart. He toured Bavaria speaking to French workers and not once was he insulted. Wearing full Waffen-SS uniform, the Frenchmen took him for a German and the Germans for a Frenchmen!

The recruiting campaign took Doutart to Göttingen, Heidelberg, Mannheim, Stuttgart, Karlsruhe, Ulm, and Sigmaringen. He arrived at Mannheim just after a daytime air raid. It was frightening. The workshops had not been hit, but the dining halls had been razed to the ground. Palpable was the hate for the Americans that filled the French workers. Here he also spoke against the terror raids.

At Sigmaringen, Doutart met many of the French exiled personalities; the chief editor of the *journal 'la France'* whose son had enlisted in the Waffen-SS; Laval; and Marcel Déat. On 30 October 1944, he held a meeting in the town's cinema. It was full to bursting. His arrival in full uniform made a strong impression. No sooner had he begun to speak than there was a power cut. Contrary to what he expected, from the audience there was not a sound, not a yell, not a whistle or an insult, just silence. When the power came back on he continued to speak, explaining the goal of 'our combat'. He included slogans heralded by Léon Degrelle in the *grand* speech he gave in April 1944 at the Palais de Chaillot, Paris.[85]

And what was the result of the recruiting campaign? The workers came to see him to sort out small problems they had with their foremen. This he did. But few volunteered there and then. And of those who did volunteer, half were 'false'; such volunteers knew full well that the medical examination would find them unfit for military service, but the enlistment process would take some ten days and that meant some ten days 'on holiday' away from life in the factories!

On 4 November 1944, Doutart was posted to the SS-Hauptamt in Berlin. Soon after, because of disciplinary reasons, he was transferred to the Franz. SS-Grenadier-Ausbildungs und Ersatz Bataillon at Greifenberg where he met his friend Paul Pignard-Berthet who he knew from the

at the local *Soldatenheim* was interrupted by SS-Oscha. Rossfelder, a former NSKK volunteer, who proposed that they join the *Lehrgang* organised at Gries for French SS volunteers of 'Charlemagne' so that the fight against Russia might be continued with the Americans! They thanked him, but declined his proposal. They had other plans on their mind.

84    Littlejohn states 2,000 (*Foreign Legions of the Third Reich: vol1*, p.165) and Saint-Loup 10,000 (*Les Hérétiques*, p.124). Also, some sources state that there were seven French companies of the NSKK (Littlejohn, *Foreign Legions of the Third Reich: vol1*, p.161, and Ory, *Les Collaborateurs*, p.265). As such this is not correct; only three companies operated at any one time.

85    After the meeting Doutart spoke with Déat for an hour. Déat spoke of the certainty of final German victory. On a large wall map, he explained how the European troops were going to attack, encircle and defeat the Allies. Also, he spoke of the V-10!

Prytanée Militaire de La Flèche. He also recalls SS-Oscha. Krusenbaum, who spoke excellent French.

### Sturmbrigade FLAK Company

From 28 April 1944 to 28 July 1944, the FLAK Company was on a training course at Munich. Each morning, FLAK Company commander Führerbewerber Guignot, called *Capitaine* which was his former rank in the French Foreign Legion, led the company onto the training ground and handed it over to the German instructors. For the rest of the day he would look on. At no time was he ever involved in its training or in its internal running! Nevertheless, he appeared at meal times. His 'lack of interest' was of little concern to the Germans who were in awe of the dazzling row of medals he wore proudly on his tunic.

Absent from the FLAK Company were platoon commanders Fayard, Ouvre and Mary, who were on a platoon commander's course. André Ouvre was born on 29 June 1918 and fought in 39-40 against the Germans. Captured, he managed to escape. Maurice Mary was born on 17 January 1916 and, like Ouvre, would have fought in 39-40 against the Germans.

At Munich, the French volunteers actively participated in the defence of the city against the Anglo-American 'terror' raids. On one occasion their barracks was bombed, but they struck back by shooting down some American aircraft. Several times, after the all-clear, the FLAK Company was also employed to repair railway bridges near its barracks (Notbrücke).

The assassination attempt on the life of Hitler on 20 July 1944 brought about a memorable day of drama and activity for the FLAK Company. Tanks of the Waffen-SS appeared throughout the city; in fear of an attempted Putsch by the Heer, the RSHA had ordered them onto the streets. German Waffen-SS soldiers left barracks Freimann to surround the barracks of the Heer, the Luftwaffe and even those of the Vlasov Army! As for the French FLAK Company, orders were received from the Kommandeur of Freimann to protect the barracks. Taking up a 'hedgehog' position around the outside of the buildings, they waited...

On 28 July 1944, after completing its training, the FLAK Company left Munich for Pomerania. The next day, it disembarked at the small town of Bruss (now Brusy) in the former Danzig corridor and was quartered in a camp.

At Bruss, the FLAK continued to train, albeit without weapons, under the supervision of Oberjunker Fayard. As for Guignot, he was impassive as ever. Sometime after, with elation, the FLAK received its full allocation of heavy and light weapons, and vehicles.

On 17 August 1944, the FLAK Company was moved to Saalesch, several kilometres from Bruss, and quartered with LVF units, who greeted its arrival with surprise and contempt. The LVF considered the FLAK as 'fanatical Nazis'.[86] But the forced cohabitation led to curiosity and then sympathy. For its part, the FLAK was not without admiration for the veterans of the Russian Front 'who recounted their adventures'.

86  *Le Schreiber*, unpublished article.

## End of the Sturmbrigade

The FLAK Company was one of the first units, if not the first unit of the SS-Sturmbrigade, to arrive in Pomerania.[87] In late August 1944,[88] its skeletal 2nd Battalion (no more than two companies) was transferred from Neweklau to the village of Schwarnegast (Swornegacie in Polish) situated west of Bruss (Brusy) and north of Könitz (Chojnice).[89]

Although the SS-Sturmbrigade commander Gamory-Dubourdeau had not been with the 1st Battalion in Galicia, he was promoted to Obersturmbannführer as a 'reward' for its impressive performance. In August 1944,[90] 'in a fit of excessive indulgence',[91] he promoted FLAK Company commander Guignot to Hauptsturmführer and placed him in command of the 2nd Battalion of the SS-Sturmbrigade. St.Ob.Ju. Fayard was slotted into the vacancy Guignot left behind and St.Ob.Ju. Pierre Vincenot, who was ex-LVF, succeeded Fayard at the head of the 1st Platoon.[92]

One of the first actions of Fayard as the new FLAK Company commander was to accelerate the pace of the training. Thus, for up to ten hours a day, the men of the FLAK Company trained and trained hard. Heavy emphasis was placed on learning the mechanics of their weapons.

From the LVF the FLAK inherited a young Russian boy by the name of Nicolas Samassoudov. He became its mascot and Fayard even promoted him to the rank of Sturmmann! He would serve with his 'adopted parents' of the FLAK Company to the end.

On 8 September 1944, Triqueneaux of the FLAK Company was promoted to Rottenführer and to Unterscharführer on 7 December 1944, even though his role of secretary was not that of an NCO.

87   Personnel of the arriving French Sturmbrigade were assigned to SS-Panzer-Grenadier Ausbildungs-und Ersatz Bataillon 35 (see the *Soldbuch* of Fenet and that of Pierre J. which appears in *39–45 magazine*, issue number 89, p.9).

88   The date the 2nd Battalion arrived at Schwarnegast is unclear; according to Mabire, *La Division Charlemagne*, p.54, days after its own arrival, the 2nd Battalion expected the survivors of the 1st Battalion who arrived on 5 September 1944. This would date the arrival of the 2nd Battalion to either late August or early September 1944. However, according to Saint-Loup, *Les Hérétiques*, pp.94-96, Gamory-Dubourdeau (and presumably the 2nd Battalion) had been at Schwarnegast 'for several weeks' before the arrival of the 1st Battalion.

89   The German name for Swornegacie is Schwornigatz. However, following the German invasion of Poland, the name was Germanized to Schwarnegast.

90   According to Soulat, *Historique de la Division Charlemagne*, p.26, Fayard took over from Guignot in August 1944. Thus, the author has reasoned that Guignot was promoted to Hauptsturmführer and placed in command of the 2nd Battalion of the Sturmbrigade that same month. Articles *Le Schreiber* (unpublished) and *La SS-Französische Flakbatterie* also suggest his date of promotion and transfer as August 1944. However, according to a non-referenced wartime command roster of 'Charlemagne', Guignot was promoted to Hstuf. on 1 July 1944. Then again this said document does contain many errors.

91   Mabire, *La Division Charlemagne*, p.135. Furthermore, the suggestion is made that Guignot's promotion to Hstuf. and his appointment to the command of the 2nd Battalion stemmed more from a shortage of officers than his ability. In fact, this may well be true. Firstly, his promotion cannot be attributed to attendance at and graduation from an SS officer training school. Secondly, after the terrible blood letting in Galicia, the French Sturmbrigade was definitely short of officers and, in particular, officers with either the training or ability to discharge command effectively at battalion level.

92   Born on 5 June 1919 in Paris, Vincenot volunteered for the LVF in May 1944 and was accepted with the rank of *Aspirant*. Sent to Greifenberg, he was still undergoing training when the LVF was withdrawn from Russia and transferred to the Waffen-SS.

On 5 September 1944, the one hundred and forty survivors of the decimated 1st Battalion joined the 2nd Battalion at Schwarnegast. A trickle then followed of those who had recovered from wounds received in Galicia. In this way, between 1,000 and 1,500 men of the two battalions of the Sturmbrigade were placed into 'Charlemagne'.[93]

On 15 September, Uscha. Bayle of the 2nd Company was sent to a hospital at Könitz to recuperate from a bad bout of dysentery. However, blood tests revealed that he also had malaria. Consequently, he was hospitalised for months.

In late September, six 'French training companies', numbering over one thousand men, arrived at Greifenberg from SS-Ausbildungslager Sennheim.[94] The convoy commander was SS-Ostuf. Laue. Some of the 'evacuees' were assigned to the Franz. SS-Grenadier Ausbildungs-und Ersatz bataillon to complete their training, but most went to the forming Waffen.Gren. Regt der SS 57 at Schwarnegast, Bruss and Leisten.

### The German Inspection

The formation and training of 'Charlemagne' continued in various locations throughout the Danzig corridor under the watchful eye of the Inspektion der französischen SS-Verbände (InF)[95] [Inspection of French SS units (infantry)] located at Leisten. At the head of the German Inspection was Brigadeführer und Generalmajor der Waffen-SS Gustav Krukenberg. In his capacity as Inspector he reported directly to the Reichsführer-SS Himmler who gave him a free hand to carry out his role.

Although regarded as an archetypal Prussian, Gustav Krukenberg was in fact born in Bonn on 8 March 1888. His father was a doctor and a professor at Bonn University. His mother was the daughter of archaeologist Alexander Conze. After passing his *Abitur*, he attended university to study law and economics, gaining a doctorate in law. Nevertheless, he saw his career as that of a military attaché.

In 1907, Krukenberg joined the Army as a Fähnrich with the 5. (Badischen) Feldartillerie-Regtiment Nr. 76. On 21 February 1911, he was commissioned as a reserve Leutnant and on 27 January 1912 switched to active duty. Briefly turning to his private life, he married in September 1912 and had two daughters, born in 1920 and 1924. Then war broke out.

His wartime posts were many. He served as an Ordnance Officer in the 3rd Guards Division, then as an adjutant in the 6th Guards Infantry Brigade and then as a corps Ia. He served on the Western Front and the Eastern Front. In 1918, after attending general staff training at Sedan, he became a Hauptmann (Captain) and a member of the Army General Staff. He served as Oberquartiermeister-Adjudant [Senior Quartermaster Adjutant] in the war history unit of the

93  Littlejohn states 'about 1,000', Bayle 1,100 and Grégory Bouysse a higher figure of 1500 (*Waffen-SS Français volume 2*).
94  Of note is that some French volunteers of the Waffen-SS remained at Sennheim until its final evacuation on 28 November 1944.
95  SS-FHA, Amt II Org. Tgb.Nr.4212/44 g.Kdos auf Befehl des Reichsführer SS am 10.10.1944. Dates vary as to when the Inspektion der französischen SS-Verbände (InF) was established: 23 September 1944 according to a note from SS-Stubaf. Dr Bruns of 25 October 1944; 24 September 1944 according to Krukenberg; and 10 October 1944 according to Mehner Kurt, *Die Waffen-SS und Polizei 1939-1945* volume 3 (Norderstedt: Militar-Verlag Klaus D. Patzwall, 1995), p.257, repeated by Michaelis, *French Units in the Waffen-SS*, p.40.

General Staff. By the end of the war, he was the recipient of various decorations, including both classes of the Iron Cross. Indeed, that of the Iron Cross 1st Class was pinned on him by Kaiser Wilhelm II.

He transferred to the *Reichswehr*, the 100,000-man post-war army, and served on the General Staff in 1919-1920 with Wehrkreiskommandos III Berlin as Generalstaboffizier (Ic).[96] He disapproved of the 1920 'Kapp Putsch', finding himself in conflict with General Hans von Seeckt, the Commander–in–Chief of the *Reichswehr*, who wished to distance the officer corps from any political view.[97] After a stint with the Reichswehministerium [Reich Ministry of Defence] as a press officer he left the military on 30 September 1920.

Krukenberg joined the civil service on 1 October 1920 and served as the principal private secretary to successive Foreign Ministers Simons and Dr. Rosen. When his contract ended at the end of 1921 he went into business.[98]

Between the years 1922 and 1923 Krukenberg was active as a representative of the Reichsverbandes der Deutschen Industrie [National Federation of German Industry]. He attended the world economy conference held in Genoa. Then he worked as a director for a German company in Holland from 1924 to 1925. In 1926, he left for Paris as part of the German delegation to the Deutsch-Französischen Studienkomitees [German-French Study Committee], becoming its *Direktor*.[99] He returned five years later with a passion for France. He now worked as a freelance speaker and publicist.

Krukenberg joined the NSDAP (with number 1,067,635) on 1 April 1932 and managed to rejoin the civil service, serving in the cabinets of von Papen (1 June-3 December 1932) and von Schleicher (3 December 1932 to 28 January 1933). From August 1932 to 31 January 1933 he held the position of Reichsrundfunkkommissar in the Reich Ministry of Interior. With Hitler's election, he became the Reichsrundfunkkommissar and Managing Director of the Reichs-Rundfunk-Gesellschaft or RRG [Reich Broadcasting Corporation]. Regarded as a conservative, his end came all too soon after a party member complained to Ministerialreferenten Metzner that Krukenberg was not suitable to hold such a position.

Again Krukenberg went into business, running a small chemical company from 1934 until he was mobilised on 28 August 1939. Meanwhile, on 30 May 1933, he joined the Allgemeine-SS with the number 116,685 and was assigned to the 6. SS-Standarte Eduard Felsen in Berlin. After a trial period he was finally accepted as a SS-Mann on 1 December 1933. Promotion followed promotion: SS-Scharführer on 8 April 1934, SS-Untersturmführer on 9 November

---

96    According to Bayle, *San et Persante*, p.153, in the post war years, Krukenberg served as a staff officer in the nationalist Brigade Reinhard (also known as Freikorps Reinhard), which helped to suppress the Spartacist uprising of January 1919 in Berlin.

97    On 13 March 1920, the Ehrhardt Brigade, one of the many armed units of the Freikorps of demobilised right-wing troops, occupied Berlin to establish Dr. Wolfgang Kapp, an ultra-right monarchist bureaucrat, as chancellor. The *Reichswehr* did not intervene.

98    Georgen, *Berlin 1945 - Sur les traces du Sturmbataillon de la Division 'Charlemagne'*, part 1, magazine *39/45*, p.21. However, according to Landwehr, *Charlemagne's Legionnaires*, p.187, Krukenberg became a bureau chief in the Foreign Ministry, whereas, according to Yerger, *Waffen-SS Commanders volume 2*, p.2, he was the ministerial office head for the Ministry of Foreign Affairs.

99    The Study Committee was also named in French *Comité Franco-Allemand d'information et de documentation* or Mayrish Committee.

1936 and SS-Hauptsturmführer on 30 January 1939. In October 1938, he took over command of the 6. SS-Standarte.

Active in the reserve Army from 1935, holding a number of positions, Krukenberg was promoted to Major d.R. [Reserve Major] on 1 October 1938. With war looming, he was recalled to full-time Army service in 1939.

At the end of the French Campaign he was appointed as deputy Chief-of Staff of Militarbefehlshaber Paris, a position he briefly held from June to July 1940. He was awarded a clasp to his WW1 Iron Cross 2nd Class on 28 July 1940. His next posting as Generalstabsoffizier Ia to the Wehrmachtbefehlshaber in the Netherlands lasted from August 1940 to February 1941. He served as a General staff officer in the German-French Waffenstillstandskommission based in Casablanca from 21 February 1941 to 17 June 1941 and then from 18 June 1941 to 1 February 1942 with Stab des Wehrmachtbefehlshabers Ostland (Riga), after which he was placed into the Führerreserve des OKH. In January 1943, he became the Chief-of-Staff of Wirtschaftsinspektion Mitte [Economy Inspection Centre] which covered occupied White Russia. This posting lasted until the end of October 1943. On 1 November 1943, he became the Chief-of-Staff of Heeresgruppenwirtschaftsführer Mitte. At the end of the month he was released from active service.

On 1 December 1943, Oberstleutant Krukenberg joined the Waffen-SS with the equivalent rank of SS-Obersturmbannführer d.R. and spent the first month with Panzer Training and Replacement Battalion 1. On 17 January 1944, he was appointed as the Chief-of-Staff of the V. SS Gebirgs-Korps [Mountain Corps], which also brought him promotion to SS-Standartenführer on the 20th.[100] However, on 7 May 1944, Corps commander Gruppenführer Phleps wrote to Himmler requesting the transfer of Krukenberg.[101] On 19 May 1944, Krukenberg was relieved of his command.[102] From 19 May to 25 June 1944, he served as Chief-of-Staff of the VI.Waffen-Armee-korps der SS (Lettisches).

On 25 July 1944, Krukenberg took up post as Befehlshaber der Waffen-SS Ostland [Waffen-SS Commander-in-Chief for Ostland] based in Riga, Latvia. He was actively involved in the mobilisation, training and reformation of Latvian Waffen-SS units, Latvian Police Battalions and Latvian Border-Guard Regiments. In early August 1944, he briefly succeeded Brigf. Ziegler as Chief-of-Staff of the III. (Germ.) SS-PanzerKorps. From 14 August to 25 August 1944 he led a unit of Kampfgruppe Jeckeln and then Kampfgruppe Krukenberg in the defence of Riga from 31 August to 23 September, winning a bar to his WW1 Iron Cross 1st Class which was awarded on 26 October 1944.

On 22 September 1944, Krukenberg was promoted to SS-Oberführer d.R., backdated to 9 May 1944, and one day later to that of SS-Brigadeführer und Generalmajor der Waffen-SS.

100   Kumm Otto, *Prinz Eugen* (Winnipeg: J.J. Fedorowicz Publishing, 1995), p.106 and Mabire, *La Division Charlemagne*, p.150. However, Krukenberg recalls in *Entretien avec le général Krukenberg, Historia* hors série 32, p.131, that he held the rank of Oberführer when appointed as the Chief-of-Staff of the V. SS Gebirgs-Korps. Unfortunately, he is mistaken. Landwehr repeats this same mistake (see *Charlemagne's Legionnaires*, p.188).
101   This was, undoubtedly, as a result of a clash between Phleps and Krukenberg.
102   Kumm, *Prinz Eugen*, p.115. Yerger dates his replacement one day earlier (*Waffen-SS Commanders volume 2*, p.43)

On 10 October 1944, he was appointed as the Inspekteur of the Inspektion der französischen SS-Verbände (InF).[103]

Krukenberg was also the holder of both classes of the Kriegsverdienstkreuz (KVK). He was an excellent choice as Inspector. He spoke the French language impeccably, had an excellent understanding of the French people, and had previous experience working and serving with foreign volunteers. Even so, while respected, he was not liked by his German subordinates according to one source.[104]

Krukenberg saw his task as follows:[105]

- Implement and supervise all the measures ordered by the OKW guaranteering the incorporation of the volunteers from various units of the Wehrmacht
- Control of the suitability of the members of the Brigade – old and new – of all ranks for [their] engagement at the front based on current requirements of combat methods
- Ensure the Brigade was armed and equipped, as well as the organisation of the supply services, which like the LVF, would remain a German responsibility
- Supervise the theoretical and practical training of former French Army officers and NCOs whose tactical training and military habits differed from German conceptions
- Establishment of a military training plan for the troops and its execution; send officers and enlisted men to attend courses in German military schools of different arms
- Familiarise psychologically those members of the Brigade who had not previously experienced the front with the defensive fighting against the Red Army

It has been suggested that Krukenberg served as the Brigade's behind the scenes commander, sidelining Puaud. Krukenberg himself refuted this suggestion:

> The commander was Colonel Puaud... He was without doubt a good Colonel. This is not the same thing as a good General... He had no idea of the actual handling of a division. It's rather complex, with artillery, armour, signals. In short, staff work. It was my speciality. I was there to help. I helped him.[106]

Krukenberg did not underestimate the task before him, though. He fully recognising that if he did not strike hard and fast then the 'wound' of French internal politics in 'Charlemagne' would hinder, if not irreparably damage, its formation and endanger the spirit of camaraderie.

---

103  Scherzer, *Sous le Signe SS*, p.149 and Michaelis, *French Units In the Waffen-SS*, p.40. The exact date of his arrival is not known, though. Scherzer dates his arrival to late September, *Sous le Signe SS*, p.150. The date of 23 September 1944 when Krukenberg was promoted to SS-Brigadeführer und Generalmajor der Waffen-SS is often cited as the date of his appointment as Inspector of the Inspektion der französischen SS-Verbände (InF).
104  Saint-Loup, *Les Hérétiques*, p.153.
105  Memorandum written by Krukenberg in 1958, see Soulat, *Historique de la Division Charlemagne*, p.14.
106  Mabire, *Entretien avec le général Krukenberg*, Historia hors série 32, p.132.

And what of the soldiers Krukenberg had to mould into a Waffen-SS formation? He thought that the legionnaires of the LVF were 'more hardened, but too undisciplined' and 'often exhausted by three years of combat and their difficult retreat'. As for those soldiers of the French SS-Sturmbrigade, he had some concerns about their political traits and said of this:

> They no longer believed in France or Germany: they spoke of a 'European nation'. For my part, I still did not believe the time had come for such an undertaking.[107]

In fact, Krukenberg wanted the volunteers to 'remain French and not be SS men speaking French'. Thus, there was no question of promoting National Socialism. Krukenberg set high standards for the French volunteers:[108] 'The honour of the French flag and the prestige of the French soldier must remain the supreme law, not only in combat, but also in behaviour towards the German civilian population.' It was a question of national pride.[109] Moreover, he would respect the religious sentiments of the French volunteers who, in his words, 'considered their engagement to be in the defence of the Christian West'. He understood the psychology of the French volunteers.

Interestingly, Krukenberg had also obtained the approval of the High Command that every volunteer 'who wanted to leave was free to do so without difficulty', but this possibility could only be used once. The reality would prove somewhat different.

Krukenberg had at his disposal a thirty-strong Inspection made up of experienced German officers. Some had already commanded or trained foreign volunteers. The Frenchmen would benefit greatly from the experience and military professionalism they had to offer.

Hstuf. Jauss was respected by all those who came into contact with him. Born on 12 December 1921 in Göppingen, Hans Robert Jauss enlisted in the Waffen-SS aged seventeen. In May 1942, he was assigned with the rank of SS-Ustuf. to 13./Frei.Legion Niederlande and, in March 1944, became the company commander of 4./SS-Freiwilligen-Panzergrenadier-Regiment 48 'General Seyffardt'. After distinguishing himself in action in Estonia, he was decorated with the German Cross in Gold. He wore several 'tank destruction' badges, denoting the single-handed destruction of an enemy tank.[110]

Orderly Officer Heinze Gehring, born on 10 February 1907 in Magdeburg, also had many years of military service behind him with SS-Polizei-Regiment 4 and SS-Polizei-Regiment 2. He was promoted to Untersturmführer on 22 July 1944. After a posting to Kienschlag as an instructor, he was assigned to the Inspection at the start of 1945.

Many other German personnel served in 'Charlemagne'. Their exact number is not known. Many, if not all, of the German Heer personnel of the LVF transferred to the Waffen-SS. For example, all of the German interpreters of the *Etat-Major de Liaison Allemand* or EMLA [German liaison headquarters] of the III/638 went across to the Brigade Headquarters Company.

---

107  Mabire, *Entretien avec le général Krukenberg, Historia* hors série 32, p.136.
108  Soulat, *Historique de la Division Charlemagne*, p.15.
109  By appealing to their national pride Krukenberg believed that the Frenchmen would fight better, Mabire, *Entretien avec le général Krukenberg, Historia* hors série 32, p.136.
110  One silver badge was awarded for each tank destroyed. Four such badges could be worn, but for five kills, a gilt badge was worn in their place. For more than five kills, additional silver badges could be added.

German personnel were found in the Engineer Company (including Edgar Becker, born on 14 Feb. 1925; Gustav Sachse, born on 31 August 1912; and Karl Sanner, born on 29 May 1920) and the Medical Company (including Johan Adlgasser, born on 13 October 1908 and Wilhelm Sack, born on 6 December 1925).[111] SS-Oscha. Hannes Berwick served as a surgeon.

Not all of those with the SS prefix to their rank were actually of German origin. SS-Uscha. Adam Wagner, born on 12 March 1911, was a *Volksdeutsche* from Hungary. He was on the German liaison staff to Waffen-Gren. Regt der SS 57.[112] SS-Uscha. Hans Wagner was Alsatian. He was a *Schirrmeister* [Technical Sergeant Major] in the I/58.

## Initial Training Courses

In late September or early October 1944, thirty French NCO candidates were sent to the SS-und Waffen Unterführerschule SS-Tr. Üb.Pl. Westpreußen at Reckow near Bütow in Eastern Pomerania for a three month long course.[113] Among the candidates were Ruskone, Boizeau[114] and Obergrenadier del Missier, who was ex-Sturmbrigade. The training was arduous.

Ruskone joined the French Brigade at Wildflecken camp on 16 December 1944 and was promoted to Unterscharführer and then quickly to Junker der Waffen-SS.[115] Del Missier was promoted to Uscha. and assigned to the Heavy Platoon of Company 8/57.

At the end of September 1944, about a dozen or twenty former officers of the LVF were sent to the SS-Unterführerschule at Lauenburg (Lebork) for a company commander's training course.[116] Among the officers were Baudouin, Defever, Falcy, Fatin, de Genouillac, Lafargue, Rigeade and Wagner. The course lasted one month and proved too demanding for four or five of their number. Good friends Falcy, de Genouillac and Rigeade, who had successfully completed the course, rejoined the French Brigade at Wildflecken camp on 11 November 1944.

In September or October 1944, the Engineer Platoon of Headquarters Company/Waffen-Gren. Regt der SS 57 as well as that of Headquarters Company/Waffen-Gren. Regt der SS 58 were dispatched to SS-Pionierschule Hradischko, one of the many training schools located within Truppenübungsplatz Beneschau, south of Prague, Bohemia-Moravia. Their escort to

---

111  Missing in action was the fate of all five.

112  Adam Wagner is listed as missing in action in Pomerania, February 1945.

113  According to Ruskone, *Stoï!*, p.245, he left for Bütow at the end of August 1944. According to del Missier, letter to the author, 12/5/1999, he attended Bütow from early October to late December 1944. He also recalls the presence of Ruskone and Boizeau at Bütow, and the three of them completing the final exam together. The author is convinced that late August is too early for the candidates to be sent to Bütow; Puaud had yet to arrive and speak to the legionnaires of the LVF about the transfer to the Waffen-SS. Curiously, according to Mabire, *La Division Charlemagne*, p.70, one hundred NCOs of the former LVF attended a Waffen-SS school but does not state which school or when the course was, other than it lasted several weeks.

114  Bernand Boizeau was ex-LVF and a holder of the KVK-II.

115  Rusco, *Stoï!*, p.248.

116  De Genouillac numbers the officers about a dozen (letter to the author) and Mabire twenty (*La Division Charlemagne*, p.67). Furthermore, Mabire suggests that this was a calculated move by the German authorities to deprive the LVF of its influential *encadrement* which might have proved troublesome over the disbandment of the LVF and the absorption of its personnel into the French Waffen-SS. This might be true but is impossible to prove.

Hradischko was SS-Rttf. Thiel, born on 7 February 1911 in Berlin.[117] At Hradischko they came into the 'care' of SS-Ustuf. Thomas. He spoke good French and had nothing but good things to say of France. Notably his young assistant with the rank of SS-Unterscharführer was from Alsace or Lorraine. He too spoke perfect French without any trace of an accent. SS-Ustuf. Hans von Twistern, who looked barely twenty years old, 'administered' political education. He spoke no French. His means of communication became a rather old interpreter who wore the uniform of the Heer and not that of the Waffen-SS. Although the interpreter admitted that he was not a National Socialist, he had not let himself slide into defeatism.

The field training was all too real. W-Strmm. Sepchat of the Engineer Platoon of the Headquarters Company/Waffen-Gren. Regt der SS 58 had this to say of the 'bunker busting':

> ...but what most impressed us was the initiation into the role played by the engineers in the clearing of fortified lines. As far as I can remember, the casemate to be neutralised was subject to a violent bombardment first. Under what still remained of the barbed-wire entanglements, an engineer, among the most daring, slid a concentrated charge (geballte Ladung) placed on a long board. Immediately after the explosion he informed his comrades that the way was clear ("Hier Gasse!"). Those rushed into the breach. One of them blinded the embrasure with a flame-thrower. Another placed on the turret the hollow charge (Hohlladung) which was going to pierce it. All of these manouevres were terribly dangerous, and more than one engineer sacrificed himself 'für Führer, Volk und Vaterland' before seeing the casemate explode, but as Ustuf. Thomas put it: "That's when the awards of the EK I are won first time!" [118]

Another training exercise required the engineers to lie down around holes, five metres in diameter and one metre deep, in which five kilograms of gelignite was exploded.

The training course at Hradischko would last some two months.

## The Panzerjäger Battalion

Hstuf. Jean Boudet-Gheusi commanded the Panzerjäger Battalion of 'Charlemagne'. Previously, he had served with the LVF. In January 1943, he received the command of the Headquarters Company of the I. Batallion and later on the 1st Company. In March 1944, he transferred to the II. Bataillon as *adjudant-major*. One month later he was recalled to France by none other than Darnand to become the *Intendant régional du Maintien de l'ordre* in Rouen. He fled to Germany before the advancing Allied armies. Appointed as the commander of the Panzerjäger Battalion, he attended a training course at SS-Panzerjägerschule Janowitz from 10 October to 11 November 1944.

On paper, the so-called 'Heavy' or 'Heavy Weapons' Battalion comprised the following elements with such commanders:

117  Roland Thiel, whose profession was teaching, later disappeared in the hell of Pomerania, February 1945.
118  Gaulois, article *Pionierarbeit*, unpublished.

- Schewe Panzerjäger-Kompanie [Tank-Hunter or Anti-Tank Company]: Ostuf. Veyrieras
- Fla.-Kompanie [FLAK Company]: Ustuf. Fayard
- Sturmgeschütz-Kompanie [Assault Gun Company]: Ostuf. Michel
- Grenadier-Begleitzug [Escort Platoon]: ?

Thirty-nine-year-old Guillaume Veyrieras was also ex-LVF. After serving with the rank of *sergent-chef* in the 3rd Company during the first winter, he was demobilised in 1942, but managed to re-enlist one year later and was appointed the commander of the 5th Company of the II. Bataillon. Transferred to the Waffen-SS, he received command of the Anti-Tank [PAK] Company of the Panzerjäger Battalion. Like Boudet-Gheusi, he attended a training course at SS-Panzerjägerschule Janowitz from 10 October to 11 November 1944, after which he was given a new assignment.

The Anti-Tank Company of the Panzerjäger Battalion was formed at Leisten. Importantly, the men were from the French Sturmbrigade company of Ostuf. Michel while the *gradés* [NCOs] were from the LVF. Uscha. Éric Labat was appointed as the commander of the 2nd Platoon. He was serving with the 9th Company of the LVF when transferred to the Waffen-SS and even though he voiced his hostility to the transfer he still received a command. Oscha. Georges Hérin was appointed as the commander of the 3rd Platoon. He was serving as Spiess of the 10th Company of the LVF when transferred to the Waffen-SS. Labat and Hérin were friends and both preferred to be addressed by their French ranks rather than their new Waffen-SS ranks.

Noting that the French Sturmbrigade of the Waffen-SS and LVF had diverging mindsets, Labat, for one, feared that their fusion into a sole unit would cause friction. However, the night before taking up command, Labat and the other NCOs agreed to 'make things work as well as possible'.[119] Concessions were forthcoming from both camps; the NCOs commanded alternately in German and French, while the young volunteers of the French Sturmbrigade started to sing the 'Panzerlied' in French. Respect was mutual. There would be no serious problems. In this way, Labat's fears were not realised.

SS-Untersturmführer Rohrer supervised the training of the Anti-Tank Company of the Panzerjäger Battalion, as well as the two regimental anti-tank companies also present at Leisten. He may have been only twenty years old, but he was highly qualified having spent the last three years on the Eastern Front. He was the holder of the Nahkampfspange [Close Combat Clasp] in silver.

In October, Labat was sent as an interpreter to SS-Panzerjägerschule Janowitz. Reluctantly, he now separated from his platoon, to whom he had started to become attached, and from Rohrer, with whom he had worked well in a spirit of perfect mutual understanding and great camaraderie. At the end of the course Labat was returned to the Brigade which had moved to Wildflecken.

Except for the anti-tank company that had its full complement of twelve towed 75mm anti-tank guns, the battalion was desperately short of equipment. Drivers did not have trucks, signallers did not have field telephones, and the Assault Gun Company under Ostuf. Michel

---

119  Labat, *Les places étaient chères*, p.258.

did not have the promised fourteen assault guns.[120] And to make matters worse, Boudet-Gheusi failed to 'stamp his authority' on the FLAK Company stationed at Saalesch.

The commanders of the two regimental anti-tank companies, also undergoing training at Leisten, had little in common. Oscha. Julien, who commanded the anti-tank company of Waffen-Gren. Regt der SS 57, was 'completely moulded by the harsh SS discipline',[121] whereas *Capitaine* Rémy, who commanded the anti-tank company of Waffen-Gren. Regt der SS 58, was ex-LVF and described as good-natured.

Born on 26 November 1917 in Grenoble, Georges Julien, a former *Milicien*, volunteered for the Waffen-SS in October 1943. He was a survivor of the battles in Galicia. Born on 3 July 1910 in Tarare, Rhône, Henri Léon Rémy was drawn to serve France on the 'high seas' rather than on solid ground, attaining the Navy rank of *Enseigne de Vaisseau de 1ére Classe* [lieutenant]. It was with the equivalent German Army rank that he entered the LVF in 1943. Trained in Poland at Kruszyna, then at Demba, he was posted to the II/638 as *officier-adjoint* to *chef de Bataillon* Tramu. At the conclusion of Operation Morocco, February 1944, he was proposed for the *Croix de guerre légionnaire*. Weeks later, at the end of March 1944, *commandant* Tramu entrusted to him the command of the 6th Company which was stationed at Scheplewitschi in a sector considered the most dangerous. By all accounts, the company was in very poor shape; demoralised and 'without spirit', it was composed of very young soldiers who had not seen action before. However, in weeks, through the personal leadership of Rémy, the company became the best in the battalion. He was tireless; he went on all patrols and operations. He received several citations for his *Croix de guerre* and was proposed for the Iron Cross 2nd Class and promotion to *Capitaine*. Transferred to the Waffen-SS, he also attended the training course at SS-Panzerjägerschule Janowitz from 10 October to 11 November 1944. Julien and Rémy, and the men they commanded, were from 'two different worlds', but soon bonded.

### Grenadier-Regiment 1 (Waffen-Grenadier-Regiment der SS 57)

As previously noted, the SS-Sturmbrigade was used as the base for Waffen-Grenadier-Regiment der SS 57. The command of the new regiment went, of course, to Ostubaf. Gamory-Dubourdeau, who was soon able to form eight companies at full strength[122] with such commanders:[123]

120 Mabire, *La Division Charlemagne* p.530. Curiously, the same author notes on p.145 of the same work that the Assault Gun Company was awaiting twelve assault guns. In response to this, an assault gun company had a theoretical establishment of fourteen and so the author has used fourteen. This number is confirmed by Lefèvre, *Axe & Alliés* hors série no 1, p.53.
121 Mabire, *La Division Charlemagne*, p.145.
122 Mabire, *La Division Charlemagne*, pp.90-91.
123 According to Mabire, *La Division Charlemagne*, p.135, as of mid-October 1944, the company commanders included Bartolomei, Brazier, Colnion, and Hennecart. In response to this, Boyer succeeded Stehli at the head of the 1/57 on 28 October 1944 but was only in post for just one week. Brazier probably succeeded Boyer. Philippe Colnion, who was born on 8 July 1926, only succeeded Raymond Gaillard at the head of 8/57 in late January or early February 1945. Likewise, Hennacart only became the head of 5/57 in February 1945.

- 1st Company:     Ustuf. Jean-Marie Stehli[124]
- 2nd Company:    Ostuf. Bartolomei
- 3rd Company:    Oberjunker Robert Lefèvre
- 4th Company:    Ustuf. James Royer
- 5th Company:    Ustuf. Aimé Berthaud
- 6th Company:    Ustuf. Pierre Albert
- 7th Company:    Ustuf. Pierre Brocard
- 8th Company:    Ustuf. Raymond Gaillard

Raymond Gaillard was ex-LVF. Jean-Marie Stehli was born on 21 March 1918 in Savièse, Switzerland, but held French nationality. Four of the company commanders, namely Stehli, Lefèvre, Berthaud and Albert had graduated of late from SS-Panzergrenadierschule Kienschlag with the rank of Oberjunker (and promoted to Untersturmführer after two months).

Faced with amalgamation, the Waffen-SS volunteers of the SS-Sturmbrigade had no crisis of conscience. But many felt great disappointment at seeing their fellow countrymen of the LVF, the Kriegsmarine and the various paramilitary organisations admitted so readily into the Waffen-SS. They, this 'new race of Franco-Boche' which the legionnaires of the LVF called the Waffen-SS volunteers of the SS-Sturmbrigade, had undergone months of rigorous selection and hardship before being accepted into the Waffen-SS.

Furthermore, the Waffen-SS volunteers of the SS-Sturmbrigade were concerned that many of their own kind now incorporated into the Waffen-SS lacked proper military training. They knew that to withstand the brutal shock of life and combat on the Eastern Front the newcomers had to be both physically and mentally tough. They doubted that the same level of training afforded to them could now be afforded to the new 'volunteers'.[125]

Also, the esprit de corps and the harsh discipline of the former Sturmbrigade that its NCOs tried to instil did not sit well with the LVF veterans who, it is said, prided themselves on their slovenliness and bawdiness. Sometimes, this led to tension between the two.[126]

Without exception, all former members of the French SS-Sturmbrigade in 'Charlemagne' continued to wear the standard SS runes right collar insignia and the SS regulation pattern national shield (or privately made versions of the national shield). As per the regulations of

---

124  According to Saint-Loup, *Les Hérétiques*, p.161, Fenet had Stehli relieved of his command. Puaud later appointed him the *officier de justice* of 'Charlemagne'.

125  In addition, Bayle points out, *San et Persante*, p.129, that the newcomers to the Waffen-SS could no longer be screened because what military or criminal records they might have had were back in France which, by now, was largely liberated. This would suggest that there may have been some concern that the newcomers from military or paramilitary formations whose standards he describes as 'more flexible' actually had criminal records that at another time would have prevented their entry into this elite corps. In response to this, it does seem doubtful that the military and paramilitary formations at which Bayle is directing his comments would recruit persons with criminal records at the expense of their reputation.

126  One former French officer of 'Charlemagne' commented to the author that accounts written of late have blown this tension out of all proportion.

15 April 1944, most, if not all, now started to wear the national shield directly under the SS eagle.[127]

In mid-October, after paying a brief visit to Ulm to speak to Darnand about the problems faced by the enlistment of his exiled *Miliciens* into 'Charlemagne', Ostuf. Fenet arrived at Schwarnegast. In his absence, he had been placed in command of the 1st Battalion of Waffen-Grenadier-Regiment der SS 57, the I/57. He was alarmed to hear that Hstuf. Guignot was in command of the II/57.

## Purge and Discipline

Puaud decided to rid himself of the 'undesirables' before the arrival of Krukenberg to take up post as Inspector of the French Waffen-SS.[128]

On 10 October 1944, SS-Ustuf. Meyer, acting as Ic of the Inspection, informed the Kommandantur of the Danzig Sicherheitspolizei of the first transport of 'undesirables' and asked if they should be sent to SS-und Polizeilager Danzig-Matzkau or to a Konzentration-Lager [concentration camp] first. The decision was made to send them to KZ Stuttof, near Danzing.[129]

On 13 October, 109 men were transported from Bruss to KZ Stutthof, arriving on the following day, 14 October.[130] 60 men were given KZ numbers.

Puaud said nothing of this transport to Krukenberg, but Mgr. Mayol de Lupé did one or two days after his arrival. Clearly Puaud was anxious to hide from Krukenberg the refusal of some legionnaires to transfer to the Waffen-SS. Thereupon, Krukenberg ordered SS-Hstuf. Schmidt to go to the concentration camp with a view to liberating them and sending them onto Arbeitsdurchgangslager [Labour transit camp] Berlin-Wilhelmshagen.[131] That same evening, Schmidt informed Krukenberg that his orders had been carried out.[132] Krukenberg concluded the matter by rebuking Puaud who, in his eyes, had overstepped his authority and acted without any formal process.

On 24 October 1944, KZ Stutthof Lagerkommandant SS-Stubaf. Paul Werner Hoppe, with the agreement of the SS-Hauptamt and the Inspektion der französischen SS-Verbände, forwarded 47 men to Arbeitsdurchgangslager Berlin-Wilhelmshagen. The 60 who were given KZ numbers stayed behind at Stuttof and were classified as political prisoners.

A further 18 men were subsequently moved to Arbeitsdurchgangslager Berlin-Wilhelmshagen. One man of the first transport died in KZ Stuttof. Rottenführer Albert Cipriano of the

---

127 The *Verordnungsblatt der Waffen-SS* of 15 April 1944. By order of the RF-SS Himmler, the national shield of units of foreign volunteers was to be worn 1.5cm below the national emblem.

128 This conclusion is reached by Krukenberg in his letter to Saint-Loup, 18/3/65.

129 Curiously, Landwehr states that those LVF legionnaires rejecting Waffen-SS service were first sentenced to a penal unit and then sent to a construction battalion on Krukenberg's orders (*Charlemagne's Legionnaires*, p.29). This is unconfirmed.

130 On 14 October, KZ Stutthof confirmed the arrival of 105 men belonging to the 'French Legion'. Two are known to have escaped en route.

131 The labour camp was often referred to more simply as Arbeitslager Wilmelmshagen in wartime documentation.

132 Krukenberg, letter to Saint-Loup, 18/3/65.

Stabskompanie of Gren.-Rgt2. was admitted into hospital on 16 December 1944 and died of heart failure on 17 January 1945.

A second transport of 75 men arrived at Stuttof on 30 October. Their expulsion had been signed off by the Brigade on 27 October. On the day after their arrival 15 men were forwarded to Arbeitsdurchgangslager Berlin-Wilhelmshagen. The others were probably due to go before SS-und Polizeigericht [SS and Police Court] Danzig. For example, Hauptscharführer Henri de Waelo was accused of murder.

Of the 187 purged, 15 were Unterführer [NCO]. Their origin is worthy of note: most were ex-LVF, ten or so were ex-Sturmbrigade and five or six were ex-Kriegsmarine. Notably, only 16 were purged because they did not want to serve with the Waffen-SS. Most were former LVF while three were Navy. The charge sheets of the others speak of indiscipline, heavy drinkers, theft, absence without leave, homosexuality, physical and moral ineptitude, and participation in preparations to desert. One of those purged was a former maquisard who was now regarded as dangerous. Three were suspected Jews. One Jew had volunteered for the Waffen-SS on 6 June 1944.[133] Eight were suspected Communists. At least five men were expelled from the Infantry Gun Company of Gren.-Rgt2. They were Rttf. Thomas, Grenadiers Dhaine, Faucher, Lerosier and Thibault.

Krukenberg was to learn much later that Puaud subsequently 'gave instructions against some of these ['undesirable'] legionnaires'.[134] Five of them ended up in concentration camp Sachsenhausen. In this way, 'Puaud kept his promise'.[135] In February 1945, Renard was transferred to concentration camp Mauthausen.[136]

On 22 October, Krukenberg met with representatives of the Hauptamt SS-Gericht [SS Court Main Office] and requested his own Divisionsgericht [Division Court]. The Hauptamt SS-Gericht supported his request and noted that the Inspector had already made use of his authority to hand over unsuitable elements to the SD, but that this could not continue. On 27 October, Krukenberg wrote to the RFSS stating that 'numerous cases of desertion, theft and other offences require immediate expiation'.

On 10 November, the SS-FHA wrote that the Inspector has the disciplinary power of a divisional commander.[137] This was not enough for Krukenberg, for on 16 December 1944, he received authority to establish a court. However, criminal matters against 'SS-Führer' would still default to Himmler.

---

133 His name was Maurice Chicheportiche. After completing his basic training at Sennheim, he was forwarded to the French Brigade. Curiously, according to Bouysse, *Waffen-SS Français*, volume 2, he was assigned to the 8th Company of the Sturmbrigade, which might refer to the 8/57. He was purged on 13 October 1944.

134 Krukenberg, letter to Saint-Loup, 18/3/65. Indeed this only came to light on the publication of Saint-Loup's *Les Hérétiques*.

135 Saint-Loup, *Les Hérétiques*, p.144.

136 Renard survived Mauthausen. When liberated he weighed only forty kilograms.

137 SS-FHA, Amt II Org/Abt. Ia/II Tgb.Nr.4212/44 g.Kdos.

**Transfer to Wildflecken Camp**

At the beginning of October, Strmm. Pillet was posted from Greifenberg to Truppenübungsplatz Wildflecken in Western Germany to serve as an instructor. Here the French Brigade was to continue its training.

Set in the picturesque setting of the wooded Rhön massif, Truppenübungsplatz Wildflecken had been built in 1936 for the German Army.[138] All roads led to a central square, Adolf Hitler Platz. Around the square were the various functional and administrative buildings, including camp headquarters. Near the Lagerkommansantur stood a high stone column. Atop was a winged eagle with a wreathed swastika in its claws. Among the firs and the larches stood the barracks constructed of stone and wood that could each house two entire companies.

In late October 1944, the entire French Brigade, no more than 5,000 men, was assembled at Bruss and dispatched to Wildflecken.[139] The first convoy left Bruss at 1400 hours on 26 October 1944 and stopped some fifty hours later at Brückenau railway station. All disembarked. Wildflecken camp was about half an hour's march away. On 31 October, the FLAK Company left Bruss. Two days later, it disembarked impeccably at Brückenau.

In late October 1944, twenty-two-year-old Jacques Bonnafont arrived at Wildflecken from France.[140] He had attended military cadet academy La Flèche and then military school Saint-Cyr, but his studies were cut short by the second disaster of November 1942. He went on to work for the Vichy Government in the murky world of counter-espionage.

In August 1944, Bonnafont thought about joining French forces in Provence, but during a mission to infiltrate a *Franc-Garde* unit was involved in a car accident, breaking his foot. He was packed off to a military hospital in Germany via Ulm. Escape was never far from his mind, but the opportunities which presented themselves had the odds stacked against them. After a number of interviews, he was sent to Wildflecken.

Bonnafont was admitted into the Waffen-SS and 'Charlemagne' with his equivalent former rank in the French Army, that of Oberjunker. Stubaf. Bridoux, the commander of Waffen-Gren. Regt der SS 58, who knew of Bonnafont and of his situation,[141] sent for him and entrusted to him the command of the anti-tank company of the regiment, which is often numbered the 10th Company and abbreviated to the 10/58.[142] In this way, Bonnafont replaced Rémy, who in the words of Bonnafont 'was political, but not a soldier and not in control of the company',

138  According to de la Mazière, *Ashes of Honour*, p.35, near the camp entrance was a large arch, supported by two pillars, on which was inscribed the Waffen-SS motto 'My Honour is Loyalty'. This is unlikely. Wildflecken was an Army camp and not a Waffen-SS camp, although Waffen-SS troops were also trained there.

139  Soulat, *Historique de la Division Charlemagne*, p.1 and Mabire, *La Division Charlemagne*, pp.152-153. However, de la Mazière, a new recruit to the French Waffen-SS, recounts that upon his arrival at Wildflecken in early October 1944 he met Zimmermann, Krukenberg and Puaud in person, and encountered sections of the French Sturmbrigade and members of the first LVF echelon. But de la Mazière, a *Milicien*, actually arrived at Wildflecken with the *Milice* in early November 1944. For whatever reason, he rewrote the date of his arrival.

140  Bonnafont was born on 14 September 1922 at Mont-de-Marsan (department Landes).

141  Bonnafont did not know how Bridoux knew of his situation and never asked him.

142  See Mabire, *La Division Charlemagne*. However, of note is that the regimental commander never used the designation 10/58 for the anti-tank company, nor did Bonnafont and nor did Girard who would later command the company.

which might explain why the company had become of great concern to Bridoux.[143] Besides, Bonnafont had been schooled in the art of anti-tank warfare. He accepted his new command with much enthusiasm.

Upon entering the anti-tank company, Bonnafont was greeted with indifference, not opposition. However, he was quick to make an impression, served well by his physical attributes; he stood one metre 82 and had a strong voice. After some initial reservations, the NCOs followed him. Problems subsided, so much so that when Oscha. Girard assumed command of the company in late January 1945 he met with no problems. However, Bonnafont would later admit:

> I felt trapped. I was no longer a handler. I had a clear notion of the German disaster, which was not the case of my entourage. I found some good comrades, courageous and resigned. Perhaps I could have helped one or two get out, the same with the men, who were not 'scumbags', contrary to what was said and is still said. They were especially naive, yet convinced, but their hands were clean.

### Walter Zimmermann

At Wildflecken, the German Inspection was joined by SS-Staf. Zimmermann. He was well known to Brigf. Krukenberg.[144] They had served together in the V. SS Gebirgs-Korps.

Walter Zimmermann was born on 1 October 1897 in Meissen, Saxony. His father was a postal secretary. On 2 September 1914, he joined the Army. In the years that followed he worked his way up through the ranks. He saw service in Lithuania, Poland and France. He won the Iron Cross 2nd Class. In March 1918, he became an officer candidate and that October was commissioned as a Leutnant d.R. with Pionier Bataillon 241.

On 1 August 1932, Zimmermann joined the NSDAP. His number was 1,378,990. Months later, on 3 January 1933, he volunteered for the Allgemeine-SS. His SS number was 59,684. He was assigned to the Engineer Platoon of the 46.SS-Standarte in Dresden. In November 1935, he moved to the recently formed Pioniersturmbann of the SS/VT and, on the 16th, was commissioned with the rank of SS-Untersturmführer. From October to December 1937, he was on a posting with the engineering section of the SS-HA [Main Office]. After a stint with the SS-Nachrichtensturmbann, he served with the staff of the SS/VT inspection and then the Kommandoamt der Waffen-SS [Command Office of the Waffen-SS] in an advisory capacity, where he remained until January 1941. By now, he held the rank of SS-Sturmbannführer.

On 20 January 1941, Stubaf. Zimmermann took command of the SS-Pionier-Ersatz-Bataillon. On 30 January 1942, he was promoted to SS-Obersturmbannführer. In April 1942, he became the first commander of SS-Geb. Pionier Bataillon 7 of the 7. SS-Freiwilligen-Gebirgs Division 'Prinz Eugen'. On 31 January 1943, he won a clasp to his World War One EK II. Klasse and, on 15 June 1943, the EK I. Klasse. He was also the recipient of the order of the crown of King Zvonimir that Ante Pavelic, the Plogavnik [leader] of Croatia, awarded him for keeping open the strategic roads of Croatia. From July 1943, he served as the Korpspionierführer [Corps

143  Also, Rémy may have been demoralised.
144  Undoubtedly Krukenberg had requested the services of Zimmermann.

Engineer Leader] of the V. SS-Freiw.-Geb.-Korps. On 20 April 1944, he was promoted to SS-Standartenführer. Then, in late September, he was placed in reserve. On 31 October 1944, SS-Staf. Zimmermann was posted to the French Brigade of the Waffen-SS at Wildflecken as its Ausbildungsführer [Training leader].

Zimmermann spoke French fluently. He carried on him a dictionary of French slang. On its cover he had drawn a tricolore.[145] Although his reputation as a cold and rather severe man instilled fear among the French trainees, he did have a charming and affable side.[146]

On one occasion, when challenged by a guard, Staf. Zimmermann had been without the password and immediately found himself against a wall with a bayonet in his back. He remained in that position for half an hour before being shown in to see Hstuf. Roy, the guard's company commander. Much to Roy's surprise, Zimmermann actually congratulated them both for 'conscientiously applying orders'.[147]

Zimmermann was one of the few Germans serving with 'Charlemagne' who wore the French national shield. In fact, he wore that of the LVF.

Many surprises awaited Strmm. Pillet at Wildflecken, none more so than the person in the next bed to his who had the typically Jewish name of Cohen![148] Nevertheless, there was nothing in a name. Many, for obvious reasons, had enlisted under *noms de guerre*. One volunteer, an electrician by trade, enlisted and served under the British name of Jack Greenhalgh.[149] However, he was certainly of French nationality; he had seen previous military service in the Armistice Army. Others with British sounding surnames included Jean-Marie Edgeworth, who was born in 1919 at Monaco and served with Waffen-Gren. Regt. der SS 58,[150] and Alfred Sunray, who was born in 1923.[151]

Later, quite by chance, Pillet was surprised to meet an old school friend. They had been together in the same class at *lycée* Carnot. Since then they had lost contact and each of them had no idea that the other had enlisted. As it turned out they met only the once. The name of Pillet's friend was Robert Blanc. He had arrived at Wildflecken with the *Milice*.

145  The author has seen the dictionary.
146  Marotin, *La Longue Marche* (Self-published), p.46. Soulat knew Zimmermann. Indeed, according to Soulat, *Historique de la Division Charlemagne*, p.4, Zimmermann was the most popular German officer among the volunteers because of his diplomacy and his knowledge of Parisian slang.
147  Gaulois, article *Mein Freund Georges*.
148  Also of interest to note is that a volunteer by the Jewish name of Goldstein served in the 1st Company of the LVF.
149  Volunteers with British names had served in the LVF. There was Alexander Hill and Richard Ryding, who was well known to Mercier. Of French nationality, 'Dick' also had British blood in him. He was perfectly bilingual and spoke with a very slight niçois accent. PPF militant, he had enlisted in the LVF at the end of 1941. However, the Germans were opposed against his going to Russia and assigned him to office duties with the Ersatz Kommando at Breslau, then Kruszyna. Ryding told Mercier that he admired the shrewdness of the Germans who feared a dangerous individual like him going to a lost corner of Russia but entrusted to him the most confidential dossiers of the regiment (Mercier, letter to the author, 24/9/2001).
150  After the Second World War, Edgeworth served with the Foreign Legion.
151  Sunray was killed at Stolpe on 5 March 1945 when 'Charlemagne' was transferred to the Eastern Front.

**9**

# Formation of 'Charlemagne' and the *Milice française*

---

## The *Miliciens* arrive

On 5 November 1944, the *Miliciens* arrived at Wildflecken and made their way to Adolf Hitler Platz in French dark-blue and khaki uniforms 'with berets pulled down over one eye'.[1] They carried captured British Sten guns, as well as 'Smith and Wesson' and American 'Colt' revolvers. At their head marched *Capitaine* Jean Bassompierre[2] and at the head of the first *Cohorte* was *Capitaine* Émile Raybaud.[3] The air of the *Miliciens* was unashamedly very anti-German.[4] Yet was this not the same *Milice* that over the past year had become closely identified in the popular mind with the Nazi cause?

1    De la Mazière, *Ashes of Honour*, p.53.
2    According to Mabire, *La Division Charlemagne*, p.168, *Capitaine* Bassompierre was wearing his former Wehrmacht field grey uniform with the tricolore badge of the LVF. This is unlikely. Bassompierre was a *milicien* through and through. He would not have 'deserted' his men in this way.
3    According to Mabire, *La Division Charlemagne*, p.168, Raybaud was wearing all his decorations. This is not true. Mabire continues on p.171 of the same work that when Raybaud collected his Waffen-SS uniform his chest was covered in decorations won in action against the Germans. This too is not true. In fact, at no time did Raybaud wear decorations in the *Milice* or in the Waffen-SS, letter from Raybaud to Mabire, 3/11/74, and for good reason; the *Croix de guerre avec palms* awarded to Raybaud at the end of the 39-40 war was not sanctioned following the intervention of his corps commander, Cdt. Carolet, because Raybaud had dissociated himself from his former military comrades when the *Armée Secrète* was formed and joined the *Milice* instead.
4    According to Saint-Loup, *Les Hérétiques*, p.145, the *Miliciens* unashamedly marched to the *chasseur* step. Some units of *franc-gardes* may have, but the majority marched to the *pas normal de l'armée française*. To explain, the *chasseur* step is very fast and requires particular training. Robert Blanc, who arrived at Wildflecken with the *Milice*, said of the step: 'My unit marched to the *pas normal de l'armée française*. Otherwise, I assure you I would have remembered it!' Also there is great debate on whether or not the *Miliciens* entered Wildflecken defiantly singing *Sambre et Meuse* and *La Madelon*. For the most part, this version is confirmed by the professional authors but is not substantiated by eyewitness accounts or Léfèvre. However, René Cessil, a *franc-garde*, remembers that *Sambre et Meuse* and *La Madelon* were sung on their entrance but remarked that this was not to defy the Germans. He explained that they were singing in French because they did not know any German songs. Curiously, according to Mabire, *La Division Charlemagne*, p.168, the *Miliciens* also sang the *Panzerlied* because 'they were proud to enter an assault unit'.

## Maintenance of Order

On 4 December 1943, Marshal Pétain was handed an ultimatum from Hitler that demanded greater action against the resistance and that Déat, Henriot and Darnand be brought into the Vichy government. Pétain bowed to these demands, though he held out against the appointment of Déat whose attacks on Vichy in *L'Oeuvre* had infuriated him.

On 30 December 1943, Darnand was named Secretary General for the Maintenance of Order. This post replaced that of the Secretary General of the Police.

Two days later, on 1 January 1944, Darnand and Henriot took up their duties. On 7 January, in an interview which appeared in the pages of *Paris-Soir*, Darnand warned that he would strike against the men of the maquis and their accomplices equally hard. He continued that the time had come for the latter to choose sides between the defenders of the national order or against them. On that same day, in *Je suis partout*, Darnand defiantly announced: 'We will continue without weakness our just reprisals... Our enemies know well that none of their crimes will go unpunished'. He asserted that France had need of the *Milice*.

Several days later, on 10 January, Darnand was granted full powers over 'all the police forces; all bodies and formations that assure public security and the internal safety of the state'. In mid-January 1944, the *Milice française* was finally authorized to extend into the North Zone. Jean Bassompierre, who Darnand had recalled from the LVF, was appointed *Inspecteur général* for the North Zone in the last days of February.

On 20 January 1944, law N° 38, signed by Pierre Laval, conferred new powers on Darnand. Under this new law, Darnand was authorised as the Secretary General for the Maintenance of Order to establish court-martials at the request of *intendants de police* to judge immediately those individuals caught in flagrante delicto committing 'assassination or murder, and attempted assassination or murder'. The first court-martial was set up in Marseille at the start of February 1944. Others followed at Angers, Annecy, Clermont-Ferrand, Lille, Limoges, Montpellier, Nice, Nîmes, Orléans and Poitiers.

As such, this new law suspended the judicial guarantees under Common Law. The proceedings were closed; the accused was not permitted a defence counsel; there was no right of appeal and the sentence, invariably execution, was discharged immediately.

To protect the identity of the three-judge panel, chosen by Darnand as 'the Secretary General for the Maintenance of Order', no transcripts were written up and the verdict was often left unsigned or signed illegibly. It is often alleged that *chefs* of the *Milice* frequently carried out this mockery of justice, but few of the judges were ever identified!

That same month, in the pages of *Combats*, the *Milice* newspaper, Darnand proclaimed: 'Do not be afraid of being only small in number. Throughout history from time immemorial it was always the handful of men who have forced destiny.' Destiny now awaited the *Milice* in Haute-Savoie.

In January 1944, Darnand initiated a police campaign against the maquis of Glières in Haute-Savoie. He nominated Colonel Lelong of the gendarmerie as the *directeur des opérations*. He had at his disposal 19 *pelotons* [platoons] *de gendarmerie*, 12 *escadrons* [platoons/squadrons] *de gardes mobiles* and, finally, 5 *escadrons de groupes mobiles de réserve* (GMR). In total, they numbered some 2,200 men.

The results of the campaign were so disappointing that Darnand sent in some 700 to 800 *Miliciens*, including some 400 *francs-gardes permanents*.[5] The *Milicens* were organised into two ad hoc battle units. The *2° unité de la Franc-Garde* (or *2° unité de Franc-Gardes*), commanded by Jacques Dugé de Bernonville, consisted of units (probably *centaine* sized) under Di Constanzo, Montgour, Perrin and de Bourmont.

Darnand appointed *Commandant de la Franc-Garde permanente* de Vaugelas to take command of the *Milice* forces engaged in Haute-Savoie 'against the outlaws'.[6] Born on 2 January 1913 in Paris, Jean de Vaugelas attended the *École de l'Air*.[7] In 1939, he was promoted to *sous-lieutenant de réserve*. His war was rather lacklustre as an administrative officer.[8] 1942 brought him promotion to *lieutenant*. Subsequently he served in Vichy's *Chantiers de la Jeunesse* but had to leave 'through lack of adapting himself to the state of spirit of this organisation'.[9] He joined the *Milice* while still in its infancy and brought his two brothers along with him. In March 1943, he attended the first training course ran at the *École des Cadres* at Uriage.

Proving to be a born leader, de Vaugelas enjoyed a meteoric rise through the ranks of the *Milice*. On 8 April 1943 he became the *chef régional* for Marseille and then, after the departure of du Vair, the *Chef de l'école* of the *École des Cadres* at Uriage. In February 1944, he took a more active role in the fight against the resistance when he left Uriage to take command of the forces of the *Franc-Garde* participating in the Maintenance of Order operations in Haute-Savoie.

A monarchist, de Vaugelas was not sentimentally or ideologically pro-German. A commander, he did not tolerate theft or breaches of discipline. This intelligent, sometimes insolent officer had character and presence, and was held in great esteem by all which somewhat displeased Darnand and the political wing of the *Milice*. Although his relationship with Darnand was often strained, he was ardently devoted to the *Milice*.[10]

At Glières, de Vaugelas was ably assisted by two career officers, *Capitaine* Victor de Bourmont and *Capitaine* Émile Raybaud.

Born on 5 May 1907 in Pontivy, Victor de Bourmont was the great grandson of Louis, comte de Ghaisnes de Bourmont.[11] In 1927, he entered the celebrated *École spéciale militaire de* Saint-Cyr. Two years later, he graduated as a *sous-lieutenant d'active* in the infantry. On 25 December 1938, he was promoted to *Capitaine* and subsequently served with the *28ᵉ régiment de tirailleurs*

5    Delperrié de Bayac, *Histoire de la Milice*, p.320. Remarkably, one source, which shall not be named, records that some 7,000 to 8,000 *Miliciens* were actually sent in!
6    See de Vaugelas' *citation à l'ordre de la Nation* published in the *Journal Officiel* of 8 July 1944.
7    According to Mabire, *La Division Charlemagne*, p.118, Jean de Vaugelas was thrown out of the *École de l'Air* after refusing to reply to a coloured officer. In a letter to the author, 20/3/97, Lefèvre states that this is untrue.
8    Research provided by Lefèvre. This corrects Giolitto's portrayal of de Vaugelas during the 1939-40 campaign as a lieutenant in a *escadrille combattante* [fighting squadron] (see *Histoire de la Milice*, p.171).
9    *Achives nationales* F 60 514.
10   According to Delperrié de Bayac, *Histoire de la Milice*, p.320, de Vaugelas had another side to his character. At the end of March 1944, after the attack on the plateau of Glières, he summarily executed a prisoner, a veteran of the 27e BCA. Later, when speaking of the execution with a *Milicien*, also of the 27e BCA and who knew the person in question, de Vaugelas told him: "What a pity. I thought he was a Communist."
11   Ghaisnes de Bourmont, who was made a *Maréchal de France*, went over to the enemy on the eve of the battle of Ligny in 1815. He served the Restoration, becoming Charles X's minister of war in 1829, and commanded the expedition that seized Algeria for France in 1830, although he later fell into disgrace.

*tunisiens*.[12] Taken prisoner in 1940, he volunteered one year later to fight in Vichy Syria. By the time he was released, the fighting was as good as over. He went instead to the Armistice Army. On its disbandment he passed to the *Milice*, attracted more by its military trappings than its political doctrines. Appointed *chef regional-adjoint* for Toulouse in March 1943, he attended the third training course at Uriage in May 1943. He was a monarchist and a legitimist. Although at times moody, he was loved by his men. Small in stature, he was overshadowed by Raybaud.

Born on 3 July 1910 in Trans,[13] Émile Raybaud attended the *École spéciale militaire de* Saint-Cyr between the years 1930-1932. Graduating as a *sous-lieutenant d'active* in the infantry, he was posted to the elite *20e BCA* (*bataillon de Chasseurs alpins*) at Antibes. On 1 April 1940, he was promoted to *Capitaine*. Two months later, he found himself on the Somme with his division, the *40e Division de Chasseurs*, fighting the Germans. In defeat, he joined the Armistice Army.[14]

Although not politically orientated, *Capitaine* Raybaud was a fervent supporter of Pétain's National Revolution that promised to rejuvenate France. He too came to the *Milice* after the Armistice Army was disbanded. After attending the second training course at Uriage, he was subsequently appointed *chef départemental-adjoint* for Basses-Alpes and, in August 1943, was appointed the *Directeur Adjoint* [assistant director] at the *École des Cadres de la Milice* at Uriage. He worked well with *directeur de l'école* de Vaugelas and, in February 1944, he left his post at Uriage to join de Vaugelas as his Chief-of-Staff for the Maintenance of Order operation in Haute-Savoie.[15]

A soldier Raybaud had been and a soldier he would remain. Side by side on his tunic, he wore the gamma of the *Milice française* and the hunting horn of the *Chasseurs alpins*. A traditional officer, he had much in common with de Bourmont. They both had nothing but contempt for the thugs, policemen and opportunists recruited of late to the *Milice*. They had little interest in political intrigues and were wary of the *partisans de la collaboration* and also of the *cagoulard* stance of some *chefs* of the *Milice*. Devoted to their men, they did not shun their responsibilities whatever the circumstances. Raybaud and de Bourmont epitomized the 'professional' side of the *Milice*.

However, the *gendarmes* of the *gardes mobiles* and the GMR at Glières did not regard the *Miliciens* as professionals, but amateurs, worse still amateurs of *style bravache*.[16] Indeed, relations between the *gendarmes* and the *Miliciens* were poor.

The combined French forces, which were in need of air support, could still not disperse the maquis by themselves. The Germans intervened and, on 26 March 1944, crushed the maquis on the plateau of Glières. The *Milice* was now relegated to the capture of isolated maquisards and the interrogation of the local population.

12  Research provided by Lefèvre. This corrects Mabire, *La Division Charlemagne*, p.115, who wrote that de Bourmont was serving in 1939 as a regular lieutenant in a Moroccan Tirailleur Regiment.
13  Research provided by Soulat. However, according to a non-referenced wartime document of German origin, his date of birth was 19 May 1910.
14  As a serving officer in the Armistice Army, Raybaud is unlikely to have been a member of the *Légion Française des Combattants* (as stated by Mabire, *La Division Charlemagne*, p.115).
15  Research provided by Lefèvre. This corrects Delperrié de Bayac, *Histoire de la Milice*, p.249, repeated by Giolitto, *Histoire de la Milice*, p.171, that Raybaud succeeded de Vaugelas as the *Chef de l'École* when he left Uriage to take command of the forces of the *Franc-Garde* participating in the Maintenance of Order operations in Haute-Savoie.
16  Delperrié de Bayac, *Histoire de la Milice*, p.322.

In a series of radio broadcasts, Philippe Henriot, the Vichy Secretary of State for Propaganda and Information, glorified the role of the *Milice* in this 'historic victory for French discipline and order' over an assortment of terrorists, assassins and cowards. Notably, not one word was mentioned of the German presence at Glières.

On 8 July 1944, the *Journal Officiel* of the French state mentioned de Vaugelas in dispatches. The citation explained that as the commander of the *Milice* forces engaged against the outlaws in Haute-Savoie he had shown tireless ardour and exemplary courage which had filled with admiration his *chefs*, his comrades and his men. As a result, he had given his troops the impetus to successfully execute the final assault against the rebels on the plateau of Glières.

The Maintenance of Order operation against the maquis in Haute-Savoie was the first of many such operations throughout the whole of France in which the *Milice* participated. The Limousin, where the maquis was great in number and active, was now targeted.

On 8 April 1944, de Vaugelas was appointed *intendant régional du Maintien de l'Ordre* for the administrative region of Limoges, which gave him authority over the Police and all Vichy forces in the Limousin. He brought along with him some two hundred *francs-gardes* who had just participated in the operation at Glières, *Capitaine* Raybaud,[17] who would be his assistant, and *Capitaine* de Bourmont.

The forces of the Maintenance of Order had a total strength of some 6,000 men. However, only the *Miliciens* were prepared to take the fight to the terrorists and they were small in number.

In April, the forces of the Maintenance of Order were organised into five groups: A, B, C, D, and E. *Capitaine* de Bourmont commanded Group E that comprised one *Franc-Garde Cohorte* and one GMR company. The *franc-gardes* numbered four hundred. Montgour commanded one of the three *centaines* of the *Franc-Garde Cohorte*.

Born on 23 April 1914 in Lyon, Marc Montgour was regarded as a fanatic of the New Order, as well as a playboy! He held the prominent post of *chef de la 1ère Cohorte de la Franc-Garde bénévole* at Lyon before passing to the *Franc-Garde permanente*.

After the mobilisation of the *forces du Maintien de l'Ordre* in June 1944, the strength of the *franc-gardes* stood at about six hundred. They were centered on Limoges with their families and faced some 8750 communist FTP[18], 4100 maquisards of the Secret Army and 1050 ORA (who rejected de Gaulle).

### The *Débarquement*

Elsewhere, the resistance continued to strike against the *Milice*, Vichy officials, other collaborators and their families. On the night of 7-8 April 1944, *Franc-Garde* Delahais, who had previously served with the LVF, was assassinated at Bobigny, thus acquiring the dubious distinction of the first *Milicien* to be killed in the North Zone. His funeral was conducted on 14 April 1944 at Pantin which was given extensive coverage in the collaborationist press. On 3 May 1944, the resistance struck again in the North Zone, killing *Milicien* Elie Penot. Darnand attended the

---

17    According to Giolitto, Raybaud only left his post at the *École des Cadres* at Uriage in May 1944. However, this is incorrect (research provided by Lefèvre).
18    The *Francs-Tireurs et Partisans* or FTP was an armed resistance movement and although most FTP groups only accepted orders from the French Communist Party they sometimes formed local alliances with the *Armée secrète*.

funeral to pay his respects. More and more *Miliciens* and family members were struck down as the prospect of an Allied invasion that summer galvanized the resistance. The *Débarquement* in Normandy on 6 June 1944 changed everything.

On 7 June 1944, in response to the Allied landing, Darnand mobilised the *Franc-Garde* in a radio speech he made to the *forces du Maintien de l'Ordre*. He stormed:

> The orders are clear. Consider as enemies of France the Franc-Tireurs and Partisans, the members of the so-called Secret Army and those bands of resistance. Attack the saboteurs, whether or not they have landed by parachute. Hunt down the traitors who are trying to sap the morale of our formations. Face them like the G.M.R. in Haute-Savoie, like the *Gardes* in the Limousin scrub. *Gardes*, gendarmes, *policies*, show that you have kept your traditions of discipline. Be soldiers without reproach.

He declared that the ranks of the forces of order are open to all Frenchmen, concluding: '*Miliciens*, Frenchmen, stand up and we will save our country. Tomorrow, the storm will have passed and order reestablished on all our soil.'

On 9 June, the RNP encouraged its militants to join the *Milice* and, three days later, Fernand de Brinon did the same with the civilian personnel of the LVF. Marcel Philippon, who had been a member of the RNP since April 1941, joined the *Franc-Garde* of the *Milice* in June 1944 and was assigned to the *3e cohorte de Versailles*. The *franciste* Bucard called on all Frenchmen who wished to take up arms to enlist in 'active formations', such as the LVF and the Waffen-SS, but made no mention of Darnand's *Milice*.

On 13 June, Darnand was finally appointed Secretary of State for the Interior. The *Franc-Garde* now numbered 6280 men in the South zone, of which 1540 were *permanents,* and 415 in the North zone. The numbers were soon swelled by the general mobilization, which lasted one month.

Darnand now issued a circular to those charged with the Maintenance of Order to stay out of the conflict between the Anglo-Americans and the Germans, reiterating that their mission was to prevent any action by the rebels. In the same circular, Darnand reminded *Miliciens* not to have contact with the occupation authorities and that regional and department *chefs* were the only ones authorized to do so under the control of the French authorities charged with the Maintenance of Order. This did not stop some *Miliciens* from closely collaborating with the SD or Gestapo, though.

For the resistance, the invasion was the cue for insurrection. The Limousin continued to be a hotbed of insurrection, which the forces of the Maintenance of Order attempted to quell. The *Franc-Garde* of the *Milice* participated in countless operations, most notably at Saint-Victurnien on 27 June 1944, at Magnac-Laval on 8 July 1944 and at Eymoutiers. The clashes were brutal and bloody. Sometimes the *Miliciens* came off better and sometimes they came off worse.[19]

That June, *Capitaine* Raybaud, who still believed in a German victory because 'morale is with us', succeeded de Vaugelas. Lieutenant Géromini replaced de Bourmont. Jean-Baptiste Géromini was born on 19 May 1914 in Corsica. After a two year stint of military service between 1935 and 1937, he re-enlisted and attended Saint-Maixent military school for officer

---

19    See Delperrié de Bayac, *Histoire de la Milice*, p.425, in particular the footnotes.

training. Subsequently promoted to *sous-lieutenant*, he was posted to the 24e BCA, where he met Darnand, describing it as a defining moment in his life. He fought bravely against the Germans and was awarded the *Croix de guerre* with two citations, one in an Army dispatch, the other in a Division dispatch. Demobilised, he met Darnand again who recruited him into the anti-Communist and anti-German *Groupes de Protection*.

In July 1941, following the collapse of the short-lived *Groupes de Protection*, Géromini resumed service with the Colonial Army and left for Senegal as an infantry lieutenant in the *1st Régiment de Tirailleurs Sénégalais*. He started out back to France less than one week before the Allied landings in North Africa. By the time he arrived back home the Armistice Army no longer existed. He now entered the *École d'administration militaire* (relocated to Marseille) where he became bored. Seeking another outlet for his patriotism, he wrote to Darnand asking for a position in the *1er Régiment de France* or in Petain's personal guard.[20] Darnand tried to convince him to come over to the *Milice* instead, offering him a post at Uriage, but he refused. Months later, Darnand was to try again and invited Géromini to Vichy. Darnand spoke to him of the *École des Cadres* at Uriage where veterans of the 24e BCA were or through which they had passed. Géromini hesitated. Darnand then asked: "Do you imagine that I want to betray France? France must be rebuilt. We will do a good job." Now troubled, Géromini still 'did not jump ship'. Darnand brought out his trump card: photos of the *franc-gardes* of the *Milice* 'with the flag'. Géromini saw *Chasseurs alpins*, his former branch in the Army. He was won over.

From the moment he arrived at Uriage, Géromini knew that his decision to join the *Milice* had not been misguided. 'He was seduced by the setting, the chateau on its spur, the ambience that reigned at the school: France to be rebuilt, the new knighthood'.[21] However, of concern were the pictures of German and Waffen-SS soldiers pinned up by the *aspirants* and trainees in the bedrooms, which he had removed. With regard the Germans, Géromini once said: 'We have a duty to keep our distance. We must keep our dignity'.[22] This he would do. He was posted to the Limousin on 24 May 1944.

Of a fiery-nature, Géromini quickly proved troublesome to his superiors and the Germans during the Maintenance of Order operations in the Limousin. Four or five of his *francs-gardes* had enlisted in the Waffen-SS without his authorisation and when they were seen dressed in German uniforms he had them arrested. A high ranking Waffen-SS officer came to see Géromini and ordered him to release the prisoners. This Géromini refused, retorting that his *francs-gardes* did not have the right to enlist in the Waffen-SS without first submitting their intentions to their commander. He won the day.

On 20 July 1944, Raybaud ordered Géromini to operate alongside the Germans against the maquis. He refused point-blank. Raybaud then replied: "You are the only one capable of preventing exactions from the Germans. It is your duty to go." Géromini agreed. A sincere patriot, he declared in 1967: 'My idea was not to fight against Frenchmen and to limit the damage.'

Three days later, Lieutenant Géromini saved thirty of his fellow countrymen at Eymoutiers from a German firing squad after the maquis had ambushed their column. On the following day, Géromini and one of his assistants intervened on behalf of a wounded terrorist who a German

20   According to Delperrié de Bayac, *Histoire de la Milice*, p.180, Darnand contacted Géromini first.
21   Delperrié de Bayac, *Histoire de la Milice*, p.250.
22   Delperrié de Bayac, *Histoire de la Milice*, p.428.

NCO was about to finish off. A fiery altercation developed. The German NCO called his men to his aid and Géromini did likewise. The two groups faced each other, with the wounded terrorist between them. A German officer was consulted who sided with Géromini, but later the Germans reproached Géromini for his incorrect attitude towards the German NCO and pressurised the appropriate French authorities to relieve him of his command. On 25 or 26 July 1944, Géromini was duly relieved of his command.

The large-scale German operation with the support of the *Milice* to destroy the FTP stronghold east of Limoges ultimately ended in failure. Admittedly, the Germans had opened roads, occupied towns and killed masquisards, but then departed. This operation cost the Germans some three hundred killed. Again, the *Milice* had only played a secondary role. Heavily outnumbered, the Germans and the forces of the Maintenance of Order could do little to quell the insurrection in the Limousin. From April to August 1944, between thirty and forty *francs-gardes* were killed in combat.

On 25 July 1944, Raybaud was promoted *adjoint* to Dr. Rainsart, *chef de la Franc-Garde de zone Nord*. He was succeeded by *chef régional* Henri Barrier. According to Barrier, Raybaud was relieved of his post at the request of the Germans. As for de Bourmont, he was appointed as the *chef régional* for Lyon, a position he would hold until the Liberation.

## Pierre Méric and the Maintenance of Order

Méric's course at the *Milice* École des cadres d'Uriage ended in late December 1943. His class was called 'Promotion Roger Franc' in memory of a comrade who had been assassinated at Thônes on 21 November 1943. Méric knew him well, for they had both attended the Fourth training course at Uriage earlier in the year.

In early 1944, Méric was posted to the *Franc-Garde* of Lot-et-Garonne stationed in chateau de Ferron, near Tonneins, some twenty kilometers from his hometown Casteljaloux. His rank was still that of *franc-garde*, even though he had been proposed as *chef de trentaine adjoint* like his comrades at the end of the course. He was assigned a role training new recruits and those mobilized by the department for a new unit. Week by week, newcomers swelled the ranks of this new unit, which was armed with weapons captured from an air drop to the Resistance, including two British Bren light machine guns, as well as conventional French small arms.

In February 1944, Méric was sent to Haute-Savoie as second in command of a *trentaine*. This was his first taste of command and he proved himself worthy of the confidence placed in him. His *trentaine* conducted patrols and manned roadblocks, which was not without risk. One of his friends from Uriage was shot and critically wounded while manning a roadblock alongside him. The aggressor was shot dead and when searched found to be carrying weapons and many interesting documents. His friend was taken to hospital and operated on. He hovered between life and death for several days, but eventually pulled through.

Late one night, Méric was called upon to assist a patrol which had got into trouble. Alerted, his unit took up a good position and, with their machine guns, managed to suppress the enemy fire, allowing their comrades to withdraw. The patrol leader turned out to be none other than de Bourmont, who was slightly wounded. De Bourmont, who was a rather reserved character, actually admitted to Méric that he would have done better to have used his *trentaine* for his *coup de main*. De Bourmont would not forget him.

At the end of the operation in Haute-Savoie, Méric attended a parade in Annecy. Before he returned to Ferron, de Bourmont summoned him, complimented him on the 'nuanced character of his action', and announced that he had proposed him for the rank of *chef de trentaine*, which was confirmed three weeks later.

In early June, Méric was ordered to operate jointly with Germans troops in the sector. This greatly troubled him, but his overriding concern was to prevent reprisals against the population. Thus, on 9 June, he presented himself to a German Captain based at Marmande and together they drew up a plan of action for the following day. They communicated through an Alsatian interpreter; Méric spoke not a word of German while the German officer could only speak a little French. The Germans would deploy one company and the *Milice* two *trentaines*. Méric left the meeting convinced that there was mutual understanding and trust between the two of them, as events would prove.

The following day, the joint operation started early in the north of the sector, towards Eymet. In mid-morning, in a village by the name of Lauzun, Méric made contact with the gendarmerie and found the gendarmes agitated. At that same moment, the *Miliciens* heard cries coming from the cells and went to investigate, releasing those locked up, 'in particular a sympathetic man, of good appearance, thirty years old, who showed us great gratitude' and 'seemed in a hurry to return home and see his wife and children again'.[23] Clearly, the gendarmes had gone over to the Resistance. Not only had they handed over their revolvers, but they were guarding prisoners for them in their cells. Méric sharply reproached the gendarmes and told them he was going to place them at the disposal of the Brigade at Marmande, which he did two hours later. He thought it better to keep the matter in-house rather than explain it to the Germans.

At Marmande, Méric met with the German Captain who told him that the maquis had just occupied Casteljaloux, Méric's hometown, and that he had decided to respond straightaway. Méric told him that this was his country and that he wanted to take the initiative. Looking at a map, they quickly drew up a battle plan: the Germans would take the main road while the *Milice* would take a route via Poussignac to intercept the fugitives.

At the top of the last hill before Casteljaloux, Méric came across some farmers who knew him and told him the stomach-churning news that the maquis had seized his father and brother, along with other townspeople. Thereupon, he raced into town with his two *trentaines*. The scene that greeted him was one full of foreboding; the Germans had already rounded up all the men they could find and had them under guard in the town centre. There was no trace of the maquisards who had left hurriedly.

Méric now intervened, for this was personal. He asked the German Captain to assemble his troops and return to Marmande, which he was not prepared to do, but he did agree to a compromise. He would withdraw his troops to a position five kilometers from the town and if Méric had not rejoined him within an hour he would return and take the matter in hand. Méric spoke to those assembled, who all knew him, and pleaded with them to make contact with the maquis and convince them to release their prisoners, in particular his father and brother, adding that if they were not released he feared quick and very heavy reprisals. After repeating his speech, he announced that they were free to go and that they knew what to do.

23   Méric was to learn later that the maquis shot this individual, although this remains unconfirmed.

With time pressing, Méric went to try and console his mother, before pushing off to the rendezvous point. The Germans and the *Milice* returned to their respective bases. Méric could congratulate himself that not a single drop of blood had been shed. The following morning, he was told that his father and brother had been released. He thanked God for their safe return.

Soon after, he was promoted to *chef de centaine*. He reported directly to the *chef de base*. Proudly, he noted that in the ranks of his unit there were a lieutenant-colonel, several majors, captains or reserve officers who had commanded under fire, some during the Great War, and yet none doubted his ability to exercise command. All had confidence in him.

More notable episodes followed. With the full knowledge of his superiors, Méric was called upon to exchange a maquis prisoner they no longer had need of for the kidnapped sister-in-law of one of those mobilized. The exchange took place without commentary or animosity from either side.

On 17 June, after receiving information that the maquis was due to attack a chateau which was *chef* Geliot's base, Méric rushed to the scene with a 'section' [probably a *trentaine*]. As the *franc-gardes* approached the chateau, they came under fire. After returning fire, the maquis fled 'the scene of the crime', leaving behind three trucks filled with plunder from the chateau. One *Milicien* by the name of Bauchet, a reservist, was seriously wounded and died during the night in the presence of Méric, who remains convinced that the bullet that killed Bauchet was accidently fired by one of their own.

Méric was posted to the Limousin with three *trentaines* from Ferron, reinforced by a *trentaine* from Gers and some elements from Agen. Their journey came to a premature end at Angoulême; the railway line to Limoges had been sabotaged. The new arrivals were greatly concerned that the local *trentaine* was too familiar with the Germans. Méric was convinced that it was better for the *Milice* to keep its independence and its autonomy, as well as jealously guard mutual respect.

While the new arrivals waited to be collected from Angoulême they trained and also participated in one operation, which proved unremarkable. Feeling useless and concerned for the safety of the families during their absence, Méric dispatched a letter to the *chef régional de la Milice* for Toulose requesting permission to return to Ferron. Days later, he received the order to return immediately.

On the return journey, while waiting for a connection at Bordeaux, Méric was welcomed and invited to dinner by Lieutenant-Colonel Franc, the *chef régional de la Milice* for Bordeaux whose son he knew and who had been assassinated in November 1943. They talked over dinner. Franc spoke of one action in which a number of young members of the maquis had been killed, including a woman he knew well and whose death he bitterly regretted. Such was the nature of civil war.

The *Milice* continued to come under attack throughout France. On 16 July 1944, near Savines in Hautes-Alpes, a convoy was ambushed. Two *miliciens* were killed, three were seriously wounded and seven others who were made prisoner were executed some days later. On 24 July, the *chef de la Milice aixoise*, Médan, a Latin teacher and lecturer, was assassinated. And yet against this backdrop of assassinations and bombings *Miliciens* continued to do their duty and were joined by new volunteers.

## The story of Émile Marotel

Émile Marotel, born on 24 October 1925 in Auxonne [department Cote d'Or], joined the *Milice de Savoie* in October 1943. The son of a career soldier, he was raised in the tradition of discipline and honour. He was heavily influenced by his parents, who detested the Popular Front and the strikes that 'paralysed our arsenals'. They admired Hitler, who was rearming and 'taking great care of his Army', unlike the Popular Front who had nothing but contempt for theirs. Nevertheless, Germany remained the hereditary enemy. They regretted that Hitler was not French!

Defeat in 1940 was bitter. Marotel described it as a 'war that nobody really wanted'. The military felt betrayed and blamed its political masters and the spinelessness of the country, but the advent of the *Maréchal* offered real hope. Marotel rejoiced: 'For some months the enthusiasm was tremendous and everything seemed possible!' And yet Vichy wrapped itself up in attentisme, 'the taste of least effort'. The German invasion of the Soviet Union changed his world:

> For me, Barbarossa was the decisive turning point. My former enemies became my friends since they were fighting against the common enemy and I could not envisage for a single moment in one way or another that I would not participate in this battle.
>
> My parents were living in a barracks which, after the dissolution of the Armistice Army in November 1942, would be occupied by the German or Italian Army. But for us they were no longer occupiers and became allies. Soon, they would be companions in arms. Among them the transformation was even quicker than among us, they truly considered us as friends! [24]

Aged seventeen, Marotel joined the *Milice* and soon passed to the *Franc-Garde permanente*. His parents and his brother were also members and so was his fiancée. Besides guard duty and patrols, he participated in maintenance of order operations.[25] As the civil war intensified during the late spring of 1944, he thought it necessary for the *Milice* to turn to the German Army and ask for help to maintain order. The assassinations of friends and their family members did not deter him. He would continue to fight to the end, which came soon enough.

## The story of Robert Blanc

Robert Blanc joined the *Milice* in April 1944. Born on 17 September 1923, he became a staunch supporter of the National Revolution. In September 1940, when he resumed studying at *Lyceé Carnot*, Paris, one of his classmates was Edmond Walter, who he described as intelligent but gruff. He had no idea that their paths would cross again many years later. In October 1941, he started to study law and at the same time entered Sciences Po [The Paris Institute of Political Studies]. *Les Décombres* by Lucien Rebatet, which denounced those responsible for France's political and military woes, captivated him, so much so that he admitted: 'Thanks to him, I became fascist and even national socialist'.

---

24    Marotel, *La longue marche*, p.9.
25    Notably, unlike some of his comrades, Marotel did not participate in the operations in Haute-Savoie in February 1944; he was kept at *départemental* headquarters, much to his chagrin.

Disgusted by the conformist and snobby ambiance of Sciences Po, Blanc walked out. He frequented Maison du Droit in Paris, run by a former career soldier and *maréchaliste*, where he met many like-minded individuals, including Jean-Marie Stehli, Charles Laschett and Bertrand Platon. [The first two would go on to join the Waffen-SS.] He was moved to action but hesitated because of his family. His father, a reserve artillery captain who fought in the Great War and in 39-40, was anti-German. The two of them argued and argued. In the end, they stopped talking. This remains one of his worst *souvenirs*.

Around the same time, Blanc met Marc Sainteuil, a young actor, who was having singing lessons with his mother. He described the meeting as fortuitous. One day, he walked on him making a call in his parents' bedroom and heard him say: '*Il faut maintenant s'engager dans les Waffen-SS et pour moi, c'est fait*'. They bonded, but Sainteuil left for the Waffen-SS soon after. Blanc continued to hesitate.

By the spring of 1944, Blanc could hesitate no more. It was now or never and he had convinced himself that if he did not 'take part and show what side he was on', he would regret it for the rest of his life. He said of his decision to join the *Milice*:

> The parties in the North zone (PPF, RNP, MSR...) did not attract me beyond a great deal of sympathy, but they were several and purely political. The *Milice* presented itself as more than just a party, but as a fighting formation based on clearly revolutionary ideas which radicalised those of the National Revolution formulated in 1940 and which many people tended to forget. The best proof was given by its enemies, who, in the South zone had from 1943 assassinated several of its members. The *Milice* was founded by a hero of the two wars, Joseph Darnand, whose past was not of a politician; then, a more particular guarantee, we learnt that one of our cousins, Henri Frossard was a member, and even responsible for Haute-Garonne.

Blanc joined the 'Students' *section* of the Paris *Franc-Garde bénévole*. His father tried to talk him out of it and also called on the services of a pastor, who knew him well. He was not to be dissuaded. Initially, he had little to do as a *milicien*, but was employed on two occasions to clear up after Allied air raids. When the *Franc-Garde* was mobilised in June he joined the *cohorte* stationed in Lycée Saint-Louis, boulevard Saint-Michel. Among his comrades were Jean Castrillo, Jacques Revel, Daniel Le Goff,[26] Jean-Pierre Lefèvre, Rochefort, whose wife the maquis had assassinated, and Chanrou, who had been moved to enlist after his daughter died in his arms during an American air raid. Blanc, Castrillo and Revel became inseparable.

Blanc received weapons training and was put on guard duty. His *trentaine* was also used to provide security for a *grand* meeting in the Palais de Chaillot at which Leon Degrelle spoke. Darnand and Noël de Tissot, who was on leave from the Sturmbrigade, came and spoke to the *miliciens* at Lycée Saint-Louis.

On 2 July, starting from the Place de l'Étoile, Blanc paraded down the Champs-Élysées with the three Paris *cohortes de la Franc-Garde* to the historic Hôtel des Invalides where they assembled in the *cour d'honneur* to be sworn in by Darnand. Blanc noted the many Germans present but thought they should have been more discreet.

---

26   Daniel Le Goff was born on 12 February 1924 in Aubervilliers in the north-eastern suburbs of Paris.

In early July 1944, Blanc volunteered for a unit of *franc-gardes* destined for Dijon. A contingent from 'barracks' Louis-le-Grand under the command of Jacques de Lafaye, who had left the Waffen-SS earlier in the year, joined this new unit.

In the early morning hours of 15 July 1944, Blanc was among the two *centaines* of *franc-gardes* sent to put down the revolt of four thousand prisoners at La Santé Prison, Paris. Jean Bassompierre led the operation and quickly managed to re-establish order. During the operation, the *franc-gardes* were fired on, but there were no casualties.[27] Two or three prisoners caught with weapons were immediately executed. The German authorities now demanded the execution of four hundred prisoners as a reprisal. Bassompierre intervened and managed to talk them down to no more than fifty, who were then lined up against a wall. There they waited for a good hour before they were led back to their cells; following the intervention of Max Knipping, the *délégué general* for the Maintenance of Order, the Germans agreed for the fifty to be courtmartialled instead.

With order re-established, the two *centaines* left the prison. A small contingent of ten *franc-gardes*, including Blanc, stayed behind to guard the court martial. Blanc believes that he was picked because of his height and serious demeanour. The court, made up of senior *chefs miliciens* Pierre Gallet, who acted as president, Max Knipping and Georges Radici,[28] questioned the fifty as well as the guards, who were very frightened and 'appeared to be questionable'.

Towards 18:00 hours, the court finally delivered its verdict, sentencing twenty-eight of the fifty to death, which was to be carried out immediately. After handing over their rifles to the firing squad of gendarmes, the *franc-gardes* looked on as the twenty-eight were executed in four groups of seven. This brought to an end the tragic 'affair' of La Santé, which left a lasting impression on Blanc. Henceforth, whenever he heard that someone should be shot, he could see the resigned and absent faces of the men facing execution. The suppression of the revolt at La Santé prison also had grave consequences for the senior *chefs miliciens* involved.

On 16 July, Blanc left Paris for Dijon where he was involved in two operations. The first was to dislodge the maquis from a farm at Flavignerot, south of Dijon, which ended in failure with three dead and several wounded, one of whom died days later. The second was against the maquis in a forest near Semur-en-Auxois. The *Miliciens* came under fire, but the maquis could not be found. This time there were no casualties.[29] Blanc now found himself caught up in the withdrawal to Germany.

## The story of Jules Dissent

Jules Dissent from Poitiers joined the *Milice* in May 1944. Born into a Catholic family, he attended college Saint Joseph de Poitiers, run by Jesuit fathers, from 1931 to 1942. His father had been a student there before him. He was admitted after his parents stated that the family were practicing Catholics, but not devout to the point of obsession.

The family believed in absolute monarchy. His father was a member of the royalist and right-wing political movement *Action Française* and read the movement's daily newspaper of the same

---

27    Conversation with Robert Blanc.
28    Georges Radici would later serve with 'Charlemagne'.
29    For more information on the Paris *franc-garde* unit sent to Dijon see Delperrié de Bayac, *Histoire de la Milice*, pp.485-492. The attack on the farm at Flavignerot took place on 30 July 1944.

name. The family detested the Republic and the shady politicians who represented it. Jules was not a member of any political party.

The family was also virulently anti-communist. In the years before the war, Jules Dissent had been appalled by the innumerable massacres and atrocities committed by the Bolsheviks against their own people. And yet the people of his generation would later claim, after the death of Stalin, that they had no such knowledge of Communist crimes.

For Jules Dissent, who was 'brought up in admiration of the heroism shown by the French Army during the First World War', the defeat of May 1940 represented a disaster of an unimaginable scale. Following the defeat of May 1940, he pledged his loyalty, like his parents, to *Maréchal* Pétain, who saved France from total collapse. For under the armistice, France retained its Navy, which he greatly admired. Indeed, he had once dreamt of becoming a naval officer.

Dissent was not anti or pro-German, but his father, a World War One infantry officer who had been captured, respected some of their qualities. The English attack on the fleet at Mers-el-Kébir turned him against a country he considered as a friend and toward that of another, Germany. Nevertheless, he was a young Frenchman who was just trying to get on with a normal life and much of his time was spent with his head in books. He passed his Baccalauréat in 1942 and went on to study medicine for two years.

He continued to follow political events, and, by the spring of 1944, a veritable climate of terror reigned in parts of France that he largely attributed to the maquis and the Communists and not to the *Milice* and not to the Germans. In the Limousin the Communists assassinated two family members on his mother's side, who had demonstrated their support for Pétain. The assassination of a well-known and devoted doctor in particularly vile circumstances angered him. His crime had been to profess anti-Communist opinions and belong to the PPF. He was moved to action.

Life as a *Milicien* was quiet, despite being mobilised after the Allied Normandy landings. He did not participate in the single operation conducted by the *Milice de Poitiers* against the maquis. Even so, he carried an old revolver but never practised with it, yet alone forced to use it in anger. Nevertheless, it gave him comfort. His duties became that of a medic, but there were 'no wounded and few sick among the young men we were'.

On 23 August 1944, Dissent departed his native Poitiers. He finally reached Ulm on 11 October. His journey had taken him via Strasbourg and Wiesbaden and not Belfort like many other *Miliciens*.

Seventeen-year-old Maurice Ranc from Avignon joined the *Milice* on 8 June 1944. He said of his decision:

> In 1943 I had a friend, with which I was at school, who lived in Avignon. His father was the person in charge of the PPF at Avignon; one day, he was kidnapped and never found... At that time the *Milice* was unarmed; often we learnt a *milicien* had been killed in such a town, in such a village. Another event which had upset me, and which perhaps was the origin of my engagement, was the affair at Voiron. In this village in Isère, the father, a *milicien*, was assassinated by *résistants*, at the same time as his wife and their baby ...[30]

30  Deloncle Luc, *Trois jeunesses provençales* (Paris: Dualpha, 2004), pp.81-82.

Moreover, he wanted to follow in the footsteps of his older brother, Paul, who had joined the *Milice* and then volunteered for the Waffen-SS. His older brother, who he admired more than anything, was his role model. Inspired by Joseph Darnand's rousing call to arms in response to the Allied invasion in Normandy, he knew that he could no longer sit by and do nothing, like the majority of people. It was time to act. With six or seven others from his close circle he enlisted in the *Milice*. However, by way of an explanation, he once stated: 'We were young, carefree, unmarried, [and] therefore freer than others'. Indeed, he told his father nothing of his decision.

Maurice Ranc soon found himself in action with the *Milice*:

> At Avignon, we were sixty strong, based first at Mistral school, then in a college on rue Jules-Verne. We were given a military training; above all we learnt how to handle weapons. We were also sent out on patrol all over the [department of] Vaucluse. We once came across *maquisards* in the countryside between Les Bouches-du-Rhône and les Basses-Alps. There was a sustained shootout. I took shelter behind a milestone, which stopped several bullets.[31]

## Pour la Milice, justice

The *Milice* was created and sponsored by a legitimate French Government. This fact was important to many who joined the *Milice*, like Pierre Méric. More often than not, the *Milice* is associated with the maintenance of order. However, the maintenance of order was not the sole responsibility of the *Milice*; the *Police Nationale* and the GMR were also charged with the maintenance of order, although they would prove more and more unreliable. Both Laval and *Maréchal* Pétain ardently supported the *Milice* in its war against the 'terrorists'. Indeed, on more than one occasion, Pétain complimented the head of the *Milice* on his success in maintaining order.

In the Maintenance of Order operations in Haute-Savoie and the Limousin the *Milice* participated in great numbers and in the manner of regular military forces. Far more often the *Milice* operated alone in small numbers. They were employed to search out, infiltrate and destroy resistance networks, round up and guard resistance suspects, and provide security for all kind of potential resistance targets.[32]

Occasionally, units of the *Franc-Garde* did find themselves on military operations fighting side by side with the German Police and Army against the maquis, but there was no common command. The *Franc-Garde* only operated under the control of the French authorities charged with the Maintenance of Order, the *intendants de police* who became *intendants du Maintien de l'Ordre* in April 1944, and possibly provincial *directeurs du Maintien de l'Ordre*. As such, *Milice* forces did not operate 'hand in glove' with the Gestapo, the SD or the German Police. In fact,

---

31   Deloncle, *Trois jeunesses provençales*, p.94.
32   According to Sweets John, *Choices in Vichy France* (New York: Oxford University press, 1986), p.95, 'the *Milice* operated in conjunction with German police or the strong-arm bands hired by the German Labor Service to track down individuals for deportation for work in Germany'. In response to Sweets, *Milicien* Robert Blanc has 'never heard of this particular mission' (letter to the author, 4/12/2004).

the *Milice* and the German authorities usually regarded each other as a mutual enemy and co-operation between the two was frowned upon without prior discussion at 'high levels'![33]

To its credit, the *Milice* handed over its prisoners to the appropriate French authorities rather than to the German authorities. However, towards the end of the occupation, maquis prisoners were actually handed over direct to the Germans, but this practice was not commonplace and often resulted from the frequent release of prisoners and suspects by the French authorities. At times, refusal by the *Milice* to hand over prisoners provoked the Germans to seize them.

Accusations of wholesale torture, murder, extortion, rape and robbery are repeatedly levelled at the *Milice*. While there were isolated instances, this cannot be denied, the criminal outrages of the maquis and the resistance certainly surpassed those of the *Milice* in scale and brutality! Furthermore, unlike the maquis, *Miliciens* were held accountable for their actions and were severely punished for breaches of discipline.

There were acts of revenge perpetrated by *Miliciens*, but this was in response to 'terrorist' outrages. Needless to say, every army at war has been guilty of acts of revenge. Assassinations of *Miliciens* were paid back in kind after November 1943 by which time thirty-three defenceless members of the *Milice française* had already been murdered, including a young woman as well as a priest. However, this was the work of individual *Miliciens* and not a policy conducted by the *Milice* as a whole.

Joseph Lécussan, the regional head of the *Milice* for Lyon, and other *Miliciens* acted on their own initiative and without orders when they murdered elderly Victor Basch, President of the League for the Rights of Man, and his wife in January 1944. When the bodies were found there was a card pinned to the clothes of Victor Basch that read: 'Terror against Terror'. For this brutal crime, Darnand dismissed Lécussan from the *Milice*.

The *chef de centre de la Milice* at Voiron, in the department of Isère, was Ernest Jourdan. On 22 March 1944, he participated in the killing of an important *résistant* from the Grenoble region. On 20 April 1944, Radio London sentenced him to death. On the evening of 20 April 1944, two students[34] from a local school, who had joined the *Milice* and gained his confidence, entered his house, shot him and his two bodyguards, and then proceeded to butcher four family members, including his daughter, aged fifteen months. The two students and their school supervisor, an accessory, were apprehended and brutally interrogated. On 3 May, the three of them appeared before the court martial of the *secrétariat général au Maintien de l'ordre* at prison Saint-Paul, Lyon and were sentenced to death.[35] Later that day, they were moved to fort Duchère, Lyon, and shot in the back by a firing squad in front of students and teachers from the same school.[36]

On 28 June 1944, Philippe Henriot, the Vichy Secretary of State for Propaganda and Information, was assassinated by resistance fighters disguised as *Miliciens* at his Ministry of Information apartment in Paris. The *Milice* took reprisals. That same day, Joannès Clavier,

---

33    For example, on two occasions, General Gleininger, the Feldkommandant at Limoges, formally requested the *direction du Maintien de l'Ordre* [the directorate of the Maintenance of Order] to sanction the intervention of the *Milice* and the forces of the Maintenance of Order and was refused.

34    Giolitto, *Histoire de la Milice*, p.271, and Delperrié de Bayac, *Histoire de la Milice*, p.266. Some internet sources state four students were directly responsible for the killings.

35    A fourth person was tried, but not sentenced to death.

36    According to Delperrié de Bayac, *Histoire de la Milice*, p.296, the onlookers were later shipped off to Germany where nearly all would die in concentration camps. Some sources, however, dispute this chain of events.

the *chef départemental* for Saône-et-Loire, had seven resistance suspects executed at Mâcon. Elsewhere, Paul Touvier, the *Chef régional du deuxième service* for Lyon, ordered the execution of seven Jews who were shot in the early hours of 29 June at a cemetery near the town of Rillieux-la-Pape. Both Clavier and Touvier acted alone when they ordered the reprisal executions.[37] Clavier and his *adjoint*, François Terrel, were arrested days later on the orders of de Bernonville, commanding the *Forces du Maintien de l'Ordre* for the region of Lyon, although the orders probably came from an incensed Laval, who fearing an adverse public reaction had reprimanded Darnand.[38]

Vichy may have prohibited all reprisals for the death of Philippe Henriot, but Francis Bout de l'An wrote in *Combats*:

> The *Milice* member Philippe Henriot is dead and it is our responsibility to safeguard his memory, to strike at those who, from nearby or far, prepared the crime. I know that he did not like bloodshed, I know that he did not like to see us multiply vengeance or reprisals, but I also know that he would not understand a curiously indulgent society only giving a few years imprisonment to such criminals.

On the night of 7 July, the notable Republican Georges Mandel, Reynaud's former Minister of the Interior and leading member of the Third Republic who had opposed both the armistice and Pétain taking power, was murdered by a *Milicien* named Mansuy. It is not known who, or if anybody, gave Mansuy the order to kill Mandel, but it was neither Darnand nor Laval. He was probably acting alone.

Between 4 and 6 July 1944, the FTP invested Magnac-Laval in the Limousin and shot twelve people accused of being hostile to the Resistance. On 8 July, in reaction to the events of the previous days, the Germans and the *Milice* arrived in force and arrested resistance suspects and sympathizers. Later that evening, while on route back to Limoges, the *Miliciens* shot the prisoners on the direct orders of *chef de trentaine* Jean Chardonneau. The number of prisoners executed varies from source to source: the highest figure is nineteen. Darnand gave the order to discipline Chardonneau for this massacre. Brought before the *tribunal du Maintien de l'Ordre de Limoges*, he was sentenced to death and shot on 22 July by a firing squad of *miliciens*. He died shouting 'Vive Darnand'. A monument was erected to the victims of the *Milice*, and rightly so, whereas the victims of the FTP are often whitewashed from the tragic events that took place in Magnac-Laval in July 1944.

According to one commentator, the violent excesses of some members of the *Milice* were 'perhaps nurtured by the circumstances in which they found themselves'.[39] The *Milicien* was

---

37   At his trial Paul Touvier claimed that upon his return to Lyon from Vichy on the afternoon of 28 June 1944 he was told by Victor de Bourmont, the *chef régional* for Lyon, that the German SIPO-SD chief for Lyon, Werner Knab, had demanded the execution of one hundred Jews in reprisal for Henriot's death. Touvier continued that de Bourmont had bargained Knab down to thirty and that they should start with just seven and see whether that would suffice. He argued at his trial that his actions at Rillieux-la-Pape had actually saved lives. However, Touvier's version of events could not be substantiated and the court concluded that Touvier had acted independently.

38   Terrel was released days before the arrival of the Allies. He fled to Germany, where he entered 'Charlemagne'.

39   Sweets, *Choices in Vichy France*, p.95.

The *Milice* newspaper *Combats* of 3 June 1944 records those killed or wounded in the line of duty. (Author)

isolated, for as the occupation wore on, support for Pétain and his National Revolution waned. Conversely support for the resistance in all its forms grew. The *Milice* did not enjoy the support of the police or the GMR when maintaining order. Moreover, support was not forthcoming from the Paris-based political parties, who feared its rise to power. Furthermore, the resistance regularly targeted *Milicens* and their families, who initially were unable to defend themselves against assassination, yet alone maintain order in the name of the National Revolution. Some *Miliciens* reacted to these circumstances 'in the manner of a trapped animal striking out in fury at his tormentors'.[40]

The *Milice française* as a whole, which numbered some 29,000 adherents at its peak, should not be judged, nor condemned, by the actions of a handful of a more violent and unsavoury disposition. More often than not, the *Milice* is portrayed as recruiting into its ranks the dregs of the French underworld and those who foresaw opportunities for booty and loot, but many of its recruits joined out of political commitment, considering themselves superpatriots who would save France from Communism and ruin. They were predominantly from the Right and the far Right but few were genuine National Socialists. A great number of *Miliciens* were, in fact, anti-German French Nationalists! Indeed, a maquis leader of the Secret Army wrote:[41]

> The majority of the *Miliciens* we captured were able to present their defence. Almost all protested their patriotism. Almost all recognised that they had helped the Germans. One said to me: "I'm anti-Communist. I believe the Communists are commanding

40    Sweets, *Choices in Vichy France*, p.96.
41    Delperrié de Bayac, *Histoire de la Milice*, p.552.

you". Another declared to me: "You have won but Europe has lost. To save Europe we had to march with Hitler".

To be a *Milicien* in 1944 was to have the courage of one's convictions. The *Milicien* was isolated. The *Milicien* aroused the hostility of most French people. The *Milicien* risked personal harm and so did his family: for example, in March 1944, *chef départmental* Denoix's wife was kidnapped and executed. There are countless more examples. It took genuine courage to stand up and be counted as a *Milicien,* more so after the Allied landing in Normandy in June 1944. Georges Cazalot of the *Avant-Garde, Centaine* 'Gascogne',[42] wrote of this new situation:

> Almost one month ago the forces of invasion landed on the Norman coasts… Parallel to this invasion the forces of subversion raised their head and left the woods and mountains where until then they had carefully been hiding, only descending into the plains and the towns very cautiously and when absolutely necessary. Now the dogs are let loose. It's not only acts of sabotage and murder attempts on isolated people and unarmed civilians, [but] ambushes on small detachments, kidnappings and assassinations of awkward notables or political opponents, indeed personal enemies who have nothing to do with the war or politics, attacks on tobacconists – tobacco and wine are, it seems, the sinews of the war for these bandits – and town halls to steal food coupons …
>
> All these bandits spread through the countryside, pillaging and plundering, raping and burning, indulging themselves, [and] sowing terror. France slowly sinks into anarchy. The majority of the *forces de police*, infiltrated, that courage is not the first virtue, that the verb 'to serve' has been banished from the list of their duties, wait to see which way the wind is going to blow, keep weapons at their feet when they don't go over to subversion, and wait to shout in chorus with the victor.
>
> Alone, courageous and lucid in this squall carrying along the homeland, the *Milice* faces [up to] things and fights. It fights against this immense rottenness spreading over us, against this havoc trying to submerge us and suffocate us, against the decay of our Society, against Bolshevism, a suppurating cancer gripping us and eating away at us.[43]

The *Milice* had the will to maintain order, but not the means. From the start of 1944, the forces of the Maintenance of Order were unable to maintain order alone and had to rely on German support more and more. Even after mobilization, they could still not maintain order.

Furthermore, the *Milice* failed to win the 'hearts and minds' of the population through its social and civic programme to deliver real change for a better society. In fact, the actions of some *Miliciens* turned the population against them.

Above all the *Milice* was a public utility French Association which was created to 'animate political life' and to be the avant-garde of the National Revolution, but it was a National Revolution that few French people wanted.

---

42   This designation may not have been the official title of his unit but was definitely used.
43   Cazalot, *Et la terre a bu leur sang!*, p.15.

## The *départ*

In the final weeks of occupation Darnand directed *Milice* units 'out in the field' to seize hostages if the local population showed itself to be hostile. One source poignantly remarks 'it was if the *Milice* were operating on foreign soil'.[44] Even Marshal Pétain, once an ardent supporter of the *Milice*, came out against its brutal methods in a letter to Laval dated 6 August 1944, protesting:

> The *Milice* has gained a hideous reputation of using methods which I knew well when they were used by the Reds in Spain. I cannot pass over in silence the tortures inflicted on victims who are often innocent, in places which, even in Vichy, are less like French State Prisons than Bolshevik Chekas. By these methods, the *Milice* has succeeded in establishing an atmosphere of police terror which has been unknown in our country till today.

On 15 August, the Allies landed in Southern France and swiftly defeated the weak German forces. Faced with the prospect of German defeat in France, Darnand ordered a general withdrawal which was broadcasted on 19 August. However, many thousands of *Miliciens* and their families were already on the road towards the East. It was chaotic and desperate. They had no illusions about their fate if they should fall into the hands of their countrymen.

Darnand sent *Commandant* of the *Franc-Garde permanente* de Vaugelas to Limoges to organise the evacuation of the encircled Vichy forces. As there was no longer any question of reaching Limoges by road, de Vaugelas arrived by plane. He was in the company of de Londaiz. Feverishly, he set about his task. At midday on 16 August 1944, a convoy of ninety-five vehicles, carrying between 400 and 500 *Miliciens*, and some 350 women and children, set off. Destination: the town of Guéret, approximately seventy kilometres away.

That same day, the convoy was ambushed twice, but managed to keep going, covering some twenty-five kilometres. On the following morning, the convoy stopped before trees placed across the road and was caught in strong crossfire: three *Miliciens* were killed and thirteen were wounded, including *chef de trentaine* Aumont.[45] Unable to pass, de Vaugelas gave the order to turn around, but they now found the way back blocked. Encircled, de Vaugelas sent out a distress call that was received by the Germans at Limoges. Troops were promised to free the convoy. The *Milice* forces dug in.

Little changed on 18 August; patrols were sent out but beat a hasty withdrawal after engaging. Then, on 19 August, the 2nd Schutzpolizei Company of Limoges came to the rescue. Assisted by the Germans, the convoy continued east and crossed the gorges of Taurion. Once on the other bank, they parted ways. Just outside Bourganeuf, the *Milice* convoy was ambushed again, losing vehicles to mines and mortars, but de Vaugelas and Géromini forced their way through to the town which was held by a small German garrison. Their roles reversed, the *Miliciens* were

---

44    Sweets, *Choices in Vichy France*, p.96.

45    Pierre Aumont was born on 24 September 1912 in Marthon (department la Charente) but spent much of his childhood in Germany and became a military instructor for the Hitler Jugend. Considered a spy, he returned to France and did his military service. Mobilised in September 1939, he saw action and won the *Croix de guerre* with a citation *à l'ordre du regiment*. For a full biography of Aumont see Bouysse, *Français sous l'uniforme allemande partie II: Sous officiers & hommes du rang de la Waffen-SS*.

now able to render assistance to the Germans and beat off a maquis attack, but one third of their vehicles had been damaged or were in tow, which took days to repair. Together the *Miliciens* and the Germans set off. Finally, on 23 August, they arrived at Guéret. It had taken eight days to cover seventy kilometres.

'Toulouse' also had a narrow escape. On 10 August, de Perricot, the *chef régional* for 'Toulouse', sent messengers to the *chefs départmentaux* with orders to assemble. In the days that followed, his forces concentrated without serious incident. He then sent the women and children ahead by train under the command of Dr. Sailhant. The *Miliciens* set out by road with the Wehrmacht, SS and Gestapo.

Harassed from the air, dogged by delays and skirmishes, they came to Montpellier where de Perricot had the unpleasant surprise of finding the train that he had sent on its way from Toulouse days earlier. Although he did not have enough vehicles to take the women and children along, the Montpellier Red Cross agreed to give them protection. However, this protection was not extended to the *Miliciens* who stayed behind with the women and children. Dr. Sailhant and seven other *Miliciens* were shot days later.

The rest continued and reached the Rhône valley where the chaos only intensified. The *Milice* forces of 'Marseille' under the command of *chef régional* Dr. Durandy[46] were already there. They went north. Machine-gunned and bombed non-stop by allied aircraft, 'Toulouse' split. The smaller group under de Perricot proceeded on the right bank to Lyon. Finally, they arrived at Belfort.

On 15 August 1944, Méric of the *Franc-Garde permanente* Lot-et-Garonne evacuated the families by train to Toulouse. 'It was a definite departure, a departure for another dramatic phase of everyone's life', he said. The following day it was his turn to depart and also that of the two hundred men who had stayed loyal to their word. He was proud of them. They left in a motor convoy.

On 17 August 1944, on leaving Agen, the motor convoy from Chateau Ferron made for Saint-Jean-de-Thurac but came across several stopped vehicles. The road ahead was blocked by the maquis, who had positioned a barricade at a junction with a minor road which crossed the nearby Canal Latéral à La Garonne and railway line on the outskirts of Saint-Jean-de-Thurac.[47] Méric admits that the maquis had chosen their ground well. Without a moment to lose, he decided to take a *trentaine* along the roadside ditches, covered by another which was to manoeuvre along the hillside.

The *Miliciens* immediately drew heavy fire but kept moving forward and managed to knock out the machine gun mounted on a pickup lorry. After a firefight lasting some twenty minutes, the maquis hastily drove off across the canal bridge. The brief engagement cost the maquis five dead and four or five wounded, whereas three *Milicens* were lightly wounded.

Méric and his *section de pointe* quickly pushed onto the hamlet of Laspeyres two kilometers away, a death trap if ever there was one. However, all was good. They continued on the road to Lamagistère, where they ran into a *trentaine* from Montauban. Unbeknown to Méric, this

---

46   Appointed *Chef régional de la Milice* on 12 January 1944, Durandy ordered a number of maintenance of order operations, some of which were accompanied by the SIPO-SD or other occupation troops. (See Margot Tiphaigne & Jean-Marie Guillon, *Provence historique* – Fascicule 252, *La Milice française dans les Bouches-du-Rhône.*)
47   The barricade was sited where the D813 meets the D114.

*trentaine*, fearing that the convoy from Ferron might run into trouble at Saint-Jean-de-Thurac, came to lend a helping hand.

Returning to Saint-Jean-de-Thurac, Méric arranged for one of his subordinates to take the maquis wounded to the hospital in Agen and contact the authorities to ensure the dead received a decent burial. The *Milicen* convoy was soon on its way again and made it to Toulouse without any further incident. A memorial now stands at the site of the engagement on the outskirts of Saint-Jean-de-Thurac.[48]

On 17 August 1944, Bassompierre, the *Inspecteur général* for the North Zone, evacuated Paris. The following day, 18 August, *Capitaine* Tonneau, *chef de la 3e cohorte de la Franc-Garde*, received the order to evacuate Versailles. One last convoy left Paris on 22 August. 'Paris' was to withdraw directly to Nancy, which was accomplished without some of the difficulties encountered by the other regions. It continued onto Belfort. Some convoys were directed onto nearby Sennheim camp.[49]

On 9 August 1944, *Franc-Garde* Marotel evacuated Savoie for Lyon. Days before the departure, a friend of his father, a former officer, had approached them about joining the maquis, guaranteeing their security, but they refused; Marotel could not betray in this way his comrades and the German soldiers who were fighting, like them, against the same enemy. Moreover, he could not betray himself and his ideals![50] Marotel left with his brother and his stepfather. His parents, his fiancée and her mother chose to remain behind.

Marotel made it to Lyon without incident where he joined a *trentaine de sécurité* charged with the evacuation and protection of families of *Miliciens*. One night the *trentaine* was deployed to chateau de Vaugneray; intelligence had been received that the maquis intended to attack the families quartered at the chateau. The attack did not materialize, and the families were evacuated to another location which was easier to guard and protect.

Emboldened, the maquis continued to strike at the *Miliciens* holed up in Lyon. Not a day passed without an incident. Nevertheless, Marotel remained optimistic. His *trentaine* was now charged with the evacuation of the families by train to Dijon. The train journey was halted numerous times due to air raids, but eventually they reached their destination. Among the last to leave Dijon, he journeyed alone to Lure and then onto Belfort.

### *Épuration* begins

Not all *Miliciens* and family members managed to escape. Many were overtaken by the liberation, unleashing the intense hatred the *Milice* had provoked in the overwhelming majority of the population. The retribution was often swift and bloody. Many *Miliciens* and family members were arrested and summarily executed by the maquis or mobs. One *chef* of the FTP declared:

---

48  Accounts of this brief engagement at Saint-Jean-de-Thurac vary greatly. Most state that the *Miliciens* ambushed the maquis and some state that the *Miliciens* finished off the wounded maquis. However, no other account makes mention of the fact that Méric arranged for the wounded maquis to be taken to Agen. Importantly, when Méric was tried after the war, the president of the court quickly passed over the incident at Saint-Jean-de-Thurac, affirming that the roles of the maquis and *Milice* were perfectly known to him. The monument lists seven killed and eight wounded.

49  See Rentano & Leguérandais, *Ces Franciliens qui ont choisi Hitler*, pp.75-76.

50  Marotel was convinced that if had gone over to the maquis he would not have survived the purge.

We did not take *Milicien* prisoners, especially at the start. They were executed as soon as they were captured. When we entered Lyon we shot about thirty.

A combined German and *Milicien* force was encircled at Estivareilles. After a brief fight, it decided to surrender. The Germans were treated as POWs whereas *chef départemental* Le Tellier, his wife, and twenty *Miliciens* were shot. They went to their death singing *La Marseillaise*.

Some *Miliciens* stayed behind in Savoie, like Colonel Carli, the former *chef départmental du 5e service* (responsible for staffing) who was known to *Franc-garde* Émile Marotel and who had received assurances of safety from his ex-army colleagues, like the one who did not want to leave his seriously ill mother and like the one who left to find his wife. All were executed.[51]

Those *Miliciens* hauled before special tribunals, court martials or resistance courts were invariably and predictably sentenced to death and executed. When the *Milice* forces of 'Annecy' could not extricate themselves the *chef départemental* negotiated surrender terms with the *Résistance* who guaranteed that the *Miliciens* were to be treated as POWs. One hundred and thirty *Miliciens*, including a number of trainees from the *École des Cadres d'Uriage*, surrendered. Contrary to the resistance promise, the *Miliciens* were brought before a tribunal on which sat three members of the F.T.P. and two of the *Armée secrète*. Seventy-four of the *Miliciens* were condemned to death and the sentences were carried out on 24 August.

Suffice to say, one commentator considered it difficult to find a city or village 'where there were *Miliciens* and where *Miliciens* were not executed in August or September 1944'.[52]

## A man for all seasons

Darnand left Paris on 17 August 1944 with a small entourage and made his way to Nancy, and then travelled onto Belfort, arriving on 22 August. Belfort was soon crowded with *Milicens* and their families, collaborationists and Vichy officials. It became a hotbed of bitterly striving and opposing factions, some of them bent on selfish power. Political intrigue filled the air. Both Pétain and Laval showed that they considered themselves as prisoners of the Germans and refused further collaboration. To prevent the 'ultras' forming a government, Laval informed Pétain that he would not resign as premier.

Hitler now intervened and invited Laval and the 'ultras' to his military headquarters in East Prussia to discuss Franco-German relations. Laval refused the invitation but sent Paul Marion as an observer. Darnand accepted the invitation and found himself on a plane to East Prussia with Déat, Marion and Otto Abetz. De Brinon and Doriot made their way there separately.

Preliminary talks between the French 'ultras' and German Foreign Minister Ribbentrop lasted days. Ribbentrop made it clear that, in his opinion, Doriot should head the French government-in-exile, but de Brinon and Déat were against giving power to their personal enemy. De Brinon countered with the idea of setting up a 'delegation' to safeguard national interests as a 'mechanism for providing a smooth transition to a Doriot government'.[53] And of

51  Marotel, *La longue marche*, p.22. Carli was sentenced to forced labour for life on 13 November 1944 by the *cour de justice* of Chambéry but was kidnapped by the maquis while being transferred on 4 December 1944 and executed near La Motte-Servolex.
52  Delperrié de Bayac, *Histoire de la Milice*, p.553.
53  Dank, *The French against The French*, p.268.

course he could head such a delegation. Déat agreed to the idea of a delegation but planned to use it as means of taking power for himself. As for Darnand, he listened to what Ribbentrop, de Brinon, Déat and Doriot had to say. He had no interest in playing their political games but agreed all the same to support the delegation.

Finally, on 1 September, Hitler received the five French collaborationists. He spoke of his strong pacifist sentiments, his regret at having to go to war, the Bolshevik menace, the new weapons to be deployed shortly which would enable him to take the offensive and throw the Anglo-Saxons back into the sea, and that 'French patriots had understood the necessity of collaboration'.

Hitler congratulated Doriot on the courage he had shown on the Eastern Front. Turning to Darnand, he said: "The men of the *Milice* died for a great cause, and, like those at Stalingrad, they did not die in vain." After listening to the translation, Darnand thanked him. No more was said about the *Milice* or its future. Darnand, de Brinon and Marion returned to Belfort on 4 September.[54]

De Brinon formed his delegation, which was soon named a 'Commission'. Both Déat and Darnand were given jobs, but Darnand had more pressing concerns on his mind: his *Miliciens* needed money, petrol and tobacco. *Miliciens*, led by Darnand, raided a petrol station. Others emptied a tobacconist and a bank. Darnand still had need of a base to assemble his growing number of *Miliciens*.

Darnand and de Brinon visited nearby Sennheim camp. The visit caused uproar among the *Miliciens* as one of their number recalls:

> Darnand, dressed in SS uniform, gathered the Waffen-SS, leaving the *miliciens* on one side. Before leaving us he said to the assembled SS: "Soon, we'll come to reinforce you." There was excitement and a certain disorder among the Versailles group. Altercations took place between the *miliciens* and officers. Two days later, the Versailles group and others were disarmed on the orders of the Germans. For three days we were forced to hear conferences conducted by *commandant* d'Armor and a SS Major in order to persuade the *miliciens* to join the SS and the Kriegsmarine. Every evening we were shown propaganda films.[55]

Clearly, Darnand had already made a decision about the future employment of the *Milice*. Indeed, on 7 September, Gauleiter Wagner reported that Darnand intended, after eliminating those unfit for military service, to integrate the *Milice* as an elite troop into the Waffen-SS or with German agreement as an autonomous French unit.[56]

On 7 September, the *Miliciens* at Belfort were assembled and told they would be leaving, although no destination was given. They departed towards Mulhouse and were quartered in

---

54   See Delperrié de Bayac, *Histoire de la Milice*, pp.556-558.
55   See Rentano & Leguérandais, *Ces Franciliens qui ont choisi Hitler*, pp.75-76. The *Milicien* dates this visit to 1 September, which is unlikely, for on this day Darnand and de Brinon met Hitler in East Prussia. Moreover, the two of them only returned to Belfort on 4 September. This visit may have taken place on 6 September when Darnand met with SS-Ogruf. Hofmann and was told that Sennheim camp could not accommodate the *Milice* because of a lack of space.
56   The addressee is an unknown Obergruppenführer (see Mounine, *Cernay 40-45*, p.344).

surrounding villages. On 10 and 11 September, they were moved northwards via Colmar to camp Natzwiller-Struthof, near the city of Schirmeck.

There was great debate about the future. Many were those who now wanted to leave the *Milice*, but only thirty or so of their number slipped away from the camp. Some would reach the Swiss frontier, where they were interned and then quickly handed over to French justice, while others were captured by the German police on the roads of Alsace and shot on the spot as 'deserters'.

Each day the French flag was hoisted over the part of the camp occupied by the *Miliciens*. Darnand came to camp Struthof to take his *Milice* in hand. He started by reducing every officer to the ranks. Only those who had proved themselves received army ranks. In this way, some *chefs* fell into disgrace. Darnand was everywhere, bawling out those with incorrectly creased uniforms, those who could not properly present arms or those who looked sleepy-eyed. It was the guardhouse for those with a button missing or with dust in a rifle barrel.

**Into Germany**

One day, Darnand called together the *Miliciens* and announced to them that they were going to cross over into Germany and that their military training would continue under French command. He added that this crossing might not be final because the Reich was preparing a great offensive and the *Milice* would return to France with the Germans.[57] The reaction was mixed. For Marotel of the *Trentaine Alpine de Savoie de la Franc-Garde permanente*, exile was of no importance. In his words:

> The same fight still continued and the objective was the same as our enemies were still the same... Thus I had no moral problems or uncertainties.[58]

His only concern was for his loved ones he had left behind in France at the mercy of 'our enemies'.

On the evening of 19 September, the *Miliciens* left Struthof on foot and embarked at Schirmeck railway station.[59] They crossed the Rhine that same day. Marotel wrote that 'they were now in a friendly country' and that 'there were no more terrorists'.[60] To celebrate, they emptied their guns into the air. The crossing affected the normally unshakable optimist Méric, who wondered if he would ever cross back the other way and in what conditions. On the 22nd, they arrived at Ulm on the Danube.

The companies disembarked in good order and went to a barracks and various schools. The 3rd *Cohorte* (Lyon) under *Capitaine* de Bourmont was quartered in a school in the heart of the city. The re-organisation, started at Struthof, continued. Discipline was very strict. Training

57    Delperrié de Bayac, *Histoire de la Milice*, p.563. However, according to Voiron, *Historia N° 40, La Milice*, p.117, Darnand left each free to decide according to their conscience, but invited all to follow him.
58    Marotel, *La longue marche*, p.36.
59    Blanc, corrections to the author, 2001, who had particular cause to remember this day well. This corrects Mabire who wrote that the *Miliciens* went over to Germany on 21 September (*La Division Charlemagne*, p.107).
60    Marotin, *La longue marche*, p.36.

resumed. Endless arms drills, parades, route marches and manoeuvres. *Jurys d'honneur* were set up to decide the cases of those *Miliciens* who 'had gone too far'. Some left the *Milice* before they were expelled.

Marotel was promoted to Sergeant, one of the few appointments made in Germany, and proudly recalls that the papers were signed by the hand of Darnand. This earned him the comical and mocking nickname of *Sergent de Darnand*! Marotel remembers that the local population adopted them and made them feel as if they were still *chez nous*.

Around 5,000 *Miliciens*, mostly *franc-gardes*, were finally assembled at Ulm. For the most part, all still remained fiercely loyal to Darnand. At their head was Jean Bassompierre. A *Milicien* through and through, he too was devoted to Darnand.

A *Franc-Garde Cohorte* of several hundred *Miliciens* under de Vaugelas was sent to Sigmaringen rather than Ulm. This *Cohorte* comprised those *Miliciens* that their *chef* had extricated from the maquis infested Limousin. Its mission at Sigmaringen, the seat of exiled French collaboration, was to uphold 'the armed presence of the *Milice* beside Marshal Pétain'.[61]

On 1 October 1944, Pétain refused to attend the raising of the tricolore over this French refuge and opted to stay in his bedroom. All the same, the ceremony went ahead with an honour guard partly supplied by the *Franc-Garde Cohorte*. Pétain had turned his back on the *Milice*. In turn, the *Miliciens* began to turn their back on their idol. Later, Pétain refused to allow a platoon of *Miliciens* to pay him tribute as he came and went from his chateau. He also refused to be guarded by them.

## Work or fight?

What now for the *Miliciens* who found themselves in exile? Since their arrival at Ulm, rumour had it that all fighting Frenchmen were to be amalgamated in a special unit. Darnand and other French *chefs collaborateurs* met several times with SS officers at Ulm to discuss the creation of what was to become 'Charlemagne'.[62]

At the end of September 1944, Darnand and SS-Ogruf. Berger of the SS-Hauptamt held preliminary discussions about the future of the *Milice*. Darnand was accompanied by his friend Henry Charbonneau who was of the opinion that the best course of action for the *Miliciens* was to enlist in the Waffen-SS and to go and fight the Reds on the Eastern Front.

Although Darnand and Berger had met several times before, Darnand was not at ease. He wished to keep the *Milice* intact for a future role when France was reconquered, but he realised that his *Miliciens* could not escape some form of mobilisation. And if or when his *Milice* disappeared, he would lose his trump card, in fact his only playing card.

Darnand was also concerned about the predominance of Doriot, his political rival. Although Berger assured Darnand that Doriot would have no role in the new French unit of the Waffen-SS, there was no mention of what his might be, if any.

Indeed, the meeting resolved little. Nevertheless, Darnand came away from the meeting certain that 'on entering the Waffen-SS, the *Miliciens* would not have to wear the runes on their

61  Mabire, *La Division Charlemagne*, p.117.
62  Eyewitness account of André Doutart who acted as an interpreter at the meetings (Mounine, correspondence to the author, 1999). Doutart did not date these meetings, though.

uniforms, but an emblem created especially for them: a sword of *Jeanne d'Arc* surrounded with two *fleurs de lys*.[63]

Beset by doubts, Darnand continued to hesitate about enlisting the *Miliciens* in the Waffen-SS.[64] In early October 1944, when Brigf. Krukenberg received Darnand in Berlin, the real negotiations about the future of the *Milice* began. They would last weeks.

Brigf. Krukenberg announced to Darnand that RF-SS Himmler had decided to call this new French unit 'Charlemagne' and that the 'Frenchmen would not wear the SS insignia on their collar patch, but a sword like that of *Jeanne d'Arc*'.[65]

Darnand pressed for an answer about his future role in this new unit and also that of Doriot. The Germans could reassure him that Doriot would not be dominant in 'Charlemagne' and that Obf. Puaud was its commander.[66] However, this did not satisfy Darnand who suspected Puaud of being in league with Doriot.

On Saturday 7 and Sunday 8 October 1944, Darnand had discussions with Brigf. Krukenberg. In a letter to Reichsführer Himmler, Darnand wrote that the following 'questions of organisation' had now been agreed:[67]

- The name of the Brigade was 'Charlemagne'.
- The badge was the sword of Joan of Arc.
- [*Milicien*] Officers and NCOs to be accepted into the Waffen-SS with the rank they held in the French Army.
- The political and social committees of the LVF and Waffen-SS to be dissolved and that, in future, the questions within their domain he would settle as *Secrétaire d'Etat*

---

63    Roch, *La Division Charlemagne*, p.29. However, of note is that Mabire and Delperrié de Bayac also write of this same meeting, but do not confirm that Darnand came away with this understanding. According to Mabire, *La Division Charlemagne*, p.122, Darnand wanted his *Miliciens* to wear another device other than that of the SS runes, but that device is not specified.

64    Indeed, according to Delperrié de Bayac, *Histoire de la Milice*, p.567, there was never any question of the *Milice* going over en bloc to the Waffen-SS!

65    Delperrié de Bayac, *Histore de la Milice*, p.568. Note the use of the word Frenchmen rather than *Miliciens*. Thus, the possibility exists that the collar patch of the 'sword of Joan of Arc' may not have been only intended for former *Miliciens* in 'Charlemagne'. And yet, according to Littlejohn, *Foreign Legions of the Third Reich volume 1*, p.172, 'Brigf. Krukenberg met Darnand's objections that his *Miliciens*, many of whom were devout Catholics, would refuse to wear the pagan runes of the SS, by saying they would not be called upon to do so but would have instead a sword like that of Joan of Arc'. This suggests that the collar patch of the 'sword of Joan of Arc' was only intended for former *Miliciens* in 'Charlemagne'.

66    Curiously, according to Delperrié de Bayac, *Histore de la Milice*, p.568, the Germans indicated that 'Charlemagne' *would be* [author's italics] commanded by *Colonel* Puaud. [Mabire and Roch repeat as much at the meeting Himmler had with Darnand later.] In response to this, Puaud received the command of 'Charlemagne' as early as August. And that is, at least, one month before these negotiations! Also, Puaud held the Waffen-SS rank of Oberführer and the equivalent French Army rank of Oberführer is not that of *Colonel*.

67    Letter of 14 October 1944 from SS-Stf. Wagner to Dr. Brandt of the Personalstab RF-SS that reproduced and commented on the undated letter from Darnand to Himmler. Regarding the letter from Darnand to Himmler, Roch dates it after the meeting between Darnand and Himmler (see *La Division Charlemagne*, p.30). However, the author believes that Darnand wrote it before he was called to meet Himmler; at their meeting, Himmler dropped the idea of the 'sword of Joan of Arc' (Delperrié de Bayac, *Histore de la Milice*, p.568).

*à l'Intérieur* and in his capacity as a member of the *commission gouvernementale française chargée de l'organisation des forces françaises nationales.*

They also agreed that the time was not right to form a pure *Milice* regiment because it might ignite the political differences. The idea of a pure *Milice* regiment was, in fact, that of Himmler. To Darnand and Krukenberg, the simplest solution seemed to maintain the two existing regiments, expand them to three battalions and divide the members of the *Milice* among the different units.

In the same letter, Darnand recognised that *Général* Puaud would command within the framework of a wholly independent military hierarchy while he 'would exercise his authority in agreement with Brigf. Krukenberg within the framework of his domain of political and social points of view over the French command of the unit'.

Of interest to note is that Darnand refers to himself again and again in no other role than that of a politician. Soon after this letter, Darnand was received by RF-SS Himmler at his headquarters at Birkenwald. The meeting lasted two hours.

RF-SS Himmler spoke about the military situation, the secret weapons and assured Darnand that the 'V' weapons would not be used against Paris. He then questioned Darnand on the strength and motives of the various collaborationist political parties. He wanted to know the number of militants Doriot had with him in Germany. They spoke of Déat and his RNP, and Bucard and his *francistes*. Himmler then questioned him on the causes that had led to the failure of the collaborationist parties. Darnand was of the opinion that the collaborationist parties had failed because, in the eyes of Frenchmen, they appeared as 'movements in the pay of the occupier, in close collaboration with the Gestapo' and thus of rather little national character. Darnand could only see a movement gaining public support if it were purely French.

Himmler recognised that the Germans had made political mistakes in France and was critical of the lack of understanding shown by the German Ministry of Foreign Affairs and the German ambassador in Paris. He declared that, in agreement with Hitler, he was prepared to support a purely national French movement which would keep its independence, its propaganda, its press, its radio and which would have sufficient broadness of outlook to assemble the Frenchmen in Germany and the opponents in France.[68] Then they came to the *Milice*.

Himmler remarked that the *Miliciens* could not remain 'unoccupied' and presented Darnand with the following solution, perhaps better described as an ultimatum: one third of the *Miliciens* would have to enlist in 'Charlemagne'; another third, the oldest and those unfit for military service, would have to go to work in the factories of the Reich; and the last third were to remain in the *Franc-Garde* and form an autonomous unit.[69] As for the women and children of the *Miliciens*, these 'guests of the Reich' would be found accommodation with German families or in camps such as Siessen or Neckargmund.

Himmler then assured Darnand that the Frenchmen of 'Charlemagne' would remain under French command, have a French chaplain and never fight against the Western powers. He

---

68    Cited from an unpublished document by Darnand appearing in *Historia N° 40, La Milice, la collaboration en uniforme* and in Delperrié de Bayac, *Histoire de la Milice*, pp.568-569. Of note is that although word for word the two quotes are not the same, they do convey a similar message.

69    The *Miliciens* of the *Franc-Garde* unit were permitted to keep their French uniform, their French arms, their French flag, their French *chefs* and their French cadres.

announced that they would now wear a tricolore shoulder badge and not the 'sword of Joan of Arc'.[70] Without any real bargaining power, Darnand had little other choice than to 'admit defeat' and accept the solution put to him.

In closing, Himmler declared that Darnand was (or could be) 'the right man for the job' despite his strong nationalism. 'He pronounced the name of Doriot and differentiated between the politicians and those who fight. After Spring, only those who fight will be valuable...'[71] Moments later, Himmler said his last words and brought the meeting to an end.

Darnand returned to Ulm. He was disappointed; Himmler had made him no promises about his own future. Now, more than ever before, he was convinced that his revolutionary *Miliciens* would end up under the control of Doriot and his PPF cadres in 'Charlemagne'. He had lost all or so he thought.

Days later, Berger invited Darnand to Berlin. Over dinner, in the company of Krukenberg, Berger promised Darnand the role of political leader in 'Charlemagne'. He added:

> Thanks to your action within the Brigade, as well as thanks to your position close to all Frenchmen at present in Germany, I hope the brigade will soon become a division. Then we will create other divisions. In this way, your soldiers will have contributed to meriting the predominant place your country has always had in Europe.[72]

Alarmed, Krukenberg intervened and explained that, for him, politics and military questions did not mix. Berger cut him short, saying that he knew what he was doing and that his decisions matched the thinking of Himmler. Overjoyed, Darnand warmly thanked Berger. Now he had to face his *Miliciens* and sell them the least unfavourable solution.

On 23 October 1944, the *Miliciens* packed into a cinema at Ulm. *Chef* of the *Milice* Robert spoke first. He explained why 'Charlemagne' was forming and why a 'unification of all revolutionary French forces at present in Germany was necessary'. Alfonsi followed him. He spoke of the necessity of both a military and a political role for the *Milice*. Then Darnand spoke.

Darnand announced that 'after careful consideration' all *Miliciens* capable of bearing arms were to be enrolled into the French unit of the Waffen-SS, adding that 'only volunteers will be accepted'. He appealed to their spirit of *catholique et français toujours* when he spoke of their conditions of service: not only would they serve under French commanders, but they would be permitted to wear the tricolore badge, and they would be ministered by Catholic chaplains. He assured: "Under no circumstances will this French unit fight on the Western Front." Then he explained:

---

70    Delperrié de Bayac, *Histoire de la Milice*, p.568. However, according to Mabire, *La Division Charlemagne*, p.123, Himmler assured Darnand that his *Miliciens* would wear the tricolore badge but did not announce that the collar badge of the 'sword of Joan of Arc' had been dropped. And, curiously, the appearance of the 'sword of Joan of Arc' on the map of collar and sleeve insignia for foreign volunteers produced in February 1945 by the SS Propaganda Department would seem to suggest that it was not dropped.
71    Cited from an unpublished document by Darnand, *Historia N° 40, La Milice, la collaboration en uniforme*. According to Mabire, *La Division Charlemagne*, p.124, Himmler is reported as saying: "We will win the war. And only those who fight will have the right to speak."
72    Delperrié de Bayac, *Histoire de la Milice*, p.570.

We cannot live like layabouts in a Germany at war against Communism and plutocracy. Our duty is to fight or work… We fought in France. We will fight again by the side of the German armies against the same enemies.

Darnand pledged to continue the fight at their head and evoked sacrifice: "If need be, we will die together". He warned them that they must be ready for the political tasks that lay ahead on their return to France. He needed them to have strength and doctrine. Bitterly, he concluded: "The French people must understand that by your discipline and your faith you have been servants of your homeland".

When Darnand finished, his *Miliciens* stood up to a man and replied by striking up the *Chant de la Milice* with a fervour that brought tears to the eyes:

> *Kneeling, we take the oath*
> *Miliciens, to die singing*
> *If need be for the new France*
> *In love with glory and grandeur*
> *All united by the same fervour*
> *We swear to remake France:*
> *Kneeling, we take the oath*

Darnand sang along with his *Miliciens*. Moved, he did not attempt to hide his emotion. Once the meeting was over the *Miliciens* headed to a stadium for a parade organised by Bassompierre, the master of ceremonies. Darnand reviewed his *Miliciens* for the last time. The *Miliciens* shouted out the *Chant des Adieux* [Goodbye Song] before falling out. Then, with a tricolore flag at their head, they paraded through the streets of the city.

There was much discussion about Darnand's announcement. The reaction was mixed. Some were enthusiastic. Many volunteered.[73] Many hesitated. Many were volunteered. Some protested.

Like most of his comrades, Robert Blanc of the Paris *Franc-Garde* was enthusiastic about entering the Waffen-SS. Darnand's announcement came as little surprise to him. There had already been talk of passing to the Waffen-SS. He had been hesitant, but that was before Jacques de Lafaye, one of the *chefs* of the Paris unit, took him to meet French Waffen-SS officers Fenet and Bonnefoy over dinner at Hotel Bahnhof. The enthusiasm and spirit with which they evoked the battles of the Sturmbrigade in the Carpathians, the feats of their men, and the Waffen-SS in general removed his scruples of a family nature, which had stopped him from leaving much earlier for the Eastern Front. His father, an *officier de réserve des deux guerres* for whom he felt great respect and affection, had asked him never to wear the German uniform. In addition, he 'had no wish to lag behind his comrades'.[74] Of his *trentaine*, on which no pressure was exerted, only three or four refused to enlist.

---

73    Various authors have stated various reasons for volunteering. According to Mabire, *La Division Charlemagne*, p.158, 'the overwhelming desire to remain together and not to abandon the struggle swept away the last doubts.' According to de la Mazière, *Ashes of Honour*, p.52, most of the young *franc-gardes* and their officers choose to be assimilated into the Waffen-SS because of their loyalty to their *chef*, Darnand.

74    Blanc, letter to the author, 14/6/2001.

The *3e Cohorte* under *Capitaine* de Bourmont volunteered for the Waffen-SS almost to a man. However, many were not so willing to volunteer. They wanted to fight but were not prepared to don the German uniform. Over and over again at meetings, Darnand and other leading *chefs* of the *Milice* attempted to sell the Waffen-SS. German officers spoke to them of the terrible new weapons that were reducing London to dust and that would ultimately guarantee them victory. Frenchmen of the former LVF and the Sturmbrigade came and extolled to them the merits and advantages of German military organisation. These efforts reaped little reward, though.[75]

On 30 October, Pierre Cance, Darnand's 'right-hand man' wounded at the head of the 1st Battalion of the Sturmbrigade in Galicia, appealed to young Frenchmen in *la France* (a collaborationist *journal*) 'to practise their politics on the battlefield'.

Jean-Pierre Lefèvre of the Paris *Franc-Garde* wrote a letter to *Capitaine* Moneuse explaining that he did not wish to go over to the Waffen-SS because of religious as well as patriotic reasons.[76] *Capitaine* Moneuse ripped up his letter and replied that it was the SS or striped pyjamas. After that, he signed on the dotted line as a volunteer.[77] He did not consider himself a volunteer but as mobilised![78]

Ordered to volunteer, *Franc-garde* Noël Cornu of the *école des cadres de la Milice* at La Chapelle en Serval obeyed.[79] For him, an order was an order. And an order was to be obeyed.

Jules Dissent of the *Milice de Poitiers* greeted the prospect of transferring to the Waffen-SS with little enthusiasm. Although it was a question of amalgamating Frenchmen from various units into one, he still had no wish to volunteer. Before leaving France, his father had told him: "Do what you're told, but don't volunteer." In this way, he let the forthcoming medical decide his destiny. Though a little short-sighted, he was declared fit for military service.

The thirty-five-year-old *chef-adjoint de la Milice de Poitiers*, who was known to Dissent, was not declared fit for military service because of a hernia and was sent to Heuberg camp where he joined the autonomous *Franc-Garde* unit.[80]

To those that protested, Darnand said:[81] "What I cannot obtain through discipline and loyalty, I can obtain through force." One by one most succumbed and fell into line. *Franc-Garde* Marcel Philippon refused to enlist in the Waffen-SS and was put in prison for eight days, where he met a member of the PPF who, on his release, handed him a pass to go to the PPF camp at

75    According to Delperrié de Bayac, *Histoire de la Milice*, p.575, volunteers were few. Whereas, according to Mabire, *La Division Charlemagne*, p.157, 'the number of volunteers for the SS remained sizeable'.

76    Born on 7th April 1925, Jean-Pierre Lefèvre joined the *Milice* in 1944. He served first with the Paris *Franc-Garde* and later in the two *Centaines* sent to Dijon that summer. His rank was *chef de dizaine*. As such, he did not serve in the *cinquième cohorte* 'Dijon' as stated by Delperrié de Bayac, *Histoire de la Milice*, p.605.

77    No *Milicien* would end up in a concentration camp as a result of refusing to 'volunteer' for the Waffen-SS, but the threat was probably all too real.

78    According to Mabire, *La Division Charlemagne*, p.159, Jean-Pierre Lefèvre was 'one of the most hostile' to the transfer to the Waffen-SS. As such, this is not correct. Yes, he was hostile, but not 'hostile enough' to be expelled from the Division.

79    Cornu was also a member of the Vichy *Équipes Nationales* composed of young volunteers who were to protect and help those civilians threatened or touched by war. See Lambert and Le Marec, *Organisations, mouvements et unités de l'état français, Vichy 1940-1944*, pp.233-246.

80    At the end of war he managed to cross back into France and enlisted in the Foreign Legion, serving five years, two in Indo-China. He would marry the sister of Jules Dissent.

81    Delperrié de Bayac, *Histoire de la Milice*, p.576.

Neustadt. He spent the rest of the war working for the PPF. Ironically he had been a member of the rival RNP since April 1941.

## The story of de Jean Chatrousse

*Chef de trentaine* Chatrousse went across to the Waffen-SS without protest. For him, 'the Waffen-SS was the only means of fighting against Bolshevism in October 1944'. Nevertheless, he was deeply unhappy that he would have to don the German uniform!

Born in Morocco in July 1921, Jean Chatrousse spent his childhood in this French protectorate where his father was an official in Native Affairs. In late September 1939, he attended the military academy of La Flèche where he made friends with Michel de Genouillac who sat next to him in the classroom and whose bed was next to his in the dormitory. They had much in common; a passion for horse-riding was but one of their shared interests. [This was the beginning of a friendship that would last some fifty years].

The *débâcle* of June 1940 distressed Chatrousse deeply. Thenceforth he bore a grudge against the Germans who had defeated and occupied his beloved France. But, by the same token, he raged at those French people responsible for the defeat: the members of Parliament, the Popular Front government, as well the Jews and the Freemasons. Also, he was fiercely critical of the British for their retreat from the Somme and their selfishness during the battle of Dunkirk. Continued British aggression at Mers-el-Kébir, then at Dakar and later in Syria only served to compound his Anglophobia. In defeat Chatrousse continued to study at Valence, then at Algiers, for the entrance examinations to the *École Spéciale militaire de Saint-Cyr*.

Finally, in 1942, Chatrousse gained admittance to Saint-Cyr where he met again his good friend de Genouillac. His attendance at Saint-Cyr was brief, coming to an abrupt end by its closure in November 1942 after the German occupation of the Free Zone and the subsequent disbandment of the Armistice Army. Demobilisation would have left him at a loose end if it were not for de Genouillac who invited him back to his parents. Weeks later, he left to try and reach North Africa via Spain. He did not get through, narrowly avoiding arrest and deportation. Where to now? Having learnt that de Genouillac was with the *Chantiers de la Jeunesse* in Haute-Savoie, he joined him. It was July 1943. For the time being, he felt at home in this patriotic and *marechaliste* [supporting the Marshal and the National Revolution] organisation, which was never actively collaborationist, but more often anti-German.

At the end of 1943, Chatrousse decided to enlist in the *Franc-Garde* of the *Milice française*. He enlisted out of a love for France and a sincere hatred for Communism. He was disgusted by the blind bombardments of the Allies that claimed more French than German victims, and also by the cowardly acts of murder perpetrated in the name of the 'Resistance'. Thus, for him, the *Franc-Garde* was the best way of fighting the Communist peril aided and encouraged by the Allies.

Appointed *chef de trentaine*, Chatrousse was posted to Rouen in Normandy where he remained from May to August 1944. His role, above all, was that of an instructor and a recruiter. In this way, the *Trentaine* of the *Franc-Garde de Normandie* became a *Centaine* whose command went to Chatrousse and with it promotion to *chef de centaine*. Life as a *franc-garde* was perilous and Chatrousse counted himself lucky when an assassin's bullet missed him one day on stepping outside of his home.

His *Centaine,* which hated the Germans occupying France as much as the Allies bombarding her, did not participate in any Maintenance of Order operations for the simple reason that there were few, or no, maquis in Normandy. But the *franc-gardes* of his *Centaine* were occupied with helping the victims of the Allied bombardments and guarding the partly destroyed houses against theft. In this way, after an air attack, his unit prevented the sacking of the office of the *Banque de France* in Rouen.

At the beginning of August, Chatrousse received permission to go on leave to Paris, but during his absence his *Centaine* was ordered to withdraw to Paris. By chance, Chatrousse met one of his *franc-gardes* who filled him in. Chatrousse was indignant; this order to withdraw smacked of flight.

In Paris, through a female associate living where he was staying, Chatrousse and a good friend, de la Mazière, met with two rather mysterious men.[82] They explained that the Allied staff was concerned about the Communist-inspired elements in the Resistance which might start fighting for Paris before receiving any order. In this way, 'the Communists could seize power and proclaim France a socialist republic'. As the Paris police were due to go on strike, the Allies were now in need of 'convinced anti-Communists' to intervene and oppose the Communists if they were to act in the way feared.

Chatrousse was then questioned about his activities and ideals. As though satisfied, the two men asked him if he would continue the fight against Communism on the Allied side! And then they asked him if he could persuade the *Miliciens* under him, described to him as an important force, to rally to the Allied side in the name of anti-Communism! He answered yes and yes. A meeting-place was arranged. Their guests left.

Thereupon, Chatrousse contacted about forty of his *franc-gardes* and asked them to assemble at a predetermined time in la place de la Concorde, Paris, at the foot of the statue of the city of Rouen. His men agreed to follow him without explanation. But one of them had no confidence in Chatrousse and informed the *État-major de la Franc Garde* of Chatrousse's plan to desert with part of the *centaine de Normandie.* Denounced, the *coup de main* was now doomed to failure.

When de Chatrousse's armed *franc-gardes* arrived at the place de la Concorde they were intercepted by the Germans summoned by some *Milice* commanders. As for Chatrousse, one of his *franc-gardes* managed to join him and warned him of the danger. He then telephoned the *chef* of the *cohorte de la Franc Garde* to which he belonged. The *chef de cohorte* agreed to release and exculpate Chatrousse's men provided that he came to him and explained himself, which he did.

The meeting with his superior proved stormy. Considering himself offended by the insulting words of his superior, Chatrousse slapped him in the face. Consequently, he was arrested and imprisoned.

Brought before a court martial, Chatrousse was sentenced to death by Bassompierre who did not even give him an opportunity to explain his point of view. No less a person than President Laval saved him from the execution squad; notified by some of Chatrousse's friends, Laval intervened and gave the order to have him released. It was Raybaud who received the order to release him and also to listen to him. At the end of the conversation, Chatrousse was free to

---

82    Little is known about these two men, although de la Mazière recounts that they were from London. See de la Mazière, *Ashes of Honour,* pp.22-25.

leave the *Milice française* or continue. With bad grace, he agreed to continue, saying: "With this departure, we're taking the way to Germany and we're leaving the way free to the Communists to take power in France." Moreover, he had no wish to abandon his men.

Thus, *chef de centaine* Chatrousse returned to his unit that had actually been preparing to liberate him by force. Weakened by desertions, the *Franc-Garde de Normandie* was amalgamated with some *franc-gardes de Bretagne* to become the *Centaine de la Franc-Garde de Normandie-Bretagne*. The retreat began.

At a barracks near Nancy, Chatrousse received a visit from Darnand who asked him about the morale of his men. In response he stated that it was not good and then evoked the 'affair' of la place de la Concorde, even remarking that Darnand had put the *Milice* under the Germans' control. At no point did Darnand say anything, but Dr. Rainsart, his *adjoint*, also present, later made Chatrousse pay for his outburst: Chatrousse found himself transferred from his unit and demoted to *chef de trentaine*. In Germany, Chatrousse was approached about returning to France as a saboteur. This he refused, preferring to fight Bolshevism as a soldier in uniform.

The medical examination before SS doctors followed. Physical fitness was demanded. Some were rejected.[83] Vilbert of the Paris *Franc-Garde* sent to Dijon, who had been seriously wounded in 1940, was refused. He cried with rage.

The number of *Miliciens* who 'volunteered' for the Waffen-SS is now considered to be 1,800, of which 300 were 'sent back' at a later date.[84] Thus, some 1,500 former *Miliciens* went on to serve in 'Charlemagne'. With them were their battle proven leaders of de Vaugelas, Bassompierre, Raybaud, de Bourmont, de Londaiz, Dr. Durandy, Géromini and de Perricot, but there were also a greater number of more elderly and less active leaders.

Of those *Miliciens* left 'unemployed', some one thousand became workers and some 700 to 800 – the youngest, the oldest, the physically unfit and the politically unreliable - were sent to Heuberg camp, near Sigmaringen, and formed into a battalion.

83   According to Mabire, *La Division Charlemagne*, p.157, those who did not want to enter the Waffen-SS could find the sympathetic ear of a French doctor.
84   Mounine and Lefèvre, correspondence to the author, 1997 and 1998, Bayle, *San and Persante*, p.125 and Bouysse (*Waffen-SS Français volume 2*). Different authors, however, have stated different figures; 2,000 (Mabire and Bassompierre); 2,500 (Saint-Loup, Delpierré de Bayac, Voiron and de la Mazière).

## *Miliciens* arrive at Wildflecken

On 4 November 1944, after parading through the streets of Ulm for the last time, shouting out German military songs, *Milice* recruits for the Waffen-SS embarked at Neu-Ulm railway station. The following day, they arrived at Brückenau railway station, disembarked, reassembled, and marched off to the camp of Wildflecken.[85] They went into barracks.[86]

The *Miliciens* received a cool welcome. The Frenchmen attired in German uniforms ridiculed the *Miliciens* because they were dressed as French soldiers and had a tendency to brandish at the slightest thing their pistols and submachine-guns.[87] They told them that they looked like gangsters and cowboys. As for the *Miliciens*, 'they felt ill-at-ease by the appearance of Frenchmen in German uniforms that looked more German than the Germans'.[88]

The *Miliciens* crossed swords with the camp staff after switching the dormitory pictures of Hitler, which they moved to a quiet corner and turned face down, with those of their leaders, Darnand or even Marshal Pétain. Aghast when they discovered this switch, the camp staff told the *Miliciens* to remove their offending French flags and 'decorations'. The *Miliciens* replied with threats that they would 'give them what for' if they tried to touch them. The camp staff prudently beat a hasty retreat.[89]

Two days after the arrival of the *Miliciens*, they were brought to Adolf Hitler Platz. The whole brigade was already assembled there. New recruits were sworn in and decorations were awarded. Blanc of the Paris *Franc-Garde* was struck by 'the scale and the reverence of the ceremonial as well as by the look of our comrades'.

85    Delpierré de Bayac, *Histoire de la Milice*, p.577, and de la Mazière, *Ashes of Honour*, p.52. However, according to Mabire, *La Division Charlemagne*, p.166, as though in quarantine, the *Miliciens* waited several days near Brückenau railway station before making their entrance into Wildflecken. Marotin, a *franc-garde* who volunteered for the Waffen-SS, agrees that there was a delay before they entered Wildflecken. In his memoirs he wrote (see *La longue marche*, p.45): 'Here we are billeted in wood huts at the foot of the mountain crowned by Wildflecken... The *franc-gardes* grow impatient. Now that the step is crossed, the decision is taken, they crave action and find it hard to understand this inaction.' In response to this, *franc-garde* Blanc cannot recall any such wait at Brückenau. Moreover, *chef* Raybaud, in his letter to Mabire of 3/11/74, cannot recall any such 'quarantine', or even a period of some days, spent outside the camp. Nevertheless, the possibility exists that part of the *Franc-Garde* was stationed at Brückenau for a number of days.

86    According to Rostaing, *Le prix d'un serment*, p.152, the *Miliciens* made their way through the camp to Adolf Hitler Platz, where they formed a square and defiantly struck up *la Marseillaise*. Brigf. Krukenberg looked on phlegmatically. Beside him was his German shepherd. However, in response to this, Robert Blanc, who arrived at Wildflecken with the *Milice*, does not recall going direct to Adolf Hitler Platz nor having sung there *la Marseillaise* (letter to the author, 2001), but added that *la Marseillaise* may have been sung out of his earshot.

87    According to Mabire, *La Division Charlemagne*, p.166, veterans of the Sturmbrigade and the LVF viewed with contempt those who only had known the Army of the defeat and the *Milice* of the civil war. Indeed, according to Krukenberg, quoted from Bayle, *De Marseille à Novossibirsk*, p.154, because of Darnand's activity as *chef de la Police de Vichy*, they feared that the presence of the *Miliciens* would tarnish the reputation of those who had volunteered to fight only Bolshevism in the East. Such sentiments, however, remain unsubstantiated (various letters to the author).

88    Delperrié de Bayac, *Histoire de la Milice*, p.578.

89    Saint-Loup, *Les Hérétiques*, p.150.

Although drafted into the Waffen-SS, the *Miliciens* were still required to swear an oath of loyalty to Hitler. Brigade headquarters agreed that Sunday 12 November 1944 was as good as any other day to conduct the ceremony. Anticipating a wave of indiscipline, Krukenberg ordered the formation of a penal platoon officered by those 'chosen for their parentage with certain ruminants'.[90]

## Enter Darnand and Cance

On 11 November 1944, Joseph Darnand arrived unannounced at Wildflecken in the uniform of a Sturmbannführer of the Waffen-SS.[91] He had come to take up his political role in 'Charlemagne' and attend the swearing-in of his *Miliciens* into the Waffen-SS. A secretary asked him for his *Soldbuch*.[92] This he did not have. The secretary explained to him that he could not be admitted into 'Charlemagne' without the appropriate paperwork. Darnand then asked for a room and a bed while the matter was cleared up. This was refused for the same reasons. Darnand got all the angrier. Informed of Darnand's arrival, Brigf. Krukenberg appeared. Undoubtedly, Krukenberg had calculated this confrontation.

Darnand declared: "I am a French Secretary of State and I ask for respect." Krukenberg replied: "Excuse me, I thought you were Sturmbannführer Joseph Darnand who has come to take his command. If you are Secretary of State Darnand, come."[93]

Krukenberg did not take his 'guest' to the officers' mess but to his personal villa outside the camp. Dinner was served during which Krukenberg fell over himself to be polite to Darnand, addressing him repeatedly as 'Mr. Secretary of State'.

Brigf. Krukenberg bluntly put it to Darnand that there was no political role or command for him in 'Charlemagne'. However, to reassure Darnand, Krukenberg confirmed that Doriot, Darnand's political rival, would also have no political role and no command in the brigade and that he would not even be coming to Wildflecken. Moreover, Doriot had drafted a letter to his militants asking them to refrain from political activity within the brigade and to do their duty as soldiers. Krukenberg then requested Darnand to do likewise.

Shortly after this tête-à-tête, Krukenberg recounted to *Capitaine* Renault, the French liaison officer to the German Inspection:

> Darnand was very annoyed when I announced to him that there was no question of him receiving any command in 'Charlemagne' or even of serving in it. He asked me if at least Pierre Cance could have an important command. I refused. We'd managed to eliminate Doriot. There was no question of accepting Darnand in the Waffen-SS. We've had enough of the political quarrels from the Frenchmen. We want soldiers, not party leaders.[94]

90  Memoirs of Soulat.
91  It should be noted that many sources state quite categorically that Darnand never donned the field-grey.
92  Mabire, *La Division Charlemagne*, p.173. Curiously, according to Delperrié de Bayac, *Histoire de la Milice*, p.579, the secretary asked Darnand for his 'certificate of cessation of pay'.
93  Delperrié de Bayac, *Histoire de la Milice*, p.579.
94  Delperrié de Bayac, *Histoire de la Milice*, p.580.

Years later, Brigf. Krukenberg reflected that Darnand took this rebuff better than he expected.

Despite his great disappointment at having lost the best elements of the *Milice* to the Waffen-SS with little to show in return, Darnand chose to stay on for the ceremony next morning at which his *Miliciens* would be sworn into the Waffen-SS.[95]

Pierre Cance, Darnand's former assistant, also came to Wildflecken for the swearing-in ceremony of the *Miliciens*.[96] Brigf. Krukenberg greatly feared his return. He was all too aware that Cance was still a close friend of Darnand and still politically pre-occupied, but he could not readily exclude him without offending the former *encadrement* of the *Milice française* and also that of the French Sturmbrigade. Cance, who had been wounded in Galicia at the head of the 1st Battalion of the Sturmbrigade, now held the rank of Sturmbannführer and, while convalescing at Sigmaringen, was appointed to command Waffen-Gren. Regt der SS 57. Thus, Krukenberg trod lightly. Cance said of his reception:

> I saw Krukenberg who invited me to dine with de Vaugelas. Krukenberg told me that he had no job for me and that I was expelled from the Brigade. Why? He believed that if I received the order to fight in the west, I might desert. I had a feeling of total uselessness. Krukenberg said that I was not physically fit to exercise a command. I had actually been wounded with the Sturmbrigade, but I had recovered. The following morning I went and had a medical examination and, as if by chance, I was declared unfit.[97]

The doctor who carried out the medical examination and declared Cance unfit was Stubaf. Schlegel of the German Inspection. Undoubtedly, the German doctor was 'under the influence' of Krukenberg to declare Cance unfit because of his serious knee injury received in Galicia. Thus, with the greatest of tact, Krukenberg had got his way again. Cance was, of course, disappointed. He went on to become an instructor at annex Neweklau of SS-Junkerschule Kienschlag. His pupils were not French, but Latvian, Estonian and Wallonie.

95  Delperrié de Bayac, *Histoire de la Milice*, pp.579-601, Mabire, *La Division Charlemagne*, pp.173-175, the memoirs of Soulat [reproduced in part by Mabire, *La Division Charlemagne*, pp.178-181] and interrogation of Jean Bassompierre, 4 December 1946. However, according to Krukenberg, Darnand arrived to assist in the swearing-in ceremony, but stayed for only a matter of hours (see *Entretien avec le général Krukenberg*, *Historia* hors série 32, p.133) or elsewhere 'arrived late and after the ceremony' (article Krukemberg, *Problemes autour de la division Charlemagne*). In reply, Krukenberg was aged 85 when interviewed for *Historia* and 92 when he wrote *Problemes autour de la division Charlemagne*. In the latter he recognised that the events were some 35 years old and that this length of time might have erased memories. So was Darnand at the ceremony or not? Swayed by the testimony of Soulat and Bassompierre, the author is convinced that Darnand attended the ceremony. Curiously, Berger wrote to Himmler on 16 December 1944 that Darnand had arrived at Wildflecken camp on 19 November 1944 only to be told that he was welcome as a Stubaf. but not as a *Secrétaire d'Etat*. The 19 was one week after the swearing in ceremony.

96  Roch, *La Division Charlemagne*, p.35, confirmed by Soulat, letter to the author, 20/2/98. This date of 'on or around' 12 November 1944 corrects that of the end of January 1945, noted by Mabire, *La Division Charlemagne*, p.233, and thus also the idea that Cance was excluded from the Brigade when Ostubaf. Gamory-Dubourdeau left for Berlin.

97  Roch, *La Division Charlemagne*, p.35.

## Oath of loyalty to Hitler

By the eve of the swearing-in ceremony, some fifty *Miliciens* had made it known that they would not swear allegiance to Adolf Hitler. The ringleaders were, it seems, André Brilland and some of his comrades of the *Avant-Garde*.[98] All had attended the *école des cadres* [training school] at La Chapelle-en-Serval. Obf. Puaud called on Hstuf. de Bourmont to 'tear a strip off' the 'draft dodgers'.[99]

De Bourmont summoned Brilland first. However, he could not convince Brilland to move from his stand that he would never wear the German uniform or swear loyalty to Adolf Hitler. De Bourmont then gave Brilland the blunt choice of 'Charlemagne' or the concentration camp. This threat still did not convert Brilland who defiantly retorted: "I prefer to be guarded by the SS rather than wear their uniform. A question of principle." Continuing, Brilland spoke of Darnand's broken promises and even questioned de Bourmont's honour. Provoked to anger, de Bourmont called Brilland a saboteur and promised him that he would find himself in Danzig-Mazkau.

Rebuffed, de Bourmont went onto the others. All ended with the same outcome. The 'draft dodgers' were locked up in the camp prison, guarded by two former soldiers of the Sturmbrigade.

Curiously, Oberjunker Bonnafont of the Panzerjäger Company of Waffen-Gren. Regt. der SS 58 refused to swear the oath of loyalty to Hitler and yet he went unpunished.

Sunday 12 November 1944 started with mass celebrated by Monseigneur Mayol de Lupé in the stable. The *Miliciens* were all there. Once mass was over they assembled on Adolf Hitler Platz for the swearing-in ceremony at 0900 hours.[100] They were still wearing their dark-blue and khaki uniforms, and *basque* berets, but the arms they had brought with them to Wildflecken had long been confiscated on the orders of Brigf. Krukenberg.

Unit by unit, the whole brigade drew up around Adolf Hitler Platz for the ceremony. It was cold and snowing. In the centre of the platz stood a rostrum flanked on each side by an anti-tank gun, a mortar and a heavy machine-gun. From three flagpoles on the platz, in front of the 'Kasino', flew the tricolore, the black SS flag and the 'war flag of the Reich'.

Standing on the rostrum were Brigf. Krukenberg, Obf. Puaud, Darnand and Ostubaf. Léon Degrelle, holder of the Knight's Cross with 'Oak Leaves' conferred on him personally by Hitler and commander of the 28. SS-Freiwilligen-Panzer-Grenadier Division 'Wallonien'. Behind them were the eighty or so officers of the brigade and those of the German inspection.

Mgr. Mayol de Lupé spoke. He stated that he had been a National Socialist since 1925. He followed up with:

> Stalin and Bolshevism represent Evil in the pure state. In the East, Good and Evil clash. You will participate in the battle against Evil in the ranks of the Waffen-SS. Be proud. Long live Führer Adolf Hitler! Long live our France-German homeland!

98    Brilland is undoubtedly a pseudonym.
99    Mabire, *La Division Charlemagne*, p.176.
100  In his memoirs, Soulat wrote that, after mass, Mgr. Mayol de Lupé gave a speech. Curiously, this speech was similar to that he gave later that day at the swearing-in ceremony (see Mabire, *La Division Charlemagne*, pp.178-179, and Saint-Loup, *Les Hérétiques*, p.581). In response to this, the author does not know if Mgr. Mayol de Lupé gave just the one speech after mass or two similar speeches.

Both Brigf. Krukenberg and Obf. Puaud gave a short speech. Then, four *Miliciens* including *Capitaine* Moneuse,[101] a decorated veteran of 1914-1918 and 1939-1940 well into his forties, took the oath in the name of all present with the left hand on a sword held out by a German officer.[102] The *Miliciens* repeated the oath in French, although 'the majority remained silent or mumbled anything'.[103] Furthermore, they should have also raised their arm but the majority did not.[104] Many had a heavy heart.

The oath sworn that day was as follows:[105] 'I swear to obey faithfully Adolf Hitler, commander of the Waffen-SS, in the struggle against Bolshevism, as a loyal soldier.' This was not the SS oath. Bassompierre, concerned that if the *Miliciens* swore an oath of loyalty to Hitler as Führer and Chancellor of the German Reich it would leave the door open for possible combat duty on the Western Front, conspired with Lieutenant Artus to swear an oath of loyalty to Hitler only in the capacity as the 'commander of the armies engaged in the struggle against Bolshevism'.[106]

For *Milicien* officer Chatrousse, his reaction to the oath was mixed:[107]

Admittedly I swore the oath without enthusiasm, but the Waffen-SS was an international European force. It was logical to recognise the authority of one military commander and only that of one military commander. The result was that I agreed to take the oath without any particular frame of mind ...

Blanc of the Paris *Franc-Garde* was not troubled by the oath. He explained:[108]

Having already agreed to fight under the command of the Fuhrer, which was a decision I had taken quite freely, it was normal that he could firmly count on me. In my mind,

---

101  The memoirs of Soulat. As a very minor point, according to Mabire, *La Division Charlemagne*, p.179, only three *Miliciens* took the oath: a *franc-garde*, an NCO and *Capitaine* Moneuse.
102  Émile Moneuse was born on 18 October, 1899. After the *Milice* was authorized to extend into the Northern Zone, he became the *inspecteur général* of the *Franc-garde permanente* for the Northern Zone.
103  Mabire, *La Division Charlemagne*, p.180.
104  Delperrié de Bayac, *Histoire de la Milice*, p.582.
105  The memoirs of Soulat, repeated by Mabire, *La Division Charlemagne*, p.180. Curiously, some days earlier, de la Mazière swore an SS oath that ran as follows: 'I swear to you, Adolf Hitler, Germanic Führer and Remaker, to be true and brave. I swear to obey you and the leaders you have placed over me until my death. May God come to my aid.'
106  Interrogation of Jean Bassompierre, 4 December 1946, repeated by Pierre Giolitto, *Histoire de la Milice*, p.492. Incredibly, according to one former French Divisional soldier, the Germans gave their word never to engage them against French troops without getting their agreement first. This is all the more remarkable because Himmler and Krukenberg were totally opposed to the employment of 'Charlemagne' on the Western Front, yet alone against their countrymen. Admittedly, foreign minister Ribbentrop was actually in favour of employing 'Charlemagne' on the Western Front but his point of view would have carried little or no weight with the then all-powerful Himmler. However, the revelation that the Germans were prepared to engage 'Charlemagne' against French troops remains unsubstantiated. Also of note is that, according to Saint-Loup, *Les Hérétiques*, p.151, Krukenberg doubted the attachment of the *Miliciens* to National Socialism and thus could not ask them to swear the *real* SS oath. Again this remains unsubstantiated.
107  Chatrousse, letter to the author, 7/1/98.
108  Blanc, letter to the author, 7/8/2001.

I swore the oath to him as the European *chef de guerre* [head of war], and not as the foreign Head of State.

Immediately after the oath, the entire brigade, more than 7,000 men, sang the 'SS-Treuelied'. On the third verse everybody automatically came to attention. The officers saluted. Commands resounded. In the thickening snow the brigade now marched past the rostrum. At its head marched Stubaf. Bridoux. The *Compagnie d'Honneur*, heartily singing the 'SS Marschiert', led the way. The companies of the two grenadier regiments and the service units of the brigade followed and then the *Miliciens*, singing 'Monika' or 'rubbish'. Grenadier Robert Soulat, who was present at the ceremony, simply remarked: 'The charm was broken.'

On seeing the 'good uniform' of the *Miliciens* parading before him, Ostubaf. Degrelle commented: "I would like to have those people with me."[109] Ambitious, he hoped to combine the Frenchmen of 'Charlemagne' with the Walloons, Flemings and Dutchmen serving in the Waffen-SS to form an army corps by the name of 'Occident'.[110]

On the command of 'head right', a platoon emphatically looked left, much to the embarrassment of those reviewing the parade. Many *Miliciens* did not know the German language.

During the ceremony Darnand's presence had paled before that of the charismatic Degrelle. In fact, he practically went unnoticed.[111] After the ceremony, he briefly visited Fenet, a former *Milicien*, who now had nothing in common with his former leader. Broken-hearted, he left Wildflecken that night (or the following day), but not before he had asked his men to be, above all, soldiers. Nevertheless, he still lived in hope.

Subsequently, Darnand wrote a strongly worded letter to SS-Ogruf. Berger of the SS-Hauptamt in which he complained that his men had not remained in a special separated unit, that the initial oath sworn to him was not satisfactory and that the German Inspection had 'taken his last combatants' from him. On Himmler's orders, Darnand had to retract his letter. He no longer interested the SS hierarchy.

109  Raybaud, letter to Bayle, 22/2/1992. Although the wording of the comment and the circumstances of its passing are different, the written interview with Raybaud in *Charlemagne's Legionnaires* confirms, as expected, that the comment was aimed at solely the *Milicens*. However, according to Saint-Loup, *Les Hérétiques*, p.151, a similar worded comment from Degrelle to Krukenberg was aimed at the Frenchmen as a whole rather than the *Miliciens* in particular.

110  Although Darnand appears to have been in agreement, the idea of an 'Occident' corps would come to nothing. Indeed, on 8/12/1944, Darnand wrote to Berger, the head of the SS-Hauptamt, stating his intention to resign his post of *Secrétaire d'Etat* from the *Commission Gouvernementale Française*, as well as requesting his transfer to 'Wallonie'. For his part, Degrelle hoped for Darnand's transfer in the expectation that he would bring with him a large number of his adherents who had just been incorporated into 'Charlemagne'. On 16/12/1944, Berger wrote to RF-SS Himmler about Darnand and warned him that 'in the eyes of many Frenchmen, Darnand had devalued himself through his widely-known project to join Degrelle' and in this way given a great political advantage to his rival Doriot. As for Degrelle's proposed 'Occident' Corps, Berger described its formation as being fraught with danger and its success doubtful. He explained that the 'antinomies between the French and the Walloons had still not been overcome' and that, even if the project were a success, 'Walloon will have drawn closer to France rather than to the Reich'. Although Berger stopped short of dismissing the project outright, 'reading between the lines', there is little doubt that he was not in favour of it. Himmler, undoubtedly, would have had similar reservations.

111  Indeed, according to Landwehr, *Charlemagne's Legionnaires*, p.90, Darnand wanted the place of honour at the ceremony, but this was given over to Degrelle. However, no other source makes mention of this.

290 For Europe Revisited

Several days later, Father Brevet, a nephew of Darnand and former chaplain of the *Milice*, turned up at Wildflecken to try his hand at talking round those *Miliciens* who had refused to swear the SS oath. He convinced over half to go over. Nineteen were left. Bassompierre tried next. He had no success.

On 15 November 1944, the nineteen were taken from Wildflecken to Sigmaringen where, five days later, Darnand spoke to them in person. He persuaded a further eight to enlist in the Waffen-SS, but he was not prepared to punish the others for a show of French patriotism. Discharged, they put on civvies and went to work for the Reich.

### The change of uniform

Meantime, back at Wildflecken, the *Miliciens* drew what uniform and kit was available, including old stocks of greenish coloured Italian overcoats that proved useless against the bitterly cold weather. Some even ended up clothed in the mustard-coloured overcoats of the SA or Organisation Todt. A steel helmet could not be found to fit Blanc of the Dijon *Franc-Garde*. Neither did he receive a mess tin!

Uscha. Mercier of Fahrschwadron A wrote that the clothing received by the *Miliciens* was 'one of the less glorious episodes'.[112] As a veteran of the LVF, he recalled the new uniforms, the new weapons, and the new equipment received in September 1941 at Deba. In contrast, the Germany Army of 1944 no longer had the means to dress its soldiers in a worthy manner. Indeed, one of Mercier's comrades, an NCO from the *Milice* of very stocky build, still did not have a uniform into which he could fit some two months later.

While most of the former *Miliciens* wore blank right collar insignia some managed to acquire and wear the standard SS runes.[113]

*Franc-garde* Maurice Ranc said of changing uniform:[114] 'It was time to abdicate, and it was without regret that I left my French uniform to put on another...' He was not alone.

Now dressed in a Waffen-SS uniform, René Cessil of the *3e Unité de Franc Garde de Lyon* felt proud to be serving with a *grande unité européenne* in the continual battle against Soviet Bolshevism.[115]

*Franc-garde* Noël Cornu donned the *feldgrau* without heartache. That he should end up in *feldgrau* came as no surprise to him. Indeed, the 'slide' had begun years before when he was with the PPF. Born on 30 August 1920 in Lillebonne in the department of Seine-Maritime, he had joined the PPF in 1941 (*section* of the 5th arrondissement in Paris) and was one of the few to pass to the *Milice*, attending the *école des cadres* at La Chapelle-en-Serval. Incredibly, while at Ulm, he recalls there were some 'small problems' due to the rivalry between the PPF and the *Milice*!

Jules Dissent found himself in a wretched Italian overcoat, which greatly displeased him. Not only was it less warm and comfortable than its German counterpart, but it made him look Italian, whose military reputation was inferior. Like most *Miliciens*, he wore blank right collar insignia. Curiously, he was not issued with a *Soldbuch*.

---

112 Mercier, letter to the author 25/10/2001.
113 Soulat, letter to the author, 21/9/98.
114 Deloncle, *Trois jeunesses provençales*, p.108.
115 René Cessil was born on 3 January 1927 in Roanne.

Pierre Méric was not that bothered at having to wear the *feldgrau*. He was more concerned that he was not issued with warm clothing and the celebrated jackboots. He was thankful that his company was not issued with the Italian overcoats, though. He said of the change of uniform: 'In short, it was not a day of glory for anyone'.

Towards the end of November 1944,[116] the *Milicien* contingent was assembled on Adolf Hitler Platz and, in a scene likened to that of a cattle market by Blanc of the Paris *Franc-Garde*, divided up among the units of 'Charlemagne'.[117] Company commanders or their delegates came to 'fish' for men, exalting the charms and merits of his unit or specialty. The patron of the Escort Platoon assured that it was the most exposed and was immediately filled up. Some decided on such and such unit to join a brother, or a cousin, or a comrade. As planned, *Franc-garde* Blanc followed the representative of Company 5/58; Platoon commander Walter was an old friend. They had studied together in 1940-41 at Lycée Carnot, Paris.[118] Blanc was accompanied by some of his closest comrades.

*Francs-gardes* from Limoges filled out the skeletal Assault Gun Company and those from the city of Chambéry the 'heavy mortars'.[119] René B., a *Milicien* from the region of Auvergne was assigned to the Assault Gun Company and then transferred to the Signals Company. *Franc-garde* Marotel was assigned to Company 4/57 and then transferred to Company 8/57, becoming its armourer. *Franc-garde* Cornu, a medical student of more than three years, was first assigned to Company 5/58 and then placed into the Medical Company.[120] *Franc-garde* Maurice Ranc was incorporated into the Artillery Battalion. However, the majority of *Miliciens* became Waffengrenadier.

*Miliciens* served in all units, although the following units benefited the most:[121]

- The Artillery Battalion
- The Anti-tank or 'Heavy' Battalion
- The two Supply columns
- The Engineer Company
- The Signals Company
- The Medical Company
- The Veterinary Company

116  Blanc, personal conversation with the author, 2001.
117  Curiously, according to Mabire, *La Division Charlemagne*, pp.166-167, some senior officers of the *Milice* came to Wildflecken hoping to form a pure *Milicien* unit within the brigade. But de Vaugelas, who had become convinced that this move would only exasperate the already serious political infighting, reached agreement with Puaud and Krukenberg to help eliminate political strife. For his part, Krukenberg considered the prospect of a wholly *Milicien* unit as a 'factor of insecurity' for the entire brigade. In return for the splitting up of the *Milicien* personnel, de Vaugelas secured from Puaud and Krukenberg that *Milicien* officers would be placed in numerous positions of command throughout the brigade. This agreement he brought back to the other officers of the *Milice* who he won over with his arguments. In response to this, if true, clearly, Darnand had not told them of the agreement he had reached with Krukenberg to divide the members of the *Milice* among the different units.
118  Blanc had not seen Walter since November 1941. Then his friend had seemed more sombre than ever.
119  Mabire, *La Division Charlemagne*, p.187. Presumably this is a reference to the organic heavy company of each grenadier battalion.
120  While Cornu was with the 5/58 his platoon commander was one Pierre Ruskone.
121  According to Blanc, the Supply Corps was not popular.

## Political infighting or not

The integration of the *Miliciens*, according to many sources,[122] intensified the political infighting, so much so that broken noses, broken teeth and stabbings settled scores. Similarly, according to another source, fights between the various factions of 'Charlemagne' became quite commonplace inside the camp and especially outside in the neighbouring small villages.[123] However, regarding this dissension and political infighting, many veterans have expressed genuine and great surprise.

Grenadier Marotel, the only *Milicien* in a small bedroom with six other NCOs, of whom five were from the SS-Sturmbrigade, recalls no such problems posed by their different origins. Moreover, while in 'Charlemagne', he had no inkling of these disputes. He commented that they were going to discover a camaraderie that was perfect.

Maurice Comte, who had arrived with the *Milice*, also recalls no such problems in his company, the 5/57, but much political discussion. Also serving in the 5/57 was *franc-garde* René Cessil. Although he was the only one of his platoon to attend mass taken by Mgr. de Mayol de Lupé, he was never ridiculed about his choice. Among his platoon there was mutual respect.

Pierre Méric, who had also arrived with the *Milice*, received the rank of Oberscharführer and was appointed as a platoon commander in Company 2/58. His platoon was made up equally of *Miliciens*, who posed him no problems, and legionnaires of the LVF, who sympathetically welcomed him, but were undecided. They were concerned that he was going to use this opportunity to advance himself and win decorations at their expense. He would soon prove to them that this was certainly not the case.

Company commander Ustuf. Rigeade cannot recall any lasting or important disputes among the men of the 3/58 of whom about half were former legionnaires of the LVF (including thirty holders of the 'Ost medialle' [East Medal] who had served during the first winter campaign in Russia). The others were former *Miliciens*, about forty in number, ex-Kriegsmarine, ex-NSKK, ex-SK der OK... but none were from the Sturmbrigade. Although Rigeade felt proud to have been 'among the first to enlist', he had no taste for snubbing, denigrating, scorning or judging the others, nor their reasons to enlist, their path or their past choices. They were now in his Company and, in his own words, 'honour to them all!'

The 4/58 also comprised 'volunteers' from the LVF, the *Milice*, the Kriegsmarine and the SK der OK. Stamping his authority, company commander Ustuf. de Genouillac made it understood to one and all that his only concern was to make them into elite combatants, that their origin or political origin would play no part in this objective, and that he would not tolerate any disruption to the cohesion of the unit. Consequently, the young *Miliciens*, who recognised that they all had to learn how to be 'veterans', posed him no problems.

Assigned to Company 5/58, *franc-garde* Robert Blanc found himself in a platoon solely made up of *Milice* recruits, except for the section commanders and platoon commander-instructor Oscha. Walter. They were ex-LVF. Nevertheless, between the two camps there was no expression of political rivalry rather esprit de corps; those from the LVF subjected the *franc-gardes* to biting remarks, even some minor ragging, but this never degenerated into insults or fights. Things would calm down some months later. Besides, the new recruits wanted to know where the

---

122  For example, see Mabire, *La Division Charlemagne*, pp.187-189, and Saint-Loup, *Les Hérétiques*, p.154.
123  Rostaing, *Le prix d'un serment*, p.152.

friendly 'pubs' were in the local villages! Of note is that Oscha. Walter remained above such 'political' problems.

Jean Castrillo of Company 5/58, who was ex-SK, recalls no such political infighting, even though the *Miliciens* from the Gers had trouble 'slipping' into the SS discipline. Assigned to the Assault Gun Company and then transferred to the Medical Company, *Milicien* Jules Dissent encountered no hostility from the other factions that made up the Brigade, but there was one occasion when he was ordered by French NCOs from the Sturmbrigade to do a series of push-ups. He no longer recalls the reason for this but felt that it was unjust and left him unhappy.

In contrast, Ustuf. Martres had cause to remember well the *Miliciens* and their ill feeling towards the Waffen-SS. For example, one day, as Unterführer vom Dienst, he officiated in German to an audience of *Miliciens*. Noting that the *Miliciens* disapproved of his use of German, he argued that 'Charlemagne' was a unit of the Waffen-SS and, as such, German would be spoken. Continuing, he told them that they were neither French nor German, but European SS.[124]

'In our unit, we had no friction between former *légionnaires*, former SS, and former *miliciens*', said Uscha. Mercier of Fahrschwadron A.[125] However, the incorporation of the *Milice* into 'Charlemagne' had not pleased him at all. He had no sympathy with the *Milice* itself, but personal contact with the *Miliciens* completely changed his opinion. He immediately developed excellent relations with them. Some became his friends (and remained so). His comrades from the *Milice* expressed themselves freely in front of him. They spoke to him of the *départ* from France and of Ulm without ulterior motive but were rather bitter when it came to evoking *chef* Darnand.

Transferred to the Headquarters Company, Soulat found himself among soldiers who were mainly ex-LVF. They warmly welcomed this young sailor. Moreover, there were never any problems because of origin.

Clearly, there was little or no political infighting. Moreover, Krukenberg would have been quick to clamp down on all political expression. However, the Waffen-SS ranks accorded to the *Miliciens*, said to be those of their equivalent former French Army rank, was greeted by concern and discontent. Uscha. Peyret, who was ex-LVF, readily admitted that he had no confidence in the abilities of the former officers of the *Milice* in front of the Russian but was not hostile to them.

Some junior ranks objected to the ranks the *Miliciens* received. Those from the Sturmbrigade had suffered one year of rigorous training before promotion to Sturmmann or Unterscharführer. Moreover, previous military service had not determined their promotion. In their eyes there was no substitute for the training received at Sennheim and Posen-Treskau.[126]

---

124 Furthermore, according to Martres, the *Miliciens* wanted to wear the Gamma badge of the *Milice française* on their uniform (personal discussion). This was not authorised. However, some foreign nationalities serving with the Waffen-SS were permitted to wear badges of a political nature.

125 Mercier, letter to the author 25/9/2001.

126 According to Saint-Loup, *Les Hérétiques*, pp.156-157, *sergents* of the LVF, who had waged war for three years against the partisans and the Red Army to gain their strips, refused to obey eighteen-year-old *aspirants* of the *Milice* whose previous military experience amounted to service in the *Chantiers de la Jeunesse*.

294    For Europe Revisited

Simply stated, many of the *Miliciens* were militarily untrained for modern warfare. Regarding this, Blanc, a *Milicien*, explained: 'We only knew guard duty and some 'operations', which despite a great willingness, did not make soldiers.' The *Miliciens* had much to learn and that included those who had formerly served in the French Army, for the training and tactics of the Waffen-SS were far removed from that of the French Army defeated in 1940. Furthermore, some *Miliciens* were too old and unfit for proper military service, and some were too political. Nevertheless, their courage was not doubted.

The ranks the *Miliciens* received were not always based on their former ranks in the French Armed Forces. For example, Pierre Méric, a former student pilot which was not a rank as such, was promoted to Oberscharführer. Arguably, he had more than proved himself worthy of command in the ranks of the *Franc-Garde permanente*, participating and commanding a number of field operations. Maurice Comte was promoted to Unterscharführer and appointed as a platoon commander and yet he had not served in the French Armed Forces in any capacity. Also and perhaps more importantly, Jean de Vaugelas was appointed Hauptsturmführer, although the highest rank he achieved in the French Armed Forces was only that of Lieutenant. Arguably, he too had more than proved himself in the heat of battle that he was capable and worthy of command, but unlike Bassompierre, de Bourmont or Raybaud, who similarly were all appointed Hauptsturmführer, he had not attended Saint-Cyr or Saint-Maixent.

As a result of the integration of the *Miliciens*, a number of changes occurred in the more senior positions. Ostuf. Fenet relinquished command of battalion I/57 to Hstuf. de Bourmont. Hstuf. Raybaud assumed command of battalion I/58. Hstuf. Bassompierre did not receive a command, though. After changing the oath of loyalty, Krukenberg had severely reprimanded Bassompierre and threatened to dismiss him. This he did not do following the intervention of Puaud, contenting himself with not giving Bassompierre a command.

Despite nullifying the political threat Darnand and Doriot had posed, Krukenberg appears to have become concerned about the political activities of Puaud. In October 1944, Krukenberg was alarmed to hear that Puaud, on his own initiative, offered Marshal Pétain a *Garde d'Honneur* from 'Charlemagne'. [The Marshal immediately refused this move.] Krukenberg said of another incident:

> One day I entered his office. He [Puaud] clumsily tried to hide a circular among his files. He eventually showed me it: he was asking the cadres in the Division for those who were interested in *postes de préfet* after the victorious return to France.[127]

Puaud was but one concern for Krukenberg. There was also the matter of the numerous 'desertions'. In less than one month, more than two hundred men, in groups of two or three, had 'deserted' to units going up to the front.[128] In this way, some of these French SS 'deserters' would actually end up serving in Waffen-SS Divisions 'Totenkopf' and 'Wiking'. And although Krukenberg would later describe the desertions as honourable because they wanted to fight, he was more concerned that 'they were very bad for the morale of their comrades' left behind.[129]

127  Mabire, *Entretien avec le général Krukenberg, Historia* hors série 32, p.133.
128  Mabire, *La Division Charlemagne*, p.192.
129  Mabire, *Entretien avec le général Krukenberg, Historia* hors série 32, p.136.

Others employed more official channels to leave. Chansarel of the Kriegsmarine discovered a make-believe Belgian ancestry and managed to get himself transferred to Waffen-SS Division 'Wallonie'. Barat, also ex-Kriegsmarine, wrote to RF-SS Himmler in person, protesting that his skills as a torpedo technician could be better employed elsewhere. Days later, he received a reply from the private secretary of the RF-SS. To the great envy of many others, he obtained satisfaction and was transferred away.

Instructor Strmm. Jean-Jaques Pillet wanted to leave the *bordel* [shambles] that was Wildflecken. He was hungry, full of lice, and disappointed that some of his compatriots were not willing to don the German uniform. Moreover, he felt undervalued as an instructor in the company commanded by Artus. In fact, his work was ridiculed.

Some deserted in the true sense of the word. A twenty-two-year-old Parisian trapped in forced labour in Germany decided to volunteer for 'Charlemagne' at the end of October 1944 with the intention of escaping at the earliest opportunity. Sent to Wildflecken, he managed to escape on 6 January 1945 and cross into Allied lines at the end of the month. During his subsequent interrogation by the Americans he disclosed that while at Wildflecken:

> In late December a list was published of names of about 20 deserters who had been caught and executed in November. The men were told that desertions, even if carried out with the intention of joining fighting units, would be punished by death.

No other source corroborates such executions for desertion, although the threat of punishment of death probably felt all too real.[130]

---

130 During his research for this work the author entered into correspodence with another deserter from 'Charlemagne', but he was not prepared to tell his story.

# 10

# Greifenberg and the Franz. SS-Grenadier-Ausbildungs und Ersatz-Bataillon

Situated at Greifenberg in Pomerania, north-western Poland, the French SS-Grenadier Training and Replacement Battalion assisted in the training of recruits and provided replacements for 'Charlemagne'. Commanded by Swiss national SS-Ostubaf. Hersche,[1] the battalion was organised with three training companies and a number of other units.

When the Ersatz Kommando of the LVF was transformed into the French SS-Grenadier Training and Replacement Battalion *Sergent* Mercier of the *Compagnie de Dépôt* was automatically transferred to the Stammkompanie. Made the temporary Rechnungsführer of one of the training companies, he was tasked with setting up its administrative structure.[2] As soon as his work was done, he left this post to a Volkdeutsche who held the rank of SS-Uscha. Health problems followed. He was sent to the SS-Erholungsheim at Bad Gleichenberg in Styrie where he spent some fifteen days.

In October 1944, all soldiers of the Stammkompanie had a medical examination.[3] Uscha. Mercier had his with Ostuf. Dr. Louis. The doctor suggested demobilising him as unfit for service. This did not correspond to his aspirations, but several of his comrades took advantage of this 'comfortable' way out from the SS. Mercier sought his own way out by requesting a transfer to the SS parachutists. He was refused on grounds of ill health. This transfer request he would later describe as a romantic gesture.

In early October, Albert Poignant of the *Compagnie de Dépôt* responded to a call for volunteers for parachute training and was accepted. (Arguably he had just signed up for the SS-Jagdverband or even the Abwehr.) Nine others also volunteered, which Poignant named as Gosset Marcel, Edeline Gustave, Daydet Roger, Pezzini, Becherault, Petit Jean, Philippe, Hosman and Walter Bizzo. On 7 October, the ten volunteers were sent to a training camp at Bruss in West Prussia, where they learnt parachuting, sabotage and map-reading. Towards the end of November, with

---

1   Hersche succeeded *Commandant* Cartaud of the LVF who had refused to pass to the SS.
2   Such was the confusion at the time of the transfer to the Waffen-SS that Mercier can no longer recall the name of the company commander. Moreover, he never saw the company commander. Nevertheless, he is convinced that it was not Ostuf. Michel who had been his company commander in 1942 when serving with the LVF. The Spiess was an old Feldwebel from the German training staff of the Ersatz Kommando. He had no idea of his function. He too may have only been temporary.
3   Mercier, letter to the author, 23/1/2002, although the date of the medical examination and the attendees are not confirmed.

their training complete, they were sent to camp Wildflecken and incorporated into the 'Special Company'. Thereafter, the thirty-one-year-old Poignant was used to train the younger recruits on how to handle automatic weapons and the theory of street-fighting.[4]

In mid-November 1944, after a long period of convalescence, Ustuf. Paul Pignard-Berthet arrived at depot Greifenberg and received the command of the Stammkompanie from W-Ustuf. Kipp.[5] The role of the depot company was twofold: in the first place, to 'process' (or bring into line) the new recruits, and, secondly, to demobilise some of the more seriously wounded or those refusing to pass to the SS. In this way, the strength of the Stammkompanie was later reduced from over 800 men to 130.

At the end of November 1944, Hstuf. Schlisler, the *officier adjoint* of the battalion, left Greifenberg for Wildflecken to take command of Fahrschwadron A of 'Charlemagne'.[6] Schlisler took a small team with him. One of those he asked to remain on his team was Uscha. Mercier, who being very attached to him, had agreed without hesitation. Once again, he was touched by Schlisler's trust. [He would follow Schlisler to the end].

With W-Hstuf. Schlisler's departure, the order of battle of the Franz. SS-Grenadier-Ausbildungs und Ersatz-Bataillon at Greifenberg was as follows:[7]

- Commander:                    SS-Ostubaf. Hersche
- Assistant:                    SS-Hstuf. Kroepsch[8]
- Training officer:             SS-Ustuf. Schueler
- Office III:                   SS-Ostuf. Dick
- Office IV/A:                  W-Ostuf. Dr. Louis[9]
- Office VI:                    SS-Ostuf. Zander
- 1. Ausbildungskompanie:       SS-Ostuf. Ludwig
- 2. Ausbildungskompanie:       W-Ostuf. Michel
- 3. Ausbildungskompanie:       SS-Ostuf. Allgeier

---

4    Rentano and Leguérandais, *Ces Franciliens qui ont choisi Hitler*, pp.114-115.
5    A Luxembourg national, Jean Kipp enlisted in the LVF and served in the 1st Company under *Capitaine* Cartaud. He won the Iron Cross 2nd Class. In September 1943, Cartaud was transferred to Kruszyna to take command of the Ersatz Kommando. Kipp went with him. In early 1944, he was promoted to *Sous-Lieutenant*. After passing his command to Pignard-Berthet, he promptly 'disappeared'. Like Cartaud, he too may have refused to pass to the SS. Indeed, he signed the soldbuch of Pierre Roselfeder with the rank of Leutnant and not Untersturmführer.
6    Schlisler once confided to Mercier that General Puaud wanted him to take command of the IV. Battalion of the LVF, which was not raised because of the events of 1944 (Mercier, letter to the author, 9/10/2001).
7    According to Scherzer, *Sous le Signe SS*, p.222, the French Grenadier Training and Replacement Battalion also fielded a fourth Ausbildungskompanie [Training Company], as well as a Genesendenkompanie [Convalescent Company]. Admittedly, each Infantry Replacement Battalion contained four training companies, and one or more convalescent and transfer companies, but that is not to say that they were raised.
8    Richard Kroepsch was born on 21 October 1895 in Riga.
9    Bayle, *San et Persante*, p.147. Curiously, Ostuf. J.M. Louis, who came to the Waffen-SS from the LVF, was a trained doctor. And, as such, one would expect to find him at the head of Office IV/B, that of medical and sanitation, rather than Office IV/A, that of uniforms, footgear and rations. In any case, he survived the war and became a surgeon.

- Stammkompanie:             W-Ustuf. Pignard-Berthet
- Ausbildungszug:[10]         W-Ostuf. Crespin

German officers Allgeier, Ludwig, and Schueler had all served as instructors at Ersatz Kommando I.R. 638. They too were transferred from the Wehrmacht to the Waffen-SS. Ludwig had been badly wounded in 1940 fighting the French and left paralysed in one arm.

Each of the three Ausbildungskompanie numbered 180 men, the Stammkompanie 825 men and the Ausbildungszug 430 men.

Transferred to Greifenberg, André Doutart recalls that Hersche kept an eye on him; because he was born in Geneva, Hersche considered him as a compatriot. Doutart was eventually promoted to the rank of Sturmmann.

At the end of December 1944, a Rekrutenkompanie (in French *compagnie de recrues)* was formed. Its command went to Ostuf. Crespin. The company was 450 strong.

In December 1944, Ustuf. Pignard-Berthet spent fifteen days at Wildflecken supervising a platoon of officer cadets. From Hstuf. Moneuse, the battalion commander of the I/58, he received the task of 'polishing up' the officer cadets and selecting those capable of attending Junkerschule Kienschlag.

While at Wildflecken, Ustuf. Pignard-Berthet also received personal instructions from Krukenberg to eliminate all those at Greifenberg whose morale would no longer withstand the new hardships or those who might exert a bad influence over their comrades. On his return, he carried out these instructions to the letter.

On 16 January 1945, the Ausbildungszug [Training platoon] was transformed into a kompanie of 250 men. Its command went to Ustuf. Pignard-Berthet. Hstuf. Flamand succeeded him at the head of the Stammkompanie.

---

10    According to Scherzer, *Sous le Signe SS*, p.222, this unit was titled Fahr-Ausbildungsschwadron.

**11**

## The Training of 'Charlemagne'

### Dispersed throughout Europe

The Third Reich still had much to offer in the way of specialist training. The following were sent to military bases and training centres throughout Europe:

- NCO candidates to SS-Unterführerschule Posen-Treskau or Paderborn
- Officer candidates to annex Neweklau of SS-Panzergrenadierschule Kienschlag
- Engineers to SS-Pionierschule Hradischko in Bohemia-Moravia
- Signallers to Sterzing-Vipiteno in South Tyrol[1]
- Mechanics to Berlin[2]
- Medical orderlies to Stettin[3]
- Interpreters to the SS-Dolmetscherschule Oranienburg near Berlin
- Company clerks to SS-Funktionsunterführerschule Breslau
- The Assault Gun Company to SS-Panzerjäger (Sturmgeschütz) Schule Janowitz
- The personnel of the Infantry Gun companies to SS-IG-Ausb. u. Ers. Btl. 1 Breslau-Lissa[4]
- Artillery officers to SS-Artillerieschule II Beneschau, Bohemia-Moravia
- Artillerymen to Josefstadt, Bohemia-Moravia
- The drivers of the horse-drawn vehicles to SS-Kavallerieschule Göttingen

Only the Waffengrenadier would stay put at Wildflecken for training.

In late November 1944, the Brigade sent some fifty officer candidates to annex Neweklau of SS-Panzergrenadierschule Kienschlag. Jean-Marie Croisile, Cossard, Lefeuvre, Jacques de

---

1 The signallers may have been sent to SS-Nachrichten-Ausbildungs-und Ersatz-Abteilung 5.
2 The mechanics may have been sent to SS-Kraftfahr-Ausbildungs-und Ersatz-Regiment (Weimar-Buchenwald) outside Berlin, but this remains unconfirmed.
3 The medical orderlies may have been sent to Sanitäts-Ausbildungs-und Ersatz-Battalion der Waffen-SS stationed at Stettin, but this remains unconfirmed.
4 *SS*-Infanteriegeschütz-Ausbildungs und Ersatz Bataillon 1 (Infantry Gun Training and Replacement Battalion 1).

Mandiargues and two or three other comrades left Wildflecken on 26 November 1944 for Kienschlag. Uscha. Yves Peyret of the Panzerjäger Kompanie/Waffen-Gren. Regt. der SS 58 and Rttf. Jean Malardier of the Headquarters Company of Waffen-Gren. Regt. der SS 58, who was fully expecting promotion to Unterscharführer, also attended the course.[5] The training officially started on 5 December 1944 and would not end until April 1945.

Walloon officer candidates also attended the same course at Kienschlag. One Walloon recalls that a French Junker was killed instantly during a shooting practice. He also recalls that one evening when the camp was plunged into darkness because of a power cut a French Junker, who was the duty officer, did not assemble the trainees in time to attend a course taken by a Walloon instructor. The following day, the French Junker was returned to 'Charlemagne'.

In late November, Section commander Rttf. Gonzales and the Engineer Company were sent to SS-Pionierschule Hradischko, one of the many training schools located within Truppenübungsplatz Beneschau, south of Prague, Bohemia-Moravia.

On his transfer to the Engineer Company, Gonzales was surprised to learn that the parents of Kompanieführer Ostuf. Roger Audibert de Vitrolles were friends and neighbours of his![6] Because of this Gonzales is convinced that Audibert asked for him to serve in his company. Audibert was elegant, but his monocled and very abrupt air reminded Gonzales of 'a certain aristocracy of French Army officers'. Nevertheless, Audibert had come up through the ranks.

Audibert had passed from the Légion Tricolore to the LVF with the rank of Oberleutenant, arriving in the field in May 1943. Wounded in August 1943, he only returned to active service in early 1944 at the head of the 7th Company of the II. Bataillon. He was still with the same company when the LVF was transferred to the Waffen-SS. He was a holder of the KVK 2. Klasse.

Gonzales had cause to remember well his company commander's assistant, Ustuf. Maile. While in Russia with the LVF, he very nearly shot him dead! As for the circumstances, well, Gonzales admits that he was completely drunk at the time. Thankfully a comrade had punched him hard and put him out for the count before he could fire again. Maile bore him no malice.

Two French NCOs of the Engineer Company were named Bohin and Anselme. Of his training at Pikowitz, Gonzales recalls the 'joys' of bridge building across the Sasau, weapons training, which included the use of flamethrowers, the placing of anti-tank mines and anti-personnel mines, and 'bunker busting'. Physical training was, of course, emphasied. They lost weight and gained strength. The training continued by night. Woken at all times of the night, Gonzales cannot forget how he and his comrades marched for kilometre after kilometre carrying two anti-tank mines on their back. Through this arduous training, some developed the sense of discipline that was lacking beforehand.

5    While at Neweklau Malardier recalls Jean-Louis de Bouge, Tristan de Bazelaire, Bonnet, Chavent, d'Abbadie, Fleury, Ginot, Jean Jacoby, Protopopoff, Jean Soupault, Marius Velet, and Georges Voiturier (letter to the author, 2/8/1999). Chavent, Ginot and Protopopoff attended the Waffen-Junker-Lehrgang. The others named by Malardier attended a Führerbewerber-Lehrgang also at Kienschlag which ran from 5 February 1945 to 14 April 1945. See the updated participants of both courses in Bouysse, Français sous l'uniforme allemand Partie II: Sous-officiers & hommes du rang de la Waffen-SS.

6    Audibert was born on 15 September 1914 in Marseille, which was also the hometown of Gonzales.

With each passing day, the engineers' proficiency improved. In addition, they began to move more and more swiftly and efficiently. Most were willing trainees, but some, for reasons best known to them, did not respond. The training course at Pikowitz would last some three months.

In December, Strmm. Sepchat of the Headquarters Company/58 joined the French artillery officers at SS-Artillerieschule Beneschau. He acted as their interpreter. The Frenchmen were part of a group that also included Flemish and Bulgarian officers. Notably, at the head of the group, for the period of the course, was Hstuf. Martin, not Hstuf. Havette, his senior and the commander of the Artillery Battalion of 'Charlemagne'. One of the instructors had considered Havette incapable of exercising this function!

One day, the trainees noted a large rectangle left in white on a map. Curious, they asked what it was. The answer came: "We cannot tell you. When certain events happen, you will understand." In this way, the myth of the secret weapons was perpetuated. Some would still believe in them to the end. On his return to Wildflecken, Sepchat was given the job of translating German artillery regulations into French. Not an easy one without a technical dictionary!

Also in December, a number of officer candidates from the former Sturmbrigade, including brothers Gastine, Piquemal, Prunennec, and Paul Viot, arrived from annex Neweklau of SS-Panzergrenadier-schule Kienschlag. Prunennec had been selected to attend by Artus.[7] The Führerbewerber-Lehrgang under Kleindienst had lasted some three months (from 24 August to 30 November 1944).[8] Strm.-F.Bew. Prunennec was assigned to the 3/57 under Ustuf. Counil.

That same month, Uscha. Christian de la Mazière[9] of the PAK Company and Hscha. Georges Blanchard de la Buharaye were sent to Panzerjägerschule Janowitz. Both had served with the *Milice*. Meeting Blanchard de la Buharaye for the first time, de la Mazière wrote:[10] 'He was a Breton with a touch of breeding. I sensed the professional soldier and was greatly taken with him'. Blanchard de la Buharaye was a product of Saint-Cyr, who had spent many years soldering in remote desert outposts.

At Janowitz, they entered a 'truly cosmopolitan milieu' and 'mingling with the various groups was like touring Europe'. There was even a Hindu in a turban. They received anti-tank theory and practice, which included all manner of anti-tank weapons, as well as physical training. They had to dig foxholes and have tanks roll over them.[11] Blanchard de la Buharaye once remarked to de la Mazière: "Do you know, I've learned more in a month here than in two years at Saint-Cyr and ten in the French Army."

---

7    Paul Viot was born on 23 September 1904 and served with the Sturmbrigade in Galicia, where he was wounded. Transferred to 'Charlemagne', he served with the 1/57, then the 5/57.

8    The author originally stated that Jacques Frantz attended this course, but now has doubts. Frantz, as stated earlier, attended the course which ran from December 1944 to April 1945. While it's possible he attended both training courses, which his timeline supports, it seems doubtful that the Reich would spend some eight months training a new recruit to be an officer at a time when manpower was desperately needed.

9    Contrary to what is written in *Ashes of Honour*, p.95 and in the article *Le Rêveur Casqué*, de la Mazière was not an officer with the rank of Untersturmführer. For whatever reason, he chose to rewrite his rank, which was that of Unterscharführer. Christian de la Mazière was born on 22 August 1922 in Tours. Notably, his father, a cavalry officer, served on the headquarters of Marshal Pilsudski in Poland against the Soviets from 1919 to 1921 and went on to become the *directeur-adjoint* of Cavalry School Naumur. Christian worked as a journalist for *Le Pays Libre*.

10   De la Mazière, *Ashes of Honour*, p.71. Blanchard de la Buharaye was born on 8 September 1915.

11   See de la Mazière, *Ashes of Honour*, pp.78-94, for his account of 'what a German training school is like'.

### The role model of the *Compagnie d'Honneur*

New recruits, be they workers or prisoners of war, as well as those who had finished convalescing from wounds received on the Eastern Front, continued to arrive at Wildflecken from Greifenberg. The reaping of Frenchmen serving in other formations of the German Army continued and together they swelled the ranks of 'Charlemagne'. Each regiment was now able to form two additional companies, called A and B. In his infinite wisdom, Puaud requested de Vaugelas to activate a third regiment, but the idea was dropped days later, which may be due in part to the protests from Fenet with support from de Vaugelas.[12]

On 10 December 1944, de Vaugelas was appointed Chief of Staff of the Brigade.[13]

On 16 December 1944, the strength of 'Charlemagne' stood at a total of 7,340. This strength probably included those in training schools.

By the middle of December 1944, Krukenberg was in a position to accelerate the military training. His training strategy revolved around the *Wach-und Ausbildungskompanie der Inspektion* (Guard and Education Company of the Inspection) which he wished to forge into an elite unit and hence a role model for the other troops.

Brigf. Krukenberg had formed the *Wach-und Ausbildungskompanie* at Leisten soon after he assumed command of the Inspection. The company reported direct to the *Inspekteur* [i.e. Krukenberg]. Oberjunker Christian Martres, who had graduated of late from SS-Panzergrenadierschule Kienschlag, was appointed its commander.[14] He was eighteen years old and 'hailed from' the Sturmbrigade. At the head of one platoon was Oscha. Roland Charles, who also hailed from the Sturmbrigade. He saw action in Galicia at the head of a platoon of the 2nd Company and was wounded.[15]

At first, the *Wach-und Ausbildungskompanie* counted three platoons of thirty men each. It was bolstered by the incorporation of two platoons of former Kriegsmarine volunteers of the 2/28 because they knew how to march and parade like Germans.

At Wildflecken, former *Miliciens* were added. In this way, the *Wach-und Ausbildungskompanie* comprised all the constituent elements of 'Charlemagne', although the French Sturmbrigade and the Kriegsmarine were well represented.

A certain Unterscharführer by the name of Eugène Vaulot, who had come to the Waffen-SS from the 2/28 of the Kriegsmarine, made such an impression on Oberjunker Martres that he requested his promotion to Oberscharführer. This, however, the Inspection refused.[16]

Trouble flared when a former *Milicien* was found in possession of a 2 Franc coin with a hole through it. This meant nothing to Martres, but to other former *Miliciens* it was a symbol of the maquis! They started to quiz the man with the coin. Nobody knew of him. Some feared he might be a maquis infiltrator. Martres never got to the bottom of it because, one or two days

---

12    Presumably these additional companies were broken up at a later date.
13    Interestingly, de Vaugelas may have commanded the Panzerjäger Battalion briefly before he was appointed as Chief-of-Staff (see Soulat, *Historique de la Division Charlemagne*, p.5).
14    This was probably early October 1944. Martres had only been out of Kienschlag a matter of weeks before he received this command.
15    Roland Charles was born on 16 June 1922 in Saint-Louis, Senegal. Interestingly, Pierre Méric is convinced that their paths had crossed at Uriage.
16    Martres believes that he had the support of Ustuf. Patzak of the Inspection, but not that of Krukenberg.

later, around the time of his promotion to Untersturmführer on 9 November 1944, a German officer by the name of Weber arrived.

Wilhelm Weber was born on 19 March 1918 in Pivitsheide, Westphalia.[17] His father was a mason. After completing his basic education, he entered the Trade School in Detmold, but as a member of the Hitlerjugend, he received an altogether different education. From 1 April 1936 to 31 March 1937, he served with the RAD [Reichs Arbeitsdienst, the Reichs Labour Service] at Bad Salzuflen. On 26 June 1937, he joined the SS-VT and was assigned to the 1st Company/ SS-Standarte 'Germania' in Hamburg. He would serve with 'Germania' until 1944.

By the time war broke out, Weber was a NCO in command of an armoured scout car. He served in the Polish Campaign of September 1939, winning the Iron Cross 2nd Class, in the Western Campaign of 1940, and then in Russia. By July 1941, he had worked his way up to the rank of SS-Oberscharführer and was now in command of a motorcycle reconnaissance platoon. From April 1942 to November 1942, he attended SS-Junkerschule Braunschweig, graduating with the rank of SS-Standartenoberjunker. Shortly afterwards, he was promoted to SS-Untersturmführer. Until 1944 he remained a platoon commander.

In August of 1944, leading a special SS Training Company in the defence of Riga, Latvia, Weber came to the attention of SS-Oberführer Krukenberg. Weber went on to command the 2nd SS Armoured Recce Training Company in Staumühle before Krukenberg requested his transfer to 'Charlemagne'.

In early November 1944, Ustuf. Weber came to Wildflecken. Brigf. Krukenberg assigned him to the *Wach-und Ausbildungskompanie*. He was to work together with Martres. However, Martres remembers well the first day Weber arrived. Weber walked straight into his office and started to go through his desk draws, as though the office and the *kompanie* was his. Martres exploded. The *kompanie* was his and his alone.

Martres and Weber continued to clash. The Inspection resolved the conflict by transferring Martres to the vacant post of Orderly Officer of Waffen-Gren. Regt. der SS 57.[18] Although disappointed, he obeyed as a good soldier. Orders are orders. Besides, he preferred this post to any other in the regiment.[19] He remained very proud of having built the base of the *Wach-und Ausbildungskompanie*.

17    According to Mabire, Weber was born three years later. This is incorrect.
18    Curiously, according to Mabire, *La Division Charlemagne*, p.203, when Kreis arrived at Wildflecken with the rank of Untersturmführer following a long period of convalescence to recover from wounds received in Galicia with the Sturmbrigade Brigf. Krukenberg decided to appoint him as the commander of the *Wach-und-Ausbildungs-kompanie*. However, like many from the Sturmbrigade, Kreis felt ill at ease in 'Charlemagne' which was no longer their 'SS'. Several days after his appointment, Weber arrived. As the two of them held the same rank, had the same bad-tempered and stubborn personality, and insisted on being its sole commander, sparks flew. Krukenberg now intervened, promoting Weber to Obersturmführer, with effect from the 9 November 1944, and dispatching Kreis as an instructor to annex Neweklau of SS-Panzergrenadierschule Kienschlag. In response to this version, at no time was Ustuf. Kreis the commander of the *Wach-und-Ausbildungskompanie* in its infancy (personal discussion with Martres). This is also confirmed by Soulat, a member of the *Wach-und-Ausbildungs-kompanie* in its infancy, who does not recall Kreis as his company commander (letter to the author, 11/6/98). Curiously, Louis Lavest, a member of the *Wach-und-Ausbildungskompanie* states that Oberjunker Kreis was his platoon commander around the end of December (*Le soleil se couchait à l'est*, p.48.) The author has not been able to explain these discrepancies.
19    This post was previously filled by Oberjunker Stehli.

Soulat also had cause to remember well the arrival of Weber: like all those who no longer satisfied the minimum height requirement for the *Wach-und Ausbildungskompanie*, Soulat was transferred out. And yet, before his arrival, Weber, who had heard good things of Soulat, had pulled a few strings to have him as his *putzer* [orderly]. Soulat went to the Headquarters Company, whereas most went to the Engineer Company and the Medical Company. Avinain took the place of Soulat. He too was former Kriegsmarine with service in the 6/28 at Sennheim and then in the 2/28 at Duisberg. The minimum height for the *Wach-und Ausbildungskompanie* was one metre seventy (or one metre seventy-five).[20]

Louis Lavest was assigned to the *Wach-und Ausbildungskompanie* because he met its height criteria: he was one metre 83 tall. Born on 13 November 1925 in Lyon, he had been shocked by the defeat of 1940 and left indignant at the illusions of French military power. From *Les Compagnons de France*, a Vichy Government approved youth movement in the Unoccupied zone, he was drawn to 'serve France against Bolshevism' in the ranks of the *Franc-Garde* of the *Milice*. Moreover, his father had been denounced for hiding a Jew but a good friend had intervened on his behalf on condition that his son joined the *Franc-Garde*. So in mid-April 1944, he joined the *Franc-Garde* in Lyon.

Thanks to Radio London, Lavest was all too aware of the risks he was now taking by joining the *Franc-Garde* and he survived two attempts to kill him: once while sat in a bistro with friends from the *Franc-Garde* and the other while on guard duty. Chaos followed the news of the débarquement, the insurrection ordered by London, and the response by Darnand to mobilize the *Franc-Garde bénévoles*. Wanting out of this chaos, he volunteered for the Waffen-SS, which was refused by his superior.

At the end of August, Lavest fled with the *Milice* to Germany and spent the month of September in Pforzheim. One morning, his *chef* asked his unit if they wish to volunteer for Waffen-SS. Only Lavest and two others did. After a medical by military doctors, he was declared 'fit for service'. He was still impatiently awaiting his transfer when he arrived at Wildflecken with the *Milice* in November 1944.

### The story of Jean-Louis Puechlong

Also assigned to the *Wach-und-Ausb.Kompanie* was Jean-Louis Puechlong, born on 20 February 1920 in Sainte-Foy-lès-Lyon (four kilometres from Lyon). His father was a career soldier, who was wounded seven times during the course of World War One. While being treated for his seventh wound in a military hospital he met a nurse who would later become his wife. By the end of the war, he held the rank of lieutenant. He left the army in 1933. A royalist, he brought his son up in the 'spirit of war for the return of the King'.

Aged fifteen, Jean-Louis Puechlong entered the world of far right politics; he joined the *Jeunesses Patriotes*. He guarded its political meetings in Lyon and the surrounding region. Although a fervent patriot, he came to admire Italy, but dare not express it at home. And then, in 1937, he accompanied a group of French scouts to a Hitler Youth camp in Bavaria. He was

---

20  Curiously, according to Mabire, *La Division Charlemagne*, p.202, this minimum height was applied from the start.

seduced by 'this active, patriotic youth, showing its will and its hope'. Nevertheless, it was with fear that he viewed the German menace becoming clearer every day.

In 1938, Puechlong enrolled in a Lyon university to study law, but in November 1939 he decided to enlist. He was posted to the *27e régiment de Tirailleurs Algériens* (27e RTA). From January to mid-May 1940, he attended E.O.R. training at camp La Courtine and, upon graduation, was commissioned as a *aspirant* with the suffix *à titre temporaire*. His twelve days of combat for France were without glory and without merit! He was retreating with his battalion to the fortress of Pont-Saint-Esprit when he learnt of the appeal from Marshal Pétain to stop fighting.[21] He cried. It was terrible.

To Puechlong, the young nationalist, the defeat of France was a catastrophe. He believed that the war was lost in advance because France did not believe in it. This was evident from the Army's lack of preparation to its lack of equipment, and from the officers' lack of morale to their lack of will. He liked order and discipline, but France was left spiritless before the will to conquer, the physical condition, and the morale of Germany.

Demobilised at the end of August 1940, Puechlong was assigned to *Groupement 15* of the *Chantiers de la Jeunesse* at Agay (Var); all men of his age, that of twenty which was the normal age of conscript service, were required by law to serve in the *Chantiers*. Over the next two years he rose through its ranks; at first *Chef d'atelier*, then *Assistant de chef de Groupe* and then *Chef de Groupe*. At the start of November 1942, he left the *Chantiers* after a bust up with a camp chaplain who was 'too attached to the values of this world when they had pretty underwear'.

On his return to Lyon, Puechlong took the advice of his father and joined the *Légion Française des Combattants*. Soon after, he passed to the *Service d'Ordre Légionnaire* where he felt at home in 'this nationalist milieu' which 'stood up to those who faced us'. He regarded as his enemies the communists, the socialists and the anarcho-syndicalists. Not so his first cousin who had joined the FTP and who was shot at Grigny after an act of sabotage carried out by his unit. He regarded him as a Hero. The German occupation of the Free Zone in November 1942 left him feeling ashamed and 'distraught that he could not do anything'.

Puechlong found himself in conflict with a Christian group of the *Jeunesse Ouvrière Christians* he belonged to after he continued to espouse his national ideas, his visceral maurrassisme and his typically French Pétainism.

In March 1943, Puechlong was called-up by the S.T.O. for work in Germany and, although the avenue of joining the maquis was very much open to him as a means of escaping it, he agreed to leave. To him, the S.T.O. was state law, even though it was in no way honorable. Moreover, his father had advised him to leave so as to avoid any possible trouble for his younger brother, then aged 18.

Puechlong was assigned to the Messerschmitt A.G. factory complex at Augsburg-Haunstetten. As an interpreter in a work camp, he made a number of good contacts with fellow workers and then with the local German population. He visited a college correspondent soon after his arrival, where he was made very welcome and asked to consider his house as his home. In this way, he grew to admire the will of the German people.

---

21    On 17 June 1940, Marshal Pétain announced to the country over the radio that the fighting must stop and that he had approached the enemy to negotiate an end to hostilities.

With politics still close to his heart, Puechlong organised a section of the SOL in the region. In May 1943, he 'converted' to the *Milice française* and was made responsible by Henri Charbonneau for the Gau [district] of Augsburg.

At the head of a thirty-strong contingent of civilian *Miliciens, Chef de centaine* Puechlong went out to spread the politics of Marshal Pétain to the kommandos of French POWs in the work camps. However, the German authorities did not always appreciate their political activity and there were some minor clashes.

Puechlong knew of the recruiting office for French volunteers of the Waffen-SS in Paris but believed his work and that of his compatriots in the camps was more useful than military service. Then came the Allied 'terror' raids on Augsburg and surrounding villages. Puechlong went to the help of the innocents. He never forgot the flames, the screams, the phosphorous, trying to get upstairs on fire, and mothers, who were trapped, throwing small children and babies from third or fourth floor windows that the rescuers, despite their best efforts, could not catch. It was terrible.

And then one Saturday afternoon the Allied bombers came back and completely destroyed the *KZ lager* next to Puechlong's camp. More than two thousand were killed. Puechlong remained convinced that he and a friend escaped almost certain death at the work camp when they went off to help the townspeople of Augsburg.

For Puechlong, the *Boche* of yesterday died in the terror bombardments, which, he reasoned, was war, undoubtedly total war, but now he too wanted to wage war, a war that was not in the west against his compatriots nor his erstwhile Allies of 1939, but a war against Russia and 'its invading tentacle of Bolshevism'.

In a gesture of European patriotism, Puechlong enlisted in the Waffen-SS. The date was late June 1944. He later explained:

> I also wanted to show a will of total war with those who appeared as though they wanted to defend, before this danger of an invasion of Europe by the Russians, our ethics [and] our concern about remaining free in a Europe without restriction. This solidarity with Germany seemed to me the only guarantee of our future liberty. At that time the Waffen-SS was the surest means to fight against the Russian invader till the end.

Puechlong believed that the SS order was born 'as a reaction against a war that was proclaimed as one of liberation and which was only an odious fight for the enslavement of the European man'.

Puechlong was sent to the *Franz. SS-Grenadier-Ausbildungs und Ersatz-Btl.* at Greifenberg. On his arrival in September 1944, he was assigned to the 1st Company of Ostuf. Ludwig. That November, he was transferred to Wildflecken. One metre seventy-eight tall, he too was assigned to the *Wach-und Ausbildungskompanie der Inspektion.*

The *Wach-und Ausbildungskompanie* was now almost two hundred-strong. With the help of some German NCOs, Weber reorganised the *Wach-und Ausbildungskompanie* into four platoons. At the head of the first platoon was Oscha. François Appolot and at that of the second was Uscha. Eugène Vaulot. Notably, the two of them were French volunteers of the Kriegsmarine who were serving in the ranks of the 2nd Company of the 28 SStA [2/28] when integrated into the Waffen-SS.

The twenty-strong sections were, for the most part, commanded by fanatical French Sturmmann who had been wounded in Galicia with the Sturmbrigade. An entire platoon, called *Jugend* [Youth], consisted solely of those under the age of eighteen. Indeed, in its ranks were some even under the age of sixteen. Because of their age they did not receive the daily ration of three cigarettes.

As his assistant Ostuf. Weber chose Oberjunker Jacques Pasquet. Born on 25 November 1913 in Tours (department of Indre-et-Loire), he was described as having been 'at various times the best athlete in Europe and, once, in the world'.[22] An exponent of physical culture, he won the title of Mr. France in 1937! He joined the *Milice* and served as the *inspecteur départemental de la Milice* for Indre and then the *sécretaire départemental de la Milice* for Maine-et-Loire. In June 1944, when a family member was abducted, he returned to Nice.

The key position of *Spiess* (Company Sergeant-Major) went to SS-Oscha. Klein, a Luxembourg national, whom Weber had brought with him. Following the reshuffle, Weber now set about moulding the *Compagnie d'Honneur* in his own image. An extraordinary individual, Weber did not ask anything of his men that he was not capable of himself.

The training programme was ferocious. Route marches of 30kms, 50kms and even 60kms. Endless arms drills. Endless combat training. Anti-tank training. Twenty-four hours a day in the freezing cold and deep snow. All commands were given in German and when Weber spoke it was never in French. He was sparing with compliments. Any error was punished with yet more exercise. Each and every day the volunteers united more and more. Their military background and political orientation became a thing of the past. They 'fought neither for France nor Germany, but for a Europe without inner borders, governed by their caste, subject to their law'.[23]

Predictably, the *Compagnie d'Honneur* was detested and taunted for being germanophile by the *Miliciens* and legionnaires. Yet its esprit de corps was envied throughout 'Charlemagne'. Gradually its volunteers were admired and emulated. In this way, Krukenberg's strategy started to pay dividends and he then made use of the company as a training tool.

In December 1944, some twenty members of the *Compagnie d'Honneur*, including Puechlong and Lavest, were sent to Paderborn for NCO training. They were assigned to the *3. Unterführer Lehrgang Kompanie* made up of two hundred trainees all hailing from different backgrounds in the Waffen-SS. The training was hard, recalls Lavest, but on a par with that in the *Compagnie d'Honneur*.

The *Compagnie d'Honneur* was not the only unit regarded as personifying the SS spirit. The FLAK Company also burned with the same spirit that was born of Fayard, its commander, the embodiment and soul of the Company, appointed to Ustuf. on 8 October 1944, and also of the independence the Company enjoyed. Identifying more with the Germans, Fayard sought to evade any dealings with the French Waffen-SS hierarchy! To this end, official paperwork from the Schreibstude [Office] of the FLAK Company had always been headed with the legend 'SS-Französische Flakbatterie'[24] and had never carried any reference to a superior corps. Indeed,

---

22   De la Mazière, *Ashes of Honour*, p.61.
23   Saint-Loup, *Les Hérétiques*, p.210.
24   Indeed, according to Soulat, *Histoire de la Charlemagne*, p.26, on 28 April 1944, the FLAK Company received final designation 'SS-Französische Flak-Batterie'. If this is correct, then the FLAK Company would have been the only French unit to carry the 'SS' and not the 'Waffen' prefix.

much of the paperwork emanating from higher echelons, especially at Wildflecken, referred to Fayard as SS-Untersturmführer. In fact, the 'SS' prefix to rank was adopted by all rather than that of 'Waffen'. And yet they did not abandon their distinctive French characteristics. They all but considered themselves as an 'Army of occupation in Germany!'

The FLAK Company was also truly cosmopolitan and integrated. There was no question of politics. If proof were needed, in early November 1944, when Ustuf. Fayard reorganised his *encadrement*, he brought in former *Miliciens* or *légionnaires* of the LVF. Of the opinion that platoon commanders Mary and Ouvre had grown too familiar, Fayard appointed former *Milicien* Hscha. Pierre Junquet[25] to the head of the 2nd Platoon and former *légionnaire* Uscha. André Masson to the head of the 3rd Platoon.

In the same reorganisation, Fayard managed to rid himself of the troublesome Rechnungsführer [Pay clerk] Hscha. Brillet, a former prisoner, to the PAK Company.[26] Rttf. Jund or Jundt, a placid Alsatian, succeeded him.

In addition, there was promotion of all from the rank of Rottenführer to Unterscharführer and of all from Sturmmann to Rottenführer. As for all those who had served in the FLAK Company since its creation, they received the rank of Oberschütze.

Around the same time, Std.Ob.Ju. Vincenot was transferred to the PAK Company. He was sorry to leave the FLAK Company. Ustuf. Fayard replaced him at the head of the 1st Platoon with Oscha. de Barthès de Montfort, who was ex-LVF.[27] Fayard was assisted by Uscha. Harry Hum.

## Gendarmerie de Brigade

General Puaud, finding himself left with a number of old LVF NCOs of little use, took the inititaive in forming a small platoon of some twenty such veterans he called the 'Gendarmerie de Brigade'. This was in addition to the military police of SS-Feldgendarmerie Trupp 57.

At the head of the Gendarmerie was Ostuf. Veyrieras, who took up this position in December 1944 after a brief stint as the company commander of the PAK Company. His assistant was Oscha. Charles Henkinett, born in 1908 in Longwy (department Meurthe-et-Moselle). He was awarded the KVK.II.

One of those assigned to the Gendarmerie de Brigade was Hscha. Albert Vianello. Italian by birth, he was granted French nationality thanks to thirteen years' service with the French Foreign Legion.[28] He enlisted in the *Légion Tricolore* in Morocco in August 1942 and passed to the LVF in 1943. He served with the I. Bataillon and survived the ambush of 13 June 1944, although seriously wounded. He only returned to service in January 1945 with an atrophied.

---

25    Pierre Junquet was born 9 September 1920 in Toulouse. He served with the rank of *aspirant* in the artillery in Syria during 1939-1940. Another individual by the name of Junquet served with the FLAK Company. His rank was Strmm.

26    Born on 30 September 1911 in La Flèche (department la Sarthe), Brillet served with the rank of *adjutant* in the *22e regiment d'infanterie* during the French campaign.

27    Articles *SS-Französische FlakBatterie* and *Le Schreiber* (unpublished). However, a document in the author's possession headed *Encadrement of the FLAK* records de Montfort at the head of the 2nd platoon and Junquet at the head of the 1st platoon.

28    Albert Vianello was born on 14 August 1906 in Venice, Italy.

## Waffen-Grenadier Regiment der SS 58

Stubaf. Bridoux, formerly of the LVF, had actively supported and encouraged its entry into the Waffen-SS three months before. However, since then, the commander of Waffen-Grenadier Regiment der SS 58 had undergone a change of heart and now anxiously sought to ensure that the military rather than the Doriotist spirit of the LVF lived on. The reasons behind his change of heart and his subsequent abandonment of post after a visit from his father, General Bridoux,[29] are not known.[30]

Without informing anybody of his decision, Stubaf. Bridoux suddenly left Wildflecken[31] the day after his father had called on him.[32] Obf. Puaud attempted to hush up his disappearance as leave but Bridoux, the respected defender of Bobr, never returned. Nevertheless, Puaud was not angry to see his most dangerous rival, one of the few career officers serving in 'Charelmagne', disappear because some German officers of the Inspection would have been happy to see Bridoux oust him and take over.[33] As for Brigf. Krukenberg, although angry on hearing the news of Bridoux's departure, he remained level-headed and argued that he only wanted volunteers and 'not those who had joined the forces of the Reich out of ambitiousness'.[34]

Brigf. Krukenberg appointed Hstuf. Émile Raybaud the new commander of Waffen-Gren. Regt der SS 58. Confronted with the situation of being a *Milicien* in command of a regiment deemed Doriotist, Raybaud held officer and NCO meetings and then assembled his whole regiment to appeal to them to drop politics and concentrate on preparing for battle. However, his appeal was not heeded by all. To curtail the political agitation of Ostuf. Auphan, his Intelligence Officer, who had built up a Doriotist network within the regiment, Raybaud had him transferred to Brigade Headquarters.

29   At the time of his visit to Wildflecken General Bridoux was concerned with military affairs and prisoners in Brinon's 'French Government in exile'.

30   Unfortunately, the instigating conversation between father and son is not known. However, Saint-Loup records Bridoux's growing unhappiness (*Les Hérétiques*, p.157): he was accused by his peers of belonging to Vichy's Deuxième Bureau and he thought he had uncovered a PPF plot against him.

31   Curiously, Landwehr states in *Charlemagne's Legionnaires*, p.58, that, after meeting with his father, Stubaf. Bridoux then joined a Battalion of SS Regiment 57, but no other source substantiates this.

32   Saint-Loup, *Les Hérétiques* p.158. However, according to Mabire, *La Division Charlemagne*, pp.217-218, Bridoux left Wildflecken that same evening after summoning many former officers of the LVF and informing them of his decision. This came as a shock to those present, reported as Oscha. Girard, company commander of the 10/58, Ustuf. Rigeade, company commander of the 3/58, and Ostuf. Fatin, company commander of the 1/58, who were all very angry and felt a great sense of betrayal. They tried their best to convince him to reverse his decision but failed. In response to this, Mabire is incorrect; in a letter to the author, 31/1/97, Rigeade states that Bridoux did not speak to him or to any other former LVF officers before departing. Nevertheless, Rigeade did say in the same letter that Mabire correctly reflected their feelings about the departure of Bridoux.

33   Soulat, *Histoire de la Charlemagne*, p.89.

34   Mabire, *La Division Charlemagne*, p.219. However, Brigf. Krukenberg may have been much more involved; some thirty years after the event, Krukenberg declared that he had learnt that as soon as it was a question of going up to the front Obf. Puaud had intended to announce to him his dismissal of Bridoux. Thereupon, Krukenberg put Bridoux in the picture and advised him to leave without delay. (See Soulat, *Histoire de la Charlemagne*, p.89.) If true, this is a most remarkable revelation and one which could be interpreted as Krukenberg actually finding himself impotent before Puaud.

'Submissive son of the Church', Hstuf. Raybaud also sought the assistance of Mgr. de Mayol de Lupé in the depoliticisation of his regiment; the prelate still retained considerable influence over his former congregation of dear Legionnaires and reassured Raybaud that he would have no problems with them. And yet, his political problems were still not laid to rest. A network of French informers was uncovered feeding back the political thoughts of their comrades to a German officer of the Inspection who was close to Brigf. Krukenberg. Raybaud went straight to Krukenberg and demanded the cessation of this activity. The Brigadeführer actually had no knowledge of this activity and agreed to Raybaud's demand. In this way, Raybaud finally became the only political leader of the regiment.

To those officers and NCOs of his regiment that might have been surprised that their new *chef* was without any war decorations, Hstuf. Raybaud explained on the occasion of a meeting the circumstances around the *Croix de guerre avec palms* awarded to him.

Waffen-Gren. Regt der SS 58 was made up of some 15% *Miliciens* and 80% legionnaires of the LVF. At the head of the 1st Battalion was Hstuf. Émile Moneuse. He was ex-*Milice*. And at the head of the 2nd Battalion was Hstuf. Maurice Berret. He was ex-LVF.

Courageous and devoted, Moneuse was a professional soldier with good military knowledge, but his age, he was well into his forties, sometimes got the better of him and his 'heavy responsibility'. His assistant was the very able W-Ostuf. Falcy who had previous military service with the *chasseurs alpins* and the LVF.[35] When the LVF was transferred to the Waffen-SS its 2nd Company became the 2/58 with Falcy still at its head. Promoted to assistant battalion commander, he had to give up his 2nd Company to Ostuf. de Rose.[36]

Raybaud placed Hstuf. de Perricot, one of his most trusted men, in command of the Headquarters Company. Born on 20 March 1893 in Damazan in the department of Lot-et-Garonne, Marc-Raoul de Perricot was called up in 1914 and went on to become an officer, serving as the *chef* of his regiment's *corps franc*. Volunteering for dangerous missions, he covered himself in glory and was awarded the *Croix de guerre* with three citations as well as the prestigious *Chevalier de la Légion d'honneur*. He finished the war as a company commander. He left the Army but was placed into the reserves. On 30 March 1924, he was promoted to the rank of *lieutenant de reserve* and, then in 1935, he switched to the *service de santé* [health service], obtaining the rank of *pharmacien lieutenant de réserve* on 11 May 1938. When war came again in 1939 he did his bit behind the front line, although he wanted a combat posting.

In the years that followed de Perricot proved himself time and time again: in March 1942 as the *chef* of the SOL for the department of Lot-et-Garonne; in 1943 as the *chef départemental* of the *Milice* for the same department; and in April 1944 as the *chef régional* for 'Toulouse'. Lastly, in September 1944, at Schirmeck, when the *Milice* was reorganized, he was appointed *chef* of one of the six Cohortes (Toulouse). His two sons, Gérard and Michel, who had also joined the *Milice*, were also now serving in 'Charlemagne'.

Raybaud's assistant was the ageing Ostuf. Marcel Baudouin, born on 11 May 1902 in Saint-Géréon (department Loire-Altantique). By October 1937, he held a commission of *lieutenant*

35    Although his exact role within the regiment remains unclear, de Genouillac believes that Falcy was the *adjoint* to the commander of the I/58. The suggestion has also been made that Falcy was even the *adjoint* to Raybaud, the regimental commander. Although Falcy was sufficiently qualified to hold either post, the author, in the face of no official documentation, has gone along with de Genouillac.
36    Born on 29th May 1914 in Paris, André de Rose joined the LVF in June 1944.

*d'active* in the infantry.[37] After the French campaign of 39-40 he became a *commissaire de police*. In 1942, he volunteered for *La Légion Tricolore* and served as *adjoint* to *Commandant* Herchin, the *chef du dépôt* of Montargis. He later transferred to the LVF and served on the headquarters staff of the II.Bn. He was a holder of the Kriegsverdienstkreuz (War Merit Cross) 2nd Class.

The company commanders of the Waffen-Gren. Regt. der SS 58 were drawn from both the LVF and the *Milice*. Their tricolore spirit did not displease Raybaud. But the combat experience of the LVF officers was in striking contrast to that of their *Milicien* counterparts.

## I. Battalion/Waffen-Gren. Regt der SS 58

The battalion was made up of four companies, numbered one to four. At the head of the 1/58 was Ustuf. Jean Fatin.[38] He was an 'old hand' of the LVF who had served on the Eastern Front since the terrible winter of 1941 and come up through the ranks. In mid-June 1944, while Obitz was on leave, he took command of the 1st Company.

Like Fatin, the four platoon commanders of the 1/58 were LVF veterans of 1941. At the head of the 1st Platoon was Oscha. Girard. At the head of the 2nd Platoon was Oscha. Froideval from the south of France, who had served as Seveau's *adjoint* in the *section de chasse*. His son, Paul Froideval, was also serving with the 1st Platoon. At the head of the 3rd Platoon was Oscha. Bonnafous, a former *gendarme*. And at the head of the 4th Platoon (heavy) was Scha. Nicolas Choumiline. A white Russian with a very strong Russian accent, he too had served in the French Army.[39] He was awarded with the *Croix de guerre légionnaire* in May 1943 for displaying a 'total disregard for danger'.

The company commander of the 2/58 was Ostuf. de Rose, also from the LVF. One of his platoon commanders was Oscha. Méric. They had met before at mass and got on well. Ostuf. de Rose would relinquish this command in mid-January 1945 to Ostuf. Géromini.

At the head of the 3/58 was Ustuf. Yves Rigeade. He too was an old hand of the LVF who had served on the Eastern Front since 1941. For three years he served with the 3rd Company, working his way up through the ranks. He was promoted to *Sous-lieutenant* on 1 April 1944. From 20 May to 12 June 1944, while *Capitaine* Martin was on leave, he took command of the 3rd Company. Following the hospitalisation of Martin on 24 June, he again took over command. Three days later, on 27 June, he was wounded at Bobr and evacuated. In August 1944, he resumed command.

Three platoon commanders of the 3/58 were also LVF veterans who had served on the Eastern Front since 1941. At the head of the 1st Platoon was twenty-six-year-old Oscha. Armani, a PPF militant, born of a Corsican father and a Madagascan mother. At the 2nd Platoon was Oscha. René Stiffler. He too was a PPF militant. He was a native of Nice. At the 3rd Platoon was Oscha. Blonay. He was a *Franciste*. Uscha. Antoine Tartaglino commanded the 4th (Mortar) Platoon.[40] He was a *Milicien* who had come to the company in November 1944. The *adjudant de compagnie* (or Spiess) was Hscha. Jean Perrigault. Born on 27 November 1898 in Cormery

37   He probably gained his commission at the *école militaire d'infanterie de Saint-Maixent*.
38   Jean Fatin was born on 4 July 1917. During the French campaign of May-June 1940 he served as an NCO with the 107e RI.
39   Jean Grenouillet, letter to the author, April 1998.
40   Antoine Tartaglino was born on 29 March 1921 in Saint-Etienne.

Rigeade of the LVF at a Russian wedding in 1943. (Rigeade)

(department of Indre-et-Loire), he was a former serviceman and had also served with the LVF since 1941 and was awarded the the *Croix de guerre légionnaire* in May 1943 for 'leading his platoon in a remarkable way'. He did not belong to any political party. By trade he was a professional draughtsman.

In late December 1944, Uscha. Blonay, who commanded an infantry platoon, was surprised that he was sent to Berlin for training to command a heavy machine-gun platoon. He believes that he was the only Frenchman on the course. His absence from his comrades was made all the more bearable by his friendship with an Austrian officer, his wife and his daughter living in Berlin. The German instructors, who were all war wounded and sometimes disabled, trained him in the use of heavy machine guns and also in anti-tank combat with the Panzerfäust and Panzerschreck. He witnessed numerous air raids on the city, which was already in ruins. In late January 1945, the course was interrupted by the arrival of the Russians at Kustrin, only some eighty kilometers away. In early February, fearing that he would be forcibly incorporated into a German unit for the defense of Berlin, he returned to Wildflecken without authorisation. On his return, he was promoted to the rank of Oberscharführer.

Ustuf. de Genouillac commanded the 4th (Heavy) Company of Battalion I/58. During the reorganisation of the LVF at Greifenberg he had been made responsible for the training of the 4th (heavy) Company of the I. Battalion which became the 4/58 in 'Charlemagne'. Three of his four theoretical platoon commanders were from the LVF: *élève-officier* Antonie Noell,[41] who he had known in Russia and who had proved himself notably at Bobr, commanded a platoon of 80mm mortars; *Adjudant-chef* Bonnefous commanded a heavy machine-gun platoon; and Jean-Louis Martin commanded the second heavy machine-gun platoon.[42] The last platoon commander, *élève-officier* Jean Chatrousse, one of his comrades from his French Army days, had arrived at Wildflecken with the *Milice*. In fact, after meeting Chatrousse quite by chance in the camp, de Genouillac had had him assigned to his company. His transfer had presented no problems. However, for the best part of the months December, January and February, the platoon commanders were away from their commands at officer training schools or on officer training courses. Some would not rejoin the company.

The Heavy Company was short of its 12cm mortars and the vehicles to tow them. Instead, it had to rely on horses, but they all had strangles and were not properly cared for. De Genouillac explained that most of the volunteers were students or workers who had no knowledge of matters equine. When he raised his concerns about the horses he was told: "But are you not a cavalry officer?" He did not reply.

On one occasion de Genouillac found himself in front of Krukenberg for not returning to him a list of German songs sung by his company. This he had completely neglected to do. With three others, he was harshly rebuked.

## II. Battalion/Waffen-Gren. Regt der SS 58

The battalion was made up of four companies, numbered five to eight. At the head of Company 5/58 was Ostuf. Georges Wagner, who had also commanded its forerunner, the 9th Company of the III/638 (LVF).[43] Platoon commanders came and went. Hscha. Edmond Walter, who was ex-LVF, was succeeded by Oscha. Blaise, also ex-LVF. It is said that Blaise had served with the Foreign Legion. Uscha. Jean-Marie Croisile, commanded the heavy machine-gun platoon. He too was ex-LVF. However, on 30 September, he requested a transfer to Regt der SS 57 to be closer to his father. On 3 October, his transfer was accepted and he left the very same day to join the 3/57. He was replaced by Uscha. René Maixendeau. Seriously wounded in Galicia with the French Sturmbrigade, he still walked with a limp. Junker Pierre Ruskone, who was ex-LVF, joined as a platoon commander in December 1944. The fourth platoon commander may have been ex-*Milice*.[44] The Company *Spiess* was Oscha. Both. He was ex-LVF. Hscha. Gobion, the LVF legend, was the company's armourer.

41  Antonie Noell was born on 20 August 1922 in Vinça (department of Pyénées-Orientales).
42  Jean-Louis Martin was born on 27 October 1907 in Lesparre (department Gironde). He was a holder of the KVK. II.
43  Various letters to the author from Blanc and Ruskone, who both served in Company 5/58. This corrects Mabire, who records Walter as the company commander (*La Division Charlemagne*, p.222). Also, according to Ruskone, letters to the author of 2/98 and 5/3/98, it was in early January 1945 that Ostuf. Wagner assumed command of the company. However, according to Blanc, letter to the author of 14/6/2001, when he was assigned to the company in November 1944 Wagner was at its head. Anyway, to end the debate, *Sergent* Jean-Marie Croisile was serving with the 9th Company of the LVF when it was absorbed into 'Charlemagne' as Company 5/58 and he states that Wagner was still at its head.
44  Curiously, Ruskone recalls that Company 5/58 had three platoons. However, the author is convinced that the company would have had four platoons. Ruskone commanded one platoon. Of the other two

Blanc of Company 5/58, who was ex-*Milice*, noted that the ex-LVF cadre had a shared nostalgia for Russia and the Russians. They would often speak of the beauty of the scenery, and of the warm and confiding welcome of the peasants. Indeed, Blaise once confided that after the war he wanted to return to Russia and get a farm there. At the time, Blanc was surprised to hear this but, much later, he would understand. Blanc's section commander was Uscha. Aimé Verstichel, who was succeeded by Gnabel.[45]

Ostuf. Louis commanded the 6/58 and, in early February 1945, he was sent to SS-Kraftfahrschule I at Sbirow.[46] Ustuf. Michel Saint-Magne, also from the LVF, replaced him in his absence. Born on 17 March 1918 in Sainte-Croix-du-Mont (department Gironde), he enlisted in the 9th R.T.A. in October 1936 and did his duty for France during the campaign of 39-40. He enlisted in the LVF with the rank of *sergent* in February 1943 and after basic training was sent to the Russian Front in July 1943 where he was assigned to the 10th Company, serving as a platoon commander.[47] He fought at Bobr in June 1944. He was later awarded the Kriegsverdienstkreuz (War Merit Cross) 2nd Class as well as the *Croix de guerre légionnaire*. He was not a member of any political party.

Saint-Magne now found himself at the head of a grenadier company that had few veterans. For the most part, the *encadrement* of its forerunner, the 10th Company of the III/638, had moved on. Nevertheless, *caporal-chef* Wassili, a former Russian partisan whom the 10th Company had adopted, continued to serve loyally in this new company.[48] He was deaf and dumb.

At the head of Company 8/58 was Ostuf. Paul Defever, who was also ex-LVF. Born on 4 October 1904 in Dunkirk, he took the path of the PMS and the EOR. In 1926, he was commissioned *sous-lieutenant de réserve*. He fought against the Germans in 39-40 and was taken prisoner.

The regiment had at its disposal an Infantry Gun Company and a PAK Company. The commander of Infantry Gun Company 9/58 was Ostuf. Jean Français. Born on 5 May 1914 in Athis-Mons (Seine department), he fought bravely as a *sergent-chef* in the 107e RI against the Germans when war came, winning the *Croix de guerre*. Taken prisoner, he was shipped off to an Oflag and was released when he volunteered for the LVF. Transferred to the Waffen-SS, he became commander of Company 9/58 in November 1944, replacing Ustuf. Briffaut, who was demobilized because of wounds received while serving with the LVF. Français was promoted to Ostuf. on 20 December 1944. His orderly was Robert Lacoste and one of his platoon commanders was *pied-noir* Oscha. Marcel Duchène, born in 1909. The three of them were inseparable. They had joined the LVF in 1943 at the same time, becoming good friends. They had served together in the same company of the LVF, the 5/638, and now, having passed to the Waffen-SS, they were serving together again in the same company.

The following also served in Infantry Gun Company 9/58:

platoon commanders, he recalls one was ex-*Milice* and one was ex-SS [undoubtedly Maixendeau]. Bouysse suggests that Marcel Carlier may have been the platoon commander, who was ex-*Milice*.

45    Aimé Verstichel was born on 21 August 1920 in Lille.
46    According to one veteran, Louis was in poor physical shape. Curiously, the same veteran recalls Louis serving in Company 5/58.
47    Saint-Magne may have also taken temporary command of the 9th Company.
48    In this way, his homeland became the 10th Company of the LVF that had welcomed him. With a French tricolore on his arm, he was killed in Pomerania.

- Grenadier Ange Bianconi
- Grenadier Henri Chignoli
- Grenadier Roman Hippolyte
- Grenadier Ange Martino
- Grenadier Victor Morini
- Rottenführer Louis Pettini
- Sturmmann Louis Savone
- Uscha. Paul Sauvageot
- Uscha. Xavier Sève

Xavier Sève, who was born on 13 November 1919 in Nice, volunteered for the LVF in 1941 and served with the 13th Company during that first winter. He was awarded the Iron Cross 2nd Class in May 1944. He may have served as a platoon commander in 9/58.[49]

Born on 12 November 1925 in Cannes, Louis Savone volunteered for the LVF in February 1944. After completing his basic training at Greifenberg, he was posted to Russia, arriving on 10 June 1944. He served briefly with the 1st Company before transferring to the 5 Company to be with his brother, Marcel. Transferred to the Waffen-SS, he was assigned to Company 9/58 and promoted to Sturmmann on 1 November 1944. His brother Marcel served with the Engineer Company and was promoted to Oberscharführer in February 1945.

The 9/58 was equipped with French 75mm mountain guns. The guns were horse-drawn.

Oberjunker Jacques Bonnafont commanded the Panzerjäger Kompanie of the regiment, often numbered 10/58. The company comprised a panzerschreck platoon, a panzerfäust platoon, and a platoon (or battery) of three 75mm anti-tank guns, which were French and pre-war. The anti-tank guns were horse-drawn, but the horses died one by one due to a contagious equine infection.

Of his platoon commanders, the company commander recalls that one 'had been with the LVF since 1941' (undoubtedly *Adjudant* Pierre), two 'came from the recruitment drive in the POW camps', and the last 'came from the *Franc-Garde* of the *Milice*'. All were apolitical, with the exception of Pierre who was former PPF. And all had previous military experience.[50]

This company was and remained essentially LVF. Only two or three NCOs from the *Milice* were assigned to the company. Uscha. Jean-Pierre Lefèvre, who was a *chef de dizaine* of the *Franc-Garde permanente*, was posted to this company, but was later selected to command the Headquarters Platoon of Company 8/58.

Oberjunker Bonnafont once incurred the displeasure of Brigf. Krukenberg, but he did bring it upon himself as he recalls:

---

49   Léguerandais, *Hitler's French Volunteers*, p.125.

50   *Sergent* Yves Peyret, who also transferred from the PAK Company of the LVF to Kompanie 10/58, was Pierre's assistant at Bobr. *Adjudant* Pierre is credited with destroying three tanks at Bobr. Transferred to the Waffen-SS, he served with the equivalent rank of Oscha. He was killed late February 1945 at Heringen, in Thuringia, Germany, when American aircraft attacked one of the many convoys transporting 'Charlemagne' to the Eastern Front. When questioned about Pierre, Bonnafont spoke highly of him. Also, Uscha. Soulé may have served as a platoon commander in the 10/58.

Brigf. Krukenberg came to inspect the company. Although it was risky, I presented the company in French and *à la française*, saluting the French salute. This did not please him and, before the men, he hurled reproaches at me in Franco-German. He summoned me and started again. I did not move nor reply ... and they did not take [my] command from me. He was not a spiteful man.

In December 1944, Oberjunker Bonnafont was selected for Kompanieführer training and attended an in-house Lehrgang supervised by SS-Hstuf. Jauss and Ustuf. Pignard-Berthet. Also attending the same Lehrgang were Jean Chatrousse, Tristian de Bazelaire,[51] Marcel Carlier,[52] Maurice Comte, Robert Girard,[53] Jean de Lacaze,[54] d'Oléon, Gérard de Perricot, Georges Girel, Lapart, Pierre Méric, Charles Roumégous[55] and François Terrel.[56] They numbered more than twenty, perhaps as many as thirty. Most were former *Miliciens* and most were NCOs. The training lasted some four weeks.

Jauss also used Bonnafont as an instructor because of his interest in anti-tank warfare and weapons. Notably, for the duration of the course, Bonnafont continued to command and train the Panzerjäger Kompanie: he worked with the NCOs in the evening and at night, leaving them to carry out his orders in the day.

One late afternoon, towards the end of the course, Oscha. Charles, who was demonstrating the use of a Teller mine, tragically met his death. Needless to say, accidents accompany realistic battlefield training. Both Méric and Comte are convinced his death was a tragic accident and their accounts of his death are similar.[57] The officer cadets were gathered around Charles who was demonstrating the use of a T-Mine, which he held out in front of him. When he connected an ignitor the mine exploded, killing him outright. Méric and Comte believe that Charles inadvertently used an instant ignitor rather than a time-based ignitor. The two of them, along with Carlier, collected the body parts scattered on the snow.

Bonnafont is not so convinced Charles' death was an accident and his account differs from those of Méric and Comte:[58]

51  The attendance of de Bazelaire is confirmed by Comte and Pignard-Berthet, correspondence with the author.

52  According to an official German document, Carlier attended Infantry School Döberitz from 28 December 1944 to 1 February 1945. In correspondence with the author, both Comte and Pignard-Berthet confirmed that Carlier attended the Lehrgang at Wildflecken. Thus the possibility exists that Carlier may have started the course and was then sent onto Döberitz. And yet, curiously, Comte recalls visiting Prague with Carlier while attending a Lehrgang at Kienschlag in January 1945, see Comte Maurice, *Une vie sous le signe de Führerprinzip* (Saint-Genis-Laval: Akriberia, 2014), p.50.

53  Bonnafont, letter to the author, 16/10/1999.

54  Jean de Lacaze was born on 10 January 1921 in Labastide-Castel-Amouroux (department Lot-et-Garonne).

55  The attendance of Roumégous is recalled by Méric who was good friends with him (correspondence with the author). In fact, Méric described him as 'the star of our group'.

56  Terrel was born on 29 December 1917 in Mâcon (department Saône-et-Loire). He was the *chef départemental-adjoint de la Milice Française* for department Saône-et-Loire.

57  Méric, interview with the author, and Comte, *Une vie sous le signe de Führerprinzip*, p.48. Admittedly, there are a few minor differences between the two accounts.

58  Bonnafont, letter to the author, 16/10/1999 and interview with Bonnafont.

Charles handled the mine despite my insistence for him not to. I knew, not him. When the mine did not explode he crawled to my hole, some six metres from the mine. I asked him to stay put. Suddenly and without reason, he left the hole and started to approach the mine. I tried to stop him by grabbing hold of his trousers, but the fabric ripped and came away in my hands. He was some three metres from the mine when it exploded. His comrades tried to accuse me of his death, but after a quick inquest Hstuf. Jauss cleared me. I still wonder if Charles did not want to commit suicide. In any case, he succeeded, completely blown to pieces. I brought him back in a tent sheet. The 'others' did not dare come forward or touch. The snow was red and grey.

Nevertheless, Charles was buried in nearby Brückenau cemetery with full military honours in the presence of de Bourmont, who seemed more sombre than ever.

**And yet more problems**

A host of problems plagued the training. To begin with, there was the chronic shortage of food supplies. To supplement their meager rations, some former legionnaires took to poaching, a habit they had picked up on the Eastern Front. The disappearance of a calf in a nearby village led to an inquiry and the military police being brought in. Subsequently, it came to light that some Frenchmen had taken, slaughtered, cut up and eaten the calf in an almost 'magical ceremony'. Krukenberg was beside himself with rage. Puaud sent the culprits to a disciplinary company and sent out notes reminding units of 'SS ideals'.[59]

The rations became so bad at one point that Ostuf. Fatin took his company back to the kitchens and gave the order to throw the contents of their mess tins across the kitchen. Ignoring the protests and the pleas of helplessness from the German cook, Ostuf. Fatin then ordered his company to occupy the kitchen until such time that the cook could come up with something edible to eat. And of course that did not prove too long! This was but one of many such instances instigated by the officers who shared the same meals as their men.

One morning, Company 2/58 under the command of Oscha. Méric along with Company 3/58 under Ustuf. Rigeade were sent by train to Fulda. The railway station area had been heavily bombed and they were put to work cleaning up. Many wagons had been ripped open, but the military police kept a close eye on them to ensure nothing went missing. The work was exhausting, yet 'willingly executed'. That evening the men assembled on the station platform for the return journey whereupon Méric noticed that their sacks seemed much heavier. He said nothing, but Rigeade then announced an impromptu search. Méric managed to talk him out of it, much to his great relief. Back at camp his men thanked him for intervening and showed their appreciation by offering him a share of their goodies, which he refused. He reflected that the incident could have turned out badly for all concerned, especially for him.

59  Saint-Loup, *Les Hérétiques*, p.159. Curiously, de la Mazière recounts an incident on Christmas Day when Krukenberg came across pork being eaten in a dining-hall instead of the veal on the menu. The pork had been brought from a local farmer and smuggled into the camp. Obviously this was strictly forbidden and yet Krukenberg took no disciplinary action in this instance.

Nevertheless, Méric became complicit in the activities of former legionnaires to find food worthy enough to celebrate Christmas. He covered up for the absence of men on their buying trips to farms far and wide. Thankfully they were never caught by the military police.

To stave off hunger, a platoon from Waffen-Gren. Regt der SS 58 assigned to remove horses that had died of impetigo fed on the rotting meat! Perhaps worse, some hungry grooms deliberately had their horse run down so as to get it put down by the veterinary surgeon and gorge themselves on the fresh meat.

Gren. Blanc and his comrades of Company 5/58 also went hungry. Conversations often returned to stories of meals. Such was their hunger that if they had been offered the choice between a snack and a good-looking woman, they would have chosen the snack! So as not to devour in the evening the entire bread ration, and thus have nothing left for the morning, Blanc confided his to a comrade on the understanding that no matter what he was not to give it back to him before the following morning. It was to Le Goff that he confided his bread, and Le Goff confided his to Blanc. This 'pact of bread' was never broken. This sort of communion was a symbol of the camaraderie existing between them. There were lighter moments as Blanc recalled:

> One evening, Jean Priot, who had left to fetch for the platoon two containers of the warm drink called coffee, was late back more than normal. Eventually, he returned and explained; passing near a building, he had heard the third movement of the Brandenburg concerto. He was still 'illuminated' and many of us envied him.[60]

There was also the problem of a shortage of equipment. What weapons were available were often rotated. The fourteen Jagdpanzers promised for the Assault Gun Company had still not arrived.[61] Each regimental commander had a light cross-country vehicle at his disposal, but no petrol for it. Neither was there petrol for the ambulances and Weber was forced to requisition a horse-drawn carriage from a village to get a wounded soldier of the *Compagnie d'Honneur* to hospital. No horses were available to pull the anti-tank guns. There was a distinct lack of practice ammunition and even personal equipment like helmets, gloves, balaclavas, spades and field glasses.

The Signals Company was also short of equipment. The company was commanded by Ostuf. Jean Dupuyau a product of military school Saint-Maixent promoted from *sergent* to active *sous-lieutenant* in December 1939.[62] He joined the *1er Régiment de France* in July 1943 and the *Milice*, making him one of the first officers and one of the few officers to do so. In October 1943, he attended a conference at Limoges in *Milice* uniform contrary to orders of his commanders in the Army and was ejected. Active in the *Milice*, he was quickly appointed to the important position of *Inspecteur général* for the South Zone. In May 1944, he was assigned to Group E of the Maintenance of Order Forces in the Limousin and took part in operations. He commanded a 'company' [probably a *centaine*] of *franc-gardes* sent to Thiviers in the Dordogne. Ten maquisards

---

60 Whenever Blanc heard this piece he would reminisce about his friend and this occasion.
61 According to Mabire, *La Division Charlemagne*, p.188, ten Tiger tanks were promised. This seems doubtful even though the brigade belonged to the elite Waffen-SS. Mabire's source was undoubtedly Soulat's *Historique de la Division Charlemagne*, which was later amended.
62 Jean Dupuyau was born on 6 September 1916 in Pau.

were captured and two were shot on the station square by a firing squad furnished by Dupuyau on the orders of his commanding officer, de Bourmont.[63] On 16 August 1944, he left Limoges for Vichy and then evacuated France. Uscha. Burtheret and Uscha. Sabiani served with the Signals Company.[64] Little else is known about the company.

Wildflecken itself was a problem. Although a modern training camp, it was, throughout the months of winter, covered with snow, sometimes two metres deep. Then there were the violent snowstorms. Indeed, according to Castrillo of Company 5/58, the weather was worse than that he had experienced with the SK in Norway. Such conditions made Wildflecken unsuitable for infantry training. Battalion and regiment maneuvers proved impossible, as well as those in conjunction with its heavy units. Oberjunker Bonnafont of the Panzerjäger Kompanie/58 recalls that the gun range was some two kilometers away through deep snow, making it difficult to access.[65]

The snow gave somebody the idea of forming a scout-ski platoon. Blanc and Le Goff of Company 5/58 were volunteered. Blanc was not asked if he was a good skier, which was not the case. In this way, they made the acquaintance of Lucien Kemarat, born of a French mother and a Thai father. He had been accepted into the ranks of the Waffen-SS when the LVF was disbanded and yet, previously, he had been denied, joining the LVF instead.

The training of the scout-ski platoon was in the hands of a former NCO of the *chasseurs alpins* by the name of Oscha. Alfred Intsaby, born on 5 May 1919.[66] He was a first-rate instructor. Almost every afternoon for a period of six weeks, the men trained. The skis provided, said to be of Norwegian origin, were not very solid and made control downhill almost impossible. The platoon was later disbanded.

Oscha. Méric of 2/58 took full advantage of the snow to go skiing, though. He went skiing on one particularly long day trip with Million-Rousseau who was an excellent skier.[67] The two of them had met at Uriage while serving with the *Milice* and become good friends.

One problem of lesser significance was the language barrier. Few were those who had full mastery of the German language. Indeed, in several units, the *Kompanie-Schreiber* [Company secretary] had little or no knowledge of German![68]

Brigf. Krukenberg remained deeply concerned that some prominent *Miliciens* still harbored political agendas and lacked the appropriate training to execute command. So, in early December, he dispatched Bassompierre and de Bourmont to Heeresschule Güstrow in Mecklenburg for a battalion commander's training course, which lasted one month.[69] Still haunted by the prospect of deployment to the Western Front, Bassompierre wrote to Darnand and called upon him to intervene vigorously to prevent such a scenario.

63    Indictment against Dupuyau, *Cour de justice du department du Cher*, Archives du Cher.
64    Born 1 November 1920 in Tananarive, Madagascar, Henri Sabiani was later proposed for the KVK II.
65    Bonnafont recalls that during one such journey to the gun range he passed La Mazière and his gun.
66    Alfred Intsaby joined the *Franc-Garde* of Basses-Pyrénées. His father and his sister were shot on 21 August 1944.
67    Méric states that Million-Rousseau had served with the *Chasseurs Alpins*, which remains unconfirmed.
68    For example, Soulat's *soldbuch* contains the spelling mistake of *Verselgung* for *Versetzung* [transfer] not once but twice.
69    Mabire, *La Division Charlemagne*, pp.197-198. Curiously, Bassompierre only returned to Wildflecken in mid-February 1945 as the Brigade was leaving for the Eastern Front.

**Headquarters Company**

Transferred to the Brigade's Headquarters Company, Soulat found himself working to SS-Uscha. Max Micholski who, before the war, had worked as the head waiter on the Orient Express! Micholski spoke seven different languages. Of late, he had served with the *Dtsch.Verb. Stab. III/Frz. I.R.638* [the German liaison staff of the III/638].

The Company commander of the Headquarters Company was W-Ostuf. Maudhuit. He reported to SS-Stubaf. Katzian, the German liaison officer.[70] Of Austrian birth, Katzian had fought with the *Gebirgsjäger* [Mountain troops] at Narvik, Norway, and in Crete. He too had served with the *Dtsch. Verb. zum Frz. I.R. 638* and transferred to the French Brigade of the Waffen-SS.

In November or perhaps as late as early December 1944, SS-Stubaf. Katzian was succeeded by the fifty-year-old SS-Stubaf. von Lölhoffel. Like Katzian, he too had served with the *Dtsch. Verb. zum Frz. I.R. 638* before his transfer to the French Brigade of the Waffen-SS.

In late December 1944, Hscha. Surrel succeeded Ostuf. Maudhuit at the head of the Headquarters Company. Born on 30 September 1910, Henri Surrel had served with the LVF, in particular the 11th Company of the III. Battalion and then the celebrated *section de chasse*.

The *Spiess* of the Headquarters Company was Hscha. Auguste Albietz. A veteran of the Great War, who was awarded the prestigious *Chevalier de la Légion d'honneur*, he served in the 2nd Company of the LVF during the first winter before Moscow.

**Fahrschwadron A**

Fahrschwadron A or Fahrschwadron I[71] began to take shape in November 1944 under the command of fifty-three-year-old W-Hstuf. Jean Schlisler. A veteran of the Great War, serving in the Air Force, and awarded the *Croix de guerre* for bravery with three citations, he had served France again in 1940 and was cited again. He went on to serve with *la Légion Tricolore* and then the *Phalange Africaine*, seeing action. On 31 May 1943, at a public ceremony, he was awarded the *Chevalier de la Légion d'honneur*. Months later he joined the LVF.

The assistant commander was W-Ustuf. Darrigade who had previously served with the *Milice*. Born on 26 September 1899 in Cap-Breton (department Landes), he served in the Army from 1919 to 1921, leaving with the rank of *adjudant*. Recalled, he fought in 39-40, was captured, but managed to escape. Like many others, he joined the LFC, transferred to the SOL, and then the *Milice*, becoming a *Chef de centaine* in the *Franc-Garde permanente*. He participated in the operations at Haute-Savoie with a small unit of at least twenty men from Haute-Garonne. As the *chef* of the *Franc-Garde permanente* for Haute-Haronne, he participated in yet more police operations in the department, as well as in Ariège. He was noted for his courage; on one occasion, storming a house held by outlaws, he was wounded twice.

---

70  The memoirs of Soulat. Because of this the possibility exists that the Headquarters Company took its orders from the German Inspection rather than from French Brigade Headquarters as one would have expected. If true, this is surprising.

71  Confusingly, Mercier of Fahrschwadron A also saw used the designation of Waffen-Grenadier-Brigade der SS 'Charlemagne' Kolonne A Fahrschwadron. Lefèvre states that its designation was Waffen-Fahrschwadron der SS 57 (*Axis & Alliés* hors série no 1, p.53).

Darrigade's orderly was Grenadier Henri Soula, who was born on 11 July 1920 in Brassac. Called up by the STO in March 1943, he joined the *Milice* of Ariège to avoid going. Called up yet again in December 1943, he spoke with his *secrétaire départemental* who advised him to join the *Franc-Garde permanente*. It was advice he decided to follow, serving as a cook. Notably, he intervened several times to get suspected resistance he knew released. Even so, he fled to Germany with the *Milice* and ended up in *feldgrau*.

The Spiess was W-Hscha. Goubin from the III. Batallion of the LVF. Fahrschwadron A was organised with three transport columns (Fahrkolonne), an escort (or combat) platoon, and an independent platoon of administrative and support staff.[72] At the head of the transport columns were W-Oscha. Hubert Carbillet and W-Oscha. Bernand. The third *chef* is not known. Hubert Carbillet was ex-LVF and was one of two brothers serving with 'Charlemagne'.[73] Bernand and the unknown *chef* were ex-*Milice*.

Uscha. Mercier, who made the journey from Greifenberg to Wildflecken with Goubin and Carbillet, was assigned to the independent platoon as Rechnungsführer.

One of the most colourful characters of Fahrschwadron A was *adjudant* Louis, who had been inherited from the Trésorerie of the I. Battalion of the LVF. Louis was a pathological liar. Because of his job within the Trésorerie he had acquired the nickname of Baron Louis in memory of the Minister of Finance of Charles X and Louis Philippe. He let it be known that his personal fortune was considerable and included, among other small things, the Lido cabaret in Paris. There was the time a soldier reported saying 'I was told to go and see baron Louis', to which he put on a saddened expression and observed, 'They call me baron when I am a marquis!'

Nobody had ever seen Louis on horseback but his knowledge of equestrian terms let the connoisseur know that he had probably been a waiter or headwaiter in a restaurant frequented by riders. He always put off until the following day the formalities that he needed to do to obtain German nationality. In fact, he thought that it was his by right, being the grandson of a German General.

Louis was idle. Hstuf. Schlisler ordered Uscha. Mercier to go over the head of Louis to organise the support services, which he did. As befitting his status, Louis continued to do nothing.[74]

Fahrschwadron A also 'inherited' Grenadier Hernu. He had once held the rank of *adjudant-chef* and been the *adjudant de battaillon* of the I. Battalion of the LVF but had got into disciplinary problems. Uscha. Mercier was asked by Oscha. Carbillet to take Hernu under his wing and appoint him to a post where he would not be ragged. Mercier had Hernu with him to the end.

Fahrschwadron A was also short of equipment, although it did receive some horse-drawn wagons bearing the inscription 'Carretta di Battaglione', which must have been scrapped before in the days of Garibaldi.

---

72  Mercier, letter to the author, 9/10/2001, although unconfirmed. The independent platoon of administrative and support staff comprised among others the Spiess, the head clerk, the secretary, liaison officers, nurses, stretcher-bearers, armourers, farriers, vets, blacksmiths, the chief accountant, and cooks.

73  Hubert Carbillet was born on 30 March 1914 in Grenoble. He was a former editor of regional daily newspaper *Le Petit Dauphiné*. His brother Marcel was born on 23 December 1915.

74  In February 1945, when 'Charlemagne' left for Pomerania, Louis remained at Wildflecken. It is not known what became of him.

## Sturmgeschütz-Kompanie (The Assault Gun Company)

Jules Dissent and René Gautier, a fellow *Milicien* he knew well, were allocated to the Assault Gun Company.[75] In the absence of assault guns, the training consisted of arms drill *à l'allemande*, exercises and some shooting practice with the old, but efficient Mauser rifle. The company sang German, as well as French songs when it marched. Towards the end of November 1944, as a medical student of one year, Jules Dissent requested a transfer to the newly formed Medical Company, but very nearly blew his chances of the transfer when one day he and two other comrades went in search of food:

> On the way back to camp, we took it in turn to carry the supplies. We were confronted by a patrol of Feldgendarmes, who opened and confiscated the packet with a promise of punishment in addition. Luckily, I was not carrying anything and thus was not worried.

On 4 December 1944, Jules Dissent celebrated a rather miserable twentieth birthday, remarking: 'I belong to a generation whose youth was not marked by many celebrations'. Later that same month, on 20 December, he was finally posted to the Medical Company.

Appointed Oberscharführer, Pierre Aumont of the *Franc-Garde permanente* briefly served with the Assault Gun Company before attending Kienschlag. Ustuf. Jacques Quantin, who attended a training course at Panzerjägerschule Janowitz from 10 October to 11 November 1944, may have also served in the Assault Gun Company.

## Waffen-Sanitäts-Kompanie der SS 57 (The Medical Company)

The Sanitäts-Kompanie and a Krankenkraftwagen-Zug [Ambulance Platoon] were ordered to form on 14 November 1944. W-Hstuf. Dr. Péribère was at the head of the Medical Company. Like many serving in the company, he too was ex-*Milice* and had 'volunteered' of late for the Waffen-SS. Born on 20 June 1896 in Aiguillon (department Lot-et-Garonne), he served in the Colonial Artillery during the Great War and was decorated with the *Croix de guerre*. He went on to study medicine, becoming a surgeon. When war came again he was mobilized as a medical *capitaine* in the 41e *régiment d'artillerie coloniale* (41e RAC). He passed from the LFC to the *Milice* where he served in a medical capacity. In early April 1944, he was made homeless when his home in Villeneuve-sur-Lot was bombed. Notably, he was against the integration of the *Milice* into 'Charlemagne', even so his son, Jacques Péribère, also a *Milicien*, joined 'Charlemagne'.[76]

Nevertheless, nearly all of the officers and NCOs were German.[77] They included Ustuf. Gerd Engel. One notable exception was Ostuf. Louis Rimaud, who must have been the oldest officer serving with 'Charlemagne'. Born on 28 March 1882 in Saint-Etienne (department of

75    Gautier was born in 1916 in Niort (department Deux-Sèvres). On 3 May 1946, the *cour de justice de Poitiers* sentenced him to five years hard labour.
76    Jacques Péribère was born on 15 October 1926 in Paris.
77    Dissent of the Medical Company recalls two German NCOs in particular with the rank of Unterscharführer and Oberscharführer, but not their names.

the Loire), Rimaud trained as a doctor and ended up as a reserve battalion commander in the Army. He was a member of the *Milice* of the Loire.[78] His son, Louis-Pierre, also served in the Medical Company.[79]

Otuf. Pierre Alaux, who was also ex-*Milice*, probably served with the Medical Company. Born on 13 July 1913 in Montauban (department Tarn-et-Garonne), Alaux trained as a pharmacist with the military. After his military service he became a pharmacist in Nérac, a small city in Lot-et-Garonne. When mobilized in March 1939 he served as a *sous-lieutenant* in the 12ᵉ RAC and later still in the 14ᵉ *Régiment d'Infanterie*, winning the *Croix de guerre* with a brigade citation.

Following an all too familiar path to the *Milice*, first the LFC and then the SOL, Alaux participated in the Haute-Savoie operations in a medical capacity. He was appointed *chef départemental-adjoint* for Tarn-et-Garonne in April 1944. Transferred to the Waffen-SS, he undoubtedly served as a pharmacist. Indeed, according to Alaux: 'In this camp [Wildflecken], I did not receive any combat training, being simply in charge of receiving and distributing medicines'. Emile Combe from Lyon, who had served with the Kriegsmarine and was good friends with Robert Soulat, was posted to the Medical Company.[80]

Transferred to the Medical Company, Jules Dissent became friends with a fellow *Milicien* by the name of Jean Georges Cardaliaguet, a Breton who had no medical knowledge. They often spent time together. He recalls that one of the French NCOs in the Medical Company was named Pierre Maurer, who became one of the pioneers of thoracic surgery. He knew him by sight.[81]

Others who served in the Medical Company included:

- Hscha. Pierre Sergent
- Uscha. André Michel
- Grenadier Roger Raffy

Hscha. Pierre Sergent, who was ex-LVF, was a medical Student. He was a holder of the KVK. II. He served with the Engineer Company before joining the Medical Company. Michel was born on 16 September 1902 in Blois (department Loir-et-Cher). Mobilized in September 1939, he was assigned to the *9e régiment de Tirailleurs Marocains* (9e RTM), winning the *Croix de guerre 39-40*. He served with the OT before becoming a free worker. Roger Raffy, who was considered to be a bit of a hot head, was transferred from a grenadier company to the Medical Company. Previously, he had served with the *Franc-Garde permanente*, attending the camp des

78  His wife and his daughter were both killed by the resistance.
79  Louis-Pierre Rimbaud survived the war unlike his father who, according to Soulat, was captured in Pomerania and died in Soviet captivity on 27 June 1945 or was killed in a Soviet air attack at Neutsrelitz on 30 April 1945.
80  Combe was born in 1927. He disappeared in the hell of Pomerania. His elder brother was an Unterscharführer in Waffen-Gren. Regt der SS 57.
81  Dissent is convinced that Maurer served with the Medical Company although most sources, not all, state that he served with the Sturmbrigade and did not pass to 'Charlemagne'. Dissent worked with Maurer's son and sent his father a letter of support following the celebrated events of 1979 when the respected Professor declared that he had enlisted in the Waffen-SS.

Calabres and Uriage, after which promotion would have followed, at least to the rank of *chef de dizaine*. He participated in operations in Haute-Savoie and later in Charente.[82]

The Medical Company was quartered in barracks at the foot of Wildflecken camp. Only the officers and some NCOs were armed. Medical staff learnt how to handle the panzerfaüst rather 'than the art of dressing wounds'.[83] Indeed, one former member of the company described it as a 'bloody shambles' and once heard a German NCO state: *"Je m'en tamponne le coquillard avec une plume de limaçon."* [I totally don't care].

Grenadier Cornu of the Medical Company left Wildflecken for driving training on 11 February 1945. Soon after, Dr. Pierre Bonnefoy, who was promoted to Hauptsturmführer on 30 January 1945, received the command of the Medical Company from the aging Hstuf. Péribère, who stayed behind at Wildflecken when 'Charlemagne' was deployed to Pomerania.[84] The reason for this may have been his advanced age. The Krankenkraftwagen-Zug was probably never formed.[85]

## Artillerie-Abteilung der SS 57 (Artillery Battalion)

Fifty-three-year-old Hstuf. Jean Havette, a highly decorated veteran of the First World War who was wounded twice, losing an eye, commanded the Artillery Battalion.[86] He was a former *Milicien*. His military branch is not known, but many of his subordinates, including his assistant, Hstuf. Martin, were professional artillerymen.[87]

Ordered to form on 1 December 1944, the Artillery Battalion consisted on paper of a Stabsbatterie and three Batterien each with four Leichte Feldhaubitze [Light Field Howitzer] or F.L.H. At the head of the Stabsbatterie was Ustuf. Jean Guénin. Born in 1905, he had served with the LVF during the first winter, been wounded and discharged in February 1942. Taking up an administrative role with the LVF, he later joined the KWM, where he served as an officer. He fled to Germany in August 1944 and was transferred to 'Charlemagne' in November 1944. He left the Brigade in January 1945 to join Jagdverband Südwest.

Oscha. Pierre Rosfelder, born on 27 November 1900 in Nancy, was assigned to the Stabsbatterie on 8th December, becoming its Spiess on 11 January 1945. He had served briefly with the artillery at the end of World War One and was mobilized in 1939 to the *184e Régiment d'Artillerie Lourde*. After a short stint with the LVF, he joined the NSKK on 25 July 1942, becoming an instructor. Dismissed from the NSKK on 26 November 1943 for answering back to a senior NSKK officer, he volunteered for the Kriegsmarine in February 1944. He worked to

---

82    Roger Raffy was born on 29 May 1921 in Montauban (department Tarn-et-Garonne).
83    Noël Cornu, correspondence to Mounine. Dissent agrees that they never practised first aid (letter to the author, 25/6/06).
84    Bonnefoy was not known to Noël Cornu, who only made his acquaintance after the war.
85    While stationed at Wildflecken with the Medical Company Noël Cornu never saw a field ambulance, confirmed by Jules Dissent, letter to the author, 25/6/2006.
86    Jean Havette was born on 19 December 1891 in Paris. During the First World War he was awarded the *Croix de guerre* with four citations, including a palm. On 16 July 1921 he was appointed *Chevalier de la Légion d'honneur*. Despite his injuries he was mobilized in 1939.
87    Martin recalls that one Battery commander was a former *Capitaine* in the French Army who had failed the entrance exam to SS-Junkerschule Tölz and whose rank was only Oberscharführer (see Chevallet & Martin, *Pour la France, pour l'Europe*, p.87).

Jean Guénin, training in Paris French volunteers of the KWM. Like his boss, he fled to Germany in August 1944 and was eventually transferred to the French Brigade of the Waffen-SS.

Oscha. Auvergne, the former *chef-départemental adjoint de la Milice* for Savoie, commanded the 1st Battery.[88] However, Oscha. Le Guichaoua took over for a period at an unknown date, signing documentation as the *Batterieführer* of the 1st Battery on 2 February 1945. Henri Le Guichaoua was well qualified for the position. Born on 24 September 1914 in Poitiers, he attended the *école militaire d'artillerie de Poitiers* during the years 1937-1938. On 15 September 1938, he was promoted to the rank of *sous-lieutenant d'active d'artillerie* and assigned to the *201ᵉ régiment d'artillerie lourde divisionnaire*. Later he joined the police. Appointed as commander of GMR group 'La Marche' on 26 June 1944, he fled to Germany with the *Milice*.

Ostuf. Salle commanded the 2nd Battery and, like Le Guichaoua, was well qualified for the position. Born on 3 January 1916, Louis Salle attended the *école militaire d'artillerie de Poitiers* and graduated in 1939 with the rank of *sous-lieutenant d'active d'artillerie*. He served in the colonial artillery. Joining *La Légion Tricolore* on 12 August 1942, he signed up for the LVF on 16 April 1943.

Ostuf. Chaufour, a former *Chef de Centaine* in the *Franc-Garde permanente* of Paris, served in the capacity as a battery commander before becoming the battalion's Orientation Officer.[89] Ostuf. James Chillou, also a former officer of the *Franc-Garde permanente* of Paris, may have served in the capacity of a battery commander.[90] The military background of both is not known.

The Artillery Battalion was eventually equipped with the 10.5cm light field howitzer, although it may not have received its full complement of twelve.[91] No tractors were supplied to tow them so they would have to be horse-drawn.

Assigned to the Artillery Battalion, Maurice Ranc was surprised when he was asked if he knew how to ride a horse.[92] He answered in the affirmative. Horse rider training followed and all too soon he was able to ride, which was in fact a secret dream of his! Disappointment awaited him, though, when he got to see and work with the horses made available to the Artillery Battalion, for they were in such poor condition. He managed to console himself with the prospect of better ones when they went up to the front. He would be disappointed again.

The Artillery Battalion was never fully formed before the Brigade was deployed: notably, many of its officers and men were dispatched to training schools and would not return to Wildflecken before it was deployed to the Eastern Front. It was probably short of ammunition.

---

88  Auvergne signed documentation as *Batterieführer* of the 1st Battery on 19 December 1944. Bouysse suggests that Auvergne only regained his post in Pomerania.

89  According to Bouysse, Chaufour may have briefly served as the commander of the 3rd Battery. Louis Chaufour was born on 25 August 1918 in Lannion.

90  According to Soulat, letter to the author, 16/7/98, James Chillou commanded the 1st Battery. Bouysse believes this might be inaccurate, although the possibility exists he commanded the battery before Le Guichaoua. Anyway, James Chillou was born on 30 November 1911 in Paris.

91  When 'Charlemagne' was deployed to the Eastern Front the Artillery Battalion took with it only eight light field howitzers.

92  Paul Ranc, Maurice's brother, also served with 'Charlemagne'. Born in 1921 in Privas, Paul Ranc served with the *Milice,* probably in the ranks of the *Franc-garde permanente*, before opting for the Waffen-SS, joining the Sturmbrigade. He was deployed to Galicia with the 1st Battalion as a medical orderly. In 'Charlemagne', he served in Company 1/57.

Consequently, the Artillery Battalion was never able to conduct exercises with other elements of the Brigade.

The Brigade and later still the Division fielded a number of other support units of which very little is known: the Bau-Kompanie [Construction Company], the Veterinär-Kompanie [Veterinary Company] and the Field Post.

Ostuf. Jean de Moroge commanded the Construction Company.[93] Born on 24 July 1887 in Autun, he was a former prominent *Milicien*, who was appointed the *chef départemental-adjoint* for Lot in early May 1944.

The Veterinary Company was also ordered to form on 1 December 1944. Pierre Briaut, a *franc-garde* de Nîmes, was assigned to the company although he lacked the necessary qualifications and was even promoted to the rank of Unterscharführer when he was put in charge of some sixty horses.[94]

## Religion still plays its part

A regular sight at Wildflecken was Monseigneur de Mayol de Lupé riding a splendid chestnut thoroughbred. Invariably he carried a revolver on his hip and around his neck was a pectoral cross. But his presence reassured many young Catholics of the *Milice* who now found themselves serving in the Waffen-SS, which they regarded as an enemy of the Church.

The riding school had been converted into a chapel and did good business. Pierre Méric regularly attended the packed Sunday morning mass celebrated by de Mayol de Lupé. Méric personally met him several times and appreciated the comfort he brought to the believers.

Blanc of the 5/58 recalls that on the first Sunday following the arrival of the *Milice* they were told that attendance at mass was obligatory, which caused widespread protests, so much so that in the end it was agreed that only those who wanted to would go. However, one Sunday morning, Walter decided to take his platoon out training. Some of his platoon uttered the word mass, whereupon Walter flew into a rage. They left without mass. The following Sundays they dare not voice their opposition when Walter wished to take them training. In this way, a few less attended mass.

Each Sunday afternoon, after mass, de Mayol de Lupé conducted a service for the few Protestants of 'Charlemagne'. Blanc of the 5/58 attended the service three or four times, meeting again old friends Jean-Marie Stehli and Claude Platon. Blanc noted that the Monseigneur had very much mastered the liturgy of the Protestant form of worship and respected the spirit perfectly. On one occasion de Mayol de Lupé even addressed a Protestant congregation as 'the elite of Christianity!'[95]

It is said the Monseigneur would have gladly converted the riding school into a Mosque, introduced Ramadan and summoned the faithful to prayer by the Muezzin call if there had been any Moslems in 'Charlemagne'.[96]

---

93    Curiously, according to Leguérandais, *Les Volontaires Français dans l'armeé Allemande*, p.123, de Moroge commanded the Compagnie technique [Technical Company] also sometimes called the Compagnie de travailleurs [Workers Company].
94    Mabire, *La Division Charlemagne*, pp.246-247.
95    This is not recalled by Blanc, though.
96    De la Mazière, *Ashes of Honour*, p.57.

Brigf. Krukenberg himself recognised the important service the Monseigneur continued to play. After the war Krukenberg said of him:[97]

> You could say that he held the Division in his hand. I have to recognise that he was the one who helped me the most to unite the so disparate elements.

Father Lara also spread the word of god at Wildflecken.[98] Of Spanish origin, he had participated in the civil war in the ranks of the Nationalists. He came to the Waffen-SS from the *Milice*.

## Christmas

In early December, morale was raised by the announcement of the Ardennes offensive. Many like Uscha. Mercier of Fahrschwadron A were still not quite convinced of Germany's defeat. He believed in the new weapons. The *Miliciens* had told him of planes 'crossing the sky of Ulm like shooting stars'. He believed that the Ardennes offensive was only the start of the recovery.

With the coming of Christmas, morale dipped again. It was a Christmas of misery and loneliness, although an end of year 'review' did provide some comic relief. Much to the delight of the audience, Desrumaux mimicked Ostuf. Defever, who was not amused. Both Desrumaux and Defever were ex-LVF.[99]

A four-page booklet was distributed for Christmas. On the first page there was the music and words of the hymn 'He was born the Holy Child'. On the evening of Christmas Eve, good friends and officers de Genouillac and Rigeade decided to visit Rigeade's brother, a prisoner of war, who was quartered in a hamlet some thirty kilometers from Wildflecken. The journey on skis proved frustrating and time consuming so much so that they actually arrived after midnight. Warmly received, they shared a few hours together. 'Delicate' subjects were avoided from either side. They set off back towards four or five in the morning.

On Christmas night, Mgr. de Mayol de Lupé celebrated the Nativity in the riding school. Nearly two thousand men, for the most part former *Miliciens*, were crowded together around the improvised altar. The aristocratic *Milice* hierarchy was there, but Puaud, Krukenberg and the officers of the Inspection were conspicuous by their absence. Assisted by Father Lara, Mgr. de Mayol de Lupé spoke of the birth of Jesus and concluded by asking the congregation to pray for 'our Führer' and for the 'final success of our crusade against atheistic Bolshevism, the enemy of Christ'! This religious ceremony did actually help to foster a sense of unity and purpose.

The Ranc brothers spent Christmas night together, thinking about their parents, their sisters and their brothers. Brigf. Krukenberg, accompanied by his blonde daughter in the uniform of the BDM, visited the assembled FLAK Company.

Oscha. Méric was invited to Christmas dinner by the men of his platoon, who had made good use of the cover provided by him to buy meat and poultry, and even acquire a little bit of

97  Mabire, *Entretien avec le général Krukenberg, Historia* hors série 32, p.133.
98  His presence at Wildflecken may have only been fleeting (Blanc, letter to the author, 31/1/2001).
99  Born on 28 October 1914 in Tourcoing (department Nord), Jean-Marie Desrumaux joined the LVF on 26 August 1941, making him among the very first to come forward, and was present at Versailles on 27 August 1941 when Laval was shot. He served on the Eastern Front during the winter of 1941 in the Signals Section of the I. Bataillon.

game. He pulled out from the bottom of his bag four packets of gauloises which he attached to the Christmas tree. The men could not quite believe it but fully appreciated the present. A good time was had by all.

On New Year's Eve, the whole Brigade was assembled in the riding school around a gigantic fir tree to celebrate the old Germanic pagan festival of Yule (or the Winter solstice). The evergreen symbolised the life force in winter promising rebirth. Poems were read out, followed by a story. Finally an officer lit one candle after another on the tree and dedicated each new flame to persons, living or dead. The highest candle was reserved for the Führer, but it would not catch light and fell to the ground. Before drawing the ceremony to an end, Krukenberg spoke briefly. Concluding, he evoked the oath sworn by all to the Führer and appealed to them all to remain faithful to the SS motto 'My honour is loyalty'.

**New Year of 1945**

Comings and goings marked January 1945. On 3 January, Brigf. Krukenberg gave the FLAK Company an operational mission: to participate in the anti-aircraft defence of Fulda from the nearby village of Bachrain. Billeted on the locals, the FLAK Company quickly forged bonds with them. Ustuf. Fayard still had his horse with him. At Wildflecken, he had managed, and nobody quite knew how, to acquire a horse for his own personal use. The liaison officer was monocled Luftwaffe Lieutenant Murmann.

While continuing to train, the FLAK Company fully played its part against the numerous Anglo-American air raids, shooting down some bombers. The FLAK Company then had to protect the bailed-out crews from the vengeful population.

On 2 January 1945, Hscha. Boyer, the commander of Pionierzug/Waffen-Gren. Regt der SS 57, and thirty men, fifteen men of his Pionierzug and fifteen men of Pionierzug/Waffen-Gren. Regt der SS 58, left Wildflecken for SS-Pionierschule Hradischko. The Pionierlehrgang, commanded by SS-Ostuf. Sapin of 'Wallonien', would last some two weeks. Here Boyer met Ostuf. Audibert de Vitrolles and Ustuf. Mailhé of the Engineer Company of 'Charlemagne' who were attending another Lehrgang. Sickness struck Boyer and he was in hospital for ten days (from 13 January to 23 January 1945).

On this same day, Uscha. Bayle rejoined his former company at Wildflecken, now numbered 2/57. He had spent the last couple of months in hospital at Könitz recuperating from a bout of malaria. At the entrance to Wildflecken he met Uscha. Vincent, a good comrade from the Sturmbrigade, who told him: "Things have changed and the atmosphere [is] very different. Be warned. It's no longer our SS." Bayle would find out soon enough.

Reporting to headquarters, he presented himself in German to an Untersturmführer still wearing the LVF tricolore who answered him: "If you're here, it's because you're French; so I only want to hear you present yourself in French!" Then the officer rudely dismissed the convalescence paperwork Bayle was holding out to him and told him he could shove it up his arse. Bayle retorted that if the officer did not understand German and did not know the ways of the Waffen-SS then courtesy could help the conversation between them. Thankfully before the conversation escalated out of control, Dr. Bonnefoy, who was within earshot and recognized Bayle, intervened and asked to take over. Dr. Bonnefoy was courteous and modest, very different from the officer that had received him. Dr. Bonnefoy had served with the Sturmbrigade. Things had definitely changed and for the worse in the opinion of Bayle.

On 3 January, Hstuf. Fenet attended the 26.Btl. und Abt.Führer Lehrgang at Heeresschule Güstrow in Mecklenburg to receive battalion commander's training. The course would last until 10 February. He graduated with glowing feedback.

On 5 January 1945, the fifty-strong Workshop Company under Ostuf. Maudhuit left Wildflecken for a training course. In its ranks was company secretary Strmm. Jean-Jacques Pillet. He had been with the Workshop Company since its formation days before. He too had responded to a circular sent to all units requesting volunteers for the company. The Workshop Company was ordered to form on 25 December 1944.

At first Strmm. Pillet believed that the Workshop Company was bound for Pomerania, but on 8 January it reached its destination of Berlin. Deloused, the company was sent on to barracks Lichterfelde-West, the home of Waffen-SS Division 'Leibstandarte SS Adolf Hitler'. Pillet for one was glad to be away from the *bordel* of Wildflecken.

The destruction of Berlin and the suffering of its inhabitants deeply affected Pillet. Each day, from his office, he watched the air raids. Each day, he noted how the first group of enemy bombers would pass over ahead in the same place. Each day, in reply, he saw explosions fill the sky. And, each day, he noted how the following groups of bombers would then turn to avoid the flak because they now knew its position.

However, his time at Berlin was not without moments of humour and surprise. He had to laugh at Ostuf. Maudhuit who, to impress the Germans, had put a nameplate of *Graf von Maudhuit* on his door! On one occasion, while eating out at a restaurant, he was surprised to meet a school friend. His surprise was all the greater at another restaurant where he met the housekeeper of a nearby household back in Paris. The two of them were in Berlin as civilian workers.

And yet his everlasting memory of Berlin was that of two German soldiers shot for desertion in the main courtyard of the barracks. Indeed, one of the soldiers was dressed up like a woman complete with robe and wig. But now he could not help wondering if this man was perhaps luckier than him and his comrades of the Workshop Company.

## Waffen-Grenadier Regiment der SS 57

Back at Wildflecken, the command of Waffen-Grenadier Regiment der SS 57 became vacant when Ostubaf. Gamory-Dubourdeau left to take up a post at the SS-Hauptampt in Berlin. His old age and his deteriorating physical state of health had conspired against him to leave him commanding his regiment in nothing more than name only. To replace him, Brigf. Krukenberg called on Hstuf. de Bourmont to become the new commander of Waffen-Grenadier Regiment der SS 57.

Preferring to be called *Mon capitaine* and not by his SS rank, de Bourmont found himself in conflict with his Orderly Officer, Ustuf. Martres, who was SS to the core. Artus mediated. This 'French war' became known throughout the whole regiment and many sided with Martres.

Hstuf. de Bourmont had at his disposal two grenadier battalions of four companies each, an Anti-Tank company, an Infantry Gun Company and various regimental units. At the head of the 1st Battalion was Ostuf. Fenet and at the 2nd Battalion Hstuf. Obitz.

Born on 9 March 1908 in Lerouville, René-André Obitz attended the infantry *École militaire de Saint-Maixent* and, in 1932, was promoted to *sous-lieutenant d'active*. He transferred from *La Légion Tricolore* to the LVF, where he served with the 1st Battalion, attaining the rank of

*Capitaine.* On 23 April 1944, he was awarded with the Iron Cross 2nd Class. Transferred to the Waffen-SS, he replaced Guignot, who was dismissed from 'Charlemagne' on 10 January 1945.

Ostuf. Paul André commanded the Headquarters Company of Waffen-Gren. Regt der SS 57. Born on 29 July 1906 in Guerville (department Seine-et-Oise), he was mobilized in 1939 as a reserve lieutenant with the *13e régiment de tirailleurs algériens* (13e RTA). He fought courageously against the Germans and was wounded. He was awarded the *Croix de guerre* with two citations. Joining the *Franc-Garde* of the *Milice*, he rose to the rank of *Chef de Trentaine*. Transferred to the Waffen-SS, he was appointed the commander of the 7/57, and then, in early 1945, the commander of the Headquarters Company.

The Headquarters Company consisted of a reconnaissance platoon, a signals platoon, and a *Pionierzug* [Engineers Platoon]. On 12 November 1944, Hscha.[100] Boyer received the command of the *Pionierzug* from Ustuf. Robert Lefèvre.[101] The *Pionierzug* numbered eighty men. Lefèvre took over the reins of the *Pionierzug* again when Boyer left the unit for training. Hscha. Boyer did not return before 'Charlemagne' was deployed to the Eastern Front. The thirty-year-old Ustuf. Jean-Pierre Labuze, also a former *Milicien*, commanded the Panzerjäger Kompanie, the 10/57.[102]

After a 'merry-go-round' of grenadier company commanders, all were soon from the Sturmbrigade. Some had only graduated of late from Kienschlag. Ustuf. Jean Brazier at the head of Kompanie 1/57 was a product of Kienschlag. Born on 4 May 1918 in Besançon (department Doubs), he joined the Air Force after attending the prestigious Saint-Cyr and the *École de l'Air* at Salon-de-Provence. PPF militant, he joined the Waffen-SS on 29 October 1943. He was promoted to Standartenoberjunker on 1 September 1944 and then Untersturmführer on 9 November 1944. He succeeded Ustuf. Jean-Marie Stehli as company commander.[103]

On 12 October 1944, Ustuf. Counil replaced Ustuf. Robert Lefèvre at the head of Kompanie 3/57. Born on 2 April 1924 in Culles-Les-Roches, Guy Counil was serving with the *Milice* when he volunteered for the Waffen-SS at the start of 1944. He too was a product of Kienschlag.

Ostuf. Charles Roumégous was at the head of Kompanie 5/57 in February 1945 when de Bourmont became the new regimental commander. Born on 26 August 1915 in Montpellier, Roumégous was ex-*Milice*. After attending Uriage, he was appointed the *chef départemental* for Gard, a position he held until the evacuation in August 1944. He attended the in-house Lehrgang at Wildflecken supervised by Jauss and Pignard-Berthet and was replaced by Oscha. Hennecart in early February when he fell sick and required hospitalization.

Ustuf. Albert at the head of Kompanie 6/57 was yet another product of Kienschalg. Born on 24 July 1922 in Claret (department Hérault), he was forced to abandon his studies for Saint-Cyr in the wake of the German invasion of the *Zone libre*. Soon after he joined the *Milice*, attending

100  Boyer was promoted to the rank of Hauptscharführer on 1 October 1944 for 'acts of war'.
101  Robert Lefèvre was born on 8 August in Brunelles (department Eure-et-Loir) and joined the Waffen-SS on 13 October 1943.
102  Jean-Pierre Labuze was born on 19 June 1914 in Saint-Junien (department Haute-Vienne). His brother, Jacques Labuze, a *Milicien de Limoges*, was captured by the F.T.P. and tortured to death.
103  According to Léguerandais, *Hitler's French volunteers*, p.134, Brazier commanded the Signals Company and became head of the 1/57 in February 1945 at Kolberg. Firstly, no other source confirms Brazier at the head of the Signals Company. Secondly, Brazier was at Kolberg but not in a command position.

the *École des cadres* d'Uriage and gained promotion to *chef de trentaine-adjoint* in the *Franc-garde permanente*.

Concerned that the *Milice* was becoming repressive, Albert decided to join the Waffen-SS like many of his *milicien* colleagues. Moreover, he feared Bolshevik Communism and vehemently believed that the ideology of National Socialism was the only possible choice to transform a decadent state into a free and strong state.

Ustuf. Philippe Colnion only replaced Ustuf. Raymond Gaillard, who was ex-LVF, at the head of Kompanie 8/57 at the end of January 1945 or early February 1945. Born on 8 July 1925 in Montray,[104] he joined the Waffen-SS on 15 October 1943. He too attended the same course at Kienschlag.

The commander of the Infantry Gun Company (9/57) was W-Ostuf. Robert Roy. Born on 13 June 1900 in Algeria, this former *Capitaine de l'artillerie coloniale française* had come to the Waffen-SS in the summer of 1943 from the NSKK.[105] He was a most remarkable character. He had a liking for good food, red wine and women. Indeed, legend has it that he smuggled his female conquests into Wildflecken in gun carriages! Although regarded as stubborn and bad tempered, he excelled as a gunner and could calculate firing distances without the use of a rangefinder. And he never made a mistake. He demanded that his subordinates call him *Mon Capitaine* rather than by his German rank and asked the Germans in his company to speak only in French! And yet he was a convinced National Socialist. Of late, he had been standing in for Fenet away on a training course. On 30 January 1945, he was promoted to the rank of Hauptsturmführer which was equivalent to his former French Army rank. Notably, he was promoted to SS-Hauptsturmführer and not Waffen-Hauptsturmführer.[106]

Georges Perret, a former artillery *sous-lieutenant de réserve* who volunteered for the Waffen-SS in August 1944, commanded the 15cm Infantry Gun Platoon of the 9/57.[107] Roy doubted Perret's national socialist convictions.

Hstuf. de Bourmont brought onto his regimental staff his friend Ostuf. de Londaiz, also a regular officer and a *Milicien*. Born on 4 November 1919 in Pau (department Basses-Pyrénées), de Londaiz was a convinced fascist who had fought on the side of the Falangists during the Spanish Civil War. In the *Milice* he held the rank of *chef de cohorte* and in June 1944 was appointed *chef regional-adjoint* for Lyon. In August 1944 he had accompanied de Vaugelas to Limoges to organise the evacuation of the encircled Vichy forces.

Much is made of the fact that Waffen-Gren. Regt. der SS 57 was considered to be an ideologically 'pure' Waffen-SS unit. This is all the more remarkable considering that the origin of much of its personnel was not the Sturmbrigade. Indeed it seems that those who were not from the Sturmbrigade had assimilated themselves body and soul into this regiment. They had responded to what the veterans of the Sturmbrigade had to offer and that was esprit de corps and unit loyalty.

---

104  This place is recorded in his SS *personakte*, but no such place exists in France.
105  According to Saint-Loup, *Les Hérétiques*, p.176, Roy was languishing in an *oflag* when he volunteered for the Waffen-SS. In response to this, he probably went to the NSKK first.
106  See the SS-Verordnungsblatt of 30 January 1945.
107  Georges Perret was born on 8 March 1905.

Nevertheless, Waffen-Gren. Regt. der SS 57 had its own problems. In January or February 1945,[108] the 'desertion' of a whole platoon from Company 2/57 complete with MG 42 machine-guns and full kit sent Brigf. Krukenberg into a rage.

Led by its commander, the platoon had left Wildflecken camp in the early hours of the morning and marched, in order and in step, to Brückenau railway station where fake movement orders were produced and stamped as being in order. The 'desertion' was, in fact, aided and abetted by the whole company; the fake movement orders had been prepared by *Spiess* Montcarnie; Vincent and his section had been on guard duty at the camp entrance; Bayle and Mauclair had been on lookout in and around the barracks.

The military police soon found the 'deserters' who had joined Leon Degrelle's 28. SS-Freiwilligen- Panzer-Grenadier Division 'Wallonien'. Brigf. Krukenberg wanted them back, but the SS-Hauptampt proved of no help to him. In the end, he had to resign himself to losing them to Degrelle whose prestige was high.

Among the 'deserters' were Strmm. Pierre Lemaire, Gren. Brousses, Gren. Eudes, Gren. Morineau, Gren. Ourgaud and Gren. Roland. They were attached to the Jungkompanie under the command of André Regibaud. Their new section commander was Uscha. Renard.[109]

More 'desertions' from Wildflecken, this 'camp of the Gauls', were planned by the entire former Sturmbrigade contingents of Company 2/57 and of neighbouring companies when their turn for guard duty came around![110] Bayle let company commander Ostuf. Bartolomei into the secret in the hope that he would follow them, but the departure to Pomerania overtook Bayle and his fellow 'conspirators'.

Also of concern were some *Miliciens*. While most had responded to their new circumstances, some had not. On 20 January 1945, company commander Coutret was thrown out of 'Charlemagne' for having 'too much bad spirit'. This former *lieutenant de chasseurs alpins de réserve* and Darnand's former *chef de cabinet* had remained a staunch supporter of Darnand and the Marshal. Sturmbrigade veterans refused to obey him because he commanded in French. Demobilised at Greifenberg, he went to Sigmaringen where Darnand sent him to Heuberg camp and the autonomous *Milice* unit.

During January 1945, a total of fifteen officers and NCOs were dismissed, although not all were former *Milicien*. The highest profile 'casualty' was undoubtedly Hstuf. Guignot, who had joined the Waffen-SS over a year before and was now serving in the capacity of a battalion commander. Ustuf. Jacques Quantin, who had served previously with the LVF, may have been dismissed at the same date, if not earlier.

---

108  This 'desertion' actually took place sometime after Bayle's arrival at Wildflecken camp on 2 January 1945 (see *De Marseille à Novossibirsk*, pp.141-143) and was not in mid-November 1944 intimated by Mabire and recorded as fact by Landwehr.

109  According to Mabire, *La Division Charlemagne*, pp.192-194, nearly all of the French 'deserters' would fall or be wounded in the Ardennes offensive. In response to this, the fate of the six Frenchmen listed was as follows; Strmm. Lemaire was wounded on the Oder front on 22 April 1945; Gren. Brousses fell in combat at Streesen on 4 March 1945; Gren. Eudes also fell in combat at Streesen on 4 March 1945; Gren. Morineau survived the war; Gren. Ourgaud was also killed at Streesen; and Gren. Roland survived the war. Also, 'Wallonien' did not see action in the Ardennes. Thus, none of these French 'deserters' actually fell in the Ardennes.

110  Bayle, *De Marseille à Novossibirsk*, pp.141-143.

Also dismissed for 'bad spirit' at a later date was Unterscharführer Yves Jahan, a former *chef de trentaine de Franc-Garde permanente* who had volunteered for the Waffen-SS in the autumn of 1943.[111] He too was sent to Heuberg and integrated into the autonomous *Milice* unit.

January 1945 also saw the completion of the in-house Junker Lehrgang supervised by SS-Hstuf. Jauss and W-Ustuf. Pignard-Berthet. At the end of the Lehrgang, most of the officer cadets went to Kienschlag where they should have attended a second Lehrgang supervised by Ustuf. Kreis, but this did not go ahead because of the rapid development of the war. Instead they received liaison officer training, lasting some fifteen days. They were taught tactics at the sand table, they were taught how to identify enemy weaponry and, from films and commentaries, they were taught the combat methods of the enemy (snipers, camouflage …).

Some of the Lehrgang were promoted to the rank of Standartenjunker. According to one participant, the training had been too short to warrant promotion to that of Standartenoberjunker.[112] Nevertheless, Pierre Méric was promoted to Standartenoberjunker. He was overjoyed of course, but a little surprised because he had struggled to answer two questions on the written test about the 'sacred dates of the fundamental laws of the National Socialist state'. Jauss told him of his promotion but also advised him to learn these dates. Méric assured him he would. Jauss never checked with Méric, which was a good thing, because he never did learn them!

### The story of Maurice Comte

At the end of the Lehrgang Std.Ju. Maurice Comte was returned to Company 5/57 and confirmed as the platoon commander of the Heavy Platoon. Thanks to the 'political' classes he attended as part of his officer cadet training he came to realise that it was no longer a question of France and its internal struggles, but the gestation of a new European order.[113] This realisation is all the more surprising because his background was that of a masquisard. Moreover, he was not an adherent of any political party.

Maurice Comte was born on 21 August 1921 in Villeurbanne (department Rhône). While studying at engineering school *Arts et Métiers* (this was from before the war to 1941) he had neither the time nor the spirit to indulge in politics. After the armistice, and despite a strong dislike of the occupying forces, he found the Germans correct, in fact, very different from the image portrayed later by the so-called 'official history'. However, at the beginning of 1943, when he was working in Grenoble, he was called up by the S.T.O. for forced labour in Germany. Not prepared to accept this eventuality, he fled, like many others, to the woods and hills, and joined the maquis.

Captured by the Mobile Guard on 7 July 1943, Comte was first imprisoned in Grenoble and then in Fort Montluc, Lyon. Tried and released on condition that he did his service with the S.T.O., he joined the maquis again, serving in the company of *Capitaine* Stéphane, regarded as one of the few officers of high moral and military worth. But he was instinctively worried

---

111  Yves Jahan was born on 26 May 1919 in Villeneuve-sur-Lot (department Lot-et-Garonne). Croisile recalls that Jahan was still at Kienschlag on 9 April 1945 when the Junkerschule was dissolved (see *Sous uniforme allemand*, p.283).
112  Comte, correspondence with the author.
113  The classes included such topics as history, the science of man and the creation of the world.

that the maquis, for the most part made up of workers, peasants and students, was led without explanation by a Communist minority, just like Stéphane himself.

And then in June 1944 the course of Comte's war as a *chef de section* in maquis Stéphane suddenly took a dramatic turn when, in stupid circumstances, he was taken prisoner by a patrol from the *École des Cadres de la Milice* at Uriage. Questioned, he told his captors as little as possible, providing them with false names and places, as well as understated numbers and weapons. They responded in kind by withholding food and water. And yet six months later Comte was in the uniform of the Waffen-SS and being put through his paces in a *Lehrgang* of officer cadets. He explained how this came about:

> Stéphane organised a *coup de main* on Uriage château; *Milicien* officer Bénézit was killed and two or three *Miliciens* were captured. Through the intermediary of a priest, one of the *chefs de la Milice* at Grenoble, Berthon, and Stéphane decided upon a meeting with a view to an exchange of prisoners. The meeting took place near Uriage in the middle of the woods. Stéphane and Berthon, whom I accompanied, talked and separated, not being able to decide without the agreement of their *chefs*. I returned to Grenoble with Berthon, still a prisoner, but treated correctly, but with a certain apprehension.
>
> The following day, back at Uriage in a car driven by Lieutenant Chabert, with political *chef* Giaume and two *Miliciens*, we were pursued, and then accosted by a car of *resistants*, armed and commanded by Lieutenant Ranavalo (grandson of the last queen of Madagascar) who I had known before the war. He also seemed to recognize me. Nobody fired. Chabert manoeuvred and escaped. We abandoned the car and set off in the direction of the château.
>
> I knew the region well. I led and proposed to my companions in adventure to go forward in the direction I indicated, and to cover them as a rearguard armed with a submachine gun. And we arrived at Uriage château to the general surprise of its occupants who saw me armed behind the four *Miliciens*, including Giaume.
>
> Immediately their attitude changed. Faces became if not friendly, at least open. De Vaugelas warmly thanked me. I was still a prisoner, but 'on parole', perfectly free to do what I pleased in the château. I was treated as a comrade. Questioned by all, we started to exchange ideas and thus I came to know another perception of the world and another perspective of the problems of the moment.
>
> The general withdrawal. I was still a prisoner on parole. Exchanges of opinions continued. And little by little, I realised that my ideas, my sentiments were very close to theirs, and that what they told me and what they thought of the problems of this world, were exactly what I felt without knowing why.
>
> We arrived at the German frontier. De Vaugelas and other *chefs de la Milice* set me free, but offered me, without constraint, to stay with them... I stayed.

Comte was not the only former maquisard to serve in 'Charlemagne'.

After his political 'conversion' he now wondered if sufficient time would be made available to instill the revolutionary ideas of a new European order.

At the end of the in-house officer-cadets' Lehrgang at Wildflecken, Oberjunker Bonnafont and Oberjunker Chatrousse were sent to Janowitz, Bohemia, for anti-tank training.[114] They never arrived. After one week of being shunted back and forth across Bavaria and Bohemia, they returned to Wildflecken.

In the absence of Oberjunker Bonnafont, Oscha. Girard succeeded Oscha. Robert at the head of the Panzerjäger Kompanie of Waffen-Gren. Regt der SS 58.[115] Some days after the return of Bonnafont to Wildflecken, Hstuf. Raybaud, with the agreement of Bonnafont, posted him back to the Panzerjäger Kompanie to *renforcer le difficile commandement*. Still not ambitious to make a career for himself, Oberjunker Bonnafont became second in command. Moreover, he got along with Girard, even though they came from two diametrically opposed horizons.[116] As for Oberjunker Chatrousse, he was assigned as Hstuf. Moneuse's Orderly Officer.[117]

Rumours continued to circulate of the employment of 'Charlemagne' on the Western Front against the Americans. There was universal uproar among the French SS volunteers. Such was the unrest that in the end Krukenberg had to put out a denial![118]

Morale nose-dived in January as Germany's military situation deteriorated: the Ardennes offensive had ended in a costly defeat and a Russian offensive had swept into East Prussia, Pomerania and Silesia.

Other factors affecting morale were a reduction in the already spartan rations, the cold, a spate of bloody accidents, and the tattooing of the blood group. 'Charlemagne' was plagued, or so it seemed, with stupid and bloody accidents. A sentry guarding men of the Penal Platoon fell on a patch of ice and his loaded rifle, pointing at them, went off. The sentry had neglected to put the safety catch on. One man was killed and another was wounded.

Then there was the armourer who foolishly tried to hammer free a shell that had become jammed in the breech of a PAK gun. The resulting explosion killed two men and wounded several others. A further two grenadier repairing damaged tracks in Fulda railway station were crushed to death by a locomotive.

The announcement of the tattooing of the blood group came as unpleasant surprise to many. The tattoo was peculiar to the Waffen-SS and was simply an indication of blood group. This information was essential for wounded requiring a blood transfusion. However, this tattoo, which was intended possibly to save life, was viewed by many with disquiet because it could equally condemn prisoners to death. This tattoo would clearly identify them as members of the Waffen-SS and it was rumoured that the Russians examined the arms of wounded and captured

114 Of note is that the two of them were graduates of Saint-Cyr. This might explain why they were sent to Janowitz rather than Kienschlag with the other officer cadets.
115 Oscha. Jacques Robert signed paperwork as the company commander of the Panzerjäger Kompanie of Waffen-Gren. Regt der SS 58 on 19 January 1945 undoubtedly in the absence of Bonnafont.
116 Bonnafont and Girard would maintain a lifelong friendship. Indeed, before answering the author's questions by mail, Bonnafont consulted with Girard.
117 As for his new appointment, Chatrousse believes that it was none other than Moneuse himself who had asked for his transfer and, although they did not know each other that well, he also believes that Moneuse held him in high regard. (Chatrousse, letter to the author, 31/8/97.)
118 In December 1944, when 'it was a question of sending us to the Western Front', one former French Divisional soldier learnt that Mgr. de Mayol de Lupé had been to see Himmler, who had asserted that 'Charlemagne' would not be deployed to the west. This is unconfirmed and may have only been rumour.

for this distinguishing mark and summarily executed those bearing the brand. Even if the tattoo was removed there would still be a telltale mark left in the same area.

The tattooing of the blood group under the left arm started in early January 1945.[119] Some men had their blood group determined and tattooed when they gave blood for the wounded. Kompanie 3/57 was tattooed by Indian doctors of the Waffen-SS. Still one-quarter of all French SS men managed to avoid being tattooed.[120] Although a non-commissioned officer who should have set an example, Uscha. de la Mazière had made up his mind to evade being tattooed and managed to on the pretext of being urgently summoned to headquarters. All the same, he felt ashamed of 'this small act of betrayal' but reasoned that if he was hit by a bullet or by a piece of shrapnel in the left arm the medical orderlies would not find his blood group in the pulp left.

Those men away in various training schools stood the best chance of not being tattooed. In this way, Henri-Georges Gonzales of the Engineer Company, away at Hradischko, was lucky enough not to be tattooed. Oberjunker Bonnafont of the Panzerjäger Kompanie of Waffen-Gren. Regt der SS 58 openly refused to have the tattoo. This came to the attention of Stubaf. Raybaud. Nevertheless, Oberjunker Bonnafont went unpunished. And yet, in contrast, some viewed the tattoo as final proof of their full integration into the Waffen-SS, 'a sort of magic sign of affiliation'.

Days after receiving the blood group tattoo, the volunteers were offered the opportunity to donate blood for those wounded at the front. In large numbers, they flocked to the collection points, but the blood they donated proved worthless; their blood was too poor. A report from the military doctors at Fulda read that 'the men are weak, overworked and anemic' and that their 'food is insufficient'. The subsequent fuss over this could not be overlooked and, as a result, rations were increased. An ironic conclusion considering that many, if not all, of the volunteers were only moved to donate blood in the first place because of the 'snack' offered to all blood donors.[121]

## Company 5/58

In early January 1945, platoon commander and instructor[122] Hscha. Walter of Company 5/58 was appointed as the company commander of the 7/58. His new appointment was well merited; Walter was a most remarkable individual. This philosophy graduate, who was married to a beautiful cinema actress by the name of Andrée Clément, joined the LVF in 1942 aged twenty and served with the 9th Company of the III. Bataillon. One year later, having worked his way up through the ranks, he was promoted to *adjudant*. A fanatical National Socialist, he seemed

---

119  This date is implied by Mabire (*La Division Charlemagne*, pp.243-244) and confirmed by de Genouillac, correspondence to the author, 1997. The turn of de la Mazière and 'his' company [the PAK Company] to be tattooed came on the day after Christmas, although he states that the tattooing 'had been announced for November'. Rostaing is alone when he records the tattooing starting in November 1944, on the 14th to be precise.

120  Mabire, *La Division Charlemagne*, p.245.

121  See Mabire, *La Division Charlemagne*, pp.245-246.

122  Blanc, letter to the author, 19/3/01. Blanc was a member of Walter's platoon. This corrects Ruskone of the same company, who, in letters to the author of 2/98 and 5/3/98, stated that Walter took care of supply problems rather than matters of training.

out of place among his tricolore compatriots of the LVF. He was, according to one commentator, the embodiment of the 'political soldier' of the time. Mercier, who was ex-LVF, said of Walter:

> Walter was my friend. When Walter was a platoon commander at Greifenberg he chose to share the barracks of his men and refused the NCO barracks allocated to him. His fanatical national socialism was not that of the party bigwigs. At Greifenberg, in 1944, we were wandering the streets on Heldengedenktag, the 'Day of Commemoration of Heroes'. One of the NCOs of the officer cadets' platoon had the wacky idea to propose to his comrades to find me and get me to play happy music on the piano of a tea room. (I no longer know who it was, but it might have been Noell.) I had barely started to play when a German NCO came over to protest that Heldengedenktag commanded reverence. I stopped my fantasias but Walter reproached me for not continuing and strongly protested that we were all veterans or future heroes and that this holiday was ours. He was a veritable non-conformist before this term was vulgarized.[123]

Transferred to the Waffen-SS, Walter was appointed as a platoon commander in Company 5/58. He was sent to Kienschlag but did not finish the course.[124] Even so, he was highly regarded by his peers, as Blanc of Company 5/58 noted: 'Walter's comrades spoke of him with respect and admiration, both for his courage and his military qualities proven in Russia, as well as for his intelligence and his culture.'

Walter was an excellent leader of men and trained his men hard, very hard. Blanc of Company 5/58, who was trained by Walter, recalls that he once said to them: "I hope that you want to kill me, because it is normal that one should want to kill one's instructor." At times they did. From seven in the morning to seven in the evening, they trained outside in sub-zero temperatures. They were without gloves, as was Walter. He did not ask anything of his men that he himself was not prepared to do. Frequent bouts of dysentery did not slacken his effort.

Each evening, weapons inspection. If the instructor found a single grain of dust in the chamber of a rifle the whole platoon was given 20 minutes to prepare for a new inspection at which all rifles were checked again. It was just too bad if the grain of dust had changed rifle. This would continue until such time as it had disappeared.

Under Walter, the men learnt collective responsibility. If a single person slipped while marching on an icy road then the whole platoon was punished by the 'stand-up, lie down' drill, preferably in a ditch and in the nastiest mud. Again, if the instructor commanded 'Panzer von links' [tank on the left] and a single person took cover to the left of the road rather than to the right then the whole platoon 'copped it'.

Walter once confided to Blanc: "Our strength lies above all in our camaraderie, because it is greater than anywhere else." It was this that Walter fostered. On one occasion, seeing that one of his men was hungry, he gave him part of his bread ration.

To toughen his men, he demonstrated that a hand grenade could be detonated atop his head, on his helmet, without harm to himself. Standing rigid, he showed that the grenade splinters traveled laterally and upwards, riddling the snow around his feet in an almost perfect circle.

---

123 Mercier, letter to the author, 20/11/2001.
124 Blanc confirms the attendance of Walter at Kienschlag, but believes he excelled there, proving himself with the ability to command a company.

One time he forgot to secure sufficiently the chinstrap of his helmet, which the grenade blast brought down on his nose and caused to swell.

Blanc recalls that Walter never joked and did not accept such behaviour from others. One day, he reproached the men for not knowing how to sing well in chorus. One of their number, Bernardini, then murmured 'Sistine Chapel'. He found himself transferred at once to the Medical Company.

Blanc liked Walter, but many of his closest comrades did not. However, Blanc later reflected that it was thanks to Walter that the men stood up well to the hardships of battle.

Jean Castrillo, Daniel Le Goff, Jean Priot, Jacques Revel, and Ducasse, who were all from the *franc-garde* of the *Milice*, also served in the same platoon. Blanc would owe two of them his life. Ducasse from Casteljaloux, who was inherently proud of being a *paysan* [farmer], had this ambition to become the mayor of his community one day. There was also Roger Wyckaert, who was good friends with Jean Castrillo.

Brothers Paul and Jacques Denamps also served in the same platoon of Kompanie 5/58, where they made the acquaintance of Robert Blanc and Jean Castrillo.[125] Paul was born on 13 August 1920 in Lille and Jacques on 12 November 1924 in Camphin-en-Carembault. Their story and that of the third brother, Louis, began in March 1943 when Paul accompanied Louis to Agen railway station. Louis, who was serving with the *Chantiers de Jeunesse*, remarked to Paul: "Tell father that I'm not going back to the *Chantiers* but to Versailles and the LVF". Family life at Tayrac was not good. Their mother had died when they were young and there was no love lost between them and father.

Paul approved of Louis' decision, for he too was a patriot. Desolated by the debacle of May 1940, Paul did not mind admitting that he cried when he first heard the news of the surrender. Thereafter he put his trust in *Marechal* Pétain, joining the LFC, passing to the SOL and then the *Franc-Garde* of the *Milice*.[126] Besides father was a member of the *Milice* and the *Franc-Garde permanente*. In May 1944, Paul Denamps was stationed at Château de Ferron, Tonneins. In July 1944, following the murder of family members of *Milicens* in the area surrounding Tayrac, Jacques, the youngest brother, joined Paul at Ferron.

In defeat, Paul and Jacques went 'into exile' in Germany where they were enrolled into the Waffen-SS and posted to 'Charlemagne' at Wildflecken, joining Louis who had passed from the LVF to the Waffen-SS months earlier, now serving with the Pionier Kompanie. Jacques was accepted even though he was only 1 metre 58 tall. He was made a runner.

Many of their fellow *Miliciens* from Lot-et-Garonne were not happy to don the German uniform. Paul recalls that company commander Wagner was a man of few words. Also rumour had it that he had wanted to join the German Army, but had not been accepted, then opting for the LVF instead.

125  Following the interview with Paul Denamps, the author was able to put Paul and Robert Blanc in contact. They had not spoken for over fifty years!
126  When the author interviewed Paul Denamps pictures of the *Marechal* still adorned the walls of his home. Paul Denamps told the author that he joined the *Franc-Garde* on 6 June 1944, whereas Bouysse states that Denamps volunteered for the *Franc-Garde permanente* in Haute-Savoie months earlier in March-April 1944.

Paul's time at Wildflecken was not an unhappy one.[127] He recalls the strong sense of camaraderie among the men. There was the time one of the de Puch brothers said to him: "One day I'm going to kill you because you are always in front." Paul Denamps and the de Puch brothers were good friends and comrades.[128]

He recalls the time part of the company was sent to Stuttgart to clean up the railway station in the wake of air raids and among the debris they found cases and cases of Cognac Martel. They were drunk for days! Then there was the time Walter lined up the company and said: "I can already see the corpses". Such was Walter's macabre humour! He recalls that they often returned from exercises with wood they had cut down, even though it was verboten. Unfortunately, there were training accidents. During a simulated attack a *Milicien* from Lot-et-Garonne by the name of Duperre was shot in the hand. Thankfully it was only a minor injury.

Uscha. Maixendeau and Junker der Waffen-SS Ruskone also served as platoon commanders in the 5/58. Both were capable. Maixendeau was in many ways the opposite of Walter and this was undoubtedly the reason they got on well. Maixendeau had style, but not the appearance of a soldier. Very cultivated, he often came and chatted with the men about literature or the cinema.[129]

Ruskone was an 'old hand' of the LVF who had served with the celebrated *section de chasse* and fought at Bobr. In July 1944, he was awarded the *Croix de guerre légionnaire* and the *Mèdaille des blesses*. His transfer at the end of August 1944 to the Waffen-SS he described as 'the consecration of his ideas' and explained that 'he joined the Legion [the LVF] to fight Communism, but he discovered another reason to fight; the creation of a New Europe'.[130] In the autumn of 1944, he attended SS-und Waffen Unterführerschule SS-Tr. Üb.Pl. Westpreußen at Reckow near Bütow and proved himself to be of NCO calibre. His arrival at Wildflecken coincided with his promotion to Uscha. and then Junker. He was posted to Company 5/58.[131]

In mid-January 1945, Ruskone was on the point of leaving for SS-Panzergrenadierschule Kienschlag when his company commander, Ostuf. Wagner, managed to pull a few strings at headquarters to keep him near with the promise that after three months at the front he would be promoted to the officer rank of Untersturmführer. Ruskone was, of course, pleased. Weeks later, before leaving for Pomerania, he was promoted to Oberscharführer and appointed his assistant.

The morale of Company 5/58 was excellent. This was due in part to Jean Castrillo, who was ex-SK. He was a sort of morale officer and political officer all rolled into one, even though his rank was that of Grenadier. He was always able to raise a laugh, even at the toughest of times, and could comfort with a wink. Each evening, after returning from training and before dinner, he taught the history of National Socialism to the men sat on stools in the corridors of the company's building. He managed to keep the exhausted men interested by incorporating

---

127 During the interview with Paul the author very much gained the impression that he had a positive disposition and that this had seen him through most things.
128 One of the de Puch brothers was named Bertrand. Through Paul Denamps, the author was put in contact with Bertrand de Puch. Born on 27 August 1925, Bertrand de Puch joined the *Milice* in April 1943 and was stationed at Château de Ferron in June 1944, where he became friends with Paul Denamps. Transferred to the Waffen-SS, Bertrand de Puch served with 7/58.
129 Maixendeau was born on 22 January 1923 in Monte-Carlo.
130 Mabire, *La Division Charlemagne*, p.243.
131 According to Rusco, *Stoi!*, p.249, as the only *gradé* present, he found himself the company commander for several weeks. However, this is not recalled by Blanc, but that is not to say that it did not happen.

humour. His reputation grew and before long he was going to neighbouring companies. Blanc regarded Castrillo as a perfect comrade, a brother. Roger Wyckaert, who, like Castrillo, was from the JPF and had served with the SK, gave him a helping hand.[132]

There was no talk of regrets and also no talk of defeat. This was in contrast to companies wholly formed of young officers of the Wehrmacht also present at Wildflecken. They were being trained again as simple recruits, why the Frenchmen did not know. Blanc recalls:

> They [the young officers] did not like us: one day, our platoon, returning from an exercise, in marching order, crossed some of them; *adjudant* Blaise saluted them as per regulations, that is to say the raised arm. Not one responded to our salute. Blaise commanded 'platoon halt', stood in front of them and addressed them in German in a ferocious tone of voice, which sounded like a row, on the theme: we are French volunteers, we are fighting like you, have the correctness to respond to our salute. Which they did eventually, but clearly their hearts weren't in it.

The 5th Company formed a sniper squad, to which Blanc and five or six other good marksmen were assigned. The squad was commanded and trained by Uscha. Le Cavelé. Blanc was issued with a semi-automatic carbine, which was shorter and lighter than the Mauser 98K, but it came without a telescope and was of dubious quality and very difficult to put together after cleaning. Nevertheless, he was very thankful for the carbine.

**January–February 1945**

The skeleton-like structure of the brigade started to flesh out late January with the return of those away on training courses. Not one of the thirty or so company clerks sent to Breslau would return to Wildflecken. They had been incorporated into the defence of the besieged fortress that would only capitulate on 7 May 1945, the same day on which General Jodl, the German Chief of Staff, signed the unconditional surrender of all German forces. Most of the Frenchmen were killed.[133]

On 1 February 1945, all grenadier with at least two years' service in the French Army or in German uniform were promoted to Rottenführer.[134] In this way, Soulat of the Headquarters Company, promoted to the rank of Sturmmann in December 1944, now found himself promoted to that of Rottenführer. Also promoted to Rottenführer was Strmm. Sepchat of the Headquarters Company/58.

A few days later, de Vaugelas, Raybaud and Boudet-Gheusi were promoted to Sturmbannführer. In fact, Raybaud continued to wear the insignia of Hstuf. while at Wildflecken and later in

---

132  Roger Wyckaert was born on 24 August 1923 in Saint-Denis.

133  Correction to original edition of *Pour L'Europe* that stated that all the Frenchmen were killed. André Coquelin and Michel Quentin were two such Frenchmen who died in the fighting for Breslau. Coquelin was born on 12 August 1923 and Quentin on 9 October 1924 in Saint-Preuil (department Charente).

134  Order SS-FHA B 12040/Amt V II b (7) Tgb. Nr 11/10835/44 geh. The automatic promotion was presented to them as a hierarchical benefit, as well as a financial benefit (de Genouillac, corrections to the author, 2000).

Pomerania. Of this, he explained that there were other more urgent concerns requiring his time and that of his staff. Curiously, Hstuf. de Bourmont was overlooked during this round of promotions. He was very piqued. Nevertheless, he too now seemed impatient to leave for the front, but which front? Marotin, like many former *francs-gardes*, still hoped that they would be leaving to liberate France alongside the German Army. However, for most, there was no question of this. And while this remained a topic of discussion, all knew with certainty that their departure was fast approaching.

On 7 February 1945, Uscha. Yves Peyret of the Panzerjäger Kompanie of Waffen-Gren. Regt. der SS 58 returned to Wildflecken camp. For the past two months he had been away on a course at Panzergrenadierschule Kienschlag. Exhausted from three long years in Russia with the LVF, he found the training mentally and physically demanding and elected to drop out before the graduation of his class. He hoped to return to Greifenberg for discharge but was sent back to Wildflecken. He left Kienschlag on 30 January 1945 and arrived in Berlin on 1 February. The following day he experienced a terrible air raid. On 4 February, in the afternoon, he left Berlin, accompanied by Mademoiselle Caubet whose brother he had met at Kienschlag and who had asked him to see her.

On his return to Wildflecken Peyret reported to Brigf. Krukenberg and explained the grounds for his decision, adding that he had little confidence in those officers of the *Milice* and the Sturmbrigade who had no experience of the Russian front. He also spoke of his regret that the *Miliciens* had been divided up among the two grenadier regiments. Of course Krukenberg did not approve of such talk, but he still acted humanely and sympathetically towards a demoralised veteran. Peyret found himself posted back to the 10/58.[135]

Peyret was not the only one to leave Kienschlag before the completion of the course. Conditions at the school were indeed tough.[136] There was no heating in this abandoned Czech village. To keep warm, the cadets had to flap their arms about every half hour. There was a lack of hot water so they shaved with their morning coffee. Hunger reigned and so did the lice. In order to study at night in their rooms, they had to fashion candles out of shoe grease. It was hell. Alfred Douroux, who attended Kienschlag, recalled:

> The instructors repeated: "You can leave when you want. The door is wide open. We don't hold back anybody". And it was true. We always had the choice, but they were even more demanding of us once we had decided to continue.

Douroux stayed put. Bellanger, Caubet, de Monfort, Vincenot and Walter chose to leave or were returned to the Brigade. Some had already served for two or three years with the LVF and 'considered it stupid to restart training from scratch'.[137] Henri Caubet had served with the III. Batallion of the LVF and had been awarded the KVK 2nd Class.[138]

---

135  Curiously, Peyret did not leave with the 10/58 to Pomerania and did not have an explanation for this other than he left *à titre isolé*.
136  See Soulat, *Historique de la Division Charlemagne*, p.87, repeated by Le Tissier Tony, *SS Charlemagne: The 33rd Waffen-Grenadier Division of the SS* (Barnsley: Pen and Sword, 2006), p.19.
137  Soulat, *Historique de la Division Charlemagne*, p.87.
138  Henri Caubet was born on 8 February 1920 in Tamatave, Madagascar.

Ustuf. de Genouillac, the company commander of the 4/58, was transferred to the post of assistant battalion commander of the II/58. He was so devastated to leave the company he had formed that he did not regard his transfer as promotion. Nobody has ever fully explained to him the reasons behind his transfer to the II/58, but he was one of the few officers of Waffen-Gren. Regt der SS 58 who could understand and speak German in a comprehensible way. Perhaps Berret, the battalion commander of the II/58, a *officier d'active Saint-Cyrien* [a regular officer who had graduated from military school Saint-Cyr], preferred an *Adjoint* with the same training as him.

In this way, the vacant command of the 4/58 went to former *Milicien* André Tardan who in the opinion of de Genouillac 'had the makings of a good officer'. But, like many *Milicien* officers, Tardan did not have the necessary military training to enable him to fulfil altogether the role assigned to him. Only time and adequate training would have provided him with all the necessary skills.

André Tardan was born on 30 September 1910 into a family from the Basque region. His family left France for Mexico around the turn of the century, built a hat factory and became very prosperous.[139] In 1940, André Tardan returned to France to do his military service. Attending *école d'officiers de reserve* [EOR] training, he was commissioned a *éléve-officier de réserve*. Thereupon, he became caught up in the vortex of the Phoney War, the *débâcle*, and, after he was unable to return to Mexico, the National Revolution. He passed from the Armistice Army to the *Franc-Garde* of the *Milice* and in early 1944 was appointed the *chéf departmentale* for Paris-Ville. Married, his wife lived in Paris, but she did not follow him into exile.

Ustuf. Philippe Rossignol was appointed the Orderly Officer of the II/58. Up to then he had been attached to the headquarters of Waffen-Gren. Regt der SS 58.[140]

In early February 1945,[141] Brigf. Krukenberg ordered Hstuf. Rémy[142] to go to depot Greifenberg in Pomerania and, from the ranks of the Franz. SS-Gren.-Ausbildungs und Ersatz-Bataillon, mobilise and take command of a Feldersatzbataillon [field replacement battalion]. Krukenberg had every confidence in Rémy who had proved himself as a very capable company commander in the LVF.

By train, Rémy journeyed to Greifenberg via the Pomeranian city of Stargard (Stargard Szczecinski) which was the base of Himmler's limited 'Sonnenwende' offensive and thus a key Soviet target. On finding the railway line cut at Stargard, he returned to Wildflecken, thereby incurring the anger of Krukenberg who immediately sent Hstuf. Bisiau in his place. Bisiau, for his part, managed to reach Greifenberg by train. His journey also took him via Stargard, but this time the railway system was up and running.

On 10 February 1945, the French Brigade of the Waffen-SS was expanded to a division with the title of the 33. Waffen-Grenadier-Division der SS 'Charlemagne' (französische Nr.1).[143] The

---

139  Indeed, according to Saint-Loup, André Tardan's father was a multimillionaire!

140  His military training was non-existent and as such would not have permitted him to discharge effectively any other function than that of a staff officer.

141  To be more precise, 'several days before the departure of 'Charlemagne' for Pomerania' (Soulat, letter to the author).

142  The precise date of Rémy's promotion to Hauptsturmführer is not known but may have been late January 1945.

143  RF-SS Feld-Kommandostelle, Adjutantur Tgb.Nr. 1698/45 geheim. This date of 10 February 1945 also appears in works by Bayle (*De Marseille à Novossibirsk*, p.77) and Yerger (*Waffen-SS Commanders*,

expansion from brigade to division status does not appear to have been widely communicated, if at all.[144] Many only learnt of the expansion postwar.[145]

## The departure for Pomerania

On 11 February 1945, Cornu of the Medical Company left Wildflecken for driving training at SS-Kraftfahrschule I Sbirow, near Pilsen, arriving some four days later. With him were Jean-François Stephanec[146] and Desrumaux who went for motor-cycle training.[147] The driving school was in a former castle. Once or twice Cornu went into Pilsen where life seemed normal and even beer was to be had. On 11 March, he left Sbirow, arriving back at Wildflecken on 17 March only to find that, in his absence, 'Charlemagne' had left for Pomerania.

In February 1945, Uscha. Mercier of Fahrschwadron A was approached about leaving for officer IV/A training. Curiously, it was Oberführer Puaud who interviewed him in German to assess his level of knowledge of the language of Goethe. Along with several others, he passed this 'exam' and was told to be ready to leave for the training course, though details of the course were withheld. Weeks later, he found himself not in a training school, but in action.

On 15 February 1945, 'Charlemagne' was assembled in the shape of a horseshoe on Adolf Hitler Platz. The spectacle was impressive. In the centre of the horseshoe stood a platform from which Mgr. de Mayol de Lupé came to celebrate mass. Then the imminent departure of 'Charlemagne' to the front was confirmed.[148]

The following day, Rttf. Soulat, a member of the Headquarters staff, learnt that 'Charlemagne' was to leave Wildflecken for Pomerania the very next day![149] However, some preparations had been going on for the past two or three days that had led him to believe that the transfer of 'Charlemagne' was imminent.

'Charlemagne' was transferred to the east at the request of Krukenberg who had become concerned about the political intrigues of the likes of Laval, Doriot, and Darnand. He was now

volume 2, Krüger to Zimmermann, p.167). However, according to an Allied Counterintelligence summary (Appendix E of Charlemagne's Legionnaires), the Division was formed on 1 February 1945, which is the same date Roch gives (La Division Charlemagne, p.41). Presumably the numerous divisional support units now acquired the number of 33 following the example of other Waffen-SS units expanded from brigade to division.

144  Indeed, after the expansion to division, the internal paperwork of 'Charlemagne' still bore the legend 'Brigade' (see the paperwork for the promotion of Soulat to Rottenführer, San et Persante, p.134). And 'Charlemagne' was still recorded as a brigade at the time of its arrival in Pomerania (see, for example, Russo-German war: 25th January to 8 May 1945, p.19 and p.35).

145  Correspondence with many veterans of 'Charlemagne', 1997-2006.

146  Born in 1927, Jean-François Stephanec joined the Avant-Garde of the Milice de Paris, passing through the école des cadres at La Chapelle-en-Serval. Transferred to the Waffen-SS, he served with the Engineer Platoon of the Headquarters Company of Waffen. Gren Regt. der SS 57.

147  Jean-Marie Desrumaux died in December 1998 (Mabire) or on 14 January 1999 at Brest (Soulat).

148  Rusco, Stoï!, p.253.

149  Soulat, letter to the author, 3/1/98. Curiously, according to Rostaing, Le Prix d'un Serment, p.158, he learnt on 9 February 1945 that 'Charlemagne' would be leaving for Pomerania in two days time. However, if a member of the Brigade's Headquarters staff only learnt of the transfer on 16 February it's very doubtful that a member of the Headquarters staff of the II/58 learnt of the transfer one week before.

convinced that the French 'government in exile' at Sigmaringen was now seeking to bring the Division under its control and engage it, in full or in part, against the 'Western Allied powers advancing on French territory'.[150]

For Krukenberg, this scenario 'would have been a catastrophe'. Yes, he would later accept that the training period was cut short,[151] but rather that than the unthinkable situation of Frenchmen fighting Frenchmen. And that was justification enough. Indeed, he was greatly concerned that if Frenchmen in German uniforms ended up fighting against their own compatriots then the German nation would have to accept the historic responsibility for it as well as sabotaging any kind of reconciliation between the two nations for an unforeseeable length of time.

On 17 February 1945, around 1400 hours, the first convoy of 'Charlemagne' left Brückenau station for Rummelsburg (Miastko), Pomerania.[152] More convoys followed that same day and continued over the next seven days. On 18 February, it was the turn of (elements of) Ostuf. Fenet's I/57. On 20 February, the Signals Company departed. On 21 February[t], the ninth convoy left. It was under W-Hstuf. Moneuse. Aboard this convoy were companies 1/58, 2/58 and 9/58 as well as elements of the divisional headquarters, W-Ostuf. Bénétoux (office II/AB) and SS-Ustuf. Büeler (office VI), in a 'special' wagon.

As the ninth convoy was leaving Bruckenau station another convoy arrived from the Protectorate of Bohemia-Moravia. This was carrying the Engineer Company of 'Charlemagne' that had just completed its training at SS-Pionierschule Hradischko. In its care was a batch of 'Charlemagne' sleevebands[153] to be delivered to Wildflecken.[154]

150 Krukenberg, cited by Soulat, *Historique de la Division Charlemagne*, p.15. However, no evidence exists, be it from World War II documentation or from credible witnesses, to substantiate the idea that the politicians of the French 'government in exile' at Sigmaringen wanted to have 'Charlemagne' engaged on the Western Front. Moreover, according to Dank, *The French against the French*, p.282, 'Doriot incurred the enmity of the RSHA through his refusal to permit the PPF men enlisted in the French Waffen-SS (Charlemagne) Division to be used on the Western Front'. The only enemy Doriot recognised was Bolshevism. Nevertheless, the fact remains that for whatever reason a political threat from the French 'government in exile' at Sigmaringen seemed all too real to Krukenberg.
151 Ibid. And yet, in contrast, according to Mabire, *La Division Charlemagne*, p.256, in February 1945 (this date is implied), Brigf. Krukenberg informed the SS-Führungshauptamt that Brigade 'Charlemagne' had received sufficient training and requested that it should be engaged as soon as possible in Pomerania. Also, according to Landwehr, *Charlemagne's Legionnaires*, p.68, 'on or about 15 February 1945, Brigf. Krukenberg decided that the training/formation process was finished, or as near to it as possible'.
152 'Charlemagne' departed to Rummelsburg not Hammerstein, for the word 'Charlemagne' can be found beside Rummelsburg on a situation map of Army Group Vistula dated 21 February 1945. According to Saint-Loup, *Les Hérétiques*, p.170, as the advance party boarded the trains, 'Charlemagne' was bound for Rummelsburg or Hammerstein. And yet, on p.175, Saint-Loup writes into a conversation between Hstuf. Moneuse and Ostuf. Métais upon their arrival at Hammerstein that 'Charlemagne' should have been equipped at Rumelsburg (sic), but the Russians had already occupied it, which is incorrect.
153 This suggests that the sleevebands were probably manufactured in Bohemia-Moravia and thus more specifically in Prague.
154 This batch of sleevebands was never delivered to Wildflecken because the convoy did not stop. It is not known what happened to the sleevebands.

Notably, the engineers were already wearing them on the left sleeve of their tunics.[155] This angered Krukenberg.[156]

On 23 February, elements of Hstuf. Berret's II/58 boarded one of the last convoys, the sixteenth.[157] On board the same convoy were elements of the FLAK Company, [158] as well as Ustuf. de Genouillac, the assistant battalion commander, armed with his chosen weapons of a Sauer pistol and an American M1 carbine. Surprised not to have a compass on him, he was shocked to learn that battalion headquarters only had one! Gren. Blanc of Company 5/58 was armed with a semi-automatic rifle, but it had no sight. Paul Denamps of the same company was only armed with a Mauser produced P08 Luger.

Fahrschwadron A went to Pomerania without much of its planned weapons and equipment. Uscha. Mercier would have left unarmed if it were not for his LVF comrade *Sergent* Labat, who had secretly given him a pistol at Greifenberg when trouble was expected in the wake of the

---

155  Witnessed by Soulat, letter to the author, 8/12/97. So was the Divisional Engineer Company the only unit of 'Charlemagne' to wear the sleeveband of the same name? To begin with, many former members of 'Charlemagne' maintained that the sleeveband was never worn, not even by the Engineer Company. Indeed, one former member of the Engineer Company cannot recall wearing the sleeveband. Much has been written about the sleeveband and according to Angolia, *Cloth Insignia of the SS*, p.491, 'some individuals from other units also acquired it'. De la Mazière of the PAK Company claims that before attending Janowitz in late December 1944 he was summoned by Krukenberg who told him: "We have just received supplies and you can sew the name of 'Charlemagne' on your uniform. Go and see Zimmermann on the way out. I want those at Yanowitz to know where you come from." According to Roch, *La Division Charlemagne*, p.53, 'Charlemagne' sleevebands were sent to Wildflecken and worn, but Krukenberg had them withdrawn. In response to this, according to Soulat, letter to the author, 20/2/98, sleevebands were never worn at Wildflecken. Roch also states that the 'Charlemagne' sleeveband was distributed to units on training courses in the region of Prague, although the Engineer Company was the only company of 'Charlemagne' to be fully kitted out. Perhaps this might explain how de la Mazière, who was at Janowitz near Prague from December to February 1945, actually acquired his sleeveband, and how, in the words of Angolia, 'some individuals from other units also acquired it'. Curiously, Martres, the Orderly Officer of Waffen-Grenadier-Regiment der Waffen SS 57, saw individuals wearing sleevebands they had made themselves, but never saw the official sleeveband. In conclusion, the Engineer Company was undoubtedly the only unit of the Division to wear the 'Charlemagne' sleeveband. However, the author is not so convinced that individuals from other units managed to acquire the sleeveband. Interestingly, those that wore the sleeveband were probably not authorised to do so.
156  Soulat, letter to the author, 20/2/98. In the same letter Soulat explained that Krukenberg objected to the wearing of the sleeveband until such time as the Division had seen battle. Mounine is also of the opinion (correspondence to the author, March 1999) that sleevebands were to be distributed once 'Charlemagne' had proved itself in battle, citing the examples of Waffen-SS Divisions 'Frundsberg' and 'Götz von Berlichingen'. While this would explain why Krukenberg was angered at the Engineer Company it does not explain why he had honoured de la Mazière with a sleeveband some two months before. Curiously, en route to Pomerania, Hstuf. Schlisler of Fahrschwadron A, who had the ear of Puaud, confided to Uscha. Mercier that 'Charlemagne' was soon to receive the sleevebands. He assumed that this would take place at a parade. There was no mention of 'Charlemagne' proving itself in battle before the sleeveband could be worn.
157  Michel de Genouillac, correspondence to the author throughout 1997. According to Rostaing, *Le prix d'un serment*, p.159, 'his' battalion, the III/58 (sic), had boarded the eleventh convoy on the 17th at 2200 hours. This date is incorrect.
158  Ibid. However, according to the article *SS-Französische Flakbatterie*, the FLAK Company received the order to embark for the Eastern Front on 25 February, which is too late.

attempt on Hitler's life on 20 July 1944. Nevertheless, Hstuf. Schlisler confirmed to his men that they would be equipped anew on their arrival. They were led to believe that this situation was normal and that 'German organisation had everything in hand'.[159] The old hands of the LVF, who had made the same journey in 1941, were not so convinced. They had different memories.

Bassompierre left on the last train. On his return to Wildflecken from Güstrow 'Charlemagne' was preparing to leave for the Eastern Front. He had presented himself to Puaud and Krukenberg who told him that he was 'assigned to the depot with the rank of *Capitaine*', but he refused to abandon his men when they were going into battle.[160] Nevertheless, he was still not given a command.

The units, manpower and weaponry of 'Charlemagne' put at the disposal of Army Group Vistula was as follows:[161]

## Units

| | |
|---|---|
| Brigadestab | Brigade Headquarters |
| 2 Gren. Rgt. mit je 2 Batl. | Two Grenadier Regiments with two Battalions |
| 2 I.G. Kompanien | Two Infantry Gun companies |
| 1 Abt. Art., 2 Battr. Je 4 L.F.H. | One Artillery Battalion, two batteries, 4 L.F.H. |
| 2 Pz.Schreck-Kompanien | Two Pz.Schreck companies |
| 1 3.7 Flak-Kp. | Anti-Aircraft Company |
| 1 Pi.Kp. | Engineer Company |
| 1 (gem.) Nachrichten-Kompanie | (mixed) Signals Company |
| 1 Feldpoststelle | Field Post Office |
| 1 Sanitätskomp. | Medical Company |
| 1 Krankenkraftwagenzug | MT Ambulance Platoon |
| 1 Feldgend.-Kompanie | Military Police Company |
| 1 Werkstattzug[162] | Workshop Platoon |

159  Mercier, letter to the author, 9/10/2001.
160  Interrogation of Bassompierre, 2 December 1946 and 4 December 1946.
161  From a non-referenced report that Soulat found by chance in the archives of Army Group Vistula. Dated '15/2', the report would not have included the *bataillon de marche de reserve* which joined 'Charlemagne' at Körlin in the first days of March 1945. Also, the *Compagnie d'Honneur* and the PAK Company of the Panzerjäger Battalion are conspicuous by their absence. The reference to a Feldgend.-Kompanie is surprising and doubted. It was normal for a division to have no more than a Feldgend.-Trupp. Lastly, the two Pz.Schreck companies are undoubtedly the two regimental anti-tank companies. To explain, at this stage of the war infantry regimental anti-tank companies had one platoon with three 7.5cm guns and two platoons (or one large platoon) with a big allotment of infantry anti-tank projectors: panzerfäust and panzerschreck (tank-terror). This was on paper and, of course, fluctuated. With that said, the anti-tank company of Waffen-Gren.Regt der SS 58 comprised one platoon with three 75mm anti-tank guns, one panzerfäust platoon, and one panzerschreck platoon.
162  Soulat doubts that a Workshop platoon accompanied the Brigade to Pomerania (personal discussion).

## Personnel

| | |
|---|---|
| Offizire | 102 |
| Unteroffizire | 886 |
| Mann | 5375 |
| | |
| Total | 6363 |

## Weaponry

| | | |
|---|---|---|
| Karabiner | 3643 | |
| Pistolen | 1030 | |
| M Pi | 538 | Machine pistol |
| 1 MG 42 | 66 | Light machine gun |
| s MG | 30 | Heavy machine gun |
| MG 34 | 31 | |
| m PAK | 3 | |
| s PAK | 3 | |
| 1.I.G. | 12 | Light infantry gun |
| s. I.G. | 5 | Heavy infantry gun |
| 3.7 cm FLAK | 9 | |
| L.F.H. | 8 | Light field howitzer |
| LKW | 44 | Trucks |
| Zgkw. | 3 | [Zugkraftwagen] |
| RSO | 3 | [Raupenschlepper Ost] Tracked tractor |
| Pferde | 1082 | Horses |
| Panzerfaüste | 872 | |
| Panzerschreck | 72 | |
| 1 Veterinär-Kompanie | | Veterinary company |

This entry in the archives of Army Group Vistula is dated '15/2'. Two days later, in response to a note from Generaloberst Weiss commanding the 2nd Army, the headquarters of Army Group Vistula announced the imminent arrival of a 'strong französischen Brigade (Division)' of '2 Regimentern zu je 2 Bataillonen, 1 Artillerie-Abt., 1 Panther-Abt., 1 Sturmgesch. Abt. und Artillerie' [two regiments of two battalions, one artillery group, one battalion of Panther tanks, one battalion of Sturmgeschütze assault guns and artillery]. Needless to say, the strength of 'Charlemagne' is grossly exaggerated! This response to Weiss was from RF-SS Himmler and signed by Ostubaf. Grothmann, his aide-de-camp.

Marotin summed up his time at Wildflecken with the words: 'I kept from Wildflecken the memory of the cold, the rain, the snow and the hunger... But also the memory of a warm camaraderie which helped us to endure the difficult moments and the rigours of our life...' Blanc was of the same opinion.

What now awaited the officers and men of 'Charlemagne' in Pomerania? They expected to receive further training before going into battle.[163] Also, they expected to receive new equipment and weapons. This was in line with current German Army practice, which was to equip new units at depots close to the front line. However, this is not what Oberjunker Bonnafont of the Panzerjäger Kompanie of Waffen-Gren. Regt. der SS 58 expected. News of the major Russian offensive had come to him from contacts made in the French POW camp near Wildflecken.[164] Because of this he became convinced that 'Charlemagne' would go straight into battle.

## Command Roster of the 33. Waffen-Grenadier-Division der Waffen SS 'Charlemagne' (französische Nr.1) mid to late February 1945 before the departure to Pomerania

### The German Inspection

| | |
|---|---|
| General-Inspector | SS-Brigf. Krukenberg |
| Orderly Officer | SS-Ustuf. Patzak |
| Orderly Officer | SS-Ostuf. Hegewald[165] |
| Orderly Officer | SS-Ostuf. Dally |
| Orderly Officer | SS-Ustuf. Gehring[166] |
| Office I/A (Operations) | SS-Hstuf. Jauss |
| Office I/B (Weapons, equipment, quarters) | SS-Ostuf. Meier |
| Office I/C (Intelligence) | SS-Hstuf. Schmidt |
| Office II/AB (Personnel) | SS-Hstuf. Pachur |
| Office III (Military justice) | SS-Ostuf. Dick |
| Office IV/A (Uniforms, clothing, rations) | SS-Hstuf. Hagen |
| • Supply Officer | SS-Hstuf. Dr. Gewecke |
| • Supply Officer | SS-Hstuf. Reinholdt |
| • Supply Officer | SS-Ostuf. Wahrlich[167] |
| Office IV/B (Medical/sanitation) | SS-Stubaf. Schlegel |
| Office IV/C (Veterinarian) | SS-Hstuf. Scheiner[168] |
| Office IV/D (Military chaplaincy) | ? |
| Office V (Vehicle) | SS-Ostuf. Neubauer |
| Office VI (Political training and activities) | SS-Ostuf. Kopp |

163 Correspondence with many veterans of 'Charlemagne'. In response to this, considering that Brigf. Krukenberg was pushing for the engagement of 'Charlemagne' without delay on the Eastern Front then this would suggest that 'Charlemagne' was not scheduled to complete its training programme or receive further training before going up to the front. It should be remembered that there had been no battalion and regimental manoeuvres, nor manoeuvres in conjunction with the heavy units.
164 Generally, the French prisoners avoided the soldiers of 'Charlemagne'.
165 Born on 14 July 1911, Rolf Hegewald was promoted to SS-Ostuf. on 1 January 1945.
166 Gehring was captured by the Soviets in March 1945 in Pomerania. His subsequent fate is not known.
167 Harald Wahrlich was born on 28 August 1904 in Merkelsdorf in Sudetenland.
168 Born on 11 October 1910 in Schaßburg, Artur Scheiner attended the SS-Veterinär-Ausbildungs und Ersatz-Abteilung Wandern in 1943.

| Training | SS-Staf. Zimmermann |
| Military Police | SS-Ostuf. Görr |
| Field Post | ? |
| French Liaison Officer | W-Hstuf. Renault |
| ? | W-Ustuf. Calot[169] |
| ? | SS-Ustuf. Friedrich |
| ? | SS-Ustuf. Zander |
| ? | SS-Ustuf. Engel |
| ? | SS-Stubaf. Katzian |

**Divisional Staff**

| Commander | W-Obf. Puaud |
| Chief of Staff | W-Stubaf. de Vaugelas |
| 1st Orderly Officer | W-Ostuf. Auphan |
| 2nd Orderly Officer | W-Std.Ob.Ju. Platon |
| Office I/A (Operations) | ? |
| Office I/B (Weapons, equipment, quarters) | ? |
| Office I/C (Intelligence) | W-Ustuf. Delile |
| Office II/AB (Personnel) | W-Ostuf. Bénétoux[170] |
| Office III (Military justice) | ? |
| Office IV/A (Uniforms,clothing, rations) | ? |
| Office IV/B (Medical/sanitation) | W-Stubaf. Dr. Lelongt |
| Office IV/C (Veterinarian) | W-Hstuf. Richert[171] |
| Office IV/D (Military chaplaincy) | W-Stubaf. de Mayol de Lupé |
| Orderly Officer | W-Ustuf. Cheveau |
| Office V (Vehicle) | ? |
| Office VI (Political training and activities) | W-Ustuf. Dr. Büeler |
| Liaison Officer | SS-Stubaf. Dr. Lölhoffel |
| | Then Major Roemheld |
| Gendarmerie de Brigade | W-Ostuf. Veyrieras |
| Assistant | W-Oscha. Henkinett |
| Civil Defence | W-Ostuf. Multrier |

**Divisional Units**

| *Compagnie d'Honneur* | SS-Ostuf. Weber |
| Assistant (*Adjoint*) | W-Std.Ob.Ju. Pasquet |

169  Notably, Robert Calot was born on 27 January 1912 in Hué (now Hanoi). He was ex-LVF.
170  Bénétoux was born on 2 November 1906 in Néré (department Charente-Inférieure).
171  Born on 3 August 1904 in Besançon (department Doubs), Jean Richert studied veterinary medicine at the *Ecole vétérinaire de Lyon*. Obtaining the *brevet de PMS de service vétérinaire*, he gained admittance to the EOR. In 1934 came his appointment to *vétérinaire sous-lieutenant de réserve*. He joined the LVF on 13 March 1944.

| | |
|---|---|
| Staff Company | W-Hscha. Surrel |
| Signals Company | W-Ostuf. Dupuyau |
| Engineer Company | W-Ostuf. Audibert de Vitrolles |
| Assistant | W-Ustuf. Mailhe |
| Medical Company | W-Hstuf. Dr. Bonnefoy |
| • Medical Officer | W-Ostuf. Pierre Alaux |
| • Medical Officer | W-Ostuf. Rimaud |
| Veterinary Company | W-Ustuf. Dr. Richter |
| Workshop Company | W-Ostuf. Maudhuit |
| Construction Company | W-Ostuf. de Moroge |
| Fahrschwadron A | W-Hstuf. Schlisler |
| Assistant (*Adjoint*) | W-Ustuf. Darrigade |
| Fahrschwadron B | W-Hstuf. Croisile |
| Assistant (*Adjoint*) | W-Ostuf. Huan[172] |

## Waffen-Grenadier-Regiment der Waffen SS 57

| | |
|---|---|
| Commander | W-Hstuf. de Bourmont |
| Assistant (*Adjoint*) | W-Ustuf. Artus |
| Orderly Officer | W-Ustuf. Martres |
| ? | W-Ostuf. de Londaiz |
| Office III (Military justice) | W-Ustuf. Stehli |
| Office IV/B (Medical/sanitation) | W-Hstuf. Dr. Leproux[173] |
| Office IV/C (Veterinarian) | W-Ostuf. Vergnaud[174] |
| Staff Company | W-Ostuf. André |
| • Reconnaissance platoon | W-Ustuf. Erdozain[175] |
| • Engineers platoon | W- Ustuf. Lefèvre |
| • Signals platoon | W-Ustuf. Brocard |
| Infantry Gun Company (9/57) | W-Hstuf. Roy |
| Anti-tank Company (10/57) | W-Ustuf. Labuze |

172 Born on 9 February 1891 in Levallois (department Seine-et-Oise), Maurice Huan was a partially disfigured and severely disabled First World War ex-serviceman who was a holder of the prestigious *la Croix de Chevalier de la Légion d' Honneur* awarded in 1921 and *Médaille Militaire*. He went to serve with the *Milice*.

173 Born on 17 August 1909 in Saint-Aubain, Pierre Leproux trained as a doctor and volunteered for the LVF on 18 December 1943. He served as a doctor with the III. Bataillon.

174 Born on 3 May 1902 in Saint-Projet-Saint-Constant in the department of Charente (which corrects he was born in Morocco), Jean Vergnaud studied veterinary medicine at the *Ecole vétérinaire de Toulouse*. Obtaining the *brevet de PMS de service vétérinaire*, he gained admittance to the EOR. In 1928, he was appointed *vétérinaire sous-lieutenant de réserve*. Mobilized, he served as a veterinarian during 39-40. He joined the *Milice*, serving with the rank of *Chef de trentaine* in the *Franc-Garde permanente*.

175 Born on 4 December 1919 at Pontoise (department Seine-et-Oise), Roger Erdozain studied at the prestigious *Prytanée national militaire* at La Fléche before entering service with the Air Force. He volunteered to go and fight in Syria against the British in 1941. On 30 October 1943, he enlisted in the Waffen-SS and, after basic training at Sennheim, he attended Posen-Treskau and then Kienschlag from 1 May to 9 September 1944. He was promoted to Untersturmführer on 9 November 1944.

## 1st Battalion (I/57)

| | |
|---|---|
| Commander | W-Ostuf. Fenet |
| Assistant (*Adjoint*) | W-Ustuf. Hug |
| Orderly Officer | W-Std.Ob.Ju. Labourdette |
| Medical Officer | SS-Std.Ob.Ju. Anneshaensel[176] |
| 1st Company | W-Ustuf. Brazier |
| 2nd Company | W-Ostuf. Bartolomei |
| 3rd Company | W-Ustuf. Counil |
| 4th Company | W-Oscha. Couvreur |

## 2nd Battalion (II/57)

| | |
|---|---|
| Commander | W-Hstuf. Obitz |
| Assistant (*Adjoint*) | W-Ostuf. Roumegous |
| Orderly Officer | ? |
| Medical Officer | W-Ostuf. Herpe[177] |
| Medical Officer | W-Ostuf. Duflos[178] |
| 5th Company | W-Oscha. Hennecart |
| 6th Company | W-Ustuf. Albert |
| 7th Company | W-Std.Ob.Ju. Million-Rousseau |
| 8th Company | W-Ustuf. Colnion |

## Waffen-Grenadier-Regiment der Waffen SS 58

| | |
|---|---|
| Commander | W-Stubaf. Raybaud |
| Assistant (*Adjoint*) | W-Ostuf. Baudouin |
| Orderly Officer | W-Std.Ju. de Vaugelas |
| Office III (Military justice) | W-Hstuf. Jautard |
| Office IV/B (Medical/sanitation) | W-Ostuf. Dr. Métais[179] |
| Office IV/C (Veterinarian) | ? |
| German liaison officer | SS-Ustuf. Goliberzuch[180] |
| Staff Company | W-Hstuf. de Perricot |
| • Reconnaissance platoon | W-Hscha. Gobion |

176  Louis Anneshaense was born in Strasbourg on 12 August 1915.
177  Marcel-Louis Herpe was born on 17 September 1895 in Plénée-Jugon (department Côtes-du-Nord). He briefly served with the LVF before enlisting in the Waffen-SS. He served with the Sturmbrigade, but did not go to Galicia with the 1st Battalion. He was promoted to Obersturmführer on 30 January 1945.
178  Roger Duflos was born on 11 August 1890. He was ex-*Milice*. He was killed in action on 6 March 1945.
179  Pierre-Marie Métais was born on 15 July 1902 in Saint-Maixent (department Deux-Sèvres). He served with the LVF as a doctor.
180  Karl Goliberzuch was born on 23 March 1909 in Dinslaken.

| | |
|---|---|
| • Engineers platoon | W-Hscha. Poletti[181] |
| • Signals platoon | W-Ustuf. Leune |
| Infantry Gun Company (9/58) | W-Ostuf. Français |
| Assistant | W-Ustuf. Pierre Werner?[182] |
| Anti-tank Company (10/58) | W-Oscha. Girard |
| Assistant | W-Std.Ob.Ju. Bonnafont |

## 1st Battalion (I/58)

| | |
|---|---|
| Commander | W-Hstuf. Moneuse |
| Assistant (*Adjoint*) | W-Ostuf. Falcy[183] |
| Orderly Officer | W-Std.Ob.Ju. Chatrousse |
| Medical Officer | W-Ostuf. Dr. Thibaud |
| 1st Company | W-Ustuf. Fatin |
| 2nd Company | W-Ostuf. Géromini |
| 3rd Company | W-Ustuf. Rigeade |
| 4th Company | W-Ostuf. Tardan |

## 2nd Battalion (II/58)

| | |
|---|---|
| Commander | W-Hstuf. Berret |
| Assistant (*Adjoint*) | W-Ustuf. de Genouillac |
| Orderly Officer | W-Ustuf. Rossignol |
| Medical Officer | W-Ostuf. Dr. Joubert |
| 5th Company | W-Ostuf. Wagner |
| Assistant | W-Oscha. Ruscone |
| 6th Company | W-Ustuf. Saint-Magne[184] |
| 7th Company | W-Hscha. Walter |
| 8th Company | W-Ostuf. Defever |

## Waffen-Panzerjäger-Abteilung der SS 57

| | |
|---|---|
| Commander | W-Stubaf. Boudet-Gheusi |

---

181 Félix Poletti who was ex-LVF, served with the 10th Company and received the EK II on 1 December 1943 at the same time as Jacques Doriot. He passed to the Waffen-SS and attended Pikowitz for engineer training. Soulat is convinced that he commanded the Engineers Platoon of the Headquarters Company (Soulat, letter to the author, 20/11/2009). His fate is not known.

182 Pierre Werner was born on 25 July 1905 in Charleville-Mézières (department Ardennes). He passed from the SOL to the *Milice*. In February 1944, with the rank of *chef de trentaine*, he led the 30 *miliciens* sent from the Gers to Haute-Savoie. His position as Français' deputy is unconfirmed, but possible because in the absence of Français he commanded Company 9/58.

183 Unconfirmed.

184 His date of promotion to Untersturmführer is not known. His grade may still have been that of Hscha.

| Assistant (*Adjoint*) | W-Std.Ob.Ju. Radici[185] |
|---|---|
| Medical Officer | W-Hstuf. Dr. Durandy |
| Supplies Officer | SS-Ostuf. Weiss |
| Anti-aircraft (FLAK) Company | W-Ustuf. Fayard |
| Anti-tank (PAK) Company | W-Ostuf. Krotoff |
| Assistant | W-Std.Ob.Ju. Vincenot |
| Assault Gun Company | W-Ostuf. Michel |
| Escort Platoon | W-Oscha. Mongour |
| German liaison Officer | SS-Hstuf. Kroepsch |

### Waffen-Artillerie-Abteilung der SS 57[186]

| Commander | W-Hstuf. Havette |
|---|---|
| Assistant (*Adjoint*) | W-Hstuf. Martin |
| Medical Officer | W-Ostuf. Dr. Fraysse[187] |
| Staff Officer | W-Ustuf. Frelut[188] |
| ? | W-Ustuf. Daffas |
| Officier d'Orientation | W-Ostuf. Chaufour |
| Supply Column | W- Std.O.Ju. Mermet[189] |
| Stabsbatterie | ? |
| 1st Battery | W-Oscha. Le Guichaoua |
| 2nd Battery | W-Ostuf. Salle |
| 3rd Battery | ? |

### Officers serving with 'Charlemagne' whose posts remain unknown:

### W-Usuf. Aimé Berthaud

Born on 13 July 1921 in Vire-en-Maçonnais (department Saône-et-Loire, he enlisted in the Waffen-SS on 28 October 1943. He attended SS-Panzergrenadierschule Kienschlag from 1 May to 9 September 1944, after which he was promoted to Untersturmführer.

---

185 Georges Radici was born on 5 January 1918 in Norgent-en-Bassigny (department Haute-Marne). During the 39-40 war, he served with the *10ème Bataillon de chars*, winning the *Croix de guerre avec palme*.
186 Soulat, letter to the author, 16/7/98 and Bouysse (*French in German Uniform part 1: Officers of the Waffen-SS*).
187 Born on 16 June 1900 in Saint-Andre Sangonis, René Fraysse studied medicine at the *Faculté de médecine de Paris*, before obtaining the *brevet de PMS* and gaining admittance to the EOR. In 1927, he received the rank of *médecin aide-major de 2° classe*. He was a member of the *Amis de la LVF*. He died on 16 August 1986.
188 Yves Frelut was born on 1 October 1919 in Montpellier.
189 This corrects previous wrong name and rank provided.

## W-Hstuf. Émile Auffray

Born on 29 August 1898 at Romagné, Auffray joined the army in April 1917 and was sent to the front that December. He was demobilized in October 1918 with the rank of *sergent*. Joining the LVF, he became the company commander of the 13th Company and fought at Bobr. He transferred to the Waffen-SS and was present at Wildflecken in November 1944, after which his whereabouts and fate remain a mystery.

## W-Ustuf. Jean Dodon

Dodon was born on 13 May 1914. He joined the LVF with the rank of *sergent-chef* and served with the PAK platoon of the I. Bataillon of the LVF, winning the *Croix de guerre légionnaire* for saving the life of his *chef* during the night of 27-28 May 1943 by killing a partisan at Sapolje. He attended SS-Panzerjägerschule Janowitz from 10 October to 11 November 1944. Given his previous military experience, it's reasonable to presume he served with Waffen-Panzerjäger-Abteilung der SS 57.

## W-Usuf. Clément Dornier

Dornier was born on 20 June 1899 in Alger. He held the rank of *Capitaine* in the French Army.

## Ustuf. Imbaud

Gilles Imbaud was born on 23 April 1916 in Bordeaux. He served as a doctor with the LVF and then with Waffen-Grenadier-Regiment der Waffen SS 58.[190] He was holder of the KVK 2nd Class.

## W-Ustuf. Labrousse

He was ex-*Milice*.

## W-Ustuf. Royer

James Royer was born on 29 October 1918 in Honfleur (department Calvados). A member of the PPF, he enlisted in the Waffen-SS in the summer of 1943 and attended Kienschlag from 1 May to 9 September 1944. He served as a company commander in Waffen-Gren. Regt. der SS 57 with the rank of Oberjunker, although the exact company is not known.[191] He was sent to Breslau, after which there is no further information.

---

190  Soulat, letter to the author dated 10/7/2006.
191  Croisile, *Sous uniforme allemand*, p.247.

## W-Ostuf. Rouzaud

Jean Rouzaud was born on 17 March 1901 in Montluçon (department Allier).

## W-Ustuf. Dr. Seigneur

Born on 22 January 1907 in Frettecuisse (department Somme), Michel Seigneur studied medicine at the *Faculté de médecine d'Amiens*. Armed with the *brevet de PMS*, he gained admittance to the EOR, graduating in 1929. Four years later, he was commissioned *sous-lieutenant de réserve*. He passed from the SOL to the *Milice*, attending the third course at Uriage. He became the *Chef départemental-adjoint* for Haute-Vienne and in May 1944 the *Chef départemental.* Given his medical background, it seems reasonable to assume he served in a medical capacity in 'Charlemagne'. He went to Pomerania with the division and was among those to come back, although he required hospitalisation.[192]

## W-Hstuf. Vincent

His precise role within 'Charlemagne' *au moment du départ au front* is not known. He may have been serving as a staff officer at divisional headquarters. He was a holder of the KVK 2nd Class. He survived the war.

---

192 Jean-Marie Croisile saw Seigneur at the SS-Polheim in Prague on 11 April 1945 (Croisile, *Sous Uniforme Allemand*, p.284).

**12**

## The Hell of Pomerania
## Part I

---

### A chance meeting

On 25 February 1945, in Berlin, Strmm. Jean-Jacques Pillet of the Workshop Company, still on a training course, met Ostubaf. Gamory-Dubourdeau quite by chance in the street. To his great surprise, he learnt that 'Charlemagne' had been engaged in Pomerania. At that moment he knew that his place and that of his company was at the front supporting the combatant elements of the division. He went at once to his company commander, Ostuf. Maudhuit and asked him if the company was leaving for Pomerania. The answer was 'No'. Strmm. Pillet then asked if the company might go to Budapest. Again the answer was 'No'.

Two days later, the sixty-strong Workshop Company left Berlin for Wildflecken camp. On 1 March 1945, the Workshop Company arrived at Fulda, where it was employed in the aftermath of an air raid. Pillet remembers bringing out bodies from a bombed house. One day later, the company was back at Wildflecken. Pillet for one could not quite believe that he had been transferred away from the fighting on the Eastern Front.

Similarly, when officer cadets Jean-Marie Croisile, Cossard, Lefeuvre and de Mandiargues, who were on a training course at Kienschlag, learnt that the division had been deployed to the Eastern Front they went to see Inspekionsführer Kleindienst and asked to be sent back to the division, explaining that they thought their duty was now to participate in the fighting with their comrades. Kleindienst replied: "Your duty is to remain here and finish this Lehrgang to become officers." They stayed.

### The military situation on the Eastern Front from January to February 1945

On 12 January 1945, the Soviets broke out of the Baranów bridgehead. This was the start of a major Soviet offensive that would extend from the Baltic to the Carpathians by 15 January. To the north the 2nd White Russian Front under Marshal Rokossovsky had been given the task of striking north-west to the Baltic coast, cutting off East Prussia and clearing the line of the lower Vistula. On Rokossovsky's left, the 1st White Russian Front under Marshal Zhukov was to break out of the Pulawy bridgehead towards Lodz, out of the Magnuszew bridgehead towards

Kutno and encircle Warsaw on its right flank. Subsequently, the Front was to drive westwards to the river Oder.

On 14 January, the 2nd White Russian Front launched its attack against the German 2nd Army. The attack met with little initial success against stiff resistance and violent counterattacks from the 'Grossdeutschland' Panzer Corps. Even so, by 18 January, the 2nd White Russian Front had still covered forty kilometres and broken the front of the German 2nd Army. By 20 January, Mlawa and Dzialdowo (Soldau) had fallen and the East Prussian border had been crossed. The 2nd White Russian Front was now poised for the dash to the coast. Allenstein (Olsztyn) and Tannenberg (Stebauk) fell on 22 January. Four days later, the Fifth Guards Tank Army reached the Baltic coast north-east of Elbing (Elblag), cutting off the 3rd Panzer Army and 4th Army in East Prussia from the rest of the Reich. The remnants of the 2nd Army fell back to the west.

Also, on 14 January, the 1st White Russian Front exploded from the Pulawy and Magnuszew bridgeheads. By the end of the day it had smashed up five divisions of the German 9th Army. Modlin was occupied on 15 January, Radom on 16 January and Warsaw on 17 January. The 1st White Russian Front then proceeded to sweep west. The right flank of the front captured Kutno on 19 January and four days later, after having covered 150 kilometres, occupied Bydgoszcz (Bromberg) without a fight. That same day, 23 January, the left flank of the front took Lodz. There was little resistance left before the Russians. On 25 January, the left flank of the 1st White Russian Front bypassed Poznan (Posen) and pushed on to the west and the Oder which was reached in the last days of January. Berlin was only 70 kilometres away.

The past three weeks had been disastrous for the Germans. The frontline, once deep in Poland, now ran along the line of the Oder and the Neisse. Losses in men and equipment had been heavy and irreplaceable. An enormous breach had been opened between the German 2nd Army, holding a front along the lower Vistula, and German forces on the Oder. The whole of Pomerania lay uncovered to the Soviet invader. To close this breach, Hitler put in the newly created Army Group Vistula (Weichsel in German) and gave its command to Himmler.

Help came to Himmler from a sudden thaw at the turn of the month that added to Zhukov's logistical problems and from the dissipating strength of the 1st White Russian Front. Zhukov had been forced to leave some of his forces to deal with the encircled garrisons at Poznan and Schneidemühl, and to divide his forces between the push into Pomerania and maintaining the bridgeheads over the Oder. By early February, Himmler had managed to erect a makeshift front.

To pinch off Zhukov's spearhead and gain time for the defence of Berlin, General Guderian, the chief of staff of the OKH, approached Hitler about a two-pronged counterattack east of the Oder. The convergent counterattack hinged upon the employment of the 6th SS Panzer Army as one attack group, but Hitler refused to sanction its commitment on this front. Thus, through lack of resources, Guderian fell back on a single-pronged attack out of the area of Stargard (Stargard Szczecinski) against Zhukov's long right flank.

Divisions were amassed for the attack, codenamed 'Soommersonnenwende' (Summer solstice), under the command of the newly created 11. SS-Panzer Armee. The III. (Germanic) SS Panzer Corps, comprising the 11. SS-Panzer-Grenadier-Freiw.-Division 'Nordland' and the 23. SS-Panzer-Grenadier-Freiw.-Division 'Nederland', was transferred from Courland to Pomerania for the attack.

But the divisions allocated to the attack had to be committed prematurely to hold the front and the assembly area in bitter fighting. Even so the attack commenced on 16 February 1945 and enjoyed initial success, lifting the siege of Arnswalde on the following day. However, by 21 February, the attack had run its course and Hitler officially ended 'Soommersonnenwende'. The 11. SS-Panzer Armee began a general withdrawal to its jump-off positions.

In the meantime the Soviet High Command had abandoned its original plan to drive onto Berlin, considering its own forces too weak and extended and the German forces too strong. Seemingly it had become concerned about the build up of the new 11. SS-Panzer Armee and the danger it posed to Zhukov's right wing. To thwart the German's plans, the Soviet High Command came up with many measures. One such measure was the deployment of the 19th Army and the 3rd Guards Tank Corps on the left flank of the 2nd White Russian Front that would drive to the Baltic Sea through Neustettin and Köslin. This would split the German forces concentrated in Pomerania. The attack was scheduled for no later than 24 February 1945.

**The first convoys**

On board the first convoy of 'Charlemagne' were elements of the divisional headquarters under Obf. Puaud, Staf. Zimmermann of the German Inspection, the *Compagnie d'Honneur*, and a small advance party under Stubaf. Boudet-Gheusi charged with organising the equipping of the division.

Boudet-Gheusi was far from happy: his Panzerjäger battalion was still not assembled. The FLAK Company, which had been participating in the defence of Fulda against Allied bombing since January, would be following later. The Assault Gun Company was still undergoing training in Bohemia. His command thus consisted of only the PAK Company with its three platoons of four 75mm guns each. And the guns were training pieces of poor quality!

The journey of the first convoy to Pomerania did not pass without incident. Towards midday on 20 February, while held up in Altdamm (Dabie) railway station, the first convoy was attacked by the Soviet Air Force. The division suffered its first casualties[1]: four or seven killed and some twelve wounded.[2] Also of note is that when the convoy set off from Altdamm it left behind ten or so luckless men of the *Compagnie d'Honneur*.[3]

Five hours later, during a stop at Gollnow station, Obf. Puaud, Staf. Zimmermann, Hstuf. Renault and Oberjunker Platon, Puaud's Orderly Officer, left the convoy and continued on their way to Rummelsburg in a cross-country vehicle. Arriving at Rummelsburg station, they learnt that their convoy and all those of the division had just been diverted to the town of Hammerstein (Czarne), also in Pomerania.[4] The large village of Hammerstein lies at the heart

---

1    Soulat, *Historique de la Division Charlemagne*, p.17, and Mabire, *La Division Charlemagne*, p.265. However, according to Bayle, *San et Persante*, p.152, the air attack that inflicted the division's first losses took place at Gollnow (Goleniów in Polish), north-east of Stettin (Szczecin in Polish). In response to this, Mabire also records an air attack on the first convoy at Gollnow, but in contrast there is no mention of losses or damage.

2    Soulat, *Historique de la Division Charlemagne*, p.17, states four killed whereas Bayle, *San et Persante*, p.152, states seven killed.

3    Soulat would meet them later at Köslin.

4    Army Group Vistula probably issued the orders that diverted 'Charlemagne' to Hammerstein.

of Pomerania, approximately one hundred kilometres from the Baltic Sea and only twenty kilometres from Neustettin.

At 0200 hours on 22 February 1945, the first convoy stopped at Hammerstein railway station. The troops disembarked and took up residence in a nearby camp. This former army camp, converted into a Stalag for POWs[5], had been evacuated of late and returned to its previous owner. And it was here that the division was to be assembled, armed and equipped before going up to the front in a week or so.[6]

The camp was empty all except for some French prisoners in khaki uniforms. There was no sign of the promised equipment. This did not unduly worry Stubaf. Boudet-Gheusi as the front was still far off. However, as the day wore on, concern grew just like that of the continuous, muffled rumbling of guns that could be heard.

The next elements of 'Charlemagne' to arrive at Hammerstein were companies 1/57, 3/57 and 4/57 of Battalion I/57.[7] On the same convoy were Hstuf. de Bourmont and Ustuf. Martres.[8] After learning of the diversion to Hammerstein de Bourmont had held an officer's briefing on the train. It is not known what was said.

## XVIII. Gebirgs-Korps

That same day, the 33. Waffen-Grenadier-Division der SS 'Charlemagne' (französische Nr.1) was subordinated to the XVIII. Gebirgs-Korps of the 2nd Army,[9] newly arrived from Lapland.[10] General Hochbaum commanded the corps whose headquarters was located at Stegers (Rzeczenica).

The situation of the XVIII. Gebirgs-Korps was not good. To defend a front running from Landeck to Konitz, almost forty-five kilometres long, the Korps had two weakened divisions: the Pomeranian 32nd Infantry Division and the 15. Waffen-Grenadier-Division der SS (lettische Nr. 1).

Commanded by Generalleuntant Boeckh-Behrens, the 32. Infanterie-Division held the sector west of Konitz. It had been transferred from Courland to Pomerania only weeks before. Although well tried, it continued to fight tooth and nail for its native land. Holding the left flank was Kampfgruppe Jutland, comprising Infanterie-Regiment 94 and 96. Holding the

---

5    Stalag II-B is situated 2.4 kilometres west of Hammerstein.

6    Soulat, *Historique de la Division Charlemagne*, p.17.

7    The exact time of their arrival is unclear. According to Bayle, *San et Persante*, p.153, the three companies of the I/57 spent the entire day of the 22 February 1945 at Hammerstein camp and were alerted around 2300 hours. Mabire is unspecific, but infers they did not arrive before midnight on 22 February (*La Division Charlemagne*, p.271). According to Saint-Loup, *Les Hérétiques*, p.175, 'SS Regiment 57' arrived in six echelons on 22 February between the hours of 0200 and 1900. This seems doubtful as both Mabire and Bayle record the arrival of elements of Waffen-Gren. Regt der SS 57 on 23 February and even as late as 24 February.

8    Martres, personal conversation with the author. Curiously, according to Mabire, *La Division Charlemagne*, p.272, regimental headquarters of the 57 was on the convoy carrying the 2/57 and the first elements of Hstuf. Obitz's II/57 that arrived the following day.

9    Soulat, letter to the author. However, according to the order of battle of Army Group Vistula on the date of 22 February 1945, 'Charlemagne' was attached directly to the 2nd Army (*Russo-German war: 25th January to 8 May 1945*, p.35).

10   The headquarters of the XVIII. Gebirgs-Korps was transferred to Pomerania on 15 February 1945.

sector north of Preussische-Friedland was Infanterie-Regiment 4, which was badly depleted. Divisional headquarters was located at Stolzenfelde, north-west of Schlochau (Czluchow in Polish).

As for the 15. Waffen-Grenadier-Division der SS (lettische Nr. 1), Grenadier Regiments 33 and 34 were in defensive positions from Rosenfelde to Landeck along Brook Dobrinka and also in a northerly direction from Landeck along Brook Küddow. Although the tired Division had been in constant action over the past month, sustaining many casualties, its Latvian troops were still full of fight and now in well constructed trenches. Also, of late, SS-Obf. Burk had taken over the command of the division from temporary commander SS-Obf. Ax, who was too inexperienced to command a division. Divisional headquarters was located at Krummensee (Krzemieniewo), north of Landeck.

Shortly before midnight on 22-23 February, Stubaf. Boudet-Gheusi assembled all officers and NCOs at Hammerstein camp to inform them that the Russians had launched a massive tank attack in the region of Schlochau only twenty kilometres east of Hammerstein. This did not bode well. And still there was no sign of its promised equipment.

Alerted, by midday on 23 February, the three companies of Fenet's I/57 had taken up a temporary position several kilometres to the south-east of Hammerstein to cover the other convoys due to arrive against a possible surprise enemy attack. A muffled rumbling could still be heard to the east and every so often the sound of tank tracks could be made out over this background noise.

23 February saw more convoys of 'Charlemagne' pull into Hammerstein railway station. They brought with them the 2/57, whose commander Ostuf. Bartolomei had already arrived, as well as elements of Hstuf. Obitz's II/57 (and perhaps the last elements of Hstuf. de Bourmont's regimental headquarters).[11] Comte and Cessil of the 5/57 disembarked in the late evening.[12] The company was sent to Hammerstein camp where it spent the night.

That same day, in his daily report to O.K.H., Colonel Eismann, the Operations Officer (Ia) of the headquarters of Army Group Vistula, indicated for 'Charlemagne' the following assembly area: Forstenau, Reichenwalde, Heinrichswalde, Klausfelde. He also signalled the arrival of the first five convoys of the Division.[13]

On 24 February 1945 at 0030 hours, General Weiss, the commander of the 2nd Army, sent a message to the headquarters of Army Group Vistula, remarking that the arrival of 'Charlemagne' would without doubt permit the reduction of the rather large front assigned to the 32. Infanterie-Division of the XVIII. Gebirgs-Korps but would not permit the release of local reserves.[14]

If General Weiss recognised that the front of the 32. Infanterie-Division was overextended, so had the Russians. At dawn on 24 February, literally hours after General Weiss sent his

11    Again the exact time of their arrival is unclear. According to Mabire, *La Division Charlemagne*, p.272, Ostuf. Bartolomei's Company 2/57, the first elements of Hstuf. Obitz's II/57, as well as regimental headquarters arrived in Hammerstein railway station before midnight on 23 February. In contrast, Bayle, a Junker der Waffen SS in the 2/57, records his arrival at Hammerstein on 24 February around 1600 hours (*De Marseille à Nowossibirsk*, p.158).
12    According to Comte, *Une vie sous le signe du Führerprinzip*, p.53, it was at the end of the day while Cessil, letter to the author, states around 2130 hours.
13    Reference I A/Br.Tgb.Nr.1842/45 geh.
14    AOK 2/Ia 365/45 G.K.Chefs.

message to Army Group Vistula, five Soviet divisions of the 19th Army, newly arrived from Finland, struck the 32. Infanterie-Division between Marienfelde and north-west of Konitz. Under this crushing blow the Russians succeeded in ripping open the front of the 32. Infanterie-Division between Marienfelde (Myśligoszcz) and Groß Jenznick (Jęczniki Wielkie). There were no reserves available to seal the breach through which the enemy now poured. Unopposed, the Soviet divisions moved towards the river Haaken along which the 2nd Army now intended to establish a defence line.

## Arrival of Stubaf. Raybaud and the I/58

Meanwhile, on the morning of 24 February 1945, two convoys, carrying elements of the I/58 and the regimental headquarters staff of Waffen-Gren. Regt. der SS 58, pulled into Hammerstein railway station.[15] Travelling with them was regimental commander Stubaf. Raybaud.[16] At Hammerstein camp, Raybaud was alarmed by the same discovery made by all others before him: the military depot was, in a word, empty.[17]

On the evening of 24 February, two more convoys carrying elements of the I/58 arrived at Hammerstein.[18] The ninth convoy, carrying companies 1/58, 2/58 and 9/58 (IG), arrived towards 1700 hours. Like its predecessors, the ninth convoy was attacked from the air en route to Pomerania. The first attack came soon after its departure on the 21 February when two Allied fighters made a single pass and put the locomotive out of action and shot up the field kitchen, causing two casualties. On the following day, 22 February, having just passed through Nordhausen station, the convoy was caught by six or seven fighters. This time the attack lasted about twenty minutes and was much more serious; the locomotive and three wagons of ammunition were destroyed, the line between Nordhausen and the next station of Halle was cut, and the dead totalled six and the wounded twenty. Thereupon, the convoy returned to Nordhausen where it spent the night. Moreover, at 1600 hours on 24 February, while stopped at Neustettin station, the ninth convoy was passed by another carrying (at least) the divisional Engineer Company.

15   Raybaud, letter to Mabire, 3/11/74, and corrections to Soulat's *Historique de la Division Charlemagne*. This corrects Mabire who states that the four companies of Moneuse's I/58 arrived throughout the night of 24-25 February (*La Division Charlemagne*, p.296). Furthermore, according to the written interview with Raybaud in Landwehr's *Charlemagne's Legionnaires*, p.98, 'his men' actually disembarked from their trains at Bärenhutte. This is incorrect.

16   Raybaud, letter to Mabire, 3/11/74. This corrects Mabire's account of Raybaud disembarking at Hammerstein with Hstuf. Berret's II/58 after the engagement of the division in the sector of Heinrichswalde and Barkenfelde. In this same letter, Raybaud also wished to set the record straight that he had not fought 'for several days' with the Zalhmeisters (quartermasters) at Wildflecken while his first battalion was in action.

17   Mabire, *La Division Charlemagne*, p.332.

18   Raybaud, corrections to Soulat's *Historique de la Division Charlemagne*. Rigeade, the company commander of the 3/58, also recalls that Battalion I/58 arrived throughout the day of 24 February (letter to the author, 31/1/97).

**Contact with the enemy!**

During the morning of 24 February, Brigf. Krukenberg held a briefing at Hammerstein camp with Obf. Puaud, Stubaf. de Vaugelas, Stubaf. Raybaud and Hstuf. de Bourmont.[19] Staf. Zimmermann assisted Krukenberg. The Brigadeführer told them that the front held by the Latvians had been ruptured[20] and that 'we will have to go and take up position immediately'.[21] Also reported was the intention of the 2nd Army to form a stop line, facing east, between Hammerstein and Schlochau. The following orders were given:[22]

- The I/57 under Ostuf. Fenet was to deploy beyond the village of Heinrichswalde (Uniechów) and take up defensive positions, facing south-east.[23]
- The II/57 under Hstuf. Obitz was to deploy towards the village of Barkenfelde (Barkowo), some twenty kilometres south-east of Hammerstein. In addition, the headquarters of Waffen-Gren. Regt der SS 57 was to establish itself in Barkenfelde (Bińcze).
- The I/58 under Hstuf. Moneuse and the headquarters of Waffen-Gren. Regt der SS 58 were to deploy to the village of Bärenhutte (Biernatka).

19    A conclusion drawn by the author, although the exact time of this briefing and its participants remain unclear. According to Soulat, *Historique de la Division*, p.29, during the morning of 24 February, 'a meeting was held at Hammerstein camp which brought together' Krukenberg, Puaud, Raybaud and de Bourmont. According to Raybaud, letter to Mabire of 3/11/74, at some point after his arrival at Hammerstein on 24 February, Brigf. Krukenberg summoned him to Hammerstein camp with de Vaugelas and perhaps de Bourmont. Although the simultaneous presence of Puaud and de Vaugelas is not reported, the author believes that this briefing, which importantly led to the engagement of 'Charlemagne', would not have gone ahead without the presence of its commander and Chief-of-Staff. Thus, the author has concluded that Soulat and Raybaud speak of the same briefing. Moreover, there is some agreement between Soulat and Raybaud on the content of this briefing.
20    Raybaud, letter to Mabire, 3/11/74. This is not strictly true. The Russians actually gained a breakthrough east of the 15. Waffen-Grenadier-Division der SS (lettische Nr. 1) in the sector of the 32. Infanterie-Division.
21    Ibid.
22    Mabire records the issuing of these orders in quite different circumstances (see *La Division Charlemagne*, pp.274-275). On the morning of 24 February, Hstuf. de Bourmont and his regimental headquarters were making their way to Barkenfelde when German liaison officers informed him that the village was in danger of being captured by the Russians! He asked about the 32nd Infantry Division and was told that it had been dispersed which was then confirmed by the sight of retreating haggard, cold and frightened German soldiers. Thereupon he decided to deploy his regimental headquarters to the village of Bärenwalde and to 'push his two battalions forward to try and get a little clarity'. While it is true that de Bourmont learnt of the danger to or even the capture of Barkenfelde while making his way there after the briefing, it appears that Mabire, who does not record the briefing at which the orders were issued, has used this particular moment of 'high drama' to introduce the orders issued to the two battalions of Waffen-Gren. Regt der SS 57, but not those of the I/58, which, according to Mabire, had still not arrived.
23    Mabire, *La Division Charlemagne*, p.280. However, according to Soulat, *Historique de la Division Charlemagne*, p.29, Fenet's I/57 was also to deploy towards the village of Barkenfelde, to the east of Heinrichswalde.

Furthermore, Stubaf. Raybaud was ordered to place the I/58 at the disposal of Waffen-Gren. Regt der SS 57 and to prepare the position of Bärenhutte while awaiting the arrival of Hstuf. Berret's II/58.[24]

For tactical reasons, Waffen-Gren. Regt der SS 57 was subordinated to the 32. Infanterie-Division whose right wing now extended to Bärenhutte railway station.[25] By 1300 hours, both battalions of Waffen-Gren. Regt der SS 57 had set off to the front.[26] And thus began the engagement of 'Charlemagne' without artillery and tank support, without heavy weapons, and without radio equipment. Indeed, some soldiers were still without a steel helmet or a spade.

Taking a route via Geglenfelde (Wyczechy), the headquarters of Waffen-Gren. Regt der SS 57 and Hstuf. Obitz's II/57 made their way to Barkenfelde. On learning that Barkenfelde was already occupied by the Russians, Hstuf. de Bourmont decided to establish his regimental headquarters at Bärenwalde, to the north of Barkenfelde.

The II/57 continued forward and made good time. Around 1500 hours, the regimental reconnaissance platoon under Ustuf. Erdozain, a former cadet at the *École militaire de La Flèche*, unexpectedly engaged an enemy detachment near Barkenfelde. It was not a detachment of Soviets, but bizarrely a detachment of 'free Germans' in German uniforms!

At the end of the afternoon of 24 February, Obitz's II/57 cautiously entered a deserted Barkenfelde, but came under accurate sniper fire from a wood and lost a dozen dead and wounded before the Russians disappeared.[27] The companies then deployed; the 5/57 took up a position some four to five kilometres from Barkenfelde near a hamlet occupied by the Russians; the 6/57 occupied some farm(house)s at the southern edge of the village; and the 8/57, with its heavy weapons, set up some two kilometres north-west of Barkenfelde across the road running from Barkenfelde to Bärenwalde.[28] All now waited.

At twilight, the Russians attacked. 'With the energy of despair', Hstuf. Obitz's battalion fought them off against great odds.[29] The machine-gunners of the Heavy Platoon of the 5/57

24  Raybaud, letter to Mabire, 3/11/74. This corrects Mabire, *La Division Charlemagne*, p.304, and Saint-Loup, *Les Hérétiques*, p.192.
25  Soulat, *Historique de la Division Charlemagne*, p.29. However, Mabire recounts, *La Division Charlemagne*, p.273, that as soon as de Bourmont disembarked from his train at Hammerstein he went to the 'headquarters of the German Division' (presumably the 32nd Infantry Division) for orders. Soon after, he returned to his headquarters with a furious air and the news that his Waffen-Gren. Regt der SS 57 was now 'integrated into' the 32nd Infantry Division. According to Lefèvre, *Axe & Alliés* no 1, p.56, headquarters and the German inspection were told at this meeting of their attachment to the XVIII. Korps.
26  According to Saint-Loup, *Les Hérétiques*, p.176, the time was 1000 hours when the state of alert was issued to all those units which had disembarked, and 1300 hours when the two battalions of Waffen-Gren. Regt der SS 57 set off to the front, the II/57 following the I/57 after an interval of minutes. According to Mabire, *La Division Charlemagne*, pp.276-280, Fenet's I/57 set off at midday. Curiously, Mabire is unspecific about Obitz's II/57. Midday is also recorded by Soulat, *Historique de la Division Charlemagne*, p.29, for the I/57, and, then on p.30, as the time the II/57 and the headquarters of Waffen-Gren. Regt der SS 57 arrived at Geglenfelde. Also of interest to note is that, according to Saint-Loup, *Les Hérétiques*, p.176, Roy's 9/57 started to disembark as the two battalions I/57 and II/57 set off to the front. However, the article *Mein Freund Georges*, recalls the company disembarking and assembling in the icy night, presumably the night of 24-25 February 1945.
27  Saint-Loup, *Les Hérétiques*, p.179. This is not recounted by Mabire.
28  Del Missier of the 8/57, map to the author.
29  Mabire registers this unequal fight at one to ten (*La Division Charlemagne*, p.277).

on the extreme left of the battalion could not bring their fire to bear because they were afraid of hitting their own troops who were engaged in hand-to-hand combat. As luck would have it, a machine gun crew was preparing a new and better emplacement when a Russian shell dropped right on the gun, destroying it completely! The 5/57 withdrew to Barkenfelde, but what was left of the company was then separated between the other units of the battalion for the defence of the village.

At nightfall, Hstuf. Obitz decided to abandon Barkenfelde and take up a position on a line of heights to the north-east of the road that runs to Bärenwalde. Closely pursued by the Russians, his battalion conducted a fighting withdrawal to this defensive position and quickly dug in. Around 1900 hours, Obitz was reinforced by the timely arrival of the Panzerjäger Battalion's PAK Company of twelve 75mm guns, as well as a battery of 105mm guns and two 88mm guns with German crews.[30]

### Heinrichswalde

Heinrichswalde is about twelve kilometres from Hammerstein and was connected by a direct dirt road, but after a recent thaw it had become nothing more than a muddy quagmire. It was along this road that Ostuf. Fenet's Battalion, the I/57, made its way to Heinrichswalde. Progress was not easy. The carts carrying the heavy weapons and ammunition sank up to their hubs which tens of men had to be detailed to get out and push along. Their horses waded about.[31] Sometimes the men suddenly sank up to their knees in muddy potholes. The battalion was then forced to advance in single file on each side of the road to allow the continuous passage of carts crowded with civilians fleeing from the Russians. That slowed its progress even more. As a result, the battalion stretched out.

In the early evening,[32] the 3/57 approached Heinrichswalde. Ustuf. Counil, the twenty-year-old company commander, despatched a patrol into the village, but it drew fire. The Russians were already occupying Heinrichswalde! Thereupon Fenet ordered Counil to attack with his company. This was repulsed. Counil reported back to Fenet that Heinrichswalde was strongly defended by the Russians who were perhaps in battalion strength. Fenet then decided to await the arrival of the other companies before proceeding with a battalion attack.[33]

Night fell, but Heinrichswalde was soon bathed in bright moonlight. Bartolomei's 2/57 would only arrive shortly before 1900 hours. Soon after Ostuf. Fenet deployed his companies: Ustuf. Brazier's 1/57 to the right, Ostuf. Bartolomei's 2/57 to the left; Couvreur's 4/57, with its machine-guns and mortars, to a pit 800 metres from the village; and Counil's 3/57 to remain in position at the western edge of the village. Fenet quickly drew up his attack plan: following a mortar barrage, Counil's 3/57 would attack through the village's entrance supported by

30   Soulat, *Historique de la Division Charlemagne*, pp.30-31.
31   Mabire, *La Division Charlemagne*, p.280. In contrast, Bayle of the 2/57, in a letter to the author, remarked that there were no horses at their disposal; they had simply not arrived yet.
32   Mabire states around 1700 hours whereas Soulat states 1900 hours, repeated by Lefèvre, *Axe & Alliés* no 1, p.57.
33   Mabire, *La Division Charlemagne*, p.282. However, Saint-Loup does not document the attack of Counil's 3/57 and according to Soulat, *Historique de la Division Charlemagne*, p.29, Ustuf. Counil estimated Russian strength at a company.

converging flank attacks from the companies of Bartolomei and Brazier.[34] The attack was set for 1900 hours.

Couvreur's mortar barrage was over in a matter minutes, his complete stock of mortar ammunition having been expended. The Russians replied with their own mortars. Supported by Couvreur's heavy machine-guns, companies 1/57 and 3/57 stormed forward. Ustuf. Counil, the company commander of the 3/57, was not wearing a steel helmet; how could he when some of his men were without one? Among the first to be wounded was section commander Strm.-F. Bew Yvon Prunennec. Hit in both arms, he was evacuated.[35]

The attack by Brazier's 1/57 came to an untimely end when the company became pinned down and started to take heavy losses. Dead and wounded littered the ground.[36]

After spending a long time in overcoming a machine gun nest, the 3/57 managed to penetrate into Heinrichswalde. Advancing towards the cemetery, Ustuf. Counil, who was two or three metres in front of his company, was killed.[37] Suddenly, the Russians launched a counterattack. Although wavering from the loss of its commander, the company, reinforced by the headquarters of the I/57 and with fire support from other units, managed to stop the Russians dead. Again the Russians came. Again they were repulsed. Again they came. And again they were repulsed. Eventually the situation stabilised.

On learning of Counil's death, Fenet ordered Oscha. Quiquempois to take over the remnants of the severely tested 3/57 and hold Heinrichswalde at all costs. Wounded of the 3/57 taken to a first aid post in a house were killed or wounded again when enemy shells smashed into it.

Meanwhile, Ostuf. Bartolomei's Company, the 2/57, had become pinned down and unable to move from its starting positions in the village cemetery. Its line of attack was across a veritable glacis, but it was lit up like day by some burning hovels and swept by well placed Russian automatic weapons. Any attempt to cross would have been murderous and Bartolomei was not going to sacrifice his men needlessly. All the same his company started to take losses. Platoon commander Oscha. André Mauclair, a former French Navy *second-maître* [Petty Officer second class], was one of the first killed.[38] A second platoon commander, Oscha. Bernand Gastine, a

34    Mabire, *La Division Charlemagne*, p.283. However, according to Saint-Loup, *Les Hérétiques*, p.182, Brazier's 1/57 was assigned to deliver the frontal attack and Ustuf. Counil's 3/57 to attack on the right wing.

35    Prunennec was evacuated to a farm serving as a field hospital that came under air attack. Riddled with shrapnel, he was further wounded in the head, the throat, the left arm and the left knee. He survived the war.

36    Mabire, *La Division Charlemagne*, pp.286-287, and Soulat, *Historique de la Division Charlemagne*, p.29. In contrast, according to Saint-Loup, *Les Hérétiques*, pp.184-185, Brazier's 1/57 advanced in successive dashes, but the supporting fire from Péléart's heavy machine-guns, was too low and brought losses. Uscha. Darat was the first to be hit and wounded by friendly fire. Undeterred, the 1/57 broke into Heinrichswalde and dislodged the Russians from a large farmhouse with grenades and then entrenched itself. The Russians counterattacked and were shot up in a hail of bullets. They came again in greater numbers. To avoid encirclement, Brazier's 1/57 was forced to fall back to its starting positions.

37    Mabire, *La Division Charlemagne*, p.285, presumably based on the eyewitness account of Roberti. However, Saint-Loup recounts, *Les Hérétiques*, pp.184-186, that Counil's 3/57, after breaking into the village, pushed on in hand-to-hand fighting and took the central crossroads of Heinrichswalde that was held for over an hour. Losses mounted and, by the time the company fell back under great enemy pressure, its *chef* was dead.

38    André Mauclair was born on 23 November 1922.

former *Milicien*, was also killed bringing orders from Bartolomei. Junker der Waffen SS Bayle took command of the platoon again.[39]

Enemy mortars zeroed in. Then, in turn, batteries of Katyusha rockets opened up. The men of the 2/57 took shelter as best they could. However, one platoon commanded by Uscha. Franchart, who was ex-Sturmbrigade, did actually attempt to attack and moved off across the fire-swept glacis. The platoon was made up of 'very young boys' and their reasons for trying to attack are not known as they were decimated in minutes. None of them would return.[40] Bartolomei's position soon became untenable and he withdrew his company to a small height to his rear.

Despite the unsuccessful attack of his battalion, Ostuf. Fenet still believed he could take and hold Heinrichswalde. But reports from Brazier and then Bartolomei, which spoke of the Russians advancing unimpeded on the flanks, left him with the realisation that the battle was beginning to turn in the favour of the Russians. Moreover, contact had still not been made with the II/57 on his left flank or with the 15. Waffen-Grenadier-Division der SS (lettische Nr. 1) on his right flank. Totally isolated, Fenet now abandoned any hope of recapturing Heinrichswalde. And although encirclement threatened he decided to hold on and 'await orders without yielding any ground'.[41] But he had no signalling equipment.

Ostuf. Fenet finally received orders from his regimental commander, Hstuf. de Bourmont, courtesy of liaison officer Ostuf. de Londaiz who arrived on horseback![42] Fenet was ordered to withdraw level to the lake midway between Barkenfelde and Bärenwalde, located two or three kilometres north-east of his current positions.[43] In turn, orders were sent to the companies, but the 2/57 had just withdrawn to avoid encirclement and could not be contacted. However, this did not unduly concern Fenet; Bartolomei was 'an old fox who knew how to avoid all the traps'.

After evacuating the wounded to the rear, Fenet withdrew.[44] There were no difficulties. By 0300 hours on 25 February, the I/57 was on its new positions, but contact could still not be made with the II/57.

---

39   Just before the departure of 'Charlemagne' from Wildflecken to Pomerania Oscha. Bernand Gastine entered the 2/57, outranking Junker der Waffen-SS Bayle who 'let Gastine have his place'. Curiously, Bayle writes, *San et Persante*, p.156, that Gastine's former *Milice* rank gave him a superior Waffen-SS rank to his. This, however, might be incorrect. Firstly, officers and NCOs of the *Milice* were admitted into the Waffen-SS with the rank they held in the French military forces and not that in the *Milice*. And any subsequent promotions came, undoubtedly, as a result of merit.

40   Saint-Loup, *Les Hérétiques*, pp.185-186. However, Bayle, who was in Kompanie 2/57 and present at Heinrichswalde, cannot recall this suicidal attack or the existence of a certain *Zugführer* [platoon commander] by the name of Franchart. But Mounine, in a letter to the author, has confirmed the existence of Franchart, his rank as that of Uscha, his company as that of the 2/57, and his death at Heinrichswalde. The author has not been able to explain this discrepancy.

41   Mabire, *La Division Charlemagne*, p.288.

42   The time of Ostuf. de Londaiz's arrival remains unclear. According to Mabire, *La Division Charlemagne*, pp.289-290, his first visit was nothing more than 'fact finding' and information share. All the same, before midnight on 24 February, de Londaiz was back with the orders. However, Saint-Loup is not in agreement and records, *Les Hérétiques*, p.186, that de Londaiz finally found the headquarters of the I/57 at 0300 hours.

43   Soulat, *Historique de la Division Charlemagne*, p.30. Mabire, for his part, details that Fenet was to withdraw two or three kilometres to the rear (*La Division Charlemagne*, p.290).

44   According to Saint-Loup, *Les Hérétiques*, p.186, when the time came for Kompanie 3/57 to withdraw from Heinrichswalde, Ustuf. Counil's body was brought along. However, this is contradicted by Mabire, *La Division Charlemagne*, pp.290-291.

Around 0715 hours on 25 February, a patrol from the 3/58 stumbled across the 2/57. An order signed by Hstuf. de Bourmont was passed onto Ostuf. Bartolomei. In this way, he learnt that 'the I/57 should have withdrawn at 0400 hours and, taking advantage of the darkness, withdrawn northwards in the direction of the level crossing situated 500 metres from Bärenwalde to receive new orders there'.[45] Alas, there was no way Bartolomei could pass on this order to Fenet, still in position north-east of Heinrichswalde, for he had lost all contact with the remainder of the battalion.

Around the same time as Bartolomei was handed de Bourmont's order, the Russian infantry hit the I/57 and punctured the company holding the centre of its disposition. To prevent being cut in two and to drive off the Russians, Ostuf. Fenet assembled all the forces of his right flank and immediately counter-attacked along the front line. This counterattack succeeded.

Ostuf. Fenet now decided to move his isolated battalion, less Bartolomei's Company, to Bärenwalde where he hoped to find Hstuf. de Bourmont and the regimental headquarters of Waffen-Gren. Regt der SS 57. Bartolomei's 2/57 was making for Hammerstein.

## Bärenwalde

Let us now return to the II/57 occupying a line of heights before Bärenwalde. During the night, the 8/57 was deployed to Bärenwalde. Towards midnight, an enemy force of company strength appeared before the 6/57. Ustuf. Albert ordered his company to let the Russians approach to within twenty metres of its well-camouflaged and concealed positions before opening fire. The Frenchmen waited. Now the Russians were within twenty metres. Fire! Many of the attackers were felled. Surprised, the Russians immediately fled in total chaos. The Frenchmen rushed after them and brought back three prisoners, who were despatched to regimental headquarters.

A little later, the Russians started to pound violently Obitz's battalion with mortars, anti-tank guns, howitzers and Stalin Organs. Hell was let loose. The unimaginable barrage lasted more than an hour, inflicting heavy casualties and totally disrupting the battalion's disposition.

At 0500 hours on 25 February, a fresh Siberian division, brought up by truck, charged the II/57.[46] It was a savage and costly struggle, but the vast Russian flood could not be stemmed. Although ordered to hold on, Obitz could do little else than retreat. And as if his battalion was not in trouble enough, but the unexpected withdrawal of a Latvian SS unit exposed its left flank. Too dispersed, the II/57 shattered. The company commander of the 7/57, Oberjunker Million-Rousseau, suddenly found himself alone in the midst of an enemy horde and had to fight his way out.

Maurice Comte, serving in the 5/57, remembers:[47]

45  Soulat, *Historique de la division Charlemagne*, p.30. And yet, curiously, according to Mabire, *La Division Charlemagne*, p.291, de Bourmont was handed an order from a patrol of Waffen-Gren. Regt der SS 57, which read: 'Order to the 1st Battalion [I/57] to withdraw northwards to the lake situated between Barkenfelde and Bärenwalde where I have established my headquarters and where I will give new orders.' This order is undoubtedly the same order Fenet received earlier that day, which, by now, had been overtaken by events.

46  Soulat, *Historique de la division Charlemagne*, p.31.

47  Comte, letter to the author. This corrects Mabire's account, *La Division Charlemagne*, pp.326-327, of the death of Artus which, for the record, describes how Artus, on learning that Russian tanks had broken through their defensive line before the Hammerstein-Bärenwalde railway and were advancing

368    For Europe Revisited

.... having been separated from my company, the 5th, I found myself withdrawing with my platoon and some stragglers in the direction of Bärenwalde where we arrived when Brigf. Krukenberg was preparing the defence. Questioned by Ostuf. Artus on what we knew of the Russian positions, I reported to him the closeness of a column of tanks. Krukenberg gave Artus the job of a reconnaissance mission on this column; Artus took what was left of my platoon [and] some others (I think Uscha. Jacques), in all around twenty lightly armed (one or two MG 42 machine guns, personal weapons and perhaps panzerfäuste). [We advanced] about twenty metres through a wood bordering and dominating the road along which the column was advancing [and made] contact, but without being spotted by the Russians. We waited for Artus' orders who, like us, was watching the column, made up of two T-34s at the front, then one Stalin, then other T-34s, and escorting infantry in file on each side without apparent worry, with weapons lowered.

At this point Comte was the nearest person to Ostuf. Artus, but still some ten to fifteen metres away from him. The Russian road column was about twenty to thirty metres away. Comte continues:

Suddenly, [an] intense bombardment. The Russians took shelter. I looked at Artus, and saw him lifeless, hit in the neck, covered with blood. One of the men said: "The Lieutenant is dead." I very clearly remember having said to the machine-gunner (Meunier I think): "Don't fire". I started to crawl towards Artus but was wounded by a piece of shrapnel to the top of my head. I passed out (perhaps some seconds or minutes) [and] was brought back by the men withdrawing to Bärenwalde. I felt fuzzy-headed. My vision and all my senses soon became sharper again.

Thus, in all probability, Artus was killed and Comte wounded by friendly artillery fire attempting to stop the Russian column.[48] Evacuated to Hammerstein, Comte was given first aid and fell into a deep sleep. The following morning, he got into a shouting match with Dr. Bonnefoy who wanted to send him to a hospital, but who gave up hours later when he showed no sign of an infection. He counted himself lucky.

All resistance was gradually submerged. The isolated companies fought a running battle at the cost of heavy losses. In desperation, 'to avoid a pointless massacre',[49] Hstuf. Obitz decided to withdraw the remnants of his battalion to the Hammerstein-Bärenwalde railway line north

on the railway station, dashed to its defence. Stalking a tank through the houses he managed to get within metres of the steel monster. Panzerfäust in hand, he took aim and fired, but nothing happened; the panzerfäust had not been primed. He was then cut down by the tank and died almost instantly.

48    The 'artillery fire' put down on the Russian column could only have come from Hstuf. Roy's 9/57 which must have been unaware of the nearby presence of friendly troops. Moreover, to reinforce the point that the artillery fire was friendly, Comte reiterated in his letter to the author that the hidden French SS soldiers were watching the Russian tank column and waiting for Artus' orders, and also that the Russians did not open fire on their positions. Comte would write later in his book that when he was treated at Hammerstein he learnt that Hstuf. Roy had fired on the column (see Comte, *Une vie sous le signe du Führerprinzip*, p.56).

49    Mabire, *La Division Charlemagne*, p.294.

of his present positions. To cover the withdrawal, the 8/57 was deployed from Bärenwalde to the railway line.

The withdrawal of the II/57 exposed the headquarters of Waffen-Gren. Regt der SS 57, which had to evacuate Bärenwalde promptly, as well as the left flank of the I/58 which had moved up into action during the night of 24-25 February 1945.

## Enter the I/58

On 24 February, soon after the arrival of Battalion I/58, Stubaf. Raybaud, Hstuf. Moneuse, the four company commanders of the I/58, Oberjunker Chatrousse, Moneuse's Orderly Officer, and (perhaps) Hstuf. de Bourmont went to a headquarters briefing by Jauss of the German Inspection in a house quite close to Hammerstein railway station. The aim of the briefing was 'to engage the I/58 as reinforcements to the I/57'.[50] After a rundown of the situation from Jauss, it was decided that companies 1/58 and the 3/58 would be committed as support behind the already engaged Waffen-Gren. Regt der SS 57. At the end, Moneuse received three maps for the whole battalion! He kept one for himself and gave another to Chatrousse who was ordered to accompany Fatin's 1/58 to its position.[51]

Waffen-Gren. Regt. der SS 58 was to be committed even though it had no heavy weapons or radio equipment. The regimental reconnaissance platoon, like that of Waffen-Gren. Regt. der SS 57, had no motorcycles, just bicycles. Stubaf. Raybaud would later compare the engagement of his regiment without support to that on the Somme in June 1940.

Stubaf. Raybaud was in Bärenhutte before nightfall and here he spent the night with his regimental headquarters, receiving a visit from de Vaugelas and Puaud. Around 0400 hours on 25 February, Raybaud woke to the sound of a Russian bombardment on Bärenwalde to the south. Undoubtedly, his thoughts would have gone out to his troops of Battalion I/58 over whom he no longer had any authority.

During the night of the 24-25 February, Moneuse's I/58 moved up to the front.[52] Compass in hand, Ustuf. Rigeade took Company 3/58 towards the front.[53] After marching a dozen or

50    Rigeade, letter to the author, 18/8/97 and Chatrousse, correspondance to the author throughout 1997. The time of this briefing for the officers of the I/58 was probably late evening. Thus, the then desperate situation of Waffen-Gren. Regt der SS 57 would not have been known and the decisions reached at this briefing for the engagement of Battalion I/58 reflect the picture known at that time. This role for Battalion I/58 of support to Waffen-Gren. Regt der SS 57 is not, as such, confirmed by Mabire who recounts, *La Division Charlemagne*, p.303 that Puaud employed Battalion I/58 to try and plug the gap that existed between Fenet's I/57 and Obitz's II/57. But these roles were defined by Puaud on the morning of the 25th! Saint-Loup, for his part, records that Rigeade's 3/58 was 'to fill out' the left flank of Battalion I/57 and that Moneuse was to plug the gap between Rigeade and Battalion II/57.

51    Chatrousse remembers, letter to the author, 20/7/97, that the third map went to Rigeade. However, he did not receive one (Rigeade, letter to the author, 18/8/97).

52    According to the written interview with Raybaud (see *Charlemagne's Legionnaires*, p.100), Battalion I/58 took up an unidentified position, 'facing east', and, at 1700 hours, was relieved by Battalion II/58. Thereupon, Battalion I/58 was sent forward to Bärenwalde to reinforce the hard pressed 'SS Regiment 57'. This is incorrect; the II/58 had not arrived yet.

53    Mabire states, *La Division Charlemagne*, p.297, that each company of the I/58 was committed individually whereas Saint-Loup, *Les Hérétiques*, p.192, pictures three of the four companies marching south-east towards the sound of the guns.

so kilometres during the night, he stopped his company at daybreak and dug in at the edge of a wood in front of a vast plain. He was on his laid down positions south-west of Bärenwalde.

Oscha. Blonay's Platoon, which was positioned in a farmhouse, chanced upon some French POWs who advised the French SS to surrender to the Russians. The SS answered by asking the POWs to join them. They refused.

Unable to find Hill 105, the planned location for his headquarters, Hstuf. Moneuse set up instead at a forest road crossing. For the time being he kept in reserve Ostuf. Géromini's Company 2/58 as well as the Headquarters Platoon and Mortar Platoon(s) of Ostuf. Tardan's Company 4/58; Fatin's 1/58 and Rigeade's 3/58 had each been reinforced by one MG Platoon of Tardan's 4/58.[54]

As for Chatrousse, after accompanying Fatin's 1/58 to its positions, he reported back to Moneuse who then asked him to set off again and make contact with Rigeade's 3/58. He would march all night through the snow-covered woods without finding a living soul.

Although Rigeade's 3/58 was in contact with the Latvians of the 15. Waffen-Grenadier-Division der SS (lettische Nr. 1) on its right, contact could not be made with Fatin's 1/58 on its left. For its part, the 1/58 managed to establish contact with Obitz's II/57 to its left, but its right flank remained wide open. Thus, a solid defensive line had still not been formed.

Towards 0600 hours on 25 February, less than an hour after the arrival of the I/58 on the front line, the first enemy activity around the positions of Company 1/58 was easily repulsed.

Three hours later, the first serious attack hit Fatin's 1/58 and was immediately repulsed, but at the cost of several dead and wounded. Around the same time, Rigeade found himself isolated; the Latvians on his right came under a ferocious artillery bombardment and quickly withdrew. In the belief that all resistance had been swept aside, the Russian infantry then advanced, but fled when the 3/58 opened up. Although better camouflaged than the Latvians, Rigeade's 3/58 had now given its position away. Their company commander knew the Russians would be back.

In the meantime, Moneuse had become increasingly concerned about his isolated situation. He still had no contact with Rigeade's 3/58, telephone lines to the command post of Waffen-Gren. Regt der SS 57 at Bärenwalde were continually cut, and runners sent in the direction of Bärenwalde never returned. To add to his despair, his command post was also coming under intense artillery fire and steadily taking casualties.

His right flank still wide open, Moneuse summoned Ostuf. Tardan and ordered him to establish contact with the 3/58. Tardan took with him his Headquarters Platoon and the crews of a 'mortar group' under Uscha. Louis Salmon, also a former *Milicien*.[55] After searching in vain for almost two hours, Tardan suddenly came across stragglers from Waffen-Gren. Regt der SS 57. For the most part, they were wounded and in a state of shock. Also, they were without weapons. Then more and more dazed Frenchmen and Latvians appeared.

Judging the situation perfectly, Ostuf. Tardan then sent his remaining mortars and crews to the level crossing between Bärenwalde and Bärenhütte where he believed resistance would be centred. He and his Headquarters Platoon returned to Moneuse's command post.

54    Chatrousse, letter to the author, 20/7/97 and Soulat, *Historique de la division Charlemagne*, p.31.
55    Soulat, *Historique de la division Charlemagne*, p.31, and Mabire, *La Division Charlemagne*, p. 300. Therefore, Saint-Loup is incorrect when he recounts that 'Tardan took the head of his company' for this mission (*Les Hérétiques*, p.193).

As the hours passed, Fatin's 1/58 was subjected to further attacks, increasing in brutality each time, but for the moment his company held the Russians in check. At some point Moneuse committed Géromini's 2/58 which may have been to the left of the 1/58.[56]

Meric's Platoon of the 2/58 encountered a Russian patrol some twenty metres away, but was the first to react, killing several men. Fearing other patrols on his right, he immediately marched his platoon in this direction. He took up position a little further and, with his machine-guns, engaged the Russian wave making for Bärenwalde, which he was able to halt for a short time. Without delay he now returned to his battalion.

When Oberjunker Chatrousse, Moneuse's Orderly Officer, returned to the command post of the I/58 he found Ostuf. Falcy questioning a Latvian SS soldier who, after being captured by the Russians, had just escaped. Like most former legionnaires of the LVF, Falcy spoke a little Russian. Notably he was wearing a Waffen-SS camouflaged smock that few possessed.[57]

Chatrousse then reported back to Moneuse that the right of their disposition was totally 'in the air'. Soon after, Moneuse learnt from runners sent to Bärenwalde that the Russians were at the village. He immediately decided to withdraw and recalled his companies.[58]

By the time the orders to withdraw reached Ustuf. Fatin he was in trouble. Contact had been severed with Obitz's II/57 and the Russians had started to infiltrate the resulting breach to his left in greater and greater numbers. In fact, faced with this deteriorating situation, he had already decided to withdraw his company with or without orders. His company was soon back with Moneuse at his command post.[59]

Hstuf. Moneuse laid down the battle plan and order: Ostuf. Géromini's company 2/58 was to be the battering ram which would open an 'escape route' and then provide flank cover for the battalion.[60] Then Ustuf. Fatin's Company 1/58 would follow echeloned in platoons.[61] Oberjunker Chatrousse was to bring up the rear with the last elements of the 1/58.

It was then that Chatrousse saw Ostuf. Français and his company arrive whose infantry guns were now being pulled by hand as the horses had been cut down by machine-gun fire. To ensure a rapid withdrawal, Français requested permission from Chatrousse to destroy and abandon the infantry guns. A hand grenade in the gun barrel was sufficient to render them unusable. Seeing

56  Soulat's wartime drawing of the 'combat de la 3/58 (Ustuf. Rigeade) à Bärenwalde' shows the 2/58 positioned to the left of the 1/58, which no other source confirms. Nevertheless, according to Saint-Loup, Les Hérétiques, pp.195-196, Moneuse despatched the 2/58 'to see what's happening' with the 1/58. Géromini found Fatin and then returned with nothing to report, even though the area was enemy-infested!
57  For example, nobody in the 1/58 possessed the camouflaged smock.
58  Saint-Loup, Les Hérétiques, p.196. However, Chatrousse cannot remember if Hstuf. Moneuse had relayed or actually given the order to withdraw (letter to the author, 20/7/97).
59  Saint-Loup, Les Hérétiques, p.196. However, according to Mabire, La Division Charlemagne, pp.309-310, when Ostuf. Fatin received orders from Hstuf. Moneuse to withdraw it was 'too late': the 1/58 was already encircled. Géromini's 2/58, described as the last reinforcements, then had to be sent to free the 1/58. As such, this 'relief' operation conducted by the 2/58 is not confirmed by any other source.
60  Soulat, Historique de la division Charlemagne, p.33. Saint-Loup confirms, Les Hérétiques, p.196, that Géromini was to be 'on the flanks', but there is no mention of spearheading the battalion's withdrawal. Oberjunker Méric states his company was on the right of the battalion and his platoon on the right of the company.
61  Chatrousse, letter to the author, 20/7/97. This corrects Saint-Loup, Les Hérétiques, p.196, which places 1/58 as the vanguard.

372 For Europe Revisited

no other alternative, Chatrousse assented to his request. Besides the company had yet to receive ammunition for the guns!

And so began the withdrawal through the enemy-infested woods to the west of Bärenwalde. Méric's Platoon of the 2/58 suddenly heard explosions and firing less than fifty metres ahead. Friendly troops fell back on the platoon that soon found itself in contact with Russians, killing several and putting the others to flight. Méric then stated what followed:

> I gave the visceral order to charge ahead shouting as loud as possible, anything. And a miracle happened. These shouts aroused us and liberated us. We also fired a lot on anything that moved and elsewhere. We pursued them into the forest for about two hundred metres shouting and firing with success, receiving almost as much fire. We neutralised the automatic weapons gunfire enfilading certain trails and rejoined the column. Luckily nothing bad happened to us ...

The platoon made it to Bärenwalde level crossing at the cost of three wounded, one seriously in the shoulder, but he was lucky enough to be evacuated. Méric would learn much later that he was proposed for the Iron Cross for his actions which saved his platoon from destruction. He never received a medal, which he would always regret. Oberjunker Chatrousse said of the retreat:

> In this retreat through the wood I served Ostuf. Falcy and witnessed his wounding by a mortar shell some metres from me. He was evacuated immediately.[62] I also served de Bourmont who was desperately trying to organise the retreat of the unit in good order.
>
> I continued to collect and rally stragglers from all manner of units as we continued to progress towards the north-west. I soon had thirty men with me, but many were wounded and had to be carried on their backs, and also few weapons. I carried Hscha. Quatennes[63] on my back. He was wounded before the breakthrough. I carried him for a very long time and was out of breath. The pace was not quick.
>
> Suddenly, the leading troops fell back on me, warning of Russians. Effectively they had outflanked us and cut off us from the rest of the battalion. There was only one

---

62  Ibid. Curiously, according to Soulat, Falcy was wounded along the Hammerstein-Bärenwalde railway line. Also, the author has a brief sighting of Falcy behind Bärenwalde level crossing (Grenouillet, letter to the author, April 1998) and he did not appear to be carrying a wound, but then again the sighting was only brief. This sighting the author has not been able to explain.

Incorrectly, according to Saint-Loup, *Les Hérétiques*, p.297, Falcy was killed along the Hammerstein-Bärenwalde railway line. Rigeade remembers meeting him in Paris shortly after the war. Falcy was arrested on 20 September 1945 and was incarcerated at Chambéry. On 6 June 1946, the *Cour de justice de Savoie* reaffirmed the judgement of May 1945 and sentenced him to death. De Genouillac met his good friend Falcy again at the start of 1947 at the camp of Carrère. He spent fifteen months in detention with Falcy. Curiously, they had often showered together and de Genouillac does not recall noticing any trace of injury on Falcy's body except two cut fingers on his left hand after being thrown onto a running circular saw by a prison warder 'anxious to prove his patriotism'. Falcy was liberated at the end of 1948. De Genouillac often met up with him in Paris until his friend's death in the 1960s.

63  Marcel Quatennes was born on 27 April 1920 at Grenay (department Pas-de-Calais). This *Sergent d'infanterie d'active* joined *La Légion Tricolore* on 2 October 1942 and signed up for the LVF on 7 September 1943. He did not survive the war. His position in 'Charlemagne' is still debated.

thing to do and that was to charge ahead immediately in the hope that the Russians were still not too thick on the ground.

It was then that I gave the order to charge, with each bawling as loud as they could more to encourage themselves than to intimidate the enemy. The Russians did not insist, leaving some corpses behind and taking flight into the forest. We reached a route that crossed the railway line via a level crossing. Russian tanks attacked us. Luckily the Anti-Tank company intervened and held them off long enough for us to take shelter behind the railway line. The wounded were evacuated. I put myself at the disposal of Tardan.[64]

And what of Ustuf. Rigeade and his 3/58? Still isolated, he and his company were oblivious of the fact that the rest of the I/58 had withdrawn. Around 1000 hours, he suddenly found himself in the path of the first brigades of enemy Russian tanks.[65] His company, having no anti-tank guns or panzerfäust at its disposal, sought to fight off the tanks by depriving them of their escorting infantry and concentrated its fire on these 'soft targets'.

Two Russian tanks made for Oscha. Blonay's Platoon. The only anti-tank weapon Blonay had been provided with was a hollow charged anti-tank hand grenade, which he used without success. The tanks continued forward. Blonay could only look on helplessly as one of the tanks crushed some comrades who had taken refuge in the roadside ditch. Never would he forget the sight of the bloody body remains stuck to the tank tracks.

Unexpectedly, the critical situation of the 3/58 was helped by flanking fire from heavy machine-guns of the arriving Battalion I/57. Contact was made and only then did battalion commander Ostuf. Fenet realise that he had rendered service to a fellow unit of 'Charlemagne'.[66] I/57 pushed on towards Bärenwalde, leaving Ustuf. Rigeade to his own means once again. Henceforth, Rigeade found himself isolated again. To stave off annihilation, he decided to withdraw his 3/58 towards Bärenwalde. But his hopes for an uninterrupted withdrawal suddenly ended with the clanking of tank treads; two Russian tanks and accompanying infantry appeared from the woods to the right of the road along which the company was withdrawing. Thankfully, his men were now armed with panzerfäuste found abandoned by a routed unit. Panzerfäust in hand, several men of the Headquarters Platoon hunted down the tanks while their compatriots with

64    Chatrousse, correspondence to the author throughout 1997. There are similarities between the accounts of Méric and Chatrousse, but the author is convinced they are two separate incidents. Saint-Loup's account of I/58's retreat is much more dramatic and includes the appearance of Méric under the pseudonym of Merin (see *Les Hérétiques*, pp.196-198). When questioned about the apparent similarities and discrepancies between his version and that of Saint-Loup, Chatrousse stated that the present version was that he had also supplied to Saint-Loup.

65    Saint-Loup, *Les Hérétiques*, p.199, and confirmed by Rigeade, letter to the author, 17/2/97. In contrast, Mabire makes no reference to enemy tanks participating in the assault on Rigeade's 3/58.

66    Mabire, *La Division Charlemagne*, p.312, and Saint-Loup, *Les Hérétiques*, p.199. Of interest to note is that, according to Soulat, *Historique de la division Charlemagne*, p.32, when Battalion I/57 regrouped near Bärenwalde and 'finally made contact with the I/58', Ostuf. Fenet learnt that orders had been issued at 0800 hours for his battalion to go to Bärenwalde. However, Rigeade had no contact with Moneuse or indeed any unit of 'Charlemagne' since his arrival at the front, so Fenet could not have learnt of this order from Rigeade. Also, the time was around 1100 hours when Fenet learnt of this order. That is around one hour after his battalion came to the timely assistance of Rigeade and would suggest that Fenet had already left him and pushed on.

automatic weapons kept down the heads of the escorting infantry. A well-aimed panzerfäuste struck home and blew apart one of the tanks.[67]

Rigeade hurried his company on towards Bärenwalde, but the Russian attack had separated him from his rearguard formed by Oscha. Blonay's 3rd Platoon.[68] Without a map, Oscha. Blonay and his platoon would only rejoin the company at Neustettin days later.

By midday, Rigeade's 3/58 had reached the Hammerstein-Bärenwalde railway line.

## Soviet forces facing 'Charlemagne'

Back at Hammerstein, Rttf. Sepchat of the Engineer Platoon/Headquarters Company/58, which had not been engaged, met Oscha. Girard, the commander of the regiment's Panzerjäger Kompanie. Sepchat knew him of old from the LVF. Then his conduct had always been exemplary, but now, in contrast, he was completely demoralised. Back from the front, he told Sepchat that they did not have the slightest chance of resisting the enemy tanks he had just observed, adding that he did not want to get himself killed.[69] Sepchat was stunned to silence. He did not ask Girard what he was doing at the rear.

So what was the size of the Soviet forces facing 'Charlemagne'? According to one source, the I/57 faced (elements of) ten Soviet Divisions and two Tank Corps whereas the II/57 was confronted by (elements of) no less than fifteen Divisions and three Tank Corps.[70] The same source also states that on 25 February 1945 the Soviets employed all available forces against 'Charlemagne' and that they amounted to four infantry divisions, two tank brigades and several regiments of artillery and mortar.[71] Another source estimates that the I/57 faced at least two Soviet regiments at Heinrichswalde and that on the morning of the 25th the II/57 faced around 10,000 Russians, which equates to the strength of two weak infantry divisions.[72]

These estimates of the Soviet forces facing 'Charlemagne' are exaggerated. Only the 19th Army and the 3rd Guards Tank Corps were tasked with the breakthrough and the drive to the Baltic coast by way of Neustettin. The organic units of the 19th Army were the 134th Guards

---

67    Presumably, as no further fighting is remarked upon, the second tank thought better of continuing the attack and turned tail.

68    Blonay, letter to the author, 16/2/2002. This corrects, firstly, Mabire, *La Division Charlemagne*, p.317, who recounts that Rigeade had ordered his company to separate into platoons for the withdrawal, secondly, Saint-Loup, *Les Hérétiques*, p.203, that the company had split into three parts by the time it was behind the Hammerstein-Bärenwalde railway line, and, lastly, company commander Rigeade, who thought that Blonay's platoon had lost its way during the retreat through the woods (Rigeade, letter to the author, 17/2/97).

69    Despite much correspondence with Sepchat the author is still not sure of the day of this meeting. Sepchat spent one day and one night at Hammerstein and evacuated Hammerstein the following morning. This suggests that he arrived on 25 February and met Girard on the morning of 26 February before evacuating Hammerstein that same morning. In response to this, the author knows of no convoys that arrived on 25 February, but that is not to say that there were none. Moreover, the bulk of 'Charlemagne' evacuated Hammerstein in the early hours of 26 February and not on the morning of the 26 February. Therefore, the author has dated this meeting to 25 February, suggesting that Sepchat arrived on 24 February along with the regimental staff of Waffen-Gren. Regt der SS 58 and the I/58.

70    Saint-Loup, *Les Hérétiques* p.191, repeated by Landwehr, *Charlemagne's Legionnaires*, p.98.

71    Saint-Loup, *Les Hérétiques* p.205.

72    Mabire, *La Division Charlemagne*, p.285 and p.293.

Rifle Corps, the 40th Guards Rifle Corps and the 8th Guards Mechanised Corps. It was also reinforced with the 3rd Guards Cavalry Corps and a number of independent rocket and artillery divisions. The two rifle corps both had the strength of three rifle divisions. The Cavalry Corps had the strength of three cavalry divisions. Thus, the 19th Army could commit no more than nine divisions at any one time. Moreover, tactically speaking, it's quite inconceivable that the Russians could and would have concentrated so large a force on such narrow frontage, which would have only invited chaos. What can be said with certainty is that 'Charlemagne' was facing vastly superior forces supported by armour, artillery and aircraft.

**Fenet's I/57**

Around midday,[73] the vanguard of Fenet's battalion was in sight of Bärenwalde and Russian tanks could clearly be seen patrolling around the village. Unaware that a defensive line had or was forming along the Hammerstein-Bärenwalde railway line, Ostuf. Fenet then decided to make an about-turn so as to try and make contact again with the I/58. Soon after, his battalion encountered some isolated and demoralised men of Waffen-Gren. Regt der SS 58 who spoke of the latest Russian attack supported by flame-throwing tanks, described as the most violent yet, which had completely disrupted the defence. The survivors were incorporated into the battalion.

Ostuf. Fenet quickly reviewed his situation; with the Russians at Bärenwalde and advancing from Heinrichswalde towards Hammerstein, encirclement was now a very real possibility. Perhaps he was already encircled. To extricate his battalion, he decided to return to Hammerstein through the woods.

The I/57 headed north-west. When the battalion came across the Hammerstein-Bärenwalde railway line in open ground, Soviet aircraft suddenly appeared at low level and machine-gunned its exposed ranks. However, no casualties are reported.

After passing Hansfelde (Nadziejewo), the I/57 entered a fir tree plantation and was engaged by an enemy patrol. The engagement was unusual, brief and costly.[74] The battalion pressed on and joined the Hammerstein-Barkenfelde road [nowadays DW201] crowded with civilians desperately fleeing before the Russians. Following another air attack, the battalion arrived at Hammerstein camp around nightfall, specified as 2100 hours.

The battalion took stock. Both the 1/57 and the 3/57 had suffered heavy losses.[75] The 4/57, although virtually intact, had lost much of its heavy equipment. Although Fenet could find no sign of any headquarters at Hammerstein, yet who should he come across? Only Bartolomei and his 2/57. It was all present and correct save one platoon.

73  Soulat, *Historique de la division Charlemagne*, p.33, and repeated by Mabire, *La Division Charlemagne*, p.313. However, according to Saint-Loup, *Les Hérétiques*, p.199, at midday, the I/57 was at Hansfelde (Nadziejewo), some five kilometres east of Hammerstein.
74  See Saint-Loup, *Les Hérétiques*, pp.200-202. This engagement is not confirmed by Mabire.
75  Indeed, according to Saint-Loup, *Les Hérétiques*, p.199, Brazier's 1/57 numbered 28 men!

## The railway line

Having arrived at Hammerstein railway station, the divisional Engineer Company of 'Charlemagne' was immediately deployed as infantry along the Hammerstein-Bärenwalde railway line. The company went into battle without much of its specialist equipment. The Company commander, Ostuf. Audibert, was later accused of 'abandoning' its flamethrowers.[76] Rottenführer Gonzales of the Engineer Company was still with his good friend Juin and recalled:

> We saw pass by from the other side of the line a whole 'armada' of cripples with barely human faces; many were wounded, they wore emergency field dressings [and] with wild eyes they shouted out to us: "Lads, we didn't half cop it! The Russians are behind us. They have tanks!" We had no artillery to oppose them apart from some panzerfaüst of limited range.

Also ordered up to the Hammerstein-Bärenwalde railway line was the one hundred and ten strong Panzerjäger Company of Waffen-Gren. Regt der SS 58, the 10/58, which had arrived at Hammerstein earlier that day. For the train journey, the company had set up its MG 42s on tripods in an anti-aircraft role, and managed to bring down one, perhaps two aircraft attacking its convoy. Nevertheless, during one attack, the wagon carrying ammunition for the battalion was destroyed, halting the convoy.

At Hammerstein, the Panzerjäger Company had to abandon its three anti-tank guns on the train; the company had no tractors and no longer any horses, dead or not yet arrived, to move them.[77] Because of this, Oberjunker Bonnafont could not help thinking that all the training at Wildflecken was 'lost'.

Bonnafont was ordered by Obf. Puaud in person to occupy positions 'in front of the battalion [the I/58] in case of tanks attacking'.[78] Puaud seemed disorientated. Bonnafont took the company forward, which was without *Kompanieführer* Oscha. Girard who had left to see Stubaf. Raybaud before Puaud appeared.[79]

The Panzerjäger Company of Waffen-Gren. Regt der SS 58 took up position north-east of the level crossing, approximately one kilometre from the railway line. As it started to dig in it came under mortar fire. Then the wounded and the survivors of Waffen-Gren. Regt der SS 57 started to arrive. They were in disorder. It was a sad sight. Stretched out before the Panzerjäger Company of Waffen-Gren. Regt der SS 58 was a huge plain where Oberjunker Bonnafont sent two or three patrols. Oberjunker Bonnafont went with the patrols. He saw Russians.

By midday on 25 February, a makeshift defensive line was beginning to form around Bärenwalde railway station and its level crossing. The defensive line extended along the railway embankment for some two kilometres either side of the level crossing. To the left of the level crossing were the remnants of the II/57, and, to the right, Moneuse's arriving I/58. Woods

---

76  André Beaurivage of the Engineer Company recalls seeing its equipment at Hammerstein railway station (see Michaelis, *French units in the Waffen-SS*, p.74).
77  Company commander Girard does not know what became of these guns.
78  Bonnafont, letter to the author, 16/10/99.
79  Bonnafont would not see Girard again until after the war.

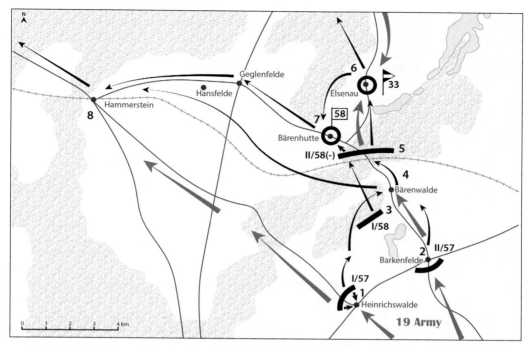

The battles south-east of Hammerstein 24-25 February 1945. 1. Battalion I/57 under Ostuf. Fenet attacks Heinrichswalde, but is repulsed. It withdraws to the north-east. 2. Battalion II/57 under Hstuf. Obitz takes up position around Barkenfelde where it comes under attack and is forced to withdraw. 3. Battalion I/58 under Hstuf. Moneuse takes up position between I/57 and II/57 and also comes under attack. 4. Barenwalde is captured by the Russians. The I/58 and the remnants of the II/57 retreat to the Hammerstein-Barenwalde railway line. 5. Various elements of 'Charlemagne' attempt to hold the railway crossing. 6. Divisional headquarters is established at Elsenau. Varous elements of 'Charlemagne', including the Compagnie d'Honneur, defend the village, but are forced to retreat. 7. The headquarters of II/58 is established at Barenhutte. Elements of the II/58, joined by those falling back from the railway line, take up defensive positions around Barenhutte. The Russians do not attack in strength, though. 8. 'Charlemagne' withdraws to Hammerstein, which it then evacuates.

enclosed the level crossing and closely lined the railway embankment. They would aid and hinder the Frenchmen.

Supporting the two badly hit grenadier battalions were the mortar platoons of the 8/57 under Uscha. Terrel, positioned just behind the railway station, the two 150mm howitzers[80] and six

---

80    Mabire, *La Division Charlemagne*, p.530. However, Saint-Loup records, *Les Hérétiques*, p.206, that Roy's batteries were made up of old 105mm guns. Also, the article *Mein Freund Georges*, based on the memoirs of a former soldier of the 9/57, also talks of 105mm howitzers. In response to this, Soulat has confirmed that the infantry guns of the 9/57 were 150mm and not 105mm howitzers. The author agrees; German Army infantry guns were of two calibres, 75mm and 150mm. Thus, a calibre of 150mm has been used.

75mm infantry guns of Hstuf. Roy's 9/57,[81] as well as a few 88mm Flak guns.[82] Also in support was the PAK Company of the Panzerjäger Battalion, commanded by Oberjunker Radici in the absence of Stubaf. Boudet-Gheusi.[83]

The headquarters of Waffen-Gren. Regt der SS 57 had relocated behind the railway line.[84] Hstuf. de Bourmont had made Ustuf. Martres, who had no troops to command, responsible for liaison between the scattered units of the regiment.

Brigf. Krukenberg directed the battle from divisional headquarters, which had been established at the village of Elsenau (Olszanowo), north of Bärenwalde.[85] He paid several visits to Stubaf. Raybaud at Bärenhutte and dismissed Hstuf. Obitz from command of the II/57. The Signals Company was deployed to Elsenau.

The violent fighting that ensued along the defensive line took place in great confusion. Moreover, many French units were already appallingly mixed. As a result, few precise and conclusive details are readily available.[86]

Russian aircraft strafed the positions of the Panzerjäger Company of Waffen-Gren. Regt der SS 58. They were so low-flying that Oberjunker Bonnafont could see the heads of the airmen. Later, at the close of day, he left his shelter to inspect the men, regain order, and position those of the 57 who were still armed and wanted to fight. He came under fire, but was not hit. He continued his work so as to encourage the men. A new wave of aircraft arrived. He came under fire once again.[87] This time he did not escape unscathed and was hit by two explosive bullets, which would have killed him outright if one had not been stopped by his holstered pistol and the other by his card wallet. Nevertheless, he was left seriously wounded and unconscious. Contrary to all expectations, he survived his terrible wounds. He owes his life to the former LVF medical officer who treated him and to two of his men who carried him, unconscious and bleeding,

81    The exact location of Roy's company 9/57 remains unclear; according to Mabire, *La Division Charlemagne*, p.318, the 9/57 had deployed in the railway station's square, not far from the level crossing. However, Saint-Loup positions two of Hstuf. Roy's batteries to the right of the level crossing and one battery at the village of Bärenhutte, north-west of Bärenwalde (*Les Hérétiques*, p.203 and 209).

82    As seen by del Missier of the 8/57 (correspondence to the author).

83    Saint-Loup, *Les Hérétiques*, p.204.

84    Raybaud, letter to Mabire, 3/11/74. This corrects Mabire who states, *La Division Charlemagne*, p.326 that de Bourmont relocated the headquarters of Waffen-Gren. Regt der SS 57 to Bärenhutte.

85    By now, according to Mabire, *La Division Charlemagne*, p.315, and Saint-Loup, *Les Hérétiques*, p.203, Krukenberg had taken command of 'Charlemagne'. However, in his letter to Mabire of 3/11/74, Raybaud wrote that he had no recollection of any note to this effect issued by divisional headquarters or of any verbal order to this effect. Moreover, de Vaugelas, with whom Raybaud had been in constant touch, had never reported to him any such takeover. Nevertheless, it would be true to say that Puaud's interest in command had waned progressively as his 'adventure' and that of his men took a greater and greater turn for the worse. Even so, it seems improbable that Krukenberg, who had proved himself a good diplomat thus far, would have publicly affronted Puaud by dismissing him from his command. Therefore, if Krukenberg was now in command, it appears to have been more of an understanding rather than in an official capacity.

86    For example, according to Mabire, *La Division Charlemagne*, p.324, the first serious Russian attack 'early in the morning' was broken up by the Frenchmen's howitzers, anti-tank guns and mortars. Indeed, Mabire pictures knocked out Russian tanks strewn in front of the French defensive line. However, no other source confirms this attack nor the losses inflicted on the Red armour.

87    Bonnafont does not know if he came under fire from the air or from Russian ground forces.

for more than ten kilometres to a medical convoy (presumably at Hammerstein).[88] He would remain in a coma for eleven or twelve days.[89]

Desperately, Ustuf. Martres of de Bourmont's headquarters staff tried to regain order, but this proved quite impossible. With him was Oberjunker Jean Ambroise of the 10/57 (anti-tank). He too was ex-Sturmbrigade. Martres escaped injury when he clumsily fell over a tree stump just as a shell landed nearby, but Ambroise was not so lucky. He was wounded in the thigh and evacuated.[90]

Oberjunker Méric of the 2/58 heard and then saw a column of five or six enemy tanks approach the level crossing. They suddenly stopped two hundred metres away: the lead tank had spotted on the snow covered road branches clumsily covering a string of Teller mines. They did not insist. Suddenly three men with panzerfauste exited the small railway station house. Méric is convinced they had been lying in ambush to bag the lead tank, describing it as an 'heroic act' because if they had managed to knock out the lead tank the others would have immediately fired on the house with little chance of them escaping from it. Tanks would later attack to his left.

Around midday, a massive Russian attack supported by tanks, as many as twenty, smashed into the flimsy French positions around the railway station and the level crossing. The battle raged.

Ustuf. Albert's 6/57, which had not yet completed its withdrawal to the railway line, was caught out of position, but defended magnificently. The hard-pressed company was only able to disengage thanks to Hstuf. Roy and his 9/57 which stopped the enemy infantry with accurate and dense defensive fire.[91] Incredibly Albert's men managed to make it back to the railway line.

Doctor Métais and a medical team went out in search of abandoned wounded. Suddenly, an enemy tank spotted them. Strangely, the tank seemed hesitant to fire on them, choosing instead to chase them with the intention of crushing them under its tracks, but Métais and his medical orderlies, yelled on by a nearby platoon in its holes, made it to the safety of the woods. Shortly after, Métais set up a medical post in a group of farmhouses some five hundred metres west of Bärenhutte. Casualties poured in.

The PAK Company reduced two tanks to scrap. A third, losing its track, 'slipped from the top of the embankment, overturned in a ploughed field below and exploded'. In return, the Russians showered death and destruction on the French PAK which fell silent. Many guns were destroyed and the crews were almost all killed or wounded. Oberjunker Vincenot of the PAK Company was seriously wounded in the ankle and evacuated.[92]

88  Bonnafont does not recall the name of the medical officer/doctor.
89  His wounds were such that three major operations and some five months in hospital awaited him.
90  His further fate is not known. Jean Ambroise was born on 7 November 1921.
91  Soulat, *Historique de la division Charlemagne*, p.33. According to Mabire, *La Division Charlemagne*, p.325, Roy managed to rescue the 6/57 when his 9/57 halted the Russian tanks making for the encircled company.
92  Soulat, *Historique de la division Charlemagne*, p.33, repeated by Mabire, *La Division Charlemagne*, p.305, who adds that Ostuf. Krotoff, the commander of the PAK Company, was hit by shrapnel at the same time as Vincenot. However, Lefèvre doubts that Krotoff was deployed to Pomerania (see Bouysse, *Encyclopaedia of the New Order: French in German Uniform Part 1: Officers*). Also of interest to note is that De la Mazière, a member of the PAK Company recalls that Oberjunker Vincenot took over command of the PAK Company at Wildflecken (see *Ashes of Honour*, p.108). This might explain why Krotoff was not deployed to Pomerania.

380 For Europe Revisited

Jean Gadeau of the PAK Company was killed. Although he ran away to join the Waffen-SS, he came to 'Charlemagne' via the Kriegsmarine. He attended Sennheim, but disappointment awaited him when he was transformed into a 'SS Frontarbeiter' and posted away to Mayence where he passed his time unloading wagons.[93] Wanting to serve in the German uniform, he 'escaped' and joined the Kriegsmarine. No doubt his joy was great when he found himself transferred back to the Waffen-SS.

Patrice Rimbert was the sole survivor of his gun 'cleaned out' by a T-34.[94] His conduct under fire was exemplary and he was later awarded the Iron Cross 2nd Class. He too was ex-Kriegsmarine. Two more tanks were knocked out; the first exploded a mine laid by the regimental engineer platoon of Waffen-Gren. Regt der SS 57; and the second Oscha. Barclay[95] accounted for with a panzerfäust.

Roy's howitzers cut deep swathes in the waves of Red infantry. Undaunted by their unconscionable losses, the Russians continued to surge forward.[96] Before long the whole defensive line was ablaze.[97] Machine gun in hand, accompanied by Stubaf. de Vaugelas and Staf. Zimmermann, Obf. Puaud went from position to position along the railway line to encourage the men. Occasionally he stopped to joke with former legionnaires of the LVF. He took so many unnecessary risks that it seemed as though he had a death wish, but he was not fated to meet his Maker quite yet.

Under tremendous pressure, the defensive line began to reel. It was now untenable. After an hour of combat, Hstuf. de Bourmont finally resigned himself to ordering general withdrawal when elements of Moneuse's I/58 started to pour back on the right.[98] Oberjunker Méric of the 2/58 was not surprised when he received the order to withdraw. He remarked: 'Before such pressure and such disproportion, all resistance became useless'.

1500 hours came and went. Soon after, the French PAK and Hstuf. Roy's infantry guns spent their last ammunition. Ordered to withdraw his infantry guns north-west to Bärenhutte, Hstuf. Roy managed to evacuate his lighter pieces by hand, but the heavier 150mm guns had to be abandoned because of the lack of tractors. They were spiked at 1515 hours.[99] The remaining PAK guns were also 'put out of action' for the same reason and the last gunners fought on as grenadiers.

93  His transfer was probably as a result of a disciplinary offence (Soulat, letter to the author, 3/8/98).
94  According to Bouysse, *Encyclopédie de l'ordre nouveau: Français sous l'uniforme allemande partie II: sous-officiers & hommes du rang de la Waffen-SS*, Rimbert served in Company 7/57.
95  Saint-Loup, *Les Hérétiques*, p.206.
96  According to Saint-Loup, *Les Hérétiques*, p.207, the Russians now attacked the railway station. Stubbornly, soldiers of the II/57 resisted the Russians every inch of the way, but were eventually dislodged in fierce hand-to-hand fighting. The defenders fell back and reformed behind the level crossing. In response to Saint-Loup, no other source confirms this fight for the railway station.
97  According to Saint-Loup, *Les Hérétiques*, p.207, the Frenchmen fought at one to ten in front of the positions of Moneuse's I/58 and at one to one hundred at the level crossing! The later is undoubtedly poetic licence.
98  Soulat, *Historique de la division Charlemagne*, p.34. Curiously, according to del Missier of Company 8/57, correspondence to the author, the order to withdraw was given around 0900 hours.
99  Saint-Loup, *Les Hérétiques*, pp.208-209. This is not confirmed by Mabire, who recounts instead, *La Division Charlemagne*, p.329, that Hstuf. Roy withdrew after nightfall.

At 1525 hours, the Russians forced their way across the level crossing. Through this breach swept its infantry and tanks like an irresistible tidal wave through a burst dam.[100] The French units withdrew. However, confusion soon overtook the withdrawal.[101] The seriously wounded had to be abandoned.

Among the last to leave the railway station was Ustuf. Colnion and the 8/57. Setting off along the road to Hammerstein, they found the Russians in their path![102] Thereupon they made for Elsenau. Along a track shielded by forest, out of sight of the Soviet tanks, they managed to reach Elsenau, arriving around 1700 hours.[103]

Company 7/57 commanded by Oberjunker Million-Rousseau, also on the left, conducted a fighting withdrawal every step of the way towards Elsenau. Strmm. Marotin of Company 8/57 found himself integrated into a small group commanded by an Untersturmführer and fought near the level crossing. They made the Russians pay dear for its capture. Their Ustuf. then gave them the order to withdraw through the woods, following a main road, perhaps that to Bärenhutte. But Marotin soon lost sight of his comrades of the 8/57 after he went off to fetch his rucksack from the building where it had been stored. In fear of losing his way in the woods, he took the road and came across some lads of Waffen-Gren. Regt der SS 57 around an anti-tank barrier. They were armed with one or two panzerfäust and some MGs. He joined them.

Soon after, an armoured Russian vanguard of three tanks with infantry support appeared before the anti-tank barrier. The first tank was destroyed by panzerfäust and the infantry were scattered by MG fire. Fortunately for the Frenchmen the other two tanks did not press home their attack; the defenders had exhausted all their panzerfäust and nearly all their MG ammunition. Other tanks and more infantry appeared hundreds of metres away. Wisely, the commanding officer gave the order to withdraw.

Company 2/58 splintered. Oberjunker Méric, with about half the company, withdrew to Bärenhutte. During this march, Méric stopped and took shelter before a stretch of road too exposed to use when he was surprised to be cordially hailed by General Puaud marching along the roadway quite at ease despite the frequent mortar explosions and sporadic machine gun bursts. Méric joined him on the road, as did the others. The General asked: *"Alors, Méric, tout va bien?"* Méric gave him a quick situation report and then the General was gone. His courage and panache, which was undeniable, greatly impressed Méric as well as his men.

The 'last obstacle', an anti-tank barrier located at a bend in the road some three hundred metres from the level crossing, fell to the Russians at the end of the day.[104] Elements of Fatin's 1/58 and Géromini's 2/58 were manning the anti-tank barrier. Soviet tanks appeared. Hit by panzerfäust, two were soon blazing wrecks. The first was probably the handiwork of Ustuf. Fatin and the second that of Uscha. Robert.[105]

100 Ibid. This rupture of the 'front' of 'Charlemagne' is possibly the same 'large breach' that Mabire recounts, *La Division Charlemagne*, p.328, as developing at the 'beginning of the afternoon'.
101 Soulat, *Historique de la division Charlemagne*, p.34. According to Mabire, *La Division Charlemagne*, p.328, 'the retreat turned into a rout'. In response to Mabire, Saint-Loup does not confirm a rout.
102 Presumably the 8/57 was withdrawing westwards along the road from Bärenwalde to Hammerstein.
103 Curiously, according to Soulat, *Historique de la division Charlemagne*, p.34, the 8/57, like the 7/57, conducted a fighting withdrawal every step of the way towards Elsenau.
104 Mabire, *La Division Charlemagne*, p.328.
105 By a strange coincidence, Grenouillet of Company 1/58 recalls the presence of two NCOs with the surname of Robert. Thus, the tank-kill cannot be credited with any real certainty.

Having now lost contact with the I/58, Fatin and Géromini followed de Bourmont who, with the remnants of the II/57, had withdrawn to Elsenau. In this way, Elsenau became an assembly point. The scenes at Elsenau were also repeated at Bärenhutte, to the north-west of the Bärenwalde level crossing, to which elements of 'Charlemagne' had also withdrawn.

## Bärenhutte

By early morning on 25 February, elements of the II/58 had arrived at Bärenhutte.[106] Later that morning, Brigf. Krukenberg ordered Stubaf. Raybaud to send one company 'midway between

106  According to Saint-Loup, *Les Hérétiques*, p.204, on the morning of 26 February the four companies of Hstuf. Berret's II/58 had arrived at Bärenhutte by forced march from Hammerstein. Mabire records, *La Division Charlemagne*, p.331, that the four companies of the II/58 disembarked at Hammerstein rail station. However, no exact date or time of arrival is provided. Mabire then details that the troops of the II/58 went up to the front 'without any support'. Soulat also records, *Historique de la division Charlemagne*, p.35, that on the morning of the 25 February the intact and complete Battalion II/58 had arrived from Hammerstein. Of the battalion, while at Bärenhutte, there are specific references to Companies 8/58 and 5/58, which formed the rearguard of the French forces when the time came to evacuate Bärenhutte. However, Ustuf. de Genouillac, the assistant battalion commander of the II/58, recalls, in correspondence to the author throughout 1997, that the battalion only arrived at Neustettin railway station on the morning of 27 February. Although he cannot confirm that his convoy was carrying the four companies of the II/58, he still believes to this very day that it was the whole battalion. This would lead to the conclusion that the II/58 could not have been at Bärenhutte as the fighting around Bärenhutte was over by the early morning hours of 26 February and this conclusion de Genouillac has confirmed. Hscha. Rostaing, also of the II/58, states, *Le prix d'un serment*, pp.160-161, that the troops of the II/58 had clambered out of their trains at the village of Neustettin (Szczecinek) around 1600 hours on 24 February 1945. Rostaing continues that they had then spent the night in the barracks situated in the city centre and were sent forward to the village of Bärenhutte on the morning of 25 February. In reply, as a member of the headquarters staff of the II/58, Rostaing almost certainly arrived at Neustettin on the same convoy as de Genouillac. Moreover, no other source confirms that the II/58 or elements of the II/58 were sent forward from Neustettin to Bärenhutte. Wagner's 5/58 arrived at Neustettin but was not sent forward to nor engaged at Bärenhutte. See Ruskone, *Stoi!*, pp.254-257, confirmed by Ruskone, letters to the author, 2/98 and 5/3/98, as well as Blanc and Castrillo of Company 5/58, correspondence to the author, 2001-2004. Raybaud, the commander of Waffen-Gren. Regt der SS 58, recalled in his letter of 3/11/74 to Mabire that the II/58 had arrived at Bärenhutte during the night of the 24-25 February or early morning on 25 Februray. In reply, it seems very doubtful that an entire battalion of around one thousand men would have been kept in reserve at Bärenhutte while their comrades were fighting desperately for their lives along the Hammerstein-Bärenwalde railway line a matter of kilometres away. Raybaud's precise memory of the detachment of the 6/58 on the morning of 25 February cannot be so readily dismissed, though. Alain Boutier of Company 7/58 recalls that his platoon was deployed between lakes Jezioro Olszanowskie and Orzechowo, southeast of Elsenau. Also, while at Neustettin, Blanc of Company 5/58 briefly met Walter, who was the company commander of the 7/58. Walter said he had seen action in front of Hammerstein and that the Russians had not lost their offensive spirit. In conclusion, despite the contradictory nature of all the sources available, it appears that elements of the II/58, at least two companies, perhaps three, did arrive at Bärenhutte on the morning of 25 February.

Bärenhutte and Elsenau'[107] to block off the road from Bärenwalde to Elsenau.[108] Raybaud was opposed to the order and protested; handicapped by a total lack of signalling equipment, he had no wish to isolate one of his companies in this way. His protests overruled, he went in person to Hscha. Saint-Magne, the company commander of the 6/58, and relayed the order. But Saint-Magne was without a map; only battalion and regimental commanders had been supplied with one. Raybaud took it upon himself to sketch one out.[109] Upon receipt of the map, Saint-Magne and his company left.

Stubaf. Raybaud said of his movements that same morning:[110]

> I made contact with de Bourmont and Artus to the north-east of the railway line, after the level crossing. I also went to divisional headquarters at Elsenau with my driver and my Orderly Officer [Oberjunker Henri de Vaugelas], without meeting a single enemy. Returning from Elsenau, I abandoned my car to make direct contact with the 6/58 which I approached, much to the surprise of Saint-Magne, from the front and not from the rear. During this morning the Brigadeführer went to our strongpoint several times by car, without apparently meeting any enemy element.

One platoon of Hscha. Walter's Company 7/58 was deployed between lakes Jezioro Olszanowskie and Orzechowo, south-east of Elsenau.[111] Gripped by a growing sense of isolation, the platoon decided to relocate position and was ambushed by the Russians. Casualties were taken. The platoon hurriedly retreated. Boutier saw his comrade Lauglanet bravely take up position against a tree to cover the retreat, but he was soon killed. Boutier managed to escape, although injured. Only two other men of his section survived.

Now that elements of 'Charlemagne' were withdrawing to Bärenhutte, Raybaud set about fortifying the village into a hedgehog position. He immediately formed four kampfgruppen; two from the II/58 whose commanders remain unknown:[112] one from the I/58, incorporating

107 Raybaud, letter to Mabire, 3/11/74. Yet, according to the written interview with Raybaud in *Charlemagne's Legionnaires*, p.100, the company was to be sent 'to the north of Bärenhutte', and, according to Mabire, *La Division Charlemagne*, p.333, 'four kilometres to the north of his disposition [Bärenhutte]'. Confusingly, this would place the company deep in woods well to the north-west of Elsenau and not even astride the road north from Elsenau to Flötenstein. In this position, the company would have served no purpose whatsoever.

108 The mission of the company has been defined as such: 'to cover Elsenau', Mabire, *La Division Charlemagne*, p.333; 'to strengthen the defence of Elsenau', Saint-Loup, *Les Hérétiques*, p.204; and 'to block off a possible route of advance for the Russians', the written interview with Raybaud in *Charlemagne's Legionnaires*, p.100. Considering the deployment of the company, its mission could be defined as blocking off the road from Bärenwalde to Elsenau and thereby strengthening the defence of Elsenau. Remarkably, Mabire described the mission as suicidal, which is far from the truth.

109 Mabire, *La Division Charlemagne*, p.333. Surprisingly, according to the written interview with Raybaud, *Charlemagne's Legionnaires*, p.100, he derided his regimental staff as incompetent when they were unable to find him a map for Saint-Magne. This is not confirmed by any other source, though.

110 Raybaud, letter to Mabire, 3/11/74.

111 Alain Boutier of Company 7/58, handwritten notes, 21/2/94. The whole company may have been deployed to this location, though.

112 According to Soulat, *Historique de la division Charlemagne*, p.35, repeated by Saint-Loup, *Les Hérétiques*, p.209, and Mabire, *La Division Charlemagne*, p.335, Berret commanded one of the two kampfgruppen of the II/58. However, Hstuf. Berret was not present. Ustuf. de Genouillac was by his side throughout

companies 2/58, 3/58 and 4/58, under Moneuse, and the last from the remnants of Waffen-Gren. Regt der SS 57 under Roy.[113] Raybaud may have carried out this reorganisation in conjunction with Obf. Puaud, also present at Bärenhutte.

The situation at Bärenhutte has been likened to that on an island surrounded on all sides by the rising flood tide.[114] Having no radio equipment, Raybaud soon lost contact with the Brigadeführer at Elsenau. Isolated and virtually helpless, his anxiety grew. Nevertheless, it soon became clear that the Bärenhutte to Hammerstein road was not a principal Soviet route of advance, although shadowy figures began to outflank the village. 'Luckily' for Raybaud, the enemy was bypassing Bärenhutte.

## Elsenau

Having rolled up the French defensive line along the Hammerstein-Bärenwalde railway line, the mighty Soviet juggernaut turned north-east. In its path lay the village of Elsenau, which numbered no more than twenty houses, where the divisional command post of 'Charlemagne' was situated. Without heavy weapons, without support, and without reserves, Brigf. Krukenberg faced a desperate situation and sent Staf. Zimmermann to the headquarters of the XVIII. Gebirgs-Korps at Stegers (Rzeczenica) to warn General Hochbaum that 'Charlemagne' would not be able to hold for more than several hours.[115] Ustuf. Patzak accompanied him on this mission.[116]

When the two German officers of the Inspection arrived by car at the chateau that served as the headquarters of the XVIII. Gebirgs-Korps they found General Hochbaum looking exhausted and rather anxious. Grabbing Staf. Zimmermann by the arm as if an old friend, the General asked: "Well, are your Frenchmen going to hold?" Avoiding the question, Staf. Zimmermann chose to remind the general that 'Charlemagne' was without anti-tank weapons, guns and tanks. Soberly, Zimmermann told the General that he was asking the impossible of

the campaign in Pomerania and at no time was Hstuf. Berret at Bärenhutte. Indeed, Hstuf. Berret only arrived in Pomerania on 27 February 1945. (De Genouillac, letter to the author, 23/2/98). Also, in a strange twist, Stubaf. Raybaud, the commander of Waffen-Gren. Regt der SS 58, was of the opinion that Hstuf. Berret had stayed behind at Wildflecken camp because of sickness. Furthermore, according to Saint-Loup, *Les Hérétiques*, p.200, Raybaud himself commanded a battlegroup, which Raybaud has not denied or acknowledged. So this might well be true.

113  According to Saint-Loup, *Les Hérétiques*, p.209, the forces at Bärenhutte totalled some 3,000 men which equates to one half of the strength of 'Charlemagne' deployed in Pomerania. This is extremely unlikely; few in number were the units of de Bourmont's Waffen-Gren. Regt der SS 57 which had withdrawn to Bärenhutte, indeed the only complete unit may have been Hstuf. Roy and his 9/57; some units of the II/58 had still not arrived at the front; at least two convoys of 'Charlemagne' were still en route to Pomerania; and, finally, to say nothing of the holes already in the ranks of 'Charlemagne'. Also, Raybaud was convinced that no elements of de Bourmont's regiment withdrew to Bärenhutte (letter to Mabire, 3/11/74).

114  Mabire, *La Division Charlemagne*, p.335.

115  Mabire, *La Division Charlemagne*, p.351. According to Soulat, *Historique de la division Charlemagne*, p.35, Zimmermann went to the headquarters of the XVIII. Gebirgs-Korps at Stegers to examine the situation with General Hochbaum.

116  Zimmermann, letter to Saint-Loup, 10/8/65. This confirms Mabire's version, *La Division Charlemagne*, p.351, and corrects that of Saint-Loup, *Les Hérétiques*, p.222, in which Brigf. Krukenberg and Hstuf. Jauss went to General Hochbaum's headquarters at Stegers on the fall of Elsenau.

them. The General would hear nothing of it and noted 'impossible is not a French word'.[117] At this, Zimmermann lost his temper and retorted that even the Pomeranians of the Wehrmacht were falling back. Again the General pressed him. Zimmermann could only conclude that they would get themselves killed, but still they would not stop the Russian onslaught.

Thereupon, General Hochbaum authorised the withdrawal of 'Charlemagne' to Stegers, where the division was to try and build a new defensive line. Divisional headquarters was to relocate to the town of Flötenstein, some fifteen kilometres north of Stegers. It was to this same location that the General had decided to re-establish corps headquarters.

As there was no time to lose, General Hochbaum hurried Zimmermann to set off back to Elsenau. Accompanied by Hochbaum, the German officers of the Inspection returned to their car parked up in the grounds. On the steps of the chateau they were horrified by the sudden appearance of a T-34 tens of metres away. The hard bark of its gun and the car burst into a ball of flames. The tank vanished as fast as it had appeared.[118]

Rather than return to Elsenau on foot, Zimmermann decided to accompany General Hochbaum and his staff officers to Flötenstein. As planned, they left at nightfall. During the night Zimmermann met by chance the Chief-of-Staff of the XVIII. Gebirgs-Korps. To the south, the sound of fighting could be heard. Zimmermann wondered how Krukenberg was still managing to hold onto Elsenau.

To defend Elsenau, Brigf. Krukenberg had at his disposal in total some four to five hundred men under Stubaf. Boudet-Gheusi, Hstuf. Renault, and Ustuf. Fatin, as well as 'his guard', the *Compagnie d'Honneur*, which eagerly awaited the Russians with a point to prove that it was not a parade unit.[119]

Commanded by Ostuf. Weber, the *Compagnie d'Honneur* arrived at Elsenau early on the 25th armed with panzerfäuste drawn at Hammerstein. As it made its way to Elsenau, the *Compagnie d'Honneur* encountered a stream of civilians mixed here and there with young, distraught-looking Latvian SS soldiers pouring back in disorder. At one point the *Compagnie d'Honneur* marched alongside the pitiful sight of a column of wounded from Waffen-Gren. Regt der SS 57. Leaning on one another, all wore blood-soaked bandages. Some were without limbs. Their eyes were widened with horror and fatigue. In similar circumstances this stark reality of battle would have totally demoralised many soldiers, but not those of the *Compagnie d'Honneur*. Weber had repeatedly given them one single choice: the wooden cross or the Iron Cross. Of the two, all knew which one they wanted.

Once at Elsenau, the *Compagnie d'Honneur* was deployed as a 'stopper to permit their comrades to withdraw'.[120] But the *Compagnie d'Honneur* was greatly understrength as many of its trainees

117 Mabire, *La Division Charlemagne*, p.352.
118 Mabire, *La Division Charlemagne*, p.353. In contrast, according to Saint-Loup, *Les Hérétiques*, p.223, a lieutenant of the headquarters staff, who had armed himself with a panzerfäust, blew apart the T-34.
119 According to Saint-Loup, *Les Hérétiques*, p.210, Krukenberg also had the troops and guns of *Capitaine* Marty at his disposal at Elsenau. Marty is undoubtedly a pseudonym for Martin, the assistant commander of the Division's artillery Battalion. His presence at Elsenau is not recorded by any other source. Moreover, according to Mabire, *La Division Charlemagne*, p.362, Hstuf. Martin would only arrive at Schlawe in Pomerania on 3 March 1945 with a one hundred strong detachment of the artillery Battalion. This has been confirmed by Mounine, letter to the author.
120 Mabire, *La Division Charlemagne*, p.343. As such, the *Compagnie d'Honneur* was the only combatant unit at Elsenau before the arrival of those retreating from the Hammerstein-Bärenwalde railway line.

had not returned and only numbered eighty men.[121] Amid this chaos the *Compagnie d'Honneur* managed to make a difference, dismantling the armoured Soviet vanguard that appeared before Elsenau.[122] It was a brave action of man against machine and one that cannot go untold, even if there is little or no agreement between the two main sources, those of Mabire and Saint-Loup, which are retold here.[123]

Firstly, Mabire recounts that the *Compagnie d'Honneur* occupied positions just outside the village perimeter, covering the road from Elsenau to Bärenwalde. Combat emplacements were dug in ditches alongside the road. Most men were armed with panzerfäuste. Weber had sited company headquarters in a small wood on a slope. To the right of the wood, across the road, was the village cemetery, which was held by the company's *section des Jeunes* [literally Youth Platoon]. To his front was a wood, through which a road ran. It was cold, yet humid. Snow covered the fields and to camouflage themselves the men had made chasubles from sheets found in the abandoned houses of the village. Supporting the *Compagnie d'Honneur* was a PAK gun that Ostuf. Weber had requisitioned from a Wehrmacht unit.[124]

In the early afternoon, Soviet aircraft suddenly swept overhead and machine-gunned the village. Their appearance was brief, but the spine-chilling shouts of 'Panzeralarm!' then rang out. The ground was vibrating.

Towards 1400 hours, the platoon held in reserve was moved up to reinforce the two others already in the front line. Unterführeranwärter [potential NCO] Louis Lavest commanded one of its sections. He had recently graduated from Paderborn and joined the *Compagnie d'Honneur* in the field. Upon leaving the village, the platoon came under fire from a T-34 that had suddenly emerged less than one kilometre away. Lavest's section was practically annihilated. Lavest wrote of this:

When my section approached the road it suddenly found itself in view of the Popovs. We could see the tanks in the open, one of which fired on us. I glimpsed the plume

---

121  Soulat, *Historique de la division Charlemagne*, p.34, repeated by Mabire, *La Division Charlemagne*, p.343. However, according to Lavest, a member of the *Compagnie d'Honneur*, the company counted 165 men (*Le soleil se couchait à l'est*, p.86) and according to Saint-Loup, *Les Hérétiques*, p.210, the company was at full strength, in total some two hundred to two hundred and fifty strong.

122  The direction from which the armoured Soviet vanguard appeared remains unclear; according to Lavest of the *Compagnie d'Honneur*, letter and maps to the author, dated 18/3/98, the Soviets came from the south, along the road from Bärenwalde. And yet, in contrast, according to Chatrousse, also present at Elsenau and in command of a group to the immediate left of the positions of the *Compagnie d'Honneur*, the Soviets attacked from the east (letter to the author dated 25/2/98).

123  See Mabire, *La Division Charlemagne*, pp.343-350 and Saint-Loup, *Les Hérétiques*, pp.210-216. Mabire's version was, undoubtedly, based on the eyewitness accounts of Boulau and Lavest of the *Compagnie d'Honneur* (and perhaps even that of Weber himself). Note that the author has supplemented Mabire's version with additional material from Lavest, correspondence to the author 1997-1998, and from Lavest's book *Le soleil se couchait à l'est* published in June 2008. However, after visiting Elsenau, the author now doubts many of the details recorded as fact by both Mabire and Saint-Loup. For example, the cemetery is probably no bigger than 20 metres by 10 metres, making it too small for elements of three companies to hold.

124  Mabire, *La Division Charlemagne*, p.346. Curiously, when the third platoon was moved up to reinforce those already in the front line, it passed a PAK gun described by the same author on p.345 as 'one of the last of the division'.

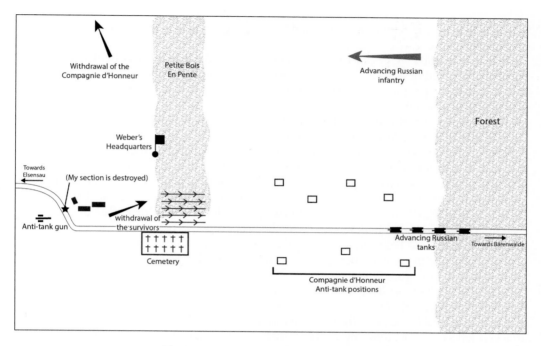

The defence of Elsenau according to Lavest.

of smoke from one of them firing. Immediately, I threw myself on the ground, as I had been taught in training. The shell exploded in the middle of the platoon and I felt a violent blow on my left ankle. With ringing eyes, I checked myself all over, lying down as I was on the reverse of the slope, helmet pulled down on the nose. Having regained my wits, I then sat up and, horror, my hands were covered in blood and brain matter ... I feverishly took my helmet off, checking my head anxiously, to note with some relief the completeness of it. I had been literally sprayed by the human remains belonging to my friend Tisseyre from Lyon[125], who was walking five metres behind me. The survivors of the section, who numbered six, were spread out either side of the road, in order to hide from the Russians. Some found refuge among the gravestones of the cemetery to the right of our position, where the youth platoon of the company was positioned. As for me, limping because of my knee, followed by three chaps, I went over the slope in the direction of a small wood perpendicular to the road. My injury caused by a stone hitting me when the shell exploded was not serious. [126]

Lavest had been lucky and reasoned that fate had protected him. Well he had been born on Friday the 13th! The survivors made it to the wood where they reported to Weber at his headquarters.

125  Alain Tisseyre was born on 10 March 1923 in Bordeaux.
126  Lavest, *Le soleil se couchait à l'est*, p.82.

Lavest could not help noting that they would make ideal targets for Russian snipers, dressed in white as they were.

Weber summoned NCO cadet Boulau and gave him orders. As soon as Boulau understood what was expected of him, he smiled and rushed off to the wood, followed by his section. In the wood he set up a tank booby trap which was quite simple, but effective. It consisted of a wire stretched across the road connected to the firing mechanisms of primed panzerfäusts, fixed firmly to tree trunks, aimed towards the middle of the road. The first tank to trigger the trip-wire would bring the hollow charges slamming into its sides.

Having completed the booby trap, Boulau and his men ran back to their positions alongside the road. It was not long before two explosions were heard. The Russian tanks responded by bombarding the wood before cautiously moving on. Fourteen tanks were counted. The tanks approached. They were almost on top of the *Compagnie d'Honneur*'s positions before Ostuf. Weber ordered 'Fire!' The PAK gun fired first and hit the lead tank that came to a stop. The men sprang up. Tank after tank was knocked out by panzerfäust, but the last two were still very much 'full of life' and began to shell the village. Weber himself dashed forward and knocked out one of them with grenade. The remaining tank continued to blast the French positions with its gun and machine-guns.

Ostuf. Weber had just devised a plan of attack to destroy this last troublesome tank when 'hundreds and hundreds' of Soviet infantrymen suddenly charged against the exposed positions of the *Compagnie d'Honneur*.[127] The German machine-guns started to rattle. Rifles cracked. The attackers fell as if mown down by a scythe. Their attack collapsed against a veritable curtain of fire. They flooded back. They came again. They were repulsed. Then again, jumping over the bodies of their comrades, they came on.

In the face of being overrun and annihilated, Weber decided to withdraw immediately and thus save his unit which had already suffered numerous dead and wounded.[128] A small ravine located to the left of the position held by his company looked as though it would afford his 'boys' shelter, but the way there was across open ground swept by Russian gunfire. Although the *Compagnie d'Honneur* had repeated this manoeuvre tens and tens of times before at Wildflecken, this time it was for real. The *Compagnie d'Honneur* emerged and dashed to the ravine. This position, however, soon became as untenable as the first and Weber ordered withdrawal again.

In the meantime, now supported by infantry, the remaining enemy tank had advanced. Armed with panzerfäust, Weber and three volunteers rushed forward to confront the steel monster. Crash. A direct hit. On fire, smoke poured from the T-34.

127  Lavest recalls, letter to the author, 15/1/98, that the Soviet infantry hit the *Compagnie d'Honneur* from both sides of the road, whereas, in his book, *Le soleil se couchait à l'est*, p.83, he wrote that the infantry attack came 'from our left'. Chatrousse, who also fought at Elsenau, does not agree (letter to the author, 25/2/98); positioned to the immediate left of the *Compagnie d'Honneur*, he and his group came under fire from Russian mortars and machine guns opposite, but were not on the receiving end of an infantry attack. Nevertheless, from his position, Chatrousse could see the Russian infantry attack the right flank of the *Compagnie d'Honneur* (on the other side of the road).
128  In contrast, according to Lavest, letter to the author, 15/1/98, the company had to abandon its positions when T-34 tanks, pushing along the road, bypassed its positions and brought them under fire from the rear.

Having destroyed the last enemy tank, Ostuf. Weber returned to his men. Disheartened, the Russians broke off their attack and dug in. The fighting fell away. Elated, Weber and his *Compagnie d'Honneur* returned to Elsenau.

Saint-Loup's storytelling is much more dramatic and questionable. The 'Brigadeführer's Guard' was in position when the first Russian tanks appeared before Elsenau. Its positions, dug in the middle of the passageways between the dunes, marshes and ponds, were good strategically, but poor tactically as the enemy tanks could only be engaged from the front rather than from the less armoured sides. Needless to say, this demanded composure and bravery. Its men were not found wanting, as one tank after another was destroyed.

One tank managed to get through but was destroyed by Soulier with a T-mine.[129] At 1615 hours, he destroyed his second by panzerfäust and his third a few minutes later. When Soulier returned to the command post to collect more panzerfäust Weber took off his Iron Cross 1st Class and pinned it on him. Soulier returned to the fighting.

The twenty-four-year-old Appolot bagged two T-34s in quick succession likewise eighteen-year-old Sturmmann Fontenay.[130] Twenty-year-old Oudin, a former student at *lycée Charlemagne*, was wounded attacking 'his' tank but refused evacuation.[131] He was killed when he missed a second tank. Eugène Vaulot got one.[132] Weber himself destroyed three T-34s.

As Soulier approached his foxhole, with Vaulot, he spotted a stationary enemy tank, a heavy 'Joseph Stalin', which appeared to have broken down.[133] Soulier and Vaulot crawled towards it and shot up the escorting infantry with their Sturmgewehrs.[134] Those that were not dead or wounded fled. Attracted by the sound of fighting, their comrades Dupuis, Garrot and Schenitz appeared. Encircled, the tank tried to keep them at bay with its machine-gun,[135] but it was in vain as Vaulot got within panzerfäust range and fired. A direct hit and it was soon blazing like a torch.

The assault group withdrew, dragging along Schenitz seriously wounded by a friendly bullet which had ricocheted off the armour plating of the Stalin. He died minutes later at the first aid post. There was no decoration for Vaulot from Weber, but a shot down German fighter pilot presented Vaulot with his own Iron Cross. Fighting side by side with the French, this downed German airmen even notched up two tanks.

129 Pierre Soulier was well known to Robert Soulat, for they had served together in the Kriegsmarine. Born in 1921 or 1922 in Alsace, Soulier volunteered for the Schutzkommando of the OT in 1943 and was posted to Russia for several months. He volunteered for the Kriegsmarine at the start of 1944.
130 Gérard Fontenay was born on 19 July 1926 in Dakar.
131 Jean Oudin was ex-LVF.
132 Vaulot may not have seen action at Elsenau. Soulat of the Headquarters Company withdrew from Neustettin to Köslin on 28 February 1945. That same day, after an air raid, he met Vaulot and a dozen men of the *Compagnie d'Honneur*, who told him that they had become separated from their convoy at Altmann following a bombardment and that they had not been engaged. This might help explain why the company was understrength and why Mabire makes no mention of Vaulot at Elsenau.
133 The author doubts the Russians employed the heavy Joseph Stalin tank at Elsenau; the terrain and roads around Elsenau are not suitable for its employment. Moreover, Lavest and Chatrousse who were present at Elsenau made no mention of its employment
134 The author, however, doubts they were armed with Sturmgewehr. No other source makes mention of this.
135 The Joseph Stalin IS-2 model was only armed with a heavy machine-gun for anti-aircraft defence.

By 1700 hours, eleven tanks had been knocked out. That figure had risen to nineteen by 1730 hours, of which seventeen were credited to the *Compagnie d'Honneur*.

But the success of the *Compagnie d'Honneur* in halting the Soviet tank vanguard had been brought at a terrible cost. Soulier was killed attacking his fifth tank. Strmm. Rouvre was killed destroying his third. Strmm. Fontenay was killed on his fourth.[136] Appolot was wounded again and evacuated. Of note is that many of the principal 'tank destroyers' were ex-Kriegsmarine.

Halted, the Russian armour then proceeded to bypass Elsenau to the east and to the west, whereas their infantry, in close line abreast, charged in turn against the village. It was literally a forest of men. Machine-guns barked out. So began the battle for Elsenau cemetery.

### Elsenau cemetery

Holding Elsenau cemetery were elements of Colnion's 8/57, Million-Rousseau's 7/57 and Fatin's 1/58.[137] They stood firm and repelled attack after attack. The Russians brought up tanks.[138] Company commander Oberjunker Million-Rousseau failed to halt the first tank when he hurriedly fired a panzerfäust and missed. The tank continued to advance. A volunteer dashed forward and managed to stop the steel mass with a rifle-grenade.

Marotin of the 8/57 found himself in Elsenau cemetery. From Bärenhutte, he had left with a group for Elsenau where he had been told he would find comrades of his battalion. He came to the cemetery and to one or two lads of his company. He commented that this cemetery 'soon became a small annex of hell'.

Armed with a French MAS 38 submachine-gun which he had brought along with him from his days with the *Milice*, Marotin fired short bursts at fleeting silhouettes in the darkness and smoke. Emptying another magazine, he suddenly realised that he would soon be out of ammunition. During a brief lull in the fighting, he picked up a Mauser 98k rifle complete with bayonet. It was not a moment too soon as a 'giant devil' suddenly appeared before him. He thrust his bayonet into the Russian; he had repeated this manoeuvre many times before, but this time it was for real. He tried to withdraw the bayonet but could not; the Russian soldier was doubled up on his weapon, which he had grabbed with both hands. In the end he had to use a foot to pull out the bayonet. He described it as 'not very elegant'. All this had only lasted a matter of seconds. He then watched silhouettes of Russian soldiers pass him on both sides.

Rifle in hand, a French POW fought stubbornly for Elsenau cemetery before succumbing in turn. His name is not known. The defenders were insulted in perfect French from either Polish regular troops or liberated French POWs serving with the Russians.

For hours the pattern of attack, defence, and renewed attack repeated itself without let up.[139] The fury of the Russian attacks grew with each passing hour. Eventually, at enormous cost, the

<hr/>

136  Fontenay was not killed at Elsenau. He would fight with the Sturmbataillon in Berlin.
137  Saint-Loup, *Les Hérétiques*, p.215, confirmed by Grenouillet, letter to the author, 12/4/98. However, the presence of Ostuf. Fatin and his 1/58 in Elsenau cemetery is not recorded by Soulat or Mabire.
138  Mabire, *La Division Charlemagne*, p.356.
139  According to Mabire, *La Division Charlemagne*, p.357, Brigf. Krukenberg also ordered Ostuf. Weber and the *Compagnie d'Honneur* into the fiercely escalating maelstrom. However, at no time did Lavest, a member of the *Compagnie d'Honneur*, find himself in Elsenau cemetery.

Russians did succeed in gaining the cemetery with their fifth attack. Enraged, the Russians put to death the helpless French wounded lying between the gravestones.

As for Marotin, he was fortunate to get out of the cemetery alive. Suddenly, he had found himself before a T-34, but moments later the tank was a ball of flames, undoubtedly the work of a panzerfäust. Then, from behind him, he heard his name shouted out. At one bound he rejoined his comrades who disengaged, abandoning the cemetery. They ran off chased by tracer bullets. He would never find out who had actually called out to him.

With the loss of the cemetery, Elsenau became untenable. Greatly outnumbered, its last defenders were outflanked, disorganised and overwhelmed. Also, they had no anti-tank weapons left. Any further resistance would serve no purpose. Some surrendered. Most choose

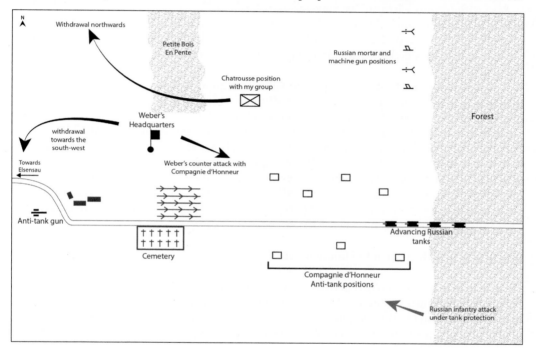

The defence of Elsenau according to Chatrousse.

to retreat. Ostuf. Weber and some twenty men of his *Compagnie d'Honneur*, including Lavest, withdrew in good order along the road to the town of Flötenstein. The losses of the *Compagnie d'Honneur* were heavy.[140]

140 According to Saint-Loup, *Les Hérétiques*, p.215, the *Compagnie d'Honneur* lost one half of its strength, thus all told some one hundred men. However, according to Soulat, *Historique de la division Charlemagne*, p.34, its losses were one quarter of its strength of eighty, thus some twenty men. And, lastly, according to Levast, Louis, *Le soleil se couchait à l'est* (Paris: Editions de l'homme libre, 2008), p.86, there were 21 survivors out of 165 men at the start of the engagement.

Eighty totally exhausted survivors, without ammunition and supplies, withdrew to the north under Ustuf. Fatin. By the time they had reached the comparative shelter of the woods, they had been joined by other individuals and groups, notably that led by Oberjunker Chatrousse, swelling their number to one hundred and twenty.

Ustuf. Fatin immediately formed three platoons whose command went to Oberjunken Chatrousse and Lapart, and Oscha. Bonnafous. He decided to return to Hammerstein, to the west, but his patrollers immediately ran into enemy infantry. Tormented by a lack of ammunition, Fatin had to avoid a pitched battle and keep moving. He now opted for the east. Thanks to the night, they made good their escape and came to a place of rest. Only then did Chatrousse realise that he had been awake, and almost in constant action, for some thirty-six hours.

Also withdrawing eastward were men from Albert's 6/57 and Million-Rousseau's 7/57. They formed a sizeable group.[141] After abandoning its equipment, the Signals Company also managed to make good its escape from Elsenau between 17:00 and 18:00 hours. It was still virtually intact, numbering a good one hundred men, but many were now without a rifle. It retreated westwards.

As for Krukenberg, he broke out of Elsenau with a group of French SS men.[142] Arriving at the town of Flötenstein on the 26th, he met Zimmermann and Patzak who had arrived before dawn that same day with General Hochbaum and his staff officers.

At Elsenau, 'Charlemagne' fought bravely and tenaciously against superior odds. Moreover, it gave the Soviets a bloody nose. Figures for Soviet tank losses at Elsenau range from only several to nineteen tanks.[143] The claim that artillery destroyed a further fourteen tanks is very doubtful or grossly inflated. Former divisional soldiers present at Elsenau do not recall the presence of friendly artillery at Elsenau or receiving artillery support. In any case, the Russians would have been quick to suppress any artillery support the defenders might well have enjoyed. Such was their superior firepower at Elsenau.

### Bärenhutte and the retreat to Hammerstein

Meantime, the isolated French garrison at Bärenhutte could only make a nuisance of itself by firing on the bumper to bumper Soviet motorised columns making for Elsenau. In this way, the last infantry and anti-tank guns under Roy, and the mortars of Tardan's 4/58 and Defever's 8/58 registered direct hit after direct hit.[144] There was little reply from the Russians other than a

141  Hstuf. Renault may have been with group.
142  Mabire, *La Division Charlemagne*, pp.367-368.
143  Each and every source records a different number of Soviet tanks destroyed at Elsenau: according to Lefèvre, several Soviet tanks were destroyed (*Axe & Alliés* no 1, p.58); according to Soulat, the *Compagnie d'Honneur* destroyed three tanks and four PAK guns destroyed several more (*Historique de la division Charlemagne*, p.36); according to Landwehr, Weber's Company halted the Soviet tank attack by destroying the entire vanguard of eighteen tanks, most of which were Stalin models (*Charlemagne's Legionnaires*, pp.78-79); according to Louis Lavest of the *Compagnie d'Honneur*, his company destroyed fourteen T-34s (letter to the author of 15/1/98); and, lastly, according to Saint-Loup, nineteen tanks were destroyed, of which the *Compagnie d'Honneur* accounted for seventeen (*Les Hérétiques*, p.214).
144  Soulat, *Historique de la division Charlemagne*, p.36, repeated by Mabire, *La Division Charlemagne*, p.337. Company 8/58 was part of Battalion II/58, elements of which arrived at Neustettin as previously

reconnaissance force which its outposts stopped, destroying a motorcar and an armoured car, as well as the occasional foray by an armoured car which Roy's guns chased off.

However, of increasing concern to the garrison were the Russian snipers that kept the village under fire. They did not give the Frenchmen a moment's peace. The German liaison officer to Waffen-Gren. Regt der SS 57 was hit by two explosive bullets in the arm and evacuated.[145]

Then the Russians mounted their first serious attack against Bärenhutte. It was contained.[146] Around 2000 hours, the infantry guns fell silent. All ammunition had been exhausted. As there were no tractors or horses available to move his guns, Hstuf. Roy had them destroyed. By now, Bärenhutte was totally encircled.

One hour later, Ostuf. Labuze, assigned a liaison mission between Bärenhutte and Hammerstein, led a patrol from his Panzerjäger Kompanie of Waffen-Gren. Regt der SS 57 into the village of Geglenfelde (Wyczechy) on the road westwards from Bärenhutte to Hammerstein.

The village was not as empty as it first seemed. An LVF veteran suddenly appeared and handed the patrol a Russian he had just taken prisoner in the village. When interrogated the prisoner indicated that several of his comrades were at an isolated farmhouse not far from the village.

Guided by the prisoner, a small group of Frenchmen made their way to the farmhouse. Covered by his men, Ostuf. Labuze curiously planted himself in front of the farmhouse and shouted out to those inside to surrender. The reply was a submachine-gun burst that killed him outright.[147]

A firefight started. The Russian prisoner was seriously wounded. Several Frenchmen also received wounds. They withdrew hurriedly. Led by a NCO, the patrol made it back to Bärenhutte and reported the 'capture' of Geglenfelde by the Russians.

By now, Stubaf. Raybaud had preparations to break out and retreat to Hammerstein well underway. He was acting on orders received from Brigf. Krukenberg.[148] The breakout plan was simple. The French forces were to take the quickest and the most direct route to Hammerstein through Geglenfelde. Hscha. Walter's 7/58 would form the rearguard. H-hour was set for

noted. The author cannot confirm if this company arrived at Hammerstein or Neustettin. If it arrived at Neustettin it would not have been engaged at Bärenhutte.

145 According to Soulat, *Historique de la division Charlemagne*, p.46, the German liaison officer to Waffen-Gren. Regt der SS 57 was an unidentified Unsturmführer with the initial of H. However, according to Mabire, *La Division Charlemagne*, p.526, SS-Ustuf. Goliberzuch, in fact an Austrian, held this position. Soulat disagrees and positions Goliberzuch as the German liaison officer to Waffen-Gren. Regt der SS 58.

146 The first Russian attack against Bärenhutte materialised during the day and not during the night (a correction penned by Raybaud to Soulat's original manuscript which, for the record, details that the Russians first launched an attack around 2300 hours.)

147 Mabire, *La Division Charlemagne*, pp.339-340, and Saint-Loup, *Les Hérétiques*, p.219. According to Raybaud, letter to Mabire dated 3/11/74, Ostuf. Labuze was killed later that night in the skirmish at Geglenfelde during the retreat from Bärenhutte to Hammerstein. In response to this, Mabire's account of the death of Labuze appears to be eyewitness based and, for that reason, has been chosen over Raybaud's recollection.

148 Raybaud, letter to Mabire dated 3/11/74. This corrects Mabire's account, *La Division Charlemagne*, p.337, that Raybaud and de Vaugelas decided among themselves to break out and withdraw to Hammerstein.

midnight. As there was no motorised transport available, all ammunition caches were destroyed and each man received a panzerfäust.

Noisily, the breakout began at midnight, not respecting Raybaud's order to observe silence, but the Russians did not intervene. Such was the din that perhaps the Soviets were convinced that the exhausted French SS units were far stronger and better equipped than they really were! Perhaps the Soviets were also exhausted and had momentarily lost their vigour. Indeed, if they had opened up on the compact and disorganised column it would have been a slaughter.

At Geglenfelde, there was a skirmish. The reconnaissance platoon of Waffen-Gren. Regt der SS 57, led by Obf. Puaud himself, immediately moved into action and neutralised the Russians blocking the way forward. The response from the French side had been so quick that the progress of the column had not been impeded.[149] Without any further incident the French SS men arrived at Hammerstein towards 0300 hours on 26 February.[150]

Hammerstein was now unrecognisable. It was a picture of panic, disorder and despair. The roads were swarming with terror-stricken civilians. POWs of numerous nationalities were wandering about and mocked the arriving columns of French SS troops. Latvian Waffen-SS troops and Germans of the Wehrmacht were looting military warehouses. Uniforms and brand new weapons littered the ground.[151] At the camp white flags abounded. There was the aroma of schnapps in the air from the hundreds of bottles broken by the looters who could not carry them off.

Some, like Marotin and his comrades of the 8/57, had arrived at Hammerstein from Elsenau. He does not recall how he found himself on the road from Elsenau to Hammerstein and in the company of some comrades, but they made haste, fearful that the Russians might cut their line of retreat.

## Hammerstein

The convoy transporting the Medical Company arrived at Hammerstein towards two in the morning on 25 February. The company was sent to the POW camp, which had been recently evacuated, and there it remained unemployed hour after hour. Dissent of the Medical Company got the distinct impression that 'nobody knew what they should do'. Eventually, in the late afternoon, the Medical Company set out on foot eastwards and took up position in a house. Several volunteers left to go and get news and orders.

In the early evening of 25 February 1945, 'Charlemagne' received orders to assemble at the city of Neustettin (Szczecinek), twenty kilometres to the west.[152] By 1900 hours, the first elements

---

149   Raybaud, letter to Mabire dated 3/11/74. Furthermore, according to Saint-Loup, *Les Hérétiques*, p.219, a medical orderly, on hearing the sound of shooting went for news and reported back to Dr. Métais that the skirmish was 'nothing'. This corrects Mabire's account, *La Division Charlemagne*, pp.340-341, of the same incident, which appears to be over-dramatised.

150   Soulat, *Historique de la division Charlemagne*, p.36. However, Saint-Loup is not in agreement and states that their arrival at Hammerstein was at daybreak, *Les Hérétiques*, p.220.

151   Saint-Loup, *Les Hérétiques*, p.220. However, this would seem to dispute the idea that the military depots were empty.

152   Mabire, *La Division Charlemagne*, p.341. However, it is not recorded who or what headquarters actually issued 'Charlemagne' orders to withdraw to Neustettin, but it was not the headquarters of the XVIII. Gebirgs-Korps. Therefore, they may have come from the 2nd Army or Army Group Vistula.

of 'Charlemagne', the motor and horse-drawn columns, were already on the road to Neustettin. Fahrschwadron A had arrived at Hammerstein earlier that same day, after a quiet journey.[153] It was still without much of its equipment and weapons. Indeed, not all of the grooms had a rifle. And few had a steel helmet.[154]

I/58 and the Engineer Company set off in turn. As the Engineer Company crossed Hammerstein its inhabitants looked on in total silence. They seemed lifeless. They knew what now awaited them.

Making his way westwards on foot to Neustettin with the Engineer Company was Rttf. Gonzales. He was upset about having to leave behind his pack at Hammerstein railway station. For his pack contained not only his changes of clothes, but also at least two hundred photographs of his time with the LVF and the two cameras, one German and one French, with which he had taken them. At ten in the evening the Medical Company set out westwards in the direction of Neustettin, arriving early next morning.

No sooner had those French troops who had made good their escape from Bärenhutte arrived at Hammerstein than they set off again to Neustettin. By 0300 hours, all had left. Behind them they left a rather unique rearguard formed at the camp on the evening of 25 February from all available personnel of the divisional Headquarters Company and the Supply Corps.

Hurriedly armed, this French kampfgruppe of 'penpushers' moved up to the front during the night of 25-26 February. In accordance with its orders to protect the flank of the French SS units withdrawing from Bärenhutte to Hammerstein, the kampfgruppe took up position in woods to the north of the road from Hammerstein to Geglenfelde.[155]

Under Stubaf. Katzian, an old Austrian officer, the kampfgruppe was made up of three platoons: the first platoon assembled German personnel of the Inspection; the second platoon consisted of tailors, orderlies, secretaries, quartermasters, interpreters and messengers of the Headquarters Company; and the third was the escort (combat) platoon of Fahrschwadron A under Ostuf. Darrigade, which had even been given one panzerfäust.

The night passed in peace. Towards 0500 hours on 26 February, Stubaf. Katzian finally issued orders to withdraw. During the withdrawal one of their number, Rttf. Soulat, became lost and, after first ending up at a Latvian SS artillery position, he returned to Hammerstein towards 1400 hours. At the camp, he came across some Germans whose field kitchen was still functioning. He took the time to eat and was amazed to see the service records of 'Charlemagne' personnel littering the corridor floors of a hut!

Rttf. Soulat then set off by foot to Neustettin. Catching up with some stragglers of 'Charlemagne', he was invited aboard the field kitchen of the divisional Signals Company by its *chef-cuisinier* [head cook]. Being exhausted, he gladly accepted this kind invitation.

The platoon under Ostuf. Darrigade rejoined Fahrschwadron A the following day.

---

153 The only incident Mercier of Fahrschwadron A recalls is of a brief stop in the suburbs of Berlin, during which kids came begging for bread. He had to refuse them. Grenadier Hernu said to Mercier that it was very sad to have to refuse them a single piece of bread in their own country.

154 Regarding this, Mercier of Fahrschwadron A said: 'At Wildflecken, I'd heard Hstuf. Croisile proudly say that an SS officer does not wear a helmet. On this point, we could have all been officers.' Mercier, letter to the author, 6/11/2001.

155 Soulat, letter to the author, 14/11/97. Curiously, according to Mabire, *La Division Charlemagne*, p.375, this French kampfgruppe took up position after a march of some ten kilometres. But the distance from Hammerstein to Geglenfelde is barely five kilometres. Thus, Mabire must be mistaken.

At 1700 hours, the first Soviet armoured columns entered Hammerstein.[156] At that same moment the bulk of the divisional Signals Company arrived. This was not its first brush with enemy armour that day. Withdrawing westwards from Elsenau, the Signals Company was stopped by a German officer of the Inspection. First he praised the fighting qualities of the Frenchmen and then ordered Dupuyau to deploy his company on a hillock as 'a sort of roadblock' against Russian forces advancing from Bärenhutte and Elsenau. Russian tanks were soon on the scene. The signalmen tried to stop them with rifles and sub-machine-guns, but it was hopeless. The enemy tanks did not even bother to engage them. The Frenchmen ran off and continued westwards. In this way, they came to Hammerstein and Soviet tanks once again! It was a slaughter. A group of telephonists was cornered and crushed by a T-34. The rest scattered and fled from Hammerstein.[157]

By midday on 26 February 1945, the bulk of 'Charlemagne' had reached Neustettin. The survivors were totally exhausted. Units were completely disorganised. The bulk of the division was quartered in one large barracks. If the Russians had intervened the consequences would have been disastrous, but fortunately they remained quiet.

## The losses

Thus ended the 'battle of Hammerstein',[158] a battle that had lasted no more than forty-eight hours for the 33. Waffen-Gren.-Division der SS 'Charlemagne' (französische Nr.1). And yet its casualty balance sheet was terrible. At Neustettin, according to Soulat of the Headquarters Company, 'out of the 4,500 men who had left Wildflecken, 3,000 replied at the roll call'. And of the difference, 1,000, including 15 officers, were missing and 500, including 5 officers, were killed. Mabire, Bayle and Landwehr repeat the same figures. However, de la Mazière records slightly higher figures of 1,000 dead and another 1,000 missing.[159] Higher still is Saint-Loup with a total figure of 3,000 dead, wounded and missing.[160] In response to the likes of Saint-Loup and de la Mazière, it is important to note that the figures Soulat cites are derived from the roll calls 'officially fed back to us [the staff of the Headquarters Company] by our *chefs*' and reproduced from memory.[161] Thus, his figures are perhaps the most accurate and 'official'.

Of the 1,000 generally accepted as 'missing', up to 300 were now withdrawing from Elsenau to the north. The balance was thus made up of those who had been wounded and evacuated, of those who had been captured, of those who were missing, of those who had taken advantage of

156 Soulat, *Historique de la Division Charlemagne*, p.36, repeated by Saint-Loup, *Les Hérétiques*, p.223. According to Silgailis Arthur, *Latvian Legion* (San Jose: Bender publishing, 1986), elements of the 15. Waffen-Grenadier-Division der SS (lettische Nr.1) occupied positions around the town of Hammerstein on the morning of 26 February. Despite beating off Russian attacks in the morning, the flanks of the Latvians were turned in the forenoon. By noon, the Russians had broken into Hammerstein. In response to this, as previously stated, Soulat left Hammerstein sometime after 1400 hours and he saw no sight of the Russians!
157 Mabire, *La Division Charlemagne*, pp.376-377. However, according to a civilian statement, Hammerstein was occupied by the Soviets without a fight. See BArch OSTDOK 1/168, fol. 169.
158 Saint-Loup, *Les Hérétiques*, p.223.
159 De la Mazière *Ashes of Honour*, p.108.
160 Saint-Loup, *Les Hérétiques*, p.223.
161 Soulat, letter to the author, dated 20/2/1998.

the chaotic situation to desert,[162] and perhaps of those who had joined German units. To be sure, the greater portion of the balance was those who had been wounded and evacuated. The number of deserters was probably small.

## Went the battle well?

Lieutenant-Colonel Harnack of Army Group Vistula wrote in a report dated 26 February 1945:

> The 15. Waffen-Grenadier-Division der SS and SS-Volunteer Brigade 'Charlemagne' have thus been split into isolated combat groups, partly losing contact with their rear, and have thus almost entirely lost their combat effectiveness.

Undoubtedly, 'Charlemagne' had lost much of its combat effectiveness as a result of battle, but it found itself in an impossible situation. It was not combat-ready. It went straight into battle off the trains. It went into battle with no knowledge of enemy strength. It went into battle without radio equipment, which was compounded by a lack of maps. It went into battle without its artillery battalion, which had not yet arrived. It received no armour or air support. Some of its soldiers went into battle without even a steel helmet and a rifle. And yes, the battle went badly, but it went down fighting.

'Charlemagne' knocked out between forty and fifty enemy tanks, destroyed a considerable quantity of motorised equipment and inflicted casualties that far outweighed its own: indeed, according to Krukenberg, sixteen enemy tanks were destroyed in less than one hour near Elsenau and Barenhütte.[163] Deeds of self-sacrifice and bravery were many: during the brief stop at Neustettin thirty Iron Crosses were awarded for various feats of arms.[164] In conclusion, 'Charlemagne' performed well under very adverse combat conditions. Realistically speaking, little more could have been expected of it.

162  For example, during the retreat from Elsenau, Lavest and the *Compagnie d'Honneur* came across two soldiers who had deserted from 'Charlemagne'. Also, during the retreat from Neustettin to Belgard, Std.Ju. Bayle of the 2/57 was approached by two former *Miliciens* who asked him about 'leaving' his platoon. He agreed to this, but not to them taking their weapons. At a roll call, he reported the disappearance of the two to *Kompanieführer* Ostuf. Bartolomei.
163  Krukenberg, order of day 27 March 1945.
164  Arguably, the number of Iron Cross and other decorations awarded at Neustettin would have been greater if it was not for the absence of part of the division.

# 13

## The Hell of Pomerania
## Part II

---

### Neustettin

According to the situation maps of Army Group Vistula, the bulk of 'Charlemagne' was southeast of Flötenstein. In reality, the bulk of the division was some thirty-five kilometres away at Neustettin!

On 26 February 1945, two convoys of 'Charlemagne' pulled into Neustettin station.[1] Aboard the first convoy, arriving in the morning, were the headquarters staff of the II/58 and elements of the II/58, including Company 5/58.[2] The day before, at Stargard (Stargard Szczecinski), the journey had been interrupted when an armoured Soviet spearhead cut the railway line.[3]

---

1   Dates of the arrival of the two convoys of 'Charlemagne' at Neustettin vary. De Genouillac and Blanc arrived at Neustettin on a convoy carrying elements of the II/58. De Genouillac believes the convoy arrived on the 27 February whereas Blanc of Company 5/58 initially believed it arrived on 28 February, but later agreed it may have been 26 February. However, according to Soulat, *Historique de la Division Charlemagne*, p.41, repeated by Mabire, *La Division Charlemagne*, p.382, and later by Lefèvre, *Axe & Alliés* No. 1, p.60, the convoy of Bassompierre arrived on 26 February 1945. In response to this, de la Mazière, present on this convoy, implies twice (*Ashes of Honour*, p.105 and p.107) that its arrival was on 27 February. According to Triqueneaux, a member of the FLAK Company, he arrived at Neustettin on 27 February but does not specify on what convoy or convoys (article *SS-Französische Flakbatterie*). Message Ia/Tgb.Nr.2143/45 geh. of 27/2/45 reported the arrival of two convoys of 'Charlemagne'. This message does not specify their arrival at Neustettin, but there can be little doubt it refers to the two convoys of 'Charlemagne' that arrived at Neustettin. This message in particular swayed the author to record the date of the arrival of the two convoys at Neustettin as 27 February. Upon reflection, this message does not state categorically that they arrived on 27 February merely that two convoys had arrived. The same message also states: 'The fighting still continues in Neustettin'. Furthermore, according to Murawski Erich, *The struggle for Pomerania* (Winnipeg: John Fedorowicz, 2016), p.156, Neustettin fell into enemy hands during the night of 27-28 February. So the author now believes that two convoys of 'Charlemagne' arrived at Neustettin on 26 February.
2   De Genouillac believes that his convoy was the sixteenth.
3   According to de Genouillac of the headquarters staff of Battalion II/58, the convoy lost a day at Stargard, whereas it was only several hours according to Blanc, Castrillo and Le Goff of Company 5/58 travelling on the same convoy (Blanc, letter to the author, 11/4/2001).

As the troops of the II/58 disembarked, the Soviet Air Force attacked,[4] but guns of Ustuf. Fayard's FLAK Company in position on flat wagons returned fire and shot down one of the attackers.[5]

Men of Oscha. Ruskone's Platoon of the 5/58 were busy unloading a small car when 'a hail of shells' suddenly rained down on the railway station. Shaken by the blast of the explosions, they let go of the car, which rolled off the wagon and onto their platoon commander. Thrown to the ground, Ruskone was badly hurt in the right knee. Although in great pain, he could still get around.

Gren. Castrillo of the 5/58 hurried off for news. He saw a train of wounded. They too were from 'Charlemagne'. In this way, Castrillo and the men of the 5/58 were shocked to learn of the 'setback' at Hammerstein.

The troops of the II/58 were then sent to a barracks in the city where they met some survivors from the earlier fighting. 'The greatest confusion reigned among these troops'. Anxious to have news of his friends serving in I/58, Ustuf. de Genouillac went from shed to shed, making inquiries, and came across Hstuf. Moneuse who was busy sawing up a telegraph post for the stove in his bedroom. He revealed to de Genouillac that he had no idea of the fate of his Orderly Officer, Oberjunker Chatrousse, nor of the overall situation, other than his battalion had 'exploded' in every sense of the word. Blanc of Company 5/58 met and briefly chatted with Hscha. Walter. He also ran into Lucien Kemarat, who was with him in the ski platoon.

That afternoon the second convoy arrived under convoy commander Hstuf. Bassompierre.[6] He had been ordered to stay behind at Wildflecken but refused. The convoy was also carrying elements of the FLAK Company, as well as eight 105mm howitzers of the Artillery Group[7] under Ustuf. Daffas.[8] The howitzers were not accompanied by their crews who were still en route to the division from Bohemia-Moravia where they had just finished their training course. In total, around one hundred and fifty men were abroad this convoy.

4    De Genouillac, letter to the author, 27/6/1997. Curiously, Blanc, Castrillo and Le Goff of Company 5/58 travelling on the same convoy do not recall this air attack (Blanc, letter to the author, 11/4/2001). Furthermore, Blanc makes the suggestion that it was another convoy, arriving before that of the II/58 and carrying elements of 'Regiment 57', which was attacked. In response to this, the author knows of no convoy carrying elements of 'Regiment 57' that arrived at Neustettin.
5    According to de Genouillac, the FLAK Company was dispersed on several of the last convoys to provide some form of protection to all (letter to the author, 15/7/97). However, Mabire and Saint-Loup imply that the entire FLAK Company arrived later on the convoy of Bassompierre. Soulat is of the same opinion (letter to the author).
6    Soulat, *Historique de la Division Charlemagne*, p.41. However, in correspondence to the author, Ruskone of the 5/58, undoubtedly on the convoy of Berret and the II/58, wrote that 'we were the last to arrive in Pomerania'. This statement the author has not been able to explain. According to Mabire, *La Divison Charlemagne*, p.382, the convoy of Bassompierre was the fifteenth and last convoy of 'Charlemagne' from Wildflecken. This convoy was, in all likelihood, the last from Wildflecken, but the fifteenth has proved impossible to confirm.
7    Soulat, letter to the author, 9/11/97. These guns are described by Saint-Loup, *Les Hérétiques*, p.256 as 'part of the guns of the artillery group' and by Mabire, *La Division Charlemagne*, p.384, as 'some infantry guns brought along from Wildflecken'.
8    According to Mabire, *La Division Charlemagne*, p.384, Ustuf. Raymond Daffas arrived in Pomerania as the commander of '*la section de commandement du régiment 58*'. This is unlikely. More likely is that he was serving with Waffen-Artillerie-Abteilung der SS 57, perhaps with the Stabsbatterie.

Shortly after arriving at the station, this convoy was 'warmly' greeted by the Soviet Air Force.[9] Two aircraft passed overhead at a low height, machine-gunning and dropping bombs. They were flying so low that Maurice Ranc of the Artillery Battalion could see the pilots! The cacophony of explosions and machine-gun fire spooked the horses in his care. The Soviet planes made a second pass, but this time they were met by two FLAK guns and quickly departed.[10] No sooner was the train empty than it was occupied again by German units that were withdrawing.

Darkness fell. That night of 26-27 February 1945, Obf. Puaud called together the officers for a meeting. Because the Russians were already threatening Neustettin a decision was made to evacuate the town and reform 'Charlemagne' at the town of Belgard (Bialogard).[11] This meant a withdrawal of eighty kilometres northwards. The withdrawal was scheduled for 0700 hours.

Towards 0100 hours on 27 February, the order was issued to reload the artillery and the Flak guns on a train bound for Belgard.[12] Shortly after, an officer woke Ustuf. Daffas with the order. Accompanied by the station master, Daffas went in search of wagons and soon located some. The loading began.

At 0300 hours, the alarm was given. The clanking of tank treads could already be heard. Under the protection of an armoured train, which had gone and taken up a position outside the railway station, the loading continued.

Towards 0700 hours, the enemy launched an attack. Because of a lack of locomotives the armoured train due to leave for Kolberg coupled the wagons of artillery and departed.[13] It was not a minute too soon. Ustuf. Fayard's FLAK Company had just finished the re-embarkation

---

9    According to de la Mazière, *Ashes of Honour*, pp.106-107, the convoy was violently attacked by a Russian advance party of armour and infantry. Jumping down from the train, he was immediately captured by two Russians who made him put up his hands! He was shoved towards a shed, the station lamp-room, but his comrades, who saw his plight, came to his assistance, killing his two captors. He then watched as the FLAK guns went into action and knocked out a T-34, setting it on fire. The others quickly made off. Suspiciously, no other source confirms this brief and violent land engagement. Also Maurice Ranc of the Artillery Battalion, who was on the last convoy, only recalls the appearance of the Soviet Air Force. Moreover, in correspondence to the author, de Genouillac considers as unlikely the appearance of Russian tanks at that moment.

10    Deloncle, *Trois jeunesses provençales*, p.125. According to de la Mazière, *Ashes of Honour*, p.87, the FLAK hit and brought down a twin-engine plane, which crashed just outside the town.

11    According to Mabire, *La Division Charlemagne*, p.386, de Vaugelas announced during this meeting that the Latvian Division, which he called their rearguard, had been swept aside by a strong Soviet attack. As such, this role of rearguard to 'Charlemagne' or indeed to any other unit is not found in Arthur Sigailis' *Latvian Legion*.

12    Lindenblatt Helmut, *Pommern 1945* (Gelbersdorf: Verlag Gerhard Rautenbeg, 1993, 2nd edition), p.188 (who cites Soulat as his source in footnote 419) and Soulat, letter to the author, 6/3/98. Curiously, de la Mazière wrote of the Flak guns, *Ashes of Honour*, p.109: 'It [the withdrawal from Neustettin] was to be covered by a dozen anti-aircraft guns, the ones we had brought on our convoy. Failing tractors to tow them, they were left on their railway trucks and the whole train with the empty wagons, moved off again to a position north of the town.' This statement the author has not been able to explain.

13    Soulat, *Historique de la Division Charlemagne* p.41. Mabire, expands, *La Division Charlemagne*, p.385, that Ustuf. Daffas could not locate at first a locomotive to pull the wagons. Then he spotted an armoured train which 'had moved several hundreds of metres away to cover the railway station with the fire of its guns and to check a possible Russian tank spearhead'. He spoke to the commander of the armoured train who had just received orders to leave Neustettin for Kolberg on the Baltic coast. Because Belgard was en route the commander of the armoured train agreed to couple the flat tractors to his train.

of its 'equipment' when it was surprised by a Russian attack.[14] Indeed, the FLAK gunners were actually in the wagons waiting to depart when the Russians suddenly appeared on the platform![15] They had to extricate themselves in hand-to-hand fighting. So instead of following their equipment, they now found themselves engaged as grenadier.

Eventually, via Bublitz (Bobolice) and Köslin (Koszalin), the armoured train reached the city port of Kolberg on the Baltic coast where the artillery pieces were subsequently employed in its defence.

At 0700 hours, as planned, the first elements of 'Charlemagne' left the barracks situated to the north of the town and set out towards Belgard.

A mood of sudden alarm was produced by the report of Russian tanks encircling Neustettin to the north, cutting the railway line to Kolberg. This changed the situation. Disaster now threatened, but the enemy was not aggressive and did not follow up.

Shortly before 0800 hours, the troops of the II/58 left the town. This was the last battalion to leave. A little later, Oberst Kopp,[16] the 'Festungskommandant' [fortress commandant] of Neustettin, who was in command of the defence of the town with elements of the Division 'Pommern', came and asked Obf. Puaud to provide him with a battalion to help him hold the town to evening and also to hold the enemy at bay so as to permit the withdrawal of the civilian population and those units not yet engaged. For Puaud, there was not too much to think about: if Neustettin fell too soon, the withdrawing division would be overtaken by disaster and crushed, but the last of its battalions had already left. Nevertheless, he agreed to supply a *bataillon de marche* or Alarm-Bataillon [Alarm Battalion].

Turning to the divisional headquarters staff around him, Obf. Puaud ordered Ostuf. Auphan, his Orderly Officer, to form a *bataillon de marche* with those units which had not already left the town. In this way, Auphan formed a weak battalion, which comprised the following companies:

- The FLAK Company under Ustuf. Fayard
- Kompanie 4/58 under Ostuf. Tardan
- The Panzerjäger Company of Waffen-Gren. Regt der SS 58 under Oscha. Girard

In total, some 250 men, but the companies commanded by Tardan and Girard had participated in the recent fighting and were completely exhausted.

The French *bataillon de marche* was assigned a sector, 1,200 metres long, between two Wehrmacht battalions. After acquainting himself with the situation of the FLAK Company, Auphan went to inspect the sector assigned to the *bataillon*. To defend the sector, he decided to deploy the FLAK Company to the east and Kompanie 4/58 to the west. His third company, the Panzerjäger Company, was to provide a 'group', perhaps a platoon, of 'tank-hunters' armed with

---

14   Soulat, *Historique de la Division Charlemagne*, p.42, repeated by Mabire, *La Division Charlemagne*, pp.389-390. The word 'equipment' presumably refers to its Flak guns. Curiously, Martres, who met Fayard at the railway station, believes that the FLAK Company did not re-embark its guns but fought with them, after which they had to abandon them.

15   Mabire, *La Division Charlemagne*, p.398.

16   Lindenblatt, *Pommern-1945*, p.189. Elsewhere his name incorrectly appears as Kropp (see Murawski, *The Struggle For Pomerania*).

panzerfäust to each of the two line companies. In this way, he would have at his disposal a small reserve of around one and a half platoons.

But first the FLAK Company, which was heavily engaged around the railway station and the artillery barracks, had to be extricated. And Auphan was all too aware that a withdrawal conducted before an aggressive and overwhelming enemy presence was not only difficult, but dangerous. To facilitate the withdrawal of the FLAK Company, he sent forward Tardan and his 4/58, which was positioned near the barracks at the western exit of the city.

Joined by the 4/58, the FLAK Company managed to extricate itself, but not without difficulty. The two companies then occupied their laid-down defensive positions in the centre of the disposition.

Elsewhere, Marotel of the 8/57 awoke to the shrill rent of the MGs and the din of the artillery. Around him men were running out of the barracks. Was this the start of their offensive? But nobody had thought to wake him from his deep sleep. He hastily equipped himself and dashed out in turn. Outside there were crowds of people around: soldiers trying to find their *gradés* and the *gradés* their men, and dazed civilians roused from sleep. The town was being evacuated.

He left the town in search of his comrades. He was stopped by a German officer who was looking for volunteers to slow down the enemy and buy enough time for the retreating columns of soldiers and civilians to put some distance between themselves and the Russian spearheads. The officer was quite insistent. Marotel joined a fifty-strong group armed with four PAK guns and some MGs for which there was little ammunition.

Two Soviet tanks appeared. Behind them followed their infantry support. The defenders stood firm and one tank fell victim to their PAK. The other tank withdrew in great haste. Their MGs shot up the exposed enemy infantry. The Russians flung themselves against this post a further two times and were repelled, but the defenders were now out of ammunition for their PAK guns and MGs.

The Russians now seized their opportunity to crush this post and reappeared with tanks from two directions. There was nothing the defenders could do this time and they withdrew in a mad rush. The Russian infantry were soon on top of them. Marotel wrote:

> A large guy was tossing grenades just anyhow... I threw myself on the ground but my mouth and eyes were full of earth and I was groggy... A German grenadier on my right cut in two this 'uncouth individual' with a precise burst.

After sharing out the last ammunition, the survivors set off on their long march to Belgard.

In the meantime, Soviet armour, stopped some 400 metres from the city, poured fire onto the anti-tank blockhouses. It was only around 1030 hours when the Soviet Air Force made an appearance and bombed the city.[17] Supported by artillery and mortar, the Soviets attempted to punch their way into the city but could make no headway. The Soviet armour was stopped by the anti-tank roadblocks while the infantry, slipping through the gardens, was halted by

---

17    Soulat, *Historique de la division Charlemagne*, p.42, repeated by Mabire, *La Division Charlemagne*, p.391. According to Saint-Loup, *Les Hérétiques*, p.257, the Soviet air strike against Neustettin began at 1200 hours and also marked the beginning of their assault against the town which would continue into the evening.

a devastating hail of fire from the defenders posted on the roofs, at the windows and at the basement windows.[18]

Having failed frontally, the Russians launched encircling attacks against the two German battalions holding the flanks of the defensive position. In this way, the French *bataillon de marche* enjoyed a spell of relative calm until 1600 hours. By that time, to the south-west, Soviet tanks had battled their way up to the barricade on Tempelburg Road where heavy fighting erupted. It was the Germans who came out on top destroying two tanks and throwing back the enemy infantry with heavy losses. On the other hand, to the north, the German battalion of territorials holding the area around the railway station had fought without ardour and had started to show the strains of battle, requiring its officers to intervene several times to get the men to hold.[19]

### The End at Neustettin

Towards 1700 hours, the end was clearly in sight for the defenders of Neustettin. To the north, the enemy managed to cross the railway bridge and capture the railway station. To the south-west, enemy cavalry was skirting around the Trzesiecko lake alongside Neustettin. Encirclement now threatened. It was now only a question of time.

Faced with encirclement and a crumbling defence, Colonel Kopp was forced to give up Neustettin to the enemy. He decided to withdraw all his units, starting with the battalion on the left flank, then the French alarm battalion and, lastly, the battalion on the right flank in echelons, to the fortified line of 'Pommern-Stellung' ten kilometres west of Neustettin. He issued orders to this effect.

Two different versions exist of what followed next.[20] The first is based on the eyewitness testimony of Ostuf. Auphan:

> As soon as the order was received, the battalion on the left retreated in disorder, while the battalion on the right, which was meant to act as the rearguard, did not even wait for the order and withdrew well before *Bataillon* Auphan which withdrew last in good order from the town. The rallying point was the command post of the German regiment five kilometres from the town on the road to Bad-Polzin (Połczyn Zdrój) where the German Colonel was to have awaited the units.
>
> The German Colonel had fled with his baggage, abandoning maps, papers and field telephone. Shortly after, the command post was hit by a volley of mortar bombs and bursts of machine-gun fire coming from the direction of the lake.
>
> Ostuf. Auphan then decided to continue the withdrawal to Bärwalde, but two sections sent ahead as scouts reported that the retreat route had been cut and that

---

18   Ibid. According to Mabire, *La Division Charlemagne*, p.391, the Frenchmen of the improvised *bataillon de marche* participated in this heavy defensive fighting. Soulat makes no mention of this, though.
19   According to Saint-Loup, *Les Hérétiques*, p.258, this exposed the flank of the FLAK Company and resulted in the full weight of the Soviet infantry falling onto Fayard whose men withdrew, contesting every building in fierce hand-to-hand fighting. However, this withdrawal by the FLAK Company is not recorded by Soulat or Mabire.
20   See Soulat, *Historique de la division Charlemagne*, pp.42-43.

the Russians were firmly holding the first village.[21] It was hardly possible to fight against them, but the railway line seemed clear and it was this route that Auphan chose. Pursued by the enemy, the battalion passed through a barrage of missiles, then splitting into two detachments; Fayard, which left on a locomotive[22] and Auphan-Tardan, which continued on foot. Both rejoined the Division at Körlin.

The second version is based on the eyewitness testimony of Ostuf. Tardan:

When the fighting started at the barricade on the road from Tempelburg Ostuf. Tardan left his command post to go there. Half an hour later, after the fighting had died down, he returned to the command post and found only his liaison staff. The heavy machine-gun platoon and the mortar group held in reserve had disappeared in the direction of Bad Polzin. There was nobody at all at Ostuf. Auphan's command post.

Ostuf. Tardan then went to the command post of the German Colonel charged with the defence of the town. Only a few officers surround the commander from whom he learnt that the Flak and the Panzerjäger Companies had left their positions to withdraw to Bad Polzin.[23]

Ostuf. Tardan would never how exactly what had happened and, as the encirclement was becoming clearer and the sounds of battle could be heard from the southwest and the west, and road to Bad Polzin was cut five kilometres from Neustettin, he then rejoined his men.

As the last of the division with seventy men of the 4/58, the commander under whose orders he had been placed having withdrawn, an entire day having been won, General Puaud having specified to him on the other hand that it was only a matter of a delaying action and not an all-out resistance, Ostuf. Tardan ordered the 4/58 to leave its positions.

Between 27 February at 18:00 hours and 1 March at 11:00 hours, the 4/58 covered sixty-three kilometres to reach Bad Polzin because of the detours required to avoid the

---

21    This village may have been Streitzig.
22    The testimony of Auphan was undoubtedly the primary source used by both Saint-Loup and Mabire when they wrote about the dramatic escape of Fayard and his FLAK Company on a locomotive from Neustettin. See Saint-Loup, *Les Hérétiques*, p.258, and Mabire, *La Division Charlemagne*, p.396. However, Auphan's testimony does not feature this dramatic escape. Because of this, the author believes that both Saint-Loup and Mabire have applied a certain amount of poetic licence when describing the escape of Fayard and his company. Moreover, the author was unable to trace any eyewitnesses who could confirm this dramatic escape. Therefore, the 'whole truth and nothing but the truth' will most likely never be known.
23    According to Mabire, *La Division Charlemagne*, p.393, on 'thinking that they had been abandoned', the men of the heavy machine-gun platoon and the mortar group [of the Panzerjäger Company] decided to withdraw westwards along the road to Bad Polzin. In response to this, Tardan was told at the German Colonel's command post that the FLAK Company and the Panzerjäger Company 'had left their positions to withdraw to Bad Polzin', which implies that the heavy machine-gun platoon and the mortar group held in reserve were acting under orders when they withdrew rather than making the decision themselves.

Russian vanguards.[24] At Bad Polzin the 4/58 was supplied with food and ammunition by the Kommandantur and rested for forty hours.

On 3 March, after having been joined by Auphan, it left at 06:00 hours for Belgard, rejoining the Division at Körlin at 16:00 hours.

The notion that Auphan was last to leave the town is disputed by one source, which states that Major Sann, who was charged with the defence of Neustettin, 'preferred to let the Frenchmen leave the city' before it was even threatened with encirclement.[25] In fact, this same source lends credence to the second version of Tardan.

For their actions at Neustettin, Auphan, with the approval of Puaud, proposed Fayard, Tardan and five other ranks for the Iron Cross 2nd Class.[26] The *bataillon de marche* had contributed to the defence of Neustettin, which managed to halt the Russian advance for some twelve hours and in so doing save the bulk of 'Charlemagne' threatened by disaster, as well as hundreds, perhaps thousands, of civilians, but it paid a heavy price. The FLAK Company lost some 40 or 50 men of its complement of 130.[27] Uscha. Christian Mathieu of the FLAK Company was reported as missing in action.[28] Kanonier Henri Catherin of the FLAK Company was wounded in the foot and evacuated.[29] While no casualty figures are available for the other two French companies of 'Charlemagne' engaged at Neustettin it does not seem unreasonable to suggest that they were on a par with those of the FLAK Company. Gérard Quagebeur of the Panzerjäger Company of Waffen-Gren. Regt der SS 58 'disappeared' at Neustettin.

One cannot conclude the battle of the French *bataillon de marche* for Neustettin without reflecting on the two different versions of its last moments. That of Auphan appears to flatter himself and his unit, which was last to leave the town after the German units had fled back in disorder without respecting the orders issued to them whereas that of Tardan is much more matter of fact and not self-praising. Both versions are plausible, although that of Tardan is perhaps the more plausible of the two. Arguably, the truth of how the battle ended for the *bataillon de marche* will never be known.

## Belgard

The Medical Company evacuated Neustettin for Belgard in the early morning hours of 27 February 1945. Some memories of this march have remained with Jules Dissent of the Medical Company:

24  And yet, in total contrast, according to Saint-Loup, *Les Hérétiques*, p.258, to cover the withdrawal of the inextricably intermingled columns of civilians and soldiers, Ostuf. Tardan imaginatively plagued the advancing Soviet tanks with groups of cyclists armed with panzerfäuste. Again and again his men successfully ambushed and halted the pursuing enemy armour. Making the most of the great confusion they had sown among the leading Russians, they jumped on their bikes and hurriedly cycled off. This version of events is undoubtedly fictitious.
25  See Lindenblatt, *Pommern-1945*, p.189. Admittedly, Sann gives no reason for this decision.
26  Auphan proposed Fayard for the EKII on 2 March 1945.
27  Soulat numbers its losses at 40 and Bayle at 50.
28  Mathieu was ex-LVF where he had been decorated with the Iron Cross 2nd Class.
29  Catherin was hospitalised in Bavaria. He was born on 18 July 1926.

Shortly after having left Neustettin, I was abroad a horse-drawn wagon when I saw pass by, on the road side, my good friend Cardaliaguet with some others; we greeted each other and he appeared in good form, then he continued, marching faster. Unfortunately, that was the last time I saw him.

While crossing a village the Medical Company became caught up in a brief air attack. All quickly dived behind what cover they could find. Towards the end of the afternoon, such was the exhaustion of Dissent and the men around him that they had to stop some moments in a house. They napped but fearing that they might fall behind and into Russian hands, set out again. And then there was a 'rather surreal vision in this world of chaos':

> The road was close to a railway line (I even think there was a railway crossing) and on these lines we saw pass by a train made up of platform wagons on which there were Panther tanks with their crews! The train seemed to be heading eastwards, thus towards the front!

Finally on the morning of 28 February, the Medical Company arrived at Belgard. The company was no longer at full strength, but was still intact and officered, including the German NCO instructors. Dissent of the Medical Company spent the day and most of the following day trying to find something to eat and sleep.

'Charlemagne' would cover the seventy-two kilometres from Neustettin to Belgard in a little less than twenty-four hours. Through a snowstorm, the exhausted and frozen men withdrew first to the west and then turned to the north at Bad Polzin (Polczyn Zdrój). Most were on foot. So was Obf. Puaud, who had handed over his Kubelwagen to the wounded. Hstuf. de Perricot was on horseback. He went up and down the column like 'a good guard dog'. At the head of the division marched Hscha. Walter's 7/58 and at the rear Wagner's 5/58.

The men were loaded with munitions. Puaud was seen to shoulder for several kilometres a machine-gun or an ammunition box that was too heavy for an exhausted gunner. But bit by bit equipment was discarded along the way. Indeed, Waffen-Gren. Regt der SS 34 of the 15. Waffen-Grenadier-Division der SS (lettische Nr.1) was able to replenish its heavily depleted weapons with those discarded.[30] Since Neustettin the morale of many former *légionnaires* of the LVF had collapsed with the news of Doriot's death on 22 February 1945. 'It was the end of their dream'.[31]

Towards 1400 hours, in the vicinity of Bärwalde, the exhausted survivors were strafed and bombed by Soviet aircraft,[32] which dropped darts and glass grenades dating from the First

30   Arthur Silgailis, *Latvian Legion*, p.176.
31   Mabire, *La Division Charlemagne*, p.400.
32   The written interview with Raybaud and Soulat, letter to the author dated 9/11/97. According to Saint-Loup, *Les Hérétiques*, the column was attacked some time later after leaving Bad Polzin. Of course, the possibility exists that the column was attacked more than once which would explain this.

World War![33] Losses were light; the Russians attacked from the sides and not down the line of the column, and the road was well protected by trees.[34]

Having no real anti-aircraft weapons with them, the soldiers struck back with machine guns, sub-machine guns and rifles. Oscha. Ruskone's platoon of Wagner's 5/58 even managed to shoot down a low-flying aircraft, which had been met by a fusillade of machine-gun fire.[35]

Night fell. An hour's rest was granted at or near the town of Bad Polzin. Belgard was now thirty kilometres away. The men fell out and collapsed onto the frozen ground. There was no shelter. The icy wind got up. Puaud tried to raise their spirits, saying to each: "I led you into this but I'll lead you out again, be sure of that". Blanc of the 5/58 entered a house in Bad Polzin to ask for water. He drank at least a litre and also filled his bottle. He also recalls: 'Women handed us chocolate bars, which was at that time a remarkable show of friendship in Germany.' The hour was over all too soon. Wearily they picked themselves up, but some had to be kicked hard to be woken. Teeth clenched, they set off again and trudged on.

Puaud seemed everywhere. While trying to sort out a bad traffic jam he was heard to say: "Ah! If only I had gendarmes!"

None of the survivors would have cared if they had been told that their division was now under the higher formation of the 3rd Panzer Army whose headquarters was far away at Plathe (Płoty).[36]

The march continued all night. The column lengthened. Blanc of the 5/58 recalls:

> Towards three in the morning, Wagner ordered a halt, we collapsed in a farmyard beside the road. I still often have a thought for little Denamps who, [as] a perfect comrade, found the strength to collect the platoon's flasks, for to go and fill them and redistribute them, before stretching out himself.[37] He would be killed some days later… We set off again.

Dawn came up. Around 0600 hours, German motorised and armoured units overtook the retreating columns of 'Charlemagne'. The march continued.

Hours later,[38] the vanguard of the column received the order to halt and bivouac several kilometres south-east of Belgard.[39] Throughout the day more and more units joined those

---

33  Saint-Loup, *Les Hérétiques*, p.261.
34  Soulat, *Historique de la division Charlemagne*, p.47, repeated by Mabire, *La Division Charlemagne*, p.397, and Saint-Loup, *Les Hérétiques*, p.261. However, the written interview with Raybaud in *Charlemagne's Legionnaires*, p.102, is the only source to claim that losses were heavy.
35  This was witnessed by Daniel Le Goff of Company 5/58.
36  The attachment of 'Charlemagne' to the higher formation of the 3rd Panzer Army probably coincided with its simultaneous attachment to ad hoc *Korps Gruppe* [Corps Group] Tettau.
37  This is a reference to Jacques Denamps, who was of short statue.
38  According to the written interview with Raybaud in *Charlemagne's Legionnaires*, p.102, the tired soldiers were finally allowed to stop at approximately 1200 hours.
39  The exact location of this bivouac is not known. According to Saint-Loup, *Les Hérétiques*, p.263, it was in the forest locality of Springkrug. However, Springkrug is about one kilometre east of the main road from Bad Polzin to Belgard and across the Neustettin-Belgard railway line. Robert Blanc of Company 5/58 does not recall leaving the main road at the end of the march from Neustettin. Also of note is that Saint-Loup states that the officers continued on for some time and arrived at the small chateau of Boissin (see *Les Hérétiques*, p.263). This is contradictory because Boissin is some two kilometres

already there. Soldiers who still had tents pitched them. Completely numbed by the cold, all tried to keep warm and fight off the hunger gnawing them. They had few supplies with them. Blanc of Company 5/58 was directed to a barn where he fell asleep, remarking: 'If we did not have lice before, we certainly picked them up from there'. Completely exhausted, Ustuf. de Genouillac let himself fall into a ditch full of snow where he went to sleep.

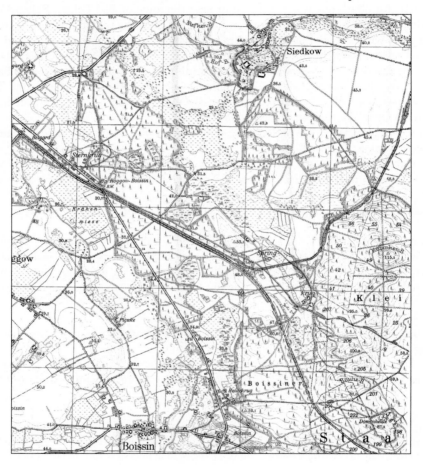

*Charlemagne* rested in this location on its way to Körlin.

south of Springkrug. There are three possible locations for the bivouac: the crossroads east of Ristow, which would enable the officers to continue on, the crossroads east of Boissin, and, lastly, the hamlet of Sternkrug (Moczylki), some four kilometres from Belgard. Blanc favours Sternkrug, the main reason being that when 'Charlemagne' left for Körlin it seemed to him that 'we only had three or four kilometres to cover before reaching Belgard' (letter to the author, 29/3/2002). *Trente Trois* numero 1 is convinced the location of the bivouac is Sternkrug and reasons 'all the veterans interviewed remember halting near a level crossing not far from Belgard'. However, Scherzer is convinced that the Division bivouacked in the woods north and northeast of Boissin called Klein-Dubberower Forst *(Sous le signe SS,* pp.333-334). One argument against this location is that it's devoid of a level crossing.

With great energy, the officers attempted to find their men and reform their commands once again. The German Inspection established itself in a small chateau in Boissin (Byszyno) nine kilometres south-east of Belgard.[40]

During the march from Neustettin to Belgard, horse-drawn Fahrschwadron A stopped three times. Uscha. Mercier of Fahrschwadron A recalls:[41]

> One of the stops was in a village where we received a visit from a Wehrmacht Lieutenant commanding a group of infantrymen in retreat. He gave us information on the Russians following him. As we had a panzerfäust at our disposal (and only one), he was so kind as to give us some advice on the efficient use of this weapon and did not linger more, being rather pressed. He wished us good luck.
>
> I recall another stop in a XVIII century chateau where the lady of the house and her butler welcomed us. *Capitaine* Schlisler, still very old-world, presented his men to this lady who put her hall at our disposal. When our *chef* protested that such luxury could only be suitable for the NCOs the butler made us realise that future customers would not have the same restraint.
>
> Another stop, probably the last, was in the house of a village burgomaster who was saddened at having his house requisitioned by several carts with houses and drivers, who spent a day waiting for orders that never came. His wife listened, incredulous, to the advice I gave her to make for the left bank of the Oder so as to be certain to see final victory. It was at this last stop that we received supplies, which I went and got.

Much to the surprise of all Brigf. Krukenberg soon joined the exhausted men at the bivouac. He had come from Flötenstein via Köslin.[42] It was at Köslin (Koszalin) near the coast that it had been planned to assemble and reform the scattered 'Charlemagne', but this had come to nothing as the Russians were already threatening the city. Nevertheless, some did make the journey to Köslin. One of those who did make the journey was Rttf. Soulat of the Headquarters Company, who left Neustettin on 28 February and arrived at Köslin that afternoon, but no sooner had he arrived than he was ordered by the German Feldgendarmerie of the Inspection to turn around the lorry and return to Belgard.[43] And yet, for several days, the situation maps of Army Group Vistula reported 'Charlemagne' in the vicinity of Köslin!

The very first volunteer that Brigf. Krukenberg came across at the bivouac was a Sturmmann of Bartolomei's Company who had bagged a doe, which he was carrying across his shoulders. Hunting, of course, was 'Verboten'. Krukenberg had him arrested and ordered him to be shot. The execution was carried out but a dummy was substituted. Once Krukenberg had gone the executed man miraculously rose from the dead and devoured the doe with his executioners!

---

40   The author originally stated that Puaud established his headquarters at Kowanz. It's more likely that Puaud also used Boissin chateau for his headquarters (see Scherzer, *Sous le signe SS*, p.334).

41   Mercier, letter to the author, 6/11/2001. However, Mercier is not sure of the location of the stops, although the last may have been before Belgard or Körlin.

42   Saint-Loup paints a rather dramatic picture of Krukenberg standing up in his car, surrounded by tank fire, as he slipped between the Russian spearheads (see *Les Hérétiques*, p.264). Undoubtedly this is apocryphal.

43   In addition to the German Feldgendarmerie of the Inspection, only some stragglers were present at Köslin.

## Reorganisation

Brigf. Krukenberg had come with the intention of completely reorganising 'Charlemagne'. For him, there was only one solution and that was to form the best elements of the division into a *Régiment de Marche* (RM) and all others into a *Régiment de Réserve* (RR).[44]

Because the situation was becoming more and more critical by the hour he ordered Stubaf. Raybaud to form the *Régiment de Marche* in three hours.[45] It took him ten hours.[46] In view of the circumstances, this was a remarkable achievement of which he remained rightly proud.

Two battalions were formed. Each battalion was made up of two grenadier companies and a support company.

The first battalion of the *Régiment de Marche*, abbreviated as the I/RM, comprised the best elements of Waffen-Gren. Regt der SS 57 and its command went to the battle-proven Ostuf. Henri Fenet. The order of battle of the I/RM was as follows:

| | |
|---|---|
| Commander: | W-Ostuf. Fenet |
| *Adjoint* (Assistant): | W-Std.Ob.Ju. Labourdette |
| 1st Company: | W-Ostuf. Roumegous |
| 2nd Company: | W-Oscha. Hennecart |
| 4th Company: | W-Oscha. Couvreur |

Both Oscha. Hennecart and Oscha. Couvreur were veterans of the Sturmbrigade who had fought in Galicia. Ostuf. Roumegous was a former *Milicien* who would never completely assimilate himself into the ways of the former Sturmbrigade perpetuated by this battalion.

Because the second battalion of the *Régiment de Marche*, the II/RM, was mainly made up of former Legionnaires of the LVF or young *Miliciens* of Waffen-Gren. Regt der SS 58, Stubaf. Raybaud picked Hstuf. Bassompierre as its commander. He was the perfect choice, having fought with both the LVF and the *Milice*, although he did not find favour with Krukenberg because of his 'Maurrasian nationalism and lack of SS spirit'.[47]

The order of battle of the II/RM was as follows:

---

44    Scherzer argues in his book that when 'Charlemagne' was reorganised the two regiments would and should have been designated SS-Divisionsgruppe 33 and Reserve-Regiment SS-Division Charlemagne rather than *Régiment de Marche* and *Régiment de Réserve* which are exclusively French military terms. Furthermore, he argues that the two battalions formed for SS-Divisionsgruppe 33 would and should have been designated SS-Regimentsgruppe 57 and SS-Regimentsgruppe 58. (See *Sous le Signe SS*, pp.336-337.) In response, no veteran of 'Charlemagne' recalls the use of such designations. In fact, RM and RR were widely used.

45    According to Mabire, *La Division Charlemagne*, pp.405-406, Stubaf. Raybaud protested that such a task would normally require at least forty-eight hours to carry out. Conceding the point, Brigf. Krukenberg granted him ten hours and not one more! However, no other source confirms such a conversation. Also, Raybaud wrote, letter to Bayle dated 22/2/92, that Mabire's account, reporting a criticism from Krukenberg, is 'simply imaginary'.

46    Soulat, *Historique de la Division Charlemagne*, p.47.

47    Saint-Loup, *Les Hérétiques*, p.267.

| Commander: | W-Hstuf. Bassompierre |
| *Adjoint* (Assistant): | W-Ostuf. Wagner[48] |
| 1st Company: | W-Hscha. Walter |
| 2nd Company: | W-Ustuf. Rigeade |
| 4th Company: | W-Ostuf. Français |

Wagner and the three company commanders were capable former Legionnaires. Ustuf. Rigeade was satisfied to see himself and his whole company incorporated into the *Régiment de Marche*.

The platoon of Company 5/58 trained by Walter was now attached to his command, the 1st Company of the II/RM.[49] There can be little doubt as to the reason for this. Moreover, the platoon was still in good shape and well-armed. The platoon commander was still Oscha. Blaise.

At this point, the *Régiment de Marche* totalled around 1,200 men. Its units were equipped with the division's last heavy weapons and panzerfäust. To the command of the *Régiment de Réserve* Brigf. Krukenberg appointed Hstuf. de Bourmont. To perpetuate the spirit of the Waffen SS, Hstuf. de Bourmont choose former Sturmbrigade veteran Hstuf. Pleyber as his assistant. His Orderly Officer remained Ustuf. Martres.

As though a mirror image of the *Régiment de Marche*, the *Régiment de Réserve* was made up of two battalions[50] of four companies each.[51] Its first battalion, abbreviated as the I/RR, was built around former members of Waffen-Gren. Regt der SS 57 whereas its second battalion, the II/RR, around those of Waffen-Gren. Regt der SS 58.

Hstuf. Moneuse, a former *Milicien*, was appointed the commander of the I/RR. The order of battle of the I/RR was as follows:

| Commander: | W-Hstuf. Moneuse |
| *Adjoint* (Assistant): | ? |
| Orderly Officer: | W-Oberjunker Méric[52] |
| 1st Company: | W-Ustuf. Erdozain |

48    Bouysse suggests that Wagner commanded the 3rd Company of the II/RM (see Partie III).
49    Blanc, conversation with the author. However, Jean Priot, also of the same platoon of the 5/58, recalls somewhat differently that Walter asked for volunteers and almost the whole platoon came forward.
50    Soulat, *Historique de la Division Charlemagne*, pp.47-48, and Mabire, *La Division Charlemagne*, p.409. However, de la Mazière, *Ashes of Honour*, p.115, and the written interview with Raybaud in *Charlemagne's Legionnaires*, p.102, depict de Bourmont's command as a battalion. The author believes this to be incorrect, although the regiment's strength may have only been that of battalion.
51    According to Mabire, *La Division Charlemagne*, p.409, the two battalions consisted of four grenadier (infantry) companies each. Traditionally, each abteilung (battalion) within an Infantry Regiment had three infantry companies and one 'heavy' company (or machine-gun company) which was numbered the fourth. This, of course, does not prove that each battalion of the RR had a heavy company, but the appointment of Hscha. Terrel to the fourth company of Battalion I/RR, theoretically the heavy company, could suggest that his past skills as a platoon commander in heavy company 8/57 were still very much in demand. Nevertheless, his new command may not have been equipped with the necessary weaponry to fulfil its role as a heavy company and was thus a heavy company in name only. Also, in correspondence to the author, de Genouillac believes that Ostuf. Devefer and his 8/58 became the heavy company of the II/RR. Again the possibility exists that the heavy company was in name only.
52    Most sources record Ustuf. Brazier as the Orderly Officer of the I/RR. The possibility exists that there were two Orderly Officers.

| | |
|---|---|
| 2nd Company: | W-Ostuf. Bartolomei |
| 3rd Company: | W-Ustuf. Hug |
| 4th Company: | W-Hscha. Terrel |

At the request of Hstuf. Moneuse, Oberjunker Méric was appointed his Orderly Officer. Told of this posting, Méric felt a sense of great pride, but it was tinged with sadness at having to part from his men who had been dispersed during the reorganisation. Moneuse warmly welcomed him. They already knew of each other and Méric held Moneuse in great esteem. Moneuse told him that he had been proposed for a decoration and congratulated him on it. Méric quickly adapted to the demands of his new charge. Hstuf. Berret, a former Legionnaire, took the head of the II/RR. Its four company commanders still remain unclear.[53]

During the reorganisation, about three hundred men may have been evacuated to Kolberg.[54] Mercier of Fahrschwadron A witnessed one soldier, whose unit was unknown to him, feign sickness in the hope of evacuation. The doctor who examined the soldier sent him packing with an almighty kick.[55] Oscha. Ruskone of Company 5/58, who was still in a great deal of pain following the accident at Neustettin, was evacuated to Kolberg.

This reorganisation took place throughout the day of 1 March 1945 (and may have only concluded in the morning hours of the following day). By now, 'Charlemagne' was attached to ad hoc Korps Gruppe [Corps Group] Tettau, named after its commander General Hans von Tettau. As of 1 March 1945, the Corps Group consisted of Wehrmacht divisions 'Pommernland'[56] and 'Bärwalde', the remnants of 15. Waffen Gren.-Division der SS (lettische Nr. 1), and lastly a kampfgruppe of 'Charlemagne'.[57]

On the evening of 1 March 1945, the Medical Company relocated from Belgard to the village of Kowanz (Kowańcz) some two kilometres due west of Körlin. The men were quartered in a cattle farm. Dissent of the Medical Company recalls how the animals suffered terribly because they were in need of milking. His company would spend two days at Kowanz. German and

53   According to de Genouillac, correspondence to the author throughout 1997, the intact II/58 was transferred en bloc to the *Régiment de Réserve* and constituted the II/RR. Nevertheless, although he cannot substantiate that the four companies of the II/58 did end up in the II/RR, to this day, 'no doubt has crossed his mind on this subject'. If true, then Walter and his company, that of the 7/58, were not transferred to the II/RM.

54   According to Saint-Loup, *Les Hérétiques*, p.266, during the reorganisation, Obf. Puaud proposed that those who wished to give up the fight would be evacuated, along with the wounded, to Kolberg. About three hundred, described as sick or malingerers, took up his offer. In this way, Obf. Puaud, whom Saint-Loup describes as 'a poor strategist but an exceptional leader of men', won a risky gamble whose repercussions could have been more serious. In response to this, Puaud's proposal is not confirmed by any other source. However, during the march of 'Charlemagne' from Neustettin to Belgard, de la Mazière makes mention of the selfsame number of 'disabled', sick and those of broken morale who would have to be evacuated (*Ashes of Honour*, p.113).

55   Mercier, letter to the author, 6/11/2001.

56   *Russo-German War, 25 January to 8 May 1945*, p.35. This division can also be found with the title of 'Pommern' (see, for example, Lindenblatt, *Pommern-1945*).

57   Ibid. Curiously, 33SS 'Charlemagne' is also shown to the rear of the 3rd Panzer Army/11th SS Panzer Army.

French SS troops left Kowanz on the morning of 4 March.[58] Kowanz was occupied by the Russians later that day.[59]

On 2 March 1945, towards 1800 hours, the German Inspection and divisional headquarters relocated to a Schloß in Kerstin, a village some four to five kilometres north-west of Körlin.[60]

Around that same time, the Division received orders from 'headquarters'[61] to move immediately to the town of Körlin (Karlino).[62] Its mission was to fortify the town and to contain the Soviet offensive as best it could, and thereby protected the retreat of the German forces towards Kolberg.[63] Some still saw and voiced the division's mission as sacrificial and by all accounts that included Krukenberg himself.[64]

## Körlin

The market town of Körlin was of great strategic importance and something of a natural strongpoint. Situated eight kilometres north-west of Belgard, Körlin commands the road to Kolberg and also the highway from Köslin to Stettin (Szczecin). Körlin is virtually enclosed by the river Persante (Parseta) that flows into the Baltic Sea, and by its tributary the Radüe (Radew). Thus, access into the town was only by way of several bridges.

Throughout the night of 2-3 March, the French SS companies set off on foot to Körlin. The night led to a certain amount of confusion, which delayed their arrival. The RM was to be centred on Körlin while the RR was to guard the crossing points over the river Persante that winds serpent-like north-west of Körlin.

When elements of the RM entered Körlin they found the town empty.[65] Thereupon, the companies were sent onto their designated positions. The staff of the *Régiment de Marche* entered the town with the rearguard. Stubaf. Raybaud was most disturbed by the apathy shown by his officers, and, to improve their efficiency, he dismissed his Chief-of-Staff[66] and replaced him with Hstuf. de Perricot. By the side of de Perricot as an interpreter was Rttf. Sepchat.

58   BArch OSTDOK, 1/155, fol. 199. Also see Lindenblatt, *Pommern-1945*, p.217.
59   BArch OSTDOK, 1/155, fol. 195.
60   Lefèvre, *Axe & Alliés* no 1, p.63, and Soulat, *Historque de la Division Charlemagne*, p.53. At some point divisional headquarters was located at Kowanz (Soulat, letter to the author, 9/11/97), but the author does not know when exactly.
61   Soulat, *Historque de la Division Charlemagne*, p.48. Unfortunately no specific headquarters is detailed.
62   Ibid. However, according to Mabire, *La Division Charlemagne*, p.411, the date of this order was 1 March 1945.
63   Ibid. However, according to Saint-Loup, *Les Hérétiques*, p.265, Brigf. Krukenberg came to Obf. Puaud's headquarters armed with similar orders: headquarters had asked him to hold Körlin for a period of twenty-four hours to 'facilitate' the withdrawal of the 32. Infanterie-Division. Responding, Puaud protested that the men were exhausted. But late on 2 March when the time came to reorganise the division and 'sell' its new mission, Puaud announced to the survivors that he had spoken to the Führer in person and, in their name, had promised him that Körlin would be defended. In response to this, while some parts may well be true, the part about Puaud speaking to the Führer is, undoubtedly, apocryphal.
64   Mabire, *La Division Charlemagne*, p.411.
65   Jean Sepchat, correspondence to the author. However, according to de la Mazière, *Ashes of Honour*, p.116, the RM found Körlin almost empty except for the main street, which was crowded with refugees.
66   The written interview with Raybaud, *Charlemagne's Legionnaires*, p.104. Presumably Raybaud was referring to his *adjoint* Ostuf. Baudouin.

Once at their positions, the Frenchmen quickly dug combat emplacements, sited machine guns and erected anti-tank barriers. German sappers mined the bridges.[67] By dawn, the *Régiment de Marche* was in position; Fenet's I/RM had been deployed to the south-east, straddling the main road from Belgard, and Bassompierre's II/RM to the north-east, straddling the road from Köslin. Regimental commander Stubaf. Raybaud, appointed Kampfkommandant [battle commandant] of Körlin, had established his headquarters in a house on the main square. At 0800 hours, the order was issued to evacuate the civilian population.

'German stragglers were stopped, interrogated, and if possible, made use of'.[68] In this way, a Tiger tank that turned up at Körlin was also pressed into its defence. The morale of the tank crew was at a low ebb, but discipline remained. This was in contrast to a Wehrmacht Infantry company Stubaf. Raybaud also had at his disposal. Its morale was poor.

Hungry, Rttf. Sepchat entered a grocery that was still open. Yes, it was stocked. And yet, because he had no coupons, the shopkeeper would not sell him anything! The shopkeeper was blissfully unaware of the tragedy of the situation.

Hstuf. de Bourmont established the headquarters of the RR in the village of Klaptow (Kłopotowo), some ten kilometres north-east of Körlin. To carry out his orders of securing the crossing points from Körlin to Gross Jestin over the river Persante, he was again forced to disperse widely his command. In this way, the two battalions of the RR had to hold a front that was twenty-two kilometres long.[69]

Battalion I/RR was deployed at crossing points over the Persante in the triangle of villages Bartin (Bardy), Mechentin (Miechecino) and Peterfitz (Piotrowice). Its 2nd Company, commanded by Ostuf. Bartolomei, held Peterfitz ten kilometres north-west of Körlin. One small consolation for the widely dispersed *Régiment de Réserve* was the Persante itself; normally a small and unimpressive river, it was swollen by a thaw.

The headquarters of the II/RR was set up in a farm. An old man came to welcome the headquarters staff. He was flabbergasted to see the French badge on their sleeves and told them

67    According to Landwehr, *Charlemagne's Legionnaires*, p.81 and p.104, the defences of both Körlin and Belgard had been laid out somewhat in advance by Staf. Zimmermann and an ad hoc construction battalion made up of French SS volunteers from various dispersed units. In response to this, there was no such ad hoc construction battalion and the division did not prepare Körlin or Belgard in advance for defence. To begin with, no other source makes reference to this advanced preparation of Körlin and Belgard for defence or to the existence of an ad hoc construction battalion. [Moreover, Soulat has confirmed, letter to the author, that there was no such ad hoc construction battalion and that no defensive positions were prepared in advance at Körlin or at Belgard.] Secondly, it was planned to reorganise 'Charlemagne' at the city of Köslin, some thirty kilometres north-east of Belgard, and this had only been dropped at the last moment. Thus there would have been very little reason for 'Charlemagne' to prepare Körlin or Belgard for defence. Thirdly, the first elements of 'Charlemagne' arrived in the town of Körlin hours after the receipt of orders to move there. Consequently, this would have allowed little or no time to prepare its defence in advance, yet alone mobilise an ad hoc construction battalion. Lastly, after the fighting south-east of Hammerstein, Staf. Zimmermann was ordered to Greifenberg to mobilise a *Bataillon de Marche*. He probably rejoined the division at Körlin with the *Bataillon de Marche*, which arrived on 3 March. And even if he did rejoin the division earlier than 3 March he would have had very little time to do anything.
68    De la Mazière, *Ashes of Honour*, p.116.
69    By now, according to Mabire, *La Division Charlemagne*, p.417, the RR was ten companies strong. This has to be a mistake.

that he could never have imagined such a scenario when he was at Verdun. He was surprised to learn from them that they were preparing for an imminent Russian attack.

The remaining 75mm guns of Roy's 9/57 were also located to Kerstin[70] and then moved to Körlin.[71] Establishing his headquarters in the house of the level crossing keeper, Roy slept on the first floor. A renowned womaniser, he soon seduced the widow of the level crossing keeper, but 'remained more reserved as regards the daughter'.[72]

## Feldersatz-Bataillon

On 3 March, 'Charlemagne' was joined at Körlin by a Feldersatz-Bataillon [Field Replacement Battalion] or *Bataillon de Marche* activated days earlier at Greifenberg. On 26 February, at Flötenstein, to fill the depleted ranks of 'Charlemagne' after the 'battle of Hammerstein', Brigf. Krukenberg ordered Staf. Zimmermann to travel to Greifenberg, where, from the ranks of the Franz. SS-Gren. A.u.E. Btl., he was to mobilise and organise the departure of a Feldersatz-Bataillon. Ustuf. Patzak, Krukenberg's Orderly Officer, went with him. The two of them managed to make it to Greifenberg whereupon they feverishly mobilised a Feldersatz-Bataillon of some five hundred men organised into three grenadier companies and an engineer platoon. The order of battle of the Feldersatz-Bataillon was as follows:

| | |
|---|---|
| Commander: | W-Hstuf. Bisiau[73] |
| Assistant: | SS-Ostuf. Ludwig |
| 1. Kompanie: | W-Ustuf. Pignard-Berthet |
| 2. Kompanie: | W-Hstuf. Flamand |
| 3. Kompanie: | W-Ostuf. de Bregeot |
| Pionierzug: | SS-? |

Bisiau and Flamand had both entered 'Charlemagne' via the LVF. Bisiau became the all-important *Regiments-Adjudant* of its III. Bataillon in March 1944. Flamand was in his forties and a veteran of the Great War. Ustuf. Pignard-Berthet had served with the Sturmbrigade. His company was that trained by Ostuf. Michel whose command he had received three days before the departure of the Feldersatz-Bataillon from Greifenberg. Pignard-Berthet recalls two

---

70  This is a conclusion drawn by the author from the relevant sections of the article *Mein Freund Georges*.
71  According to the article *Mein Freund Georges*, the 9/57 moved to Belgard and dug in. However, the author is convinced that the 9/57 moved to Körlin. To explain: throughout 4 March 1945, the Wehrmacht forces holding Belgard were engaged in heavy defensive fighting, but in the end could not prevent the Russians from taking the city later that night. Curiously, the article *Mein Freund Georges* makes no mention of the company being drawn into this fierce fighting either on that date or on any other. Also, the same article alleges that while the 9/57 was at Belgard Staf. Zimmermann went about distributing the contents of a tobacco shop to his grenadiers. Regarding this, neither Staf. Zimmermann or elements of 'Charlemagne' were at Belgard at a time when the Russians were 'close', as stated by the article. Arguably, Zimmermann 'played the supply officer' at Körlin.
72  Article *Mein Freund Georges*.
73  Curiously, the texts of Bayle and Mabire record Hstuf. Rémy as the commander of the Feldersatz-Bataillon and yet their respective command rosters record Hstuf. Bisiau. In fact, it was Hstuf. Bisiau who was the commander.

of his platoon commanders: Oscha. Breuvart and Uscha. Jacquet. He knew Jacquet from his Sturmbrigade days. Then Jacquet had commanded the 2nd Section of his 1st Platoon in the 1st Company. The two of them had been wounded on the first day of combat in Galicia. Ostuf. Maurice de Bregeot was a former tank *Capitaine de réserve* and, of late, a prisoner of war in Stalag III/B in Fürstenberg.[74] His company was that trained by Ostuf. Ludwig. A German officer commanded the Engineer Platoon, but his name is not known.[75]

The Feldersatz-Bataillon left Greifenberg by train on 27 February[76] and travelled through Treptow (Trzebiatów) and Kolberg.[77] While stopped at Gross Jestin (Goscino) railway station a French POW volunteered his services and was warmly welcomed aboard. Close to Körlin, the Feldersatz-Bataillon disembarked and continued on foot, arriving in the evening of 3 March.

Pignard-Berthet's Company was sent straight to divisional headquarters. Deprived of the *Compagnie d'Honneur* since the battle at Elsenau, Brigf. Krukenberg was in need of a new 'guard'. The company was divided into two.

On Krukenberg's orders, the Feldersatz-Bataillon was broken up and shared out.[78] Ostuf. Ludwig, the German liaison officer to the Feldersatz-Bataillon, went across to Krukenberg's headquarters staff. Hstuf. Flamand's 2nd Company was placed at the disposal of Bassompierre's II/RM and Ostuf. de Bregeot's 3rd Company at Fenet's I/RM. Following the arrival of the Feldersatz-Bataillon, 'Charlemagne' numbered some three thousand five hundred men, perhaps as many as four thousand men.

Hstuf. Durandy and his secretary Oberjunker Marchèse joined 'Charlemagne' at Körlin.[79] They had been in Berlin to procure and arrange the transportation of medical supplies, but thought their place was with their comrades at the front.

As the day wore on liaison had become an increasing problem for both regiments. Telephone lines were being constantly cut by saboteurs and since radios were not always available couriers had to be employed and relied upon. Concerned, Ostuf. Fenet complained to his regimental commander, Stubaf. Raybaud, that he could no longer command his battalion because he had been forced by orders to disperse it over too wide an area. As a result, having no means of communication, some of his platoons had now become isolated. Overruling Krukenberg's orders, Raybaud authorised him to tighten his disposition. Fenet established his command post

74    Maurice de Bregeot was born on 21 May 1900 in Pouliguen (department Loire-Inférieure).

75    SS-Ustuf. Hegewald may have commanded the Engineer Platoon at Körlin.

76    Saint-Loup, *Les Hérétiques*, p.253. However, Scherzer dates the departure of the battalion from Greifenberg to 2 March 1945 but adds the caveat 'probably' (*Sous le Signe SS*, p.340).

77    Saint-Loup, *Les Hérétiques*, p.253. However, according to Mabire, *La Division Charlemagne*, p.413, the *Bataillon de Marche* came up from the depot of Greifenberg by forced march. This is incorrect (letter to the author from Pignard-Berthet).

78    It is not known to which command Hstuf. Bisiau was transferred. Also of note is that, according to Mabire, *La Division Charlemagne*, p.413, when Brigf. Krukenberg broke up the Feldersatz-Bataillon he put Hstuf. Rémy at the disposal of Obf. Puaud because he doubted Rémy's capability, which stemmed undoubtedly from Rémy's aborted mission to Greifenberg.

79    Born on 27 January 1918 in Monaco, Philippe Marchèse was a former *Milicien*, attending Uriage in June 1943 and went on to serve as the *secrétaire régional de la Milice* at Marseille. According to Bouysse, *Français sous l'uniforme allemand partie II*, Marchèse held the rank of Scharführer. Pierre Méric, who knew him well, states that Marchèse had the same rank as him, that of Oberjunker.

in the village of Redlin and then, as a priority, gave himself over to maintaining contact with his companies and his platoons.[80]

Meanwhile, over the last few days, the military situation in Pomerania had quickly deteriorated and it must have been with great anxiety that 'Charlemagne' headquarters had viewed the developments.

On 1 March, the Russians crossed the road and railroad east of Köslin, cutting the German 2nd Army's last land communications with the rest of the Reich. That same day, Zhukov launched an offensive into Western Pomerania. His 1st White Russian Front ripped open the German front at Reetz (Recz) and the 1st Guards Tank Army raced due north towards Kolberg. The Russian momentum could not be halted.

On the following day, the Russians struck the German forces of the X. SS Corps and adjacent Corps Group Tettau to the east of the breakthrough. The Russians continued to press forward on 3 March. It would be no exaggeration to say that the situation map at the headquarters of Army Group Vistula looked terrible. There were breakthroughs everywhere. Henceforth, 'Charlemagne', positioned in and around Körlin, could expect the Russians from the north-east, as well as from the south-east!

On the morning of 3 March, the Soviets reached Gut Schwartow and the village of Garchen (Garnki).[81] At 14:30 hours, they were in front of Kowanz, which was only three and a half kilometres from Kerstin, where Charlemagne divisional headquarters was located. Around 1800 hours, divisional headquarters was informed of a strong concentration of Russian mechanised and motor forces in the region of Stolzenberg (Slawoborze) only twenty kilometres south-west of Körlin. Two hours later, a Soviet armoured column of ninety tanks and two motorised regiments was reported on the move northwards from Stolzenberg in the direction of Kolberg. This spelt danger; if the Russians could not be halted then 'Charlemagne' would soon find itself in the grip of the Soviet pincers.

## Gross Jestin

With each passing hour of the night 3-4 March 1945 the fate of 'Charlemagne' was sealed tighter and tighter. Shortly after 0200 hours on 4 March 1945, Soviet tanks of the 45th Guards Tank Brigade crashed into the village of Gross Jestin (Goscino), fifteen kilometres west of Körlin. Stationed there were various rear and support elements of 'Charlemagne' under the overall command of Stubaf. Katzian. These elements comprised the *automobile train* with its last motor vehicles, divisional service units including the Feldpost, the Headquarters Company and the Engineer Platoon of the Feldersatz-Bataillon that had arrived from Greifenberg.

The Soviet armoured column swept through Gross Jestin, easily overrunning the French units and, after pausing outside the village, continued on its way to Kolberg, only fifteen kilometres away. Even though the Soviets were literally in and out of Gross Jestin like a shot, leaving a trail

---

80  Mistakenly, Mabire records that Fenet established his command post in the small village of Denzin, which is several kilometres due south of Belgard (see *La Division Charlemagne*, p.419).

81  Scherzer, *Sous le Signe SS*, p.349. According to a local civilian, '4 Frenchmen and 2 Wachleute [watchmen] were dragged along by the Russians and shot' and buried by a local farmer, see BArch OSTDOK 1/155, fol. 131. Although there is no mention of the Frenchmen being soldiers or SS, there's a strong possibility that they were.

of death and destruction in their wake, many Frenchmen were captured. Ostuf. Bénétoux, in charge of headquarters Department II A/B (Personnel), was actually taken prisoner by Polish partisans and then handed over to a Soviet officer. After a brief interrogation, Bénétoux was placed in charge of a convoy of captured Frenchmen which was made up of French Waffen-SS volunteers of 'Charlemagne', as well as French 1939-1940 POWs and French STO labour conscripts! However, the Frenchmen in civilian clothes and khaki uniforms were furious at being associated with their compatriots in field-grey. Not wishing to remain a prisoner, Bénétoux slipped away and miraculously managed to make it through to German lines two days later.

Soviet infantry did not immediately follow up the armour to secure the village. This at least gave the many Frenchmen left in the village a chance to get out of there and make it to safety. Hurriedly the last trucks were loaded. A motor column, carrying some two hundred men, left Gross Jestin sometime after 0200 hours and made for Treptow. Bringing up the rear in a Kübelwagen was Ostuf. Meier, in charge of headquarters Department I/B (equipment). His fellow passengers sprayed the roads of Gross Jestin behind them so as to keep down the heads of possible Polish partisans or Russians disguised in civilian clothing.

At 0500 hours on 4 March 1945, the Russians reached the south-west suburb of Kolberg. Short of fuel, ammunition and above all infantry support, the Red armour stopped. By now, 'Charlemagne' had been turned and was in mortal danger.

### Encirclement and the first attack

Meantime, during the night of 3-4 March, the command of the II/RR changed hands. A French POW employed on the farm used by the II/RR as headquarters came and informed the French SS officers present that a *pauvre monsieur* was lying on the front steps. The *pauve monsieur* proved to be none other than battalion commander Hstuf. Berret, who had just returned from a reconnaissance on horseback along the Persante.

At first, many, including Ustuf. de Genouillac, thought Berret had been assassinated, but he carried no visible sign of an injury. A doctor examined him and had him evacuated on account of exhaustion. Informed, Hstuf. de Bourmont appointed Ustuf. de Genouillac the battalion commander of the II/RR. Obf. Puaud confirmed this appointment on the following day.[82]

The night of 3-4 March 1945 also saw Brigf. Krukenberg alert Obf. Puaud's headquarters. Henceforth, their headquarters at Kerstin, north-west of Körlin, could be taken any moment by Soviet tanks which had smashed through Gross Jestin. Puaud decided to up and move to the centre of Körlin, which was quickly followed by a move to Schloß Fritzow (Wrzosowo), some

---

82  Correspondence with de Genouillac throughout 1997. This corrects Soulat, *La Historique de la Division Charlemagne*, p.54, repeated by Mabire and Saint-Loup, that Ostuf. Defever, the former commander of Heavy Company 8/58 succeeded Berret. But there is also Rostaing's account of Berret's evacuation to consider. Called to the chateau of the German Inspection, Rostaing was met by Stubaf. Katzian of the German Inspection who told him that Berret had been found on the steps unconscious with a wound to the head. However, Rostaing did not get to speak to Berret before the latter was hurriedly evacuated from the spot to the rear. Thus, he was not to know that what he had been told was, in fact, incorrect. Curiously, according to Rostaing, Ostuf. Leune, who up to then 'had been commanding the heavy company', succeeded Berret. In response to this, Leune did not succeed Berret and nor was he the heavy company commander.

ten kilometres north of Körlin.[83] In the meantime, Krukenberg may have decided to remain at Kerstin,[84] but eventually he too abandoned Kerstin and moved to Schloß Fritzow.[85]

Taking stock of the deteriorating military situation, Krukenberg decided to draw 'Charlemagne' tighter around Körlin which would become the centre of resistance. Orders were sent out to this effect.

Ustuf. Martres visited Fritzow and recalls on the walls lists of companies with their commanders and men. He was principally employed on liaison duties. On his travels he met Fayard who had one or two guns with him.

Back at Körlin, in the early morning, Rttf. Gonzales, now of the *Régiment de marche*, was awoken by the cannonade which was getting closer and closer. He joined Hstuf. Bassompierre at his command post, a great building in the centre of town, which was probably that of the mayor. Bassompierre was in the company of Stubaf. de Vaugelas. Both were leant over a military map of the area. Bassompierre was very happy to see his former orderly from his LVF days; they had not seen each other for over a year.

Gonzales asked 'his *Capitaine*' if he could use the small amphibious car parked outside in the road. The keys were immediately handed over to him. He would spend the whole day driving around. He soon realised that the bulk of the Russian forces were bypassing the city.

Around mid-morning on 4 March, a most extraordinary incident happened at Körlin. A Leutnant of the Wehrmacht Company assembled his platoon. He put it to his men that they had nothing in common with 'these strangers' [the Frenchmen] who wanted to fight it out at Körlin and proposed that they should withdraw to Kolberg. One NCO protested and this carried the others. They remained.[86]

Around midday, Stubaf. Raybaud made his way towards the bridge over the Persante to the west of Körlin. He intended to remind the German engineers charged with its destruction not to proceed without a formal order from him; this bridge was necessary for the withdrawal of the division's outposts of around company strength on the other side of the river, and also for the imminent entry into Körlin of the promised reinforcements of German armour.

When Stubaf. Raybaud arrived at the bridge the only enemy activity he noted was heavy small-arms fire against a building surmounted by a bell-turret some eighty to one hundred metres to his left. With the naked eye no enemy tanks were visible on the horizon. Besides, the outposts had not given the alarm. However, with binoculars, he spotted about one kilometre away a tank under cover but could not make out if it was Russian or German. Suddenly, at that

83    Soulat, *La Historique de la Division Charlemagne*, p.54. Scherzer makes no mention of Puaud relocating to Körlin before moving onto to Fritzow Schloß (*Sous le Signe SS*, p.350). Also, according to Saint-Loup, Puaud and his headquarters staff were still at Kerstin when dawn broke on 4 March (*Les Hérétiques*, p.285).

84    See Mabire, *La Division Charlemagne*, p.422.

85    Mabire, *La Division Charlemagne*, p.432.

86    The conduct of the Heer Leutnant was reported to the SS Führungshauptamt. At the beginning of April 1945, RF-SS Himmler punished the Leutnant when he stripped him of his rank and posted him as a simple grenadier to 'Charlemagne' at Carpin. See Saint-Loup, *Les Hérétiques*, p.290. No other source confirms this incident, though.

same moment, a shell exploded near him and he crumpled to the ground, badly wounded. His right knee was crushed and his left tibia fractured in two places.[87]

Hstuf. de Perricot rushed over to Stubaf. Raybaud. Although in great pain, Raybaud ordered that the command of the *Régiment de Marche* be passed to Hstuf. Bassompierre. While awaiting the arrival of Bassompierre, de Perricot took command temporarily.[88]

Because there was little that could be done for Stubaf. Raybaud, Hstuf. Dr. Durandy decided to have him evacuated.[89] That night, Oberjunker Platon drove Raybaud to Kolberg.[90] Days later, Raybaud was evacuated by boat.[91]

The explosion that seriously wounded Raybaud killed de Perricot's driver and also wounded Oscha. Marcel Savone of the divisional Engineer Company.[92] Hit in the leg by shrapnel, he too was evacuated to Kolberg.

Soon after the wounding of Stubaf. Raybaud, around 1230 hours, the Soviets launched an attack on Körlin from the south-west with a force estimated at twenty-five tanks and two companies of infantry.[93] The Persante Brücke [bridge] was blown. Rttf. Sepchat recalled:

> When the German officer told him that the bridge over the river at the far end of the fairground was to be blown, Hstuf. de Perriot turned towards me: "Tell him that I will blow his brains out if one single man is left on the other bank when the bridge is blown." I could not bring myself to translate it all and contented myself with pointing out that nobody should be on the other bank when the bridge is blown. The Heer Oberleutnant replied to me by quoting the maxim: "Difficulties are made to be overcome." The strength of a company crossed the bridge at the double. There were no latecomers. The bridge was blown. Very proud of the result, the Heer Oberleutnant could not stop himself (from) proclaiming: "Pionierarbeit!" [Engineer's work].[94]

87   Raybaud's memoirs written in 1946, supplemented by additional material from Soulat, *Historique de la Division Charlemagne*, p.54. This corrects the accounts by Saint-Loup and Mabire of Raybaud's wounding. Also it's not known whether tank or artillery fire actually wounded Raybaud.

88   Incorrectly, the written interview with Raybaud in *Charlemagne's Legionnaires*, p.104, states that Hstuf. de Perricot now took command of the *Régiment de Marche*. Rttf. Sepchat heard Raybaud hand over command to Bassompierre.

89   Soulat, *Historique de la Division Charlemagne*, p.54. However, according to Saint-Loup, *Les Hérétiques*, p.291, Stubaf. Raybaud was evacuated to the medical post north of Körlin where Dr. Métais gave him the best medical attention he could.

90   Yves Peyret recorded in his *Journal de marche*: 'Towards midnight, I meet *commandant* Raybaud who is being taken to Kolberg by *aspirant* Platon. He is seriously wounded'. Peyret was at Klaptow. This corrects Mabire, *La Division Charlemagne*, p.435, and Saint-Loup, *Les Hérétiques*, p.291, who both record that Raybaud was evacuated by ambulance soon after his wounding.

91   The *souvenirs* of René M. (as told to Mounine). Indeed, it could be said that Raybaud saved the life of René M.; recognising René M. among the wounded, Raybaud had him evacuated from the encircled port along with him.

92   Marcel Savone was born on 24 June 1922 in Cannes.

93   Saint-Loup, *Les Hérétiques*, p.290, Mabire, *La Division Charlemagne*, p.433 and Lefèvre, *Axe & Alliés* no 1, p.63. However, Rttf. Jean Sepchat, who was still at the disposal of Hstuf. de Perricot, does not recall any such attack from the south-west (letter to the author). Indeed, while at Körlin, he saw only one single Russian tank and that approached from Belgard. A German tank destroyed it.

94   The bridge was initially identified as that over the Radüe. However, this bridge was not blown. See Scherzer, *Sous le Signe*, p.397. The author now assumes that Sepchat was referring to the bridge over

Hstuf. de Perricot was lightly wounded in the head by a piece of stone from the explosion. A Tiger tank immobilised through lack of petrol set ablaze three or four Russian tanks within a short period.[95] This brought the attack to a halt, albeit momentarily. The Soviet armour then responded by laying down intensive fire on the southern sector of Körlin that prevented any movement in the roads or across the road bridge to Belgard, the Radüe-Brücke (or Belgarder Brücke).

To shore up the defences to the west of Körlin, Brigf. Krukenberg fed in Flamand's Company and de Bregeot's Company which had both arrived with the Feldersatz-Bataillon from Greifenberg and been assigned as reinforcements to the two battalions of the RM.[96]

Then, around 1430 hours, several platoons of Russian infantry managed to get across the Persante and gain a foothold on the right bank. This spelt great danger for the defenders of Körlin; not only were the Russians now in the rear of Fenet's I/RM around the village of Redlin, but also behind the south-east defences of the town.[97]

Galvanised into action, Fenet immediately improvised a counterattack with Hennecart's Company and all the stragglers he could round up.[98] The counterattack hit the Russian infantry in the flank and threw them back, despite their supporting fire. In this way, for the present, the danger had been averted. The counterattack also permitted the withdrawal behind the Persante of the advanced French units that had found it impossible to disengage and pull back.[99] Thereupon, Fenet's I/RM returned to its original positions around Redlin.

Around 1600 hours, part of the horse-drawn train was sent to Kolberg. The road from Körlin to the city port was open, although nobody knew for how long. This news had been brought back to Fritzow by a mounted patrol from the Artillery Group which had reached the very gates of Kolberg two hours earlier where weak Russian elements were already holding the mill and the bridge over the first branch of the Persante. Proudly, the patrol also reported the destruction of a Russian tank with panzerfäuste. The 'tank destroyers' were Oscha. Pierre Ranc[100] and gunners Blaise and Hoinard.

the Persante.

95    Lefèvre makes the point that the Tiger tank may have been an assault gun or PzKpfw III or IV, *Axe & Alliés* no 1, p.63. Scherzer doubts that there was a tank battle as such and provides eyewitness statement that there was a 3.7cm FLAK gun stationed near the bridge (*Sous le Signe SS*, p.356), which presumably engaged the Soviet tanks. As stated earlier, Martres recalls that 'Fayard had one or two guns with him'. Perhaps this FLAK gun was manned by men of the FLAK Company.

96    Soulat, *Historique de la Division Charlemagne*, p.54. According to Mabire, *La Division Charlemagne*, p.439, these companies were formed into an improvised battalion. In response to this, no other source states the formation of such a battalion. Furthermore, Mabire does not even record the name of the battalion commander, which the author finds suspicious.

97    Soulat, *Historique de la Division Charlemagne*, p.54. The author included in his original depiction of this action material from both Saint-Loup and Mabire, which, upon reflection, now seems exaggerated. Consequently, the author has stripped back his depiction of this action to the original source, that of Soulat.

98    Mabire, *La Division Charlemagne*, p.437.

99    Scherzer questions the intensity of this battle and whether or not it took place at all, citing a number of German civilian eyewitnesses (see *Sous le Signe SS*, pp.357-358).

100   Pierre Ranc was born on 6 October 1916 in Nîmes. He passed from the *Milice* to the Waffen-SS and served with the Artillery Battalion.

By the afternoon of 4 March, the *Régiment de Réserve* had responded to the changing circumstances and had taken up improvised and flimsy positions on the other bank of the Persante, facing westwards. De Bourmont relocated the headquarters of the *Régiment de Réserve* from Klaptow to the village of Alt Marrin (Mierzyn), some nine kilometres north of Körlin. Hstuf. Moneuse's I/RR still remained widely dispersed along the Persante while Ustuf. de Genouillac's II/RR was either side of a railway bridge over the Persante.[101] The headquarters of the II/RR was now located in a small gatekeepers house some two hundred metres from the bridge.[102] Alt Marrin was occupied by the Soviets on the afternoon of 5 March 1945, by which time the French had left.[103]

Ostuf. Bartolomei's Company of the I/RR relocated from Peterfitz to the village of Bartin on the other bank of the Persante.[104] A courier on horseback from Gross Jestin brought Bartolomei news of what had happened there during the night. He now realised that he could be attacked from the east as well as the west. Hstuf. Moneuse, his battalion commander, ordered him to move his company to the village of Mechenthin (Miechecino).[105]

Reacting in turn, Bartolomei despatched runners who discovered that many combat emplacements were already deserted. Due to a total breakdown in liaison, many platoon and section commanders had felt abandoned and thus under no obligation to await orders that might never come. So they had simply decided to try their luck and make for Kolberg under their own steam.

1800 hours. A meeting at divisional headquarters brought together Brigf. Krukenberg, Obf. Puaud, Stubaf. de Vaugelas, Hstuf. Schlisler, Hstuf. de Perricot and other German and French officers, which included Ostuf. Tardan, Ostuf. Huan and Ostuf. de Rose. It was decided to hold Körlin at all costs. Undoubtedly, this decision had been influenced by the order received at divisional headquarters earlier that afternoon from Reichsführer-SS Himmler which had

101  Soulat states, *Historique de la Division Charlemagne*, p.54, that the II/RR under Ostuf. Defever 'came to reinforce the defences to the west of Körlin where the danger was urgent'. According to Mabire, *La Division Charlemagne*, p.439, the four ill-equipped and understrength companies of the II/RR were rushed to the west of Körlin to meet an attack developing from the south-west. They arrived, of course, just in the nick of time. In response to this, the battalion commander of the II/RR, Ustuf. de Genouillac, does not concur. And although he cannot substantiate that none of his companies were engaged, to this day he is convinced that none saw action at Körlin as he would have been informed of this and then gone to their positions. This alone is sufficient to cast serious doubt on the redeployment of the II/RR to the west of Körlin as stated by Soulat and repeated by Mabire.

102  De Genouillac, correspondence to the author. This is at variance with Soulat, who records the headquarters of the II/RR at Alt Marrin (*Historique de la Division Charlemagne*, p.55, which is repeated by the likes of Mabire and Scherzer). Alt Marrin is some five kilometres from the Persante at its nearest point. Perhaps the headquarters of the II/RR moved to a new location when the headquarters of the RR 'took up residence' in Alt Marrin.

103  A German civilian eyewitness has confirmed that the French were still at Alt Marrin in the early morning hours of 4 March 1945 (Scherzer, *Sous le Signe SS*, p.356) while another German civilian eyewitness has stated that he saw French soldiers in defensive positions near Alt Marrin at 02:00 hours on 5 March 1945 (Scherzer, *Sous le Signe SS*, p.379).

104  Bartin was occupied by the Soviets on 5 March 1945, see BAarch OSTDOK, I/155, fol. 45.

105  According to Mabire, *La Division Charlemagne*, p.432, Moneuse ordered Bartolomei to withdraw to Körlin and gave Mechenthin as the first stop. This seems doubtful. Saint-Loup's explanation of a 'safer position to spend the night' seems more likely (see Saint-Loup, *Les Hérétiques*, p.287).

simply read: 'The town must be held at all costs!' And yet, notably, the option of a withdrawal to Kolberg was still a very real possibility at that time.

At the meeting the question may have been asked of the whereabouts of the 10. SS-Panzer-Division 'Frundsberg' and whether or not it was still coming to their rescue.

**Pignard-Berthet Mission**

Towards 2100 hours on 3 March, Brigf. Krukenberg personally ordered the newly arrived Ustuf. Pignard-Berthet to take two platoons of his company to the hamlet of Neuland, south-west of Körlin at the junction of roads Körlin-Plathe and Kolberg-Schivelbein, where he was to make contact with a Pionier Kompanie and elements of the III. (Germanisches) SS-Panzer Korps.[106] Together, they were to stop the Soviet vanguards and, in this way, keep open a line of communication to the rear. The two platoons set out on foot and not in lorries as planned.[107]

Towards 0900 hours on 4 March, when Ustuf. Pignard-Berthet and the two platoons of his company approached Neuland crossroads there was no sign of the pioneers, only the Russians whose units were advancing north to Kolberg. However, east of the crossroads, they came across a friendly motorised reconnaissance detachment of three armoured cars from the III. (Germanisches) SS-Pz.-Korps.[108] The commanding officer with the rank of Obersturmführer and the crews were Dutch. They passed on yet more bad news to their French comrades of the Waffen-SS. The III. (Germanisches) SS-Pz.-Korps. was without fuel and would not be coming to the aid of 'Charlemagne' or to the other encircled forces.

The Frenchmen and Dutchmen teamed up. They built a roadblock across the road along which Pignard-Berthet had come. Suddenly, a Russian column of lorries loaded with troops appeared. The armoured cars immediately engaged the enemy, destroying two lorries. The others about-turned, but Russian tanks soon joined the fight. Their appearance changed the odds drastically. Thereupon, Ustuf. Pignard-Berthet ordered his men to withdraw eastwards, back to Körlin, but half of his command had disappeared in the confusion of the engagement. The Dutchmen then decided to take on board their remaining comrades-in-arms and together they raced off. In vain they repeatedly tried to call the headquarters of the III. (Germanisches) SS-Pz.-Korps. and Brigf. Krukenberg at Körlin.

At a crossroads three kilometres from Körlin, they came face to face with Russian tanks coming from Stolzenberg by way of an adjacent road and lost one armoured car in a brief, one-sided firefight. After picking up those who had dismounted from the destroyed armoured

106  Saint-Loup's account of the mission to Neuland, *Les Hérétiques*, p.285, is riddled with inaccuracy; to begin with, he incorrectly identifies the company ordered to Neuland as that of Million-Rousseau and then lists Pignard-Berthet as a platoon commander. He also incorrectly records that Puaud gave Pignard-Berthet the orders.
107  According to Saint-Loup, *Les Hérétiques*, p.285, and Mabire, *La Division Charlemagne*, p.443, the two platoons were fifty-strong whereas Soulat states, *Historique de la Division Charlemagne*, p.56, eighty men.
108  Mabire, *La Division Charlemagne*, p.442, and Pignard-Berthet, letter to the author. However, according to Soulat, *Historique de la Division Charlemagne*, p.56, repeated by Saint-Loup, *Les Hérétiques*, p.285, the reconnaissance detachment was somewhat larger and also included one radio car and two *voitures-canon* [cars or armoured cars equipped with a cannon].

424     For Europe Revisited

car, the other two made off across country to a nearby wood situated to the north, where they took shelter.[109]

Accepting that the road to Körlin was now cut by the Russians,[110] Ustuf. Pignard-Berthet and the Dutch Obersturmführer decided to try their luck northwards. So they belted towards Kolberg, but their luck was short-lived as one armoured car after another ran out of petrol. After blowing up the armoured cars, they continued on foot and, at nightfall, bivouacked in a wood. By then, the group was about forty-strong, half Dutch and half French.

Hours later, the group was 'joined' by a Soviet patrol. Both sides soon realised that they were not alone. Because the situation was so confused nobody dare fire. They fought hand-to-hand.

Like all in that wood, Ustuf. Pignard-Berthet was completely lost. On hearing the Dutch SS officer shout *Sammlung* he started out towards him. Suddenly, in front of him, he saw the shadow of a man appear. In the belief that it was one of his men, he grabbed hold of him by the belt and tapped him on the shoulder only to discover that it was a Soviet soldier! He wrestled himself free from the clutches of his adversary and ran off in the direction of the Dutch SS officer. Along with ten others he hid away and tried to keep silent. Shots rang out, but they became less and less frequent.

At nightfall, the group set off. Kolberg was only fifteen kilometres away. When the group dispersed Ustuf. Pignard-Berthet found himself in the company of three others, two Frenchmen and one Dutchman, who wanted to make for Cammin, but he still favoured Kolberg. So Kolberg it was. Well he was their superior. Besides, Kolberg was the nearer of the two.

Avoiding contact with the Russians, they continued northwards and were joined, much later, by some Latvian SS troops. On one occasion they could not refuse combat when they suddenly came face to face with a Soviet armoured reconnaissance detachment. In a matter of minutes, they managed to knock out three tanks with panzerfäuste and kill ten or so Russians before quickly disappearing into nature, chased by gunfire.

In the evening, they slipped into a village held by the Russians. While they slept German peasants mounted guard, but their presence was detected and they took to the fields and woods again. Finding their way north barred by an increasing concentration of Soviet artillery, they took cover and decided to turn westwards and to the Oder. They waited for nightfall before making their move.

Progress was slow, but each day brought the fugitives closer to the Oder. At dawn on 10 March,[111] near the banks of the Oder, they were facing danger once more; a regiment of Cossacks started to pass tens of metres away from the edge of the wood where they were hiding.

109 Pignard-Berthet, letter to the author, 1997. However, according to Mabire Jean, *Mourir pour Dantzig* (Paris: L'Aencre, 1995), p.60, after this engagement Uscha. Jacquet had found himself isolated with ten or so men. This would seem to suggest that all the men were not picked up. Subsequently these men were hunted down.

110 According to Saint-Loup, *Les Hérétiques*, p.286, the rationale for this assumption was that all the bridges over the Persante had been blown. This is impossible. When Ustuf. Pignard-Berthet and the two platoons of his company left Körlin on this mission the bridges over the Persante would still have been standing because the Russians at that time were not a threat. Besides, as previously recounted, the bridge over the Persante to the west of Körlin was blown shortly after 1230 hours on 4 March. Having no radio contact, the mixed detachment could not have known this.

111 Pignard-Berthet, letter to the author. This corrects Saint-Loup, *Les Hérétiques*, p.287, who states his capture on 7 March, and Mabire (*Mourir pour Dantzig*, pp.62-68), who implies 7 March.

They 'flattened themselves and tried to make themselves invisible'. Squadron followed squadron. Stragglers brought up the rear. They seemed half-asleep. Suddenly, one stopped his horse, dismounted and walked over towards their hide-out. He was on the point of urinating when he spotted them only metres away. The shots that killed him also awoke the other Russians to their presence. So this was the beginning of the end. And yet capture did not bring death.

The prisoners were marched towards Greifenberg. Night started to fall when Pignard-Berthet made good his escape by slipping into a copse.

After another night in the open, Pignard-Berthet was making his way towards Plathe (Ploty) when he was stopped by some Poles who took him on as a cook. Changing into civilian clothes, he made good his escape once again only to be stopped by a Russian patrol. Revelling in victory, the happy Russians actually handed him a pass! However, several kilometres later, this pass did not get him through Polish partisans.

Eventually, Ustuf. Pignard-Berthet was taken to a POW repatriation camp and, soon after his arrival, denounced as an officer of the SS and *chef* of the *Milice* by one of his compatriots from 'Charlemagne'. He was handed over to the Russians. Would his fate await all those still entrenched at Körlin?

## Breakout

On the evening of 4 March, Ustuf. de Genouillac was visited by Obf. Puaud at his headquarters in a small gatekeepers house two hundred metres from a bridge over the Persante. The battalion commander of the II/RR thought that Puaud seemed to be at a loose end and complained to him that he had no means of blowing up the bridge or even of securing the approach road. Moreover, his battalion had handed over all their panzerfaust to the RM. He also mentioned to Puaud that he had not eaten since the day before. Puaud promptly returned with a Tellermine and a smoked herring. As soon as the herring was consumed, de Genouillac left and, by the light of a torch, mined the bridge himself.

A little later, following a radio conversation with Reichsführer-SS Himmler at the headquarters of Army Group Vistula, Brigf. Krukenberg and Obf. Puaud 'decided to break out to the west in several echelons'.[112]

Now that the route to Kolberg seemed cut and with Russian forces holding positions to the west of Körlin, the breakout would be attempted via Belgard still held by the Wehrmacht. From Belgard, the division was to bear west, reach the river Rega, traverse it and then make for the river Oder via Plathe or Greifenberg. If the dangerous withdrawal was to have any chance of success the Frenchmen would have to avoid the main roads criss-crossed by enemy columns, go across country, hide in the woods, live off the land, march at night and travel light. This was most important. Nothing should be carried to slow the withdrawal down.

---

112 Soulat, *Historique de la Division Charlemagne*, p.56. However, the time and the contents of this radio conversation remain unknown. According to Mabire, *La Division Charlemagne*, p.444, RF-SS Himmler authorised the breakout. Curiously, at 1820 and then again at 1840, General Krebs, the chief of operations of the OKH, signalled to Lieutenant-General Kienzel at the headquarters of Army Group Vistula that, by order of the Führer, Group von Tettau was to hold its position. Undoubtedly, Himmler would have known or been made aware of this order.

The order of march was laid down at once: Ostuf. Fenet's I/RM and divisional headquarters was to be the vanguard, followed by de Hstuf. Bourmont's *Régiment de Réserve*. Hstuf. Bassompierre's II/RM was to be the rearguard. The assembly area was Körlin. The breakout was scheduled for 2300 hours. Hstuf. Jauss had suggested breaking out in four kampfgruppen side by side at the same time, but Brigf. Krukenberg had overruled him, ordering the three battalions to follow the vanguard 'in single file'.[113]

After finalising the details, Brigf. Krukenberg, Staf. Zimmermann and Hstuf. Jauss drove to Redlin to join Fenet. Obf. Puaud was not with them; he had refused to join the vanguard because he wished to remain at Körlin 'until the departure of his last elements'.[114] The time was now around 1900 hours.[115] Fahrschwadron A, which was already on the road to Kolberg, was ordered to turn around and return to Körlin.

On the morning of 4 March, the Medical Company crossed Körlin and took up a position on the road to Kolberg. At the end of the afternoon, the soldiers of the Medical Company were told that the Division was going to try and cross the Russian lines towards the west. They were ordered to carry as little as possible, which did not bother Dissent because he only had on him a haversack holding a little food, as well as a bayonet, used for the most part to open tinned food!

Obf. Puaud and Hstuf. de Bourmont visited the headquarters of the II/RR. They told Ustuf. de Genouillac that, at 0200 hours on 5 March, the *Régiment de Réserve* was to set off 'to break through the encirclement'.[116] The battalion commander's hunger suddenly disappeared. He was told to abandon all vehicles, all heavy equipment and all the wounded. The last was painful to hear. After explaining the details of the plan his visitors left.

For de Bourmont, problems arose well before the hour of the breakout. Very few of his runners had returned and some units of Moneuse's I/RR were still far from Körlin. At 2100 hours, he decided to fetch the battalion himself. He came across Bartolomei's Company, which had just reached Mechentin and was beginning to dig in. Ostuf. Bartolomei was ordered to withdraw to Körlin and to abandon all heavy equipment on the spot. However, horses were to be kept to transport the wounded. Bartolomei then assembled all the French SS troops around him. Only twenty were from his company. Most were stragglers or those who had become detached from their parent units. Hurried by Bartolomei, they arrived at Körlin shortly before midnight.

Bartolomei wasted precious time before he found headquarters, where he was greeted by Obf. Puaud who informed him that they would not be leaving straight away![117] And yet the breakout

---

113 Westemeier Jens, *Hans Robert Jauss Konstanz Jugend, Krieg und Internierung* (University Konstanz, 2015), p.102. Jauss would later blame Krukenberg for the massacre, stating: 'The vanguard escaped without caring about those that followed'. The two did not like each other and this was undoubtedly said with the benefit of hindsight.

114 Soulat, *Historique de la Division Charlemagne*, p.56. Curiously, according to Mabire, *La Division Charlemagne*, p.446, Puaud came to see Krukenberg and told him that he would be leaving with the *Régiment de Réserve*, for the most part *légionnaire*, and not with the true 'SS' of the *Régiment de Marche*. This is unconfirmed.

115 Mabire, *La Division Charlemagne*, p.447.

116 The memoirs of de Genouillac. Yet, according to Mabire, *La Division Charlemagne*, p.447, by midnight of 4-5 March 1945, Brigf. Krukenberg expected no French SS troops to be left in Körlin.

117 Mabire, *La Division Charlemagne*, pp.448-449, presumably based on the eyewitness account of Bartolomei. The delay brought about by Puaud to the withdrawal of the *Régiment de Réserve* has never been fully explained and will forever remain a mystery. Saint-Loup explains, *Les Hérétiques*, p.295, that Puaud had wanted to hold Körlin twenty-four hours longer than that asked of him by the Germans.

depended upon time and speed. In one corner Bartolomei saw Moneuse. He looked aged and exhausted.

As planned, the vanguard consisting of Ostuf. Fenet's I/RM and divisional headquarters left Redlin noiselessly at 2300 hours. As per orders, all heavy equipment had been abandoned. By 0200 hours, the vanguard was in sight of Belgard, ablaze from end to end.[118] The Wehrmacht was still holding the town and stubbornly resisting the Russians. The vanguard crossed the cemetery on the northern outskirts, then skirted round the town and proceeded south-east.[119] The thick woods swallowed them up.

Doubting the information he was receiving, Hstuf. Moneuse sent Oberjunker Méric in the direction of Belgard to report on the breakout. Méric jumped into an Opel passenger car with three others and took off into the night. The wiper blades struggled to deal with the falling snow. They caught up with and passed the first companies of the RM. As they approached Belgard, an NCO warned them to be careful because Russian infiltrators had been reported up ahead. They continued forward and ran into a group of Russians, who fired off a few isolated shots. The Frenchmen returned fire with their machine pistols through open windows as the driver managed to do a U-turn on the road without losing control and sped off, getting them out of the mess they had got into. Méric congratulated the driver on this manoeuvre which had undoubtedly saved his life. The others also came of it unscathed, but the car was riddled with bullet holes. They returned to Körlin in the full knowledge that Moneuse would have his information.

Towards 0100 hours on 5 March, Obf. Puaud had a sudden change of heart and took off by car with de Vaugelas and Renault to 'catch up' the vanguard.[120] But the car broke down and they returned on foot to Körlin and the assembling *Régiment de Réserve*.[121]

118 Some doubt that 'Belgard was ablaze'. As a prisoner Sepchat happened to cross Belgard along the railway line from north to south shortly after the capitulation. He saw no visible trace of fire. Moreover, he spent the best part of a day (and perhaps the following night) in one of the two rail stations and it was completely intact. (Letter to the author, 14/6/99.)
119 According to Scherzer, *Sous le Signe SS*, p.379, Fenet's Battalion crossed the Persante on the bridge north of Denzin (Dębczyno) and swung west to the village of Roggow (Rogowo). His reasoning is based on a civilian eyewitness who saw 'a lot of military, Latvian and French soldiers' pass through the village, which is ambiguous to say the least. How many soldiers represent a lot? When did the soldiers pass through? This report could equally refer to men of the RR or the II/RM.
120 According to a former member of 'Charlemagne,' Puaud 'gave away some of his baggage and kept only the legion flag, which he wrapped around his body beneath his uniform' (Michaelis, *French units in the Waffen-SS*, p.77). In response, this is not substantiated by any other source.
121 Soulat, *Historique de la Division Charlemagne*, p.57, repeated by Mabire, *La Division Charlemagne*, p.453. However, Ustuf. de Genouillac was to meet Obf. Puaud, Stubaf. de Vaugelas, Hstuf. Renault, and Ustuf. Delile later that same night near the Persante. And this is what he learnt from them. To join the retreating troops, the four of them had left Körlin in a Volkswagen car driven by Delile. Travelling without lights, Delile had crashed into an abandoned vehicle, throwing Puaud into the windscreen. After abandoning their wreck, they had set off across country in search of de Bourmont's column and this is how they chanced upon de Genouillac and the two men with him. Delile was the only one of the four to be armed. The group would cross the Persante and find de Bourmont's column. Regarding this, undoubtedly, Soulat and de Genouillac are referring to the same departure of Puaud by car from Körlin, but importantly the memoirs of de Genouillac suggest that at no time was Puaud with de Bourmont's column on the east bank of the Persante. Clearly, this contrasts with the presence of Puaud with de Bourmont's regiment before Belgard (Mabire, *La Division Charlemagne*, pp.453-455) or in

## Medical Company

On the evening of 4 March 1945, the Medical Company crossed the town of Körlin once more and took the road to Belgard.[122] Jules Dissent of the Medical Company believes that his company followed in the wake of the I/RM and the divisional headquarters and was not with the RR. His company crossed Belgard to the south, bore south-west, followed a pathway along the Persante on its right bank and then crossed over a bridge 'in the middle of the country'.

Daybreak found the company in front of a road it had to cross, but it was a road traversed by Russian trucks.[123] The order was thus given to cross in small groups and as quickly as possible. This was carried out, but the company, which had kept its cohesion up to this point, now started to break up. Dissent said of what happened next:

> Shortly after crossing the road, we reached a small wood with the hope of resting there awhile; but barely had we stopped when several mortar shells fell on the wood, forcing us to set off again. It was in fact the start of the end. Finding myself close to two German NCOs of my company with the ranks of Oberscharführer and Unterscharführer, I then decided to follow them, thinking that they were perhaps the most capable ones of getting out of this spot (and me with them). We ran to the edge of the wood as shooting started from all sides and bullets whistled unpleasantly above our heads. I heard shouted at a certain point 'The Sturmbannführer is dead'[124] and I ended up flat on my stomach between the two Germans at the top of a wooded slope. One had a rifle and the other a sub machine-gun (my only weapon was a bayonet!) and they exchanged fire with the Russians. A moment later, which seemed a long time when bullets are whistling above your head making a very particular sound, I noticed that they were no longer firing: the Unterscharführer was dead and the Oberscharführer seriously wounded in the arm. I saw the Russians come out of the wood and come towards me, with weapons pointed and shouting... I then got up and said: 'Comrade!'
>
> They approached, took the weapons, including my bayonet that they casually threw away; one of them immediately stole my watch. I then tried hard to bandage the wounded German who was saying nothing but who must have been suffering greatly because a bullet had certainly fractured the humerus. I then helped him walk to some nearby buildings where they separated us. I still don't know if he pulled through.
>
> A little later, on a small road, I found myself with other prisoners and 'Davai... Davai', we started to march. We passed in front of several T-34s before reaching a property whose outbuildings were going to serve as shelter for some hours. Our guards

Belgard cemetery (Saint-Loup, *Les Hérétiques*, pp.297-298.) In response to both Mabire and Saint-Loup, if Puaud was with de Bourmont's column he did not march beside de Bourmont; de Genouillac was beside de Bourmont and does not recall the presence of Puaud. In conclusion, the author has reservations about the presence of Puaud and the command group with de Bourmont's column before Belgard cemetery and on the east bank of the Persante but has not been able to substantiate that they were not.

122  Jules Dissent is convinced of the date; he made notes at the time.
123  Dissent believes the road was that from Belgard to Standemin.
124  Dissent believes this may have been SS-Stubaf. Schlegel who was at the head of Bureau IVB.

kept us locked up in a shed first where I met several comrades, but we were packed like sardines in a tin! We could just about sit, but certainly not stretch out.

Best of all, a Russian tank crewman entered who was very agitated and brandishing a pistol that he waved in the face of several prisoners demanding in a threatening air: "Du? SS?" But luckily he confined himself to threats and ended up leaving. We learnt later that his tank had been hit by a panzerfaust which had unleashed his anger.

### Régiment de Réserve

Towards 0200 hours, the II/RR left its position along the Persante, joined the rest of the regiment[125] at Körlin and took the road to Belgard.[126] At the head of the column marched Hstuf. de Bourmont, the commander of the RR, and, beside him, Ustuf. de Genouillac, the battalion commander of the II/RR. Confusion overtook the *Régiment de Réserve*, which had disregarded Krukenberg's orders and marched with horse-drawn wagons and much of its unnecessary heavy equipment. All units were completely disorganised.

Belgard was not far off when Hstuf. de Bourmont called the *Régiment de Réserve* to a halt. The city was still ablaze from end to end and the continuing sounds of battle could be heard. He told Ustuf. de Genouillac to take a patrol into Belgard and find a bridge over the Persante.

Accompanied by the first two soldiers he met, Ustuf. de Genouillac penetrated into the city centre as far as a large bridge over the river Persante and came under heavy fire. 'Convinced that the din they had unleashed was every bit as good as a progress report', they hurried out of the city.[127] Skirting round the city, they came again to the Persante that they followed westwards in search of a bridge. It was dark and snowing lightly. They were alone; de Bourmont had not waited for their return.

In the cold, the *Régiment de Réserve*, halted two kilometres before Belgard, had waited and waited. Small groups started to leave the column and push on. Others bunched around their best hope: former NCOs of the LVF. Some others even tried to get their heads down. Officers tried to get some order into their companies, but officers and men alike were totally spent. Then the order to about-turn went down the column.[128]

In ever increasing confusion the disintegrating column backtracked to Körlin. Carts overturned. Horses bolted. Then another order was received. The *Régiment de Réserve* was to

---

125  The *Régiment de Réserve* numbered more than 2,000 men (Mabire, *La Division Charlemagne*, p.453) or 3,000 men (Soulat, *Historique de la Division Charlemagne*, p.57).
126  De Genouillac, letter to the author, 29/4/1997.
127  Schwerzer doubts de Genouillac's testimony and refers to two German civilian eyewitnesses who both state that there was no fighting for Belgard (see *Sous le Signe*, p.379).
128  And yet, according to Saint-Loup, *Les Hérétiques*, p.295, towards 0400 hours, the men of the *Régiment de Réserve* appeared before Belgard cemetery, where they were greeted by Russian machine-gun fire. The Frenchmen attacked and took the cemetery but suffered heavy casualties. Puaud was lightly wounded in the calf. Saint-Loup continues that the Frenchmen split up and went in different directions. The bulk went to the west of Belgard and continued southwards. Some also ventured into Belgard itself and came upon the scene of a horrific massacre of civilians. In response to this, no other source confirms this action in the cemetery. Also, the notion that elements of the RR entered and actually captured Belgard from the Russians is disputed by de Genouillac (letter to the author, 26/5/97). Moreover, Mabire suggests that the RR gave wide berth to Belgard.

cross the Persante between Körlin and Belgard and continue its march south-east on the left bank.[129] Men hurried off in search of crossing points. Like many, Hstuf. de Bourmont, the regimental commander, was overcome by despair.

For over an hour, de Genouillac and his two companions walked alongside the Persante searching for a way to cross. Suddenly, to his right, de Genouillac saw some silhouettes running towards them. Fearing that they were Russians, he called out to them in a combination of Russian and French dialects: "*Stoi Halte*". When the silhouettes revealed themselves he saw the faces of Obf. Puaud, Stubaf. de Vaugelas, Hstuf. Renault and Ustuf. Delile. Embarrassed about scaring them to death, he offered Puaud his apologies. Nevertheless, the newcomers were not altogether displeased to come across some armed individuals because Delile was the only one of them carrying a weapon.

The group continued along the Persante for some time without finding a bridge. Suddenly Ustuf. de Genouillac spotted an iron boat aground in the rushes less than two metres away from the river bank. Unfortunately, de Genouillac could not reach the boat with the end of his rifle. It was just too far away. As he tried desperately to reach out he let go of the person holding him and plunged headfirst into the river, after which collecting the boat posed no problem! Using their rifle butts as oars, they managed to get the heavy skiff moving and across to the other bank. As they were disembarking it stopped snowing and the fog lifted, revealing in the early morning light a long column crossing the river four or five hundred metres away.[130] It was de Bourmont! They had found him.

De Bourmont and the *Régiment de Réserve* pressed on. For the time being there was no question of stopping to rest. Only the woods far off offered the dead tired men relative security.

The going got more and more difficult and very time consuming. All kinds of obstacles had to be crossed: streams, hedges, barbed wire fences and water holes. Progress was slow, much too slow.

By daybreak, the *Régiment de Réserve* was only in the woods near Zarnefanz (Czarno-węsy) to the south-west of Belgard which was still burning. Thick fog had come down, affording the regiment some protection.

Among those to make it out of Körlin and into the woods was Uscha. Mercier of Fahrschwadron A. As per orders, Fahrschwadron A had abandoned all heavy equipment. Mercier travelled light. He had distributed the few provisions he had (tins of food and sausage) and gave to those who wished them the things that up to now he had guarded jealously but kept in his pockets the unit's records. A little later, one of his comrades, a *Milicien* NCO, exploded with anger when he noted that he had lost his camera 'because of those bloody records'.

129 According to Scherzer, *Sous le Signe SS*, p.381, de Bourmont was ordered to cross at the village of Rostin (Rościno), some seven kilometres from Belgard.
130 According to Scherzer, *Sous le Signe SS*, p.381, de Bourmont crossed the bridge near Rostin which leads to Kamissow (Kamosowo) which was known to parts of 'Charlemagne' which had attempted to cross days before, citing the testimony of a member of the Volkssturm who guarded the bridge, BArch OSTDOK 2/126, fol. 588.

Mercier followed his *chef,* Hstuf. Schlisler. Along with some comrades, he 'played the sheep dog', encouraging those of his column to keep grouped and moving. The route that his column took was first along a main road and then through a wood.[131]

The horses slowed the progress of the column. Despite his perfect ignorance of matters equestrian, Mercier gave advice to the former drivers on the subtle manoeuvre required to get the horses to cross the ditches. Day broke. There was thick fog. Those leading the horses by the bridle were repeatedly told that on no account were they to mount them, but they could not be stopped from leaving the wood to walk more easily.[132]

**Massacre**

Towards 0800 hours, under the cover of the fog, the *Régiment de Réserve* started to move across a vast and bare plain. The troops were dangerously crowded together. Marching within earshot of Obf. Puaud was Ostuf. Dr. Métais, who heard Puaud ask: "What's happening? It's crazy! Who's in front?" The reply was "De Bourmont." Puaud then turned to Stubaf. de Vaugelas and ordered: 'Take a horse. Tell him to find an unoccupied wood immediately, stop there and organise protection.'

As Stubaf. de Vaugelas galloped off towards the head of the column, Obf. Puaud exclaimed: 'It's crazy. And yet I had recommended hiding away in the woods during the day. If this continues, we're heading for a massacre!'[133]

Moments later, the thick fog suddenly lifted, exposing the regiment to daylight and presenting a perfect target for nearby Russian columns of armour and motorised artillery on the move.[134]

There was no cover for the Frenchmen. Russian mortars and machine guns poured murderous fire onto the Frenchmen and in minutes hundreds were dead and wounded. Tanks rumbled towards them. One eyewitness to the massacre wrote of at least fifty T-34/85s with all guns blazing in an unbroken line.[135] Anti-tank weapons might have turned the tables, but the *Régiment de Réserve* had handed theirs over to the rearguard at Körlin. Nothing could now stop

131  Mercier, letter to the author, 6/11/2001. Mercier does not know to which column he belonged but curiously he cannot recall crossing the Persante. In this same column was Rttf. Sepchat of the Headquarters Company/RM. He recalls an advance solely through woods (letter to the author, 12/1/2001). He can neither recall the about-turn on the road to Belgard, nor the search for a bridge over the river Persante, nor the presence of streams, hedges, and holes of water to get round or cross. Because of this he is now convinced that his column had followed a totally different route to that of the bulk of the division. Thus, the possibility exists that a third column evacuated Körlin during the night of 4-5 March 1945. The composition of this third column is not known, but when the column was sighted and overrun by the Russians Sepchat was captured and taken to a barn where prisoners from various units were assembled. There were medical and supply personnel, engineers, and German 'support' personnel, who were known to Sepchat from his LVF days. This suggests that the column comprised the support services.

132  Mercier still regrets that they had kept the horses, which 'loaded us down, delayed us and, later, got us spotted' (letter to the author, 6/11/2001).

133  Soulat, *Historique de la Division Charlemagne*, p.57, based on the eyewitness account of Métais, which is repeated by Saint-Loup, *Les Hérétiques*, p.299, although there are one or two minor changes of words.

134  Some have questioned the site of the massacre. In a letter to Mounine, dated 29/7/99, Sepchat suggests further west near Natztow (Nasutowo), which is nine kilometres west of Belgard.

135  Bayle, *De Marseille à Novossibirsk*, p.163.

them. The tanks crushed into pulp everything in their path. It was a massacre. The Frenchmen fled and made for the shelter of the woods.

The few dramatic and terrible accounts that exist of the massacre are worth recording here. Jacques C., a former *Milicien*, had this to say of the massacre:

> We didn't know where we were going and I think our *chefs* no longer knew. With this fog and the snow it was difficult to find our way. We heard the sound that the tank tracks were making. When the fog lifted, we noticed that we were advancing right in the middle of T-34 columns. Immediately shells started to rain down on us. There was no organised resistance. We simply tried not to be caught. I was taken prisoner around 1100 hours or midday.[136]

Marching at the head of the *Régiment de Réserve* on Belgard plain, Uscha. Bayle found himself less than twenty metres away from a line of tanks when the fog started to lift.[137] The tanks opened up. Bayle ran to the right of the road towards an embankment, climbed it 'without knowing where he was going' and hid in a grove. Joined by some comrades who had followed him, they watched the massacre unfold.

As for Hscha. Rostaing, he was stretched out on the ground under a fir sharing the last piece of black bread he had with his orderly, Martinet, when the silence was broken by an explosion. He scrambled to his feet, machine pistol in hand. Unsure of what was happening, he went to the edge of the wood. There was a second explosion in the exact spot he had just left. The fir he had been under moments earlier had been uprooted.

Rostaing was convinced that they had been spotted and decided to make for a small village in the distance. Followed by his men, he raced across the vast glacis between the hamlet and the wood. When the fog suddenly lifted Russian tanks were only four hundred metres behind them. An unequal battle began. Shells crashed murderously into the French troops who had no cover at all on the flat ground. Rostaing tried to run faster. He was out of breath. His orderly was hit by a machine-gun burst and went down. Rostaing did not stop. His fear of capture by the Russians drove him forward. He kept running and running. Shells were exploding around him. Some even ricocheted off the frozen ground. He could not help thinking that the next was for him. It seemed impossible for anybody to survive. All that mattered was getting out of this hell.

Finally he reached the village only to discover that it was occupied by the Russians! The battalion was following on his heels. Firing to his right and left, he crossed the village. Bullets mewed all around him, but his luck held. Some were less fortunate. He climbed up a slope, crossed its crest, hurtled down the other side and rushed into the woods. Puaud, de Vaugelas, Renault and other officers did the same to his left. Some one hundred and twenty men managed to finish this 'race of hope'. Turning round, he saw thirty of his comrades, who could not follow, stop and raise their arms.

Ustuf. de Genouillac was also caught up in the massacre. He was sat at the foot of a fir tree, trying to empty his boots of water, when an explosion rang out nearby. This was followed by

---

136  Delperrié de Bayac, *Histoire de la Milice*, p.606.
137  Curiously, according to Bayle, *De Marseille à Novossibirsk*, p.162, 'Barto', his company commander had ordered Bayle and his platoon to march at the head of the RR and yet his company formed the rearguard of the RR.

the crack, then the din of a large fir tree smashing its way to the ground through the branches of its neighbours. This caused great panic among the troops who fled in all directions and de Genouillac found himself swept along in the middle of a terrorised crowd. Almost immediately the true nature of the danger facing them revealed itself in all its horror: hell was unleashed.

Going in what seemed the opposite direction to this inferno, de Genouillac then found himself outside of the wood on a ploughed field covered with snow. His boots became ice-blocks that make it difficult to run. Regardless, he continued to press on. It started to snow again. Now and then he was passed by silhouettes that were going in every direction, except his.

The snow then stopped 'as if raising the curtain on a theatre scene': hundreds of grey silhouettes made their appearance on a vast plain. Up to then the Russians had been firing blind, but now they could choose their targets. Transfixed, de Genouillac came under fire and watched the earth and snow dance around him. It did not occur to him to fall to the ground and feign death. Somehow he made it to the first trees of the forest bordering Belgard plain. He was out of breath and at the end of his strength. He saw some buildings. As he moved towards them he encountered once again the command group of Puaud, de Vaugelas, Renault and Delile.

Offering to walk point, Ustuf. de Genouillac led the command group deeper into the forest and to a narrow track which he surveyed through binoculars. To his left about two hundred metres away there was a suspicious looking object that brought him to shout: "Tank to the left!" Nevertheless, the tank was stationary and relatively blind in such surroundings. He cleared the track at one jump and then yelled to the others that they could cross. Nothing stirred.[138] After waiting several minutes he pressed on.

Pierre de Séverin said of the massacre:

> It's hell for two hours. We are mercilessly shot like rabbits. Instinctively I lie down playing dead. My comrades who continue to run are machine-gunned or crushed by tank tracks. I raise my head sometimes and I see small groups managing to find shelter in the forest. Some will then break through the enemy's barriers, displaying admirable courage. I still did not move in this snow covered with the blood of my comrades. Some metres from me, one of my companions in arms, his belly ripped open, pleaded for somebody to shoot him. Another, his legs crushed, called for help. Tens of bodies around me seemed lifeless. [139]

And there Pierre de Séverin lay until nightfall, whereupon he 'came to life' and found refuge in a nearby wood. Russian patrols were scouring the area but did not spot him. He was still armed and had no intention of surrendering. Cold and hungry, he continued on his way.

Uscha. Mercier of Fahrschwadron A was in a wood when the fog lifted. He recalls what happened next:

> We heard a fusillade in the plain on our right. With *Capitaine* Schlisler, we observed what was happening in the plain and saw many Russian tanks approach. We were not

138  De Genouillac would meet de Vaugelas, Renault and Delile three weeks later at Lensberg camp and none of them could recall why they had not followed him. He added: 'Anyway, it would not have changed the final result'.

139  Lormier, *SS Français*, p.60.

434     For Europe Revisited

armed to face them and the only solution was to take advantage of the thickness of the bush to conceal us and wait for the Russians to go away. At first, there was some panic. Men ran in every direction. Some shouted 'Les Soldbuch! Les Soldbuch!' and started to tear them up. *Capitaine* Schlisler was against this, saying to them: 'You have nothing to hide!' And he restored calm [by] promising them that he would get them out of this spot, which was perhaps a bit optimistic.

Lieutenant Darrigade left with one member of the escort (combat) platoon and tried his luck at another end of the wood. Some were killed or captured in the plain stretching out on our right.Two steps from me, a man of Fahrschwadron A committed suicide by firing a Mauser bullet into his mouth. I knew him by sight since 1941. He belonged to the *train de combat* of the 3rd Company of the I. Battalion of the LVF. In 'Charlemagne', he was a driver. I think he was a Sturmmann. He was rather silent, but I believe that, if before his desperate gesture, I had spoken to him with one of our ritual gibes, such as 'Well, old man! It's always the same', I may have influenced his fate. I still regret this. He was called Roche.

The Russians undertook to clean up the plain and started to take care of the forest, but the vegetation was dense enough to enable us to camouflage ourselves. It is difficult for me to estimate how long we remained hidden in the bushes. Nothing was happening. And then, a Russian, who could not have been any older than fifteen, entered the wood yelling 'Komm! Komm!' He saw nobody and, when he passed beside me, I had the ludicrous idea to shoot him down, without imagining that the slightest gunfire would have alerted the Russians outside the wood and caused a massacre. Luckily, my pistol jammed.

My LVF comrade *Sergent* Godart, one of the old brigade [LVF veteran of 1941], applied the partisans' method and climbed a tree.[140] He was to be flushed out shortly after and was shot in the leg to help him down. Most fortunately, the wound was slight, but made him suffer at the start of his captivity.

And then other Russian soldiers entered the wood. We could no longer remain (where we were) and *Capitaine* Schlisler took us (off) in a breakthrough attempt across the plain. Suddenly, we found ourselves facing about thirty tanks. *Capitaine* Schlisler gave the signal for surrender and angrily threw down his submachine gun. I expected to be shot in the nape of the neck and wished to die with dignity. I was greatly surprised to note that the Krasnoïarmist who took charge of me did not experience an immediate need to make me pass from life to death, but was concerned above all with getting my watch … I had much to learn.[141]

Unbeknown to Mercier, Uscha. Jean-Pierre Lefèvre, who became a good friend after the war, was beside him when Sturmmann Roche committed suicide.

After serving first with the 10/58, Lefèvre came to Pomerania as the *chef* of the command section of the 8/58. Made de Bourmont's bodyguard for the retreat from Körlin, he lost him in the chaos following a Soviet bombardment with mortars and Stalin's organs. He searched for

---

140  Godart was born in 1911 in Gagny in the Eastern suburbs of Paris.
141  Mercier, letter to the author, 12/10/2001.

de Bourmont, but it was as though he had vanished into thin air. On Belgard plain when the Russian tanks emerged he took to the woods and hid.

Russian tanks and infantry approached. Lefèvre destroyed his Soldbuch and his papers, only keeping a photo of his parents and a picture of La Sainte Vierge. The Russians now started to comb the woods. A soldier near Lefèvre fired a bullet into his mouth. (This was Sturmmann Roche.) With no means of escape, he surrendered.[142]

Capture was also the fate of Rttf. Sepchat. He said this of how his adventure came to an end:

> Suddenly, as day was breaking, we discovered that we were in contact with the enemy. Immediately, an officer on horseback that I did not know ordered: "Direction due north". I followed another in the direction of the south-east. This was to throw myself into the lion's jaw. I soon heard pleas of "Friend! Friend!" And had as neighbours only a young Feldwebel, smoking a cigarette peacefully and, a little further, a Major, who seemed as relaxed.
>
> A Russian soldier appeared and disappeared. I brought him to the attention of the Major who advised me not to bother him: "I'm a doctor." A Russian tank approached and went away. I noticed a sheet of water and immersed myself in it up to my nostrils. For whole hours I heard bursts from submachine guns. One of them had 'my number on.' I felt nothing and only saw the leggings and boots of the gunner, but later I counted a good half-dozen small tears on the collar of my greatcoat.
>
> When the calm returned, interested by the faraway rumbling of the cannonade, I got out of my bath with the intention of approaching it. I did not get far. Suddenly, behind me, I heard cries of rage. A patrol of two men and a twelve-year-old kid had caught me. I was presented to an officer who interrogated me in perfect German.
>
> The officer asked: "Why did you continue to fight since you know that the war is lost?" I replied: "You're a soldier, *mon capitaine*. I'm a soldier too. When an order is given, it must be executed." He followed up: "How many are you in your Division?" I replied: "I am not allowed to say." Probably on his order, I was badly beaten up.

The following day, Sepchat escaped from a column of prisoners and met by chance the brother of a Knight's Cross holder, who told him that the Gauleiter of Schwede-Koburg revealed to the troops under his command that they had to evacuate Köslin because they would soon use a new explosive capable of destroying everything within a two mile radius and that they would return.

Eventually, the two of them came to an abandoned village. Gnawed by hunger, they searched each and every house but could not find anything to eat. During the night they heard the never ending sound of heavy vehicles crossing the village. The next day, a small lost German boy named Siegfried told them that he had seen Russians in the village. They waited for night to move on and find a new hiding place, which turned out to be the barn of an isolated farm. The

---

142  For accounts of Lefèvre's capture see Mabire, *La Division Charlemagne*, p.465-466, and Delperrié de Bayac, *Histoire de la Milice*, pp.605-606. There are, however, differences between the two sources, one of which is noteworthy. According to Mabire, Lefèvre was on Belgard plain when disaster overtook the *Régiment de Réserve* whereas Delperrié de Bayac suggests that 'Jean-Pierre L.' was not with the main body. In response to this, de Bourmont was with the *Régiment de Réserve*, which was the main body of 'Charlemagne'.

farmer was accommodating but feared reprisals if he was caught hiding them. So they entrusted Siegfried to him and continued on their way.

Sepchat and the German soldier stopped at the edge of a wood, through which ran a stream. His comrade, suffering from a frostbitten foot, could no longer walk long distances so they decided to stay put and wait for the counter-offensive announced by the Gaultier. Besides they had matches on them and knew where to get supplies. And here they waited until the day they were discovered by a Russian soldier and a Polish partisan. The Pole told the Russian that undoubtedly they were SS. The Russian seemed to reassure the Pole, though. They were sent to Köslin where they were put to work.

Stubaf. de Vaugelas and several other divisional officers were also taken prisoner. Although beaten up, de Vaugelas was not put to death. For those who went undetected, the fate that awaited them was death or capture, days if not weeks later. In small groups, sometimes in pairs or even singly, they tried to make their way westwards to the Oder through enemy territory. Few would rejoin the German front. Not only were the survivors of the massacre pursued by the Russians, and later by their Polish allies of the 1st Polish Army, the cold, the snow and the wind were also on Stalin's side. Weakened by dysentery and a lack of food, wounds and fatigue took their toll. Little help was forthcoming from the terrorised local population. Danger lurked everywhere. The fate of many is just not known.

Ostuf. de Londaiz, the cavalryman and former *Milicien*, who had made himself the commander of the remnants of the 'regimental engineer platoon', was marching at the head of the *Régiment de Réserve* when the fog lifted. He was so close to the Russians that it proved relatively easy to burst through their thin 'cordon' and slip undetected into the woods.

Around him Ostuf. de Londaiz formed a small group which was determined to wage war. As luck would have it, they came upon an isolated farmhouse and food. They ate and drank in peace. Suddenly there was a shout from the lookout posted outside the farmhouse. The Russians were coming. In fact they turned out to be Polish regulars.[143] They had an armoured car with them. Strangely, de Londaiz, machine pistol in hand, went alone to confront them and was killed outright by a machine gun burst. His men returned fire. The Poles replied. Abandoning the farmhouse, the Frenchmen made off through the woods. Some of the group would later make it back to the Oder.

Hstuf. Croisile of Fahrschwadron B was captured on 7 March 1945 at Lipin.[144] On that same day, Uscha. Jean Bertrand, a former *Chef de main de la Franc-Garde permanente* Tarn-et-Garonne, and five others were captured by the Russians as they were about to cross the river Rega.

Uscha. Bayle and two other men were captured by Poles on 8 March 1945 ten kilometres south-east of Körlin. A group of around ten men had formed around him after the massacre on Belgard plain. Not one was former Sturmbrigade or LVF. They set off towards Stolzenberg and met along the way a group of fifteen Latvian Waffen-SS soldiers, who put themselves at the disposal of Bayle, calling him *Vadonis* [Leader] rather than Unterscharführer. They continued on and were able to release a number of Latvian prisoners held by the Russians in a clearing. 'Overjoyed' at his release, Stubaf. Veidenbaums awarded Bayle with his Iron Cross 1st Class

143 Saint-Loup, *Les Hérétiques*, p.325. However, according to Mabire, *La Division Charlemagne*, p.468, the Russians turned out to be Polish partisans.
144 Croisile records his place of capture as Lepin, Lipin in Pomerania is more likely.

as well as his Nahkampfspange. Now that the group had grown too large for its own good, Bayle and Veidenbaums decided to split up by nationality again and go their separate ways. The Frenchman came across some horrible sights as they continued on.[145] They had several brushes with the enemy, but the inevitable happened when they were spotted attempting to cross a road. One of the Polish soldiers took from Bayle the Iron Cross Veidenbaums had given to him.

Ustuf. de Genouillac came so near to freedom: on or around 13 March 1945, he was captured at Cammin on the shores of the Oder. After the massacre on Belgard plain he came across isolated groups which followed him for several days. In this way, his group may have grown to around forty, but he lost them all crossing a road along which enemy convoys were travelling. Fortunately, on that same day, two Wehrmacht soldiers joined him and followed him until their capture by Polish troops. He was not ill-treated by them or by the Russians to whom he was handed over.

On 14 March 1945, Hstuf. Renault was captured by Soviet troops in front of Kolberg. Two French SS men, one from Hstuf. Roy's 9/57, were captured after spending four days on the run. Fearing the worse because of their SS collar insignia, they were dragged before two Russian officers who, as luck would have it, had studied in Paris and spoke French! The officers integrated the two of them into their unit as cooks. However, one month later, the officers warned them that their unit was leaving for the front and that, consequently, they could no longer keep them. Thus, the two French prisoners found themselves handed over to NKVD troops.[146]

The ultimate fate of the commander of 'Charlemagne' still remains a mystery. Nevertheless, Puaud did not meet his death on Belgard plain; he was seen on horseback by some soldiers around 1400 hours on that tragic day of 5 March 1945. Wounded in the shoulder, he ordered them to try and reach the west.[147] Of Puaud's subsequent movements, Ostuf. Multrier has stated the following:

> General Puaud, wounded in the leg, was dragging himself along a road. A French NCO met him and sat him on the rear seat of a motorcycle. But they were attacked by Russian snipers. General Puaud was wounded again. Too serious to continue on. Approaching Greifenberg, the NCO left his commander in a hotel and placed him in a ground floor room where other wounded were already. Then he went off on foot. This NCO would return the following day in civilian clothes, although the Russians had seized the town. He then saw that the ground floor room where he left General Puaud was empty. But the ground and the walls were bloodstained.[148]

This version of Puaud's disappearance was recounted by the NCO, a former *Milicien*, to Multrier, also a former *Milicien*, at Prague in the last days of the war. Multrier then wrote down the story

---

145  See Bayle, *De Marseille à Novossibirsk*, pp.170-171.
146  Unpublished article *Mein Freund Georges*.
147  Soulat, *Historique de la Division Charlemagne*, p.58.
148  Landemer, *L'internationale SS, Histoire* hors série 32, p.135. However, according to Léguerandais, *Hitler's French volunteers*, p.122, Puaud was injured in the shoulder at Belgard cemetery, where he remained, issuing his final instructions, and was later reported missing, presumed dead, 'due to either his injuries or from the heavy Soviet artillery fire that was bombarding his last known position'. This, of course, conflicts with the testimonies of de Genouillac, Rostaing and Multrier.

exactly as he heard it from the mouth of the NCO whose identity still remains unknown.[149] There are no reasons to discount this version, even if sixty kilometres separate Greifenberg from Belgard over poor and icy side roads. Thus, along with the other non-transportable wounded at the hotel, Puaud may have been murdered by the Russians who were probably unaware that he was a General because even at this late stage of the war the Russians still prized the capture of a General. That said, the possibility also exists that Puaud died of his wounds while in captivity.

After the war there were many reported sightings of Puaud. Marcel H. of *La Milice d'Angers* claims that he saw Puaud alive and well in a POW camp at the start of May 1945 and, then later, in Russia in the uniform of a Red Army officer.[150] Puaud was also sighted in the uniform of a NKVD officer in East Berlin![151] Indeed, it was even claimed that Puaud became the head of the Russian police in Berlin![152] Undoubtedly all such sightings were rumours or wishful thinking. And although Puaud's ultimate fate has never been substantiated the only conclusion that can be reached is that he lost his life somewhere in Pomerania.

Although a doctor, Hstuf. Bonnefoy realised that his life was in the balance when he was captured with a group of German policemen and Ukrainians of the 'Vlasov army' who could expect no mercy from the Soviets. They were loaded onto an American lorry and driven away. As expected, retribution followed swiftly. Now and then the lorry stopped and each time two prisoners were made to kneel at the roadside and summarily executed. It was now only a matter of time before it was his turn. It came all too soon when he was lined up with nine others near a forest.

Suddenly, a staff car drew up and out stepped a high-ranking officer. An argument ensued between him and the officer in charge of the transport. While this was going on, a female soldier, who was with the high-ranking officer, came over to the prisoners. Bonnefoy did not know why she appeared to be especially interested in him and him alone. She then pointed Bonnefoy out to the other Russians and told them that he was a doctor and was not to be executed. It was only then that he understood that the female soldier was a doctor too. He was saved.

Bonnefoy was taken before the high-ranking Soviet officer who, on noticing his French armshield, tried to converse with him in broken French. Bonnefoy had much to say, but the Soviet officer seemed to understand little, if anything, of the replies he gave. As the Soviet officer returned to his car the nine other prisoners were put to death. Indeed life had become a lottery! Spared, Bonnefoy got back on the lorry, which continued eastwards. He ended up in a POW camp at Posen.

Hstuf. Durandy was killed in an engagement during the retreat. Oberjunker Marchèse, who was near him, was wounded and later captured.[153]

---

149 This same testimony is retold by Saint-Loup, *Les Hérétiques*, p.518, and Mabire, *La Division Charlemagne*, pp.473-474, as that of '*commandant* M.' However, there are differences between all three versions, although they are of little significance: according to Mabire, the NCO returned to Greifenberg in the company of a comrade from 'Charlemagne', whereas Saint-Loup has the NCO returning to Greifenberg days later and as a prisoner. In addition, Saint-Loup states that after the NCO saw the hospital empty and covered with blood he came to the conclusion that all the wounded there had been put to death.
150 Delperrié de Bayac, *Histoire de la Milice*, p.606.
151 Saint-Loup, *Les Hérétiques*, p.518.
152 Landemer, *L'internationale SS*, *Historia* hors série no 32, p.135.
153 The author does not know the unit in which Durandy and Marchèse left Körlin.

## Out of hell

Against all the odds, Ostuf. Fenet managed to bring his entire battalion to Meseritz (Międzyrzecz). As dawn was breaking on 5 March, Brigf. Krukenberg had the men of Ostuf. Fenet's I/RM hide in the woods, but they could not rest because it was that cold and still snowing continuously. There was, of course, no question of lighting a fire or even a cigarette.

Hours later, Brigf. Krukenberg held a *petit conseil de guerre* with Staf. Zimmermann, Hstuf. Jauss and Ostuf. Fenet. Concerned that his men would be frozen stiff by a whole day of keeping still and thus in no condition to set off again, Fenet insisted that they should not wait till night to push on. Besides, there was no time to lose. He proposed that they conduct a daytime march by taking advantage of the vast forest extending westwards and the disorder in the wake of the Russian advance. Krukenberg was won over by reason. His overriding desire was to save the men to fight for another day. Suddenly, all could hear the sounds of battle from the region of Zarnefanz, Ristow and Boissin. They had no inkling that it was the main body of the division.

Towards 0900 hours, the men of the I/RM started out again. Ostuf. Fenet himself was at their head. Silently they marched on and on. In this way, they came to the Rambin (Rąbino)-Belgard road and also danger; the Russians had lined the road with watch posts. There was no way forward without being spotted and being drawn into a fight. They detoured and crossed at a point out of sight of the Russian watch posts.

As night fell they suddenly lost the cover of the woods. They took a chance on the cover of darkness and marched on. After skirting round the village of Stolzenberg (Sławoborze) from the south, they came to the main Schievelbein-Kolberg road. From roadside ditches, they watched a continual stream of Russian tanks and trucks pass by. Between convoys, small groups of Frenchmen dashed across the road, hid away on the other side and waited for others to cross. All made it safely across. They continued on.

Unseen, the French column crossed a village occupied by the headquarters of a Russian regiment, but when several men of the rearguard under Hstuf. Jauss entered a house in search of something to drink they woke the Russians there. Shots were fired. The Frenchmen made off. Fortunately, casualties were not heavy.

The column then came to the village of Falkenberg (Jastrzębniki) which was strewn with the debris of war: burnt out tanks, disfigured corpses, abandoned rifles, tent sheets, equipment and ammunition. The smell of death hung in the air. Hurried by their officers, they quickly crossed the village. On they went.

At 0400 hours, the column reached the village of Schlenzig (Słowieńsko), which was only some six kilometres away. By now, the men were totally spent and Brigf. Krukenberg finally granted a three-hour rest. It was over all too soon and the I/RM continued on its way again. At this point Greifenberg was still its destination.

In the morning, Krukenberg and Zimmermann learnt from German peasants that the Russians were at Plathe (Płoty), fifteen kilometres south-east of Greifenberg, and that Greifenberg itself was totally encircled. This was worrying. Fenet and Jauss were immediately informed, but it was thought better not to let the men know this bad news just yet. Undaunted, they pushed on, keeping to the forests and the woods. The snow was still falling and the temperature was still well below zero centigrade.

Brigf. Krukenberg then decided to head north to the village of Petersfelde (Poradz). They arrived in the afternoon. Unoccupied, the village now awaited the Russians with white flags from every window. Some Frenchmen were angered by this sight and wanted to tear them down, but their NCOs pushed them on.

Once again, the civilians were the best source of information. From them, the Frenchmen learnt that a Wehrmacht Army Corps was regrouping at Meseritz (Miedzyrzecze), some ten kilometres away. After nightfall, the I/RM arrived at Meseritz. The remnants of General Munzel's Corps Group were camped in the village and around the grounds of the chateau in which the General had established his headquarters.

For bringing the I/RM out of hell, Brigf. Krukenberg decided to award Ostuf. Fenet with the Iron Cross 1st Class.[154] Unable to obtain the relevant decoration for Fenet, Krukenberg went to General Munzel with his predicament to which the General replied by unhooking his and handing it over. Some moments later, in a brief ceremony, the Brigadeführer decorated Fenet.

However, not all those with Fenet had made it out. The day of the 5th had presented Ustuf. Fayard and his FLAK Company with few problems, but then, on the morning of 6 March, he and his men had suddenly found themselves encircled in a wood. It was each for his own. Some were captured. Others escaped and managed to dress in civilian clothes thanks to the help of German refugees. This was how Stabsscharführer Hscha. Lenoir, Uscha. Lhomme, Gefechtsschreiber Uscha. Triqueneaux, Schirmeister Uscha. Deschamps, tailor Ob.Schutz Chomy, telephonist Cardet and the young Russian Samassoudov, the company mascot, escaped.

Ustuf. Fayard was captured but he too, with some others, managed to escape.[155] Days later, they came across Lenoir and the others with him. One by one they went their own way. A detachment led by Ustuf. Fayard joined up with a Volkssturm Company but were captured on 7 March by Russian tanks.[156]

At Meseritz or near to Greifenberg, a group of survivors from the massacre on Belgard plain led by Ustuf. Leune joined Fenet. It had all started in a small wood some hours after the massacre on Belgard plain when Ustuf. Leune took command of a group which numbered sixty or one hundred[157], including officers Ostuf. Métais, Ustuf. Herpe, and Ostuf. Tardan. Leune was not the most senior officer present, although he was the most experienced, having served in the Merchant Navy and the LVF.[158] Leune led the group westwards.

Three different accounts exist of how Leune guided these men to safety. The three sources are Saint-Loup, Rostaing, who marched with this group, and Soulat.[159] While there is some agreement between the accounts there is little or none between all three. Two of the accounts

154  Mabire, *Mourir A Berlin*, p.17. However, according to Saint-Loup, *Les Hérétiques*, p.327, it was General Munzel who, on the basis of a report submitted by Krukenberg, conferred on Fenet his own Iron Cross.
155  Unpublished article *La SS-Französische Flakbatterie*.
156  Soulat, *Historique de la Division Charlemagne*, p.58, repeated by Bayle, *San et Persante*, p.179.
157  Soulat numbers the group sixty (*Historique de la Division Charlemagne*, p.58) and Saint-Loup one hundred (*Les Hérétiques*, p.321).
158  Maxime Laune was born on 7 April 1909 in Pontoise. He was ex-LVF. According to Bouysse, *Encyclopaedia of the New Order: French in German Uniform Part 1: Officers*, he commanded the 7/58 from September 1944 to January 1945 when Walter took over.
159  See Saint-Loup, *Les Hérétiques*, pp.320-324, Rostaing, *Le prix d'un serment*, pp.170-173, and Soulat, *Historique de la Division Charlemagne*, p.58 and p.89. There are two other accounts: first, Mabire (see *Mourir A Berlin*, p.9), but his source, undoubtedly Soulat's *Histoire de la Charlemagne*, p.67, was later amended because it was inaccurate; and second, Scherzer, *Sous le Signe SS*, p.384, who simply states that Leune joined Fenet on the morning of the 7 March at a hunting lodge deep in a forest near Natelfitz (Natolewice).

lack detail while elements of Rostaing's are questionable.[160] However, what can be said is that with a good deal of luck and with the help of civilians along the way a group of survivors led by Leune joined Fenet's Battalion.[161] Leune was not decorated for the feat of bringing 'his' group of survivors out of hell, even though it was merited.

Hstuf. Roy and Ustuf. Martres joined Fenet at Meseritz. After the massacre they had started out with a group that was one hundred-strong and led by a French Haupsturmführer.[162] As the group made its way westwards through a gauntlet of hell it lost men in ambushes and to wounds and exhaustion. Before long Roy and Martres were alone. As luck would have it, they met a platoon of Sturmgeschütze that took them all the way to Meseritz.

Another group did make it 'out of hell'. On the morning of 5 March,[163] some one hundred and fifty French and German stragglers assembled around three assault guns at Fritzow (Wrzosowo) and struck north to Kolberg. Halfway there, in a small village, the group was engaged by Soviet tanks, but still managed to pass and then break through the enemy investment of the city.

## Bartolomei's Company

The fate of the *Régiment de Réserve* on Belgard plain was not shared by its rearguard, the ninety or two hundred men of Ostuf. Bartolomei's 2nd Company of the I/RR.[164] Two kilometres before Belgard, Bartolomei's Company was ordered to halt and cover the retreat of the *Régiment de Réserve*. Hstuf. de Perricot's parting words were: 'Only set off again on a new order. *Général* Puaud will not forget about you.'[165]

From Belgard came the noise of battle. Hours passed and still no new orders. Towards 0700 hours, feeling abandoned and sensing the growing anxiety of his men, Bartolomei gave the order to start out to Belgard. Suddenly they came under mortar fire. The fog lifted. A Russian tank emerged some tens of metres away and opened up. Panic-stricken, they scattered. They too were without anti-tank weapons. To escape the Russians, many ran back towards Körlin.

Ostuf. Bartolomei managed to assemble several men around him and set off back to Körlin where the II/RM should still be. Approaching Körlin, they came under violent fire again; by now, the Russians had completely invested the town. They turned around and took refuge in a copse.

160 For example, according to Rostaing, they chanced upon a village, which was a picture of peace and quiet, and whose occupants were coming and going about their daily business. And it was in 'this small corner of paradise' they took the opportunity to shave, eat and sleep off their tiredness before pushing on to Greifenberg. To honour the uniform they were wearing, they wanted to make a dignified entry into the town!
161 Instead, according to Soulat, their guardian angel was a French prisoner of war they met quite by chance, who fed them, dissuaded them from staying on the same route, a route which would have led them straight into the Russians, and, finally, showed them a pathway through the undergrowth, which enabled them to find *bataillon* Fenet that same evening.
162 Martres cannot recall the name of the French Hauptsturmführer.
163 The date is unconfirmed (Soulat, *Historique de la Division Charlemagne*, p.58).
164 Soulat numbers the Bartolomei's Company ninety (*Historique de la Division Charlemagne*, p.57) whereas Mabire two hundred (*La Division Charlemagne*, p.463).
165 Mabire, *La Division Charlemagne*, p.463.

Following the Persante, they went back up to Belgard in the hope of rejoining de Bourmont and the *Régiment de Réserve*. By means of a footbridge, they got across onto the left bank. Trying to avoid the open fields, they slipped from wood to wood.

The time was around midday when, in a wood, Bartolomei's group met up with three officers and one hundred or one hundred fifty men who had escaped the morning massacre on Belgard plain.[166] They were led by Hstuf. de Bourmont. Thereupon, they decided to make for the region of Stettin by night marches. To march by day in a region filled by the rumbling of Russian tanks would be suicide.

A snowstorm set in and Bartolomei found himself separated from the other group. He continued on. As for de Bourmont, Bartolomei was the last person to see him alive. And although de Bourmont was never heard of again, there is little doubt that he met his death in Pomerania.[167]

Bartolomei's group, now of platoon strength,[168] spent the whole of the following night of 5-6 March marching to the south-west. At dawn on 6 March, Bartolomei took shelter in the loft of a farmhouse. He was disturbed by the farm owner fetching hay for his livestock with a pitchfork! Almost immediately a Russian submachine-gun barked and bullets passed near him. He desperately tried to get his boots on, but one fell through the hay trap door into the cowshed. He retrieved it and dashed off to the woods. It would have been useless, no suicidal, to continue on without boots.

With a small number of comrades, Bartolomei waited until nightfall before starting out on the way again. Direction: Greifenberg. Towards midnight, they came across a forest chalet and settled down for the night. At 0500 hours on 7 March, fifty men led by Ustuf. Rigeade suddenly joined them. Nearly all were LVF veterans who did not seem to be unduly concerned by their present situation. The chalet, on their way, seemed the ideal place to treat a soldier, named Clabots, who had been wounded during an engagement.[169]

Bartolomei and his men continued on through the woods. They encountered others.[170] They too were half-starved and cold. Many no longer had weapons. On the morning of 8 March, they came to a farmhouse. Was it deserted? Bartolomei and two men, named as Guillemert and Derbaeke, went off to investigate. They spoke to a Ukrainian prisoner of war-cum-labourer and the German farmer who gave them some supplies, biscuits, pots of conserve, and milk. The latter invited them back in the afternoon for hot milk. The small group of Frenchmen would

---

166 Saint-Loup numbers this group of survivors one hundred (*Les Hérétiques*, p.299) and Soulat one hundred and fifty (*Historique de la Division Charlemagne*, p.57).

167 According to Landwehr, *Charlemagne's Legionnaires*, p.85, de Bourmont was one of the first to be killed on this tragic day. This is incorrect.

168 Saint-Loup, *Les Hérétiques*, p.312.

169 According to Saint-Loup, *Les Hérétiques*, p.312, the newcomers noisily made themselves at home so much so that Bartolomei eventually gave the place over to them! Saint-Loup goes on to imply that Bartolomei's decision resulted from the infighting between the different factions within 'Charlemagne'. However, Rigeade, in a letter to the author, 17/2/97, said of this implication: 'It's sheer lunacy!' Yes, while it's true that some were unhappy about being woken up, there was definitely no factional squabbling.

170 According to Soulat, *Historique de la Division Charlemagne*, p.127, by the morning of 8 March, Bartolomei had four men with him, named as Jullian, Guillemert, Verlecoq and Carrier. Mabire repeats that Bartolomei found himself with three or four men. And yet, according to Saint-Loup, *Les Hérétiques*, p.313, Bartolomei and his small group were joined by others, including 'Brochart and two *caporaux*' from column Bassompierre 'wheeling about' not far from there.

not get to enjoy his hospitality because he denounced them to the Russians. Surrounded by a Russian company, the group surrendered.[171]

To the victors went the spoils of war: Bartolomei's group was robbed of wedding rings, watches, compasses, in fact all manner of personal possessions. Suddenly, not far away, gunfire was heard. It did not last long.[172] Soon after, part of the Russian company reappeared with two dead and one wounded. They were furious. The Ukrainian farmhand was shot in cold blood and the prisoners were asked to present their soldbuchs. The SS insignia on them provoked a fit of rage and a political commissar struck two of the prisoners in the face with a pistol. The Cossacks then had their prisoners kneel alongside a ditch. The Frenchmen thought death was at hand, but they were 'only' struck across the back of their heads with a pistol. Blood flowed. Yet they were still alive!

The prisoners were then sent to the village of Zarnefanx (Czarno-węsy).[173] On their arrival they were hit and spat at by Soviet rearward personnel. The female soldiers proved more aggressive than their male counterparts and gashed the prisoners' faces with their nails.

Bartolomei was then brought before a Soviet Colonel whose questions an interpreter put to him in German. Wishing 'to be more French than ever', the French officer left the questions unanswered. As the interpreter could not speak French, the Colonel did not insist and dismissed him. Nevertheless, the Colonel had food and glasses of schnapps brought to the prisoners. He toasted them all one after the other. Guillemert did not drink fast enough and was struck around the head again!

Again the prisoners were robbed. This time it was their soap, razors, belts and wallets. They were left with absolutely nothing of value. On joining a column of prisoners, mostly from 'Charlemagne', Bartolomei and his men noticed that 'many had swollen faces'.

Oberjunker Méric, Moneuse's Orderly Officer, believes he broke out of Körlin on the same day of the massacre but much later and after nightfall. His route took him along the railway line with Belgard on his left, before entering the forest, where his column quickly fragmented into small groups. Quite by chance, he met an old comrade from Uriage by the name of Bonnefond, also a platoon commander. The two of them shared the firm hope of getting out of this alive. Méric also ran into Moneuse and joined a group numbering over one hundred men.[174]

---

171 Soulat, *Historique de la Division Charlemagne*, p.127. According to Saint-Loup, *Les Hérétiques*, p.313, the Ukrainian POW came and collected the small group of Frenchmen in the evening. He brought them back to the farmhouse and just as they arrived so did a company of Cossacks! They ran back to the woods, chased by bullets. Bartolomei fell into a pond, hauled himself out, and ran off again. Finally he managed to reach cover and counted himself fortunate to evade capture, but one of their number by the name of Julian (pseudonym) was not so. The Cossacks then put those hiding in the woods in a terrible situation; unless they surrendered, their compatriot would be put to death. They came out. In response to Saint–Loup, again he writes with a sense of drama, but this might be how the adventure of Bartolomei and the men with him came to an end.

172 It is believed by Soulat, *Historique de la Division Charlemagne*, p.127, repeated by Mabire and Saint-Loup, that the Russians had engaged elements of 'Charlemagne', perhaps those of Bassompierre's Battalion.

173 Soulat, *Historique de la Division Charlemagne*, p.127, repeated by Mabire, *La Division Charlemagne*, p.471. The same location is identified by Saint-Loup, *Les Hérétiques*, p.314, as a big market town.

174 The author is convinced that Méric did not leave Körlin with the II/RM. Méric is adamant that Belgard was on his left. The II/RM broke out with Belgard on its right. Also, as a member of the RR, it seems doubtful that Méric would have stayed behind with the II/RM.

## Rearguard at Körlin

Brigf. Krukenberg had 'suggested' to Hstuf. Bassompierre that Körlin be held for twenty-four hours after the withdrawal of the *Régiment de Réserve*, but Puaud had 'outbid' him with forty-eight hours.[175] It may have been this conversation that pinned the 500 to 750 men[176] of the II/RM to Körlin and which greatly reduced their already slim chances of making it to the Oder and safety.[177] Indeed, it could be said that after 0200 hours on 5 March, by which time the bulk of 'Charlemagne' had evacuated Körlin, the presence of Bassompierre and the rearguard at Körlin served little or no meaningful purpose. Surely, it would have been better to break out there and then, but orders are orders.

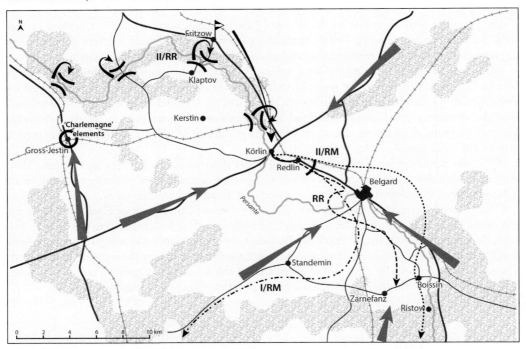

Körlin, March 1945.

Bassompierre positioned his forces: Walter's Company to the north and Rigeade's Company to the east. Rigeade quartered in the station hotel. The men dug in. With Bassompierre at

175  De la Mazière, *Ashes of Honour*, p.128.
176  Saint-Loup states 500, *Les Hérétiques*, p.300, Soulat 600, *Historique de la Division Charlemagne*, p.74, and de la Mazière 750, *Ashes of Honour*, p.128.
177  If Brigf. Krukenberg had expected no French SS troops to be left in Körlin by midnight of 4-5 March, then it seems doubtful that he would have suggested to Hstuf. Bassompierre that he hold Körlin for twenty-four hours.

Körlin were officers Baudouin, Français, Joubert, Moneuse, Rémy, Rigeade, Wagner, Walter and Werner.

Sent to get supplies, Blanc of Walter's Company ran into Ostuf. Joubert. A former *chef* of the *Avant-Garde de la Milice*, Joubert had led into the ranks of the Waffen-SS many very young students from the *École des cadres* at Chapelle-en-Serval.[178]

Accounts of the rearguard action of the II/RM at Körlin vary dramatically, so much so that they have proved irreconcilable. First off, a number of German civilian eyewitness accounts exist which speak of little or no fighting for Körlin, which was occupied by the Russians on 6 March.[179]

Blanc of Walter's Company recalled:

> Our section (8 to 10 men in total) took up four successive positions over the days of the 3rd, 4th, 5th and 6th March. Until the 5th we were positioned in a house to the north of the town in front of a group of trees, slightly raised. It was peaceful. The other elements of Walter's Company were not far from us. Headquarters was inside Körlin.
>
> Perhaps on the day of 5 March we were moved to another position in the north of the town and came under mortar fire. Bassompierre paid us a brief visit. Indifferent to the firing, he stopped beside me to examine the terrain. I presented myself, reminding him of the *affaire* of la Santé and asked him if he had any news of Agnély. We could hear the sounds of battle taking place elsewhere.
>
> On the morning of 6 March (day had still not broken) we were moved to a position at the foot of the slope on which the road to Köslin passed, facing north. Here we could hear the sounds of tank tracks and engines which knotted our stomachs.
>
> Then we were moved to a position along the pathway connecting the cemetery to the town, facing east. We did not directly participate in the retaking of the famous cemetery, nor the bayonet charge. We came under constant machine-gun fire, though. I cannot tell you for how long because I admit I fell asleep (we had not slept for two days). On the other hand, I saw a Russian prisoner pass, and then we learnt of the death of Uscha. René Maixendeau and another young NCO by the name of Guillarme.[180]

René Maixendeau who was killed in Körlin cemetery.
(Blanc)

178  Philippe Joubert was born on 15 November 1918 in Nîmes.
179  BArch OSTDOK 1/155, fol. 179, fol. 173, fol. 181, fol. 185, fol. 187 and 2/136, fol. 579. Also see Scherzer, *Sous le Signe SS*, pp.391-396.
180  Blanc, letter to the author, 11/4/01, with input from Jean Castrillo and Daniel Le Goff.

Castrillo of Walter's Company, who served in the same section as Blanc, recalls:

> During the night our company was outflanked on the right by Russian armoured cars. I was well placed against a low wall of earth and I fired a panzerfäust at the first one, which stopped it dead. As we ran to the rear I turned around to see a thick smoke pouring out of the armoured car I had hit.
>
> The following day, we were in position around a cemetery where there was serious hand to hand fighting. Suddenly, I found myself opposite a gigantic Russian descending upon me. I had in my hand a P38 pistol, which I had got from a wounded NCO. I raised my weapon and, turning my head away, fired without taking aim. The Russian fired at the same time. When I looked back I saw the Russian stretched out, stone dead. In short a lucky break.

Castrillo had been lucky indeed, more so because he admitted he was a poor shot with a revolver.

In the fighting in the cemetery Paul Denamps and de Puch of Walter's Company captured a Russian soldier, who they held for two or three hours before handing him over to an officer. Denamps reflected, 'What could I do with a prisoner when I was more or less a prisoner myself'. [This prisoner may have been the one seen by Blanc.] Sadly, a few days earlier, his brother Jacques Denamps, a runner in the same company, was killed by a Russian sniper who had killed three or four others serving in the same capacity.[181] Rigeade and his company did not see action.[182] And yet, in contrast, many French sources speak of a full-blown battle for Körlin. For example, de la Mazière, who was with the rearguard at Körlin, wrote:

> Six hours, twelve hours, twenty-four hours... we still held out. It was an intoxicating and desperate show. We hurled grenades over our heads, we vied with each other in machine-gunnning. Clinging to the ruins, each of us fought his own fight. We were far beyond forming an organised group. We were all sorts of people scattered over too large a battlefield. We had, however, a real leader in Bassompierre – the last to arrive, he was also the last to leave.
>
> The Russian corpses piled up, but they were continually replaced by new waves of 'Ivan' attackers... As evening approached we knew that the end was near. The Russians, attacking from all sides simultaneously, would overrun us the next day. Our fighting strength had suffered bloody losses; of the seven hundred and fifty men, only about three hundred and fifty remained.[183]

181 According to Bouysse, *Encyclopédie de l'ordre nouveau: Français sous l'uniforme allemande partie II: sous-officiers & homes du rang de la Waffen-SS,* Jacques Denamps was killed on 2 March 1945. Paul said that Jacques had stupidly got himself killed.
182 According to Mabire, *La Division Charlemagne,* p.493, Rigeade's Company of the II/RM, to the east of the town, 'hung on to the ground as fiercely' as that of Walter's Company. This is incorrect. While at Körlin Ustuf. Rigeade's Company was not attacked (Rigeade, letter to the author, 10/4/97).
183 De la Mazière, *Ashes of Honour,* pp.129-130. However, according to Soulat, *Historique de la Division Charlemagne,* p.74, Bassompierre still had 500 men with him when the II/RM broke out of Körlin.

Mabire wrote of a fierce see-saw battle for the cemetery north of Körlin that raged all morning. Indeed, shortly after dawn on 6 March, Russian infantry supported by armour retook the cemetery. Walter counterattacked *à la baïonnette* and in savage hand-to-hand fighting managed to recapture the cemetery for a second time. A few minutes later, hell was let loose. Multiple rockets rained in and massive explosions ripped gravestones and crosses into pieces. In the face of this hellish barrage, Walter ordered a withdrawal. As rockets continued to explode all around, the company returned to its starting positions. The time was now 1100 hours.[184]

Mabire continues that on the afternoon of 6 March the bombardment intensified on Körlin. Shells and rockets tore into buildings. Fires broke out and blazed. Forced to abandon their positions, the French SS troops pulled back to the inner suburbs. Men armed with panzerfäust managed to destroy several tanks at the entrance to the town, which barred access to the others.[185]

In response to de la Mazière and Mabire, there were skirmishes in and around Körlin which resulted in losses but based on the eyewitness accounts of German civilians and the likes of Blanc, Castrillo and Rigeade clearly there was no full-blown battle for Körlin, which involved tanks, artillery and 'Stalin's Organs'.[186]

Calling several officers together, Bassompierre announced that he had decided to try and break out, but it would be a breakout into uncertainty. Nobody knew where the German lines were. His plan was to leave Körlin to the east, follow the Körlin-Belgard railway line to the south-east, cross the Persante between Körlin and Belgard, and then march westwards.

Ustuf. Rigeade asked why they weren't breaking out towards Kolberg. This seemed the most logical direction, but Bassompierre replied that the port had already fallen to the Russians. This was tragically inaccurate. Rigeade's Company was assigned the role of vanguard and Walter's Company that of rearguard. H hour was set for nightfall.

The companies silently abandoned their positions and hurriedly assembled east of Körlin near the railway line. The less seriously wounded, basically those who stood a chance of surviving the journey, were fastened to horses whose shoes were covered with rags to prevent them making a noise. The more seriously and the non-transportable wounded were stripped of their military uniforms and papers and left in the care of the civilian representative of the German Red Cross.[187] Several medical orderlies volunteered to stay behind with them. Nevertheless, for all concerned, it was still a painful decision to leave the non-transportable wounded behind.

Orders to destroy all heavy equipment were carried out to the letter. The men would march light. Indeed, no provisions were to be carried. Some men volunteered to stay behind and man the combat posts to keep the Russians guessing about their intentions. They were to disengage in turn.

184 Mabire, *La Division Charlemagne*, pp.490-493. Furthermore, according to Saint-Loup, *Les Hérétiques*, p.300, by nightfall, Walter had retaken the cemetery four times.
185 Mabire, *La Division Charlemagne*, pp.493-494. This was undoubtedly based on Soulat, who wrote that the II/RM continued to hold Körlin in the face of enemy forces 'very superior in number and material' and that it was 'violently bombarded by Russian tanks and mortars', see *Historique de la Division Charlemagne*, p.74
186 This conclusion is reached by Scherzer, *Sous le Signe SS*, p.396.
187 Soulat, *Historique de la Division Charlemagne*, p.75.

In the evening of 5 March, the breakout began.[188] Many, like Blanc of Walter's Company, knew nothing of their destination, but assumed it was Kolberg, where they could embark for safety. After a thick hot soup and a cup of watered down coffee, he set off too into the unknown.

Following the Körlin-Belgard railway line in a south-easterly direction, the battalion's vanguard, Rigeade's Company, passed the railway station and crossed the tributary Radüe over the railway bridge. Its movement went unnoticed thanks to the night and a diversion in the west sector, a barrage laid down by all remaining heavy weapons to expend the last of the ammunition. Besides, the movement had been quite noiseless. But it could be said that luck was with the battalion as it now filed out of Körlin; the town was lit up like the middle of the day by a bright moon and by burning buildings. At 2200 hours, the last elements left Körlin. Now and then the Russians sent a shell into the town at random. There was no reply.

Luck was still very much with Bassompierre's battalion when Rigeade's Company overran sleeping Soviet infantry and armour in its path.[189] Bassompierre forced the pace. There was a brief engagement with a Russian patrol, which brought about casualties on both sides. The battalion marched on. Later, it was joined by those who had stayed behind at Körlin to cover the breakout. While evacuating Körlin one group had inadvertently walked into a minefield sown by engineers of 'Charlemagne'. Roger Wyckaert of Walter's Company was gashed in the leg by shrapnel. Hastily dressed, he had limped on.

After following the railway line towards Belgard for some four kilometres, Bassompierre's Battalion then went across country. The going was tough. Between each field there was barbed-wire fencing and no wire cutters were to be had. Boots quickly became waterlogged.

The men were so exhausted that they started to hallucinate. Blanc of Walter's Company thought he saw ship masts, which convinced him that they had reached the port of Kolberg. Only later did he learn that Kolberg was not their destination.

Blanc passed his water bottle to NCO Verstichel to take a drink, who sincerely thanked him. That was the last time Blanc would see him. When dawn came up the battalion took to the woods and hid away. The battalion's hiding place may have been the forest of Nassow, north of Belgard.[190]

---

188  Different authors, however, have recorded various times and dates. Mabire states, *La Division Charlemagne*, p.498, that the II/RM left the town during the night of 6-7 March but started before 1900 hours. Rigeade, in a letter to the author, 17/2/97, states the date of 6 March and the time of evening. Delperrié de Bayac states, *Histoire de la Milice*, p.607, the early hours of 6 March. Saint-Loup writes, *Les Hérétiques*, p.301, that at midnight of the night 5-6 March, 'they abandoned their positions'. Saint-Loup continues that, two hours later, 'a column of ghosts' was passing along the railway line southwards. Landwehr states, *Charlemagne's Legionnaires*, p.86, the night of 5-6 March. Soulat states, *Historique de la Division Charlemagne*, pp.74-75, 1900 hours on 7 March. De la Mazière implies in *Ashes of Honour* both the evening of 6 March and night of 6-7 March. Lefèvre states 7 March between 1800 and 2200 hours, *Axe & Alliés* no 1, p.66. Michaelis states the night of 7 March, *French Units In The Waffen-SS*, p.78. Scherzer confidently states on the night of 4-5 March, *Sous le Signe SS*, p.396. Regarding this, the author has been swayed in particular by the German civilian eyewitness accounts that Körlin was occupied on 6 March, even if a newspaper report dates its capture to 5 March. Moreover, the breakout would not have gone unnoticed if the Russians had occupied the town.

189  In a letter to the author, Rigeade recalls a very quick engagement which is far removed from de la Mazière's account, *Ashes of Honour*, pp.132-133, of a 'pitched battle' which lasted almost half an hour.

190  Blanc, letter to the author, 6/6/2002, and personal conversation. According to de la Mazière, *Ashes of Honour*, p.133, progress during the first night was good. He goes on to imply that the battalion reached

The men rested. In the afternoon, a German plane flew over at low level. Some got up to cheer it, but it did not have German markings. They wondered if the plane was really German or 'under new management', that of the Russians.

Walter, who had somehow managed to find a civilian coat, went on reconnaissance. On his return he assembled his company, which was still some one hundred strong. He announced that at nightfall they would 'set off again in the direction of the coast'.[191] He finished with a few words of encouragement. They still had hope.

The breakout had succeeded, but it was not a breakout to freedom. The ensuing days and weeks were a confusing succession of marches, detours, and violent engagements, perhaps fifteen in total.[192] Death or capture awaited all. As a result of the battalion's fate, it has been difficult, at times impossible, to reconcile the different accounts. What follows is the tragedy of Bassompierre's battalion presented in the form of 'snapshots' (although they may not appear in strictly chronological order and some of the participants may not have started out with Bassompierre).

On the evening of 7 March, the battalion set out again in single file. The rearguard was formed by Oscha. Blaise's platoon of Walter's Company. All went well for the first hour, but then, while crossing open ground, the battalion was suddenly exposed by flares. Mortars immediately opened up and crashed down on the frozen ground. The troops dived for cover. Darkness returned when the flares burnt out. The firing stopped.

It was then that the men of the rearguard realised they were alone. As they raced back to the woods several others joined them. They too were lost. They numbered thirty or so. Overcome by fatigue, they immediately fell asleep in the woods. Next morning, they awoke to find themselves buried under snow. Oscha. Blaise and Uscha. Le Cavelé went on reconnaissance. The two of them were never heard from again. This left them without an officer or a NCO.

Their objective remained Kolberg, but they had neither map nor compass. They would walk round and round for days. Cold, thirsty and famished, such was their hunger that they risked detection when they shot a doe. One of them drank the warm blood from the wound and felt better for it.

They encountered the Russians and lived to fight another day. They were walking in single file along a forest track when a lorry loaded with Russian soldiers suddenly appeared. Those at the head of the file shouted 'Russians, Russians' and fell back. But those following them misheard 'hives'[193] for the shouts of 'Russians' and rushed forward screaming: "We're going to eat honey!" Curiously, the Russians did not give battle and drove off.

To reach Kolberg, they had to cross the Persante, which was in spate, but the bridges were guarded and they were too few to overcome the guards. They built a raft but they were so weak

---

and crossed the Persante south of Belgard. If true, then the progress of Bassompierre's battalion during that first night was truly remarkable; the men were exhausted and cold; the route was to the east of Belgard; the route was through forests; and the last units of the battalion did not leave Körlin until around 2200. For these reasons, the author has concluded that the battalion was still on the 'wrong' bank of the Persante (Mabire, *La Division Charlemagne*, p.504) after its first night 'on the run'. Also, according to Mabire, *La Division Charlemagne*, p.503, during that first night the battalion went round and round in circles.

191  Blanc, personal conversation.
192  Soulat, *Historique de la Division Charlemagne*, p.75.
193  The French word for hives is ruches.

from not having eaten for three or four days that they could not carry it to the water's edge. Moreover, a Russian patrol arrived on the opposite bank.

They pushed further east. They came to a road and watched a stream of Russian vehicles pass before crossing at one bound. Still cold, thirsty and hungry, gunfire could still be heard in all directions. This gave them hope. Thus, nothing was finished. There was no talk of surrender. Besides, they had grave doubts about the fate that the Russians had reserved for the SS that they captured.

By now, they numbered eight or nine. They had started with thirty or so, but one by one they had disappeared. In this way, good friends Blanc and Castrillo were separated. Finally, one evening, they came across a deserted forest cabin and here they stayed. After some days of rest two or three men went their own way. They were never heard from again. Some, however, were in no condition to continue. Two brothers by the name of Hovelaque left.[194] The youngest one, who was barely eighteen, had frostbite to some toes, but was convinced that they should push on. Now they were five. There was Jean Priot and Jacques Revel, who were still able, and Blanc, Rimbert, and Désigot, who were not. Blanc was suffering from frostbite to his feet.

The cabin was known locally. A group of German women courageously came to feed them and look after them a number of times. Then, one evening, they heard women shouting and bursts from automatic weapons not far away. They never saw the women again.

The three *invalides* survived on the food foraged nightly by Jean Priot and Jacques Revel, but as the weeks passed they weakened.[195] They dreamt of food and, when awake, they talked of little else but food.

On 18 April 1945, after five weeks in the cabin, the Russians discovered them. Jean Priot and Jacques Revel, who were outside, shouted a warning and disappeared, but there was no escape for the *invalides*.[196] They saw two young Russian soldiers push open the door and aim their submachine guns at them. Blanc said of what happened next:

> We did not move (how could we?), them neither. I waited for the small flame to appear suddenly from the gun since I was certain that they were going to kill us; I thought about my parents with sadness because they would never know where, how and when I died, nor that I had so much sadness for them. That was all that was in my mind, but the curious thing is that I had absolutely no fear. The small flame did not come. They were joined by an officer, who looked at us with a sort of pity, perhaps contempt, but also disgust (we smelt bad and he saw that we had lice, which the Russians fear because of typhus). He murmured in German 'Kindersoldaten', then in Russian 'Fransouski'.[197]

194  Michel Hovelaque was born on 11 November 1926 in Paris and René Hovelaque was born on 16 February 1925 in Paris. Both joined the *Franc-Garde Permanente* of the *Milice* in Lot-et-Garonne. Their father was also a *Milicien*. Transferred to the Waffen-SS, the brothers served in the 7/58. Captured, they were handed over to the French authorities in Berlin in July 1945. Michel was acquitted by the *Cour de justice* of Agen, while René was sentenced to six months in prison and national indignity for life.
195  Jean Priot recalls 'visiting' the neighbouring villages of Pustchow and Buchhorst. This would place the cabin in the forest of Nassow, north of Belgard.
196  Jean Priot and Jacques Revel were captured one week later.
197  Personal conversation with the author, 2001.

The Russians left, convinced that the Frenchmen were not going to escape. They returned one or two hours later with a horse and cart driven by a civilian. The Frenchmen were brought out. The civilian lit a fire, helped them undress and burnt their rags. Then he shaved them all over. Disgusted, the Russians looked on from a distance. To warm himself up, Blanc crawled to the edge of the fire but got too close, badly burning his knees. In the following months, this would cause him more trouble than the frostbite and amputations.

Placed onto the cart, the Frenchmen were taken to a medical post, where they were treated. Each of them had a bed and a guard. 'Perhaps they are frightened that we might escape', Rimbert commented. They remained feverish.

They had time to reflect. They had survived. And it was because of Jean Priot and Jacques Revel that they had survived. Bonded by camaraderie, Jean Priot and Jacques Revel had not deserted them in their hour of need. Blanc's good friend Jean Castrillo said of his ending:

> In the last engagement fifteen of us were cut off from the rest of the column. I remained all night with three or four comrades, including Roger Wyckaert whose feet were totally frozen and unable to move them. We carried him to a building beside a railway line where he stayed with two men. The rest of the group were all groggy by three nights without sleep and battle. Two or three of us were seriously wounded. The able-bodied went on their way with their weapons. As for me, I stayed with a single comrade from the town of Mirepoix.[198] I was in bad shape. I had a piece of shrapnel in the groin and was losing a lot of blood. The Russians caught me on a railway track motorcar with my comrade and I ended up with other German and Russian wounded in the city of Köslin where a Soviet Major operated on me in quite a rustic field hospital.

Wyckaert was captured three weeks later by a Russian patrol. Transported to Belgard hospital, he had both legs amputated on Palm Sunday.[199]

Death could strike at any time as Robert Lacoste of Ostuf. Français' Kompanie recalled:

> We were marching in column at the edge of a wood; the Russians had occupied the main roads. Ostuf. Français was bringing up the rear of the column. A shot [rang out]. A Russian sniper hiding in the trees shot him in the back. He gave a squall and collapsed. I turned to give him help, but alas he was already dead. I took his identity disc and pistol and set off on my way again with the column, abandoning the body beside the path.[200]

Français was his friend.

---

198  His name may have been Cabirol.
199  Repatriated to France at the end of August 1945, Roger Wyckaert went before the courts and was sentenced on 3 April 1946. Years in prison followed. Freed, 'he devoted his life to helping his former comrades in combat and captivity even more disadvantaged than himself' (Mabire, *La Division Charlemagne*, p.468). He died on 11 February 1973.
200  Lacoste, letter to the author, 3/12/2002. This corrects Mabire who implies that Ostuf. Français was killed when the battalion crossed the Körlin-Belgard road (see *La Division Charlemagne*, p.502).

Hstuf. Rémy was also killed. Hstuf. Bassompierre had known him from his LVF days and held him in great respect. Thus, at Körlin, Rémy had found himself back under Bassompierre and serving in the II/RM. And when the time came for the II/RM to evacuate Körlin and retreat westwards, Bassompierre entrusted Rémy with the command of the rearguard. Oscha. Duchène wrote of Rémy's death:

> At the beginning of the morning we were a handful of men, hidden in a forest closely watching the movements of the enemy tanks. Beside me were *Capitaine* Bassompierre, *Adjudants-Chefs* Gaubion [Gobion—the author] and Cabannes (the latter from Lyon I think) and men that I did not know from disparate units. Over one hundred metres in front of us [was] a big copse in which were two men, *Capitaine* Rémy and his orderly. I got the information from a runner that this *Capitaine* Rémy, on an order from *Capitaine* Bassompierre, had advanced up to there in order to observe better the Russian armour. Personally I disapproved of his presence in the copse.
>
> Actually some moments later, I saw a member of the crew get out of a Russian tank, imprudently as only Russians can be, submachine-gun in hand. He looked intently towards the place occupied by your husband while I aimed at the man a rifle that I borrowed from a man hidden beside me.
>
> The Russian ran forward bent double, submachine-gun ready to fire. I took aim at my man, and when he went down on his knees, behind and against a slight mound, his gun went off and I pressed the trigger some tens of seconds slower than him. The delay, pardon me Nadaine, cost the *Capitaine* his life. If it can come as a consolation, I'll have you know that the Russian was also dead on the spot.
>
> After the Russian's burst, we saw the *Capitaine*'s orderly leave the grove and return in our direction under the fire of the tanks, running until he was out of breath. I sent for him to ask him for information: the *Capitaine* was realising with binoculars the encirclement of which we were victims when, suddenly, a submachine-gun burst coming from their right, struck down the officer.[201]

The thirty-four-year-old Henri Rémy left behind a wife and three children.

Oscha. Robert, who had come to the Waffen-SS from the LVF,[202] saved the battalion, pursued by Soviet tanks, when he knocked out two of them with panzerfäuste.[203]

Lacoste of Ostuf. Français' Kompanie could march no more. His feet were frostbitten. He was with a group, which had become separated from the battalion. He recollected:

---

201  Duchène, letter to Nadine Rémy, the wife of Henri, 28/8/50. According to Mabire, *La Division Charlemagne*, p.503, Bassompierre learnt of the death of Rémy after the road crossing which had cost Hstuf. Moneuse his life. This may be true, but it should be clarified that Rémy was not killed during this very same road crossing.

202  In 'Charlemagne', his unit may have been the 3/58.

203  According to Saint-Loup, *Les Hérétiques*, p.311, Bassompierre's battalion was being tracked down by a Soviet armoured brigade when Oscha. Robert saved the day. Realistically speaking, it seems inconceivable that the Soviets would employ and tie up a whole brigade pursuing a battalion that numbered no more than three hundred at this stage unless the Soviets believed the French SS troops were far stronger than they really were.

I asked *mon adjudant* Marcel Duchène,[204] who commanded the group, to abandon me. He refused. With incredible courage for several days he carried me on his shoulders. We were in the vicinity of Belgard when we were made prisoner by the Russians in a beetroot silo, where we were hiding. We were on our knees and going to be shot when a Russian woman officer arrived, shouting not to fire. Then we joined the great column of prisoners.

Lacoste was to witness the unbelievable group rape of a small girl by some ten Russians, after which the victim was disembowelled.

Unable to face his battalion disintegrating around him, Hstuf. Bassompierre sent his assistant, Hstuf. de Perricot, in search of two lost detachments.[205] Off he went with two liaison officers. They did not find those they were looking for and eventually became lost in turn. They marched westwards, hoping to find the Persante. The Russians seemed everywhere.

Near the Persante, de Perricot was seriously wounded; a bullet entered through his hip and lodged itself under his breastbone. Convinced that he was near to death, de Perricot told, then ordered, the two liaison officers to try and rejoin the column. They left. Much to his surprise, he did not draw his last breath. After tearing up his Soldbuch and his *carte de chef Milicien* and burying the pieces in the snow, he got to his feet and headed to the Persante, one of the few landmarks in the snow-covered region. He suddenly came upon a Russian soldier and fled as fast as his legs would carry him. When he stopped, out of breath, he suddenly realised that for a man in agony he had run quickly and for a good length of time!

Like many, Hstuf. de Perricot walked round in circles but was lucky enough to come across his two liaison officers who were as lost as him. They tried in vain to find Bassompierre's column. However, they did discover a forest house where 'Charlemagne' had sited a small supplies depot. Here they spent four or five days and were only spotted and captured by the Soviets after one of the liaison officers had foolishly lit a fire to get warm; the smoke from the fire had given them away. They surrendered without a fight. He ended up in a POW camp at Posen.

After skirting around Belgard to the east, Bassompierre suddenly changed direction to the west. In this way, the battalion came to the Persante and a footbridge, which was still intact, but guarded. Even so, the Frenchmen were wary. 'For safety's sake', half of the men took to the river and swam across to the other bank. As for the others, they used the footbridge after dispatching the Russians guarding it. They too made it across. So it was not a trap after all. Again they took to the forests which should have meant security.[206]

Bassompierre became more and more demoralised. Bassompierre approached Rttf. Gonzales, his former orderly in the LVF, and asked him: "What do you think of the situation?" Gonzales

---

204 Soulat believes that Duchène's final rank was that of Hauptscharführer (see Bouysse, *Encyclopédie de l'ordre nouveau: Français sous l'uniforme allemande partie II: sous-officiers & hommes du rang de la Waffen-SS*).

205 While there is great similarity between Mabire's and Delperrie de Bayac's accounts of Hstuf. de Perricot's misadventure, they do not agree on the date and the time of these events; Mabire is unspecific and Delperrie de Bayac details the dawn of 6 March 1945.

206 The date of this crossing remains unclear; de la Mazière's account implies the same night as the breakout from Körlin. However, Mabire writes, *La Division Charlemagne*, pp.504-505, that when the first dawn 'on the run' came up the battalion was still on the 'wrong' bank of the Persante.

replied: 'It's all over. We must no longer have illusions the secret weapons will arrive too late. The best troops have too many fronts to hold.'

That same evening, tragedy over took the battalion on attempting to cross a major road.[207] Quietly, the Frenchmen had crept up to within fifty yards of the road. From roadside ditches they waited for an opportune moment to cross. They watched two or three light convoys pass. And then a column of T-34s, 'Joseph Stalin' tanks and truck-borne infantry appeared. Their lights blazed. Gripped by the fear of being spotted, they waited and watched. The minutes passed agonisingly. Ten. Twenty. Thirty. Those who were crushed by fatigue fell off to sleep, but for most the waiting became harder by the minute. However, it now seemed as though the convoy might pass without spotting them. Suddenly, a 'Joseph Stalin' tank came to a stop and its turret started to turn towards them

Panzerfäust in hand, Hscha. Walter jumped up and ran forward through the bursts of machine gun fire around him. He fired and destroyed the tank. The Russians responded with flares to illuminate the night. And so began the battle. Those with panzerfäuste raced towards the enemy tanks. Moments later, two more were ablaze. These 'kills' are credited to Gabin and Krebs.[208] Gabin survived, but Krebs was killed. Many trucks and other kinds of vehicles were also destroyed.[209]

The fighting became hand-to-hand. Some Russians turned out to be women who were 'as furious as the men'. They were shot down without a second thought.[210] There was total confusion amongst the Russians, enabling the Frenchmen to cross the road and reach the forests again. Indeed, a picket of Russians deployed on the plain between the road and the forests melted away.[211] Under the false impression that the few Frenchmen who had got through thus far were just a small 'advance-guard', an insignificant number not worth bothering about, the Russians went off for the 'rich pickings' among the larger force which had to be to the rear.

The Frenchmen paid a terrible price to forge this road crossing: around one hundred men, including Hstuf. Moneuse who was hit in the chest and died almost instantly.[212] Bassompierre,

---

207  The date and location of this tragic road crossing varies. First, according to Mabire, *La Division Charlemagne*, p.501, the tragedy over took the battalion during the night of the breakout when it attempted to cross the Körlin-Belgard road clogged by a constant stream of Soviet convoys. Second, according to Saint-Loup, *Les Hérétiques*, p.311, and Delpierré de Bayac, *Histoire de la Milice*, p.607, the location was the Belgard-Stolzenberg road, on the other bank of the Persante, and days later. Third, de la Mazière, an eyewitness, describes the road as 'an important artery with three carriageways leading to Stettin and Frankfurt-on-the-Oder' (*Ashes of Honour*, p.174), possibly the Körlin-Plathe highway, and times this tragic road crossing days after the breakout from Körlin. Fourth, Rigeade, also an eyewitness, in his letter to the author of 5/3/97, suggests a road south of Belgard or further west, dating the road crossing to the night of the breakout from Körlin, noting it was much later than that recounted by Mabire.

208  Saint-Loup, *Les Hérétiques*, p.312. Paul Denamps of Walter's Company believes that his brother Louis of the Engineer Company knocked out a Russian tank with a panzerfaust during this engagement.

209  De la Mazière, *Ashes of Honour*, p.139. Soulat specifies, *Historique de la Division Charlemagne*, p.75, that ten or so trucks and other vehicles were destroyed with panzerfäuste. These same figures are repeated by Saint-Loup, *Les Hérétiques*, p.312.

210  De la Mazière, *Ashes of Honour*, p.138. Curiously, Mabire also writes, *La Division Charlemagne*, pp.510-511, of an engagement in which three tanks were destroyed and Russian women soldiers appear, but this engagement postdates that of de la Mazière and was not the result of a 'failed' road crossing.

211  De la Mazière, *Ashes of Honour*, p.139.

212  Before Moneuse died, Comte believes that Moneuse murmured 'Je suis touché'.

Std.Ju. Comte and Oberjunker Méric were all beside him. Comte, Méric and two others, one of whom Méric believed to be Hscha. Walter, wrapped his body in a tent sheet and carried it to a nearby ditch. Méric recalls: 'Moneuse was a colossus and he was very heavy. But there was nothing else we could do'.[213] Moneuse was buried in a shallow grave because the ground was frozen solid. Méric, who had taken his papers, handed them to the person he believed to be Walter, thus his superior. Among those who disappeared during this violent engagement was Ostuf. Dr. Philippe Joubert of the II/58.[214]

After dressing the wounded and regrouping, Bassompierre's Battalion if such it could be termed, marched on. Where possible the worn out survivors kept to the forests. Spotted by Russian patrols time and time again, some ran as fast as their legs would carry them whereas some fought it out.[215] A wound meant almost certain death. Some vowed never to surrender after they came across a pile of SS corpses; the Soviets had killed all of these wounded prisoners with a bullet in the back of the neck. They were also pitted against the elements.

Dying of thirst, many took to sucking snow, which burnt certain parts of the system and increased their thirst. All were hungry and they raided farms and hamlets in search of food. Infested with lice, it could be said that many were more dead than alive The wounded had to be abandoned.[216] One soldier, wounded in the leg, said to Bassompierre with a smile: *"Au revoir, mon capitaine*, don't forget to tell my family that I did my duty to the end and that I fought so that they would not know it [Bolshevism]. *Vive la France!"* Bassompierre would not forget him or his words.[217]

Some of the wounded took their own lives, but many could not bring themselves to pull the trigger. They lived in the hope that the Russians would attend to them, honouring their promises broadcasted at Körlin, but others, physically unable to kill themselves, pitifully begged their comrades to put them out of their misery. On the whole this wish was fulfilled.

The 'battalion' continued to disintegrate. Two or three days after the road crossing, one such group to become separated from Bassompierre counted Rttf. Gonzales and six others: Robert Maurel, Favier (a *sergent* originating from Marseille), Robert (whose brother, an officer in the *Milice*, was shot at liberation), Micha (a small Russian who had served with the 1st Battalion of the LVF) and two other comrades not known to Gonzales.

Gonzales was lightly wounded, carrying a piece of mortar shrapnel in the calf of his left leg, but he could still run. He and the others made their way westwards. He recalled:

---

213 Gonzales may have also been beside Hstuf. Moneuse when he was killed. He recalls in his *souvenirs* that a certain *Capitaine* Demessine, who was a colossus, was hit in the head when attempting to cross a road. Demessine actually served with the LVF and did not serve with the Waffen-SS.

214 Soulat, *Historique de la Division Charlemagne*, p.75. However, Blanc of Walter's Company believes that Joubert stayed behind at Körlin with the non-transportable wounded. He would meet Joubert's parents years later, but there was little he could tell them of their son's fate.

215 De la Mazière exaggerated when he wrote the enemy tanks fired directly at them, one shell per man (see *Ashes of Honour*, p.140).

216 De la Mazière explains that it became necessary to abandon the seriously wounded when the remaining horses were shot for food (De la Mazière *Ashes of Honour*, p.136).

217 Bassompierre, *Frères ennemis*, p.157.

We tried to cross a bridge over the Rega[218] (a small river in the neighbourhood of Greifenberg) because we still had a mind to pass through the Russian lines to find the Oder; the bridge was guarded by a platoon of Russian soldiers… thus impossible to cross.

We went along the river and we arrived in sight of a forest house (numerous in the region). Nobody in sight, apart from a horse all on its own, abandoned in a place adjoining the house. We were starving, having not eaten anything for several days. Thus we decided to kill the animal. I fired a bullet from my P38 between its eyes first. It was still standing looking at me! I fired a second bullet and it was still looking at me… Thus I decided to use a third bullet; this time behind the head, level with the cerebellum. It fell down in a heap … I still regret having killed it.

A little later we arrived near a great farm. After many precautions, assuring us that there were no enemy soldiers, we were welcomed by several women, most of whom were young and of Russian and Polish origin. They gave us some eggs and milk. The invaders had still not passed through there because there wasn't a main road nearby.

A little further, as we neared a small house, we heard a bizarre noise certainly coming from the said house. Cautiously we approached. When we arrived in front of the door, we heard a significant grunting; it was a pig that had been shut up there! I killed this one this time with no regrets because in Russia we were in the habit of appropriating a pig from time to time. This one was quickly jointed. We took the two rear legs and liver because we could not carry everything, still having some horsemeat steaks.

That same day, at nightfall, after perhaps fifteen or twenty days spent behind Russian lines, I started to limp. My wound started to become seriously infected. All the more because an abscess formed inside my thigh. And to crown it all, I fell in a ditch full of water. I could not go on any more and I felt that I was becoming a 'heavy weight' for my comrades, delaying our march.

During the night we saw a light coming from a small maisonette, some one hundred metres away. We approached, still with caution, and through the glass window we saw that some women and children, as well as a man in civilian clothes who was missing an arm occupied this dwelling place. Exhausted, we decided to go inside. We were made very welcome because we had an abundance of food that we hastened to cook on the cooker. We shared all that with the occupants, after which, exhausted, we were ready to sleep. The civilian [man], certainly a Pole, left to go and 'spend a penny'.

Unbeknown to Gonzales and his comrades, the Pole went and denounced them to the Russians. At dawn, Russian soldiers surrounded the house. Machine-guns covered the only exit out of the house. The Russians put to the Frenchmen inside that if they did not surrender then they would have to massacre the women and children also inside. They could do nothing else but surrender. Fearing the worst, they were surprised when the Sergeant commanding the Russians pulled out a bottle of Vodka and asked them to drink with him. In reply, Gonzales offered him a box

---

218  In his memoirs Gonzales names the river as the Persante. The author believes that Gonzales is mistaken and has corrected the name of the river to the Rega.

of cigars that he had acquired at Körlin. To him, this was no great loss as he could have taken it anyway. They talked. It was very cordial. The Russian Sergeant was from Smolensk, also the birthplace of Micha who was still with his comrades of 'Charlemagne'. The Russian Sergeant advised them to burn their *Soldbuch* and tear off their SS collar insignia. They did. They were then sent to Greifenberg, which was only some three kilometres away.

Paul Denamps of Walter's Company walked with his brother Louis. Eventually, they parted. The last time he saw Louis he noted that his brother was exhausted. Paul continued on. He was soon alone. At one point he was forced to hide in a bush from approaching Russians or Poles. However, close by was a female wild pig with her babies. Frightened that the sow would attack or give his presence away, he left and pressed on. He came across other comrades and walked for roughly ten days through the forest before they came to a railway line. Many of his comrades had swapped their uniform for civvies. Only three remained in uniform. Soon after, cold, hungry and suffering from frostbite, he was captured.[219]

Comte lost contact with Méric but joined up with Carlier. They came to an exposed incline some two to three hundred metres wide which a Russian light tank prevented from crossing. Carlier managed to disable the tank with a Mauser grenade launcher, depriving it of mobility, which enabled them to cross. They continued on. Comte suddenly had a sinister premonition and dived for cover. He raised his head tens of seconds later to see six comrades who were in front of him now lying dead. Clearly, it was not his time.

All too soon, Comte lost Carlier and rejoined Bassompierre, who called together the men still with him and told them to split up into smaller groups and make their way back to the German lines as best they could. Bassompierre asked Comte to stay with him, which he did.

Like many of his men, Bassompierre was suffering from severe frostbite to his toes. On or around 16 March 1945, the twenty or thirty survivors with Bassompierre stopped in a farmhouse where they managed a find a little to eat. They melted snow and heated the water. Crushed by fatigue, they fell asleep. Comte recalls what happened the following morning:

> I went out early to go pee and then I saw riders quietly approaching the farm. Well, I went back in and said to Bassompierre, [after] I woke him up: "Haupsturmführer, I think we're surrounded." He answered: "We resist my little one, we resist!" I said: "Yes with what?" We had nothing left. I still had my P38 with a magazine, he had his. We had nothing more. Well, he said to me: "Get a white sheet and go outside."

They surrendered to Polish cavalry who treated them correctly.[220] Bassompierre was taken to a camp at Arnswalde (Choszczno).

Marching with Hscha. Walter's Company was Uscha. Pierre Briault[221] of the Veterinary Company. He had 'changed employment' at Körlin when the last of the horses in his care

---

219 Paul Denamps told the author he was captured on 23 or 24 March 1945, whereas Bouysse records the date of his capture a little earlier on 15 or 16 March 1945, *Encyclopédie de l'ordre nouveau: Français sous l'uniforme allemande partie II: sous-officiers & hommes du rang de la Waffen-SS.*

220 In his book *Frères ennemis*, Bassompierre does not mention the location of his capture, however, according to Saint-Loup, *Les Hérétiques*, p.312, Bassompierre and the men left around him were captured in the region of Schivelbein.

221 Pseudonym.

were slaughtered for food. However, after a brief and violent engagement with the Russians, he now suddenly found himself alone in a forest and on the receiving end of an enemy artillery bombardment. He took shelter under several tree trunks. For around half an hour, shrapnel whistled all around him, but his mind was taken off the bombardment and the cold when he discovered nearby a comrade, like him a former *franc-garde* of the *Milice*, with whom he exchanged words about bullfighting.

And then the shelling ceased and the Russian infantry came on. At least two platoons. Advancing from fold to fold, they approached the two Frenchmen. Their situation looked black and minutes later a wounded Briault was captured. However, this was not the end of his odyssey. He managed to escape but was recaptured. This happened again and again, perhaps five or six times in total. In this way, he drew nearer and nearer to the Oder and was only about a dozen kilometres away when he was found 'half dead' on a dung heap by Polish partisans. By now, he was in terrible physical shape: his feet were bleeding, he was suffering from exposure, hunger and exhaustion, and he was carrying a serious wound to his shoulder.

The partisans took Briault to their commander who spoke French well. 'Struck by the Frenchmen's courage', the Polish officer asked him if he wished to fight under his command. The former *Milicien* hailing from Nîmes declined his offer.[222]

As for Hscha. Walter, he met his death bravely attacking a tank.[223] Rumour has it that an NCO by the name of Verstichel, a *lillois*, who had served with Walter in Company 5/58 and greatly admired him, committed suicide when Walter was killed.[224]

Oberjunker Méric was on the run for over a week. He recalls the cold, the snow, the hunger and the constant feeling of tiredness. Early one morning his group, which included Gérard de Perricot, stumbled upon a horrible sight:

222  Mabire, *La Division Charlemagne*, pp.511-513. However, there is a certain similarity between the odysseys of both Briault and that of Alain D. which appears in *Historia* hors série 32, p.180. Both individuals were from Nîmes, both have a passion for bull-fighting, both were captured five times and both escaped five times, both were 'finally' captured by Polish partisans, both were brought before a Polish officer, both were asked by the Polish officer to fight under him, and both replied with the same words which declined the offer. Notwithstanding the numerous similarities, there are a host of insignificant differences between the two accounts, but the account of Alain D. contains two 'extra' episodes of note that do not appear in that of Briault. Firstly, Alain D. was captured in the evening of 'the hell of Belgard', briefly interrogated by a Russian officer and when he confirmed that he was French he was allowed to go free! And yet the German SS prisoners with him were shot on the spot. Secondly, after speaking with the Polish officer, he was again allowed to go free! He set off again. On foot and alone, he made his way through Germany and then France, before crossing into Spain where he took refuge in the Baleares to await the end of the political 'storm'. Alain D. is described as twenty-five, a specialist in the use of the bayonet and 'a hero of Charlemagne'. Also of note is that Alain D. could not have been with Walter's Company if he was captured in the evening of 'the hell of Belgard'; as part of the II/RM, Walter's Company had remained at Körlin after the departure of the I/RM and the RR. Thus, Walter's Company was not with the RR on Belgard plain when disaster overtook it.
223  Mabire, *La Division Charlemagne*, p.516. However, according to Paul Denamps of Walter's Company, Walter was wounded and could not walk any more, after which he said he would never be taken as a prisoner and killed himself with a grenade. Furthermore, Paul Denamps is convinced that his brother Louis was killed on the same day Walter was wounded. The family gravestone records Louis' date of death as 10 March 1945.
224  Paul Denamps of Walter's Company knew Verstichel and was surprised to learn that he killed himself.

We discovered a convoy of refugees, or what was left of it, seven or eight corpses, including four women and two babies. The women had been raped and shot on the spot, several days previously. Frightened we had to continue on our way.

The group made it to the town of Meseritz. The last few days had been hard, with more and more frequent clashes with the enemy. All of them felt that it was the end. So they decided to stop in a manor house which they searched for food, discovering enough for a veritable feast. They ate their fill. They also discovered in a building occupied by prisoners a stock of civilian clothes that could still be used. They all agreed to end their adventure and try and pass themselves off as workers. They carefully hid their tunics away, but still kept their weapons close to hand. The disguise was not convincing, though; Méric was still in his feldgrau trousers!

They fell asleep on real beds and slept like they had not slept for a long time, only to be brutally awoken by Polish horsemen the following morning. They were led to a corner of the yard and lined up unceremoniously against the wall to be shot. Méric shouted out: "Shit, it's a shame to shoot guys like that." Thereupon, the Polish officer in command halted the execution, pulled out a packet of cigarettes from his pocket and offered them round. He explained that he had once worked at Béthune in the north of France and wanted to help them, but had to speak to the Russian commanding officer, who was sat a few metres away. The Polish officer went to the Russian officer who gave him carte blanche to do what he wanted with the prisoners. The Polish officer stated that he would hand them over to the first passing convoy of prisoners. He was as good as his word. Méric felt good to still be alive, but little did he know that he swapped one hell for another.

Ustuf. Rigeade's Company broke up when it attempted to cross a road along which Soviet convoys of tanks and trucks were moving. It had been decided to cross this road in groups of roughly ten men each during the breaks in the traffic and then regroup on the other side, but the crossing did not go as planned. Rigeade's group made it across and entered the forest, but no other groups followed. Rigeade believes that the group following his must have moved away from the road and in this way lost contact with his group as well as the following group. One of the groups was never heard from again, although it is easy to imagine the ultimate fate of its men.[225] Among the group were Hscha. Perrigault, Prevost, Scheyder and Ferrer. All were LVF veterans of 1941 and very dear to Rigeade who now found himself with just six of his men (Armani, Leonard, Reynier, Sage, Seurre? and one other). They continued westwards.

Separated from Rigeade when the company had attempted to cross the road carrying Soviet convoys, Oscha. Blonay and his platoon, joined by French, German and Latvian escapers, tried to make for the Oder. They marched by night and tried to rest by day. They were not only cold, but also hungry. There was no escape from the frost, which struck at limbs. Fingers and toes froze. But they too continued to push westwards. Day after day passed. They neared Stolzenberg. Blonay said of his capture:

On the morning of 17 March 1945, [suffering from] frostbitten feet for the second time (the first time was in 1941 before Moscow), I could march no more. I asked Ostuf.

---

225 Rigeade, letter to the author, 17/2/97. This corrects Mabire's account, *La Division Charlemagne*, p.515, that the group disappeared from a column of prisoners Rigeade had joined after his capture.

Veyrieras who was with me to take command of the group, which he did, deciding to leave the wood in broad daylight. A hill hid a road along which a Polish convoy was passing. Spotted, the group surrendered, signalling my presence in the wood, thanks to which I was saved.

A medical officer, a Polish Jew, had me transported on a cart pulled by German prisoners. Speaking French, he told me that his regiment was composed of compatriots deported to Siberia following the Soviet occupation of part of Poland under the German-Soviet Pact of 1939, which partitioned Poland. They had to enlist in the Red Army so that they could return to their country. I was sent to Greifenberg and then to a field hospital in Pulawy, Poland, where a German medical officer amputated the toes of my left foot.

Tracked by a large group of Polish troops, Rigeade's group could not shake them off. And then, at dawn one morning, it was surrounded in a small wood. As there was little point in fighting it out, Ustuf. Rigeade ordered his men to surrender. They had covered some fifty kilometres on foot and reached Greifenberg, but in the end it had all been in vain.

Much to the surprise of Rigeade, he and the men with him were treated well. Other prisoners arrived. Separated into small groups, all were herded eastwards. The Frenchmen soon found themselves among thousands of German prisoners which the Russians 'goaded' on.

Rigeade was to witness the roadside summary execution of a young German SS soldier walking near him. He only escaped this same end because he was no longer wearing his distinctive SS collar patches, which he had torn off as a precaution against retribution.

Eventually Rigeade would join the group of captured officers of 'Charlemagne' and share their fate.

Separated from Rigeade when the company had attempted to cross the road carrying Soviet convoys, Oscha. Girard managed to lead twenty men, mostly from the Panzerjäger Kompanie of Waffen-Gren. Regt der SS 58, all the way back to the Oder, but they were unable to cross over and all were captured.

Hscha. Gobion, perhaps the most decorated former NCO of the LVF, also managed to reach the Oder. He had ten men with him. However, no boats could be found. On the night of 23-24 March 1945, the group attempted to cross a partly destroyed bridge at Wollin (Wolin), but was spotted by the Russians. Three men were hit. Two of them had to be abandoned when the group gave up the idea of crossing and withdrew under fire.

From the west bank, German soldiers, attracted by the fusillade, pointed to rubber dinghies hidden on a river island. An LVF veteran then tried to swim across and reach them, but he got cramp in the icy water and had to give up. Hope faded. At dawn on 24 March, after an artillery duel, the Reds attacked and Polish soldiers captured the nine survivors of 'Charlemagne' in a potato silo.

Pierre de Séverin managed to reach the Oder and make it across, but his joy was short-lived. Taken to the closest German command fire, he came under Russian artillery fire and was seriously wounded by shrapnel in his right leg. He lost consciousness and awoke in a makeshift German field hospital. His war was over.[226]

And yet the trek still continued for some. According to former *Milicien* Marcel H:

> We marched all night. During the day we hid in the woods. We tried to eat in abandoned farms. Tanks and Russian and Polish cavalry tracked us down. I had lost my company. We were thirty Frenchmen commanded by a former Lieutenant of the Sturmbrigade, Bergeat [de Bregeot].[227] We wanted to reach the Baltic and try and go over to Sweden from there. In fact we went through Stettin, in flames, and we had continued westwards, still on foot, still pursued. We were captured by Polish cavalry just at the end on 2 May 1945 in a village beyond the Sprée.[228]

226 Pierre de Séverin was transferred to a military hospital on the outskirts of Berlin. Such was the seriousness of his wound, which had become infected, that he feared the worst, but a German managed to save his leg, for which he was thankful. Evacuated to Magdeburg, he was captured by the Americans at the start of May 1945.
227 According to Lefèvre, de Bregeot was a former member of the *Milice*, see Bouysse, *Encyclopaedia of the New Order: French in German Uniform Part 1: Officers*.
228 Delperrié de Bayac, *Histoire de la Milice*, p.7.

**14**

# The Hell of Pomerania
# Part III

In the fierce fighting at Bärenwalde and Elsenau on 25 February 1945 'Charlemagne' splintered. A number of groups withdrew to the north-east and into the forming Danzig defensive pocket. Some of the groups were no longer composed of soldiers from one specific unit. On 28 February, the Soviets entered Flötenstein from the south, but were thrown back by a counterattack launched by tanks and 1 Kompanie 'Charlemagne'.[1] This company remains unidentified.

### 'Corsair' Gagneron[2]

Some of the groups teamed up with German units. One such group was that led by Oscha. Jacques Gagneron, who was ex-LVF and a recipient of the KVK II.[3] It consisted of the forty or so men of his almost intact platoon of the 1/58.

After the fighting in Elsenau cemetery, the platoon suddenly found itself separated from Ustuf. Fatin and the company, and withdrew northward, passing through Flötenstein on 28 February. The following day, at the village of Falkenhagen (Milocice), the Frenchmen chanced upon an intact German unit of eight assault guns, which was operating independently. The crews were young, their morale was high, and the commanding officer, a young Hauptmann, was in need of infantry support. Thereupon, Oscha. Gagneron offered the services of the French platoon. Besides, the German unit was well equipped with provisions! The platoon had not eaten properly for three days. Together they set off to the north. The Frenchmen, now elevated to the role of Panzergrenadiere, were sat on the superstructure of the assault guns.

Gagneron was a legionnaire of old who knew well the partisan war of 'hit and run' and it was the same tactics the armoured group was to employ. After nightfall, they came to the town of Rummelsburg (Miastko) which was occupied by nearly forty Russian tanks. Within gun range,

---

1   Lindenblatt, *Pommern 1945*, p.191.
2   See Saint-Loup, *Les Hérétiques*, pp.270-277.
3   Saint-Loup, *Les Hérétiques*, p.271. However, his rank appears as Untersturmführer in *Der Freiwillige* 10/97 and Léguerandais, *Hitler's French volunteers*, p.133. This is unlikely. In the LVF he served as a NCO, not an officer. According to Bouysse, whose source was Lefèvre, Gagneron acquired the rank of Oberjunker, but the date of this promotion is not known.

they took up positions around the town and waited for dawn to attack. All night long they listened to the screams of women being raped and the muffled shouts of wounded being finished off. This, of course, enraged them. And it was only the first gun shot that released their pent-up rage. In minutes, one third of the Soviet armour was knocked out. The other tanks fled, leaving its infantry support to its own devices. Gagneron's men then efficiently cleaned out the town of drunken Russians. By midday, the town was in their hands.

The smell of death hung in the air. Dozens and dozens of disembowelled women lay in the middle of the roads. Clearly, some, after being raped, had been thrown out of windows to their death.

Adhering to the tactics of 'hit and run', the German armour and Gagneron's men evacuated the town before the arrival of considerable Soviet forces from the direction of Baldenburg (Bialy Bor). They went east towards Radensfelde, arriving at 1700 hours, and here they rested.

Whilst on sentry duty Gagneron stopped a column of twenty-four French POWs making their way to the Russians and liberation. He advised them to think again and not to set foot in Rummelsburg but they did not heed his advice, replying that they had nothing to fear from the Russians. He let them pass.

Later that night, the German unit received orders to retake Rummelsburg and hold it for twenty-four hours to allow the passage of an armoured train. A German company of infantry was detailed to support the attack. The 'illegal' presence of the Frenchmen was not disclosed in case they would have to part ways.

As to be expected, the reception was considerably 'hotter' this time. Although two assault guns were lost, one to tank fire and the other to a mine, Rummelsburg was retaken. Again they discovered in the town what the Russians were capable of: the twenty-four French POWs that Gagneron had spoken to earlier that day had all been killed, either bayoneted in the stomach or shot in the head.

After seeing through the armoured train, the mixed force moved to Bütow (Bytów), but their time together was now over. With the 'illegal' presence of the Frenchmen reported, the *kommandantur* of Bütow forced them to go their separate ways.

Singing in full voice, Gagneron's Platoon set off on foot to the north and was picked up by a convoy of German trucks that conveyed it all the way to Schlawe (Slawno). Gagneron was later wounded and hospitalised, losing his right arm.

### Compagnie d'Honneur

Following the fighting at Elsenau which had been costly for the *Compagnie d'Honneur*, Ostuf. Weber had assembled his command and led it to the village of Flötenstein, where it spent the best part of a day, time enough to rest and find something to eat, before pushing on to Kolberg in the evening. It now had orders to make for Greifenberg, orders that Brigf. Krukenberg had left in his wake.

At dawn the next day, the *Compagnie d'Honneur* was crossing a village when refugees suddenly appeared from all sides, repeating the same warning: "The Russians are coming". This was not their imagination at play as minutes later Russian tanks materialised. Two Sturmgeschütze moved into action and fought off the T-34s. Relieved, the *Compagnie d'Honneur* continued on its way to the Baltic Sea.

Refugees and their baggage crowded the road. Crushing everything in their path, Russian tanks soon caught up with the *Compagnie d'Honneur* again. Taking a calculated risk that the tanks would not follow him across country, dotted with frozen ponds and marshes that might give way, Weber ordered his men to continue their withdrawal parallel to the road. At a distance of several hundred metres from the road, the retreating *compagnie* was only inconvenienced by the occasional short burst of machine gun fire. Even so Weber hurried his exhausted and frozen men; the Russian infantry might not be that far behind.

And then, some fifteen kilometres from Flötenstein, the *Compagnie d'Honneur* came to a village and, unbelievably, a train bound for Kolberg sitting in its railway station. It boarded and found itself in the presence of other elements of 'Charlemagne'. They numbered a good one hundred. That same evening, the *Compagnie d'Honneur* was installed in a lavish officers' casino in Kolberg. The following day, a train took the *Compagnie d'Honneur* along the coast to Greifenberg.

## Greifenberg

Before the Soviet advance through Pomerania, the *französischen Ausbildungs-und-Ersatz-Bataillon* [Franz. A.-u.-E. Btl.] evacuated Greifenberg and relocated to Wildflecken camp.[4] However, elements may have seen action in the defence of Greifenberg.

### The motor convoy

The motor convoy of the Headquarters Company and divisional service units under Stubaf. Katzian also made good their escape from Pomerania. Leaving Gross Jestin at 0200 hours on 4 March, it made good time and, at daybreak, entered the town of Treptow-an-der-Rega (Trzebiatów), where it stopped.

From the back of a truck an armed Russian suddenly appeared; he must have jumped aboard in the belief that the truck was friendly. There was great surprise, even panic. A driver shot the Russian dead as he was about to fire. The other trucks were immediately searched. No more unwelcome passengers were found, but the rumbling of enemy tanks could be heard distinctly. At 0600 hours, the convoy left Treptow. Destination: Swinemünde (Swinoujscie) at the mouth of the Oder.

Around 1000 hours, in the region west of Treptow, a Russian tank column appeared and gave chase to the convoy. The drivers put their foot down, leaving behind the enemy tanks which fired wildly at the convoy. Thankfully rain covered the convoy from air attack. Its progress often slowed to walking pace as the roads became more and more congested with refugees and littered with wreckage. Crossing the island of Wollin (Wolin), the convoy finally came to Swinemünde at 1100 hours on 6 March. And it was here that Rttf. Soulat rejoined his French and German comrades of the divisional *Stabskompanie* with the motor convoy. He was overjoyed. He had come from Kolberg, via Cammin and Wollin, and on foot most of the way! He was not the only one to join the motor convoy, which was now ferried across the city to the island of Uznam.

4    At Wollin station, Soulat of the Headquarters Company saw some wagons full of French volunteers. He went to investigate. They were from Greifenberg and, according to the officer in charge, bound for Wildflecken. Soulat noted that all had new equipment.

On 7 March, the survivors, who now numbered two hundred, left Swinemünde for Jargelin, near Anklam in Western Pomerania. However, they were minus all their equipment; they had been required to hand it over. Also Ustuf. Sarrailhé was missing. Stubaf. Boudet-Gheusi was absolutely furious. However, the recalcitrant was found hiding away in a barracks and brought along. Sarrailhé explained he preferred to stay behind and participate in the defence of Swinemünde rather than leave with them. The following day, at 1600 hours, they arrived at Jargelin and found themselves billeted in a barn full of holes. Their straw litter was vermin infested.

They passed the time delousing themselves. To relieve the monotony, some of the NCOs put the exhausted and demoralised survivors through the joys of close order drill again. There was little else to do. On 14 March, they were moved to Menzlin, three kilometres from Jargelin. Their thoughts went out to their comrades still trapped in the 'hell of Pomerania'.

## The Danzig pocket

Forced to withdraw to the north-east and into the forming Danzig pocket were the groups led by Ustuf. Fatin and Oberjunker Chatrousse. Many of the men under Fatin belonged to his own company, the 1/58, which, despite many MIAs, was one of the few units to have retained some form of cohesion. Following Fatin's group was that under Chatrousse of which only a few were still armed and able-bodied. While continuing to reassemble his men Chatrousse strove to maintain contact with Fatin.

At 0500 hours on 3 March, after an exhausting night march, the group under Ustuf. Fatin arrived in Schlawe (Slawno), where he was surprised to learn that other French SS troops, some three hundred in total, were already there. For the most part, they were from the II/57 under Hstuf. Obitz. Elements of the Signals Company had also managed to make it to Schlawe. Oberjunker Chatrousse and his group arrived soon after Fatin.

That same day also saw the arrival by train of a one hundred strong detachment of the Division's Artillery Battalion under Hstuf. Martin, which had just completed its training in Bohemia–Moravia.

At 1600 hours, Hstuf. Obitz, the senior officer, took command of the various isolated elements of 'Charlemagne' at Schlawe. All told, he had the command of some five hundred men. Wishing to move the men and equipment by train, he requisitioned railway wagons, but the lack of a locomotive thwarted that idea. Nevertheless, the ever resourceful Frenchmen used the wagons as sleeping accommodation.

The following day at dawn, Hstuf. Obitz assembled all officers and passed on to them the news that the last railway links with the main force of Army Group Vistula had just been broken to the east of Köslin. In fact, this news was days old. They were cut off. Henceforth, there was no longer any hope of reaching Greifenberg as per orders. Obitz could do little else for the time being other than order the officers to take their men in hand again. Thus, the day was made over to cleaning weapons, repairing equipment, and searching for food, but mainly the latter.

That same day, Uscha. del Missier and the twelve men of his section of the 8/57 arrived at Stolp, east of Schlawe. They had walked there all the way from Elsenau. As the day of 4 March passed Hstuf. Obitz grew more and more restless. Night fell. Dawn broke. By now, Obitz could bear it no more and placed his detachment at the disposal of the headquarters of the 4.

SS-Polizei-Panzer-Grenadier Division, which enjoined him to take his command to Neustadt a.d. Rheda (Wejherowo), some one hundred kilometres to the east.[5]

As if by a miracle, an old locomotive was found and, at midday, Hstuf. Obitz and his detachment left Schlawe. Towards midnight, the train pulled into Stolp (Slupsk) station. Progress had been slow, taking the best part of twelve hours to cover the twenty-five kilometres between the two major towns.

While sat in Stolp station disaster suddenly struck: a single Russian fighter-bomber swept overhead and dropped three or four bombs. All were direct hits. The effect in the packed railway cars was devastating: fifty men were killed and sixty were wounded.[6] Among the dead was Ustuf. Colnion, the commander of Company 8/57. Among the wounded were Hstuf. Obitz and Ostuf. Salle who had only arrived at the front with the artillery group days before.[7]

Command of the French detachment now went to Hstuf. Martin, who formed a *bataillon de marche* of three combat companies of some one hundred and twenty men each.[8] As his assistant he chose Ustuf. Fatin who would prove to be the real commander of the battalion. The command of the companies went to Oberjunker Chatrousse, Oberjunker Lapart, and Oscha. Bonnafous.

Oberjunker Chatrousse was the former Orderly Officer of Hstuf. Moneuse. Oberjunker Lapart was ex-LVF and had attended the same Lehrgang as Chatrousse at Wildflecken.[9] Oscha. Bonnafous was also ex-LVF and had served on the Eastern front since the first winter. In 'Charlemagne', he became the commander of the 3rd Platoon of the 1/58.

In the evening of 6 March, the French Battalion continued its journey by train and finally arrived at Neustadt. The three companies were then sent to billets in three separate villages north of Neustadt. Even so the companies were no more than three kilometres apart.

On 6 March, thanks to the personal leadership of Uscha. Georges Racine, a small group of French SS soldiers also arrived at Neustadt. Racine first served France in the ranks of the Air Force and then, from 1941, in the LVF. A very capable and resourceful NCO, Racine was appointed the commander of the 1st Platoon of the 1/58 after the departure of Oscha. Girard to command the Panzerjäger Kompanie of Waffen-Gren. Regt der SS 58.

---

5    Soulat, *Historique de la Division Charlemagne*, p.80. However, according to Mabire, *La Division Charlemagne*, p.106, Obitz went off to find someone who would give him orders and when he came across an officer of the 4. SS-Polizei-Panzer-Grenadier Division he put his command at his disposal. Naturally this officer had no specific orders for Obitz but decided to send him and his command to the depot of the 4. SS-Polizei-Panzer-Grenadier Division at Neustadt a.d. Rheda (Wejherowo). The officer was sure that the Division could make use of them.

6    Mabire, *La Division Charlemagne*, p.107, and del Missier of the 8/57 who was present at Stolp at the time of the attack (correspondence to the author). However, according to Soulat, *Historique de la Division Charlemagne*, p.80, eight men were killed, including Frezard, who was ex-LVF (Soulat, letter to the author, 22/11/2007).

7    On 12 March 1945, Hstuf. Obitz was evacuated by sea from the port of Gotenhafen, but his ship was torpedoed by a Russian submarine and went down with all hands.

8    Chatrousse, letter to the author, 31/8/97. This corrects Mabire who details the formation of this same *bataillon de marche* at Neustadt one day later.

9    Born on 28 August 1920 in Paris, Maurice Lapart enlisted in the LVF in 1941 with his father. Transferred to the Waffen-SS, he served in Company 5/57. His father Joseph held the rank of Lieutenat in the LVF and his party, the RNP, issued a *document de propaganada* based on what 'he saw in Russia' with the LVF.

After Elsenau some twenty men assembled around Racine. He hoped to join another Waffen-SS unit and go back up to the front again, but this proved impossible! When they tried to integrate themselves into a company of the 4. SS-Polizei-Panzer-Grenadier Division they were told that all French stragglers had to be sent to collection stations at either Stolp or Neustadt. As they marched eastward their number grew. In this way, they became forty-strong. Finally, the group led by Racine managed to board a train bound for Danzig.

The journey was brought to a sudden halt when the train came under fire. All out! Officers of the 4. SS-Polizei-Panzer-Grenadier Division appeared and formed a *unité de marche* made up of Latvian SS troops also on the train. Racine offered the services of the Frenchmen, but this was declined as the only orders they had for them stated that they were to be sent to Neustadt to be regrouped. And the orders were definite. They felt all the more redundant on learning that their train journey was suspended temporarily. Thus, they took up residence in the cinema of a small village to while away the hours of waiting. Exhausted, some soon fell off to sleep.

In the evening, a Waffen-SS NCO informed the Frenchmen that the Germans were pulling back and that they had best leave on foot as the train was now out of the question. So at nightfall they set out. Some 'clever dicks' were even on bicycles. Finally they came to the city of Lauenburg between Stolp and Neustadt. And as luck would have it another train took them the rest of the way to Neustadt, which they reached hours later.

Uscha. Racine went straight to the headquarters of the 4. SS-Polizei-Panzer-Grenadier Division and was told of the whereabouts of other French SS troops in villages north of Neustadt. It was added that he should really go and get some sleep before joining his compatriots the next day. The group was sent to a barracks where warm soup and clean bedsteads awaited.

In the early morning hours of 7 March, Hstuf. Martin and Ustuf. Fatin went by car to Danzig to make contact with a Waffen-SS headquarters. During their absence the Russians unexpectedly attacked Neustadt but met stiff resistance from tanks of the 7th Panzer Division, which had been dug in through lack of petrol. So rather than continue this investment which had already cost them several tanks and numerous other vehicles, they decided to skirt around the city to the north. In their path lay the weak French SS companies of the *bataillon de marche*.

On learning from a German motorcyclist that the Russians were turning north after being repulsed at Neustadt, Oberjunker Chatrousse came to the conclusion that the only way of reaching Danzig and of finding Ustuf. Fatin was to march due east. Oberjunker Lapart and Oscha. Bonnafous converged with Chatrousse to go in this direction. They decided to await nightfall before setting out.[10]

---

10    According to Mabire, *Mourir pour Dantzig*, p.115, the French SS companies quartered north of Neustadt repulsed Soviet spearheads with rifle and machine gun fire. Thereupon, the three French SS company commanders 'improvised a resistance to delay the enemy and give their men time to withdraw to the east'. However, the notion that the three French SS companies fought north of Neustadt is disputed by Chatrousse (letter to the author, 3/8/97). Also, if there was no fighting, then it is doubtful that Oscha. Bonnafous 'disappeared in the fighting' (as recorded by Mabire, *Mourir pour Dantzig*, p.115). Furthermore, Chatrousse has confirmed that Bonnafous, Lapart and himself were in contact during this period and during the retreat later that night. Curiously, according to Saint-Loup, *Les Héretiques*, p.277, detachments *Chartrons* and *Labart* were 'set up as a rearguard'. In reply, the French SS companies were alone and without orders. Thus, the role of rearguard remains unconfirmed.

Aided by night, the three companies set off and marched eastwards. By now, whether they realised it or not, they were, in fact, encircled.[11] Compass in hand, Oberjunker Chatrousse guided them to within sight of the sea whereupon the lights of a powerful lighthouse became their new guide to the south.

And then, quite suddenly, they found themselves in front of positions held by a German armoured unit and were greeted by gunfire.[12] Making themselves known, they came forward. The Germans were full of apologies and explained to Chatrousse that they had been expecting to see the Russians appear at any moment. This misunderstanding was soon forgotten about when a lift was secured for the whole *bataillon* on a lorry convoy of a bridging unit en route to Danzig. On arriving at Danzig, the *bataillon* was billeted in a school and it was here that Fatin rejoined the *bataillon*.

When tallied the *bataillon* was still some 250-300 strong and, despite the very difficult night march, it had retained its cohesion.[13] But the *bataillon* had a great many wounded and was without much of its weaponry.[14]

As for the French SS troops led by Uscha. Racine, they were thrown into the battle at Neustadt. Requisitioned at Neustadt barracks with other stranded French SS soldiers, Sturmmann André Bourreau of the 7/57[15] found himself sent up to the front and guarding a sort of public garden from a hole he had hastily dug in the frozen ground. Several metres from him Bourreau thought he recognised a comrade from the *Compagnie d'Honneur*. The situation was so confused that he watched the Russians arrive by lorry barely one hundred metres away and disembark without attempting to camouflage themselves.

It was around six in the evening when Bourreau heard, then caught sight of German troops slipping from tree to tree. Were they changing position or withdrawing? Soon after, he heard the sound of footsteps on dead leaves just in front of him. He cocked his machine pistol. This time it was the Russians who were coming!

Bourreau then spotted a Russian well beyond his position. The young *Milicien*[16] thought that he was done for; the Russians seemed everywhere. Firing a short burst, he brought down the Russian. He let off another burst somewhat at random, and, out of fear, began to shout. Thereupon, he became convinced that the more he shouted, the more he would instil fear in the

11   Saint-Loup, *Les Hérétiques*, p.277. Although the battalion was encircled, there was no such break through as stated by Mabire, *Mourir pour Dantzig*, p.115. (Chatrousse, correspondence to the author.)
12   In correspondence to the author, Chatrousse positions the German armoured unit 'on the main road connecting Danzig to Hela'. This 'main road', now multilane highway 6, runs the whole length of Gotenhafen and exits the city to the north-west. Thus, the German armoured unit and the French *bataillon*, which had not yet reached the city of Gotenhafen, were somewhere north-west of Gotenhafen when they 'met'.
13   A figure of 'approximately three hundred' is recorded by Mabire, *Mourir pour Dantzig*, p.116, whereas that of two hundred and fifty is recorded by Chatrousse, letter to the author, 22/9/97.
14   Soulat records, *Historique de la Division Charlemagne*, p.80, one third of the *bataillon* as able-bodied and armed, another third as able-bodied, but not armed, and the last third as wounded. Mabire, *Mourir pour Dantzig*, p.116, and Saint-Loup, *Les Hérétiques*, p.277, repeat one third of the *bataillon* as able-bodied and armed, but record the wounded respectively as over half and two-thirds of the *bataillon*.
15   Article 'André Bourreau' and Mabire, *La Division Charlemagne*, p.536. And yet, curiously, according to Mabire, *Mourir pour Dantzig*, p.109, Bourreau served with the 8/57.
16   Article 'André Bourreau'. Bourreau served first with the *Franc-Garde permanente* of Paris and transferred to that of Seine-Inférieure. He was born on 29 May 1923 in Paris.

Russians. In response, he heard shouts and explosions. Then, some one hundred metres away, he recognised the unmistakable sound of a German machine gun joining in. 'Surprised by this unexpected resistance', the Russians fell back. Silence returned.

In the early morning hours, Bourreau and his comrade from the *Compagnie d'Honneur* cleared off and crossed Neustadt. Stopped by a German NCO of the 'Polizei' who wanted to send them back to the front, they 'played dumb'. Baffled by their reply, the German NCO spoke sternly and then let the matter drop. Besides, he had to stop others now arriving from Neustadt.

Bourreau and his compatriot then found themselves with a mixed unit composed of Wehrmacht troops and Russian volunteers of the Vlasov Army who had no desire to fall into the hands of the Red Army. Soon after, they met up with the other Frenchmen that Uscha. Racine had brought to Neustadt the day before. Uscha. Racine was still at their head. Of the forty men with him the day before, he now had twenty. He pushed them along the road to Gotenhafen where they would eventually join the other French SS volunteers trapped in the Danzig pocket.

The 'Waffen-SS Headquarters at Danzig' decided to rest and rearm those Frenchmen still capable of continuing the fight. Deloused, they were quartered in accommodation that overlooked port Gotenhafen and the Baltic Sea. While waiting to go back up to the front line the Frenchmen were employed digging combat emplacements and taking prisoner shot down Soviet airmen, about ten a day. Old reflexes soon reappeared.

A small group of four French SS soldiers arrived at Gotenhafen from the Hela (Hel) peninsula. Led by Uscha. Vasseur, this small group was the perfect cross section of the diverse elements that had gone to make up 'Charlemagne'; there was René Cessil of the 5/57, a former *franc-garde*; Chauvin, a former LVF *legionnaire*;[17] and a former volunteer of the NSKK. The group came to Hela by train via Stolp.[18] From Hela, a motor launch brought the Frenchmen across the bay of Danzig to Gotenhafen. Inseparable, the four Frenchmen would participate in the heavy defensive fighting for the port city of Gotenhafen. They would remain totally independent of the other French Waffen-SS personnel in the 'Danzig pocket'.

The small group led by Uscha. Vasseur was not the only one to make it to Gotenhafen under its own steam. Another such group was that led by Uscha. Grenouillet of the 1/58. He had fifteen men with him. And he knew not one. He found himself in their company after the fierce fighting in Elsenau cemetery which had seen his platoon, the 1st, shatter. It was to a small hamlet beside Rummelsburg that the group withdrew.

At the end of several days without orders and supplies, Grenouillet sent a grenadier to Rummelsburg for news. He reported back that there was no one left in the city. Thereupon, the group left to the north and Stolp. Its stay in the small hamlet had lasted between eight to ten days. At this moment Grenouillet still did not know that he and his group were in a great 'pocket'. From Stolp, he hoped to withdraw to the west.

Arriving at Stolp, Grenouillet learnt that a withdrawal to the west was now out of the question; the German Second Army, holding Eastern Pomerania, had been cut off in its entirety, and was falling back east towards Danzig and Gotenhafen. The group went east too, following the coast as though a handrail. At Danzig, feldgendarmen sent the group onto Gotenhafen.

---

17  Charles Chauvin was born on 27 December 1927 in Bourg-la-Reine in the southern suburbs of Paris.
18  While at Stolp railway station the group witnessed a violent Soviet air strike. Presumably this was the very same air strike that had inflicted terrible losses on those French SS troops making their way to Neustadt by train.

At the *Kommandantur* of Gotenhafen, Grenouillet met Uscha. Racine, his platoon commander. They fell into each other's arms. The two of them were on the verge of tears. They had not seen each other since becoming separated in Elsenau cemetery.

Racine told Grenouillet that Fatin, their company commander, and others of the 1st Platoon were two kilometres from here in a villa beside the Baltic Sea. The others with Grenouillet, of various units, did not share his joy or that of Racine. With a joyous heart, the two of them made their way to the villa and Fatin. At an open door there Fatin stood. For the first time, looking him straight in the eyes, Fatin shook his hand. Grenouillet was overjoyed. He had found his family again. Uscha. Guilcher, a Breton and also of the 1st Platoon of the 1/58, then came towards him. Grenouillet was now back home. He felt a sort of relief, although his thoughts were still very much with those he would never see again: the missing and the fallen.

Uscha. del Missier arrived at Danzig from Hela and was incorporated into the 4. SS-Polizei-Panzer-Grenadier Division. Forty-eight hours after his arrival, he was sent to Praust (Pruszcz Gdanski) some ten kilometres south of Danzig. He would fight under a German officer.

On 11 March 1945, the seventeen men of a platoon under Uscha. Combin,[19] all from Fatin's 1/58, lost their way while on reconnaissance south-east of Gotenhafen. The frozen corpses of deserters and civilian looters hung from the branches of trees along the road and swayed in the wind. This was the work of the merciless Feldgendarmerie. To avoid a similar fatal meeting with the military police, the French platoon integrated itself into a column of German pioneers.

The French platoon was assigned a mill to defend. Later, the Frenchmen noticed that the Germans had pulled back without informing them. Faced with little other choice, Uscha. Combin decided to try and make it back to Gotenhafen. First their route lay through large woods deep in snow and sometimes under foot were the frozen bodies of women or peasants. Then they came to a vast plain. Alarm bells started to ring. Cautiously they advanced across, observing the terrain. Convoys could be seen far off, but whose were they? They approached the road. Suddenly a machine gun opened up and only missed them by a fraction. The convoys were Russian! Two tanks came straight for them. It was the end. They had gambled and lost. Now they were prisoners. A Soviet gestured to the Frenchmen to climb aboard. They obeyed.

The eight prisoners aboard one tank expected the worst when the tank stopped in the remote corner of a wood. The Soviet tank commander, pistol in hand, called the first down. Uscha. Combin complied. The pistol was brought down on his nape and then his valuables were stolen – wedding ring, watch and pen. The next was called down and he too was hit and robbed. This was repeated a further six times. It was only then that Ivan concerned himself with the weapons the prisoners were still carrying! They set off again. The Frenchmen could not believe that they were still alive.

As for the other nine prisoners who had clambered aboard the second Soviet tank, they were never heard from again.

---

19   This might be a pseudonym.

On 20 March 1945, all combat worthy French SS troops within the Danzig pocket were reformed into a SS-Ersatz-Bataillon[20] and deployed to the front north-west of Gotenhafen.[21] It was in the third line of defence behind German and Latvian troops. Trenches were built.

SS-Ersatz-Bataillon Martin[22] was no more than three hundred-strong and remained subordinated to the 4. SS-Polizei-Panzer-Grenadier Division. Attached to the French battalion were three German NCOs who had served in the Foreign Legion, spoke perfect French and were veterans of the Eastern Front, but Ostuf. Fatin resented this outside interference. [23]

From 21 to 30 March, the front was rather calm.[24] However, on 31 March, the Russians broke through the first two defensive lines. The Frenchmen waited for the battle to begin, which started with infernal artillery and mortar bombardments. During one such mortar shower Oberjunker Chatrousse was wounded in the heel by a piece of shrapnel measuring 2cms by 1cm. He was evacuated.

And then, in the early morning hours of 1 April 1945, the Russians attacked.[25] The number of T-34 tanks could not even be counted! Nevertheless, the tank attack collapsed under the watchful eye of three Tiger tanks whose long-barrel 88mm guns knocked out the T-34s one after the other. Eleven Russian tanks were soon blazing before the Tigers were called to another sector. Calm returned. And although SS-Ersatz-Bataillon Martin had managed to hold its ground and halt the Russians with 'a bloody nose', its own losses had been heavy, in fact crippling.

The Russians then turned to a war of words. By means of leaflets and powerful loudspeakers, they invited the Frenchmen to surrender or face the attack of several divisions. Nobody went over. Again the Russians unleashed a violent hurricane of steel on their positions. Shells and rockets churned up the ground. Defensive positions caved in.

Finally, SS-Ersatz-Bataillon Martin received orders to prepare for a night-time embarkation.[26] Night came and the remaining Frenchmen withdrew to the Baltic shoreline. From a small creek offering some protection from Russian fire, they were evacuated by all manner of boats

20    The battalion may have only counted two companies (memoirs of Grenouillet) or three companies (Mabire, *Mourir pour Dantzig*, p.119).
21    According to Soulat, *Historique de la Division Charlemagne*, p.87, its positions may have been the villages of Kielau, Ciessau and Sagorsch. One French grenadier of Battalion Martin recalls that its positions were between Oxhöft and Rewa. According to Mabire, *Mourir pour Dantzig*, p.119, the French *bataillon de marche* took up positions along an airfield whose runways and hangars had been destroyed by heavy bombardments, and then deployed to new positions, not far from the sea, overlooking a sort of plateau, possibly Oxhöfter Kämpe. However, Mabire does not date the movement of the *bataillon* into these two positions.
22    Mabire, *Mourir pour Dantzig*, p.120.
23    Chatrousse had one of the German NCOs attached to his company (correspondence to the author throughout 1997).
24    Soulat, *Historique de la Division Charlemagne*, p.82, and the *souvenirs* of a French grenadier of SS-Ersatz-Bataillon Martin (as told to Mounine). This corrects Landwehr, *Charlemagne's Legionnaires*, p.26, who states that the battalion 'soon' faced a powerful Communist assault.
25    Mabire, *Mourir pour Dantzig*, p.120. However, one French SS-grenadier of SS-Ersatz-Bataillon Martin recalls that the tank attack took place during the night of 31 March-1 April 1945.
26    The memories of a French grenadier of SS-Ersatz-Bataillon Martin (as told to Mounine). However, according to Mabire, *La Division Charlemagne*, p.121, orders were received around midday 'to withdraw and reach the shore' and goes on to suggest there was little or no delay between the receipt of the orders and the embarkation.

and transported across the bay to the sandy Hela peninsula where the defenders of the Danzig pocket were now being assembled for sea evacuation.

Late on 2 April 1945, the Frenchmen boarded a former British cargo ship, converted of late by the Kriegsmarine into a troop ship.[27] Bound for Denmark, the ship was crowded with civilian refugees of all ages and wounded soldiers.[28]

Three days later, on 5 April 1945, the ship docked at Copenhagen. At 1600 hours, the Frenchmen disembarked. They endured three days of delousing before enjoying the delights the Danish capital had to offer. It seemed as though the Danish capital had been spared the ravages of war. On 9 April, they were ferried to Fredericia where they enjoyed six days of paradise. On 16 April, they entrained for Neustrelitz where 'Charlemagne' was reforming. Attacked by British aircraft, they had to change train. They finally reached Neustrelitz on 19 April.[29]

Of the five hundred French SS men assembled at Schlawe one month earlier, only one hundred rejoined 'Charlemagne' at Neustrelitz. Thus, the losses of Martin's battalion amounted to around eighty per cent, and while many had been wounded or were missing, many had indeed 'died for Danzig'.

Among the wounded was Oberjunker Chatrousse. From Copenhagen, he was conveyed by hospital train to a hospital at Halle. En route, the hospital train, which was clearly marked with the Red Cross, was machine-gunned by the Allied Air Force. After only two days in hospital, he was sent on his way to Austria of all places. It was explained to him that nobody knew where 'Charlemagne' was and that the Russians were closing in from the East and the Allies from the West. From Austria, he went on to Italy, arriving on 3 May 1945. The day after, he 'vanished into thin air'.

Some Frenchmen 'fought for Danzig' independent of SS-Ersatzbataillon Martin. On 26 March 1945, Uscha. del Missier, fighting at Praust with 'SS-Polizei', was wounded in the head by mortar shrapnel. It could be said that he was 'lucky' because the other two men with him were killed. Evacuated to the peninsula of Hela, he was shipped on the General Sankt Martin to Copenhagen, Denmark, arriving on 1 April 1945. He was then taken by hospital train to Saxony and hospitalised in a converted school at Ernsthal, some twelve kilometres south-west of Chemnitz. At the end of April, he left hospital and set out for home.

On 28 March 1945, after several days of hard and violent defensive fighting for Gotenhafen, the three-man group led by Uscha. Vasseur was evacuated from the city to the collection point of Hela.[30] In turn, the group was shipped westwards. Before docking at the port of Stralsund, Germany, the ship had had to wait out to sea for a decision where to disembark. It was now early April 1945.

After spending five days at Stralsund, the group was issued a travel warrant to return to Wildflecken. By train, the four Frenchmen journeyed back through a devastated Germany;

---

27  Ibid and Soulat, *Historique de la Division Charlemagne*, p.82.
28  In all likelihood the wounded Chatrousse was aboard this same ship.
29  See the notes of Robert Soulat which appear in *Pour La France, Pour L'Europe*, pp.91-93. These notes are for the most part based on his *Historique de la Division Charlemagne*, which records the French survivors finally reaching Neustrelitz on the 10th. This date of the 10th was repeated by Mabire (*Mourir A Berlin*, p.78) and the present author.
30  Most sources record that the Soviets took Gotenhafen on this day.

first, Stettin; then Berlin; Leipzig; Munchen; Ulm; and, finally, by the end of April 1945, Sigmaringen. The war was soon over.

Still as a group, they headed south and, after destroying their weapons, separated at Konstanz near the Swiss border. Thanks to some French POWs, they were now in civilian clothes. As for René Cessil, he crossed into France via Bale. He did not know what became of his comrades.

Ostuf. Auphan very nearly made it out of Pomerania with an incredible story to tell:

> In March 1945, during the Division's retreat, after being bombed in the direction of Danzig, where *Adjutant* Marmejant [Mermet] met his death, I managed to change into civilian clothes and merge into a column of French prisoners. Thus I found myself in civilian clothes with my former orderly von Hoeke who spoke Polish fluently, personally I had some knowledge of Russian, and the two of us entered the Polish circles of the PPR, Polska Partia Robotnicza [Polish Workers' Party]. I must say I had been an officer-instructor of Polish airmen in 39-40 at Aulnat base, so I had notions of the language. Thus I worked on the material organisation and installation of this party, as some sort of deputy chief at Deutsch Krone for the ruling party in Poland. On 11 April, I was recognised by French prisoners and arrested on 22 May. On that date I was handed over to the Russian authorities at their request. Since then I spent time in different POW camps in Russia.[31]

He was finally released in September 1945 by the Russians after declining offers to attend classes at a political school in Moscow and then an instructor's post in the Soviet Air Force.

**Siege of Kolberg**

It has been estimated that some six hundred Frenchmen of 'Charlemagne' managed to reach Kolberg before the Baltic Sea port was completely encircled on 7 March 1945. All were billeted on the ground floor of the Casino Municipal. Many were from the divisional staff and support units, but there was also a sprinkling of those from the elite *Compagnie d'Honneur* and the *Régiment de Marche*. Nevertheless, a good number of them were totally demoralised and unfit for combat duty.

At their head was ageing Hstuf. Havette, the commander of Waffen-Artillerie-Abteilung der SS 33. His assistant was the sixty-three-year-old Ostuf. Multrier, a veteran of World War One, responsible for civil defence at Wildflecken.[32] But the two officers were as exhausted and demoralised as the troops. Two 'Charlemagne' officers, Ostuf. Ludwig and Ustuf. Büeler, not of French origin but German and Swiss respectively, were still very much full of fight, though. They had arrived at Kolberg on 5 March 1945. Of late, Ludwig had been attached to Krukenberg's headquarters and Büeler to that of Puaud.

---

31   Post-war interview with Military Security, reproduced in Rentano & Leguérandais, *Ces Franciliens qui ont choisi Hitler*, p.112.
32   Maurice Multrier was born on 14 May 1882 in Dunkirk. He joined the French Army in October 1902, went on to attend Saint-Cyr and graduated with the rank of *sous-lieutenant*. He fought bravely in the Great War, winning the *Croix de guerre* and *Chevalier de la Légion d'honneur* (awarded on 30 October 1915). He left the army as a battalion commander. He joined the SOL and passed to the *Milice*.

At first the Frenchmen were gainfully employed on constructing anti-tank obstructions. When Oberst [Colonel] Fritz Fullriede, the town commander, asked Havette and Multrier to man these same defences with Frenchmen they replied that they could not with so many men that were non-combatant. Hence, it came down to Ludwig and Büeler to assemble those French volunteers determined to fight on. Between two and three hundred men came forward to fight.[33] In this way, a reinforced *compagnie de marche* of three platoons was raised and added to the defence of the city.[34] At the head of the company was Ostuf. Ludwig. His *adjoint* was Ustuf. Büeler.[35] The French *compagnie de marche* was attached to Battalion Hempel.[36]

Among those to come forward to fight was Oberjunker Claude Platon, Puaud's Orderly Officer.[37] Notably, his father was Admiral Jean Platon.[38] Brothers Louis and Marcel Savone, who was wounded, also came forward to fight, probably in the ranks of the French *compagnie de marche*. Soon after, they were wounded by the same shell and evacuated together by ship to Swinemünde.[39] As for those Frenchmen who stayed put at the Casino, they were disarmed. All the same, they agreed to continue building fortifications and assist in the evacuation of civilians and soldiers.

To defend the city packed with refugees, Oberst Fullriede had at his disposal a motley force from all branches of service. Total military personnel amounted to some 3,300 men, one third of which were Volkssturm organised into two battalions. Heavy weapons were scarce: eight 105mm howitzers, whose previous owner was 'Charlemagne';[40] seven heavy and eight light FLAK cannons; eight tanks of Panzer Division 'Holstein' sent to Kolberg for repair, supplemented on 5

33    Mabire states two hundred (*Mourir pour Dantzig*, p.85) and Saint-Loup three hundred *(Les Hérétiques*, p.302).

34    Soulat, *Historque de la Division Charlemagne*, p.61, Saint-Loup, *Les Hérétiques*, p.302, and Mabire, p.86. However, in Bayle's book *San et Persante*, p.180, an eyewitness with the initials of 'AA' gives a very brief account of the fighting at Kolberg and talks of two French companies taking up positions facing the enemy. The notion of two French companies is repeated by Scherzer (*Sous le Signe SS*, pp.451-452) who adds that they were commanded by Ostuf. Ludwig and Ustuf. Büeler.

35    According to Mounine Henri, *Kolberg* (Paris: Éditions de l'Homme Libre, 2009), p.48, Büeler commanded the 1st Platoon and very quickly replaced Ludwig. Büeler was succeeded by Grenadier Armé-Blanc (pseudonym). The rank of Armé-Blanc is incorrect.

36    The *compagnie de marche* was probably raised on 5 March and attached to Battalion Hempel that same day. It should be recalled that Ostuf. Ludwig and Ustuf. Büeler only arrived at Kolberg on 5 March. (See Saint-Loup, *Les Hérétiques*, p.301). Interestingly, Scherzer makes the point that this battalion must have had a high proportion of Waffen-SS personnel because the Polish First Army actually referred to it as SS-Bataillon Hempel (see *Sous le Signe SS*, p.451).

37    Claude Platon was born on 2 March 1918 in Cherbourg. He joined the *Milice* in August 1943 with the rank of *chef de trentaine* in the *Franc-Garde bénévole* of Toulouse and was sent to Haute-Savoie on 5 March 1944 with the same rank in the *Franc-Garde permamente*. At the end of May 1944, he was incorporated into the *Franc-Garde permamente* of Ariège, receiving promotion to *chef de centaine-adjoint*, and participated in the maintenance of order operations against the maquis. Ill-discipline saw him demoted to *chef de trentaine* and posted back to Toulouse.

38    Considered 'ultracollaborationist', Admiral Platon was the former Vichy minister for the Colonies, before Pétain dismissed him from the government for his views. Arrested by the Resistance, he was brought before a military tribunal of the F.F.I. at Limoges. Condemned to death on 24 July 1944, he was shot or barbarically quartered on 18 August 1944.

39    Louis Savone died of his wounds on 21 March 1945. Marcel Savone had his leg amputated, after which he was evacuated to Bavaria. He survived the war and died on 3 September 2009 at Nice.

40    These were the same howitzers that 'Charlemagne' sent by train from Neustettin to Belgard.

March by the arrival of a further seven;[41] one armoured train which arrived on 4 March; and one Volkssturm rocket battery with 800 rounds. However, his trump card was the Kriegsmarine. From 7 March, the defenders could call upon destroyers Z-34 and Z-43 and their 150mm guns. Their fire support would smash up tank attacks and knock out artillery batteries.

At first fortress Kolberg and its 'garrison' faced the Soviet 45th Guards Tank Brigade and the 272nd Infantry Division of the First Guards Tank Army. When these two units were withdrawn the 6th and 3rd Infantry Divisions of the First Polish Army took their place.

At 0600 hours on 6 March, Battalion Hempel launched a counterattack along Treptower straße [now Trebiatowska] to redress a dangerous situation that had arisen during the night. The counterattack was irresistible and Neugeldern, beyond the city perimeter to the south-west, was regained. Karlsberg could not be retaken, though. The French *compagnie de marche* may have been engaged.[42]

The French *compagnie de marche* was deployed along Kösliner straße and Körliner straße.[43] Fierce street battles ensued.[44] On the evening of 7 March, the Soviets attacked along Treptower straße [now Trebiatowska] and initially made some progress but were eventually contained by a company of Battalion Hempel. On 8 March, they attacked the district of Lauenburg along Körliner straße [now Grochowska] and penetrated into the area of the gas works.

The following day, 9 March, the Soviets and the newly arrived Polish 7th Infantry Regiment continued to attack against the district of Lauenburg but were met by repeated and fierce counterattacks in the sector of the gas works. Battalion Hempel struck along Treptower straße and captured twenty-four heavy weapons.

For its part, the French *compagnie de marche* was moved to a position north of the gas works and went over to the attack.[45] Two sections of its 2nd Platoon received orders to retake St.-Georgs [Saint George's] cemetery, not far from the gas works, alongside the railway line.[46] With fixed bayonets, the sections of SS-Oscha. Francke and W-Uscha. Aimé-Blanc charged forward.[47]

41 Soulat, *Historque de la Division Charlemagne*, p.61. However, according to Saint-Loup, *Les Hérétiques*, p.302, Oberst Fullriede had at his disposal six damaged Tiger tanks that had to towed about and employed in a fixed position.

42 According to Scherzer, *Sous le Signe SS*, p.454, Saint-Loup, *Les Hérétiques*, pp.303-306, Mounine, *Kolberg*, pp.47-48, the French *compagnie de marche* was engaged. Furthermore, Scherzer and Mouine specify that two platoons of the French Company were engaged. However, Soulat and Mabire make no mention of the French Company's involvement.

43 Saint-Loup, *Les Hérétiques*, pp.303-306, and Mounine, *Kolberg*, p.62.

44 See Mabire, *Mourir pour Dantzig*, p.86.

45 Soulat, *Historque de la Division Charlemagne*, p.62, although the cemetery is not specified, and Saint-Loup, *Les Hérétiques*, p.306. However, Mabire dates the counterattack one day later (*Mourir pour Dantzig*, p.87). Mounine makes no mention of this attack on 9 March, although he does state there was fierce fighting for the gas works and Saint-George's cemetery (*Kolberg*, p.62).

46 Ibid. Again Mabire is at variance and records that the 1st and 2nd platoons of the *compagnie de marche* took part in the attack (*Mourir pour Dantzig*, p.87).

47 Ibid. Once again Mabire is at variance and states, *Mourir pour Dantzig*, p.87, that Ustuf. Büeler and Oscha. Francke were in command of those units which went over to the attack. However, of interest to note is that Mabire states the names of *Franc* and *Ayme-Blot* (pseudonyms) in his earlier work *Mourir À Berlin*. Arguably, as *adjoint* of the *compagnie de marche*, Ustuf. Büeler may well have co-ordinated and overseen the attack.

They swept aside the Russians and retook the cemetery. Support arrived. Now began the battle for the cemetery.

Gren. Marotel of the 8/57 also fought in Kolberg cemetery, but not in the ranks of the *compagnie de marche* Ludwig. Arriving at Kolberg, he was sent to the casino where he met up with two comrades. Like many, he was suffering from dysentery but still wished to remain a soldier. The spectacle of defeat and rancour prevailing at the casino disgusted Marotel all the more. The three of them left and chanced upon a patrol from a *demie compagnie* of the 4. SS-Polizei-Panzer-Grenadier Division. Taking to each other, the Frenchmen incorporated themselves. At this point Marotel still did not know that there were other Frenchmen at Kolberg besides the sick and wounded at the casino.

The sixty-strong 'SS-Polizei' half-company commanded by a very young Untersturmführer 'in a warm ambience of camaraderie' was employed by headquarters as a sort of 'fire brigade' wherever the need was greatest. The half-company was committed to the fighting in the cemetery, where Marotel now met Frenchmen of the *compagnie de marche*. To find other Frenchmen who still wanted to fight pleased him. Moreover, two of them even had news of his brother.

Soviet artillery sprayed the cemetery with shellfire. Marotel wrote that 'the bombardment mixed dead and alive in a great fraternal dance'.[48] Furiously, the Frenchmen of the *compagnie de marche* and their German comrades in arms fought for the cemetery, but the enemy pressure was too great and the defenders were forced to give ground step after step. Yet they managed to hold the cemetery for twenty-four hours before being thrown out. The *compagnie de marche* then withdrew to a new defence line which ran along Köslinerstrasse from the gasometer.[49]

The losses of the *compagnie de marche* numbered five killed and three wounded. Again they were losses it could ill-afford. For this action, three men received the Iron Cross, of which one was 1st Class and awarded posthumously.

Elsewhere the fighting continued unabated. Volkssturm Battalion Pfeiffer, to the west of the city, was offering stubborn resistance and succeeded in throwing back a powerful attack. Also, on this day, Hempel was proposed for the Knight's Cross.

During lulls in the fighting, the Russians turned to a war of words. In French, loudspeaker broadcasts invited the Frenchmen to stop fighting and surrender. Nobody is reported as having been persuaded into going over.

Day after day the defenders fought desperately to buy the time to complete the sea evacuation of all civilians within the city. The Polish forces were heavily reinforced with an additional infantry division, the 4th, and with the 4th Heavy Tank Regiment as well as regiments of artillery and mortars to bring about the swift capture of Kolberg.

On the morning of 13 March, the Poles mounted another attack. For the first time they sent in all their forces. The attack was opened with a violent bombardment from all guns. The defenders yielded. Events took a dangerous turn; the Poles captured the gas works and penetrated towards the harbour on both sides of the Persante.

On 14 March, after heavy fighting in the morning, the Polish commander used the open radio at 1530 hours and again at 1600 hours to demand the surrender of Kolberg. The 'invitations'

48   Marotel, *La longue marche*, p.72.
49   Saint-Loup, *Les Hérétiques*, p.306.

went unanswered. The fighting began again in all its fury. By now, it was impossible for the defenders to dig trenches because the water table was so high.

On 15 March, the Poles continued to gain ground despite the defenders contesting every single yard. Shielded from view by thick fog, two companies of Festungs-regiment 5 [Fortress Regiment 5] were landed without opposition from the Polish artillery. The newcomers immediately counterattacked in the sector of the railway station. They suffered heavy losses.[50] That same day, a communiqué from the headquarters of Army Group Vistula laudatory cited the elements of the 33. SS-Waffen-Gren.Div (franz.) 'Charlemagne' fighting at Kolberg.[51] According to the communiqué, they had fought in a remarkable manner.

During the night of the 15-16 March the last of the women and children were evacuated. Their suffering would have been made worse, if that was possible, by the arrival that day of the 6th Rocket Artillery Brigade whose Katyushas pounded the small perimeter now held by the defenders.

To Marotel, still with his 'newlyweds' of the 'SS-Polizei', the days became indistinguishable, a succession of patrols, missions and violent engagements. One such mission was to protect the armourers and the explosive experts ordered to blow up a munitions depot of large calibre naval shells. Just as they were completing the demolition preparations the Soviets appeared. The engineers and their escort withdrew in haste. The depot was blown. It was like a crash of thunder. The ground opened beneath the Soviets. The Germans were thrown to the ground. They had been a bit too close!

Marotel had a brush with death. Coming back from patrol, he stopped to talk to some Feldgendarmen. His comrades went on without him. A brief conversation later, he hurried off to rejoin them. In front of him marched two lads of the Wehrmacht. Suddenly a mortar shell landed in the street, throwing him high into the air. He blacked out. The very next thing he remembered was his comrades, who had returned for him when he did not rejoin them, 'shaking him like a plum tree to see if he had anything broken'.[52] Although covered in blood, remarkably he was not wounded, only dazed. He looked around; the two soldiers of the Wehrmacht lay flat on the ground, dead. Pieces of shrapnel were everywhere; his greatcoat had taken the blast. All the same he continued to fight on.[53] Only later, when back in France, did he learn that several ribs had, in fact, been broken.

During the night of 16-17 March the embarkation began of male civilians, railwaymen, those of the paramilitary organisations, and soldiers without arms. In this way, the first Frenchmen from those residing at the casino may have been evacuated. By now, the conditions at the casino were terrible. Their straw bedding was filthy. Water was in such short supply that they had to drink the foul water of the Persante polluted upstream by human and animal corpses.

---

50   Soulat, *Historique de la Division Charlemagne*, p.62. This is possibly the same fortress infantry unit that, according to Saint-Loup, *Les Hérétiques*, p.306, became lost in the maze of roads and 'disappeared, decimated by enemy fire'. Indeed, according to Duffy, *Red Storm on the Reich*, p.234, the low-grade newcomers proved 'useless' in the intense fighting.

51   Ia/Nr. 3191/45 geh.v. 15.3.45.

52   Marotel, *La longue marche*, pp.74-75.

53   Ibid. However, according to Mabire, *Mourir pour Dantzig*, p.88, Marotel played no further part in the fighting and lapsed in and out of consciousness over the next few days before being evacuated.

On the morning of 17 March, the French *compagnie de marche* took up defensive positions in front of the railway station. It was now commanded by Ustuf. Büeler[54] and its strength stood at between fifty and sixty men.[55] By the time the company received orders to withdraw to the port and make ready for embarkation, it totaled thirty-three men.[56]

At 1700 hours, redoubt Waldenfels fell. This was a disaster. From there, the Poles could bring fire to bear on the whole east bank of the Persante, the port entrance and the remaining artillery positions. The end was clearly in sight; the defenders were now left holding a strip of land 1,800 metres long and 400 metres deep on the east bank of the Persante. The only heavy weapons they still had with them were three light FLAK cannons, two mortars and one gun. The pressure was such that the *compagnie de marche* had to be committed to the fighting once more. In hand-to-hand fighting it retook some houses next to the wood bordering the beach.

With the assistance of Hstuf. Havette and Oscha. Dufresnoy, Ostuf. Ludwig formed a platoon to reinforce the engaged *compagnie de marche* from the two hundred Frenchmen still at the casino. Moments later, while making its way to the positions held by its compatriots, the platoon was caught in a 'Stalin Organ' barrage and totally annihilated. All but four were killed.

The *compagnie de marche* continued to counterattack till nightfall. Receiving orders to embark, the company was relieved by German troops. It now counted no more than twenty men![57] At midnight, Ostuf. Ludwig guided the survivors to the port where they embarked.

At 0630 hours on 18 March, after beating off a final attack, Lieutenant Hempel and the small rearguard were evacuated.[58] While on the bridge of a destroyer Büeler was approached by Fullriede, Hempel and Ludwig. Full of praise, Hempel congratulated him on the performance of 'his' Frenchmen.

On 19 March, the survivors disembarked at Swinemünde. They were sent back to Wildflecken. As for Marotel, he said of the last days at Kolberg:

> It was time we evacuated this main road which leads to the harbour station from the north-east and withdraw towards the mouth of the Persante, commanded by the tower of fort 'Münde' which raised its red bricks over the Baltic.
>
>      Ivan broke through along the Persante where the avenue is very large and where the railway lines of the harbour station converge. Two times the Soviets would attack the barricades at the end of the avenue, they would take them once which would be retaken from them... I found some Frenchmen again on the beach... with them we would participate in the holding of this avenue... Our strength melted like snow in the

---

54    Mabire, *Mourir pour Dantzig*, p.89 and Soulat, letter to the author, 17/4/98. It appears that Ostuf. Ludwig had burnt himself out and 'could not take it any longer' (see Mabire, *Mourir pour Dantzig*, p.89). Nevertheless, Ludwig joined Fullriede's command staff at the town hall. Curiously, according to Saint-Loup, *Les Hérétiques*, p.308, the company was under Lieutenant Erdmann of Feld-Ausbildung-Regiment Pz.A.O.K.3.

55    Saint-Loup, *Les Hérétiques*, p.308.

56    Mabire, *Mourir pour Dantzig*, p.92.

57    Saint-Loup, *Les Hérétiques*, p.309.

58    Duffy, *Red Storm on the Reich*, p.235. However, according to Saint-Loup, *Les Hérétiques*, p.309, Fullriede was among the last group to leave at 0430 hours. Incorrectly, according to Mabire, the company received orders to withdraw on the morning of 18 March and was later evacuated in the early hours of 19 March.

sun... But we were still there... There were old men of the Volkssturm with us... I had lost several comrades I knew... The *demi-compagnie* of the 'SS-Polizei' no longer had twenty able-bodied men fit for combat duty ... Our Ustuf. and about ten of them were still going to disappear in this avenue and on the beach.

At night, on the night of the 17th to the 18th I believe, we withdrew to the beach, facing the fort. The Volkssturm were holding the last barricades... The boats approached but they could not come to the beach and we had to take a sort of long footbridge made of shaky planks. Without panic the men ran... arched... In front of me, an unknown soldier fell into the water without (letting out) a shout![59]

He embarked on a sort of troop transporter armed with a captured French 75mm gun and was taken out to sea.

Once sixty-strong, the *demi-compagnie* of 'SS-Polizei' could now be counted on the fingers of one hand! As for the *compagnie de marche* of 'Charlemagne', its losses amounted to ninety per cent.[60] Yet the contribution made by the *compagnie de marche* of 'Charlemagne' and also by the *demi-compagnie* of 'SS-Polizei' to the defence of Kolberg brought about the successful evacuation of some 35,000 local residents, more than 50,000 refugees, numerous wounded and nearly all of the surviving soldiers. Thus their sacrifice had not been in vain. Indeed, it could be said that the impossible had been pulled off.

In addition, the defenders of Kolberg had killed and wounded thousands and thousands of Russians and Poles, and destroyed as many as thirty tanks, some of which were credited to the French *compagnie de marche*.[61] Fullriede, who would finish the war with the rank of Generalmajor a.D., later noted that the French volunteers had also fought extremely well.[62]

## Escape

Not all of the Frenchmen at Kolberg received the order to evacuate. Among those left behind was eighteen-year-old François de Lannurien.[63] François was the youngest of three sons. His oldest brother, Henri, had joined the LVF in September 1941 and was seriously wounded on the first day he saw action in December 1941. He was subsequently repatriated and demobilised in June 1942. Encouraged by his father, who worked out of Rennes recruiting French volunteers for the struggle against Bolshevism, François volunteered for the Waffen-SS in June 1944.

---

59  Marotel, *La longue marche*, p.76.
60  Saint-Loup, *Les Hérétiques*, p.310. It should be noted that the losses of the defenders as a whole amounted to fifty per cent. Bataillon Hempel which numbered 400 men on 4 March, counted 150 men on 18 March.
61  At least three different figures exist of the number of tanks the enemy lost. Saint-Loup states, *Les Hérétiques*, p.310, twenty-four. Soulat states, *Historique de la Division Charlemagne*, p.62, twenty-eight, and Mabire states, *Mourir Pour Dantzig*, p.93, thirty. Additionally, Saint-Loup credits four tank kills to the *compagnie de marche*, while Mabire credits three tank kills to Oberjunker Platon alone. Bouysse credits three tanks each to both Claude Platon and Bertrand Platon.
62  Voelcker, *Kolberg*, p.180.
63  François de Lannurien was born on 22 July 1926 in Paris. Notably, he was the nephew of *général* Barazer de Lannurien, a prominent figure in the MSR.

Arriving at the depot of Greifenberg, François de Lannurien was assigned to Ostuf. Michel's training company, which became that of Ustuf. Pignard-Berthet and was sent to the front as part of the Feldersatz-Bataillon. Losing his unit during one of the first engagements near Neuland crossroads, he joined a group of German panzerjägers. Evacuated to Cammin, then onto Kolberg, he was among those Frenchmen who came forward as combatants for *compagnie de marche* Ludwig.

In a hole three or four kilometres from the city centre, de Lannurien was overwhelmed by the sudden silence that reigned. The guns of the Kriegsmarine covering the embarkation could no longer be heard and those of the Russians had fallen silent in turn. Suddenly, enemy tanks and thousands of infantry approached. Escape was out of the question. It was all over. The young Breton put his hands up. To his great surprise, he was not shot dead.

Brought to a forest, de Lannurien joined several hundred other prisoners held there. It was twelve degrees below zero and all were cold. The wakeful nights and days of savage fighting had also left the vanquished hungry and exhausted. Although guarded, the prisoners were able to come and go as they pleased in this forest. In this way, de Lannurien came across one of the panzerjäger with whom he had fought in the sector of Neuland.

The two of them had escape on the mind. The panzerjäger explained his plan: since the Russians had not counted their prisoners all they would have to do was to hide themselves away and then wait for the guards and the other prisoners to leave the forest. A simple plan, but was it good enough to succeed?

A group of four, including de Lannurien, took to a shell hole which comrades covered over with branches and snow. Moments earlier, he had asked some of his compatriots to accompany him, but all had replied that he was mad.

All day long the four hid away in their hideout. They remained undetected when the other prisoners were assembled at nightfall and marched away. The plan had worked like a dream. Nevertheless, to be on the safe side, they only emerged from their hideout four or five hours after their comrades had left.

Luckily, one member of the group, a Kriegsmarine officer, had managed to keep hold of a compass. He took his three companions to the west. For fifteen nights they travelled and for fifteen days they camouflaged themselves in groves and ricks. Villages were avoided as all were Russian occupied. Still in jackets and shirts, they suffered horribly from the cold. They had no food on them and had to suck on frozen snow that resulted in raging dysentery. But on they went. In this way, they eventually reached the banks of the Oder at Stepenitz (Stepnica). The western bank was still in German hands. There lay salvation.

The small group encountered hundreds of soldiers who, like them, had managed to escape from the enemy, but could not cross the final obstacle of the Oder. The Russians had yet to clean out its banks and had taken up position on cliffs from where they could watch over the river and intervene against all crossings. However, one lifeline for those stranded on the 'wrong' bank was the small boats, skippered by civilians, which slipped across from the western bank each night. Indeed, the small boats had kept coming to their help night after night, but this lifeline was, of course, full of danger. To reach a boat, the escapers had to dash across several hundred metres of sand lit up by enemy flares and swept by mortars and gunfire. And then and only then, in the full view of an alert enemy, could the crossing begin.

Nights later, the four, with many others, tried their luck. Under fire, all dashed towards a boat. Those who still had weapons tried to cover them. The young de Lannurien, who against orders had removed his boots, outran the others with him, dived into the river, swam to the boat and hauled himself abroad, but the boat was hit and started to sink. There he was in the water again. He could have quite easily given up and returned to the east bank, but he swam off to the west bank.

The Oder is more than two kilometres wide but dotted with numerous islands and sandbanks. It was these that de Lannurien used to rest and get his breath back before swimming on. Finally he came to the west bank where he was joined by two Germans who had also managed to swim across. All were rudely welcomed by gunfire. They dived for cover and started shouting to persuade this welcoming committee of their identity. Eventually, their shouts were understood and their saviours approached. His strength failing him, de Lannurien fainted.

The young Breton was admitted to hospital. He was in need of treatment for a bullet he now carried in his back, as well as for a piece of shrapnel in his foot, and for frostbite, but he had escaped from the hell of Pomerania. Two or three weeks later, after regaining his strength, he asked to rejoin his French comrades of 'Charlemagne'. No less dramatic was the escape of Fenet's I/RM.

### Fenet's Battalion

As many as eight hundred men of 'Charlemagne' managed to reach Meseritz. Ostuf. Fenet had them assembled into four *compagnies de marche* of nearly two hundred men each.[64] What now? This was the same difficult question that General von Tettau was asking himself. For in his hands was the fate of those units of his Army Corps and of the X. SS-Armee-Korps encircled in Pomerania. He had intended to make for Schmalentin (Smolecin) and, from there, onto the island of Wollin via the city of Cammin (Kamien Pomorski), but on 6 March he learnt that Cammin had fallen to the Soviets. As a result, he now inclined north towards the coast and the small port of Horst from where he hoped to be evacuated by sea.

Towards midnight on the night of 6-7 March, after several hours' sleep, the Frenchmen of 'Charlemagne' set off again. In the early morning hours, they arrived at Pinnow. Continuing on, they came to Natelfitz (Natolewice), about ten kilometres from Greifenberg, where it was learnt that forces of Corps Group von Tettau were to launch an attack to free the encircled garrison of Greifenberg. The attack went ahead without the French Battalion which was completely exhausted. From its starting point of Natelfitz, the attack gained three kilometres before grinding to a standstill.

Battalion Fenet then set off again to reach the new rallying point of Cammin[65] on the east bank of the Oder. In the evening of 7 March, the French column arrived at Wendisch Pribbernow (Przybiernowo), where it rested for the night. At dawn, the battalion continued its march to the north-west. Soon after, civilians supplied the news that the Russians were already at Cammin. Its direction of march remained the same.

The battalion came to the river Rega. A bridge was found intact but guarded by two T-34s. Because the enemy tank crews were playing cards on the riverbank, the Frenchmen could have quite easily dealt with them and then passed, but they still remained under strict orders to

---

64   Saint-Loup, *Les Hérétiques*, p.330, and Mabire, *Mourir A Berlin*, p.29.
65   Soulat, *Historique de la Division Charlemagne*, p.70, and repeated by Mabire, *Mourir A Berlin*, p.29.

avoid any contact with the enemy.[66] Thus, they steered well clear of this bridge. Ten kilometres upstream, south of Treptow, they found another bridge and crossed over without incident. Then, on the road from Treptow to Greifenberg, a vehicle exploded a mine and wounded seven men.

In the afternoon, battle raged around the villages of Görke (Górzyca) and Woedtke (Otok). The latter was recaptured from the Soviets who had already given themselves over to pillage and violence.[67] During the day, Staf. Zimmermann assembled the men to wish Brigf. Krukenberg a happy birthday. He was fifty-seven-years-old. Krukenberg seemed touched and gave a brief speech, congratulating them on their discipline and performance, and then gave the order to march on. In the early evening, the battalion arrived at Groß-Zapplin (Czaplin Wielki) and settled down for the night.[68]

Throughout 9 March the battalion continued its march northwards, arriving at the small fishing port of Horst (Niechorze) late into the night. Exhausted, the men collapsed on bare shopfloors and fell off to sleep.[69] On the afternoon of 10 March, the battalion left Horst for Rewahl (Rewal) along the coast, arriving around 1700 hours.

Uscha. Peyret of the Panzerjäger Kompanie of Waffen-Gren. Regt der SS 58 wrote of his journey to Rewahl in the notebook he carried:

**5 March:** At Belgard, it's a scattering! The last elements disperse around 0700 hours. In the evening, I make my way towards the Russian lines with a group of three men (including *sergent* COMTE) to try and break through them.
**6 March:** After having marched all night in the direction of Greifenberg with my compass as the only means of orientation, we stop in a small wood besides a village occupied by the Russians. Exhausted.
**7 March:** Numb with cold, we go up and install ourselves in a mirador to spend here our second day. At night, we enter a house where a small, old man, happy to see Frenchmen, all the more reason if they are wearing the field-grey uniform, literally filled us to bursting. We had eaten nothing for three days!

Around midnight, we come upon a German column withdrawing from Greifenberg (about fifteen kilometres from here) which, they announce to us, has just fallen into the hands of the Russians.
**8 March:** After having spent some hours in a stable, we wander through the Russian lines. We cross the Rega around 1500 hours. In the evening, we halt in a village.
**9 March:** Departure around 0700 hours. We are surrounded by the Russians. We break through thanks to the flak (20mm and 88mm pieces). For an hour and a half, I come within a hair's breadth of death under machine-gun and mortar fire.

66    Saint-Loup, *Les Hérétiques*, p.332.
67    Soulat, *Historique de la Division Charlemagne*, p.70. Of note is that there is no mention of Battalion Fenet participating in the fighting. However, according to Mabire, *Mourir A Berlin*, pp.20-21, Battalion Fenet did sweep aside the Russians in both villages. In response to this, Soulat mentions the recapture of one village, but not both. Also, Scherzer doubts that a battle took place at Woedtke as described by Soulat (see *Sous le Signe SS*, p.420, footnote 524).
68    According to Mabire, *Mourir A Berlin*, p.22, the battalion rested at the village of Zappten.
69    Soulat, *Historique de la Division Charlemagne*, p.70. However, according to Saint-Loup, *Les Hérétiques*, p.334, when part of the battalion could not find sufficient space available at Horst it continued on its way to the seaside resort of Rewahl.

Avoiding Horst, I make my way to Rewahl and Hoff where I meet friends again. We spend the night in a stable. At 2100 hours, alert! Withdrawal to Rewahl and Horst.

## Breakthrough to Dievenow (Dziwnów)[70]

And what of the encircled forces under General von Tettau pinned against the Baltic Sea in the area around the coastal resorts of Hoff and Horst? Disappointed in his hopes of being evacuated by sea, he had decided to break through by land to a bridgehead still held around Dievenow (Dziwnów).

At 2200 hours on 10 March, the breakthrough to the west began. The spearhead of the forces breaking out was composed of the Fusilier Battalion of Panzer Division 'Holstein' and Regiment 'Buchenau'. At 0200 hours on 11 March, after piercing the Soviet ring, the first German elements arrived at Dievenow, but in their wake the Russians penetrated into the escape corridor.

For 'Battalion Fenet' the day of 11 March was spent resting and preparing for its all-important mission. Through Staf. Zimmermann's personal friendship with von Tettau, the mission of the French Battalion was upgraded from covering the retreat to spearheading 'the last breakthrough, along the shore, so as to clear the way for five thousand refugees'.[71] H-hour was set for midnight.

Sporadic shelling caused casualties among the hapless refugees crowded in Rewahl. For the breakthrough, Battalion Fenet was split into two. The first group, under Ostuf. Fenet, was to pass along the beach at the water's edge. The second group, smaller than the first, with Hstuf. Roy, Ustuf. Leune and Ostuf. Darrigarde, was to escort the convoy of civilians and wounded along the coastal road at the top of the cliffs. Armour was to precede this convoy. Warships of the Kriegsmarine were to support the breakthrough.[72]

Towards H-Hour, the refugees and their French escort under Ostuf. Fenet lined up on the beach. The battalion was now to escort some ten thousand refugees, double the number than that first planned. At midnight, all set off along the beach.[73]

---

70   Soulat and Mabire record that the breakthrough was from Rewahl to Dievenow. This is confirmed, for example, by *Russo–German war: 25 January to 8 May 1945*, p.22, and *Red Storm over the Reich*, Duffy, pp.197-198. However, Saint-Loup details, *Les Hérétiques*, p.339, that the journey from Rewahl to Dievenow had presented few problems for 'Battalion Fenet' and that the breakthrough was from Dievenow to Swinemünde (Swinoujscie). This would suggest that the Russians had got across the river Oder and onto the island of Wollin in sufficient strength to encircle the German forces holding the bridgehead around Dievenow. This is not true. With that said, it should be noted that there is great similarity between the accounts of the breakthrough recounted by Saint-Loup and Mabire.

71   Soulat, *Historique de la Division Charlemagne*, p.70.

72   In the afternoon, according to Saint-Loup, *Les Hérétiques*, p.340, a young SS General arrived by Fieseler Storch on Dievenow beach to discuss the details of the breakthrough with Krukenberg.

73   According to Rostaing, *Le prix d'un serment*, p.176, a five-hour artillery and naval barrage preceded the breakthrough. However, this seems rather doubtful as, firstly, no such prolonged barrage is recorded by either Mabire or Saint-Loup and, secondly, the element of surprise, a key precondition to the breakthrough, would have been sacrificed. Indeed, Krukenberg had dispensed with the idea of a covering detachment at the top of the high dunes running along the beach 'in order to avoid alerting the suspicions of enemy patrols and look-outs' (Soulat, *Historique de la Division Charlemagne*, p.70).

At their head, pistol in hand, marched Hstuf. Jauss.[74] Also among the twenty-strong vanguard armed with panzerfäust was Staf. Zimmermann. An engineer of old, he was on the lookout for mines. Ustuf. Martres was with the rearguard that also comprised troops of the 4. SS-Polizei-Panzer-Grenadier Division.

The vanguard came to and easily overwhelmed the first Soviet outpost. Prisoners were taken. Staf. Zimmermann was slightly wounded in the foot by a piece of grenade shrapnel but marched on in a pair of slippers. The element of surprise was now lost, though.

The beach was so narrow in places that the troops and refugees could only advance in single file. Sometimes they even had to take to the water. Hence, the advance slowed. This gave the alerted Soviets time to intervene. From the cliffs, they harassed the column with machine-gun fire and grenades that exploded with devastating effect. The French soldiers urged the civilians on.

Suddenly, Kreigsmarine heavy cruiser Admiral Scheer and torpedo boat T-33, out to sea, opened up and shells now started to rain down on those on the beach; the naval support had mistaken them for Russians. Some were wounded. Jauss reacted immediately and fired multi-coloured flares skywards that silenced the guns. They hurried on.

Three times they found their route barred and three times they had to smash their way through. Every now and then they stumbled across dead and wounded from the fighting of the day before. At the approach of the column the wounded woke and cried out pitifully to be taken along, but that was quite impossible.

All of a sudden the cliffs levelled off and gave way to beaches lined with villas. This spelled danger. Enemy machine guns barked out. All threw themselves onto the sand. Minutes later, mortars showered death on the Frenchmen. There was no escape from the shrapnel on this flat beach. Jauss signalled for the naval support. With deadly accuracy, it crashed down among the Soviet-held positions. Galvanised by this, the Frenchmen went over to the attack. Led by Jauss, they dashed towards a Russian Maxim heavy machine gun positioned in the middle of the beach. It was destroyed by rifle grenade launchers. Casualties mounted on both sides, but the attack continued. They knew what was at stake if the attack bogged down.

Hstuf. Jauss charged towards another Maxim in a villa. With a grenade, he put an end to the enemy machine gun and its crew. In close quarter fighting, the Frenchmen proceeded to clean out the villas. The column could now continue on its way. Again the cost was dear, yet more dead and wounded. Among the wounded was Gilles of the 1/57 who had been hit by a piece of mortar shrapnel.[75] He was brought to an improvised first aid post, also shelled, and then evacuated by sea on a patrol boat.

The fighting was not over yet. There were countless more skirmishes and losses. Std.Ob.Ju. Dr. Anneshaensel was last seen alive treating the wounded. It is said that he was, in turn, seriously wounded and would succumb to his wounds while being transferred to a field hospital in the rear.[76] Brigf. Krukenberg subsequently awarded him a posthumous Iron Cross 1st Class.

74    Saint-Loup, *Les Hérétiques*, p.341.
75    Saint-Loup, *Les Hérétiques*, p.343.
76    Mabire, *Mourir A Berlin*, p.32. However, according to Saint-Loup, *Les Hérétiques*, p.346, Dr. Louis Anneshaensel went 'missing' during the breakthrough along the coastal road and not along the beach. (Presumably this was based on the eyewitness account of Dr. Métais.) Furthermore, according to

At 0400 hours, Battalion Fenet affected a junction with German forces, north of the village Raddack (Radawka).[77] Ustuf. Martres with the rearguard could not quite understand how the battalion had managed to break through. Anyway, he and the battalion pushed onto Dievenow. There was no sign of the column that had attempted to break through along the coastal road. The hours rolled by and still no sign of it.

The two accounts of what happened to the column which took the coastal road differ. According to Mabire,[78] the column made good initial progress thanks, in the main, to the escorting Tiger and Panther tanks that had opened up the coastal road. But the escorting armour proved a double-edged sword: they also awoke the Russians to their presence. By 0500 hours, the column had a fight on its hands against Soviet motorised elements and took to the wood for refuge. However, the fighting continued in the undergrowth. It was savage. Finally, around 1000 hours, with the support of German paratroopers, the Luftwaffe and the Kriegsmarine out to sea, the column swept aside the enemy and got moving again. It was around 1400 hours when the column rejoined the battalion at Dievenow.

According to Saint-Loup,[79] columns under Hstuf. Roy and Ustuf. Leune set off at 0200 hours in an indescribable disorder.[80] The column under Ustuf. Leune comprised seriously wounded on carts. Cover was provided by French SS troops and a German company. The night was still except for the cries of the wounded. Progress was good for the first three kilometres, but then the scenery changed theme. Now in its path lay broken telegraph poles that slowed progress. The ruins of a village could be seen in the distance and on the horizon flames danced briefly. The rumbling of enemy guns could be heard. Many of the escorting German and French SS troops got jumpy and dashed off.

Suddenly shots rang out. The column came to a halt. More of the escort disappeared. Night started to draw to a close. Uncertainty heightened. Ustuf. Leune ordered the column to a wood ahead, but when it entered gunfire erupted from all directions. The Russians were already there. The French and German troops panicked and fled. Many of them were battle-hardened veterans, but they could not take it anymore. Their nerves had finally gone to pieces. Leune and Dr. Métais were carried along by this rout.

Then German officers suddenly appeared, pistol in hand, shouting: "Forward! Forward!" The fleeing troops hesitated, stopped, about-turned, reassembled and went back to the battle. The fusillade stopped as suddenly as it had broken out. The column continued forward, straight over the dead and wounded lying across the road. The important thing was to keep going. The escape route might only remain open for hours, perhaps even for a matter of minutes.

---

*Siegrunen VIII. Nos 5 and 6*, Dr. Anneshaensel was listed as MIA at Heinrichswalde. This has to be incorrect.

77  Saint-Loup, *Les Hérétiques*, p.343. According to Soulat, *Historique de la Division Charlemagne*, p.74, it was around 0800 hours when Battalion Fenet arrived at Dievenow. This is possible. It should be recalled that German forces were holding a bridgehead around Dievenow that extended for up to five kilometres. However, Mabire recalls, *Mourir A Berlin*, p.33, that the time of 0800 hours was when the battalion affected a junction with 'German Waffen-SS troops who were coming from Dievenow to meet their French comrades.' This has to be incorrect.

78  Mabire, *Mourir A Berlin*, p.35.

79  Saint-Loup, *Les Hérétiques*, pp.343-348. It should be noted that this account is similar to that of Rostaing, *Le Prix d'un serment*, pp.176-178.

80  Of note is that there is no mention of escorting tanks.

The column came to two T-34s on fire. Smoke poured from them. Further on was a gutted Russian lorry which Ustuf. Leune stopped beside. He was approached by Oscha. Boucret, who offered him rich foodstuffs all the way from America! A Russian convoy, unbelievably full of American goodies, had just been intercepted. After stuffing themselves, they set off again. They marched on and on. Towards 1500 hours, the survivors finally re-established contact with the German front line.

Dr. Métais was stopped by Brigf. Krukenberg who admonished him for being improperly dressed; he had bandages stuffed in his tunic pockets! Krukenberg then questioned him about his gloves. Métais replied that he had left them behind at Körlin. By way of conclusion, Krukenberg remarked that an officer of the Waffen-SS had to remain impeccably turned out at all times whatever the circumstances.

Regrouped, Battalion Fenet set off towards Kolzow (Kolczewo). At its head marched Fenet and an impeccably dressed Krukenberg complete with gloves. Despite a foot wound, Zimmermann was still with them. He had refused to be evacuated. Crossing the pontoon bridge at Dievenow over the Oder, the survivors now set foot on the island of Wollin, which confirmed their final deliverance from the hell of Pomerania.

By the evening of 12 March, the last units of Corps Group von Tettau had reached Dievenow. The seashore behind them presented an appalling sight. The coast was littered with corpses, abandoned and destroyed military vehicles, overturned carts of the refugees and dead horses. Battalion Fenet made its way across the island of Wollin. Staf. Zimmermann came into possession of a bicycle and pedalled along.

Late on 13 March, the battalion reached Swinemünde. Along the way, Staf. Zimmermann went to the headquarters of General Aiching at Misdroy where his Chief-of-Staff congratulated him on the spirit and the fine appearance of the battalion. The General had seen the battalion on the road withdrawing in good order and singing.[81]

The battalion was forced to hand over its weapons, although some gradés [officers and NCOs] were permitted to retain their personal sidearm.[82] Oberst Eismann, the Operations Officer of Army Group Vistula, later informed the 3. Pz.-Armee that the Reichsfuhrer-SS had taken the arms of the Latvian and French SS-Verbände for Gruppe Ansat.[83]

On 13 March 1945, Army Group Vistula recorded the strength of 'Charlemagne' as 300.[84] This is undoubtedly an understatement. A communiqué from 'General Headquarters' was

---

81   Soulat, *Historique de la Division Charlemagne*, p.74, repeated by Mabire, *Mourir A Berlin*, p.37, whereas, according to Saint-Loup, *Les Hérétiques*, p.349, it was General Aiching who actually congratulated Staf. Zimmermann on the spirit and appearance of the French Battalion. Indeed, the General said that it had been a long time since he had last seen men march past that still resembled soldiers! Mabire repeats this same comment, but attributes it to the General's Chief-of-Staff.

82   Mabire, *Mourir A Berlin*, p.37. This order is said to have exasperated the survivors who, during the past weeks of battle and long marches, had carried their weapons to safeguard them. And yet, in contrast, according to Soulat, *Historique de la Division Charlemagne*, p.74 General Aiching, let the battalion retain its weapons rather than hand them over. The memorandum Oberst Eismann – Oberst Ludendorff of 14 March 1945 makes it clear that the battalion had its weapons taken.

83   Memorandum Oberst Eismann – Oberst Ludendorff of 14 March 1945.

84   See *DEUTSCH-RUSSISCHES PROJEKT ZUR DIGITALISIERUNG DEUTSCHER DOKUMENTE IN ARCHIVEN DER RUSSISCHEN FÖDERATION* <https://wwii.germandocsinrussia.org/de/pages/301344/map> (accessed 16 January 2021).

to recognise the important part they had played in the breakthrough to Dievenow.[85] From Swinemünde, the battalion left for Jargelin in the vicinity of Anklam where the other survivors of 'Charlemagne' were assembling and arrived around midday on 16 March.

85   Saint-Loup, *Les Hérétiques*, p.348. The headquarters referred to is possibly OKH, which was responsible for directing Eastern Front operations.

**15**

## Reformation of 'Charlemagne'

---

### Anklam

The survivors were sent to Jargelin, north-west of Anklam, where they were to assemble. Some two hundred men of the divisional Headquarters Company, divisional service units and the *Compagnie d'Honneur* arrived on 8 March 1945. Every day saw the arrival of more and more survivors.

Headquarters was established in a vestibule of a large country residence crowded with civilians. The clerical staff worked from two tables in front of the window. Because it was necessary for the clerical staff and runners to be there night and day, they decided to make themselves a bed of straw under the gigantic billiard table cluttering the vestibule. When Rttf. Soulat went for straw the German owner of the property confronted him. Soulat was furious. He had fought to defend Germany and Europe and shouted as much to the German, who shouted back, then turned on his heels and walked away. As he did so Soulat warned him that the Russians would not ask his permission first before helping themselves.

Brigf. Krukenberg and the 23 *Führer* and 701 *Mann* of Battalion Fenet arrived on 16 March.[1] With them was Ostuf. Bénétoux, who had managed to escape from Soviet captivity.

Two days later, on 18 March, the map of Army Group Vistula showed '33. SS Charlemagne' as Army Group reserve in a position south of Neubrandenburg astride Reichsstrasse 96.[2]

On the same day, Brigf. Krukenberg visited the field headquarters of Reichsführer-SS Himmler near Prenzlau to report on the performance of 'Charlemagne' in Pomerania.[3] On his return, later that day, Krukenberg bestowed a number of promotions and decorations on the

---

1 Biographical report of Brigf. Krukenberg sent by Hstuf. Pachur to SS-Hauptamt. Later Krukenberg would put the number as high as 1000.
2 See *Российско-Германский проект по оцифровке германских документовв архивах Российской Федераци* <https://wwii.germandocsinrussia.org/pages/291483/map> (accessed 16/01/2021). Jargelin is some seventy kilometres from the area indicated on the map.
3 Mabire, *Mourir A Berlin*, p.40, undoubtedly based on the eyewitness testimony of Soulat. However, Scherzer doubts that Krukenberg saw Himmler who was not even at his headquarters, see *Sous le Signe SS*, pp.465-466. The possibility exists that Krukenberg told the survivors that he had seen Himmler in person to boast their morale.

survivors. For the first time, Rttf. Soulat noticed that Krukenberg was wearing the *tricolore écusson* [badge]. At an awards ceremony, for his exceptional bravery, Fenet was promoted to Hauptsturmführer.[4] Labourdette, his assistant, was promoted from Standartenoberjunker to Untersturmführer.[5]

Bigf. Krukenberg then presented the Iron Cross 1st Class to newly promoted Ustuf. Labourdette, and the Iron Cross 2nd Class to Ustuf. Martres and some fifteen men. Also awarded were a far greater number of posthumous decorations. Thereupon, Krukenberg spoke briefly and passed on a message of congratulations from the Reichsführer-SS.[6] These awards were not final. In the following weeks more awards were issued.

That same day, SS-Stubaf. Katzian left for Wildflecken. He had orders to return from there with the French *Ausbilungs-und-Ersatz-Bataillon*. Also, Staf. Zimmermann[7] finally went into hospital to receive treatment for his foot wound suffered in Pomerania.[8]

On 19 March, RF-SS Himmler spoke to his private physician, Dr. Felix Kersten, about his Waffen-SS and its losses. The Reichsführer informed Kersten that of the 6,000 Danes, 10,000 Norwegians, 75,000 Dutch, 25,000 Flemings, 15,000 Walloons and 22,000 French in the Waffen-SS, one in three was killed in action. He added that the losses of the volunteers hailing from the Baltic States, the Ukrainians and the Galicians were higher. Praise indeed, but his figure of 22,000 Frenchmen in the Waffen-SS is pure fantasy.

On 21 March, the survivors gathered at Anklam town railway station to await transportation to their new billets in Mecklenburg. Because no trains were running they set off on foot. Marching in quick time, they sung out loudly.

Passing Anklam airfield, they saw lines of impeccably camouflaged German fighter planes, which were all grounded through lack of fuel. They marched on. Their first stop was the village of Schwerinsburg, where they were quartered in the great room of a requisitioned inn whose previous occupants were prisoners of war.

The following day, they set off at dawn. They passed through the villages of Sarnow, where supplies of foul-tasting biscuits were received, and then Friedland before being split up for the night in various locations. The divisional Headquarters Company spent the night in Schönbeck school.

23 March was good to them, starting with milk in the morning. Towards 1600 hours, they arrived at the village of Bredenfelde, where they rested. Suddenly two enemy aircraft flew

---

4    Fenet was actually promoted to Hauptsturmführer on 1 March 1945 (Message Tgb.Nr.1380/45 and Soldbuch of Fenet).

5    Mabire, *Mourir A Berlin*, p.41. Labourdette was not appointed to Obersturmführer as stated by Landwehr.

6    Soulat, *Historique de la Division Charlemagne*, p.72, and Mabire, *Mourir A Berlin*, p.40. According to Saint-Loup, *Les Hérétiques*, p.370, the awards ceremony took place at Carpin on 27 March 1945.

7    Curiously, according to Mabire, *Mourir A Berlin*, p.39, and Landwehr, *Charlemagne's Legionnaires*, p.108, Zimmermann was now at the head of Waffen-Grenadier Regiment der SS 'Charlemagne'. However, according to official documentation, 'Charlemagne' was not ordered to convert to a regiment until 25 March 1945.

8    According to Mabire, *Mourir A Berlin*, p.79, Zimmermann was hospitalised at Anklam, whereas, according to Soulat, *Historique de la Division Charlemagne*, p.96, he was hospitalised at Neustrelitz. Curiously, according to Scherzer, Zimmermann only went into hospital on 29 April (see *Sous le Signe*, p.687).

overhead but did not interfere with them. In the evening, having covered over twenty kilometres, they came to Stolpe and a 'feast of potatoes'. Indeed, the day had been good to them.

On 24 March, they arrived in the region of Neustrelitz and were billeted in surrounding villages. The headquarters staff went to the village of Carpin. Brigf. Krukenberg established divisional headquarters in castle Carpin, a rather grandiose title for nothing more than a rather large farmhouse, but it was one of the few to have electricity.

**Reorganisation**

The day of 25 March, a Sunday, was given over to delousing. Also, on this day, the SS-FHA ordered the 33. Waffen-Grenadier Division der SS 'Charlemagne' to reorganise into a Grenadier Regiment with a structure based on the 'Type 45' (1945) Infantry Division of 2 Grenadier Battalions and 1 Schweres Bataillon [Heavy Battalion] of:[9]

| | |
|---|---|
| 1 Panz.Jäg. Kp. | [Tank Destroyer Company] |
| 1 Jagdpanzer-Kp. | [Assault Gun Company] |
| 1 Fla-Kp. of 1-2 batteries | [Flak Company] |

In addition, the division was to have the support elements of:

| | |
|---|---|
| 1 Nachr.Zg. | [Signals Platoon] |
| 1 Pi.Zg. | [Engineers Platoon] |
| 1 Verpfl.Kol. | [Supply Column] |
| 1 Werkst.Zg. | [Workshop Platoon] |

This order was to be executed by 15 April 1945. This reorganisation was to take place using 'all remnant elements of the division and incorporating all trained personnel of the Franz. SS-Grenadier. Ausb.u.Ers.Btl., Wildflecken'. To this effect, the Franz.SS-Grenadier. Ausb.u.Ers.Btl. at Wildflecken was to dispatch all trained personnel to the 'division' by 31 March 1945. As such, the division was not officially disbanded and remained subordinated to the 3rd Panzer Army of Army Group Vistula.

According to this order, the role of division headquarters will be assumed by the inspectorate. Brigf. Krukenberg responded by naming Staf. Zimmermann as the commander of Waffen-Grenadier Regiment der SS 'Charlemagne' and also by forming three battalions for the Regiment:

SS-Bataillon 57 under Hstuf. Fenet
SS-Bataillon 58 under Ostuf. Géromini
Heavy Battalion under Stubaf. Boudet-Gheusi

---

9    SS-FHA Amt II Org. Abt.Ia/II Tgb.Nr.2354/45 gkdos. Curiously, according to Landwehr, *Charlemagne's Legionnaires*, p.108, on 15 March 1945, the Division was reorganised as Waffen-Grenadier Regiment der SS 'Charlemagne' at Anklam. In response to this, the author believes that Landwehr may have misinterpreted Mabire. (See *Mourir A Berlin*, p.39)

The nucleus of SS-Bataillon 57 was the former regiment of the same number. Hence SS-Bataillon 57 was the direct heir of the French SS-Sturmbrigade. Fenet, of course, retained its command. In its ranks remained many men who had enlisted in the Waffen-SS during the summer of 1943 and who, one year later, went on to fight in Galicia.

For the time being, SS-Bataillon 57 remained at Bergfeld with its command post in the five-building 'Familie Kunitz-Gusthof Kunitz' and its three assigned grenadier companies in nearby farms. At the head of the 1st Company was Ostuf. Roumegous. However, he was so demoralised that, in the end, Hstuf. Fenet had him relieved of his command. He was put at 'the disposal of the division'. Ustuf. Labourdette took over.

SS-Bataillon 58 was born of the former regiment of the same number. The morale of its former LVF legionnaires and *Miliciens* was not as high as that of their counterparts in SS-Bataillon 57. The baptism of fire in Pomerania had been particularly hard on those from the *Milice*. The difficult job of commanding SS-Bataillon 58 went to Ostuf. Géromini, himself a former *Milicien*. Although regarded as outspoken and temperamental, this Corsican had proved himself a courageous and popular company commander in Pomerania. He was still full of fight, but all was not well with him, which culminated in a scene with Brigf. Krukenberg who abruptly cut him short and asked him to leave his office. Even so Géromini remained at the head of SS-Bataillon-58 billeted around the village of Grünow, five kilometres west of Carpin.

The fifty-strong *Compagnie d'Honneur* was quartered at first in the village of Ollendorf, some four kilometres north-east of Carpin, but was quickly moved to Georgenhof, due north of Carpin.[10] It was still under the command of Ostuf. Weber who immediately resumed his harsh training programme.[11] Days after arriving near Carpin, Louis Lavest was overjoyed to be promoted to Sturmmann.

Uscha. Puechlong rejoined Weber and the *Compagnie d'Honneur*. Much to his disappointment, he had missed Pomerania. Towards the end of February 1945, he was hospitalised following a training accident at Paderborn. During an exercise to occupy and leave a Tiger tank with great speed he fell and dislocated his right hip. He called himself clumsy and stupid, all the more so when his fellow countrymen at the training school were recalled to Wildflecken and from there sent on to Pomerania.

After three weeks in hospital, Puechlong was discharged. He returned to Wildflecken. Assigned to Kreis' Company, he was entrusted with the task of accompanying to Sigmaringen a convoy of some one hundred *Miliciens* who had refused to serve in the Waffen-SS. This he performed. From Sigmaringen, he then journeyed northwards to Carpin where 'Charlemagne' was reforming. It proved a most difficult journey, taking days to complete, but it mattered not because he was back with Weber and his beloved *Compagnie d'Honneur*.

At Carpin, Puechlong was again the victim of bad luck. A candle with which he was reading fell into straw and set fire to a barn in which some of his compatriots were sleeping. On Weber's

---

10   Soulat, *Historique de la Division Charlemagne*, p.83, and repeated by Mabire, *Mourir A Berlin*, p.51. And yet, according to Lavest of the *Compagnie d'Honneur*, the company was stationed for three or four days at Georgenhof then at Ollendorf.

11   According to Lavest, letter to the author and later still in his book *Le soleil se couchait à l'est*, p.97, 'general headquarters' [OKH?] mentioned the *Compagnie d'Honneur* in dispatches for its success at Elsenau, awarding it the War Merit Cross. That same day, the Propaganda-kompanie or PK photographed the assembled company for the magazine Signal. This, however, Soulat does not recall (letter to the author).

orders, he was transferred to Labourdette's 1st Company. He found it impossible to hide the humiliation of the transfer.

On 27 March, Brigadeführer Krukenberg issued an order of the day. He spoke of the 'combative spirit' and discipline of the Frenchmen which had brought about success in the fighting in Pomerania. He hoped that General Puaud and other heroic combatants would soon rejoin them. He asserted that all Frenchmen who wanted a new European order would look at them with pride. Again he invoked their spirit, which, in days to come, would lead them again to new successes 'until the long awaited day when we will take part in the liberation of our country'. He concluded: 'Alongside our German comrades fighting for the same ideal we follow the Führer, the liberator of Europe'.

More French volunteers continued to arrive at Carpin. Among them were returning wounded and various trainees and specialists who had been away on courses while the division had been engaged in Pomerania. Yet there were also new recruits from the French community in exile. Many believed that the front could not be any worse than life in the German cities under air raids. Also, some were under the rather naive impression that they would eat better as members of the Waffen-SS than they would as civilians. Their illusions were soon shattered.[12] Inexplicably, the survivors of Kolberg, who had disembarked at Swinemünde, were sent straight to the French *Ausbildungs-und-Ersatz-Bataillon* at Wildflecken.

As the strength of 'Charlemagne' grew, its billets, which had not been very conducive to training in the first place, became more and more overcrowded. As a result, SS-Bataillon 57 was relocated from Bergfeld to a former training camp at Fürstensee, eight kilometres south-west of Carpin, whereas SS-Bataillon 58 went to the village of Wokuhl, eight kilometres due south of Carpin.

Military training was accelerated, but the morale of some continued to fluctuate and cause problems. Disheartened former *franc-gardes* vented their bitterness against the Germans. Former members of the Sturmbrigade confronted them and accusations were angrily traded.

In early April 1945, a Wehrmacht staff group commanded by Oberst von Massow reconnoitred the region of Neustrelitz with a view to preparing secondary defensive positions. The French SS soldiers were ordered to begin work on fortifications and anti-tank obstructions. However, the demeaning order was met with little enthusiasm. Hstuf. Fenet, who regarded such work as demoralising, was well aware that he had been given an order and that it was an order he would have to carry out like any other.

To win his men over to the order, Fenet successfully employed the approach of 'actions speak louder than words'. On the morning the work was to begin, he appeared in front of his assembled men, took off his shirt, asked for a shovel and started to dig. He laboured in silence for hours and one by one all his men joined him

### A question of discipline

Breaches of discipline remained an ongoing problem even though the smallest breach inevitably resulted in harsh punishment. An order circulated from the Führer himself set out the penalty

---

12  According to Delperrié de Bayac, *Histoire de la Milice*, p.610, six to seven hundred German SS soldiers were 'added' to 'Charlemagne'. This remains unconfirmed.

of death for deserters, looters and thieves. To ensure that all his men had read this order, Hstuf. Fenet had them sign it.

Days later, a worried Ustuf. Labourdette reported an incident of petty theft to Hstuf. Fenet. A farmer had complained that the NCOs billeted with him had stolen some light bulbs. An investigation was conducted and the culprits were brought before Fenet. Well aware of the Führer's order, they expected to be shot, but a lenient Fenet only scolded them.

Not all would be so lucky. After refusing to obey his platoon commander during the construction of the anti-tank ditches, Uscha. Émile Girard, a former *franc-garde de* Nice born on 14 September 1920 in Le-Canet, found himself on a charge of deserting his post at Elsenau even though it had passed off in silence at the time. Court-martialled, Girard was found guilty and sentenced to death. The *Compagnie d'Honneur* supplied the firing squad and at the head of the firing squad was Oscha. Apollot. During the night of the 19-20 April, Girard was executed by firing squad in Carpin cemetery.

Two deserters arrested in Berlin wearing civilian clothes were brought to Carpin for court-martial. They had been encouraged to desert by some Belgian women with whom they had set up house.[13] The names and rank of the two deserters were Sturmmann Turco and Grenadier Harel. The former, a veteran of the Sturmbrigade, had fought in the ranks of its 1st Battalion in Galicia. In the eyes of Fenet, this made him all the more culpable.

The two deserters were brought before a court martial over which Stubaf. Boudet-Gheusi presided. The court martial found them guilty of desertion but did not sentence them to death as ordered of late by the Führer. Brigf. Krukenberg was furious. In his opinion the deserters were either guilty and should be shot or they were innocent and should be acquitted. No other outcome was acceptable.

The two sentences were quashed. The two deserters were judged again before another court martial over which Ustuf. Labourdette of SS-Bataillon 57 presided.[14] This time, on 12 April, the court martial sentenced them to death by firing squad. The execution was set for the following morning. Soulat, who witnessed their execution on 13 April at Carpin, wrote:

> Two deserters arrested in civilian clothes in Berlin, Sturmmann Turco and Grenadier Harel (I knew the latter in the Kriegsmarine), condemned to death yesterday by the court martial are due to be shot this morning. They spent the night drinking, smoking and eating as they pleased. Assembly at 04:30 hours before the Kommandant. Compulsory attendance for all. The condemned flanked by the firing squad made up of volunteers lead the way. The execution post is erected in a grove five hundred metres north of Carpin. Ustuf. Verney administers the last rites to the condemned. I realise with surprise that they were to be shot almost at point-blank range. At 05.00 hours, the salvo cuts them down. They had time enough to shout "Vive la France!" Ostuf. Görr of

13    Mabire, *Mourir A Berlin*, p.68. However, Scherzer doubts that the two deserters would have been brought all the way from Berlin to Carpin for justice but provides no evidence to support this (see *Sous le Signe*, p.476).
14    Mabire, *Mourir A Berlin*, p.68. Presumably, it was Krukenberg who quashed the two sentences and ordered a retrial.

the Feldgendarmerie administers the coup de grâce and all Germans and Frenchmen alike acknowledge their courageous attitude before the execution.[15]

One night, a Luftwaffe supply depot near to Fürstensee, guarded by French SS troops from Bataillon 57, was looted. 'A weeks ration for a whole battalion' was taken. In response, Ustuf. Labourdette was ordered to conduct an investigation, which he entrusted to his *adjudant de compagnie*, a certain Uscha. Girald.[16] His investigation proved damning: not only were pots of margarine from the Luftwaffe depot found in the battalion's billets, but the four-man guard on duty that night was in fact responsible for the looting. Indeed, the *chef de poste* [post commander], Uscha. Gastine,[17] had broken open the warehouse door and then actively encouraged the looting. Furthermore, he had even let his accomplices call four of their comrades to share the 'loot'. The culprits were arrested, but Uscha. Gastine had flown. The accused were brought to Carpin. Two versions of the court proceedings exist, although the final sentences meted out are the same.

According to Mabire,[18] Brigf. Krukenberg insisted that the accused must be judged by their unit, that of SS-Bataillon 57. An order laid down the make-up of the court: Fenet would preside, and Labourdette and a private would assist. The three men on guard duty and their four accomplices appeared before the court. The Führer's order countersigned by the three men on guard duty was produced. From that moment on there was only one possible sentence for them and all three were sentenced to death.

Hours after sentence was passed on the three, Gastine was brought back to the camp and put on trial. Also charged with desertion, he was found guilty on both counts. He too was sentenced to death by firing squad, but 'higher authorities of the division' requested that his sentence be changed to death by hanging. This Fenet rejected outright. In reply, Fenet requested that one of the condemned, an officer's son who was 'crushed by having failed to keep honour', be sent to a 'special unit' [penal unit?] to meet a soldier's death. This was rejected by 'Division'. As for the four accomplices, they were not sentenced.

According to Saint-Loup,[19] Brigf. Krukenberg immediately brought the four accused before a court martial over which Stubaf. Boudet-Gheusi presided. Assisting him was *officier de justice* Ustuf. Stehli and defending the accused was *lieutenant* Sabatieri.[20] Boudet-Gheusi employed all his skills as a lawyer to save Gastine and the three sentries on duty, named as Labarret, Dreveau and Beynac,[21] from the death sentence, although Gastine, the instigator, was sentenced alone to twenty years hard labour. However, Krukenberg immediately quashed the sentence and replaced Boudet-Gheusi with Fenet as the presiding judge for a new court martial. Subsequently the four accused were found guilty and sentenced to death.

Chaplain Verney came to comfort and administer the last rites to the four condemned men. Shortly before sunrise, the condemned were brought before a firing squad of twelve volunteers

---

15   Soulat's notes written while in prison in 1948.
16   Might be a pseudonym.
17   Born on 28 June 1923, Jacques Gastine enlisted in the Sturmbrigade with his brother Bernand. He attended a training course at Neweklau and was promoted to Standartenjunker, but Oscha. Hennecart demoted him for bad conduct during the retreat through Pomerania
18   See Mabire, *Mourir A Berlin*, pp.71-72.
19   See Saint-Loup, *Les Hérétiques*, pp.377-378.
20   Sabatieri is undoubtedly a pseudonym.
21   All three names might be pseudonyms.

picked from the more than fifty who had come forward. Waiting to witness the execution at Fürstensee was the entire Bataillon 57. The condemned were not tied to posts and stood in front of trees. A shout of "Aim! Fire!" Once again the salvo of the firing squad resounded. They fell without crying out. An Oberscharführer administered the coup de grâce. It was a needless formality. All four were dead. Lost in thought, the companies silently returned to their barracks. Three others went to the firing squad for looting.[22]

Ostuf. Audibert of the Engineer Company also found himself before a court martial. He was charged with having abandoned on Bärenwalde platform station the equipment of the Engineer Company, in particular its most recent model flamethrowers, which fell into the hands of the Russians. Vigorously, he contested the charge. Covered by an order from Obf. Puaud, he managed to exonerate himself. He was acquitted.

### Rebuilding 'Charlemagne'

By early April 1945, the strength of 'Charlemagne' had grown to around one thousand men.[23] RF-SS Himmler and Brigf. Krukenberg now decided to reorganise 'Charlemagne' by culling those who did not want to continue the fight to the very end. They would be formed into a Construction Battalion (Bau-bataillon). Krukenberg assembled the survivors and told them:[24]

> I only want volunteers. You may abandon the armed fight. You will remain in the SS, but as workers. I only want to have combatants with me now.

22  Soulat, *Historique de la Division Charlemagne*, p.96, repeated by Saint-Loup, *Les Hérétiques*, p.377. Scherzer is not totally convinced that French SS soldiers were executed in and around Carpin in April 1945 (see *Sous le Signe SS*, pp.475-477). He argues that Krukenberg, who was the 'supreme judge of his division', makes no mention of the various court hearings or the sentences and also that no French citizens are buried in Carpin or Fürstensee, except for a French POW of 1940 who died of natural causes in 1942. Scherzer then dismisses his own argument by adding that deserters were not normally buried in a cemetery anyway! In response to Scherzer, Soulat actually witnessed the execution of Harel and Turco. Scherzer goes on to suggest that Soulat actually crafted the story of Labourdette's death in Berlin so as to protect Labourdette in case he survived the war and was in need of a new identity because he would have found no mercy before the French courts, having sat on the court martial which sentenced Harel and Turco to death. The 'evidence' presented by Scherzer is flimsy to say the least. Finally, Scherzer argues that the names of others shot are not known or appear as pseudonyms which prove that the French veterans were 'trying to cover up something'. Again this is not true. Saint-Loup and Mabire extensively employed the use of pseudonyms throughout their respective works and that included the names of some of those shot. The author repeated some of those names in earlier versions of this work.

23  Scherzer estimates that 'Charlemagne' numbered no more than 850 men which was made up as follows: 300 men Krukenberg brought back from Pomernia, 100 men with Martin from Gotenhafen, 200 who crossed the Oder with Katzian plus 250 new recruits and recovered men for a total of 850 men (*Sous le Signe*, p.482). However, Scherzer provides no evidence whatsoever to support the notion that 250 new recruits and recovered men actually joined 'Charlemagne'.

24  Mabire, *Entretien avec le général Krukenberg, Historia* hors serie 32, p.136.

To a man, the *Compagnie d'Honneur* chose to fight on.[25] For Uscha. Puechlong, he had sworn an oath of loyalty and he for one was going to remain faithful to it. Moreover, he could not demean himself in this way. Lavest, also of the *Compagnie d'Honneur*, said:[26]

> Although we knew full well that the war was lost we choose to continue the fight so as not to fall into the hands of the Russians alive. In spite of everything we believed in the new weapons.

Seventy-five percent of the men of Fenet's SS-Bataillon 57 and 50% of those of Géromini's SS-Bataillon 58 chose the rifle rather than the pick and shovel. As for Soulat, although he realised the war was nearing its end, the choice of 'keeping out of things' appeared to him shameful when so many of his comrades had disappeared in Pomerania. In total, one officer and around four hundred men opted for the Construction Battalion.[27] Many were former *Miliciens*. Uscha. Peyret of the Panzerjäger Kompanie of Waffen-Gren. Regt der SS 58, who was ex-LVF, went across to the Construction Battalion. His adventure in Pomerania had annihilated him both physically and morally.

To the command of the Construction Battalion Brigf. Krukenberg appointed Hstuf. Roy, which he greatly resented. Nevertheless, Krukenberg was not punishing him; he had need of solid officers for the battalion and in Pomerania Roy had fought with tenacity, skill and courage. Krukenberg also transferred Ustuf. Martres to the Construction Battalion. This he too resented, but orders are orders. When the Construction Battalion was activated on 10 April 1945 its order of battle was as follows:

| | |
|---|---|
| Commander: | W-Hstuf. Roy |
| Assistant: | W-Ustuf. Martres[28] |
| 1 Kompanie: | W-Ostuf. Roumégous |
| 2 Kompanie: | W-Ostuf. Géromini |
| 3 Kompanie: | W-Ostuf. Darrigade |

Notably the three company commanders were former *Miliciens*. Ustuf. Saint-Magne, who was ex-LVF and had fought in Pomerania at the head of the 6/58, also joined the Construction Battalion.[29]

Three different accounts exist of how Ostuf. Géromini ended up as a company commander in the Construction Battalion. According to one account,[30] Géromini actually volunteered to continue the fight at the head of Btl. 58, but found himself instead demoted to a company

25  According to Levast, *Le soleil se couchait à l'est*, p.97, the question of continuing the fight or not was not even put to the *Compagnie d'Honneur*.
26  Lavest, letter to the author.
27  Mabire, *Mourir A Berlin*, p.78. This figure has been confirmed by Soulat, letter 9/11/97. According to Saint-Loup, *Les Hérétiques*, p.370, the figure was three hundred.
28  According to Soulat, *Historique de la Division Charlemagne*, p.96, Martres held the position of Orderly Officer and Hstuf. Martin that of *adjoint*. In response to this, Martres does not recall Martin serving with the Bau-Bataillon and his position was not that of the O.O. (letter to the author, 12/7/99).
29  The author does not know if this posting was through choice.
30  Mabire, *Mourir A Berlin*, p.80.

commander in the Construction Battalion, finally paying the price of his all too regular outspoken views in the presence of Krukenberg. In contrast, according to another account,[31] Géromini actually resigned his command to take up that of a Construction Company. The last and third account begins when Brigf. Krukenberg called together the officers at Carpin late March and declared:[32]

> I only want volunteers in the 'Charlemagne' Regiment, real volunteers, and people who want to fight. Some came to Wildflecken against their will. I no longer want them. They may go.

Krukenberg continued by slandering the former PPF militants, the former *Miliciens* and Darnand. After this outburst, he told the officers: "Those who want to fight, to the right; those who do not want to fight, to the left." Only Ostuf. Géromini went to the left. A lively tête-à-tête followed between Géromini and Krukenberg that confirmed yet again Krukenberg's view of Géromini as a troublemaker.[33] In keeping with his temperament, Ostuf. Géromini would prove as troublesome to Hstuf. Roy as he was to Brigf. Krukenberg.

The Construction Battalion was quartered in the vicinity of the village of Drewin. Its morale was, at best, low. Its commander, Roy, although a convinced National Socialist, doubted the existence of the much vaunted secret weapons. Indeed, during a discussion about the secret weapons, Ustuf. Martres, his assistant, recalls how Roy brought out a small knife, claiming it was a secret weapon!

Throughout its short existence the Construction Battalion had little, or no, contact with the 'fighting' elements of 'Charlemagne'. Ustuf. Martres had at his disposal a section of ten soldiers and, notably, they were the only men in the whole battalion to carry arms. This was, of course, unofficial. As for those who volunteered to fight on, they were required to sign an 'oath form' which pledged unconditional loyalty to the Führer till death. For some, it was the third oath they had sworn to Hitler. One such volunteer was Hscha. Rostaing who commented that he was not even a National Socialist. He was driven by one desire alone: to fight Communism, 'the enemy of every civilisation'.[34]

Following the cull, the already high morale of SS-Bataillon 57, still stationed at Fürstensee, rose. The order of battle of SS-Bataillon 57 was as follows:

| | |
|---|---|
| Commander: | W-Hstuf. Fenet |
| Assistant: | ? |
| 1 Kompanie: | W-Ustuf. Labourdette |
| 2 Kompanie: | W-Hscha. Hennecart |
| 3 Kompanie: | ? |
| 4 Kompanie: | W-Oscha. Ollivier |

---

31  Landwehr, *Charlemagne's Legionnaires*, p.114.
32  Delperrié de Bayac, *Histoire de la Milice*, pp.609-610.
33  The details of this lively tête-à-tête supplied by Delperrié de Bayac seem repeated and expanded by Mabire, *Mourir A Berlin*, p.58, in a similar confrontation. Unfortunately Mabire does not date the confrontation.
34  Rostaing, *Le prix d'un serment*, p.180.

The three company commanders were battle-proven.

Born in 1917, Jean Ollivier fought in 1940, winning the *Croix de guerre*. He passed from the SOL to the *Milice* but volunteered for work in Germany in June 1943. One month later, he volunteered for the Waffen-SS at Vienna. He served with the 9/57 in Pomerania as a platoon commander before going on to serve with the 6/58.

The cull left SS-Bataillon 58 seriously depleted, but it had its desired effect. The battalion was now made up of a hardcore of battle-proven LVF veterans who were still full of drive and fight. Many of them had served on the Eastern Front since the first winter of 1941/1942.

The order of battle of SS-Bataillon 58 was as follows:

| | |
|---|---|
| Commander: | SS-Hstuf. Jauss |
| 5 Kompanie: | W-Std.Ju. Aumont |
| 6 Kompanie: | W-Hscha. Rostaing |
| 7 Kompanie: | W-Ostuf. Fatin |
| 8 Kompanie: | W-Ustuf. Sarrailhé |

However, the new commander of the battalion, Hstuf. Jauss, was not the same courageous individual who had acted alternately with Fenet as a guide for the 1/RM across Pomerania or who had been at the forefront during the break through to Dievenow. He had become disenchanted, silent for long periods of time, and had let his appearance go.

Two of the company commanders had similar credentials to their men, namely Ostuf. Fatin and Hscha. Rostaing. Both had served and made their mark in the LVF. Of late, Fatin had been promoted to the rank of Obersturmführer and won the Iron Cross 1st Class for his part in the defence of Gotenhafen.

Rostaing had served with the celebrated *section de chasse*. Transferred to the Franz. Brigade der SS, he served on the headquarters staff of the II/58. Attending SS-Unterführerschule Lauenberg, Pomerania, he regained the enthusiasm of his youth and wanted to prove to his German comrades that he was their worthy equal. Unsurprisingly he graduated, retaining his former rank. His time at Wildflecken camp holds very few memories.[35] In February 1945, Rostaing found himself in the 'hell of Pomerania', but he was one of the few to return. In the wake of the creation of the Construction Battalion, Hstuf. Jauss appointed Hscha. Rostaing to the head of the 6th Company. In this way, Rostaing replaced Ustuf. Leune who was posted to the Engineer Platoon.

The *Compagnie d'Honneur*, by now some eighty-strong[36] and renamed the Kampfschule [Combat School], was unaffected by the reorganisation. Weber's boys had literally laughed at the order offering them the option to become rear area construction troops. They were proud and fanatical. Indeed, they had been first to receive the camouflaged uniforms on 1 April 1945. That same day, which was Easter day, the company was invited in small groups to have lunch with the inhabitants of a nearby village. Shortly after, the company was moved to new quarters in Carpin.

---

35  See Rostaing, *Le prix d'un serment*, pp.151-158. There are so few personal details of his time at Wildflecken camp.
36  Lavest, letter to the author, 1998.

The reputation of the Kampfschule continued to grow when one morning the men paraded without belt buckles for a German officer of the Inspection. Calmly, Weber explained to the staff officer that the Kampfschule had only received Wehrmacht belt buckles with the inscription "Gott mit uns" [God is with us] which, of course, were not suitable for members of the Waffen-SS! He then added that they had no need of God! The staff officer was stunned to silence. Shortly after, the appropriate belt buckles bearing the Waffen SS motto were received.

Theoretically speaking, the Kampfschule was directly answerable only to the German Inspection, but Brigf. Krukenberg had become more and more distant for those Frenchmen in its ranks, who now only obeyed Weber and him alone.[37]

Also reassembled were the support elements of Regiment 'Charlemagne', which comprised one engineer platoon, one signals platoon, one horse-drawn supply column, one motor column, and a repair workshop. All were under-strength and desperately short of equipment. The engineer platoon had no equipment to its name. The signals platoon was without radio sets and had to make do with some poor field telephones. All were stationed at the village of Zinow, some five kilometres due west of Carpin.

The so-called Heavy Battalion, located in Goldenbaum, had the strength of a reinforced company. Many of its men had gone across to the Construction Battalion. The 'Battalion' was armed with light machine-guns, mortars, panzerfäust and panzerschreck, but no PAK guns.

The medical and veterinary staff were merged together under a German doctor transferred from the 3. SS-Panzer-Division 'Totenkopf'.

Headquarters still waited impatiently the arrival of the 1,200 French SS troops under SS-Ostubaf. Hersche who had set out on foot from Wildflecken camp during the night of 30-31 March. There was no news of their progress. Also expected was the Assault Gun Company that was away on a training course in Bohemia-Moravia.

More awards were issued. Ostuf. Dupuyau and Std.Ju.Ob. Radici received the Iron Cross 2nd Class. Many individuals were also awarded the Wounded Badge and nominated for the Assault Badge and the Close Combat Clasp. Shortly after, Radici was promoted to Untersturmführer.

Toward mid-April, the headquarters staff of 'Charlemagne' underwent a number of changes to look as follows:[38]

| | |
|---|---|
| Commander: | SS-Brigf. Krukenberg |
| Assistant and Office IA: | SS-Hstuf. Pachur |
| Orderly Officer: | SS-Ustuf. Hegewald |
| Kommandant Stabsquartier: | SS-Ostuf. Ruhnow |
| Office IB: | SS-Ostuf. Meier |
| Office IC: | SS-Ostuf. von Wallenrodt |
| Office IIA/B: | SS-Hstuf. Pachur |
| Office IVA: | SS-Hstuf. Hagen |
| Office IVB: | SS-Stubaf.Dr. Schlegel |
| Office IVD: | W-Ustuf. *Abbé* Verney |
| Office V: | SS-Ustuf. Datum |
| Felgendarmerie: | SS-Ostuf. Görr |

37  Mabire, *Mourir A Berlin*, p.84.
38  Soulat, *Historique de la Division Charlemagne*, p.92. Scherzer positions SS-Neubauer at the head of Office V rather than SS-Ustuf. Herbert Datum (see *Sous le Signe*, p.484).

Even though the Regiment had its own commander, namely Staf. Zimmermann and in his absence Hstuf. Kroepsch, it was Brigf. Krukenberg and 'his' headquarters that exercised control, perhaps total control, over its subordinate units. It appears that at no time was Kroepsch opposed to Krukenberg.[39]

Krukenberg's new assistant, Hstuf. Pachur, a Berliner, was very much after his own heart.[40] The headquarters staff under Ostuf. Ruhnow were stationed at Carpin. Ostuf. Görr and his Military Police were at the village of Thurow, about six kilometres north-west of Carpin.

On 14 April 1945, some thirty five French officer candidates[41] rejoined Regiment 'Charlemagne' at Carpin. They had just completed their training course at annex Neweklau of SS-Panzergrenadierschule Kienschlag. The course had moulded their minds and bodies, and they now burned with fanaticism and idealism. The arrival of these officer candidates would contribute greatly to bringing the regiment to a state of combat readiness and to strengthening the regiment's spirit of determination by moulding their troops in their own image. Indeed, their impatience to fight had to be quelled.

The officer candidates came from no one particular origin. The majority of the new officers who had served with the LVF were assigned to Bataillon 58. Oberjunker Baumgartner,[42] St.Ju. Chavent, St.Ju. Dumoulin[43] and Oberjunker Ginot were assigned to Rostaing's 6th Company. Gaston Baumgartner and Jean Dumoulin were known to Rostaing from the days of the LVF. Baumgartner had served with the 9th Company of III/638. Ginot, who was from Paris, had served with the 5th Company of II/638. Jacques Chavent had fought at Bobr and been decorated with the Iron Cross 2nd Class for bravery.

Also out of Kienschlag was Jean Malardier who had been promoted to the rank of Unterscharführer. Ex-LVF, he was assigned to Rostaing's 6th Company and served as the *adjoint* to a section commander of the 1st Platoon now commanded by Oberjunker Ginot.

SS-Bataillon 57 also benefited from the influx of new officers. Assigned to Labourdette's company were Oberjunker Boulmier,[44] St.Ju. Cossard, Oberjunker Croisile, Oberjunker Maxime de Lacaze and St. Ju. Le Maignan de Kérangat. Boulmier and Jean Cossard were ex-LVF.

The twenty-year-old Maxime de Lacaze was ex-*Milice*.[45] He joined the *Franc-Garde permanente* of Lot-et-Garonne and, during the summer of 1943, he and his brother, Jean, received officer candidate training at the *École des cadres de la Milice* at Uriage. One of their instructors was Pignard-Berthet. With the rank of *chef de dizaine*, he trained new recruits and participated in several operations against the terrorists. In November 1944, the two brothers entered 'Charlemagne'.

---

39    Arguably, a French regimental commander, whatever his rank, may have had 'much more to say'.
40    Paul Pachur was born on 27 October 1909 in Berlin. His Nazi Party number was 452 329 and his SS number 36 617. He was commissioned as an Untersturmführer on 30 January 1938. Promotions followed over the years. Finally, he was promoted to Hstuf. on 20 April 1944.
41    See Bouysse, *Français sous l'uniforme allemande partie II: Sous-officiers & hommes du rang de la Waffen-SS*.
42    Mabire employs a pseudonym of Gardinier for the same individual. Born in 1914 in Paris, Baumgartner enlisted in the LVF in February 1943.
43    Jean Dumolin was born on 29 June 1917 in Amiens.
44    His brother was also serving in 'Charlemagne'.
45    Maxime de Lacaze was born on 14 August 1924 in Labastide-Castel-Amouroux (department Lot-et-Garonne).

Jacques Le Maignan de Kérangat, who was also twenty years old, had 'deserted' the cause of the NSKK for that of the Waffen-SS in the late summer of 1943. Ollivier's 4th (heavy) Company received St.Ju. Sellier and St.Ju. Serge Protopopoff. In late 1943, 'Prince' Protopopoff attended the *École des cadres* of the LVF at Montargis near Orleans. Posted to Russia, he was assigned to the II. Bataillon.

Fenet took Oberjunker Douroux as an Orderly Officer. Born on 12 September 1920 in Paris, Alfred Douroux volunteered for the LVF at the start of 1943. He too attended the *École des cadres* of the LVF at Montargis. At the end of the year, he was posted to the Eastern Front and incorporated with NCO rank into the 6th Company of II/638. He too was transferred from the LVF to the Waffen-SS and 'Charlemagne'.

The following also returned from Kienschlag with the rank of Oberjunker: Frantz, Le Brun, Maisse, Néron, Piffeteau, and Poupon, a *franciste*. The following returned with the rank of Standarten-Junker: Billot, Catta, Conte, Deconynck, Fortis, Garrabos, Hardy, Lefeuvre, Noell, and Robelin. They too came from very different backgrounds.

Born on 7 March 1925 in Boulogne-Billancourt, Jacques Frantz volunteered for the Waffen-SS in the early summer of 1944 and underwent his basic training at Sennheim in the ranks of the 1st Company. Raymond Poupon, who was born on 25 July 1921 in Dijon, came to 'Charlemagne' via the LVF and served with 4/57 when transferred to the Waffen-SS. Pierre Maisse was born on 22 November 1919 in Lyon. He too came to 'Charlemagne' via the LVF, but previously he had briefly served with the *Milice*, attending Uriage, followed by his appointment as the *chef du 2eme Service de la Milice* for the Rhône department. Albert Robelin came to 'Charlemagne' via the *Milice*.

Pierre-Henri Fortis was a highly decorated former *chef de bataillon*. Born in 1892, he fought in the trenches of 1914-1918, winning 17 citations and the *Légion d'Honneur*, and suffering 7 wounds. France applauded him as a hero. In 39-40, he commanded a battalion in the 139° *Régiment d'Infanterie* and was taken prisoner. In March 1944, rather than remain a prisoner any longer, he enlisted in the Waffen-SS.[46]

The planned Third French Waffen-Junker-Lehrgang at Kienschlag (15 April to 15 August 1945) did not go ahead because the military situation was desperate. April also saw the return of the Assault Gun Company from its course at Votice, Bohemia-Moravia. It had been equipped with Jagdpanzer 38(t) Hetzers,[47] but en route the assault guns were 'confiscated' by Army Group Schoerner.[48] Because of this, the men of the Assault Gun Company would now have to fight as grenadier.

Shortly after the integration of the new Oberjunker and NCOs into Regiment 'Charlemagne', Ostuf. Pierre Michel, one of their former instructors, arrived at Neustrelitz.[49] Assigned to

---

46    On 14 November 1945, the *tribunal* [court] of Marseille sentenced Fortis to five years hard labour. He died in 1955 from an illness resulting from his old wounds.

47    Soulat, letter to the author, 11/1/99, and Mabire, *Mourir A Berlin*, p.90.

48    Soulat, letter to the author, 19/2/99.

49    Different sources provide various dates as to when Michel attended SS-Panzergrenadierschule Kienschlag as an instructor. According to his SS personnel file, Michel was transferred to Kienschlag as an Inspektionschef on 1 March 1945. However, according to Soulat, *Historique de la Division Charlemagne*, p.87, Michel was an instructor at Kienschlag until December 1944. And, lastly, according to Lefèvre, magazine *Uniforms* numéro 300, Michel took up post at Kienschlag in January 1945.

SS-Bataillon 57, he received from Hstuf. Fenet the command of the 2nd Company, displacing Hscha. Hennecart who was transferred to battalion headquarters.

The 2nd Company had a solid core of leadership in platoon commanders Oberjunker Neron, Oscha. Montgour and St.Ju Hardy. Néron, a *pied-noir*, had left his native Algeria to study history at Lyon.[50] Anti-Communist, he enlisted in the LVF in January 1944 and was sent to Greifenberg. After receiving NCO training, he was promoted to *Sergent*. He passed to the Waffen-SS and served with 2/57. Marc Montgour, a native of Lyon, was a former *chef de centaine de la Milice* who had participated in the maintenance of order operations in the Limousin. Of late, he had received assault gun training in Bohemia-Moravia. St.Ju Hardy, who was seriously wounded in the spring of 1944 while training with the Sturmbrigade in Bohemia-Moravia, is described as an 'excellent instructor'.[51]

And yet Brigf. Krukenberg's problems were still not at an end. Hstuf. Jauss, the young commander of SS-Bataillon 58, had become more and more disillusioned.[52] This, of course, Krukenberg could tolerate no longer. He had to protect the exceptional spirit of the seven hundred combatants from corruption and erosion. In a report addressed to the SS-Führungshauptamt or SS-FHA, he wrote:[53] 'Hstuf. Jauss is perhaps perfect to supervise a Junkerschaft of officer cadets but his place is not with the French volunteers.' This was tantamount to requesting his transfer. Jauss was duly transferred.[54]

### Calm before the storm

On the morning of 16 April 1945, the Soviets launched a massive offensive against the German 9th Army and 4th Panzer Army along the river Oder. The Germans fought back with stubborn resistance. However, by 19 April, the Soviets had broken through the German lines and were racing to encircle Berlin. And yet for 'Charlemagne' this period was one full of almost comic moments.

To supplement the poor rations of his company employed on building anti-tank obstructions, Hscha. Rostaing had a doe shot daily. This he had continued even after a rebuke from battalion commander Hstuf. Jauss; hunting was forbidden by law on Reich property. And then one day the forest warden of Wokuhl confronted him.

Wild with anger, the forest warden kicked in the door to Rostaing's office. He then blurted out that he had caught one of Rostaing's men, an LVF veteran by the name of Minot, killing a doe. And when he had approached the soldier he had fired over his head.

In an attempt to cover up the incident, Rostaing angrily retorted to the forest warden that he must be mistaken, adding that he reigned over his men with an iron discipline. Unconvinced, the forest warden kept on. Rostaing, whose patience was short, abruptly jumped up, grabbed

---

50    Jean-Philippe Neron was born on 26 July 1923 in Philippeville, Algeria.
51    Mabire, *Mourir A Berlin*, p.91.
52    Indeed, according to Saint-Loup, *Les Hérétiques*, p.376, Jauss was now going round 'making the worst accusations against Krukenberg'. Moreover, it appears that Krukenberg and Jauss had never quite seen eye to eye.
53    Memoirs of Soulat. Mabire has slightly different wording.
54    The date of his transfer may have been 17 April. See Westemeier, *Hans Robert Jauss Konstanz Jugend, Krieg und Internierung*, pp.103-104.

hold of the forest warden's rifle and violently threw it on the ground. It smashed. At this, the forest warden's anger suddenly died away and his eyes filled with tears. He retreated. The following day, in a gesture of friendship, he sent Rostaing a stag he had just killed.[55]

And then it was the turn of Ostuf. Fatin to be confronted by a forest warden! Angrily, the forest warden complained to Fatin: "Your men are cutting down trees in the forest." Yes they were, but Fatin explained that they needed them for anti-tank obstructions. Remarkably, the forest warden reacted with the words: "But they're felling without authorisation and that is a crime against the Greater Reich!" Fatin went red, then pale. However, as a compromise, the forest warden suggested that Fatin could fell only those trees that were 'administratively designated'. At this, Fatin exploded. Seizing the forest warden by the collar, Fatin ejected him.[56]

And then one day two volunteers of the Indische Freiwilligen-Legion der Waffen-SS (Indian Legion of the Waffen-SS) arrived at 'Charlemagne' headquarters. It turned out that they had actually been sent there by mistake! Soulat of the headquarters staff got talking to one of them who knew some German. He was surprised to learn that they were in fact English soldiers captured in Egypt by the Africa Korps!

Finally, on 19 April, the survivors of Bataillon Martin, which had fought in the area of Gotenhafen, joined Regiment 'Charlemagne'. Most of them opted for the Construction Battalion, though. Uscha. Jean Grenouillet decided to fight on and joined SS-Bataillon 58 (probably with Fatin).

20 April 1945 was a memorable day for many reasons. In the first place, it was Hitler's fifty-sixth birthday. At 1700 hours, a simple ceremony was held at the anti-tank ditch at Georgenhof. Ustuf. Bender gave a short speech in French and then in German. This was followed by a rendition of the 'Treuelied'. Krukenberg was next to speak. After hinting at the coming final battle, he evoked the fallen. By now, Soulat of the headquarters staff was so lost in thought that he did not hear the rest of the speech that brought the ceremony to a close.

When the Frenchmen returned to their billets each received a modest present 'containing objects of use': a razor and blades, a comb, a mirror, a notebook, a small phial of schnapps and a small piece of marzipan. Those of office IIA/B also received from Hstuf. Pachur a modern German novel inscribed by him.

In the second place, new weaponry arrived for the seven hundred men of 'Charlemagne' determined to continue the fight. They received MG 42 heavy calibre machine guns, the redoubtable Sturmgewehr 44 assault rifles and panzerfäuste. In this way, their training was finally enriched with weapons.

Also, that same day, Rttf. Soulat was proposed for the KVK II. Klasse because he was only one at headquarters without it. The course of events was such that he would never receive this award.

In the late morning of 21 April 1945, on hearing of the murder of the forest warden (or game warden) of Serahn, a small hamlet in the woods five kilometres from Carpin, Brigf. Krukenberg immediately ordered Stubaf. Boudet-Gheusi to lead a manhunt for the killers, said to be two

---

55   Rostaing, *Le prix d'un serment*, p.182. However, according to Saint-Loup, *Les Hérétiques*, p.372, the ending was more civil.

56   Saint-Loup, *Les Hérétiques*, p.375. Rostaing also recollects a similar 'visit' from a forest warden with the self-same complaint. And although Rostaing treated his visitor with more respect than Fatin, the forest warden threatened to make him pay for his crime! His words of warning would come to nothing.

deserters from the Stettin front, one of whom spoke no German and the other only badly. The story went that the two deserters had called on a neighbour of the forest warden, begging for bread, and that he had urged them to follow him and the warden to the Feldgendarmerie at Carpin. The deserters agreed, but on the way they pulled out a gun they had hidden, killed the warden and disappeared.

All available units of 'Charlemagne' were alerted and despatched on a concentric sweep. During the sweep the headquarters staff of SS-Bataillon 57 visited the warden's house to pass on their condolences to the family. Admitted, they were greeted by a sombre scene. They felt ill at ease. Fenet spoke with the daughter of the family. She was touched by his sympathy and wished him well before returning to her grieving mother.

After a sweep of five kilometres through the woods, the French Waffen-SS units returned to their billets empty-handed.[57] Later, from a reliable source, Soulat was to learn that the two deserters were, in fact, a Polish paratrooper (or parachutist) and a soldier of the 3/57, who had met him by chance in the woods. It was the Pole who had pulled the trigger. Frightened, the Frenchman had cleared off and returned to his billets without saying anything to anybody.

On 22 April 1945, 'Charlemagne' Headquarters at Carpin received reports of enemy paratroopers in the sector. As proof, a peasant from Goldenbaum brought along with him a parachute that he claimed he had discovered in his fields.[58]

Now to 23 April 1945 and remarkably the arrival of a new French recruit! Hstuf. Fenet received him. A former prisoner of war, he had grown to love Germany and, now that Germany was in her hour of need, he wanted to come to her defence. So he had enlisted in the Waffen-SS. Told to report to the nearest unit, instead he went in search of 'Charlemagne'. And one month later here he was.

Although Fenet was convinced that the new recruit was genuine, he decided that he could not accept his sacrifice. So he turned him down gently. After pointing out that they were busy at the moment and that the enlistment office was not open, he told him to go home and wait to be called up, which would only be in a matter of days. The recruit clicked his heels, saluted and left.[59]

**The Mission**

During the night of 23-24 April 1945, Brigf. Krukenberg was ordered to Berlin to assume a new command. He would be accompanied by a French battlegroup from 'Charlemagne'.

Much has been written of what transpired that night, but what is the truth?

57   The *souvenirs* of Soulat. However, according to Mabire, *Mourir A Berlin*, p.105, it was on the evening of 23 April that the headquarters staff of SS-Bataillon 57 visited the warden's house.
58   According to Mabire, *Mourir A Berlin*, p.102, and [repeated by?] Landwehr, *Charlemagne's Legionnaires*, p.117, reports of enemy paratroopers trigged the employment of companies from both SS-Bataillon 57 and SS-Bataillon 58 in search of them. This is not confirmed by Soulat.
59   Saint-Loup, *Les Hérétiques*, pp.375-376. However, according to Mabire, *Mourir A Berlin*, p.99, and repeated by Landwehr, *Charlemagne's Legionnaires*, p.117, Fenet told the new recruit that he was too late because he had no military training and 'Charlemagne' no longer had [any] training units. The new recruit asked: "You really don't have any place for me?" The answer was no. Thereupon he left.

According to Krukenberg,[60] he received two telephone calls one after the other around 0400 hours on 24 April 1945. The first was from the Personalamt [Personnel Office] der Waffen-SS (of the SS-FHA) near Fürstenberg and the second from the headquarters of Army Group Vistula near Prenzlau.

Both calls transmitted the order of the OKW to proceed rapidly to Berlin where he would receive the command of a division whose commander had fallen ill. Also, upon his arrival in Berlin, he was to report to Colonel-General Krebs, the Army Chief-of-Staff, and to Ogruf. Fegelein, the liaison officer of the Waffen-SS to the headquarters of the Führer, who were both at the Reichs Chancellery.

Krukenberg asked about the situation in Berlin. He was told that the Russians had broken through the defensive front along the river Oder and were advancing in two columns on Berlin. It might only be a matter of hours before Berlin was encircled. A Panzer Corps (the LVI Panzer-Korps), to the east of the city, had been thrown back into the suburbs and was now engaged in hard defensive fighting.

However, the situation was not without hope. It was explained to Krukenberg that 'our commander' had made contact with the 'commander of our enemies in the West'. The Americans were already on the river Elbe and all resistance had been ceased against them so that they could continue to advance and occupy Berlin first or at the same time as the Soviets. Also, in the region of Rathenow-Genthin, a Panzer Corps (the XXXXI Panzer-Korps, although it was a Panzer Corps in name only) with General Wenck (the commander of the 12th Army) had received orders to advance in the direction of Potsdam. It was to open a passage for the Americans into West Berlin so that they could occupy from there the other quarters of the city.

Momentarily, Krukenberg became lost in thought. He asked himself the question: how was the defence of a city with several million inhabitants possible? In June 1940, France had declared Paris an 'open city', sparing its inhabitants the horrors of street battle. But the Red Army had raped, pillaged and looted its way through West Prussia and Pomerania. If Berlin fell to the Red Army, then the same excesses awaited its inhabitants. But the capital city had been declared a *Festung* [fortress] on 1 February 1945 and ever since work had been continuing on its defence. So perhaps the city could be defended.

Because the situation awaiting him in Berlin appeared so very unclear, Krukenberg, also prompted by past experiences, asked for permission to take with him to his new posting 'one part of his usual headquarters and an escort detachment of about ninety men'. The headquarters of Army Group Vistula agreed to his requests and added that the route to Berlin via Oranienburg and Frohnau, 'still clear of the enemy', was the most suitable.

According to Soulat,[61] at 0030 hours, Brigf. Krukenberg received a telegram ordering him to 'form a Sturmbataillon [Assault Battalion] with the remnants of 'Charlemagne' on receipt of this order, equip it ready for action and take it immediately and via the shortest routes to Berlin' where he was to report to the Chancellery for orders.[62]

60   In 1964, Krukenberg wrote his account of the battle of Berlin under the title 'Battle for Berlin'.
61   Soulat, *Historique de la Division Charlemagne*, p.100 and his *souvenirs*, which is repeated by Saint-Loup, *Les Hérétiques*, p.381.
62   Of note is that Soulat actually laid eyes on the telegram. He remembers it well because it was so extraordinary.

A Sturmbataillon was immediately formed. It comprised the entire SS-Bataillon 57,[63] the Kampfschule, as well as one company of SS-Bataillon 58.[64] Rostaing and his company felt proud to be the only company of SS-Bataillon 58 chosen to leave for Berlin. All other combatant units of 'Charlemagne' were readied to follow in a second echelon the very next day.[65]

So did Brigf. Krukenberg receive a telegram ordering Division 'Charlemagne' to Berlin? And was his escort ninety-strong or of battalion strength? Ostuf. Weber also saw a telegram ordering Division 'Charlemagne' to Berlin.[66] The telegram was from the *Führerhauptquartier* and signed by Adolf Hitler. Its existence was confirmed after the war by Stubaf. Günsche, an SS officer in Adolf Hitler's immediate entourage, who also declared to Weber that he dispatched the telegram. Therefore, it can be concluded that a telegram was sent and received by Brigf. Krukenberg ordering 'Charlemagne' to Berlin.

According to many French and German survivors of all ranks, the so-called escort that accompanied Brigf. Krukenberg to Berlin was of battalion strength.[67] Furthermore, to settle the debate once and for all, a report from Pz.AOK 3 [3rd Panzer Army] dated 24 April 1945, states that, from its rear zone, the headquarters and '1 Batl. 33. SS-WGD. 'Charlemagne' have set out direction Berlin'. Therefore, it appears that the 'escort' Brigf. Krukenberg took to Berlin was of battalion strength.

Brigf. Krukenberg assembled all officers at his headquarters in Castle Carpin. Hstuf. Fenet was the first to arrive. A 'smiling' Krukenberg greeted him. He was briefed about Berlin.[68] His reaction was one of joy. The officers assembled one by one and were conversing in hushed tones when Krukenberg made his entrance.[69] Without preamble, he started by telling them that the Russians would soon invest Berlin. Continuing, he told them that he had been called to Berlin to receive a new command and that they were coming along with him to defend the capital. He concluded by detailing the proposed route to Berlin: via the city of Oranienburg, north of Berlin.

Open-mouthed, the French Waffen-SS officers had listened to him in total silence. Suddenly it dawned on them what destiny had in store for them: Berlin, the Chancellery, the last battle. However, that was not to be the destiny of all those present. Ustuf. Chaplain Verney and Ostuf. Dr. Métais were left unsure whether or not they would be leaving for Berlin. Verney went

---

63   According to Soulat, *Historique de la Division Charlemagne*, p.100, and also letter to the author, 19/2/99, on its departure from Carpin, SS-Bataillon 57 counted four companies; Company 3/57 had been placed under the command of Ostuf. Fatin.

64   According to Soulat, letter to the author, 19/2/1999, Hennecart was with the 6/58.

65   It appears that sufficient transport could not be made available to move the whole of 'Charlemagne' as one. According to Mabire, *Mourir A Berlin*, p.111, the first echelon was to comprise the three companies of SS-Bataillon 57, its staff, and Weber's Kampfschule, but space could be found for a further one hundred men. Thereupon, headquarters decided to include one company from SS-Bataillon 58. The 6th Company commanded by Rostaing, deemed the most solid and combat ready, was chosen. However, for his part, Rostaing recalls that he was not just an 'afterthought'.

66   See Saint-Loup, *Les Hérétiques*, p.382 and Mabire, *Mourir A Berlin*, p.110. Curiously, each author reproduces the text of the telegram, but the wording differs.

67   For example, Puechlong of Labourdette's Company recalls that the same Company went to Berlin eighty-five to ninety strong including officers and NCOs. (Letter to the author, 24/11/97.)

68   Mabire, *Mourir A Berlin*, p.110.

69   According to Saint-Loup, *Les Hérétiques*, p.381, Zimmermann was present. This is incorrect. Zimmermann was still in a hospital at Anklam. (Zimmermann, letter to Saint-Loup, 10/9/65.)

straight up to Krukenberg and asked him outright. He would be leaving. Métais tried his luck but was not so fortunate; Krukenberg had no need of his services because the German doctor from 'Division' (presumably Schlegel) and Ostuf. Dr. Herpe of SS-Bataillon 57 were already leaving, and this he considered sufficient.

The news of the mission to Berlin spread like wildfire through the billets. The men may have had the choice of leaving for Berlin or remaining behind.[70]

Ammunition and weaponry were distributed. Nearly all grenadier of SS-Bataillon 57 were armed with a Sturmgewehr. Those of Rostaing's company were not quite so fortunate; 'only' one in three held a Sturmgewehr in their hands. Every section was equipped with at least one MG 42 machine-gun, some with two. The redoubtable Panzerfäust was not forgotten. For the first and last time, rations were issued generously, but many troops preferred to draw ammunition. The 4th Company of SS-Bataillon 57, the so-called 'Heavy Company', left behind its 81mm mortars and infantry guns.

The Sturmbataillon assembled. To Soulat, his comrades had never looked in such fine form. Indeed, their enthusiasm reminded him of 'those victorious German soldiers of the first years of the war'. Their morale was excellent. He saw, for the first time, a strange flame burn in their eyes.

At 0530 hours, the French Sturmbataillon left Carpin for Alt-Strelitz. It was from here at 0830 hours that Brigf. Krukenberg had decided to leave for Berlin. The column consisted of several private cars and seven or eight trucks.[71]

70  According to Saint-Loup, *Les Hérétiques*, p.382, at the briefing, Brigf. Krukenberg ordered Fenet, company commanders Labourdette, Michel, Ollivier, Rostaing and Weber to assemble their commands immediately and explain to their men what awaited them and offer them the choice of leaving for Berlin or remaining behind with the Heavy Company (sic). The reason given for this decision was that not enough weapons were available to arm everyone. Krukenberg's orders were carried out, although the way in which the company commanders went about it were quite different. Weber simply ordered his men to assemble at 0745 hours to leave for Berlin. Labourdette and Michel carried out Krukenberg's orders to the letter, explaining the mission entrusted to them. A single command was put to the assembled company: "Volunteers for Berlin, one step forward!" The two companies advanced to a man. Rostaing said to his company: "Lads, we're leaving to defend Berlin! I hope that nobody of the 6th Company will chicken out. Volunteers, one step forward." Without a moment's hesitation, the 125 soldiers of his company all advanced as one. Also, according to a certain Oberjunker of Rostaing's Company (undoubtedly Ginot), the choice was given of leaving for Berlin or remaining behind. Brigf. Krukenberg assembled the companies of the *bataillon de marche* going to Berlin and told them that the 'supreme moment had come [and] the Führer had called the French units to him'. Continuing, he spelled out that 'he wanted only volunteers for this mission' and that they should take one step forward. All did. See Roch, *La Division Charlemagne*, p.130. This choice, however, is not confirmed by any other source. Moreover, according to Lavest, a member of the *Kampfschule*, Brigf. Krukenberg addressed the company and announced that it had the distinguished honour of participating in the defence of Berlin with the other companies of 'Charlemagne', but there was no mention of a choice.
71  Soulat, *Historique de la Division Charlemagne*, p.100. However, the exact number of vehicles will probably never be known; for example, according to Krukenberg, the column consisted of two saloon cars and three trucks; Mabire, *Mourir A Berlin*, p.110, states 'ten Luftwaffe trucks with several private cars'; Charles Georgen states at least two cars and nine trucks that carried up to 45 men each (*Sur les traces du Sturmbataillon de la division 'Charlemagne'*, magazine 39/45, part 1); and according to an Oberjunker of Rostaing's Company (see Roch, *La Division Charlemagne*, p.131), each truck carried one platoon packed tight. Assuming that each of the five companies leaving for Berlin had a minimum of three platoons each, then the column counted fifteen trucks.

While the French SS volunteers were assembling at the Marktplatz of Alt-Strelitz they saw a black Mercedes approaching the column at great speed.[72] At the wheel of the car was Reichsführer-SS Himmler himself. Krukenberg, his assistant Pachur and his Orderly Officer Patzak threw themselves to attention. Passing the column, the Mercedes did briefly slow down but did not stop. In fact, Himmler did not even look their way. The Mercedes disappeared. There was great surprise and obvious disappointment; the Reichsführer had not stopped, even though he had not inspected members of 'Charlemagne' before. Then they went back to the job in hand.

Krukenberg recollected after the war:

> Later I discovered that Himmler had just met Bernadotte in Lübeck. As he knew all about our orders and seeing that he had been trying to negotiate a surrender, he ought, in all conscience, to have stopped us from going on to Berlin or at least have informed me about the situation. I have no doubt that, by driving straight past us, Himmler was trying to avoid this painful necessity.

At 0830 or 0900 hours on 24 April 1945,[73] the column of trucks and private cars carrying some 400 to 500 French volunteers of the Waffen-SS set off southwards to Berlin, around 100 kilometres away as the crow flies.[74] Also with the convoy was Ostuf. Fatin.[75]

---

72    Mounine, correspondence to the author, 1998. Incorrectly, Rostaing states that the French *bataillon de marche* boarded at the *grand-place* [main square] of Neustrelitz (see *Le prix d'un serment*, p.186). 'South of Neustrelitz' and 'the southern road out of Alt-Strelitz' have also appeared as the embarkation point.
73    Mabire and Krukenberg state 0830 hours, and Saint-Loup 0900 hours.
74    Different authors have stated various figures. Georgen, *Sur les traces du Sturmbataillon de la division 'Charlemagne'*, magazine 39/45, part 1, p.19, no more than 410 to 420, Mabire, *Mourir A Berlin*, p.110, around 350, Landwehr, *Charlemagne's Legionnaires*, p.118, 350, Roch, *La Division Charlemagne*, p.131, 400, and, lastly, Soulat, *Historique de la Division Charlemagne*, p.100, 500.
75    Undoubtedly, Fatin did not accompany the Sturmbataillon to Berlin at the head of Company 3/57. There are two possibilities, which might explain his presence with the convoy. First, he went to Berlin as Fenet's assistant. Two months before, at Gotenhafen, he had proved himself admirably in such a capacity. Second, he was brought along to 'support' the three company commanders of the Sturmbataillon, namely Labourdette, Ollivier and Rostaing, who, although able, had only been company commanders for little more than one month and had yet to lead their commands in combat. He was more than 'qualified' for such a role; his military record made excellent reading and his credentials as a battle proven company commander were second to none.

**16**

## First Days in Berlin

---

### To Berlin

The convoy carrying the French *bataillon de marche* made its way southwards, encountering more and more convoys of refugees heading north, which often slowed its pace to a crawl. It also passed prisoners from concentration camps Oranienburg and Ravensbrück. Civilians and soldiers alike were surprised to see a convoy heading in the opposite direction to them.

Brigf. Krukenberg stopped one vehicle of soldiers and questioned them on the whereabouts of the Russians. He was told that Russian armour had already been sighted not far from Oranienburg. Thus the route to Berlin via Frohnau was now out of the question. Thereupon Krukenberg decided to try another route via Neuruppin.

Near Löwenberg, Krukenberg gave the order to proceed westwards in the hope of reaching Fehrbellin and from there Friesack where the convoy would pick up the highway from Hamburg that leads straight into Berlin.[1]

As they continued, fighting against traffic jams in every village and at every crossroads, they passed all manner of troops. From the Waffen-SS, they saw only the Signals Battalion of the Scandinavian 11. SS-Freiwilligen-Panzer-Grenadier-Division 'Nordland' which, according to its commander, had been ordered to Holstein. Its morale and discipline were still intact. They encountered police battalions. And although they looked rested, their vehicle convoys were in the greatest disorder. Several times, they also ran into groups of dishevelled, but joyous German soldiers singing at the top of their voices, who now believed they were saved; because of agreements made between the Allies, the Soviets could not follow them any further and the western powers would immediately demobilise them!

At Friesack, the convoy came upon a police battalion manoeuvring in impeccable order and singing 'as if it had reached the gates of Moscow'.[2] Whilst crossing the town of Nauen the column was strafed by a Soviet aircraft, but escaped without damage. It proceeded on to Wustermark. Finding the route blocked at Wustermark by enemy artillery fire, Krukenberg searched his

---

1    Now Durchgangsstrabe 5.
2    Saint-Loup, *Les Hérétiques*, p.387.

memory of the outskirts of Berlin and then decided to turn back and take the country road to Ketzin. From there, they would proceed to Marquardt. The time was now around midday.

The convoy covered six kilometres without problem. Suddenly Soviet troops were spotted cautiously converging on the road from the south-west, from the region of Paretz, and also from the north-east, from the region of Priort. They were small in number and without heavy weapons. Undoubtedly they were just patrols from the spearheads of the Soviet formations encircling Berlin, but once they linked up, Berlin would be cut off from the outside world.

In turn, the Soviet troops spotted the convoy. They halted and took cover in small copses. Krukenberg thought over his next move. Should they turn back? There was absolutely no question of this until every available option had been expended. Orders are orders. Should they go on? There was much to consider. Firstly, as the Russians had not yet linked-up, the route ahead was their last chance to get into Berlin. But what if they continued? They would have to face the Russians, growing in number by the minute, and cross the canal near the farms of Falkenrehde. Was the canal bridge still standing? This he did not know. What if they continued and the canal bridge was down? They might not be able to continue to Berlin or turn back and the Russians were not far away. Then again, what of the telephone conversations earlier that day? He was convinced that the Americans and the English would never abandon Berlin to their Communist allies, but 'we', its defenders, would have to hold out until such time as they arrived. His decision was to keep going forward.

The convoy continued on quietly. By holding fire, Krukenberg hoped to mislead the Russians into believing that the convoy was one of theirs. His ruse worked. And the road ahead was clear. Henceforth, the convoy was dogged by all kinds of misfortune. To the rear of the convoy, the truck carrying Oberjunker Ginot's Platoon of Rostaing's Company suddenly broke down. Luckily, Ginot managed to convey his plight to the truck in front. A towrope was attached and he was soon on his way again. Window down, leaning out the door, he kept a constant watch on the towrope, his lifeline to the battalion and Berlin.

Two other trucks were no longer with the convoy. Remarkably, they would make it back to Carpin. On board were officers Ostuf. Fatin, Ostuf. Herpe, Ustuf. Verney, and St.Ju. Chavent's 3rd Platoon of Hscha. Rostaing's 6th Company.[3]

Around 1500 hours, the convoy reached Falkenrehde canal bridge. It was still intact! Krukenberg's gamble had paid off and in less than an hour the convoy would be in Berlin. But first a flimsy anti-tank obstruction thrown across the entrance to the bridge had to be dismantled. Troops were detailed to clear this 'slight inconvenience'. Some headquarters staff of SS-Bataillon 57 also ventured onto the bridge.

Suddenly the bridge blew up in their faces! The force of the explosion literally picked men up and threw them in all directions. Some landed in the canal. Although nobody was killed, one grenadier, standing near Krukenberg, was seriously wounded in the legs and several others were lightly wounded, including Krukenberg. Also, the explosion immobilised his saloon car.

Nineteen-year-old Uscha. Roberti, one of 'Fenet's gang', whom the explosion had thrown into the canal, swam to the bank and was pulled out by two men. Although temporary blinded and deafened, he refused to be evacuated.

3    Rostaing would only see Chavent again in 1946 in Fresnes prison.

Badly damaged, the canal bridge was now impassable to vehicles but not to pedestrians. Quickly recovering from the shock of the explosion, Krukenberg ordered all supplies and equipment unloaded from the trucks. They would continue on foot. The trucks and the badly wounded man were sent back to Neustrelitz via the same route they had come between the two Soviet spearheads. Some hours later and without incident they arrived back.

The troops started to cross the damaged bridge and several trips had to be made to bring across all the ammunition. On the other bank, three old men of the Volkssturm [Home Guard] approached Brigf. Krukenberg and confessed to blowing up the bridge. Ordered to destroy the bridge at the approach of the enemy, they had acted accordingly in the belief that the convoy was Russian. They were blameless. Strangely enough, in the space of hours, troops from both sides had mistaken the French SS troops for Russians!

Berlin was still twenty kilometres away. Rapidly assembled, the column, loaded down by weapons and ammunition, now set off at a brisk pace. At its head marched Brigf. Krukenberg, Hstuf. Fenet and the runners. Krukenberg marched with a limp; he had leg problems. Millet and Bicou guided Roberti along by the arm.[4] Behind them came Weber's Kampfschule, then the companies of Michel, Rostaing, and Ollivier. Labourdette brought up the rear, picking up the stragglers.

They went east. They covered kilometre after kilometre. The ammunition and weapons grew heavy. They became drenched in sweat and white with dust. To subdue their impatience at not having reached Berlin yet, they sang. They passed columns of civilians evacuating the capital. At one stop, Krukenberg called together the platoon commanders and ordered them to stop singing because it was having an adverse effect on the civilians! All the same they continued to sing.

They came to the unfinished Ringbahn, which they were able to make use of for several kilometres. On and on they marched. Remarkably, a Supply Corps officer approached Brigf. Krukenberg and tried to persuade him to let the Frenchmen 'plunder' his dump. Krukenberg refused point-blank and gave as a pretext that they were pressed for time. Even so Rostaing sent some of his men to stock up.

In the opposite direction fled more and more columns of civilians and servicemen who wore the face of the vanquished. And then it was the turn of a group of French 39-40 prisoners of war. They actually applauded their compatriots and wished them luck! Some young lads even threw them chocolate and American chewing gum.

Night started to fall. Berlin was still far off or so it seemed. They passed through Gross Glienicke, Gatow and Pichelsdorf. Along the way they came across no defenders except for three Hitler Jugend boys on bicycles each armed with a panzerfäust. Finally they came to the Freybrücke road bridge which carries the Heerstrasse [East-West Axis] over the river Havel. The bridge was closed by roadblocks, but unguarded. They crossed.

Towards 2200 hours, they arrived at the Reichssportfeld [Olympic stadium]. It had been a long and very exhausting march of more than twenty kilometres there. Nearby was an unguarded, but full Luftwaffe supply depot. Brigf. Krukenberg ordered his men to go and help themselves but their reaction was one of horror: that was tantamount to looting! To ease their conscience,

4    Nicknamed Bicou, Guy Lacombe was born on 18 September 1922 in Toulouse. He enlisted in the Waffen-SS on 9 October 1943, completed his basic training at Sennheim and attended Posen-Treskau. He fought in Galicia with the 2nd Company of the Sturmbrigade.

he requisitioned the depot! It was full of chocolate and those who ate too much would remain awake all night.

Staff of various services occupied the houses lining the road. Judging by the noise and the music that could be heard, they seemed untroubled by the situation.

Krukenberg confiscated one of the many civilian cars parked up in front of the houses. Only then did he order his 'escort' to rest under trees to avoid being spotted by enemy aircraft. They bivouacked for the night on the slopes of Grunewald forest overlooking the river Havel. The Freybrücke was about one hundred metres away.

### Brigadeführer Krukenberg and his first night in Berlin

Around midnight,[5] Brigf. Krukenberg and his adjutant, Hstuf. Pachur, jumped into the requisitioned car. At its wheel was Ustuf. Patzak. They drove off to the Reichs Chancellery. Their journey took them across Adolf Hitler Platz, down Bismarckstrasse, under the Brandenburg Gate, across Pariser Platz, down Wilhelmstrasse and into Vossstrasse, where they pulled up on the footpath at the entrance to the Chancellery Bunker. Surprisingly, the journey had only taken half an hour. Furthermore, they had not been stopped once along the way. Berlin was literally deserted and an uneasy silence hung over the city, occasionally broken by the distant rumbling of Russian artillery. Of great concern was that the city was devoid of any defensive works and yet at the beginning of February 1945 Hitler had declared Berlin a Festung [Fortress].

Krukenberg and Pachur now made their way down the few steps to the Bunker guarded by sentries. Krukenberg asked to meet with General Krebs, and although completely unknown to the sentries, he was admitted. Nevertheless, the General was absent for the time being and they were asked to sit down in a communications room. The minutes ticked by as they waited for the General. Krukenberg called his old Army Group Headquarters at Prenzlau to report his safe arrival in Berlin. The minutes became hours.

In the oppressive and warm atmosphere of the signals room they reflected on Berlin's apparent lack of preparedness to receive the Russian onslaught. Indeed, a Soviet commando team could easily have captured the bunker and the Führer himself in a surprise attack! Finally, towards 0330 hours, some three hours after arriving at the Bunker, Krukenberg was shown in to see General Krebs who he knew from 1943 when he was serving in the Wehrmacht with von Kluge's Army Group Centre. With General Krebs was General Burgdorf, Hitler's Chief Adjutant and committed National Socialist. The two generals were very surprised to see him. Krebs explained that forty-eight hours ago they had ordered a whole string of officers and units positioned around Berlin to come to the defence of the capital immediately. And so far he was the only one to have arrived!

Krebs then briefed him on the situation. And it was a briefing all too similar to that he had received before his departure. Krebs talked of little else other than the future help of the Western powers and the approach of Army Wenck.

When Krukenberg described his experiences near Ketzin Krebs answered that the Soviet spearheads were certainly weak in strength and added that Wenck's Army, coming to the rescue of Berlin, would easily brush them aside.

5    Mabire states just before night (*Mourir A Berlin*, p.133), Saint-Loup 0030 hours (*Les Hérétiques*, p.409).

Krebs then ordered Krukenberg to report in the morning to General Weidling who had become the overall Commandant of the Berlin Defence Area the day before, 24 April 1945. Krebs let it be known that it was Weidling who had personally asked for him and that he would explain why. His command post was to be found on Fehrbelliner Platz on the Hohenzollerndamm in the former Headquarters of the peacetime III Corps and the wartime Deputy III Corps. Krukenberg knew it well.

Before leaving, Krukenberg asked as to the whereabouts of SS-Ogruf. Fegelein, Himmler's liaison officer to the Führer, to whom he was also supposed to report. When Fegelein could not be found he was told to return to the Chancellery in the next couple of days.

Shortly after 0400 hours on 25 April, Krukenberg and Pachur left the Chancellery. The roads proved just as empty on the return journey. Again there was no sign of defensive troops. Towards 0500 hours, they arrived back at the Reichssportfeld. The sun was coming up. The sky was clear.

The Frenchmen were still asleep. Most had enjoyed an unbroken night's sleep despite the sound of concentrated Russian artillery fire pouring down on the nearby Freybrücke.

Krukenberg was welcomed back by Fenet who was impatient for orders. Krukenberg told him that he was to see General Weildling that morning and that as soon as he knew in what sector they were to be engaged he would send Ustuf. Patzak to collect them. Fenet would have to wait. Krukenberg and Pachur now rested.

One by one, the men of the French SS-Sturmbataillon were pulled from their slumber by officers and NCOs going from group to group. A roll call was taken. Not a single Frenchman was missing. The last of the stragglers had rejoined their comrades during the night. They now prepared themselves for the coming battle; after washing in the Havel, they shaved, brushed down their uniforms and polished their equipment. To pass the time and take heart, they sang.

Hstuf. Fenet reorganised the units available to him into the Franz. SS-Sturmbataillon, which looked as follows:[6]

| | |
|---|---|
| Battalion commander | W-Hstuf. Fenet |
| Assistant and V.O. | SS-Ostuf. von Wallenrodt |
| Orderly Officer 1 | W-Std.Ob.Ju. Frantz |
| Orderly Officer 2 | W-Std.Ob.Ju. Douroux |
| **1st Company** | |
| Commander | W-Ustuf. Labourdette |
| Assistant | W-Std.Ju. Cossard |
| Assistant | W-Std.Ob.Ju. Croisile |
| Platoon commander | W-Std.Ob.Ju. Boulmier |
| Platoon commander | W-Std.Ob.Ju. de Lacaze |
| Platoon commander? | W-Std.Ob.Ju. Le Maignan de Kérangat |

6    This reorganisation may have amounted to nothing more than the designation of numbers to the four companies that had got through to Berlin.

**2nd Company**

| | |
|---|---|
| Commander | W-Ostuf. Michel |
| Platoon commander | W-Std. Ju. Hardy |
| Platoon commander | W-Std.Ob.Ju. Néron |
| Platoon commander | W-Oscha. Montgour |

**3rd Company**

| | |
|---|---|
| Commander | W-Hscha. Rostaing |
| Assistant | W-Std.Ju. Dumoulin |
| Platoon commander | W-Std.Ob.Ju. Ginot |
| Platoon commander | W-Std.Ob.Ju. Baumgartner |

**4th Company**

| | |
|---|---|
| Commander | W-Oscha. Ollivier |
| Assistant | W-Std.Ju. Protopopoff |
| Platoon commander | W-Uscha. Fieselbrand |
| Platoon commander | W-Std.Ju. Sellier |
| Platoon commander | W-Uscha. Sauvageot[7] |

**Kampfschule**

| | |
|---|---|
| Commander | SS-Ostuf. Weber |
| Platoon commander | W-Oscha. Pierre Bousquet |
| Platoon commander | W-Uscha. Aimé-Blanc |
| Platoon commander | W-Uscha. Fontenay |

Also serving with the French Sturmbataillon in Berlin were the following W-Std. Ob.Ju.: Garrabos, Maisse and Poupon.[8] Notably many platoons were still commanded by non-commissioned officers. This was especially true of the Kampfschule. Twenty-four-year-old Uscha. Aimé-Blanc had fought with the French *Marschkompanie* at Kolberg.[9] Uscha. Fontenay was eighteen years old.[10] Oscha. Klein was still with the Kampfschule as *Spiess*.

Throughout the coming battle, Krukenberg would have a number of German headquarters staff with him as well as a small French Begleitkommando. The composition and strength of the escort has been impossible to determine, although some were from the Kampfschule.[11]

SS-Uscha. Max Walter of the Staff Company also came to Berlin with the Sturmbataillon.[12]

After a few hours rest, Brigf. Krukenberg journeyed through the city to Weidling's command post on Hohenzollerndamm. With him were Pachur and Patzak. By now, a few patrols and barricades had appeared in the streets, but there was still no sign of any defensive troops. A

---

7    Paul Sauvageot was ex-LVF. Transferred to the Waffen-SS, he served with the 9/58.
8    W-Std.Ob.Ju. Lebrun may have also been with the French SS-Sturmbataillon in Berlin.
9    Jean Aimé-Blanc was born on 19 December 1920.
10   Fontenay would survive the 'holocaust' of Berlin; Puechlong would meet him in Paris in 1946 or 1947.
11   One such Frenchman of the Begleitkommando was Lavest of the Kampfschule.
12   A translator, he was, undoubtedly, attached to Fenet or Krukenberg. Seriously wounded in the fighting, he died on 15 September 1945 in Halle hospital.

closed Soldbuch got them through the sentries and into corridors full of officers, as well as civilians and secretaries.

Krukenberg was taken to Oberst [Colonel] von Dufving first. He was the Chief-of-Staff of the LVI Panzer Corps. Krukenberg was then introduced to General Weidling who struck him as a man totally without confidence. They were left alone to talk.

Weidling told Krukenberg that he had been brought to Berlin two days previously and, despite his conflicting ideas for its defence, appointed the 'battle commandant' of the city. The forces General Weidling had at his disposal to defend Berlin were wholly inadequate. Besides his old command, the LVI Panzer Corps, which had suffered greatly in the recent fighting,[13] there were the badly armed units of the Volkssturm and the hurriedly formed alarm units from the administrative services, Luftwaffe auxiliaries and the Hitler Jugend. Although they showed a great willingness to fight and die, they were of dubious military value.[14] Weidling spoke of his predecessor, General Reymann, whom the Party had removed from post.[15] Lines of command were confused. Also his request to have sole authority for the issue of orders for its defence had been ignored![16]

In the presence of his Chief-of-Staff who had joined them, Weidling told Krukenberg that the south-east of the city, designated Defence Sector C, had been assigned to the 11. SS-Freiwilligen-Panzer-Grenadier-Division 'Nordland' under Brigf. Ziegler. As of late, Ziegler had become very troublesome and seemed to have lost control of his division. He himself had met members of the division throughout the various western districts of Berlin. He wanted Ziegler removed from command and he had brought Krukenberg to Berlin to replace him.

Concerned that his orders were verbal, Krukenberg asked Weidling for a written order to present to Ziegler. This Weidling penned and signed. Furthermore, Ziegler was instructed, as soon as he handed over command to Krukenberg, to report to the Reich Chancellery.[17]

13  The strength of the LVI Panzer Corps was around 13-15,000 men. Its component forces were the relatively intact 18th Panzergrenadier Division, the severely reduced 20th Panzergrenadier Division, the 'Müncheberg' Panzer Division, of which only one-third would participate in the fighting, the badly battered and reduced 9th Parachute Division and the 11.SS-Freiwilligen-Panzer-Grenadier-Division 'Nordland' under Brigf. Ziegler.

14  Weidling also had at his disposal the Waffen-SS units under SS-Brigf. Mohnke that amounted to the strength of half a division. They included the Berlin-based regiment of the 1. SS-Panzer-Division 'Leibstandarte Adolf Hitler' which provided Hitler's ceremonial bodyguard. The regiment consisted of some 1,200 troops. All told, Weidling had under his command some 60,000 men with only some 50-60 tanks. The LVI Panzer Corps and the Waffen SS units were the only forces that could be considered cohesive and reasonably equipped. As for artillery, Weidling had at his disposal the integral units of three divisions, the city's FLAK batteries and some locally raised units. This local artillery consisted of fourteen batteries of foreign guns 'manned by Volkssturm and soldiers of all arms, but few gunners' and a further six batteries of German guns. Ammunition was in short supply and only 100 rounds per battery were available for the foreign guns. As most of the guns were flat-trajectory they were sited in the Tiergarten and some of the larger squares.

15  Reymann was appointed in March 1945 and Hitler dismissed him on 22 April 1945 for defeatism.

16  Weidling was further handicapped by poor communications. It could take runners hours just to cover a few hundred metres as the roads were now under shellfire and choked by debris.

17  According to Mabire, *Mourir A Berlin*, p.140, Krukenberg then asked about his French Waffen-SS troops. Weidling replied that they could constitute an 'independent assault battalion within the 'Nordland' Division'. Curiously, the memoirs of Krukenberg do not substantiate this attachment.

Although all telephone contact with the divisional headquarters of 'Nordland' had been lost for some time, its location was thought to be on Hasenheide, between the suburbs of Neukölln and Kreuzberg. Krukenberg proceeded there immediately.

## 'Nordland'

When Krukenberg came to Hasenheide he found the divisional headquarters of 'Nordland' without difficulty from the many vehicles quite openly parked around it. Unfortunately, the Soviet Air Force had also spotted the same telltale signs and just bombed it. Clouds of dust were still pouring out of the building. Its upper floors had been destroyed. Disorder reigned on the ground floor where the command post was. Wounded were lying about everywhere and among them, in a corner, was Ziegler.

The two Generals knew each other. Their paths had crossed in the second half of 1944 in the Baltic States. Krukenberg informed Ziegler that he was here to replace him. This Ziegler was expecting. As a comrade, he warned Krukenberg that he too would not be in post more than twenty-four hours.

According to Ziegler, the defence of Berlin was an impossible mission and that is why those 'at the top' were out for scapegoats. Krukenberg asked him what forces he had deployed in the front line and was shocked when Ziegler quoted him a figure of seventy men! The rest were too exhausted and resting. Indeed, the two grenadier regiments of 'Nordland' each had the strength of a strong company or, at best, that of a weak battalion! 'Nordland' still had some tanks and assault guns at its disposal but was desperately short of petrol. The Artillery Regiment was also a shadow of its former shelf. On orders from Corps, its few guns had been sited in the Tiergarten. In addition, 'Nordland' had no contact with the Volkssturm or the neighbouring sectors.

Krukenberg sent Ustuf. Patzak and trucks back to collect 'his detachment' from the Reichssportfeld complex. Meanwhile, Pachur set about reorganising the command post.

At midday, Ziegler took his leave and left by car for the Reich Chancellery. On his arrival, he was placed under arrest on a charge of failing to hold the defence line along the Spree and then the Teltow canal.

Still very much 'in the dark', Krukenberg walked towards the front to learn more of the situation. By now, the Hasenheide was under light artillery fire. Guarding the Hasenheide and the neighbouring terrain from possible surprise attack were small alarm units of 'Nordland'. Surprisingly, in the foremost positions, Brigf. Krukenberg only found members of the Volkssturm. Sent into battle armed with a wide selection of captured French, Belgian, Czech or Italian rifles, and already short of ammunition, 'they seemed lost and confused'.[18] Krukenberg said of them: 'These men cut rather poor figures.' He went in search of their commander.

Krukenberg found the local Volkssturm commander, a Kreisleiter [NSDAP District Leader], in a large building on Hermannplatz at the corner of Hasenheide and Kottbuser Damm. From the first floor, the Kreisleiter had an excellent view of the whole south-eastern suburb of the city.

The Kreisleiter complained that the Volkssturm had been engaged 'alone' and without contact with regular troops. He reported that the Soviets were advancing from the east and the district of Treptow had already fallen the day before. He had posted weak elements on Urbandam and

---

18   Krukenberg, chapter *Battle Memoir*, *Charlemagne's Legionnaires*, p.155.

First Days in Berlin



Sonnenallee but, with only a few machine-guns and very little ammunition at their disposal, they were expected to offer little resistance.

As for his neighbouring sectors, the Kreisleiter stated he was in telephone contact with the sector of Görlitzer Bahnof [railway station] on his left and had just learnt that Reichsleiter Hilgenfeld had fallen in combat two hours previously. His only news of Tempelhof airfield on his right came from refugees, who told him a violent tank battle was raging.

While they were talking two Soviet tanks suddenly appeared on the opposite side of Hermannplatz and opened fire. As the tanks were not supported and alone, Krukenberg thought the chances of fighting them in close combat were good.

After telling the Kreisleiter that 'he was going to do something' to relieve his men, Krukenberg returned to the Hasenheide and 'Nordland' divisional command post. On the way back, he was nicked in the face by shrapnel. Back at the command post, Pachur greeted him with the good news that the French SS-Sturmbataillon had just arrived safely from the Reichssportfeld. Tightly packed together in tucks, the Frenchmen had crossed the city saluting and singing.

In the late afternoon,[19] the French SS-Sturmbataillon arrived in the sector of Neukölln and found 'lodgings' in the quarter to the north of the Hasenheide between Hermannplatz and the church on Gardepionierplatz. Rostaing's Company took up residence in a pub cellar, which, fortunately, was stocked with beer. The Kampfschule went to a pub on Hermannplatz, but theirs was dry. The men of Michel's Company accommodated themselves on the ground floor of a carpet warehouse and made themselves comfortable among precious oriental carpets and rugs.

No sooner had Weber's Kampfschule arrived than it was employed at a road barricade alongside the Feldgendarmerie checking the papers of soldiers and civilians alike. The Frenchmen were relieved in the evening and returned to the pub on Hermannplatz.

All companies were ordered to send out patrols. Oscha. Ollivier, the commander of the 4th Company, insisted on taking out a patrol himself. The patrol, consisting of Sauvageot's Platoon, ventured towards Tempelhof airport across the Hasenheide. The noise of battle drew closer. The patrol came across an old Berliner sitting on a bench who seemed to have died peacefully from a heart attack. The dead man was found to be carrying some provisions on him. This find would go some way to subduing their pangs of hunger, for no rations had been made available to them yet. A little later, and without further incident, the patrol returned to its billets.

Oscha. Montgour led one of the patrols conducted by Ostuf. Michel's 2nd Company. He took his twenty-strong platoon out on patrol with him and although many were young and had never been in action they seemed eager for battle.

At the head of the patrol marched Grenadier François Laplaud[20] and his section commander, Uscha. Fodé.[21] The light was fading and the roads seemed strangely deserted. Laplaud heard machine-gun fire and explosions whose location he could not pinpoint, but the Russians were thought to be near. Suddenly shots rang out. The troops closely hugged the walls. Montgour shouted out orders. Fire was returned at random. Suddenly it dawned on Laplaud and Fodé that

19    Mabire, *Mourir A Berlin*, p.151. In contrast, according to Krukenberg, *Combat pour Berlin*, p.8, the French detachment was found quarters in Gneisenau barracks.
20    Laplaud was born on 21 June 1924 in La Meyze. He was a *chef de trentaine de la Franc-Garde de Limoges*.
21    Bernard Fodé was born on 28 October 1923 in Nancy. He was a member of the *Franc-Garde de Haute-Vienne*.

they were alone. Footsteps were heard close by and they called out in hushed voices. The reply was in Russian! The two Frenchmen hid themselves behind a fence and, through gaps, watched the Russians pass by and then return to a tank which was 'waiting in ambush' not far away. Minutes later, they spotted a second tank near to the first. As the Russian crews were off their guard, they decided to 'deal' with them after nightfall; the two of them were armed with the redoubtable panzerfäust. It proved a nerve-racking ordeal to wait quietly.

Sometime after 0300 hours, Laplaud and Fodé crept out of their hiding place and along the houses towards the two Russian tanks. All was silent except for the sound of a crackling tank radio set. The Russians seemed to be either asleep or dead drunk. They fired, threw away the empty tubes and dashed off. Behind them they left two tanks consumed in flames. Minutes later, they ran into a patrol from their platoon. Oscha. Montgour informed them that they were going to counterattack at dawn which was now only hours away. Laplaud and Fodé were not the first French volunteers of the Waffen-SS to knock out a Russian tank in Berlin.[22] That honour went to Grenadier Ronzier, also of the 2nd Company.[23]

### Krukenberg and the afternoon of the 25th

The immediate priority for Krukenberg was to relocate the divisional headquarters of 'Nordland' from the Hasenheide. The aerial bombardment had so devastated the building that it was no longer usable. He decided to relocate to Gneisenau barracks, reported to him as a possible place of refuge by elements of his headquarters already 'in residence'. This police barracks was nearby, completely intact and, importantly, had excellent communication facilities, because the absence of its Signals Battalion, sent to Holstein, was being sorely felt.

At Gneisenau barracks, Krukenberg sought and received from the headquarters of the LVI Panzer Corps authorisation for the relocation. He also requested to be freed from the responsibility for Sector 'C' and to be assigned a more central district for the regrouping of 'Nordland'. This was granted when he reported the presence of two well-equipped, fresh police battalions at Gneisenau barracks that could handle the 'Nordland' sector. The two police battalions appeared to have been forgotten about!

'Nordland' was assigned the district around Gendarmenmarkt in the city centre. Thereupon Brigf. Krukenberg chose the cellars of the Opera House as his temporary headquarters. Summoned to the headquarters of the LVI Panzer Corps, now sited more centrally on Bendlerstrasse, Krukenberg arrived at the appointed time of 2000 hours. The Chief-of-Staff of the LVI Panzer Corps ordered him to engage 'Nordland' in Defence Sector 'Z' by midday next day.[24] The commander of this defence sector was a certain Oberstleutnant [Lieutenant Colonel]

22    According to Krukenberg, *Combat pour Berlin*, p.8, he immediately deployed half of the 'French anti-tank group' under Fenet against the Soviet armour sighted on Hermannplatz and he also attached Weber to Fenet. In the course of the evening and the night, the Frenchmen managed to shoot up fourteen Soviet tanks in close combat, 'forcing the enemy to abandon its pressure in this sector'.
23    Jacques Ronzier was born on 4 June 1923 in Paris.
24    According to Krukenberg, the 'Z' stood for Zentrum [Centre] whereas, according to Le Tissier Tony, *The battle of Berlin 1945* (London: Jonathan Cape, 1988), the 'Z' was for 'Zitadelle' [Citadel].

Seifert of the Luftwaffe whose headquarters was located in the Air Ministry.[25] Krukenberg went at once to report to him.

The corridors of the Air Ministry were full of Luftwaffe soldiers, but Krukenberg noted that none were officers. Seifert received Krukenberg in the presence of an orderly officer who, incredibly, was the sum total of the headquarters staff for his Defence Sector!

Oberstleutnant Seifert proved extremely hostile towards Krukenberg, 'Nordland' and the Waffen-SS in general. Bluntly, he told Krukenberg that he had no need of his regimental commanders or their headquarters staff because he had been told that the fighting strength of each regiment was no more than that of a battalion. Krukenberg defended 'Nordland'. He argued that sector 'Z' would become the centre of resistance and that greater the number of proven officers available greater the resistance. This fell on deaf ears, though.

In reply, Seifert stated that the defence of the district had already been organised and that, as such, he had no need of support. Pulling out a map, he showed Krukenberg the machine-gun posts and the other combat positions. Krukenberg offered Seifert the services of one or two of those with him to reinforce his headquarters staff. This he refused. Curtly, he also refused Krukenberg's next offer to place himself at his disposal to advise him on the defence plan. Seifert wanted to hear nothing of it. Such was his prejudice against the Waffen-SS that nothing could shake. Krukenberg pointed out that he had transferred to the Waffen-SS about a year previously and that he had been on the Army General staff during the First World War, but Seifert was still not won over. His distrust of the Waffen-SS was too deep-rooted.

Towards 2300 hours, Krukenberg returned to his new command post in the Berlin Opera House. The meeting with Seifert had left him with a 'very bad feeling'. Before getting some sleep he relayed the orders from Corps to the commanders of regiments 'Danmark' and 'Norge'. Also, such was his concern about Seifert that he informed them of his hostile attitude. The night of 25-26 April Krukenberg remembers as calm.

**Battle for Neukölln**

On 26 April, well before daybreak, the companies of the French SS-Sturmbataillon assembled and set off from their billets north of the Hasenheide and silently made their way towards Neukölln town hall. At 0500 hours, from Neukölln town hall, the French SS-Sturmbataillon was to counterattack along Berlinerstrasse. 'Nordland' was to advance on its left along the Landwehr canal and provide tank support. Fenet wrote of the tank support:[26]

> The tanks were already there: on a street corner, an enormous Königstiger, massive on its wide tracks, extended its interminable 88mm gun; further, they were the Panthers with their fine silhouette, then stocky Sturmgeschütze with their squat 75mm. The crews were quietly waiting for the departure time, a little as if they were going for a drive. Together, we worked out the plan of attack down to the last detail: the grenadiers will advance along the avenues, clearing the houses and sideroads, and covering the tanks, which in turn will provide them with covering fire.

25    According to Mabire, *Mourir A Berlin*, p.147, Krukenberg complained of finding himself subordinated to a Luftwaffe officer who was not even a Colonel!

26    Fenet, *Die letzte Runde*, p.5.

Uscha. Georg Diers of schwere SS-Panzer-Abteilung 503 [Heavy SS Panzer Battalion 503] commanded the Königstiger [King Tiger].[27] The Sturmgeschütze assault guns and possibly the Panthers belonged to SS-Pz.Abt.11/Nordland.

Shortly before 0500 hours, the French SS-Sturmbataillon was in position. Fenet planned to attack with Rostaing's 3rd Company and Michel's 2nd Company. The 4th Company commanded by Ollivier was held in reserve. Battalion Headquarters was established in Neukölln town hall. The 1st Company was not available to Fenet. It had been placed at the disposal of the Tempelhof sector.

Daybreak was ushered in by the roar of Russian artillery. The platoon held in reserve in the cemetery at the corner of crossroads Berliner-Hermannstrasse was hit and suffered some losses.[28] Time fast approached H Hour, but the order to attack had still not been received. 0500 hours came and went... nothing. The district was still wrapped in silence. The minutes ticked by. And still nothing at 0530 hours. The troops grew impatient. The day brought promise of good weather. The blue sky was cloudless. Finally, shortly before 0600 hours, the order to attack arrived.

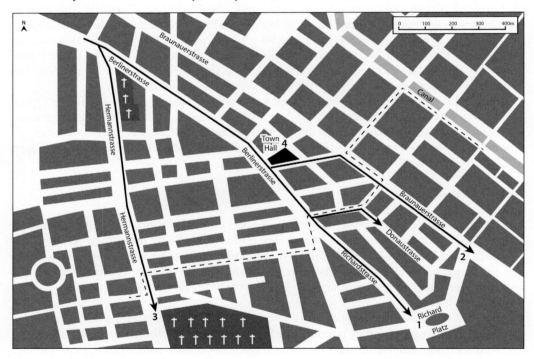

Battle for Neukölln, 26 April 1945. 1. The 2nd Company under Ostuf. Michel attacks along Berlinerstrasse. 2. The 3rd Company under Hscha. Rostaing attacks along Braunauerstrasse. 3. Elements of Weber's Kampfschule, held in reserve at Hermannplatz, are committed along Hermannstrasse. 4. When the Russians go over to the attack the French forces withdraw to the town hall, which is turned into a centre de résistance. They hold out until retreat becomes inevitable.

27   Archer, Kraska & Lippert, *Panzers in Berlin 1945*, p.13.
28   Saint-Loup, *Les Hérétiques*, p.420. However, this is not confirmed by any other source.

The columns of waiting French SS troops rushed forward, closely followed by the tanks. Opposite nothing stirred. This, however, was short-lived. Maxim heavy machine guns were the first to wake. And then the anti-tank guns with their raucous bark. As if on exercise, the French SS troops dashed from doorway to doorway, jumping over walls and debris, and flushing out Red snipers.

## Attack of the 3rd Company

Rostaing's 3rd Company advanced along Braunauerstrasse.[29] It had the support of the Königstiger. However, due to a lack of petrol, the tank could not accompany the advance. Thus, from afar, it would cover the advance.

Advancing on the left was Oberjunker Baumgartner's Platoon. And on the right Hscha. Rostaing, his assistant Std.Ju. Dumoulin, liaison officer Pilsin and Oberjunker Ginot with his 1st Platoon. Suddenly a burst of gunfire rang out and Std.Ju. Dumoulin, standing beside Rostaing, crumpled to the ground. He was dead. Rostaing immediately ordered the 1st Platoon forward, but had to replace Oberjunker Ginot, its commander, who was paralysed by fear. The troops pushed forward. Ahead, in the middle of the avenue, stood a German anti-tank barricade that was now held by the Russians. Some fifty metres from the barricade Rostaing came to a transverse road. Before crossing, he glanced down the road on his right. He drew back. A T-34 was parked up about ten metres away. And its dismounted crew had caught sight of him. He opened fire with his Sturmgewehr, killing two, but the other three managed to find shelter in the porch of a block of flats. Rostaing then gestured to his *pourvoyeur* to pass him a panzerfäust. Taking aim at the tank, he fired, hitting it just below the turret. A massive explosion blew apart the tank; the panzerfäust round had struck the tank's ammunition. Debris and metal fragments were scattered in every direction. Rostaing's *pourvoyeur,* who was leaning out to watch him, was decapitated by a piece of sheet metal. Rostaing was hit in the right temple by metal fragments and collapsed.

Rostaing soon came round. Wearily, he got up and brushed himself down. He turned round and, to his horror, he saw the dead bodies of twelve of his men sprawled on the pavement. A survivor, seriously wounded, was crying out for his mother. He wondered how this had happened. The other platoons had seen and heard nothing.

Rostaing looked around closely. Suddenly, only metres away, he noticed the doors of a portal slowly open and then the barrel of a Maxim machine gun appear. He threw himself forward, rolled into the road and opened fire, killing the three Russians around the Maxim. Waiting in ambush, the Russians had opened up as each of his men had passed the porch. They had gone unnoticed because the terrible din coming up from the city had drowned out the noise of the machine gun.

Carefully, Rostaing's 3rd Company now pressed on along the road, but already, in less than an hour, it had lost more than one quarter of its strength. Casualties continued to mount. One man crumpled to the ground every five minutes. All were victims of snipers. Platoon Commander Oberjunker Baumgartner and his assistant, Oscha. Verfaillie,[30] were both hit in

29  Now Sonnen Allee.
30  Of Belgian nationality, Roland Verfaillie was among the first to volunteer for the LVF and had served during that first winter. After the war, he too went on trial in France. When asked by the chairman

the ankle. Oberjunker Ginot was wounded in the elbow but refused orders to be evacuated. He had regained his spirit and his sangfroid.[31]

A bullet tore through Rostaing's trousers above his right knee without injuring him. His good luck had not deserted him. Two of his four runners became casualties. One of the remaining two had also been hit in the ankle but continued to carry orders and messages. Purposely, Rostaing entrusted him with a message to battalion headquarters at Neukölln town hall in the hope that he would get himself attended to and evacuated if need be. Rostaing never saw him again.

Rostaing now felt isolated. His only support came from the immobilised 'Nordland' Tiger that had knocked out two T-34s in his path. Later, after finding himself outflanked, Rostaing was forced to withdraw. However, it was only a temporary setback. His troops reorganised and pushed forward once again, clearing out room after room, apartment after apartment, and building after building in brutal hand-to-hand fighting. A young soldier beside Rostaing was hit right between the eyes and crumpled to the ground face down. Believing he was dead, Rostaing turned him over to collect his Soldbuch, but the soldier smiled at him, sat up and asked for a cigarette. He was evacuated to the rear for treatment. Rostaing thought that was the last he would see of him. He was wrong. For most of the following day, Rostaing saw him glued to the turret of a tank. His head was bandaged and he was still smoking!

Mortar bombs rained down in the avenue. Against all the odds, the counterattack was vigorously pressed home. The barricade fell to the Frenchmen. Rostaing ordered grenadier Tillier, a strapping Norman, and one of his comrades to clear the ground floor of a house where he wanted to take up position. They entered a room that looked out onto a square not far from the spot where the Russian machine gun nest had inflicted such a grievous 'body blow' on the Company. His comrade left the room. Tillier made himself comfortable. Suddenly he noticed about six Russians in the square only metres away. Without hesitation he fired his rifle grenade at them. The Russians scattered and withdrew. Informed of this incident, Rostaing decided to change buildings and make for another across the road.

To distract the Russians while they crossed, Rostaing had a panzerfäust fired in their direction. But, as the Frenchmen crossed, they received sniper fire from across the road. Oscha. Dedieu was killed by a bullet in the middle of the head.[32] Spotting the sniper, Rostaing pointed toward a window and shouted to Tillier to place a grenade inside. It took him three attempts. The Russian sniper fell silent. When they entered the building Tillier came face to face with a Russian, a very small Mongol, who disappeared 'like through a trap door'.[33]

Rostaing's Company worked its way forward to Richard Platz but could not debouch because a Russian anti-tank gun had the square covered. An assault gun was brought up. A shot on target and the enemy anti-tank gun 'barked' no more. However, a Maxim heavy machine gun continued to hold up Rostaing's troops, now sheltering in porches.

Stealthily, Rostaing made his way towards the Russian machine gun nest. A grenade tossed by him put an end to it. Triumphantly, his company followed him onto the square. Even though

of the court why he had enlisted in the LVF he 'disarmed' him by replying that it was to gain French nationality.

31    Unable to fire his Sturmgewehr, Ginot was eventually persuaded to go and get himself attended to.
32    Born on 29 June 1918 at Toulouse, Guy Dedieu served with the *Milice* and was transferred to the Waffen-SS.
33    Mabire, *Mourir A Berlin*, pp.163-164.

he had lost contact with battalion headquarters, he now decided to press on with the attack towards the Tempelhof-Treptow 'S-Bahn' line.

Suddenly one of the men with Rostaing called Arbonnel started to sob heavily. He was convinced he had been wounded in the stomach. Rostaing examined him. He had been hit, but in the belt buckle! The impact had led him to believe that he was done for. Rostaing slapped him several times which brought him back to his senses. Arbonnel set off again.

## Attack of the 2nd Company

Company commander Ostuf. Michel was missing one of his platoons when his company prepared to attack. Contact had been lost with Oscha. Hardy's Platoon of fifteen or so men while on patrol in an enemy infested district.

On hearing a curious loud sound of hammering Hardy took his platoon to investigate. They came to an immobilised Russian tank, which the crew was hurriedly trying to repair. Hardy called upon a certain grenadier by the name of Dispans to deal with the sitting target.

A former *chef* of the *Jeunesse catholique de* Seine-et-Oise, Dispans had enlisted in the Waffen-SS at the age of eighteen. He saw action at Kolberg in the ranks of Ludwig's *compagnie de marche* and now desperately wanted to open his 'account'.

Approaching the tank, Dispans was suddenly disturbed by a Russian soldier. He had to silence him and quietly or else the alarm would be raised. Dispans launched himself at the Russian and eventually overcame him, not before the Russian had almost bitten off a thumb. He had nearly howled out in pain, but that would have 'given the game away'. Excited, he rushed back to his comrades to tell them loudly of his victory in this most primeval of contests: hand-to-hand combat. Hardy told Dispans to keep quiet and get back to the task in hand. Dispans took up position within panzerfäust range, carefully took aim and fired, 'scoring a hit'.

Hardy and his platoon quickly made off, but the Russians seemed everywhere now. They took to a house. From the attic, they were amazed to see hundreds of Russians sitting on a waste piece of ground who were all armed with a mortar! Their situation looked hopeless and clearly it was. Hours later, they were taken prisoner. Dispans talked himself and his comrades out of a bullet in the back of the neck by claiming that they had been deported for work and then mobilised by the Germans. They were sent to the rear.

The 2nd Company attacked along Berlinerstrasse[34] that runs parallel to Braunauerstrasse. At the head of the 2nd Company advanced Oscha. Montgour's Platoon. The Russians were quick to lay down a curtain of defensive fire. Bullets whistled all around. Hell had supplanted peace. Among the first to fall was company commander Ostuf. Michel. Seriously wounded in the face, he was evacuated to a cellar.[35]

The curtain of fire brought the advance to a halt. Pinned down, the attackers took shelter. They could not emerge. In this way, platoons became cut off from the company and the sections from the platoons.

---

34  Now Karl Marx Strasse.
35  Although the ultimate fate of Michel is unknown, the severity of his wounds leaves little doubt that he would die of them. Even so some have claimed that Michel survived the war and later served in the *Sécurité militaire*, but the physical description of a certain '*Capitaine* Michel' does not agree at all with that of Ostuf. Michel.

Some men of Montgour's Platoon, including Uscha. Fodé and Gren. Laplaud, found themselves in a 'sort of hangar' cut off from the rest of the platoon. A liaison officer went off to the rear but was back minutes later. Several houses away, he had come face to face with a Russian. They had fought with their bare hands. And then, strangely, each had let go of the other and run off to their respective sides.

Again the Russians seemed to be everywhere. The men around Fodé came to realise that they were isolated, perhaps even encircled. Fodé quickly organised them into defensive positions. Tanks, which they presumed Russian, could already be heard. Tiredness overcame Laplaud and he fell asleep; he had been on his feet three days and two nights. When he woke, just moments later, Fodé had gone. He was all alone.

Algerian-born platoon commander Oberjunker Néron of the 2nd Company was seriously injured by shrapnel in the legs and neck. Evacuated to a field aid post, he was decorated by a German officer with the Iron Cross 2nd Class. According to his own testimony, he had destroyed four or five Russian tanks with panzerfaust.

## The 4th Company

Although held in reserve, the 4th Company of the Sturmbataillon commanded by Osha. Ollivier, was struck by disaster when it came under fire from either an enemy anti-tank gun or a captured 'Nordland' tank.[36] Fenet hastened to the scene of what he described as a 'devastating blow'. Broken-hearted, he counted the bodies on the roadway. He was joined by an officer of Nordland who loudly expressed his sorrow.

Many were killed, fifteen or more, as well as wounded.[37] All told, the 4th Company had just lost over one third of its strength. Platoon commander Uscha. Fieselbrand had his right leg almost severed above the ankle. His comrades had to complete the amputation with a knife while waiting for an ambulance to arrive. Company commander Ollivier had a piece of shrapnel lodged in the chest between two vertebras and shrapnel had gashed his right hand. He passed command of the 4th Company to Std.Ju. Protopopoff. An ambulance evacuated him and three other seriously wounded men.

At some point the 4th Company was called upon to shore up the advancing companies experiencing more and more difficulties.

36 According to Fenet, À Berlin, jusqu'au bout, p.158, a salvo of anti-tank shells massacred a reserve platoon that, thinking itself safe, had carelessly assembled. According to Saint-Loup, Les Hérétiques p.425, the reserve platoon, which had carelessly assembled in the middle of crossroads Donaustrasse-Schönstedt, was hit by four anti-tank shells. According to Soulat, Historique de la Division Charlemagne, p.103, Ollivier was giving orders to his platoon commanders around him when the company was 'taken to task' by a Russian anti-tank gun. In contrast, according to Mabire, Mourir A Berlin, p.160, Oscha. Ollivier was giving orders to his adjoint and his three platoon commanders when a 'Nordland' tank, parked up nearby, suddenly opened fire with all guns on his company. Men of Sellier's platoon attacked without hesitation, silencing the tank with panzerfäust, but it had already wrought carnage. Ollivier was convinced that the Russians had captured the tank and without a sound. And although this version of events seems improbable, it cannot be dismissed because Mabire interviewed Ollivier for Mourir A Berlin.
37 Saint-Loup and Fenet number the killed at fifteen, Mabire and Soulat at seventeen.

## Ollivier's travels

Evacuated to one of Berlin's many medical posts, Jean Ollivier, the commander of the 4th Company, had his hand wound bandaged up and the shrapnel in his chest removed. Impatient to return to his unit, he left as soon as the doctors had finished with him. He found himself in the sector of the Tiergarten and decided to report to a nearby Waffen-SS artillery unit in the hope that it would give him a helping hand back to the Sturmbataillon in Neukölln. Unexpectedly, on entering the command post, he came face to face with SS-Hstuf. Heller who he knew. Their paths had crossed at the Waffen-SS Infantry Gun School at Breslau. Then Heller was an instructor and Ollivier his pupil.

Far from giving Ollivier a helping hand, Heller immediately put him in command of a battery of two 150mm infantry guns served by recruits of the 2. SS-Panzer-Division 'Das Reich' who had no artillery training. Nevertheless, they were very willing. Two Rottenführer served as both gun commander and gun-layer. The battery was motorised; two converted private cars towed the guns and a Citröen P.45 van was the ammunition carrier!

Ollivier and his battery were immediately sent into action. He was to secure an important crossroads. After much difficulty, the two guns were eventually unlimbered and positioned in an avenue some 500 metres from the crossroads. Ollivier only had to wait fifteen minutes for the first Russian tank to appear. This was destroyed. The young Germans rejoiced. Needless to say, this tank was not alone. A further eight tanks would appear and all were destroyed one after the other, but it was impossible to keep the guns camouflaged. The Russians unleashed 'Stalin's Organs'. One gun was destroyed and the crew killed. The Citröen van was blown to bits in turn. Even so Ollivier decided to fight on.

Ollivier managed to knock out three more tanks by constantly changing the position of his second gun. This was as much as he could do. Not only had the last rounds been expended due to the loss of the ammunition carrier, but also the gun had become a sitting target; by now, the ground was so churned up that the gun could not be moved.

After rendering the second gun useless, Ollivier assembled the few survivors and led them back to the command post of the Waffen-SS artillery unit. Although Heller was still not prepared to let Ollivier go just yet, sending him on patrol in the sector of the Reich Chancellery, he did promise him that he would eventually rejoin his compatriots.

## Confusion

Shortly after midday, one 'combat group' of Weber's *Kampfschule*, held in reserve at Hermannplatz, was committed on the right flank of Fenet's positions, not far from Tempelhof airport. The combat group was commanded by an unidentified Oberscharführer, who was ex-LVF.

Supported by a Sturmgeschütz assault gun, the French combat group, now mixed with other 'units', moved down Hermannstrasse. For an unknown reason, after several hundred metres, the assault gun suddenly abandoned the Frenchman to their fate. They pressed on, reaching one of the many cemeteries around the airport and came under intense mortar fire, forcing them to shelter in doorways from the lethal razor-sharp shrapnel.

Once the mortar fire had finished the group continued along Hermannstrasse and took up position in a small pub, from where the Frenchmen could support two nearby tanks.[38] The rest of the night passed off peacefully. The following morning Lavest was sent out on patrol, after which he was sent back to the pub on Hermannplatz to get orders and reinforcements.[39] He managed to find the pub, but nobody was there so he returned to his group. Towards the end of the afternoon, his group lost the support of the two tanks when they were called to another sector. Besides, they had little ammunition left. Lavest and his group would now have to fend for themselves and withdrew during the night

Back at Neukölln town hall, Hstuf. Fenet had become more and more concerned about the growing isolation of his battalion. Friendly troops should have been on their flanks, but the Russians were infiltrating almost at will, making life extremely hazardous.

Suddenly a strange order arrived from Division: 'If the attack has not already begun, stop and come and get new orders; if it has, then do your best!' Perplexed, Hstuf. Fenet immediately sent his assistant, Ostuf. von Wallenrodt, to 'Nordland' divisional headquarters to seek clarification. He returned 'much later'.[40] He was the bearer of grave news.

The situation was black. Earlier that morning, just as the French SS-Sturmbataillon and 'Nordland' had started to counterattack into Neukölln, the Russians had resumed their drive to the centre of Berlin with overwhelming forces. The main defensive ring had already started to crack. Fenet was infuriated. History was repeating itself. It was like Heinrichswalde two months before. Then his I/57 had been three hours into a successful assault when he had to fall back because there was no liaison on either flank or to the rear.

Phlegmatically, von Wallenrodt asked: "What do we do?" In the hope that the situation on their flanks could be restored, Fenet sent orders to the three companies to hold where they were and to avoid being encircled. It was a forlorn hope.

The Sturmbataillon now formed a salient in Russian lines. Contact with friendly units to the left and to the right was broken. From patrols and runners who managed to return to battalion headquarters all reported that the Russians were everywhere. The situation now demanded that troops be withdrawn from the tip of the advance to reinforce the threatened flanks. The city hall was made into the *centre de résistance*.

Reinforcements arrived. They were from the Hitler Jugend and all were aged between fourteen and seventeen. They numbered several hundred and burned with an indescribable enthusiasm to emulate the exploits of their elders, even though the panzerfäuste and Mauser rifles they carried were sometimes as big as they were. They seemed wholly impervious to danger and would pay the price for their youthful naivety. Fenet wrote:[41] 'In these hours of supreme danger, Berlin resorts to the supreme sacrifice, the most cruel, but the most highly symbolic: the flower of its youth ...'

The Sturmbataillon continued to hold its ground. Fenet claims that the 'tanks and the grenadiers had destroyed about thirty tanks' which seems exaggerated. Thanks to its runners, battalion headquarters managed to keep up communication with the attacking companies.

38    Levast identifies the two tanks as Panthers, whereas Mabire identifies them as Tigers.
39    Levast, *Le soleil se couchait à l'est*, p.109. Mabire implies that the events that befell Lavest and this combat group of the Kampfschule all happened on one day (see *Mourir A Berlin*, pp.174-178).
40    Fenet, *Die letzte Runde...*, p.6.
41    Fenet, *Die letzte Runde...*, p.7.

Since dawn, Rottenführer Millet, the section commander of the runners, had run the most important and dangerous assignments himself. Each time Millet entered the ruins for a run Fenet feared that would be the last he would ever see of him, but the cheerful Millet had always returned, cool and calm, to report: "Mission carried out!"

In the afternoon, accompanied by Rttf. Millet, Hstuf. Fenet toured the companies. The situation had not improved. They returned to the town hall. As they were crossing the road to enter the headquarters they suddenly came under fire. Millet was hit and killed. He was only twenty years old and had fought in Galicia and Pomerania.

At the very same moment Fenet felt a burning sensation in his left foot. He too had been hit. Carried inside the town hall, he was treated by a German doctor. A bullet had gone straight through his left foot without hitting bone. Like Rostaing, luck had not abandoned him. He could only reflect, 'This is a fine time to get a bullet through the foot!'

Firing continued outside. So the Russians were much nearer than first thought, perhaps some fifty metres to the rear of the town hall. With the Russians now so close to the town hall and behind their positions, the battle had taken a dramatic turn. There was no time to lose.

To avert encirclement, Fenet ordered Oberjunker Douroux, his Orderly Officer who still carried an injury, to clear the Russians from the immediate vicinity. To make matters worse, French SS and some bewildered Germans were 'surging back' in disorder.[42] The situation had to be redressed immediately or else disaster would be inescapable.

Pistol in hand, Douroux assembled all those around him and set about freeing the immediate vicinity from Russian possession. In vicious hand-to-hand fighting with hand grenades and bayonet they cleared out house after house. In less than quarter of an hour, the Russians attempting to take the Frenchmen from the rear were either dead or had turned tail. But this failure seemed to make the Russians all the more determined to capture the town hall and they now made a frontal attack, sparing on neither men nor ammunition.

The Frenchmen and the boys of the Hitler Jugend defended like devils. When the Russians seemed to hesitate, the defenders, led by Oberjunker Douroux, launched a counterattack in force and drove the Russians out of the immediate vicinity. The Russians replied with tanks along Berlinerstrasse. Up to now the face of the fighting had been inside blocks of houses between infantry, but that all changed when the T-34 tanks arrived in single file. Panzerfäuste accounted for one or two, but the others rolled on unchecked.

The Königstiger was alerted. Taking up position in Jägerstrasse, perpendicular to Berlinerstrasse, it waited in ambush. Not far from the tank, Fenet and Douroux could hear the 'march of the red armour'. The sound of the tank tracks approached. When the leading T-34 showed its turret to the Königstiger the German tank fired. The T-34 stopped in its tracks. With weapons raised, the Frenchmen watched and waited for the Russian crew to emerge from the hatches, but nobody left the 'iron coffin'.

The body of Millet lay close by, which some of his comrades carried under cover. The tall nineteen-year-old black-haired Roger Roberti took the place of Millet who Fenet described as being fanatical to the core. In the coming days, he would display extraordinary courage time and time again. Indeed, 'his prodigious contempt for anything that might smack of half-heartedness,

42   Mabire, *Mourir A Berlin*, p.184.

mediocrity, or weakness, his worship of loyalty and camaraderie, the nobility and purity of his ideals', made him, in the opinion of Fenet, the 'SS type'.

As the afternoon wore on the situation at the town hall became more and more critical. The front to the left and to the right had completely given way and the Russians were pouring through. Unstable on his legs, Fenet continued to direct the defence of the town hall from a chair. In the opinion of Douroux, Fenet 'embodied the very soul of the resistance'. For his part, Fenet commented that he managed to hold this breakwater thanks only to the drive and exceptional fighting spirit of his troops.

One such example, among many, was Uscha. Claude Capard of Flemish origin who had traded his secretary's desk pad for a machine gun and was holding a road all by himself.[43] He fired on everything that moved opposite with a precision and a rapidity that clearly disconcerted the Russians. Each and every time the Russians spotted him and tried to silence him, he seemed to change position 'just in the nick of time'. It was as though he was one step ahead of them.

Fink joined Capard. He too was a secretary at battalion headquarters. He had been helping Fenet to get about until he grabbed a passing teenager from the Hitler Jugend to take his place. Taking turns, Capard and Fink would hold the road until evening without letting the Russians advance a single step.

By 1700 hours, the French Sturmbataillon was all alone and jutting out from the main line. Those 'Nordland' tanks short of ammunition and fuel had withdrawn. Cut off from Division, Fenet decided to stay put at the town hall as long as there still remained a withdrawal route to friendly lines. Besides, he had not received orders to withdraw. And yet, curiously, at 1700 hours, Rostaing, who commanded the 3rd Company, received orders from Fenet to fight on a little longer, then withdraw to his headquarters at Neukölln town hall. Rostaing was mad with rage. Because of the other companies he now had to stop his successful 'offensive'.[44]

The Russians desperately and obstinately continued to attack frontally and from the flanks, even though a small and determined number, say fifty, could have easily outflanked the defenders and cut off their line of retreat. This time they employed combined arms, but their attacks still came to nothing; as soon as their infantry appeared they found themselves targeted by a deadly hail of bullets and were cut to pieces. As for their 'big brothers', there was no hiding from the panzerfäuste.

The Russians then unleashed a hurricane of fire over Neukölln, which grew in intensity. It deafened and stretched the nerves of the defenders towards breaking point. For some, it was all too much.[45] They were either too young or too old. Suddenly, Oberjunker Douroux saw about one hundred men appear from roads near to the town hall. They were in flight and throwing away their weapons. Pistol in hand, he rushed among them. He knew that he had to check their stampede or else they would spread panic before them. However, a gigantic blond German, standing in the middle of the road, legs apart, firing on the enemy with an MG 42 held at hip level, also saw the flight. He turned around and fired a long burst just over their heads. When this had no effect he did not hesitate to fire lower and shorter, which stopped them dead. Panic over, he then went back to firing on the enemy along Berlinerstrasse. Douroux rounded the men

---

43   Born on 12 November 1924 in Casablanca, Claude Capard enlisted in the LVF, then the NSKK and finally the Waffen-SS.
44   Rostaing, *Le prix d'un serment*, p.193.
45   Saint-Loup, *Les Hérétiques*, p.430.

up and pushed them forward. Then a 'Nordland' Tiger tank commander approached Oberjunker Douroux and presented him with his Iron Cross 1st Class. Taken aback and touched, Douroux thanked him vaguely. Impractical to wear the decoration on his battle dress, he shoved it into his pocket with great respect.[46]

Towards 1900 hours, runners reported that Soviet tanks were approaching Hermannplatz, some nine hundred metres to the rear! That left only two roads, Hermannstrasse and Berlinerstrasse, open for a withdrawal. And they would not remain open for long. The fate of the Sturmbataillon and its comrades in arms from the Hitler Jugend now hung in the balance: if the Russians managed to take Hermannplatz then there was no way out for them. It was the law of numbers making itself felt again. This time there was really only one decision Fenet could make and, reluctantly, he ordered the general withdrawal back to Hermannplatz. Any delay now could lead to disaster.

During a lull in the fighting Fenet quickly regrouped the SS and HJ for the withdrawal. Rostaing's 3rd Company would bring up the rear. Covered by 'Nordland' Panther and Tiger tanks, they withdrew to Hermannplatz. The withdrawal was orderly and did not meet with any interference along the way. It took them quarter of an hour to reach Hermannplatz. By then, darkness had set in.

Feverishly, the French Sturmbataillon and the HJ organised defensive positions behind barricades of paving stones. It was not a moment too soon; Soviet tanks were held at bay barely one hundred metres from the square and, minutes after the arrival of the Sturmbataillon, all roads east of the square fell into enemy hands.

Time and time again Soviet tanks attempted to emerge onto Hermannplatz from Brauerstrasse and Weserstrasse. Sturmgeschütze beat them back, scoring a bull's-eye with each and every shot. The night was lit up like day from all these burning tanks which noisily exploded one after the other. Fenet called the battle 'a veritable massacre of Red tanks'. Indeed, in less than an hour, some forty Soviet tanks were destroyed on the approaches to Hermannplatz.[47] The Soviet infantry did not show themselves.[48]

Hennecart took the sorely tired 2nd Company in hand. Finding himself quite by chance under the 88mm barrel of a Tiger tank just as a round was loosed off, he was left deaf for twenty-four hours. Towards midnight on 26-27 April 1945, Fenet received the order to withdraw. On the way they were joined by Labourdette and his 1st Company.

## The 1st Company

Since early morning the fifty-strong 1st Company under Ustuf. Labourdette had been at the disposal of the German commander of sector Tempelhof and spent most of the day in reserve. This inaction gave rise to a growing sense of impatience among the officer cadets to do battle.

46   See Saint-Loup, *Les Hérétiques*, p.431.
47   Saint-Loup, *Les Hérétiques*, p.432.
48   Fenet, *Die letzte Runde...*, p.10. In contrast, according to Saint-Loup, *Les Hérétiques*, pp.432-433, when the Russians submerged the barricade on Weserstrasse the Frenchmen, side by side with 'Nordland', the Hitler Jugend, the Volkssturm and the Kriegsmarine, counterattacked. Shouting like madmen, they stormed the strongly defended barricade and overwhelmed the Russians, but casualties were appalling, especially among the Hitler Jugend.

Eventually, the 1st Company was deployed. It occupied a defensive line between Tempelhof airport and one of the many neighbouring cemeteries. Individual holes were dug and machine guns were sited. Nobody knew quite where the Russians were until they started to appear and establish themselves in position hundreds of metres away. The Frenchmen fired on them to make their presence known as well as their intention to hold the ground.

Labourdette dispatched Uscha. Puechlong to find and make contact with Fenet at Neukölln town hall. Unfortunately, Labourdette had no map of Berlin to give Puechlong. In fact, he only had a sketch map of the city himself! Thus it is no wonder that Puechlong soon became lost in the labyrinth of roads. Fired on by friend and foe alike, he made his way across a cemetery. For once, as luck would have it, he met some comrades who pointed him in the right direction of the town hall. On his arrival he reported to Fenet who seemed pleased to have news of Labourdette and the 1st Company. Fenet then briefed him on his unfavourable situation and gave him a message to pass on to Labourdette: if he has to break off the action then he could rejoin the Sturmbataillon at Hermannplatz.

Puechlong immediately set off. He came to the same cemetery and got lost again. Everything looked the same. He wandered round the deserted cemetery for ages before finding his way again. He reported back to Labourdette. In his absence, the situation of the 1st Company had deteriorated. Labourdette left him in no doubt about its seriousness. He had no contact to the left or to the right and the Russians were infiltrating. Encirclement was looming.

Suddenly, the roar of guns and the crump of mortars interrupted the conversation. Shells crashed down all around. The intensity of the Soviet bombardment grew and grew. It was hell. Shrapnel filled the air. Uscha. Gérard[49] was badly wounded in the buttocks and evacuated to the rear by a group led by Puechlong.

Quite unexpectedly the group chanced upon an ambulance but the German medical orderlies did not want to know. After making all kind of feeble excuses, they concluded by pointing out that the doors of the ambulance were locked. Seeing red, Puechlong blasted the lock with his Sturmgewehr. Turning to the medical orderlies, he told them to evacuate his wounded comrade to a first aid post and threatened that if they refused then he would kill them. That did the trick. As soon as the ambulance was on its way, the group returned to the defensive positions of the 1st Company. The constant need to maintain contact came at a heavy price: Oberjunker Cossard was killed on a liaison mission and St.Ju. Lefeuvre disappeared on another.[50]

The Russians continued to bombard Tempelhof airport. This bombardment would only abate in the late evening, which was followed by an infantry assault. They infiltrated houses to the north-east of the positions held by the 1st Company. From there, the Russians now overlooked the airfield. This gave the Russians a distinct tactical advantage that they were quick to exploit. Labourdette saw disaster coming and withdrew his company to the cemetery.

Oberjunker Croisile accompanied Oberjunker Boulmier's Platoon into the cemetery where it came under fire from an enemy machine gun. Boulmier panicked and handed over his platoon

---

49   Gabriel Gerard was born on 6 October 1923 in Bourg (department Gironde).
50   Robert Lefeuvre was ex-LVF and had served in the celebrated *section de chasse*. He attended Kienschalg from the end of November 1944 to March 1945.

to Croisile, who managed to lead it out of the cemetery and into a new position without loss. Croisile never saw Boulmier again.[51]

Once in the cemetery the 1st Company was immediately set upon by hordes of Russians screaming 'Urra!' There was great confusion. Desperately the Frenchmen fought back. Russian pressure mounted by the minute. Death swept over that cemetery again and again. With an enormous effort the Frenchmen extricated themselves and sought out new positions easier to defend.[52] The survivors received an order to assemble and take up position at the corner of Hermannstrasse and Flughafenstrasse.

Labourdette now decided to occupy and fortify a block of houses. He then set about assembling his disorganised Company, which had lost many men. Finally, in the late evening, Labourdette and his 1st Company rendezvoused with Fenet at Hermannplatz. There was considerable joy at their return.

As the Sturmbataillon withdrew, the 1st Company was once again requisitioned to seal a new breach in the front. Fenet had need of the 1st Company, the only relatively fresh unit left in the Battalion, to make up his losses. He went to the sector commander to protest and ask him to let the last survivors of the French Division fight together, but the sector commander was insistent about requisitioning the 1st Company. Because the situation had become catastrophic in their sector, Fenet agreed to the limited employment of the 1st Company while the rest of the Battalion could rest for several hours.

Fenet sought out Labourdette before he parted. He wrote of their brief farewell:[53]

I recommended to Labourdette that he should not let himself become involved and to return at all costs at the agreed time. 'You can count on me', he replied, but hearing him I was gripped by a painful premonition. I took him by the shoulder: 'You must return with the guys, you must return, do you hear me?'

There was a brief silence.

'Don't worry, I will return', he finished by saying in a distant and somewhat hesitant voice, as if the words were refusing to come out his mouth.

'Right, see you soon!'

'See you soon, Hauptsturmführer'.

We shook hands and he left with his men into the night. I watched his black silhouette fade with a pang of anguish: his attitude worried me. It was that of a man going into battle knowing that he won't return... But no, this was ridiculous. I shrugged my shoulders, furious with myself for letting myself have these dark thoughts. What a stupid premonition! My nerves were undoubtedly strained and the fault lay with this ridiculous wound which made me walk with crutches. No, Labourdette would return, he must return, he's always so sure, so punctual.

Roger interrupted my thoughts by bringing a chair and urging me to rest. 'Not now, Roger!' Now a place had to be found where my men could sleep for several hours.

51　According to Bouysse, *French in German uniform Part 1: Officers of the Waffen-SS*, Boulmier was wounded and captured by the Soviets.
52　Mabire, *Mourir À Berlin*, p.197. In contrast, Croisile does not recall this fierce fighting in the cemetery.
53　Fenet, *Die letzte Runde...*, p.11.

Out of the darkness appeared von Wallenrodt. He had found sleeping accommodation for part of the Sturmbataillon in the Thomas Keller brewery opposite Anhalter Bahnhof. The others would lodge with Weber and the Kampfschule at the Opera house. Fenet told his German assistant to take the exhausted men to their accommodation and join him later in the morning at 'Nordland' divisional headquarters, where he had decided to return to straight away.

For those Frenchmen of the Sturmbataillon who had not been able to make it out of Neukölln, for whatever reason, death or capture was their only certainty. In such a predicament were the ten men of Montgour's Platoon of the 2nd Company.

Bypassed by Russian troops, the ten French men had remained holed up in a big factory in Neukölln. Food was the least of their worries; German civilians came and fed them. Night fell and they were still there. Also hiding out in the same cellar was a French POW who they had immediately adopted, calling him 'old man' because he was at least thirty! He had ended up as a free worker in Berlin, which he knew quite well now. Like the SS, he too was in no hurry to surrender; some of his friends had warned him about the Russians.

The Frenchmen discussed their situation. It was hopeless. They had no heavy weapons and very little ammunition. Their best chance of escape was through the labyrinth of interconnected cellars that now existed underground. Several months before, as a precaution against being buried alive in the event of air raids or artillery bombardments, the inhabitants of Berlin had been ordered to connect cellars. The prisoner offered to act as a guide, but this he would only do if they stripped to pass themselves off as foreign workers.

Only Laplaud removed his tunic, all of the others hesitated. They seemed too exhausted and afraid to try and escape. Laplaud stayed close to the prisoner as they made their way from cellar to cellar. Just in case, he kept a pistol in his pocket. They became covered in dust and plaster. This combination masked the prisoner's khaki and Laplaud's field-grey uniform trousers.

When the two of them emerged from the cellars and went out into a road they sighted Russian tanks fifteen to twenty metres away. The crews glanced at the newcomers and, after reassuring themselves that the newcomers were not armed, they seemed to pay them no further attention. Laplaud then saw German prisoners of war being escorted to the rear. Among them he recognised some of his comrades who had stayed behind at the factory not so long ago. In turn they saw Laplaud and the prisoner but did not give them away with any show of emotion. Laplaud would never see any of them again.

Together they hurried on, but a Russian, who had spotted Laplaud's field-grey trousers, approached them. To his question of whether or not they were Germans, they replied they were French. He let them continue.[54] The two merged into the grey throng of civilians beginning to emerge from the cellars of Neukölln. The fighting was definitely over.

It was now time to reflect and count the cost. For the Sturmbataillon, the outcome of the battle must have been a bitter disappointment. Not only had its counterattack, which had started so promisingly, been forced to a halt, but its attempt to hold onto Neukölln had ultimately been in vain. And yet its counterattack was one of the few during the battle of Berlin that had actually pushed the Russians back. This achievement in the face of greater enemy numbers and power was a source of pride to many, but pride tinged with deep sadness at their losses.

---

54    Laplaud was sentenced to one year in prison on 24 January 1946 by the *Cour de justice* of Limoges.

Rostaing's 3rd Company, which had started the day with some eighty men, now only counted thirty. Ollivier's 4th Company now counted twenty. As for the 2nd Company, hit as hard as the 4th Company, it would be reasonable to assume that it suffered the same high percentage of casualties. The 1st Company was some forty-strong when requisitioned for the second time. All told, the French SS-Sturmbataillon may have numbered no more than one hundred and fifty 'effectives' after the battle for Neukölln. Thus, the casualty balance sheet of Neukölln was between 150 and 200 men.

The cost to the Sturmbataillon was high, in fact very high, but it had dealt out death and destruction upon the Russians out of proportion to its limited resources fielded. The Frenchmen 'scrapped' fourteen T-34s.[55] Gren. Aubin is credited with one, Uscha. Lacombe with one, Oscha. Apollot with one, and Uscha. Vaulot with two. The number of Russian dead and wounded was untold. However, it seemed as though the Russians had a never-ending supply of men and material to replace their losses.

Taking their leave of von Wallenrodt and the Sturmbataillon, Fenet and Douroux went in search of a car to take them to the city centre. Supporting himself on Douroux, Fenet was still limping badly. They came to the command post of Regiment 'Danmark' and were warmly welcomed by the Scandinavian and German staff. Unfortunately, they could not oblige the two French SS officers with transport to the city centre: yes, they had vehicles but not a single drop of fuel. Fenet asked about the whereabouts of Brigf. Krukenberg and was informed 'Nordland' divisional command post had just moved again, but its new location was not known.

Accepting an invitation to get some rest, the two French SS officers were put up on mattresses in the medical post. A badly burned Panzer crewman was brought in and laid beside them. In terrible pain, he called out for his mother and begged them to finish him off.

Meanwhile, north-east of Neukölln, some five hundred metres from the French SS-Sturmbataillon, a Frenchman, dressed in the uniform of the LVF, continued to fight his own war. His name was Pierre Soulé. This was the same individual who, some eight months earlier, had refused to pass to the Waffen-SS and, as a result of his protest, been sent to Danzig-Matzkau.

On his release, Soulé was sent to Berlin and demobilised as a free worker. However, he was not prepared to stop fighting for Europe and, in November 1944, decided to join a commando unit under the control of Otto Skorzeny.[56] He was wounded. His hands were so badly burnt that he had to spend some six weeks in hospital and, at the end of March 1945, he was released. Thereupon he left for Berlin in search of another combat post. With difficulty, he got through to the German capital.

Soulé joined a makeshift group of Hitler Jugend and Volkssturm organised by a SS-Sturmbannführer of 'Nibelungen' who had released himself from hospital in order to fight. Soulé commanded fourteen boys of the Hitler Jugend. One by one he lost twelve of them in the fighting, but they destroyed seven tanks. The Stubaf. awarded the Iron Cross 2nd Class to Soulé and to the last two kids with him who were both wounded but fighting on.

55    Saint-Loup, *Les Hérétiques*, p.430.
56    Presumably Soulé joined one of the SS Jagdverband.

## Krukenberg and the 26 April 1945

Towards midday, the commanders of SS-Panzer-Grenadier-Regiment 23 'Norge' and SS-Panzer-Grenadier-Regiment 24 'Danmark' reported to Brigf. Krukenberg that they each had about six to seven hundred combat troops at their disposal. Krukenberg ordered them to place one-third of these troops at the disposal of Defence Sector 'Z' and continue equipping and preparing the rest for combat. As such the Scandinavian Waffen-SS troops of 'Nordland' should now have passed to the direct control of the Wehrmacht and the obdurate Seifert, but Krukenberg also ordered the two regimental commanders to remain responsible for their commands even if the Sector 'did not wish to hear of them'.

Towards 1900 hours that evening, the two regimental commanders reported back that they had found nobody at the front apart from their panzergrenadiers. They were alone. Moreover, Defence Sector 'Z' was totally devoid of the prepared defensive positions that Seifert had shown Krukenberg on a map. Krukenberg was now convinced that all the defence plans for Sector 'Z' only existed on paper. He then understood why Seifert had refused all his offers of help. Because of this he decided not to put off any longer his introduction to Ogruf. Fegelein. And although he did not know Fegelein he believed that he could interest him 'in the peculiarities of our engagement'.[57]

Later that evening, Brigf. Krukenberg went to the Führerbunker. Once again, on entering, he was not challenged. Escorted through the busy rooms and corridors of the Bunker, he noticed officers as well as NSDAP party members of various ranks. One stocky individual in the uniform of the Party attracted his attention: as he passed him, he was dictating to his secretary the following words: '… and relieved of his duties with immediate effect…" He asked his guide who this person was. Surprised at the question, his guide replied: "What, you don't know Reichsleiter Martin Bormann?'[58] No, he did not.

Krukenberg was shown to a long room where Ogruf. Fegelein came to meet him. He urged Fegelein to support him in his efforts to prevent the scattered employment of the only Waffen-SS division in the defensive zone of Berlin. He complained that Defence Sector 'Z', where 'Nordland' was to be engaged, was 'only ready on paper'. He warned Fegelein that the removal of the regimental commanders from 'Nordland', coming after the dismissal of Ziegler, might be fraught with consequences. Worse still, he foresaw the Waffen-SS blamed for the failure of the defence in Sector 'Z'!

At that same moment General Weidling entered the room. Krukenberg repeated to him what he had told Fegelein. Krukenberg appealed to Weidling to engage 'Nordland', the only unit he stressed in the city centre with combat experience, under its own officers. Weidling did not look pleased. This gave Krukenberg the impression that Weidling wanted 'Nordland' engaged without its officers.

Nevertheless, Weidling eventually gave in, assigning the command of Defence Sector 'Z' to Brigf. Mohnke of the Waffen-SS and announcing the creation of two Sub-Sectors. Oberstleutant Seifert, located in the Air Ministry building, would command the Western Sub-Sector and Brigf. Krukenberg the Eastern Sub-Sector. The demarcation line was Wilhelmstrasse. Furthermore,

57   Krukenberg, *Combat pour Berlin*, p.10.
58   Mabire, *Mourir A Berlin*, p.202.

'Nordland' was now to be engaged and also under its own officers in the Eastern Sub-Sector. Lastly, those units of 'Nordland' already under Seifert were to remain in his sector until such time as they could be relieved and handed back to Krukenberg. Then General Weidling left. That was the last contact Krukenberg had with him, verbal or otherwise.

Just as Krukenberg was about to leave, Dr. Goebbels, the Reich Minister of Public Enlightenment and Propaganda, arrived. Krukenberg had worked with Goebbels in the Propaganda Ministry, but in the spring of 1933 they had clashed and Krukenberg had resigned his post. Now, as Gauleiter of Berlin and Reichs Commissar for Defence, Goebbels had a direct responsibility for the defence of the capital and it was a task he had gone about with the same drive and efficiency he applied to his Ministry.

Goebbels asked Krukenberg for his unvarnished view of the morale of the troops placed under him. In his reply, he talked of their origin, of their fighting qualities, of their resolve to fight on, and of their recent battles, concluding that they would hold the sector assigned to them until the arrival of western troops.

Goebbels responded that negotiations with the West were well under way and that Army Wenck was fast approaching the Havel. Thus, the garrison of Berlin would only have to hold out for several more days. Krukenberg had no reason to doubt him. Later, he was to find out it was all propaganda. By 0100 hours on Friday 27 April 1945, Krukenberg was back at his command post in the Opera House. The rest of the night passed quietly.

# 17

## To the Death

---

### Krukenberg and 27 April 1945

Friday 27 April proved relatively quiet. In the early morning, Brigf. Krukenberg held a briefing of 'Nordland' officers at his command post in the Opera House. Hstuf. Fenet arrived late. Earlier that morning, a German officer came to collect Hstuf. Fenet from the 'Nordland' regimental medical post where he had spent the night. The German officer had a car with him, but rubble-strewn roads cut short their journey. The three officers then continued on foot.

The German officer, an elderly Berliner twice the age of Fenet, continually lamented at the sight of the city's ruins. To him, this was the end of the world. He considered himself too old to ever see better days again but foresaw them for the youth. The Russians interrupted him with a violent artillery barrage. Caught out in the open, the officers found temporary shelter in the basement of the Imperial Castle.

Shells rained down on the entire quarter. It was a veritable hurricane of steel. The ground trembled under the explosions. Walls collapsed. Fenet reflected, 'if we had only half the ammunition that these savages waste shelling deserted squares and ruined monuments'. Eventually, he made it to the briefing.

At the briefing, Krukenberg reviewed the situation. He declared himself satisfied with the operations that 'Nordland' and the French Sturmbataillon had conducted yesterday. He seemed more relaxed, even jovial, which was in sharp contrast to the austere face he normally wore. He granted the Sturmbataillon a day of rest, after which it would be engaged as an 'anti-tank *Kommando*'.[1]

Leaving his subordinates to continue preparing 'Nordland' for its engagement at midday, Brigf. Krukenberg went to report to Brigf. Mohnke at the Chancellery. Krukenberg did not know him. Not far from the entrance to the Chancellery, he ran into General Krebs. They

---

1   Krukenberg, *Combat pour Berlin*, p.12. According to Saint-Loup, *Les Hérétiques*, p.442, Krukenberg also spoke of a counterattack planned for the night of 27-28 April 1945 to relieve the great pressure on the city centre from the direction of the Spittalmarkt to the east. This counterattack did not materialise for several reasons: the Russians blew the bridges over the river Spree to cover themselves, Russian strength tripled during the course of the day, and, lastly, there was a lack of operational co-operation between the Party-sponsored Volkssturm and the Army.

talked. Krebs told him that the leading elements of Army Wenck had just reached Werder, west of Potsdam. When Krukenberg questioned him about the negotiations with the West he could tell him nothing new but added that the Americans were posed to cover the 90 kilometres between the Elbe and Berlin in very little time and restore the situation in the city. Krebs then turned to the subject of the troops' morale just as a Police General passed them, who he named as Gestapo chief Heinrich Muller. They parted.[2]

Krukenberg reported to Mohnke, who promised him all possible support for his 'difficult mission'. Krukenberg expanded on his difficulties. 'Nordland' was new to him, their paths having not crossed before. On the other hand, he had the advantage of being extremely familiar with his defence sector as well as the squares and roads of Berlin, but the air raids had changed the face of the city. To find one's bearings, even for him, was not easy.

Mohnke surprised Krukenberg by placing at his disposal a company of naval infantrymen that had been airlifted into Berlin the night before, but they were armed with Italian rifles and lacked experience as combat infantry. Its commander was summoned, who made an excellent impression. Also Mohnke agreed to keep at Krukenberg's disposal schwere SS-Panzer-Abteilung 503 [Heavy SS Panzer Battalion 503] which still numbered eight 'runners'. Krukenberg now left.

That morning, 'Nordland' occupied its new defensive sector without any problems. Outposts were established along the Landwehr Kanal. Brigf. Krukenberg divided his command into three. One third he assigned to the foremost lines in the ruins south of Hollmannstrasse. It was to observe the enemy and contain its patrols, but in the event of an enemy attack in force, it was under orders to fall back slowly to the principal line of defence along Besselstrasse and Ritterstrasse.

The next third was to be formed into shock troops and held in reserve near regimental and battalion command posts ready to move forward quickly and seal off enemy penetrations. The last third, still needing rest and recuperation, was to remain in houses along Leipzigerstrasse.[3]

The few remaining tanks, short of petrol, were concentrated on Leipzigerstrasse, which offered them some degree of movement other than in single file and promised the support of groups of French tank hunters.[4]

Concerned that the artillery of 'Nordland' was poorly positioned, Krukenberg had it moved from the Tiergarten to the rear of his sector. The guns were now deployed at the entrance of streets leading onto the Unter den Linden in such a way that they could deal with enemy tanks arriving from the north, the Reichstag and Schlossplatz because, despite repeated demands, he still knew little of the situation in these areas.

2    Krukenberg, *Combat pour Berlin*, p.12. Curiously, according to Saint-Loup, *Les Hérétiques*, p.443, Brigf. Krukenberg struck up a conversation with Krebs in the presence of Mohnke.
3    According to the chapter *Battle Memoir*, *Charlemagne's Legionnaires*, p.161, the last third was to be held in emergency reserve. However, this is unconfirmed.
4    The *Battle Memoir* recounts that the French SS troops found themselves heavily engaged in the northern sector of Zitadelle under Seifert (see *Charlemagne's Legionnaires*, p.161). This too is unconfirmed.

Krukenberg was still missing part of his command; Seifert was proving slow in returning those forces put at his disposal. Indeed, some he would keep hold of.[5] Nevertheless, Krukenberg continued to receive reinforcements, who were for the most part volunteers of the Waffen-SS.

The enemy was quiet along the 'Nordland' front. Some isolated soldiers were reported approaching the canal at Hallesche Tor. Krukenberg decided, with the support of the naval infantrymen, to launch a counterattack against them. The counterattack, he hoped, would 'reawaken the feeling of superiority' in a unit that over the past few days had conducted one retreat after another. Orders were given. However, when the Russians were first sighted approaching the 'bridge over the canal', presumably the Hallesche Tor bridge, Volkssturm personnel, still operating independently, blew it. In this way, the counterattack had to be scrapped.

All morning the Soviet bombardment on the Opera House, the Imperial Castle and the surrounding area continued unabated. Reaching a punishing intensity, the bombardment forced Krukenberg to move the divisional command post. During the first lull in the shelling, the headquarters staff left the Opera House and made for the Schauspielhaus, a theatre, on Schillerplatz between the 'French' and 'German' cathedrals.

On the way, Dr. Zimmermann, a 'Nordland' doctor, informed Fenet that they were on Französischestrasse [French Street], named after the Huguenot émigrés who had settled in this quarter two hundred and fifty years earlier. Fenet thought to himself, 'We're fighting in the ruins of this capital that they helped to build'. Zimmermann added: 'Henceforth, this road will also be in your honour.'

During the afternoon, 'Nordland' division headquarters relocated from the Schauspielhaus to Stadtmitte underground station.

That afternoon, Krukenberg went to his newly designated command post in Stadtmitte underground station and was shocked to discover that the so-called headquarters of the central sector of *Festung* Berlin was nothing more than an abandoned underground railway car with broken windows and no electricity or telephones.[6] However, his assistant, Pachur, 'worked miracles' to bring organisation to the command post.

The ceiling of the underground station was so thin that a Soviet artillery shell pierced it, exploded and wounded some fifteen men. Dr. Zimmermann, now working out of a railway car crudely converted into a first-aid post, promptly treated them. Some were evacuated by ambulance to the medical post in the air-raid shelter of Hotel Adlon on Pariser Platz.

Food supplies were readily available from grocery shops in the nearby Gendarmenmarkt. To prevent pillaging, all were put under guard. And in the interest of discipline, the drinking of alcohol remained banned. Ammunition had to be fetched from far-off police barracks and the lack of panzerfäuste was a cause for concern until a cache was 'found' at the Reich Chancellery.[7]

5    Curiously, according to Krukenberg, *Combat pour Berlin*, p.13, one part of the French volunteers would remain under Seifert to the end.
6    This was all too typical of the lack of preparations which Krukenberg would complain about after the war.
7    Krukenberg was convinced that without this find of panzerfäuste his troops would have gone without (see *Combat pour Berlin*, p.14).

That same afternoon, von Wallenrodt brought the French Sturmbataillon from the Opera House and the Thomas Keller brewery to Stadtmitte underground station.[8] Not far from the Reich Chancellery, von Wallenrodt was caught in a violent bombardment and forced to take shelter in a launderette where he was recognised by Oscha. Ollivier of the French Sturmbataillon, who raced over towards him. The launderette was the headquarters of 'Group Heller'.[9]

Ollivier was desperate to rejoin his former command. Von Wallenrodt spoke to the commanding officer, who now agreed to release him. Von Wallenrodt took him to the 4th Company sheltering and resting in the machinery cellar of a theatre. He was shocked and dismayed to find the 4th Company no more than twenty strong.

Irritated by two Soviet observation aircraft circling the district in search of targets, Ollivier had two machine-guns set up in an anti-aircraft role. Flying at roof level, the Soviet aircraft returned. Std.Ju. Protopopoff immediately ordered one of the machine-gunners out of his seat, sat down and, when one of the slow moving aircraft came well within range, loosed off burst after burst, hitting it. The aircraft nose-dived and crashed behind a block of houses with a muffled explosion. The second aircraft quickly disappeared.

Shortly after the arrival of von Wallenrodt and the battalion at the Stadtmitte underground command post, Krukenberg held a brief ceremony to award those Frenchmen with the Iron Cross won the day before at Neukölln.[10] Among the recipients were Oscha. Hennecart, decorated with the Iron Cross 1st Class, and Uscha. Claude Capard, decorated with the Iron Cross 2nd Class. Fenet wrote of this:

> We were very happy to be together again and this break of several hours had been most welcome for us all. The men gathered around me, jostling to fill my pockets with bonbons, chocolate and cigarettes that they had just been given. We sang in the underground carriages, everybody was happy. Nevertheless, the party was incomplete, for the 1st Company had still not returned. What the hell was Labourdette doing?[11]

The first to return was a group led by Std.Ju. Robelin,[12] followed later that evening by Oberjunker de Lacaze and his platoon, but there was still no sign of Labourdette and the platoon under Oberjunker Croisile.[13]

8    Fenet, chapter *À Berlin, jusqu'au bout*, *Historia* hors série no 32, p.161. And yet, according to Rostaing, *Le prix d'un serment*, p.195, he and his company spent the entire day at the Opera House. Also, according to Georgen, *Sur les traces du Sturmbataillon de la division 'Charlemagne'*, magazine 39/45, part 1, p.25, the Sturmbataillon assembled in the cellars of the Schauspielhaus.

9    Soulat, *Historique de la Division Charlemagne*, p.104. In contrast, according to Mabire, *Mourir A Berlin*, p.230, Ollivier had found himself at the launderette by pure chance, being as good as any other place to rest.

10   The exact number is not known.

11   Fenet, *Die letzte Runde…*, p.13.

12   According to Georgen, *Sur les traces du Sturmbataillon de la division 'Charlemagne'*, magazine 39/45, part 1, p.25, Robelin commanded the *section de canons d'infanterie du bataillon* [the battalion's infantry gun platoon] before the depart for Berlin.

13   According to Fenet, on the return of de Lacaze he reported that Labourdette had entered the underground system with a few men and also ordered him to bring back the company in due course if he had not returned himself (see Fenet, *Die letzte Runde…*, p.13). However, this contrasts with the

## The 1st Company, Croisile and the death of Ustuf. Labourdette

Requisitioned again, the 1st Company, which was down to some forty men, was deployed by platoon earlier in the day. The platoon under Oberjunker de Lacaze was assigned to the defence of a barricade while the platoon under Oberjunker Croisile, who was joined by his company commander Labourdette, was deployed to an underground station to prevent possible Soviet infiltration through the tunnels.[14]

Croisile, accompanied by some grenadiers, went on a reconnaissance mission. They marched quite a long way before they were stopped by a barricade of timber and barbed wire across the tunnel. Croisile decided to go no further and returned to the underground station. The streets above were empty and the platoon under de Lacaze had disappeared. Forgotten about and alone, Labourdette decided to leave the underground station and rejoin the others.

Eventually Labourdette, Croisile and his platoon met up with a small group under St.Ju. Robelin. He was known to Croisile, who had attended the same course at Kienschlag. Convinced that the bulk of the battalion had withdrawn to the Reich Chancellery, Labourdette decided to try and make it there. They hurried off. They came under sporadic artillery fire which seemed to be directed by a light aircraft that flew over them at regular intervals. In this way, several men were wounded. They were left at makeshift first aid posts. The shelling became heavier, but they kept going.

Towards midday, near S-Bahn station Yorckstrasse, the Frenchmen were requisitioned by a Major of the Wehrmacht. One grenadier, who had just had his leg severed by a piece of shrapnel, was left at a first aid post. The Wehrmacht Major intended to use the Frenchmen to mount a counterattack so that he could evacuate the first aid post.

Labourdette ordered Std.Ju. Robelin and his small group to rejoin Fenet to keep him updated about the situation of his company. They made it back.[15] By now, Croisile's Platoon counted no more than fourteen men, plus one soldier of the Wehrmacht, one airman, and one member of the Volkssturm. It still had one machine-gun. Towards 1400 hours, the Frenchmen were called upon to counterattack, but a line of seven Russian tanks then appeared along Yorckstrasse supported by large numbers of infantry. The Wehrmacht Major ordered a withdrawal of 500 metres and the Frenchmen to hold up the Russians. This was easier said than done because they

testimony of Croisile of the 1st Company who stated that Labourdette lost contact with de Lacaze's platoon (see Croisile, *Sous Uniforme Allemand*, p.300).

14  According to Georgen, *Sur les traces du Sturmbataillon de la division 'Charlemagne'*, magazine 39/45, part 1, p.23, de Lacaze's Platoon was assigned to defend a barricade around Belle-Alliance-Platz while Croisile's Platoon was deployed to borough Schöneberg in south-west Berlin. Some five kilometres separate Belle-Alliance-Platz and Schöneberg. Croisile's testimony suggests that the two platoons were deployed much closer together (see Croisile, *Sous Uniforme Allemand*.) Moreover, when Labourdette and Croisile's Platoon were forced to withdraw they were requisitioned near S-Bahn station Yorckstrasse, which is nearer Schöneberg than Belle-Alliance-Platz across the Landwehr Kanal.

15  According to Soulat, *Historique de la Division Charlemagne*, p.124, they were never heard from again and yet, according to Georgen, *Sur les traces du Sturmbataillon de la division 'Charlemagne'*, magazine 39/45, part 3, p.25, they did make it back to Fenet. The author has used Georgen's version. Also, according to Bouysse, *Français sous l'uniforme allemande partie II: Sous-officiers & hommes du rang de la Waffen-SS*, Robelin was killed on 29th April 1945.

did not have any anti-tank weapons. So they opened fire on the infantry, who seemed hesitant anyway. The Major managed to evacuate the wounded before the Frenchmen retreated in turn.

The Major set up his headquarters on the first floor of a building. The Frenchmen occupied the ground floor. They repulsed two or three infantry attacks, after which the tanks advanced a little further forward, blasting the buildings on either side of the road which caught fire. A German military lorry suddenly appeared and was blown apart. The Russians then sent forward five or six men pulling a cart disguised as civilians. Fired on, they fled.

An old gentleman then came and asked Labourdette to remove the boxes of munitions cluttering up his flat on the fifth floor. When opened they contained panzerfäuste. That evening, the Russian tanks attacked. One tank stopped almost in the centre of the crossroads. Oberjunker Croisile and the Wehrmacht soldier with his platoon grabbed panzerfäust. Croisile fired and hit the tracks, without any effect, but the *Landser* hit the turret and the tank exploded. The Russians pulled back.

Night fell. It proved to be a quiet night. On the morning of the 28th, the Major sent for Labourdette and Croisile. Labourdette was fast asleep and could not be woken by Croisile so he went alone to see the Major, who ordered him to participate in an attack on nearby buildings the Russians had started to infiltrate. Croisile returned to the ground floor. Finding Labourdette still fast asleep, Croisile organised the necessary support fire and set off with a small group. At a street corner he was seriously wounded in the head. Two comrades brought him back to headquarters where medical orderly Bourrier attended to him. Croisile was evacuated to the nearest first-aid post. His war was over.

Company commander Labourdette would never return to Fenet, who would learn later[16] that he met his death in an underground tunnel covering his men.[17]

News came through to Fenet that Army Wenck had reached the area around Potsdam. On the other hand, the Russians had launched a great offensive across the river Oder south of Stettin and had already reached Prenzlau. Fenet thought of his comrades at Neustrelitz waiting to join those already at Berlin. Convinced that they were now in the middle of a battle, he knew that they would not be coming. He overheard one of his men say: "What a pity for them. They'll have missed a fine occasion."

## Saturday 28 April 1945

In the early morning hours of 28 April 1945, the Russians managed to throw pontoon bridges across the Landwehr kanal near the Hallesches Tor and then proceeded to send over a large number of tanks. In their path was Belle-Alliance-Platz. From this square emanated three key roads that led to the Reich Chancellery.

---

16  According to Saint-Loup, *Les Hérétiques*, p.449, Fenet received news of Labourdette's death on 30 April.
17  See Fenet, chapter *À Berlin, jusqu'au bout*, *Historia* hors série no 32, p.161, Fenet, *Die letzte Runde…*, p.13, and Mabire, *Mourir À Berlin*, p.232. All three sources date Labourdette's death to 27 April. However, according to the testimony of Croisile, *Sous Uniforme Allemand*, p.307, Labourdette was still very much alive on the morning of 28 April. Furthermore, according to Georgen, *Sur les traces du Sturmbataillon de la division 'Charlemagne'*, magazine 39/45, part 3, p.25, Fenet only learnt at the end of the battle that Labourdette had been killed on 28 April in a U-Bahn tunnel.

During the night the Sturmbataillon sent two anti-tank commandos to Belle-Alliance-Platz. The first commando, assembled and on its way within quarter of an hour of the request from 'Nordland', was commanded by Ostuf. von Wallenrodt.[18] Oscha Hennecart commanded the second, requested one hour after the first.[19] Aged thirty-seven, Lucien Hennecart was like an old man to the youngsters around him. Hands in pockets, he was celebrated for coming through storms of bullets and shrapnel without picking up a scratch. Fenet thought that Hennecart should have received his epaulettes of Untersturmführer a long time ago, having earned them a hundred times! After repeating his orders back to Fenet, Hennecart took his leave and disappeared into the night. The hours passed by. No one returned.

A direct order from 'Nordland' also brought Weber's Kampfschule to Belle-Alliance-Platz.

When dawn came up 'Nordland' requested more reinforcements for the same sector. The last of the Sturmbataillon was now to be engaged. Douroux took Fenet to Krukenberg who explained the situation to him in detail. Fenet recalls:

> The whole battalion was to be engaged together near Belle-Alliance-Platz to prevent access by the tanks and infantry to the Reich Chancellery via Wilhelmstrasse and Friedrichstrasse. I got up to go. 'Where are you going?' asked the Brigadeführer.
>
> 'To get the rest of the Battalion going in ten minutes, then we'll be gone.'
>
> 'I don't want you to move from here, you can't stand. Issue your orders and keep quiet at the headquarters!'
>
> 'Brigadeführer, it's impossible to remain here, while all of my men are in action.'
>
> 'I consider it above all impossible for you not to obey my orders', replied the Brigadeführer curtly, 'Don't insist!'[20]

Fenet went and sat in a corner where he quickly scribbled out orders for von Wallenrodt and handed them to Douroux to take to him.

With panzerfäuste, the French SS troops shot up one tank attack after another. Each time they broke up an attack the Russians would instantly renew a punishing artillery bombardment. Their ammunition stocks seemed inexhaustible. Time and time again the defenders were buried when roofs caved in, when floors gave way, and when buildings collapsed, but they seemed spirited as ever.

Uscha. Puechlong of the 1st Company decided to rejoin Weber. Previously, he had served with the *Compagnie d'honneur*. Liaison had become a serious problem again. To redress this, Weber ordered a patrol to reconnoitre Wilhelmstrasse in the direction of the Chancellery. Volunteers immediately came forward and one of them was Puechlong, who wanted to 'stretch his legs a bit'. A German NCO, who knew the capital well, led the patrol.

---

18    Fenet, *Die letzte Runde…*, p.14. However, according to Georgen, *Sur les traces du Sturmbataillon de la division 'Charlemagne'*, magazine 39/45, part 1, p.26, von Wallenrodt led a patrol towards Wilhelmstrasse to establish a picture of the situation.

19    Fenet, *Die letzte Runde…*, p.14, repeated by Mabire, *Mourir A Berlin*, p.234. However, according to Saint-Loup, *Les Hérétiques*, p.450, Rostaing commanded the second (anti-tank) commando despatched to Belle-Alliance-Platz, but Rostaing makes no mention of this assignment in his book.

20    Fenet, *Die letzte Runde…*, p.14. For the record, both Mabire and Saint-Loup have slightly different wording for the conversation.

In single file, the patrol left. Suddenly it came under fire from a Soviet anti-tank gun only eighty to one hundred metres away. Caught in the open, the patrol was decimated: of the eight men, only two escaped death and they were seriously wounded.

Puechlong was one of the 'lucky' two. When he came round he was lying in the middle of the road and so he tried to make for cover under a porch but crumpled to the ground again. It was only then that he realised the extent of his injuries. Shrapnel had lacerated his leg and his foot was virtually hanging off. Blood was pouring along his leg. Calmly, he took a leather lace from his belt and tied it around his leg as a tourniquet.

Puechlong was joined by another French SS soldier, whose chest had been ripped open by shrapnel. They called out to their comrades, perhaps some 200 to 300 metres away, to come and collect them, but they could not make themselves heard over the din of battle. The sound of explosions and gunfire were their only company.

Still out in the open, Puechlong tried to drag himself to shelter, but the fear of losing his foot was too great and he stopped. A boy suddenly appeared, looked at them and ran off.

Then an old, fragile woman showed her face. Although Puechlong could not make himself understood she dragged the two of them into the corridor of a house and then fetched a blanket, but that was as much as she could do for them.

Puechlong gave the old woman his Soldbuch and that of his compatriot, identifying them as SS; they were as good as dead if the Russians found such documents on them. With a puzzled air, she looked at the papers. Puechlong could not explain to her what to do with them. Like his badly wounded comrade, he lost consciousness.

Puechlong awoke to the sound of battle drawing closer. He saw Russian soldiers suddenly appear and as they passed they kicked him to make sure he was dead. Holding his breath, he made no sound. The Russians quickly checked the house and moved on. By now, Puechlong had lost all hope and made up his mind to commit suicide. He searched for his pistol and came across instead the rosary from his first communion that his mother had asked him to keep with him at all times. Hope flooded back and he decided to wait. He was in more and more pain. By now, his comrade beside him was awake. Again the sound of battle could be heard getting louder and louder.

More shadows appeared in the corridor. This time they were Rumanian or Hungarian SS troops. As one, Puechlong and his compatriot cried out to them. Saved, they were carried out to a tank in the road and set down on the ground beneath its gun barrel. Their suffering was still not at an end; the fighting was continuing and the infernal noise of the gun firing to cover the withdrawal burst their eardrums.

Finally, the two wounded were lifted onto the tank. Puechlong desperately tried to convince himself that he was not going to lose his foot. The tank set off and so began a long journey of confusion, noise and fear. They were left at a medical post. Eventually, a nurse attended to Puechlong. She did what she could for him: his leg was put in an iron splint and fastened by paper. Several days later, Puechlong underwent an operation to save his leg. Anaesthetic was in such short supply that he only received a reduced dosage. As a result, Puechlong came round too early and heard the doctor amputating his leg with a saw.

Back at Stadtmitte underground station, Fenet and Krukenberg continued to monitor the course of the battle north of Belle-Alliance-Platz by means of runners who bravely risked their lives time and again in their work of liaison. A veil of thick smoke hanging over the city did not help matters. It was all too easy to end up lost.

Time hung heavy for Fenet impatient to rejoin his troops. Nevertheless, he now felt better for the rest. He finally made up his mind to try his luck with Krukenberg who seemed better disposed towards him and who was clearly pleased with the battalion's activities. This time Krukenberg allowed Fenet to leave. After saluting, he turned and quickly made off just in case Krukenberg changed his mind.

Before setting forth to the front line Fenet and Douroux visited Oscha. Hennecart who had just been wounded and evacuated. Hit in the leg and knee during a bombardment, he could no longer stand and was disappointed to be out of action. They promised to keep him some Russians for when he returned!

By now, the French SS troops were in position along Hedemannstrasse. Their right flank extended to Mockernstrasse. Thus, they closed off the three key roads from Belle-Alliance-Platz to the Chancellery, those of Friedrichstrasse, Wilhelmstrasse and Saarlandstrasse.[21]

Led by Fink, Fenet and Douroux made their way through the underground to Kochstrasse station. Surfacing, they cut across blocks of houses in ruins and then down a ladder to a yard below where Weber warmly welcomed them. He showed Fenet into a low-roofed room overlooking Wilhelmstrasse. Putting a finger to his lips, Weber took Fenet by the arm and led him towards a hole in the wall. He said: "Look!" Three metres away stood a knocked out Soviet T-34. The turret bore the fatal hole of the panzerfäust. Flames suddenly appeared from the underside and slowly licked away at the steel carcass. Weber quietly asked: "Isn't it beautiful?" This tank was his handiwork.

Weber reported that so far today five or six Soviet tanks had been destroyed with panzerfäuste and that numerous infantry attacks had been repelled with heavy losses. And all this had been achieved with only Sturmgewehr, panzerfäuste and some MG 42s. The Frenchmen no longer had at their disposal a single tank, a single anti-tank gun, a single howitzer, a single mortar or even a single grenade-launching rifle. In contrast, the Russians seemed to have never-ending squadrons of tanks. To say nothing of their considerable and formidable artillery arm upon which they could always call. On the other hand, their infantry, although great in number, had been rather timid up to now. Fenet found battalion headquarters in a neighbouring room, where he was greeted with cries of joy from the couriers under Roberti who dashed over, surrounded him and started to recount their latest exploits. There seemed to be no stopping them.

Roberti's actions that day once again proved the extraordinary talent he had for close combat. He was soon off. He and his acolytes had spotted a large building occupied by the Russians in numbers. Entering a sewer in Hedemannstrasse, they slipped undetected through a series of interconnecting cellars into the basement of the building, where they started a fire, after which they retired and took up position. Patiently, with Sturmgewehrs trained on the exits, they waited for the building to go up in flames. Minutes later, the building was engulfed in flames and the Russians hurriedly evacuated, but they had reckoned without the waiting Sturmgewehrs that now barked from all sides. Tens of Russians were cut down. It was a veritable slaughter. Grenades 'encouraged' the remainder out who were trying to hide in the building. They too were greeted by Sturmgewehr. All fell one after the other. Over fifty corpses were now scattered

---

21    According to Saint-Loup, *Les Hérétiques*, p.452, 'Weber, Rostaing and de Lacaze' clashed with small enemy units coming up Wilhelmstrasse and drove them back to Belle-Alliance-Platz, but the square was teeming with Russian tanks, guns and troops. Because an attack on the square was out of the question, Hedemannstrasse was then made into a 'line of resistance'.

all around the building and in its entrance. All at battalion headquarters were jubilant. They embraced each other and slapped each other on the back. On his return, Roberti declared: "It's better than the cinema." Fenet called life fine.

A few minutes later, the fifty or so corpses strewn over the road were crushed under the tracks of T-34s launched in another attack that would be 'as furious as it was in vain'.

Reinforcements arrived: some one hundred Main Security Office officials. Most were between the ages of fifty and sixty and yet they were not found wanting in willingness, discipline or courage. This was in sharp contrast to the officers with them, three or four Sturmbannführer, two Hauptsturmführer and five or six other officers, who seemed only capable of traffic control rather than the command of men in street fighting.[22] The reinforcements, although armed with outdated rifles, were a most welcome sight and permitted the French battalion to flesh out its disposition noticeably.

Enemy snipers continued to exact their deadly toll. Appearances at windows and porches, however fleeting, immediately drew fire. The slightest careless movement brought death or serious injury. Oberjunker de Lacaze, who had replaced the missing Labourdette at the head of the 1st Company, fought with 'with astonishing confidence for a debutant' and broke up Russian infantry attacks time and time again, but was stopped by a sniper's bullet that seriously wounded him. Dragged under cover, he was evacuated to a medical post.[23]

Uscha. Roberti and his inseparable 'accomplice' Bicou, who was eighteen and hence the youngest NCO in the Sturmbataillon, ventured onto the rooftops to do battle with Russians snipers overlooking their position. Fenet met the pair when they returned from one foray to stock up on grenades. They explained to Fenet that they had just dislodged several Russian snipers but had run out of grenades to engage the others. As the two of them spoke to Fenet of their rooftop action, they stuffed egg-shaped grenades into their pockets, hung stick grenades from their tunic buttons and slipped them under their belts.

The two NCOs then rushed back to the roofs where they took on a group of Russians hiding behind a line of small chimneys. The Russians gave in first and withdrew, covering themselves with grenades. One exploded near Roberti, wounding him. Blood poured from the grenade splinter he had 'taken' just under his right eyelid. He could barely see. The roof seemed to sway beneath him and he thought he was going to fall into the street below.

Bicou brought Roberti back to battalion headquarters and sat him down in an armchair. Fenet noted that Roberti looked more pale than normal. Although in pain, Roberto soon dozed off. A little later, Bicou took Roberti to the first-aid post with a convoy of wounded. The doctor told Bicou that the right eye was lost and that he did not know if he could save the other. Bicou vowed to make the Russians pay for this. For Roger Roberti, the war was now over.

After returning from the first-aid post, Bicou took up position behind a barricade of rubble. With his finger wrapped around the trigger of a Sturmgewehr, he kept watch. Suddenly, a

22    Mabire, *Mourir A Berlin*, p.251.
23    Fenet, *Die letzte Runde…*, p.19, repeated by Mabire, *Mourir A Berlin*, p.252. However, the manner of de Lacaze's wounding may have been quite different, for according to Saint-Loup, *Les Hérétiques*, p.465, de Lacaze was riddled by hundreds of grenade fragments while attempting to clear the Russians from the first floor of a house whose ground floor the French were holding. Before passing out, he found the strength to pull from his finger the emblazoned signet ring he wore and throw it into the rubble around him to conceal it from the Russians.

Soviet anti-tank shell smashed into the barricade and he was knocked unconscious. His section of runners thought it had just lost its third commander after Millet and Roberti, but Bicou soon came round. After resting for an hour, he was back on watch over a night that proved rather quiet towards its end. Yes, he'd had more than his fair share of luck!

The road outside battalion headquarters was deserted[24] except for the T-34 destroyed by Weber, which continued to burn. Long flames now danced around the steel carcass, 'projecting their violent light against the darkness of the sky that the rose-coloured halo of the fires above the roofs could not dissipate'.

## Sunday 29 April 1945

The onset of daylight brought the Soviet tanks again. The noise from the engines gave them away. Well-placed panzerfäuste quickly brought the first wave to a bloody halt. The success of the Frenchmen was also due in part to the Russians themselves; they continued to commit tanks spaced well apart and this gave the Frenchmen time enough to see them coming and prepare a 'warm' reception for each of them.

After the failure of the first wave, the Russians reverted to blasting at point-blank range those houses occupied by the Frenchmen. Walls collapsed, roofs caved in on the stalwart defenders and, sometimes, a well-placed shot through a window or entrance showered them with earth and debris and plunged them into dusty darkness for minutes. The curtain was now going up on the last act as the Russians attacked all-out. The defenders, pounded non-stop by mortars, tanks and anti-tank guns, had to face several tank attacks per hour. There was no respite as the fighting flared to new heights of ferocity. Nevertheless, the Frenchmen did not lose morale. Defeatism did not exist for them, although they were well aware of how desperate their situation was becoming.

Weber and the men of the Kampfschule struck back at the tank columns again and again. Weber presented Uscha. Vaulot to Fenet. Vaulot already had four tank kills to his name.[25] On a score of three was Uscha. Albert-Brunet. A native of Dauphiné, Roger Albert-Brunet joined the *Milice* in early 1943, attending its national *École des cadres* at Uriage, but in the autumn of the same year he decided to volunteer for the Waffen-SS. He fought in Galicia with the Sturmbrigade[26] and came to Berlin with the *groupe des liaisons* of the Sturmbataillon.

Loudly, Albert-Brunet insisted on laying claim to the next tank to appear. A score of four would equal that of his friend Vaulot. Each wanted his own tank but there were no longer enough panzerfäuste to go round and arguments ensued. The never-ending anxiety over the lack of panzerfäuste necessitated costly sorties to the Reich Chancellery to replenish their supply.

---

24    Fenet, *Die letzte Runde...*, p.19. In contrast, according to Rostaing, *Le Prix d'un Serment*, p.196, the city came to life after the Russian offensive stopped at 2100 hours. Civilians came out of cellars and shelters 'like rats abandoning a ship in distress'. Mindful of the Russians using any guise or means to fall on their positions, Rostaing fired a few bursts into the air to clear the civilians from the road. This would prevent the Russians from mingling with them and turning their positions when they were least expecting it.

25    According to Fenet, *Die letzte Runde...*, p.20, all four had been knocked out in the last twenty-four hours.

26    According to Lefèvre, *Axe & Alliés*, hors-série 1, Albert-Brunet served with the 5th Company.

Audry, an LVF veteran getting on for forty, was mortally wounded attacking his third tank towards the end of the afternoon. He died during his evacuation to the medical post at Stadtmitte underground station.

The harder the Frenchmen resisted the greater the firepower the Russians visited upon them. Fenet's command post became the main bastion of the defence and its walls were expected to fall in on their heads at any moment. The whole house seemed to sway under the impact of each shell. Fenet bowed to the inevitable and the inevitable was that sooner or later they would have to evacuate this increasingly untenable building before they were all crushed or buried. But he delayed the withdrawal for as long as possible because it would have serious consequences; the configuration of the quarter was such that the whole front would have to be pulled back fifty metres and that brought the Russians fifty metres nearer to the Chancellery. And the Chancellery was now only some hundreds of metres away.

Thinking that the Frenchmen were dead, the Russians came with tanks again, but this time without a preparatory artillery barrage. Tens and tens of tanks converged on Hedemannstrasse at the same time. The Russians realised their mistake when two tanks went up in flames and a third was badly damaged. They about-turned and, as soon as they were sat out of panzerfäust range, they began to blast the French positions. Also brought to bear were all their barrels in the sector. Under this avalanche of fire floors disintegrated and caved in. The rooms of Fenet's command post filled with thick dust that gave rise to breathing problems and reduced visibility to fifty centimetres! Parts of the ceiling collapsed, wounding several men.

By now, a gaping hole had appeared in a wall that was right in the Russian tanks' line of fire. This spelled the end. Moreover, the Russians were infiltrating on the left flank and the command post was already under fire from snipers in a large building opposite. Fenet could delay his withdrawal no more but was concerned that he had left it too late.

A Russian oversight answered that concern. The Frenchmen discovered that 'Ivan' had neglected to occupy the basement of the building opposite where large stocks of paper were stored. Couturin, a former Parisian fireman, set fire to the paper with hand grenades. The fire soon caught hold of the building and while the Russians 'played the fireman' the Frenchmen made off.

Although greeted by gunfire and grenades from the Russians in the burning building, the Frenchmen made it across the strip of ruins separating them from their new positions without suffering any losses. Clearly, as hoped, the fire had distracted the Russians. The Frenchmen dug in along Puttkamerstrasse. In this quarter, one house in three remained standing.

Fenet told grenadier Lavest of the Kampfschule to take a badly wounded man to Stadtmitte U-Bahn station and while there to ask Krukenberg for reinforcements and ammunition. Lavest made it over to the underground station, confided his wounded comrade to 'Nordland' medics and passed on Fenet's request to the Brigadeführer, who promised the few resources he still had available and that included a Tiger tank.

Lavest and some comrades boarded the tank loaded with boxes of ammunition and panzerfäuste. The tank rumbled off towards the buildings occupied by Fenet and the Sturmbataillon. The roads were deserted. Suddenly, the tank rocked violently; a large calibre mortar shell had just fallen close by. The blast shredded the Frenchmen at the rear of the tank. Lavest was hit in the small of his back. Jumping from the tank, he accidentally put his right hand on the exhaust pipe, horribly burning himself.

Prostate on the road, Lavest noticed that he was covered in blood; one of his comrades whose face had been blown off had fallen on him. A comrade picked him up, helped him to a house and down steps to a cellar where he fainted. When he came round a young Belgian of the Luftschutz[27] offered to help him get back to Stadtmitte.

The two of them left the cellar and crossed the road, leaping from shell hole to shell hole. They came to the corner of Kochstrasse and Wilhelmstrasse and were about to make their way to shelter behind a destroyed machine-gun carrier when a shell crashed down and exploded on that very spot. Eventually, they made it to Stadtmitte where Lavest was left in the hands of a medic, who gave him an injection. Soon after, he was awarded the Iron Cross 2nd Class and the Wound Badge.

Loaded onto an ambulance, he was transported to another building and taken down to a vast shelter serving as a medical post where he was examined and given yet more injections. He fell into a deep sleep and awoke to a great commotion; the building was on fire and an opaque smoke was filling the room. He was evacuated to the vaults of a neighbouring building, which Lavest believes were those of the Reichsbank. The vaults were full of wounded, including two other lightly wounded Frenchmen, as well as Weber's orderly who was riddled with shrapnel. Days later, after silence descended, he was captured by the Russians.

In haste, the Frenchmen organised combat positions. The new front along Puttkamerstrasse would be easier to defend because a network of inner courtyards provided the Frenchmen with an excellent means of communication that was under cover from the enemy. However, there was one weak spot and that was a house in ruins at the corner of Friedrichsstrasse. It was difficult to watch over and thus quite open to infiltration.

To straighten the front, Fenet counterattacked with the elderly officials of the Sichereitshauptamt. Supported by fire from the Frenchmen, they drove back the Russian infantry infiltrating through the ruins. In the total absence of heavy weapons support, they suffered very heavy losses.

While this furious infantry battle was going on the Russians unleashed another massive tank attack. This time the Russians employed a new tactic. Having realised their error of the previous days, they attacked no longer in staggered single file but in packs of seven or eight abreast, almost track to track. It was a veritable wall of steel. Fortunately for the Frenchmen the rubble strewn on the road reduced the thoroughfare to two tanks at a time and it was at this very spot that Weber's men, panzerfäuste in hand, awaited their arrival. And when the time came his bleary-eyed tank hunters were not found wanting, destroying first time the two lead tanks and so blocking the way to the others following which about-turned. However, the Russians were not done. Moments later, they tried to tow the wrecks to the rear in order to clear the road for the next attack. The shelling resumed. It was heavier than ever. The fighting continued.

Ill at ease, Oscha. Ollivier decided to take up a more advantageous position in a building on the other side of the road. With Strmm. Coulomb and six or so men from his 4th Company, he attempted to cross, but was caught in a violent bombardment. Ollivier and Coulomb found themselves buried under a pile of bricks. Nevertheless, Ollivier managed to pull himself partly

---

27    Either the Luftschutzdienst [Air-raid Protection Service] or Luftschutz Warndienst [Air-raid Warning Service].

out of the rubble, but he was in a bad way: his nose was fractured and his knees crushed. He warned those who rushed over to help him to proceed with great care; he and Coulomb were 'live bombs' for they had on them a primed panzerfäust and grenades that any false movement might explode.

Anxiously, the rescuers started to clear away the bricks one by one. They expected, at any moment, to be blown to bits. After what seemed an eternity to all, the trapped men were free. Coulomb was also in a great deal of pain; his legs had been mutilated. They were evacuated to a medical post located in a hospital basement. Ollivier was operated on. Conducting the operation was a British doctor serving in the Wehrmacht. He did what he could for Ollivier, but this time Ollivier would not be returning to take the head of his company again

## Rostaing uses another of his nine lives

Again there was that distinctive rattle of tank tracks. This time it was a heavy 'Joseph Stalin' tank coming up Friedrichstrasse. From his observation post on the second floor of the building serving as the battalion's command post, Hscha. Rostaing watched this approaching steel monster. He shuddered with fear: only the 88mm gun could penetrate its heavy armour and the Frenchmen only had panzerfäuste. The enemy tank closed rapidly and was only thirty metres away when four pear-shaped panzerfäust cones crashed simultaneously into its tracks. The very next moment the building 'caved in'. Hit on the head by a large beam, he collapsed and was buried alive by the falling rubble. He passed out not before he heard the characteristic sound of the Sturmgewehr.

Because there was no sign of life from Rostaing he was believed to be dead. Rostaing's comrades reported to Fenet that their company commander had just been killed. It was a blow to Fenet who went in person to the scene. He too was now convinced that Rostaing was dead, but he too was wrong.

When Rostaing came round he tried to move his arms and legs. All responded. Thankfully nothing seemed broken. With his hands and feet, he dug himself out of the rubble, emerging to darkness and a sky full of stars. Nobody was about, yet he could still hear the sounds of battle. He wandered around for minutes trying to work out what had happened. He started by thinking that when the tank had exploded it had brought down the building but concluded that the tank had fired at the same moment as it was hit by the panzerfäuste. And the tank shell had smashed into the facade and totally demolished the floor, burying him. Luck, his faithful companion, had not deserted him. It never would.

Rostaing glanced into the road. It was empty and calm. He was at a loss what to do next, but there was no question of surrender. He made out voices coming from the basement and, on recognising that of his old LVF comrade Protopopoff, he hurtled down the stairway and into the battalion's command post.[28] In a rare show of affection, Fenet embraced him. Fenet

---

28 Rostaing, *Le Prix d'un Serment*, pp.199-201. Mabire, Fenet and Saint-Loup also recount the 'death' of Rostaing, but all differ. Firstly, according to Mabire, *Mourir A Berlin*, p.271, both Rostaing and the young de Lannurien were buried alive. In fact, after freeing himself from the rubble, Rostaing dug out his companion. He too was more stunned than wounded. Also, Saint-Loup confirms that both Rostaing and de Lannurien were buried, although the circumstances of the burying differ and no awards ceremony followed their reappearance at battalion headquarters (*Les Hérétiques*, p.474). And

expressed the surprise of all present and offered him a cup of coffee to 'get him back on his feet again before the harsh fighting awaiting them'. Fenet then arranged a brief ceremony to award Rostaing the Iron Cross 1st Class.[29] Rostaing said of this ceremony: "Even today when I think about these moments I get a lump in my throat and my eyes fill with tears. It was marvellous... I will never forget it and I will carry the memory of it to my grave."

Before his comrades, standing to attention impeccably, Rostaing received from Fenet the Iron Cross 1st Class. Fenet, taking three paces back, saluted. Rostaing returned his salute. His comrades responded in kind and then struck up the *Horst Wessel Lied* in French.[30] Uscha. Albert-Brunet, who had just destroyed his fourth tank, was decorated with the Iron Cross 1st Class.[31]

Prior to their parting another tornado hit the building, raising clouds of dust so thick that all were left blind and suffocating, and unable to speak or move. Dazed, they were unsure of where they were. It was minutes before they regained the use of their senses. By now, the Frenchmen had taken on a new appearance. It was not human. Their eyes, deep-set, were bright with fever and their faces, hollowed with tiredness, were caked with dirt and dust.

Water was in short supply. There was little enough for drinking, yet alone for washing or shaving. Supplies from division had been few and far between. Thus, 'they ate what they found when they found it and when they could'. Nevertheless, because of their feverish state, hunger did not torment them.

The past few days of hell had turned them into automatons. Everything they now did seemed as natural to them as any action in everyday life. They snatched sleep when they could and minutes of 'shut eye' seemed like hours to them. Nevertheless, their aggressiveness survived the exhaustion, the hunger and the thirst.

By now, they had lost all notion of time. Dust and clouds of smoke had blanketed the sky. Since the early morning hours of 28 April 1945 they had fought non-stop. Their world was one of endless alerts, bombardments, explosions, fires and ruins. For them, the problem of the future no longer arose. They saw no other future than that to destroy tanks, fire on the Red infantry,

yet, curiously, according to Malardier of the Sturmbataillon, letter to the author, 11/10/98, he met Rostaing shortly after his 'wakening' and Rostaing was all alone. Also, Malardier was beside Rostaing when he rejoined his comrades and de Lannurien was not present. The dates of the 'death' of Rostaing also differ: Saint-Loup and Rostaing record this episode taking place on 30 April 1945 rather than the 29 April as stated by Mabire and Fenet

29   According to Rostaing, *Le Prix d'un Serment*, p.200, Fenet asked him: "Tell me, do you not have the Iron Cross?" His answer was yes, explaining that although he had the certificates for both classes of the Iron Cross he still did not have the medals themselves. However, according to Mabire, *Mourir A Berlin*, p.271, after his 'wakening', Fenet told him that he had just been awarded the Iron Cross 1st Class.

30   According to Rostaing, *Le prix d'un serment*, p.200, the awards ceremony was held in a library and that Fenet was wearing around his neck the Knight's Cross which Brigf. Krukenberg had presented to him. Rostaing is incorrect; Krukenberg disputes the award of the Knight's Cross to Fenet and Fenet is silent about the award of the Knight's Cross in his memoirs of the battle for Berlin.

31   Fenet, *Die letzte Runde...*, p.22, repeated by Mabire, *Mourir A Berlin*, p.271. More French volunteers of the Waffen-SS may have been decorated during this ceremony: Oberjunker Douroux had the Iron Cross confirmed which the 'Nordland' officer had presented to him; Std.Ju. Protopopoff was posthumously awarded the Iron Cross (Saint-Loup, *Les Hérétiques*, p.476); and SS-Ostuf. von Wallenrodt may have received the Iron Cross 1st Class (Georgen, *Sur les traces du Sturmbataillon de la division 'Charlemagne'*, magazine 39/45).

and throw hand grenades... All their energy and all their strength was channelled into holding out and not letting the enemy pass. That was their reason to both live and die.

## French holders of the Knight's Cross

Back at Stadtmitte underground station, Krukenberg felt a growing sense of unease and loneliness: neither he nor Brigf. Mohnke had been summoned to any briefings at Weidling's Headquarters. He did not even have a radio set. His only outside communication and intelligence came from Fenet and Weber who kept him in the picture about the 'front' along Puttkamerstrasse. On learning that Uscha. Vaulot of the Kampfschule had just shot up his eighth tank within twenty-four hours, Krukenberg recommended him for the Knight's Cross.

Born in Paris on 1 June 1923,[32] Eugène Vaulot was among the first to volunteer for the LVF in August 1941.[33] He served with the 1st Company (1942-1943), gaining NCO rank[34], and winning the Iron Cross 2nd Class. While on leave in April 1944 he deserted the LVF for the Kriegsmarine and trained with the 6th Company of Schiffsstammabteilung 28.[35]

Transferred to the forming Franz. Brigade der SS in the autumn of 1944, Vaulot was assigned to the *Compagnie d'Honneur*. He held the rank of Unterscharführer. He went to Pomerania and saw action at Elsenau and Kolberg. Distinguishing himself, he was decorated with the Iron Cross 1st Class. He came to Berlin as the 6th Truppführer [section commander] of the Kampfschule.

During the afternoon of 29 April 1945 Krukenberg bestowed the Knight's Cross upon Vaulot. He conducted the awards ceremony in the presence of his staff and some of Vaulot's comrades assembled in his candle-lit command post at Stadtmitte underground station. In a short address in French, he said that 'the bearing of this young volunteer was what we had come to expect of French soldiers, men who had won their spurs on the battlefields throughout the world'.

After the ceremony, Vaulot said to Rostaing: "I fought with a single desire: to get this decoration. Now it's done. I can die."[36] The newly decorated Vaulot was ordered to lead a patrol to Kaiserhof Hotel in search of table linen for Krukenberg's command post! The Russians were still bombarding the area when the patrol emerged from the underground station and set off to the ruins of the Hotel. On the way, a Sturmmann was hit by shrapnel and taken to a cellar, where the Russians would capture him three days later. The mission went on. The patrol reached

32   The *Journal officiel* of 2/3/48 and birth certificate. According to Landwehr, *Charlemagne's Legionnaires*, p.192, Vaulot was born in 1921. This is incorrect.
33   His occupation has been stated as a plumber-heating engineer (Georgen and Mabire, *Mourir A Berlin*, p.272), an electrician (Landwehr) and a metallurgist (Bouysse).
34   Vaulot gained the NCO rank of Obergefreiter (Landwehr), Sergeant (Mabire) or Caporal (Bouysse).
35   Bouysse, *Encyclopédie de l'ordre nouveau: Français sous l'uniforme allemande partie II: sous-officiers & hommes du rang de la Waffen-SS*, citing Lefèvre. Therefore, Vaulot was not invalided out as a result of sickness or wounds (see Mabire, *Mourir A Berlin*, p.272, and Landwehr, *Charlemagne's Legionnaires*, p.192).
36   Rostaing, *Le prix d'un serment*, p.194. However, Rostaing is mistaken about Vaulot's name, rank and the circumstances of his death. Curiously, according to Saint-Loup, *Les Hérétiques*, p.469, Rostaing was full of bitterness at not receiving the same decoration.

the Hotel from where it returned with dozens of serviettes for Krukenberg, as well as several good bottles of wine that were kept from him.[37]

Krukenberg also said of 29 April: 'The commander of SS-Panzer Abteilung 503, 'Major' [Stubaf.] Herzig, also received the Knight's Cross from the hands of "Major-General" [Brigf.] Mohnke. These were the last two such decorations in this war.'

However, according to one well-respected source,[38] on that same day of 29 April 1945, three other awards of the Knight's Cross also went to members of the French SS-Sturmbataillon, namely Hstuf. Fenet, Ostuf. Weber and Oscha. Appolot. However, in the post-war years, Krukenberg has questioned the authenticity of these awards, awards for which no official wartime documentation exists.

Much has been said of the disputed awards of the Knight's Cross to Fenet, Weber and Appolot. The following three sources are perhaps the most important as they may have been based on eyewitness testimony: Georgen (Lefèvre), Mabire and Saint-Loup.

According to Georgen,[39] Weber was wounded on 29 April and evacuated to the field hospital beneath the Reich Chancellery. 'Like the majority of officers coming down from the front', he too gave a brief description of the situation along the front to Brigf. Mohnke, the commander of Sector 'Z', whose headquarters was in the next room. After hearing Weber's report, Mohnke went to General of Infantry Burgdorf, the chief of the Heerespersonalamt or HPA,[40] and proposed the awarding of the Knight's Cross to several officers and NCOs of the French Sturmbataillon. That same day, General Burgdorf signed off the appropriate 'paperwork' and handed Brigf. Mohnke the certificates and medals. In this way, no more than a few hours after the nominations had gone forward to the chief of the HPA, Brigf. Mohnke decorated Weber with the Knight's Cross.[41]

According to Saint-Loup,[42] Weber was wounded in the early morning of the 30th and evacuated to the 'bunker of the Reichsführer SS' and from there onto the Führerbunker itself. This was his sixth wound of the war. Mohnke came to visit him and told him that Vaulot had received the Knight's Cross and that he, along with Fenet and Appolot, had been awarded the Knight's Cross. Mohnke added that Krukenberg would receive 'the papers' the following day.[43]

Mabire, for his part, recounts that on the afternoon of 29 April, a Scandinavian Obersturmführer from 'Nordland' (possibly Ostuf. Christensen) visited the command post of the French SS-Sturmbataillon. Full of praise for his 'singular neighbours', the 'Nordland' Obersturmführer handed round some bottles of wine he had brought along as a present. He then whispered to Oberjunker Douroux that Hstuf. Fenet had been proposed for the Knight's Cross, but cautioned him not to tell Fenet because it was not yet official. However, Douroux did

---

37    Fenet was only informed on the night of 1-2 May 1945 by one of his runners (Fournier) that Vaulot had been decorated with the Knight's Cross.

38    See Krätschmer, *Die Ritterkreuzträger der Waffen-SS.*

39    See Georgen, *Sur les traces du Sturmbataillon de la division 'Charlemagne'*, magazine 39/45, part 3, which was presumably based on the eyewitness accounts of Brigf. Mohnke, Hstuf. Pachur and Ostuf. Weber.

40    The HPA was the Army Personnel Office. Burgdorf committed suicide on 2 May 1945.

41    Curiously, according to Krukenberg, *Combat pour Berlin*, p.15, on one of the last days of battle, Weber received 'The German Cross in Gold' for destroying his fifth enemy tank in this war.

42    See *Les Hérétiques*, pp.477-478.

43    Saint-Loup explains that the papers were lost en route or never sent (see *Les Hérétiques*, p.478).

tell him (presumably before the end of the war). Fenet would hear no more of a Knight's Cross until years after the war.[44]

Like Vaulot, Robert Appolot was ex-Kriegsmarine, but first he had fought the Germans, going into captivity in that infamous month of June 1940 as a *Sergent-chef* in the *28e régiment d'infanterie de forteresse*. Towards the end of 1942, Appolot became a *Freiarbeiter* [free worker]. He worked at Pillau and Königsberg, but one afternoon his *Schichtmeister* [shift supervisor] caught him with his wife when he came home one hour earlier than normal. Thereupon, he was offered the choice of either joining the Wehrmacht or being sent to a concentration camp. Instead he opted for the Kriegsmarine.[45] Assigned to the 6th Company of Schiffsstammabteilung 28, he underwent basic training at Sennheim from May to June 1944 and then at Duisberg where the company was renumbered 2/28.[46]

In September 1944, Appolot was transferred to the forming Franz. Brigade der SS and assigned to the *Wach-und-Ausb.Kp*. He received the rank of Oberscharführer and the command of a section. He went to Pomerania, where he ably demonstrated his skills as a soldier and as a leader of men, and also proved himself in battle as a man of great personal courage. He came to Berlin as the 2nd Truppführer of the Kampfschule.[47] He was awarded the Knight's Cross for knocking out six Russian tanks.

Although most commentators have him meeting his death in Berlin, Appolot did, in fact, survive the war, keeping a low profile. Remarkably, Appolot was a card-carrying member of the *Parti Communiste Français*.

## The fighting continues

The defensive line either side of the French positions had now been pushed back, leaving them in a salient in the shape of a clenched fist. The Russians stepped up their attacks against the defenders in frequency, ferocity and strength. Dropping with fatigue, the Frenchmen stemmed the northward surge of the Russians time and time again. They no longer kept count of the tank attacks. The Russian infantry, more and more aggressive, abandoned frontal attacks and now attempted to dislodge the defenders by infiltration with grenades and flame-thrower.

If Russian losses were heavy, so were those of the Frenchmen. All had lost friends and companions to death. Only the seriously wounded were evacuated for good: 'the others made do with a makeshift dressing and continued to fight on or would rest several hours at the medical post before returning to take their place'.[48]

The *Junkers* and *Oberjunkers* of the French Sturmbataillon, for the most part very young, had paid a particularly heavy tribute. Labourdette, Le Maignan de Kérangat (1st Company), Cossard, Dumoulin, Billot (2nd Company) and Robelin had been killed. Among the wounded

---

44    Notably, Fenet was silent about the award of the Knight's Cross in his memoirs of the battle for Berlin and later in the article *A Berlin Jusqu'au Bout, Historia* hors série no 32.
45    Gaulois, magazine *Der Freiwillige*, issue 3/97, confirmed by Lefèvre.
46    According to Landwehr, *Charlemagne's Legionnaires*, p.184, Appolot was a platoon commander. In reply, Landwehr is incorrect. While training at Duisburg no Frenchman of the 2/28 was promoted (Soulat, corrections to the author, 2006).
47    According to Landwehr, *Charlemagne's Legionnaires*, p.184, Appolot came to Berlin as a platoon commander in the *Kampfschule*. Again this is incorrect (Puechlong, letter to the author, 24/11/97).
48    Fenet, *Die letzte Runde...*, p.23.

were Michel, de Lacaze, Ginot, Ollivier, Baumgartner, Hennecart, Croisile, Fieselbrand, Frantz, and Boulmier. Frantz was hit by mortar shrapnel in a courtyard and then evacuated in a tent sheet. Douroux and Protopopoff may have been the only French *Junkers* to come this far without a scratch.[49] There was also von Wallenrodt, of late a war correspondent, who, in the words of Fenet, 'remained very calm and very at ease in all this din' and had 'acquitted himself remarkably in his new role as adjutant'.[50] In the opinion of Fenet, his Iron Cross 1st Class was well-deserved. Furthermore, twenty-four-year-old Uscha. Aimé-Blanc, a platoon commander in the Kampfschule was injured and evacuated after a balcony collapsed on him.

Lying in ambush, de Lannurien of the 3rd Company[51] watched a number of Russian tanks approach. He knocked out a Josef Stalin heavy tank with a panzerfaust, but the T-34 following it spotted his firing position on the second floor and fired. The floor collapsed beneath his feet and he ended covered with rubble. Comrades dug him out and were flabbergasted that he was still alive, although he had injuries to his right hand and back. He was taken to the medical post at Stadtmitte, where Krukenberg awarded him the Iron Cross 1st Class.[52]

The fighting did not abate. That evening, Fenet relocated his command post once more, this time to the basement of a library that held magnificent art books.[53] One of the runners discovered a colour book dedicated to Spain, which became the main source of entertainment for those who came, in turn, to rest awhile. They would leaf through its pages of sunny landscapes as if in search of an antidote to their 'visions of hell'. As a former *Khâgneux*, Fenet was furious at the thought of all these books ending up consumed by fire or, worse still, ripped to shreds, trampled underfoot by a band of drunken Mongols.

The battle continued to rage throughout the night, but what was night? Fenet wrote of this:

> Darkness, chased away by this huge inferno that Berlin had become, has totally vanished and only the colour of light varies by the hour. The burning houses and tanks are our torches, and Berlin is illuminated in the fire devouring it. A sinister clarity hangs over the whole city, now suffused with a reddish halo on which the flames rise

49   Dates of Protopopoff's death vary. According to Georgen, *Sur les traces du Sturmbataillon de la division 'Charlemagne'*, magazine 39/45, part 3, p.55, and Bouysse, *Encyclopédie de l'ordre nouveau: Français sous l'uniforme allemande partie II: sous-officiers & hommes du rang de la Waffen-SS*, Protopopoff was killed on the 29 April, according to Mabire, *Mourir A Berlin*, pp.284-285, and Saint-Loup, *Les Hérétiques*, p.479, it was on 1 May 1945, and, lastly, according to Rostaing, *Le prix d'un serment*, pp.201-202, it was on 31 April 1945 (sic). In reply, the author has been swayed in particular by Mabire's account of Protopopoff questioning the prisoner on 30 April and has dated his death after that event but acknowledges that he might have been killed on 29 April instead.
50   Fenet, *Die letzte Runde...*, p.23.
51   Lannurien, François de, *Le sublime et la mort* (Paris: Editions de l'homme libre, 2009) p.123, although he wrote that Rostaing commanded the company after the loss of Michel. To add to the confusion, Mabire states that de Lannurien served with the Kampfschule (*Mourir A Berlin*) whereas Lefèvre believes he served with the 1st Company.
52   De Lannurien, *Le Sublime et la Mort*, pp.117-118. De Lannurien dates these events to 29 April. The author originally reproduced what Mabire wrote of these events (*Mourir A Berlin*, pp.296-297), but the two versions differ: for example, Mabire makes no mention of de Lannurien knocking out a Josef Stalin tank. Also, according to Mabire, it was Weber who pulled him from the rubble. De Lannurien makes no mention of Weber, probably with good reason, because on this same day Weber was wounded.
53   Fenet, *Die letzte Runde...*, p.23.

all around us shedding their violent light. Beneath this tragic fairytale light, the ruins, standing out against the incandescent sky, take on unreal and mind-blowing shapes.[54]

Fenet poetically recounts that the Frenchmen had become actors starring in a cosmic drama. The enemy opposite them were no longer men, but dancing silhouettes with gigantic shadows that the dry crack of their bullets spun round before crashing to the ground, while all around rumbled the noise of battle. The setting of this drama had nothing earthly about it. Sometimes they had the impression that the ground was going to open up and that everything was going to return to chaos ...

With greater and greater fierceness, the Frenchmen fought on in this duel to the death. The Russians brought up more and more tanks and more and more men and fired more and more shells. The air was thick with exploding shells from mortar and artillery bombardments. Although death, injury or captivity seemed the only certainties for the Frenchmen, an almost superhuman determination to hold drove them on. Hold. HOLD. That was the only thought in their minds and on their lips. They would fight to the bitter end.

## Monday 30 April 1945

Although sleep weighed heavy on the most exhausted, those at the library had remained awake and alert all night thanks to the endless hot drinks prepared by the two women they had come across on their arrival at the library.

The Russians started early again. They came with tanks. Panzerfäust in hand, standing in windows, the Frenchmen awaited them. A Russian T-34 charged up Friedrichstrasse. One well-aimed panzerfäust tore the tank apart. It went up in a ball of flame. Then another tank came. It too exploded into a flaming pyre. By the end of the day, Rostaing counted no less than twenty-one burning hulks around the library. Moreover, this cemetery of Russian armour, a barrier of steel and flames, now protected the Frenchmen better than if they were entrenched in a blockhouse.

This victory gave the Frenchmen heart and a victory it was. The Russians had lost twenty-one tanks to a group of men that numbered no more than 25 or 26,[55] but it was to a group of men that, as Rostaing remembers, had defended 'with an energy that I can barely imagine today'. The Russians also had troubles of their own. Fenet recalled:

On the evening of 30 April a Russian is brought to the command post, who had let himself be captured without difficulty: he's a Ukrainian NCO, a big, well fed lad. He brings with him several loaves of bread, which the men share between them with pleasure, because they have not seen the like for several days: in exchange the prisoner is given cigarettes, which seems to please him. Very talkative, he explains to the interpreter that he's Ukrainian and not Russian. Forcibly mobilised, and a ferocious adversary of bolshevism, so much so that we could not have a better friend than himself in the Red Army. Of course we are under no illusions about the sincerity of his good

---

54  Fenet, *Die letzte Runde...*, p.24.
55  Rostaing, *Le prix d'un serment*, p.198. His own command, around eighty-strong six days earlier, now counted six men.

will, but we pretend to listen with interest. Having gained his confidence, he chats with the interpreter, responding at length to the questions casually put to him during the course of the conversation. Today a communiqué has been distributed to the Red lines announcing imminent victory: there's only one square kilometre of Berlin left to conquer, and this last bastion must be taken for tomorrow in honour of the 1 May. Great hilarity greets the translation of these last words: 'Tomorrow, we'll still be here, my friend, and your buddies will be received as usual when they try to pass!'[56]

He recognises that we are giving them a hard time and that morale in his sector leaves much to de desired, but we cannot believe our ears when he adds that the tank crews will only board at pistol point. The interpreter asks with good humour if he's making fun of us. 'Niet! Those getting into lead tanks know that they will not be coming back!'

The Soviet offensive to conquer the last square kilometre of Berlin began in earnest and continued throughout the night and into the morning of 1 May.[57] So the Ukrainian prisoner had not been lying!

The Soviets came with tanks and infantry. The French SS troops let the T-34s approach; they could only engage them at point-blank range. So they poured fire from their Sturmgewehr on the supporting infantry, pinning them down. The Soviet soldiers tried to advance further but did not get far. Helpless, the unshaven and grimy defenders observed the Russians concentrate their tanks barely three hundred metres away. Peacefully, in the shelter of this steel barrier, their infantry now assembled. The defenders bemoaned the lack of guns, mortars and MGs with which they could have broken up the Russians positioning themselves for the kill. All knew what was at stake if they were overwhelmed and crushed: the Reich Chancellery. Even though more and more of their comrades were dead or dying the will to resist of most Frenchmen remained unshaken. For some, however, like *sergent* G. and his friend P., the time had now come to 'demobilise themselves'.[58]

During a particularly violent assault a T-34 managed to break through. For seconds, a terrible anguish gripped the defenders, 'as if a chasm had opened beneath their feet', but the tank was stopped some thirty metres behind their 'line' by a volunteer with a well-aimed panzerfäust shot.

During a quiet moment Rostaing and his friend Protopopoff went out for a breath of fresh air in the ground to the rear of the library. Walking side by side, they chatted away and agreed that they were the last two from the LVF still fighting in the Waffen-SS. Suddenly, Rostaing heard the distinct whistling of an incoming mortar shell. As he took cover he yelled to Protopopoff to flatten himself. The shell fell in the courtyard and exploded. The barrel, behind which Rostaing

56   Fenet, *Die letzte Runde…*, p.25. According to Mabire, *Mourir A Berlin*, p.281, it was Std.Ju. Protopopoff who questioned the prisoner whereas according to Saint-Loup, *Les Hérétiques*, p.485, it was Pachur.

57   Fenet, *Die letzte Runde…*, pp.25-26, and Mabire, *Mourir A Berlin*, p.282. However, not all sources are in agreement. The *Battle Memoir* in *Charlemagne's Legionnaires* and Le Tissier's *The Battle For Berlin* speak of the battle suddenly quietening down at midnight on 30 April and then continuing in a desultory fashion, 'sometimes building up briefly and then dying down again'.

58   Fenet, article *À Berlin, jusqu'au bout, Historia* hors série no 32, p.175. *Sergent* G. was a former legionnaire of the LVF transferred to the Waffen SS.

had taken shelter, was riddled with shrapnel. Uninjured, he got up and saw that his friend was lying on his side, motionless. Rostaing knelt beside him. Protopopoff muttered: "You're the last left." And then he died.[59]

Told of Protopopoff's death, Fenet went at once to the scene of his death where he performed a brief 'funeral' ceremony: he broke in half Protopopoff's identity disc, took his *Soldbuch* and saluted. That was all. Fenet returned to the battle. Protopopoff, is credited with the destruction of five tanks at Berlin, for which he was awarded the Iron Cross 1st Class posthumously.

Death had been the constant companion of the Frenchmen for the past week. The day of 30 April was costly: Protopopoff, Mazoué, the son of a Sorbonne professor, Jacquier, Funel, Duchot... all dead.[60] Few were now left.[61]

## Malardier accompanies Krukenberg to the Reich Chancellery[62]

Hscha. Rostaing had employed Jean Malardier more as a runner than a section commander. Notably, he knew the local area well, having spent over two months (April 1944 to 6 June 1944) hospitalised at Berlin Lazaret Wilmersdorf for bronchial-pneumonia. Malardier had stuck close to Rostaing as though he was his shadow, except for the times Rostaing sent him on secondment as a runner for Krukenberg.

On the late afternoon of 30 April, Malardier was summoned to headquarters. At Stadtmitte, Hstuf. Pachur, Krukenberg's assistant, told him: "We'll escort the Brigadeführer to the Reich Chancellery for the daily conference at 19:00 hours." But then added in a worried tone: "Something bad must have happened at the Reich Chancellery because Brigadeführer Mohnke has specified that not only should the sector commanders attend as normal, but also all the commanders of the fighting units." Listening to Pachur, Malardier also concluded that this smelt of disaster.

On their exit from station Kaiserhof at the corner of Vossstrasse and Wilhemstrasse, they threw themselves on the ground, which experience of the past few days had taught them to do. They picked themselves, bounded forward and threw themselves on the ground again. Shells passed overhead, but some exploded in the street, but they were not hit.

Malardier thought that they were going to enter the new Reich Chancellery through the former at the corner of Vossstrasse and Wilhemstrasse, which was only a matter of tens of metres from station Kaiserhof. But the Führerbunker and the bunkers of the government officials were located behind the former Reich Chancellery, some one hundred and twenty metres away, a distance which seemed endless. He feared that they would be going round in circles in the debris, leaving them exposed.

59   Rostaing, *Le prix d'un serment*, pp.201-202.
60   Saint-Loup, *Les Hérétiques*, p.479. Billot, Cossard and Dedieu are also listed, but Fenet and Mabire have already registered the death of all three earlier in the fighting. Also Mazoué was known to Jacques Evrard of the 3rd Company who was forced to abandon his body on a pavement (see Georgen, *Sur les traces du Sturmbataillon de la division 'Charlemagne'*, magazine 39/45, part 3, p.57).
61   No more than twenty according to Rostaing, *Le prix d'un serment*, p.203, or as many as fifty according to Saint-Loup, *Les Hérétiques*, p.493.
62   Malardier, letter to the author, 31/8/1998. This letter, which counted eighteen pages, would later form the basis of pages 467-490 of his book *Combats pour l'honneur*, although they are differences.

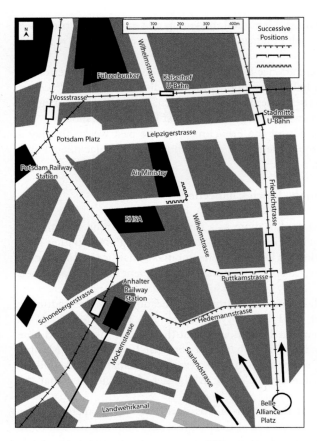

The defence of the Führerbunker, Berlin,
28 April - 2 May 1945

Eventually the three of them made it to the entrance of the Chancellery and were allowed to pass without their identities being checked. After brushing themselves down, they went down the stairs to the underground bunkers, took a gallery on the right in which, after about ten metres, a corridor opened and stopped outside an office bearing a copper plate for Brigadeführer Wilhelm Mohnke where Malardier was told to wait until the end of the conference.

Exhausted, Malardier had to bend himself against the wall so as not to collapse. He then looked around for a seat to rest on for a few moments but could not see any. Too tired to go and look for a seat, he let himself slide down the wall and then stretched out his poor legs across the hallway. As he rested, he was kicked a couple of times in the shins by incessant passerby. He thought it better to get up and resume position, just as an officer appeared through a door at the end of the corridor. Moments later, the officer was upon him. Malardier wanted to jump up and salute him, but he was incapable. The officer was a very young Untersturmführer of the Leibstandarte who was impeccably dressed.

Malardier presented himself to the officer and clarified how he found himself to be here. Expecting to be rebuked for his lack of uniform, he was thunderstruck to hear him say: "Komm mit, Kamerad!" He followed the officer to the door he had left open and found himself before Obersturmbannführer Franz Schädle, the commander of the *Führerbegleitkommando* or FBK, who he instantly recognised from Signal or some other magazine. Malardier presented himself again and repeated the reason for his presence. Schädle beckoned him to sit as he picked up the phone and spoke to Mohnke, telling him that he had the Frenchman with him and then asking him to pass on his compliments to Krukenberg for his success at Neükolln. Malardier no longer had any need to worry.

Schädle asked Malardier for his Soldbuch, which he leafed through. Malardier heard him say 'Was für ein mutiger Kerl!' [What a courageous lad!] to the Untersturmführer, who immediately translated it for Malardier. A conversation followed between the two of them. Schädle complimented Fenet on his tactics near Belle-Alliance-Platz and then Malardier for passing from the LVF to the Waffen-SS without hesitation. Schädle held out his Soldbuch to him. Malardier wanted to get up to receive it, but was told to stay put, after which Schädle complimented the Frenchmen and their comrades in 'Nordland' on a fantastic job 'without which the Russians would already be here'.

Schädle then presented Malardier with a pig skin toiletries bag 'in memory of their meeting', which Malardier warmly thanked him for. With sadness in his voice, Schädle then evoked imminent defeat, describing it as 'the bitter end', an expression he would never forget. There was a moment's silence, which, for Malardier, seemed to last a very long time. Finally, Schädle announced that the Führer had committed suicide earlier that day around 15:30 hours.

The commander of the FBK held out his hand, which Malardier shook with emotion, and murmured: "Gott grüsse sie, mein lieber kamerad!" Malardier returned his salute, but, regulations are regulations, followed up with a Nazi salute and 'Heil Hitler'. Malardier then returned to his post. He would never see Schädle or the young Untersturmführer again. Shortly thereafter, Pachur reappeared. Brigadeführer Krukenberg was going to stay on and the two of them should return to headquarters. Pachur did not speak of Hitler's death and nor did Malardier.

## Tuesday 1 May 1945

At 0700 hours on Tuesday 1 May 1945, Brigf. Krukenberg received a call on his recently installed field telephone at Stadtmitte underground station. On the other end was Brigf. Mohnke. He opened with the news that during the night Colonel-General Krebs, Oberst von Dufving and Lieutenant-Colonel Seifert had crossed the front lines in the sector of Seifert with a view to opening negotiations with the Soviets but could not be more precise about their mission.[63] This, of course, came as a great surprise to Krukenberg.

Mohnke had more bad news: Army Wenck had ceased its attack towards Berlin in face of superior enemy forces and was withdrawing to the river Elbe in very heavy defensive fighting. Also, Krebs and his companions, given a free pass to come and go by the Russians, were not back yet. Mohnke thought that they might be under interrogation in which case the Russians

---

63  Krukenberg, *Combat pour Berlin*, p.17, repeated by Mabire, *Mourir A Berlin*, p.284. However, according to Le Tissier, *The Battle For Berlin*, p.207, with Krebs was von Dufving and an interpreter by the name of Neilands. Also, according to the *Battle Memoir, Charlemagne's Legionnaires*, p.164, Krebs had gone to the Soviet command centre to discuss the surrender of the city. In fact, 'Krebs was to give the Soviet High Command the following information: the Führer's suicide, the contents of his will, a request for an armistice, and the government's wishes to open negotiations with the Russians for the surrender of Germany' (Weidling, diary entry for 30 April).

now knew of the weak spots in the city's defence. One such weak spot was Potsdamer Platz underground station. Still not closed off, it offered an approach to the Reich Chancellery via Vossstrasse. This subway route Mohnke ordered Krukenberg to bar. In addition to this, Krukenberg was ordered to go to the Air Ministry and assume command of 'sub-sector Seifert' that was now without its commander.[64]

As the afternoon wore on the situation of the French SS troops deteriorated. The large building, almost intact when first occupied, was now falling in ruins. Long floorboards hung from the floors into the road, presenting a perfect target for the Russian flame-thrower teams infiltrating through the ruins. Weak on the ground, the French had not been able to stop them nor keep them at distance. After several unfruitful attempts, the Russians finally managed to set fire to this pyre 'so kindly offered to them'. The building was tinder-dry and the flames spread.

Georges, the radio operator and a former Paris fireman, tried to fight the flames as best he could, but without a drop of water he never had a chance. The flames seared through the building. Fenet bowed to the inevitable later rather than sooner: the flames were approaching the last exit when, reluctantly, he gave the order to withdraw. It was now 1800 hours.

The Frenchmen now took up position some tens of metres away in the Sicherheitshauptamt [Main Security Office] at the corner of Wilhelmstrasse and Prinz-Albrechtstrasse. Although this large building was in ruins, its cellars, opening out onto Prinz-Albrechtstrasse, were still very much intact and useable as shelters and gun positions. Soon after, the sounds of a violent infantry battle could be heard from the direction of Saarlandstrasse and Anhalter railway station on their right. The battle ebbed back and forth, but there was only ever going to be one outcome. Nightfall found the French SS troops still ensconced in the Main Security Office. Fenet had installed himself in a vault that served as both a shelter and a place of rest.

In the light of a candle burning on a *Julleuchter*, a Jul Candlestick,[65] symbolising the never dying sunlight,[66] Fenet decorated a number of comrades with the Iron Cross.[67] Although simple, the ceremony that evening seemed all the more extraordinary.

Meanwhile, Krukenberg had been busy. After his early morning conversation with Mohnke, he set about securing his rear area, sending a section of 'Nordland' engineers to block the underground tunnel running from Potsdamer Platz which had been left wide open. Then he left for the Air Ministry. With him was an escort of German and French SS troops. The journey was one fraught with danger.

---

64    Curiously, according to Mabire, *Mourir A Berlin*, p.284, on drawing his telephone call to a close, Brigf. Mohnke commanded that Krukenberg must hold out, stating that they were the Führer's orders. This Krukenberg does not confirm.

65    The *Julleuchter* was a traditional folklore candlestick used throughout the year to mark celebrations, such as New Year's Eve and the Summer Solstice, and commemorations. For more information about the *Julleuchter* as an essential symbol of the SS, see Barger Charles, *The SS family* (Epsom: Ulric, 1998), which is an English translation of the book *The Celebration of Special Festivities in the life of the SS-family* written just after the outbreak of war.

66    Barger, *The SS family*, p.34. For Fenet, the flame of the *Julleuchter* symbolised the victory of light over darkness as well as hope over death (see Fenet, *Die letzte Runde...*, p.27, and Mabire, *La Brigade Frankreich*, p.27).

67    According to Mabire, *Mourir A Berlin*, p.287, the awards came from Krukenberg via a runner. This, however, Krukenberg does not confirm.

As Krukenberg and his small escort crossed Wilhelmplatz they were caught in a violent artillery bombardment, but still managed to make it across. Continuing along Wilhelmstrasse, they drew fire, but again passed unscathed. They came to the Ministry. Outside stood some wagons of infantry munitions, which were not camouflaged. Hit by enemy fire, two of them exploded, showering their contents in all directions.

To the great surprise of Krukenberg, the Air Ministry was not guarded, even though the Russians were only hundreds of yards away. They went down into the cellars and found asleep more than one hundred soldiers of the Luftwaffe under the command of an old General, who was also asleep. Woken, he stated that he obeyed only Luftgau-Kommando Berlin and not the Army Corps of Weidling.

Krukenberg asked the General where the Luftgau-Kommando was. He replied: "At Neustadt-an-der-Dosse." [Neustadt-an-der-Dosse is some seventy kilometres northwest of Berlin!] Krukenberg made him aware of the situation and the immediate Russian threat on his doorstep. Only then did the General post guards.

Krukenberg continued on and came across a young Wehrmacht Hauptmann [Captain] who told him that he had been attached the day before to the headquarters of the Sub-Sector at the Air Ministry and yet Seifert had told him that he had no need of anybody. Anyway, Seifert had locked himself away in an office with his Orderly Officer and was probably busy destroying papers and documents.

Together they went to the sector headquarters, where they could only locate a Luftwaffe Leutnant, the same one Krukenberg had already met on the evening of 25 April. A lively discussion ensued, but the Leutnant refused to tell Krukenberg what had happened the day before or tell him the whereabouts of Seifert even after he had explained his mission to him. However, at that moment, Seifert entered the room, flanked by two French NCOs of Krukenberg's escort, who had found him in another part of the building.

Seifert was 'saved' by a telephone call from Mohnke's headquarters, revoking the order Krukenberg had received earlier that morning.[68] It was all a misunderstanding! Krukenberg returned to his sector towards 1000 hours, not before he had written up a short report on the events of today and asked Seifert once again for the return of the 'Nordland' troops and the French detachment still under his command. In reply, Seifert gestured his helplessness. Contrary to all expectations, 1 May remained quiet in the sector of 'Nordland'. Towards midday, Brigf. Mohnke commandeered the last 'Nordland' Tiger tank.[69]

At 1900 hours, Krukenberg attended the Führerbunker for a real briefing, the word 'real' stressed by the order that summoned him. He took with him the Ia of 'Nordland' and his assistant, Pachur. Brigf. Ziegler, who was still under 'house arrest', greeted him in the antechamber of Mohnke's headquarters and quickly brought him up to date about the latest developments. The Führer had committed suicide yesterday afternoon. Before his suicide he had married Eva Braun, the sister-in-law of Ogruf. Fegelein, who had attempted to flee from

---

68    Krukenberg, *Combat pour Berlin*, p.17. Curiously, according to Mabire, *Mourir A Berlin*, p.295, which is repeated in the *Battle Memoir*, *Charlemagne's Legionnaires*, p.165, the telephone call was from Mohnke.
69    Krukenberg, *Combat pour Berlin*, p.18, Mabire, *Mourir A Berlin*, p.296 and the *Battle Memoir*, p.166. However, according to Saint-Loup, *Les Hérétiques*, p.490, the call came earlier at 1000 hours, and the Tiger tank was not the last.

the Chancellery in civilian clothes and been shot.[70] Joseph Goebbels and his family had also committed suicide. This shocked Krukenberg. Worse still, Army Wenck had stalled days before and the negotiations with the Western allies had ended in total failure. Clearly, this was the end. Krukenberg felt deceived and was to write years later: 'All the sacrifices made by the troops had been in vain. The idealism of the volunteers had been abused in the worst possible way.'

After a long wait, Brigf. Mohnke entered the room, accompanied by Reichsjugendführer Axmann and several others who were not known to Krukenberg. In several short sentences, he confirmed what Brigf. Ziegler had just told him. Then he spoke of General Kreb's night-time attempt to obtain an immediate cease fire in Berlin to prevent any further shedding of blood. This proposal the Soviets had refused, demanding unconditional surrender. Mohnke then asked Krukenberg, as the most senior officer present, if he would continue to assure the defence of the city centre, in which case all available forces would be placed under his command. He refused, describing it as a 'mad idea'.[71]Mohnke raised no objection. Continuing, he explained that there was nothing else to do other than follow an order from Weildling that the Berlin garrison was, in small groups, to try and break through the Soviet encirclement.[72] Each unit would be on its own, moving in the general direction of Neuruppin and then north-west. There would be no rearguard. To prevent chaos, the news of Hitler's death was not to be made public before 2100 hours that evening. Lastly, 'in accordance with General Weidling's order communicated to all sectors', the fighting was to cease at 2300 hours.[73] Deciding to break out with his old command, Ziegler returned with Krukenberg to Stadtmitte underground station. Noting the preparations to evacuate Stadtmitte, de Lannurien, a wounded Frenchmen of the Sturmbataillon, grew worried.

### Night of 1-2 May 1945 and the breakout[74]

Assembling all officers in his underground command post for one last briefing, Brigf. Krukenberg told them that even if they had to split up into small groups to facilitate their breakout then each

---

70    Fegelein was shot on the Führer's orders.
71    Krukenberg, *Combat pour Berlin*, p.18. According to Saint-Loup, *Les Hérétiques*, p.491, Krukenberg refused because he was still very bitter at being excluded from the briefings by Mohnke and Weidling over the past few days. Curiously, a different reason appears in *Battle Memoir, Charlemagne's Legionnaires*, p.166, for 'he was in no mood for any more useless sacrifices'.
72    Ibid. And yet, the *Battle Memoir, Charlemagne's Legionnaires*, p.166, credits Krukenberg with suggesting the breakout in small groups to which Mohnke and Ziegler agreed. However, this claim does not concur with other sources consulted, for example, Le Tissier and Trevor-Roper Hugh, *The last days of Hitler* (London: Macmillan, 1947). In fact, Hitler had given his formal approval for a breakout on the night of 29-30 April. Indeed, Brigf. Mohnke was ready to breakout from the Reich Chancellery the following night, that of 30 April-1 May, but had delayed the attempt by twenty-four hours when the Russians cut the East-West axis on 30 April.
73    Krukenberg, *Combat pour Berlin*, p.18. However, such an order would clearly have placed those attempting to break out in an impossible situation. Indeed, Weidling held back his surrender negotiations until after midnight in order to give the cover of darkness to those attempting to break out (Weidling, pp.173-174). Thus, if such an order was issued, it was not issued by Weidling.
74    The events that transpired during the night of 1-2 May 1945 differ in every source. Needless to say, this will come as no great surprise. Those who attempted to break out were desperate and worn out. It was a question of survival, not of putting pen to paper. Moreover, many of those attempting to break

officer was to remain with his unit. Now that the situation was so critical comradeship was more important than ever.

The commanders were given carte blanche to withdraw their troops from 2300 hours onwards and assemble on Leipzigerstrasse. The frontline posts were to remain manned until midnight so as to mask from the enemy the total evacuation of its positions. At midnight, 'Nordland' was to strike northwards via Charlottenstrasse, Friedrichstrasse and Reinhardstrasse. Use of the underground system was not ruled out, even though Krukenberg regarded it as a 'mantrap'.[75] However, a solid grille prevented passage via the S-Bahn under the river Spree.[76] Once across the Spree, the troops were to pause near the Deutsches Theater in order to regroup and decide the next move. Krukenberg would take up position in Albrechtstrasse and attempt to work out the possibilities with officers who knew the area well.

A little before midnight, Krukenberg set off.[77] With him were his headquarters staff and his French escort. He sent Ustuf. Patzak to the Air Ministry in order to bring back the soldiers of 'Nordland' and the Frenchmen still in this sector. Patzak knew Berlin well, for it was his native city. However, Fenet did not receive Krukenberg's orders to break off the battle and attempt to break out northwards; Patzak disappeared en route from Stadtmitte U-Bahn station to the Air Ministry. The ultimate fate of Patzak is not known.

The roads were choked off with rubble and debris. Vehicles could not pass. Without noise and in good order, 'Nordland' withdrew northwards. Once across the Spree Krukenberg sent two officers, both born locally, to make a reconnaissance, but neither of them returned.[78]

Around 0300 hours, Krukenberg decided to go on reconnaissance himself with his French escort. He thought about going through the Charité Hospital, then along the north bank to Rehberge and exiting the city via Jungfernheide. This idea came to nothing after a doctor came to see him in Schumannstrasse and explained to him that the hospital director had made an

out did not know Berlin and probably did not have maps of the city. Communications, as well, were non-existent. Consequently, to reconstruct a definitive account of that night is now impossible. What follows is Krukenberg's account of that night from *Combat pour Berlin*, which is 'unblemished'. As noted earlier, some sources differ and their version of events can be found in the footnotes.

75   Krukenberg, *Combat pour Berlin*, p.19. Curiously, the *Battle Memoir*, which was based on letters from and an interview with Krukenberg, contradicts *Combat pour Berlin*! According to the *Battle Memoir*, *Charlemagne's Legionnaires*, p.167, Krukenberg 'ruled against its use [the subway] because he was fearful his men might be totally entrapped therein'. In response to this, such a decision to avoid the underground tunnels would seem rather ironic considering that those breaking out of the Chancellery planned to make full use of the U-Bahn and S-Bahn tunnels.

76   Ibid. Of interest to note is that when the first group to break out of the Chancellery, led by Mohnke, came to pass under the Spree through the very same S-Bahn tunnel it found itself stopped by two transport authority watchmen guarding a bulkhead that they refused to unlock. And although armed, Mohnke's group accepted the situation and returned to Friedrichstrasse station to seek another route across the Spree.

77   According to Le Tissier, *The Battle of Berlin 1945*, p.217, Krukenberg was extremely furious at Mohnke who had attempted his breakout before he had been able to fully assemble and brief his troops. Now that the Russians had been alerted, he opted to break out with those troops on hand. Also, according to Georgen, article *Sur les traces du Sturmbataillon de la division 'Charlemagne'*, magazine 39/45, Krukenberg and an advance party moved off very promptly at 2300 hours.

78   According to the Georgen, *Sur les traces du Sturmbataillon de la division 'Charlemagne'*, part 4, magazine 39/45, Brigf. Krukenberg and the advance party reached Weidendamm Bridge, crossed, turned left along the bank of the Spree and then turned up a side street to await the scouts sent out on reconnaissance.

agreement with the Russian command to declare the hospital a neutral zone. So Krukenberg now decided to go via Chausseestrasse and met up with elements of 'Nordland' led by Brigf. Ziegler. In this group were no fewer than four or five holders of the Knight's Cross, including Uscha. Vaulot.

In the meantime, day started to break, exposing the column to enemy artillery. Drawing intense fire, it about-turned in the hope of breaking out via Gesundbrunnen, towards Pankow and from there towards Wittenau. Initially all went well as the column followed Brunnenstrasse north, but when it reached the turning with Lortzingstrasse it was suddenly hit by a barrage of well-aimed mortar fire. They sought refuge in the courtyard of a block of flats only to come under an ever more violent fire. Brigf. Ziegler, who was beside Krukenberg, was mortally wounded by shrapnel and died almost immediately.[79] Others were wounded.

Concerned that they would endanger the inhabitants hiding away in the cellars if they stayed here long, the Scandinavian and French SS volunteers split up and set out again. The group which included Krukenberg and his assistant suddenly came under sniper fire. Faced with no way forward, they made their way back towards the city centre in order to get away from the enemy fire and consider their options.[80] By Ziegelstrasse, Krukenberg came upon the burnt out carcass of the 'Nordland' Tiger tank he had despatched to Mohnke the day before.[81] There was no trace of the crew.

The whole area, including Weidenhammer Bridge, was still clear of the enemy at 0900 hours. To greatly improve their chances of escape, Krukenberg and his men slipped into civilian clothes. It was now 1000 hours.[82] They went north via Schönhauser Allee. And as they made their way out of the city centre they passed one Soviet patrol after another. Wearing identical clothes, they fully expected to arouse the suspicions of the Soviets, but the Soviets took no notice of them; all eyes were fixed on the fronts of the houses from where they seemed to fear some surprise.

In Pankow, Krukenberg entered the house of a railwayman to exchange clothing. Minutes later, after finding something suitable to wear, he went back outside only to discover that his companions were not there. A woman was who told him that the Russians had taken all of them away. And, on the other side of the road, were two Soviets waiting for him. Krukenberg went straight up to them and dangled before them a gold bracelet-watch. They could not resist it and while they argued over possession as he hoped they would he took off, disappearing in the direction of Schönholzer Park, where, for more than an hour, he searched, in vain, for his men. This convinced him that they had been taken prisoner.

Alone, Krukenberg continued on in the direction of Wilhelmsruh, but was stopped and arrested by Soviet artillerymen around 1300 hours. He was taken to the cellar of a nearby house, where a NCO took hold of his Soldbuch and ripped it up, saying: "Not good!" Thereupon, he decided not to disclose his rank or his role in the defence of Berlin.

---

79  Le Tissier and Mabire do not agree; Ziegler is placed with Mohnke's group and his death on either Invalidenstrasse (Le Tissier, *The Battle of Berlin 1945*, p.217) or Albrechtstrasse when advancing behind an assault gun (Mabire, *La Division Nordland*, p.429).

80  Le Tissier is the only source to recount that Krukenberg and the survivors of his group actually joined Mohnke's group in a disused goods yard by Stettiner Railway station sometime in the morning (see Le Tissier, *The Battle of Berlin 1945*, p.220).

81  Both Mabire and Saint-Loup record that this tank was indeed the one behind which Reichsleiter Bormann and his companions took shelter during their attempted breakout.

82  According to Saint-Loup, *Les Hérétiques*, p.465, Krukenberg 'changed identity' at 0800 hours.

After crossing the Spree, those with Krukenberg separated into groups of platoon strength.[83] One such group comprised Weber, twelve or so Frenchmen, including Appolot, Vaulot, and Rttf. Evrard of the 3rd Company, as well as German and Scandinavian SS troops. They went west. Accompanying them were two Tiger tanks.[84] They crossed the Tiergarten but ran into strong Russian resistance along the main road through Charlottenburg. The tanks smashed through, but Vaulot was killed.[85] The survivors dispersed.

Evrard clung to Weber. He had joined him in the belief that his chances of escape would be better with a German commander, who would not know his way about Berlin. Weber now ordered those still with him to take to the ruined buildings. All too soon they found themselves encircled. Their situation was hopeless. After holding off the Russians for several hours, they made their bid to escape. Some got through the Russian net and out of Berlin. Others were not so lucky. As for Evrard, he dashed across the road, rushed into a house, went down a corridor and opened a door only to find a Russian seated peacefully. Surprise was total and mutual. By the time the Russian reacted and fired a burst in his direction, he was already back across the road and running towards the house where he had been holed up since dawn.

In the course of the afternoon a Soviet tank took up position in front of the house defended by the German and French SS troops. The tank brought its gun to bear, but inexplicably seemed hesitant to fire. German civilians suddenly appeared from the cellars, surrounded the SS soldiers and beseeched them to cease fighting. Rather than fight on, they choose to lay down their weapons. Evrard had thought of changing into civilian clothing but dismissed the idea in favour of remaining together with his fellow compatriots in uniform. After destroying arms and ammunition, they went out to surrender.

## The strange case of Reichsleiter Bormann[86]

Still in great pain, François de Lannurien decided to go to the Chancellery to get his hand treated, which proved relatively easy to reach. Admitted to the Führerbunker, he was bandaged up, although nobody was presently available to remove the grenade splinters from his hand that were causing him more and more pain.

Two nurses brought in a stocky man who had just been seriously wounded in the face, near an eye, and who was bleeding profusely. De Lannurien noted that this newcomer was given

83  Saint-Loup, *Les Hérétiques*, p.494.
84  Saint-Loup, *Les Hérétiques*, p.495.
85  Ibid. According to the *Battle Memoir, Charlemagne's Legionnaires*, p.167, Vaulot fell victim to a sniper's bullet.
86  Mabire, *Mourir A Berlin*, pp.308-310, and personal conversation with de Lannurien. Years later, following his death, de Lannurien's autobiography *Le sublime et la mort* was published. However, many of the details differ from those told to the author and presumably Mabire. For example, in his autobiography, de Lannurien claims he met Adolf Hitler briefly, who congratulated him on his courage and that of his compatriots, and also exchanged some words with Martin Bormann, who, very soon after, invited him to join his entourage attempting to breakout sheltered behind a tank, whose designation is not named. Anyway, in response to his autobiography, the author has amended some details of de Lannurien's story but has not reproduced those which seem a figment of his ghost writer's imagination.

precedence over the other wounded. De Lannurien did not know the newcomer, but a soldier beside him told him that the newcomer was Reichsleiter Bormann. He was still none the wiser!

Loneliness suddenly gripped de Lannurien. Quite convinced that some of his comrades would still be roaming about in the vicinity of Stadtmitte station, the rallying point, he left the Führerbunker and went in search of them. Shortly after, he joined a small group of men advancing behind a Tiger tank. In the group he thought he recognised this Reichsleiter Bormann.

Combat experience had taught de Lannurien not to stay too close to a tank in battle, an obvious and irresistible target for enemy gunners and tanks. Thus, he followed the Tiger tank at a distance of some twenty metres.

Suddenly, the Tiger tank took a direct hit and exploded. De Lannurien was thrown to the ground, but those nearer the tank were killed, including the individual he believed to be Reichsleiter Bormann. His throat had been ripped wide open by a piece of shrapnel, practically severing the head from the body. De Lannurien decided to make his way to Stadtmitte which took some time.

When he finally reached Stadtmitte he noted that there no guards. Inside the station he came across a wounded Frenchmen who told him that Krukenberg and all the able-bodied men had left and that they were authorised to disguise themselves as civilians. He also came across his good friend Jean-Claude Delage, who he first met and befriended when they were training together at Greifenberg. Delage was in a bad way; his leg was completely mangled.

De Lannurien managed to drag and then carry Delage to a nearby cafe-bar. Delage lowered himself into the cellar while de Lannurien went outside to look for a change of uniform and as chance would have it he came across two dead soldiers of the Wehrmacht. He removed their tunics, after which he scampered back to Delage, who had lost consciousness in the meantime. De Lannurien feared the worst but was very relieved when his friend answered him. Now dressed as soldiers of the Wehrmacht, they awaited their fate. Captured soon after, they were moved to Hotel Adlon, which had been made into a makeshift hospital.[87]

**Fenet and 2 May 1945**

The night of 1-2 May 1945 proved relatively quiet for Fenet and the surviving Frenchmen ensconced in the buildings of the Main Security Office. They had occupied the sector of a neighbouring company, presumably of 'Nordland', which 'had gone on an assignment' for the Chancellery. Douroux was sent to the headquarters of 'Nordland' now located in the Reich Chancellery and reported back that 'all is well'. That evening, they had celebrated the award of the Knight's Cross to Vaulot. 1 May had passed off much more successfully for the Frenchmen than the captured Ukrainian prisoner had predicted the previous evening.

Towards the end of the night, the Frenchmen found themselves out on their own again. Patrols were sent out. They confirmed beyond all doubt that nobody was to their left or their right. Somewhat later, another patrol brought back the alarming news that the front line was now running level with the Luftfahrministerium [Air Ministry] at the corner of Wilhelmstrasse

---

87   Jean-Claude Delage had his leg amputated and went into exile to Córdoba, Argentina in the late 1950s, where he died shortly after.

and Leipzigerstrasse behind them. Exposed, Fenet took the decision to pull back to the Air Ministry, 'the last defendable position before the Chancellery'.[88]

Carrying what arms and ammunition they could, the Frenchmen pulled back to the Air Ministry. No problems were encountered. Contact was made with the forces of the Luftwaffe holding the building. No sooner had they taken up position than cars appeared from enemy lines flying white flags. Sat side by side in the cars were German and Soviet officers. They spoke of capitulation. Unarmed Red Army soldiers then approached them, offering cigarettes. Some Luftwaffe soldiers even started to fraternise. Other Reds appeared from behind German lines.[89]

The Luftwaffe Major commanding the soldiers in the Air Ministry went up to Fenet and announced his intentions to surrender. "It's all over", he added. "The capitulation has been signed." Fenet could not believe that it was all over. That was impossible. Nevertheless, despite a quite magnificent display of dedication and bravery, they had lost.

Fenet decided to go and see at firsthand what was happening at the Reich Chancellery. Defiantly, he thought to himself, 'And if there is one last square to form, it's there that we will form it.' Besides, to remain at the Air Ministry would be to foolishly invite capture.

Again they picked up their weapons and boxes of ammunition. Each carried a panzerfäust across his shoulder. They left the building without responding to the Russians warmly calling out to them to lay down their weapons. An unnerving silence had descended over the city. The road was swarming with civilians and unarmed German soldiers. Fenet took to the ruins to avoid contact with marauding Russian patrols.

Bringing up the rear was Rostaing. Suddenly a Russian appeared beside him. Lost in thought, he had not seen or heard him approach. The Russian ordered him to throw down his weapon. His response was to run off in the direction taken by his comrades.[90] There was no shot. He rejoined Fenet and continued on through the silent ruins.

Via an air vent, they entered the underground system that offered them their best chances of survival and also of reaching the Reich Chancellery undetected. In this way, they came to Stadtmitte U-Bahn station, of late Krukenberg's command post. There was not a living soul to be seen. They continued on to Kaiserhof U-Bahn station, across from the Chancellery.

Arriving at the station, they noted an iron ladder that went all the way up to a ventilation grill at road level. Fenet went up first and recalled:

88  Saint-Loup, *Les Hérétiques*, p.493.
89  Fenet, *Die letzte Runde...*, p.29, and repeated by Mabire, *Mourir A Berlin*, p.315. However, according to Saint-Loup, *Les Hérétiques*, pp.499-501, when Fenet arrived at the Air Ministry, it was packed full of military, paramilitary and party personnel in a rainbow of uniform colours, but all seemed to be without fight. Told that the Führer was dead, Fenet answered haughtily that he did not believe a word of it. Then he went off to speak to the commanding officer, a Colonel, about organising the fight. He found him busy getting a white flag sewn together. The Colonel told him the war was over, adding they would capitulate at 0800 hours. Overwhelmed, Fenet returned to his men. Behind a pillar he surprised two of them burning their papers. He said nothing. Day broke. The roads started to fill with civilians. Then the Red Army soldiers approached them, offering cigarettes.
90  Rostaing, *Le prix d'un serment*, p.205. Also, according to Saint-Loup, *Les Hérétiques*, p.502, Rostaing lost his revolver to the Russian. It was a magnificent American colt which he had 'spirited away' from a *Milicien* at Wildflecken.

Going up, I listen attentively in hope of hearing the sounds of battle, but there's only a confused sound of klaxons and moving trucks. Still some steps, but at last I can see! With my hands clasping the ladder, my eyes absorb this spectacle ahead from which my whole body retracts. As far as the eye can see, Russians, vehicles with the Red star going in all directions. Not a single shot, the Chancellery walls are mute. There's nobody around. It's all over.[91]

Fenet came back down without saying a word. For those below, it had been an agonising wait for news. They surrounded Fenet, who announced that the Russians were everywhere and that the Führer was certainly dead. Their heads lowered silently.

Despair gripped some. A young Uscha. asked Rostaing if they should don civilian clothes. His reply was typical of the professional soldier he was: "We did not come here to disguise ourselves." Even so, the realisation of defeat had brought him to tears. Nevertheless, he added: "We will continue."

For Fenet, the only solution was to get out of here and then to try and break out in the direction of Potsdam where Army Wenck should be. He intended to make use of the underground system for as long as he possibly could and then take advantage of night to complete the rest of the journey. All agreed with him. They still lived in hope: the distance from the Chancellery to Potsdam was less than that from Körlin to the river Oder.[92]

Without making the slightest noise, they now made for Potsdamer Platz. They had to climb over fallen debris and sometimes dig their way through collapsed sections with hand or bayonet, but they kept going. At Potsdamer Platz, a 'cruel deception' awaited them: scouts reported that the underground continued over ground, making it impossible to follow because it would soon be midday. And so it was decided to hide out in this underground maze and wait for nightfall before trying their luck again.

The Frenchmen split into small groups and vanished from sight one after another. One of the tunnels opening under a bridge arch cluttered with fallen debris and assorted objects offered them excellent hiding places. Some old men of the Volkssturm arrived, who had the same idea as the Frenchmen. Slow to hide, they attracted the attention of a Soviet patrol that arrived unexpectedly moments later. The first to be captured cried out: "Don't shoot! Don't shoot!" The Russians then proceeded to search the whole area and small groups of Frenchmen were discovered one after another.

The search, however, was not thorough. Fenet, von Wallenrodt, Douroux, Georges Giana[93] and Bicou went undiscovered: cleverly, they had hidden themselves behind a pile of wicker baskets. From there, with their heart in their mouth, they had witnessed the capture of their comrades. All of a sudden the wicker baskets parted and Albert-Brunet slipped in beside them, murmuring: "I want to stay with you. This is not the time to leave!" He stayed. The search was continuing. They held their breath each time the Russians passed by. Their hearts were racing.

91   Fenet, *Die letzte Runde…*, p.28.
92   Ibid. However, according to Rostaing, *Le prix d'un serment*, p.206, the Russians had invested the underground system and were firing on them. This left the French survivors with no other choice than to disappear into the underground tunnels. Furthermore, Rostaing writes that they were pursued part of the way.
93   Georges Giana was born on 20 April 1920 in Agen (department Lot-et-Garonne). He was ex-LVF.

On several occasions the Russians actually stopped before this pile of wicker basket but looked no further. Fink was captured in turn some ten metres from them and was heard to shout out to his comrades: 'Surrender as National Socialists.'

The prisoners were assembled, counted and recounted by a Russian officer and then marched off. Fenet looked at his watch: only one hour had passed. He wondered when night would fall. Suddenly, the sound of footsteps and voices: yet more Russians. The enemy was returning. This time the search was much more thorough. Nonetheless, twice they passed the hideout of Fenet and the other survivors. Squeezed up against one another, the six Frenchmen felt like hunted animals. However, they did not give up hope.

The end came very suddenly. With rifle butts and boots, the Russians smashed their way through the shield of wicker baskets and 'pounced' on the six Frenchmen. They were searched and stripped of their possessions: watches first, then weapons! The time was after 1500 hours.[94]

The prisoners were dragged outside. Lorries full of Russian troops, who were singing and playing the accordion, were criss-crossing Potsdamer Platz. Groups were staggering about blind drunk. One Russian called out to the French SS prisoners as they passed by: 'Hitler kaputt!" With a bitter grin, von Wallenrodt replied: 'Ja, Hitler kaputt!' Another promised them the charms of Siberia. Others pretended to shoot them down with invisible rifles, yelling: 'SS ... Puk! Puk! Kaputt!' Yet another, who noticed that Fenet was limping, deplored his comrade who had only managed to wound Fenet in the foot instead of blowing his head off. 'The scalp dance begins', commented Fenet.[95]

The guards marched the prisoners away. Marching beside Fenet was Albert-Brunet. A drunken Red grabbed him by the arm and dragged him off towards a neighbouring house, but one of the guards was quick to intervene and brought his prisoner back to the column.[96] Albert-Brunet said to Fenet: 'I had a narrow escape.'

The drunken Russian, however, was not to be denied his revenge and came running back, grabbed hold of the young Frenchmen once again, drew his pistol and, screaming: 'SS! SS!', fired point-blank. Albert-Brunet fell at Fenet's feet with a hole in his temple. Noting that the prisoners were slowing, the guards hurriedly pushed them forward. The prisoners continued on their way.

The prisoners were marched past the Chancellery, 'their last hope', which was being looted by Red Army soldiers. Hundreds and hundreds of tanks flying Red flags were parading from the Tiergarten to the Brandenburg Gate whose disfigured silhouette defiantly reared up towards the grey sky.

Rostaing and sixteen other French survivors were captured at Potsdamer Platz around midnight. A voice woke them with an ultimatum: either they surrender or the station would be blown up. When they did not reply the ultimatum was repeated in French. They looked at each

94    Saint-Loup, *Les Hérétiques*, p.508.
95    Fenet, *Die letzte Runde...*, p.30.
96    According to Saint-Loup, *Les Hérétiques*, p.509, Albert-Brunet had drawn attention to himself because he was wearing on his (right upper) sleeve four silver emblems each denoting the single-handed destruction of an enemy tank or other armoured fighting vehicles. So frightful had been the Russian losses in tanks and crews during the Battle of Berlin that the sight of these emblems would have incensed their comrades.

other. There was nothing else to do. With arms raised, they came out of hiding. This was not the time to antagonise the battle-happy Russian soldiers.

Their watches were taken first, followed by everything in their pockets: papers, photos, money, and jewellery. Their captors repeatedly asked if they were SS or had destroyed tanks. They gave no reply. Hours before, they had ripped off their collar insignia and arm badges, but one of them had forgotten to remove two silver 'tank destruction' emblems on his sleeve. A Soviet NCO saw them and flew into a towering rage, screaming at him, and then punching and kicking him. Suddenly, he drew his pistol and executed him with a bullet in the head.

As for the other prisoners, they were lined up against a wall, convinced that their last hour had come. Rostaing was strangely calm. To his right was an eighteen-year-old volunteer by the name of Kapar. He was crying. He had shown exceptional courage throughout the battle for Berlin, but now his nerves had gone to pieces. Rostaing tried to reassure him.

Just then a drunken Russian officer entered the courtyard, holding a bottle at arms-length. Staggering across, he finally stopped before Rostaing and started to question him in Russian. Thankfully, Rostaing knew the language and explained that they were Frenchmen who had been forced to serve alongside the Germans. Rostaing must have been convincing as the officer ordered those with raised weapons to lower them and move away. The officer then told Rostaing to get his men into a column and follow him. He was only too happy to oblige.[97]

By way of a conclusion, years later, Krukenberg summed up the contribution of the French Waffen SS volunteers to the defense of Berlin:[98] 'Without the Frenchmen, the Russians would have taken Berlin eight days sooner...' Praise indeed, but they are credited with knocking out some fifty Red Army tanks.[99]

97    Rostaing, *Le prix d'un serment*, pp.211-213.
98    Mabire, Chapter *Entretien avec le général Krukenberg*, *Historia* hors série 32, p.137.
99    Krukenberg, *Combat pour Berlin*, p.15. This number, however, does not include those knocked out after 29 April. Thus, the final tally was undoubtedly higher. Indeed, according to Mabire, *Mourir A Berlin*, p.321, in one week of battle for Berlin, Waffen-SS troops knocked out some 800 Russian tanks and armoured vehicles.

**18**

## 'Charlemagne' and its end in Mecklenburg

On the morning of 24 April 1945, with the return of two lorries that failed to make it through from the Berlin-bound convoy, 'Charlemagne' totalled some 700 men garrisoned in and around Neustrelitz.[1] Of this number, 300 were combatants of SS-Bataillon 58 as well as headquarters and support staff. The remaining 400 were workers of the Baubataillon [Construction Battalion]. The revised structure and command of 'Charlemagne' was as follows:[2]

| | |
|---|---|
| Commander: | SS-Staf. Zimmermann |
| Adjoint: | W-Stubaf. Boudet-Gheusi |
| V.O. and office I/C: | SS-Ustuf. Bender |
| Office II/AB: | W-Ostuf. Bénétoux |
| ? | W-Ostuf. Audibert |
| ? | W-Ustuf. Radici (Orderly Officer of Boudet-Gheusi) |

**SS-Bataillon 58**

| | |
|---|---|
| Commander: | SS-Hstuf. Kroepsch |
| Assistant: | Haensel |
| Kompanie 5/58: | W-Std.Ju. Aumont |
| Kompanie 7/58: | W-Ostuf. Fatin |
| Kompanie 8/58: | W-Ustuf. Sarrailhé |

**Baubataillon (unchanged since its formation)**

| | |
|---|---|
| Commander: | W-Hstuf. Roy |
| Assistant: | W-Ustuf. Martres |
| 1 Kompanie: | W-Ostuf. Roumégous |
| 2 Kompanie: | W-Ostuf. Géromini |
| 3 Kompanie: | W-Ostuf. Darrigade |

1  According to Halard, letter to the author of 26/9/98, he left in a second small convoy to Berlin, but got no further than Oranienburg. Thereupon the Frenchmen formed a kampfgruppe with comrades from 'Nordland'. In response to this, curiously, no authors or any other veterans questioned by the author have made mention of a second convoy to Berlin. However, if true, then the figure would be less than that quoted.
2  Soulat, *Historique de la Division Charlemagne*, p.118.

**San-und Vet-Staffel**
Office IV/B:                    W-Ostuf.Dr. Métais
Office IV/D:                    W-Ustuf. Verney

**Fahrkolonne**
Office IV/A:                    SS-Hstuf. Hagen
Office I/B:                     SS-Ostuf. Meier

With Staf. Zimmermann still hospitalised, Stubaf. Boudet-Gheusi commanded the Regiment, which still remained subordinated to the 3rd Panzer Army of Army Group Vistula.

Orders were received to man the anti-tank positions around Carpin and Fürstensee. One company of SS-Bataillon 58 was deployed to Carpin and the two others to barriers at Fürstensee across the Berlin-Neustrelitz road, south of Neustrelitz.[3]

On the morning of 25 April, at anti-tank positions around Drewin, St.Ju. Deconynck and twenty men of the Baubataillon were working away when up drew a convoy of some twenty trucks and out of a car stepped RF-SS Himmler in person. Deconynck presented his men to Himmler who gave him some words of support and encouragement.[4]

On the evening of 26 April, the 3rd Panzer Army radioed 'Charlemagne' that the Soviets had reached the line Prenzlau-Pasewalk. The following day, on 27 April, the front was pierced at Prenzlau. At 1000 hours, Soviet armour was reported in the region of Woldeck, thirty kilometres north-east of Carpin, and Feldberg, fifteen kilometres east of Carpin. In the late afternoon, Stubaf. Boudet-Gheusi relocated 'Charlemagne' headquarters five kilometres westwards from Carpin to the town of Zinow, behind the anti-tank positions. That same day of 27 April, the Construction Battalion was sent to Malchin.

On the morning of 28 April, Rttf. Soulat of the headquarters staff was heartened by the appearance of a Heer panzer division moving forward to Carpin. However, its counterattack towards Woldeck came to nothing. The Soviets continued to advance. That evening at 1800 hours, they occupied the former 'Charlemagne' garrison town of Bergfeld. Thereupon, the headquarters staff filled their last remaining truck with munitions and sent it to the three companies of Bataillon Kroepsch.

Towards 1900 hours, Stubaf. Boudet-Gheusi assembled and separated the sixty men still with him. Thirty or so immediately left on foot through the woods to join Roy and the Baubataillon in the region of Malchin. The remaining thirty awaited the return of the truck to transport them to Neustrelitz. They would not have to wait long.

At 2100 hours, Stubaf. Boudet-Gheusi withdrew 'Charlemagne' headquarters to Neustrelitz and sent the company manning the anti-tank positions around Carpin, now relieved by the Wehrmacht, to rejoin the main body of Bataillon 58 around Drewin and Fürstensee.

The situation was now critical. The Soviets were closing in on Neustrelitz from the south-east and the north. SS-Bataillon 58 or Bataillon Kroepsch started the day of Sunday 29 April positioned as follows:

3    The date of deployment is not known. It may have been as late as 27 April.
4    *Souvenirs* of Soulat.

| Kompanie 5/58: | manning the anti-tank barricades south of Fürstensee across the Berlin-Neustrelitz main road, facing south, with the support of one of the last 15cm S.I.G. [Infantry Gun] |
| Kompanie 7/58: | to the left of Kompanie 5/58 |
| Kompanie 8/58: | facing east astride the road from Fürstensee to Wokuhl |

Kompanie 8/58 saw action, destroying 2 or 3 Soviet tanks.[5] Casualties were taken.[6]

Stubaf. Boudet-Gheusi went to speak with the *Kampfkommandant* of Neustrelitz. He took along Rttf. Soulat of the headquarters staff as an interpreter. However, his services were not required. To their great surprise, the *Kampfkommandant* was, in fact, Oberst von Massow who spoke French. He authorised the withdrawal of Bataillon Kroepsch but insisted that Boudet-Gheusi also obtain the prior agreement of the *Kommandeur* of the German division holding the sector. However, his whereabouts was not known. So off went Boudet-Gheusi in search of him and this phantom division! He was back one hour later. The withdrawal could now go ahead.

Bataillon Kroepsch was duly relieved and, at 1400 hours, left Neustrelitz via the road to Wesenberg. This was the only 'escape route' left open to it. Westwards it retreated, with the Russians in pursuit. Air attacks were also the 'constant companion' of Bataillon Kroepsch.[7]

Jean Favereau, who was wounded with the Sturmbrigade in Galicia and no longer fit for combat, said of the battle around Neustrelitz and the end of his unit:[8] 'When the Russians arrived, the rest of my company, eighteen men commanded by *lieutenant* Leune,[9] tried to resist, but many of us were killed and the rest had to withdraw through Germany to Goldensädt where we were made prisoner by the Americans on 1 May 1945.'

Also 'on the road' was the headquarters staff and the *train auto*. The plan was to reach the region of Schwerin and from there continue onto Lübeck and perhaps even Denmark. They managed to make it to Wesenberg where they came under attack from enemy aircraft. Boudet-Gheusi decided to press on, but the airstrikes had inflicted numerous civilian casualties, which Dr. Métais attended. Once he was done, the headquarters staff climbed into the truck and continued on their way to Waren. Enemy planes forced them to stop and hide in a forest where

---

5    Soulat, *Historique de la Division Charlemagne*, p.118. Of note is that Marotel of an unidentified 'combatant' company (presumably of Bataillon 58 because he was armed) and a small group of artillerymen still with artillery guns did brief battle with the Russians at nightfall on 28 April and managed to immobilise a tank before withdrawing (see *La longue marche*, p.79). However, it is not known if these engagements are one and the same.

6    Indeed, according to Landwehr, *Siegrunen* Number 80, at least 133 members of 'Charlemagne' died in combat north of Berlin in April 1945. This remains unconfirmed, but seems extremely high considering that the Regiment could only field 300 combatants.

7    According to Landwehr, *Siegrunen* Number 80, located along the road from Neustrelitz to Wesenberg are at least three mass graves of these victims of the Soviet onslaught. One of them, located next to the roadside contained the bodies of 86 people including 16 French volunteers from SS-Untersturmfuhrer Sarraihlé's 2nd Company/SS-Kampf Btl. 58. It is thought that they had been probably killed in an enemy air attack.

8    Testimony of Jean Favereau which appears in *Ces Franciliens qui ont choisi Hitler*, p.128.

9    Soulat mentions a company commanded by Leune in his memoirs and that Sarrailhé was Kroepsch's assistant. He would go on to state this in *Historique de la Division Charlemagne*, p.118, but would later amend it. The testimony of Favereau supports the notion that Leune commanded a company. Leune died on 12 February 1996.

they met Kroepsch and the companies of his battalion. They pressed on and would drive all night.[10]

The roads were full of soldiers wearing all manner of uniform. It seemed as though every military and paramilitary organisation of the Third Reich was represented. They too were retreating westwards away from the Russians. On the morning of 30 April, 'Charlemagne' headquarters staff and the *train auto* stopped beside a column of concentration camp inmates. There were a number of Frenchmen among them who, after noting their French arm badges, entered into friendly conversation. The prisoners asked for bread, but their compatriots also had none and gave them tobacco and cigarettes instead. One of the prisoners, a former gendarmerie officer deported for belonging to the Resistance, told them: "You are soldiers who risk your life for your ideals". The soldiers informed them that they would soon be liberated by the Russians. They parted.

At midday, 'Charlemagne' headquarters staff and the *train auto* arrived at the town of Malchow. Boudet-Gheusi and Bender went to speak to somebody in authority, who might have information, but could not find such a person. They carried on their way to Nossentin Hütte, some six kilometres to the north-east, where the headquarters of Wallonie was located. Degrelle had already left. Boudet-Gheusi now sent Audibert to make contact with the Baubataillon. Soulat performed night guard duty near the truck. The following morning, the Frenchmen were very much alone, Wallonie having left. Automatic weapons could be heard no more than four kilometres away.

The retreat westwards continued on Tuesday 1 May 1945 under increasing attacks from the air. By that evening, 'Charlemagne' headquarters staff, the *train auto* and Bataillon Kroepsch had reached the region of Schwerin.

In a village east of Lake Schwerin, the headquarters staff were approached by 'POWs of 1939-40'. Wearing a mocking smile across their face, the POWs were quick to inform the headquarters staff that the English had launched an offensive across the River Elbe and that 'the English radio' (arguably the BBC world service) now reported them some thirty kilometres away. After thanking them for the information, the headquarters staff responded that the Russians were only ten kilometres away, which wiped the smile off their face. They too did not want to fall into Russian hands! They ran off to warn their colleagues.

At nightfall, the headquarters staff continued on. Two hours later, the convoy stopped for the night in a village near Bad Kleinen, north of Schwerin.

Early next morning, a German Oberscharführer of the Inspection brought Stubaf. Boudet-Gheusi the news that the English had occupied Bobitz which was only three kilometres away. If true, Lübeck was now of the question. It was. This meant that 'Charlemagne' was completely encircled in a vast pocket between the English and the Russians. And the pocket was contracting by the hour.

Then, via radio, came the OKW announcement that the Führer had just died in Berlin during the fighting for the Chancellery. For Soulat, with the Führer dead, the war was definitely lost. He no longer wished to fight on.

---

10    According to Landwehr, *Siegrunen* Number 80, in a nearby cemetery, there are the bodies of 2 French volunteers that served in the Military Construction Battalion and are thought to have been killed in captivity since they were unarmed.

At 0900 hours, Stubaf. Boudet-Gheusi assembled the fifty Germans and Frenchmen of the headquarters staff still with him. He ordered the Germans to 'try and join any formation of the Wehrmacht' or alternately to try and reach German lines. Soulat wondered to himself where they were going to find German lines. As for the Frenchmen, Stubaf. Boudet-Gheusi gave them the option of surrendering to the English with him or of putting on civilian clothes and trying to pass themselves off as prisoners or repatriated workers.

With emotion, Soulat shook hands with the *Spiess* of the *Stabsquartier*, he had always been decent, and with several other loyal comrades. He chose to surrender in uniform whereas nearly all of the Frenchmen put on civilian clothes. Besides, he bore the SS tattoo which would be discovered sooner or later.

Arms and ammunition that the Germans could not take with them was disposed of in a marsh. Off went the Germans in the direction of nearby woods. At their head was Swiss Ustuf. Bender. They were swallowed up.

In turn, 'the civilians' dispersed. Eight Frenchmen in uniform remained behind in the village to await the enemy. They were Stubaf. Boudet-Gheusi, Ostuf. Bénétoux and Métais, Ustuf. Radici, Hscha. Sergent, Rttf. Mignol[11] and Soulat, and the orderly of Boudet-Gheusi. The hours passed by. Stubaf. Boudet-Gheusi took out his soldbuch and ripped out the page with the Führer's portrait, declaring: "It's better". Then, turning to all, he said: "Be sure to say that you are not SS but *légionnaires*." Soulat, for one, did not have the heart to reply to him but was quite determined to do nothing of the sort. He was SS. Besides, the enemy knew that most of the French volunteers were Waffen-SS.

In the early afternoon, Boudet-Gheusi decided to make haste to Bobitz and surrender to the English. The Russians were just too close to comfort and he had no wish to fall into their hands. The eight Frenchmen followed the railway line to Bobitz. At 1500 hours, they came to Bobitz railway station and a motorcyclist of the English Army who did not even look at them until Boudet-Gheusi called out to him in English. The motorcyclist told them to continue along the same way. Soulat noted to himself that for the second time in five years he was on the side of the defeated.

At the level crossing, they came upon a column of tanks. Presenting himself to an English tank officer as the *chef* of the *Légion des Volontaires Français contre le Bolchevisme*, Boudet-Gheusi asked to be taken to an English General as he wished to defend the interests of his men held as prisoners. He and Radici, a good friend whom he chose to accompany him, were actually taken before a Major who exploded, saying: 'Since you are the *commandant* of the *légion française antibolcheviste*, we're going to take you to Wismar [and] to the Russians who have just occupied the city and you will sort it out with them.'

In disbelief, Boudet-Gheusi even asked himself if this was a joke. However, it seemed all too real when he found himself aboard the superstructure of a tank taking him and Radici to the Communist lines. It was dark now. Needless to say, the two French SS officers decided to escape. Boudet-Gheusi was the first to make a move. He jumped and ran off into the night. Radici was about to follow him but held back after noticing that the following tank had seen Boudet-Gheusi make his escape. The column came to a stop and went in search of Boudet-Gheusi, but he was long gone. As for Radici, reasoning that he was only a simple second Lieutenant and thus

---

11   Victor Mignol was born in 1911 in Charité-sur-Loire (department Nièvre).

of little or no interest, the English released him. Thereafter the two officers joined the mass of anonymous prisoners of war.

And what became of the other elements of 'Charlemagne' on the run from the Russians? Kompanie 5/58 was still some sixty-strong when it arrived south of Schwerin. By now, it was literally sandwiched between the Americans and the Soviets. On 1 or 2 May 1945, after firing off its last bullets at the Soviets, it turned and surrendered to the Americans.

On 1 May 1945, two inhabitants of Neustrelitz came across the lifeless corpses of two Waffen-SS soldiers. Their throats had been cut which suggests that they had been killed after their capture by the Soviets. The two Waffen-SS soldiers were undoubtedly Frenchmen of 'Charlemagne'.[12]

## End of the Construction Battalion

For Ustuf. Martres, life at Drewin with the Construction Battalion was like a prison sentence. He had wanted to go to Berlin, but orders are orders. However, later on, if it were not for his personal intervention then the name of 'Charlemagne' could have been tainted with war crimes. This situation arose when a train from the Swedish Red Cross stopped quite unexpectedly beside the camp of the Construction Battalion and down stepped SS auxiliaries and female deportees from concentration camp Ravensbrück. They started to look around. Martres looked on from the camp. The deportees, wearing blue and white striped suits, seemed in good health. Even so, their arrival disturbed him, for he had no wish to leave himself open to prosecution as a war criminal. He took action. Gun in hand, he led his armed guard of ten men out to confront the SS auxiliaries. He told them that there was nothing for them here and that if they did not move on he would fire. And yes, he meant it. They did not argue. The train whistled. All boarded. The train continued to the north.

During the night of 27-28 April 1945, the Construction Battalion withdrew to Waren, north-west of Neustrelitz. During the exhausting march, Victor Degraeve of its 2nd Company deserted with another Frenchman by the name of Willy Rostopelli. After obtaining civilian clothes from German refugees, they accompanied them to Krakow-am-See, near Güstrow. He went into hiding, and removed his blood group tattoo, even though it left a tell-tale sign.

From Waren, the Construction Battalion retreated westwards through Güstrow. Air attacks inflicted losses. With the Americans and Russians closing in, Hstuf. Roy, on the advice of Ostuf. Géromini, decided to disband the battalion.[13] At that very same moment, American tanks appeared. The battalion scattered. It suffered yet more losses. Another group was surprised and overrun by a Russian vanguard. Such was the ironic end of those who had chosen to continue with the pick and shovel in their hands rather than weapons. René B. of the Construction

---

12    Research provided by Soulat, letters to the author, 5/2/98 and 12/2/98.
13    Soulat was to meet in prison members of the *Baubataillon* who assured him that Roy had already started to negotiate the embarkation of his unit for Sweden with the Swedish consul at Schwerin, but the Russian advance had put paid to its realisation (*souvenirs* of Soulat.) In response to this, Martres, who was with Roy throughout the retreat and when the *Baubataillon* was disbanded, has no recollection of Roy entering into any such negotiations. Undoubtedly, this was nothing more than rumour or wishful thinking.

Battalion was captured by the Americans on 30 April at Bad Kleinen on the north bank of Lake Schweriner See.

In the evening of 1 May 1945, Uscha. Peyret of the Construction Battalion arrived at Schwerin, where he spent the night in a bunker. The following day, he learnt of the Führer's death. Continuing westwards, he was captured by the Americans ten kilometres west of Schwerin. At the end of May, he was handed over to the British at the former concentration camp of Neuengamme.

Unable to make it through a cordon of sentries, Hstuf. Roy and Ustuf. Martres went into British captivity at Bad Kleinen, north of Schwerin. This, however, was not the end of their adventure. Handed a change of clothes and identity papers by German prisoners of war who knew of their situation, they managed to make good their escape. They tried to make it back to France, but four or five days later they were recaptured by French forces. This time it was the end. Martres was to reflect, years later, that he should have stayed and hid out in Germany until such time as the 'coast was clear' to return home.

### To the end with 'Horst Wessel'?

On 20 April 1945, a group of French volunteers of the Waffen-SS joined a kampfgruppe of 'Horst Wessel' commanded by SS-Hstuf. Heinz Dittmann.[14] Unfortunately, no other information has surfaced about this group.

14   See Tieke & Rebstock, *Im letzten Aufgebot 1944-45* volume 1. Dittmann died on 15 June 1998.

# 19

# The French Waffen-SS in the West

## Reorganization at Wildflecken

Having supplied a Feldersatz-Bataillon [Field Replacement Battalion] to fill the depleted ranks of 'Charlemagne', the resultant order of battle of the *französische Ausbildungs-und Ersatz-Bataillon*, also called the *Franz. SS-Grenadier Ausbildungs-und Ersatz-Bataillon*, garrisoned at Greifenberg was as follows:

| | |
|---|---|
| Commander: | SS-Ostubaf. Hersche |
| 1. Ausbildungskompanie: | SS-Ustuf. Schueler |
| Stammkompanie: | SS-Ostuf. Allgeier |
| Rekrutenkompanie: | W-Ostuf. Crespin |

Before the Soviet advance through Pomerania, the French SS Training and Replacement Battalion evacuated Greifenberg and relocated to Wildflecken camp.

At Wildflecken, the battalion joined other various elements of 'Charlemagne' that had not been sent to Pomerania or were still in training. After purging itself of some 250 'undesirable and doubtful' men,[1] the battalion was still some 400 strong.

Strmm. Doutart was transferred from Greifenberg to Wildflecken, arriving on 1 March 1945. At Wildflecken he was surprised to encounter men of the Indian Volunteer Legion of the Waffen-SS, as well as Indian prisoners of war. He noted that there was no animosity between the two groups.

The elderly Ostuf. Louis and some twenty to thirty men from various units returned to Wildflecken on 17 March 1945 after attending a driver's course at SS-Kraftfahrschule I Sbirow in Bohemia.

On 18 March 1945, Feldkommandostelle RF-SS [Field Command Post of the RF-SS] ordered that after four weeks of basic training personnel in the French SS Training and Replacement Battalion at Wildflecken are to be transferred to the field replacement unit of *33. Waffen-Grenadier-Division der SS 'Charlemagne' (franz. Nr. 1)*.

---

1    Soulat, *Historique de la Division Charlemagne*, p.49.

On 20 March 1945, the forty-strong Workshop Company was sent to Fulda railway station, where it was employed to keep the heavily bombed railway system operational. It worked alongside Hungarian soldiers and French POWs. Then, on 22 March, the Frenchmen in field-grey and also in khaki attended to a bombed train carrying cheese. There was cheese everywhere. Of course, all helped themselves: they were hungry and they were French too! However, the scene turned ugly when, for whatever reason, a French SS officer shot dead a French POW. The officer then phoned Wildflecken camp and attempted to justify his shooting of the POW by stating that all his soldiers were stealing cheese. Thus, on the return of the Company to Wildflecken late that night, all were searched. And all, with the exception of one or two men who had come to learn of the officer's phone call and rightly feared repercussions, were found with cheese on them. In this way, almost to a man, the entire Workshop Company was transferred to the Penal Company.

On 25 March 1945, Reichsführer-SS Himmler ordered all trained personnel of the Franz. SS-Gren. Ausb.u.Ers.Btl. at Wildflecken to join the *33. Waffen-Grenadier-Division der SS 'Charlemagne' (franz. Nr. 1)* in the area east of Neustrelitz. This order was to be executed by 31 March 1945.

Meanwhile, the Western Front had collapsed and American forces were fast approaching the camp. On the night of 22 March 1945, the first elements of General Patton's Third Army crossed the Rhine between Mainz and Worms, which was some 130 kilometres away.

On 29 March 1945, the French SS Training and Replacement Battalion was ordered to evacuate Wildflecken.[2] Ostubaf. Hersche, who still intended to try and reach the Division at Neutrelitz, organised the estimated 1,200 French volunteers[3] of the Waffen-SS at Wildflecken into the following units:[4]

- *Marschbataillon* (in French *Bataillon de Marche*) under SS-Stubaf. Katzian made up of five battle-ready companies
- *Sonderbataillon* (in French *Bataillon spécial*)[5] under SS-Stubaf. von Lölhöffel made of an infantry platoon,[6] two *compagnies de travailleurs* [Construction Companies],

2  Soulat, *Historique de la Division Charlemagne*, p.91, Lefèvre & Pigoreau, *Bad Reichenhall*, p.88, Mabire, *Mourir A Berlin*, p.333, Saint-Loup, *Les Hérétiques*, p.393, and Landwehr, *Charlemagne's Legionnaires*, p.170. Furthermore, according to Lefèvre & Pigoreau, *Bad Reichenhall*, p.88, the order was received by telephone to join the remnants of the Division at Neustrelitz.
3  Scherzer states that this number is understandable, although he adds it's 'somewhat high' (see *Sous le Signe SS*, pp.488-489). However, his reasoning is flawed. In his calculation of the number he assumes that the Medical Company and Workshop Company were at full strength. This is unlikely. The Medical Company was destroyed in Pomerania and not fully rebuilt, whereas the Workshop Company remained understrength throughout its existence.
4  Scherzer claims that Hersche reorganised the French Waffen-SS units at Wildflecken as part of Aktion Leuthen of 21 March 1945 (see *Sous le Signe SS*, pp.488-489). No evidence exists to substiante this claim, though.
5  Soulat, *Historique de la Division Charlemagne*, p.112. However, different authors have employed different titles for this battalion: according to Scherzer, *Sous le Signe SS*, p.489, its title was *Rekruten-Bataillon*, according to Saint-Loup, *Les Hérétiques*, p.393, its title was *Bataillon de travailleurs* [Construction Battalion], according to Landwehr, *Charlemagne's Legionnaires*, p.170, its title was 'Special Use'.
6  Lefèvre & Pigoreau, *Bad Reichenhall*, p.89. This same infantry platoon is designated by Oertle, *Volontaires suisses*, p.308, as a *Divisions-Kampfzug* (or in French *section de combat divisionnaire*). Presumably it was

the Penal Company as well as a medical unit[7]

- *Train de combat* and the Workshop Company still under Ostuf. Maudhuit[8]

Counted among the five battle-ready companies of the *bataillon de marche* were the two depot and education companies which had been based at Greifenberg and relocated to Wildflecken late February 1945. The company commanders were SS-Ustuf. Heinrich Büeler, Ustuf. Kreis, Ostuf. Dupeyron and Oberjunker Louis Barellon.[9]

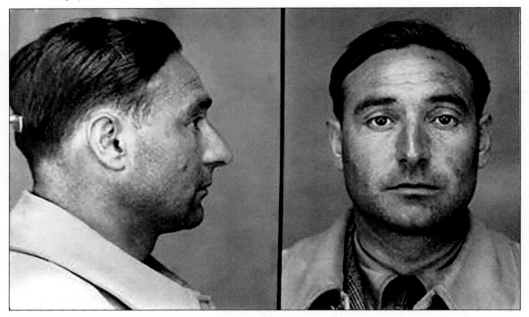

Henri Dupeyron.

Henri Dupeyron was born on 7 August 1909 in Sfax, Tunisia and, in 1936, was commissioned *sous-lieutenant* in the reserves. He was the *inspecteur général* of the *Avant-Garde* of the *Milice* for the North Zone. Transferred to the Waffen-SS, he served with the FLAK Company, but was not deployed to the front. Sent to the *französischen Ausbildungs-und-Ersatz-Bataillon*, he became Hersche's deputy.

---

the only unit of the *Sonderbataillon* to be armed.

7    Ostuf. de Moroge may have commanded the 1st Construction Company.

8    According to Soulat, *Historique de la Division Charlemagne*, p.91, Maudhuit had reached the rank of Hauptsturmführer. However, Bouysse considers this promotion unlikely. See Bouysse, *Encyclopaedia of the New Order: French in German Uniform Part 1: Officers*.

9    According to Bouysse, *Encyclopédie de l'ordre nouveau: Français sous l'uniforme allemande partie II: sous-officiers & hommes du rang de la Waffen-SS*, Barellon commanded the 5th Company. Soulat was unsure (undated letter to the author).

Louis Barellon was the former *chef départemental-adjoint de la Milice* for Jura and had participated in maintenance of order operations.[10] He had welcomed his entry into the Waffen-SS and was sent for artillery training at Beneschau. Assigned to Waffen-Artillere Abteilung der SS 33, he was deployed to Pomerania and fought for Danzig. Evacuated by sea, he was returned to Wildflecken.

Barellon's *adjoint* was Hscha. Marc Dufresnoy, also a former *Milicien*, who may have attained the rank of *chef de trentaine*. He too was assigned to Waffen-Artillere Abteilung der SS 33, deployed to the Eastern Front and fought for Danzig.

The 'Special' Battalion was some 400 strong, but only equipped with two spades and four picks![11] Its morale was low.[12] Ostuf. Henri Victor Louis commanded the Penal Company. Born on 5 February 1898 in Lot-et-Garonne, he joined the LVF in 1944 and was transferred to the Waffen-SS. As previously noted, he was away on a training course when the Division was deployed to the Eastern Front. Of late, the Penal Company had shed itself of fifty men by lorry to Dachau.

Hersche also had at his disposal French officers Ostuf. Dupuyau, Ostuf. Raillard and Ostuf. de Rose. Ostuf. Dupuyau was the former commander of the divisional Signals Company of 'Charlemagne'. He counted himself among those who had managed to make it out of the 'hell of Pomerania' unscathed.

Gaston Raillard was born on 17 December 1911 in Bitche (department Moselle). He entered the *Ecole militaire d'infanterie de Saint-Maixent* in 1936 and graduated with the rank of *sous-lieutenant d'active*. In 1939, he was not mobilised because of poor health. He joined the SOL in November 1942 and passed to the *Milice*. From June 1943 to February 1944, he served as the *Chef départmental-adjoint du Cher* for the South Zone. Transferred to the Waffen-SS, he was appointed Ostuf. on 4 December 1944. He attended Kienschlag from 26 December 1944 to early March 1945, after which he was sent to Wildflecken.

The two battalions and 'odds and ends' have appeared under different titles: *régiment N° 59*,[13] *59e régiment d'infanterie*,[14] SS March Regiment 'Charlemagne'[15] and perhaps *Französisches Ausbildungs-Regiment der SS*.[16] However, none of these titles are supported by official documentation.

---

10   Louis Barellon was born on 24 October 1915 in Saint-Étienne (department Loire). His younger brother, Marc Barellon, served with the *Compagnie d'honneur*.

11   Saint-Loup, *Les Hérétiques*, p.394.

12   According to Scherzer, *Sous le Signe SS*, p.489, new recruits with less than four weeks training were placed into this battalion.

13   While based at Carpin Soulat recalls having heard this designation during a telephone conversation he had with Wildflecken (letter to the author of 8/9/98). Also, see Soulat, *Historique de la Division Charlemagne*, p.91.

14   Saint-Loup, *Les Hérétiques*, p.393.

15   Landwehr, *Charlemagne's Legionnaires*, p.170.

16   Scherzer, *Sous le Signe SS*, p.489, although he accepts that this title is supposition.

## March of the Motorised Column

During the night of 28-29 March 1945, a motorised column under German SS-Ustuf. Neubauer, comprising the *Train de combat* and the Workshop Company, evacuated Wildflecken.[17] The march of this column was as follows:[18]

- Night of 28-29 March: depart Wildflecken camp. Cross the communities of Oberbach, Bad Kissingen and Schweinfurt.
- 3 April: stop at Bamberg.
- 4-12 April: stationed at Bayreuth.
- Evening of 12 April: stop in a village situated 10 kilometres from Truppenübungsplatz Grafenwöhr, north-east of Nuremberg.
- 13 April: Direction Weiden, stop at Schwandorf, where the Frenchmen fraternised with British POWs, after which Neubauer disarmed them and handed their weapons to the local Volkssturm.
- 16 April: Regensburg.
- 17 April: Egmuhl.
- 18-23 April: stop in a village close to Ergolsbach.
- Evening of 23 April: Direction Landshut.
- 24 April: arrive at Landshut.

At Landshut, Neubauer told the Frenchmen that they were going to be put at the disposal of the 38. SS-Grenadier-Division 'Nibelungen' to fight against the French and the Americans. Horrified, Hscha. Boyer decided to desert with two comrades, Oscha. Jean Bordes and Uscha. Claude Willaume.[19] They made their way towards Regensburg and settled down for the night in a barn. In the morning, a French POW surprised them and advised them to get rid of their uniforms. They donned civilian clothes they had on them. Stopped and arrested by suspicious feldgendarmes at Schweinbach, they were not held for long thanks to a false alarm for enemy armour which saw their guards scarper. They continued on foot to Regensburg, meeting American troops on 29 April 1945. They passed themselves off as workers.

## March of Battalion Katzian

During the night of 30-31 March 1945, Battalion Katzian left Wildflecken for Neustrelitz where 'Chalemagne' was reforming. The 'Regiment' was on foot. American armour was now

---

17    According to Scherzer, *Sous le Signe SS*, p.494, the SS-FHA ordered the Workshop Company transferred to SS-Division 'Junkerschule Tolz' [later 38. SS-Grenadier Division 'Nibelungen'] which had been deployed of late to Truppenübungsplatz Grafenwöhr. He explains that the Workshop Company had become redundant now that 'Charlemagne' only consisted of infantry. No other source confirms this, even though the *Train de Combat* and the Workshop were later attached to 'Niebelungen', which might have been more of an impromptu arrangement that circumstances dictated.

18    Courtesy of Henri Mounine. The information is based on the unpublished memories of Émilien Boyer.

19    Born on 20 May 1925, Claude Willaume, a former *Milicien*, served with the 2nd Company in Galicia and later as either a section commander or platoon commander in 2/57. He fought at Kolberg and was evacuated.

less than twenty kilometres away. It retreated to the north-east in the direction of Eisenach. The Battalion marched as follows:

- Bischofsheim an der Rhön
- Weisbach
- Sondheim (possible first stop)
- Ostheim
- Stockheim
- Mellrichstadt
- Eußenhausen (stop)

The Battalion then continued to the north-east through:

- Henneberg
- Bauerbach

On 31 March 1945, Hersche ordered Büeler to cover the 'Regiment' with his company. During the night, Katzian arrived and brought the bad news that Mellrichstadt, barely ten kilometres away, had already fallen to the Americans. He ordered Büeler to check the information. The company moved to Ritschenhausen, arriving at three in the morning. His exhausted men were quartered in a barn. They had lost all fight.

Hearing artillery and tank fire, Büeler went to a vantage point in the church bell tower and spotted American forces coming along the road from Mellrichstadt. Numerous Germans appeared with white flags out of the woods bordering both sides of the approach road and surrendered to the Americans. He sent a runner to his assistant, a young German Untersturmführer, with orders to evacuate to a nearby wood, but the Frenchmen refused to move, such was their exhaustion. The runner reported back. He then decided to change tack. He sent word to his men to stay calm and hide in the hay in the hope that the Americans might roll through the village. Besides he considered resistance pointless and would only result in the village being set alight.

The Americans crossed Ritschenhausen without stopping for over an hour. Suddenly Büeler heard rocket fire from the direction of Suhl. The Americans now stopped. Gunfire resounded. Thereupon, the Americans started to comb the village. Büeler could only look on helplessly as some of his men were taken prisoner.

Still in the bell tower, Büeler received a visit from two young Germans who, fearing reprisals, implored him to give up or, failing that, leave the church; the Americans had made it known that they would burn down the houses of those harbouring German soldiers. Towards midday on the 2 April, he fled the village and reached the nearby woods. As he made his way southwards, at Römhild, he came across some fifty men of his company, as well as German soldiers and two tanks. He took command of them and hastily erected an anti-tank barrier. One or two days later, the panzers left. On the following day, 3 or 4 April, the Americans attacked the roadblock. Pushed aside, Büeler ordered his Frenchmen to surrender and fled south-eastwards.

Büeler managed to reach the Danube, which he swam across, and was captured at Münsterkirchen at the end of April 1945.

Meanwhile, the Battalion continued to withdraw northwards. Realising that the way northwards was now blocked, Hersche went south/south-east.[20] By forced march day and night, and by evading the main roads interdicted by enemy air attacks, the Battalion managed to stay ahead of the American armour. The march of the Battalion continued through:[21]

- Ritschenhausen
- Leutersdorf
- Themar
- Rappelsdorf (third stop)
- Eisfeld
- Sonneberg
- Stockheim
- Reitsch (fourth stop)
- Kronach
- Oberrodach
- Zeyren
- Wallenfels
- Bernstein
- Schwarzenbach
- Culmitz (fifth stop)
- Naila
- Selbitz
- Hof

The Battalion arrived at Hof on 13 April.[22] The exhausted companies now marched southwards to Marktdrewitz, stopping at Niederlamitz and Wunsiedel along the way. On the following day, 14 April, the Battalion took a train from Marktredwitz to the town of Regensburg on the Danube[23] where it was reunited with the Special Battalion. Hersche had received orders from Ogruf. Berger, chief of the SS Hauptamt, to go to the 'Alpine Redoubt'.[24]

20   On 2 April 1945, elements of the American 11th Armored Division bypassed Meiningen, which was attacked and captured on 5 April 1945.
21   Lefèvre & Pigoreau, *Bad Reichenhall*, Chapter 4. However, according to Oertle, *Volontaires suisses*, p.308, after leaving Ritschenhausen, the battalion went to Meiningen. According to Soulat, letter to the author of 29/7/99, after Ritschenhausen, the French column went to Römhild.
22   According to Scherzer, *Sous le Signe SS*, p.495, the rest of the French Regiment was now transferred, like the Workshop Company, to SS-Division 'Junkerschule Tolz'. Again no other source confirms this.
23   Mabire, *Mourir À Berlin*, p.332. According to Saint-Loup, *Les Hérétiques*, p.401, the column boarded a train at Bayreuth, but this is now considered unlikely.
24   According to Mabire, *Mourir À Berlin*, p.333, on 13 April 1945, at Hof, Berger spoke in person to the French SS troops and announced that they would not be going to Mecklenburg, but instead to Bavaria. According to Lefèvre & Pigoreau, *Bad Reichenhall*, p.103, Berger met Hersche on the same day at Marktredwitz. Kreis was undoubtedly Mabire's source. However, his claims should be taken with a pinch of salt. According to Saint-Loup, *Les Hérétiques*, p.402, the attempt to reach Krukenberg at Neustrelitz failed because of the breakdown of the railway network.

## March of the Special Battalion and the medical unit

The medical unit under Hstuf. Dr. Robert Péribère was attached to the *Sonderbataillon*, the Special Battalion. The march of the medical unit, and presumably also that of the Special Battalion, was such:[25]

- Night of 30-31 March: depart Wildflecken. Stop at Nordheim.
- Night of 31 March-1 April (Sunday): stop at Bauerbach
- Night of 1-2 April: Kloster Veβra
- Night of 2-3 April: Crock (Brünn)
- Evening of 3 April: embark at Eisfel-then Sonneberg, Pressig, Naila
- Night of 4-5 April: Naila, Langenbach. Here to Sunday 8 April.
- Night of 8-9 April: Bad Steben, then Bug on Bruck
- Night of 11-12 April: Hof. Depart in the afternoon of 12 April.
- 13 April: embark at Kirchenlamitz, south of Hof, then Weiden, Schwandorf, Regensburg. That same evening arrive at Obertraubling.
- Night of 13-14 April: Obertraubling

By now, the strength of the two French battalions may have dwindled to around six hundred men. It would be unfair to contribute this reduction solely to desertions. The general confusion and the arduous march would have also taken their toll. Battalion Katzian had lost Company Büeler of some 150 to 200 men in a rearguard action. Some, like twenty-year-old Roland Albert, who did not want to go into battle with a company of mainly young and untrained recruits, had deserted to fight with another unit of their choosing. Some sick would have been evacuated. And, lastly, some Frenchmen stayed behind at camp Wildflecken.[26]

The French units separated and continued south. One column with the headquarters staff marched in the direction of Mainburg via Lindkirchen. Some units were billeted around Mainburg, most notably in the village of Sandelzhausen from 17 April. The medical unit had arrived there the night before after two days on the road:

- 14 April to the evening: depart Obertraubling, arrive at Alteglossheim.
- 15 April: Alteglossheim.
- Night of 15-16 April: stop unknown.
- Night of 16-17 April: Sandelzhausen.

The medical unit stayed at Sandelzhausen until the night of 24-25 April.

On 18 April, the Penal Company was disbanded.[27] Strmm. Jean-Jacques Pillet now marched with the 1st Company. On the night of 24-25 April, the medical unit departed Sandelzhausen

---

25  The testimony of Noël Cornu of the medical unit.
26  According to Saint-Loup, *Les Hérétiques*, p.394, the Special Battalion and Penal Company disintegrated. 400 strong at Meiningen, there were 300 left at Eisfeld and 200 at Sonneberg.
27  On that same day, according to Soulat, *Historique de la Division Charlemagne*, p.91 and Oertle, *Volontaires suisses*, p.309, French units fought a delaying action near Wartenberg. Wartenberg is south of Moosburg where French units would only see action on 29 April.

and moved to Mainburg. On the night of 27-28 April, it departed Mainburg and went south to Moosburg. The one hundred men billeted in Sandelzhausen left during the night of 27-28 April 1945, whereas the remnants of the Special Battalion around Mainburg only set off on the afternoon of 28 April. They went southwards, crossing Moosburg to bivouac two to three kilometres south of the town. One column arrived at Moosburg via Landshut to the north-east.

## Moosburg

Moosburg is a small town at the confluence of rivers Isar and Amper. On the night of 28-29 April, two companies of Battalion Katzian, those under Dupeyron and Barellon, reinforced elements of 'Nibelungen' guarding a bridge over the Amper.[28] The Frenchmen were exhausted and badly equipped.

Towards 0900 hours, the first American tank of the 47th Tank Battalion attempted to cross the bridge and was destroyed by SS-Ostuf. Burkhardt of 'Nibelungen' with a panzerfäust.[29] The Americans fired on the other bank with all they had got. Hscha. Albert Vianello of Company Dupeyron, who was armed with a 08/15 machinegun dating from the First World War with only eight cartridges, was wounded again and evacuated.[30]

Several American infantrymen on the bridge were wounded by the first bursts of fire. After they were evacuated, the American tanks of the 47th Tank Battalion and supporting infantry pushed across the bridge, forcing the Frenchmen to retreat. One group of Frenchmen, positioned in a farmhouse, were killed or captured when they attempted to flee. The Americans would later acknowledge that 'resistance was stiff, even fanatic, but short lived' and by 1030 hours '... the SS were lying dead in their foxholes or going to the rear a prisoner ...'[31]

The Americans now entered Moosburg, taking more prisoners, and raced to the bridge over the Isar, which was blown as they approached.[32] Some 6000 German soldiers, including many SS, were taken prisoner at Moosburg. The French units shattered and now went their own way.

Strmm. Pillet, who fought at Moosburg, remembers 30 April well. He was near Erding. Exhausted, he and a good friend took to a farm to rest and changed into civilian clothes. There were also four or five Italian and Russian POWs present. His feet were a bloody pulp, for which the farmer brought him warm water. The following day, the Americans overran Pillet and his

---

28    Lefèvre & Pigoreau, *Bad Reichenhall*, p.117. According to Saint-Loup, *Les Hérétiques*, p.402, Kreis commanded one of the two companies.

29    Soulat, *Historique de la Division Charlemagne*, p.92. However, according to Historian Jim Lankford, as the first tank attempted to move across the bridge it was met with intense small arms fire from SS troops positioned 'on the far side of the stream' and from behind the railway embankment. Thereupon the supporting infantry took cover behind the tank, while the other tanks and infantry took up positions along the bank of the river and returned fire. See Jim Lankford, *The Liberation of Stalag VIIA* and Carter, *History of the 14th Armoured Division, 47th Tank Battalion*, p.37.

30    Soulat, undated letter to the author. According to Bouysse, *Français sous l'uniforme allemande partie II: sous-officiers & hommes du rang de la Waffen-SS*, Vianello was serving with the 5th Company.

31    Carter, *History of the 14th Armoured Division, 47th Tank Battalion*, p.37.

32    Lefèvre & Pigoreau, *Bad Reichenhall*, p.121. Curiously, according to Saint-Loup, *Les Hérétiques*, p.402, the Americans found both French SS companies in position along the Isar and with ammunition for their machine-guns. Saint-Loup continues that they managed to hold for twenty-four hours before they were forced to withdraw. Undoubtedly, some Frenchmen were present when the Americans attempted to take the bridge over the Isar by coup de main, but not two full well-armed companies.

comrade. Pillet noted that the Americans were sympathetic and one of them even told Pillet of his sorrow at what they had done to the German cities, adding that he did not understand why. They advised him to say he was in the German Army! They even asked him to ask the Russian POWs to clean the farm for them. Pillet left the farm on 5 or 6 May 1945.

Grenadier Noël Cornu of the medical unit recalls his continuing march as follows:

- Sunday 29 April: disengage. Towards 2300 hours, depart. Direction Dorfen. Stop from 8 hours to 14 hours - Haaz.
- 30 April: arrive at Wasserburg.
- 1 May: in the vicinity of Rosenheim. Dispersion.

Teaming up with Hscha. Pierre Caucia,[33] Ostuf. Pierre Normand and one other, Cornu went south into the mountains. Their route was:

- 3 May: cross Kufstein, stop in Zillertal
- 5 May: stop at Ginsly
- 6 May: cross into Italy Val di Vizze
- 8 May: Vipiteno, Mezzaselva
- 9 May: Bressanone
- 10 May: Bolzano

Meanwhile, on 4 May, Hstuf. Péribère, the commander of the medical unit who had been hospitalised at Isling, was captured by the Americans.

On 5 May, one group, comprising the remnants of the *Sonderbataillon*, Ostuf. Maudhuit, Ostuf. de Rose and some fifty men who had made for Innsbruck, via Wasserburg am Inn, were captured by the Americans on the east bank of the Chiemsee.[34]

Another group, including Ustuf. Kreis, made for Italy. Ostubaf. Gamory-Dubourdeau, attached of late to the SS Hauptamt in Berlin, joined the group at Innsbruck. Together Gamory-Dubourdeau and the group travelled through the Brenner Pass and onto Bolzano in the South Tyrol.

Oberjunker Barellon, Hscha. Dufresnoy and some comrades also made it to Bolzano via Innsbruck. On the morning of 2 May, Bout de l'An met Barellon and told him that the last *franc-gardes* were fighting against the Italian partisans. He also handed Barellon money for his men. That same day, another group arrived at Bolzano, which included Uscha. Illarthein.[35] They had taken the same route as Barellon. In this way, the number of Frenchmen present at Bolzano numbered around one hundred.

33  PPF member Pierre Caucia volunteered for the LVF and was admitted with the rank of *adjudant-chef*. Notably, he attended and was photographed at the burial of Doriot on 25 February 1945.
34  Soulat, *Historique de la Division Charlemagne*, p.92.
35  Born on 18 May 1907 in Paris, Roger Illarthein joined the MSR in 1941 and volunteered for the KMW two years later. He fled to Germany and transferred to the Waffen-SS. In September 1946, he was sentenced to ten years hard labour by the *Cour de justice* of Charente-Maritime. Released in November 1948, he died in Paris.

588    For Europe Revisited

On 4 May, the Americans entered the city, which was in chaos, and employed German and French Waffen-SS to maintain order, in particular against the threat posed by Communist partisans. On 13 May, the Americans disarmed the French Waffen-SS and put them in a school. Among those present were Ostubaf. Gamory-Dubourdeau, Ostuf. Louis, who Gamory-Dubourdeau proposed for the KVK II on 8 May, Ostuf. Raillard,[36] Ostuf. Normand, Ustuf. Kreis, Oberjunker Barellon,[37] Hscha. Dufresnoy, Hscha. Caucia and Grenadier Cornu.[38]

On 18 May, Cornu was transferred to Bordighera and that night to Nice. On 19 May, he was moved to the repatriation centre at Villefranche-sur-Mer. The *cour de justice* awaited him. One group, comprising elements of Battalion Katzian and the headquarters staff, including Staf. Hersche,[39] went Traunstein, Salzburg, Hallein, Bad Reichenhall, Lofer and Reit im Winkel, where on the night of 8-9 May 1945 it went into American captivity.[40]

Not all of the Frenchmen at Wildflecken went with Hersche. One of those 'left behind' was Strmm. André Doutart, who remembers:[41]

> Towards 15 or 16 April, I ended up isolated with two other comrades as a rear echelon at Wildflecken. There was nothing to do. We then decided to don the tracksuit after having of course unstitched the SS runes.
>
> The American troops approached. We thus left due west hoping to slip through the net and get back to France. One early afternoon, from afar I hear a radio from which was coming the music of Benny Goodman. Being a great lover of Jazz, I had immediately recognised [him]. I approach and see that it is a jeep with 2 or 3 G.I.s. My comrades remain hidden and I go up to the Americans. They are the first who are surprised to 'see' a European speak to them of Benny Goodman and others. So at once he gave me a pass in due form.

And thanks to this pass Doutart managed to make it back to Paris. He was arrested one year later at his home.

36    Interestingly, when captured, Raillard said his unit was the 1st Battalion of Regiment 57.
37    Condemned to death by the *cour de justice* of Besançon on 12 February 1946, Louis Barellon's sentence was later commuted. He was finally released in 1955 and died on 13 October 1993.
38    According to Landwehr, *Charlemagne's Legionnaires*, Gamory-Dubourdeau surrendered to the Americans at Bolzano, having first obtained a concession that none of them would be handed over to their compatriots for one year and implies that the Americans were as good as their word. As such, this is not true: for example, Cornu was handed straight over to his compatriots. However, Ostuf. Raillard was held prisoner by the British for one year and handed over to French authorities in April 1946.
39    Hersche was promoted to Standartenführer on 1 May 1945. On this same day, he was awarded the EK II and also the KVK II.
40    Oertle, *Volontaires suisses*, p.309.
41    Letter to the author via Mouine. However, according to Bouysse, *Encyclopédie de l'ordre nouveau: Français sous l'uniforme allemande partie II: sous-officiers & hommes du rang de la Waffen-SS*, Doutart left Wildflecken with the Franz. A.-u.-E. Btl on 30 March 1945 and took advantage of the situation to desert on 15 or 16 April 1945.

## The Black Forest

In late April 1945, French SS soldiers may have also seen action against the 1st French Army in the Black Forest. The *Journal de Marche* [unit war diary] of the *1e Régiment de Cuirassiers* reads:[42]

> [E]ntering Brotzingen, it is French SS soldiers or French *Miliciens* who 'set upon' *Capitaine* Dorance's tanks, the *Légionnaires* and the infantrymen of the *Bataillon de Choc*. The fire is accurate and the infantry losses are heavy. Leaving Brotzingen, the situation gets worse: the infantry can no longer keep level with the first tanks. At 1500 hours, *Capitaine* Dorance is killed by a sniper, a bullet right in the head, [while] in his turret... The losses are heavy: twenty or so killed, including *Capitaine* Dorance (commanding the *2e escadron*), eighty wounded ...

The possibility exists that the 'French SS soldiers' were Frenchmen of the Brandenburg Division or of SS-Jagdverband Süd-West.

Also, several French SS soldiers fought with SS-Kampfgruppe Schleuter in Montreux-Chateau and Brebotte against the 1st French Army. Stubaf. Max Lelongt, the chief Medical Officer of 'Charlemagne', surrendered to the Americans in Salzburg, Austria in July 1945 and was repatriated to France.

## Bad Reichenhall[43]

On the morning of 8 May 1945, around 1000 hours, twelve French SS troops surrendered without a fight to American troops in Bavaria, who immediately handed them over to the *2ème Division Blindée de les Forces Françaises Libres* (2nd Armoured Division of the Free French Forces) or *2e D.B.* under General Leclerc.[44] The *2e D.B.* was attached to the XXI US corps under General Milburn.

42  This entry was probably based on the report from the *2e escadron du 1e Régiment de Cuirassiers* which reads: 'Entering Brotzingen, numerous sniper fire: it is French SS soldiers or French *Miliciens*. The fire is remarkably accurate and the losses of our infantry are enormous'.

43  Much has been written about Bad Reichenhall, but what follows is solely based on eyewitness accounts. Of note is the inclusion of three such eyewitness accounts not cited before. The first is a letter written in 1985 from former Second Lieutenant Florentin, a platoon commander in the 4th Company/1st Battalion/*Régiment de marche du Tchad* of the *2e D.B.* who witnessed the execution of the prisoners. The second is the transcript of an interview conducted in 1984 with Serge des Bruères, a former serviceman of the *compagnie de commandement* of the *2e D.B.* who guarded the prisoners, albeit briefly, witnessing General Leclerc's interrogation of the prisoners. The third is from a civilian who witnessed the execution of the prisoners. Also, it should be noted that the author has used material from the excellent book *Bad Reichenhall* by Lefèvre & Pigoreau.

44  Letter of 7/2/1946 from *Père* Gaume, former chaplain of the *2e D.B.*, to a country priest in which he forwarded the last letter from Serge Krotoff, one of those murdered at Bad Reichenhall, to his wife. However, according to X.R., article *Fusillés sans jugement, Historia* hors série 32, p.182, the Americans held the Frenchmen with German prisoners in Gebirgsjäger Kaserne [Mountain Troops Barracks] Bad Reichenhall, but on hearing that their guards were to be relieved by the Gaullists, the Frenchmen decided to escape. Crossing the barracks' fence, they made it to a nearby wood, but their escape was

Among the twelve were Ostuf. Serge Krotoff, Ustuf. Robert Daffas, Ustuf. Paul Briffaut, Uscha. Jean Robert and Gren. Raymond Payras.[45] Some, such as Krotoff, were members of the Franz. A.u.E. Bataillon and had undergone the long march from Wildflecken. Likewise, Briffaut had 'marched' from Wildflecken.[46] Others were outpatients from Bad Reichenhall military hospital and carried evacuation cards on their uniform.[47]

The prisoners were brought to General Leclerc's advanced headquarters,[48] which had been set up in a villa in Bad Reichenhall. General Leclerc turned up in person to speak to the twelve French prisoners and reproached them for wearing the German uniform. Words were exchanged.[49] Photographer Henri Malin took five photos of the twelve men.

A Sergeant and Serge des Bruères of the Headquarters Company of the *2e D.B.* were then made responsible for guarding the prisoners and ordered not to speak to them. Even so Serge des Bruères spoke to two or three of the prisoners, most notably Krotoff, warning him: "You are mad to surrender to Frenchmen. Anything might happen! You should put on civilian clothes and try and return to France!" With extraordinary dignity, Krotoff replied: "We are soldiers fighting for their ideals and we will not put on civilian clothes." Indeed, with the exception of perhaps one or two, the prisoners made the best impression on Serge des Bruères. And it was with dignity that all of them faced up to things. They would guard them for about two hours. By now the time was around 1400 hours.

The order was given to have them shot, but it is not known who gave the order.[50] Undoubtedly, the order was given in the full knowledge that the capitulation had been signed at Reims the day

quickly discovered. Two companies of the *2e D.B.* surrounded the wood and recaptured them. In response, this version of events is unconfirmed.

45    Some sources state thirteen men surrendered and were subsequently handed over to the *2e D.B.*, but one of them was spared execution. Allegedly the son of a senior French Army officer, who counted General Leclerc among his friends, he was spirited away by Leclerc in the greatest secrecy and sent back to his father. However, all eyewitness accounts speak of twelve prisoners (Florentin, Serge des Bruères and Gaume). Therefore, there was no thirteenth prisoner.

46    Letters from Mme. Wüthensohn to Mme. Briffaut, January and February 1948, in which she specifies that Paul Briffaut arrived at Sandelzhausen with some one hundred men on 17 April, that he 'lodged' with her, and that he departed for Moosburg during the night of 27-28 April. Therefore, he had not 'retired' to the headquarters of the PPF on the banks of Lake Constance (as stated by Mabire, *Mourir A Berlin*, p.335).

47    Mabire, *Mourir A Berlin*, p.335, and Soulat, *Historique de la Division Charlemagne*, p.124, however the evacuation cards are not visible on the photographs that exist of the twelve prisoners.

48    Of interest to note is that eyewitness *Père* Gaume of the *2e D.B.* wrote the following to doctor Lelongt who had served with the LVF and 'Charlemagne' (letter of 19/4/1958): 'Your comrades surrendered to the Americans who 'found' nothing better than to hand them over to the French... who were, believe it, greatly embarrassed.'

49    Various versions exist of what was said. However, two are important. The first is by Serge des Bruères serving with the Headquarters Company of the *2e D.B.*, an eyewitness, who states that 'the interrogation by Leclerc went off as correctly as possible'. The second is by Father Fouquet also of the *2e D.B.*, the divisional Chaplain, who may have been 'in the know' because of his position and his later involvement. (See the article which appeared in *Deutsche Wochenzeitung*, N° 47, November 1981.) He stated: 'The French SS men had a particularly arrogant air. To a French officer, who had reproached them for having put on the *boche* uniform, they had replied that he himself seemed to be very comfortable in an American uniform.'

50    Many sources claim that General Leclerc gave the order to have the prisoners shot when he met them, but there are no eyewitness accounts to substantiate this claim. However, regarding the order, three

before and hostilities were due to cease later that day at 2300 hours. There was no trial before a military court. The prisoners, however, were granted the succour of a Catholic priest.

On hearing of the decision to shoot the prisoners, Serge des Bruères of the Headquarters Company went with some others to the *2e Bureau* to get them to think it through. The decision was not reversed. Serge des Bruères was later rebuked for his action.

It proved 'one hell of a job' forming a firing squad.[51] Even veterans of the International Brigades refused.[52] Nevertheless, the 4th Company of the 1st Battalion of the *Régiment de marche du Tchad* under Lieutenant Ferrano supplied the firing squad.[53] In the ranks of the 4th Company were many Spaniards of the defeated Republican Army.[54] The 1st Platoon of the 4th Company under Second Lieutenant Florentin was put in charge of guarding and transporting the prisoners to the place chosen for the execution, a clearing in the locality of Kugelbach.

Platoon commander Morvan of the 4th Company told his men:[55] "We have received an order from the headquarters of the division. They are traitors, [and] they have been condemned to death.[56] We are charged with the execution." And so, in the late afternoon,[57] the prisoners were trucked the short distance from Bad Reichenhall to the village of Karlstein and then taken on foot to the clearing. Second Lieutenant Florentin got talking to a *petit gradé* [NCO] and asked him what had prompted him to enlist in the LVF. He replied:

accounts from former servicemen of the *2e D.B.* do exist and are worth recording. First, according to Serge des Bruères of the Headquarters Company of the *2e D.B.*, General Leclerc contacted Paris for orders and received an evasive response. Second, *Père* Fouquet, the divisional Chaplain, told one of the families of the executed that the 'decision was taken at Headquarters by an officer, whose name was not known to him, and after a telephone conversation with General Leclerc' (Soulat, *Historique de la Division Charlemagne*, p.124). Third, according to Boch, also a veteran of the *2e D.B.*, de Gaulle phoned Leclerc to order him to have the prisoners shot for political reasons (see *Le guet-apens de Bad Reichenhall*).

51  Interview conducted with Serge des Bruères of the Headquarters Company of the *2e D.B.*, 13/12/1984.
52  Composed of volunteers from around the world, the multinational International Brigades fought on the side of the Republicans in the Spanish Civil War.
53  Florentin wrote in his letter of 27/5/1985: '*Sur ordre du Lieutenant Ferrano des groupes de quatre furent constitués et les chefs de section désignés.*' Unfortunately, this sentence is ambiguous, but one suggestion is that the firing squad was formed from 'groups of four' soldiers from each of the three platoons of the 4th Company and that each 'group of four' was commanded by its respective *chef de section* [platoon commander]. The three *chefs de section* of the 4th Company were *Sous-Lieutenants* Florentin of the 1st Platoon, Morvan of the 2nd Platoon and Bell of the 3rd Platoon. Lefèvre & Pigoreau state that each of the three platoon commanders commanded a firing squad and that each platoon supplied a firing squad (*Bad Reichenhall*, p.210).
54  Bayle, *De Marseille à Novossibirsk*, p.240, although unconfirmed.
55  Notin Jean-Christophe, *Leclerc* (Paris: Éditions Perrin, 2005), p.332.
56  No written documentation has been found to confirm that the twelve were judged before a military court.
57  Interview conducted with Serge des Bruères of the Headquarters Company of the *2e D.B.*, 13/12/1984. Also Father Gaume wrote to the family of the victims that the execution took place on 8 May 1945. However, in contrast, according to two eyewitnesses whose accounts have appeared since the Helion Books publication of *For Europe*, the twelve were locked up for the night before their execution the following day and the 4th Company of the I/RMT left Bad Reichenall on the morning of 8 May (see Lefèvre & Pigoreau, *Bad Reichenhall*, p.154). Such differences are irreconcilable, but the author is swayed in particular by the accounts of Serge des Bruères and Father Gaume, who, arguably, acted correctly.

My father was killed during the 1914-1918 war on the Belgian front and my mother abandoned me. Taken in by an elderly person living in Lyon, I enlisted in the LVF to help her out financially as best as possible. What I can tell you is that I fought against the Reds but I did not fire on Frenchmen.

This *petit gradé* asked Florentin if he had English cigarettes on him, because he had never smoked them before, and 'if he wished to give him one'. Florentin handed him one.

The prisoners were shot about 1700 hours. According to Serge des Bruères,[58] the execution was 'rotten, very rotten'. The prisoners protested vehemently.[59] One officer shouted: "You do not have the right to shoot me. I'm married. I'm not even French…" Another officer questioned Lieutenant Ferrano on what right they were to be shoot, adding that 'being an officer and responsible for these men he should be shot first'. Second Lieutenant Florentin said of this officer [possibly Briffault]: 'He was an example of courage for all'. And later as this same officer stood before the execution squad he encouraged his men to sing loudly with him the *Marseillaise*.[60]

Of the 'shooting', Catholic priest Maxime Gaume, the chaplain of the XI/64e R.A. of the *2e D.B.*, later declared to one of the families of the executed:

After the decision was made at divisional headquarters to shoot the prisoners without trial, Father Fouquet, the divisional Chaplain, gave me the order to comfort them in their last moments. The young Lieutenant who received the order to command the firing squad did not come from my unit and was completely panic-stricken at having to carry out such an order, even wondering if he wasn't going to refuse to obey. He then made up his mind to do at least all in his power to comfort the last moments of the victims and even received communion with them before the execution.

The eleven [twelve—the author] men were taken by truck from Bad Reichenhall, where the headquarters of the *2e D.B.* was, to Karlstein. Only one refused the help of religion; three of them declared that they had no message to pass on to their family.

The shooting was carried out three times: by groups of four in such a way that the last living fell on their comrades under their (very) eyes. All refused to be blindfolded and bravely fell with cries of '*Vive la France*'. Among the last four were lieutenant Briffaut and, probably, soldier Payras. Following the orders received, I left the corpses there, but I spoke to American soldiers billeted in the vicinity, recommending them to bury the corpses, which was done some days later.[61]

---

58    Interview conducted with Serge des Bruères of the Headquarters Company of the *2e D.B.*, 13/12/1984.
59    Indeed, according to Soulat, *Historique de la Division Charlemagne*, p.124, when the prisoners were told that they were to be shot in the back they protested violently and were allowed to face their executioners. However, the original source of this information is not known. It may well have been Gaume.
60    Letter from Florentin, 27/5/1985.
61    Article *Fusillés sans jugement*, *Historia* hors série 32, p.183. An abridged version of this testimony also appears in Mabire's *Mourir A Berlin*, p.336.

Gaume would later write:[62] 'They were executed simply, without hate, by respectful and distressed soldiers.' Gaume also provided writer René Bail with more details of the execution.[63] One of the twelve men refused 'the help of religion', explaining to Gaume that although he was a believer he had lived his life as a non-believer and that he intended to die as he lived. Also, of the three who had no message to pass on to their family, one stated that he had no parents or friends to write to while another said that he preferred that his family did not know what became of him.

Finally, 'on the day before his departure from Bad Reichenhall, Gaume contacted the local mayor to have the corpses buried, but the mayor wanted to do nothing and sent the *père* back to the American authorities. The US liaison officer to the *2e D.B.* would 'sort out the matter'.'

The execution was witnessed by a local woman, Marianne Fuchs, aged twenty-three, who later testified:

> They arrived with two cars and I thought, my God, what are they going to do? I was with soldiers that I had hidden in my house; they said to me: don't go. But me, I thought why not go and see what's happening...
>
> While hiding, I slipped into the ditch... Two young men asked for [some] water and wood to make a cross. One of them did not want to be blindfolded, the others yes; then they fired. It was terrible. I cried out; fortunately they did not hear me because of the shots, otherwise they may have also killed me...

Notably this testimony contradicts that of Gaume, who testified that all of the prisoners refused to be blindfolded. Today, such contradictions remain irreconcilable.

By the evening of 10 May, the last units of the *2e D.B.* had left Bad Reichenhall. American forces replaced them. Finally, in the presence of an American military chaplain, American soldiers buried the bodies of the twelve.[64] The names of the executed were inscribed on wooden crosses.

Rumours circulating among the civilian population of Bad Reichenhall that a dozen or so French SS soldiers had been shot in the region of Karlstein prompted the local German police to investigate, who confirmed the rumours, naming those responsible as the Gaullist troops of the *2e D.B.* Nevertheless, the police file was closed.

Soon after the shooting, Mgr de Mayol de Lupé and his orderly Henri Cheveau, who were in hiding at Bad Reichenhall, came to Kugelbach and blessed the burial places.[65]

---

62    Gaume, letter to doctor Lelongt of 18/4/1958.

63    See Roch, *La Division Charlemagne*, pp.162-164. There are, however, doubts about the validity of some of the 'new' details. According to Bail, while Father Gaume heard the confession of one prisoner the others chatted with the soldiers of the firing squad 'in an atmosphere of quasi camaraderie'. This is not true. As stated by Second Lieutenant Florentin, the prisoners protested vehemently. Also, according to Bail, a lorry full of troops of the *2e D.B.* appeared during the executions and when one prisoner of the third group cried out '*Vive la France!*' one of the occupants of the lorry thought it good to retort: "Ours is not the same." Others considered this remark out of place. Again this is not true, confirmed by Bail to Paul Briffaut junior in 2004.

64    According to Soulat, *Historique de la Division Charlemagne*, p.124, the bodies went unattended and unburied for three days. If true, this would date the burial to 11 May, the day after the Americans replaced the French at Bad Reichenhall.

65    Bail, *Monseigneur*, *Historia* hors série 32, p.143, and Roch, *La Division Charlemagne*, pp.164-165.

During the winter of 1945-1946, the crosses 'disappeared'. The circumstances are not sinister. The forest around the clearing was the site of considerable felling of trees and unfortunately the trunks were rolled over the graves, crushing or burying the crosses that nobody at the time bothered to replace.

In February 1946, some nine months after the 'shooting', Maxime Gaume contacted the families of the executed direct or through an intermediary to pass on their last letters.[66]

On 6 December 1948, an inquest opened at the demand of Mme Briffaut who was advised by Mme Wüthensohn, with whom her son Paul Briffaut had 'lodged' briefly at Sandelzhausen during the march from Wildflecken. The outcome was inconclusive; nothing precise was obtained concerning the capture and the interrogation of the victims, nor the circumstances preceding and accompanying their deaths.

Finally, on 2 June 1949, the bodies were exhumed from the clearing at Karlstein and transferred to a common grave (with plot number Grupp 11, Reihe 3, Nr. 81 und 82) at Sankt Zeno cemetery, Bad Reichenhall. Inscribed on the graveside cross were four names: Lt Paul Briffault, Lt Robert Stoffart, Sd Raymond Payras and Sd Sergey Krotoff. Notably, only one name is correct: Raymond Payras. Personal belongings found on the exhumed bodies were handed over to the local police.

On 6 July 1963, the bodies were exhumed again and buried this time in front of a wall close to the monument commemorating the dead of the First World War. A commemorative plaque was fixed to the monument and carries the five names of Paul Briffaut, Robert Doffat, Serge Krotoff, Jean Robert, and Raymond Payras. This time, only Doffat is incorrect.

On 25 October 1981, a commemorative cross was erected at the site of the execution.

Of those executed, only five have been positively identified.[67] They are:

W-Ostuf. Serge Krotoff
W-Ustuf. Paul Briffaut
W-Ustuf. Raymond Daffas
W-Gren. Raymond Payras
W-Uscha. Jean Robert

Briffaut was ex-LVF, who went on to command the Infantry-Gun Kompanie of Waffen-Gren. Regt. der SS 58, but in December 1944, due to his war wounds, he was demobilised. When executed he was still in the uniform of the Wehrmacht worn by the LVF. He was a holder of the Iron Cross 2nd Class.

Serge Krotoff was born on 11 October 1911 in Tananarive, Madagascar.[68] Paris was his home. By the time he volunteered for the Waffen-SS, he had behind him years of service at sea as an

---

66    Gaume contacted families Briffaut and Krotoff through the intermediary of a local clergyman. Also, according to X.R., article *Fusillés sans jugement, Historia* hors série 32, p.183, the Catholic priest gave to Mme. Briffaut two small photographs of *général* Leclerc in the presence of the twelve Frenchmen. This is not true. In fact, she received two photographs from Serge des Bruères, which, curiously, were dated 7 May 1945 on the reverse.

67    One of the others executed was known by sight to Mercier, but alas not by name. He too had served with the LVF.

68    As such, Krotoff was not of Russian origin, as stated by most sources. One of his ancestors, attached to the court of the Emperor, acquired French nationality in 1805.

officer in the Merchant Navy. He underwent basic training at Sennheim and then officer training at Kienschlag, graduating in September 1944. He may have been deployed to Pomerania with 'Charlemagne' at the head of the Anti-tank (PAK) Company of the Panzerjäger or 'Heavy Weapons' Battalion.

Born on 13 April 1908 in Auch (department Gers), Raymond Daffas did his military service with the *73e régiment d'artillerie*. Called up when war was declared, he was assigned to the *29e escadron du train* in the Levant, where he was working. After serving two months in prison for his anglophilia, he was demobilised and returned to France. He volunteered for the LVF in November 1941 and was given the rank of *adjutant*. Arriving at the front in May 1942, he was assigned to the Headquarters Company of the III. Batallion. In November of that same year, he was promoted to *adjudant-chef*. Promotion to *Sous-lieutenant* followed in July 1944, after Bobr. Transferred to the Waffen-SS and 'Charlemagne', he was eventually assigned to the Artillery Battalion and saw action in Pomerania.

Raymond Payras was born on 16 December 1922 in Colombo, Sri Lanka. Called up by the STO, he ended up working in Austria. For unknown reasons, he decided to enlist in the Waffen-SS in January 1945. Sent to Greifenberg and assigned to the *compagnie de dépôt*, he was evacuated to Wildflecken. His parents formally identified him.

Jean Robert, who was born on 1 February 1915 at Lyon, enlisted in the *117e régiment d'infanterie* in February 1933, but one month later was discharged because of health problems. Even so he was still mobilised in October 1939. He probably did not see action. After his marriage failed, he moved to La Rochelle and in early 1943 joined the KMW. When hopes of reconciling his marriage were dashed he signed on the dotted line for the LVF on 14 December 1943. His movements thereafter are not known.

In 1979, Pierre Jacques Ponneau, whose rank is unknown, was tentatively identified from a photo of the victims prior to their killing.[69] However, this was later proved to be incorrect.[70] Georges de Taxis du Poet has also been proposed as one of those executed.[71]

In conclusion, the facts are that on 8 May 1945 the *2e D.B.* under General Leclerc did commit a war crime at Bad Reichenhall, however there remain a number of unanswered questions, including:

- Who gave the order to have the prisoners shot?
- Why were the prisoners not judged before any form of military court?
- Did the fact that hostilities were due to stop on 8 May 1945 at 2300 hours actually hasten the decision to have the prisoners shot?
- What did the Americans know of the shooting?

---

69    Brooks, article *Death at Bad Reichenhall, Charlemagne's Legionnaires*, p.178. Pierre Jacques Ponneau was born on 5 February 1924 at Paris. His last known whereabouts are Paderborn, March 1945.
70    Lefèvre & Pigoreau, *Bad Reichenhall*, p.244. Curiously, Scherzer remains convinced that one of those shot 'could have been Pierre Ponneau.
71    See Scherzer, *Sous le Signe SS*, pp.600-601. His unit was the Infantry Gun Company of Waffen-Gren. Regt der SS 58, which Scherzer incorrectly numbers as the 13th. Georges de Taxis du Poet was born on 9 June 1926 in Saigon, Indochina.

Today, the whole truth will never be known. Bad Reichenhall may not have been the only war crime committed by the Western Allies against Frenchmen of the Waffen-SS. On 1 April 1945, according to Uscha. Illarthein, a platoon of the *battalion de marche* was encircled in a barn by American troops, who burnt the occupants alive and shot down any who tried to escape.[72]

72  Lefèvre & Pigoreau, *Bad Reichenhall*, p.96, footnote. Of interest is that de Gaulle's troops were responsible for other murders (see Scherzer, *Sous le Signe SS*, p.603).

# 20

## Prisoners

---

### In the East

On the morning of 5 March 1945, in Pomerania, Uscha. Mercier of Fahrschwadron A followed his *Capitaine* into captivity. They were joined in captivity by the men hiding with them in the woods and sent to a village where the victors were quartered.

Mercier was like in a dream. He had but one thought in his mind and that was his uniform. He was convinced, and he does not know why, that the Soviets would liquidate the officers, but keep the men who would make excellent slaves for their camps. So, if he was going to be shot, at least he would stand upright and the survivors would bear witness to it.

The prisoners then arrived in a sort of farmyard. Mercier thought he was going to be shot in the nape of the neck, but to his great amazement the prisoners were greeted with jibes from a group of kids and women in uniform. A Soviet NCO restored a little order by saying to the prisoners: "Franzous-Pétain-Laval" and made *Capitaine* Schlisler, who was at the head of the prisoners, leave the ranks.

At Schlisler's request, Mercier accompanied him as a French-German translator. His knowledge of Russian, like that of the majority of his comrades from the LVF, was very broken. His appearance was such that the Soviet NCO realised that he was dealing with an important person who should be forwarded to a higher echelon. They were taken to a Colonel, who was relatively young. The Colonel was with two or three officers and a private who was an interpreter.

To the great surprise of Mercier, the Colonel said that it was lunchtime and that they could continue the conversation over the table. The Soviet interpreter remained standing, but Mercier was invited to sit beside Schlisler. The Soviet Colonel, who had gone into raptures over Schlisler's decorations, asked for their names and origins. He only moved on after getting it confirmed that the originals were still in France. Mercier expected a classic military interrogation, but not a society conversation. Above all the Colonel wanted to know how they had ended up as French soldiers dressed in German uniforms. Schlisler answered: 'Order from our government.'

The Colonel said: 'But you fought against the Germans in 1939, since you have a decoration.' To which Schlisler replied: "Yes, we prepared for years to fight against the Germans and during this time the French Communists were anti-militarist. In 1939, the French Communists were against our war and in 1940 our English allies abandoned us."

The Colonel did not seem to understand until he had spoken in private with one of his assistants. The conversation then turned for a rather long time on the details of European and American diplomacy.

Mercier was very careful to be as faithful as possible to the subtleties of the words of Schlisler, who broadly claimed total obedience to the orders of the legal government of France.

At one point, with the Russians surprised at Franco-German rapprochement, Schlisler said that the alliance of the Soviets with American capitalism was as abnormal. For the first time, this triggered off a movement of irritation from the Soviet Colonel who energetically asserted that the Americans did not command in the Soviet Union.

Having come to the end of the meal, the Colonel said to them that the war was almost finished and he suggested to Schlisler that he finish it at his side as an advisor. Still very much 'old France', Schlisler replied that he appreciated this offer, but that military honour made it his duty to remain with his men. Then, turning towards Mercier, the Colonel said to him: "And you?" Mercier replied that his duty was to remain with his *Capitaine*.

At the end of the conversation, the Frenchmen asked what had become of their soldiers. There must have been some confusion in the translation because the Colonel replied: "None of today's prisoners have been shot." They pressed the Colonel for more information. He became very evasive. Evidently he knew nothing. However, he said to Mercier that they had been following his unit for the past week and they were the first prisoners they had taken.

Schlisler told Mercier to thank the Colonel for his courtesy. The interpreter replied to Mercier: "Das Oberst sagt: ich bin Graf." [The Colonel says: I am a count.] Schlisler added: "Je suis cavalier." Schlisler and Mercier rejoined their comrades. Now real captivity began.

Days later, they were marched off to Arnswalde. It was a march of several days. To lighten his load and deprive the Russians of booty, Mercier followed the sound words of advice from his friend Henri Bellanger to throw away everything. Mercier thought about escape, which was a real possibility, but the total absence of a civilian population augured ill.

At Arnswalde, the men were separated from the officers. Mercier saw for the first time Germans of Freies Deutschland. He was horrified. And yet, despite everything, he kept faith in the cause and never lost hope.

Days after arriving at Arnswalde, Mercier was on the move again. First to Landsberg, then by train to Posen (Poznan), where he learnt of Roosevelt's death, and finally by train to Voronèje and work camp 82/4. Soon after his arrival, one morning the camp commandant assembled all the prisoners and solemnly told them that the capitulation had been signed.

Voronèje was hell. Put to work under the supervision of Latvians and Bessarabians, Mercier was kicked, beaten, and starved. He is convinced that he would have 'thrown in the towel' if it were not for the friendship of a veritable saint, Uscha. Jean Fauconnier, who was ex-*Milice*.[1] Weeks later, he hit rock bottom when Fauconnier was struck down with dementia. The Soviets had cared for him by putting him in the dungeon next to the morgue. He would have died but for the Russian doctor who took an interest in his case and cured him… by feeding him normally. Mercier would later reflect such was the Russia of contrasts. The country of Ilya

---

1    Jean Fauconnier is not to be confused with Le Fauconnier, the hero of Saint-Loup's *Les Volontaires*. Born in 1923, Fauconnier was a fervent catholic.

Ehrenbourg and Ivan the Terrible, but also of Tolstoî and Soljenitsine. He survived the hell of Voroneje through faith, hope eternal and the support of comrades.

Curiously, Mercier was paid at Voronèje. One night, he saw some comrades waiting for something in front of a door. One comrade told him to be quiet and wait. Shortly after, he was shown into an office where an officer asked him for his name and handed him some roubles *contre signature*. This was quite by chance and never happened to him again.

In August 1945,[2] Mercier left Voronèje for camp 188, that of Rada, near Tambov, commonly called camp Tambov. He was interrogated several times about the smallest of things. For example, did he own a pet? Did his parents own a pet? At Tambov, he was surprised to meet comrades of the LVF captured in 1944 and who had spent the previous winter in appalling conditions. He then realised, 'If we have to spend the winter in Tambov our chances of survival were slim'. For some French POWs, Tambov was their final resting place.

Taken prisoner, Ustuf. de Genouillac was sent to a POW camp at Arnswalde, where he was nearly strung up. To gain the favour of the victors, a French soldier had made totally unfounded accusations against each and every officer present in the camp. The French soldier responsible was undoubtedly a *Milicien* because he had made a particular point of accusing the *chefs miliciens* who had participated in the *opérations du maintien de l'ordre* in France and notably against the Communist maquis, but these events had left the Soviets completely indifferent. On the other hand, they were very interested by the account of a massacre of Russian prisoners at Hammerstein whose responsibility the informer laid at the feet of de Genouillac. The Soviets interrogated him and then, thankfully, took the time to confirm his statement. When they were convinced that he was not present at the scene of the crime they very kindly provided him with the identity of the one 'who had wasted their time just in case he came across him in the future!'

At Arnswalde, de Genouillac joined a group of 'Charlemagne' officers captured in Pomerania. On 14 April 1945, the group was moved to Landsberg (Gorzow Wlkp) and then, on 24 April, to Posen.

The French SS officers at Posen that May were Alaux, André, Bartolomei, Bassompierre, Baudouin, Bonnefoy, Defever, Delile, de Genouillac, Labrousse, de Perricot, Renault, Rigeade, Rossigneux, Rouzaud, Schlisler, Tardan, de Vaugelas, Vergniaud and Veyrieras. Also with the group of French SS officers were a Luxembourg national by the name of Ambrosini, as well as four *malgré-nous*[3] of the Wehrmacht: Jules Vilbois, a native of Lorraine, Alsatians Schottlé and Würfel, and Müller.

While the group was at Posen there were two departures; seriously ill, Labrousse was transferred to a hospital as a patient whereas Bonnefoy, a doctor, was transferred to a hospital to ply his trade.

On 12 August 1945, the group left Posen and headed east, arriving five days later at Walka in Lithuania. Held at Walka until 23 December 1945, the group was then moved to Tapa, Estonia.

On 27 January 1946, the group of French SS officers boarded a goods wagon which was to return them to France. Each had been handed a *certificat de libération*. For the journey, Stubaf. de Vaugelas was made to sign a receipt for various items: a 100 litre can which was quickly

2    Unconfirmed.
3    Literally 'against-our-wills', this expression was used to signify those Frenchmen forced into German service.

converted into a stove; a large pile of yellow stones which actually turned out to be oil shale; a barrel of herrings pickled in brine; and two or three potato sacks filled with slices of dry bread.

The goods wagon was to be their 'palace' for the next twenty-two days. To combat the cold, they burned the 'yellow stones'. At one point the wagon was attached to a convoy which went east. This was not reassuring. They journeyed via Dortpat, Vitebsk, Mogilev, Zhitomir, Tarnopol, Lemberg, Stanislav, Voronenka and Bacicoi. Finally, on 17 February 1946, they came to Sighet in Transylvania and one more POW camp.

In exchange for the remnants of their military dress, the French SS officers were given disparate and faded civilian clothes. Only the headdress was uniform: caps with earflaps still displaying the metallic insignia of the Feldgendarmerie.

On 27 March 1946, the French SS officers found themselves again aboard a train. After travelling through Satumare, Debrecen, Cegled, Budapest, Veszprem, Szombathely, Vienna, and Saint-Polten, they arrived at Saint-Valentin, Austria, where they entered yet one more POW camp. It was 2 April 1946.

At Saint-Valentin, the officers were joined by some one thousand Frenchmen who, for the most part, came from a POW camp at Kursk. Of the one thousand, some one hundred were former 'Charlemagne', the others were Alsatians or *Lorrains*.

The Russian camp commander, a jovial giant of a man, had a liking for military music and had formed a military orchestra from Russian nationals in transit through his camp to forced labour in Siberia. Each and every day, the Frenchmen were invited to march past a platform where the orchestra was standing. And each and every day, because of the lamentable spectacle they gave, the Frenchmen were subjected to the vehement reproaches of the camp commander who went as far as to say that it was appropriate that soldiers who paraded so bad had lost the war. For their part, the Frenchmen, tired of hearing about the wrongdoings of Prussian militarism, had no wish to fall back into its ways.

On 2 May 1946, a detachment of French soldiers came to the camp to take charge of the French nationals present. Before boarding the goods wagons, the camp commander had the French prisoners assembled in front of the 'band stand' for a farewell ceremony. He spoke for a long time, but only the most gifted among the prisoners could understand him. His speech was cordial. After wishing them well on their return, he invited the prisoners to parade one last time, in his words, 'as a slap in the face to your fellow citizens who have just come to collect you and who certainly do not know how to parade'.[4]

The orchestra then struck up the 'Friedrich-der-Grosse-Marsch'. Moved by the camp commander's speech, the prisoners responded by executing a left turn perfectly and then proceeded to parade in a manner as to give the camp commander the fright of his life! Indeed, a few would have attempted the 'Parade Marsch' if they had not feared losing their clogs in doing so. With his hand on the peak of his cap, the joyful-looking camp commander shouted to the prisoners: "Karacho, karacho, dos vidania" [It's good, goodbye!].

The prisoners were then made to board the wagons. Thereupon the French servicemen disappeared to the front car, and Russian sentries came and sat on the edge of the sliding doors left open.

4    *Souvenirs* of de Genouillac.

Pushed slowly by a locomotive, the convoy headed west, towards the demarcation line of the river Enns. When the lead car entered the American zone of Occupation the locomotive retired with the Russian sentries, leaving the convoy unguarded on the railway bridge. And there it stood for nearly an hour before a locomotive from the American side appeared. By then Bassompierre and de Vaugelas had taken advantage of this unexpected opportunity and made good their escape. No other officer followed the example of Bassompierre and de Vaugelas.

After passing through Linz, Salzburg, Innsbruck, Bregenz, and Donaueschingen, the prisoners came to Strasbourg and again a POW camp. It was 5 May 1946. Two days later, they were sent on to Paris. Prison awaited them.[5]

Maurice Comte was captured by Polish cavalry and sent to a POW camp where he was fed soup and black bread, describing it as a veritable feast. The following day he was moved to another camp where he was overjoyed to meet Carlier and Duchène, who was walking around barefoot on the frozen ground because his boots were that worn and hurting him. They were marched to another camp, which took days and then onto a 'large assembly area', which Comte believes was at Woldenberg [Dobiegniew],[6] where he was deloused. They were moved again, ending up at Posen.

Captured at Meseritz, Oberjunker Méric spent two or three days with his Polish captors before he was handed over to a column of German prisoners. The guards played games with them. Now and then they forced the prisoners to march quickly for quarter of an hour and then trot for five minutes. This was repeated three times. Those who fell behind were shot. The guards had the power of life and death over them as Méric recalled:

> I saw several times executions that were for their pleasure. I still remember a German sergeant, good looking, who, wounded, struggled along, helped by his comrades. One of these savages pulled him from the ranks and without wasting time shot him in cold blood on the road side, with a bullet in the temple. Without hatred displayed, without indifference.

Méric was then handed over to another group guarded by Cossacks and feared for the worst, but they arrived at Greifenberg the following day without incident. Two days later, a Russian officer told him he was to take fifteen men to Deutsch Krone [Wałcz], some one hundred and thirty kilometres away, and handed him a document giving safe conduct. He could not quite believe it.

Led by Méric, the group set off. Among the group was Gérard de Perricot and two or three former NSKK. Three of the group, whose feet were frozen and unable to walk, soon gave up and stayed behind in the hope of receiving care. The group foraged for food in this empty region and most of the time there was little to be had. One time, the group feasted on grilled meat from a stray horse one of them had found and shot. Arms were easier to find than food!

In a small village the group watched a column of prisoners pass. Méric recognised two men from his troop at Ferron, including the tall Bertrand de Puch. They also spotted him and suddenly burst out singing 'Ne pleure pas, Jeannette', which they had learnt together.[7]

---

5    The *malgré-nous* officers were not repatriated because the Russians had decided that they were Germans. They were repatriated in July 1946 (de Genouillac, telephone conversation with Vilbois, 18/2/2000).
6    Comte may be referring to the former German POW Camp Oflag II-C.
7    'Ne pleure pas, Jeannette' is a traditional children's song.

After some fifteen days on the road the group finally made it to Deutsch Krone. Three days later, it was marched to the railway station and put on a train to Posen. On arrival Méric and Gérard de Perricot were placed with other French Waffen-SS officers and officer cadets, which included Pignard-Berthet, Comte, Marchèse, Auphan,[8] Carlier, Aymar, Salmon, Wagner and Pasquet. Also with this group were Alsatians Amman and Guichard,[9] as well as Oberleutenant Jentgen, a Luxembourg national.

Méric knew Philippe Marchèse, who he had first met at the Milice's *École des Cadres* at Uriage and later at Vichy when he joined the *Franc-Garde*. They would become the best of friends.

At Posen Comte and Carlier were picked for a work detail, carrying 40 kilogramme bags of sugar from a warehouse to a train of platform wagons. It was back-breaking. Thankfully, the work detail did not last long and at its end they filled their water bottles with sugar, which the Russians did not discover when they were searched. They shared the sugar with their comrades.

From Posen, the group of French officers and officer cadets was transferred by train to Kissilowka, stopping en route at Brest-Litovsk where there were two huge portraits of Stalin and Molotov on the station wall with an enormous inscription, which roughly translated as 'Here starts the land of liberty'.

From Kissilowka, via Moscow, the Frenchmen were transferred to camp Rada, near Tambov. They were greeted with the sinister sight of prisoners pushing and pulling a cart stacked with naked corpses towards the forest for burial. They were separated from the other prisoners and confined in an enclosure surrounded by barbed wire, or as Méric described it 'le camp du camp', but soon permitted to wander around the camp.

In contrast to the hostility of the Alsatians, the Frenchmen were warmly welcomed by the Hungarian officers who had somehow managed to keep their magnificent cavalry boots and even their orderlies! The Frenchmen enjoyed many long conversations with the Hungarians who spoke correct French which they had learnt at school. The Hungarians showed a sincere admiration for France.

Like all that passed through Tambov, the camp left an inedible impression on Méric and Comte; the lack of food, the lice, the filthy 'latrines' and Barracks 22, the morgue. The Frenchmen all lost weight. They became concerned about Pignard-Berthet, who lost some thirty kilos. Comte asked all to give a 'little of their daily pittance' to Pignard-Berthet to save him. All agreed except one... Pignard-Berthet! Outvoted, Pignard-Berthet acquiesced and ate what amounted to almost another complete ration. The 'latrine' was a disgusting septic ditch in which Oberjunker Laschett fell and drowned.

The politruk took a particular interest in Comte and tried over and over again to 'convert' him, but Comte politely refused each and every time. The politruk even claimed that he had been deported to concentration camp Buchenwald where he had witnessed the SS execute Léon Blum, the former Prime Minister of France. Much to his surprise, Comte was to discover later that Blum was alive and well and back in the government!

Méric and Comte had nothing but praise for the female Russian doctor in her fifties who worked day and night at the infirmary and who did her best for the sick with what she had

---

8    Auphan may have joined the group later.
9    Pignard-Berthet, letter to the author. Guichard is probably a pseudonym for Quichaud.

available. Indeed, many comrades saw her openly cry at the bedside of a dying man. Comte described her as much 'more than a doctor, a mother!'

Distractions from the misery of camp life were few and far between. Méric and Comte both recall the visit of six female instructors to the camp to test and perfect their knowledge of French. Their visit lasted three days. Marchèse, who also spoke English and Germany, was named as the liaison between the group of instructors and the Frenchmen. Moreover, he was probably the most diplomatic, although he could be outspoken on occasion. One day, Marchèse asked Méric to show the instructors a picture of his wife in her wedding dress, which he had managed to keep with him. Marchèse also showed them a picture of his wife in her wedding dress. The instructors were surprised to learn that the wedding dress was only worn once and commented that this was typical of capitalism and explained that is why they had lost the war! Méric also fondly remembers the time he attended a concert staged by the Hungarians, which quickly transported him away from captivity.

The months passed. The Frenchmen feared spending a winter in Tambov. Thankfully, that October, they were repatriated in two convoys, the second one leaving eight days after the first. On the first were those whose names started from A to L and on the second those from M to Z. When it was announced at roll call that they would be leaving the Alsatians reacted angrily, shouting: "They're SS, they should stay." Comte left on the first convoy with Ammann, Auphan, Carlier and Jentgen. Méric and his friend Philippe Marchèse left on the second.[10]

The first convoy arrived at Valenciennes on 10 November 1945 towards 2300 hours. All spent the night in the train. The following morning they were handed over to the authorities and arrested. Carlier was sent on to Lille, Auphan to Paris and Comte was imprisoned locally because he did not appear on the list of collaborators. Méric and Marchèse were also arrested at Valenciennes when they arrived. The following day they were moved to Douai and locked up together.

Pignard-Berthet and Pasquet, who were probably on the same convoy as Méric and Marchèse, were arrested by French *Sécurité militaire* at Wolfsburg in Germany on 3 or 4 November 1945 and taken to Niemberg. Pignard-Berthet was questioned extensively about the Red Army before he was finally repatriated to France in June 1946.

Captured three kilometres from Greifenberg, Rttf. Gonzales was first moved to Plathe in a column of prisoners who were mostly German. There were a sprinkling of other Frenchmen and Gonzales recalls seeing the son of *Commandant* Fleury, who was seriously wounded in both legs, hobbling along using two pieces of wood as crutches. En route he stopped at a hole full of water to fill up his canteen only to discover a very young blonde girl, naked, legs apart, eyes gouged out, who had definitely been raped. He would never forget this horrific sight. He ran back to find his place. Those who fell behind to the back of the column were often run over by the vehicles following them. In the late evening the column arrived at Plathe.

The following morning, after a brief assembly and a ladle of thin soup, Gonzales received treatment for his leg wound, which was causing him a great deal of pain. After putting him under with chloroform, Russian medical staff operated on his leg. When he finally came round

10    Méric made no mention of the other French Junkers who may have been travelling in a different wagon.

he noted a summary dressing on his leg and the pain had gone. Thankfully, he was able to rest for one day before being moved on.

The new destination was Arnswalde. Gonzales only managed to make it there thanks to his comrade Robert Maurel who supported him when the pain from his leg wound returned. At Arnswalde, he was able to receive medical care from a German Medical Officer, who did the best he could for him. He was thankful for the attention and for several days of much needed rest.

Gonzales was then sent to Posen. He was still with Robert Maurel. Because they had met no other Frenchmen they thought they were the only ones to have been captured! In great pain from his knees, Gonzales was admitted into the camp infirmary, which was basic, but then again he did receive some sort of herbal tea twice a day. Also, he greatly benefited from the spinach soup, which was served daily, convinced that it combated dysentery. Days later, he was discharged, but in the meantime his friend Robert Maurel had been sent on to Odessa. Not long after came his transfer.

Along with fifty others, Gonzales was crammed into a railway horse wagon with a single opening for air and another in a corner for their needs. Thankfully, he found himself once more in the company of a fellow countryman whose name was Labonne.

The convoy departed Posen. For the prisoners, not told of their destination, it was a journey into the unknown. Gonzales tried to follow the route of the convoy from the place names of the stations. Those of Minsk, Borisov, Orscha and Smolensk were well known to him from his LVF days. By now, he was of the opinion that the convoy was making for Moscow. It was, but Moscow was not its destination. The convoy continued eastwards. Siberia beckoned.

Fed one piece of bread daily, hunger became the constant companion of the prisoners. Finally, after a journey that had lasted one month, the convoy shed its cargo of prisoners at Asbest. Thankfully, the camp was nearby. Exhausted and unsteady on their feet, few of the prisoners could have gone far. The prisoners were counted. Of those in the same wagon as Gonzales, three or four had died along the way. A shower was next, but it too had its price as the prisoners were stripped of the last personal objects they could not hide. In this way, Gonzales came to part with a small *bossu* [a coin of Napoleon I], a memento given to him by his maternal grandfather that had been with him through the 14-18 war.

After the shower, the prisoners were shaved all over. The blunt razors cut the skin again and again. There was literally blood everywhere. Because Gonzales could speak Russian well he was assigned to the kitchens. On the other hand, his friend Labonne was sent to work in the asbestos mines, where he would work without the protection of a facemask.[11]

Gonzales spent two months in the camp and, because he was working in the kitchens, not once did he go hungry. He also made use of his situation to steal pieces of bread for his comrade. For two months he had no news of the outside world, which he found hard to bear, but that was until the day a Russian woman doctor turned up at the camp to examine the prisoners. She told them that they were going to be repatriated to their respective countries of origin. Good news indeed, but alas this did not happen immediately.

Finally, Gonzales and Labonne were moved to another camp, not far from the first, where they found themselves among the likes of Bulgarians, Hungarians and Rumanians. Days later,

---

11   Labonne would later die of tuberculosis.

in the company of a Russian NCO, the two of them started out by train to Tambov, some 400 kilometres south of Moscow.

At Moscow, they had to change trains, but their connection was not due for hours. To kill the time, the Russian NCO, along with his two prisoners, went to visit his parents in the suburbs! During the journey Gonzales had the chance to speak to a Russian woman of Jewish origin. She spoke good French and deeply regretted that she did not have the freedom to go to France. At that she embraced him. Her eyes then filled with tears.

That same evening, they continued on to Tambov. Many were the stops that presented Labonne with opportunity after opportunity to improve their lot by plying his former occupation of circus showman. Before an audience of peasants who had come to sell or trade their goods to passing travellers he would eat glass or razor blades. For his show he was given eggs, glasses of milk or black bread.

It took two days to reach camp Tambov. Called the 'camp of the Frenchmen', its inmates were, for the most part, Alsatians. Once more Gonzales felt quite alone, especially when Labonne entered the infirmary. Conditions at Tambov were terrible. Typhus was rampant. Gonzales had no need to fear this sickness, having contracted it some months beforehand. However, there was no escape whatsoever from the terrible black-coloured parasites called *Gimelanke*. More vicious than any lice or bugs Gonzales had known before, one of these irritants would prevent sleep. Also of nuisance at night-time were the fleas living in the bark of the logs used as beds. Not wanting to become a host for them, he was forever shaking his shirt outside his hut. And then there was the hunger.

Weeks, perhaps months later, Gonzales, along with a group of Alsatians, numbering twenty or so, was moved a matter of kilometres to another camp, much smaller, situated in the middle of a huge peat bog.[12] Notably two Alsatians ran the camp. Gonzales likened them to comedians Laurel and Hardy, but Laurel was without joy. In fact, he was rather hard-hearted. In contrast, the Russian guards were rather friendly.

Coming forward as a carpenter, Gonzales was assigned to the construction of a small guard post at the entrance to the camp. Yes, this work, of course, was less tiring than the digging of the peat, but for Gonzales, he also got to go out to the forest with the other prisoners to cut wood for the proposed guard post. Generally a guard who had lost an arm in the war accompanied them. On more than one occasion, he had an opportunity to talk to him freely. To the great surprise of Gonzales, the guard confessed to him that he was not in agreement with the Communist regime, explaining that after his discharge from his regiment he had requested a patch of land and a cow, but this had been refused.

Gonzales was at this camp for some two months. In all that time, he never once received a meal that varied from cabbage soup, a handful of small fish and a piece of black bread. The monotony of camp life was broken once by a visiting troop of comedians and performers. A light tenor brought tears to the eyes of the prisoners at the end of a quite beautiful song entitled 'The return of the prisoner'.

Then came the day Gonzales was moved back to Tambov to prepare for his repatriation to France. He was shocked to lay eyes on a deserter from his former LVF unit, the 2nd Company,

12  Gonzales called this camp 'Raja'. Presumably he was referring to Rada. Arguably, this 'new' camp was part of or an annex of camp Rada.

in the uniform of a Red Army Sergeant.[13] Nevertheless, as he counted down the days to repatriation he got to meet more and more French POWs, including Jean Pierre Lefèvre.

Days before the prisoners left Tambov for France their rations suddenly improved. Obviously Russia was desperate to show the world that it fed its prisoners well. And so, in October 1945, began the train journey back 'home'. Mercier of Fahrschwadron A and Émile Schwaller were on the same train.[14] The stops were frequent. The train had to make way for those bound for Russia. At each stop, the prisoners were free to descend and walk about. In this way, quite unbelievably, Gonzales actually missed his train that suddenly departed. He went to a smaller station nearby where he caught another westward. He was soon back on the 'right' train.

At each stop, Gonzales found himself opposite, more often than not, a convoy of Russian prisoners who had fought under the German sponsored General Vlasov. The Allies were exchanging them for their own nationals. Apprehension was written all over their faces.

While stopped at Radom, Poland, the train was visited by a detachment of the French Red Cross. Three or four ladies distributed cigarettes. One French prisoner was pacing up and down the platform smoking away when, passing by the ladies, he heard one of them say to the others: 'If we'd known that they were volunteers...' Without hesitating, the prisoner held out his half smoked cigarette with the words: 'Take it, it's not finished!'

At Berlin, during one more stop, Gonzales assisted in the burial of a Russian General. The coffin was open. The face of the deceased was completely swollen and scarlet. It appeared as though excessive eating and drinking had struck him down.

The very next day, the train crossed into Holland, but it was the British Army to which the prisoners were handed over. First they were deloused. Then they were fed. However, the food proved too rich for many and they were sick, including Gonzales.

Soon after, the prisoners were sent on to Bruxelles where the Belgium Red Cross gave them a warm welcome. This was in contrast to the French Red Cross that received them 'like dogs'. Finally, in early November 1945, they crossed into France, arriving at Valenciennes. The French 'authorities' were somewhat confused when they realised that the convoy comprised not only martyrs from Alsace-Lorraine and Luxembourg, but also suspects. Ironically, the *Marche Consulaire* blared from a loudspeaker welcoming the repatriates.[15]

The newly arrived were screened in a hasty manner and 'those comrades not from Alsace-Lorraine' isolated. Next they heard an appeal for volunteers to take the repatriates to 'village

13  This LVF deserter was also well known to Mercier, who in 1942 had served with him in the same platoon of the 2nd Company.
14  Born on 8 October 1911, Schwaller enlisted in the LVF with the rank of *sergent* and fought in the first winter before Moscow. With the rank of *adjudant-chef*, he was declared unfit on 8 April 1943, whereupon he took a desk job as the *secrétaire départemental* de la LVF for department Ille-et-Vilaine in the region of Brittany. Joining the *Franc-Garde permanente of Bretagne*, he actively participated in operations against the maquis, earning him a sinister reputation and eventual promotion to *chef de cohorte*. He fled to Germany and served with 'Charlemagne', although his role and rank are not clear. He was condemned to death on 12 July 1946 by the *Cour de justice* of Rennes and executed on 5 November 1946.
15  When Jacques Benoist-Méchin conceived the *Légion Tricolore* he decided that its official anthem would be the *Marche Consulaire*, which he considered as 'the most beautiful anthem after the *Marseillaise*'.

nègre'.[16] The escort appeared and asked if there was an officer among them. In this way, Pierre Million-Rousseau, probably the 'most senior officer with the highest rank', took command of the manoeuvre. And it was as soldiers that the veterans of the LVF, SS, and *Milice* went from the station to the barracks, despite their rags and their skeletal appearance.

Mercier thought the worst was now over. He had always kept faith and hope of seeing better days and he was never short of friends. Gonzales, in contrast, thought that their troubles were only just beginning!

Robert Blanc of Walter's Company, who spent some five and a half months in Russian captivity, was treated well. In terrible physical condition and suffering from frostbite when captured, he was taken to a hospital in Köslin and went to the operating table. Under local anaesthetic, the dead parts of his feet were amputated.

Blanc went back to the operating table a further two times. During one operation another Frenchman was brought in. His name was Nöel V. and he was from the same origin as Blanc, who could now hear the sound of the saw amputating his countryman's legs below the knees.

Blanc and his comrade Patrice Rimbert shared the same hospital room. A good drawer, Rimbert was popular as a portraitist with the nurses. When one of the nurses brought them a collection of post cards of Paris Blanc gave them all a talk and for this he drew a sort of map of Paris to position the different views. He had a great deal of trouble getting them to accept that the Sacré-Coeur was not a mosque!

Blanc was moved to a ward mainly of Soviet nationals. Not once was he made an object of hostility. One day, the surgeon, who also spoke a little French, asked Blanc what would please him. Modest in his demands, Blanc requested a drink weaker than the daily vodka ration, which he then replaced with du Dubonnet. Also, there was no reading material to be had. The surgeon brought him *Nouvelle Héloïse* by Jean-Jacques Rousseau, of which he read twenty pages out of courtesy.

At the end of about a month, Blanc, Desigaud,[17] Rimbert, and Nöel V. were moved to a field hospital in Bromberg. Separated from his comrades, Blanc found himself in a hut with some French POWs of 40, who soon learnt that he was SS whereupon the atmosphere took a turn for the worse. The following morning, the French POWs denounced Blanc to the medical officer and asked him to rid them of him. The medical officer, who spoke a little French, put them in their place: "You, you let yourself be captured. At least, he fought." Blanc was not troubled again.

More surprises awaited Blanc at Bromberg. One morning, a giant of a man, whom Blanc believed to be of high rank judging by the size of his epaulettes, accompanied the medical officer on his round. At the foot of each bed the giant acquainted himself with the case and the situation of the occupant. Then he came to Blanc, who distinctly heard "Fransouski SS", but understood little of what else was said. Nevertheless, he still thought to himself that the good life was now over and that he was going to find himself God knows where. When the dialogue ended, to the great surprise of Blanc, the *haut gradé* took him by the hand, squeezed it and shook it vigorously, and said to him in French these few simple words: "*Maréchal Pétain, grand soldat!*" Then he quickly passed to the next bed.

16    'Village nègre' translates as 'Negro village' and in this instance appears to have been used as a code name.
17    Jean Desiguad was born on 31 July 1924 in Lyon.

Desigaud died suddenly. His family would have no news of him; his compatriots had not thought of asking him for his address when he was still in possession of his mind. One month later, Blanc was transferred to a third and last hospital in Thorn. The hospital, which ad-joined a huge POW camp, had some one thousand patients. In the same room as Blanc were two Italian soldiers and five Frenchmen, of whom three were 'POWs of 40' and two were STO. Again Blanc was well cared for. Each day he was taken to the treatment room, where his feet were examined by a doctor and bandaged by a nurse. The food was adequate. He regained his strength and started to walk.

Blanc, who made no secret that he was SS, soon discovered that the two STO were in fact also SS. They were Truchet, who was in his forties, and Jacques A., who was the same age as Blanc and also ex-*Milice*; he had followed his father and elder brother into the *Milice*, the latter being killed in a terrorist ambush. The *Milice* led him to the Waffen-SS. He served with the Artillery Battalion of 'Charlemagne'. Seriously wounded at Danzig, he was evacuated to the city's military hospital, where he witnessed some horrifying scenes when the Russians arrived. From the top floor, all the SS patients were systematically defenestrated.[18] He had escaped a similar fate quite by chance; he had not responded to the call of his name, which the Russians, trapped by their Cyrillic alphabet, had mispronounced.

With nothing to do and nothing to read at Thorn, the days were long. Blanc tried to learn Russian. He gleaned very many words, but his request for more formal learning was politely but firmly refused. Perhaps the Russians feared that it would make a spy of him.

In September 1945, along with Jacques A., Truchet, Nöel V. and two or three other comrades, Blanc was repatriated.[19] Blanc would later reflect that he had fought Bolchevism, but not the Russians who had cared for him with such kindness and concern.

Captured in the vicinity of Standemin, Jules Dissent of the Medical Company was first marched to a camp at Arnswalde, which took twelve days. He joined up with Yves Morel and Fauconnier. On a road near Deutsch Krone, they marched past an 88m flak gun and ten or so destroyed T-34 lined up one behind the other. 'It was the one of the rare occasions where we had the opportunity to rejoice', Dissent commented. Finally, on the afternoon of 19 March 1945, his column of POWs arrived at Arnswalde, where he remained until 10 April 1945. Thankfully, the three weeks he spent in this camp enabled him to regain his strength and rest his feet from the rigours of his tour of Pomerania.

From Arnswalde Dissent was moved to Landsberg, where he spent three nights, and then by train to Posen. On 20 April 1945, he left for Russia. He was determined not to give up and there were times he encouraged friends, convinced that they would never see France again, to keep up their morale. His destination was Voronej Camp 4 on the left bank of the Don.

On 8 May 1945, the end of the war was announced and Dissent, like many others, believed that his chances of seeing France again had just improved. He was put to work moving sand. One time he was made to bury three skeletal German POWs who had just died, after which he feared spending a winter in a camp. On 31 May, he was on his way again to another camp called 'Electro-Signal', where he was questioned about his family and ancestors. Again he was put to

18   One of Blanc's comrades witnessed similar scenes at Swinemünde.
19   There was a French Waffen-SS nurse by the name of Truchet, who was born in 1924, but the two of them were not related.

work, getting the camp ready to house an influx of prisoners, who turned out to be from Breslau and Courland. And it was in this camp that he started to develop symptoms of tuberculosis.

Sent on to yet another camp, this time Voronej Camp 2, Dissent was examined by a German doctor who diagnosed him with full-blown tuberculosis and had him admitted into the camp's basic hospital. This came as a shock to him, but, afterwards, he would often reflect that he owed his life to this German doctor; the two months he spent in hospital enabled him to grow stronger and avoid the hell of Tambov. On 30 September 1945, he began the return journey home. He was very ill but, as ever, determined to see France again and more importantly his parents.

Hungry, exhausted and suffering from frostbite, Paul Denamps of Walter's Company was marched first to Plathe (Ploty). He was in the company of de Puch and Figuié.[20] Arriving at Plathe, the prisoners were housed in the New Castle, which was originally the seat of the Von Bismarck family. Forty to fifty prisoners were crammed into a small room, where they rested for the night. Denamps managed to find a cabinet without a door and fell asleep inside. The following morning he awoke to discover de Puch dead in his arms; during the night he had died from exhaustion. De Puch was buried in the grounds of the castle.

Paul Denamps was marched to Poznan. Hospitalised, he was operated on by German medics, who amputated two frostbitten toes on his right foot. Toilet paper was used to bandage the wounds. One morning he heard a fellow Frenchmen scream in disgust when he discovered a maggot eating the flesh of his feet. He checked his feet and found more. A German doctor quickly attended him and told him not to remove the maggots because they were eating away the rotten flesh!

On 5 May 1945, Denamps learnt from his Russian captors that Germany had capitulated. There was no Red Cross and he now feared, like many of his comrades, that they would be shot or sent to the far reaches of Siberia where they would be worked to death.

Denamps was marched from Poznan to Pulawy, arriving on 21 June 1945, where he found himself grouped with some sixteen other Frenchmen, two of whom would die of dysentery. Every ten days they were permitted to shower and their clothes were steamed, but it did not kill all the lice. Pulawy was a mixing pot of nationalities and Denamps recalls meeting a few Englishmen, and even some Indians who were supporters of Indian nationalist Chandra Bose.

Denamps was interned at Pulawy until 15 September 1945. Soon after, he was put on a train and sent to Berlin where he was handed over to the British. The sunflower bread provided for the journey, which Denamps jokingly dated from the Sino-Russian war, could not be eaten as it was infested with some kind of weevil. Thankfully, at each stop, potatoes were also provided. Even so he was desperately underweight when he arrived at Berlin. German women approached them for information about loved ones, but invariably they had to disappoint. The prisoners were

---

20  Born on 20 October 1911 in Agen, Georges Figuié fought with the 24e BCA during 1939-40, in Syria against the Allies in 1941 and with the LVF before Moscow in 1941. Demobilised, he went to work in Germany, but when he learnt of the existence of the *Franc-Garde permanente* he decided to 'desert' and made his way back to Agen to join up. Stationed at Château de Ferron, he participated in maintenance of order operations. Exiled, he transferred to the Waffen-SS and was assigned to the PAK Company with the rank of Unterscharführer. He attended a training course at Janowitz in Bohemia-Moravia. The paths of Denamps and Figuié had undoubtedly crossed at Château de Ferron while serving with the *Franc-Garde*. Denamps would meet Figuié again after the war in Agen.

surprised to swap potatoes for apples, which seemed much more abundant. Denamps was sent on to France and arrested on his arrival.

**In the West**

Rttf. Soulat was held first in a camp at Gadebusch. Joined by others of 'Charlemagne', they soon counted 20. Of the 20, whose average age was 27, 3 were married (2 with children) and 17 were single. As for their background, 3 came from the LVF, 3 from the Kriegsmarine, 2 from the SS, and 12 from the *Milice*. Notably, twenty-one-year-old *milicien* André D. was in fact a 'converted' maquisard. The professions of the twenty was split; 6 were students, 4 were farmers, 2 were mechanics, 2 were bakers, 2 were 'employees', 1 was a driver, 1 was a typographer and 2 had no profession.

On 25 May 1945, Soulat and the other French POWs of 'Charlemagne' were moved to SS-POW-Camp 357 at Fallingbostel, Hanover.[21] They remained 20 in number until the arrival of a second group of 150 with *aspirant* de Vaugelas junior and 4 or 5 *adjudants*. Also with this second group was Uscha. Yves Peyret.

Days after their arrival, a list was circulated calling for volunteers to fight with the American Army of the Far East against the Japanese.[22] Soulat signed up. However, nothing came of his gesture, a gesture he was to later call low and ill-timed because he would have ended up serving against a courageous people one hundred times better than the Americans. This he regretted.

There was much talk of the Americans shooting Ostuf. Herpe and Ustuf. Sarraillé at Schwerin on 2 May in 'strange circumstances', but this proved to be nothing more than hearsay.

On 20 September, Soulat and the third and last detachment of French Waffen-SS POWs left the camp by truck for France. Two days later, they arrived at Lille. All out! As they got out one of them hummed:

> *SS Marschiert*
> *In Feindesland ...*

On 16 May 1945, at former concentration camp Neuengamme, Staf. Zimmermann symbolically dissolved 'Charlemagne' in the presence of Martin, Roumegous, Platon, another French officer, 'some lads from the Brigade', and about a dozen German officers. His Tricolore badge, respectfully kept, served as a miniature flag in the middle of the worn-out circle on the grass. Martin gave a resumé, presumably of the history of 'Charlemagne', while Zimmermann pronounced his acknowledgements. Hail to Franco-German camaraderie.[23]

21  SS-POW-Camp 357 was later renamed Civilian Internment Camp (C.I.C.) 3.
22  Of interest to note is that a rumour at the time had it that the survivors were going to be sent to fight side by side with the Americans against the Japanese.
23  Zimmermann, letter to Saint-Loup, 10/8/65.

**21**

*Le Bataillon d'Infanterie légère d'Outre-Mer*[1]

As the war in Indo-China dragged on France became desperate more than ever for fresh manpower. The politicians came to consider the many thousands of prisoners the country was then holding as an acceptable and accessible source of manpower.

On 27 May 1948, André Marie, the Minister of Justice, issued a circular to the regional directors of the Prison Service asking for the number of prisoners who wished to enlist in Far East combat units in order to 'make amends vis-à-vis the nation'. The politicians then went to the military, which drew up proposals to raise a *demi-brigade* of three battalions of political prisoners. So as not to alarm the public unduly it was decided to raise one battalion first. Thus, on 6 July 1948, the Minister of the Armed Forces communicated the decision to create the *1er Bataillon d'Infanterie légère d'Outre-Mer* [Overseas Light Infantry Battalion] or BILOM to the general headquarters of the Armed Forces.

The BILOM was to be composed exclusively of political prisoners capable of military service overseas. For those volunteering, there would be no question of amnesty, but merely of a suspensive pardon. They would wear no insignia and have no pennant. They were not eligible for promotion; all leadership positions were to be filled by Colonial troops.

The political prisoners in question were veterans of the LVF and the Waffen-SS who had survived the fighting on the Eastern Front, as well as those who had advocated a New Order and who had survived the court martials and summary sentences that came with 'Liberation'.

Among those accepted was the apolitical Gino Valle born of Italian and Austrian parents. Life had been hard for him. Throughout his youth he had dreamt of being French, the country which had given him security and bread. When he was eighteen he opted for French nationality, but the civil servants attempted to dissuade him. Convinced that there was no better way of being French than by fighting Bolshevism, he enlisted in the LVF in May 1944. Besides, he craved adventure and the idea of a Europe of united nations in the same battle appealed to him. He enjoyed soldiering and wanted to be among the best. Thus, his transfer to 'Charlemagne' in September 1944 did not trouble him. He was proud to fight in the Waffen-SS that had the reputation of being an elite unit.

---

1   See Muelle Raymond, *Le Bataillon des réprouvés* (Paris: Presses de la Cité, 1990).

At Wildflecken, Valle was assigned to 'the heavy company of Waffen-Gren. Regt der SS 58' and tattooed.[2] Seriously wounded in Pomerania, he was evacuated by ship to Bremerhaven via Copenhagen. Although his wounds were far from healed he was sent to the depot of 'Charlemagne'.[3] When the Russians launched their 'Berlin' offensive he fled west and surrendered to the British in May 1945. Sentenced to ten years hard labour, he often thought of escape, but knew that he could go nowhere without money and an escape network. For him, volunteering for Indo-China was an escape. Besides, he was a *homme de guerre*.

Some volunteers were from military families. Jehan Proton de la Chapelle's father was a hero of the First World War. As a nationalist and royalist, reserve Captain Proton de la Chapelle did not welcome favourably the idea of his son Jehan donning the uniform of the *Légion Tricolore* to fight bolshevism and forbid him. It was this refusal that incited his son to action. Aged seventeen, he enlisted in the Waffen-SS instead.[4]

Arriving at Sennheim in the autumn of 1943, Jehan Proton de la Chapelle drew attention to himself through his knowledge of the German language and also his enthusiasm, but his individualism was of concern. After recruit training, he attended the Signals training school in the Tyrol, then the Interpreters school at Oranienburg near Berlin.

Transferred from the French Sturmbrigade to 'Charlemagne', Strmm. Jehan Proton de la Chapelle served in Waffen-Gren. Regt der SS 57 and saw action in Pomerania as a liaison officer. Captured by Polish partisans, he was hidden by French POWs, but handed over to the Russians by STO 'volunteers'. He was sent to a camp at Poltava. To embarrass the Soviet authorities into releasing him, he bombarded them with complaint after complaint and request after request. Some were ludicrous. He even requested asylum, claiming that his life would be in danger if he was returned to France. This received no reply, but one day he was set free. Making his way through Germany, he was denounced to the British by a catholic priest of whom he had asked hospitality. In turn, the British handed him over to the French authorities.

In early 1946, when brought before the *tribunal militaire* of Landau, Proton de la Chapelle was acquitted, because 'he had not come of age at the time of the events'. He was subsequently sentenced to twenty years hard labour. Desperate to get out of prison, he volunteered for the BILOM and managed to get himself accepted even though he was medically unfit: he had lost several toes to frostbite in Pomerania.

Cottelowe and Forrez were inseparable. Their journey to the BILOM began together with the rank of *quartiers-maître* [leading seaman] aboard the *Bretagne* at the time of the English attacks at Mers-el-Kébir. They survived, but many of their comrades were killed. Soon after, they enlisted in the LVF. The Russian winters and combat did not diminish their memories of their comrades who had fallen one summer's day at the foot of the mountain of Santa-Cruz. Their transfer to 'Charlemagne' did not pose them problems, nor did it weaken their determination to fight the Soviets allied with the English, the hereditary enemy.[5] They both became model NCOs. They remained inseparable; they were decorated at the same time, and judged and sentenced together. They decided to continue their brotherly crusade in the BILOM.

---

2    Muelle, *Le Bataillon des réprouvés*, p.19, possibly the 4/58 or 8/58.
3    Ibid, p.22, possibly Neusterlitz.
4    Jehan Proton de la Chapelle was born on 12 July 1927 in Pau.
5    Muelle, *Le Bataillon des réprouvés*, p.126.

Pierre Laurion was one of the oldest. A romantic adventurer and convinced anti-Communist, he had fought on the side of Franco. The nationalists made him an officer and decorated him for his courage under fire. In September 1939, when storm clouds gathered over Europe, he returned to France. In May 1940, with the rank of *maréchal des logis* [sergeant] serving in a reconnaissance group, he fought the Germans.

Like many from his generation, Laurion was impressed by his victors. They exuded order, force and faith in an ideal 'already glimpsed' in Spain. He was drawn to the infectiousness of the unknown and 'the passionate liturgy of the elite troops at the disposal of a new order' to reverse the decay of the old worm-eaten world. And yet he hesitated to don the uniform of the enemy of yesterday. But the death of his mother in an English air raid swept away any last reservations. He passed from the LVF to the Waffen-SS and fought in Pomerania. At the end of the war, he attempted to flee west by passing himself off as a STO conscript, but the blood group tattoo gave him away. He was sentenced to fifteen years hard labour, had his property confiscated and was ordered to pay costs. Now, the BILOM offered him adventure and the opportunity to continue the fight against a detested ideology.

Also concerned about the 'menace coming from the East' was Robert Cousin. In March 1942, not yet aged eighteen, he enlisted in the LVF. By that October, he was in action against the Soviet partisans in the forests. He joined an autonomous fifty-man commando of Frenchmen, Germans and Poles engaged most of the time as *enfants perdus* against the Soviet parachutists who trained and supervised the partisans. And then, one day, he met some French volunteers of the Waffen-SS. They suggested he should join. The idea did not displease him and his request for a transfer was agreed. He fought in Galicia with the Sturmbrigade, winning the Iron Cross 2nd Class.

Sturmmann Cousin saw subsequent action in Pomerania. Finding himself at Kolberg, he managed to escape from the city in the company of a handful of other exhausted men. Withdrawing westwards, they were captured by Polish troops near to the town of Wollin (Wolin). He spent the next one and a half years in various prison camps throughout Russia before being repatriated in the summer of 1946. He was sentenced to 5 years in prison.

Others, like Marc Barellon, had jumped at the opportunity to regain their freedom by means of enlisting in the BILOM. He had served with the *Milice*, like his older brother Louis Barellon, and been transferred to the Waffen-SS in November 1944.[6] Assigned to the *Compagnie d'Honneur*, he was wounded in Pomerania.

Towards the end of the war, Barellon was still convalescing in Berlin with either Latvian or Dutch SS and was transported out and to the west on one of the last trains, but his train journey was violently halted by an air attack. Captured by the British, he escaped, reached his region in France and was promptly denounced. In July 1945, he was sentenced to twenty years imprisonment. Many others of those accepted had served in 'Charlemagne':

- Amar Illoul: served briefly with the Waffen-SS before joining Skorzeny[7]
- Bordon: *adjudant d'artillerie* in 'one of the heavy companies'
- Dante Giorgi
- Daniel Le Goff: Grenadier, Company 5/58

6    Marc Barellon was born on 28 January 1924 in Saint-Étienne.
7    Amar Illoul was born on 17 February 1920 in Algeria.

- Francis Quagebeur: served with the Sturmbrigade
- Germain Brandt: Alsatian, he held the rank of Unterscharführer
- Henri Catherin: Oberkanonier, FLAK Company
- Jean Peloux: Sturmmann[8]
- Michel Robert: Served with the 2/57 and then assigned to the *Compagnie d'Honneur*
- Pierre Ringue: *Milicien de* Lyon, he served in 'Charlemagne with the rank of Sturmmann
- Roger Boulin: Headquarters Company of Regiment 58, Oberscharführer[9]
- Roland Albert: Sturmmann, assigned to the Franz. SS-Grenadier-Ausbildungs und Ersatz-Bataillon
- Yves Parot: Oberjunker in the Signals Platoon of a regimental Headquarters Company

A small number of volunteers had served and seen action in other branches of the German war machine:

- René Hanin: Kriegsberichter [war correspondent] with the 3. SS-Panzer-Division 'Totenkopf'[10]
- Hervé Cormatin: Served with Skorzeny
- Rambert: Served with *Bezenn Perrot* composed of extremist Breton separatists[11]

Also many were those who had not donned the *feldgrau*. André Cantelaube had been a prominent figure in the *jeunesse franciste*.[12] Sentenced to fifteen years imprisonment, he was one of those who wanted out of prison at any cost.

By late August 1948, a little less than five hundred volunteers had been accepted. Of note is that none had been the leading lights of collaboration; the powers that be had kept them under lock and key.

---

8   Jean Peloux was born on 6 March 1925 in Bordeaux. Unemployed and penniless, he enlisted in the LVF on 9 September 1943. He would pass to the Waffen-SS.
9   Born in 1917, Roger Boulin enlisted in the Air Force in 1936 and worked his way up to the rank of *sergent*. He enlisted in the LVF on 21 September 1941 with the rank of *caporal-chef* and was assigned to the 13th Company. He served with the LVF for the next three years in various capacities.
10   Born on 25 October 1921, Hanin was a member of the royalist *Action Française*. He arrived at Sennheim on 13 August 1943 and left in February 1944 for Orianenburg where he was trained as a war correspondent.
11   Rambert is undoubtedly a pseudonym. The name *Bezenn Perrot* was derived from father Jean-Marie Perrot, the parish priest of Scrignac, assassinated by terrorists on 12 December 1943. He was an outspoken advocate of collaboration with the Germans as a road to Breton separatism. The *Bezenn Perrot* was no more than one hundred strong and wore the *feldgrau*. Armed with weapons captured from the terrorists, it took part in operations against the maquis. Rambert was arrested in May 1945 at Rabastens-de-Bigorre and sentenced to life imprisonment on 21 September 1945.
12   According to Bouysse, *Waffen-SS Français* volume 2, Cantelaube served briefly with 'Charlemagne'.

Many of the volunteers could not understand the irony of their new situation; they could 'make amends' by fighting international Communism and yet they had been languishing in prison for years because they had fought against Communism![13]

The volunteers were brought together at Fréjus, where they were dressed and armed, albeit poorly. The military training posed few problems. In fact, their young *encadrement* [Officers and NCOs], except for the *adjudants* and *adjudants-chefs* from the Colonial troops, had limited military experience and thus little to teach. Some were even former members of FFI units!

*Adjudant-chef* Pierre Duthilleul was posted to the BILOM as a '*tour colonial*'. A seasoned soldier, he had fought in North Africa in 1942, in the Italian Campaign with the 1st French Mountain Division as a gunner, in Provence in the late summer of 1944, ending WWII in Germany. In the BILOM, he served in the *section de commandement* as paymaster. He regarded and treated the volunteers as fellow serviceman, although his first impression of them was not good and he thought some were scoundrels. He would enjoy a good relationship with the volunteers.

## Indo-China

Meantime, the Communist Party had orchestrated a press campaign against this project, calling for vengeance, justice and punishment of the 'collabos', but France had need of *soldats* for Indo-China.

Finally, on 11 December 1948, the 1st Company of the BILOM, otherwise the 1/BILOM, 4 officers, 20 NCOs and 148 men, and elements of battalion headquarters, 5 officers and 5 NCOs, boarded the *Pasteur* bound for Indo-China. *Adjudant-chef* Duthilleul was satisfied with the preparation and the combat readiness of the volunteers. Fifteen days later, on 26 December, they disembarked at Saigon.

From 3 January to 17 March 1949, the 1/BILOM was stationed in Cambodia and suffered its first losses. On 18 March, the 1/BILOM was transferred to Sud Annam in the sector of Nha Trang. For the *réprouvés* [outcasts] of the BILOM, the war was one of patrols, ambushes, sudden and violent engagements, exhausting 'combing' operations, booby traps, malaria, dysentery … and death. Losses mounted, but they were not found wanting, proving themselves time and time as *soldats de qualité*.

On 6 April 1949, at Marseille, the first detachment of the 2/BILOM, 2 officers, 6 NCOs and 57 men, boarded SS *Compiègne*. This detachment arrived at Saigon on 8 May and joined the 1/BILOM nine days later. A further detachment of the 2/BILOM, 5 NCOs and 24 men, arrived in June.

The 20 June 1949 marked a milestone in the history of the BILOM. For the first time, the *réprouvés* of the BILOM were decorated with the *Croix de guerre*. This was proof, if proof was needed, of acts of courage. *Adjudant-chef* Duthilleul thought the decorations were merited. All now hoped for respect.

On 2 July 1949, by order of the *général commandant en chef les Forces armées d'Extrême-Orient*, the 1/BILOM was dissolved to form the *1re Compagnie de Marche du Sud Annam*, otherwise the

---

13    The irony of this was also not lost on a former company commander of the 2BEP who served at Dien Bien Phu (letters to the author) whose older brother had joined the Waffen-SS and died in Russian captivity. Both had fought Communism, and yet one was lauded as a hero, the other was regarded as a traitor.

1/CMSA, and the 2/BILOM the 2/CMSA. As a seasoned soldier, *Adjudant-chef* Duthilleul was little concerned with the dissolution of the BILOM. The former prisoners were told that henceforth they were soldiers in regular units of the *Corps expéditionnaire* and French soldiers in the service of their country. Nevertheless, it was not yet a question of discharge or the erasing of sentences.

The CMSAs would be hybrid, comprising 75 percent local and 25 percent European personnel. The surplus Europeans would form a commando, a shock unit, for each company. For the first time, some ex-prisoners were promoted to NCO rank. Also, some were assigned to positions of responsibility in the support services throughout Sud Annam. In this way, the process of their fragmentation began, but France was desperately short of *gradés* of worth.

On 1 January 1950, the 1/CMSA became the *3e Compagnie du 6e bataillon de marche d'Extrême-Orient* (BMEO) and the 2/CMSA the *4e Compagnie du 6e BMEO*.[14] In February, some one hundred former BILOM soldiers of the 3rd and 4th Companies of the 6/BMEO were posted to other units: eighty went to other BMEOs, most notably the 3/BMEO, the 4/BMEO and the 5/BMEO, with the remainder to different units and support services of the *Forces terrestres des Plateaux*. Thus, the spirit of the BILOM lived on throughout the whole of Sud Annam. And yet there was still no prospect of a pardon or amnesty on the administrative horizon.

On 31 December 1950, the BMEOs became *Bataillons montagnards*. In March 1951, the first repatriations of former BILOM personnel started. Some would remain or return to Indo-China.

Giorgio Valle spent more than three years in Indo-China and it took the intervention of his superiors to get him, by now a Sergeant, to agree to leave his unit. Earning his paratrooper wings in France, he quickly returned to the Far East, winning more citations, the Military Medal and the respect of his *chefs*. In Algeria, the Red Berets made him an officer.

Amar Irguiz earnt his strips of *adjudant* and won the Military Medal. After a second tour of duty in Indo-China, he served in black Africa in 'confidential jobs'.

Cantelaube returned to Indo-China for his second tour of duty and came back a sergeant. Marc Barellon was not in France long; he went straight off to fight Communism in Korea and when that war finished he set sail back to Indo-China. Sergeant Barellon was taken prisoner in July 1954 in the region of Ankhé and marched to a camp in Tonkin. He survived. Liberated, he then went to the war in Algeria that was just beginning. After Algeria was granted independence, he left the army and attempted to join the gendarmerie, which was denied.[15]

Robert Cousin would remain loyal to the French Colonial Army for fifteen years. After Indo-China, he served in Algeria as a paratrooper with the Red Berets, and then in Cameroon. He finished his military career in a unit born of the *2e D.B.*

*Adjudant* Hervé Cormatin became an excellent and respected NCO in Indo-China. He stepped on a mine in East Algeria and died hours later in a Parisian hospital. He was decorated with the *Croix de chevalier de la Légion* on his deathbed.

For historical clarity, it should also be mentioned that some former volunteers of the LVF and the Waffen-SS fought on the side of the Viet Minh. One even became an officer! Also, to put their past behind them, some collaborators, including those who had volunteered for and served in the ranks of the Waffen-SS, chose to join the Foreign Legion. They too saw service in Indo-China.

14    The BMEOs were created in response to the Viet-Minh threat on the mountains and plateaux of Sud-Annam.
15    Marc Barellon died on 3 June 1987.

# 22

# After the Fire

**Audibert, Roger.** Brought before the courts, he was one of the few to be acquitted.

**Appolot, François.** Contrary to popular belief, Appolot did not die in Berlin. Captured by the Soviets and sent to Odessa, he was repatriated, imprisoned and tried. He was released in 1947. His family was unaware of his story, except for his son who, after reading a book by Mabire, put two and two together and then spoke at length to his father. He lived somewhere in the east of France.

**Bartolomei, Yvan.** Sentenced to five years in prison by the *Tribunal militare permanent* of Toulouse on 7 January 1947, he was released in July 1948. Died on 10 February 1996 at the grand age of ninety-nine.

**Bassompierre, Jean.** After giving his captors the slip, he crossed France. He passed into Italy with the help of Mme de S.[1] From Naples, he hoped to embark for the safe haven of South America. Under the false name of Joseph Bassemart he managed to obtain travel documents for Buenos Aires. However, after meeting up again with his comrade Jean de Vaugelas, also in a similar situation but without travel documents, he handed his over to him. On 28 October 1945, Bassompierre was arrested aboard a boat that would have taken him to South America. Brought back to France, he was locked up in *la Santé* prison. Hauled before *la Cour de justice de la Seine*,

---

**FANTAISISTE de la collaboration Audibert est acquitté par la Cour de justice**

DEPUIS qu'il moisit dans une cellule de Fresnes, Roger Audibert a eu le temps de réfléchir, et, comme c'est un économiste distingué, ses réflexions se sont orientées vers de très graves problèmes.

Enchaîné mais l'esprit libre, Audibert, dans l'ombre de son cachot, a écrit un ouvrage respectable sur le progessisme communautaire. Il a, d'autre part, jeté les bases d'un parti qui rassemblerait ses adeptes dans un nouvel État.

Ce philosophe dont les différents examens menteaux souligent l'exubérance méridionale, doublée d'une tendance paranoïaque, est un ancien délégué à la propagande de Vichy ; mais devant la 12ᵉ sous-commission de la Cour de justice où il est poursuivi pour intelligences avec l'ennemi, il assure qu'il avait « une âme de résistant ».

**L. V. F. et résistant ?**

« J'ai été en rapport avec le commandant Loustaneau-Lacau, et lorsque je proposais à la Légion Tricolore la création de corps francs tunisiens c'était pour jouer le double jeu ».

En tout cas, les sentiments d'Audibert évoluaient rapidement puisqu'on l'a retrouvé, en 1943, à la tête d'une compagnie de la L.V.F. devant Orel, où il participa à de sanglants combats.

Peu après, au cours d'une permission à Paris, il rencontrait Jean Harold-Paquis, avec qui il étudia un important projet de « lutte contre le maquis ».

« Il est permis d'être illuminé, mais il y a des limites », lui fait observer le président Castel.

« Oh ! c'est en qualité de résistant que j'ai pris contact avec le chroniqueur de « Radio-Paris », réplique Audibert, de plus en plus dans les nuages.

Il redescend sur terre pour entendre son acquittement, les jurés ayant estimé qu'il avait fait du noyautage au sein de la L.V.F.

Report in newspaper *Combat* of 20-21 October 1946 on the acquittal of Audibert, who claimed he was playing a double game.

---

1     A former *résistante*, Mme de S. first came to the assistance of the vanquished in 1945 as they sought to vanish from Europe and escape vengeance. In this way, she would help many other former members of 'Charlemagne'. It should also be noted that the case of Mme de S. was not unique. To cite one example of many, at Bordeaux, in peacetime, a former lieutenant of the F.F.I., considered 'a real hero', hid and helped several fugitives to escape. For more such examples see Piverd, Chapter *Le sauve qui-peut des maudits*, *Historia* hors série, 32, p.180.

Bassompierre was charged on three counts: his attitude as *inspecteur général de la Milice* in the North Zone, his role in the assassination of Georges Mandel, as well as that in the repression of the mutiny at *la Santé* prison, Paris. The case against him was flimsy and soon hinged on the third count: his role in the repression that followed at the prison of *la Santé*. On the evening of 13 July 1944, 'common criminal' prisoners at *la Santé* mutinied. The following morning units of the Paris *Franc Garde* led by Bassompierre restored order. As punishment, the German authorities wanted four hundred prisoners executed, which would have included 'political prisoners' (that is to say *Résistants*) who had refused to join in the mutiny, but Bassompierre talked them down to fifty. He was preparing their execution when Knipping, the *délégué secrétaire d'Etat pour L'Intérieur en zone nord*, arrived and intervened. Knipping negotiated with the German authorities that the fifty would not be summarily executed but appear before a court martial. On the court martial sat *chefs milicien* Pierre Gallet, who was president, Max Knipping and Georges Radici [who would later serve with 'Charlemagne']. Forty-five common law criminals appeared before the court, of which seventeen were exonerated. Half an hour after the proceedings ended, the executions began by the police with guns supplied by the *Franc Garde* units present.

Despite the fact that Bassompierre had saved considerable life 'by opposing the murderous fury of the Germans',[2] two witnesses, Goujet, the *sous-directeur de la Santé* prison, and Vanegue, the *directeur adjoint de la police municipal*, swore on oath that Bassompierre had resigned himself to the execution of fifty mutineers. Following the dispositions of Goujet and Vanegue, the government commissioner concluded that 'Bassompierre had not attempted to lighten the sanctions and was willing to shoot as many Frenchmen as the Germans demanded', which is not true. Bassompierre pleaded his innocence in this bloody affair, reminding this court that he was not a member of the court martial that had handed down the death sentences. Bassompierre's barrister, Charles-Ambroise Colin, opened the speeches for the defence and tried to prove that his client did not have blood on his hands and that he was an 'honourable, ardent and sincere man'. He spoke of the loyalty Bassompierre had sworn to the Maréchal, which 'he had kept to the end', and of the despair which had seized him after the armistice, later leading him to become a soldier. On 17 January 1948, the jury, after just minutes of deliberation, sentenced Bassompierre to death. He replied: "The man you have just sentenced to death is not a criminal or a traitor to his country." Despite pleas for mercy, despite the newspaper *L'Époque* publishing lists of former *résistants* ready to intervene on behalf of Bassompierre, despite a request from Reverend Father Bruckberger to *président* Auriol to take the place of the condemned, 'the only response was the salvo of the execution squad'. In the early morning hours of 20 April 1948, Bassompierres was brought to fort de Montrouge for the execution of his sentence. At 0700 hours, accompanied by his Chaplain, he was marched before the butt. After receiving absolution, Bassompierre let himself be tied to the execution post but refused the blindfold. Bassompierre smiled to Bruckberger, who was now on his knees begging and crying, and then shouted out: "May God protect my family! May God protect France!" The firing squad, made up of *chasseurs alpins*, Bassompierre's former regiment, fired. A NCO administered the *coup de grâce*. It was a needless formality. Bassompierre was dead. He was buried in the cemetery of the *condamnés à mort* at Thiais. Later, he was moved and laid to rest in the family plot in Auteuil cemetery, Paris, under a marble cross carrying the inscription 'J.B. 1914-1948'.

2    Giolitto, *Histoire de la Milice*, p.540.

**Baudouin, Marcel.** Died on 26th January 1969 in Bordeaux.

**Bisiau, Michel.** He was murdered on 15 June 1953 in Ugarteche, Argentina. His killers were never found.

**Blanc, Robert.** On his return to France he was locked up in Fresnes. On 18 May 1946, he was tried at the *Cour de justice*. There was brief mention of his service with the *Milice* in Paris, but nothing about Dijon. He was sentenced to six months in prison and ten years 'national unworthiness'. He was released that same day, having already served seven and a half months. He regretted nothing, except for the grief and the worry he caused his parents, who saw him leave for a cause that they hated and saw as lost. Died on 20 June 2017.

**Blonay, Georges.** Died on 20 January 2016.

**Bonnafont, Jacques.** Died on 29 August 2017 in Paris.

**Boudet-Gheusi, Jean.** Died on 19 December 1969 in Cagnes-sur-Mer.

**Boyer, Emilien.** He was sentenced to hard labour for life by the *Cour de justice* of Montellier which was later commuted. He was released in 1951 and died on 2 January 1995.

**Bridoux, Jean.** It is said that he committed suicide on 14 July 1945 in Eichstätt prison following a visit from one of his former comrades of Saint-Cyr who had lent him his pistol. However, some believe that he was killed *sans jugement*. He is buried in Treuchtlingen cemetery.

**Cance, Pierre.** On 19 February 1947 he was sentenced to death by the *Cour de justice* of Montellier, which was later commuted. He was released on 17 October 1950. Died in August 1988.

**Castrillo, Jean.** In August 1946, he was brought to trial at the *Cour de justice*. Before the verdict the presiding judge asked him if he had any regrets. He replied: *"Monsieur le Président*, I have only one regret and it's losing the war." Reproached for swearing an oath of loyalty to Hitler, he was sentenced to four years in prison and 'national unworthiness' for life. Died in January 2012.

**Cessil, René Jean.** Denounced on his return to France, he was sentenced to two years in prison, plus banishment to Algeria for one year. Died on 15 April 2000.

**Chatrousse, Jean**. The Paris *cour de Justice* sentenced him to two years in prison on 6 October 1947. Died on 11 July 2010.

**Cornu, Noël.** On 18 May 1945, he was arrested at Bordighera. On 24 July, the *Cour de justice du Havre* sentenced him to ten years hard labour, later commuted to five years. Released in 1948, he continued to study medicine. Died on 19 August 2016.

**Croisile, Jean.** Hospitalised by the Soviets in Schievelbein for shrapnel wounds to his leg, he left on 19 April 1945 and changed into civilian clothes. Repatriated, he was arrested at Lille and interned at caserne Vandamme; his blood group tattoo, which he had tried to remove, had been his undoing. On 29 October 1945, the *Cour de justice* of Colmar sentenced this highly decorated veteran of 14-18 and 39-40 to five years in prison and national indignity for life. His son Jean-Marie was sentenced on the same day. He was released in August 1949 and died in 1961 in Casablanca.

**Croisile, Jean-Marie.** Taken captive, he was eventually hospitalised in Lichtenrade, Berlin. He was in poor shape, feeling 'almost paralysed'. An x-ray revealed that he had shrapnel lodged between his first and second cervical vertebrae. The German doctor treating him seemed astonished that he was still alive. It took the doctor two operations to remove the shrapnel, after which he was discharged. By train and on foot, he made his way westwards and crossed into Alsace on 27 July 1945. Questioned at Strasbourg repatriation centre, he explained that he had been forcibly conscripted into the Wehrmacht. His cover story was helped by the simple fact that he had not been tattooed with his blood group which would have identified him as Waffen-SS; he was away at Neweklau when his battalion was tattooed. Released, he decided to travel to Colmar in the hope of finding his parents and made the journey in the company of a person called Renault who he met by chance and who invited him to stay. At Colmar, he could find no trace of his parents. On 2 August, Renault, denounced as a *milicien* on his return, was arrested at home, along with Croisile, who now decided to confess all. On 29 October 1945, the *Cour de justice* of Colmar sentenced him to two years in prison and national indignity for ten years. Died on 5 April 2011.

**Denamps, Paul.** On 16 May 1946, he was sentenced to seven years hard labour. On the family gravestone at Tayrac is a rather large plaque in memory of his two brothers, Jacques and Louis, who were killed in Pomerania while serving with 'Charlemagne'. The plaque reads that they died with 'the LVF on the Eastern Front in March 1945'. Paul admitted that when he learnt of Louis' death he felt more as though he had lost a comrade rather than a brother. The death of his brother would only hit him later, much later. Died on 19 October 2016.

**Désiré, Norbert.** Died in May 1968 in Bordeaux aged fifty-nine.

**Dissent, Jules.** On his return to France, he was still suffering from tuberculosis and was hospitalised for a further two months. On 14 January 1946, he learnt that he had been released conditionally. He may have been free, but his health still continued to fail him and he spent two months in a Paris hospital, which was followed by two years in a sanatorium. In 1950, he was granted an amnesty without going before the courts. He resumed his medical studies and became a doctor.

**Doutart, André.** Tried by a military tribunal, he was acquitted. His love of Jazz never left him. Died on 10 September 2008 in Paris.

**de Genouillac, Michel.** On 3 August 1946, the *Cour de justice d'Orléans* sentenced him to two years in prison and a 50,000 Franc fine for harming the national defense. He served his sentence, which was not reduced at any time, and paid the fine to the last centime before a law of amnesty around 1950.

**de Lacaze, Maxime.** Wounded in Berlin, he was captured in hospital by the Russians. Although still weak, he escaped at night and wandered around the city before occupying an abandoned house in the quarter of Moabit. The following day, he found himself in danger yet again; the Russians had taken over the vacant apartments above and below his. Thereupon he decided to 'move house'. He made his move in the middle of the night. After feeling his way down the building's stairway, he was on the landing when a grenade fell out of his pocket, noisily rolled down the steps and exploded in the road. Riddled with shrapnel, he was very lucky to be alive. His Russian 'neighbours' dashed to his assistance and, without asking him any questions, took him to a hospital. Even though he bore the tell-tale tattoo, he must have counted himself very fortunate that nobody actually thought of checking for this brand when he passed himself off as a conscripted worker. Repatriated to France, he spent five months in Foch de Suresnes hospital and was then moved, still incognito and still 'carrying' pieces of shrapnel, to the Côte d'Azur for convalescence. At Nice, he was introduced to the former *résistante* Mme de S. who had already helped certain *vaincus de la Libération* escape from France. After recounting his story, she smuggled him into Italy at night in her motorboat. His next guardian was a Jesuit who took him in. Sometime later, he managed to reach South America where he started a new life in Argentina. Died on 20 June 2017.

**de Lupé, Jean de Mayol.** The end of the war found de Lupé and his ever faithful Orderly Officer Henri Caux in the American Zone of Occupation. Ignorant of the terrible political climate reigning in France, de Lupé wrote to his family and immediately received a reply from his nephew, Jacques de Mayol de Lupé, telling him to stop all correspondence. But his warning came too late; de Lupé had already sent a post card to his home address on avenue Émile-Accolas, Paris, and was immediately denounced to the Police by the concierge with whom he had been on good terms. In September 1946, de Lupé and Caux were arrested by the Americans. Transferred to Munich, de Mayol de Lupé and Caux were handed over to the French police, who kept them under 'lock and key' for one month before sending them back to France. Upon their arrival, they were both incarcerated in Fresnes. Caux was the first of the two to be tried. The Monseigneur came to his defence and maintained that his secretary had only ever acted on his orders. In February 1947, Caux received a two-year suspended sentence. On 13 May 1947, de Mayol de Lupé appeared before the *cour de justice de Paris*. Struck down by illness months before, the seventy-four-year-old Monseigneur had to be brought into the courtroom on a stretcher carried by four guards. Yet the press immediately accused him of trying to move the public and the judges to pity. He was accused of collaboration, of being a National Socialist apologist and of wearing an enemy uniform and decorations. In the face of government commissioner Coyssac demanding a sentence of hard labour for life, de Lupé's barrister, Mr. Véron, conducted a most brilliant defence with the help of numerous witnesses. Nevertheless, de Mayol de Lupé still received a fifteen-year prison sentence, the general confiscation of his possessions and the loss of (state) rights. He was interned in camp Châtaigneraie at La Celle-Saint-Cloud, where, in June 1950, he celebrated his sacerdotal jubilee. On 24 December 1950, his great-nephew, Luigi de Lupé, of late ordained a priest, celebrated his first mass in the Monseigneur's cell. In May 1951, four years into his sentence, de Lupé was released on parole.[3] He retired to his home on avenue Émile-Accolas where he died on 23 June 1955. At his burial six former POWs who owed their release to him carried the coffin.

**del Missier, Jean.** Against all the odds, he slipped home undetected shortly after the end of the war. In June 1945, his mother reported him to the police. On 25 October 1945, he was sentenced to 20 years hard labour and the confiscation of means present and future. He spent almost three years 'inside': Fresnes (from July 1945 to 6 January 1946), Clairvaux (January 1946 to 15 April 1946), camp Struthof (April 1946 to November 1947), Baugé (November 1947 to January 1948) and, lastly, camp Vierge at Epinal. On 8 May 1948, he was released conditionally. Died on 6 July 2013.

**de Rose, André.** Died on 26 July 1982.

**de Vaugelas, Jean.** After making good his escape from the train returning him to France, he managed to reach Buenos Aires in 1948 under a Red Cross passport and then took refuge in Argentina, where he built up a successful wine business by the name of *Les Caves franco-argentines*. In 1957, he died from injuries received in a car accident near Mendoza, despite an operation to save him.[4]

**Fayard, René.** He managed to reach Spain in 1945 and from there Argentina. He went into partnership with de Vaugelas in *Les Caves franco-argentines* and took over from him at the head of the firm after his death in 1957. Sometime later, he escaped an assassination attempt and, in early 1960, discovered that his car had been sabotaged. On 3 March 1960, he was playing bridge with his wife and friends out in the garden of his home in San Rafael, near Mendoza, when assassinated with a bullet in the nape of the neck.[5] The assassin has never been traced, but many believe that this was the work of the French *2e Bureau*.

**Evrard, Jacques.** After the war he became a *chef de service* (departmental head) in a Paris hospital. Died in December 1994.

---

3    According to Landwehr, *Charlemagne's Legionnaires*, p.192, de Lupé was released because of continuing bad health.
4    However, claims have been made that de Vaugelas was murdered and his death made to look as though it was a car accident. See *L'Express*, 12 August 1993, which states that around ten Frenchmen were silently 'neutralised' in South America without any fuss and made to look as though it was natural death or the result of an accident, including de Vaugelas. Also, in a broadcast of *A la recontre de Monsieur X* on the French radio station *France-Inter*, late September 1997, an 'official' said: 'You know, we murdered Jean de Vaugelas in Argentina!' But such claims are false. Told of the accident, Madame de Vaugelas rushed to her husband's side. She was able to speak to him before and after the operation and at no time did he think that the accident was the result of a 'deliberate wish to kill him'. (*Récit de la Mort de Jean de Vaugelas*, from Madame de Vaugelas to a family friend, 2000, which is in the author's possession.) Moreover, she is convinced that if her husband had any suspicions of malevolence towards him he would have told her.
5    *L'Aurore*, March 1960. This article, titled 'A game of bridge, an assassin and a death', claims that Fayard was a former member of the Gestapo, which is untrue, and that he had swindled 30 million Francs out of his firm, which has never been substantiated.

**Faroux, François**. The end of the war found him in Austria. He decided to return to France and said of this: 'I attempted to make my way into Germany across the bridge over the river Inn at Passau. Because there were American and Allied checkpoints everywhere I decided to say I had no papers and explain the reasons for this. I was made prisoner, though more or less free. Then I was transported to a camp at Bamberg. Some French soldiers were there, but still I was free. And so it was until my return to France in the middle of June. I was brought back on a train with civilians, mostly from Alsace. After two days and two nights we arrived at Longuyon, along the border with Luxembourg, and a camp under the control of the FTP [Communists]. And so began two days of appalling ill treatment. Jail, but twenty to a cell… made to hold a can of shit above our head and then run like that… cigarettes extinguished on our skin (I still carry the marks sixty-one years later). Forty-eight hours later, I was taken to Nancy and the *Sécurité Militaire*. I was interrogated courteously by a Lorrain who had served in the German Army! He told me that I had only to enlist in the French Army for three years and go and fight in Indochina. Then he made me sign up for a regiment that was normally stationed near where my family lived. I was given thirty days to report to the regiment at Rambouillet. This I did, but it was a trap. Two or three days later I was arrested and jailed again. I appeared on the list of 'wanted' and in this way I had given them time enough to find out. Besides if I had not reported then I could have easily been traced in my department, caught and jailed and, if I was not 'wanted', then service for three years.

Anyway, other recruits came to see the jailed *Boche*. The following day, I was transported to Versailles. Two more days of ill treatment at the hands of the police followed before I was presented to a judge. I was sentenced to a 'stretch' of six months, plus fifteen years of national indignity (no rights and more taxes to pay!) because I had not come of age when I enlisted… A lucky man!' Faroux would later reflect that he may have joined and served with the French Army, albeit for a matter of days, but he never wore its uniform, the very same uniform worn by those responsible for the murder of twelve of their fellow countrymen at Bad Reichenhall.

Bartolomei (left) and Fenet (right) May 1985 at a veteran's meeting.

**Fenet, Henri Joseph.** Fenet's stay in Soviet captivity was short-lived. First he was taken to a POW camp and then admitted into a hospital north of Berlin for his foot wound. Days later, he was returned to the POW camp, but in the meantime it had been evacuated. Remarkably, the local Russians provided him with civilian clothes and let him go free. Thereupon he joined a group of French repatriates in south Berlin. Crossing into France at Valenciennes, he was arrested because he bore the telltale blood group tattoo. The soldier who caught him told him: 'This letter is the insignia of killers, the most dangerous killers'.[6] Sentenced to twenty years hard labour, Fenet was released at the end of 1949. Died on 14 September 2002 in Paris.

Henri Fenet (right) at a veteran's meeting.

**Ferber, Jean.** He joined the *Milice* in Paris and was incorporated into the Waffen-SS, serving with the Artillery Battalion. Most notably, he's remembered for escaping during a session with an examining magistrate in Paris by jumping through a window and leaning up against a tree to hide the big red PG markings on the back of his jacket and trousers. Eventually recaptured, he spent time in Struthof and was released on 19th April 1947. Died on 5 March 2011.[7]

**Ginot, Raoul.** Died on 5 June 2011 and was buried on 10 June 2011.

**Gonzales, Henri-Georges.** From Valenciennes, he was moved to Douai prison, dating from the time of Napoleon, and then to his native Marseille. Processed through the Law Courts, he was sentenced in his absence to death, which was later commuted to four years imprisonment.

6    Roch, *La Division Charlemagne*, p.149.
7    Newsletter, NK 33, July 2011.

His time in prison was hard but made bearable thanks to the support from his parents. On 29 June 1948, after some two and a half years in prison, he was released conditionally. Died on 27 December 2017.

**Grenouillet, Jean.** The *Cour de Justice* of Bordeaux sentenced him to three years in prison and ten years loss of national rights. He was released on 12 May 1948 and granted an amnesty in 1950. At that time the French Army was in need of junior *cadres*, and although exempt from military service, he was at the end of 1951 called before the Military Authorities, who proposed that he undertake training of his own free will to become an *sous-officier de réserve*. He agreed to this. He enlisted at the end of July 1952 and was appointed *sergent* one month later, then *sergent-chef* in the reserves at the end of 1955. In June 1956, he asked to serve in Algeria where he would remain on active service until March 1957. On 1 October 1956, he was appointed *sous-lieutenant de réserve*. After Algeria he continued to train in the reserves, reaching the rank of *chef de bataillon*. As a member of a combatant unit in Algeria, he was decorated with the *Croix de la Valeur Militaire*. Died on 25 June 2007.

**Halard, Jean.** Not tattooed, he managed to make it back to France by passing himself off as an S.T.O. deportee. Called up, he found himself back in uniform! He chose to go to Indo China for the duration of his military service. That was two years. On his return to France in 1947 he was arrested by the Military Police; the Czechs had passed to France all the dossiers of the French volunteers of the Waffen-SS held in Prague. He was brought before a *Tribunal pour enfants* [Juvenile court] - he was a minor when he enlisted - but the charges against him of harming the national defence were dropped because of the *loi d'amnistie* [law of amnesty] of 1947. He remained very proud of having fought for Europe in the ranks of the Waffen-SS.

**Hennecart, Lucien.** Died on 18 June 1996 in Avignon.

**Hersche, Heinrich.** He spent two and a half years in American captivity, passing through thirteen POW camps. On 27 September 1947, the Americans freed him and gave him the choice of staying in the US zone or returning to Switzerland. He chose the latter. On his return home, he was tried and sentenced to one year in prison and loss of citizen rights for two years. Died on 9 February 1971.

**Hug, Pierre.** After the war he exiled himself to Argentina. Died on 21 October 1991.

**Jauss, Hans Robert.** After the war he studied philosophy and history at Heidelburg where he became a professor in 1957. One of the founders of the University of Constance, he obtained in 1966 the chair of Romance literature. Died on 1 March 1997.

**Kreis, Henri.** Died on 9 May 1990.

**Krukenberg, Gustav.** On 9 May 1945, Krukenberg and ten other prisoners were brought before a Soviet Lieutenant who, to the great surprise of all, asked them if anybody could play an accordion he had just found in his lodgings. One man came forward and, after a one hour long concert, the Soviet officer freed them all, including Krukenberg. He went north to Wittenau where they had agreed to meet up, but 'nobody else was there'. Then he made his way to the suburbs to the west of Berlin. In Dahlem he rested at a friend's residence. Krukenberg had much to think about: he had seen a poster from the Soviet *Kommandantur* of Berlin ordering all German officers to come forward. What should he do? While convinced that he could get through to the west he chose to share the fate of the European volunteers placed under him at Berlin.[8] He felt morally bound in particular to the French volunteers who had held to the end beside him. So, on 12 May 1945, Krukenberg presented himself of his own free will to the Russian authorities at Berlin-Steglitz, indicating his rank and service record. A Soviet military tribunal sentenced him to the loss of liberty for twenty-five years.[9] His crime was 'damages caused to the Red Army by his military resistance in Pomerania and Berlin'. After eleven years in Soviet captivity in East Berlin, including three in solitary confinement, he was finally released.[10] In the years that followed, Krukenberg continued to work for reconciliation between Germany and France. Died on 23 October 1980 in Bonn.

**Lacoste, Robert.** He was in the camp at Thorn with Robert Blanc and was repatriated by the French Red Cross. He was also locked up in Fresnes.

**Lavest, Louis.** Captured in Berlin, he passed himself off as a worker who was injured when his factory was bombed and ended up in a camp in Biesdorf, East Berlin, where he came across a comrade from the *Compagnie d'honneur*, as well as Marc Montgour, one of his former *chefs de centaine* in the *Franc-Garde*. Montgour did not recognise him at first. They went their separate ways. Moved to Magdeburg, he was handed over to the Americans and then repatriated to Charleville-Mézières. He stuck to his story until he was asked to raise his left arm which revealed his tattoo. Arrested and hospitalised, after which he was sent to Paris with seven other SS and incarcerated in la Santé for one night, followed by Fresnes. In October 1945, he was moved to Lyon and incarcerated in Saint-Paul. In January 1946, he fell ill and was admitted into the prison hospital and administered aspirin. Lavest wrote of his poor treatment:[11] 'The administration preferred to see the sick die, rather than send them to [the hospital at] Antiquaille, a scandal which has never been mentioned.' After several days on aspirin, his fever dropped, but it came back again worse than ever whereupon the medical staff finally took his illness seriously. He managed to survive this illness, later diagnosed as pleurisy, thanks more to his strong constitution than medication. On 3 April 1946, he was sentenced by the *Cour de justice de Lyon* to eighteen months in prison and national indignity for life, although his assets

8    According to Saint-Loup, *Les Hérétiques*, p.495, Krukenberg was naive to surrender. This is incorrect, for he knew full well what awaited him in Soviet captivity (Krukenberg, *Combat pour Berlin*, p.21).

9    Krukenberg, *Combat pour Berlin*, p.22, Mabire, *Mourir À Berlin*, p.313, and Mabire, chapter Entretien avec le général Krukenberg, *Historia* hors série 32, p.137. However, according to Saint-Loup, *Les Hérétiques*, p.496, and Landwehr, *Charlemagne's Legionnaires*, p.169, Krukenberg was sentenced to twenty-five years hard labour.

10   Krukenberg, *Combat pour Berlin*, p.22, Mabire, *Mourir À Berlin*, p.313, Bouysse, *Encyclopaedia of the New Order: French in German Uniform Part 1: Officers* and Landwehr, *Charlemagne's Legionnaires*, p.169. Incorrectly, his time in captivity has appeared as thirteen years (Saint-Loup, *Les Hérétiques* p.496, and Mabire, chapter Entretien avec le général Krukenberg, *Historia* hors série 32, p.137).

11   Levast, *Le soleil se couchait à l'est*, p.156.

were not confiscated being a minor 'at the time of the facts'. This left him with four months to serve, but one month later he was granted conditional release. Died on 31 December 2005.

**Lefèvre, Jean-Pierre.** From his release to his death of a heart attack on 26 February 1994, he devoted himself to the care of his former comrades in arms.

**Louis, Henri.** Died on 22 December 1979.

**Mailhe, Jean.** Died on 12 June 1997 in Paris.

**Malardier, Jean.** Captured in Berlin, he was repatriated to France where he was sentenced to two and a half years imprisonment. He served his sentence in full, refusing conditional release; he spent more than one year in Cuincy, near Valenciennes, and the remainder at Noë. He was released in March 1948. Died in 2018.

**Marotel, Emil**. Sentenced to ten years hard labour, he was released on 14 July 1949. Died on 12 January 1996.

**Martres, Christian.** Handed over to the French Army, he was transported under escort to Lille. He was in the company of a deportee. His true identity was not known until his tattoo was discovered. On his arrival at Lille, he was locked up in a cage at the zoo. People from the local area came to insult and spit at him and the other prisoners. And then one day a 'visitor' to the zoo approached his cage and pointed him out as the 'biggest bastard' whereupon he was pulled from his cage by a large crowd and badly beaten up, describing it as a 'monumental correction'. The guards did not intervene. Only then was Martres transferred to prison Loos-les-Lille. Martres was tried before the *tribunal militaire de Paris*. He feared the worst when he learnt that the representative for the prosecution was a Communist whose son had been executed by German Waffen-SS Division 'Das Reich' in the Limousin. The defence argued that Martres was very young and likened 'Charlemagne' to the Brigade 'Jeanne d'Arc' [that had fought on the side of Franco during the Spanish Civil War]. He was sentenced to seven years imprisonment. Surprisingly, his property - as an only child he had inherited the property of his parents killed by an English bomber shot down by FLAK - was not confiscated. Was this an oversight? The answer is undoubtedly yes. He served two years in a number of prisons - *la Santé* in Paris, Fresnes,[12] Versailles and le Struthof - before his release at the end of 1947. The BILOM approached him, but he did not want to fight, calling it a 'regiment of forced combat'. He had no regrets. Died on 27 July 2003.

**Mercier, Raymond.** From Valenciennes, he was moved to Douai prison, where he was imprisoned on 27 November 1945. Compared to the Soviet camps he had been through, Douai, although rather rustic, was paradisiacal. The food was spartan but compared to the menu at Tambov it was abundant. At first, the prisoners shared five to a cell, which later became three. Mercier shared with Std.Ju. Louis Salmon and Charles M. (ex-LVF of the 3rd Company, captured

12   Martres was at Fresnes when Laval was shot.

at Bobr) who continued to support him. On 28 May 1946, *la Cour de Justice de Valenciennes* sentenced Mercier to four years in prison and 'national unworthiness'. In early 1947, Mercier was transferred to Noé prison. For the journey he was chained to Paul Viaud, a former *Milicien* who was also 'Charlemagne'.[13] Once again he found himself among friends: Blonay, Enselme, Edmond Faudemay (Sturmmann, Company 8/58), Malardier, Raoul Martin,[14] Pierre Million-Rousseau, Vincenot and many others. Never would he forget *la messe des Rameaux* [Palm Sunday] at Noé that year, for the Gospel of the Passion was read by Robert Le Vigan, one of the greatest actors of French pre-war cinema. Little by little, prison life became more civilised and during the summer they could even take advantage of the sun. In August 1947, he was moved to a new prison: Saint-Sulpice la Pointe in the Tarn. It came as a great surprise to him to find that the men who ran the prison were intelligent and humane, more so because the prison governor was a communist militant. There was much talk of Quiquempois, the Spiess of Fahrschwadron B, who had made good his escape from the camp and then sent a postcard to the prison governor on the day of his departure for South America![15] With over half his sentence served, Mercier was released conditionally on 23 February 1948, but asked and obtained permission to leave the next morning so that he could spend one last evening with the comrades whose friendship and loyalty had got him through captivity. He may have gained liberty, but *rien n'était fini*. He entered a world that he had left some seven years before and which he no longer knew. Died on 24 February 2015, aged 93. He was buried in the family plot at Bois Le Roi cemetery.

**Méric, Pierre.** On 21 January 1946, Méric was transferred from Douai to Agen. On 17 May 1946, he was brought before the *Cour de Justice* of Agen. His last words to the court were: 'At all times I had the certainty of doing my duty'. The court disagreed and sentenced him to death by firing squad, whereupon he was put in chains. Sixty-two days later, on 17 July 1946, he was told that his sentence had been commuted to twenty years hard labour. He was moved to the Maison centrale d'Eysses in Lot-et-Garonne, where he would spend almost three years. Moved to Saint-Sulpice la Pointe in the Tarn, he was released conditionally on 23 October 1949. That same day, his father and his father-in-law came to collect him. Pierre Méric died on 19 May 2008.

**Métais, Pierre-Marie.** Died in Bayonne on 13 September 1973.

**Montgour, Marc.** In 1946, he was shot in Lyon for his activities in the *Milice*.

**Nelly.** In November 1944 she was sent to a hospital in Bavaria where she met and befriended a young Flemish girl. At the end of the war they fled to Austria and took to the hills with soldiers. Captured by the English, they were made prisoners on parole because the English 'did not want to believe that they were volunteers'! The English left and were followed by the Americans who handed them over to the French on île de Mainau, lake Constance. Her Flemish friend was

---

13    Viaud would later present Mercier to his family as his *compagnon de chaine*.
14    Born on 2 February 1923 at Menton (department Alpes-Maritimes), Raoul Martin enlisted in the Kriegsmarine in 1944 and was transferred to 'Charlemagne' where he served in the Engineer Company.
15    Sentenced on 4 January 1946 to twenty years in prison, national indignity for life and confiscation of all means by the *Cour de justice* of Toulouse, Quiquempois made good his escape from Saint-Sulpice la Pointe on 8 June 1946.

handed over in turn to the Belgians. Transported to Lyon, she was incarcerated in Fort Paillet in a dungeon and chained to a young Alsatian girl: 'The handcuffs rather amused us. Well we were young and idealists'. Four or five months later, thanks to her lawyer, a close family friend, she was transferred to Paris and Fresnes. After finding herself in a cell with six others, a situation that lasted a matter of days, she shared a cell with the niece by marriage of General de Lattre de Tassigny. The cell was so cold that one sudden warm night waterlogged their straw mattress. When brought before the courts she could not keep quiet, remarking that she regretted nothing. This drove her lawyer to despair, but eventually he managed to get her out because of her fragile health. She looked like a skeleton. Months later, she appeared before a civic court at which only her lawyer had the right to speak. Found guilty of collaboration, she was sentenced to 20 years of 'national unworthiness' and the confiscation of possessions. This sentence did not concern her. She had taken the nationality of her wartime fiancé, that of Denmark, and being rather spendthrift, she had few belongings. She moved to Germany and regretted nothing.

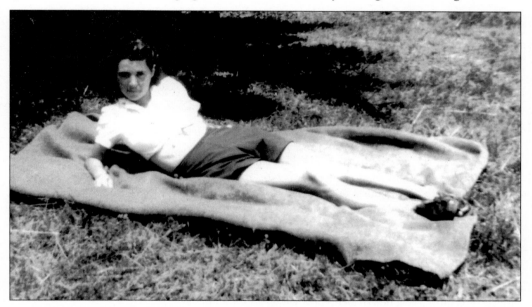

Nelly after her release from prison. (Nelly)

**Peyret, Yves.** From Neuengamme, he was transferred to SS-POW Camp 357 at Fallingbostel. On 15 September 1945, he was handed over to the French authorities. On 13 March 1946, the *Cour de Justice de Poitiers* sentenced him to 20 years hard labour, later commuted to a prison sentence of five years. In August 1948, he was released conditionally. Died on 18 November 2017.

**Pignard-Berthet, Paul.** In June 1946, after one week in Fallingbostel POW camp, he was repatriated to France via Strasbourg, ending up at Chambéry where at the start of September 1946 he was tried and sentenced to five years hard labour. Imprisoned at Mauzac, his sentence was later commuted to three years. In mid-October 1948, he was released conditionally. Died on 24 May 2010.

**Pillet, Jean-Jacques.** Escaping from the Americans, he chose to go straight back home to his parents, arriving in Paris on 21 May 1945. He had wanted to stay in German but could not speak the language and was concerned about the constant threat of being 'shopped'. Died on 21 September 2009.

**Prunennec, Yvon.** Died on 2 April 2015.

**Puechlong, Jean-Louis.** On 24 June 1945, because of his severe injuries, he was repatriated. He was hospitalised in Paris and underwent further surgery 'to regularise' the stump. In mid-August 1945, he escaped from the hospital. Remaining in Paris, he went underground. At the end of September 1946, he was arrested and imprisoned in Fresnes. Brought before the *Tribunal militaire de Paris*, he received a two-year prison sentence. He served his sentence in full. Died on 3 August 2002.

**Radici, Georges.** Sentenced to death by the *cour de justice de la Seine* for his activities in the *Milice* on 7 January 1947, he was shot on 24 July 1947 at Fort Montrouge.

**Raybaud, Emile.** Captured and repatriated to France, where he was tried and sentenced to death for his service in the *Franc-Garde de la Milice*. He was imprisoned at Limoges and found himself in the same cell with four or five prisoners, including some notable *chefs de la Milice*, including Dr. Lejeune, the *chef départemental de la Milice* for Corrèze who was involved in the events that transpired at Tulle in June 1944. During the night of 8 September 1946, an armed mob (undoubtedly communists or former FTP) broke into the jail and forced the guards to take them to the cell of the condemned to death. When the cell door was opened, one of the prisoners by the name of Delaplace rushed one of the assailants armed with a machine-gun. The two fought while the others in the cell barricaded themselves. Moments later Delaplace fell, riddled with bullets, but his sacrifice saved the others.[16] According to a newspaper report which appeared in *La Croix*, 'The perpetrators of the attack left without having been identified'. Raybaud's sentence was not executed. Pardoned, he was released after serving six years in prison.

> **Des inconnus en armes envahissent la prison de Limoges et tuent un milicien**
>
> Dans la nuit de jeudi à vendredi, une quinzaine d'individus armés ont réussi à se faire ouvrir la porte de la prison de Limoges et, sous la menace de leurs armes, ont obligé les gardiens à les conduire à la cellule des condamnés à mort où étaient enfermés cinq miliciens notoires, notamment de Bary, inspecteur régional, et Barbier, chef départemental de la Milice en Haute-Vienne, ainsi que le Dr Lejeune, chef départemental de la Milice de la Corrèze.
>
> Lorsque la porte fut ouverte, le milicien Delaplace, se rendant compte de ce qui attendait les condamnés, engagea la lutte avec un homme porteur d'une mitraillette. Les autres détenus profitèrent de cette bagarre pour se barricader à l'intérieur de leur cellule.
>
> Quelques instants après, Delaplace tombait, criblé de balles de mitraillette, et les autres détenus échappaient de justesse aux nombreuses balles tirées par la lucarne de la cellule.
>
> Les auteurs de l'attentat quittèrent la prison sans avoir été identifiés.

Newspaper *La Croix* reports that an armed mob forced its way into Limoges prison, which resulted in the death of a *Milicien*.

---

16    Delaplace, a former communist militant from Soissons who had converted to the cause of the PPF, served with the LVF, where he was promoted to *Sergent* and also awarded with the Iron Cross 2nd class. Wounded and brought back to France for recuperation, he then decided to offer his services to the SiPo-SD (Security Police).

In 1970, much to his surprise, he learnt from a former secretary serving on the headquarters staff of Waffen-Gren. Regt der SS 58 that late into the Pomeranian campaign he had been promoted to the rank of Obersturmbannführer and awarded the Iron Cross 1st Class. This Krukenberg confirmed. Died on 7 September 1995.

**Rigeade, Yves.** Died on 5 August 2005.

**Rossignol, Philippe.** Died on 20 September 2006.

**Ruskone, Pierre**. Died on 7 July 2005.

**Salle, Louis.** He was sentenced to death in absentia by the *Cour de justice* of Toulouse on 6 February 1946. Died in 1953 in Briançon, in the department of Hautes-Alpes.

**Sainteuil, Marc.** In early May 1945, dressed as a civilian, he set off back to France, but without identity papers he did not get far. Crossing the Rhine, he was stopped at a police checkpoint and questioned. He explained that his identity papers had been stolen, which were kindly replaced in a Breton name, made up by him, and with a place of birth in a village near Brest whose town hall he knew had been bombed and set on fire by the Anglo-Americans, destroying all records. En route for Brittany, he decided to stop in the town of a fellow countryman by the name of Lucien he had met in Germany some weeks before.[17] Lucien had championed the politics of the 'New Europe' in this town and had left with the Germans in August 1944. Sainteuil hoped for help from Lucien's family, whose address Lucien had given him to pass on news. What innocence! Lucien's wife greeted Sainteuil with the 'welcome': "If you knew what trouble Lucien caused us I would rather that he were dead." She went and denounced him to the police. That evening, he went in search of female company and 'scored', spending that night and most of the following day in the bedroom of a small hotel. Almost dark when they left, they failed to spot that they were being followed. Two plain-clothes policemen arrested them and took them to the local police station for questioning. Knowing that the woman was married, he wanted to protect her honour and see her go free with the minimum of fuss and delay. He thought about persisting with his Breton identity, but that meant the police would keep hold of her until such as time as he checked out. He thought about escaping at night, but that meant leaving her in the hands of the police. And so rather than give his real identity he gave a second false name, that of a Swiss man, also an actor, well known in the theatre circle of Paris, who had enlisted in the Waffen-SS at the same time as him. Sainteuil was aware that this Swiss man, full of Nietzschean ideas, had asked Hersche after fifteen days at Sennheim to leave and return to Switzerland, which was granted. To support his new identity, Sainteuil even gave the police the address of this Swiss man's mother in Paris, which by chance he had remembered. When the police phoned 'his' mother in front of him she confirmed that her son had enlisted in the Germany Army and that he was in flight. Thus, the police could not prove any connection between the woman and this Swiss man. Asked how they knew each, Sainteuil replied by way of an explanation that they had met quite by chance in the street. And so she was released after some two hours in detention. As

---

17    Lucien is a pseudonym.

for Sainteuil, he spent the night at the police station to the outside accompaniment of car horns, laughter and lights to celebrate victory. It was the 7 May 1945 and Germany had just capitulated. The following day, he was handcuffed and moved to the town's prison. Finally, he admitted his real identity. One month later, he was transferred to Fresnes. Once at Fresnes, through his lawyer, he requested of the Ministry of Justice authorisation to fight in the war in Indo-China, which had just started. The response came: "Your client must be judged first." With disappointment, Sainteuil reflected: 'In this way, France refused to turn the page, to reinstate into the national community a young Frenchman who perhaps had made a wrong choice, but who was ready to risk his life to show quite simply that he was a Frenchman'. Moreover, he thought it ironic that at the same time the Foreign Legion was opening its ranks to hundreds of Germans from the Wehrmacht and the Waffen-SS with 'no questions asked'. In early 1946, Sainteuil was tried. When asked by the judge 'if the accused had anything to add' he spoke of his convictions and reasons for enlistment in May 1944 when victory was not assured. This he did in reaction to those also in the dock who 'rewrote history' to get out of this spot. Sentenced to ten years in prison, he was unexpectedly released in early October 1946. He had his lawyer to thank who, in collusion with his parents, had conspired to prove that he was mentally ill. Nevertheless, he had already served some sixteen months at Fresnes. Sainteuil returned to acting, but then one day the police arrested him again. Due to an administrative error, his name still figured on a wanted list. While the matter was sorted he spent four days in *la Santé* prison, which was worse than the five hundred or so of his first captivity. But his secret was now out and the Communist *Union des Artiste* made sure that he never set foot on the boards again. Bitterly, he recalls that his second arrest took away from him another love, that of the theatre.

**Sepchat, Jean.** Died on 22 May 2011.

**Simon, Henri.** He was sentenced to fifteen years of hard labour by the *Cour de justice* of Orléans on 20 September 1945. Died on 24 April 1997.

**Soulat, Robert**. Died on 14 July 2015 in Paris.

**Soulé, Pierre.** Wearing a Russian jacket and chapka, he made it out of Berlin, passing himself off as a French partisan. Captured by the Americans, he escaped and made his way to the region of Innsbruck-Salzburg where he joined up with 'elements of all nationalities determined to continue the fight'. From the mountains, they harassed the Russians, inflicting some damage. Out of ammunition and hungry, they surrendered to the Americans, but the Americans refused to take them prisoner because the POW camps had been emptied. Soulé was given a German identity card and taken on as an auxiliary. 'Weary of their congenital stupidity', he left them and made it back to France. Denounced, charged, sentenced, he served one year in prison. Died on 22 December 1992 in his native Bordeaux.

**Triqueneaux, Bernard**. Wearing civilian clothes, he was repatriated via Odessa, landing at Marseille on 10 May 1945. He managed to slip through the 'mesh' of the D.S.T. [*Direction de la Surveillance du Territoire*] and went into hiding, moving between different convents in Brittany thanks to his very catholic family. Eventually he gave himself up at Marseille on 21 December 1945. In the meantime, on 19 November 1945, he had been sentenced in absentia to twenty years hard labour. He was fortunate to be tried by the Military Tribunal of Nancy which, on 16 March 1946, sentenced him to three years in prison for acts likely to harm the National Defense. Transferred to Haut Close de Troyes, he found himself among friends. On 8 June 1947, his youngest brother, a newly ordained priest, celebrated his first mass before the detainers. Transferred on 10 May 1948 to Camp de la Viege at Epinal, he was released on 28 June 1948 after his sentenced was suspended following the intervention of a powerful *Conseiller d'Etat* [Councillor of State], who was a family friend. He was granted amnesty in 1949. He married again and moved to Belgium, where died on 4 May 1997.

**Verney, Albert.** On 16 January 1946 he was sentenced to five years hard labour but was released on 12 February 1949. Died on 20 July 1965 in Carpentras.

**Vincent, Roger.** Died on 2 September 1974 in Strasbourg.

Tricolore arm shield worn by Jules Dissent of the Medical Company.

# Bibliography

## Unpublished Manuscripts

Cera, Jean-François, 'Les raisons de l'engagement des volontaires français sous l'uniforme allemand, juillet 1941 mai 1945' (1992)

Marotin, *Émil*, 'La longue marche' (published in 2007)

Roch, Sabine, 'La Division Charlemagne' (1990)

Soulat, Robert, 'Historique de la Division Charlemagne'

Soulat, Robert, 'Histoire des volontaires français dans l'armée allemande 1940-1945'


## Books

Angolia, John, *Cloth Insignia of the SS* (San Jose: Bender publishing, 1983, 2nd printing)

Archer, Lee, Kraska, Robert & Lippert, Mario, *Panzers in Berlin 1945* (Old Heathfield:
Panzerwrecks, 2019)

Armani, Yves, *Les pendues de Wildflecken* (Paris: Éditions de l'Homme Libre)

Aron, Robert, *The Vichy regime 1940-44* (London: Putnam, 1958)

Auvray, Jacques, *Les derniers grognards* (Paris: Editions Irminsul, 1999)

Barger, Charles, *The SS family* (Epsom: Ulric, 1998)

Bassompierre, Jean, *Frères ennemis* (Paris: Amiot-Dumont, 1948)

Bayle, André, *De Marseille à Novossibirsk*, (Histoire et Tradition, 1992)

Bayle, André, *San et Persante* (Self-published, 1994)

Bender, Roger James and Taylor, Hugh Page, *Uniforms, organization and history of the Waffen-SS*,
volume 4 (San Jose: Bender publishing, 1982)

Bene, Krisztián, *La collaboration militaire française dans la Seconde Guerre mondiale* (Éditions
Codex, 2011)

Bene, Krisztián, *Les archives de la a collaboration militaire française dans la Seconde Guerre mondiale*
(Éditions Codex, 2015)

Boch, Charles, *Le guet-apens de Bad Reichenall* (Paris: Les Éditions du Lore, 2008)

Bouysse, Grégory, *Encyclopaedia of the New Order: French in German Uniform Part 1: Officers*
(Lulu, 2018)

Bouysse, Grégory, *Encyclopédie de l'ordre nouveau: Français sous l'uniforme allemande partie II:
sous-officiers & hommes du rang de la Waffen-SS* (Lulu, 2019)

Bouysse, Grégory, *Encyclopédie de l'ordre nouveau: Histoire du SOL, de la Milice française & des mouvements de la collaboration volume* 8 (Lulu, 2020)

Bouysse, Grégory, *Encyclopédie de l'ordre nouveau: Français sous l'uniforme allemande partie III: LVF* (Lulu, 2020)

Brunet, Jean-Paul, *Jacques Doriot* (Paris: Balland, 1986)

Cazalot, Georges, *... Et la terre a bu leur sang!* (Paris: Éditions de l'Homme Libre, 2005)

Charbonneau, Henry, *Le roman noir de la droite française* (Robert Desroches, 1969)

Chevallet, Franck and Martin, Gérard, *Pour la France, pour l'Europe* (Amazon, 2018)

Colin, Charles Ambroise, *Sacrifice de Bassompierre* (Paris: Amiot-Dumont, 1948)

Comte, Maurice, *Une vie sous le signe de Führerprinzip* (Saint-Genis-Laval: Akriberia, 2014)

Conway, Martin, *Collaboration in Belgium* (New Haven and London: Yale University Press, 1993)

Costabrava, Fernand, *Le soldat Baraka* (Self-published, 2007)

Croisile, Jean-Marie, *Sous Uniforme Allemand* (Paris: Nimrod, 2018)

Cullen, Stephen, *World War II Vichy French Security Troops* (Oxford: Osprey Publishing, 2018)

Dank, Milton, *The French against the French* (London: Cassell, 1978)

Davis, Brian Leigh, *German uniforms of the Third Reich* (London: Blandford Press, 1980)

Davies, W.J.K., *German Army handbook 1939-1945* (London: Purnell Book Services, 1974)

Delarue, Jacques, *Trafics et crimes sous l'Occupation* (Fayard, 1968)

Deloncle, Luc, *Trois jeunesses provençales* (Paris: Dualpha, 2004)

Delperrié, de Bayac Jacques, *Histoire de la Milice* (Paris: Fayard, 1969)

Deniau, Jean-François, de l'Académie française, *Mémoires de 7 vies* (Paris: Plon, 1954)

Deniel, Alain, *Bucard et le Francisme* (Paris: Jean Picollec, 1979)

Duffy, Christopher, *Red storm over the Reich* (New York: Atheneum, 1991)

Dupont, Pierre, *Au temps des choix héroiques* (Paris: Editions de l'homme libre, 2002)

Duprat, François, *Les campagnes de la Waffen-SS*, two volumes (Paris: Les Sept Couleurs, 1992 and 1993)

Ertel, Heinz and Schule-Kossens, Richard, *Europäische Freiwillige im Bild* (Osnabrück: Munin Verlag, 1986)

Fenet, Henri, *Berlin: Derniers témoignages* (Paris: Éditions de l'Homme Libre)

Fosten, D.S.V. and Marrion, R.J., *Waffen-SS* (London: Almark publications, 1974, 4th edition)

Fournier-Foch, Henry, *Tovarich Kapitaine Foch* (Paris: La Table Ronde, 2001)

Gaultier, Léon, *Siegfried et le Berrichon* (Paris: Perrin, 1991)

Germain, Michel, *Histoire de la Milice et des forces du maintien de l'ordre en Haute-Savoie 1940-1945* (Montmélian: La Fontaine de Siloé, 1997)

Giolitto, Pierre, *Histoire de la Milice* (Paris: Perrin, 1997)

Giolitto, Pierre, *Volontaires français sous l'uniforme allemand* (Paris: Perrin, 1999)

Hirschfeld, Gerhard & Marsh, Patrick, *Collaboration in France* (Oxford: Berg, 1989)

Jurado, Carlos, *Foreign volunteers of the Wehrmacht* (Oxford: Osprey Publishing, 1983)

Jurado, Carlos, *Resistance warfare 1940-1945* (Oxford: Osprey Publishing, 1985)

Kedward, Harry, *Occupied France Collaboration and Resistance 1940-1944* (Oxford: Basil Blackwell Ltd, 1985)

Klietmann, Dr. K.-G., *Die Waffen-SS eine Dokumentation* (Osnabrück: Verlag 'Der Freiwillige' G.m.b.H. 1965)

Kumm, Otto, *Prinz Eugen* (Winnipeg: J.J. Fedorowicz Publishing, 1995)

La Mazière, Christian de, *Ashes of Honour* (London: Tattoo, 1976)

Labat, Eric, *Les places étaient chères* (Paris: La Table Ronde, 1953)

Lambert, Pierre P. and Le Marec, Gérard, *Organisations, mouvements et unités de l'état français, Vichy 1940-1944* (Paris: Jacques Grancher, 1992)

Lambert, Pierre P. and Le Marec, Gérard, *Partis et mouvements de la collaboration, Paris 1940-1944* (Paris: Jacques Grancher, 1993)

Lambert, Pierre P. and Le Marec, Gérard, *Les Français sous le casque allemand* (Paris: Jacques Grancher, 1994)

Landwehr, Richard, *Charlemagne's Legionnaires* (Silver Spring: Bibliophile Legion Books, 1989)

Lannurien, François de, *Le sublime et la mort* (Paris: Editions de l'homme libre, 2009)

Littlejohn, David, *Foreign legions of the Third Reich*, volume 1 (San Jose: Bender publishing, 1979)

Le Tissier, Tony, *The battle of Berlin 1945* (London: Jonathan Cape, 1988)

Le Tissier, Tony, *SS Charlemagne: The 33rd Waffen-Grenadier Division of the SS* (Barnsley: Pen and Sword, 2006)

Lefèvre, Eric and Mabire, Jean, *La LVF 1941: Par-40° devant Moscou* (Fayard, 1985)

Lefèvre, Eric and Mabire, Jean, *La Légion perdue* (Paris: Jacques Grancher, 1995)

Lefèvre, Eric and Mabire, Jean, *Sur les pistes de la Russie centrale* (Paris: Jacques Grancher, 2003)

Lefèvre, Eric and Mabire, Jean, *Par-40° devant Moscou Les Français de la L.V.F. 1941* (Paris: Grancher, 2004)

Lefèvre, Eric and Oliver, Pigoreau, *Bad Reichenhall* (Paris: Grancher, 2010)

Léguerandais, Christophe, *Hitler's French volunteers* (Barnsley: Pen & Sword Military, 2016)

Léguerandais, Christophe, *Les Volontaires français dans l'armée allemande* (Memorabilia, 2020)

Levast, Louis, *Le soleil se couchait à l'est* (Paris: Editions de l'homme libre, 2008)

Lindenblatt, Helmut, *Pommern 1945* (Gelbersdorf: Verlag Gerhard Rautenbeg, 1993, 2nd edition)

Logusz, Michael, *The Waffen-SS 14th Grenadier Division 1943-1945* (Atglen: Schiffer publishing, 1997)

Lormier, Dominique, *SS Français* (Paris: Éditions Jourdan, 2018)

Lupo, Georges, *Levée d'écrou* (1948)

Mabire, Jean, *La Brigade Frankreich* (Fayard, 1973)

Mabire, Jean, *La Division Charlemagne* (Fayard, 1974)

Mabire, Jean, *Mourir à Berlin* (Fayard, 1975)

Mabire, Jean, *Mourir pour Dantzig* (Paris: L'Aencre, 1995)

Mabire, Jean, *La Division Nordland* (Fayard, 1982)

Madeja, W. Victor, *Russo-German war 25 January to 8 May 1945* (Valor publishing company, 1987)

Malardier, Jean, *Combats pour l'honneur* (Paris: Editions de l'homme libre, 2007)

Malbosse, Christian, *Le soldat traqué* (Paris: La Pensée moderne, 1971)

Martelli, Paul, *On the Devil's tail* (Solihull: Helion & Company, 2015)

Marotin, Émil, *La longue marche* (Paris: Arctic, 2007)

Mehner, Kurt, *Die Waffen-SS und Polizei 1939-1945* volume 3 (Norderstedt: Militar-Verlag Klaus D. Patzwall, 1995)

Michaelis, Rolf, *French units in the Waffen-SS* (Atglen: Schiffer Military History, 2016)

Mollo, Andrew, *Uniforms of the SS volume 7* (London: Historical research unit, 1976)

Mounine, Henri, *Cernay 40-45* (Ostwald: Éditions du polygone, 1999)

Mounine, Henri, *Kolberg* (Paris: Éditions de l'Homme Libre, 2009)

Muelle, Raymond, *Le Bataillon des réprouvés* (Paris: Presses de la Cité, 1990)

Munoz, Antonio, *The forgotten legions: obscure formations of the Waffen-SS, 1943-1945* (New York: Paladin Press, 1991)

Munoz, Antonio, *Hitler's Eastern Legions volume 1: The Baltic Schutzmannschaft* (New York: Axis Europa)

Munoz, Antonio, *The East Came West: Muslim, Hindu and Buddist volunteers in the German Armed Forces 1941-1945* (New York: Axis Europa Books, 2002)

Murawski, Erich, *The struggle for Pomerania* (Winnipeg: John Fedorowicz, 2016)

Neulen, Hans, *Europas verratene Söhne* (Bastei Lubbe, 1980)

Notin, Jean-Christophe, *Leclerc* (Paris: Éditions Perrin, 2005)

Oertle, Vincenz, *Volontaires suisses* (Thesis-verlag, 1997)

Ophuls, Marcel, *The sorrow and the pity* (St. Albans: Paladin, 1975)

Ory, Pascal, *Les collaborateurs* (Paris: Le Seuil, 1977)

Lavigne-Delville, *Pour la Milice, justice* (Paris: Editions Etheel, 1955)

Penot, Christian, *Histoire de la milice en Creuse* (La Crèche: La Geste, 2019)

Rentano, Bruno & Léguerandais, Christophe, *Ces Franciliens qui ont choisi Hitler* (Les Éditions du Lore, 2015)

Rostaing, Pierre, *Le prix d'un serment* (Paris: La Table ronde, 1975)

Rusco, Pierre, *Stoï!* (Paris: Jacques Grancher, 1988)

Saint-Loup, *Les Volontaires* (Paris: Presses de la Cité, 1963)

Saint-Loup, *Les Hérétiques* (Paris: Presses de la Cité, 1965)

Scherzer, Veit, *Sous le Signe SS* (Bayreuth: Verlag Veit Scherzer, 2018)

Schneider, Jost W., *Their honor was loyalty* (San Jose: Bender publishing, 1993, 2nd edition)

Schneider, Russ, *Götterdämmerung 1945* (Philomont: Eastern Front Warfield Books, 1998)

Schulze-Kossens, Richard, *Militärischer Führernachwuchs der Waffen-SS Die Junkerschulen* (Osnabrück: Munin Verlag, 1987, 2nd edition)

Silgailis, Arthur, *Latvian Legion* (San Jose: Bender publishing, 1986)

Slowe, Peter and Woods, Richards, *Battlefield Berlin* (London: Robert Hale, 1988)

Soucy, Robert, *French fascism: The second wave 1933-1939* (London: Yale University Press, 1995)

Stahel, David, *Joining Hitler's Crusade* (Cambridge: Cambridge University Press, 2018)

Sweets, John, *Choices in Vichy France* (New York: Oxford University Press, 1986)

Terrisse, René, *La Milice à Bordeaux* (Bordeaux: Éditions Aubéron, 1997)

Thomas, Nigel, *Wehrmacht Auxiliary Forces* ((Oxford: Osprey Publishing, 1992)

Tieke, Wilhelm and Rebstock, Friedrich, *Im letzten Aufgebot 1944-1945, band 1* (T.K. 18/33, 1994)

Tieke, Wilhelm, *Horst Wessel* (Winnipeg: J.J. Fedorowicz Publishing, 2015)

Trevor-Roper, Hugh, *The last days of Hitler* (London: Macmillan, 1947)

Trigg, Jonathan, Hitler's Gauls (Stroud: Spellmount, 2006)

Valla, Jean-Claude, *La Milice. Lyon 1943-1944* (Paris: Pygmalion, 2000)

Viel, Hugues, *Darnand la mort en chantant* (Paris: Jean Picollec, 1995)

Westemeier, Jens, *Hans Robert Jauss Konstanz Jugend, Krieg und Internierung* (University Konstanz, 2015)

Williamson, Gordon, *The Waffen-SS (4) 24 to 38 Divisions, & Volunteer Legions* (Oxford: Osprey Publishing, 2004)
Yerger, Mark, *Waffen-SS commanders, Krüger to Zimmermann* (Atglen: Schiffer, 1999)

## Periodicals and Articles

*Les Archives Keystone sur la LVF* (Paris: Editions Grancher, 2005)
*Armes Militaria* No 119 (Paris: Histoire & Collections, 1995)
*Axe & Alliés, hors-série* 1 (Eguilles: Éditions du Paladin, 2007) by Éric Lefèvre
*Axis Europa*, various issues (New York: Axis Europa)
*The Axis Forces* 6 (Soldiershop Publishing, April 2018)
*The Axis Forces* 9 (Soldiershop Publishing, February 2019)
*der Freiwillige*, various issues
*Devenir numéro* 1 to 5
*Les Dossiers de l'Histoire* No 92 (Paris: Société de Presse 92)
*The European Volunteer* 0 (December 2015)
*The European Volunteer* 1 (March 2016)
*Historia hors-série* 21, 32 and 40 (Paris: Éditions Tallandier)
*Historia Special* No 31 - *Collaboration et collaborateurs* (Paris: Éditions Tallandier, 1994)
*Histoire pour tous* N° 95, (Paris: Éditions Rouff, 1968)
*Histoire pour tous* No 177 (Paris: Éditions Rouff, 1975)
Revue d'histoire de la Deuxième Guerre Mondiale
*Siegrunen*, various issues
*Trente Trois*, numéro 1 (2009)
*Trente Trois*, numéro 2 (2010)
*Uniforms Hors-Série* no 29 (December 2011)
*39-45 Magazine* numéro 34, 288, 296, 312, 313 and 335 (Bayeux: Editions Heimdal)

The author remains interested in obtaining copies of the following:

Unpublished memoirs of *abbé* Vernay
Unpublished memoirs of Dr. Métais
Unpublished memoirs of Emilien Boyer